The 2007 Pulitzer Prize for Editorial Cartooning was awarded to Walt Handelsman of *Newsday* (Long Island, N.Y.) for his stark, sophisticated cartoons and his impressive use of zany animation. In fact, this was the first time in which animated cartoons won the Pulitzer. Here are examples of each, drawn from the ten cartoons and ten animations he entered for the competition.

★ Chapter 1, "Freedom, Order, or Equality?," discusses the National Security Agency's surveillance of American citizens as part of the war on terrorism. Cartoonist Handelsman questions whether the increased security is worth the infringement on personal freedom.

★ In this animation, Handelsman plays on the name of a popular movie to criticize the Bush administration's interpretation of the Constitution, which is analyzed (objectively) in Chapter 3. To view his animation, go to <http://www.pulitzer.org/> and scroll on the top banner to the year 2007. Choose "Editorial Cartooning" from the menu. Then choose "works" and click on the pirate image at the bottom.

We bring the news to you!

In partnership with one of the world's most trusted news sources—The Associated Press—Houghton Mifflin Political Science is proud to bring you this 2008 Update Edition.

We've collected some of the AP's top news stories and powerful images that have shaped American government in the past twelve months. This *Year in Review* is designed to foster critical thinking, spark classroom debate, and provide timely and relevant illustrations of the major concepts from this textbook.

HM *NewsNow*
Powered by **AP** Associated Press

Bring the news right into your classroom! Students and instructors alike may access a live newsfeed to The Associated Press by logging onto our textbook website. Better yet, take a class poll or engage in a lively debate related to these stories through our HM NewsNow PowerPoint slides, which may be downloaded from our password-protected instructor website. No in-class Internet connection required!

HM *Interactives*
Powered by **AP** Associated Press

These multimedia learning tools walk students through the history of a present-day conflict or debate, and include visuals, animations, and questions for further discussion or research.

Note: The following Associated Press news stories have been edited for length by Houghton Mifflin.

"The way to stop discrimination on the basis of race is to stop discriminating on the basis of race."

— SUPREME COURT CHIEF JUSTICE JOHN ROBERTS, writing the majority opinion that public school districts in Louisville and Seattle cannot consider race as a factor in determining students' school assignments

"I don't know that it makes sense to have people running for president answering questions posed by snowmen."

— REPUBLICAN PRESIDENTIAL CANDIDATE MITT ROMNEY, referencing a video from the CNN/YouTube Democratic debate where a snowman asked candidates to discuss global warming

"Tonight, I have a high privilege and distinct honor of my own— as the first president to begin the State of the Union message with these words: Madam Speaker."

— GEORGE W. BUSH, congratulating Nancy Pelosi on her election as the first female Speaker of the House, during his 2007 State of the Union address

DECEMBER 7, 2006

Bush gives chilly response to some recommendations of Iraq Study Group

PRESIDENT BUSH GAVE A CHILLY response to the Iraq Study Group's proposals for reshaping his policy Thursday, objecting to talks with Iran and Syria, refusing to endorse a major troop withdrawal, and vowing no retreat from embattled U.S. goals in the Mideast.

British Prime Minister Tony Blair, an unflagging ally in the unpopular war, stood with Bush and wholeheartedly supported his determination to fight to victory in Iraq and spread democracy across the Middle East. "The vision is absolutely correct," Blair said at a news conference where the two leaders agreed, nevertheless, on a need for new approaches in Iraq.

"I thought we would succeed quicker than we did," Bush said. "And I am disappointed by the pace of success." When a reporter suggested Bush was denying even to himself how bad things are, the president tartly replied, "It's bad in Iraq. That help?"

The president and prime minister met a day after a bipartisan commission, in a blistering assessment, warned that "the situation in Iraq is grave and deteriorating" and recommended fundamentally different U.S. policies. Its key recommendations called for direct engagement with Iran and Syria as part of a new diplomatic initiative and a pullback of all American combat brigades by early 2008, barring unexpected developments.

While calling the report constructive, Bush and Blair took an unapologetic, almost defiant tone about their decisions and their resolve to keep up the struggle against extremists. The two leaders did not appear to agree with the commission's conclusion that America's ability to shape outcomes was diminishing and time was running out.

"We're going to succeed," the president said. "I believe we'll prevail." . . . Battered in the polls, Bush and Blair have paid a heavy price for the war. The Democratic takeover of Congress was attributed in large measure to voters' unhappiness with Bush and his Iraq policy. But the two leaders said it was essential to support moderates and reformers across the Middle East and to back the Iraqi government led by Prime Minister Nouri al-Maliki at a time of increasing sectarian violence.

> "The situation in Iraq is grave and deteriorating."

U.S. Army soldiers examine the wreckage from a car bomb attack that injured a woman in the Harithiyah neighborhood of western Baghdad, Iraq, Monday, July 9, 2007. Attacks in Baghdad killed 13 people. *(AP Photo/Khalid Mohammed)*

Army secretary steps down in wake of scandal at Walter Reed Hospital

IT BEGAN WITH REPORTS OF MICE and moldy plaster, but after two weeks of outrage, the scandal over poor conditions at Walter Reed Army Medical Center has claimed several careers—including the secretary of the Army's.

Secretary Francis J. Harvey's abrupt dismissal Friday came under withering criticism from Pentagon chief Robert Gates, who said the Army's response to the substandard conditions for the war-wounded was defensive, and not aggressive enough. And it left the door open for more personnel changes, as investigations continue and Congress prepares for hearings next week.

> "So I figured, what the heck, if I offer my resignation that may stop all this bleeding."

Harvey's departure was the most dramatic move during two weeks of furor over the treatment of soldiers at one of the military's highest-profile and busiest medical facilities.

President Bush has ordered a comprehensive review of conditions at the nation's network of military and veteran hospitals, which has been overwhelmed by injured troops from the wars in Iraq and Afghanistan.

Gates said Harvey had resigned, but senior defense officials, speaking on condition of anonymity, said Gates had privately demanded that Harvey leave. Gates was displeased that the officer Harvey had chosen as interim commander of Walter Reed—Lt. Gen. Kevin Kiley, the current Army surgeon general and a former commander of Walter Reed—has been accused by critics of long knowing about the problems there and not improving outpatient care.

"I am disappointed that some in the Army have not adequately appreciated the seriousness of the situation pertaining to outpatient care at Walter Reed," Gates said

in the Pentagon briefing room. He took no questions from reporters.

Harvey was at Fort Benning, Ga., on Friday morning when he cut short his visit to return to Washington to meet with Gates.

In an interview in his office shortly after the announcement, Harvey said he offered Gates his resignation because he believed the Army had let the wounded soldiers down. He said the furor has depressed the staff at Walter Reed, and he wanted to prevent any others from leaving or being fired.

"We can't have them leave," he said. "We can't have them be so demoralized that they leave. So I figured, what the heck, if I offer my resignation that may stop all this bleeding, and it was accepted."

Acting Army Undersecretary Raymond DuBois, left, addresses a House Oversight and Government Reform subcommittee hearing at Walter Reed Medical Center in Washington, Monday, March 5, 2007, on conditions of wounded soldiers at the hospital.
(AP Photo/Dennis Cook)

APRIL 5, 2007

Obama campaign take of $25 million grabs attention of Iowa political activists

IF MONEY TALKS in presidential politics, Sen. Barack Obama has 25 million reasons why skeptical Democrats should start to listen.

The $25 million in campaign contributions the Illinois Democrat reported collecting in the first three months of this year was just $1 million less than rival Hillary Rodham Clinton's record haul and was a remarkable feat for a novice in national politics. "He was the newcomer, he was the outsider, and this shows he's a serious candidate," said Ron Parker, a Democratic strategist in Iowa, home of the nation's first nominating caucuses. "It shows he can do a lot more than draw big crowds."

Fundraising by Clinton and Obama, combined with healthy donations to their party rivals, helped Democratic presidential candidates outraise Republicans $80 million to just over $50 million, a surprising role reversal for the usually well-funded GOP.

"That should send a pretty clear signal that people are looking for a change," said another Iowa Democratic activist, Carl Grover. While he hasn't donated money to Obama, Grover said, "I'm definitely thinking about it."

Obama backers also were cheering the fact that $23.5 million of the $25 million they raised is targeted at what's shaping up to be a competitive primary fight. Clinton has not disclosed how much of her money is targeted at the primary and how much must be held for general election use, should the New York senator be the nominee.

Obama told The Associated Press on Wednesday that his fundraising reflects the growing enthusiasm for his bid.

"It indicates that people are really engaged and enthusiastic, and the crowds we've been attracting, I think, are indicative of a broad base of support across the country," Obama said just before speaking to a raucous crowd of more than 2,500 at a community college.

Asked if the financial disclosures left the fight for the Democratic nomination between Clinton and himself, Obama demurred.

"It's way too early," he said, but added: "We're proud of the fact that we were able to do this without any money from federal lobbyists or PACs."

Obama wrote in an e-mail to supporters that Wednesday's fundraising report was "an unmistakable message to the political establishment in Washington about the power and seriousness of our challenge."

> "He was the newcomer, he was the outsider, and this shows he's a serious candidate."

Democratic presidential hopeful Sen. Barack Obama, D-Ill., makes remarks during a fundraiser, Monday, July 9, 2007, in Birmingham, Ala. *(AP Photo/Rob Carr)*

CBS fires Don Imus over racial comments about Rutgers team

DON IMUS' RACIST REMARKS got him fired by CBS on Thursday, the finale to a stunning fall for one of the nation's most prominent broadcasters.

Imus was initially suspended for two weeks after he called the Rutgers women's basketball team "nappy-headed hos" on the air last week. But outrage kept growing and advertisers kept bolting from his CBS radio show and its MSNBC simulcast, which was canceled Wednesday.

"There has been much discussion of the effect language like this has on our young people, particularly young women of color trying to make their way in this society," CBS President and Chief Executive Officer Leslie Moonves said in announcing the decision. "That consideration has weighed most heavily on our minds as we made our decision."

Imus, 66, had a long history of inflammatory remarks. But something struck a raw nerve when he targeted the Rutgers team—which includes a class valedictorian, a future lawyer, and a musical prodigy—after they lost in the NCAA championship game.

A spokeswoman for the team said it did not have an immediate comment on Imus' firing. But Imus was scheduled to meet with the team Thursday evening at the governor's mansion in Trenton, N.J.

He was fired in the middle of a two-day radio fundraiser for children's charities. CBS announced that Imus' wife, Deirdre, and his longtime newsman, Charles McCord, will host Friday's show.

The cantankerous Imus, once named one of the 25 Most Influential People in America by Time magazine and a member of the National Broadcasters Hall of Fame, was one of radio's original shock jocks. His career took flight in the 1970s and with a cocaine- and vodka-fueled outrageous humor. After sobering up, he settled into a mix of highbrow talk about politics and culture, with locker room humor sprinkled in.

He issued repeated apologies as protests intensified. But it wasn't enough as everyone from Hillary Clinton to Barack Obama to Oprah Winfrey joined the criticism.

The Rev. Al Sharpton and Jesse Jackson met with Moonves on Thursday to demand Imus' removal.

Jackson called the firing "a victory for public decency. No one should use the public airwaves to transmit racial or sexual degradation."

> Outrage kept growing and advertisers kept bolting.

Radio personality Don Imus appears on the Rev. Al Sharpton's radio show, in New York on April 9, 2007. *(AP Photo/Richard Drew)*

APRIL 12, 2007

Strained Army extends Iraq tours to 15 months for active-duty soldiers

STRETCHED THIN BY FOUR YEARS of war, the Army is adding three months to the standard yearlong tour for all active-duty soldiers in Iraq and Afghanistan, an extraordinary step aimed at maintaining the troop buildup in Baghdad.

The change, announced Wednesday by Defense Secretary Robert Gates, is the latest blow to an all-volunteer Army that has been given ever-shorter periods of rest and retraining at home between overseas deployments. Rather than continue to shrink the at-home intervals to a point that might compromise soldiers' preparedness for combat, Gates chose to lengthen combat tours to buy time for units newly returned from battle. The longer tours will affect about 100,000 soldiers currently in Iraq and Afghanistan, plus untold thousands more who deploy later. It does not affect the Marine Corps or the National Guard or Reserve.

> "Our forces are stretched, there's no question about that."

"Our forces are stretched, there's no question about that," Gates said.

The extended tours are a price the Army must pay to sustain the troop buildup that President Bush ordered in January as part of his rejiggered strategy for stabilizing Baghdad and averting a U.S. defeat. Troop levels are being boosted from 15 brigades to 20 brigades, and in order to keep that up beyond summer the Army faced harsh choices: Either send units to Iraq with less than 12 months at home, or extend tours.

The decision also underscores the political cost the administration has had to pay in order to keep alive its hope that higher troop levels in Iraq, combined with a push for Iraqi political reconciliation, will finally produce the stability in Baghdad that experts say is needed before U.S. troops can begin going home.

In recent days, the Pentagon has notified National Guard brigades from four states that they are in line to deploy to Iraq for a second time, eliciting complaints from governors. Also, the Pentagon poured more than $1 billion into bonuses last year to keep soldiers and Marines in the military in the face of an unpopular war.

At a Pentagon news conference, Gates said that it was too early to estimate how long the troop buildup would last but that his new policy would give the Pentagon the capability to maintain the higher force levels until next April.

Families run to greet their returning soldiers Thursday, July 26, 2007, as the soldiers of E Company of the 134th Brigade Support Battalion return home to Camp Ripley near Little Falls, Minn., after two years of deployment in Iraq. *(AP Photo/St. Cloud Times, Kimm Anderson)*

Female candidates face pressure from female voters to meet high standards

FOR THE FIRST TIME IN HISTORY, a woman has the visibility, the reputation and the cash to make a serious run at the presidency.

It would seem that Sen. Hillary Rodham Clinton, the Democratic front-runner, would be in a solid position to parlay the female vote into success against an all-male field in 2008.

> "Most of the male candidates running wouldn't be running if they were women."

But women running for office face an unusual political conundrum: Women sometimes set exceedingly high standards for female candidates.

It's in part because some expect the first female president to be a reflection of them, only better, said Marie Wilson, president of the White House Project, a group that aims to encourage women to lead in business and politics.

"We look at them and we say 'We want them to be perfect....' We hold them to a higher standard because they do represent us," she said. "Most of the male candidates running wouldn't be running if they were women. A woman John McCain's age would have a hard time, a woman with Barack Obama's experience would have a hard time."

As a result, female candidates are more scrutinized, an extension of gender-specific criticism still part of American culture, experts say.

"It's as if each woman is forever competing to be the prom queen, or the wife, and every other women is a competitor, so if she wins it means you lose, instead of experiencing the woman's victory as a group," said Phyllis Chesler, psychologist and author of "Women's Inhumanity to Women."

Women aren't necessarily against female candidates.

An AP analysis of data from the 2006 American National Election Study Pilot Test found that when it came to selecting a candidate for president, gender matters more for women than for men. But it's a two-way street; women are more likely to vote for a candidate because she is female, and also more likely to dismiss a candidate because of her gender, according to the analysis.

While women have made great strides in advancing through the political ranks in recent decades, they still make up just over 16 percent of Congress and a similar number at the state legislature level.

Democratic presidential hopeful Sen. Hillary Rodham Clinton, D-N.Y., right, talks with supporters after her address at the California Democratic Convention in San Diego. *(AP Photo/Denis Poroy)*

Republican candidates embrace Reagan legacy in first debate

TEN REPUBLICAN presidential candidates wanting to succeed President Bush embraced a more popular president, conservative icon Ronald Reagan, at every turn in their first debate of the 2008 race.

"Ronald Reagan was a president of strength," Mitt Romney intoned. "Ronald Reagan used to say, we spend money like a drunken sailor," said John McCain. And Rudy Giuliani praised "that Ronald Reagan optimism."

> "They went out of their way on multiple occasions, no matter the question, to associate themselves with Reagan."

The world, however, is far different today than it was some 25 years ago when the nation's 40th president relaxed at his retreat in the rolling hills of southern California.

Iraq and terrorism now are top issues, support for Bush is at a low point, and Republican hopefuls find themselves trying to prove to the party's base that they're conservative enough to be the GOP nominee—on social matters as well as the economic and security issues Reagan championed.

The three leading candidates—Giuliani, McCain and Romney—and their seven lesser-known rivals attempted to do just that Thursday at the Ronald Reagan Presidential Library. They debated for 90 minutes in the shadow of the late president's Air Force One suspended from above and before Reagan's widow, Nancy, who sat in the front row of the audience.

They stressed the importance of persisting in Iraq and defeating terrorists, called for lower taxes and a muscular defense, and supported spending restraint.

One by one, they invoked Reagan 19 times. In contrast, Bush's name was barely uttered; the president's job approval rating languishes in the 30s.

"They went out of their way on multiple occasions, no matter the question, to associate themselves with Reagan," said Mitchell McKinney, a political communication professor at the University of Missouri-Columbia. "They tried their best to not be explicitly bashing or attacking Bush. Most of them tried, in some way, to take a pass on that." . . .

Each largely stuck to their talking points—and often reverted to their stump speeches—as they sought to present themselves as the most conservative candidate in the pack, and a worthy heir to the political legacy of Reagan.

Republican presidential candidates during their debate in the Air Force One Pavilion at the Ronald Reagan Presidential Library in Simi Valley, Calif., on Thursday, May 3, 2007. The debate focused on foreign policy questions, abortion and the legacy of Ronald Reagan.
(AP Photo/Mark J. Terrill)

Lawmakers pledge to make Capitol complex carbon neutral in battle against climate change

Congress says it is going to join the war against global warming by cleaning up its own backyard, now cluttered with a coal-burning power plant, a fleet of fuel-inefficient vehicles and old-fashioned lights.

House Speaker Nancy Pelosi has set a goal of making House operations carbon neutral during this session of Congress, meaning the House would remove as much carbon dioxide from the atmosphere as it adds by the end of next year.

"The House must lead by example and it is time for Congress to act on its own carbon footprint," Pelosi said in announcing the initiative that would also shift the House to 100 percent renewable electric power.

Sen. John Kerry, D-Mass., has sponsored legislation with the long-term aim of making the entire Capitol complex, 23 buildings where some 15,000 people work, carbon neutral by 2020.

Currently the Capitol complex, which includes office buildings, the Library of Congress, the Botanic Garden and the Government Printing Office, accounts for about 316,000 metric tons of greenhouse gas emissions a year, the same as 57,455 cars.

About one-third of that comes from the combustion of fossil fuels at the 97-year-old Capitol Power Plant, the only coal-burning facility in the District of Columbia.

> "The House must lead by example and it is time for Congress to act on its own carbon footprint."

In addition, the Government Accountability Office said in a recent report, there is not one hybrid-electric vehicle in the legislative branch fleet of more than 300 vehicles. The fleet, mostly light-duty trucks, has only 35 vehicles that use alternative fuels, although the Architect's Office has ordered that almost all newly acquired vehicles be alternative-fuel compatible.

House workers have taken the immediate step of converting 2,000 desk lamps to more efficient compact fluorescent lamps. Within six months the remaining 10,000 desk lamps will switch to CFLs, saving the House $245,000 a year in electric power costs.

House Chief Administrative Officer Daniel Beard, in a report to Pelosi, said the House side of the Capitol, which includes four large office buildings, was responsible for 91,000 tons of greenhouse gas in the fiscal year ending last September, equivalent to annual carbon dioxide emissions of 17,200 cars.

With the Capitol looming in the background, a coal-fired power plant is seen in Washington, Thursday, May 31, 2007.
(AP Photo/Susan Walsh)

Virginia Tech's Norris Hall reopens

BULLET HOLES HAVE BEEN PATCHED, walls freshly painted off-white, doors, ceilings and floors replaced. Nearly two months later, there is no visible evidence of student Seung-Hui Cho's shooting rampage in a Virginia Tech classroom building that left 31 dead, including himself.

University officials on Thursday gave news media tours of Norris Hall, which has been locked since the April 16 shootings in which Cho also killed two students in a dormitory. The tours came in advance of reopening the classroom building next week for the use of engineering program laboratories and offices.

> "A horrendous and heinous crime occurred on our property."

"A horrendous and heinous crime occurred on our property," university spokesman Larry Hincker said, and officials did not want victims' families subjected to images of the crime scene soon after the shootings.

"It needed to be remediated," he said.

Furniture has been removed from the second-floor classrooms where Cho killed 25 students and five professors and 25 were injured, some as they jumped out windows to safety. University officials have said classes will no longer be held in the building.

Relatives of 18 of the injured or dead have had private visits in the building, Hincker said.

All the families were contacted before the announcement last week that the building would reopen.

Cho fired 174 shots from two handguns in nine minutes in four classrooms, two on each side of a hallway.

"The shootings were concentrated in the classrooms themselves" rather than the hallway, Virginia State Police spokeswoman Corinne Geller said. Police have not said where individual victims were found or how many were in each classroom out of consideration for their families, she said.

Cho fired his weapons in two engineering classes, a French class and a German class. There has been no indication of why he chose those classrooms.

He took his own life at 9:51 a.m. as police climbing the stairwell closed in, and his body was found in one room among his victims. Police have not said which one.

One family member who toured Norris last week was Virginia Tech professor Bryan Cloyd, whose daughter, Austin, was killed.

"Even though I've been and taught in the building recently, I almost didn't recognize my own classroom," Cloyd said. "It's changed that much."

Flowers and beads grace one of the 33 stones placed near a makeshift memorial in front of Burruss Hall on the campus of Virginia Tech in Blacksburg, Va. (AP Photo/Chuck Burton)

Immigration bill crushed as supporters fall 14 votes short of keeping it alive

PRESIDENT BUSH'S IMMIGRATION PLAN to legalize as many as 12 million unlawful immigrants while fortifying the border collapsed in the Senate on Thursday, crushing both parties' hopes of addressing the volatile issue before the 2008 elections.

The Senate vote to drive a stake through the delicate compromise was a stinging setback for Bush—who had made reshaping immigration laws a centerpiece of his domestic agenda—engineered by members of his own party. It could carry heavy political consequences for Republicans and Democrats, many of whom were eager to show they could act on a complex issue of great interest to the public.

"Legal immigration is one of the top concerns of the American people and Congress' failure to act on it is a disappointment," a grim-faced president said after an appearance in Newport, R.I. "A lot of us worked hard to see if we couldn't find common ground. It didn't work."

Sen. Edward M. Kennedy, D-Mass., his party's lead negotiator on the bill, called its defeat "enormously disappointing for Congress and for the country." But, he added: "We will be back. This issue is not going away."

The bill's Senate supporters fell 14 votes short of the 60 needed to limit debate and clear the way for final passage of the legislation. The tally was 46 to 53, with three-quarters of the Senate's Republicans voting to derail the bill.

Lawmakers in both parties said further action was unlikely this year, dooming its prospects as the political strains of a crowded presidential contest get louder.

Only 13 percent of those in a CBS News Survey taken earlier this week said they supported passage of the bill. Almost three times that number, 35 percent, opposed it. Even more, 51 percent, said they did not know enough about the immigration legislation to say whether they supported passage.

"I believe that until another election occurs, or until something happens in the body politic, that what occurred today was fairly final," said Sen. Mel Martinez, R-Fla., the GOP chairman.

> "A lot of us worked hard to see if we couldn't find common ground. It didn't work."

Jesus Rocha, 10, third from right, his brother Eric Rocha, 14, and father Delfino Rocha, right, listen from an overflow area during a local government meeting in Manassas, Va., Tuesday, July 10, 2007. The Prince William County board of supervisors listened to public comment on a proposed mandate aimed at discouraging illegal immigrants from settling in the county. *(AP Photo/Jacquelyn Martin)*

AP

JULY 11, 2007

Bush refuses to explain clemency order for Libby as House panel opens probe

PRESIDENT BUSH REFUSED to explain to Congress on Wednesday why he commuted the prison sentence of former White House aide I. Lewis "Scooter" Libby.

The husband of the CIA agent outed in the case testified during a House hearing that the clemency grant had cast a pall of suspicion over the presidency.

In a letter to House Judiciary Committee Chairman John Conyers, D-Mich., Bush counsel Fred Fielding said Congress had no authority to review a presidential clemency decision.

"To allow such an inquiry would chill the complete and candid advice that President Bush,

> Bush counsel Fred Fielding said Congress had no authority to review a presidential clemency decision.

and future presidents, must be able to rely upon in discharging their constitutional responsibilities," he wrote.

The letter came in the middle of a politically charged hearing by the Judiciary panel on Bush's move last week to erase Libby's 2½-year prison sentence. Libby, a former top aide to Vice President Dick Cheney, was convicted of obstructing justice in a federal probe of the leak of former CIA agent Valerie Plame Wilson's identity.

When he issued the commutation July 2, Bush said in a statement that he respected the jury's verdict but thought the prison term was too harsh.

The hearing's star witness was her husband Joseph C. Wilson IV, a former diplomat whose 2003 newspaper column challenging Bush's case for the Iraq war precipitated Plame's unmasking and the resulting investigation that ensnared Libby.

"In commuting Mr. Libby's sentence, the president has removed any incentive for Mr. Libby to cooperate with the prosecutor. The obstruction of justice is ongoing, and now the president has emerged as its greatest protector," Wilson testified.

Wilson said Bush "at the very least owes the American people a full and honest explanation of his actions and those of other senior administration officials in this matter, including but not limited to the vice president."

Conyers said he recognized Bush's constitutional right to grant clemency, but he argued that using the power to benefit a former aide who was in a position to incriminate other administration officials was suspect.

Former White House aide I. Lewis "Scooter" Libby walks towards his car outside federal court in Washington, Tuesday, June 5, 2007, after he was sentenced to 2½ years in prison for lying and obstructing the CIA leak investigation.
(AP Photo/Charles Dharapak)

Gonzales resigns, bringing GOP relief, Democratic vows to continue probes

ATTORNEY GENERAL Alberto Gonzales' resignation Monday after months of draining controversy drew expressions of relief from Republicans and a vow from Democrats to pursue their investigation into fired federal prosecutors.

President Bush, Gonzales' most dogged defender, told reporters he had accepted the resignation reluctantly. "His good name was dragged through the mud for political reasons," Bush said.

The president named Paul Clement, the solicitor general, as a temporary replacement. With less than 18 months remaining in office, there was no indication when Bush would name a successor—or how quickly or easily the Senate might confirm one.

Apart from the president, there were few Republican expressions of regret following the departure of the nation's first Hispanic attorney general, a man once hailed as the embodiment of the American Dream.

"Our country needs a credible, effective attorney general who can work with Congress on critical issues," said Sen. John Sununu of New Hampshire, who last March was the first GOP lawmaker to call on Gonzales to step down. "Alberto Gonzales' resignation will finally allow a new attorney general to take on this task."

Sen. Chuck Grassley, R-Iowa, added, "Even after all the scrutiny, it doesn't appear that Attorney General Gonzales committed any crimes, but he did make management missteps and didn't handle the spotlight well when they were exposed."

Democrats were less charitable.

Under Gonzales and Bush, "the Department of Justice suffered a severe crisis of leadership that allowed our justice system to be corrupted by political influence," said Sen. Patrick Leahy, D-Vt., who has presided over the investigation into the firings of eight prosecutors whom Democrats say were axed for political reasons.

Majority Leader Harry Reid, D-Nev., said the investigation would not end with Gonzales' leaving.

"Congress must get to the bottom of this mess and follow the facts where they lead, into the White House," said the Nevada Democrat.

> Apart from the president, there were few Republican expressions of regret.

Then U.S. Attorney General Alberto Gonzales addresses the National Association of Attorneys General at the association's summer meeting in Atlanta, Ga., Thursday, June 21, 2007. *(AP Photo/W. A. Harewood)*

SEPTEMBER 6, 2007

Fred Thompson makes his candidacy for the Republican US presidential nomination official

FRED THOMPSON OFFICIALLY ENTERED a wide-open Republican presidential race Thursday, vowing to invigorate a dispirited Republican Party and promising to thwart another Clinton from capturing the presidency.

The former senator harkened to the Republican glory days of 1994 when he and other Republicans seized control of Congress and established an equal counterpoint to Democrat Bill Clinton in the White House. In the 2008 campaign, former first lady Hillary Rodham Clinton is among the leading Democratic candidates.

Thompson, now an official candidate for the Republican nomination, has promised to return the party to better times.

"In 1992, we were down after a Clinton victory," Thompson said in a 15-minute Webcast that laid out the rationale for the candidacy he also declared on television talk show "The Tonight Show with Jay Leno."

> "If you can't get your message out in a few months, you're probably not ever going to get it out."

"In 1994, our conservative principles led us to a comeback and majority control of the Congress. Now, you don't want to have to come back from another Clinton victory. Our country needs us to win next year, and I am ready to lead that effort," he said.

Thompson also swiped at his leading Republican rivals, Rudy Giuliani and Mitt Romney, without naming them, saying: "In 1994, when I first ran, I advocated the same common-sense conservative positions that I hold today."...

Today, some conservatives question Giuliani's and Romney's credentials—and Thompson sees an opening for his candidacy.

An actor for decades, Thompson is perhaps best known as the gruff district attorney Arthur Branch on NBC's "Law & Order," and for his roles in more than a dozen movies....

After months of playing coy, the veteran actor launched his candidacy Hollywood style and with a multiphase campaign roll out. He confirmed his bid on television Wednesday in Los Angeles—"I'm running for president of the United States"—while his eight rivals gathered in New Hampshire to debate without him. Then, he released the online video. A tour of early primary states begins Thursday afternoon in Iowa.

On "The Tonight Show," Thompson called Giuliani, Romney and Sen. John McCain formidable but added: "I think I will be, too" as he rejected the notion that he was jumping in too late for the 2008 election. Poking at his rivals, who have been running since January, he added: "If you can't get your message out in a few months, you're probably not ever going to get it out."

Former U.S. Sen. Fred Thompson, left, talks with host Jay Leno after announcing that he is formally joining the 2008 White House race, during the taping of "The Tonight Show with Jay Leno" at the NBC Studios in Burbank, Calif., Wednesday, Sept. 5, 2007.
(Paul Drinkwater/NBC Universal/Getty Images)

Bush approves gradual troop cuts

PRESIDENT BUSH, DEFENDING AN unpopular war, ordered gradual reductions in U.S. forces in Iraq on Thursday night and said, "The more successful we are, the more American troops can return home."

Yet, Bush firmly rejected calls to end the war, insisting that Iraq will still need military, economic and political support from Washington after his presidency ends.

Bush said that 5,700 U.S. forces would be home by Christmas and that four brigades—for a total of at least 21,500 troops—would return by July, along with an undetermined number of support forces. Now at its highest level of the war, the U.S. troop strength stands at 168,000.

"The principle guiding my decisions on troop levels in Iraq is: return on success," the president said, trying to summon the nation's resolve once again to help Iraq "defeat those who threaten its future and also threaten ours."

With no dramatic change in course, Bush's decision sets the stage for a fiery political debate in Congress and on the 2008 presidential campaign trail. Democrats said Bush's modest approach was unacceptable.

"An endless and unlimited military presence in Iraq is not an option," said Sen. Jack Reed of Rhode Island, a former Army Ranger, who delivered the Democratic response.

"Democrats and Republicans in Congress—and throughout the nation—cannot and must not stand idly by while our interests throughout the world are undermined and our armed forces are stretched toward the breaking point," Reed said. "We intend to exercise our constitutional duty and profoundly change our military's involvement in Iraq."

The reductions announced by Bush represented only a slight hastening of the originally scheduled end of the troop increase that Bush announced in January. When the cutbacks are complete, about 132,000 U.S. forces will be in Iraq.

Bush's speech was the latest turning point in a 4½-year-old war marred by miscalculations, surprises and setbacks.

Almost since the fall of Baghdad, in April 2003, U.S. commanders and administration officials in Washington mistakenly believed they were on track to winding down U.S. involvement and handing off to the Iraqis. Instead, the insurgency intervened and the reality of a country in chaos conspired to deepen the U.S. commitment.

> "The more successful we are, the more American troops can return home."

President Bush arrives at Al-Asad Airbase in Anbar province, Iraq, as Gen. David Petraeus, commanding general of the multinational forces in Iraq, left, and CENTCOM commander Adm. William Fallon, right, look on, Monday, Sept. 3, 2007. The president made an unannounced visit to Iraq to meet with Petraeus, Ambassador to Iraq Ryan Crocker, Iraqi leaders, and U.S. troops.

(AP Photo/Charles Dharapak)

"We're saying to the world, if you want to create goods and products for American consumers, you'll need to meet the expectations for safety and quality that American consumers have."

— HEALTH AND HUMAN SERVICES SECRETARY MICHAEL LEAVITT, addressing concerns about the safety of Chinese imports after a wave of problems with products ranging from toys to toothpaste

"I see problems with both. Obama because he's black and Hillary because she's a woman. Are we ready? Is America ready to go there?"

— AN UNDECIDED SOUTH CAROLINA DEMOCRAT, pondering which candidate would be most likely to beat a Republican challenger in the 2008 presidential election

"None of us is indispensable or unreplaceable except [President Bush] and Dick Cheney, and they ain't going anywhere."

— KARL ROVE, longtime advisor to George W. Bush, after resigning from his job at the White House

"This is now a greedy, stupid process."

— FORMER SPEAKER OF THE HOUSE NEWT GINGRICH, on the increasing competition among states to hold one of the first primary elections in the nation

"We're on dry land, recovering . . . the federal government still knows you exist."

— GEORGE W. BUSH, speaking in New Orleans about continuing efforts to rebuild the city after the devastation of Hurricane Katrina

"It is not often in the law that so few have so quickly changed so much."

— SUPREME COURT JUSTICE STEPHEN BREYER, speaking after a conservative majority ruled that public school districts in Louisville and Seattle cannot consider race when determining students' school assignments

"I love the earth, I love the environment, I love nature. And it's so important."

— METALLICA GUITARIST KIRK HAMMETT, after performing at a Live Earth concert organized by former Vice President Al Gore

"We have never received death threats before like I received. It is unbelievable how this has inflamed the passions of the American people."

— REPUBLICAN PRESIDENTIAL CANDIDATE JOHN McCAIN, speaking about the controversy over illegal immigration, and the public reaction to his views on the subject

"Jon makes these guys feel comfortable. He provides them with an opportunity to reach an audience they don't always reach, which is young men."

— MICHELE GANELESS, executive vice president and general manager of Comedy Central, explaining why so many presidential candidates appear on "The Daily Show" with host Jon Stewart

"This court has shown the same respect for precedent that a wrecking ball shows for a plate-glass window."

— RALPH G. NEAS, president of the liberal organization People for the American Way, objecting to the decisions rendered by the Supreme Court during its 2006 session

The Challenge of Democracy

2008 Update Edition

The Challenge of Democracy

Government in America

Ninth Edition

Kenneth Janda
Northwestern University

Jeffrey M. Berry
Tufts University

Jerry Goldman
Northwestern University

Houghton Mifflin Company   Boston   New York

To our students in the United States and abroad who have assisted us with their questions and suggestions.

Publisher: Suzanne Jeans
Senior Sponsoring Editor: Traci Mueller
Marketing Manager: Edwin Hill
Senior Development Editor: Lisa Kalner Williams
Senior Project Editor: Christina Horn
Senior Art and Design Coordinator: Jill Haber
Cover Design Manager: Anne Katzeff
Senior Photo Editor: Jennifer Meyer Dare
Composition Buyer: Chuck Dutton
New Title Project Manager: James Lonergan
Editorial Assistant: Evangeline Bermas
Marketing Assistant: Samantha Abrams
Editorial Assistant: Anne Finley

Cover image: © Randy Faris/CORBIS.

Printed in the U.S.A.

Library of Congress Control Number: 2006935030

Instructor's Exam Copy:
ISBN-13: 978-0-547-05156-7
ISBN-10: 0-547-05156-5

For orders, use Student Text ISBNs:
ISBN-13: 978-0-618-99094-8
ISBN-10: 0-618-99094-1

123456789-CRK-11 10 09 08 07

★ Brief Contents

Contents

Compared with What?

Looking to the Future

Politics in a Changing World

Features

★ Preface

★ *The Challenge of Democracy, 2008 Update Edition:* Bringing Currency to Your Classroom

The Challenge of Democracy, 2008 Update Edition, provides coverage of the key news stories that have shaped our nation over the past twelve months, giving students a unique lens through which to examine the current state of American politics and the upcoming 2008 elections.

Key Content Updates

The text includes coverage of the latest political events that have emerged since the publication of the last edition. Key updates include discussion of the following:

- The latest developments in the Iraq war, including updated figures on U.S. deaths.
- The current Congress, Nancy Pelosi as the first female Speaker of the House and Harry Reid as the new Senate Majority Leader, and President Bush's relationship with the Democratic Congress.
- The 2008 presidential primary season, including new Internet campaigns, new DNC rules for early caucuses and primaries, and new contribution limits.
- The conviction of Lewis "Scooter" Libby and the subsequent commutation of his sentence.
- Justice Department firings of U.S. attorneys, which led to Attorney General Alberto Gonzales's resignation.
- The dismissal of Donald Rumsfeld and the appointment of Robert Gates as secretary of defense.
- Recent Supreme Court actions and the Court's shift in a more conservative direction, including its reversed courses on abortion and school segregation.
- The latest developments surrounding same-sex marriage in the states.
- The failure of immigration law reform in 2007.
- The recent increase in the minimum wage.

Still, no textbook can ever be completely up-to-date; as soon as a book goes to the printing plant, new, important developments are sure to emerge. Yet textbooks, and especially new editions of existing books, must consist of much more than an updating of recent events. In the best of all possible worlds, an American government textbook should provide a context for students to examine current events on their own. In this respect, we think *The Challenge of Democracy* excels.

Partnership with The Associated Press

Current news stories, videos, and images are available from The Associated Press for use in your classroom.

- *Year in Review.* We have collected some of the AP's top news stories and powerful images that have shaped American government in the past twelve months. This Year in Review, located at the beginning of this text, is designed to foster critical thinking, spark classroom debate, and provide timely and relevant illustrations of the major concepts from this textbook.

- *HM NewsNow (powered by The Associated Press).* Bring the news right into your classroom! Students and instructors alike may access a live newsfeed to The Associated Press by logging onto our textbook website. Better yet, take a class poll or engage in a lively debate related to these stories through our HM NewsNow PowerPoint slides, which may be downloaded from our password-protected instructor website at **college.hmco.com/ pic/jandaupdate9e**. No in-class Internet connection required!

- *HM Interactives (powered by The Associated Press).* These multimedia learning tools walk students through the history of a present-day conflict or debate, and include visuals, animations, and questions for further discussion or research. Marginal icons throughout the text point students to relevant HM Interactives, which are accessible at **college.hmco.com/ pic/jandaupdate9e**.

★ Thematic Framework

Through all nine editions, we have striven to write a book that students will actually read, so we have sought to discuss politics—a complex subject—in a captivating and understandable way. American politics isn't dull, and its textbooks needn't be either. Equally important, we have sought to produce a book that students would credit for stimulating their thinking about politics. While offering all of the essential information about American government and politics, we feel that it is important to give students a framework for analyzing politics that they can use long after their studies have ended.

To accomplish these goals, we built *The Challenge of Democracy* around three dynamic themes that are relevant to today's world: the *clash among the values of freedom, order, and equality;* the *tensions between pluralist and majoritarian visions of democracy;* and the fundamental ways that *globalization* is changing American politics.

Freedom, Order, and Equality

The first theme is introduced in Chapter 1 ("Freedom, Order, or Equality?"), where we suggest that American politics often reflects conflicts between the values of freedom and order and between the values of freedom and equality.

These value conflicts are prominent in contemporary American society, and they help to explain political controversy and consensus in earlier eras.

For instance, in Chapter 3 ("The Constitution") we argue that the Constitution was designed to promote order and that it virtually ignored issues of political and social equality. Equality was later served, however, by several amendments to the Constitution. In Chapter 15 ("Order and Civil Liberties") and Chapter 16 ("Equality and Civil Rights") we demonstrate that many of this nation's most controversial issues represent conflicts among individuals or groups who hold differing views on the values of freedom, order, and equality. Views on issues such as abortion are not just isolated opinions; they also reflect choices about the philosophy citizens want government to follow. Yet choosing among these values is difficult, sometimes excruciatingly so.

Pluralist and Majoritarian Visions of Democracy

The second theme, introduced in Chapter 2, asks students to consider two competing models of democratic government. One way that government can make decisions is by means of *majoritarian* principles—that is, by taking the actions desired by a majority of citizens. A contrasting model of government, *pluralism,* is built around the interaction of decision makers in government with groups concerned about issues that affect them.

These models are not mere abstractions; we use them to illustrate the dynamics of the American political system. In Chapter 12 ("The Presidency") we discuss the problem of divided government. More often than not over the past forty years, the party that controlled the White House did not control both houses of Congress. When these two branches of government are divided between the two parties, majoritarian government is difficult. Even when the same party controls both branches, the majoritarian model is not always realized. In Chapter 10 ("Interest Groups") we see the forces of pluralism at work. Interest groups of all types populate Washington, and these organizations represent the diverse array of interests that define our society. At the same time, the chapter explores ways in which pluralism favors wealthier, better-organized interests.

Globalization's Impact on American Politics

The third theme, the impact of globalization on American politics, is introduced in Chapter 1 and then discussed throughout the text. The traditional notion of national sovereignty holds that each government is free to govern in the manner it feels best. As the world becomes a smaller place, however, national sovereignty is tested in many ways. When a country is committing human rights violations—putting people in jail for merely disagreeing with the government in power—should other countries try to pressure it to comply with common norms of justice? Do the democracies of the world have a responsibility to use their influence to try to limit the abuses of the powerless in societies where they are abused? These are just a few of the questions we explore.

Throughout the book we stress that students must make their own choices among the competing values and models of government. Although the three of us hold diverse and strong opinions about which choices are best, we do not believe it is our role to tell students our own answers to the broad questions we pose. Instead, we want our readers to learn firsthand that a democracy requires thoughtful choices. That is why we titled our book *The Challenge of Democracy.*

Our framework travels well over time. The civil rights struggles of the 1960s exemplified the utility of our theme emphasizing equality, as do more contemporary controversies surrounding gay rights, the rights of the disabled, and affirmative action. We're just beginning to understand the privacy and personal freedom issues involving the Internet. Our theme of pluralism versus majoritarianism remains compelling as well. Pluralist images of America predate the adoption of the Constitution. In his defense of the proposed Constitution, James Madison defended the pursuit of self-interested goals by various groups in society, each looking out for its own good. A contrary view of democracy—majoritarian government—emphasizes control of government by majorities of voters through our party system. But the party system sometimes has a hard time channeling a majority of voters into majority rule. Prior to the Civil War, fissures in the party system made it difficult to understand exactly where the majority stood. More recently, in the 2000 election, Democrat Al Gore won more popular votes than Republican George Bush, but Bush won a majority of the electoral college, and that's the majority that counts. Since the mid-1950s, more often than not, we've had divided government where one party controls the White House but the other controls at least one of the two houses of Congress. Which majority should be followed in such instances?

Our framework also travels well over space—to other countries with very different political heritages. One of the most important aspects of globalization is the number of countries that have recently made a transition to democracy or are currently trying to make that change. The challenge of democratization, however, is illustrated by recent developments in Iraq. Elections have been held, but democracy has been hindered by the lack of order. The relevance of our other major theme is illustrated as well. One of the most difficult problems faced by those who wrote the country's new constitution was the dispute between the majority Shiites, who, not surprisingly, wanted a government that facilitates majority rule, and the minority Sunnis and Kurds, who wanted a more pluralistic system with firm protections against majority dominance.

One of our greatest satisfactions as authors of a book on American democracy is that it has been used in a number of countries where democracy has at least a foothold, if it hasn't yet fully flowered. Houghton Mifflin has donated copies of earlier editions of our book to English-speaking faculty and students in Bulgaria, Croatia, the Czech Republic, Georgia, Ghana, Hungary, Kenya, Poland, Romania, Russia, Slovakia, and South Africa. Moreover, the brief edition of our text has been translated into Russian, Hungarian, Georgian, Czech, and Korean. We are pleased that *The Challenge of Democracy* is now available to many more students in these countries—students who have been confronting the challenge of democracy in times of political transition.

⭐ Substantive Features of the Update Edition

Chapter-Opening Vignettes

As in previous editions, each chapter begins with a vignette to draw students into the chapter's substance while exploring one of the book's themes. Chapter 1, "Freedom, Order, or Equality?," opens with discussion of President Bush's authorization of eavesdropping of Americans' phone calls by the National Security Agency without court-approved warrants. Was this an appropriate response to maintain order, or an unnecessary infringement on our freedom? Chapter 2, "Majoritarian or Pluralist Democracy?," considers President

Bush's goal of promoting democracy around the world. His policies echo Woodrow Wilson's, who proclaimed in 1917 that "the world must be made safe for democracy." Chapter 3, "The Constitution," begins with an examination of the European Union and its trouble in creating a constitution because of adverse votes by member states. In Chapter 8, "Political Parties," we identify some minor parties in the United States, such as the Libertarian, Green, and American Independent Parties and explain why it is that third parties have such difficulty in gaining support in our system. Some of the scandals surrounding lobbyist Jack Abramoff are highlighted in the beginning of Chapter 10, "Interest Groups."

"Politics in a Changing World"

In light of the growing emphasis in our book on globalization, we initiated a set of boxed features on "Politics in a Changing World" in the Seventh Edition. In these boxes we examine various elements of political change—some troubling, some hopeful. Some of the PCW boxes focus on the United States, while others involve other countries. We continue with these boxes in the Update Edition, and, again, many of these are new or updated to take recent events and trends into account. In a new PCW in Chapter 11, "Congress," we look at political representation and the increasing numbers of African American and Hispanic legislators. In Chapter 14, "The Courts," the PCW concerns the touchy subject of the right to die. Do the terminally ill have a right to have a physician assist them in ending their life? Chapter 17, "Policymaking," uses the tragic story of the late Terri Schiavo, the brain-dead woman kept alive through a feeding tube, as a means of examining the process by which issues emerge on the national agenda.

"Looking to the Future"

In the Eighth Edition we introduced an entirely new set of boxed features, "Looking to the Future." These features invite students to anticipate how the political world might look if some current and rather intriguing trends are extrapolated. Accompanying each "Looking to the Future" box are provocative questions about whether the trend is likely to continue as extrapolated or not—and why. In Chapter 10, "Interest Groups," we document the steady decline in the percentage of workers who belong to labor unions. Will this trend adversely affect the quality of life for working-class Americans? Chapter 16 examines the rise in the percentage of Americans who do not fit our conventional set of racial categories. As our population includes increasing percentages of those of mixed-race ancestry, what are the implications for American society? In Chapter 18, "Economic Policy," we look at the increasing share of the national debt that is being financed by foreigners. Americans are increasingly buying more goods and services from other countries than we are selling to them. When these trends are projected out over time, they're quite unsettling. These "Looking to the Future" boxes generally alternate with "Politics in a Changing World" features.

"Compared with What?"

We firmly believe that students can better evaluate how our political system works when they compare it with politics in other countries. Once again, each chapter has at least one boxed feature called "Compared with What?" that treats its topic in a comparative perspective. Which democracies are the most pluralistic? How does India implement affirmative action? How does the public in different countries regard the war in Iraq? Which countries are most satisfied with their form of democracy? How are the United States and President Bush evaluated by our European allies?

"Can you explain why . . . "

Periodically in the margins of each chapter, we pose a question to students. Each begins "Can you explain why . . ." and then completes the sentence with a query that highlights some feature of our system of government that may seem counterintuitive. For example, we ask students, "Can you explain why the United States might oppose an International Criminal Court?" Or, "Can you explain why some of the nation's founders thought that adding a bill of rights to the Constitution might actually limit individual rights?" In each case, the accompanying text offers material that should help the reader formulate an answer to the question. We hope students will find these questions in the margins provocative and interesting.

"In Our Own Words"

We have enriched the close connection that we initiated in previous editions between the words in our text and technology. Each chapter opens with information on "In Our Own Words," downloadable audio files that speak of the major objectives of each chapter. In this edition, we've also dramatically increased the number of marginal callouts that tie in chapter content to the self-test at the award-winning IDEAlog website. (See "For the Student: Effective Learning Aids" later in the preface for more information on "In Our Own Words" and IDEAlog.)

Additional Resources for Students

Each chapter concludes with a brief summary. At the end of the book, we have included the Declaration of Independence, an annotated copy of the Constitution, and a glossary of key terms.

★ For the Instructor: Innovative Teaching Tools

Our job as authors did not end with writing this text. From the beginning, we have been centrally involved with producing a tightly integrated set of instructional materials to accompany the text. With help from other political scientists and educational specialists at Houghton Mifflin, these ancillary materials have grown and improved over time.

Teaching Support

- *Online Instructor's Resource Manual.* This resource provides instructors with material that relates directly to the thematic framework and organization of the book. Revised and updated for this edition by Mary

Beth Melchior, it includes learning objectives; chapter synopses; detailed full-length lectures (including a lecture format that encourages class participation); ideas for class, small group, and individual projects and activities; and Internet resources. Media Lectures are available for every relevant chapter. These lecture activities help students connect the material in the text with music and television programming they are exposed to every day. Too access this manual, visit the password-protected instructor website at **college.hmco.com/pic/jandaupdate9e**.

■ *HMTesting Instructor CD.* Thoroughly updated by P. S. Ruckman of Rock Valley College, this CD-ROM provides over 1,500 test questions in identification, multiple-choice, and essay formats. HMTesting provides instructors with all the tools they need to create, author, edit, customize, and deliver multiple types of tests. Instructors can import questions directly from the Test Bank, create their own questions, or edit existing algorithmic questions.

■ *PowerPoint Slides.* PowerPoint slides, which include figures from the text and brief outlines of chapter content, are available on the password-protected instructor website at **college.hmco.com/pic/jandaupdate9e**.

■ *In-Class "Clicker" Quizzes.* Multiple-choice quizzes, delivered in PowerPoint format and compatible with "clicker" technology, are available for download on the password-protected instructor website. Each clicker quiz consists of ten questions, and there is one quiz for every chapter in the text. As a motivator for students, half of the questions are available on the student website as pre-class quizzes; students who make an effort to answer these questions ahead of time are rewarded by being better prepared for in-class quizzes.

■ *HM NewsNow (powered by The Associated Press).* Bring the news right into your classroom! Students and instructors alike may access a live newsfeed to The Associated Press by logging onto our textbook website. Better yet, take a class poll or engage in a lively debate related to these stories through our HM NewsNow PowerPoint slides, which may be downloaded from our password-protected instructor website at **college.hmco .com/pic/jandaupdate9e**. No in-class Internet connection required!

■ *HM Interactives (powered by The Associated Press).* Delivered in PowerPoint format, these multimedia learning tools walk students through the history of a present-day conflict or debate, and include visuals, animations, and questions for further discussion or research. HM Interactives PowerPoint slides may be downloaded from our password-protected instructor website at **college.hmco.com/pic/jandaupdate9e**.

■ *uspolitics.org.* The 2008 Update Edition continues to be supported by **uspolitics.org**, Kenneth Janda's personal website for *The Challenge of Democracy*. His site offers a variety of teaching aids to instructors who adopt any version of *The Challenge of Democracy* for courses in American politics. It is divided into two sides: the student side is open to all users, but the instructor side is limited to teachers who register online at **uspolitics.org** as *Challenge* adopters. The site offers some material not contained in Houghton Mifflin's own website, yet it also provides convenient links to the publisher's site.

Online Learning

Houghton Mifflin now offers three exciting options for online learning.

- *AmericansGoverning.org*. Encourage in-class discussion through **AmericansGoverning.org**. Correlated to the 20 chapters in the text and fully customizable by instructors, this site provides online videos such as interviews, campaign ads, and short-form documentaries; interactive simulations; and quality writing and homework assignments. The site also helps students stay current with daily headlines from the *Washington Post* and the *New York Times*. An online Notebook allows instructors to track which assignments the students have completed. To learn more and to set up a course, visit **AmericansGoverning.org**.

- *Eduspace*. Houghton Mifflin's Eduspace® for American Government provides a customizable course management system powered by Blackboard® along with interactive homework assignments that engage students and encourage in-class discussion. Assignments include gradable homework exercises, writing assignments, primary sources with questions, simulations with quizzing and discussion questions, and HM Interactives. Eduspace also provides a gradebook and communication capabilities, such as synchronous and asynchronous chats and announcement postings. To learn more, visit **www.eduspace.com**.

- *Challenge of Democracy Blog*. Do you blog? We know that one of the biggest challenges of teaching with blogs is finding new content to keep your site fresh and your students engaged. The authors of *The Challenge of Democracy* as well as our blogmaster post new and provocative content that will generate discussion and get your students to think critically about current events. To learn more, and for instructions on how to create your own blog, visit **challengeofdemocracy.com**.

For information on the teaching tools that accompany *The Challenge of Democracy*, please contact your Houghton Mifflin sales representative.

★ For the Student: Effective Learning Aids

- *Student Website*. The student website, accessible at **college.hmco.com/pic/jandaupdate9e**, offers a wide array of resources for students. Included are ACE Practice Tests, material from the *Study Guide* written by Kevin Davis of North Central Texas College–Corinth, chapter outlines, Internet exercises, and selected readings. Online appendices, such as *Federalist* Nos. 10 and 51, the Articles of Confederation, Presidents of the United States, Justices of the Supreme Court Since 1900, and Party Control of the Presidency and Congress, are available as general resources for students. The student website also hosts "In Our Own Words," a new audio feature. Spoken in the voice of the textbook authors, "In Our Own Words" provides insight into each chapter that will help students prepare for class.

    IDEAlog 8.0, an earlier version of which won the 1992 Instructional Software Award from the American Political Science Association, is also available on the student website and is closely tied to the text's "value conflicts" theme. IDEAlog 8.0 first asks students to rate themselves on the two-dimensional tradeoff of freedom versus order and freedom versus equality. It then presents them with twenty questions, ten dealing with the conflict of freedom versus order and ten pertaining to freedom versus equality. Students' responses to these questions are classified according to libertarian, conservative, liberal, or communitarian ideological tendencies.

■ *AmericansGoverning.org.* Instructors may assign students online videos, interactive simulations, or writing and homework assignments from AmericansGoverning.org. A student passkey for AmericansGoverning .org comes packaged with new copies of this textbook. To purchase access with a used book, please visit **AmericansGoverning.org**.

We invite your questions, suggestions, and criticisms of the teaching/ learning package and *The Challenge of Democracy*. You may contact us at our respective institutions or through our collective e-mail address <cod@ northwestern.edu>.

★ Acknowledgments

All authors are indebted to others for inspiration and assistance in various forms; textbook authors are notoriously so. Our biggest debt in producing this edition is to Patricia Conley, a Visiting Professor at the University of Chicago. Professor Conley contributed many creative ideas and helped us update a number of chapters. We again want to single out Professor Paul Manna of the College of William and Mary, who has assisted us in many different ways. We are grateful to Professor Timothy R. Johnson of the University of Minnesota,

Kenneth Janda, Jeffrey Berry, and Jerry Goldman in front of the Jay Pritzker Pavilion, designed by Frank Gehry, in Chicago's Millennium Park.

who offered several valuable suggestions. Our thanks go to Stu Baker, head of Northwestern Library Management Systems, and to Claire Stewart, head of Northwestern's Marjorie Mitchell Digital Media Services, for their generous assistance. Andrew Suprenant provided support for the new and improved version of IDEAlog. We also wish to express our gratitude to Julieta Suarez-Cao and Andrew Gruen of Northwestern and to Matthew Wolfe and Tom Wyler of Tufts for their timely research assistance.

We have been fortunate to obtain the help of many outstanding political scientists across the country who provided us with critical reviews of our work as it has progressed through nine separate editions. We found their comments enormously helpful, and we thank them for taking valuable time away from their own teaching and research to write their detailed reports. More specifically, our thanks go to the following:

David Ahern
University of Dayton

Philip C. Aka
University of Arkansas at Pine Bluff

James Anderson
Texas A&M University

Greg Andranovich
California State University, Los Angeles

Theodore Arrington
University of North Carolina, Charlotte

Denise Baer
Northeastern University

Richard Barke
Georgia Institute of Technology

Linda L. M. Bennett
Wittenberg University

Stephen Earl Bennett
University of Cincinnati

Elizabeth Bergman,
California State Polytechnic University, Pomona

Thad Beyle
University of North Carolina, Chapel Hill

Bruce Bimber
University of California–Santa Barbara

Michael Binford
Georgia State University

Bonnie Browne
Texas A&M University

Jeffrey L. Brudney
University of Georgia

J. Vincent Buck
California State University, Fullerton

Gregory A. Caldeira
University of Iowa

David E. Camacho
Northern Arizona University

Robert Casier
Santa Barbara City College

James Chalmers
Wayne State University

John Chubb
Stanford University

Allan Cigler
University of Kansas

Stanley Clark
California State University, Bakersfield

Ronald Claunch
Stephen F. Austin State University

Guy C. Clifford
Bridgewater State College

Gary Copeland
University of Oklahoma

Ruth A. Corbett
Chabot College

W. Douglas Costain
University of Colorado at Boulder

Cornelius P. Cotter
University of Wisconsin–Milwaukee

James L. Danielson
Minnesota State University, Moorhead

Christine L. Day
University of New Orleans

David A. Deese
Boston College

Victor D'Lugin
University of Florida

Douglas C. Dow
University of Texas at Dallas

Art English
University of Arkansas

Tim Fackler
University of Texas, Austin

Dennis Falcon
Cerritos Community College

Henry Fearnley
College of Marin

Elizabeth Flores
Del Mar College

Patricia S. Florestano
University of Maryland

Richard Foglesong
Rollins College

Steve Frank
St. Cloud State University

Mitchel Gerber
Hofstra University

Dana K. Glencross
Oklahoma City Community College

Dorith Grant-Wisdom
Howard University

Paul Gronke
Duke University

Sara A. Grove
Shippensburg University

David J. Hadley
Wabash College

Kenneth Hayes
University of Maine

Ronald Hedlund
University of Wisconsin–Milwaukee

Richard Heil
Fort Hays State University

Beth Henschen
The Institute for Community and Regional Development, Eastern Michigan University

Marjorie Randon Hershey
Indiana University

Roberta Herzberg
Indiana University

Jack E. Holmes
Hope College

Peter Howse
American River College

Ronald J. Hrebenar
University of Utah

James B. Johnson
University of Nebraska at Omaha

William R. Keech
Carnegie Mellon University

Scott Keeter
Virginia Commonwealth University

Sarah W. Keidan
*Oakland Community College
(Michigan)*

Linda Camp Keith
Collin County Community College

Beat Kernen
Southwest Missouri State University

Haroon Khan
Henderson State University

Dwight Kiel
Central Florida University

Nancy Pearson Kinney
Washtenaw Community College

Vance Krites
Indiana University of Pennsylvania

Clyde Kuhn
*California State University,
Sacramento*

Jack Lampe
Southwest Texas Junior College

Brad Lockerbie
University of Georgia

Joseph Losco
Ball State University

Philip Loy
Taylor University

Stan Luger
University of Northern Colorado

David Madlock
University of Memphis

Michael Maggiotto
University of South Carolina

Edward S. Malecki
*California State University,
Los Angeles*

Michael Margolis
*University of Cincinnati–McMicken
College of Arts and Sciences*

Thomas R. Marshall
University of Texas at Arlington

Janet Martin
Bowdoin College

Steve J. Mazurana
*University of Northern
Colorado*

Wayne McIntosh
University of Maryland

David McLaughlin
*Northwest Missouri State
University*

Don Melton
Arapahoe Community College

Dana Morales
Montgomery College

Jim Morrow
Tulsa Junior College

David Moskowitz
*The University of North Carolina,
Charlotte*

William Mugleston
Mountain View College

William Murin
University of Wisconsin–Parkside

David A. Nordquest
Pennsylvania State University, Erie

Bruce Odom
Trinity Valley Community College

Laura Katz Olson
Lehigh University

Bruce Oppenheimer
University of Houston

Richard Pacelle
Indiana University

William J. Parente
University of Scranton

Tony Payan
University of Texas, El Paso

Robert Pecorella
St. John's University

James Perkins
San Antonio College

Denny E. Pilant
Southwest Missouri State University

Curtis Reithel
University of Wisconsin–La Crosse

Russell Renka
Southeast Missouri State University

Chester D. Rhoan
Chabot College

Michael J. Rich
Emory University

Richard S. Rich
Virginia Tech

Ronald I. Rubin
*Borough of Manhattan Community
College, CUNY*

Gilbert K. St. Clair
University of New Mexico

Barbara Salmore
Drew University

Todd M. Schaefer
Central Washington University

Denise Scheberle
University of Wisconsin–Green Bay

Paul R. Schulman
Mills College

William A. Schultze
San Diego State University

Thomas Sevener
Santa Rosa Junior College

Kenneth S. Sherrill
Hunter College

Sanford R. Silverburg
Catawba College

Mark Silverstein
Boston University

Charles Sohner
El Camino College

Robert J. Spitzer
SUNY Cortland

Terry Spurlock
*Trinity Valley Community
College*

Candy Stevens Smith
Texarkana College

Dale Story
University of Texas at Arlington

Nicholas Strinkowski
Clark College

Neal Tate
University of North Texas

James A. Thurber
The American University

Ronnie Tucker
Shippensburg University

Eric M. Uslaner
University of Maryland

Lawson Veasey
Jacksonville State University

Charles E. Walcott
Virginia Tech

Richard J. Waldman
University of Maryland

Thomas G. Walker
Emory University

Benjamin Walter
Vanderbilt University

Shirley Ann Warshaw
Gettysburg College

Gary D. Wekkin
University of Central Arkansas

Jonathan West
University of Miami

John Winkle
University of Mississippi

Clifford Wirth
University of New Hampshire

Ann Wynia
*North Hennepin Community
College*

Jerry L. Yeric
University of North Texas

Finally, we want to thank the many people at Houghton Mifflin who helped make this edition a reality. There's not enough room here to list all the individuals who helped us with the previous eight editions, so we say a collective thank you for the superb work you did on *The Challenge of Democracy*. Traci Mueller, senior sponsoring editor at Houghton Mifflin, was new to this edition but quickly became an enthusiastic champion of our book. Senior development editor Lisa Kalner Williams had day-to-day responsibility for this project and was a model of professionalism in the way she managed unruly authors, unrealistic deadlines, and mangled prose. Senior project editor Christina Horn worked with us again on the Update Edition and was the creative force on the art and style facets of the book. Thanks, too, to marketing manager Edwin Hill and the sales representatives who do such a terrific job of bringing each new edition of *The Challenge of Democracy* to the attention of those who might use it.

Others who made important contributions to the Update Edition are Lisa Ciccolo, senior media producer; Peter Schott, web project manager; Martha Shethar, photo researcher; Janet Theurer, designer and art editor; Susan Zorn, copyeditor; Linda McLatchie and Angela Morrison, proofreaders; and Carrie Parker and Anne Finley, editorial assistants.

K.J. J.B. J.G.

1 Freedom, Order, or Equality?

(© Douglas Kirkland/Corbis)

Online Study Center
This icon will direct you to resources
and activities on the website
college.hmco.com/pic/jandaupdate9e

"I have no greater responsibility than to protect our people, our freedom, and our way of life," declared President George W. Bush in his radio address of December 17, 2005. Later in the address, Bush disclosed having "authorized the National Security Agency, consistent with U.S. law and the Constitution, to intercept the international communications of people with known links to Al Qaeda and related terrorist organizations."

President Bush was responding to a front-page story the previous day in the *New York Times*, which described his action differently: "Months after the Sept. 11 attacks, President Bush secretly authorized the National Security Agency to eavesdrop on Americans and others inside the United States to search for evidence of terrorist activity without the court-approved warrants ordinarily required for domestic spying."[1]

According to the Foreign Intelligence Surveillance Act of 1978, the government must obtain search warrants from a special court prior to eavesdropping on people suspected to be enemies of the state. Based in Washington, the Foreign Intelligence Surveillance Court continually reviews requests for warrants and rarely turns any down. The court's annual summaries show that it received 10,617 requests from 1995 to 2004 and approved all but 4. In 2004 alone, it had 1,758 requests for warrants and "did not deny, in whole or in part, any application submitted by the government."[2] Moreover, in an emergency the government can initiate electronic surveillance immediately and obtain a warrant up to seventy-two hours later.

President Bush's acknowledgment that he authorized electronic surveillance without warrants sparked debate about whether the president had exceeded his authority—if in fact he broke the law. Concern came not only from Democrats but also from Republicans who favor limited government. David Keene, chair of the American Conservative Union, viewed the spy program as "presidential overreaching." Conservative columnist George Will wrote that conservatives lose their "wholesome wariness of presidential power" when their people hold the office of president. Some Republican members of the House and Senate spoke out against "big brother" electronic snooping and called for congressional hearings. More revelations about the scope of government surveillance soon followed: the major telephone providers (AT&T, Verizon) regularly cooperated on wholesale government wiretapping; the FBI after 9/11 monitored activities of activist groups like People for the Ethical Treatment of Animals (PETA) and Greenpeace; and the government eavesdropped on some purely domestic phone calls, not just international calls.[3] Less than a week after the president's radio address, one of the eleven judges on the Surveillance Court even resigned in protest.

In his radio address, President Bush stressed that because we confront a global threat in the war on terrorism, we need "to uncover links between terrorists here at home and terrorists abroad." He defended the government surveillance program as "a vital tool in our war against the terrorists," saying, "The American people expect me to do everything in my power under our laws and Constitution to protect them and their civil liberties." Bush's critics—on the left and on the right—charged that he infringed too much on people's civil liberties in pursuing his vow to protect them from terrorism. Did he? It is not an easy question to answer. ★

Our main interest in this text is the purpose, value, and operation of government as practiced in the United States. As President Bush noted, however, we face a global threat and live in an era of **globalization**—a term for the increasing interdependence of citizens and nations across the world. So we must also consider the political, economic, and even social policies of other nations as they affect us and we them.

We probe the relationship between individual freedoms and personal security, as well as how government ensures security by making and enforcing laws to establish order. We also examine the relationship between individual freedom and social equality as reflected in government policies, which often confront underlying dilemmas such as these:

Which is better: to live under a government that fiercely protects individual freedom or under one that infringes on freedom while fiercely guarding against threats to public security? *Which is better:* to let all citizens keep the same share of their income or to tax wealthier people at a higher rate to fund programs for poorer people? These questions pose dilemmas tied to opposing political philosophies that place different values on freedom, order, and equality.

This book explains American government and politics in light of these dilemmas. It does more than explain the workings of our government; it encourages you to think about what government should—and should not—do. And it judges the American government against democratic ideals, encouraging you to think about how government should make its decisions. As its title implies, *The Challenge of Democracy* argues that good government often involves difficult choices.

College students often say that American government and politics are hard to understand. In fact, many people voice the same complaint. More than 60 percent of a national sample interviewed after the 2000 presidential election agreed with the statement "Politics and government seem so complicated that a person like me can't understand what's going on."[4] We hope to improve your understanding of "what's going on" by analyzing the norms, or values, that people use to judge political events. Our purpose is not to preach what people ought to favor in making policy decisions; it is to teach what values are at stake.

Teaching without preaching is not easy; no one can completely exclude personal values from political analysis. But our approach minimizes the problem by concentrating on the dilemmas that confront governments when they are forced to choose between important policies that threaten equally cherished values, such as freedom of speech and personal security.

A prominent scholar defined "politics" as "the authoritative allocation of values for a society."[5] Every government policy reflects a choice between conflicting values. All government policies reinforce certain values (norms) at the expense of others. We want you to interpret policy issues (for example, should assisted suicide go unpunished?) with an understanding of the fundamental values in question (freedom of action versus order and protection of life) and the broader political context (liberal or conservative politics).

By looking beyond the specifics to the underlying normative principles, you should be able to make more sense out of politics. Our framework for analysis does not encompass all the complexities of American government, but it should help your knowledge grow by improving your comprehension of political information. We begin by considering the basic purposes of government. In short, why do we need it?

IN OUR OWN WORDS

Listen to Kenneth Janda discuss the main points and themes of this chapter.

Online Study Center
Improve Your Grade

globalization The increasing interdependence of citizens and nations across the world.

⭐ The Globalization of American Government

Most people do not like being told what to do. Fewer still like being coerced into acting a certain way. Yet billions of people in countries across the world willingly submit to the coercive power of government. They accept laws that state on which side of the road to drive, how many wives (or husbands) they can have, what constitutes a contract, how to dispose of human waste—and how much they must pay to support the government that makes these coercive laws. In the first half of the twentieth century, people thought of government mainly in territorial terms. Indeed, a standard definition of **government** was the legitimate use of force—including firearms, imprisonment, and execution—within specified geographical boundaries to control human behavior. Since the Peace of Westphalia in 1648 ended the Thirty Years' War in Europe, international relations and diplomacy have been based on the principle of national sovereignty, defined as "a political entity's externally recognized right to exercise final authority over its affairs."[6] Simply put, **national sovereignty** means that each national government has the right to govern its people as it wishes, without interference from other nations.

Some scholars argued strongly early in the twentieth century that a body of international law controlled the actions of supposedly sovereign nations, but their argument was essentially theoretical.[7] In the practice of international relations, there was no sovereign power over nations. Each enjoyed complete independence to govern its territory without interference from other nations. Although the League of Nations and later the United Nations were supposed to introduce supranational order into the world, even these international organizations explicitly respected national sovereignty as the guiding principle of international relations. The U.N. Charter, Article 2.1, states: "The Organization is based on the principle of the sovereign equality of all its Members."

As we enter into a world of increasing globalization in the twenty-first century, human rights weigh more heavily in international politics. Consider what Kofi Annan, then secretary general of the United Nations, said in support of NATO airstrikes against Serbian forces to stop the ethnic cleansing in Kosovo in 1999. In a speech to the U.N. Commission on Human Rights, he warned rogue nations that they could no longer "hide" behind the U.N. Charter. He said that the protection of human rights must "take precedence over concerns of state sovereignty."[8]

The world's new concern with human rights is not limited to rogue nations; all nations are grappling with international law. In late 2000, the Japanese government admitted violating a 1907 Hague Convention on prisoners' rights in wartime and gave a cash settlement to survivors of one thousand Chinese prisoners forced to work under harsh conditions in World War II, the first time that Japan awarded compensation for a violation of international law.[9] National laws in Europe are increasingly being brought into line with laws of the European Union. For example, rulings of the European Court of Human Rights in 1999 led Britain to end its ban on gay men and women in the military.[10]

Our government, you might be surprised to learn, is worried about this trend of holding nations accountable to international law. In fact, in 2002, the United States "annulled" its signature to the 1998 treaty to create an International Criminal Court that would define and try crimes against humanity.[11] Why would the United States oppose such an international court? One reason

> **? Can you explain why . . .**
> the United States might oppose an International Criminal Court?

government The legitimate use of force to control human behavior; also, the organization or agency authorized to exercise that force.

national sovereignty "A political entity's externally recognized right to exercise final authority over its affairs."

Sealand Website
The Principality of Sealand is perched on a World War II military platform approximately six miles off the southeastern coast of England. Located in international waters, the platform was acquired in 1967 by Paddy Roy Bates, a retired British officer who declared it a sovereign nation and lived there with his family for decades. In 2000, he leased it to an Internet firm, HavenCo <http://www.havenco.com>, which is headed by an American citizen. HavenCo claims "unsurpassed physical security from the world, including government subpoenas and search and seizures of equipment and data." *(Leighton/ Network/Saba)*

is its concern that U.S. soldiers stationed abroad might be arrested and tried in that court.[12] Another reason is the death penalty, which has been abolished by more than half the countries in the world and all countries in the European Union. Indeed, in 1996, the International Commission of Jurists condemned the U.S. death penalty as "arbitrarily and racially discriminatory," and there is a concerted campaign across Europe to force the sovereign United States to terminate capital punishment.[13]

The United States is the world's most powerful nation, but, as the events of September 11 proved, it is not invulnerable to attack from the outside. While not the most "globalized" nation (see "Politics in a Changing World: The Globalization of Nations"), the United States is nevertheless vulnerable to erosion of its sovereignty. As the world's superpower, should the United States be above international law if its sovereignty is threatened by nations that don't share *our* values? What action should the United States follow if this situation occurs?

Although this text is about American national government, it recognizes the growing impact of international politics and world opinion on U.S. politics. The Cold War era, of course, had a profound effect on domestic politics because the nation spent heavily on the military and restricted trading with communist countries. Now, we are closely tied through trade to former enemies (we now import more goods from communist China than from France and Britain combined) and thoroughly embedded in a worldwide economic, social, and political network. (See Chapter 20, "Global Policy," for an extended treatment of the economic and social dimensions of globalization.) More than ever before, we must discuss American politics while casting an eye abroad to see how foreign affairs affect our government and how American politics affects government in other nations.

IDEAlog.org
Our IDEAlog.org self-test poses twenty questions about political values seen in Figure 1.2. One of the questions in the IDEAlog self-test is about imposing the death penalty. Take the quiz and see how you respond.

Politics in a Changing World

The Globalization of Nations

The text presents a working definition of *globalization* as "the increasing interdependence of citizens and nations across the world." But citizens and nations differ in their degree of global interdependence. Scholars measure the extent of globalization in different nations by combining various indicators of personal contact across national borders, international financial transactions, and use of international communication through technology. Here is a ranking of the "global top twenty" according to a recent study. Nations were scored on the basis of four sets of indicators: (1) *Economic integration* combines data on trade and foreign direct investment inflows and outflows. (2) *Personal contact* tracks international travel and tourism, international telephone traffic, and cross-border remittances and personal transfers (including worker remittances, compensation to employees, and other person-to-person and nongovernmental transfers). (3) *Technological connectivity* counts the number of Internet users, Internet hosts,

and secure servers through which encrypted transactions are carried out. (4) *Political engagement* includes each country's memberships in a variety of representative international organizations, personnel and financial contributions to U.N. peace-keeping missions, ratification of selected multilateral treaties, and amounts of governmental transfer payments and receipts. According to these measures, three other nations are more globalized than the United States. Singapore, an island-state in the South China Sea centered on shipping, heads the list. Ireland, which hosts many international companies like Microsoft and Intel, also ranks higher than the United States, as does Switzerland in the middle of Europe. Relative to other globalized nations, Americans have little economic integration with other countries. Of course, the large population of the United States contributes to its domestic self-sufficiency, but the process of globalization seems inevitable.

★ The Purposes of Government

Governments at any level require citizens to surrender some freedom as part of being governed. Although some governments minimize their infringements on personal freedom, no government has as a goal the maximization of personal freedom. Governments exist to control; *to govern* means "to control." Why do people surrender their freedom to this control? To obtain the benefits of government. Throughout history, government has served two major purposes: maintaining order (preserving life and protecting property) and providing public goods. More recently, some governments have pursued a third purpose, promoting equality, which is more controversial.

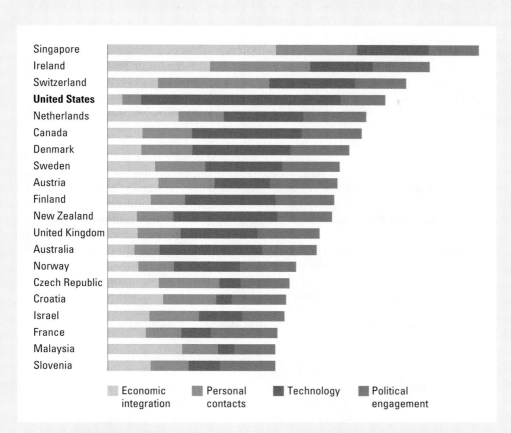

Economic integration | Personal contacts | Technology | Political engagement

Source: Adapted from A. T. Kearney, "Measuring Globalization," *Foreign Policy*, May–June 2005, p. 52. Copyright 2005, A. T. Kearney, Inc. and the Carnegie Endowment for International Peace. All rights reserved. A. T. Kearney is a registered service mark of A. T. Kearney, Inc. Foreign Policy is a trademark of the Carnegie Endowment for International Peace.

Maintaining Order

Maintaining order is the oldest objective of government. **Order** in this context is rich with meaning. Let's start with "law and order." Maintaining order in this sense means establishing the rule of law to preserve life and protect property. To the seventeenth-century English philosopher Thomas Hobbes (1588–1679), preserving life was the most important function of government. In his classic philosophical treatise, *Leviathan* (1651), Hobbes described life without government as life in a "state of nature." Without rules, people would live as predators do, stealing and killing for their personal benefit. In Hobbes's classic phrase, life in a state of nature would be "solitary, poor, nasty, brutish, and short." He believed that a single ruler, or sovereign, must possess unquestioned authority to guarantee the safety of the weak, to protect them from the attacks of the strong. Hobbes named his all-powerful government "Leviathan," after a biblical sea monster. He believed that complete obedience to Leviathan's strict laws was a small price to pay for the security of living in a civil society.

order The rule of law to preserve life and protect property. Maintaining order is the oldest purpose of government.

Most of us can only imagine what a state of nature would be like. But in some parts of the world, whole nations have experienced lawlessness. It occurred in Liberia in 2003, when both rebel and government forces, consisting largely of teenage and preteen children, plunged the country into chaos before international forces restored a semblance of order. However, international forces did not end the lawlessness in the Darfur region of Sudan, where many thousands fled before armed militias or were killed over a period of three years starting in 2003. Throughout history, authoritarian rulers have used people's fear of civil disorder to justify taking power. Ironically, the ruling group itself—whether monarchy, aristocracy, or political party—then became known as the *established order.*

Hobbes's conception of life in the cruel state of nature led him to view government primarily as a means of guaranteeing people's survival. Other theorists, taking survival for granted, believed that government protects order by preserving private property (goods and land owned by individuals). Foremost among them was John Locke (1632–1704), an English philosopher. In *Two Treatises on Government* (1690), he wrote that the protection of life, liberty, and property was the basic objective of government. His thinking strongly influenced the Declaration of Independence; it is reflected in the Declaration's famous phrase identifying "Life, Liberty, and the Pursuit of Happiness" as "unalienable Rights" of citizens under government. Locke's defense of property rights became linked with safeguards for individual liberties in the doctrine of **liberalism,** which holds that the state should leave citizens free to further their individual pursuits.[14]

Not everyone believes that the protection of private property is a valid objective of government. The German philosopher Karl Marx (1818–1883) rejected the private ownership of property used in the production of goods or services. Marx's ideas form the basis of **communism,** a complex theory that gives ownership of all land and productive facilities to the people—in effect, to the government. In line with communist theory, the 1977 constitution of the former Soviet Union declared that the nation's land, minerals, waters, and forests "are the exclusive property of the state." In addition, "The state owns the basic means of production in industry, construction, and agriculture; means of transport and communication; the banks, the property of state-run trade organizations and public utilities, and other state-run undertakings." Years after the Soviet Union collapsed, the Russian public remains deeply split over abandoning the old communist-era policies to permit the private ownership of land. Even outside the formerly communist societies, the extent to which government protects private property is a political issue that forms the basis of much ideological debate.

Providing Public Goods

After governments have established basic order, they can pursue other ends. Using their coercive powers, they can tax citizens to raise money to spend on **public goods,** which are benefits and services that are available to everyone, such as education, sanitation, and parks. Public goods benefit all citizens but are not likely to be produced by the voluntary acts of individuals. The government of ancient Rome, for example, built aqueducts to carry fresh water from the mountains to the city. Road building was another public good provided by

liberalism The belief that states should leave individuals free to follow their individual pursuits. Note that this differs from the definition of *liberal* later in the chapter.

communism A political system in which, in theory, ownership of all land and productive facilities is in the hands of the people, and all goods are equally shared. The production and distribution of goods are controlled by an authoritarian government.

public goods Benefits and services, such as parks and sanitation, that benefit all citizens but are not likely to be produced voluntarily by individuals.

freedom in this sense means immunity from discrimination, you can see that it comes close to the concept of equality.[16] In this book, we avoid using *freedom* to mean "freedom from"; for this sense, we simply use *equality*. When we use *freedom*, we mean "freedom of."

Order

When *order* is viewed in the narrow sense of preserving life and protecting property, most citizens would concede the importance of maintaining order and thereby grant the need for government. For example, "domestic Tranquility" (order) is cited in the preamble to the Constitution. However, when *order* is viewed in the broader sense of preserving the social order, people are more likely to argue that maintaining order is not a legitimate function of government (see "Compared with What? The Importance of Order and Freedom in Other Nations"). *Social order* refers to established patterns of authority in society and to traditional modes of behavior. It is the accepted way of doing things. The prevailing social order prescribes behavior in many different areas: how students should dress in school (neatly, no purple hair) and behave toward their teachers (respectfully); who is allowed to marry (single adults of opposite sexes); what the press should not publish (sexually explicit photographs); and what the proper attitude toward religion and country should be (reverential). It is important to remember that the social order can change. Today, perfectly respectable men and women wear bathing suits that would have caused a scandal a century ago.

A government can protect the established order by using its **police power**—its authority to safeguard residents' safety, health, welfare, and morals. The extent to which government should use this authority is a topic of ongoing debate in the United States and is constantly being redefined by the courts. In the 1980s, many states used their police powers to pass legislation that banned smoking in public places. In the 1990s, a hot issue was whether government should control the dissemination of pornography on the Internet. After September 11, 2001, new laws were passed increasing government's power to investigate suspicious activities by foreign nationals in order to deter terrorism. Despite their desire to be safe from further attacks, some citizens feared the erosion of their civil liberties. Living in a police state—a government that uses its power to regulate nearly all aspects of behavior—might maximize safety, but at a considerable loss of personal freedom.

Most governments are inherently conservative; they tend to resist social change. But some governments intend to restructure the social order. Social change is most dramatic when a government is overthrown through force and replaced. This can occur through an internal revolution or a "regime change" effected externally. Societies can also work to change social patterns more gradually through the legal process. Our use of the term *order* in this book encompasses all three aspects: preserving life, protecting property, and maintaining traditional patterns of social relationships.

Equality

As with *freedom* and *order, equality* is used in different senses, to support different causes. **Political equality** in elections is easy to define: each citizen has one and only one vote. This basic concept is central to democratic theory, a

police power The authority of a government to maintain order and safeguard citizens' health, morals, safety, and welfare.

political equality Equality in political decision making: one vote per person, with all votes counted equally.

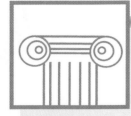

The Four Freedoms

Norman Rockwell became famous in the 1940s for the humorous, homespun covers he painted for the *Saturday Evening Post,* a weekly magazine. Inspired by an address to Congress in which President Roosevelt outlined his goals for world civilization, Rockwell painted *The Four Freedoms,* which were reproduced in the *Post* during February and March 1943. Their immense popularity led the government to print posters of the illustrations for the Treasury Department's war bond drive.

The Office of War Information also reproduced *The Four Freedoms* and circulated the posters in schools, clubhouses, railroad stations, post offices, and other public buildings. Officials even had copies circulated on the European front to remind soldiers of the liberties for which they were fighting. It is said that no other paintings in the world have ever been reproduced or circulated in such vast numbers as *The Four Freedoms.*

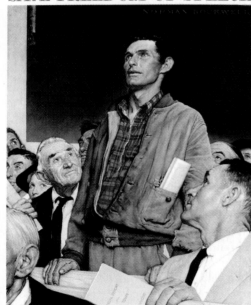

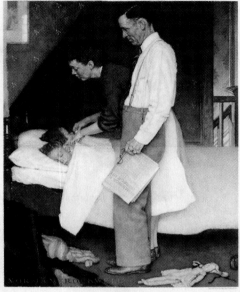

(© Swim Ink 2, LLC/Corbis)

subject explored at length in Chapter 2. But when some people advocate political equality, they mean more than one person, one vote. These people contend that an urban ghetto dweller and the chairman of the board of Microsoft are not politically equal, despite the fact that each has one vote. Through occupation or wealth, some citizens are more able than others to influence political decisions. For example, wealthy citizens can exert influence by advertising in the mass media or by contacting friends in high places. Lacking great wealth and political connections, most citizens do not have such influence. Thus, some analysts argue that equality in wealth, education, and status—that is, **social equality**—is necessary for true political equality.

There are two routes to promoting social equality: providing equal opportunities and ensuring equal outcomes. **Equality of opportunity** means that each person has the same chance to succeed in life. This idea is deeply ingrained in American culture. The U.S. Constitution prohibits titles of nobility and does not make owning property a requirement for holding public office. Public schools and libraries are free to all. For many people, the concept of social equality is satisfied by offering equal opportunities for advancement; it is not

social equality Equality in wealth, education, and status.

equality of opportunity The idea that each person is guaranteed the same chance to succeed in life.

Compared with What?

The Importance of Order and Freedom in Other Nations

Compared with citizens in twenty-nine other nations, Americans do not value order very much. The World Values Survey asked respondents to select which of four national goals was "very important":

- Maintaining order in the nation
- Giving people more say in important government decisions
- Fighting rising prices
- Protecting freedom of speech

The United States tied with New Zealand for twenty-second place in the list. While American citizens do not value government control of social behavior as much as others, Americans do value freedom of speech more highly. Citizens in only three countries favor protecting freedom of speech more than citizens in the United States.

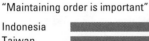

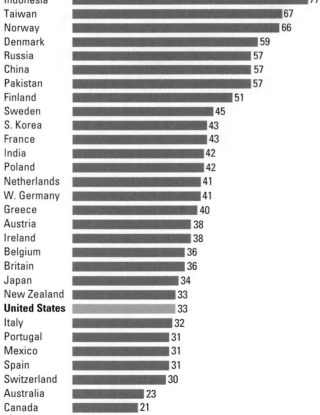

"Maintaining order is important"

Country	
Indonesia	77
Taiwan	67
Norway	66
Denmark	59
Russia	57
China	57
Pakistan	57
Finland	51
Sweden	45
S. Korea	43
France	43
India	42
Poland	42
Netherlands	41
W. Germany	41
Greece	40
Austria	38
Ireland	38
Belgium	36
Britain	36
Japan	34
New Zealand	33
United States	33
Italy	32
Portugal	31
Mexico	31
Spain	31
Switzerland	30
Australia	23
Canada	21

Percentage of respondents
who value "order"

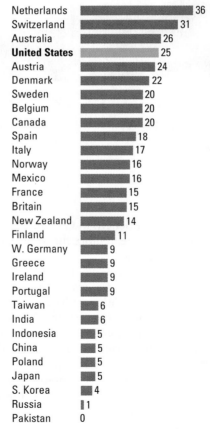

"Freedom of speech is important"

Country	
Netherlands	36
Switzerland	31
Australia	26
United States	25
Austria	24
Denmark	22
Sweden	20
Belgium	20
Canada	20
Spain	18
Italy	17
Norway	16
Mexico	16
France	15
Britain	15
New Zealand	14
Finland	11
W. Germany	9
Greece	9
Ireland	9
Portugal	9
Taiwan	6
India	6
Indonesia	5
China	5
Poland	5
Japan	5
S. Korea	4
Russia	1
Pakistan	0

Percentage of respondents
who value "freedom"

Source: World Values Survey. Most countries were surveyed around 1999–2001. These data were kindly provided by Ronald Inglehart at the University of Michigan.

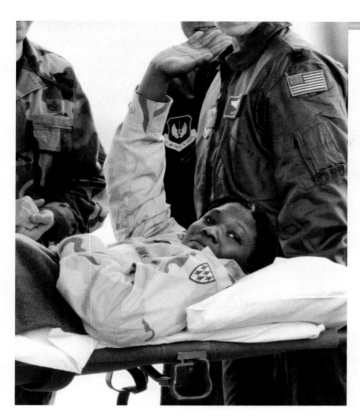

Equality in the Military
Army Specialist Shoshanna Johnson was serving in Iraq with the 507th maintenance company when her group was ambushed and captured in March 2003. Johnson and six other prisoners of war were rescued in April and flown to Germany for medical treatment. Equality for women in the military has its price: more U.S. women soldiers have died in the Iraq war than in any other war since World War II, including the more deadly Korean and Vietnam wars. *(AP/Wide World Photos)*

essential that people actually end up being equal. For others, true social equality means nothing less than **equality of outcome.**[17] President Lyndon B. Johnson expressed this view in 1965: "It is not enough just to open the gates of opportunity. . . . We seek . . . not just equality as a right and a theory but equality as a fact and equality as a result."[18] According to this outlook, it is not enough that governments provide people with equal opportunities; they must also design policies that redistribute wealth and status so that economic and social equality are actually achieved. In education, equality of outcome has led to federal laws that require comparable funding for men's and women's college sports. In business, equality of outcome has led to certain affirmative action programs to increase minority hiring and to the active recruitment of women, blacks, and Latinos to fill jobs. Equality of outcome has also produced federal laws that require employers to pay men and women equally for equal work. In recent years, the very concept of affirmative action has come under scrutiny. In 2003, however, the U.S. Supreme Court supported affirmative action in the form of preferential treatment to minorities in college admissions.

Some link equality of outcome with the concept of government-supported **rights**—the idea that every citizen is entitled to certain benefits of government, that government should guarantee its citizens adequate (if not equal) housing, employment, medical care, and income as a matter of right. If citizens are entitled to government benefits as a matter of right, government efforts to promote equality of outcome become legitimized.

Clearly, the concept of equality of outcome is quite different from that of equality of opportunity, and it requires a much greater degree of government

equality of outcome The concept that society must ensure that people are equal, and governments must design policies to redistribute wealth and status so that economic and social equality is actually achieved.

rights The benefits of government to which every citizen is entitled.

activity. It also clashes more directly with the concept of freedom. By taking from one to give to another, which is necessary for the redistribution of income and status, the government clearly creates winners and losers. The winners may believe that justice has been served by the redistribution. The losers often feel strongly that their freedom to enjoy their income and status has suffered.

★ Two Dilemmas of Government

The two major dilemmas facing American government early in the twenty-first century stem from the oldest and the newest objectives of government: maintaining order and promoting equality. Both order and equality are important social values, but government cannot pursue either without sacrificing a third important value: individual freedom. The clash between freedom and order forms the original dilemma of government; the clash between freedom and equality forms the modern dilemma of government. Although the dilemmas are different, each involves trading some amount of freedom for another value.

The Original Dilemma: Freedom Versus Order

The conflict between freedom and order originates in the very meaning of government as the legitimate use of force to control human behavior. How much freedom must a citizen surrender to government? The dilemma has occupied philosophers for hundreds of years. In the eighteenth century, the French philosopher Jean Jacques Rousseau (1712–1778) wrote that the problem of devising a proper government "is to find a form of association which will defend and protect with the whole common force the person and goods of each associate, and in which each, while uniting himself with all, may still obey himself alone, and remain free as before."[19]

The original purpose of government was to protect life and property, to make citizens safe from violence. How well is the American government doing today in providing law and order to its citizens? More than 35 percent of the respondents in a 2005 national survey said that there were areas within a mile of their home where they were "afraid to walk alone at night."[20] Simply put, Americans view crime (which had decreased before rising recently) as a critical issue and do not believe that their government adequately protects them.

Contrast the fear of crime in urban America with the sense of personal safety while walking in Moscow, Warsaw, or Prague when the old communist governments still ruled in Eastern Europe. Then—but not now—it was common to see old and young strolling late at night along the streets and in the parks of these cities. The formerly communist regimes gave their police great powers to control guns, monitor citizens' movements, and arrest and imprison suspicious people, which enabled them to do a better job of maintaining order. Police and party agents routinely kept their citizens under surveillance—eavesdropping on phone conversations, opening foreign mail—to ensure that they were not communicating privately with the capitalist world outside of official channels. Communist governments deliberately chose order over freedom. But with the collapse of communism came the end of strict social order in all communist countries. Even in China, which still claims to be communist but where the majority of people now work in the private economy, there has been an increase in crime, notably violent crime.[21]

? **Can you explain why . . .** crime rates rose in communist countries after they abandoned communism?

The crisis over acquired immune deficiency syndrome (AIDS) adds a new twist to the dilemma of freedom versus order. Some health officials believe that AIDS, for which there is no known cure, is the greatest medical threat in the history of the United States. By the end of 2005, more than 988,000 cases of AIDS had been reported to the Centers for Disease Control, and more than 550,000 of these people died.[22]

To combat the spread of the disease in the military, the Department of Defense began testing all applicants for the AIDS virus. Other government agencies have begun testing current employees. And some officials are calling for widespread mandatory testing within the private sector as well. Such programs are strongly opposed by those who believe they violate individual freedom. But those who are more afraid of the spread of AIDS than of an infringement on individual rights support aggressive government action to combat the disease.

The conflict between the values of freedom and order represents the original dilemma of government. In the abstract, people value both freedom and order; in real life, the two values inherently conflict. By definition, any policy that strengthens one value takes away from the other. The balance of freedom and order is an issue in enduring debates (whether to allow capital punishment) and contemporary challenges (whether to allow art galleries to display sexually explicit photographs). And in a democracy, policy choices hinge on how much citizens value freedom and how much they value order.

The Modern Dilemma: Freedom Versus Equality

Popular opinion has it that freedom and equality go hand in hand. In reality, the two values usually clash when governments enact policies to promote social equality. Because social equality is a relatively recent government objective, deciding between policies that promote equality at the expense of freedom, and vice versa, is the modern dilemma of politics. Consider these examples:

During the 1960s, Congress (through the Equal Pay Act) required employers to pay women and men the same rate for equal work. This legislation means that some employers are forced to pay women more than they would if their compensation policies were based on their free choice.

During the 1970s, the courts ordered the busing of schoolchildren to achieve a fair distribution of blacks and whites in public schools. This action was motivated by concern for educational equality, but it also impaired freedom of choice.

During the 1980s, some states passed legislation that went beyond the idea of equal pay for equal work to the more radical notion of pay equity—that is, equal pay for comparable work. Women had to be paid at a rate equal to men's even if they had different jobs, providing the women's jobs were of "comparable worth." For example, if the skills and responsibilities of a female nurse were found to be comparable to those of a male laboratory technician in the same hospital, the woman's salary and the man's salary would have to be the same.

During the 1990s, Congress prohibited discrimination in employment, public services, and public accommodations on the basis of physical or mental disabilities. Under the 1990 Americans with Disabilities Act, businesses with twenty-five or more employees cannot pass over an otherwise qualified disabled person in employment or promotion, and new buses and trains have to be made accessible to them.

These examples illustrate the challenge of using government power to promote equality. The clash between freedom and order is obvious, but the clash between freedom and equality is more subtle. Americans, who think of freedom and equality as complementary rather than conflicting values, often do not notice the clash. When forced to choose between the two, however, Americans are far more likely to choose freedom over equality than are people in other countries.

The conflicts among freedom, order, and equality explain a great deal of the political conflict in the United States. The conflicts also underlie the ideologies that people use to structure their understanding of politics.

★ Ideology and the Scope of Government

People hold different opinions about the merits of government policies. Sometimes their views are based on self-interest. For example, most senior citizens vociferously oppose increasing their personal contributions to Medicare, the government program that defrays medical costs for the elderly, preferring to have all citizens pay for their coverage. Policies also are judged according to individual values and beliefs. Some people hold assorted values and beliefs that produce contradictory opinions on government policies. Others organize their opinions into a **political ideology**—a consistent set of values and beliefs about the proper purpose and scope of government.

How far should government go to maintain order, provide public goods, and promote equality? In the United States (as in every other nation), citizens, scholars, and politicians have different answers. We can analyze their positions by referring to philosophies about the proper scope of government—that is, the range of its permissible activities. Imagine a continuum. At one end is the belief that government should do everything; at the other is the belief that government should not exist. These extreme ideologies, from the most government to the least government, and those that fall in between are shown in Figure 1.1.

Totalitarianism

Totalitarianism is the belief that government should have unlimited power. A totalitarian government controls all sectors of society: business, labor, education, religion, sports, the arts. A true totalitarian favors a network of laws, rules, and regulations that guides every aspect of individual behavior. The object is to produce a perfect society serving some master plan for "the common good." Totalitarianism has reached its terrifying full potential only in literature and films (for example, in George Orwell's *1984,* a novel about "Big Brother" watching everyone), but several real societies have come perilously close to "perfection." One thinks of Germany under Hitler and the Soviet Union under Stalin. Not many people openly profess totalitarianism today, but the concept is useful because it anchors one side of our continuum.

Socialism

Whereas totalitarianism refers to government in general, **socialism** pertains to government's role in the economy. Like communism, socialism is an economic system based on Marxist theory. Under socialism (and communism), the scope

political ideology A consistent set of values and beliefs about the proper purpose and scope of government.

totalitarianism A political philosophy that advocates unlimited power for the government to enable it to control all sectors of society.

socialism A form of rule in which the central government plays a strong role in regulating existing private industry and directing the economy, although it does allow some private ownership of productive capacity.

FIGURE 1.1   Ideology and the Scope of Government

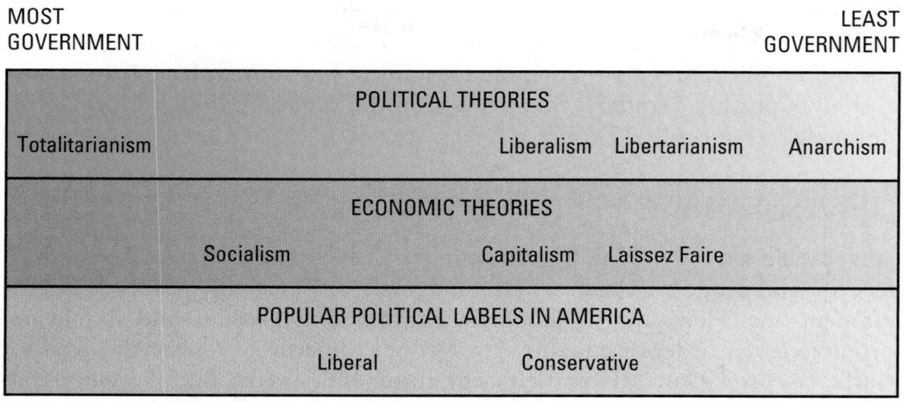

MOST
GOVERNMENT

LEAST
GOVERNMENT

POLITICAL THEORIES			
Totalitarianism	Liberalism	Libertarianism	Anarchism

ECONOMIC THEORIES		
Socialism	Capitalism	Laissez Faire

POPULAR POLITICAL LABELS IN AMERICA	
Liberal	Conservative

We can classify political ideologies according to the scope of action that people are willing to allow government in dealing with social and economic problems. In this chart, the three rows map out various philosophical positions along an underlying continuum ranging from "most" to "least" government. Notice that conventional politics in the United States spans only a narrow portion of the theoretical possibilities for government action. In popular usage, liberals favor a greater scope of government, and conservatives want a narrower scope. But over time, the traditional distinction has eroded and now oversimplifies the differences between liberals and conservatives. See Figure 1.2 for a more discriminating classification of liberals and conservatives.

of government extends to ownership or control of the basic industries that produce goods and services. These include communications, mining, heavy industry, transportation, and power. Although socialism favors a strong role for government in regulating private industry and directing the economy, it allows more room than communism does for private ownership of productive capacity. Many Americans equate socialism with the communism practiced in the old closed societies of the Soviet Union and Eastern Europe. But there is a difference. Although communism in theory was supposed to result in what Marx referred to as a "withering away" of the state, communist governments in practice tended toward totalitarianism, controlling not just economic life but both political and social life through a dominant party organization. Some socialist governments, however, practice **democratic socialism.** They guarantee civil liberties (such as freedom of speech and freedom of religion) and allow their citizens to determine the extent of the government's activity through free elections and competitive political parties. Outside the United States, socialism is not universally viewed as inherently bad. In fact, the governments of Britain, Sweden, Germany, and France, among other democracies, have at times since World War II been avowedly socialist. More recently, the formerly communist regimes of Eastern Europe have abandoned the controlling role of government in their economies in favor of elements of capitalism.

Capitalism

Capitalism also relates to the government's role in the economy. In contrast to both socialism and communism, **capitalism** supports free enterprise—private businesses operating without government regulation. Some theorists, most notably economist Milton Friedman, argue that free enterprise is necessary for free politics.[23] This argument, that the economic system of capitalism is essential to democracy, contradicts the tenets of democratic socialism. Whether it is valid depends in part on our understanding of democracy, a subject discussed in Chapter 2. The United States is decidedly a capitalist country, more so than Britain or most other Western nations. Despite the U.S. government's enormous

democratic socialism A socialist form of government that guarantees civil liberties such as freedom of speech and religion. Citizens determine the extent of government activity through free elections and competitive political parties.

capitalism The system of government that favors free enterprise (privately owned businesses operating without government regulation).

budget, it owns or operates relatively few public enterprises. For example, rail-roads, airlines, and television stations are privately owned in the United States; these businesses are frequently owned by the government in other countries. But our government does extend its authority into the economic sphere, regulating private businesses and directing the overall economy. American liberals and conservatives both embrace capitalism, but they differ on the nature and amount of government intervention in the economy that is necessary or desirable.

Libertarianism

Libertarianism opposes all government action except what is necessary to protect life and property. **Libertarians** grudgingly recognize the necessity of government but believe that it should be as limited as possible and should not promote either order or equality. For example, libertarians grant the need for traffic laws to ensure safe and efficient automobile travel. But they oppose as a restriction on individual actions laws that set a minimum drinking age, and they even oppose laws outlawing marijuana and other drugs that are illegal to possess now. Libertarians believe that social programs that provide food, clothing, and shelter are outside the proper scope of government. Helping the needy, they insist, should be a matter of individual choice. Libertarians also oppose government ownership of basic industries; in fact, they oppose any government intervention in the economy. This kind of economic policy is called **laissez faire,** a French phrase that means "let (people) do (as they please)." Such an extreme policy extends beyond the free enterprise advocated by most capitalists.

Libertarians are vocal advocates of hands-off government, in both the social and the economic spheres. Whereas those Americans who favor a broad scope of government action shun the description *socialist*, libertarians make no secret of their identity. The Libertarian Party ran candidates in every presidential election from 1972 through 2004. However, not one of these candidates won more than 1 million votes.

Do not confuse libertarians with liberals—or with liberalism, the Locke-inspired doctrine mentioned earlier. The words are similar, but their meanings are quite different. *Libertarianism* draws on *liberty* as its root (following Locke) and means "absence of governmental constraint." While both liberalism and libertarianism leave citizens free to pursue their private goals, libertarianism treats freedom as a pure goal; it's liberalism on steroids. In American political usage, *liberalism* evolved from the root word *liberal* in the sense of "freely," like a liberal serving of butter. Liberals see a positive role for government in helping the disadvantaged. Over time, *liberal* has come to mean something closer to *generous*, in the sense that liberals (but not libertarians) support government spending on social programs. Libertarians find little benefit in any government social program.

Anarchism

Anarchism stands opposite totalitarianism on the political continuum. Anarchists oppose all government in any form. As a political philosophy, anarchism values freedom above all else. Because all government involves some restriction on personal freedom (for example, forcing people to drive on one side of the

libertarianism A political ideology that is opposed to all government action except as necessary to protect life and property.

libertarians Those who are opposed to using government to promote either order or equality.

laissez faire An economic doctrine that opposes any form of government intervention in business.

anarchism A political philosophy that opposes government in any form.

Anarchists in Action
Anarchism as a philosophy views government as an unnecessary evil used by the wealthy to exploit the poor. In June 2007, scores of young anarchists were among hundreds in the streets of the German city, Rostock, protesting against the G8 summit meeting of leaders of wealthy nations in nearby Heiligendamm. *(AP Photo/Markus Schreiber)*

road), a pure anarchist would object even to traffic laws. Like totalitarianism, anarchism is not a popular philosophy, but it does have adherents on the political fringes.

Anarchists sparked street fights that disrupted meetings of the World Trade Organization (WTO) in Seattle (1999), Prague (2000), and Montreal (2003). Labor unions protested meetings of the WTO, which writes rules that govern international trade, for failing to include labor rights on its agenda; environmental groups protested for promoting economic development at the expense of the environment. But anarchists were against the WTO on *principle*—for concentrating the power of multinational corporations in a shadowy "world government." Discussing old and new forms of anarchy, Joseph Kahn said, "Nothing has revived anarchism like globalization."[24] Although anarchism is not a popular philosophy, it is not merely a theoretical category.

Liberals and Conservatives: The Narrow Middle

As shown in Figure 1.1, practical politics in the United States ranges over only the central portion of the continuum. The extreme positions—totalitarianism and anarchism—are rarely argued in public debates. And in this era of distrust of "big government," few American politicians would openly advocate socialism (although one did in 1990 and won election to Congress as an independent candidate). On the other hand, almost 150 people ran for Congress in 2004 as candidates of the Libertarian Party. Although none won, American libertarians are sufficiently vocal to be heard in the debate over the role of government.

Still, most of that debate is limited to a narrow range of political thought. On one side are people commonly called *liberals;* on the other are *conservatives.* In popular usage, liberals favor more government, conservatives less.

This distinction is clear when the issue is government spending to provide public goods. Liberals favor generous government support for education, wildlife protection, public transportation, and a whole range of social programs. Conservatives want smaller government budgets and fewer government programs. They support free enterprise and argue against government job programs, regulation of business, and legislation of working conditions and wage rates.

But in other areas, liberal and conservative ideologies are less consistent. In theory, liberals favor government activism, yet they oppose government regulation of abortion. In theory, conservatives oppose government activism, yet they support government surveillance of telephone conversations to fight terrorism. What's going on? Are American political attitudes hopelessly contradictory, or is something missing in our analysis of these ideologies today? Actually, something *is* missing. To understand the liberal and conservative stances on political issues, we must look not only at the scope of government action but also at the purpose of government action. That is, to understand a political ideology, it is necessary to understand how it incorporates the values of freedom, order, and equality.

★ American Political Ideologies and the Purpose of Government

Much of American politics revolves around the two dilemmas just described: freedom versus order and freedom versus equality. The two dilemmas do not account for all political conflict, but they help us gain insight into the workings of politics and organize the seemingly chaotic world of political events, actors, and issues.

Liberals Versus Conservatives: The New Differences

Liberals and conservatives *are* different, but their differences no longer hinge on the narrow question of the government's role in providing public goods. Liberals do favor more spending for public goods and conservatives less, but this is no longer the critical difference between them. Today, that difference stems from their attitudes toward the purpose of government. **Conservatives** support the original purpose of government: maintaining social order. They are willing to use the coercive power of the state to force citizens to be orderly. They favor firm police action, swift and severe punishment for criminals, and more laws regulating behavior. Conservatives would not stop with defining, preventing, and punishing crime, however. They tend to want to preserve traditional patterns of social relations—the domestic role of women and business owners' authority to hire whom they wish, for example. For this reason, they do not think government should impose equality.

Liberals are less likely than conservatives to want to use government power to maintain order. In general, liberals are more tolerant of alternative lifestyles—for example, homosexual behavior. Liberals do not shy away from using government coercion, but they use it for a different purpose: to promote equality. They support laws that ensure equal treatment of homosexuals in employment, housing, and education; laws that require the busing of schoolchildren to achieve racial equality; laws that force private businesses to hire and promote women and members of minority groups; laws that require public transportation to provide equal access to the disabled; and laws that order

? Can you explain why . . . conservatives might favor *more* government than liberals?

conservatives Those who are willing to use government to promote order but not equality.

liberals Those who are willing to use government to promote equality but not order.

FIGURE 1.2 Ideologies: A Two-Dimensional Framework

The four ideological types are defined by the values they favor in resolving the two major dilemmas of government: How much freedom should be sacrificed in pursuit of order and equality, respectively? Test yourself by thinking about the values that are most important to you. Which box in the figure best represents your combination of values?

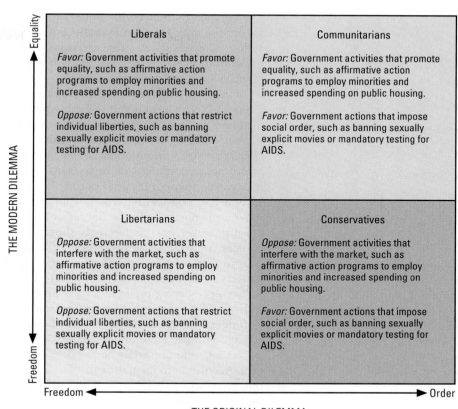

Liberals

Favor: Government activities that promote equality, such as affirmative action programs to employ minorities and increased spending on public housing.

Oppose: Government actions that restrict individual liberties, such as banning sexually explicit movies or mandatory testing for AIDS.

Communitarians

Favor: Government activities that promote equality, such as affirmative action programs to employ minorities and increased spending on public housing.

Favor: Government actions that impose social order, such as banning sexually explicit movies or mandatory testing for AIDS.

Libertarians

Oppose: Government activities that interfere with the market, such as affirmative action programs to employ minorities and increased spending on public housing.

Oppose: Government actions that restrict individual liberties, such as banning sexually explicit movies or mandatory testing for AIDS.

Conservatives

Oppose: Government activities that interfere with the market, such as affirmative action programs to employ minorities and increased spending on public housing.

Favor: Government actions that impose social order, such as banning sexually explicit movies or mandatory testing for AIDS.

THE MODERN DILEMMA · Equality · Freedom

Freedom ◄——————————————► Order

THE ORIGINAL DILEMMA

cities and states to reapportion election districts so that minority voters can elect minority candidates to public office. Conservatives do not oppose equality, but they do not value it to the extent of using the government's power to enforce equality. For liberals, the use of that power to promote equality is both valid and necessary.

A Two-Dimensional Classification of Ideologies

To classify liberal and conservative ideologies more accurately, we have to incorporate the values of freedom, order, and equality into the classification. We can do this using the model in Figure 1.2. It depicts the conflicting values along two separate dimensions, each anchored in maximum freedom at the lower left. One dimension extends horizontally from maximum freedom on the left to maximum order on the right. The other extends vertically from maximum freedom at the bottom to maximum equality at the top. Each box represents a different ideological type: libertarians, liberals, conservatives, and communitarians.[25]

Libertarians value freedom more than order or equality. (We will use this term for people who have libertarian tendencies but may not accept the whole philosophy.) In practical terms, libertarians want minimal government intervention in both the economic and the social spheres. For example, they oppose affirmative action and laws that restrict transmission of sexually explicit material.

Liberals value freedom more than order but not more than equality. Liberals oppose laws that ban sexually explicit publications but support affirmative action. Conservatives value freedom more than equality but would restrict freedom to preserve social order. Conservatives oppose affirmative action but favor laws that restrict pornography.

Finally, we arrive at the ideological type positioned at the upper right in Figure 1.2. This group values both equality and order more than freedom. Its members support both affirmative action and laws that restrict pornography. We will call this new group **communitarians.** The *Oxford English Dictionary* (1989) defines a communitarian as "a member of a community formed to put into practice communistic or socialistic theories." The term is used more narrowly in contemporary politics to reflect the philosophy of the Communitarian Network, a political movement founded by sociologist Amitai Etzioni.[26] This movement rejects both the liberal–conservative classification and the libertarian argument that "individuals should be left on their own to pursue their choices, rights, and self-interests."[27] Like liberals, Etzioni's communitarians believe that there is a role for government in helping the disadvantaged. Like conservatives, they believe that government should be used to promote moral values—preserving the family through more stringent divorce laws, protecting against AIDS through testing programs, and limiting the dissemination of pornography, for example.[28] Indeed, some observers have labeled President George W. Bush a communitarian.[29]

The Communitarian Network is not dedicated to big government, however. According to its platform, "The government should step in only to the extent that other social subsystems fail, rather than seek to replace them."[30] Nevertheless, in recognizing the collective nature of society, the network's platform clearly distinguishes its philosophy from that of libertarianism:

> It has been argued by libertarians that responsibilities are a personal matter, that individuals are to judge which responsibilities they accept as theirs. As we see it, responsibilities are anchored in community. Reflecting the diverse moral voices of their citizens, responsive communities define what is expected of people; they educate their members to accept these values; and they praise them when they do and frown upon them when they do not.[31]

Although it clearly embraces the Communitarian Network's philosophy, our definition of communitarian (small *c*) is broader and more in keeping with the dictionary definition. Thus, communitarians favor government programs that promote both order and equality, somewhat in keeping with socialist theory.[32]

By analyzing political ideologies on two dimensions rather than one, we can explain why people can seem to be liberal on one issue (favoring a broader scope of government action) and conservative on another (favoring less government action). The answer hinges on the purpose of a given government action: Which value does it promote, order or equality? According to our typology, only libertarians and communitarians are consistent in their attitude toward the scope of government activity, whatever its purpose. Libertarians value freedom so highly that they oppose most government efforts to enforce either order or equality. Communitarians (in our usage) are inclined to trade

communitarians Those who are willing to use government to promote both order and equality.

freedom for both order and equality. Liberals and conservatives, on the other hand, favor or oppose government activity depending on its purpose. As you will learn in Chapter 5, large groups of Americans fall into each of the four ideological categories. Because Americans increasingly choose four different resolutions to the original and modern dilemmas of government, the simple labels of *liberal* and *conservative* no longer describe contemporary political ideologies as well as they did in the 1930s, 1940s, and 1950s.

Summary

The challenge of democracy lies in making difficult choices—choices that inevitably bring important values into conflict. This chapter has outlined a normative framework for analyzing the policy choices that arise in the pursuit of the purposes of government.

The three major purposes of government are maintaining order, providing public goods, and promoting equality. In pursuing these objectives, every government infringes on individual freedom. But the degree of that infringement depends on the government's (and, by extension, its citizens') commitment to order and equality. What we have, then, are two dilemmas. The first—the original dilemma—centers on the conflict between freedom and order. The second—the modern dilemma—focuses on the conflict between freedom and equality.

Some people use political ideologies to help them resolve the conflicts that arise in political decision making. These ideologies define the scope and purpose of government. At opposite extremes of the continuum are totalitarianism, which supports government intervention in every aspect of society, and anarchism, which rejects government entirely. An important step back from totalitarianism is socialism. Democratic socialism, an economic system, favors government ownership of basic industries but preserves civil liberties. Capitalism, another economic system, promotes free enterprise. A significant step short of anarchism is libertarianism, which allows government to protect life and property but little else.

In the United States, the terms *liberal* and *conservative* are used to describe a narrow range toward the center of the political continuum. The usage is probably accurate when the scope of government action is being discussed. That is, liberals support a broader role for government than do conservatives.

But when both the scope and the purpose of government are considered, a different, sharper distinction emerges. Conservatives may want less government, but not at the price of maintaining order. In other words, they are willing to use the coercive power of government to impose social order. Liberals, too, are willing to use the coercive power of government, but for a different purpose—promoting equality.

It is easier to understand the differences among libertarians, liberals, conservatives, and communitarians and their views on the scope of government if the values of freedom, order, and equality are incorporated into the description of their political ideologies. Libertarians choose freedom over both order and equality. Communitarians are willing to sacrifice freedom for both order and equality. Liberals value freedom more than order, and equality more than freedom. Conservatives value order more than freedom, and freedom more than equality.

The concepts of government objectives, values, and political ideologies appear repeatedly in this book as we determine who favors what government action and why. So far, we have said little about how government should make its decisions. In Chapter 2, we complete our normative framework for evaluating American politics by examining the nature of democratic theory. There, we introduce two key concepts for analyzing how democratic governments make decisions.

2

Majoritarian or Pluralist Democracy?

(Andrew Parsons/Pool/AP/Wide World Photos)

"The survival of liberty in our land increasingly depends on the success of liberty in other lands." So said President Bush in his 2005 Inaugural Address. Accordingly, he announced, "It is the policy of the United States to seek and promote the growth of democratic movements and institutions in every nation and culture, with the ultimate goal of ending tyranny in our world."

Bush's words recalled President Woodrow Wilson's in 1917: "The world must be made safe for democracy. Its peace must be planted upon the tested foundations of political liberty." The two presidents' pronouncements differed significantly, however. Wilson asked Congress to declare war against Germany, whose submarines were sinking U.S. ships supplying Britain and France (two other democracies) fighting Germany. To Wilson, "making the world safe for democracy" meant that democracies had to fight for peace. To Bush, tyranny would end and peace would reign only if all countries became democratic.

President Bush backed up his promise with personal diplomacy. He actively promoted democracy in public statements and in meetings with political leaders from countries (especially in the Middle East) whose democratic credentials were lacking. He even lobbied leaders of the world's most populous democracy. During his 2006 visit to India, he lectured, "As a global power, India has an historic duty to support democracy around the world" and used *democracy* sixteen times in one speech.[1] The next day at a joint news conference with President Pervez Musharraf of Pakistan, a country rated "not free" by the nonpartisan group Freedom House, Bush said, "I believe democracy is Pakistan's future" (presumably not its present). In defense, Musharraf said, "Unfortunately, we are accused a lot on not moving forward on democracy." Then he explained what has been done "in line with democracy to introduce sustainable democracy in Pakistan."[2] Meanwhile, some of Musharraf's political opponents (including a member of parliament) were held in detention, rounded up before the news conference for fear of leading anti-Bush demonstrations.[3]

President Musharraf's idea of democracy appeared to differ from that practiced by most democratic nations. That leads us to the question: What *is* democratic government? ★

★ The Theory of Democratic Government

The origins of democratic theory lie in ancient Greek political thought. Greek philosophers classified governments according to the number of citizens involved in the process. Imagine a continuum running from rule by one person, through rule by a few, to rule by many.

At one extreme is an **autocracy,** in which one individual has the power to make all important decisions. The concentration of power in the hands of one person (usually a monarch) was a more common form of government in earlier historical periods, although some countries are still ruled autocratically. Iraq under Saddam Hussein was an example.

IN OUR OWN WORDS

Listen to Jeffrey Berry discuss the main points and themes of this chapter.

Online Study Center
Improve Your Grade

autocracy A system of government in which the power to govern is concentrated in the hands of one individual.

Cowboy and Indians
President Bush inspects an honor guard of Indian troops at a welcoming ceremony in New Delhi. During this recent visit, the president visited India (the world's most populous democracy) and Pakistan (rated "not free" in Freedom House's Global Survey). Bush courted India for its economic power and Pakistan for its role in fighting terrorism. He told India to work harder at promoting democracy elsewhere and exhorted Pakistan to practice democracy. *(Charles Dharapak/AP/Wide World Photos)*

Oligarchy puts government power in the hands of an elite. At one time, the nobility or the major landowners commonly ruled as an aristocracy. Today, military leaders are often the rulers in countries governed by an oligarchy.

At the other extreme of the continuum is **democracy,** which means "rule by the people." Most scholars believe that the United States, Britain, France, and other countries in Western Europe are genuine democracies. Critics contend that these countries only appear to be democracies: although they hold free elections, they are actually run by wealthy business elites, out for their own benefit. Nevertheless, most people today agree that governments should be democratic.

The Meaning and Symbolism of Democracy

Americans have a simple answer to the question "Who should govern?" It is "The people." Unfortunately, this answer is too simple. It fails to define who *the people* are. Should we include young children? Recent immigrants? Illegal aliens? This answer also fails to tell us how the people should do the governing. Should they be assembled in a stadium? Vote by mail? Choose others to govern for them? We need to take a closer look at what "government by the people" really means.

The word *democracy* originated in Greek writings around the fifth century B.C. *Demos* referred to the common people, the masses; *kratos* meant "power." The ancient Greeks were afraid of democracy—rule by rank-and-file citizens. That fear is evident in the term *demagogue*. We use that term today to refer to a politician who appeals to and often deceives the masses by manipulating their emotions and prejudices.

Many centuries after the Greeks defined democracy, the idea still carried the connotation of mob rule. When George Washington was president, opponents of a new political party disparagingly called it a *democratic* party. No one would do that in politics today. In fact, the term has become so popular that the names of more than 20 percent of the world's political parties contain some variation of the word *democracy*.[4] But although nearly all Americans (94 per-

oligarchy A system of government in which power is concentrated in the hands of a few people.

democracy A system of government in which, in theory, the people rule, either directly or indirectly.

FIGURE 2.1   Public Support for U.S. Policy of Promoting Democracy Abroad

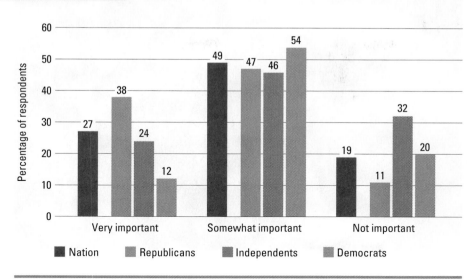

In his January 2005 Inaugural Address, President Bush said, "It is the policy of the United States to seek and promote the growth of democratic movements and institutions in every nation and culture, with the ultimate goal of ending tyranny in our world." In September 2005, respondents in the United States were asked whether they thought "helping to bring a democratic form of government to other nations" was "very important" as a foreign policy goal, "somewhat important," or "not an important goal at all." Fewer than 30 percent of respondents agreed that spreading democracy was "very important" as a foreign policy goal, and almost 20 percent thought it not important at all. Republicans were more likely to favor the goal than Democrats.

Source: PIPA/Knowledge Networks and Chicago Council on Foreign Relations Poll, "Americans on Democratization and U.S. Foreign Policy," 15–21 September 2005. Sample size of 808.

cent in a 2004 survey) regarded democracy as "the best form of government," less than 30 percent wanted the United States to promote democracy to other countries as a foreign policy goal, as President Bush proposed (see Figure 2.1).[5] Perhaps Americans value democracy but do not fully understand it or agree on what it entails.

There are two major schools of thought about what constitutes democracy. The first believes democracy is a form of government. It emphasizes the procedures that enable the people to govern: meeting to discuss issues, voting in elections, running for public office. The second sees democracy in the substance of government policies, in freedom of religion and the provision for human needs. The procedural approach focuses on how decisions are made; the substantive approach is concerned with what government does.

The Procedural View of Democracy

Procedural democratic theory sets forth principles that describe how government should make decisions. The principles address three distinct questions:

1. *Who* should participate in decision making?

2. *How much* should each participant's vote count?

3. *How many* votes are needed to reach a decision?

According to procedural democratic theory, all adults should participate in government decision making; everyone within the boundaries of the political community should be allowed to vote. If some people, such as recent immigrants, are prohibited from participating, they are excluded only for practical or political reasons. The theory of democracy itself does not exclude any adults from participation. We refer to this principle as **universal participation.**

procedural democratic theory A view of democracy as being embodied in a decision-making process that involves universal participation, political equality, majority rule, and responsiveness.

universal participation The concept that everyone in a democracy should participate in governmental decision making.

First Mopeds, Next iPods?
Some years ago citizens on picturesque Block Island, off the state of Rhode Island, were buzzed by summer vacationers riding rented mopeds. Denied by their state legislature the right to regulate moped rentals, the citizens voted in a town meeting to secede and join the neighboring state of Connecticut. The Rhode Island legislature grudgingly gave in to the rebellion and granted Block Island the right to restore peace, quiet, and public order. (© Jack Spratt/The Image Works)

How much should each participant's vote count? According to procedural theory, all votes should be counted *equally*. This is the principle of **political equality.**

Note that universal participation and political equality are two distinct principles. It is not enough for everyone to participate in a decision; all votes must carry equal weight. President Abraham Lincoln reportedly once took a vote among his cabinet members and found that they all opposed his position on an issue. He summarized the vote and the decision this way: "Seven noes, one aye—the ayes have it."[6] Everyone participated, but Lincoln's vote counted more than all the others combined. (No one ever said that presidents have to run their cabinets democratically.)

Finally, how many votes are needed to reach a decision? Procedural theory prescribes that a group should decide to do what the majority of its participants (50 percent plus one person) wants to do. This principle is called **majority rule.** (If participants divide over more than two alternatives and none receives a simple majority, the principle usually defaults to *plurality rule,* under which the group does what most participants want.)

A Complication: Direct Versus Indirect Democracy

The three principles—universal participation, political equality, and majority rule—are widely recognized as necessary for democratic decision making. Small, simple societies can meet these principles with a direct or **participatory democracy,** in which all members of the group, rather than representatives they elect to govern on their behalf, meet to make decisions, observing political equality and majority rule. The origins of participatory democracy go back to the Greek city-state, where the important decisions of government were made by the adult citizens meeting in an assembly. The people ruled themselves rather than having a small number of notables rule on their behalf. (In Athens, the people who were permitted to attend the assemblies did not include women, slaves, and those whose families had not lived there for generations. Thus, par-

political equality Equality in political decision making: one vote per person, with all votes counted equally.

majority rule The principle—basic to procedural democratic theory—that the decision of a group must reflect the preference of more than half of those participating; a simple majority.

participatory democracy A system of government where rank-and-file citizens rule themselves rather than electing representatives to govern on their behalf.

ticipation was not universal. Still, the Greek city-state represented a dramatic transformation in the theory of government.)[7]

Something close to participatory democracy is practiced in some New England towns, where rank-and-file citizens gather in a town meeting, often just once a year, to make key community decisions together. A town meeting is impractical in large cities, although some cities have incorporated participatory democracy in their decision-making processes by instituting forms of neighborhood government. For example, in Birmingham, Alabama; Dayton, Ohio; Portland, Oregon; and St. Paul, Minnesota, each area of the city is governed by a neighborhood council. The neighborhood councils have authority over zoning and land use questions, and they usually control some funds for the development of projects within their boundaries. All adult residents of a neighborhood may participate in the neighborhood council meetings, and the larger city government respects their decisions.[8] In Chicago, the school system uses participatory democracy. Each school is primarily governed by a parents' council, not by the citywide school board.

Philosopher Jean Jacques Rousseau contended that true democracy is impossible unless all citizens gather to make decisions and supervise the government. Rousseau said that decisions of government should embody the general will, and "will cannot be represented."[9] Yet in the United States and virtually all other democracies, participatory democracy is rare. Few cities have decentralized their governments and turned power over to their neighborhoods.

Participatory democracy is commonly rejected on the grounds that in large, complex societies, we need professional, full-time government officials to study problems, formulate solutions, and administer programs. Also, the assumption is that relatively few people will take part in participatory government. This, in fact, turns out to be the case. In a study of neighborhood councils in the cities mentioned above, only 16.6 percent of residents took part in at least one meeting during a two-year period.[10] In other respects, participatory democracy works rather well on the neighborhood level. Yet even if participatory democracy is appropriate for neighborhoods or small towns, how could it work for the national government? We cannot all gather at the Capitol in Washington to decide defense policy.

The framers of the U.S. Constitution were convinced that participatory democracy on the national level was undesirable and instead instituted **representative democracy.** In such a system, citizens participate in government by electing public officials to make decisions on their behalf. Elected officials are expected to represent the voters' views and interests—that is, to serve as the agents of the citizenry and to act for them.

Within the context of representative democracy, we adhere to the principles of universal participation, political equality, and majority rule to guarantee that elections are democratic. But what happens after the election? The elected representatives might not make the decisions the people would have made had they gathered for the same purpose. To account for this possibility in representative government, procedural theory provides a fourth decision-making principle: **responsiveness.** Elected representatives should respond to public opinion—what the majority of people wants. This does not mean that legislators simply cast their ballots on the basis of whether the people back home want alternative A or alternative B. Issues are not usually so straightforward. Rather, responsiveness means following the general contours of public opinion in formulating complex pieces of legislation.[11]

representative democracy A system of government where citizens elect public officials to govern on their behalf.

responsiveness A decision-making principle, necessitated by representative government, that implies that elected representatives should do what the majority of people wants.

By adding responsiveness to deal with the case of indirect democracy, we have four principles of procedural democracy:

■ Universal participation

■ Political equality

■ Majority rule

■ Government responsiveness to public opinion

The Substantive View of Democracy

According to procedural theory, the principle of responsiveness is absolute. The government should do what the majority wants, regardless of what that is. At first, this seems to be a reasonable way to protect the rights of citizens in a representative democracy. But think for a minute. Christians are the vast majority of the U.S. population. Suppose that the Christian majority backs a constitutional amendment to require Bible reading in public schools, that the amendment is passed by Congress, and that it is ratified by the states. From a strictly procedural view, the action would be democratic. But what about freedom of religion? What about the rights of minorities? To limit the government's responsiveness to public opinion, we must look outside procedural democratic theory to substantive democratic theory.

Substantive democratic theory focuses on the *substance* of government policies, not on the procedures followed in making those policies. It argues that in a democratic government, certain principles must be incorporated into government policies. Substantive theorists would reject a law that requires Bible reading in schools because it would violate a substantive principle, freedom of religion. The core of our substantive principles of democracy is embedded in the Bill of Rights and other amendments to the Constitution.

In defining the principles that underlie democratic government—and the policies of that government—most substantive theorists agree on a basic criterion: government policies should guarantee civil liberties (freedom of behavior, such as freedom of religion and freedom of expression) and civil rights (powers or privileges that government may not arbitrarily deny to individuals, such as protection against discrimination in employment and housing). According to this standard, the claim that the United States is a democracy rests on its record of ensuring its citizens these liberties and rights. (We look at how good this record is in Chapters 15 and 16.)

Agreement among substantive theorists breaks down when the discussion moves from civil rights to social rights (adequate health care, quality education, decent housing) and economic rights (private property, steady employment). They disagree most sharply on whether a government must promote social equality to qualify as a democracy. For example, must a state guarantee unemployment benefits and adequate public housing to be called democratic? Some insist that policies that promote social equality are essential to democratic government. Others restrict the requirements of substantive democracy to those policies that safeguard civil liberties and civil rights. Americans differ considerably from the citizens of most other Western democracies in their view of the government's responsibility to provide social policies. In most other Western democracies, there is much more support for the view that jobs and incomes for the unemployed are a right.[12]

IDEAlog.org
Should the government try to improve the standard of living for all poor Americans? Take IDEAlog's self-test.

substantive democratic theory The view that democracy is embodied in the substance of government policies rather than in the policymaking procedure.

A theorist's political ideology tends to explain his or her position on what democracy really requires in substantive policies. Conservative theorists have a narrow view of the scope of democratic government and a narrow view of the social and economic rights guaranteed by that government. Liberal theorists believe that a democratic government should guarantee its citizens a much broader spectrum of social and economic rights. In later chapters, we review important social and economic policies that our government has actually followed over time. Keep in mind, however, that what the government has done in the past is not necessarily a correct guide to what a democratic government should do.

Procedural Democracy Versus Substantive Democracy

The problem with the substantive view of democracy is that it does not provide clear, precise criteria that allow us to determine whether a government is democratic. It is, in fact, open to unending arguments over which government policies are truly democratic. Substantive theorists are free to promote their pet values—separation of church and state, guaranteed employment, equal rights for women—under the guise of substantive democracy.

The procedural viewpoint also has a problem. Although it presents specific criteria for democratic government, those criteria can produce undesirable social policies, such as those that prey on minorities. This clashes with **minority rights,** the idea that all citizens are entitled to certain things that cannot be denied by the majority. Opinions proliferate on what those "certain things" are, but nearly everyone in the United States would agree, for example, on freedom of religion. One way to protect minority rights is to limit the principle of majority rule—by requiring a two-thirds majority or some other extraordinary majority for decisions on certain subjects, for example. Another way is to put the issue in the Constitution, beyond the reach of majority rule.

The issue of prayer in school is a good example of the limits on majority rule. No matter how large, majorities in Congress cannot pass a law to permit organized prayer in public schools because the U.S. Supreme Court has determined that the Constitution forbids such a law. The Constitution could be changed so that it would no longer protect religious minorities, but amending the Constitution is a cumbersome process that involves extraordinary majorities. When limits such as these are put on the principle of majority rule, the minority often rules instead.

Clearly, then, procedural democracy and substantive democracy are not always compatible. In choosing one instead of the other, we are also choosing to focus on either procedures or policies. As authors of this text, we favor a compromise. On the whole, we favor the procedural conception of democracy because it more closely approaches the classical definition of democracy: "government by the people." And procedural democracy is founded on clear, well-established rules for decision making. But the theory has a serious drawback: it allows a democratic government to enact policies that can violate the substantive principles of democracy. Thus, pure procedural democracy should be diluted so that minority rights and civil liberties are guaranteed as part of the structure of government. If the compromise seems familiar, it is: the approach has been used in the course of American history to balance legitimate minority and majority interests.

? **Can you explain why . . .** theorists disagree whether political rights include basic human needs?

minority rights The benefits of government that cannot be denied to any citizens by majority decisions.

★ Institutional Models of Democracy

A small group can agree to make democratic decisions directly by using the principles of universal participation, political equality, and majority rule. But even the smallest nations have too many citizens to permit participatory democracy at the national level. (The accompanying photo shows how citizens of the smallest canton—akin to a township—in Switzerland overflow the square at their annual town meeting.) If nations want democracy, they must achieve it through some form of representative government, electing officials to make decisions.[13] Even then, democratic government is not guaranteed. Governments must have a way to determine what the people want, as well as some way to translate those wants into decisions. In other words, democratic government requires institutional mechanisms—established procedures and organizations—to translate public opinion into government policy (and thus be responsive). Elections, political parties, legislatures, and interest groups (which we discuss in later chapters) are all examples of institutional mechanisms in politics.

Some democratic theorists favor institutions that closely tie government decisions to the desires of the majority of citizens. If most citizens want laws banning the sale of pornography, the government should outlaw pornography. If citizens want more money spent on defense and less on social welfare (or vice versa), the government should act accordingly. For these theorists, the essence of democratic government is majority rule and responsiveness.

Now *That's* a Town Meeting

For almost 600 years, citizens of Appenzell Inner-Rhodes, the smallest canton (like a township) in Switzerland, have gathered in the town square on the last Sunday in April to make political decisions by raised hands. At a recent meeting, Appenzellers adopted a leash law for dogs, approved updating property files on a computer, chose a new building commissioner, and acted on other public business before adjourning until the next year. *(Marc Hutter/Appenzell)*

Other theorists place less importance on the principles of majority rule and responsiveness. They do not believe in relying heavily on mass opinion; instead, they favor institutions that allow groups of citizens to defend their interests in the public policy–making process. Health care is a good example. Everyone cares about it, but it is a complex problem with many competing issues at stake. What is critical here is to allow differing interests to participate so that all sides have the opportunity to influence policies as they are developed.

Both schools hold a procedural view of democracy, but they differ in how they interpret "government by the people." We can summarize the theoretical positions by using two alternative models of democracy. As a model, each is a hypothetical plan, a blueprint for achieving democratic government through institutional mechanisms. The majoritarian model values participation by the people in general; the pluralist model values participation by the people in groups.

The Majoritarian Model of Democracy

The **majoritarian model of democracy** relies on our intuitive, elemental notion of what is fair. It interprets "government by the people" to mean government by the *majority* of the people. The majoritarian model tries to approximate the people's role in a direct democracy within the limitations of representative government. To force the government to respond to public opinion, the majoritarian model depends on several mechanisms that allow the people to participate directly.

The popular election of government officials is the primary mechanism for democratic government in the majoritarian model. Citizens are expected to control their representatives' behavior by choosing wisely in the first place and by reelecting or voting out public officials according to their performance. Elections fulfill the first three principles of procedural democratic theory: universal participation, political equality, and majority rule. The prospect of reelection and the threat of defeat at the polls are expected to motivate public officials to meet the fourth criterion: responsiveness.

Usually we think of elections only as mechanisms for choosing among candidates for public office. Majoritarian theorists also see them as a means for deciding government policies. An election on a policy issue is called a *referendum*. When citizens circulate petitions and gather a required minimum number of signatures to put a policy question on a ballot, it is called an *initiative*. Twenty-one states allow their legislatures to put referenda before the voters and give their citizens the right to place initiatives on the ballot. Five other states provide for one mechanism or the other.[14] Sixteen states also allow for the *recall* of state officials, a means of forcing a special election for an up or down vote on a sitting governor or state judge. Like initiatives, a specified percentage of registered voters must sign a petition asking that a vote be held. If a recall election is held, a majority vote is necessary to remove the officeholder. Recalls were put into state constitutions as a safety valve to enable voters to remove an incumbent who proved to be dishonest or truly incompetent.[15] Recalls are not utilized nearly as often as initiatives or referenda but became a subject of widespread discussion when a recall petition to remove Governor Gray Davis of California received sufficient support, and a special election was called for October 2003. Davis was, in fact, recalled and movie star Arnold Schwarzenegger was elected to take his place (see "Politics in a Changing World: Too Much Direct Democracy in California?").

majoritarian model of democracy The classical theory of democracy in which government by the people is interpreted as government by the majority of the people.

Politics in a Changing World

Too Much Direct Democracy in California?

California is known for using the tools of direct democracy. In the past century, its voters have enacted hundreds of initiatives they placed on the ballot by petition. Yet since 1911, when the recall provision was put into the state's constitution, no statewide official had been recalled until October 2003, when Democrat Gray Davis was ousted from the governor's office in a special recall election. (See page 37 for the origin of the initiative petition and recall election, and Chapter 7 for thorough coverage of the referendum, initiative, and recall mechanism.)

Although Governor Davis had just won reelection in 2002, he was broadly disliked in California. The recession that gripped the country seemed to hit California especially hard. Davis was seen as unable to stop the state's downward spiral, and his handling of the state's massive $38 billion deficit riled voters. Many believed he hadn't been candid about the deficit during the 2002 campaign, and when part of the subsequent deficit reduction package was a 200 percent increase in car licensing fees, voter anger sizzled.

Even so, no recall would have occurred without the efforts of Darrell Issa, a wealthy Republican member of the House of Representatives who bankrolled the first stage of the recall. Issa hired people to collect signatures across the state for a recall election. Under California's constitution, 12 percent of those who voted in the previous gubernatorial election needed to sign. Issa's collectors obtained 1.6 million signatures, far above the minimum.

With his work done, Issa declared his candidacy for the recall election. Then the action-movie star Arnold Schwarzenegger announced—on NBC's *The Tonight Show*—that he would also run. In a tearful press conference, Issa withdrew—terminated by the "Terminator."

Schwarzenegger's celebrity candidacy as a moderate Republican was so compelling that it was hard for other candidates to gain any attention. Yet this did not stop many from trying. Unlike regular elections in California, recall elections have a very low threshold for candidates to qualify, and 135 got on the ballot. Along with Schwarzenegger and a half-dozen other serious candidates for governor of California were adult film actress Mary Carey, *Hustler* magazine publisher Larry Flynt, and former child TV star Gary Coleman.

Schwarzenegger's lack of political experience didn't seem to damage him. Here

Statewide initiatives and referenda have been used to decide a wide variety of important questions, many with national implications. Although they are instruments of majoritarian democracy, initiatives are often sponsored by interest groups that speak for a minority sector of the population and are trying to mobilize broad-based support for a particular policy.[16] States sometimes move in different directions when they vote on the same policy issue. In the 2002 election, voters in Massachusetts voted in favor of an initiative designed to end bilingual education. Voters in Colorado turned down a similar initiative there.[17]

In the United States, no provisions exist for referenda at the federal level. Some other countries do allow policy questions to be put before the public. In

was an intelligent man who had masterminded a brilliant career, first as a bodybuilder and then as a movie star, but his grasp of the issues was weak. He avoided press conferences, and his campaign speeches never reached beyond the most general of platitudes. As support for his candidacy began to swell, the campaign's momentum was broken by allegations of sexual harassment. With the strong public support of his wife, Maria Shriver (the niece of President John Kennedy and Senator Ted Kennedy), Schwarzenegger did not appear to be badly hurt by the numerous charges. In October 2003, voters approved the recall of Governor Davis 55 to 45 percent on one part of the ballot. On the other part, the replacement election, Schwarzenegger easily won with 49 percent of the vote.

Whatever Davis's failings as governor, many dispassionate observers were uneasy about the California recall. If the nation recalled every officeholder who had disappointed the electorate, there would be special elections every year. If incumbent governors were afraid of being recalled, they might not take unpopular actions in office. But unpopular policies, such as tax increases, are sometimes necessary. Moreover, the recall election was a disturbing reminder of the strong role of money in politics. The recall took place because a rich California congressman wanted to be governor and had the money to go out and hire people to gather the necessary signatures for the recall.

During his first year in office, Schwarzenegger lived up to his billing, reaching an approval rate of 69 percent. He also had some early stumbles and found himself in fights with public employee unions (especially the teachers angered over funding issues). With his approval

(Childers Michael/Corbis)

rating dropping, some wondered if Schwarzenegger's career in politics would be a short one. Yet over time his moderate, pragmatic approach to policymaking and his deal making with Democrats in the California state legislature impressed voters and observers nationwide. He ran again for governor in the regular 2006 election and walloped his Democratic opponent by close to 1.5 million votes. His vindication in the election called to mind his promise in *The Terminator:* "I'll be back."

2001, Irish voters decided to prohibit any mention of the death penalty in the country's constitution. Although the death penalty had not been used in Ireland for decades, voters apparently wanted to make sure that the government did not use existing provisions in the constitution that permitted capital punishment on matters of national security.[18]

Americans strongly favor instituting a system of national referenda. In a survey, 65 percent of those queried indicated that voters should have a direct voice on some national issues. Only 25 percent felt that we should leave all policymaking decisions to our elected representatives.[19] The most fervent advocates of majoritarian democracy would like to see modern technology used to maximize the government's responsiveness to the majority. Some have proposed incorporating public opinion polls, first used regularly in the 1930s, in government decision making. More recently, some have suggested using computers for referenda. For instance, citizens could vote on an issue by inserting plastic identification cards in computer terminals installed in all homes. But Americans are decidedly cool toward electronic democracy. Roughly two-thirds of the public don't believe that instant computer voting on referenda would improve our democratic process.[20]

The majoritarian model contends that citizens can control their government if they have adequate mechanisms for popular participation. It also assumes that citizens are knowledgeable about government and politics, that they want to participate in the political process, and that they make rational decisions in voting for their elected representatives.

Critics contend that Americans are not knowledgeable enough for majoritarian democracy to work. They point to research that shows that only 26 percent of a national sample of voters said that they "follow what's going on" in government "most of the time." More (32 percent) said that they followed politics "only now and then" or "hardly at all."[21] Two scholars who have studied citizens' interest in politics conclude that most Americans favor "stealth" democracy—like a B-2 bomber that exists but is not routinely visible.[22] They say, "The kind of government people want is one in which ordinary people do not have to get involved."[23] If most citizens feel that way, then majoritarian democracy is not viable, even with the wonders of modern information technology.

The call for enhancing majoritarian democracy through interactive electronic technology raises other concerns. Some believe that instead of quick and easy mass voting on public policy, what we need is more deliberation by citizens and their elected representatives. In this view, the government works best by depending on policymakers who immerse themselves in the substance of public policy problems.

Defenders of majoritarian democracy respond that although individual Americans may have only limited knowledge of or interest in government, the American public as a whole still has coherent and stable opinions on major policy questions. One study concluded that people "do not need large amounts of information to make rational voting choices."[24]

An Alternative Model: Pluralist Democracy

For years, political scientists struggled valiantly to reconcile the majoritarian model of democracy with polls that showed widespread ignorance of politics among the American people. When 40 to 50 percent of the adult population doesn't even bother to vote in presidential elections, our form of democracy seems to be "government by *some* of the people."

The 1950s saw the evolution of an alternative interpretation of democracy, one tailored to the limited knowledge and participation of the real electorate, not an ideal one. It was based on the concept of *pluralism*—that modern society consists of innumerable groups that share economic, religious, ethnic, or cultural interests. Often, people with similar interests organize formal groups—the Future Farmers of America, chambers of commerce, and the Rotary Club, for example. Many social groups have little contact with government, but occasionally they find themselves backing or opposing government policies. When an organized group seeks to influence government policy, it is called an **interest group.** Many interest groups regularly spend much time and money trying to influence government policy (see Chapter 10). Among them are the International Electrical Workers Union, the American Hospital Association, the Associated Milk Producers, the National Education Association, the National Association of Manufacturers, and the National Organization for Women.

The **pluralist model of democracy** interprets "government by the people" to mean government by people operating through competing interest groups. According to this model, democracy exists when many (plural) organizations operate separately from the government, press their interests on the government, and even challenge the government. Compared with majoritarian thinking, pluralist theory shifts the focus of democratic government from the mass electorate to organized groups. The criterion for democratic government changes from responsiveness to mass public opinion to responsiveness to organized groups of citizens.

The two major mechanisms in a pluralist democracy are interest groups and a decentralized structure of government that provides ready access to public officials and that is open to hearing the groups' arguments for or against government policies. In a centralized structure, decisions are made at one point: the top of the hierarchy. The few decision makers at the top are too busy to hear the claims of competing interest groups or to consider those claims in making their decisions. But a decentralized, complex government structure offers the access and openness necessary for pluralist democracy. For pluralists, the ideal system is one that divides government authority among numerous institutions with overlapping authority. Under such a system, competing interest groups have alternative points of access for presenting and arguing their claims.

Our Constitution approaches the pluralist ideal in the way it divides authority among the branches of government. When the National Association for the Advancement of Colored People (NAACP) could not get Congress to outlaw segregated schools in the South in the 1950s, it turned to the federal court system, which did what Congress would not. According to the ideal of pluralist democracy, if all opposing interests are allowed to organize and if the system can be kept open so that all substantial claims are heard, the decision will serve the diverse needs of a pluralist society.

Although many scholars have contributed to the model, pluralist democracy is most closely identified with political scientist Robert Dahl. According to Dahl, the fundamental axiom of pluralist democracy is that "instead of a single center of sovereign power there must be multiple centers of power, none of which is or can be wholly sovereign."[25] Some watchwords of pluralist democracy, therefore, are *divided authority, decentralization,* and *open access.*

On one level, pluralism is alive and well. As will be demonstrated in Chapter 10, interest groups in Washington are thriving, and the rise of many citizen groups has broadened representation beyond traditional business, labor, and professional groups.[26] But on another level, the involvement of Americans in their groups is a cause for concern.[27] Political scientist Robert Putnam has documented declining participation in a wide variety of organizations (see Figure 2.2). Americans are less inclined to be active members of civic groups like parent-teacher associations, the League of Women Voters, and the Lions Club. Civic participation is a fundamental part of American democracy because it generates the bonding or social "glue" that helps to generate trust and cooperation in the political system.[28] In short, pluralism is working well in terms of

interest group An organized group of individuals that seeks to influence public policy. Also called a *lobby.*

pluralist model of democracy An interpretation of democracy in which government by the people is taken to mean government by people operating through competing interest groups.

tifiable ruling elite usually gets its way. Not surprisingly, elite theorists reject this view. They argue that studies of decisions made on individual issues do not adequately test the influence of the power elite. Rather, they contend that much of the elite's power comes from its ability to keep issues off the political

elite theory The view that a small group of people actually makes most of the important government decisions.

FIGURE 2.2 **America the Disengaged**

Membership across a wide

agenda. That is, its power derives from its ability to keep people from questioning fundamental assumptions about American capitalism.[32]

Consequently, elite theory remains part of the debate about the nature of American government and is forcefully argued by some severe critics of our political system.[33] Although we do not believe that the scholarly evidence supports elite theory, we do recognize that contemporary American pluralism favors some segments of society over others. On one hand, the poor are chronically unorganized and are not well represented by interest groups. On the other hand, business is very well represented in the political system. As many interest group scholars who reject elite theory have documented, business is better represented than any other sector of the public. Thus, one can endorse pluralist democracy as a more accurate description than elitism in American politics without believing that all groups are equally well represented.

Elite Theory Versus Pluralist Theory

The key difference between elite and pluralist theory lies in the durability of the ruling minority. In contrast to elite theory, pluralist theory does not define government conflict in terms of a minority versus the majority; instead, it sees many different interests vying with one another in each policy area. In the management of national forests, for example, many interest groups—logging companies, recreational campers, and environmentalists, for example—have joined the political competition. They press their various viewpoints on government through representatives who are well informed about how relevant issues affect group members. According to elite theory, the financial resources of big logging companies ought to win out over the arguments of campers and environmentalists, but this does not always happen.

> **Can you explain why . . .**
> America can be considered democratic when a small group of people has much more in the way of resources and influence than the rest of us?

On Tonight's Menu, Lots of Green
Elitist critics of American government point to the advantages that the wealthy have in our political system. The campaign finance system contributes to this belief. This Washington fundraiser gives lobbyists and wealthy donors a chance to mingle with policymakers and remind them who supports them financially. *(Rob Crandall/The Image Works)*

with another type of democracy. The citizens who live in states that have the initiative and use it frequently do not demonstrate different levels of trust in government from other states.[50]

This evaluation of the pluralist nature of American democracy may not mean much to you now. But you will learn that the pluralist model makes the United States look far more democratic than the majoritarian model would. Eventually you will have to decide the answers to three questions:

1. Is the pluralist model truly an adequate expression of democracy, or is it a perversion of classical ideals, designed to portray America as democratic when it is not?

2. Does the majoritarian model result in a "better" type of democracy?

3. If so, could new mechanisms of government be devised to produce a desirable mix of majority rule and minority rights?

These questions should play in the back of your mind as you read more about the workings of American government in meeting the challenge of democracy.

Summary

Is the United States a democracy? Most scholars believe that it is. But what kind of democracy is it? The answer depends on the definition of *democracy*. Some believe democracy is procedural; they define democracy as a form of government in which the people govern through certain institutional mechanisms. Others hold to substantive theory, claiming that a government is democratic if its policies promote civil liberties and rights.

In this book, we emphasize the procedural concept of democracy, distinguishing between direct (participatory) and indirect (representative) democracy. In a participatory democracy, all citizens gather to govern themselves according to the principles of universal participation, political equality, and majority rule. In an indirect democracy, the citizens elect representatives to govern for them. If a representative government is elected mostly in accordance with the three principles just listed and also is usually responsive to public opinion, it qualifies as a democracy.

Procedural democratic theory has produced rival institutional models of democratic government. The classical majoritarian model, which depends on majority votes in elections, assumes that people are knowledgeable about government, that they want to participate in the political process, and that they carefully and rationally choose among candidates. But surveys of public opinion and behavior, and voter turnout, show that this is not the case for most Americans. The pluralist model of democracy, which depends on interest group interaction with government, was devised to accommodate these findings. It argues that democracy in a complex society requires only that government allow private interests to organize and to press their competing claims openly in the political arena. It differs from elite theory—the belief that America is run by a small group of powerful individuals—by arguing that different minorities win on different issues.

In Chapter 1, we discussed three political values: freedom, order, and equality. Here we have described two models of democracy: majoritarian and pluralist. The five concepts are critical to an understanding of American government. The values discussed in this chapter underlie the two questions with which the text began:

• Which is better: to live under a government that allows individuals complete freedom to do whatever they please, or to live under one that enforces strict law and order?

• Which is better: to let all citizens keep the same share of their income or to tax wealthier people at a higher rate to fund programs for poorer people?

The models of democracy described in this chapter lead to another question:

• Which is better: a government that is highly responsive to public opinion on all matters, or one that responds deliberately to organized groups that argue their cases effectively?

These are enduring questions, and the framers of the Constitution dealt with them too. Their struggle is the appropriate place to begin our analysis of how these competing models of democracy have animated the debate about the nature of our political process.

Internet activities and reading suggestions for this chapter are available on the *Online Study Center*

To complete the multimedia assignments for this chapter, go to AmericansGoverning.org.

3

The Constitution

(William Thomas Cain/Getty Images)

Online Study Center
This icon will direct you to resources
and activities on the website
college.hmco.com/pic/jandaupdate9e

"You are the 'Conventionists' of Europe. You therefore have the power vested in any political body: to succeed or to fail," claimed Chairman Valéry Giscard d'Estaing in his introductory speech on February, 26, 2002, to the members of the Convention on the Future of Europe. The purpose of the convention, according to Giscard d'Estaing, was for the members to "agree to propose a concept of the European Union which matches our continental dimension and the requirements of the 21st century, a concept which can bring unity to our continent and respect for its diversity." If the members succeeded, he reassured them, no doubt they would in essence write "a new chapter in the history of Europe."[1] Integrating and governing twenty-five nation-states with a total population of 500 million is, to say the least, a daunting task, especially considering that many of those nation-states at one time or another were bitter enemies.

Over two centuries earlier, on March 31, 1787, from his home at Mount Vernon, George Washington penned a letter to James Madison. "I am glad to find," Washington wrote, "that Congress have recommended to the States to appear in the Convention proposed to be holden in Philadelphia in May. I think the reasons in favor, have the preponderancy of those against the measure."[2] Roughly two months later, in May, Washington would be selected by a unanimous vote to preside over the Constitutional Convention, known then as the Federal Convention, which was charged with revising the Articles of Confederation. Acting beyond its mandate, the body produced instead a new document altogether, which remains the oldest operating constitution in the world.

The delegates to the Convention on the Future of Europe produced a constitution that met the high expectations of Chairman Giscard d'Estaing. On July 18, 2003, after toiling for over a year, members of the convention submitted to the European Council the fruits of their labors: a draft treaty to establish a constitution for Europe. The process that produced the document differed significantly from the behind-closed-doors work in Philadelphia that Washington, Madison, and the other founders toiled to complete in their day. The European convention's meetings were open to the public; its official documents were posted to a website, which received thousands of hits per month; and it solicited and received feedback from hundreds of nongovernmental organizations, leaders in business and academia, and religious groups.[3]

The hope for a European constitution collapsed in May 2005. Many substantial hurdles stood in the path of a final version. Would nations forgo their own tax, foreign, and defense policies in favor of a single European voice? Would the current unanimity voting principle be replaced with a less restrictive rule, which would have to be adopted unanimously? In a single week, France and the Netherlands, two of the European Union's founding nations, rejected the scheme by large majorities. Fifty-five percent of French voters and 62 percent of Dutch voters turned the constitution down.

The opponents, who ranged across the ideological spectrum, rallied young and old to attack the constitution.[4] The French version weighed in at nearly two hundred pages and contained more details than voters could grasp. These factors, combined with current economic and political issues, probably made the constitution an easy target.

Although the process in 1787 on one side of the Atlantic may have differed from that on the other side in 2002, the political passions that these efforts spawned were equally intense and highlight the fragility inherent in designing a constitution. And no wonder. The questions that challenged America's founders and that now confront the women and men charged with setting a future course for Europe do not have easy or obvious answers. Dr. Guenter Burghardt, head of the European Commission delegation to the United States, noted several parallels in a speech in Berlin on June 6, 2002. Today, he remarked, Europeans are asking the same kinds of questions that confronted the delegates at Philadelphia: "How can a balance be achieved in the representation of large and small states? How much power should be conferred upon the federal level and what should be the jurisdiction of the EU today? What fundamental set of values underpins political unity? Is there a European equivalent to 'life, liberty and the pursuit of happiness'?"[5] Answers remain in doubt for a unified Europe. In spite of France and the Netherlands, sixteen countries have ratified the constitution, but all twenty-seven must still agree. A new document may yet emerge, assembled from pieces of the failed effort. ★

The American experience is sure to shed light on the answers confronting Europe. In fact, the American experience may yet *presage* the European story, since Americans' first step toward unity resulted in failure and then an effort at redesign that ultimately proved successful. This chapter poses questions about the U.S. Constitution. How did it evolve? What form did it take? What values does it reflect? How can it be altered? Which model of democracy—majoritarian or pluralist—does it fit better? In these answers may lie hints of the formidable tasks facing the European Union.

IN OUR OWN WORDS

Listen to Jerry Goldman discuss the main points and themes of this chapter.

Online Study Center
Improve Your Grade

★ The Revolutionary Roots of the Constitution

The U.S. Constitution contains just 4,300 words. But those 4,300 words define the basic structure of our national government. (In contrast, the proposed European constitution was more than 60,000 words long.) A comprehensive document, the Constitution divides the national government into three branches, describes the powers of those branches and their connections, outlines the interaction between the government and the governed, and describes the relationship between the national government and the states. The Constitution makes itself the supreme law of the land and binds every government official to support it.

Most Americans revere the Constitution as political scripture. To charge that a political action is unconstitutional is akin to claiming that it is unholy. So the Constitution has taken on symbolic value that strengthens its authority as the basis of American government. Strong belief in the Constitution has led many politicians to abandon party for principle when constitutional issues are at stake. The power and symbolic value of the Constitution were forcefully

The Bloom Is Off This Rose
A constitution for the European Union was not to be. Voters in France and the Netherlands defeated the plan in 2005. German Chancellor Angela Merkel, pictured here receiving flowers from European Commission President José Manuel Barroso in 2007, had reason to smile. Merkel forged a deal with EU members on a blueprint for a treaty to replace the failed constitution. The treaty is shorter than the constitution, but contains most of its essential parts. For most member states, the treaty will be submitted for ratification to individual legislatures rather than to voters, who are often skittish about EU policy. *(Dominique Faget/ATP/Getty Images)*

demonstrated in the Watergate affair. (See the feature "Remembering Watergate and the Constitution.")

The U.S. Constitution, written in 1787 for an agricultural society huddled along the coast of a wild new land, now guides the political life of a massive urban society in the postnuclear age. The stability of the Constitution—and of the political system it created—is all the more remarkable because the Constitution itself was rooted in revolution.

The U.S. Constitution was designed to prevent anarchy by forging a union of states. To understand the values embedded in the Constitution, we must understand its historical roots. They lie in colonial America, in the revolt against British rule, and in the failure of the Articles of Confederation that governed the new nation after the Revolution.

Freedom in Colonial America

Although they were British subjects, American colonists in the eighteenth century enjoyed a degree of freedom denied most other people in the world. In Europe, ancient customs and the relics of feudalism restricted private property, compelled support for established religions, and limited access to trades and professions. In America, landowners could control and transfer their property at will. In America, there were no compulsory payments to support an established church. In America, there was no ceiling on wages, as there was in most European countries, and no guilds of exclusive professional associations. In America, colonists enjoyed almost complete freedom of speech, press, and assembly.[6]

By 1763, Britain and the colonies had reached a compromise between imperial control and colonial self-government. America's foreign affairs and overseas trade were controlled by the king and Parliament, the British legislature; the rest was left to colonial rule. But the cost of administering the colonies was substantial. The colonists needed protection from the French and their American Indian allies during the Seven Years' War (1756–1763), which was an expensive undertaking. Because Americans benefited the most from that protection, their English countrymen argued, Americans should bear the cost.

The Road to Revolution

The British believed that taxing the colonies was the obvious way to meet the costs of administering the colonies. The colonists did not agree. They especially did not want to be taxed by a distant government in which they had no representation. Nevertheless, a series of taxes (including a tax on all printed matter) was imposed on the colonies by the Crown. In each instance, public opposition was widespread and immediate.

A group of citizens—merchants, lawyers, and prosperous traders—created an intercolonial association called the Sons of Liberty. This group destroyed taxed items (identified by special stamps) and forced the official stamp distributors to resign. In October 1765, residents of Charleston, South Carolina, celebrated the forced resignation of the colony's stamp distributor by displaying a British flag with the word *Liberty* sewn across it. (They were horrified when a few months later local slaves paraded through the streets calling for "Liberty!"[7])

Women resisted the hated taxes by joining together in symbolic and practical displays of patriotism. A group of young women calling themselves the Daughters of Liberty met in public to spin homespun cloth and encourage the elimination of British cloth from colonial markets. They consumed American food and drank local herbal tea as symbols of their opposition.[8]

On the night of December 16, 1773, a group of colonists in Massachusetts reacted to a British duty on tea by organizing the Boston Tea Party. A mob boarded three ships and emptied 342 chests of that valuable substance into Boston Harbor. The act of defiance and destruction could not be ignored. "The die is now cast," wrote George III. "The Colonies must either submit or triumph."[9] In an attempt to reassert British control over its recalcitrant colonists, Parliament passed the Coercive (or "Intolerable") Acts (1774). One act imposed a blockade on Boston until the tea was paid for; another gave royal governors the power to quarter British soldiers in private American homes. The taxation issue became secondary; more important was the conflict between British demands for order and American demands for liberty. The Virginia and Massachusetts assemblies summoned a continental congress, an assembly that would speak and act for the people of all the colonies.

All the colonies except Georgia sent representatives to the First Continental Congress, which met in Philadelphia in September 1774. The objective was to restore harmony between Great Britain and the American colonies. In an effort at unity, all colonies were given the same voting power—one vote each. A leader, called the president, was elected. (The terms *president* and *congress* in American government trace their origins to the First Continental Congress.) In October, the delegates adopted a statement of rights and principles; many of these later found their way into the Declaration of Independence and the

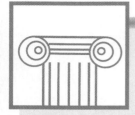

Remembering Watergate and the Constitution

The Watergate affair remains the most serious constitutional crisis since the Civil War. Yet today, two-thirds of Americans admit they don't know the basic facts.[1] It began when midnight burglars made a small mistake: they left a piece of tape over the latch they had tripped to enter the Watergate office and apartment complex in Washington, D.C. A security guard found their tampering and called the police, who surprised the burglars in the offices of the Democratic National Committee at 2:30 A.M. The arrests of the five men—four Cuban exiles and a former CIA agent—in the early hours of June 17, 1972, triggered a constitutional struggle that eventually involved the president of the United States, the Congress, and the Supreme Court.

The arrests took place a month before the 1972 Democratic National Convention. Investigative reporting by Carl Bernstein and Bob Woodward of the *Washington Post,* and a simultaneous criminal investigation by Assistant U.S. Attorney Earl J. Silbert and his staff, uncovered a link between the Watergate burglary and the forthcoming election.[2] The burglars were carrying the telephone number of another former CIA agent, who was working in the White House. At a news conference on June 22, President Richard Nixon said, "The White House has had no involvement whatsoever in this particular incident."[3]

At its convention in July, the Democratic Party nominated Senator George McGovern of South Dakota to oppose Nixon in the presidential election. McGovern tried to make the break-in at the Democratic headquarters a campaign issue, but the voters either did not understand or did not care. In November 1972, Richard Nixon was reelected president of the United States, winning forty-nine of fifty states in one of the largest electoral landslides in American history. Only then did the Watergate story unfold completely.

Two months later, seven men answered in court for the break-in. They included the five burglars and two men closely connected with the president: E. Howard Hunt (a former CIA agent and White House consultant) and G. Gordon Liddy (counsel to the Committee to Re-Elect the President, or CREEP). Five, including Hunt, entered guilty pleas. Liddy and James McCord (one of the burglars) were convicted by a jury. The Senate launched its own investigation of the matter. It set up the Select Committee on Presidential Campaign Activities, chaired by a self-styled constitutional authority, Democratic senator Sam Ervin of North Carolina.

A stunned nation watched the televised proceedings and learned that the president had secretly tape-recorded all of his conversations in the White House. (Although presidents dating to Franklin Roosevelt had tape-recorded conversations in the White House, Nixon's system for recording was by far the most comprehensive.[4]) The Ervin committee asked for the tapes. Nixon refused to produce them, citing the separation of powers between the legislative and the executive branches and claiming that "executive privilege" allowed him to withhold information from Congress.

Nixon also resisted criminal subpoenas demanding the White House tapes. Ordered by a federal court to deliver specific tapes, Nixon proposed a compromise: he would release written summaries of the taped conversations. Archibald Cox, the special prosecutor appointed by the attorney general to investigate Watergate and offenses arising from the 1972 presidential election, rejected the compromise. Nixon retaliated with the "Saturday night massacre," in which Attorney General Elliot L. Richardson and his deputy resigned, Cox was fired, and the special prosecutor's office was abolished.

The ensuing furor forced Nixon to appoint another special prosecutor, Leon Jaworski, who eventually brought indictments against Nixon's closest aides. Nixon himself was named as an unindicted co-conspirator. Both the special prosecutor and the defendants wanted the White House tapes, but Nixon continued to resist. Finally, on July 24, 1974, the Supreme Court ruled that the president had to hand over the tapes. At almost the same time, the House Judiciary Committee voted to recommend to the full House that Nixon be impeached for, or charged with, three offenses: violating his oath of office to faithfully uphold the laws, misusing and abusing executive authority and the resources of executive agencies, and defying congressional subpoenas.

The Judiciary Committee vote was decisive but far from unanimous. On August 5, however, the committee and the country finally learned the contents of the tapes released under the Supreme Court order. They revealed that Nixon had been aware of a cover-up on June 23, 1972, just six days after the break-in. He ordered the FBI, "Don't go any further in this case, period!"[5] Now even the eleven Republican members of the House Judiciary Committee, who had opposed impeachment on the first vote, were ready to vote against Nixon.

Faced with the collapse of his support and likely impeachment by the full House, Nixon resigned the presidency on August 9, 1974. Vice President Gerald Ford stepped in. Ford had become the nation's first unelected vice president in 1973 when Nixon's original vice president, Spiro Agnew, resigned amid his own personal scandal. Ford then became the first unelected president of the United States. A month later, acting within his constitutional powers, Ford granted private citizen Richard Nixon an unconditional pardon for all crimes that he may have committed. Others were not

so fortunate. Three members of the Nixon cabinet (two attorneys general and a secretary of commerce) were convicted and sentenced for their crimes in the Watergate affair. Nixon's White House chief of staff, H. R. Haldeman, and his domestic affairs adviser, John Ehrlichman, were convicted of conspiracy, obstruction of justice, and perjury. Other officials were tried, and most were convicted, on related charges.[6]

The Watergate affair posed one of the most serious challenges to the constitutional order of modern American government. The incident ultimately developed into a struggle over the rule of law, between the president, on the one hand, and Congress and the courts, on the other. In the end, the constitutional principle separating power among the executive, legislative, and judicial branches prevented the president from controlling the Watergate investigation. The principle of checks and balances allowed Congress to threaten Nixon with impeachment. The belief that Nixon had violated the Constitution finally prompted members of his own party to support impeachment, leading the president to resign. In 1992, 70 percent of Americans still viewed Nixon's actions as having warranted his resignation.[7] In some countries, an irregular change in government leadership provides an opportunity for a palace coup, an armed revolution, or a military dictatorship. But here, significantly, no political violence erupted after Nixon's resignation; in fact, none was expected. Constitutional order in the United States had been put to a test, and it passed with high honors.

1. ABC News Poll, June 17, 2002 (telephone interview of 1,004 participants).

2. Carl Bernstein and Bob Woodward, *All the President's Men* (New York: Warner, 1975); Stanley I. Kutler, *The Wars of Watergate* (New York: Knopf, 1990).

3. Bernstein and Woodward, *All the President's Men*, p. 30.

4. William Doyle, *Inside the Oval Office: The White House Tapes from FDR to Clinton* (New York: Kodansha International, 1999), p. 169.

5. *The Encyclopedia of American Facts and Dates* (New York: Crowell, 1979), p. 946.

6. Richard B. Morris (ed.), *Encyclopedia of American History* (New York: Harper & Row, 1976), p. 544.

7. Gallup Organization, *Gallup Poll Monthly* (June 1992): 2–3.

Uniquely American Protest

Americans protested the Tea Act (1773) by holding the Boston Tea Party (*background, left*) and by using a unique form of painful punishment, tarring and feathering, on the tax collector (see "STAMP ACT" upside-down on the Liberty Tree). An early treatise on the subject offered the following instructions: "First, strip a person naked, then heat the tar until it is thin, and pour upon the naked flesh, or rub it over with a tar brush. After which, sprinkle decently upon the tar, whilst it is yet warm, as many feathers as will stick to it." *(Courtesy of the John Carter Brown Library at Brown University)*

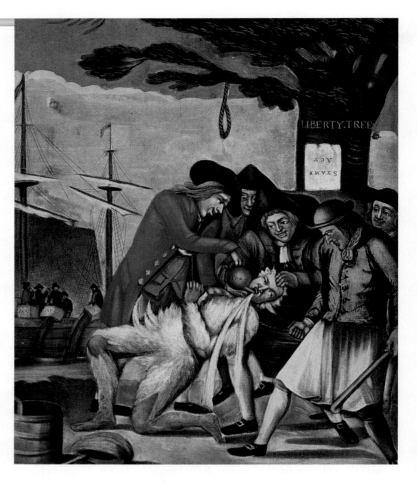

Constitution. For example, the congress claimed a right "to life, liberty, and property" and a right "peaceably to assemble, consider of their grievances, and petition the king." Then the congress adjourned, planning to reconvene in May 1775.

Revolutionary Action

By early 1775, however, a movement that the colonists themselves were calling a revolution had already begun. Colonists in Massachusetts were fighting the British at Concord and Lexington. Delegates to the Second Continental Congress, meeting in May, faced a dilemma: Should they prepare for war, or should they try to reconcile with Britain? As conditions deteriorated, the Second Continental Congress remained in session to serve as the government of the colony-states.

On June 7, 1776, owing in large part to the powerful advocacy of John Adams of Massachusetts, a strong supporter of independence, the Virginia delegation called on the Continental Congress to resolve "that these United Colonies are, and of right ought to be, free and Independent States, that they are absolved from all allegiance to the British Crown, and that all political connection between them and the State of Great Britain is, and ought to be, totally dissolved." This was a difficult decision. Independence meant disloyalty to Britain and war, death, and devastation. The congress debated but did not immediately adopt the resolution. A committee of five men was appointed to prepare a proclamation expressing the colonies' reasons for declaring independence.

The Declaration of Independence

Thomas Jefferson, a young farmer and lawyer from Virginia who was a member of the committee, became the "pen" to John Adams's "voice."[10] Because Jefferson was erudite, a Virginian, and an extremely skilled writer, he drafted the proclamation. Jefferson's document, the **Declaration of Independence,** was modestly revised by the committee and then further edited by the congress. It remains a cherished statement of our heritage, expressing simply, clearly, and rationally the many arguments for separation from Great Britain.

The principles underlying the Declaration were rooted in the writings of the English philosopher John Locke and had been expressed many times by speakers in the congress and the colonial assemblies. Locke argued that people have God-given, or natural, rights that are inalienable—that is, they cannot be taken away by any government. According to Locke, all legitimate political authority exists to preserve these natural rights and is based on the consent of those who are governed. The idea of consent is derived from **social contract theory,** which states that the people agree to establish rulers for certain purposes, but they have the right to resist or remove rulers who violate those purposes.[11]

Jefferson used similar arguments in the Declaration of Independence. (See the appendix.) Taking his cue from a draft of the Virginia Declaration of Rights,[12] Jefferson wrote,

> We hold these truths to be self-evident, that all men are created equal, that they are endowed by their Creator with certain unalienable rights, that among these are life, liberty, and the pursuit of happiness. That to secure these rights, governments are instituted among men, deriving their just powers from the consent of the governed. That whenever any form of government becomes destructive of these ends, it is the right of the people to alter or to abolish it, and to institute new government, laying its foundation on such principles, and organizing its power in such form, as to them shall seem most likely to effect their safety and happiness.

He went on to list the many deliberate acts of the king that had exceeded the legitimate role of government. The last item on Jefferson's original draft of the Declaration was the king's support of the slave trade. Although Jefferson did not condemn slavery, he denounced the king for enslaving a people, engaging in the slave trade, and proposing that the slaves be freed to be able to attack their masters. When South Carolina and Georgia, two states with an interest in continuing the wretched practice, objected, Jefferson and the committee dropped the offending paragraph. Finally, Jefferson declared that the colonies were "Free and Independent States," with no political connection to Great Britain.

The major premise of the Declaration of Independence is that the people have a right to revolt if they determine that their government is denying them their legitimate rights. The long list of the king's actions was evidence of such denial. So the people had the right to rebel, to form a new government.

Declaration of Independence Drafted by Thomas Jefferson, the document that proclaimed the right of the colonies to separate from Great Britain.

social contract theory The belief that the people agree to set up rulers for certain purposes and thus have the right to resist or remove rulers who act against those purposes.

Toppling Tyrants: Then and Now
A gilded equestrian statue of George III (*left*) once stood at the tip of Manhattan. On July 9, 1776, citizens responded to the news of the Declaration of Independence by toppling the statue. It was melted down and converted into musket balls. In 2003—with a little help from American soldiers—Iraqi citizens (*right*) toppled a statue of their deposed leader, Saddam Hussein. *(left: Lafayette College Art Collection; right: Patrick Robert/Sygma Collection/Corbis)*

On July 2, 1776, the Second Continental Congress finally voted for independence. The vote was by state, and the motion carried 11–0. (Rhode Island was not present, and the New York delegation, lacking instructions, did not cast its yea vote until July 15.) Two days later, on July 4, the Declaration of Independence was approved, with few changes. Several representatives insisted on removing language they thought would incite the colonists. In the end, even though Jefferson's compelling words were left almost exactly as he had written them, the adjustments tugged at the Virginian's personal insecurities. According to historian Joseph Ellis, while the congress debated various changes to the document, "Jefferson sat silently and sullenly, regarding each proposed revision as another defacement."[13]

By August, fifty-five revolutionaries had signed the Declaration of Independence, pledging "our lives, our fortunes and our sacred honor" in support of their rebellion against the world's most powerful nation. This was no empty pledge: an act of rebellion was treason. Had they lost the Revolutionary War, the signers would have faced a gruesome fate. The punishment for treason was hanging and drawing and quartering—the victim was first hanged until half-dead from strangulation, then disemboweled, and finally cut into four pieces while still alive. We celebrate the Fourth of July with fireworks and flag waving, parades, and picnics. We sometimes forget that the Revolution was a matter of life and death.

The war imposed an agonizing choice on colonial Catholics, who were treated with intolerance by the overwhelmingly Protestant population. No other religious group found the choice so difficult. Catholics could either join the revolutionaries, who were opposed to Catholicism, or remain loyal to England and risk new hostility and persecution. But Catholics were few in number, perhaps twenty-five thousand at the time of independence (or 1 percent of the population). Anti-Catholic revolutionaries recognized that if Catholics opposed independence in Maryland and Pennsylvania, where their numbers were greatest, victory might be jeopardized. Furthermore, enlisting the support of Catholic France for the cause of independence would be difficult in the face of strong opposition from colonial Catholics. So the revolutionaries wooed Catholics to their cause.[14]

The War of Independence lasted far longer than anyone expected. It began in a moment of confusion, when a shot rang out as British soldiers approached the town of Lexington, Massachusetts, on April 19, 1775. The end came six and a half years later with Lord Cornwallis's surrender of his six-thousand-man army at Yorktown, Virginia, on October 19, 1781. It was a costly war: a greater percentage of the population died or was wounded during the Revolution than in any other U.S. conflict except the Civil War.[15]

With hindsight, of course, we can see that the British were engaged in an arduous and perhaps hopeless conflict. America was simply too vast to subdue without imposing total military rule. Britain also had to transport men and supplies over the enormous distance of the Atlantic Ocean. Also, the Americans' courtship of Britain's rivals, owing in large part to the indefatigable advocacy and diplomacy of John Adams,[16] resulted in support from the French navy and several million dollars in Dutch loans that helped to bolster General Washington's Revolutionary forces. Finally, although the Americans had neither paid troops nor professional soldiers, they were fighting for a cause: the defense of their liberty. The British never understood the power of this fighting faith or, given the international support for the American cause, the totality of the forces arrayed against them.

> **?** **Can you explain why . . .**
> the War of Independence was one of the gravest conflicts in the United States?

★ From Revolution to Confederation

By declaring their independence from England, the colonists left themselves without any real central government. So the revolutionaries proclaimed the creation of a **republic.** Strictly speaking, a republic is a government without a monarch, but the term had come to mean a government based on the consent of the governed, whose power is exercised by representatives who are responsible to them. A republic need not be a democracy, and this was fine with the founders; at that time, democracy was associated with mob rule and instability (see Chapter 2). The revolutionaries were less concerned with determining who would control their new government than with limiting its powers. They had revolted in the name of liberty, and now they wanted a government with strictly defined powers. To make sure they got one, they meant to define its structure and powers in writing.

The Articles of Confederation

Barely a week after the Declaration of Independence was signed, the Second Continental Congress received a committee report entitled "Articles of Confederation and Perpetual Union." A **confederation** is a loose association of independent states that agree to cooperate on specified matters. In a confederation, the states retain their sovereignty, which means that each has supreme power within its borders. The central government is weak; it can only coordinate, not

republic A government without a monarch; a government rooted in the consent of the governed, whose power is exercised by elected representatives responsible to the governed.

confederation A loose association of independent states that agree to cooperate on specified matters.

Voting for Independence

The Second Continental Congress voted for independence on July 2, 1776. John Adams of Massachusetts viewed the day "as the most memorable epocha [significant event] in the history of America." In this painting by John Trumbull, the drafting committee presents the Declaration of Independence to the patriots who would later sign it. The committee, grouped in front of the desk, consisted of (*from left to right*) Adams, Roger Sherman (Connecticut), Robert Livingston (New York), Thomas Jefferson (Virginia), and Benjamin Franklin (Pennsylvania).

Trumbull painted the scene years after the event. Relying on Jefferson's faulty memory and Trumbull's own artistic license, the scene bears little resemblance to reality. First, there was no ceremonial moment when the committee presented its draft to the congress. Second, the room's elegance belied its actual appearance. Third, the doors are in the wrong place. Fourth, the heavy drapes substitute for actual venetian blinds. And, fifth, the mahogany armchairs replaced the plain Windsor design used by the delegates. Nevertheless, the painting remains an icon of American political history. (© Francis G. Mayer/Corbis)

Articles of Confederation
The compact among the thirteen original states that established the first government of the United States.

control, the actions of its sovereign states. Consequently, the individual states are strong.

The congress debated the **Articles of Confederation,** the compact among the thirteen original colonies that established the first government of the United States, for more than a year. The Articles were adopted by the Continental Congress on November 15, 1777, and finally took effect on March 1, 1781, following approval by all thirteen states. For more than three years, then, Americans had fought a revolution without an effective government. Raising money, troops, and supplies for the war had daunted and exhausted the leadership.

The Articles jealously guarded state sovereignty; their provisions clearly reflected the delegates' fears that a strong central government would resemble British rule. Article II, for example, stated, "Each state retains its sovereignty, freedom, and independence, and every power, jurisdiction, and right, which is not by this Confederation expressly delegated to the United States, in Congress assembled."

Under the Articles, each state, regardless of its size, had one vote in the congress. Votes on financing the war and other important issues required the consent of at least nine of the thirteen states. The common danger, Britain, had forced the young republic to function under the Articles, but this first effort at government was inadequate to the task. The delegates had succeeded in crafting a national government that was largely powerless.

The Articles failed for at least four reasons. First, they did not give the national government the power to tax. As a result, the congress had to plead for money from the states to pay for the war and carry on the affairs of the new nation. A government that cannot reliably raise revenue cannot expect to govern effectively. Second, the Articles made no provision for an independent leadership position to direct the government (the president was merely the presiding officer of the congress). The omission was deliberate—the colonists feared the reestablishment of a monarchy—but it left the nation without a leader. Third, the Articles did not allow the national government to regulate interstate and foreign commerce. (When John Adams proposed that the confederation enter into a commercial treaty with Britain after the war, he was asked, "Would you like one treaty or thirteen, Mr. Adams?")[17] Finally, the Articles could not be amended without the unanimous agreement of the congress and the assent of all the state legislatures; thus, each state had the power to veto any changes to the confederation.

The goal of the delegates who drew up the Articles of Confederation was to retain power in the states. This was consistent with republicanism, which viewed the remote power of a national government as a danger to liberty. In this sense alone, the Articles were a grand success. They completely hobbled the infant government.

Disorder Under the Confederation

Once the Revolution had ended and independence was a reality, it became clear that the national government had neither the economic nor the military power to function effectively. Freed from wartime austerity, Americans rushed to purchase goods from abroad. The national government's efforts to restrict foreign imports were blocked by exporting states, which feared retaliation from their foreign customers. Debt mounted and, for many, bankruptcy followed.

The problem was particularly severe in Massachusetts, where high interest rates and high state taxes were forcing farmers into bankruptcy. In 1786, Daniel Shays, a Revolutionary War veteran, marched on a western Massachusetts courthouse with fifteen hundred supporters armed with barrel staves and pitchforks: they wanted to close the courthouse to prevent the foreclosure of farms by creditors. Later, they attacked an arsenal. Called Shays's Rebellion, the revolt against the established order continued into 1787. Massachusetts appealed to the confederation for help. Horrified by the threat of domestic upheaval, the congress approved a $530,000 requisition for the establishment of a national army. But the plan failed: every state except Virginia rejected the request for money. Finally, the governor of Massachusetts called out the militia and restored order.[18]

The rebellion demonstrated the impotence of the confederation and the urgent need to suppress insurrections and maintain domestic order. Proof to skeptics that Americans could not govern themselves, the rebellion alarmed all American leaders, with the exception of Jefferson. From Paris, where he was serving as American ambassador, he remarked, "A little rebellion now and then is a good thing; the tree of liberty must be refreshed from time to time with the blood of patriots and tyrants."[19]

★ From Confederation to Constitution

O rder, the original purpose of government, was breaking down under the Articles of Confederation. The "league of friendship" envisioned in the Articles was not enough to hold the nation together in peacetime.

Some states had taken halting steps toward encouraging a change in the national government. In 1785, Massachusetts asked the congress to revise the Articles of Confederation, but the congress took no action. In 1786, Virginia invited the states to attend a convention at Annapolis, Maryland, to explore

? Can you explain why . . .
the Articles of Confederation made the states strong and the nation weak?

The Articles of Confederation are available on the

Online Study Center
General Resources

revisions aimed at improving commercial regulation. The meeting was both a failure and a success. Only five states sent delegates, but they seized the opportunity to call for another meeting—with a far broader mission—in Philadelphia the next year. That convention would be charged with devising "such further provisions as shall appear . . . necessary to render the constitution of the Federal Government adequate to the exigencies of the Union." The congress later agreed to the convention but limited its mission to "the sole and express purpose of revising the Articles of Confederation."[20]

Shays's Rebellion lent a sense of urgency to the task before the Philadelphia convention. The congress's inability to confront the rebellion was evidence that a stronger national government was necessary to preserve order and property—to protect the states from internal as well as external dangers. "While the Declaration was directed against an excess of authority," observed Supreme Court Justice Robert H. Jackson some 150 years later, "the Constitution [that followed the Articles of Confederation] was directed against anarchy."[21]

Twelve of the thirteen states named seventy-four delegates to convene in Philadelphia, the most important city in America, in May 1787. (Rhode Island, derisively renamed "Rogue Island" by a Boston newspaper, was the one exception. The state legislature sulkily rejected participating because it feared a strong national government.) Fifty-five delegates eventually showed up at the statehouse in Philadelphia, but no more than thirty were present at any one time during that sweltering spring and summer. The framers were not demigods, but many historians believe that such an assembly will not be seen again. Highly educated, they typically were fluent in Latin and Greek. Products of the Enlightenment, they relied on classical liberalism for the Constitution's philosophical underpinnings.

They were also veterans of the political intrigues of their states, and so were highly practical politicians who knew how to maneuver. Although well versed in ideas, they subscribed to the view expressed by one delegate that "experience must be our only guide, reason may mislead us."[22] Fearing for their fragile union, the delegates resolved to keep their proceedings secret.

The Constitutional Convention, at the time called the Federal Convention, officially opened on May 25. Within the first week, Edmund Randolph of Virginia had presented a long list of changes, suggested by fellow Virginian James Madison, that would replace the weak confederation of states with a powerful national government rather than revise it within its original framework. The delegates unanimously agreed to debate Randolph's proposal, called the **Virginia Plan.** Almost immediately, then, they rejected the idea of amending the Articles of Confederation, working instead to create an entirely new constitution.

The Virginia Plan

The Virginia Plan dominated the convention's deliberations for the rest of the summer, making several important proposals for a strong central government:

- That the powers of the government be divided among three separate branches: a **legislative branch,** for making laws; an **executive branch,** for enforcing laws; and a **judicial branch,** for interpreting laws.

- That the legislature consist of two houses. The first would be chosen by the people, the second by the members of the first house from among candidates nominated by the state legislatures.

Virginia Plan A set of proposals for a new government, submitted to the Constitutional Convention of 1787; included separation of the government into three branches, division of the legislature into two houses, and proportional representation in the legislature.

legislative branch The law-making branch of government.

executive branch The law-enforcing branch of government.

judicial branch The law-interpreting branch of government.

- That each state's representation in the legislature be in proportion to the taxes it paid to the national government or in proportion to its free population.

- That an executive, consisting of an unspecified number of people, be selected by the legislature and serve for a single term.

- That the national judiciary include one or more supreme courts and other, lower courts, with judges appointed for life by the legislature.

- That the executive and a number of national judges serve as a council of revision, to approve or veto (disapprove) legislative acts. Their veto could be overridden by a vote of both houses of the legislature.

- That the scope of powers of all three branches be far greater than that assigned the national government by the Articles of Confederation, and that the legislature be empowered to override state laws.

By proposing a powerful national legislature that could override state laws, the Virginia Plan clearly advocated a new form of government. It was to have a mixed structure, with more authority over the states and new authority over the people.

Madison was a monumental force in the ensuing debate on the proposals. He kept records of the proceedings that reveal his frequent and brilliant participation and give us insight into his thinking about freedom, order, and equality.

For example, his proposal that senators serve a nine-year term reveals his thinking about equality. Madison foresaw an increase "of those who will labor under all the hardships of life, and secretly sigh for a more equal distribution of its blessings. These may in time outnumber those who are placed above the feelings of indigence."[23] Power, then, could flow into the hands of the numerous poor. The stability of the senate, however, with its nine-year terms and election by the state legislatures, would provide a barrier against the "sighs of the poor" for more equality. Although most delegates shared Madison's apprehension about equality, the nine-year term was voted down.

The Constitution that emerged from the convention bore only a partial resemblance to the document Madison wanted to create. He endorsed seventy-one specific proposals, but he ended up on the losing side on forty of them.[24] And the parts of the Virginia Plan that were ultimately included in the Constitution were not adopted without challenge. Conflicts revolved primarily around the basis for representation in the legislature, the method of choosing legislators, and the structure of the executive branch.

James Madison, Father of the Constitution
Although he dismissed the accolade "Father of the Constitution," Madison deserved it more than anyone else. As do most fathers, he exercised a powerful influence in debates (and was on the losing side of more than half of them).
(© Bettmann/Corbis)

The New Jersey Plan

When in 1787 it appeared that much of the Virginia Plan would be approved by the big states, the small states united in opposition. They feared that if each state's representation in the new legislature was based only on the size of its population, the states with large populations would be able to dominate the new government and the needs and wishes of the small states would be ignored. William Paterson of New Jersey introduced an alternative set of resolutions, written to preserve the spirit of the Articles of Confederation by amending rather than replacing them. The **New Jersey Plan** included the following proposals:

New Jersey Plan Submitted by the head of the New Jersey delegation to the Constitutional Convention of 1787, a set of nine resolutions that would have, in effect, preserved the Articles of Confederation by amending rather than replacing them.

- That a single-chamber legislature have the power to raise revenue and regulate commerce.

- That the states have equal representation in the legislature and choose its members.

- That a multiperson executive be elected by the legislature, with powers similar to those proposed under the Virginia Plan but without the right to veto legislation.

- That a supreme tribunal be created, with a limited jurisdiction. (There was no provision for a system of national courts.)

- That the acts of the legislature be binding on the states—that is, that they be regarded as "the supreme law of the respective states," with the option of force to compel obedience.

The New Jersey Plan was defeated in the first major convention vote, 7–3. However, the small states had enough support to force a compromise on the issue of representation in the legislature. Table 3.1 compares the New Jersey Plan with the Virginia Plan.

The Great Compromise

The Virginia Plan provided for a two-chamber legislature, with representation in both chambers based on population. The idea of two chambers was never seriously challenged, but the idea of representation according to population stirred up heated and prolonged debate. The small states demanded equal representation for all states, but another vote rejected that concept for the House of Representatives. The debate continued. Finally, the Connecticut delegation moved that each state have an equal vote in the Senate. Still another poll showed that the delegations were equally divided on this proposal.

A committee was created to resolve the deadlock. It consisted of one delegate from each state, chosen by secret ballot. After working straight through the Independence Day recess, the committee reported reaching the **Great Compromise** (sometimes called the Connecticut Compromise). Representation in the House of Representatives would be apportioned according to the population of each state. Initially, there would be fifty-six members. Revenue-raising acts would originate in the House. Most important, the states would be represented equally in the Senate, with two senators each. Senators would be selected by their state legislatures, not directly by the people.

The delegates accepted the Great Compromise. The small states got their equal representation, the big states their proportional representation. The small states might dominate the Senate and the big states might control the House, but because all legislation had to be approved by both chambers, neither group would be able to dominate the other.

Compromise on the Presidency

Conflict replaced compromise when the delegates turned to the executive branch. They did agree on a one-person executive, a president, but they disagreed on how the executive would be selected and what the term of office would be. The delegates distrusted the people's judgment; some feared that

Great Compromise Submitted by the Connecticut delegation to the Constitutional Convention of 1787, and thus also known as the Connecticut Compromise, a plan calling for a bicameral legislature in which the House of Representatives would be apportioned according to population and the states would be represented equally in the Senate.

TABLE 3.1	Major Differences Between the Virginia Plan and the New Jersey Plan	
Characteristic	**Virginia Plan**	**New Jersey Plan**
Legislature	Two chambers	One chamber
Legislative power	Derived from the people	Derived from the states
Executive	Unspecified size	More than one person
Decision rule	Majority	Extraordinary majority
State laws	Legislature can override	National law is supreme
Executive removal	By Congress	By a majority of the states
Courts	National judiciary	No provision for national judiciary
Ratification	By the people	By the states

popular election of the president would arouse public passions. Consequently, the delegates rejected the idea. At the same time, representatives of the small states feared that election by the legislature would allow the big states to control the executive.

Once again, a committee composed of one member from each participating state was chosen to find a compromise. That committee fashioned the cumbersome presidential election system we still use today, the **electoral college.** (The Constitution does not use the expression *electoral college.*) Under this system, a group of electors would be chosen for the sole purpose of selecting the president and vice president. Each state legislature would choose a number of electors equal to the number of its representatives in Congress. Each elector would then vote for two people. The candidate with the most votes would become president, provided that the number of votes constituted a majority; the person with the next-greatest number of votes would become vice president. (The procedure was changed in 1804 by the Twelfth Amendment, which mandates separate votes for each office.) If no candidate won a majority, the House of Representatives would choose a president, with each state casting one vote.

The electoral college compromise eliminated the fear of a popular vote for president. At the same time, it satisfied the small states. If the electoral college failed to elect a president, which the delegates expected would happen, election by the House would give every state the same voice in the selection process. Finally, the delegates agreed that the president's term of office should be four years and that presidents should be eligible for reelection with no limit on the number of terms any individual president could serve.

The delegates also realized that removing a president from office would be a serious political matter. For that reason, they involved both of the other two branches of government in the process. The House alone was empowered to charge a president with "Treason, Bribery, or other high Crimes and Misdemeanors" (Article II, Section 4), by a majority vote. The Senate was given the sole power to try the president on the House's charges. It could convict, and thus remove, a president only by a two-thirds vote (an **extraordinary majority,** a majority greater than the minimum of 50 percent plus one). And the chief justice of the United States was required to preside over the Senate trial. In

electoral college A body of electors chosen by voters to cast ballots for president and vice president.

extraordinary majority A majority greater than the minimum of 50 percent plus one.

1998, the Congress considered whether President Bill Clinton's denial, under oath, of a sexual relationship with a White House intern, who later admitted their affair, fit the constitutional standard of impeachment for "high Crimes and Misdemeanors." Although the House of Representatives voted to impeach President Clinton, the Senate, in a trial presided over by Chief Justice William H. Rehnquist, did not convict him.

★ The Final Product

Once the delegates had resolved their major disagreements, they dispatched the remaining issues relatively quickly. A committee was then appointed to organize and write up the results of the proceedings. Twenty-three resolutions had been debated and approved by the convention; these were reorganized under seven articles in the draft constitution. The preamble, which was the last section to be drafted, begins with a phrase that would have been impossible to write when the convention opened. This single sentence contains four elements that form the foundation of the American political tradition:[25]

- *It creates a people:* "We the people of the United States" was a dramatic departure from a loose confederation of states.

- *It explains the reason for the Constitution:* "in order to form a more perfect Union" was an indirect way of saying that the first effort, the Articles of Confederation, had been inadequate.

- *It articulates goals:* "[to] establish Justice, insure domestic Tranquility, provide for the common defence, promote the general Welfare, and secure the Blessings of Liberty to ourselves and our Posterity"—in other words, the government exists to promote order and freedom.

- *It fashions a government:* "do ordain and establish this Constitution for the United States of America."

The Basic Principles

In creating the Constitution, the founders relied on four political principles—republicanism, federalism, separation of powers, and checks and balances—that together established a revolutionary new political order.

Republicanism is a form of government in which power resides in the people and is exercised by their elected representatives. The idea of republicanism may be traced to the Greek philosopher Aristotle (384–322 B.C.), who advocated a constitution that combined principles of both democratic and oligarchic government. The framers were determined to avoid aristocracy (rule by a hereditary class), monarchy (rule by one person), and direct democracy (rule by the people). A republic was both new and daring: no people had ever been governed by a republic on so vast a scale.

The framers themselves were far from sure that their government could be sustained. They had no model of republican government to follow; moreover, republican government was thought to be suitable only for small territories, where the interests of the public would be obvious and where the government would be within the reach of every citizen. After the convention ended, Benjamin Franklin was asked what sort of government the new nation would have. "A republic," the old man replied, "if you can keep it."

republicanism A form of government in which power resides in the people and is exercised by their elected representatives.

Federalism is the division of power between a central government and regional governments. Citizens are thus subject to two different bodies of law. Federalism can be seen as standing between two competing government schemes. On the one side is unitary government, in which all power is vested in a central authority. On the other side stands confederation, a loose union of powerful states. In a confederation, the states surrender some power to a central government but retain the rest. The Articles of Confederation, as we have seen, divided power between loosely knit states and a weak central government. The Constitution also divides power between the states and a central government, but it confers substantial powers on a national government at the expense of the states.

According to the Constitution, the powers vested in the national and state governments are derived from the people, who remain the ultimate sovereigns. National and state governments can exercise their power over people and property within their spheres of authority. But at the same time, by participating in the electoral process or by amending their governing charters, the people can restrain both the national and the state governments if necessary to preserve liberty.

The Constitution lists the powers of the national government and the powers denied to the states. All other powers remain with the states. Generally, the states are required to give up only the powers necessary to create an effective national government; the national government is limited in turn to the powers specified in the Constitution. Despite the specific lists, the Constitution does not clearly describe the spheres of authority within which the powers can be exercised. As we will discuss in Chapter 4, limits on the exercise of power by the national government and the states have evolved as a result of political and military conflicts; moreover, the limits have proved changeable.

Separation of powers and checks and balances are two distinct principles, but both are necessary to ensure that one branch does not dominate the government. **Separation of powers** is the assignment of the lawmaking, law-enforcing, and law-interpreting functions of government to independent legislative, executive, and judicial branches, respectively. Separation of powers safeguards liberty by ensuring that all government power does not fall into the hands of a single person or group of people. However, the Constitution constrained majority rule by limiting the people's direct influence on the electoral process (see Figure 3.1). In theory, separation of powers means that one branch cannot exercise the powers of the other branches. In practice, however, the separation is far from complete. One scholar has suggested that what we have instead is "separate institutions sharing powers."[26]

Checks and balances is a means of giving each branch of government some scrutiny of and control over the other branches. The aim is to prevent the exclusive exercise of certain powers by any one of the three branches. For example, only Congress can enact laws. But the president (through the veto power) can cancel them, and the courts (by finding that a law violates the Constitution) can strike them down. The process goes on as Congress and the president sometimes begin the legislative process anew, attempting to reformulate laws to address the flaws identified by the Supreme Court in its decisions. In a "check on a check," Congress can override a president's veto by an extraordinary (two-thirds) majority in each chamber. Congress is also empowered to propose amendments to the Constitution, counteracting the courts' power to invalidate. Figure 3.2 depicts the relationship between separation of powers and checks and balances.

federalism The division of power between a central government and regional governments.

separation of powers The assignment of lawmaking, law-enforcing, and law-interpreting functions to separate branches of government.

checks and balances A government structure that gives each branch some scrutiny of and control over the other branches.

FIGURE 3.1   The Constitution and the Electoral Process

The framers were afraid of majority rule, and that fear is reflected in the electoral process for national office described in the Constitution. The people, speaking through the voters, participated directly only in the choice of their representatives in the House. The president and senators were elected indirectly, through the electoral college and state legislatures. (Direct election of senators did not become law until 1913, when the Seventeenth Amendment was ratified.) Judicial appointments are, and always have been, far removed from representative links to the people. Judges are nominated by the president and approved by the Senate.

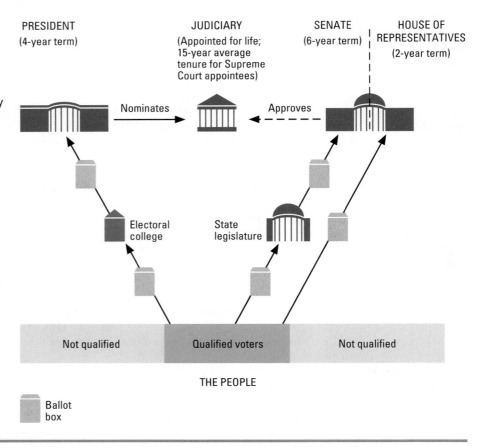

The Articles of the Constitution

In addition to the preamble, the Constitution contains seven articles. The first three establish the separate branches of government and specify their internal operations and powers. The remaining four define the relationships among the states, explain the process of amendment, declare the supremacy of national law, and explain the procedure for ratifying the Constitution.

Article I: The Legislative Article.   In structuring their new government, the framers began with the legislative branch because they considered law-making the most important function of a republican government. Article I is the most detailed, and therefore the longest, of the articles. It grants substantial but limited legislative power to Congress (Article I begins: "All legislative Power herein granted. . . ."). It defines the bicameral (two-chamber) character of Congress and describes the internal operating procedures of the House of Representatives and the Senate. Section 8 of Article I articulates the principle of **enumerated powers,** which means that Congress can exercise only the powers that the Constitution assigns to it. Eighteen powers are enumerated; the first seventeen are specific powers. For example, the third clause of Section 8 gives Congress the power to regulate interstate commerce. (One of the chief shortcomings of the Articles of Confederation was the lack of a means to cope with trade wars between the states. The solution was to vest control of interstate commerce in the national government.)

enumerated powers The powers explicitly granted to Congress by the Constitution.

FIGURE 3.2 Separation of Powers and Checks and Balances

Separation of powers is the assignment of lawmaking, law-enforcing, and law-interpreting functions to the legislative, executive, and judicial branches, respectively. The phenomenon is illustrated by the diagonal from upper left to lower right in the figure. Checks and balances give each branch some power over the other branches. For example, the executive branch possesses some legislative power, and the legislative branch possesses some executive power. These checks and balances are listed outside the diagonal.

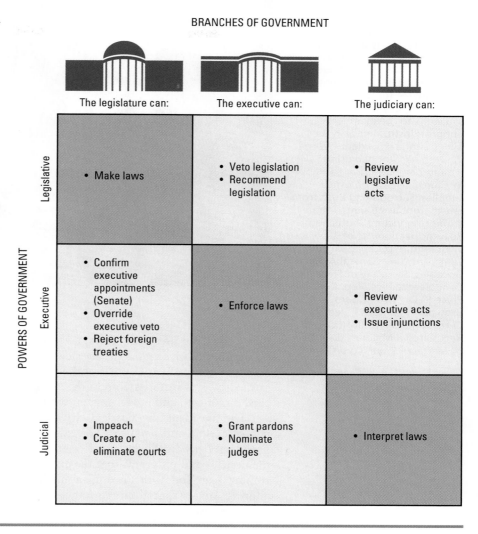

BRANCHES OF GOVERNMENT

POWERS OF GOVERNMENT

	The legislature can:	The executive can:	The judiciary can:
Legislative	• Make laws	• Veto legislation • Recommend legislation	• Review legislative acts
Executive	• Confirm executive appointments (Senate) • Override executive veto • Reject foreign treaties	• Enforce laws	• Review executive acts • Issue injunctions
Judicial	• Impeach • Create or eliminate courts	• Grant pardons • Nominate judges	• Interpret laws

The last clause in Section 8, known as the **necessary and proper clause** (or the elastic clause), gives Congress the means to execute the enumerated powers (see the appendix). This clause is the basis of Congress's **implied powers**—those powers that Congress needs to execute its enumerated powers. For example, the power to levy and collect taxes (clause 1) and the power to coin money and regulate its value (clause 5), when joined with the necessary and proper clause (clause 18), imply that Congress has the power to charter a bank. Otherwise, the national government would have no means of managing the money it collects through its power to tax. Implied powers clearly expand the enumerated powers conferred on Congress by the Constitution.

Article II: The Executive Article. Article II grants executive power to a president. The article establishes the president's term of office, the procedure

necessary and proper clause The last clause in Section 8 of Article I of the Constitution, which gives Congress the means to execute its enumerated powers. This clause is the basis for Congress's implied powers. Also called the *elastic clause*.

implied powers Those powers that Congress needs to execute its enumerated powers.

Saving Office Supplies

A president gives his approval to legislation by signing it into law. Beginning in the 1960s, the bill-signing ceremony became an art form, garnering much press attention. The president would typically employ many pens in small strokes for his signature and then distribute the pens as souvenirs to the members of Congress instrumental in the bill's passage. President George W. Bush has stopped using a multi-pen signature, perhaps in a move to save on office supplies. Surrounding Bush from left to right as he signed the Trafficking Victims Protection Reauthorization Act of 2005, in Washington, D.C., January 10, 2006: Attorney General Alberto Gonzales, Secretary of State Condoleezza Rice, Rep. Deborah Pryce (R-Ohio), Sen. Sam Brownback (R-Kans.), Rep. Christopher Smith (R-N.J.), and Rep. Carolyn Maloney (D-N.Y.). *(© Martin H. Simon/Corbis)*

for electing the president through the electoral college, the qualifications for becoming president, and the president's duties and powers. The last include acting as commander in chief of the military; making treaties (which must be ratified by a two-thirds vote in the Senate); and appointing government officers, diplomats, and judges (again, with the advice and consent of the Senate).

The president also has legislative powers—part of the constitutional system of checks and balances. For example, the Constitution requires that the president periodically inform Congress of "the State of the Union" and of the policies and programs that the executive branch intends to advocate in the coming year. Today, this is done annually in the president's State of the Union address. Under special circumstances, the president can also convene or adjourn Congress.

The duty to "take Care that the Laws be faithfully executed" in Section 3 has provided presidents with a reservoir of power. President Nixon tried to use this power when he refused to turn over the Watergate tapes despite a judicial subpoena in a criminal trial. He claimed broad executive privilege, an extension of the executive power implied in Article II. But the Supreme Court rejected his claim, arguing that it violated the separation of powers, because the decision to release or withhold information in a criminal trial is a judicial, not an executive, function.

Article III: The Judicial Article. The third article was left purposely vague. The Constitution established the Supreme Court as the highest court in the land. But beyond that, the framers were unable to agree on the need for a national judiciary or on its size, its composition, or the procedures it should follow. They left these issues to Congress, which resolved them by creating a system of federal (that is, national) courts, separate from the state courts.

Unless they are impeached, federal judges serve for life. They are appointed to indefinite terms "during good Behaviour," and their salaries cannot be reduced while they hold office. These stipulations reinforce the separation of powers; they see to it that judges are independent of the other branches and that they do not have to fear retribution for their exercise of judicial power.

Congress exercises a potential check on the judicial branch through its power to create (and eliminate) lower federal courts. Congress can also restrict the power of the federal courts to decide cases. And, as we have noted, the president appoints, with the advice and consent of the Senate, the justices of the Supreme Court and the judges of the lower federal courts. Since the 1980s, especially, the judicial appointment process has become highly politicized, with both Democrats and Republicans accusing each other of obstructionism or extremism in several high-profile confirmation debates.

Article III does not explicitly give the courts the power of **judicial review,** that is, the authority to invalidate congressional or presidential actions because they violate the Constitution. That power has been inferred from the logic, structure, and theory of the Constitution and from important court rulings, some of which we will discuss in subsequent chapters.

The Remaining Articles. The remaining four articles of the Constitution cover a lot of ground. Article IV requires that the judicial acts and criminal warrants of each state be honored in all other states, and it forbids discrimination against citizens of one state by another state. This provision promotes equality; it keeps the states from treating outsiders differently from their own citizens. For example, suppose Smith and Jones both reside in Illinois, and an Illinois court awards Smith a judgment of $100,000 against Jones. Jones moves to Alaska, hoping to avoid payment. Rather than force Smith to bring a new lawsuit against Jones in Alaska, the Alaska courts give full faith and credit to the Illinois judgment, enforcing it as their own. The origin of Article IV can be traced to the Articles of Confederation.

Article IV also allows the addition of new states and stipulates that the national government will protect the states against foreign invasion and domestic violence.

Article V specifies the methods for amending (changing) the Constitution. We will have more to say about this amendment process shortly.

An important component of Article VI is the **supremacy clause,** which asserts that when the Constitution, national laws, and treaties conflict with state or local laws, the first three take precedence over the last two. The stipulation is vital to the operation of federalism. In keeping with the supremacy clause, Article VI requires that all national and state officials, elected or appointed, take an oath to support the Constitution. The article also mandates that religious affiliation or belief cannot be a prerequisite for holding government office.

Finally, Article VII describes the ratification process, stipulating that approval by conventions in nine states would be necessary for the Constitution to take effect.

The idea of a written constitution seems entirely natural to Americans today. Lacking a written constitution, Great Britain has started to provide written guarantees for human rights (see "Compared with What? Britain's Bill of Rights"). And after failing to rekindle efforts to forge a constitution, European leaders took a different tack in 2007 when they agreed to draft a treaty and ratify it by 2009. The issues that animated our Constitutional Convention in

judicial review The power to declare congressional (and presidential) acts invalid because they violate the Constitution.

supremacy clause The clause in Article VI of the Constitution that asserts that national laws take precedence over state and local laws when they conflict.

Compared with What?

Britain's Bill of Rights

Britain does not have a written constitution, that is, a deliberate scheme of government formally adopted by the people and specifying special processes for its amendment. In Britain, no single document or law is known as "the constitution." Instead, Britain has an "unwritten constitution," an amalgam of important documents and laws passed by Parliament (the British legislature), court decisions, customs, and conventions. Britain's "constitution" has no existence apart from ordinary law. In contrast to the American system of government, Britain's Parliament may change, amend, or abolish its fundamental laws and conventions at will. No special procedures or barriers must be overcome to enact such changes.

According to government leaders, Britain has done very well without a written constitution, thank you very much. Or at least that was the position of Prime Minister Margaret Thatcher when she was presented with a proposal for a written constitution in 1989. Thatcher observed that despite Britain's lack of a bill of rights and an independent judiciary, "our present constitutional arrangements continue to serve us well. . . . Furthermore, the government does not feel that a written constitution in itself changes or guarantees anything."

In 1995, a nationwide poll revealed that the British people held a different view. Three-fourths of British adults thought that it was time for a written constitution, and even more maintained that the country needed a written bill of rights. These high levels of public support and the election of a new government in 1997 helped to build momentum for important changes in Britain's long history of rule by unwritten law. In October 2000, England formally began enforcing the Human Rights Act, a key component of the government's political program, which incorporated into British law sixteen guarantees of the European Convention on Human Rights drafted by the Council of Europe, a group founded to protect individual freedoms. (The charter was enacted earlier in Scotland, which, along with England, Wales, and Northern Ireland, makes up Great Britain.) Thus, the nation that has been the source of some of the world's most significant ideas concerning liberty and individual freedom finally put into writing guarantees to ensure these fundamental rights for its own citizens. Legal experts hailed the edict as the largest change to British law in three centuries.

It remains to be seen whether the Human Rights Act will, in the words of one former minister in the Thatcher government, "rob us of freedoms we have had for centuries" or, as British human rights lawyer Geoffrey Robertson sees it, "help produce a better culture of liberty." Perhaps the track record of the United States and its nearly 220 years of experience with the Bill of Rights will prove useful to our British "cousins," who appear ready to alter their system of unwritten rules.

Sources: Andrew Marr, *Ruling Britannia: The Failure and Future of British Democracy* (London: Michael Joseph, 1995); Will Hutton, *The State We're In* (London: Cape, 1995); Fred Barbash, "The Movement to Rule Britannia Differently," *Washington Post*, 23 September 1995, p. A27; "Bringing Rights Home," *The Economist*, 26 August 2000, pp. 45–46; Sarah Lyall, "209 Years Later, the English Get American-Style Bill of Rights," *New York Times*, 2 October 2000, p. A3; Suzanne Kapner, "Britain's Legal Barriers Start to Fall," *New York Times*, 4 October 2000, p. W1.

1787 seem all too familiar to us on this side of the Atlantic. Balancing power between a central government and the individual nation-states and agreeing to the core powers of the central government were but two of the big issues that derailed European constitutionalism.

The Framers' Motives

Some argue that the Constitution is essentially a conservative document written by wealthy men to advance their own interests. One distinguished historian who wrote in the early 1900s, Charles A. Beard, maintained that the delegates had much to gain from a strong national government.[27] Many held government securities dating from the Revolutionary War that had become practically worthless under the Articles of Confederation. A strong national government would protect their property and pay off the nation's debts.

Beard's argument, that the Constitution was crafted to protect the economic interests of this small group of creditors, provoked a generation of historians to examine the existing financial records of the convention delegates. Their scholarship has largely discredited his once-popular view.[28] For example, it turns out that seven of the delegates who left the convention or refused to sign the Constitution held public securities worth more than twice the total of the holdings of the thirty-nine delegates who did sign. Moreover, the most influential delegates owned no securities. And only a few delegates appear to have directly benefited economically from the new government.[29] Still, there is little doubt about the general homogeneity of the delegates or about their concern for producing a stable economic order that would preserve and promote the interests of some more than others.

What did motivate the framers? Surely economic considerations were important, but they were not the major issues. The single most important factor leading to the Constitutional Convention was the inability of the national or state governments to maintain order under the loose structure of the Articles of Confederation. Certainly, order involved the protection of property, but the framers had a broader view of property than their portfolios of government securities. They wanted to protect their homes, their families, and their means of livelihood from impending anarchy.

Although they disagreed bitterly on the structure and mechanics of the national government, the framers agreed on the most vital issues. For example, three of the most crucial features of the Constitution—the power to tax, the necessary and proper clause, and the supremacy clause—were approved unanimously without debate; experience had taught the delegates that a strong national government was essential if the United States were to survive. The motivation to create order was so strong, in fact, that the framers were willing to draft clauses that protected the most undemocratic of all institutions: slavery.

The Slavery Issue

The institution of slavery was well ingrained in American life at the time of the Constitutional Convention, and slavery helped shape the Constitution, although it is mentioned nowhere by name in it. (According to the first national census in 1790, nearly 18 percent of the population—697,000 people—lived in slavery.) It is doubtful, in fact, that there would have been a Constitution if the delegates had had to resolve the slavery issue, for the southern states would have opposed a constitution that prohibited slavery. Opponents of slavery were in the minority, and they were willing to tolerate its continuation in the interest of forging a union, perhaps believing that the issue could be resolved another day.

The question of representation in the House of Representatives brought the slavery issue close to the surface of the debate at the Constitutional Convention, and it led to the Great Compromise. Representation in the House was to be based on population. But who counted in the population? States with large slave populations wanted all their inhabitants, slave and free, counted equally; states with few slaves wanted only the free population counted. The delegates agreed unanimously that in apportioning representation in the House and in assessing direct taxes, the population of each state was to be determined by adding "the whole Number of free Persons" and "three fifths of all other Persons" (Article I, Section 2). The phrase "all other Persons" is, of course, a substitute for "slaves."

The three-fifths formula had been used by the 1783 congress under the Articles of Confederation to allocate government costs among the states. The rule reflected the view that slaves were less efficient producers of wealth than free people, not that slaves were three-fifths human and two-fifths personal property.[30]

The three-fifths clause gave states with large slave populations (the South) greater representation in Congress than states with small slave populations (the North). If all slaves had been included in the count, the slave states would have had 50 percent of the seats in the House, an outcome that would have been unacceptable to the North. Had none of the slaves been counted, the slave states would have had 41 percent of House seats, which would have been unacceptable to the South. The three-fifths compromise left the South with 47 percent of the House seats, a sizable minority, but in all likelihood a losing one on slavery issues.[31] The overrepresentation resulting from the South's large slave populations translated into greater influence in selecting the president as well, because the electoral college was based on the size of the states' congressional delegations. The three-fifths clause also undertaxed states with large slave populations.

Another issue centered around the slave trade. Several southern delegates were uncompromising in their defense of the slave trade; other delegates favored prohibition. The delegates compromised, agreeing that the slave trade would not be ended before twenty years had elapsed (Article I, Section 9). Finally, the delegates agreed, without serious challenge, that fugitive slaves would be returned to their masters (Article IV, Section 2).

In addressing these points, the framers in essence condoned slavery. Tens of thousands of Africans were forcibly taken from their homes and sold into bondage. Many died on the journey to this distant land, and those who survived were brutalized and treated as less than human. Clearly, slavery existed in stark opposition to the idea that all men are created equal. Although many slaveholders, including Jefferson and Madison, agonized over it, few made serious efforts to free their own slaves. Most Americans seemed indifferent to slavery and felt no embarrassment at the apparent contradiction between the Declaration of Independence and slavery. Do the framers deserve contempt for their toleration and perpetuation of slavery? The most prominent founders— George Washington, John Adams, and Thomas Jefferson—expected slavery to wither away. A leading scholar of colonial history has offered a defense of their inaction: the framers were simply unable to transcend the limitations of the age in which they lived.[32]

Nonetheless, the eradication of slavery proceeded gradually in certain states. Opposition to slavery on moral or religious grounds was one reason. Economic forces, such as a shift in the North to agricultural production that was less labor intensive, were a contributing factor too. By 1787, Connecticut, Massachusetts, New Jersey, New York, Pennsylvania, Rhode Island, and Vermont had abolished slavery or provided for gradual emancipation. No southern states followed suit, although several enacted laws making it easier for masters to free their slaves. The slow but perceptible shift on the slavery issue in many states masked a volcanic force capable of destroying the Constitutional Convention and the Union.

★ Selling the Constitution

Nearly four months after the Constitutional Convention opened, the delegates convened for the last time, on September 17, 1787, to sign the final version of their handiwork. Because several delegates were unwilling to sign the document, the last paragraph was craftily worded to give the impression of unanimity: "Done in Convention by the Unanimous Consent of the States present." Before it could take effect, the Constitution had to be ratified by a minimum of nine state conventions. The support of key states was crucial. In Pennsylvania, however, the legislature was slow to convene a ratifying convention. Pro-Constitution forces became so frustrated at this dawdling that they broke into a local boardinghouse and hauled two errant legislators through the streets to the statehouse so the assembly could schedule the convention.

The proponents of the new charter, who wanted a strong national government, called themselves Federalists. The opponents of the Constitution were quickly dubbed Antifederalists. They claimed, however, to be the true federalists because they wanted to protect the states from the tyranny of a strong national government. Elbridge Gerry, a vocal Antifederalist, called his opponents "rats" (because they favored ratification) and maintained that he was an "antirat."[33] Such is the Alice-in-Wonderland character of political discourse. Whatever they were called, the viewpoints of these two groups formed the bases of the first American political parties, as well as several enduring debates that politicians have wrestled with as they have attempted to balance the tradeoffs between freedom, order, and equality.

The *Federalist* Papers

The press of the day became a battlefield of words, filled with extravagant praise or vituperative condemnation of the proposed constitution. Beginning in October 1787, an exceptional series of eighty-five newspaper articles defending the Constitution appeared under the title *The Federalist: A Commentary on the Constitution of the United States.* The essays bore the pen name Publius (for a Roman emperor and defender of the Republic, Publius Valerius, who was later known as Publicola); they were written primarily by James Madison and Alexander Hamilton, with some assistance from John Jay. Reprinted extensively during the ratification battle, the *Federalist* papers remain the best single commentary we have on the meaning of the Constitution and the political theory it embodies.

Not to be outdone, the Antifederalists offered their own intellectual basis for rejecting the Constitution. In several essays, the most influential published under the pseudonyms Brutus and Federal Farmer, the Antifederalists attacked the centralization of power in a strong national government, claiming it would obliterate the states, violate the social contract of the Declaration of Independence, and destroy liberty in the process. They defended the status quo, maintaining that the Articles of Confederation established true federal principles.[34]

Of all the *Federalist* papers, the most magnificent and most frequently cited is *Federalist* No. 10, written by James Madison (see the appendix). He argued that the proposed constitution was designed "to break and control the violence of faction." "By a faction," Madison wrote, "I understand a number of citizens, whether amounting to a majority or minority of the whole, who are united and actuated by some common impulse of passion, or of interest, adverse to the rights of other citizens, or to the permanent and aggregate interests of the community." No one has improved upon Madison's lucid and compelling argument, and it remains the touchstone on the problem of factions to this day.

What Madison called factions are today called interest groups or even political parties. According to Madison, "The most common and durable source of factions has been the various and unequal distribution of property." Madison was concerned not with reducing inequalities of wealth (which he took for granted) but with controlling the seemingly inevitable conflict that stems from them. The Constitution, he argued, was well constructed for this purpose.

Through the mechanism of representation, wrote Madison, the Constitution would prevent a "tyranny of the majority" (mob rule). The people would not control the government directly but indirectly through their elected representatives. And those representatives would have the intelligence and the understanding to serve the larger interests of the nation. Moreover, the federal system would require that majorities form first within each state and then organize for effective action at the national level. This and the vastness of the country would make it unlikely that a majority would form that would "invade the rights of other citizens."

? Can you explain why . . . having many factions reduces the danger of factions?

The purpose of *Federalist* No. 10 was to demonstrate that the proposed government was not likely to be dominated by any faction. Contrary to conventional wisdom, Madison argued, the key to mending the evils of factions is to have a large republic—the larger, the better. The more diverse the society, the less likely it is that an unjust majority can form. Madison certainly had no intention of creating a majoritarian democracy; his view of popular government was much more consistent with the model of pluralist democracy discussed in Chapter 2.

Madison pressed his argument from a different angle in *Federalist* No. 51 (see the appendix). Asserting that "ambition must be made to counteract ambition," he argued that the separation of powers and checks and balances would control efforts at tyranny from any source. If power is distributed equally among the three branches, he argued, each branch will have the capacity to counteract the others. In Madison's words, "usurpations are guarded against by a division of the government into distinct and separate departments." Because legislative power tends to predominate in republican governments, legislative authority is divided between the Senate and the House of Representatives, which have different methods of election and terms of office. Additional protection arises from federalism, which divides power "between two distinct governments"—national and state—and subdivides "the portion allotted to each . . . among distinct and separate departments." Madison called this arrangement of power, divided as it was across and within levels of government, a "compound republic."

The Antifederalists wanted additional separation of powers and additional checks and balances, which they maintained would eliminate the threat of tyranny entirely. The Federalists believed that such protections would make decisive national action virtually impossible. But to ensure ratification, they agreed to a compromise.

A Concession: The Bill of Rights

Despite the eloquence of the *Federalist* papers, many prominent citizens, including Thomas Jefferson, were unhappy that the Constitution did not list basic civil liberties—the individual freedoms guaranteed to citizens. The omission of a bill of rights was the chief obstacle to the adoption of the Constitution by the states. (Seven of the eleven state constitutions that were written in the first five years of independence included such a list.) The colonists had just rebelled against the British government to preserve their basic freedoms. Why did the proposed Constitution not spell out those freedoms?

The answer was rooted in logic, not politics. Because the national government was limited to those powers that were granted to it and because no power was granted to abridge the people's liberties, a list of guaranteed freedoms was not necessary. In *Federalist* No. 84, Hamilton went even further, arguing that the addition of a bill of rights would be dangerous. To deny the exercise of a nonexistent power might lead to the exercise of a power that is not specifically denied. For example, to declare that the national government shall make no law abridging free speech might suggest that the national government could prohibit activities in unspecified areas (such as divorce), which are the states' domain. Because it is not possible to list all prohibited powers, wrote Hamilton, any attempt to provide a partial list would make the unlisted areas vulnerable to government abuse.

But logic was no match for fear. Many states agreed to ratify the Constitution only after George Washington suggested adding a list of guarantees through the amendment process. Well in excess of one hundred amendments were proposed by the states. These were eventually narrowed to twelve, which were approved by Congress and sent to the states. Ten became part of the Constitution in 1791, after securing the approval of the required three-fourths of the states. Collectively, the ten amendments are known as the **Bill of Rights**. They restrain the national government from tampering with fundamental rights and civil liberties and emphasize the limited character of the national government's power (see Table 3.2).

Ratification

The Constitution officially took effect upon its ratification by the ninth state, New Hampshire, on June 21, 1788. However, the success of the new government was not ensured until July 1788, by which time the Constitution was ratified by the key states of Virginia and New York after lengthy debate.

The reflection and deliberation that attended the creation and ratification of the Constitution signaled to the world that a new government could be

? Can you explain why . . . some of the nation's founders thought that adding a bill of rights to the Constitution might actually limit individual rights?

IDEAlog.org
Are you for or against restricting violence and sex on cable television? Take IDEAlog's self-test.

Bill of Rights The first ten amendments to the Constitution. They prevent the national government from tampering with fundamental rights and civil liberties, and emphasize the limited character of national power.

TABLE 3.2 The Bill of Rights

The first ten amendments to the Constitution are known as the Bill of Rights. The following is a list of those amendments, grouped conceptually. For the actual order and wording of the Bill of Rights, see the appendix.

Guarantees	Amendment
Guarantees for Participation in the Political Process	
No government abridgement of speech or press; no government abridgement of peaceable assembly; no government abridgement of petitioning government for redress.	1
Guarantees Respecting Personal Beliefs	
No government establishment of religion; no government prohibition of free religious exercise.	1
Guarantees of Personal Privacy	
Owner's consent necessary to quarter troops in private homes in peacetime; quartering during war must be lawful.	3
Government cannot engage in unreasonable searches and seizures; warrants to search and seize require probable cause.	4
No compulsion to testify against oneself in criminal cases.	5
Guarantees Against Government's Overreaching	
Serious crimes require a grand jury indictment; no repeated prosecution for the same offense; no loss of life, liberty, or property without due process; no taking of property for public use without just compensation.	5
Criminal defendants will have a speedy public trial by impartial local jury; defendants are informed of accusation; defendants may confront witnesses against them; defendants may use judicial process to obtain favorable witnesses; defendants may have legal assistance for their defense.	6
Civil lawsuits can be tried by juries if controversy exceeds $20; in jury trials, fact-finding is a jury function.	7
No excessive bail; no excessive fines; no cruel and unusual punishment.	8
Other Guarantees	
The people have the right to bear arms.	2
No government trespass on unspecified fundamental rights.	9
The states or the people retain all powers not delegated to the national government or denied to the states.	10

launched peacefully. The French observer Alexis de Tocqueville (1805–1859) later wrote:

> That which is new in the history of societies is to see a great people, warned by its lawgivers that the wheels of government are stopping, turn its attention on itself without haste or fear, sound the depth of the ill, and then wait for two years to find the remedy at leisure, and then finally, when the remedy has been indicated, submit to it voluntarily without its costing humanity a single tear or drop of blood.[35]

★ Constitutional Change

The founders realized that the Constitution would have to be changed from time to time. To this end, they specified a formal amendment process, and one that was used almost immediately to add the Bill of Rights. With the passage of time, the Constitution has also been altered through judicial interpretation and changes in political practice.

The Formal Amendment Process

The amendment process has two stages, proposal and ratification; both are necessary for an amendment to become part of the Constitution. The Constitution provides two alternatives for completing each stage (see Figure 3.3). Amendments can be proposed by a two-thirds vote in both the House of Representatives and the Senate or by a national convention, summoned by Congress at the request of two-thirds of the state legislatures. All constitutional amendments to date have been proposed by the first method; the second has never been used.

FIGURE 3.3 **Amending the Constitution**

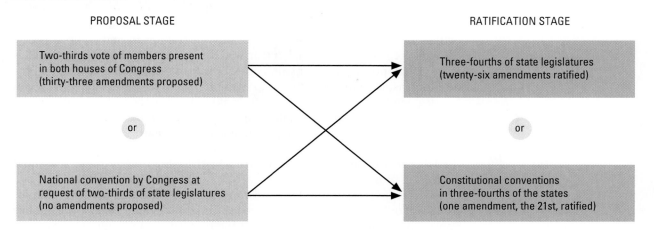

Amending the Constitution requires two stages: proposal and ratification. Both Congress and the states can play a role in the proposal stage, but ratification is a process that must be fought in the states themselves. Once a state has ratified an amendment, it cannot retract its action. However, a state may reject an amendment and then reconsider its decision.

A proposed amendment can be ratified by a vote of the legislatures of three-fourths of the states or by a vote of constitutional conventions held in three-fourths of the states. Congress chooses the method of ratification. It has used the state convention method only once, for the Twenty-first Amendment, which repealed the Eighteenth Amendment (prohibition of intoxicating liquors). Congress may, in proposing an amendment, set a time limit for its ratification. Beginning with the Eighteenth Amendment, but skipping the Nineteenth, Congress has set seven years as the limit for ratification.

Note that the amendment process requires the exercise of extraordinary majorities (two-thirds and three-fourths). The framers purposely made it difficult to propose and ratify amendments (although nowhere near as difficult as under the Articles of Confederation). They wanted only the most significant issues to lead to constitutional change. Note, too, that the president plays no formal role in the process. Presidential approval is not required to amend the Constitution, although the president's political influence affects the success or failure of any amendment effort.

Calling a national convention to propose an amendment has never been tried, and the method raises several thorny questions. For example, the Constitution does not specify the number of delegates who should attend, the method by which they should be chosen, or the rules for debating and voting on a proposed amendment. Confusion surrounding the convention process has precluded its use, leaving the amendment process in congressional hands.[36] The major issue is the limits, if any, on the business of the convention. Remember that the convention in Philadelphia in 1787, charged with revising the Articles of Confederation, drafted an entirely new charter. Would a national convention called to consider a particular amendment be within its bounds to rewrite the Constitution? No one really knows.

Most of the Constitution's twenty-seven amendments were adopted to reflect changes in political thinking. The first ten amendments (the Bill of Rights) were the price of ratification, but they have been fundamental to our system of government. The last seventeen amendments fall into three main categories: they make public policy, they correct deficiencies in the government's structure, or they promote equality (see Table 3.3). One attempt to make public policy through a constitutional amendment was disastrous. The Eighteenth Amendment (1919) prohibited the manufacture or sale of intoxicating beverages. Prohibition lasted fourteen years and was an utter failure. Gangsters began bootlegging liquor, people died from drinking homemade spirits, and millions regularly broke the law by drinking anyway. Congress had to propose another amendment in 1933 to repeal the Eighteenth. The states ratified this amendment, the Twenty-first, in less than ten months, less time than it took to ratify the Fourteenth Amendment, guaranteeing citizenship, due process, and equal protection of the laws.

Since 1787, about ten thousand constitutional amendments have been introduced; only a fraction have survived the proposal stage. Once Congress has approved an amendment, its chances for ratification are high. The Twenty-seventh Amendment, which prevents members of Congress from voting themselves immediate pay increases, was ratified in 1992. It had been submitted to the states in 1789 without a time limit for ratification, but it languished in a political netherworld until 1982, when a University of Texas student, Gregory D. Watson, stumbled upon the proposed amendment while researching a paper. At that time, only eight states had ratified the amendment. Watson took up

Down the Drain
The Eighteenth Amendment, which was ratified by the states in 1919, banned the manufacture, sale, and transportation of alcoholic beverages. Banned beverages were destroyed, as pictured here, by federal agents from the Treasury Department, which enforced prohibition. The amendment was spurred by moral and social reform groups, such as the Woman's Christian Temperance Union, founded by Evanston, Illinois, resident Frances Willard in 1874. The amendment proved to be an utter failure. People continued to drink, but their alcohol came from illegal sources. (© Bettmann/ Corbis)

the cause, prompting renewed interest in the idea. In May 1992, ratification by the Michigan legislature provided the decisive vote, 203 years after congressional approval of the proposed amendment.[37] Only six amendments submitted to the states have failed to be ratified.

Interpretation by the Courts

In *Marbury* v. *Madison* (1803), the Supreme Court declared that the courts have the power to nullify government acts that conflict with the Constitution. (We will elaborate on judicial review in Chapter 14.) The exercise of judicial review forces the courts to interpret the Constitution. In a way, this makes a lot of sense. The judiciary is the law-interpreting branch of the government; as the supreme law of the land, the Constitution is fair game for judicial interpretation. Judicial review is the courts' main check on the other branches of government. But in interpreting the Constitution, the courts cannot help but give new meaning to its provisions. This is why judicial interpretation is a principal form of constitutional change.

What guidelines should judges use in interpreting the Constitution? For one thing, they must realize that the usage and meaning of many words have changed during the past two hundred years. Judges must be careful to think about what the words meant at the time the Constitution was written. Some insist that they must also consider the original intent of the framers—not an easy task. Of course, there are records of the Constitutional Convention and of the debates surrounding ratification. But there are also many questions about the completeness and accuracy of those records, even Madison's detailed notes. And at times, the framers were deliberately vague in writing the document. This may reflect lack of agreement on, or universal understanding of, certain

TABLE 3.3	Constitutional Amendments: 11 Through 27			
No.	Proposed	Ratified	Intent*	Subject
11	1794	1795	G	Prohibits an individual from suing a state in federal court without the state's consent.
12	1803	1804	G	Requires the electoral college to vote separately for president and vice president.
13	1865	1865	E	Prohibits slavery.
14	1866	1868	E	Gives citizenship to all persons born or naturalized in the United States (including former slaves); prevents states from depriving any person of "life, liberty, or property, without due process of law," and declares that no state shall deprive any person of "the equal protection of the laws."
15	1869	1870	E	Guarantees that citizens' right to vote cannot be denied "on account of race, color, or previous condition of servitude."
16	1909	1913	E	Gives Congress the power to collect an income tax.
17	1912	1913	E	Provides for popular election of senators, who were formerly elected by state legislatures.
18	1917	1919	P	Prohibits the making and selling of intoxicating liquors.
19	1919	1920	E	Guarantees that citizens' right to vote cannot be denied "on account of sex."
20	1932	1933	G	Changes the presidential inauguration from March 4 to January 20 and sets January 3 for the opening date of Congress.
21	1933	1933	P	Repeals the Eighteenth Amendment.
22	1947	1951	G	Limits a president to two terms.
23	1960	1961	E	Gives citizens of Washington, D.C., the right to vote for president.
24	1962	1964	E	Prohibits charging citizens a poll tax to vote in presidential or congressional elections.
25	1965	1967	G	Provides for succession in event of death, removal from office, incapacity, or resignation of the president or vice president.
26	1971	1971	E	Lowers the voting age to eighteen.
27	1789	1992	G	Bars immediate pay increases to members of Congress.

*P: amendments legislating public policy; G: amendments correcting perceived deficiencies in government structure; E: amendments advancing equality.

provisions in the Constitution. Some scholars and judges maintain that the search for original meaning is hopeless and that contemporary notions of constitutional provisions must hold sway. Critics say that this approach comes perilously close to amending the Constitution as judges see fit, transforming law interpreters into lawmakers. Still other scholars and judges maintain that judges face the unavoidable challenge of balancing two-hundred-year-old constitutional principles against the demands of modern society.[38] Whatever the approach, unelected judges with effective life tenure run the risk of usurping policies established by the people's representatives.

Political Practice

The Constitution is silent on many issues. It says nothing about political parties or the president's cabinet, for example, yet both have exercised considerable influence in American politics. Some constitutional provisions have fallen out of use. The electors in the electoral college, for example, were supposed to exercise their own judgment in voting for the president and vice president. Today, the electors function simply as a rubber stamp, validating the outcome of election contests in their states.

Meanwhile, political practice has altered the distribution of power without changes in the Constitution. The framers intended Congress to be the strongest branch of government. But the president has come to overshadow Congress. Presidents such as Abraham Lincoln and Franklin Roosevelt used their formal and informal powers imaginatively to respond to national crises. And their actions paved the way for future presidents, most recently George W. Bush, to enlarge further the powers of the office.

The framers could scarcely have imagined an urbanized nation of 300 million people stretching across a landmass some three thousand miles wide, reaching halfway over the Pacific Ocean, and stretching past the Arctic Circle. Never in their wildest nightmares could they have foreseen the destructiveness of nuclear weaponry or envisioned its effect on the power to declare war. The Constitution empowers Congress to consider and debate this momentous step. But with nuclear annihilation perhaps only minutes away and terrorist threats a regular occurrence since September 11, 2001, the legislative power to declare war is likely to give way to the president's power to wage war as the nation's commander in chief. Strict adherence to the Constitution in such circumstances could destroy the nation's ability to protect itself.

★ An Evaluation of the Constitution

The U.S. Constitution is one of the world's most praised political documents. It is the oldest written national constitution and one of the most widely copied, sometimes word for word. It is also one of the shortest, consisting of about 4,300 words (not counting the amendments, which add 3,100 words). The brevity of the Constitution may be one of its greatest strengths. As we noted earlier, the framers simply laid out a structural framework for government; they did not describe relationships and powers in detail. For example, the Constitution gives Congress the power to regulate "Commerce . . . among the several States" but does not define interstate commerce. Such general wording allows interpretation in keeping with contemporary political, social,

Politics in a Changing World

A New Birth of Freedom: Exporting American Constitutionalism

When the founders drafted the U.S. Constitution in 1787, they hardly started from scratch. Leaders like James Madison and John Adams drew on the failed experiences of the Articles of Confederation to chart a new course for our national government. They also leaned heavily on the ideas of great democratic thinkers of the past. Today, given the more than two-hundred-year track record of the United States, it is no wonder that many other nations have looked to the American experience as they embark on their own democratic experiments.

In the past ten years especially, democratizing countries on nearly every continent have developed new governing institutions by drawing at least in part on important principles from the U.S. Constitution and Bill of Rights. This is certainly the case in the former communist countries of Eastern Europe, most of which have entered their second decade of newly established democratic rule. Enshrining democratic ideals in a written constitution corresponds to the ascendancy of freedom worldwide (see the accompanying figure).

Echoing the U.S. Declaration of Independence and the Constitution's preamble, for example, Article 2 of the Lithuanian constitution declares unequivocally, "Sovereignty shall be vested in the people." To protect the rights of citizens and to prevent power from becoming too concentrated, many Eastern European nations have designed government institutions to allocate and share power among different branches paralleling the legislative, executive, and judicial arrangement of the American experience.

Specific guarantees protecting individual rights and liberties are also written in great detail in the constitutions of these new democracies. The Romanian constitution, for example, takes a strong stand on the defense of personal ideas, stating that "freedom of expression of thoughts, opinions, or beliefs, and freedom of any creation by words, in writing, in pictures, by sounds or other means of communication in public are inviolable." Similarly, the constitution of Bulgaria details important restrictions on government action against the nation's citizens. Protections regarding

and technological developments. Air travel, for instance, unknown in 1787, now falls easily within Congress's power to regulate interstate commerce.

The generality of the U.S. Constitution stands in stark contrast to the specificity of most state constitutions and the constitutions of many emerging democracies. The constitution of California, for example, provides that "fruit and nut-bearing trees under the age of four years from the time of planting in orchard form and grapevines under the age of three years from the time of planting in vineyard form . . . shall be exempt from taxation" (Article XIII, Section 12). Because they are so specific, most state constitutions are much longer than the U.S. Constitution.

The constitution of the Republic of Slovenia, adopted in December 1991, prevents citizens from being "compelled to undergo medical treatment except in such cases as are determined by statute." In the Republic of Lithuania, the

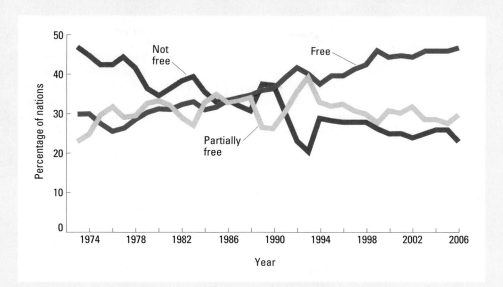

cruel and unusual punishment, unreasonable detention or search, and privacy within one's home and personal correspondence are just a few of the Bulgarian constitution's guarantees.

Because there is no ready-made formula for building a successful democracy, only time will tell whether these young constitutions will perform well in practice. A generation ago, humorists asked: "What is the difference between the Soviet constitution and the U.S. Constitution?" The answer: "Under the Soviet constitution, there is freedom of speech and freedom of thought. But under the U.S. Constitution there is freedom *after* speech and freedom *after* thought!" The point

is that putting democracy into practice is much harder than theorizing about democracy. Undoubtedly, success will be the product of many factors, including the courage to resist past totalitarian practices, the willingness to make important adjustments to national institutions when the need arises, and, perhaps most important, a measure of good luck.

Sources: International Institute for Democracy, *The Rebirth of Democracy: Twelve Constitutions of Central and Eastern Europe,* 2nd ed. (Amsterdam: Council of Europe, 1996); A. E. Dick Howard, "Liberty's Text: Ten Amendments That Changed the World," *Washington Post,* 15 December 1991, p. C3; Freedom House, "Freedom in the World 2007," available at <http:www.freedomhouse.org/uploads/press_release/fine07_charts.pdf>.

national constitution, adopted in October 1992, spells out in significant detail some of the free-speech rights of its citizens, including the protection that "citizens who belong to ethnic communities shall have the right to foster their language, culture, and customs."[39] The U.S. Constitution remains a beacon for others to follow (see "Politics in a Changing World: A New Birth of Freedom: Exporting American Constitutionalism").

Freedom, Order, and Equality in the Constitution

The revolutionaries' first try at government was embodied in the Articles of Confederation. The result was a weak national government that leaned too much toward freedom at the expense of order. Deciding that the confederation was beyond correcting, the revolutionaries chose a new form of government—

a federal government—that was strong enough to maintain order but not so strong that it could dominate the states or infringe on individual freedoms. In short, the Constitution provided a judicious balance between order and freedom. It paid virtually no attention to equality.

Consider social equality. The Constitution never mentioned the word *slavery*, a controversial issue even then. In fact, as we have seen, the Constitution implicitly condones slavery in the wording of several articles. Not until the ratification of the Thirteenth Amendment in 1865 was slavery prohibited.

The Constitution was designed long before social equality was ever even thought of as an objective of government. In fact, in *Federalist* No. 10, Madison held that protection of the "diversities in the faculties of men from which the rights of property originate" is "the first object of government." More than a century later, the Constitution was changed to incorporate a key device for the promotion of social equality—a national income tax. The Sixteenth Amendment (1913) gave Congress the power to collect an income tax; it was proposed and ratified to replace a law that had been declared unconstitutional in an 1895 Supreme Court case. The income tax had long been seen as a means of putting into effect the concept of progressive taxation, in which the tax rate increases with income. The Sixteenth Amendment gave progressive taxation a constitutional basis.[40] Progressive taxation later helped promote social equality through the redistribution of income; that is, higher-income people are taxed at higher rates to help fund social programs that benefit low-income people.

Social equality itself has never been, and is not now, a prime constitutional value. The Constitution has been much more effective in securing order and freedom. Nor did the Constitution take a stand on political equality. It left voting qualifications to the states, specifying only that people who could vote for "the most numerous Branch of the State Legislature" could also vote for representatives to Congress (Article I, Section 2). Most states at that time allowed only taxpaying or property-owning white males to vote. With few exceptions, blacks and women were universally excluded from voting. These inequalities have been rectified by several amendments (see Table 3.3).

Political equality expanded after the Civil War. The Fourteenth Amendment (adopted in 1868) guaranteed all persons, including blacks, citizenship. The Fifteenth Amendment (ratified in 1870) declared that "race, color, or previous condition of servitude" could not be used to deny citizens the right to vote. This did not automatically give blacks the vote; some states used other mechanisms to limit black enfranchisement. The Nineteenth Amendment (adopted in 1920) opened the way for women to vote by declaring that sex could not be used to deny citizens the right to vote. The Twenty-fourth Amendment (adopted in 1964) prohibited the poll tax (a tax that people had to pay to vote and that tended to disenfranchise poor blacks) in presidential and congressional elections. The Twenty-sixth Amendment (adopted in 1971) declared that age could not be used to deny citizens eighteen years or older the right to vote. One other amendment expanded the Constitution's grant of political equality. The Twenty-third Amendment (adopted in 1961) allowed residents of Washington, D.C., who are not citizens of any state, to vote for president.

The Constitution and Models of Democracy

Think back to our discussion of the models of democracy in Chapter 2. Which model does the Constitution fit: pluralist or majoritarian? Actually, it is hard to

this distinction between different sovereignties becomes murkier because many decisions were supposed to be shared by different levels of government. Evacuation, for instance, was a responsibility shared by both the state and national authorities. Ideology—the belief in maintaining strict controls on the powers of the national government—cast a shadow on the catastrophe. Generally, conservatives tend to be more reluctant to exercise national power in matters such as public health, safety, and welfare.

Sovereignty also affects political leadership. A governor may not be a president's political equal, but governors have their own sovereignty apart from the national government. Regarding the political response to the damage caused by Hurricane Katrina, the national government blamed the state government for failing to request the specific help needed or to give up command and control. The state government underlined the inability of FEMA to deal with the necessities of the displaced population.[3] And local officials stressed the fact that national and state authorities seemed preoccupied with the press. Unfortunately, for the people of New Orleans who were left behind in this tragedy, the same questions will keep on resonating in their heads: "Is anybody out there listening? Does anybody out there care?"[4] ★

In this chapter, we examine American federalism in theory and in practice. Is the division of power between the nation and states a matter of constitutional principle or practical politics? How does the balance of power between the nation and states relate to the conflicts between freedom and order and between freedom and equality? Does the growth of federalism abroad affect us here at home? Does federalism reflect the pluralist or the majoritarian model of democracy?

IN OUR OWN WORDS

Listen to Jerry Goldman discuss the main points and themes of this chapter.

Online Study Center
Improve Your Grade

★ Theories and Metaphors

The delegates who met in Philadelphia in 1787 were supposed to repair weaknesses in the Articles of Confederation. Instead, they tackled the problem of making one nation out of thirteen independent states by doing something much more radical: they wrote a new constitution and invented a new political form—federal government—that combined features of a confederacy with features of unitary government (see Chapter 3). Under the principle of **federalism,** two or more governments exercise power and authority over the same people and the same territory.

For example, the governments of the United States and Pennsylvania share certain powers (the power to tax, for instance), but other powers belong exclusively to one or the other. As James Madison wrote in *Federalist* No. 10, "The federal Constitution forms a happy combination . . . [of] the great and aggregate interests being referred to the national, and the local and particular to state governments." So the power to coin money belongs to the national government, but the power to grant divorces remains a state prerogative. By contrast, authority over state militias may sometimes belong to the national government and sometimes to the states. The history of American federalism

sovereignty The quality of being supreme in power or authority.

federalism The division of power between a central government and regional governments.

Blame Game

FEMA head Mike Brown won undeserved praise from President Bush in the immediate aftermath of Hurricane Katrina. New Orleans mayor Ray Nagin and Louisiana governor Kathleen Babineaux Blanco accused Brown of incompetence. He in turn blamed state and local officials for inadequate disaster preparation. Within days, Brown resigned. Subsequent investigations cast blame in all directions but a large share rested with Brown's failure of leadership. *(Mike Keefe/The Denver Post, © 2005)*

Federalist No. 10 is available on the

Online Study Center
General Resources

reveals that it has not always been easy to draw a line between what is "great and aggregate" and what is "local and particular."*

Nevertheless, federalism offered a solution to the problem of diversity in America. Citizens feared that without a federal system of government, majorities with different interests and values from different regions would rule them. Federalism also provided a new political model.

The history of American federalism is full of attempts to capture its true meaning in an adjective or metaphor. By one reckoning, scholars have generated nearly five hundred ways to describe federalism.[5] Perhaps this is not surprising given one scholar's view that the American federal system "is a highly protean form, subject to constant reinterpretation. It is long on change and confusion and very low on fixed, generally accepted principles."[6] Still, before complicating the picture too much, it will be useful to focus on two common representations of the system: dual federalism and cooperative federalism.

Dual Federalism

The term **dual federalism** sums up a theory about the proper relationship between the national government and the states. The theory has four essential parts. First, the national government rules by enumerated powers only. Second, the national government has a limited set of constitutional purposes. Third, each government unit—nation and state—is sovereign within its sphere. And fourth, the relationship between nation and states is best characterized by tension rather than cooperation.[7]

Dual federalism portrays the states as powerful components of the federal system—in some ways, the equals of the national government. Under dual federalism, the functions and responsibilities of the national and state govern-

dual federalism A view that holds that the Constitution is a compact among sovereign states, so that the powers of the national government and the states are clearly differentiated.

---

*The phrase Americans commonly use to refer to their central government—*federal government*—muddies the waters even more. Technically, we have a federal system of government, which encompasses both the national and state governments. To avoid confusion from here on, we use the term *national government* rather than *federal government* when we are talking about the central government.

FIGURE 4.1 Metaphors for Federalism

The two views of federalism can be represented graphically.

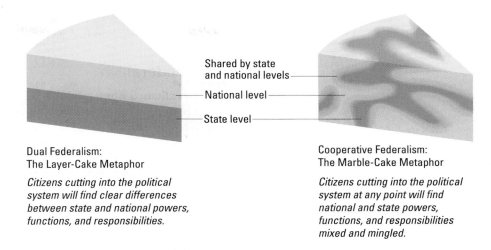

Shared by state and national levels

National level

State level

Dual Federalism:
The Layer-Cake Metaphor

Citizens cutting into the political system will find clear differences between state and national powers, functions, and responsibilities.

Cooperative Federalism:
The Marble-Cake Metaphor

Citizens cutting into the political system at any point will find national and state powers, functions, and responsibilities mixed and mingled.

ments are theoretically different and practically separate from each other. Of primary importance in dual federalism are **states' rights,** which reserve to the states all rights not specifically conferred on the national government by the Constitution. According to the theory of dual federalism, a rigid wall separates the nation and the states. After all, if the states created the nation, by implication they can set limits on the activities of the national government. Proponents of states' rights believe that the powers of the national government should be interpreted narrowly.

Debates over states' rights often emerge over differing interpretations of a given national government policy or proposed policy. Whether the Constitution has delegated to the national government the power to make such policy or whether it remains with the states or the people is often an open and difficult question to answer. States' rights supporters insist that the activities of Congress should be confined to the enumerated powers. They support their view by quoting the Tenth Amendment: "The powers not delegated to the United States by the Constitution, nor prohibited by it to the States, are reserved to the States respectively, or to the people." Conversely, those people favoring national action frequently point to the Constitution's elastic clause, which gives Congress the **implied powers** needed to execute its enumerated powers.

Regardless of whether one favors national action or states' rights, political scientists use a metaphor to describe the idea of dual federalism. They call it *layer-cake federalism* (see Figure 4.1) in which the powers and functions of the national and state governments are as separate as the layers of a cake. Each government is supreme in its own layer, its own sphere of action. The two layers are distinct, and the dimensions of each layer are fixed by the Constitution.

Dual federalism has been challenged on historical grounds. Some critics argue that if the national government is really a creation of the states, it is a creation of only thirteen states—those that ratified the Constitution. The other thirty-seven states were admitted after the national government came into being and were created by that government out of land it had acquired. Another challenge has to do with the ratification process. Remember that special

states' rights The idea that all rights not specifically conferred on the national government by the U.S. Constitution are reserved to the states.

implied powers Those powers that Congress needs to execute its enumerated powers.

conventions in the original thirteen states, not the states' legislatures, ratified the Constitution. Ratification, then, was an act of the people, not the states. Moreover, the preamble to the Constitution begins, "We the People of the United States," not "We the States." The question of just where the people fit into the federal system is not handled well by dual federalism.

Cooperative Federalism

Cooperative federalism, a phrase coined in the 1930s, is a different theory of the relationship between the national and state governments. It acknowledges the increasing overlap between state and national functions and rejects the idea of separate spheres, or layers, for the states and the national government. Cooperative federalism has three elements. First, national and state agencies typically undertake government functions jointly rather than exclusively. Second, the nation and states routinely share power. And third, power is not concentrated at any government level or in any agency; the fragmentation of responsibilities gives people and groups access to many venues of influence.

The bakery metaphor used to describe this type of federalism is a *marble cake* (see Figure 4.1).* The national and state governments do not act in separate spheres; they are intermingled in vertical and diagonal strands and swirls. In short, their functions are mixed in the American federal system. Critical to cooperative federalism is an expansive view of the Constitution's supremacy clause (Article VI), which specifically subordinates state law to national law and charges every government official with disregarding state laws that are inconsistent with the Constitution, national laws, or treaties.

Some scholars argue that the layer-cake metaphor has never accurately described the American political structure.[8] The national and state governments have many common objectives and have often cooperated to achieve them. In the nineteenth century, for example, cooperation, not separation, made it possible to develop transportation systems, such as canals, and to establish state land-grant colleges. Overall, then, the layer cake might be a good model of what dual federalists think the relationship between national and state governments *should* be, but several examples reveal how it does not square all that well with recent or even distant American history.

A critical difference between the theories of dual and cooperative federalism is the way they interpret two sections of the Constitution that define the relationship between the national and state governments. Article I, Section 8, lists the enumerated powers of Congress and then concludes with the **elastic clause,** which gives Congress the power to "make all Laws which shall be necessary and proper for carrying into Execution the foregoing Powers" (see Chapter 3). The Tenth Amendment reserves for the states or the people powers not assigned to the national government or denied to the states by the Constitution. Dual federalism postulates an inflexible elastic clause and a capacious Tenth Amendment. Cooperative federalism postulates suppleness in the elastic clause and confines the Tenth Amendment to a self-evident, obvious truth.

? Can you explain why . . . the Tenth Amendment and the necessary and proper clause of Article I might contradict one another?

cooperative federalism A view that holds that the Constitution is an agreement among people who are citizens of both state and nation, so there is much overlap between state powers and national powers.

elastic clause The last clause in Section 8 of Article I of the Constitution, which gives Congress the means to execute its enumerated powers. This clause is the basis for Congress's implied powers. Also called the *necessary and proper clause.*

---

*A marble cake is a rough mixture of yellow and chocolate cake batter resembling marble stone. If you've never seen or eaten a slice of marble cake, imagine mixing a swirl of vanilla and chocolate soft freeze ice cream at Dairy Queen.

Federalism's Dynamics

Although the Constitution establishes a kind of federalism, the actual and proper balance of power between the nation and states has always been more a matter of debate than of formal theory. Three broad principles help to underscore why. First, rather than operating in a mechanical fashion, American federalism is a flexible and dynamic system. The Constitution's inherent ambiguities about federalism, some of which we have discussed already, generate constraints but also opportunities for politicians, citizens, and interest groups to push ideas that they care about. Second, because of this flexibility, both elected and appointed officials across levels of government often make policy decisions based on pragmatic considerations without regard to theories of what American federalism should look like. In sum, politics and policy goals rather than pure theoretical or ideological commitments about federalism tend to dominate decision making. Third, there is a growing recognition among public officials and citizens that public problems (such as questions involving trade-offs between freedom, order, and equality) cut across governmental boundaries. This section develops the first claim, and we explore the other two in later sections of this chapter.

The overall point these three claims illustrate is that to understand American federalism, one must know more than simply the powers that the Constitution assigns the different levels of government. Real understanding stems from recognizing the forces that can prompt changes in relationships between the national government and the states. In this section, we focus on four specific forces: national crises and demands, judicial interpretations, the expansion of grants-in-aid, and the professionalization of state governments.

National Crises and Demands

The elastic clause of the Constitution gives Congress the power to make all laws that are "necessary and proper" to carry out its responsibilities. By using this power in combination with its enumerated powers, Congress has been able to increase the scope of the national government tremendously during the previous two centuries. The greatest change has come about in times of crisis and national emergencies, such as the Civil War, the world wars, the Great Depression, and the aftermath of September 11, 2001. As an example, consider the Great Depression.

The Great Depression placed dual federalism in repose. The problems of the Depression proved too extensive for either state governments or private businesses to handle, so the national government assumed a heavy share of responsibility for providing relief and pursuing economic recovery. Under the New Deal, President Franklin D. Roosevelt's response to the Depression, Congress enacted various emergency relief programs designed to stimulate economic activity and help the unemployed. Many measures required the cooperation of the national and state governments. For example, the national government offered money to support state relief efforts; however, to receive these funds, states were usually required to provide administrative supervision or contribute some money of their own. Relief efforts were thus wrested from the hands of local bodies and centralized. Through the regulations it attached to funds, the national government extended its power and control over the states.[9]

IDEAlog.org

Do you prefer a bigger government with more services or a smaller government with fewer services? Take IDEAlog's self-test.

All Eyes on New Orleans

Hurricane Katrina devastated Louisiana and New Orleans. Less than a month later, a more powerful hurricane named Rita seemed headed on the same path of destruction. This time, all levels of government—state, local, national—attended a briefing aboard the USS *Iwo Jima* in advance of the powerful storm. From left to right: New Orleans mayor Ray Nagin, Louisiana governor Kathleen Babineaux Blanco, President George W. Bush, Lt. General Russell Honoré (responsible for military relief in the aftermath of Katrina), and Rear Admiral Larry Hereth (the principal federal official for Hurricane Rita). Rita landed west of New Orleans with less impact than Katrina. Still, the storm caused $10 billion in damage. *(© Jason Reed/Reuters/Corbis)*

Some call the New Deal era revolutionary. There is no doubt that the period was critical in reshaping federalism in the United States. The national and state governments had cooperated before, but the extent of their interactions during President Franklin Roosevelt's administration clearly made the marble-cake metaphor the more accurate description of American federalism. In addition, the size of the national government and its budget increased tremendously. But perhaps the most significant change was in the way Americans thought about their problems and the role of the national government in solving them. Difficulties that at one time had been considered personal or local were now viewed as national problems requiring national solutions. The general welfare, broadly defined, became a legitimate concern of the national government.

In other respects, however, the New Deal was not so revolutionary. For example, Congress did not claim any new powers to address the nation's economic problems. Rather, the national legislature simply used its constitutional powers to suit the circumstances. Arguably those actions were consistent with the overall purpose of the U.S. Constitution, which, as the preamble states, was designed in part to "insure domestic Tranquility . . . [and] promote the general welfare."

More recently, concerns over terrorist attacks on U.S. soil have expanded national power. In the month after the events of September 11, 2001, the Congress swiftly passed and the president signed into law the USA-Patriot Act (Public Law 107-56). Among other provisions, the law expanded significantly the surveillance and investigative powers of the Department of Justice. After some disagreement about its structure and organization, federal policymakers created the Department of Homeland Security in 2002, a new department that united over twenty previously separate federal agencies under a common administrative structure. In a move to further expand domestic surveillance activities, President Bush gave approval to wiretaps without warrants of American citizens suspected of terrorist ties. Congress had established a process for obtaining judicial warrants before or after such surveillance, but the president maintained that he had inherent power as commander in chief to act without regard to the congressional act.[10]

NSA = No Such Agency *or* National Security Agency?
The National Security Agency is the national government's largest intelligence service, much larger than the CIA. NSA is responsible for the worldwide collection and analysis of foreign communications. Its eavesdropping covers every type of communication medium, from mobile phone and radio to instant messaging and e-mail. For a long time, the NSA's existence was not acknowledged by the national government. NSA's domestic mission had been confined to court-warranted communications of foreign agents on American soil. In an effort to unearth evidence of terrorist activities following September 11, however, President George W. Bush relaxed these domestic restrictions to allow warrantless monitoring of people in the United States who placed international calls and engaged in Internet communications. President Bush defended his action as crucial to national security. His critics claimed his actions were lawless invasions of constitutionally protected liberties. *(Evan Vucci/AP/Wide World Photos)*

The role of the national government has also grown as it has responded to needs and demands that state and local governments were unwilling or unable to meet. Legislation is one prod the national government has used to achieve goals at the state level. The Voting Rights Act of 1965 is a good example. Section 2 of Article I of the Constitution gives the states the power to specify qualifications for voting. But the Fifteenth Amendment (1870) provides that no person shall be denied the right to vote "on account of race, color, or previous condition of servitude." Before the Voting Rights Act, states could not specifically deny blacks the right to vote, but they could require that voters pass literacy tests or pay poll taxes, requirements that virtually disenfranchised blacks in many states. The Voting Rights Act was designed to correct this political inequality (see Chapter 7).

The act gives the national government the power to decide whether individuals are qualified to vote and requires that qualified individuals be allowed to vote in all elections, including primaries and national, state, and local elections. If denial of voting rights seems to be widespread, the act authorizes the appointment of national voting examiners to examine and register voters for *all* elections. By replacing state election officials with national examiners, the act clearly intrudes on the political sovereignty of the states. The constitutional authority for the act rests on the second section of the Fifteenth Amendment, which gives Congress the power to enforce the amendment through "appropriate legislation."

Judicial Interpretation

How federal courts have interpreted the Constitution and federal law is another factor that has influenced the relationship between the national government and the states. Continuing with the example of the Voting Rights Act, it is important to remember that the law was not universally acclaimed when it was originally passed. Its critics used the language of dual or layer-cake federalism to insist that the Constitution gives the states the power to determine voter qualifications. The act's supporters claimed that the Fifteenth Amendment guarantee of voting rights should take precedence over states' rights and thus gives the national government new responsibilities.

The U.S. Supreme Court, the umpire of the federal system, ultimately resolved this dispute. It upheld the act as an appropriate congressional enforcement of the Fifteenth Amendment.[11] The Court settles disagreements over the powers of the national and state governments by deciding whether the actions of either are unconstitutional (see Chapter 14). In the nineteenth and early twentieth centuries, the Supreme Court often decided in favor of the states. Then, for nearly sixty years, from 1937 to 1995, the Court almost always supported the national government in contests involving the balance of power between nation and states. After 1995, a conservative U.S. Supreme Court tended to favor states' rights, but not without some notable and important exceptions. Exploring the Court's federalism jurisprudence provides a useful window on changes to the system that have transpired since the nation's founding.

Ends and Means. Early in the nineteenth century, the nationalist interpretation of federalism prevailed over states' rights. In 1819, under Chief Justice John Marshall (1801–1835), the Supreme Court expanded the role of the national government in the landmark case of *McCulloch* v. *Maryland*. The Court was asked to decide whether Congress had the power to establish a national bank and, if so, whether states had the power to tax that bank. In a unanimous opinion that Marshall authored, the Court conceded that Congress had only the powers conferred on it by the Constitution, which nowhere mentioned banks. However, Article I granted Congress the authority to enact all laws "necessary and proper" to the execution of Congress's enumerated powers. Marshall adopted a broad interpretation of this elastic clause: "Let the end be legitimate, let it be within the scope of the constitution, and all means which are appropriate, which are plainly adapted to that end, which are not prohibited, but consist with the letter and spirit of the constitution, are constitutional."

The Court clearly agreed that Congress had the power to charter a bank. But did the states (in this case, Maryland) have the power to tax the bank? Arguing that "the power to tax involves the power to destroy," Marshall insisted that states could not tax the national government because the powers of the national government came not from the states but from the people.[12] Marshall was embracing cooperative federalism, which sees a direct relationship between the people and the national government, with no need for the states to act as intermediaries. The framers of the Constitution did not intend to create a meaningless document, he reasoned. Therefore, they must have meant to give the national government all the powers necessary to carry out its assigned functions, even if those powers are only implied.

Especially from the late 1930s to the mid-1990s, the Supreme Court's interpretation of the Constitution's **commerce clause** was a major factor that increased the national government's power. The third clause of Article I, Section 8, states that "Congress shall have Power . . . To regulate Commerce . . . among the several States." In early Court decisions, beginning with *Gibbons* v. *Ogden* in 1824, Chief Justice Marshall interpreted the word *commerce* broadly to include virtually every form of commercial activity. But later courts would take a narrower view of that power.

Roger B. Taney became chief justice in 1836, and during his tenure (1836–1864), the Court's federalism decisions began to favor the states. The Taney Court took a more restrictive view of commerce and imposed firm limits on the

commerce clause The third clause of Article I, Section 8, of the Constitution, which gives Congress the power to regulate commerce among the states.

powers of the national government. As Taney saw it, the Constitution spoke "not only in the same words, but with the same meaning and intent with which it spoke when it came from the hands of its framers and was voted on and adopted by the people of the United States."[13] In the infamous *Dred Scott* decision (1857), for example, the Court decided that Congress had no power to prohibit slavery in the territories.

The judicial winds shifted again during the Great Depression. After originally disagreeing with FDR's and the Congress's position that the economic crisis was a national problem that demanded national action, the Court, with no change in personnel, began to alter its course in 1937 and upheld several major New Deal measures. Perhaps the Court was responding to the 1936 election returns (Roosevelt had been reelected in a landslide, and the Democrats commanded a substantial majority in Congress), which signified the voters' endorsement of the use of national policies to address national problems. Or perhaps the Court sought to defuse the president's threat to enlarge the Court with justices sympathetic to his views. ("The switch in time that saved nine," rhymed one observer.) In any event, the Court abandoned its effort to maintain a rigid boundary between national and state power.

The Umpire Strikes Back. One scholar has gone so far as to charge that the justices have treated the commerce clause like a shuttlecock volleyed back and forth by changing majorities.[14] Looking at the period from the New Deal through the 1980s, the evidence to support that claim appears rather unconvincing. However, in the 1990s, a series of important U.S. Supreme Court rulings involving the commerce clause suggested that the states' rights position was gaining ground. The Court's 5–4 ruling in *United States* v. *Lopez* (1995) held that Congress exceeded its authority under the commerce clause when it enacted a law in 1990 banning the possession of a gun in or near a school. A conservative majority, headed by Chief Justice William H. Rehnquist, concluded that having a gun in a school zone "has nothing to do with 'commerce' or any sort of economic enterprise, however broadly one might define those terms." Justices Sandra Day O'Connor, Antonin Scalia, Anthony Kennedy, and Clarence Thomas—all appointed by Republicans—joined in Rehnquist's opinion, putting the brakes on congressional power.[15]

Another piece of gun-control legislation, known as the Brady bill, produced similar eventual results. Congress enacted this law in 1993. It mandated the creation by November 1998 of a national system to check the background of prospective gun buyers in order to weed out, among others, convicted felons and those with mental illness. In the meantime, the law created a temporary system that called for local law enforcement officials to perform background checks and report their findings to gun dealers in their community. Several sheriffs challenged the law.

The Supreme Court agreed with the sheriffs, delivering a double-barreled blow to the local-enforcement provision in June 1997. In *Printz* v. *United States* (1997), the Court concluded that Congress could not require local officials to implement a regulatory scheme imposed by the national government. In language that seemingly invoked layer-cake federalism, Justice Antonin Scalia, writing for the five-member conservative majority, argued that locally enforced background checks violated the principle of dual sovereignty by allowing the national government "to impress into its service—and at no cost to itself—the police officers of the 50 States." In addition, he wrote, the scheme violated the principle of separation of powers by congressional transfer of the

IDEAlog.org

One of the questions in the IDEAlog self-test deals with stricter gun-control laws. How did you answer that question?

president's responsibility to faithfully execute national laws to local law enforcement officials.[16]

Federalism's Shifting Scales. In what appeared to signal the continuation of a pro–states' rights trajectory, in 2000 the justices struck down congressional legislation that had allowed federal court lawsuits for money damages for victims of crimes "motivated by gender." The Court held that the Violence Against Women Act violated both the commerce clause and Section 5 of the Fourteenth Amendment. Chief Justice Rehnquist, speaking for the five-person majority, declared that "the Constitution requires a distinction between what is truly national and what is truly local."[17]

But just as an umpire's strike zone can be ambiguous—is it knees to belt or knees to letters?—the Court more recently has veered from its states' rights direction on federalism. Perhaps the best-known decision in this vein is *Bush* v. *Gore,* the controversial Supreme Court decision resolving the 2000 presidential election. That tight election did not result in an immediate winner because the race in Florida was too close to call. Florida courts, interpreting Florida election law, had ordered ballot recounts, but a divided Supreme Court ordered a halt to the process and gave George W. Bush the victory. In an unrelated case from 2003, the Court also ruled against the states when it declared unconstitutional, by a 6–3 vote, a Texas law that had outlawed homosexual conduct between consenting homosexual adults. In the process, the decision also overturned a prior Court decision from the 1980s that had upheld Georgia's right to maintain a similar law.[18]

In two recent death penalty cases, the Court reflected the ambiguity and dynamic nature that frequently characterize the American federal system. In 2002, the Court denied state power to execute a defendant who was mentally disabled, reasoning that because many states had deemed such a practice inappropriate, "evolving standards of decency" in the nation suggested it was time to halt the practice.[19] In 2005, the Court again relied on evolving standards of decency to strike down a state death penalty for seventeen-year-olds.[20] In both cases, the Court acted against the policy of individual states by asserting national power to declare that the death penalty amounted to cruel and unusual punishment and thus violated the Constitution.

Grants-in-Aid

Since the 1960s, the national government's use of financial incentives has rivaled its use of legislation and court decisions as a means of influencing its relationship with state governments. Simultaneously, state and local governments have increasingly looked to Washington for money. Leaders at these lower levels of government have attempted to push their own initiatives by getting leverage from new national interest in a variety of policy areas. Thus, if governors can somehow convince national policymakers to adopt laws that buttress state priorities, then these state officials can advance their own priorities even as Washington's power appears to grow. Through a sort of back-and-forth process of negotiation and debate, the dynamics of the American federal system are revealed yet again. The principal arena where many of these interactions take place is in debates over federal grants-in-aid.

A **grant-in-aid** is money paid by one level of government to another level of government to be spent for a given purpose. Most grants-in-aid come with

grant-in-aid Money provided by one level of government to another to be spent for a given purpose.

standards or requirements prescribed by Congress. Many are awarded on a matching basis; that is, a recipient government must make some contribution of its own, which the national government then matches. For example, the nation's primary health-care program for low-income people, Medicaid, works on this sort of matching basis. Grants-in-aid take two general forms: categorical grants and block grants.

Categorical grants target specific purposes, and restrictions on their use typically leave the recipient government relatively little formal discretion. Recipients today include state governments, local governments, and public and private nonprofit organizations. There are two kinds of categorical grants: formula grants and project grants. As their name implies, **formula grants** are distributed according to specific rules that define who is eligible for the grant and how much each eligible applicant will receive. The formulas may weigh factors such as state per capita income, number of school-age children, urban population, and number of families below the poverty line. Most grants, however, are **project grants,** which are awarded through a competitive application process. Recent project grants have focused on health (substance abuse and HIV-AIDS programs); natural resources and the environment (radon, asbestos, and toxic pollution); and education, training, and employment (for the disabled, the homeless, and the aged).

In contrast to categorical grants, Congress awards **block grants** for broad, general purposes. They allow recipient governments considerable freedom to decide how to spend the money. Whereas a categorical grant promotes a specific activity—say, developing an ethnic heritage studies curriculum in public schools—a block grant might be earmarked only for elementary, secondary, and vocational education more generally. The state or local government receiving the block grant would then choose the specific educational programs to fund with it. The recipient might use some money to support ethnic heritage studies and some to fund consumer education programs. Or the recipient might choose to put all the money into consumer education programs and spend nothing on ethnic heritage studies.

Grants-in-aid are a method of redistributing income. Money is collected by the national government from the taxpayers of all fifty states. The money is then funneled back to state and local governments. Many grants have worked to reduce gross inequalities among states and their residents. But the formulas used to redistribute income are not impartial; they are highly political, established through a process of congressional horse-trading.

Although grants-in-aid have been part of the national government arsenal since the early twentieth century, they grew at an astonishing pace in the 1960s, when grant spending doubled every five years. Presidents Nixon and Reagan were strong advocates for redistributing money back to the states, and political support for such redistribution has remained strong. Controlling for inflation, in 1990 the national government returned $172 billion to the states. By 2006, the amount had increased to $363 billion.[21] The main trend, as illustrated in Figure 4.2, is an enormous growth in health-care spending, which now approaches 50 percent of all national grant funds to the states.[22]

Whatever its form or purpose, grant money comes with strings attached. Some strings are there to ensure that recipients spend the money as the law specifies; other regulations are designed to evaluate how well the grant is working. To these ends, the national government may stipulate that recipients follow certain procedures. The national government may also attach restrictions

categorical grants Grants-in-aid targeted for a specific purpose by either formula or project.

formula grants Categorical grants distributed according to a particular set of rules, called a formula, that specify who is eligible for the grants and how much each eligible applicant will receive.

project grants Categorical grants awarded on the basis of competitive applications submitted by prospective recipients to perform a specific task or function.

block grants Grants-in-aid awarded for general purposes, allowing the recipient great discretion in spending the grant money.

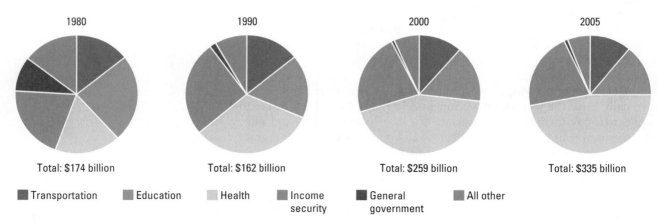

FIGURE 4.2 Trends in National Government Grants to States and Localities, FY 1980 to 2005

1980 — Total: $174 billion
1990 — Total: $162 billion
2000 — Total: $259 billion
2005 — Total: $335 billion

■ Transportation   ■ Education   ■ Health   ■ Income security   ■ General government   ■ All other

National government grants to states and localities vary substantially. In 1980, education programs accounted for the biggest slice of the national government pie. In 1990, grants for health programs, reflecting the expanding costs of Medicaid, took the biggest slice, reaching more than 30 percent of all national government grants to state and local governments. By 2000, health grants exceeded 43 percent of all such national government spending. By 2005, health grants exceeded 47 percent of national government grants to the states.

Source: Historical Tables, *Budget of the United States Government,* FY2005, Table 12.3. Dollar amounts are in billions of constant FY1996 dollars.

designed to achieve some broad national goal not always closely related to the specific purpose of the grant. Consider the issue of drunk driving, for example.

The use of highway construction funds has proved an effective means to induce states to accept national standards. Congress threatened to reduce millions of dollars in these funds if states did not agree to prohibit the purchase or consumption of alcoholic beverages by persons under the age of twenty-one. Some states objected, claiming that the Tenth and Twenty-first amendments assigned them responsibility for matters such as alcoholic beverage consumption. In *South Dakota* v. *Dole* (1987), the Supreme Court conceded that direct congressional control of the drinking age in the states would be unconstitutional. Nevertheless, the Constitution does not bar the indirect achievement of such objectives. The seven-member majority argued that, far from being an infringement on states' rights, the law was a "relatively mild encouragement to the States to enact higher minimum drinking ages than they would otherwise choose." After all, Chief Justice William H. Rehnquist wrote, the goal of reducing drunk driving was "directly related to one of the main purposes for which highway funds are expended—safe interstate travel."[23] By 1988, every state in the nation had approved legislation setting twenty-one as the minimum drinking age.

In October 2000, following a three-year battle in Congress, President Bill Clinton signed new legislation establishing a tough national standard of .08 percent blood-alcohol level for drunk driving. Thirty-one states define drunk driving at the .10 percent standard or do not set a specific standard. States that now refuse to impose the lower standard stand to lose millions in government highway construction money.[24] The restaurant industry was not cheering the result.

It characterized the law as an attack on social drinkers, who are not the source of the drunk-driving problem. The lure of financial aid has proved a powerful incentive for states to accept standards set by the national government, especially when those standards are aligned with priorities that the states and their citizens generally accept (here, reducing the incidence of drunk driving).

Professionalization of State Governments

A final important factor that has produced dynamic changes in the American federal system has been the emergence of state governments as more capable policy actors than they were in the past. While political scientists generally agree that the rise of competitive party politics in the South (see Chapter 8), the expansion of the interest group system (Chapter 10), and the growth of money in elections (Chapter 9) have all produced significant changes in American politics, nevertheless, many scholars and students rarely consider the expanded capabilities of state governments in the same light. That oversight is important, especially when one considers how far the states have come during the past four decades and how their progress has influenced the shape of American federalism.

It was not long ago that states were described as the weak links in the American policy system. Despite the crucial role that they played in the nation's founding and the legacy of dual federalism, observers both inside and outside the government were skeptical of their ability to contribute actively and effectively to national progress in the post–World War II era. In an oft-quoted book, former North Carolina governor Terry Sanford leveled heavy criticisms at the states, calling them ineffective, indecisive, and inattentive organizations that may have lost their relevance in an increasingly complicated nation and world.[25] Writing nearly twenty years earlier, in 1949, journalist Robert Allen was even less kind; he called the states "the tawdriest, most incompetent, most stultifying unit in the nation's political structure."[26]

But since the 1960s especially, states have become more capable and forceful policy actors. These changes have created better policy outcomes that have benefited citizens across the United States while simultaneously contributing to dynamic changes in the American federal system. If the situation was so bleak less than four decades ago, what happened to bring about the change? Several factors account for the change in perspective.[27]

First, the states have made many internal changes that have fostered their capabilities. Both governors and state legislators now employ more capably trained and experienced policy staff rather than part-time assistants with responsibilities across a wide range of policy areas. Second, legislatures now meet more days during the year, and elected officials in states receive higher salaries. Third, the appeal of higher salaries, in particular, has helped to attract more highly qualified people to run for state office. Fourth, the increasing ability of states to raise revenue, as a result of state tax and budgetary reforms that have transpired since the 1960s, has also given states greater leverage in designing and directing policy, rather than previous generations, where local property taxes played a more significant role in relation to state budget and tax policy. And, fifth, the unelected officials who work in state departments and administer state programs in areas such as transportation, social services, and law enforcement have become better educated. For instance, the proportion of state administrators possessing a graduate degree increased

Can you explain why . . . you have to be twenty-one to drink in all fifty states, even though Congress has never passed a law declaring a national drinking age?

from 40 to 60 percent during the period from 1964 to 1994. At the same time, administrators with only some college or less education dropped from 34 percent to just 7 percent.[28]

As evidence of the dynamic relationships between the national government and the states, changes in national policy have also helped the states to develop. Many federal grants-in-aid include components designed explicitly to foster capacity-building measures in state governments. Because the national government recognizes—often for political or practical reasons—that several of its domestic initiatives depend on capable implementation from state actors, members of Congress and presidents often design national laws with these capacity-building elements in mind.

One example is the Elementary and Secondary Education Act (ESEA), which became law in 1965. This act, passed as part of President Lyndon Johnson's Great Society effort, was designed to provide federal assistance to the nation's disadvantaged students. Though it is often overlooked, Title V of the law contained several provisions designed to strengthen state departments of education, the agencies that would be responsible for administering the bulk of other programs contained in the ESEA. Thus, although the law was often portrayed as an assertion of national power (which it was), it also helped to set in motion changes that would allow state governments to improve their capabilities to make and administer K–12 education policy. Those new capabilities, which subsequent federal laws and internal state efforts have fostered, continued to influence the shape of both federal and state education policy, especially during the most recent revision of the ESEA as the No Child Left Behind Act of 2001.[29]

All of this is not to say that the states are without problems of their own. In some ways, they have been victims of their own success. Now that state capitals have become more viable venues where citizens and interest groups can agitate for their causes, the states have begun to face ever-increasing demands. Those requests can strain state administrators and legislative or gubernatorial staffs, who, while better educated and equipped than their predecessors, still struggle to set priorities and please their constituents.

★ Ideology, Policymaking, and American Federalism

As the previous section illustrated, American federalism appears to be in constant motion. This is due in large part to what some political scientists call **policy entrepreneurs:** citizens, interest groups, and officials inside government who attempt to persuade others to accept a particular view of the proper balance of freedom, order, and equality. The American federal system provides myriad opportunities for interested parties to push their ideas.

In essence, the existence of national and state governments—specifically, their executive, legislative, and judicial branches, and their bureaucratic agencies—offers these entrepreneurs venues where they can attempt to influence policy and politics. Sometimes when doors are closed off in one place, opportunities may be available elsewhere. The most creative of these entrepreneurs can work at multiple levels of government simultaneously, sometimes coordinating with one another to score political and policy victories.

policy entrepreneurs Citizens, members of interest groups, or public officials who champion particular policy ideas.

In this section, we explore how views about American federalism can influence the shape of the nation's politics and policy. We also relate these issues to our ongoing discussion of political ideology, which we introduced in Chapter 1 (see Figure 1.2).

Ideology, Policymaking, and Federalism in Theory

To begin our discussion in this section, it will be helpful to return to the cake metaphors that describe dual and cooperative federalism. Looking at those models of the nation's federal system helps to capture some of what could be considered conventional wisdom about political ideology and federalism—in particular the views of conservatives and liberals. In their efforts to limit the scope of the national government, conservatives are often associated with the layer-cake metaphor. In contrast, it is often said that liberals, believing that one function of the national government is to bring about equality, are more likely to support the marble-cake approach and more activism from Washington. Let's explore each of these general claims in a bit more detail.

Conservatives are frequently portrayed as believing that different states have different problems and resources and that returning control to state governments would actually promote diversity. States would be free to experiment with alternative ways to confront their problems. States would compete with one another. And people would be free to choose the state government they preferred by simply voting with their feet and moving to another state. An additional claim frequently attributed to the conservative approach to federalism is that the national government is too remote, too tied to special interests, and not responsive to the public at large. The national government overregulates and tries to promote too much uniformity. States are closer to the people and better able to respond to specific local needs. (Consider "Looking to the Future: Water Wars Among the States?")

In contrast, pundits and scholars often argue that what conservatives hope for, liberals fear. Liberals remember, so the argument goes, that the states' rights model allowed extreme political and social inequalities and that it supported racism. Blacks and city dwellers were often left virtually unrepresented by white state legislators who disproportionately served rural interests. The conclusion is that liberals believe the states remain unwilling or unable to protect the rights or provide for the needs of their citizens, whether those citizens are consumers seeking protection from business interests, defendants requiring guarantees of due process of law, or poor people seeking a minimum standard of living.

Looking in general terms at how presidents since the 1960s have approached federalism issues seems to provide some support for these descriptions of liberals and conservatives.

President Lyndon Johnson's efforts to forge a Great Society are often characterized as the high-water mark of national government activism. With the range of programs in housing, education, and urban renewal developed during Johnson's tenure and his extensions of FDR's New Deal, it was clear to many observers that the marble cake seemed to dominate LBJ's thinking about federalism. In 1969, Richard Nixon advocated giving more power to state and local governments. Nixon wanted to decentralize national policies through an effort dubbed New Federalism. The president's New Federalism called for

Looking to the Future

Water Wars Among the States?

We take water for granted in much of the United States, but it has become scarce in some areas, and not just in the desert regions of the West. Drought, over-allocation and overuse, aging infrastructure, and land development threaten water supplies, and population growth and trends in water usage increase the demand on water resources.

Conflicts loom within and between states as demand for potable water exceeds existing and anticipated supplies. The states can address some of the supply problems by promoting the transfer of water rights, discouraging overuse, and creating drought plans. On the demand side, states can meter water use for everyone and adjust the price of water to promote efficient landscaping and recycling.

Here is one prediction in the form of a map of the areas in the western United States where water is likely to be a source of growing conflict. The map highlights areas of potential conflict, as water becomes an increasingly scarce commodity. By 2025, continued explosive population growth in the western states, coupled with their naturally arid climate, will combine to strain existing water supplies. Continued severe drought in the region will only make the problem worse. The current infrastructure of water storage and delivery is well past its useful life, relying on nineteenth-century technology to meet the demands of the twenty-first century. Of course, if the drought ends or the population growth slows, then the areas most at risk of conflict over water usage might never materialize into conflict.

Is it in a state's interest to encourage or discourage population growth without considering the need for adequate water supplies? How should a state balance the needs of its citizens against the water needs of other vital consumers (such as farmers and water-dependent industries)? Do we need to establish a water bank where surplus water can be "deposited" and "withdrawn" at a price?

Source: Council for State Governments, *Water Wars. Trends Alert: Critical Information for State Decision-Makers* (July 2003). Map from <http://www.doi.gov/water2025>.

combining and reformulating categorical grants into block grants. The shift had dramatic implications for federalism. Block grants were seen as a way to redress the imbalance of power between Washington and the states and localities. Conservatives in Washington wanted to return freedom to the states. New Federalism was nothing more than dual federalism in modern dress.

After the term of President Jimmy Carter, who made some headway in reorganizing federal efforts in domestic policy but by no means supported the extensive block-grant approach of Nixon, Ronald Reagan took office in 1981. Charging that the federal system had been bent out of shape, Reagan promised what to some could be called "new New Federalism" to restore a proper constitutional relationship among the national, state, and local governments. The national government, he said, treated "elected state and local officials as if they were nothing more than administrative agents for federal authority."[30]

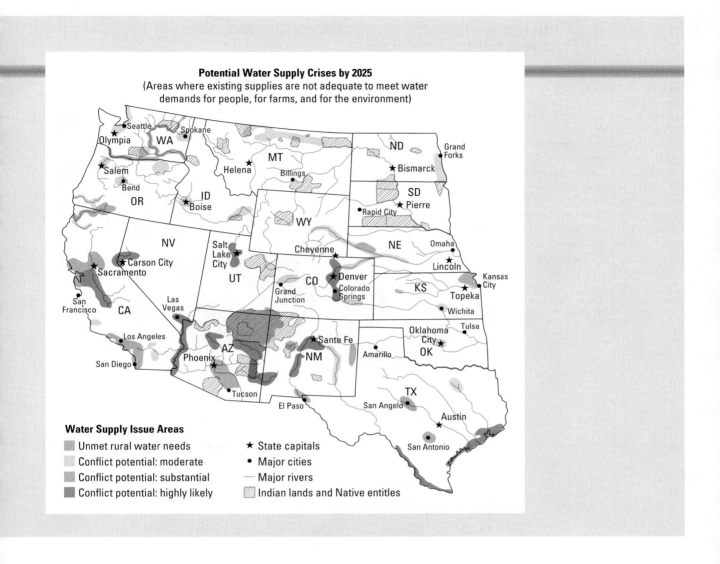

Potential Water Supply Crises by 2025
(Areas where existing supplies are not adequate to meet water demands for people, for farms, and for the environment)

Water Supply Issue Areas

- Unmet rural water needs
- Conflict potential: moderate
- Conflict potential: substantial
- Conflict potential: highly likely
- ★ State capitals
- • Major cities
- — Major rivers
- Indian lands and Native entitles

Reagan's commitment to reducing federal taxes and spending meant that the states would have to foot an increasing share of the bill for government services (see Figure 4.3). In the late 1970s, the national government funded 25 percent of all state and local government spending. By 1990, its contribution had declined to roughly 17 percent. By the end of 2000, that figure had increased again, inching up to about 23 percent, where it remains.

While it would be inaccurate to describe Clinton and Lyndon Johnson as liberals cut from the same cloth, President Clinton, unlike Nixon and Reagan, saw much more potential for the national government to produce policy successes, especially in areas such as education and environmental protection. Clinton's approach might be described as seeing the national government as a policy guru, guiding and encouraging states to experiment with vexing problems.

FIGURE 4.3 The National Government's Contributions to State and Local Government Expenditures

In 1960, the national government contributed roughly 11 percent of total state and local spending. After rising in the 1960s and 1970s, that total stood at almost 25 percent by 1980. The national share declined during the 1980s, and by 1990 it was not quite 17 percent. By 2000, the national government share had moved up to 23 percent, and by 2004, it had grown still higher, to 27 percent. In 2006, it dropped to 24 percent.

Source: Calculations from Historical Tables, *Budget of the United States Government,* FY2006, Table 15.2 (adjusted to 1996 dollars).

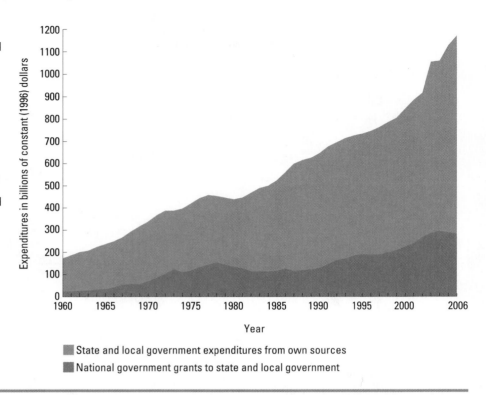

State and local government expenditures from own sources

National government grants to state and local government

When George W. Bush took the White House in 2000, there appeared to develop yet another bend in the nation's federalism road. Generally, Bush, who described himself as a "compassionate conservative" both on the campaign trail and during his term, has sought to embrace the states' rights perspective but in a tempered fashion. That approach signaled a move away from the Republican effort in 1994 to scale back the national government while ignoring the potential costs—in human and social terms, for example—of their proposals.

Ideology, Policymaking, and Federalism in Practice

Despite the apparent consistencies between presidential preferences regarding federalism and refrains such as "liberals love the national government" and "conservatives favor states' rights," these simplifications are only sometimes correct and, in fact, are often misleading. Recall our admonition from Chapter 1 that to grasp the differences between conservatives and liberals, one needs to understand not only these general labels but also the purposes of government under discussion. One illustration emerges from debates over the federal preemption of state power.

National Intervention in State Functions. The power of Congress to enact laws that have the national government assume total or partial responsibility for a state government function is called **preemption.** When the national government shoulders a new government function, it restricts the discretionary power of the states.

Preemption is a modern power. Congress passed only fourteen preemptive acts before 1900. By 1988, Congress had preempted the power of states to legislate in certain areas 350 times, and 186 of these acts were passed between 1970 and 1990.[31] The pace of preemption has accelerated. From 2001 to 2006, twenty-seven new laws have preempted state authority.[32] For example, under the Nutrition Labeling and Education Act of 1990, the national government established food-labeling standards and simultaneously stripped the states of their power to impose food-labeling requirements. The act therefore prevents the states from providing added protections for health-conscious consumers. Industry groups, such as the Grocery Manufacturers of America, favored preemption because uniform labeling would be cheaper than following fifty different state labeling guidelines.[33]

Congressional preemption statutes infringe on state powers in two ways: through mandates and restraints. A **mandate** is a requirement that a state undertake an activity or provide a service, in keeping with minimum national standards. For example, through the Medicaid program, the national government requires states to provide their low-income citizens with access to some minimal level of health care. Although Medicaid is a program funded jointly by the national government and the states—in 2005, it cost $298 billion—it has grown to become the second largest item in state budgets, trailing only education. The overall cost of funding and managing this program was one of the reasons that in 2002 and 2003, amid punishing budget crises, several states began to cut back on medical services that their Medicaid programs would cover, and they clamored for more financial support from the national government.[34]

In contrast, a **restraint** forbids state governments from exercising a certain power. Consider bus regulation, for example. To ensure bus service to small and remote communities, in the past some states would condition the issuance of bus franchises on bus operators' agreeing to serve such communities, even if the routes lost money. But in 1982, Congress passed the Bus Regulatory Reform Act, which forbade the states from imposing such conditions. Many states now provide subsidies to bus operators to ensure service to out-of-the way areas.

Whether preemption takes the form of mandates or restraints, the result is additional costs for state and local government and interference with a fundamental government task: setting priorities. Furthermore, the national government is not obliged to pay for the costs it imposes. As preemption grew in the 1980s, the national government reduced spending in the form of grants to the states. For example, the 1988 Family Support Act required states to continue Medicaid coverage for a year to families who left welfare for jobs, but the states had to pick up the tab.

Constraining Unfunded Mandates.

State and local government officials have long objected to the national government's practice of imposing requirements without providing the financial support needed to satisfy them. By 1992, more than 170 congressional acts had established partially or wholly unfunded mandates.[35]

One of the early results of the Republican-led 104th Congress (1995–1997) was the Unfunded Mandates Relief Act of 1995. The legislation requires the Congressional Budget Office to prepare cost estimates of any newly proposed

Label Me
Food labeling follows a single national standard today as a result of the Nutrition Labeling and Education Act of 1990. The act preempted the states from imposing different labeling requirements. (© Sara-Maria Vischer/The Image Works)

preemption The power of Congress to enact laws by which the national government assumes total or partial responsibility for a state government function.

mandate A requirement that a state undertake an activity or provide a service, in keeping with minimum national standards.

restraint A requirement laid down by act of Congress, prohibiting a state or local government from exercising a certain power.

national legislation that would impose more than $50 million a year in costs on state and local governments or more than $100 million a year in costs on private business. It also requires a cost analysis of the impact of new agency regulations on governments and private businesses. Congress can still pass along to the states the costs of the programs it mandates, but only after holding a separate vote specifically imposing a requirement on other governments without providing the money to carry it out. It is important to note that the law does not apply to legislation protecting constitutional rights and civil rights or to antidiscrimination laws.

The act's critics argue that large proportions of state appropriation budgets still must cover the costs of programs imposed by the national government. The National Conference of State Legislatures estimated, for example, that Mississippi spent at least 8 percent of its appropriations budget on federal programs in 2004.[36] The president of the conference complained that "unfortunately for states, the federal government continues to overstep its bounds by imposing its will on state governments."[37] But the act's defenders found little overreaching. Only 44 of 377 congressional enactments in 2001 and 2002 contained mandates, and only five mandates met or exceeded the act's cost thresholds.[38]

Ideology and Unfunded Mandates. Anecdotally, the previous paragraph suggests that Republicans, typically the more conservative of the two major political parties, would be more likely than their liberal Democratic counterparts to support states' rights. A more systematic examination, however, reveals that this is not always the case. Rather, liberal or conservative support for federal mandates tends to depend on the interaction of ideology *and* the purposes of government being considered. Consider the following evidence from recent research on presidential and congressional policymaking.

If conservative presidents are more likely to support states' rights, then one would expect them to defend state interests when opportunities arise. One such possibility exists in federalism cases before the U.S. Supreme Court. When the U.S. government is not a party in a case, the U.S. Department of Justice is allowed to file a brief either supporting or opposing state interests. In a study of these briefs from federalism cases during the 1980s and 1990s, one scholar found that Ronald Reagan's Justice Department filed briefs in twenty cases supporting the national government and eight supporting the states. The corresponding numbers for Bill Clinton were seven and five, respectively.

On their face, these numbers are somewhat puzzling. If Reagan was indeed a conservative and Clinton was more liberal, then how could it be that both of them—and overwhelmingly so in Reagan's case—favored national government interests over state interests in these cases? According to the author of the study, "The explanation seems to lie in the Reagan administration's willingness to support business interests when pitted against state administrative agencies, especially in environmental cases. . . . In contrast, the Clinton administration often aligned itself with a state or local government when such a party collided in court with a business group."[39] Thus, ideology explains only part of the story; an added component is the policy context and different views of the proper way to use federalism to balance freedom, order, and equality.

Evidence from congressional roll call voting from the period 1983 to 1990 (the 98th through 101st Congresses) reveals a similar set of findings. In a study that examined the factors that predict a House or Senate member's likelihood of voting to support a federal mandate, one congressional scholar found that the link between ideology or partisanship and willingness to support federal mandates varied a great deal by policy area. Thus, sometimes liberals were more likely to support mandates, other times conservatives were, and at other times still, ideology appeared to have no measurable effect. This finding led the author to conclude that "federalism is largely a secondary value, overshadowed and often overwhelmed by other, more primary goals." In short, "roll call voting is largely prompted by the underlying policy issue involved, not by the principle of federalism at stake."[40]

The findings from these studies of presidential and congressional behavior underscore two of the major principles that we outlined earlier in this chapter. The flexibility of the American federal system creates significant opportunities for policymakers and other policy entrepreneurs to accomplish their goals. And given those opportunities, it is not surprising that pragmatic considerations about the substance of policy, rather than fealty to a principled view of federalism, tend to dominate the behavior of public officials and their supporters.

Federalism and Electoral Politics

In addition to affecting the shape of American public policy, federalism also plays a significant role in electoral politics. We will have much more to say about elections in Chapter 9. For now, we focus on the ways that federalism is related to the outcome of both state and national elections.

National Capital–State Capital Links

State capitals often serve as proving grounds for politicians who aspire to national office. After gaining experience in a state legislature or serving in a statewide elected position (governor or attorney general, for example), elected officials frequently draw on that experience in making a pitch for service in the U.S. House, Senate, or even the White House. The role that state political experience can play in making a run for the presidency seems to have become increasingly important in recent decades. Consider that four of the previous five candidates to be elected to the highest office in the land, a period dating back to 1976, had formerly served as governors: Jimmy Carter (Georgia), Ronald Reagan (California), Bill Clinton (Arkansas), and George W. Bush (Texas). George H. W. Bush is the lone exception to this otherwise long streak. Today, several prominent members of Congress also have past experience in statewide offices. Examples include Senator Judd Gregg, former governor of New Hampshire; Representative Michael Castle, former lieutenant governor and governor of Delaware; and Senator Claire McCaskill, former state auditor of Missouri.

It is hard to underestimate the value of previous political experience in attempting to mount a campaign for national office. In addition to learning the craft of being a politician, experience in state politics can be critically important for helping a candidate to build up a network of contacts, die-hard constituents, and potential fundraisers. Past governors also have the benefit of being plugged into organizations such as the National Governors' Association and the Republican and Democratic governors' groups, which can help to cultivate national-level name recognition, friendships, and a reputation in Washington. Finally, considering that presidential elections are really a series of fifty different state-level contests, given the structure of the electoral college, a candidate

Win One for the Gripper
Presidents routinely come to the aid of fellow office seekers, hoping to increase their party's fortunes in local and statewide races. In 2006, President George W. Bush campaigned to re-elect Republican senator Jim Talent of Missouri. Talent lost his bid. Democrats defeated all six Republican incumbents. President Bush acknowledged that "it was a thumping." (© Shawn Thew/epa/Corbis)

for the White House can benefit tremendously from a friendly governor who can call into action his or her own political network on the candidate's behalf.

If state-level experience and friends can sometimes catapult an individual to national office, once secure in the Congress or the White House, national-level politicians frequently return to the states to stump for local favorites. In the 2002 election cycle, with a closely divided House and Senate, President George W. Bush and his key political strategist, Karl Rove, adopted an aggressive approach to the midterm election campaign. The president traveled across the country speaking on behalf of Republican candidates, increasing the party's majority by eight seats in the House and four in the Senate. But the same strategy proved disastrous for Bush and fellow Republicans in the 2006 elections. Republicans lost thirty seats and their majority in the House; they lost six seats and their majority in the Senate. And Democrats claimed a majority of gubernatorial elections. Presidential popularity (and unpopularity) cuts both ways.[41]

Congressional Redistricting

Perhaps even more important than activities on the campaign trail is the decennial process of congressional redistricting, which reveals crucial connections between federalism and the nation's electoral politics. Most generally, **redistricting** refers to the process of redrawing boundaries for electoral jurisdictions. This process, which occurs at all levels of government, becomes an extremely high-stakes game in the two years after each decennial national census in the United States. During that window of time, the U.S. Census Bureau produces and releases updated population counts for the nation. Those numbers are used to determine the number of seats that each state will have in the U.S. House, which are apportioned based on population.

While it is relatively straightforward to determine how many seats each state will have, where the new district lines will be drawn is a hugely complicated and political process. Even in states that may not have lost or gained seats but have had population shifts—some areas grow at a rapid rate while

redistricting The process of redrawing political boundaries to reflect changes in population.

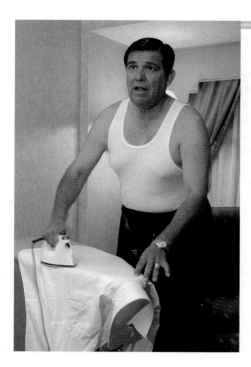

Ironing Out Legislative Wrinkles
Hoping to stall a Republican effort to reopen the congressional redistricting process in Texas, Democrats left the state to deny the legislature a quorum. Here, Democratic state senator Eddie Lucio irons his shirt in Albuquerque, New Mexico, in the summer of 2003. Eventually the Democrats returned, and the Republicans won their redistricting battle. *(AP/Wide World Photos)*

others lose population, for example—the task of redistricting carries huge stakes. In large part, this is because state legislatures typically have the task of drawing the lines that define the congressional districts in their states. Given that this process happens only once every ten years and that the careers of U.S. House members and their party's relatively long-term fortunes in Congress can turn on decisions made in these state-level political debates, it is no wonder that the redistricting process commands significant national attention.

Evidence that federalism has become increasingly intertwined with the politics of congressional redistricting emerged in Texas in 2003. Frustrated by the lack of Republican representation in his state's congressional delegation and hoping to increase the GOP majority in Congress, U.S. House majority whip Tom DeLay worked with legislators in Texas's Republican-controlled state legislature to reopen the redistricting question that had been settled prior to the 2002 midterm elections. Given their minority status in the Texas legislature, state Democrats took drastic measures to deny the state house a quorum—by fleeing to an undisclosed location outside Texas, some on state representative James E. "Pete" Laney's private plane—to turn back the offensive of their partisan adversaries. Shortly after this turn of events, it was learned that DeLay, who had risen to House majority leader, had called to service the Federal Aviation Administration and the Department of Homeland Security, the latter the new office designed to protect the nation against terrorist attacks, to track down Laney's plane and pinpoint the location of the Texas Democrats. Republicans tended to defend DeLay as simply performing constituent service by intervening as he did, while Democrats assailed DeLay's effort as an inappropriate use of the nation's resources, especially during a time of war and heightened concerns over terrorism.[42] DeLay was indicted in 2005 for money laundering. He stepped down from his leadership position in 2006.

A final way that federalism can influence redistricting is through a process called *preclearance*. Under Section 5 of the Voting Rights Act, several states are required to submit their redistricting plans to the U.S. Department of Justice for approval. The process is quite complicated, but in essence it requires that states show how their proposed plans will not be "retrogressive in purpose or effect," meaning they will not dilute minority voting strength. Passing the test of preclearance, however, does not mean that a state's redistricting plans cannot be challenged for civil rights purposes or other grounds as defined in federal law and court decisions, such as rulings affirming the one person–one vote principle.

In short, both the politics of drawing congressional boundaries and the interactions between Justice Department officials and state legislators responsible for preclearance reveal the intimate connections between federalism and the redistricting process.[43]

★ Federalism and the American Intergovernmental System

We have concentrated in this chapter on the links between the national and state governments in the federal system. Although the Constitution explicitly recognizes only national and state governments, the American federal system has spawned a multitude of local governments as well. It is worth considering these units because they help to illustrate the third main principle that we outlined near the beginning of this chapter: a growing recognition among public officials and citizens that public problems cut across governmental boundaries. Finding the right mix of national, state, and local involvement is a perennial challenge that dogs even the most savvy and experienced public officials.

Thousands of Governments

Based on data from 2002, the most recent year available, the U.S. Census Bureau estimates that in addition to the one national government and fifty state governments, the United States is home to over 87,500 local governments of different sorts.[44] These governments are mainly the product of the previous century of American history, with nearly all coming into existence during the 1900s.

Americans are citizens of both a nation and a state, and they also come under the jurisdiction of these various local government units. These units include **municipal governments,** the governments of cities and towns. Municipalities, in turn, are located in (or may contain or share boundaries with) counties, which are administered by **county governments.** (Sixteen states further subdivide counties into *townships* as units of government.) Most Americans also live in a **school district,** which is responsible for administering local elementary and secondary educational programs. They may also be served by one or more **special districts,** government units created to perform particular functions, typically when those functions, such as fire protection and water purification and distribution, spill across ordinary jurisdictional boundaries. Examples of special districts are the Port Authority of New York and New Jersey, the Chicago Sanitation District, and the Southeast Pennsylvania Transit Authority.

Local governments are created by state governments, either in their constitutions or through legislation. This means that their organization, powers, re-

municipal governments
The government units that administer a city or town.

county governments The government units that administer a county.

school district The government unit that administers elementary and secondary school programs.

special districts Government units created to perform particular functions, especially when those functions are best performed across jurisdictional boundaries.

Whose Rules?
Grand Staircase–Escalante National Monument in southern Utah was established by presidential decree in 1996. It sits on 1.7 million acres of austere and rugged land. The decree irked local residents, who had hoped for greater industrial development that is now barred. They have fought back by claiming ownership of hundreds of miles of dirt roads, dry washes, and riverbeds in the monument. The conflicting signs illustrate the controversy. On the left, the local government, Kane County, approves use of all-terrain vehicles. On the right, the national government signals just the opposite. (Kevin Maloney for The New York Times)

sponsibilities, and effectiveness vary considerably from state to state. About forty states endow their cities with various forms of **home rule**—the right to enact and enforce legislation in certain administrative areas. Home rule gives cities a measure of self-government and freedom of action. In contrast, county governments, which are the main units of local government in rural areas, tend to have little or no legislative power. Instead, county governments ordinarily serve as administrative units, performing the specific duties assigned to them under state law, such as maintaining roads and administering health programs.

How can the ordinary citizen be expected to make sense of this maze of governments? And do these governments really benefit ordinary citizens?

In theory at least, one advantage of localizing government is that it brings government closer to the people; it gives them an opportunity to participate in the political process, to have a direct influence on policy. Localized government conjures visions of informed citizens deciding their own political fate—the traditional New England town meeting, repeated across the nation. From this perspective, overlapping governments appear compatible with a majoritarian view of democracy.

The reality is somewhat different, however. Studies have shown that people are much less likely to vote in local elections than in national elections.[45] In fact, voter turnout in local contests tends to be quite low (although the influence of individual votes is thus much greater). Furthermore, the fragmentation of powers, functions, and responsibilities among national, state, and local governments makes government as a whole seem complicated, and hence incomprehensible and inaccessible, to ordinary people. In addition, most people have little time to devote to public affairs, which can be very time-consuming. These factors tend to discourage individual citizens from pursuing politics and augment the influence of organized groups, which have the resources—time, money, and know-how—to sway policymaking (see Chapter 10). Instead of bringing government closer to the people and reinforcing majoritarian democracy, the system's enormous complexity tends to encourage pluralism.

Still, the large number of governments makes it possible for government to respond to the diversity of conditions in different parts of the country. States

home rule The right to enact and enforce legislation locally.

A Grisly Record
In two separate attacks about two hours apart on April 17, 2007, Seung-hui Cho killed thirty-two people and wounded twenty-five on the campus of Virginia Tech. Campus, city, state, and federal police forces converged on the campus to track the killer and minister to the wounded. Pictured here: State police gather on the campus in Blacksburg, Virginia (*left*). Agents from the federal Bureau of Alcohol, Tobacco, Firearms, and Explosives (ATF) enter Norris Hall, scene of many campus deaths (*right*). This was the deadliest shooting in American history. *(left: © Matthew Cavanaugh/epa/Corbis; right: AP photo/Charles Dharapak)*

Can you explain why . . .
Americans generally believe that government should be close to the people, yet so few citizens vote in local elections?

and cities differ enormously in population, size, economic resources, climate, and other characteristics—the diverse elements that French political philosopher Montesquieu argued should be taken into account in formulating laws for a society. Smaller political units are better able to respond to particular local conditions and can generally do so more quickly than larger units. Nevertheless, smaller units may not be able to muster the economic resources to meet some challenges. And in a growing number of policy areas, from education to environmental protection to welfare provision, citizens have come to see the advantages of coordinating efforts and sharing burdens across levels of government.

Crosscutting Responsibilities

The national government continues to support state and local governments. Yet spending pressures on state and local governments are enormous. The public demands better schools, harsher sentences for criminals (and more prisons to hold them), more and better day care for children, and nursing home assistance for the elderly. Bolstered by a strong national economy, many states cut income and business taxes in 2006. Other states provided local property tax relief. Overall, state and local governments still managed to increase their tax revenue despite rate cuts in many places.[46]

In addition to ongoing policy development and financing the activities of government, sometimes crises press different levels of government into duty together. A tragic turn of events in October 2002 provides a case in point. During that month, the Washington, D.C., metropolitan area found itself under siege from what appeared to be random, yet chillingly precise, attacks from a rifle-wielding sniper. Before the assailants had been captured, ten people were killed and four others injured. Law enforcement agents also suggested that the Washington killings may have been related to similar murders in Alabama and Louisiana.

Officials at all levels of government in several states participated in what became a massive hunt for the killers. As the investigation unfolded, the local face that Americans became familiar with was Montgomery County (Maryland) police chief Charles Moose. His office exchanged a handful of messages with the assailants, and the chief became a regular figure on nightly news programs. Because some of the attacks also took place in Virginia, members of the Old Dominion State's local law enforcement and state police also contributed their efforts. Finally, because the sniper killings came roughly one year after the attacks of 9/11, which raised the specter that they were connected to terrorism, and owing to the interstate nature of the crimes, federal law enforcement officials, including Attorney General John Ashcroft, also participated in the hunt. Over the course of the investigation, apprehension, and into the trial phase of the case, the overlapping responsibilities and jurisdictions involved in the case revealed some of the strengths and weaknesses of the American federal system in action. Although many citizens were pleased to see such a comprehensive effort to halt the shootings, inevitably turf battles emerged between the various jurisdictions involved, as officials in national, state, and local government jockeyed with one another, sometimes to push for their own theories of how the case was unfolding, and, inevitably given the bright spotlight on the whole affair, to score political points with their constituents and the public at large.[47]

★ Federalism and the International System

In today's increasingly interconnected world, it is perhaps not surprising that federalism is more than simply a local curiosity for citizens of the United States. The dynamics of American federalism, in addition to helping shape the nation's politics, have begun to have more noticeable impacts in the international arena as well. And federalism as a system of government and governance is becoming increasingly important across the globe. In this section, we relate federalism to several evolving international issues and events.

American Federalism and World Politics

American federalism can have important impacts on how the United States deals with other nations, even in areas that clearly seem to be the prerogative of the national government. Trade policy is one good example.

Article I, Section 8, of the U.S. Constitution declares that the legislative branch shall have the power "to regulate Commerce with foreign Nations," and Section 10 prohibits individual states from entering "into any Treaty, Alliance, or Confederation," or, without Congress's consent, from laying "any Imposts or Duties on Imports or Exports, except what may be absolutely necessary for executing its inspection Laws." And even those imposts and duties "shall be for the Use of the Treasury of the United States." Article II, Section 2, reserves to the president the power to make treaties with other nations with the advice and consent of the Senate. These constitutional provisions provide the national government, but not the states, with significant justification and formal authority to develop foreign trade agreements and regulate imports and exports.

The national government also commands significant capacity to act in trade policy. The U.S. Department of Commerce, the Office of the U.S. Trade

Representative, and the formal roles that the United States plays in international bodies such as the World Trade Organization provide federal officials with significant access to data and even formal decision-making power over trade-related issues on the domestic and global stage.

Despite what appears to be a clear mismatch between national and state officials on trade, state leaders do develop and advance their own trade agendas. It may come as a surprise to some readers, but trade policy has a noticeable intergovernmental component. In summarizing developments in state politics, two scholars recently noted that states have become more aggressive in establishing their own outposts, so to speak, in other countries.[48] In 2006, thirty-nine states[49] employed international trade directors, and these officials coordinate several activities through an umbrella group called the State International Development Organizations (SIDO), an affiliate of the Council of State Governments. SIDO is like many other state-level groups that lobby Washington policymakers. However, the group also plays a more formal role by participating on a joint advisory panel with the U.S. Department of Commerce to help coordinate national and state export activities. Certainly, when national government officials advance agendas that would expand or restrict trade, states may see their own agendas to promote exports bolstered or challenged. Members of SIDO and other state leaders can advance their own state trade agendas by using and helping to shape federal agendas in this area.[50]

State activities in the international arena extend beyond export promotion. Other dimensions of trade policy illustrate in an interesting way that state and local governments can have noticeable impacts on American foreign policy. For example, a small but not insignificant number of state and local jurisdictions have become more assertive in using their own trade activities to advance international human rights positions. A recent case involved Massachusetts, which in 1996 adopted a law that banned its state agencies from contracting with U.S. or foreign corporations that do business in Myanmar, an Asian nation previously known as Burma. The law was designed to signal Massachusetts's displeasure with the human rights conditions in that country. A unanimous U.S. Supreme Court declared the law unconstitutional in 2000 on the basis of the Constitution's supremacy clause, holding that a federal law placing sanctions on Myanmar preempted the state law. Despite this setback for Massachusetts, arguably the existence of the law itself, the groups that supported it, and the publicity that followed helped embolden national policy entrepreneurs who wanted to use Washington's power to pressure Myanmar over human rights.[51]

Federalism Across the Globe

Supreme Court Justice Anthony Kennedy once observed that "federalism was our Nation's own discovery. The Framers split the atom of sovereignty. It was the genius of their idea that our citizens would have two political capacities, one state and one federal, each protected from incursion by the other."[52] Federalism is not an obsolete nineteenth-century form of government inappropriate in the contemporary world. In fact, the concept of the nation-state, developed in the seventeenth century, may be heading for the dustbin. (A *nation-state* is a country with defined and recognized boundaries whose citizens have common characteristics, such as race, religion, customs, and language.)

Compared with What?

Iraqi-Style Federalism

In October 2005 the Iraqi people approved a new constitution that established a federal system with separate legislative, executive, and judicial functions. Whereas the United States made its transition from a highly dispersed system under the Articles of Confederation to a more centralized federal arrangement, Iraq has now moved from a highly centralized and unitary system under dictator Saddam Hussein to a more distributed federal system under its new constitution.

The situation in Iraq is very complicated. Ethnic, tribal, and religious groups demand resources, territory, and autonomy. Arabs, Kurds, and Turkomen are the main ethnic groups. Although the population is almost entirely Muslim, the people divide into majority Shiite and minority Sunni sects. The Sunnis held sway under Saddam Hussein. Now the Shiites dominate.

Too little acknowledgment of group demands risks violent disruption. But giving too much authority to the various groups and the regions where they concentrate will fuel the very nationalisms that will divide Iraq. The fine line between too little and too much requires compromises in reallocating economic resources, dividing power between regional and central authority, and introducing a version of democracy that rules out extremists rooted in ethnic or religious intolerance.

Former U.S. ambassador to Croatia Peter Galbraith, a critic of the Bush administration's Iraq policy but a strong defender of the new constitution, argues that "the constitution reflects the reality of the nation it is meant to serve." "There is," he says, "no meaningful Iraqi identity. In the north, you've got a pro-Western Kurdish population. In the south, you've got a Shiite majority that wants a 'pale version of an Iranian state.' And in the center you've got a Sunni population that is nervous about being trapped in a system in which it would be overrun."

These divisions over ethnic and religious lines were expressed in parliamentary elections and constitutional craftsmanship. The Kurds chose pro-autonomy leaders and opted for a constitution with strong regional control. The Shiites voted for religious parties and supported a decentralized republic along the lines of the early U.S. confederation. Many Sunnis who initially opted out of elections supported a strong central government, fearing that the Kurds and Shiites might marginalize them. In such a context, federalism is the best political tool to accommodate conflicting interests. Indeed, the Iraqi constitution provides the foundations for a loose federal system in which only fiscal and foreign affairs will be handled by the national government.

The challenge of democracy is to find that delicate balance ensuring enough regional autonomy to satisfy ethnic or religious solidarity but not so much autonomy as to splinter the entire enterprise. American views of democracy may complicate the situation. An Iraq that emulates America's free-style democracy may promote the seeds of its own destruction by giving every zealot a forum. But constraining Iraqi democracy by ruling some extreme viewpoints out of bounds may call into question one of the reasons America intervened in Iraq in the first place: to plant a viable democracy in the Middle East.

Sources: Edward Wong, "The World: New Wars in Iraq; Making Compromises to Keep a Country Whole," *New York Times,* 4 January 2004, sec. 4, p. 4; David Brooks, "Divided They Stand," *New York Times,* 25 August 2005; "Iraq's Constitution," *Wall Street Journal,* 15 October 2005, p. A5.

Some scholars have noted that we may be moving from a world of sovereign nation-states to a world of diminished state sovereignty and increased interstate linkages of a constitutionally federal character. Among the 195 politically sovereign states in the world today, 25 are federations that together embrace about 2.5 billion people, or 40 percent of the world population. About 480 constituent or federated states serve as the building blocks of these 25 federations.[53] New versions of the federal idea continue to arise (see "Compared with What? Iraqi-Style Federalism"). One is the European Union, "where individual federations, unions and unitary states have 'pooled their sovereignty' (as they express it) in a hybrid structure which has come to involve elements of confederation and federation."[54]

The creation of a European superstate—in either a loose confederation or a binding federation—demonstrates the potential for federalism to overcome long-held religious, ethnic, linguistic, and cultural divisions. The economic integration of such a superstate would create an alternative to the dominant currency, the U.S. dollar. And the creation of a single and expanding European market would serve as a magnet for buyers and sellers. But lingering doubts among some nations regarding a common currency (the euro) and power sharing (reductions in veto power for any member) have halted for now the creation of such a superstate, generating strains similar to the ones America endured more than two hundred years ago when it sought to govern itself. The colossal political endeavor of a unified Europe will continue to draw its organizational inspiration from the federal arrangement of power that the United States has successfully exported worldwide.

★ Federalism and Pluralism

At the nation's founding, the federal system of government in the United States was designed to allay citizens' fears that they might be ruled by a majority in a distant region with whom they did not necessarily agree or share interests. By recognizing the legitimacy of the states as political divisions, the federal system also recognizes the importance of diversity. The existence and cultivation of diverse interests are the hallmarks of pluralism.

Both of the main competing theories of federalism that we have explored support pluralism, but in somewhat different ways. The layer-cake approach of dual federalism aims to maintain important powers in the states and to protect those powers from an aggressive or assertive national government. The theory recognizes the importance of local and national standards, but it maintains that not all policy areas should be considered the same; some are more amenable to decision making and standards closer to home, while others are more appropriately national. Preserving this possible variety at the state level allows the people, if not a direct vote in policymaking, at least a choice of policies under which to live.

In contrast, the marble cake of cooperative federalism sees relations between levels of government in more fluid terms and is perfectly willing to override state standards for national ones depending on the issues at stake. Yet this view of federalism, while more amenable to national prerogatives, is highly responsive (at least in theory) to all manner of pressures from groups and policy entrepreneurs, including pressure at one level of government from those that might be unsuccessful at others. By blurring the lines of national and state responsibility, this type of federalism encourages petitioners to try their luck at whichever level of government offers them the best chance of success, or simultaneously to mount diverse sets of strategies across levels of government.

Summary

The government framework outlined in the Constitution is the product of political compromise, an acknowledgment of the original thirteen states' fear of a powerful central government and frustrations that the Articles of Federation produced. The division of powers sketched in the Constitution was supposed to turn over "great and aggregate" matters to the national government, leaving "local and particular" concerns to the states. The Constitution does not explain, however, what is "great and aggregate" or "what is local and particular."

Federalism comes in many varieties, two of which stand out because they capture valuable differences between the original and modern vision of a national government. Dual, or layer-cake, federalism wants to retain a strong separation between state and national powers, which, in essence, provides the states with a protective buffer against national encroachments. Cooperative, or marble-cake, federalism sees national and state government working together to solve national problems. In its own way, each view supports the pluralist model of democracy.

One of the enduring features of American federalism has been the system's great ability to adapt to new circumstances. Several factors have produced changes in the nature of the system. National crises and demands from citizens frustrated with the responsiveness of state governments, judicial interpretations of the proper balance between states and the national government, changes in the system of grants-in-aid, and the professionalism of state governments have all contributed to changes in American federalism.

Because the Constitution treats federalism in an ambiguous and sometimes seemingly contradictory way, it is difficult to pin clear ideological labels on particular theories of federalism. Although it is common to hear political pundits and politicians associate conservatism with dual federalism and liberalism with cooperative federalism, in practice these labels do not tend to correlate as well as casual glances would suggest. Rather, it is the combination of ideology and the specific policy context—how one prioritizes freedom, order, and equality—rather than ideology alone that drives conceptions of the proper national-state balance across several policy areas.

Although it is accurate to say that the national government's influence has grown significantly since the New Deal of the 1930s and the Great Society of the 1960s, it is also the case that citizens and elected officials alike have come to appreciate the intergovernmental nature of problems confronting the nation. Today, the answer to the question "Which level of government is responsible?" is frequently, "All of them." Certainly there exists some separation between the national government and states—the flavors of the marble cake have not swirled together so much that they are indistinguishable. Still, given the mixed messages present in the Constitution and debates that date to the country's founding over the proper role for the national government and the states, for better or for worse it is likely that American federalism will remain in constant flux well into the future.

Internet activities and reading suggestions for this chapter are available on the *Online Study Center*

To complete the multimedia assignments for this chapter, go to AmericansGoverning.org.

5 Public Opinion and Political Socialization

(Jeff Chiu/AP/Wide World Photos)

Online Study Center
This icon will direct you to resources
and activities on the website
college.hmco.com/pic/jandaupdate9e

Officials in Arnold Schwarz- enegger's hometown of Graz, Austria, removed the giant metal letters spelling out his name on the local soccer stadium in the middle of the night.[1] Graz, whose official slogan is "City of Human Rights," took the name off at the request of the California governor himself. Schwarzenegger wanted his name removed before local opposition had the chance. But why would the locals want to renounce their famous son?

Most residents of Graz (and Austria) oppose the death penalty. And in December 2005, Governor Schwarzenegger refused to stay the execution of Stanley Tookie Williams. Convicted for the murders of four people, the fifty-one-year-old founder of the Crips gang maintained his innocence until the very end. In prison, Williams became an antiviolence crusader, writing children's books denouncing gang life. Williams had the ardent support of celebrities and peace activists, such as the rapper Snoop Dogg, the actor Jamie Foxx, the Reverend Jesse Jackson, and South African bishop Desmond Tutu.[2]

Governor Schwarzenegger, however, said that Williams failed to atone for his crimes. He called the Crips "a notorious street gang that has contributed and continues to contribute to predatory and exploitive behavior."[3] Though Schwarzenegger's decision in the Williams case was controversial, his general support of the death penalty does not put him at odds with the American people. Public opinion polls show consistently high support for the death penalty. In 2006, 65 percent of all respondents were in favor of the death penalty for murder, while only 28 percent were opposed.[4]

We can learn much about the role of public opinion in America by reviewing how our government has punished violent criminals. During most of American history, government execution of people who threatened the social order was legal. In colonial times, capital punishment was imposed not just for murder but also for antisocial behavior—denying the "true" God, cursing one's parents, committing adultery, practicing witchcraft, even being a rebellious child.[5] In the late 1700s, some writers, editors, and clergy argued for abolishing the death sentence. The campaign intensified in the 1840s, and a few states responded by eliminating capital punishment. Interest in the cause waned until 1890, when New York State adopted a new, "scientific" technique, electrocution, as the instrument of death. By 1917, twelve states had passed laws against capital punishment. But the outbreak of World War I fed the public's fear of foreigners and radicals, leading to renewed support for the death penalty. Reacting to this shift in public opinion, four states restored it.

The security needs of World War II and the postwar fears of Soviet communism fueled continued support for capital punishment. After anticommunist hysteria subsided in the late 1950s, public opposition to the death penalty increased. But public opinion was neither strong enough nor stable enough to force state legislatures to outlaw it. In keeping with the pluralist model of democracy, efforts to abolish the death penalty shifted from the legislative arena to the courts.

The opponents argued that the death penalty is cruel and unusual punishment and is therefore unconstitutional. Certainly the public in the 1780s did not consider capital punishment either cruel or unusual. But nearly two hundred years later, opponents contended that execution by the state was cruel and unusual by contemporary standards. Their argument apparently had some effect on public opinion: in 1966, a plurality of respondents opposed the death penalty for the first (and only) time since the Gallup Organization began polling the public on the question of capital punishment.

The states responded to this shift in public opinion by reducing the number of executions, until they stopped completely in 1968 in anticipation of a Supreme Court decision. By then, however, public opinion had again reversed in favor of capital punishment. Nevertheless, in 1972, the Court ruled in a 5–4 decision that the death penalty as imposed by existing state laws was unconstitutional.[6] The decision was not well received in many states, and thirty-five state legislatures passed new laws to get around the ruling. Meanwhile, as the nation's homicide rate increased, public approval of the death penalty jumped almost ten points and continued climbing.

In 1976, the Supreme Court changed its position and upheld three new state laws that let judges consider the defendant's record and the nature of the crime in deciding whether to impose a sentence of death.[7] The Court also re-jected the argument that punishment by death in itself violates the Constitution, and it noted that public opinion favors the death penalty. Through the end of the 1970s, however, only three criminals were executed. Eventually, the states began to heed public concern about the crime rate. Over one thousand executions have taken place since the 1976 Supreme Court ruling.[8]

Although public support for the death penalty remains high, Americans are concerned that innocent persons have been executed.[9] Indeed, since 1973, over one hundred death row inmates have been exonerated of their crimes with the help of DNA testing.[10] In Illinois, the exoneration of thirteen death row inmates led Governor George Ryan to institute a state moratorium on the death penalty in 2000. Ryan eventually cleared death row in Illinois by pardoning or commuting the death sentences of all death row inmates in 2003. Thirty-eight states have capital statutes, but only twenty-nine have executed criminals since 1977.[11] Fifty percent of these executions have taken place in Texas, Virginia, and Oklahoma.[12] ★

IN OUR OWN WORDS

Listen to Kenneth Janda discuss the main points and themes of this chapter.

Online Study Center
Improve Your Grade

public opinion The collected attitudes of citizens concerning a given issue or question.

Does the death penalty deter people from killing? A majority of the public thinks it does. **Public opinion** is simply the collective attitude of the citizens on a given issue or question. The history of public thinking on the death penalty reveals several characteristics of public opinion:

1. *The public's attitudes toward a given government policy can vary over time, often dramatically.* Opinions about capital punishment tend to fluctuate with threats to the social order. The public is more likely to favor capital punishment in times of war and when fear of foreign subversion and crime rates are high.

2. *Public opinion places boundaries on allowable types of public policy.* Stoning criminals is not acceptable to the modern American public (and surely not to courts interpreting the Constitution), but administering a lethal injection to a murderer is.

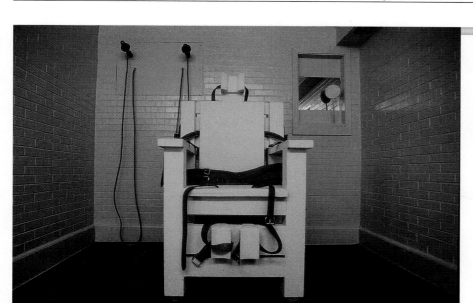

The Death Chamber
This is the electric chair in an Alabama state prison. It dramatizes the ultimate power that government has to control behavior. Capital crimes may draw capital punishment.
(A. Ramey/Stock Boston)

INTERACTIVE 5.1

 1000th Execution

3. *If asked by pollsters, citizens are willing to register opinions on matters outside their expertise.* People clearly believe execution by lethal injection is more humane than electrocution, asphyxiation in a gas chamber, or hanging.

4. *Governments tend to respond to public opinion.* State laws for and against capital punishment have reflected swings in the public mood. The Supreme Court's 1972 decision against capital punishment came when public opinion on the death penalty was sharply divided; the Court's approval of capital punishment in 1976 coincided with a rise in public approval of the death penalty.

5. *The government sometimes does not do what the people want.* Although public opinion overwhelmingly favors the death penalty for murder, there were only sixty executions in 2005 (but over sixteen thousand murders that year).

The last two conclusions bear on our understanding of the majoritarian and pluralist models of democracy discussed in Chapter 2. Here, we probe more deeply into the nature, shape, depth, and formation of public opinion in a democratic government. What is the place of public opinion in a democracy? How do people acquire their opinions? What are the major lines of division in public opinion? How do individuals' ideology and knowledge affect their opinions?

IDEAlog.org

One of the questions in the IDEAlog self-test asks about the death penalty. After reading the information about the death penalty here, would you answer that question differently now? Take IDEAlog's self-test.

⭐ Public Opinion and the Models of Democracy

Opinion polling, which involves interviewing a sample of citizens to estimate public opinion as a whole (see the feature "Sampling a Few, Predicting to Everyone"), is such a common feature of contemporary life that we often forget it is a modern invention, dating only from the 1930s (see Figure 5.1). In fact, survey methodology did not become a powerful research tool until the advent of computers in the 1950s. Before polling became a common part of the American scene, politicians, journalists, and everyone else could argue about what the people wanted, but no one really knew. Before the 1930s, observers of America had to guess at national opinion by analyzing newspaper stories, politicians' speeches, voting returns, and travelers' diaries. What if pollsters had been around when the colonists declared their independence from Britain in July 1776? We might have learned (as some historians estimate) that "40 percent of Americans supported the Revolution, 20 percent opposed it, and 40 percent tried to remain neutral."[13]

When no one really knows what the people want, how can the national government be responsive to public opinion? As we discussed in Chapter 3, the founders wanted to build public opinion into our government structure by allowing the direct election of representatives to the House and apportioning representation there according to population. The attitudes and actions of the House of Representatives, the framers thought, would reflect public opinion, especially on the crucial issues of taxes and government spending.

In practice, bills passed by a majority of elected representatives do not necessarily reflect the opinion of a majority of citizens. This would not have bothered the framers because they never intended to create a full democracy, a government completely responsive to majority opinion. Although they wanted to provide for some consideration of public opinion, they had little faith in the ability of the masses to make public policy.

The majoritarian and pluralist models of democracy differ greatly in their assumptions about the role of public opinion in democratic government. Ac-

In Search of Public Opinion
Pollsters sometimes catch respondents wherever they can, but such "parking lot polls" often yield unreliable results. To draw valid inferences from samples with known estimates of error, every person in the population must have an equal chance of selection. True random sampling cannot be done by catching people in parking lots. It requires other methods (such as random-digit dialing). *(Billy E. Barnes/PhotoEdit)*

FIGURE 5.1 Gallup Poll Accuracy

One of the nation's oldest polls was started by George Gallup in the 1930s. The accuracy of the Gallup Poll in predicting presidential elections over sixty years is charted here. Although not always on the mark, its predictions have been fairly close. Gallup's final prediction for the 2000 election declared the race "too close to call." Indeed, the race in the electoral college remained too close to call for weeks after the election. The poll was most notably wrong in 1948, when it predicted that Thomas Dewey, the Republican candidate, would defeat the Democratic incumbent, Harry Truman, underestimating Truman's vote by 5.4 percentage points. In 1992, the Gallup Poll was off by a larger margin, but this time it identified the winner: Bill Clinton. Although third-party candidate Ross Perot was included in the presidential debates and spent vast sums on his campaign, Gallup kept with historical precedent and allocated none of the undecided vote to Perot. As a result, they overestimated Clinton's share.

Source: Gallup Organization, <www.gallup.com/poll/trends/ptaccuracy.asp>.

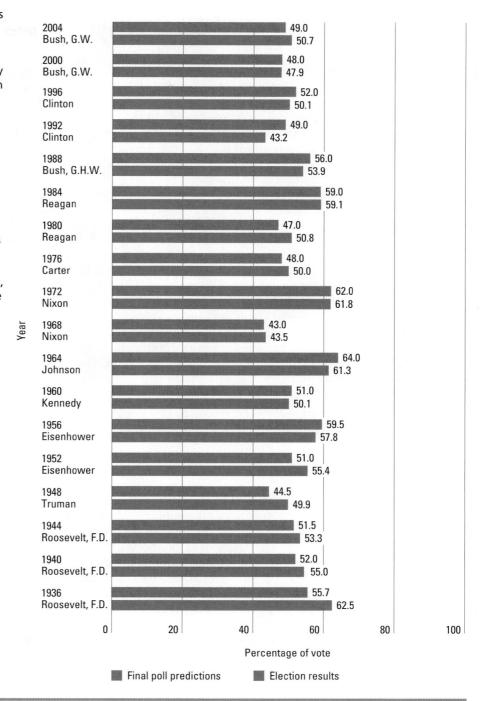

Final poll predictions ■   Election results ■

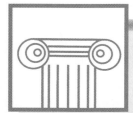

Sampling a Few, Predicting to Everyone

How can a pollster tell what the nation thinks by talking to only a few hundred people? The answer lies in the statistical theory of sampling. Briefly, the theory holds that a sample of individuals selected by chance from any population is representative of that population. This means that the traits of the individuals in the sample—their attitudes, beliefs, sociological characteristics, and physical features—reflect the traits of the whole population. Sampling theory does not claim that a sample exactly matches the population, only that it reflects the population with some predictable degree of accuracy.

Three factors determine the accuracy of a sample. The most important is how the sample is selected. For maximum accuracy, the individuals in the sample must be chosen randomly. Randomly does not mean "at whim," however; it means that every individual in the population has the same chance of being selected.

For a population as large and widespread as that of the United States, pollsters first divide the country into geographical regions. Then they randomly choose areas and sample individuals who live within those areas. This departure from strict random sampling does decrease the accuracy of polls, but by only a relatively small amount. Today, most polls conducted by the mass media are done by telephone, with computers randomly dialing numbers within predetermined calling areas. (Random dialing ensures that even people with unlisted numbers are called.)

The second factor that affects accuracy is the size of the sample. The larger the sample is, the more accurately it represents the population. For example, a sample of four hundred randomly selected individuals is accurate to within six percentage points (plus or minus) 95 percent of the time. A sample of six hundred is accurate to within five percentage points.

cording to the classic majoritarian model, the government should do what a majority of the public wants. Indeed, polls show that 70 percent of Americans think that the views of the majority should have "a great deal" of influence on the decisions of politicians.[14] In contrast, pluralists argue that the public as a whole seldom demonstrates clear, consistent opinions on the day-to-day issues of government. At the same time, pluralists recognize that subgroups within the public do express opinions on specific matters—often and vigorously. The pluralist model requires that government institutions allow the free expression of opinions by these "minority publics." Democracy is at work when the opinions of many different publics clash openly and fairly over government policy.

Sampling methods and opinion polling have altered the debate about the majoritarian and pluralist models of democracy. One expert said, "Surveys produce just what democracy is supposed to produce—equal representation of all citizens."[15] Now that we know how often government policy runs against majority opinion, it becomes harder to defend the U.S. government as

(Surprisingly, the proportion of the sample to the overall population has essentially no effect on the accuracy of most samples. A sample of, say, six hundred individuals will reflect the traits of a city, a state, or even an entire nation with equal accuracy. Why this statement is true is better discussed in a course on statistics.)

The final factor that affects the accuracy of sampling is the amount of variation in the population. If there were no variation, every sample would reflect the population's characteristics with perfect accuracy. The greater the variation is within the population, the greater is the chance that one random sample will be different from another.

The Gallup Poll and most other national opinion polls usually survey about fifteen hundred individuals and are accurate to within three percentage points 95 percent of the time. As shown in Figure 5.1, the predictions of the Gallup Poll for seventeen presidential elections since 1936 have deviated from the voting results by an average of only −1.0 percentage point. Even this small margin of error can mean an incorrect prediction in a close election. But for the purpose of esti-

mating public opinion on political issues, a sampling error of three percentage points is acceptable.

Poll results can be wrong because of problems that have nothing to do with sampling theory. For example, question wording can bias the results. In surveys during the 1980s concerning aid to the Nicaraguan contras fighting the Sandinista government, questions that mentioned President Reagan's name produced more support for increased aid by almost five percentage points.[1] Survey questions are also prone to random error because interviewers are likely to obtain superficial responses from busy respondents who say anything, quickly, to get rid of them. Recently, some newspaper columnists have even urged readers to lie to pollsters outside voting booths, to confound election night television predictions. But despite the potential for abuses or distortions, modern polling has told us a great deal about public opinion in America.

1. Brad Lockerbie and Stephen A. Borrelli, "Question Wording and Public Support for Contra Aid, 1983–1986," *Public Opinion Quarterly* 54 (Summer 1990): 200.

democratic under the majoritarian model. Even at a time when Americans overwhelmingly favored the death penalty for murderers, the Supreme Court decided that existing state laws applying capital punishment were unconstitutional. Even after the Court approved new state laws as constitutional, relatively few murderers were actually executed. Consider, too, the case of prayer in public schools. The Supreme Court has ruled against clergy-led prayers at public school graduations. Yet surveys continually show that a clear majority of Americans (75 percent) do not agree with that ruling.[16] Because government policy sometimes runs against settled majority opinion, the majoritarian model is easily attacked as an inaccurate description of reality.

The two models of democracy make different assumptions about public opinion. The majoritarian model assumes that a majority of the people holds clear, consistent opinions on government policy. The pluralist model assumes that the public is often uninformed and ambivalent about specific issues, and opinion polls frequently support that claim. What are the bases of public opinion? What principles, if any, do people use to organize their beliefs and

Stop the Presses! Oops, Too Late . . .

As the 1948 election drew near, few people gave President Harry Truman a chance to defeat his Republican opponent, Thomas E. Dewey. Polling was still new, and almost all the early polls showed Dewey far ahead. Most organizations simply stopped polling weeks before the election. The *Chicago Daily Tribune* believed the polls and proclaimed Dewey's victory before the votes were counted. Here, the victorious Truman triumphantly displays the most embarrassing headline in American politics. Later, it was revealed that the few polls taken closer to election day showed Truman catching up to Dewey. Clearly, polls estimate the vote only at the time they are taken. *(Bettmann)*

attitudes about politics? Exactly how do individuals form their political opinions? We will look for answers to these questions in this chapter. In later chapters, we assess the effect of public opinion on government policies. The results should help you make up your own mind about the viability of the majoritarian and pluralist models in a functioning democracy.

★ The Distribution of Public Opinion

A government that tries to respond to public opinion soon learns that people seldom think alike. To understand and then act on the public's many attitudes and beliefs, government must pay attention to the way public opinion is distributed among the choices on a given issue. In particular, government must analyze the shape and the stability of that distribution.

Shape of the Distribution

The results of public opinion polls are often displayed in graphs such as those in Figure 5.2. The height of the columns indicates the percentage of those polled who gave each response, identified along the baseline. The shape of the opinion distribution depicts the pattern of all the responses when counted and plotted. The figure depicts three patterns of distribution: skewed, bimodal, and normal.

Figure 5.2a plots the percentages of respondents surveyed in 2005 that favored or opposed imposing the death penalty for a person convicted of murder. The most frequent response ("favor") is called the *mode*. The mode produces a prominent "hump" in this distribution. The relatively few respondents who didn't know or were opposed to the death penalty lie to one side, in its "tail." Such an asymmetrical distribution is called a **skewed distribution.**

skewed distribution An asymmetrical but generally bell-shaped distribution (of opinions); its mode, or most frequent response, lies off to one side.

FIGURE 5.2   **Three Distributions of Opinion**

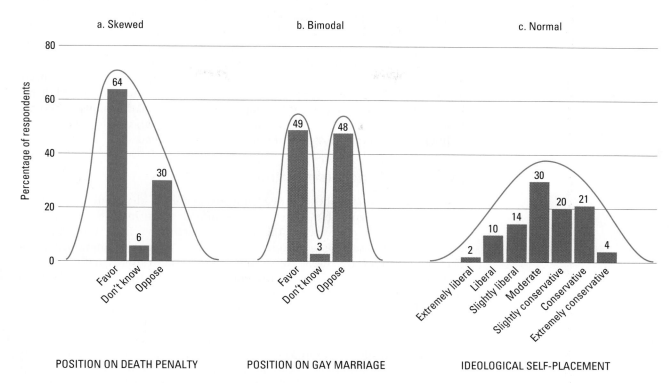

POSITION ON DEATH PENALTY   POSITION ON GAY MARRIAGE   IDEOLOGICAL SELF-PLACEMENT

Here we have superimposed three idealized patterns of distribution—skewed, bimodal, and normal—on three actual distributions of responses to survey questions. Although the actual responses do not match the ideal shapes exactly, the match is close enough that we can describe the distribution of (a) thoughts on the death penalty as skewed, (b) opinions on gay marriage as bimodal, and (c) ideological attitudes as approximately normal.

Sources: (a) Gallup Poll, 13–16 October 2005, <http://www.gallup.com>; (b) Gallup Poll, 2–4 May 2004, <http://brain.gallup.com/documents/topics.aspx>; (c) 1996 National Election Study, Center for Political Studies, University of Michigan.

Figure 5.2b plots responses on the issue of gay marriage. These responses fall into a **bimodal distribution:** respondents chose two categories with equal frequency, dividing almost evenly over whether homosexual couples should be allowed to form civil unions with the same legal rights as married heterosexual couples.

Figure 5.2c shows how respondents to a national survey in 1996 were distributed along a liberal–conservative continuum. Its shape resembles what statisticians call a **normal distribution**—a symmetrical, bell-shaped spread around a single mode, or most frequent response. Here, the mode ("moderate") lies in the center. Progressively fewer people classified themselves in each category toward the liberal and conservative extremes.

When public opinion is normally distributed on an issue, the public tends to support a moderate government policy on that issue. It will also tolerate policies that fall slightly to the left or to the right as long as they do not stray too far from the moderate center. In contrast, when opinion is sharply divided

bimodal distribution A distribution (of opinions) that shows two responses being chosen about as frequently as each other.

normal distribution A symmetrical bell-shaped distribution (of opinions) centered on a single mode, or most frequent response.

in a bimodal distribution, as it is over homosexuality, there is great potential for political conflict. A skewed distribution, on the other hand, indicates that most respondents share the same opinion. When consensus on an issue is overwhelming, those with the minority opinion risk social ostracism and even persecution if they persist in voicing their view. If the public does not feel intensely about the issue, however, politicians can sometimes discount a skewed distribution of opinion. This is what has happened with the death penalty. Although most people favor capital punishment, it is not a burning issue for them. Thus, politicians can skirt the issue without serious consequences.

Stability of the Distribution

A **stable distribution** shows little change over time. Public opinion on important issues can change, but it is sometimes difficult to distinguish a true change in opinion from a difference in the way a question is worded. When different questions on the same issue produce similar distributions of opinion, the underlying attitudes are stable. When the same question (or virtually the same question) produces significantly different responses over time, an actual shift in public opinion probably has occurred.

We have already discussed Americans' long-standing support of the death penalty. People's descriptions of themselves in ideological terms are another distribution that has remained stable. Chapter 1 argued for using a two-dimensional ideological typology based on the tradeoffs of freedom for equality and freedom for order. However, most opinion polls ask respondents to place themselves along only a single liberal–conservative dimension, which tends to force libertarians and communitarians into the middle category. Nevertheless, we find relatively little change in respondents' self-placement on the liberal–conservative continuum over time. Even in 1964, when liberal Lyndon Johnson won a landslide victory over conservative Barry Goldwater in the presidential election, more voters described themselves as conservative than liberal. Indeed, the ideological distribution of the public has been skewed toward conservatism in every presidential election year since 1964.[17] Despite all the talk about the nation's becoming conservative in recent years, the fact is that most people did not describe themselves as liberal at any time during the past thirty years. People's self-descriptions have shifted about five percentage points toward the right since 1964, but more people considered themselves conservative than liberal to begin with.

Sometimes changes occur within subgroups that are not reflected in overall public opinion. College students, for example, were far more liberal in the 1970s than they are today (see "Politics in a Changing World: Are Students More Conservative Than Their Parents?"). Moreover, public opinion in America is capable of massive change over time, even on issues that were once highly controversial. A good example is racially integrated schools. A national survey in 1942 asked whether "white and Negro students should go to the same schools or separate schools."[18] Only 30 percent of white respondents said that the students should attend schools together. When virtually the same question was asked in 1984 (substituting *black* for *Negro*), 90 percent of the white respondents endorsed integrated schools. Nevertheless, only 23 percent of the whites surveyed in 1984 were in favor of busing to achieve racial balance. And whites were more willing to bus their children to a school with a few blacks than to one that was mostly black.[19] So although white opinion changed dra-

stable distribution A distribution (of opinions) that shows little change over time.

Politics in a Changing World

Are Students More Conservative Than Their Parents?

Do you remember filling out a questionnaire when you enrolled in college? If it asked about your political orientation, you may be represented in this graph. For about three decades, researchers at the University of California at Los Angeles have collected various data on entering freshmen, including asking them to characterize their political views as far left, liberal, middle of the road, conservative, or far right. In contrast to Americans in general, who have shown little ideological change over time, college students described themselves as markedly more liberal in the early 1970s than they do now.

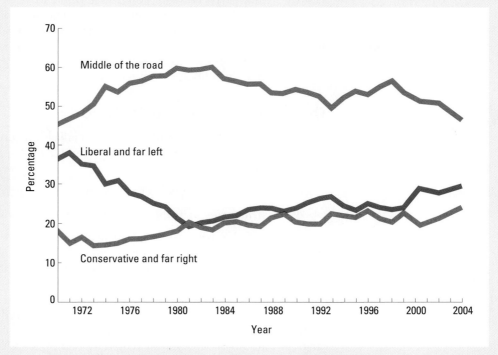

Sources: Higher Education Research Institute, University of California, Los Angeles, "The American Freshman: National Norms for 2004," <http://www.gseis.ucla.edu/heri>.

matically with regard to the principle of desegregated schools, whites seemed divided on how that principle should be implemented.

In trying to explain how political opinions are formed and how they change, political scientists cite the process of political socialization, the influence of cultural factors, and the interplay of ideology and knowledge. In the next several sections, we examine how these elements combine to create and influence public opinion.

★ Political Socialization

Public opinion is grounded in political values. People acquire their values through **political socialization,** a complex process through which individuals become aware of politics, learn political facts, and form political values. Think for a moment about your political socialization. What is your earliest memory of a president? When did you first learn about political parties? If you identify with a party, how did you decide to do so? If you do not, why don't you? Who was the first liberal you ever met? The first conservative?

Obviously, the paths to political awareness, knowledge, and values vary among individuals, but most people are exposed to the same sources of influence, or agents of socialization, especially from childhood through young adulthood: family, school, community, peers, and, of course, the media.

The Agents of Early Socialization

Like psychologists, scholars of political socialization place great emphasis on early learning. Both groups point to two fundamental principles that characterize early learning:[20]

- *The primacy principle.* What is learned first is learned best.

- *The structuring principle.* What is learned first structures later learning.

The extent of the influence of any socializing agent depends on the extent of our exposure to it, our communication with it, and our receptivity to it.[21] Because most people learn first from their family, the family tends to be an important agent of early socialization.

Family. In most cases, exposure, communication, and receptivity are highest in parent-child relationships. From their parents, children learn a wide range of values—social, moral, religious, economic, and political—that help shape their opinions. It is not surprising, then, that most people link their earliest memories of politics with their family. Moreover, when parents are interested in politics and maintain a favorable home environment for studying public affairs, they influence their children to become politically interested and informed.[22]

One of the most politically important things that many children learn from their parents is party identification. They learn party identification in much the same way as they do religion. Children (very young children, anyway) imitate their parents. When parents share the same religion, children are almost always raised in that faith. When parents are of different religions, their children are more likely to follow one or the other than to choose an entirely different religion. Similarly, parental influence on party identification is greater when

political socialization The complex process by which people acquire their political values.

both parents strongly identify with the same party.[23] Overall, more than half of young American voters identify with the political party of their parents. Moreover, those who change their partisanship are more likely to shift from being partisan to independent or from independent to partisan than to convert from one party to the other.[24]

Two crucial differences between party identification and religion may explain why youngsters are socialized into a religion much more reliably than into a political party. The first is that most parents care a great deal more about their religion than about their politics, so they are more deliberate about exposing their children to religion. The second is that religious institutions recognize the value of socialization; they offer Sunday schools and other activities that reinforce parental guidance. American political parties, in contrast, sponsor few activities to win the hearts of little Democrats and Republicans, which leaves children open to counterinfluences in their school and community.

School.   According to some researchers, schools have an influence on political learning that is equal to or greater than that of parents.[25] Here, however, we have to distinguish between elementary and secondary schools, on the one hand, and institutions of higher education, on the other. Elementary schools prepare children in a number of ways to accept the social order. They introduce authority figures outside the family: the teacher, the principal, the police officer. They also teach the nation's slogans and symbols: the Pledge of Allegiance, the national anthem, national heroes and holidays. And they stress the norms of group behavior and democratic decision making: respecting the opinions of others, voting for class officers. In the process, they teach youngsters about the value of political equality.

Children do not always understand the meaning of the patriotic rituals and behaviors they learn in elementary school. In fact, much of this early learning—in the United States and elsewhere—is more indoctrination than education. By the end of the eighth grade, however, children begin to distinguish between political leaders and government institutions. They become more aware of collective institutions, such as Congress and elections, than do younger children, who tend to focus on the president and other single figures of government authority.[26] In sum, most children emerge from elementary school with a sense of national pride and an idealized notion of American government.[27]

Although newer curricula in many secondary schools emphasize citizens' rights in addition to their responsibilities, high schools also attempt to build "good citizens." Field trips to the state legislature or the city council impress students with the majesty and power of government institutions. But secondary schools also offer more explicit political content in their curricula, including courses in recent U.S. history, civics, and American government. Better teachers challenge students to think critically about American government and politics; others focus on teaching civic responsibilities. The end product is a greater awareness of the political process and of the most prominent participants in that process.[28] Despite teachers' efforts to build children's trust in the political process, outside events can erode that trust as children grow up. For example, urban adolescents have been found to have a more cynical view of both the police and the president than nonurban youth have.[29]

In general, people know far more about the politics of the era in which they grew up than they know about the politics of other generations' formative years. A 1996 study of a group of people who graduated from high school in 1965 and their parents revealed that over 90 percent of the parents knew that President Franklin D. Roosevelt had been a Democrat, but only about 70 percent of their children did. However, two-thirds of this younger generation could name a country bordering Vietnam, compared with fewer than half of their parents. The author explained that for the parents, "the FDR years formed a core part of their autobiographies," whereas "the class of 1965 was inevitably affected by the [Vietnam] war and the controversy surrounding it."[30]

Political learning at the college level can be much like that in high school, or it can be quite different. The degree of difference is greater if professors (or the texts they use) encourage their students to question authority. Questioning dominant political values does not necessarily mean rejecting them. For example, this text encourages you to recognize that freedom and equality, two values idealized in our culture, often conflict. It also invites you to think of democracy in terms of competing institutional models, one of which challenges the idealized notion of democracy. These alternative perspectives are meant to teach you about American political values, not to subvert those values. College courses that are intended to stimulate critical thinking have the potential to introduce students to political ideas that are radically different from those they bring to class. Most high school courses do not. Still, specialists in socialization contend that taking particular courses in college has little effect on attitude change, which is more likely to come from sustained interactions with classmates who hold different views.[31]

Community and Peers. Your community and your peers are different but usually overlapping groups. Your community is the people of all ages with whom you come in contact because they live or work near you. Peers are your friends, classmates, and coworkers. Usually they are your age and live or work within your community.

The makeup of a community has a lot to do with how the political opinions of its members are formed. Homogeneous communities—those whose members are similar in ethnicity, race, religion, or occupation—can exert strong pressures on both children and adults to conform to the dominant attitude. For example, if all your neighbors praise the candidates of one party and criticize the candidates of the other, it is difficult to voice or even hold a dissenting opinion.[32] Communities made up of one ethnic group or religion may also voice negative attitudes about other groups. Although community socialization is usually reinforced in the schools, schools sometimes introduce students to ideas that run counter to community values. (One example is sex education.)

For both children and adults, peer groups sometimes provide a defense against community pressures. Adolescent peer groups are particularly effective protection against parental pressures. In adolescence, children rely on their peers to defend their dress and their lifestyle, not their politics. At the college level, however, peer group influence on political attitudes often grows substantially, sometimes fed by new information that clashes with parental beliefs. A classic study of students at Bennington College in the 1930s found that many became substantially more liberal than their affluent and conservative parents. Two follow-up studies twenty-five and fifty years later showed that most retained their liberal attitudes, in part because their spouses and friends (peers) supported their views.[33] Other evidence shows that the baby boomers who

Katrina Swamps Public Opinion

On August 29, 2005, Hurricane Katrina slammed into the shores of southern Louisiana and Mississippi. The high winds and flooding left thousands of people dead or displaced from their homes. The slow response on the part of the federal government, particularly to the plight of poor people stranded in the flooded city of New Orleans, enraged many, and moved public opinion. Before Hurricane Katrina, Americans named the war in Iraq, terrorism, and economic woes as the nation's most important problems. After Katrina, respondents identified natural disaster relief and funding as the second most important problem after the war in Iraq, more important than the threat of terrorism. *(Data from Joseph Carroll, "American Public Opinion About the Most Important Problem," 27 September 2005, <http://gallup.com>. Photo: James Nielsen/AFP/Getty Images)*

went to college during the late 1960s and became the affluent yuppies of the 1980s (perhaps your parents) became more liberal on social issues than their high school classmates who did not go to college. However, yuppies were about as conservative as nonyuppies on economic matters.[34]

Continuing Socialization

Political socialization continues throughout life. As parental and school influences wane in adulthood, peer groups (neighbors, coworkers, club members) assume a greater importance in promoting political awareness and developing political opinions.[35] Peers exert a strong influence on attitudes, despite a marked decline in trust in other people over the past few decades (see "Looking to the Future: Will No One Trust Anyone by 2060?"). Because adults usually learn about political events from the mass media—newspapers, magazines, television, radio, and the Web—the media emerge as socialization agents. Older Americans are more likely to rely on newspaper and television news for political information, while younger Americans are more likely to turn to radio, magazines, or the Internet.[36] The mass media are so important in the political socialization of both children and adults that we devote a whole chapter—Chapter 6—to a discussion of their role.

Looking to the Future

Will No One Trust Anyone by 2060?

In periodic surveys from 1964 to 2002, the National Opinion Research Center at the University of Chicago asked national samples of respondents: "Would you say most people can be trusted?" For almost four decades, the trend of the "Yes" responses has been steadily downward. If this trend line is extrapolated over the future, no citizen in the year 2060 will feel that he or she can trust most other citizens. So if you are reading this as a college student in the first decade of the twenty-first century, by the time you retire from working you may find yourself in a suspicious society in which few citizens trust others.

What explains this decrease in trust over the last forty years? Will this trend continue? If not, why not?

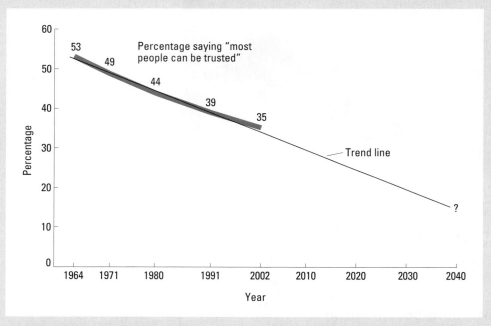

Source: Data from Greg Burns, "America's Motto: In Few We Trust," *Chicago Tribune*, 7 June 2003, p. 1.

Regardless of how people learn about politics, they gain perspective on government as they grow older. They are likely to measure new candidates (and new ideas) against those they remember. Their values also change, increasingly reflecting their own self-interest. As voters age, for example, they begin to see more merit in government spending for Social Security than they did when they were younger. As social norms change, generational differences in values translate into different public policy preferences (see Figure 5.3). Finally, political education comes simply through exposure and familiarity. One exam-

FIGURE 5.3 Socialization, Age, and Public Opinion

As noted in Figure 5.2, public opinion on the issue of gay marriage is bimodal. However, the distribution of opinion for the public as a whole masks important generational differences. Consider the same question broken down by age categories. The public appears evenly divided, though subgroups of the population are not. Young Americans are clearly more tolerant of gay marriage than older Americans are.

Source: Frank Newport, "Public Shifts to More Conservative Stance on Gay Rights," Gallup Poll Analyses, July 30, 2003, <http://gallup.com/poll/release/pr030730.asp>.

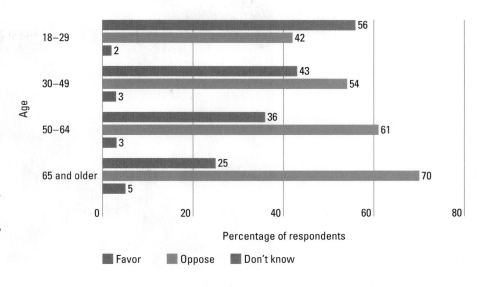

Percentage of respondents

■ Favor   ■ Oppose   ■ Don't know

ple is voting, which people do with increasing regularity as they grow older: it becomes a habit.

★ Social Groups and Political Values

No two people are influenced by precisely the same socialization agents or in precisely the same way. Each individual experiences a unique process of political socialization and forms a unique set of political values. Still, people with similar backgrounds do share similar experiences, which means they tend to develop similar political opinions. In this section, we examine the ties between people's social background and their political values. In the process, we examine the ties between background and values by looking at responses to two questions posed by the 2004 National Election Study, administered by the University of Michigan's Center for Political Studies. Many questions in the survey tap the freedom-versus-order or freedom-versus-equality dimensions. The two we chose serve to illustrate the analysis of ideological types.

The first question dealt with abortion. The interviewer said, "There has been some discussion about abortion during recent years. Which opinion on this page best agrees with your view? You can just tell me the number of the opinion you choose":

1. "By law, abortion should never be permitted" [13 percent agreed].

2. "The law should permit abortion only in cases of rape, incest, or when the woman's life is in danger" [32 percent agreed].

3. "The law should permit abortion for reasons other than rape, incest, or danger to the woman's life, but only after the need for the abortion has been clearly established" [18 percent agreed].

You're in Good Hands

A person's "religiosity" may be as important as his or her denominational identification in predicting political opinions. One measure of people's religiosity in a Christian-Judaic society is their opinion about the Bible. When asked about the nature of the Bible in 2005, about 32 percent of respondents said it was the actual word of God. About 47 percent regarded it as inspired by God but believed it should not be taken literally. The remaining 18 percent viewed it as an ancient book of history, legends, fables, and moral precepts recorded by humans. Those who believed that the Bible is the literal word of God strongly favored government action to limit abortion. They were also much more likely to think that "creationism," a theory of the origin and development of life on Earth based on a strict reading of the Bible, should be taught in public schools alongside the theory of evolution. (*Data from Gallup Poll news service, <http://poll.gallup.com>. Photo: Stephen Morton/Getty Images*)

IDEAlog.org

What are your views on abortion? Take IDEAlog's self-test.

4. "By law, a woman should be able to obtain an abortion as a matter of personal choice" [37 percent agreed].[37]

Those who chose the last category most clearly valued individual freedom over order imposed by government. Evidence shows that pro-choice respondents also tend to have concerns about broader issues of social order, such as the role of women and the legitimacy of alternative lifestyles.[38]

The second question posed by the 2004 National Election Study pertained to the role of government in guaranteeing employment:

Some people feel the government in Washington should see to it that every person has a job and a good standard of living. Suppose that these people are at one end of the scale. . . . Others think the government should just let each person get ahead on his own. Suppose these people were at the other end. . . . Where would you put yourself on this scale, or haven't you thought much about this?

Excluding respondents who "hadn't thought much" about this question, 34 percent wanted the government to provide every person with a living, and 19 percent were undecided. That left 47 percent who wanted the government to leave people alone to "get ahead" on their own. These respondents, who opposed government efforts to promote equality, apparently valued freedom over equality.

Overall, the responses to each of these questions were divided approximately equally. Somewhat fewer than half the respondents (37 percent) felt that the government should not set restrictions on abortion, and just short of a majority (47 percent) thought the government should not guarantee people a job and a good standard of living. However, sharp differences in attitudes emerged for both issues when the respondents were grouped by socioeconomic factors: education, income, region, race, religion, and sex. The differences are shown in Figure 5.4 as positive and negative deviations from the national average for each question. Bars that extend to the right identify groups that are more likely than most Americans to sacrifice freedom for order (on the left-hand side of the figure) or equality (on the right-hand side). Next, we examine the opinion patterns more closely for each socioeconomic group.

Education

Education increases people's awareness and understanding of political issues. Higher education also promotes tolerance of unpopular opinions and behavior and invites citizens to see issues in terms of civil rights and liberties. This result is clearly shown in the left-hand column of Figure 5.4, which shows that people with more education are more likely to view abortion as a matter of a woman's choice.[39] When confronted with a choice between personal freedom and social order, college-educated individuals tend to choose freedom.

With regard to the role of government in reducing income inequality, the right-hand column in Figure 5.4 shows that people with more education also tend to favor freedom over equality. The higher are their levels of education, the less likely respondents were to support government-guaranteed jobs and living standards. You might expect better-educated people to be humanitarian and to support government programs to help the needy. However, because educated people tend to be wealthier, they would be taxed more heavily for such government programs. Moreover, they may believe that it is unrealistic to expect government to make such economic guarantees.

Income

In many countries, differences in social class, based on social background and occupation, divide people in their politics.[40] In the United States, the vast majority of citizens regard themselves as "middle class." Yet, as Figure 5.4 shows, wealth is consistently linked to opinions favoring a limited government role in promoting order and equality. Those with a higher income are more likely to favor personal choice in abortion and to oppose government guarantees of employment and living conditions. For both issues, wealth and education have a similar effect on opinion: the groups with more education and higher income favor freedom.

FIGURE 5.4 Deviations of Group Opinion from National Opinion on Two Questions of Order and Equality

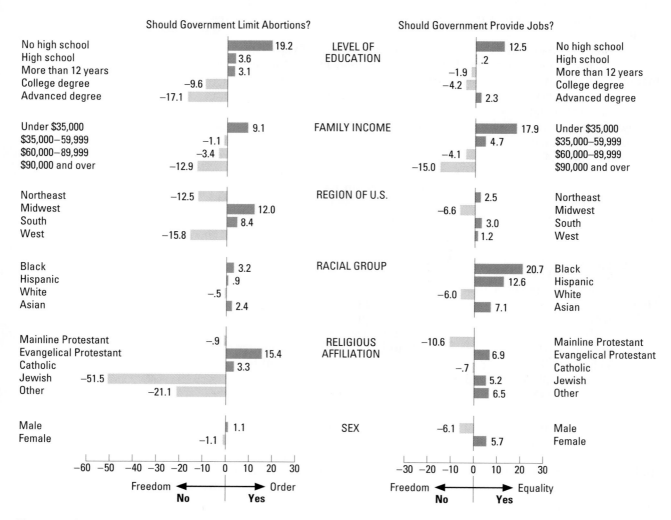

Two questions—one posing the dilemma of freedom versus order (regarding government limits on abortion) and the other the dilemma of freedom versus equality (regarding government guarantees of employment)—were asked of a national sample in 2004. Public opinion across the nation as a whole was sharply divided on each question. These two graphs show how respondents in several social groups deviated from the national mean for each question. The longer the bars are next to a group, the more its respondents deviated from the overall sample's view. Bars that extend to the left show opinions that deviate toward freedom. Bars that extend to the right show deviations away from freedom, toward order (in the left-hand graph) or equality (in the right-hand graph).

Source: Data from 2004 National Election Study, Center for Political Studies, University of Michigan.

Region

Early in our country's history, regional differences were politically important—important enough to spark a civil war between the North and South. For nearly a hundred years after the Civil War, regional differences continued to affect American politics. The moneyed Northeast was thought to control the purse strings of capitalism. The Midwest was long regarded as the stronghold of isolationism in foreign affairs. The South was virtually a one-party region, almost completely Democratic. And the individualistic West pioneered its own mixture of progressive politics.

In the past, differences in wealth fed cultural differences between these regions. In recent decades, however, the movement of people and wealth away from the Northeast and Midwest to the Sunbelt states in the South and Southwest has equalized the per capita income of the various regions. One result of this equalization is that the formerly "solid South" is no longer solidly Democratic.[41] In fact, the South has tended to vote for Republican presidential candidates since 1968, and the majority of southern congressmen are now Republicans.

Figure 5.4 shows greater differences in public opinion on social issues than on economic issues in the four major regions of the United States. Respondents in the Northeast and West were more likely to support personal choice than were residents of the South and Midwest, where they were more likely to favor restricting abortion. People in the Northeast were somewhat more supportive of government efforts to equalize income than were people elsewhere.

Race and Ethnicity

Over the course of American history, individuals of diverse racial and ethnic backgrounds have differed with respect to political values and opportunities. In the early twentieth century, the major ethnic minorities in America were composed of immigrants from Ireland, Italy, Germany, Poland, and other European countries who came to the United States in waves during the late 1800s and early 1900s. These immigrants entered a nation that had been founded by British settlers more than a hundred years earlier. They found themselves in a strange land, usually without money and unable to speak the language. Moreover, their religious backgrounds—mainly Catholic and Jewish—differed from that of the predominantly Protestant earlier settlers. These urban ethnics and their descendants became part of the great coalition of Democratic voters that President Franklin Roosevelt forged in the 1930s. And for years after, the European ethnics supported liberal candidates and causes more strongly than the original Anglo-Saxon immigrants did.[42]

From the Civil War through the civil rights movement of the 1950s and 1960s, African Americans fought to secure basic political rights such as the right to vote. Initially mobilized by the Republican Party—the party of Lincoln—following the Civil War, African Americans also forged strong ties with the Democratic Party during the New Deal era. Today, African Americans are still more likely to support liberal candidates and identify with the Democratic Party. African Americans constitute almost 13 percent of the population, with sizable voting blocs in southern states and northern cities.

Hispanics are the most rapidly growing racial or ethnic group in American society, surpassing African Americans as the largest U.S. minority group,

Waiting for the President

Cindy Sheehan, whose twenty-four-year-old son Casey was killed in Iraq, gained national attention by holding a vigil outside President Bush's Texas ranch in the summer of 2005. Sheehan wanted to meet Bush personally to hear his justification for the ongoing war in Iraq. "He said my son died in a noble cause, and I want to ask him what the noble cause is." Though many soldiers' families criticized Sheehan for voicing opposition to the war, public opinion polls showed that 90 percent of the public agreed that it's okay for opponents of the war to publicly share their concerns about the conflict. *(Data from "Poll: 90 Percent Support Right to Protest War," Associated Press, 26 August 2005, <http://msnbc.com>. Photo: Mandel Ngan/AFP/Getty Images)*

according to the Census Bureau.[43] Hispanics are commonly but inaccurately regarded as a racial group, for they consist of both whites and nonwhites. People of Latin American origin are often called Latinos. If they speak Spanish (Haitians and Brazilians usually do not), they are also known as Hispanics. At the national level, Hispanics (consisting of groups as different as Cubans, Mexicans, Peruvians, and Puerto Ricans) have lagged behind African Americans in mobilizing and gaining political office. However, although Hispanics make up only 14 percent of the nation's population, they constitute over 30 percent of the population in California, Texas, and New Mexico.[44] In these communities, Hispanics are being wooed by non-Hispanic candidates and are increasingly running for public office themselves.

Both Asians and Native Americans account for another 5 percent of the population. Like other minority groups, their political impact is greatest in cities or regions where they are concentrated and greater in number. For instance, Asian Americans constitute 12 percent of the population of California; Native Americans make up 10 percent of the population of New Mexico.[45] Scholars have recently started to conduct more surveys of minority groups in order to have large enough numbers of respondents to make generalizations about racial and ethnic differences in public opinion and political values.[46]

We do know that blacks and members of other minorities display somewhat similar political attitudes on questions pertaining to equality. The reasons are twofold.[47] First, racial minorities (excepting second-generation Asians) tend to have low **socioeconomic status,** a measure of social condition that includes education, occupational status, and income. Second, minorities have been targets of prejudice and discrimination and have benefited from govern-

socioeconomic status Position in society, based on a combination of education, occupational status, and income.

ment actions in support of equality. The right-hand column in Figure 5.4 clearly shows the effects of race on the freedom-equality issue. All minority groups, particularly African Americans, are much more likely than whites to favor government action to improve economic opportunity. The abortion issue produces less difference, although minority groups favor government restrictions on abortion slightly more than whites do.

Religion

Since the last major wave of European immigration in the 1930s and 1940s, the religious makeup of the United States has remained fairly stable. Today, 53 percent of the population is Protestant, 25 percent is Catholic, 2.6 percent is Jewish, and about 19 percent deny any religious affiliation or choose some other faith.[48] For many years, analysts found strong and consistent differences in the political opinions of Protestants, Catholics, and Jews.[49] Protestants were more conservative than Catholics, and Catholics tended to be more conservative than Jews.

As Figure 5.4 indicates, religiosity has little effect on attitudes about economic equality but has a powerful influence on attitudes about social order. Evangelicals (Baptist and Pentecostal churches) strongly favor government action to limit abortion. Jews overwhelmingly favor a woman's right to choose. Differences among religious groups have emerged across many contemporary social and political issues. Evangelical Protestants are also more likely than members of other religious groups to oppose gay marriage and support the death penalty. Evangelicals and Jews are more likely to express support for Israel in Middle Eastern politics. Religious beliefs have been at the center of national and local debates over issues such as stem cell research, human cloning, and the teaching of evolution or creationism as the appropriate explanation for the development of life on Earth.[50]

Gender

Men and women differ with respect to their political opinions on a broad array of social and political issues. As shown in the right-hand column of Figure 5.4, women are more likely than men to favor government actions to promote equality. Men and women differ less on the abortion issue (see the left-hand column in Figure 5.4). Surveys show that women are consistently more supportive than men are of both affirmative action and government spending for social programs. They are consistently less supportive of the death penalty and of going to war.[51]

Since gaining the right to vote with the passage of the Nineteenth Amendment in 1919, women have been mobilized by the major political parties. Contemporary politics is marked by a "gender gap": women tend to identify with the Democratic Party more than men do (see Figure 8.5 on page 248), and they are much more likely than men to vote for Democratic presidential candidates. In the 2000 presidential election, 54 percent of female voters supported Democratic candidate Al Gore, and 43 percent of female voters supported George Bush.[52] During his 2004 reelection campaign, President Bush made a special effort to gain the votes of "security moms," white suburban women with children, whose top issue priority was terrorism. In 2004, Bush narrowed the gender gap, winning 48 percent of the female vote.

★ From Values to Ideology

We have just seen that differences in groups' responses to two survey questions reflect those groups' value choices between freedom and order and between freedom and equality. But to what degree do people's opinions on specific issues reflect their explicit political ideology (the set of values and beliefs they hold about the purpose and scope of government)? Political scientists generally agree that ideology influences public opinion on specific issues; they have much less consensus on the extent to which people think explicitly in ideological terms.[53] They also agree that the public's ideological thinking cannot be categorized adequately in conventional liberal–conservative terms.[54]

The Degree of Ideological Thinking in Public Opinion

Although today's media frequently use the terms *liberal* and *conservative,* some people think these terms are no longer relevant to American politics. Even President Clinton said, "The old labels of liberal and conservative are not what matter most anymore."[55] But when did they ever matter "most"? When asked to describe the parties and candidates in the 1956 election, only about 12 percent of respondents volunteered responses that contained ideological terms (such as *liberal, conservative,* and *capitalism*).[56] Most respondents (42 percent) evaluated the parties and candidates in terms of "benefits to groups" (farmers, workers, or businesspeople, for example). Others (24 percent) spoke more generally about "the nature of the times" (for example, inflation, unemployment, and the threat of war). Finally, a good portion of the sample (22 percent) gave answers that contained no classifiable issue content. Even more than four decades ago, most voters did not use ideological labels when discussing politics.

So perhaps we should not make too much of recent findings about the electorate's unfamiliarity with ideology. In one poll, voters were asked what they thought when someone was described as "liberal" or "conservative."[57] Few responded in explicitly political terms. Rather, most people gave dictionary definitions: "'liberals' are generous (a *liberal* portion). And 'conservatives' are moderate or cautious (a *conservative* estimate)." The two most frequent responses for *conservative* were "fiscally responsible or tight" (17 percent) and "closed-minded" (10 percent). For *liberal* the top two were "open-minded" (14 percent) and "free-spending" (8 percent). Only about 6 percent of the sample mentioned "degree of government involvement" in describing liberals and conservatives.

Ideological labels are technical terms used in analyzing politics, and most citizens don't play that sport. But if you want to play, you need suitable headgear. Scales and typologies, despite their faults, are essential for classification. No analysis, including the study of politics, can occur without classifying the objects being studied. The tendency to use ideological terms in discussing politics grows with increased education, which helps people understand political issues and relate them to one another. People's personal political socialization experiences can also lead them to think ideologically. For example, children raised in strong union households may be taught to distrust private enterprise and value collective action through government.

True ideologues hold a consistent set of values and beliefs about the purpose and scope of government, and they tend to evaluate candidates in ideo-

? Can you explain why . . . the "moderate" ideological category may be overstated?

logical terms.[58] Some people respond to questions in ways that seem ideological but are not because they do not understand the underlying principles. For example, most respondents dutifully comply when asked to place themselves somewhere on a liberal–conservative continuum. The result, as shown earlier in Figure 5.2, is an approximately normal distribution centering on "moderate," the modal category. But many people settle on moderate when they do not clearly understand the alternatives, because moderate is a safe choice. A study in 2004 gave respondents another choice—the statement, "I haven't thought much about it"—which allowed them to avoid placing themselves on the liberal–conservative continuum. In this study, 20 percent of the respondents acknowledged that they had not thought much about ideology.[59] The extent of ideological thinking in America, then, is even less than it might seem from responses to questions asking people to describe themselves as liberals or conservatives.[60]

The Quality of Ideological Thinking in Public Opinion

What people's ideological self-placement means in the early twenty-first century also is not clear. At one time, the liberal–conservative continuum represented a single dimension: attitudes toward the scope of government activity. Liberals were in favor of more government action to provide public goods, and conservatives were in favor of less. This simple distinction is not as useful today. Many people who call themselves liberal no longer favor government activism in general, and many self-styled conservatives no longer oppose it in principle. As a result, many people have difficulty deciding whether they are liberal or conservative, whereas others confidently choose identical points on the continuum for entirely different reasons. People describe themselves as liberal or conservative because of the symbolic value of the terms as much as for reasons of ideology.[61]

Studies of the public's ideological thinking find that two themes run through people's minds when they are asked to describe liberals and conservatives. People associate liberals with change and conservatives with tradition. The theme corresponds to the distinction between liberals and conservatives on the exercise of freedom and the maintenance of order.[62]

The other theme has to do with equality. The conflict between freedom and equality was at the heart of President Roosevelt's New Deal economic policies (Social Security, minimum wage legislation, farm price supports) in the 1930s. The policies expanded the interventionist role of the national government to promote greater economic equality, and attitudes toward government intervention in the economy served to distinguish liberals from conservatives for decades afterward.[63] Attitudes toward government interventionism still underlie opinions about domestic economic policies.[64] Liberals support intervention to promote economic equality; conservatives favor less government intervention and more individual freedom in economic activities.

In Chapter 1, we proposed an alternative system of ideological classification based on people's relative evaluations of freedom, order, and equality. We described liberals as people who believe that government should promote equality, even if some freedom is lost in the process, but who oppose surrendering freedom to government-imposed order. Conservatives do not necessarily oppose equality but put a higher value on freedom than on equality when the two conflict. Yet conservatives are not above restricting freedom when threatened with the loss of order. So both groups value freedom, but one is more willing to trade freedom for equality, and the other is more inclined to trade freedom for order. If you have trouble thinking about these tradeoffs on a single dimension, you are in good company. The liberal–conservative continuum presented to survey respondents takes a two-dimensional concept and squeezes it into a one-dimensional format.[65]

Ideological Types in the United States

Our ideological typology in Chapter 1 (see Figure 1.2) classifies people as liberals if they favor freedom over order and equality over freedom. Conversely, conservatives favor freedom over equality and order over freedom. Libertarians favor freedom over both equality and order—the opposite of communitarians. By cross-tabulating people's answers to the two questions from the 2004 National Election Study about freedom versus order (abortion) and freedom versus equality (government job guarantees), we can classify respondents according to their ideological tendencies. As shown in Figure 5.5, a substantial portion of respondents falls within each of the quadrants. This finding indicates that people do not decide about government activity according to a one-dimensional ideological standard. Figure 5.5 also classifies the sample according to the two dimensions in our ideological typology. (Remember, however, that these categories—like the letter grades A, B, C, and D for courses—are rigid. The respondents' answers to both questions varied in intensity but were reduced to a simple yes or no to simplify this analysis. Many respondents would cluster toward the center of Figure 5.5 if their attitudes were represented more sensitively.) The conservative response pattern was the most common, followed by the communitarian pattern. The figure suggests that three-quarters of the electorate favor government action to promote order, increase equality, or both. The results resemble earlier findings by other researchers who conducted more exhaustive analysis involving more survey questions.[66]

Respondents who readily locate themselves on a single dimension running from liberal to conservative often go on to contradict their self-placement when answering questions that trade freedom for either order or equality.[67] A two-dimensional typology such as that in Figure 5.5 allows us to analyze responses more meaningfully.[68] Although a slight majority of respondents in the 2004 survey (55 percent) expressed opinions that were either liberal (23 percent) or conservative (32 percent), many expressed opinions that deviated from these familiar ideological types.

The ideological tendencies illustrate important differences between different social groups. Communitarians are prominent among minorities and among people with little education and low income, groups that tend to look favorably on the benefits of government in general. Libertarians are concentrated among people with more education and higher income, who tend to be suspicious of government interference in their lives. Though geographically dispersed, libertarians tend to be located in western states and a handful of northeastern states such as New Hampshire. People in the southern states tend to be communitarians, those in the Midwest tend to be conservatives, and those in the Northeast are inclined to be liberals. Men are more likely to be conservative or libertarian than women, who tend to be liberal or communitarian.[69]

FIGURE 5.5   Respondents Classified by Ideological Tendencies

In the 2004 election survey, respondents were asked whether abortion should be a matter of personal choice or regulated by the government, and whether government should guarantee people a job and a good standard of living or people should get ahead on their own. (The questions are given verbatim on pages 141–142.) These two questions presented choices between freedom and order and between freedom and equality. People's responses to the two questions showed no correlation, demonstrating that these value choices cannot be explained by a simple liberal–conservative continuum. Instead, their responses can be analyzed more usefully according to four different ideological types.

Source: 2004 National Election Study, Center for Political Studies, University of Michigan.

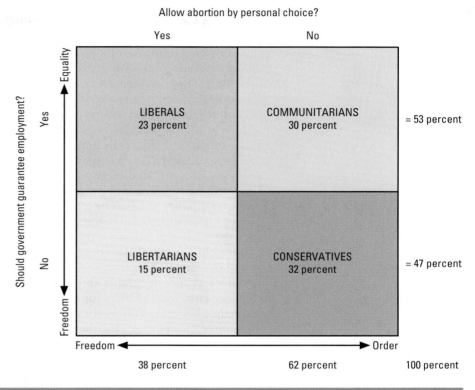

This more refined analysis of political ideology explains why even Americans who pay close attention to politics find it difficult to locate themselves on the liberal–conservative continuum. Their problem is that they are liberal on some issues and conservative on others. Forced to choose along just one dimension, they opt for the middle category, moderate. However, our analysis also indicates that many people who classify themselves as liberal or conservative do fit these two categories in our typology. There is value, then, in the liberal–conservative distinction as long as we understand its limitations.

★ Forming Political Opinions

We have seen that people acquire their political values through socialization and that different social groups develop different sets of political values. We have also learned that some people, but only a minority, think about politics ideologically, holding a consistent set of political attitudes and beliefs. But how do those who are not ideologues—in other words, most citizens—form political opinions? As noted at the start of the chapter, the majoritarian and pluralist models of democracy make different assumptions about public opinion. Are most people well informed about politics? What can we say about the quality of public opinion in America?

Political Knowledge

It seems reasonable to ask whether most Americans are ideologically unsophisticated yet still well informed about politics. In the United States today, education is compulsory (usually to age sixteen), and the literacy rate is relatively high. The country boasts an unparalleled network of colleges and universities, entered by two-thirds of all high school graduates. American citizens can obtain information from a variety of daily and weekly news sources in print and on the Web. They can keep abreast of national and international affairs through cable and television news programs, which bring live coverage of world events via satellite from virtually everywhere in the world.

In a study of political knowledge, political scientists Delli Carpini and Keeter collected thirty-seven hundred individual survey items that measured some type of factual knowledge about public affairs.[70] They focused on over two thousand items that clearly dealt with political facts, such as knowledge of political institutions and processes, contemporary public figures, political groups, and policy issues. The authors found that "many of the basic institutions and procedures of government are known to half or more of the public, as are the relative positions of the parties on many major issues."[71]

Yet political knowledge is not randomly distributed within our society. "In particular, women, African Americans, the poor, and the young tend to be substantially less knowledgeable about politics than are men, whites, the affluent, and older citizens."[72] Education is the strongest single predictor of political knowledge, but other cultural or structural factors prevent women and blacks, for example, from developing the same levels of general political knowledge as white males.[73]

Researchers have not found any meaningful relationship between political sophistication and self-placement on the liberal–conservative continuum. That is, people with equivalent knowledge of public affairs and levels of conceptualization are equally likely to call themselves liberals or conservatives.[74] However, individuals who strongly believe in certain causes may be impervious to information that questions their beliefs; they may even create false memories that support their beliefs. For instance, researchers found that individuals who thought the war in Iraq was fought to eliminate that country's weapons of mass destruction were more likely to think that these weapons had been found after the start of the war.[75] They were less sensitive to news information that contradicted their initial beliefs.

Even if a portion of the public is uninformed, some researchers hold that the *collective* opinion of the public, which balances off random ignorance on both sides of an issue, can be interpreted as stable and meaningful. Political scientists Benjamin Page and Robert Shapiro analyzed the public's responses to 1,128 questions that were repeated in one or more surveys between 1935 and 1990.[76] They found that responses to more than half of the repeated policy questions "showed no significant change at all"—that is, they changed no more than six percentage points.[77] Moreover, Page and Shapiro concluded that when the public's collective opinion on public policy changes, it changes in "understandable, predictable ways."[78]

Costs, Benefits, and Cues

Perhaps people do not think in ideological terms or know a wide variety of political facts, but they can tell whether a policy is likely to directly help or hurt them. The **self-interest principle** states that people choose what benefits them personally.[79] Self-interest plays an obvious role in how people form opinions on government policies with clear costs and benefits.[80] Taxpayers tend to prefer low taxes to high taxes. Smokers tend to oppose bans on smoking in public places. Gun owners are less likely to support handgun control. Some people evaluate incumbent presidents according to whether they are better or worse off financially than they were four years ago. Group leaders often cue group members, telling them what policies they should support or oppose. (In the context of pluralist democracy, this often appears as grassroots support for or opposition to policies that affect only particular groups.[81])

In some cases, individuals are unable to determine personal costs or benefits. This tends to be true of foreign policy, which few people interpret in terms of personal benefits. Here, many people have no opinion, or their opinions are not firmly held and are likely to change quite easily given almost any new information. For example, public approval of the war in Iraq and of Bush's handling of the war has varied with positive news such as the Iraqi elections and negative news such as the number of military casualties. (To learn more about the perceived impact of the war in Iraq in other countries, see "Compared with What? Opinions on a World Without Saddam Hussein.")

Public opinion that is not based on a complicated ideology may also emerge from the skillful use of cues. Individuals may use heuristics—mental shortcuts that require hardly any information—to make fairly reliable political judgments.[82] For instance, citizens can use political party labels to compensate for low information about the policy positions of candidates. Voters may have

Can you explain why . . . self-interest might *not* influence public opinion on some issues?

self-interest principle The implication that people choose what benefits them personally.

Compared with What?

Opinions on a World Without Saddam Hussein

Americans, as well as citizens in other countries, will freely offer an opinion about world events. Respondents from seventeen countries were asked in spring 2005 about whether or not they felt that the world was a safer or more dangerous place after the war with Iraq that removed Saddam Hussein from power. Only the United States and India had near ma-jorities of respondents who felt that the world is a safer place. Respondents in every other country felt the world is more dangerous. Respondents living in countries that joined the U.S.-led "coalition of the willing"—Great Britain, Canada, and Poland—were more likely to believe the world is better off than respondents in Asia and the Middle East.

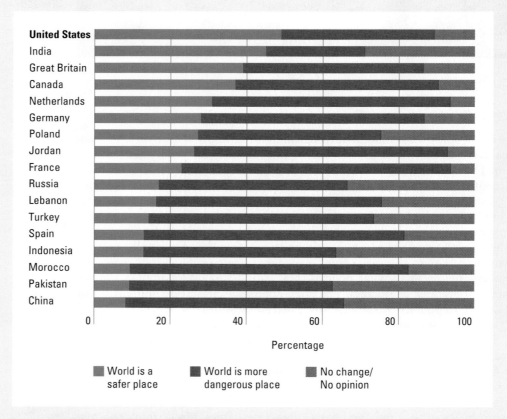

Source: Pew Global Attitudes Project, Spring 2005 Seventeen Nation Survey, <http://pewglobal.org>.

INTERACTIVE 5.2

 Reactions to the Death of Saddam Hussein

well-developed expectations or stereotypes about political parties that struc-ture the way they evaluate candidates and process new information.[83] They as-sume that Democrats and Republicans differ from each other in predictable ways. Similarly, citizens take cues from trusted government officials and inter-est groups regarding the wisdom of bills pending in Congress or the ideology of Supreme Court nominees.

Political Leadership

Public opinion on specific issues is molded by political leaders, journalists, and policy experts. Politicians serve as cue givers to members of the public. Citizens with favorable views of a politician may be more likely to support his or her values and policy agenda. In one study, 49 percent of respondents were uncomfortable with the statement, "I have never believed the Constitution re-quired our schools to be religion free zones," when it was presented anony-mously; only 34 percent claimed to be uncomfortable when the statement was attributed to former president Bill Clinton.[84] In a different study, African Americans were presented with a statement about the need for blacks to rely more on themselves to get ahead in society; respondents agreed with the state-ment when it was attributed to black politicians (Jesse Jackson and Clarence Thomas) and disagreed when the statement was attributed to white politicians (George H. W. Bush and Ted Kennedy).[85]

Politicians routinely make appeals to the public on the basis of shared political ideology and self-interest. They collect and share information about social trends, policy options, and policy implementation. Competition and controversy among political elites provide the public with a great deal of in-formation. But politicians are well aware that citizen understanding and sup-port for an issue depend on its framing. In **issue framing,** politicians define the way that issues are presented, selectively invoking values or recalling history in the presentation. For example, opinion leaders might frame a reduction in taxes as "returning money to the people" or, quite differently, as "reducing government services." Politicians and other leaders can frame issues to change or reinforce public opinion. Such framing is sometimes referred to as "spin," and "spin doctors" are those who stand ready to reinforce or elaborate on the spin inherent in the framing.[86]

The ability of political leaders to influence public opinion has been en-hanced enormously by the growth of the broadcast media, especially television.[87] The majoritarian model of democracy assumes that government officials re-spond to public opinion, but the evidence is substantial that this causal se-quence is reversed—that public opinion responds to the actions of government officials.[88] If this is true, how much potential is there for public opinion to be manipulated by political leaders through the mass media? We examine the ma-nipulative potential of the mass media in the next chapter.

issue framing The way that politicians or interest group leaders define an issue when presenting it to others.

Summary

Public opinion does not rule in America. On most issues, it merely sets general boundaries for government policy. The shape of the distribution of opinion (skewed, bimodal, or normal) indicates how sharply the public is divided. Bimodal distributions harbor the greatest potential for political conflict. The stability of a distribution over time indicates how settled people are in their opinions. Because most Americans' ideological opinions are normally distributed around the moderate category and have been for decades, government policies can vary from left to right over time without provoking severe political conflict.

People form their values through the process of political socialization. The most important socialization agents in childhood and young adulthood are family, school, community, and peers. Members of the same social group tend to experience similar socialization processes and thus to adopt similar values. People in different social groups that hold different values often express vastly different opinions. Differences in education, race, and religion tend to produce sharper divisions of opinion today on questions of order and equality than do differences in income or region.

Most people do not think about politics in ideological terms. When asked to do so by pollsters, however, they readily classify themselves along a liberal–conservative continuum. Many respondents choose the middle category, moderate, because the choice is safe. Many others choose it because they have liberal views on some issues and conservative views on others. Their political orientation is better captured by a two-dimensional framework that analyzes ideology according to the values of freedom, order, and equality. Responses to the survey questions we used to establish our ideological typology illustrate that the American electorate may be usefully classified as liberals, conservatives, libertarians, and communitarians.

In addition to ideological orientation, many other factors affect the process of forming political opinions. When individuals stand to benefit or suffer from proposed government policies, they usually base their opinions of these policies on their own self-interest. Citizens use heuristics like political party labels to compensate for their lack of detailed information about pending legislation or political candidates. In the absence of information, respondents are particularly susceptible to cues of support or opposition from political leaders, communicated through the mass media.

Which model of democracy, the majoritarian or the pluralist, is correct in its assumptions about public opinion? Sometimes the public shows clear and settled opinions on government policy, conforming to the majoritarian model. However, public opinion is often not firmly grounded in knowledge and may be unstable on given issues. Moreover, powerful groups often divide on what they want government to do. The lack of consensus leaves politicians with a great deal of latitude in enacting specific policies, a finding that conforms to the pluralist model. Of course, politicians' actions are closely scrutinized by journalists' reporting in the mass media. We turn to the effect on politics of this scrutiny in Chapter 6.

Internet activities and reading suggestions for this chapter are available on the *Online Study Center*

To complete the multimedia assignments for this chapter, go to AmericansGoverning.org.

6

The Media

(Courtesy Fox News)

Online Study Center
This icon will direct you to resources
and activities on the website
college.hmco.com/pic/jandaupdate9e

The Fox News Cable Channel was not shy about making judgments when covering the war on terrorism after September 11, 2001. Fox newscasters referred to "our troops" fighting "terror goons" in Afghanistan and spoke of "homicide bombers" rather than "suicide bombers" in Israel.[1] Meanwhile, at CNN, then the established leader in cable news, anchors reported news more objectively, but with less audience appeal. By January 2002, Fox had jumped past CNN to first place in the cable news ratings.

After the fall of Baghdad in 2003, a Fox news anchor sneered at citizens who opposed the war—"You were sickening then, you are sickening now"—while another anchor hoped that Iraq's reconstruction would not be left to "the dopey old U.N."[2] Meanwhile, at MSNBC, third among the cable news channels, Fox's rapid rise in ratings was not unnoticed. MSNBC's two new commentators, hired shortly before the Iraqi war, described antiwar protesters as "leftist stooges for anti-American causes" who were "committing sedition, or treason." MSNBC's ratings in the week after the war began rose even faster than CNN's ratings.[3]

This shift to the political right in cable news coverage, known as the "Fox effect," introduced both more colorful commentary in news coverage and commentary with a conservative rather than liberal perspective.[4] For its part, Fox claimed to offer "fair and balanced" news as an alternative to the bias in the "liberal media"— meaning the three major networks, ABC, CBS, and NBC, which had long led the industry.[5] As recently as 1993, 60 percent of the public watched the nightly news programs on these three networks. A decade later, viewership had dropped to 32 percent, virtually the same as the 33 percent said to watch cable news.[6]

Mostly, the public was in tune with Fox's approach. In a 2003 poll, 45 percent of the respondents viewed the news media as too liberal, compared with 14 percent who saw it as too conservative.[7] In addition, over 70 percent of the respondents "thought it was good for news outlets to take a strong pro-American point of view." At the same time, 64 percent also wanted news coverage of the war on terrorism to be neutral.[8] The public apparently thought that the media could be both pro-American and neutral while covering international news.

Who runs Fox News, and who deserves credit for its popularity? Its chairman is Roger Ailes, a former political consultant to President Reagan and to President George H. W. Bush. However, the Fox cable network is only one part of the global News Corporation run by Australian-born Rupert Murdoch, now a U.S. citizen. Murdoch also owns controlling interests in 124 American radio stations; in the prestigious *Wall Street Journal,* the *New York Post,* and the *Weekly Standard;* in several major newspapers in Australia and Britain; and in other television news channels in Britain, India, and China.[9] To varying degrees, all of these outlets in his global media empire reflect an aggressive conservative variant of economic libertarianism that Murdoch shared with his friend and supporter, former British prime minister Margaret Thatcher, and that he introduced into the American media.[10]

This vignette about cable news trends in the United States foreshadows the topics addressed in this chapter. Freedom of the press is essential to the governing process, but what consequences, if any, flow from liberal or conservative biases in the media? What are the "media" anyway? Who uses which media, and what do they learn? Do the various media promote or frustrate democratic ideals? Does the concept of freedom of the press inhibit the government's effort to secure order? Do the media advance or retard equality in society? Does the Internet pose spe-cial problems concerning freedom of the press? What new problems flow from globalization generally of the news media? In this chapter, we describe the origin and growth of the media, assess their objectivity, and examine their influence on politics. ★

★ People, Government, and Communications

IN OUR OWN WORDS

Listen to Kenneth Janda discuss the main points and themes of this chapter.

Online Study Center
Improve Your Grade

"**W**e never talk anymore" is a common lament of couples who are not getting along very well. In politics, too, citizens and their government need to communicate to get along well. *Communication* is the process of transmitting information from one individual or group to another. *Mass communication* is the process by which information is transmitted to large, heterogeneous, widely dispersed audiences. The term **mass media** refers to the means for communicating to these audiences. The mass media are commonly divided into two types:

- *Print media* communicate information through the publication of words and pictures on paper. Prime examples of print media are daily newspapers and popular magazines. Because books seldom have a large circulation relative to the general population, they are not typically classified as a mass medium.

- *Broadcast media* communicate information electronically, through sounds and images. Prime examples of broadcast media are radio and television. The worldwide network of personal computers commonly called the Internet can also be classified as broadcast technology, and the Internet has grown in size so that it also qualifies as a mass medium.

Our focus here is on the role of the media in promoting communication from government to its citizens and from citizens to their government. In totalitarian governments, information flows more freely in one direction (from government to the people) than the other. In democratic governments, information must flow freely in both directions; a democratic government can respond to public opinion only if its citizens can make their opinions known. Moreover, the electorate can hold government officials accountable for their actions only if voters know what the government has done, is doing, and plans to do. Because the mass media (and increasingly the group media) provide the major channels for this two-way flow of information, they have the dual capability of reflecting and shaping our political views.

The media are not the only means of communication between citizens and government. As we discussed in Chapter 5, various agents of socialization (especially schools) function as "linkage mechanisms" that promote such communication. In the next four chapters, we will discuss other mechanisms for communication: voting, political parties, campaigning in elections, and interest

mass media The means employed in mass communication; often divided into print media and broadcast media.

You've Got Mail . . . in Africa!
Suppose you're in Ghana, traveling from the city of Kumasi to the capital, Accra, and want to check your e-mail. Just stop at this cyber café and log in. The Internet is truly international. *(Linking Agricultural Research for Rural Radio in Africa Project Team)*

groups. Certain linkage mechanisms communicate better in one direction than in the other. Primary and secondary schools, for example, commonly instruct young citizens about government rules and symbols, whereas voting sends messages from citizens to government. Parties, campaigns, and interest groups foster communication in both directions. The media, however, are the only linkage mechanisms that specialize in communication.

Although this chapter concentrates on political uses of five prominent mass media—newspapers, magazines, radio, television, and the Internet—political content can also be transmitted through other mass media, such as recordings and motion pictures. Rock acts such as Green Day and U2 often express political ideas in their music, as do rappers such as the late Tupac Shakur and Gangsta N.I.P. At a London concert in March 2003, Dixie Chicks' singer Natalie Maines spoke out against President Bush's push for military action against Iraq, saying, "We're ashamed the president of the United States is from Texas," which caused the group's songs to be pulled temporarily from many country music stations. Motion pictures often convey particularly intense political messages. The 1976 film *All the President's Men,* about the two *Washington Post* reporters who doggedly exposed the Watergate scandal, dramatized a seamy side of political life that contrasted sharply with an idealized view of the presidency. Michael Moore's *Fahrenheit 9/11,* filmed in documentary style, was a blistering attack on the Bush presidency that won the top honor at the 2004 Cannes Film Festival.

★ The Development of the Mass Media in the United States

Although the record and film industries sometimes convey political messages, they are primarily in the business of entertainment. Our focus here is on mass media in the news industry—on print and broadcast journalism. The growth of the country, technological inventions, and shifting political attitudes about the scope of government, as well as trends in entertainment, have shaped the development of the news media in the United States.

Newspapers

When the Revolutionary War broke out in 1775, thirty-seven newspapers (all weeklies) were publishing in the colonies.[11] They had small circulations, so they were not really mass media but group media read by economic and social elites. The first newspapers were mainly political organs, financed by parties and advocating party causes. Newspapers did not move toward independent ownership and large circulations until the 1830s.

According to the 1880 census, 971 daily newspapers and 8,633 weekly newspapers and periodicals were published in the United States. Most larger cities had many newspapers: New York had twenty-nine papers; Philadelphia, twenty-four; San Francisco, twenty-one; and Chicago, eighteen. Competition for readers grew fierce among the big-city dailies. Toward the latter part of the nineteenth century, imaginative publishers sought to win readers by entertaining them with photographs, comic strips, sports sections, advice to the lovelorn, and stories of sex and crime.

By the 1960s, under pressure from both radio and television, intense competition among big-city dailies had nearly disappeared. New York had only three papers left by 1969, and this pattern was repeated in every large city in the country. By 2004, only thirty-one U.S. towns or cities had two or more competing dailies under separate ownership.[12] The net result is that newspaper circulation as a percentage of the U.S. population has dropped almost 50 percent since 1950.[13]

The daily paper with the largest circulation in 2005 (about 2.3 million copies) was *USA Today,* the only paper designed for national distribution and sold at gasoline stations and convenience stores across the country. The *Wall Street Journal,* which appeals to a national audience because of its extensive coverage of business news and close analysis of political news, was second (2 million). The *New York Times,* which many journalists consider the best newspaper in the country, sells about 1.1 million copies, placing it third in circulation (see Figure 6.1). In comparison, the weekly *National Enquirer,* which carries stories about celebrities and true crime, sells about 1.3 million copies. Neither the *Times* nor the *Wall Street Journal* carries comic strips, which no doubt limits their mass appeal. They also print more political news and news analyses than most readers want to confront.

Magazines

Magazines differ from newspapers not only in the frequency of their publication but also in the nature of their coverage. Even news-oriented magazines cover the news in a more specialized manner than do daily newspapers. Many magazines are forums for opinions, not strictly for news. Moreover, magazines dealing with public affairs have had relatively small circulations and select readerships. The earliest public affairs magazines were founded in the mid-1800s, and two—*The Nation* and *Harper's*—are still publishing today. Such magazines were often politically influential, especially in framing arguments against slavery and later in publishing exposés of political corruption and business exploitation. Because these exposés were lengthy critiques of the existing political and economic order, they found a more hospitable outlet in magazines of opinion than in newspapers with big circulations. Yet magazines with limited readerships can wield political power. Magazines may influence **attentive policy elites**—group leaders who follow news in specific areas—and thus influence mass opinion indirectly through a **two-step flow of communication.**

As scholars originally viewed the two-step flow, it conformed ideally to the pluralist model of democracy. Once group leaders (for instance, union or

attentive policy elites Leaders who follow news in specific policy areas.

two-step flow of communication The process in which a few policy elites gather information and then inform their more numerous followers, mobilizing them to apply pressure to government.

FIGURE 6.1 Audiences of Selected Media Sources

Different media appeal to different audiences, and what news people learn depends on their sources. The big story is the enormous growth in the Internet news audience. About two-thirds of the 130 million Americans who accessed the Internet in 2004 used it for news, weather, or sports, but only about 11 percent (mainly younger people) got news mainly over the Internet. Even limiting the audience to that 11 percent, about 14 million Americans constitute the Internet news audience, vaulting that source ahead of the audience for network television news. The major news magazines (published weekly) tend to have more readers than newspapers do, but newspapers are published daily and there are more of them. Opinion magazines reach only a small fraction of the usual television news audience.

Sources: Information on television audiences comes from Journalism.org, "The State of the News Media 2005." Newspaper circulation comes from Joseph T. Hallinan, "Newspaper Circulation Declines 1.9%," *Wall Street Journal,* 3 May 2005, p. B4. Magazine circulation comes from *Standard Periodical Directory* (New York: Oxbridge Publishing, 2005). Internet news audience estimate is based on U.S. Census Bureau, *Statistical Abstract of the United States, 2006,* Tables 1118 and 1147, and the Pew Research Center for the People and the Press Survey of June 2005, released June 26.

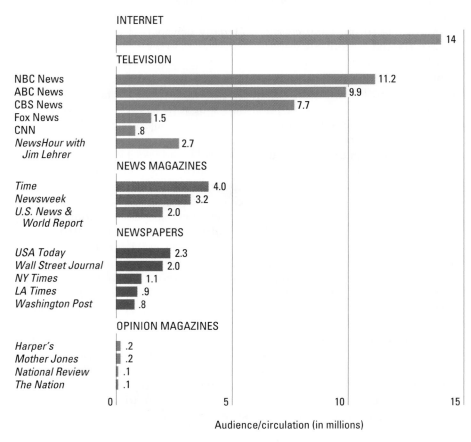

industry leaders) became informed of political developments, they informed their more numerous followers, mobilizing them to apply pressure on government. Today, according to a revised interpretation of the two-step flow concept, policy elites are more likely to influence public opinion (and not just their followers) and other leaders by airing their views in the media. In this view, public deliberation on issues is mediated by these professional communicators who frame the issues in the media for popular consumption (as discussed in Chapter 5 on page 155)—that is, define the way that issues will be viewed, heard, or read.[14]

Three weekly news magazines—*Time* (founded in 1923), *Newsweek* (1933), and *U.S. News & World Report* (1933)—enjoy big circulations in the United States (2.0 million to 4.0 million copies in 2005). Although these news magazines can be considered mass media, their audience is tiny compared with the 10 million readers of *Reader's Digest.* In contrast to these mainstream, "capitalist" publications, a newer, "alternative" press is more critical of the prevailing power structure. Such periodicals as *Mother Jones* have spearheaded investigations into possible corporate-government deals, as in its September–October 2002 issue on "The Security Industrial Complex" disclosing who profits from homeland defense programs.

Radio

Regularly scheduled, continuous radio broadcasting began in 1920 on stations KDKA in Pittsburgh and WWJ in Detroit. Both stations claim to be the first commercial station, and both broadcast returns of the 1920 election of President Warren G. Harding. The first radio network, the National Broadcasting Company (NBC), was formed in 1926. Soon four networks were on the air, transforming radio into a national medium by linking thousands of local stations. Millions of Americans were able to hear President Franklin D. Roosevelt deliver his first "fireside chat" in 1933. However, the first coast-to-coast broadcast did not occur until 1937, when listeners were shocked by an eyewitness report of the explosion of the dirigible *Hindenburg* in New Jersey.

Because the public could sense reporters' personalities over radio in a way they could not in print, broadcast journalists quickly became household names. Edward R. Murrow, one of the most famous radio news personalities, broadcast news of the merger of Germany and Austria by short-wave radio from Vienna in 1938 and during World War II gave stirring reports of German air raids on London. Today, radio is less salient for live coverage of events than for "talk radio," often criticized for polarizing politics by publicizing extreme views.[15]

Television

Experiments with television began in France in the early 1900s. By 1940, twenty-three television stations were operating in the United States, and—repeating radio's feat of twenty years earlier—two stations broadcast the returns of a presidential election, Roosevelt's 1940 reelection.[16] The onset of World War II paralyzed the development of television technology, but growth in the medium exploded after the war. By 1950, ninety-eight stations were covering the major population centers of the country, although only 9 percent of American households had televisions.

The first commercial color broadcast came in 1951, as did the first coast-to-coast broadcast: President Harry Truman's address to delegates at the Japanese peace treaty conference in San Francisco. That same year, Democratic senator Estes Kefauver of Tennessee called for public television coverage of his committee's investigation into organized crime. For weeks, people with televisions invited their neighbors to watch underworld crime figures answering questions before the camera. And Kefauver became one of the first politicians to benefit from television coverage. Previously unknown and representing a small state, he nevertheless won many of the 1952 Democratic presidential primaries and became the Democrats' vice-presidential candidate in 1956.

By 1960, 87 percent of U.S. households had televisions. By 2004, the United States had more than 1,200 commercial and 300 public television stations, and virtually every household (98 percent) had television. Today, television claims the biggest news audience of all the commerical media (see Figure 6.1). From television's beginnings, most stations were linked into networks founded by three of the four major radio networks. Many early anchors of

Watching the President on Television

Television revolutionized presidential politics by allowing millions of voters to look closely at the candidates' faces and judge their personalities in the process. This close-up of John Kennedy during a debate with Richard Nixon in the 1960 campaign showed Kennedy to good advantage. In contrast, close-ups of Nixon made him look as though he needed a shave. Kennedy won one of the closest elections in history; his good looks on television may have made the difference. (*Corbis/Bettmann*)

INTERACTIVE 6.1

 JFK Assassination: Sounds and Images

television network news programs came to the medium with names already made famous during their years of experience as radio broadcast journalists. Now that the news audience could actually see the broadcasters as well as hear them, the lead network news announcer became its "anchorman." Dan Rather, Tom Brokaw, and Peter Jennings—the anchors for CBS, NBC, and ABC— became celebrities during their decades of personifying network television news. By 2005, all three were gone, ending an era. The three broadcast networks still had huge audiences, but millions of viewers drifted to alternative media, mainly cable news and the Internet. Still, some researchers have disputed citizens' "mass migration" from traditional media, concluding instead that alternative news sources, particularly the Internet, supplement rather than displace print and broadcast sources.[17]

The Internet

What we today call the Internet began in 1969 when, with support from the U.S. Defense Department's Advanced Research Projects Agency, computers at four universities were linked to form ARPANET, which connected thirty-seven universities by 1972. New communications standards worked out in 1983 allowed these networks to be linked, creating the Internet. In its early years, the Internet was used mainly to transmit e-mail among researchers. In 1991, a group of European physicists devised a standardized system for encoding and transmitting a wide range of materials, including graphics and photographs, over the Internet, and the World Wide Web (WWW) was born. Now anyone with a computer program called a "browser" can access Web "pages" on the Internet from around the world. In January 1993 there were only 50 websites in existence.[18] Today there are over 350,000 sites and over a billion Web users. (See "Compared with What? Top Thirty Nations in Internet Penetration.")

The Internet was soon incorporated into politics, and today virtually every government agency and political organization in the nation has its own website. In recent years, private citizens have begun operating their own websites on politics and public affairs, daily posting their political thoughts and critical comments. These so-called **blogs** (for weblogs) have had dramatic effects on news reporting. In 2004, conservative "bloggers" exposed flaws in a *CBS Evening News* broadcast that questioned whether George W. Bush had served as claimed in the Texas Air National Guard. The blogs criticizing the network's reporting were publicized in the established media. Subsequently, Dan Rather, the anchorman at CBS with the longest tenure in network news, was forced to depart, short of completing twenty-five years in the chair. In early 2005, Eason Jordan, the chief news executive at CNN, resigned after bloggers assailed him for suggesting in a speech in Switzerland that the U.S. military deliberately targeted and killed journalists.[19] Bloggers promise to have a continuing impact on American politics.

Are bloggers themselves journalists? In 2005, Apple Computer sued a blogger to reveal who leaked information about Apple's new products. In court, the blogger claimed protection under the First Amendment freedom of the press. As a journalist, he could not be compelled to reveal his source.[20] In 2006, a state appeals court decided that bloggers enjoyed the same protections against divulging sources as established media organizations. If this decision holds in higher courts, some fear a "wild west atmosphere" in which untrained private individuals can broadcast what they wish online to millions of readers without professional, organizational, or legal concerns about its source.[21] However, the First Amendment does not provide even accredited journalists with major newspapers complete protection against revealing a source. Judith Miller of the *New York Times* spent eighty-five days in jail before agreeing to reveal who in the White House illegally gave her the name of a CIA operative.[22]

blogs A form of newsletter, journal, or "log" of thoughts for public reading, usually devoted to social or political issues and often updated daily. The term derives from we**blog**.

Compared with What?

Top Thirty Nations in Internet Penetration

Compared with other major countries in the world, the United States does not have the highest percentage of the population with Internet access. In fact, it ranks seventh. Moreover, broadband service in many countries in Europe and Asia is cheaper and faster in both download and upload speeds. People all over the world are going "online" and enjoying rates and speeds that U.S. Internet users envy.

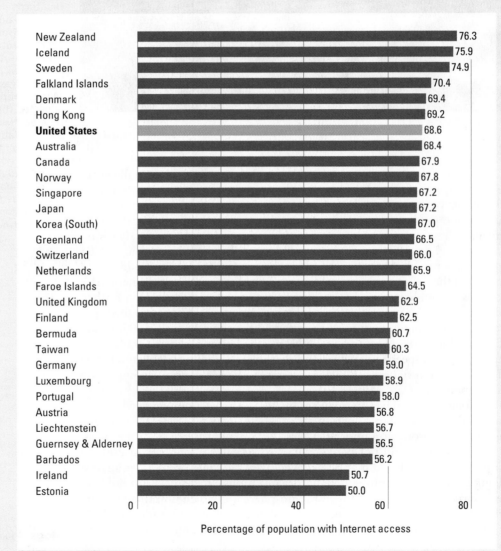

Percentage of population with Internet access

Sources: Internet data at <www.internetworldstats.com/top25.htm>; Jesse Drucker, "For U.S. Consumers, Broadband Service Is Slow and Expensive," *Wall Street Journal*, 16 November 2003, p. B1.

★ Private Ownership of the Media

In the United States, people take private ownership of the media for granted. Indeed, most Americans would regard government ownership of the media as an unacceptable threat to freedom that would interfere with the marketplace of ideas and result in one-way communication: from government to citizens. The American Internet search company Google even resisted government requests for records of user search queries in pornography investigations.[23] When the government controls the news flow, the people may have little chance to learn what the government is doing or to pressure it to behave differently. Certainly that was true in the former Soviet Union. China offers another illustration of arbitrary government control of the media. The Chinese government employs thousands of Internet police to prevent "subversive content" from being disseminated to about 100 million Web users. Among other things, the police look for phrases like "human rights" and "Dalai Lama."[24] Although Google resisted U.S. government requests for users' search records, Google agreed to limit the blogging and e-mail functions on its computer servers in China when launching *Google.cn* to serve that lucrative and fast-growing market.[25] Another search company, Yahoo, gave Internet records to the Chinese government that led to citizen arrests. Both companies (and Microsoft) were summoned before Congress for acting as "surrogate government censors." As private companies, they defended their Chinese business policies as serving their stockholders' financial interests. Moreover, they also argued that developing the Internet in China does more good than harm.[26]

In other Western democracies, the print media (both newspapers and magazines) are privately owned, but the broadcast media often are not. Before the 1980s, the government owned and operated the major broadcast media in most of these countries. In Western Europe, government radio and television

Internet Fortune Cookie
Google, an American company and the world's largest Internet search service, disabled its e-mail and blog capabilities on its Chinese computer servers (at the request of China's government) in order to enter potentially the world's largest market of Internet users. *(Mike Ramirez/ Investors Business Daily, © 2006)*

stations now compete with private stations, but throughout the rest of the world, the state owns from 60 to 70 percent of the broadcast media.[27] In the United States, except for about 300 public television stations (out of about 1,500 total) and 400 public radio stations (out of about 10,000), the broadcast media are privately owned.

The Consequences of Private Ownership

Just as the appearance of the newscaster became important for television viewers, so did the appearance of the news itself. Television's great advantage over radio—that it shows people and events—accounts for the influence of television news coverage. It also determines, to some extent, the news that television chooses to cover. In fact, private ownership of the mass media ensures that news is selected for its audience appeal.

Private ownership of both the print and broadcast media gives the news industry in America more political freedom than any other in the world, but it also makes the media more dependent on advertising revenues to cover their costs and make a profit. Because advertising rates are tied to audience size, the news operations of the mass media in America must appeal to the audiences they serve.

The average American spends four hours watching television every day, but only about half the adult population watches any kind of news for a half hour or more.[28] About 55 million newspapers circulate daily, but more than 60 percent of their content is advertising. After fashion reports, sports, comics, and so on, only a relatively small portion of any newspaper is devoted to news of any sort, and only a fraction of that news—excluding stories about fires, robberies, murder trials, and the like—can be classified as political. In terms of sheer volume, the entertainment content offered by the mass media in the United States vastly overshadows the news content (see Figure 6.2). In other words, the media function to entertain more than to provide news. Entertainment increases the audience, which increases advertising revenues. Thus, the profit motive creates constant pressure to increase the ratio of entertainment to news or to make the news itself more "entertaining."

You might think that a story's political significance, educational value, or broad social importance determines whether the media cover it. The sad truth is that most potential news stories are not judged by such grand criteria. The primary criterion of a story's **newsworthiness** is usually its audience appeal, which is judged according to its potential impact on readers or listeners, its degree of sensationalism (exemplified by violence, conflict, disaster, or scandal), its treatment of familiar people or life situations, its close-to-home character, and its timeliness.[29]

The importance of audience appeal has led the news industry to calculate its audience carefully. (The bigger the audience, the higher the advertising rates.) The print media can easily determine the size of their circulations through sales figures, but the broadcast media must estimate their audience through various sampling techniques. Because both print and broadcast media might be tempted to inflate their estimated audience (to tell advertisers that they reach more people than they actually do), a separate industry has developed to rate audience size impartially. These ratings reports have resulted in a "ratings game," in which the media try to increase their ratings by adjusting the delivery or content of their news. Within the news industry, the process has

newsworthiness The degree to which a news story is important enough to be covered in the mass media.

FIGURE 6.2 Getting the News: Consider the Source

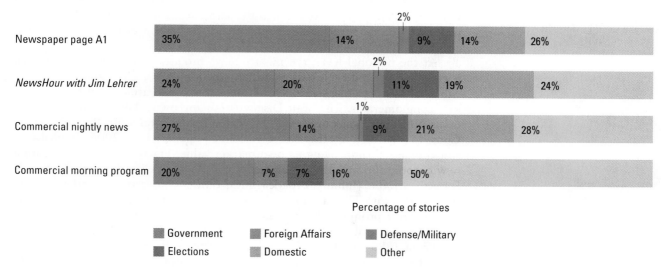

If you want news about government and politics, read a newspaper. That was suggested by an analysis of 16,800 stories that were reported in 2005 on the front pages of sixteen daily newspapers and on the major national television news programs. About 60 percent of all the front-page newspaper stories dealt with government and politics, followed closely by 57 percent of stories throughout the hour-long broadcasts of PBS's *NewsHour with Jim Lehrer.* The average half-hour commercial nightly news devoted 51 percent of its stories to government and politics. The morning news programs (such as *Good Morning America* and *Today*) served only 34 percent news at breakfast. Americans encountered more news about government and politics by scanning the front pages of their newspapers than by watching a half hour of evening news.

Source: "The State of the News Media, 2005: Network TV," published by *journalism.org* and available at <http://www.stateofthemedia.com/2005/printable_networkTV_contentanalysis.asp>.

been termed **market-driven journalism**—that is, both reporting news and running commercials geared to a target audience.[30] For example, the *CBS Evening News,* which has the oldest viewing audience among all network television news programs (30 percent over sixty-five years of age), nearly always features a health-related story and runs one or more commercials related to prescription drugs.

More citizens report watching local news than national news, and local news epitomizes market-driven journalism by matching audience demographics to advertising revenue while slighting news about government, policy, and public affairs. According to a 2005 report on American journalism, local television stations across the nation practice a "hook and hold" approach in their newscasts. They hook viewers at the start by airing eye-catching, alarming, and supposedly "live" stories based on incidents of crime, accidents, fires, and disasters. The middle of the broadcast has informative news stories about business, education, science, technology, and politics that are not considered good

market-driven journalism
Both reporting news and running commercials geared to a target audience defined by demographic characteristics.

viewing. To hold viewers to the end, stations tease them by promising funny or unusual videos about soft topics on pop culture, human interest, and perhaps medical news or novelties. As a result, local news broadcasts from Boston, to Omaha, to Sacramento look much the same, fronted by socially diverse (but remarkably familiar) personalities dispensing political, weather, sports, and social news.[31]

At the national level, the nightly news broadcasts were once the crown jewels of independent broadcasting companies—ABC, CBS, and NBC—and valued for their public service. Now these broadcasts are cogs in huge corporate conglomerates. The Walt Disney Company owns ABC, General Electric owns NBC, and Viacom owned CBS (along with Paramount Pictures, MTV, Comedy Central, and other entertainment companies) until 2006. To please its stockholders by improving its own market value, Viacom split off CBS into a new corporation including cable networks (Showtime), publishing (Simon & Schuster), radio (Infinity Broadcasting), outdoor advertising, and television (CBS, UPN, and TV stations).[32] Television nightly news is no longer a public service, but a profit center. Moreover, the financial reports from network news broadcasts are not good.

From 1980 to 2007, ABC, CBS, and NBC suffered severe losses in their prime-time programming audience, dropping from 52 million viewers to 21 million—despite an increase in population.[33] Increasingly, viewers turned to watching cable stations or videotapes instead of network programs. Audience declines brought declining profits and cutbacks in network news budgets. As their parent corporations demanded that news programs "pay their way," the networks succumbed to **infotainment**—a mix of information and diversion oriented to personalities or celebrities, not linked to the day's events, and usually unrelated to public affairs or policy.[34] One media analyst argued that politically unengaged consumers of soft news—such as *Regis & Kelly* and *Entertainment Tonight*—tend to follow foreign policy crises more than those who avoid even soft news. This argument that "very little" information is better than "nothing at all" was tested by another analyst, who found very little evidence that those who consumed only soft news actually learned about politics.[35]

Network television in particular has begun offering more soft news to bolster sagging ratings. In early 2006, CBS nightly news even began to invite viewers to vote over the Internet on which of three soft news topics they would like to see featured the next week. (See the photo on page 171.) Newspapers too are inviting their readers to decide what to cover and even to participate in writing the paper. Commenting on this trend to cater to viewers and readers, Ted Koppel, the former anchor of ABC's *Nightline*, drew a distinction between entertainment and journalism. "It is the journalist who should be telling their viewer what is important, not the other way around." However, he said, "right now, the main agenda is to give people what they want."[36]

The Concentration of Private Ownership

Media owners can make more money by increasing their audience or by acquiring additional publications or stations. There is a decided trend toward concentrated ownership of the media, increasing the risk that a few owners could control the news flow to promote their own political interests—much as political parties influenced the content of the earliest American newspapers. In fact, the number of *independent newspapers* has declined as newspaper chains

infotainment A mix of information and diversion oriented to personalities or celebrities, not linked to the day's events, and usually unrelated to public affairs or policy; often called "soft news."

 **SOYBEAN-POWERED CARS**

Meet the brain trust behind an ingenious new soybean-powered car. The twist: These guys aren't in the auto business -- they're in high school.

 **VARSITY BOWLING**

There's nothing like a varsity letter to impress the girls in high school. But lettering in Bowling? Who knew? We'll investigate what is now the fastest growing high school varsity sport.

 **SUDOKU TEAM**

Forget the Olympics - we need to find America's six best Sudoku players. The world championships are just around the corner. We report on the search for the latest USA Dream Team.

> SUBMIT

Vote for This Week's News

The *CBS Evening News* once relied on its reporters across the world to identify newsworthy events, collect the facts, and report important stories for broadcasting to viewers eager to learn the news. In 2006, CBS reinterpreted its role in journalism by launching a new weekly feature, "Assignment America," that invited viewers to choose what "soft news" CBS would cover. Viewers (voters) chose "Soybean-Powered Cars" for broadcast on February 17, 2006. *(CBS News)*

(owners of two or more newspapers in different cities) have acquired more newspapers. Most of the more than 100 newspaper chains in the United States today are small, owning fewer than ten papers.[37] Some are very big, however. The Gannett chain, which owns *USA Today,* which has the biggest daily circulation in the nation, also owns nearly 100 other newspapers throughout the United States. Only about 400 dailies are still independent; many of these papers are too small and unprofitable to invite acquisition.

At first glance, concentration of ownership does not seem to be a problem in the television industry. Although there are only three major networks, the networks usually do not own their affiliates. About half of all the communities in the United States have a choice of ten or more stations.[38] This figure suggests that the electronic media offer diverse viewpoints and are not characterized by ownership concentration. As with newspapers, however, chains sometimes own television stations in different cities, and ownership sometimes extends across different media. As mentioned earlier, none of the three original television networks remains an independent corporation. And, as mentioned at the start of this chapter, Rupert Murdoch's News Corporation, which has worldwide interests, owns the newer Fox network.[39]

★ Government Regulation of the Media

Although most of the mass media in the United States are privately owned, they do not operate free of government regulation. The broadcast media operate under more stringent regulations than the print media, initially because of technical aspects of broadcasting. In general, government regulation of the mass media addresses three aspects of their operation: technical considerations, ownership, and content.

Technical and Ownership Regulations

In the early days of radio, stations that operated on similar frequencies in the same area often jammed each other's signals, and no one could broadcast clearly. At the broadcasters' insistence, Congress passed the Federal Radio Act (1927), which declared that the public owned the airwaves and private broadcasters could use them only by obtaining a license from the Federal Radio Commission. So, government regulation of broadcasting was not forced on the industry by socialist politicians; capitalist owners sought it to impose order on the use of the airwaves (thereby restricting others' freedom to enter broadcasting).

Seven years later, Congress passed the Federal Communications Act of 1934, a more sweeping law that regulated the broadcast and telephone industries for more than sixty years. It created the **Federal Communications Commission (FCC)**, which has five members (no more than three from the same political party) nominated by the president for terms of five years. The commissioners can be removed from office only through impeachment and conviction. Consequently, the FCC is considered an independent regulatory commission: it is insulated from political control by either the president or Congress. (We discuss independent regulatory commissions in Chapter 13.) By law, its vague mandate is to "serve the public interest, convenience, and necessity." Accordingly, the FCC must set the social, economic, and technical goals for the communications industry and deal with philosophical issues of regulation versus deregulation.[40] Today, the FCC's charge includes regulating interstate and international communications by radio, television, telephone, telegraph, cable, and satellite.

For six decades—as technological change made television commonplace and brought the invention of computers, fax machines, and satellite transmissions—the communications industry was regulated under the basic framework of the 1934 law that created the FCC. Pressured by businesses that wanted to exploit new electronic technologies, Congress, in a bipartisan effort, swept away most existing regulations in the Telecommunications Act of 1996.

The new law relaxed or scrapped limitations on media ownership. For example, broadcasters were previously limited to owning only twelve television stations and forty radio stations. The 1996 Telecommunications Act eliminated limits on the number of television stations one company may own, just as long as their coverage didn't extend beyond 35 percent of the market nationwide. As a result, CBS, Fox, and NBC doubled or tripled the number of stations that they owned to cover or even exceed 35 percent of the viewing market allowable by law.[41] The 1996 law also set no national limits for radio ownership and relaxed local limits. As a result, Clear Channel Communica-

Federal Communications Commission (FCC) An independent federal agency that regulates interstate and international communication by radio, television, telephone, telegraph, cable, and satellite.

tions corporation, which owned 36 stations, gobbled up over 1,100, including all 6 stations serving Minot, North Dakota.[42] For some local TV stations and for many local radio stations, the net effect of relaxation on media ownership was to centralize programming in one city and feed the same signals to local affiliates.[43] In addition, the FCC lifted rate regulations for cable systems, allowed cross-ownership of cable and telephone companies, and allowed local and long-distance telephone companies to compete with one another and to sell television services.[44]

Thanks to the relaxed rules, media groups entered the third millennium in a flurry of megamergers. The Federal Trade Commission approved the largest of these, the $183 billion purchase of Time Warner by America Online, in 2000. The AOL/Time Warner deal merged the nation's largest Internet service provider with the second largest cable system (which had already merged with one of the biggest publishers in the United States). The resulting conglomerate (renamed Time Warner in 2003) started with 24 million Internet customers (nearly half of the U.S. market), 12.6 million cable subscribers, and "breathtaking reach in films, music, and publishing." Backed by its parent company, General Electric, NBC in 2003 merged with Vivendi Universal, giving the nation's largest network control of a major film studio. Critics might view this as the vindication of a prediction made over a decade before: a special issue of the opinion magazine *The Nation* warned of the dangers of an impending "National Entertainment State," in which the media would be controlled by a few conglomerates.[45] The industry countered with the argument that diversity among news sources in America is great enough to provide citizens with a wide range of political ideas.[46]

Regulation of Content

The First Amendment to the Constitution prohibits Congress from abridging the freedom of the press. Over time, *the press* has come to mean all the media, and the courts have decided many cases that define how far freedom of the press extends under the law. Chapter 15 discusses the most important of these cases, which are often quite complex. Although the courts have had difficulty defining obscenity, they have not permitted obscene expression under freedom of the press. In 1996, however, a federal court overturned an attempt to limit transmission of "indecent" (not obscene) material on the Internet, calling the attempt "profoundly repugnant to First Amendment principles."[47]

Usually the courts strike down government attempts to restrain the press from publishing or broadcasting the information, reports, or opinions it finds newsworthy. One notable exception concerns strategic information during wartime: the courts have supported censorship of information such as the sailing schedules of troop ships or the planned movements of troops in battle. Otherwise, they have recognized a strong constitutional case against press censorship. This stand has given the United States some of the freest, most vigorous news media in the world.

Because the broadcast media are licensed to use the public airwaves, they have been subject to some additional regulation, beyond what is applied to the print media, of the content of their news coverage. The basis for the FCC's regulation of content lies in its charge to ensure that radio (and, later, television) stations would "serve the public interest, convenience, and necessity." For years, the FCC operated under three rules to promote the public interest concerning political matters. The *fairness doctrine* obligated broadcasters to provide fair coverage of all views on public issues. The *equal opportunities rule* required any broadcast station that gave or sold time to a candidate for a public office to make an equal amount of time available under the same conditions to all other candidates for that office. The *reasonable access rule* required that stations make their facilities available for the expression of conflicting views on issues by all responsible elements in the community.

In 1987, under President Reagan, the FCC repealed the *fairness doctrine*. One media analyst noted that the FCC acted in the belief that competition among broadcasters, cable, radio, newspapers, and magazines would provide a vibrant marketplace of ideas. He feared, however, that the FCC had overestimated the public's demand for high-quality news and public affairs broadcasts. Without that demand, the media were unlikely to supply the news and public affairs coverage needed to sustain a genuine marketplace.[48] Moreover, because broadcasters no longer needed "to provide fair coverage of all views," they could express ideological viewpoints, leading many stations to air conservative views on talk radio without a need to offer liberal views.[49]

Then in 2000, a U.S. Court of Appeals struck down both of the other longstanding FCC rules governing media content. Although these regulations to ensure "equal opportunities" and "reasonable access" seemed laudable, they were at the heart of a controversy about the deregulation of the broadcast media, which the FCC was intent on pushing. Note that neither of these content regulations was imposed on the print media, which have no responsibility to give equal treatment to political candidates or to express conflicting views from all responsible elements of the community. In fact, one aspect of a free press is its ability to champion causes that it favors without having to argue the case for the other side. The broadcast media have traditionally been treated differently because they were licensed by the FCC to operate as semimonopolies. With the rise of one-newspaper cities and towns, however, competition among television stations is greater than among newspapers in virtually every market area. Advocates of dropping all FCC content regulations argued that the broadcast media should be just as free as the print media to decide which candidates they endorse and which issues they support.

In the United States, the mass media are in business to make money, which they do mainly by selling advertising. To sell advertising, they provide entertainment on a mass basis, which is their general function. We are more interested here in five specific functions the mass media serve for the political system: *reporting* the news, *interpreting* the news, *influencing* citizens' opinions, *setting the agenda* for government action, and *socializing* citizens about politics.[50]

★ Functions of the Mass Media for the Political System

Most journalists consider "news" (at least *hard* news) as an important event that has happened within the past twenty-four hours. A presidential news conference or an explosion in the Capitol qualifies as news. And a national political convention certainly qualifies as news, although it may not justify the thousands of media representatives present at the 2004 party conventions. Who decides what is important? The media, of course. In this section, we discuss how the media cover political affairs, what they choose to report (what becomes "news"), who follows the news, and what they remember and learn from it.

Reporting the News

All the major news media seek to cover political events with firsthand reports from journalists on the scene. Because so many significant political events occur in the nation's capital, Washington has by far the biggest press corps of any city in the world—nearly 7,000 congressionally accredited reporters: 2,000 from newspapers, 1,800 from periodicals, 2,500 from radio and television, over 300 photographers. Only a few of these reporters (and at least one blogger on a daily pass in 2005)[51] are admitted to fill the fifty seats of the old White House briefing room (built in 1969 over an indoor swimming pool), set to be remodeled but not expanded in 2007. Since 1902, when President Theodore Roosevelt first provided space in the White House for reporters, the press has had special access to the president. As recently as the Truman administration, reporters enjoyed informal personal relationships with the president. Today, the media's relationship with the president is mediated primarily through the Office of the Press Secretary.

To meet their daily deadlines, White House correspondents rely heavily on information they receive from the president's staff, each piece carefully crafted in an attempt to control the news report. The most frequent form is the news release—a prepared text distributed to reporters in the hope that they will use it verbatim. A daily news briefing enables reporters to question the press secretary about news releases and allows television correspondents time to prepare their stories and film for the evening newscast. A news conference involves questioning high-level officials in the executive branch—including the president, on occasion. News conferences appear to be freewheeling, but officials tend to carefully rehearse precise answers to anticipated questions.

Occasionally, information is given "on background," meaning the information can be quoted, but reporters cannot identify the source. A vague reference—"a senior official says"—is all right. (When he was secretary of state, Henry Kissinger himself was often the "senior official" quoted on foreign policy developments.) Information disclosed "off the record" cannot even be printed. Journalists who violate these well-known rules risk losing their welcome at the White House. In a sense, the press corps is captive to the White House, which feeds reporters the information they need to meet their deadlines and frames events so that they are covered on the evening news. Beginning with the Nixon White House, press secretaries have obliged photographers with "photo opportunities," a few minutes to take pictures or shoot film, often of the president with a visiting dignitary or a winning sports team. The photographers can keep their editors supplied with visuals, and the press secretary ensures that the coverage is favorable by controlling the environment.

Most reporters in the Washington press corps are accredited to sit in the House and Senate press galleries, but only about 400 cover Congress exclusively. Most news about Congress comes from innumerable press releases issued by its 535 members and from an unending supply of congressional reports. A journalist, then, can report on Congress without inhabiting its press galleries.

Not so long ago, individual congressional committees allowed radio and television coverage of their proceedings only on special occasions—such as the

Kefauver committee's investigation of organized crime in the 1950s and the Watergate investigation in the 1970s. Congress banned microphones and cameras from its chambers until 1979, when the House permitted live coverage (though it insisted on controlling the shots being televised). Nevertheless, televised broadcasts of the House were surprisingly successful, thanks to C-SPAN (the Cable Satellite Public Affairs Network), which feeds to 90 percent of the cable systems across the country and has a cultlike following among hundreds of thousands of regular viewers.[52] To share in the exposure, the Senate began television coverage in 1986. C-SPAN coverage of Congress has become important to professionals in government and politics in Washington—perhaps more so than to its small, devoted audience across the country. Even members of the Washington press corps watch C-SPAN.

In addition to these recognized sources of news, selected reporters occasionally benefit from leaks of information released by officials who are guaranteed anonymity. Officials may leak news to interfere with others' political plans or to float ideas ("trial balloons") past the public and other political leaders to gauge their reactions. At times, one carefully placed leak can turn into a gusher of media coverage through "pack journalism"—the tendency of journalists to adopt similar viewpoints toward the news simply because they hang around together, exchanging information and defining the day's news with one another.

Interpreting and Presenting the News

Media executives, news editors, and prominent reporters function as **gatekeepers** in directing the news flow: they decide which events to report and how to handle the elements in those stories.[53] Only a few individuals—no more than twenty-five at the average newspaper or news magazine and fifty at each of the major television networks—qualify as gatekeepers, defining the news for public consumption.[54] They not only select what topics go through the gate but also are expected to uphold standards of careful reporting and principled journalism. So where were the gatekeepers during the media's feeding frenzy over the presidential sex scandal in 1998? The president of an editors' association lamented, "We spout off all these high ideals and goals of journalism, and then you get a story where the principal characters are of questionable character, and the details have a salacious aspect, and the whole blasted thing is based on anonymous sources."[55] Some journalists attributed the "collapse of all balance and judgment" in the mainstream media to lowered standards "in the face of the information free-for-all that has resulted from the rise of the Internet, talk radio, and 24-hour cable news."[56] Many people expected that these new media would raise the level of public discourse by increasing the amount and variety of news available, but it has become apparent that they also spread "news" of dubious quality. The Internet, in particular, has no gatekeepers and thus no constraints on its content.

The established media cannot communicate everything about public affairs. There is neither space in newspapers or magazines nor time on television or radio to do so. Time limitations impose especially severe constraints on television news broadcasting. Each half-hour network news program devotes only about twenty minutes to the news (the rest of the time is taken up by commercials), and there is even less news on local television (see Figure 6.2). The average story lasts about one minute, and few stories run longer than two minutes.

? Can you explain why . . . the traditional role for gatekeepers has declined in the media?

gatekeepers Media executives, news editors, and prominent reporters who direct the flow of news.

The typical script for an entire television news broadcast would fill less than two columns of one page of the *New York Times*.

A parade of unconnected one-minute news stories, flashing across the television screen every night, would boggle the eyes and minds of viewers. To make the news understandable and to hold viewers' attention, television editors and producers carefully choose their lead story and group stories together by theme. The stories themselves concentrate on individuals because individuals have personalities (political institutions do not—except for the presidency). A careful content analysis of network news coverage of the president, Congress, and the Supreme Court in 2003–2004 found that 52 percent of the stories were about the presidency, compared with 37 percent on Congress and 10 percent on the Court.[57] Moreover, when television does cover Congress, it tries to personify the institution by focusing on prominent, quotable leaders, such as the Speaker of the House or the Senate majority leader. Such personification for the purpose of gaining audience appeal tends to distort the character of Congress, which harbors competing views among different powerfully placed members.

During elections, personification encourages **horse race journalism,** in which media coverage becomes a matter of "who's ahead in the polls, who's raising the most money, who's got TV ads and who's getting endorsed." A study of network news coverage of the 2004 presidential campaign found the horse race covered as much as the issues, and horse race content increased in the later months as election day approached. Journalists cover the horse race because it offers new material daily, whereas the candidates' programs remain the same.[58] Other countries give more attention to issues in their election coverage. U.S. television presents elections as contests between individuals rather than as confrontations between representatives of opposing parties and platforms.

Political campaigns lend themselves particularly well to media coverage, especially if the candidates create a **media event**—a situation that is too "newsworthy" to pass up. One tried-and-true method is to conduct a statewide walking campaign. Newspapers and television can take pictures of the candidate on the highway and conduct interviews with local folks who just spoke with the political hiker. (See Chapter 9 for further discussion of the media in political campaigns.) Television is particularly partial to events that have visual impact. Organized protests and fires, for example, "show well" on television, so television tends to cover them. Violent conflict of any kind, especially unfolding dramas that involve weapons, rate especially high in visual impact.

Where the Public Gets Its News.

Until the early 1960s, most people reported getting more of their news from newspapers than from any other source. Television nudged out newspapers as the public's major source of news in the early 1960s. Over the recent decade, however, people have relied less on television for their primary news source; the figure dropped from 82 percent in 1992 to 70 percent in 2000.[59] As found in the surveys described in Figures 6.3 and 6.4, people are far more interested in local news than in national news. The survey also found that the believability of both the networks and their news anchors eroded during the 1990s. Television's dominance as a news medium is eroding, and we should inquire into the public's specific sources of news.

In a 2004 survey of news media usage, 71 percent of respondents said that they start their morning with some type of news. The same survey found that only about 65 percent follow national, international, or local news "very"

horse race journalism
Election coverage by the mass media that focuses on which candidate is ahead rather than on national issues.

media event A situation that is so "newsworthy" that the mass media are compelled to cover it. Candidates in elections often create such situations to garner media attention.

FIGURE 6.3 Who Knows the News?

Page 179 describes four questions asked in a national survey in the summer of 2004. Each respondent was scored from 0 to 100 for percentage of correct responses. Respondents were then grouped and analyzed as consumers of different news sources. This table reports the mean correct response for those who were regular viewers, readers, or listeners in each category, compared with the average for all respondents. Because relatively few respondents relied on the specialized news sources near the top of the chart, their higher percentages of correct answers were outweighed in computing the mean by the many more consumers of television toward the bottom.

Source: Pew Research Center for the People and the Press, "News Audience Increasingly Politicized," press release, 8 June 2004. National survey of 3,000 respondents during April and May 2004.

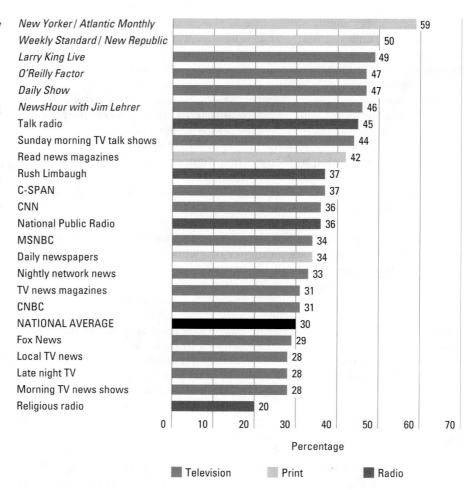

Source	Percentage
New Yorker / Atlantic Monthly	59
Weekly Standard / New Republic	50
Larry King Live	49
O'Reilly Factor	47
Daily Show	47
NewsHour with Jim Lehrer	46
Talk radio	45
Sunday morning TV talk shows	44
Read news magazines	42
Rush Limbaugh	37
C-SPAN	37
CNN	36
National Public Radio	36
MSNBC	34
Daily newspapers	34
Nightly network news	33
TV news magazines	31
CNBC	31
NATIONAL AVERAGE	30
Fox News	29
Local TV news	28
Late night TV	28
Morning TV news shows	28
Religious radio	20

Percentage

■ Television   ■ Print   ■ Radio

or "somewhat" closely.[60] The survey described half the population as news "grazers"—those who check the news from time to time rather than read, watch, or listen at regular times. Almost 70 percent of young respondents (ages eighteen to twenty-four) were news grazers, in contrast to almost 70 percent of old respondents (age sixty-five and over) who followed news regularly. News grazers said they followed stories only when dramatic events occurred, and they lost interest otherwise because they didn't know enough. The survey report noted a sort of catch-22: "The fact that news grazers follow the news intermittently has prevented them from developing a base of knowledge that would help them to more easily follow news stories."[61] Getting news from late-night talk television might be the ultimate form of news grazing; see Figure 6.5.

What People Remember and Know. If, as surveys indicate, about 75 percent of the public read or hear the news each day, how much political in-

FIGURE 6.4 Interest in the News

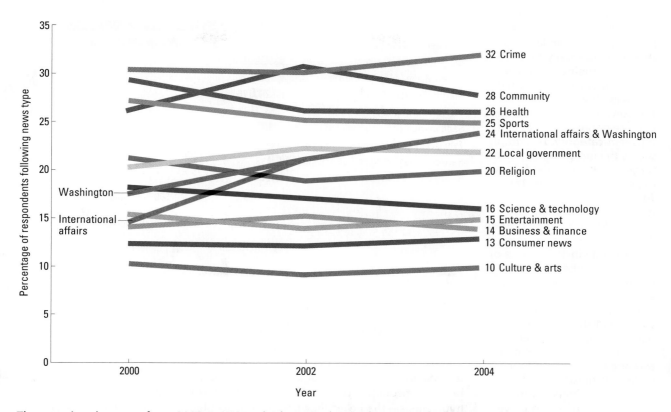

Three national surveys from 2000 to 2004 asked respondents what type of news they followed "very closely," accepting more than one response. The graph shows remarkable stability over the years in news interest by type. Crime, community, health, and sports topped the list every year. However, a major change occurred following September 11, 2001, and the Iraq war in 2003. Respondents began following "hard" news about Washington and international affairs more closely.

Source: Pew Research Center for the People and the Press, "News Audience Increasingly Politicized," press release, 8 June 2004. National survey of 3,000 respondents during April and May 2004.

formation do they absorb? By all accounts, not much. Interviewed in the summer of 2004, more respondents knew that Martha Stewart was found guilty in her recent trial (79 percent) than could name either Osama bin Laden or Al Qaeda as responsible for the September 11, 2001, attack on America (71 percent). Although 56 percent correctly said that the Republicans (not the Democrats) controlled the House of Representatives, 50 percent could have guessed correctly by chance. Asked how many U.S. soldiers had been killed over the first year of the Iraq war (under 500, 500–1,000, 1,000–2,000, over 2,000?), 55 percent correctly guessed 500–1,000. (By 2007, the number had grown to over 3,500.) Given four choices, 25 percent would have been correct

FIGURE 6.5 Gagging on Late-Night TV

Polls show that about 10 percent of Americans get their political news from late-night television, primarily from hosts who open their programs with monologues laced with political jokes. *The Daily Show*, with Jon Stewart, reports fake news in more detail, so it falls in a different category. This graph shows the most frequent joke targets in 2005 on the following popular programs: *The Tonight Show, The Late Show with David Letterman,* and *Late Night with Conan O'Brien.* For the first time since this count began in 1989, three of the top five joke targets were not politicians but entertainers, perhaps because 2005 was not an election year. Figure 6.3 shows that those getting their news from late-night television performed below the national average in answering four news quiz questions, while those getting news from *The Daily Show* scored far above average.

Source: "2005 Late-Night Comics' Ticket: Dubya/Jaco," Center for Media and Public Affairs, Washington, D.C., press release, 22 December 2005.

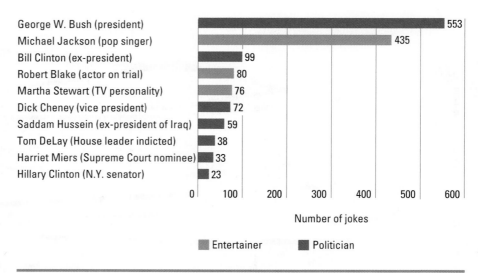

Joke target	Number of jokes
George W. Bush (president)	553
Michael Jackson (pop singer)	435
Bill Clinton (ex-president)	99
Robert Blake (actor on trial)	80
Martha Stewart (TV personality)	76
Dick Cheney (vice president)	72
Saddam Hussein (ex-president of Iraq)	59
Tom DeLay (House leader indicted)	38
Harriet Miers (Supreme Court nominee)	33
Hillary Clinton (N.Y. senator)	23

Number of jokes

■ Entertainer   ■ Politician

television hypothesis The belief that television is to blame for the low level of citizens' knowledge about public affairs.

by chance.[62] (More people guessed lower than higher; the ratio was nearly 3 to 1. For more information, see Figure 6.3.)

Numerous studies have found that those who rely on television for their news score lower on tests of knowledge about public affairs than those who rely on print media. Among media researchers, this finding has led to the **television hypothesis**—the belief that television is to blame for the low level of citizens' knowledge about public affairs.[63] This belief has a reasonable basis. We know that television tends to squeeze public policy issues into one-minute or, at most, two-minute fragments, which makes it difficult to explain candidates' positions. Television also tends to cast abstract issues in personal terms to generate the visual content that the medium needs. Thus, viewers may become more adept at visually identifying the candidates and describing their personal habits than at outlining their positions on issues. Finally, because they are regulated by the FCC, the television networks may be more concerned than newspapers, which are not regulated, about being fair and equal in covering the candidates. Recent research, however, suggests that newspapers differ from television less in content of coverage than in the amount; newspapers simply cover campaigns more extensively and intensively than television.[64] Whatever the explanation, the technological wonders of television may have contributed little to citizens' knowledge of public affairs. Indeed, electronic journalism may work against providing the informed citizenry that democratic government requires. (See "Looking to the Future: Who Will Be Last to Read a Newspaper?")

"For most of us," according to two media scholars studying news of election campaigns, "the mediated reality portrayed by the television networks is the reality we perceive."[65] These scholars concluded that candidates and campaigns put out more and better information than is reported on television news and that print sources also did a better job of informing the public about election campaigns. Some recent research has questioned the hypothesis that

Looking to the Future

Who Will Be Last to Read a Newspaper?

In a survey taken in the spring of 2002, only 41 percent of the respondents said that they had read a daily newspaper "yesterday." As shown in the accompanying graph, those thirty years old or younger were far less likely to have read a newspaper than those seventy years or older. Given the current trend, will anyone be reading newspapers in a generation or two?

Will Internet news replace news in daily papers? Is a decline in reading the newspaper inevitable, or will something slow the trend? Is the aging process itself (not the year of birth) related to newspaper reading? As you think about this, be advised that most major newspaper companies posted strong economic gains, not losses, in 2003.

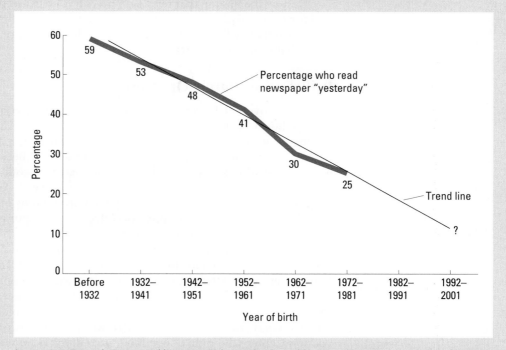

Sources: Pew Research Center, "Public's News Habits Little Changed by September 11," press release, 9 June 2002; "Newspaper Companies' Net Increases," *Wall Street Journal*, 15 October 2003, p. A8.

television is a poor medium for disseminating information on public affairs other than election campaigns. One study found that respondents learned differently from television, newspapers, and news magazines according to their cognitive skills, or ability to learn. People with high cognitive skills learned equally well from all three media, but those with average or low skills learned the most from television and the least from newspapers. The authors' key finding was that "television was more successful in communicating information about topics that were of low salience [significance] to the audience, while print media were superior in conveying information about topics that had high salience."[66] Conceding that people who rely on television for news score lower on political knowledge tests than people who rely on print media, the researchers argued that those who knew more tended to select the print media in the first place. Could it be that the media do not inform people as much as informed people seek out the media? One study designed to test that possibility confirmed the traditional assumption, that media usage increases knowledge more than knowledge leads to media usage.[67]

Despite the finding that television news has value for topics of low salience and for people with limited cognitive skills, the point remains that people with high cognitive skills prefer newspapers. Perhaps they are searching for something that other people aren't.

Influencing Public Opinion

Americans overwhelmingly believe that the media exert a strong influence on their political institutions, and nearly nine out of ten Americans believe that the media strongly influence public opinion.[68] However, measuring the extent of media influence on public opinion is difficult.[69] Because few of us learn about political events except through the media, it could be argued that the media create public opinion simply by reporting events. Consider the dismantling of the Berlin Wall in 1989. Surely the photographs of joyous Berliners demolishing that symbol of oppression affected American public opinion about the reunification of Germany.

The media can have dramatic effects on particular events. Television images in 2005 of the chaos in New Orleans after Hurricane Katrina conflicted with government officials' reports that they were in control of the situation. Chris Wallace of Fox News asked Michael Chertoff, secretary for homeland security, "Mr. Secretary, how is it possible that you could not have known on late Thursday, for instance, that there were thousands of people in the Convention Center who didn't have food, who didn't have water, who didn't have security, when that was being reported on national television"?[70]

Documenting general effects of the media on opinions about more general issues in the news is difficult. Doris Graber, a leading scholar on the media, reported several studies that carefully documented media influence. For example, more pretrial publicity for serious criminal cases leads to full trials rather than settlement through plea-bargaining; media attention to more obscure foreign policy issues tends to force them on the policy agenda.[71] Also, television network coverage of the returns on the night of the 2000 presidential election may have profoundly affected public opinion toward both major candidates. In a report commissioned by cable news network CNN, three journalism experts concluded that the networks' unanimous declarations of George W. Bush's victory that night "created a premature impression" that he had defeated Al Gore before the Florida outcome had been decided. The impression carried through the postelection challenge: "Gore was perceived as the challenger and labeled a 'sore loser' for trying to steal the election."[72] All the networks studied their coverage and vowed to be more careful the next time.

Setting the Political Agenda

Despite the media's potential for influencing public opinion, most scholars believe that the media's greatest influence on politics is found in their power to set the **political agenda**—a list of issues that people identify as needing government attention. Those who set the political agenda define which issues government decision makers should discuss and debate. Like a tree that falls in the forest without anyone around to hear it, an issue that does not get on the political agenda will not get any political attention. Sometimes the media force the government to confront issues once buried in the scientific community, such as AIDS, global warming, and cloning. Other times the media move the government to deal with unpleasant social issues, such as child abuse and wrongful execution of the death penalty. However, the media can also keep high on the agenda issues that perhaps should attract less public resources.[73]

Crime is a good example. In 2004, local television news covered crime twice as much as any other topic, continuing a long-standing pattern.[74] Given that fear of crime today is about the same as it was in the mid-1960s, are the media simply reflecting a constantly high crime rate? Actually, crime rates by then had fallen in every major category (rape, burglary, robbery, assault, murder) since the 1980s.[75] As one journalist said, "Crime coverage is not editorially driven; it's economically driven. It's the easiest, cheapest, laziest news to cover."[76] Moreover, crime provides good visuals. ("If it bleeds, it leads.") So despite the falling crime rate, the public encounters a continuing gusher of crime news and believes that crime has increased over time.

One study found varying correlations between media coverage and what the public sees as "the most important problem facing this country today," depending on the type of event. Crises such as the Vietnam War, racial unrest, and energy shortages drew extensive media coverage, and each additional news magazine story per month generated an almost one percentage point increase in citations of the event as an important problem. But public opinion was even more responsive to media coverage of recurring problems such as inflation and unemployment. Although these events received less extensive coverage, each magazine story was linked with an increase in public concern of almost three percentage points.[77] What's more, evidence shows that television networks, in particular, tend to give greater coverage to bad economic news (which is more dramatic) than to good economic news.[78] This tendency can have serious consequences for an incumbent president, whose popularity may fall with bad economic news. The media's ability to influence public opinion by defining "the news" makes politicians eager to influence media coverage. Politicians attempt to affect not only public opinion but also the opinions of other political leaders. The president receives a daily digest of news and opinion from many sources, and other top government leaders closely monitor the major national news sources. Even journalists work hard at following the news coverage in alternative sources. In a curious sense, the mass media have become a network for communicating among attentive elites, all trying to influence one another or to assess others' weaknesses and strengths. If the White House is under pressure

political agenda A list of issues that need government attention.

on some policy matter, for example, it might supply a cabinet member or other high official to appear on one of the Sunday morning talk shows, such as *Meet the Press* (NBC), *This Week* (ABC), or *Face the Nation* (CBS), or on the week-night *NewsHour with Jim Lehrer* (PBS). These programs draw less than half the audience of the network news shows, but all engage the guest in lengthy discussions. The White House's goal is to influence the thinking of other insiders, who faithfully watch the program, as much as to influence the opinions of the relatively small number of ordinary citizens who watch that particular newscast.[79] Of course, other political leaders appear on these programs, and criticism of the administration's policies in one medium, especially from members of the president's own party, emboldens others to be critical in their comments to other media. In this way, opposition spreads and may eventually be reflected in public opinion.

Socializing the Citizenry

The mass media act as important agents of political socialization, at least as influential as those described in Chapter 5.[80] Young people who rarely follow the news by choice nevertheless acquire political values through the entertainment function of the broadcast media. From the 1930s to the early 1950s, children learned from dramas and comedies on the radio; now they learn from television. The average American child watches about 19,000 hours of television by the end of high school—and sees a lot of sex and hears countless swear words in prime time.[81] What children learned from radio was quite different from what they are learning now, however. In the golden days of radio, youngsters listening to the popular radio drama *The Shadow* heard repeatedly that "crime does not pay . . . the *Shadow* knows!" In program after program—*Dragnet, Junior G-Men, Gangbusters*—the message never varied: criminals are bad; the police are good; criminals get caught and are severely punished for their crimes.

Television today does not portray the criminal justice system in the same way, even in police dramas. Consider programs such as *24* and *In Justice*, which have portrayed law enforcement officers and government agents as law-breakers. Other series, such as *Law and Order, Prison Break*, and *The Shield*, sometimes portray a tainted criminal justice system and institutional corruption.[82] Perhaps years of television messages conveying distrust of law enforcement, disrespect for the criminal justice system, and violence shape impressionable youngsters. Certainly, one cannot easily argue that television's entertainment programs help prepare law-abiding citizens.

Some scholars argue that the most important effect of the mass media, particularly television, is to reinforce the hegemony, or dominance, of the existing culture and order. According to this argument, social control functions not through institutions of force (police, military, and prisons) but through social institutions, such as the media, that cause people to accept "the way things are."[83] By displaying the lifestyles of the rich and famous, for example, the media induce the public to accept the unlimited accumulation of private wealth. Similarly, the media socialize citizens to value "the American way," to be patriotic, to back their country, "right or wrong."

So the media play contradictory roles in the process of political socialization. On one hand, they promote popular support for government by joining in the celebration of national holidays, heroes' birthdays, political anniversaries, and civic accomplishments. On the other hand, the media erode public confidence by detailing politicians' extramarital affairs, airing investigative reports of possible malfeasance in office, and even showing television dramas about crooked cops.[84] Some critics contend that the media also give too much coverage to government opponents, especially to those who engage in unconventional opposition (see Chapter 7). However, strikes, sit-ins, violent confrontations, and hijackings draw large audiences and thus are "newsworthy" by the mass media's standards. In the aftermath of September 11, nearly half the respondents in a 2005 national survey thought that news organizations were "weakening the nation's defenses" by criticizing the military while the country was involved in a global war on terror.[85]

★ Evaluating the Media in Government

Are the media fair or biased in reporting the news? What contributions do the media make to democratic government? What effects do they have on the pursuit of freedom, order, and equality?

Is Reporting Biased?

News reports are presented as objective reality, yet critics of modern journalism contend that the news is filtered through the ideological biases of the media owners and editors (the gatekeepers) and the reporters themselves.

The argument that news reports are politically biased has two sides. On one hand, news reporters are criticized in best-selling books for tilting their stories in a liberal direction, promoting social equality and undercutting social order.[86] On the other hand, wealthy and conservative media owners are suspected—in other best-selling books—of preserving inequalities and reinforcing the existing order by serving a relentless round of entertainment that numbs the public's capacity for critical analysis.[87] Let's evaluate these arguments, looking first at reporters.

Although the picture is far from clear, available evidence seems to confirm the charge of liberal leanings among reporters in the major news media. In a 2004 survey of 547 journalists, 34 percent of the national press considered themselves "liberal," compared with only 7 percent who said they were "conservative."[88] Content analysis of the "tone" of ABC, CBS, and NBC network coverage of presidential campaigns from 1988 to 2004 concluded that Democratic candidates received much more "good press" than Republicans in every election but 1988, when the Republican candidate (Bush) benefited from better press.[89] However, one news medium—talk radio—is dominated by conservative views. Rush Limbaugh alone broadcasts to more than 14 million listeners over six hundred stations. Other prominent conservative radio hosts—such as Sean Hannity and Michael Savage—reach millions more.[90] Liberal views were not widely broadcast on talk radio until 2004, when "Air America Radio," featuring comic Al Franken, was launched on a few metropolitan stations. Whether America is ready for liberal talk on the radio remains to be seen. Franken left in 2007 to run for the Senate from Minnesota in 2008.

The counterargument is that working journalists in the national and local media often conflict with their own editors, who tend to be more conservative. This was demonstrated in a recent study of news executives in national and

> **? Can you explain why . . .** newspaper reporters and their editors may balance out ideological bias in the news?

local media.[91] The editors, in their function as gatekeepers, tend to tone down reporters' liberal leanings by editing their stories or not placing them well in the medium. Newspaper publishers are also free to endorse candidates, and almost all daily newspapers once openly endorsed one of the two major party candidates for president. In fifteen of seventeen elections from 1932 to 1996, newspaper editorials favored the Republican candidate. Again in 2000, more papers endorsed George W. Bush than Al Gore. In 2004, however, more editorials backed challenger John Kerry (208) than Bush (189), and the papers backing the Democrat had larger circulations (21.8 million) than those favoring the Republican (14.4 million).[92] Always of questionable value, newspaper endorsement carries even less value given the decline in newspaper readers.

Without question, incumbents—as opposed to challengers—enjoy much more news coverage simply from holding office and issuing official statements. The less prominent the office, the greater the advantage from such free news coverage. Noncampaign news coverage leads to greater incumbent name recognition at election time, particularly for members of Congress (see Chapter 11). This coverage effect is independent of any bias in reporting on campaigns. For more prominent offices such as the presidency, however, a different news dynamic may come into play. When a powerful incumbent runs for reelection, journalists may feel a special responsibility to counteract his or her advantage by putting the opposite partisan spin on the news.[93] Thus, whether the media coverage of campaigns is seen as pro-Democratic (and therefore liberal) or pro-Republican (and therefore conservative) depends on which party is in office at the time. A study of newspaper stories written in the last weeks of the 2000 presidential campaign, when there was no incumbent, showed that both major party candidates received negative coverage. Fifty-six percent of the stories written about the Democratic heir apparent, Al Gore, were negative. George W. Bush received negative coverage in 51 percent of the stories.[94]

Of course, bias in reporting is not limited to election campaigns, and different media may reflect different understandings of political issues. An important series of surveys about perceptions of the Iraq war were taken over the summer of 2003, after Bush had announced the end of combat. Substantial portions of the public held erroneous understandings of the war just ended. For example, 27 percent in the September survey thought that world opinion supported the U.S. war against Iraq (when world opinion opposed the war); 21 percent thought that Iraq had been directly involved in the 9/11 attack (which our government never claimed and President Bush denied at a news conference),[95] and 24 percent thought that the United States had already found Iraqi weapons of mass destruction (when it had not). The researchers then analyzed which respondents held all three misperceptions by their primary source of news. Respondents who relied on the commercial television networks (Fox, CBS, ABC, CNN, or NBC) held the most misperceptions, with 45 percent of Fox viewers making all three mistakes compared with only about 15 percent for the other networks. Just 9 percent of those who relied on print media erred on all three facts. Broadcast media, per se, were not to blame, for a scant 4 percent of PBS viewers or listeners to National Public Radio were wrong on all items.[96]

Even the nation's outstanding newspapers display biases in reporting news. Scholars analyzed the content of thirty days' coverage of the Palestinian-Israeli conflict during ten months of 2000 and 2001 printed in the *New York Times, Washington Post,* and *Chicago Tribune.* The *Post* and the *Tribune,* while covering the conflict differently, were more similar to each other than to the *Times,* which was "the most slanted in a pro-Israeli direction, in accordance with long-standing criticisms of a pro-Israeli bias leveled against the American media by observers around the world."[97] Presumably such reporting biases affect newspaper readers.

Contributions to Democracy

As noted earlier, in a democracy, communication must move in two directions: from government to citizens and from citizens to government. In fact, political communication in the United States seldom goes directly from government to citizens without passing through the media. The point is important because news reporters tend to be highly critical of politicians; they consider it their job to search for inaccuracies in fact and weaknesses in argument—practicing **watchdog journalism.**[98] Some observers have characterized the news media and the government as adversaries—each mistrusting the other, locked in competition for popular favor while trying to get the record straight. To the extent that this is true, the media serve both the majoritarian and the pluralist models of democracy well by improving the quality of information transmitted to the people about their government.

The mass media transmit information in the opposite direction by reporting citizens' reactions to political events and government actions. The press has traditionally reflected public opinion (and often created it) in the process of defining the news and suggesting courses of government action. But the media's role in reflecting public opinion has become much more refined in the information age. Since the 1820s, newspapers conducted straw polls of dubious quality that matched their own partisan inclinations.[99] After commercial polls (such as the Gallup and Roper polls) were established in the 1930s, newspapers began to report more reliable readings of public opinion. By the 1960s, the media (both national and local) began to conduct their own surveys. In the 1970s, some news organizations acquired their own survey research divisions. Occasionally, print and electronic media have joined forces to conduct major national surveys.

The media now have the tools to do a better job of reporting mass opinion than ever before, and they use those tools extensively, practicing "precision journalism" with sophisticated data collection and analysis techniques. The well-respected *New York Times*/CBS News Poll conducts surveys that are first aired on the *CBS Evening News* and then analyzed at length in the *Times*— same for the NBC News/*Wall Street Journal* poll. Citizens and journalists alike complain that heavy reliance on polls during election campaigns causes the media to emphasize the horse race and slights the discussion of issues. But the media also use their polling expertise for other purposes, such as gauging support for going to war and for balancing the budget. Although polls sometimes create opinions just by asking questions, their net effect has been to generate more accurate knowledge of public opinion and to report that knowledge back to the public. Although widespread knowledge of public opinion does not guarantee government responsiveness to popular demands, such knowledge is necessary if government is to function according to the majoritarian model of democracy.

Effects on Freedom, Order, and Equality

The media in the United States have played an important role in advancing equality, especially racial equality. Throughout the civil rights movement of the

INTERACTIVE 6.2

 Struggle for Peace in the Middle East

watchdog journalism Journalism that scrutinizes public and business institutions and publicizes perceived misconduct.

1950s and 1960s, the media gave national coverage to conflict in the South as black children tried to attend white schools or civil rights workers were beaten and even killed in the effort to register black voters. Partly because of this media coverage, civil rights moved up on the political agenda, and coalitions formed in Congress to pass new laws promoting racial equality. Women's rights have also been advanced by the media, which have reported instances of blatant sexual discrimination exposed by groups working for sexual equality, such as the National Organization for Women (NOW). In general, the mass media offer spokespersons for any disadvantaged group an opportunity to state their case before a national audience and to work for a place on the political agenda. Increasingly, members of minority groups have entered the media business to serve the special interests and needs of their group.

Although the media are willing to encourage government action to promote equality at the cost of some personal freedom, journalists resist government attempts to infringe on freedom of the press to promote order.[100] While the public tends to support a free press in theory, public support is not universal and wavers in practice. Asked whether it is more important "that the government be able to censor news stories it feels threaten national security OR that the news media be able to report stories they feel are in the national interest," about one-third in a 2006 national survey favored government censorship. The public backed the government even more on the surveillance issue raised to open Chapter 1. Asked whether "it is generally right or generally wrong for the government to monitor telephone and e-mail communications of Americans suspected of having terrorist ties without first obtaining permission from the courts," more respondents (54 percent) thought it was generally right than wrong (43 percent).[101]

The media's ability to report whatever they wish and whenever they wish certainly erodes efforts to maintain order. For example, sensational media coverage of terrorist acts gives terrorists the publicity they seek; portrayal of brutal killings and rapes on television encourages copycat crimes, committed "as seen on television." The chaos that erupted among Muslims in 2006 over Islamic cartoons published in Danish newspapers to test freedom of expression resulted in deaths and destruction across the world. Freedom of the press is a noble value and one that has been important to democratic government. But we should not ignore the fact that democracies sometimes pay a price for pursuing it without qualification.

INTERACTIVE 6.3

 Understanding Islam

Summary

The mass media transmit information to large, heterogeneous, and widely dispersed audiences through print and broadcasts. The mass media in the United States are privately owned and in business to make money, which they do mainly by selling space or airtime to advertisers. Both print and electronic media determine which events are newsworthy largely on the basis of audience appeal. The rise of mass-circulation newspapers in the 1830s produced a politically independent press in the United States. In their aggressive competition for readers, those newspapers often engaged in sensational reporting, a charge sometimes leveled at today's media, including the broadcast media and especially television.

The broadcast media operate under technical, ownership, and content regulations imposed by the government; but over the past two decades, the FCC has relaxed its rules limiting media ownership and ensuring fair and balanced representation of competing views. The main function of the mass media is entertainment, but the media also perform the political functions of reporting news, interpreting news, influencing citizens' opinions, setting the political agenda, and socializing citizens about politics.

The major media maintain staffs of professional journalists in major cities around the world. Washington, D.C., hosts the biggest press corps in the world, but only a portion of those correspondents concentrate on the presidency. Because Congress is a more decentralized institution, it is covered in a more decentralized manner. What actually gets reported in the established media depends on media gatekeepers: the publishers and editors. Professional journalists follow rules for citing sources, and these also guide their reporting, but on the Internet and in talk radio, there are few rules concerning what is covered. We are entering an era in which the gatekeepers have less control over what poses as news, both in terms of what subjects are reported on and in terms of the veracity of the reports.

Americans today get more news from television than from newspapers. Although increasing numbers of citizens turn to the Internet for news, a far smaller proportion of the public relies on online sources than on television and newspapers. Compared with television, newspapers usually do a more thorough job of informing the public about politics. Despite heavy exposure to news in the print and electronic media, the ability of most people to retain much political information is shockingly low. The problem appears to be not in the media's ability to supply quality news coverage but in the lack of demand for it by the public. The media's most important effect on public opinion

is in setting the country's political agenda. The role of the news media may be more important for affecting interactions among attentive policy elites than in influencing public opinion. The media play more subtle, contradictory roles in political socialization, both promoting and undermining certain political and cultural values.

Reporters from the national media tend to be more liberal than the public, as judged by their tendency to vote for Democratic candidates and by their own self-descriptions. Journalists' liberal leanings are checked somewhat by the conservative inclinations of their editors and publishers. However, if journalists systematically demonstrate any pronounced bias in their news reporting, it may be against incumbents and front-runners, regardless of their party, rather than a bias that favors liberal Democrats. Numerous studies of media effects have uncovered biases of other forms, as in reporting the Iraq war and conflict in the Middle East.

From the standpoint of majoritarian democracy, one of the most important roles of the media is to facilitate communication from the people to the government through the reporting of public opinion polls. The media zealously defend the freedom of the press, even to the point of encouraging disorder by granting extensive publicity to violent protests, terrorist acts, and other threats to order.

Internet activities and reading suggestions for this chapter are available on the *Online Study Center*

To complete the multimedia assignments for this chapter, go to AmericansGoverning.org.

7 Participation and Voting

(© Fred Prouser/Reuters/Corbis)

Online Study Center
This icon will direct you to resources
and activities on the website
college.hmco.com/pic/jandaupdate9e

Terrorists are "cold-blooded killers," said President Bush. "That's all they are. They hate Freedom. They love terror."[1] Bush spoke after the 2003 terrorist attacks in Baghdad on the first day of Ramadan, the Islamic holy month. Within the span of one hour, suicide bombers killed some thirty-five people and wounded two hundred in coordinated attacks on the Red Cross headquarters in Iraq and on four separate Iraqi police stations. The terrorists in Baghdad, like those who plowed airplanes into the World Trade Center two years earlier, were willing to kill innocent people. But do terrorists only want to kill people, or do they have political objectives?

Suicide bombers, experts agree, are not simply crazed psychopaths. Typically they are intelligent, zealous partisans who have been indoctrinated to sacrifice their lives for a greater good.[2] According to one expert adviser to the Bush administration, "Terrorism has a purpose. Writing it off as mindless and irrational is not useful."[3] Indeed, the U.S. legal code defines **terrorism** as "premeditated, politically motivated violence perpetrated against noncombatant targets by subnational groups or clandestine agents, usually intended to influence an audience."[4]

The immediate purpose behind the suicide attacks in Baghdad, according to news reports, was to "demoralize Iraqi citizens and officials, drive away international aid workers and unsettle the American soldiers, who are routinely blamed for failing to prevent the attacks."[5] The ultimate purpose, of course, was to oust the coalition forces from Iraq, humiliating the U.S. government in the process.

Not all terrorism involves suicide bombers, but all terrorism involves violence. The threat of violence is not sufficient. Violence must be employed, or the threat will lose credibility. In fact, the basis of terrorism is fear—such as dying from anthrax—spread by the media. Terrorism cultivates fear and depends in large part on the media to spread credible threats of harm. Timothy McVeigh, a decorated veteran of the 1991 Gulf War, chose to bomb the federal building in Oklahoma City in 1995 because it would provide good camera coverage. Executed in 2001 for taking 168 lives, McVeigh said he bombed the building because the federal government had become a police state hostile to gun owners, religious sects, and patriotic militia groups.[6]

Governmental officials tend to portray terrorism simply as criminal violence—assaults on society that cannot be justified as serving a political cause. Nevertheless, terrorist violence typically has a political objective. That makes terrorism a perverse form of political behavior practiced by individuals and groups that are excluded from or shun normal modes of political participation. While this chapter discusses common modes of participation that occur in democratic politics, we should be aware of the violence that can occur when democratic politics breaks down.

Although most people immediately think of political participation in terms of voting, far more vigorous forms of political activity lie within the bounds of democracy. How politically active are Americans in general? How do they compare with citizens of other countries? How much and what kind of participation sustains the pluralist and majoritarian models of democracy? ★

I n this chapter, we try to answer these and other important questions about popular participation in government. We begin by studying participation in democratic government, distinguishing between conventional forms of political participation and unconventional forms that still comply with democratic government. Then we evaluate the nature and extent of both types of participation in American politics. Next, we study the expansion of voting rights and voting as the major mechanism for mass participation in politics. Finally, we examine the extent to which the various forms of political participation serve the values of freedom, equality, and order and the majoritarian and pluralist models of democracy.

★ Democracy and Political Participation

G overnment ought to be run by the people. That is the democratic ideal in a nutshell. But how much and what kind of citizen participation is necessary for democratic government? Neither political theorists nor politicians, neither idealists nor realists, can agree on an answer. Champions of direct democracy believe that if citizens do not participate directly in government affairs, making government decisions themselves, they should give up all pretense of living in a democracy. More practical observers contend that people can govern indirectly, through their elected representatives. And they maintain that choosing leaders through elections—formal procedures for voting—is the only workable approach to democracy in a large, complex nation.

Elections are a necessary condition of democracy, but they do not guarantee democratic government. Before the collapse of communism, the former Soviet Union regularly held elections in which more than 90 percent of the electorate turned out to vote, but the Soviet Union certainly did not function as a democracy because there was only one party. Both the majoritarian and pluralist models of democracy rely on voting to varying degrees, but both models expect citizens to participate in politics in other ways. For example, they expect citizens to discuss politics, form interest groups, contact public officials, campaign for political parties, run for office, and even protest government decisions.

We define **political participation** as "those activities of citizens that attempt to influence the structure of government, the selection of government officials, or the policies of government."[7] This definition embraces both conventional and unconventional forms of political participation. In plain language, *conventional behavior* is behavior that is acceptable to the dominant culture in a given situation. Wearing a swimsuit at the beach is conventional; wearing one at a formal dance is not. Displaying campaign posters in front yards is conventional; spray-painting political slogans on buildings is not.

Figuring out whether a particular political act is conventional or unconventional can be difficult. We find the following distinction useful:

- **Conventional participation** is a relatively routine behavior that uses the established institutions of representative government, especially campaigning for candidates and voting in elections.

- **Unconventional participation** is a relatively uncommon behavior that challenges or defies established institutions or the dominant culture (and thus is personally stressful to participants and their opponents).

terrorism Premeditated, politically motivated violence perpetrated against noncombatant targets by subnational groups or clandestine agents.

political participation Actions of private citizens by which they seek to influence or support government and politics.

conventional participation Relatively routine political behavior that uses institutional channels and is acceptable to the dominant culture.

unconventional participation Relatively uncommon political behavior that challenges or defies established institutions and dominant norms.

What Motivates a Suicide Bomber?

In her farewell video, a twenty-two-year-old Palestinian woman and mother of two pledged to use her body as shrapnel to kill Israelis. In mid-January 2004 Reem al-Riyashi carried out a suicide bombing, killing three Israeli soldiers and a security guard and wounding nine others. Her husband and other family members said they were unaware of her plans. In her video, she professed love for her daughter, age one, and son, age three, and said, "I am convinced that God will help and take care of my children." Reem al-Riyashi is only one of many worldwide who have sacrificed themselves for political causes in recent years. *(Handout/Reuters Newmedia Inc./Corbis)*

Voting and writing letters to public officials illustrate conventional political participation; staging sit-down strikes in public buildings and chanting slogans outside officials' windows are examples of unconventional participation. Joining a militia group and training in the woods is unconventional, but the aim is often political. Although the militia movement in the United States peaked at 858 groups in 1996 and has fewer than 200 groups today, it remains deadly serious in pledging to defend its view of freedom against all enemies, foreign or domestic.[8] Other democratic forms of participation, such as political demonstrations, can be conventional (carrying signs outside an abortion clinic) or unconventional (linking arms to prevent entrance). Various forms of unconventional participation are often used by powerless groups to gain political benefits while working within the system.[9]

Unconventional methods of participation figure in popular politics as disadvantaged groups resort to them in lieu of more conventional forms of participation used by most citizens. Let us look at both kinds of political participation in the United States.

★ Unconventional Participation

On Sunday, March 7, 1965, a group of about six hundred people attempted to march fifty miles from Selma, Alabama, to the state capitol at Montgomery to show their support for voting rights for blacks. (At the time, Selma had fewer than five hundred registered black voters, out of fifteen thousand eligible.)[10] Alabama governor George Wallace declared the march illegal and sent state troopers to stop it. The two groups met at the Edmund Pettus Bridge over

March for Freedom, Forty Years Later

On Sunday, March 6, 2005, thousands marched across the Edmund Pettus Bridge outside Selma, Alabama, to commemorate the "Bloody Sunday" forty years earlier when people were beaten during a voting rights protest. *(David Bundy/The Montgomery Advertiser)*

the Alabama River at the edge of Selma. The peaceful marchers were disrupted and beaten by state troopers and deputy sheriffs—some on horseback—using clubs, bullwhips, and tear gas. The day became known as Bloody Sunday.

The march from Selma was a form of unconventional political participation. Marching fifty miles in a political protest is certainly not common; moreover, the march challenged the existing institutions that prevented blacks from voting. But they had been prevented from participating conventionally—voting in elections—for many decades, and they chose this unconventional method to dramatize their cause.

The march ended in violence because Governor Wallace would not allow even this peaceful mode of unconventional expression. In contrast to demonstrations against the Vietnam War later in the 1960s, the 1965 civil rights march posed no threat of violence. The brutal response to the marchers helped the rest of the nation understand the seriousness of the civil rights problem in the South. Unconventional participation is stressful and occasionally violent, but sometimes it is worth the risk. In 2005, thousands of blacks and whites solemnly but triumphantly reenacted the march on its fortieth anniversary.

Support for Unconventional Participation

Unconventional political participation has a long history in the United States. The Boston Tea Party of 1773, in which American colonists dumped three car-

FIGURE 7.1 What Americans Think Is Unconventional Political Behavior

A survey presented Americans with five different forms of political participation outside the electoral process and asked whether they "have done," "might do," or "would never do" any of them. The respondents disapproved of two forms overwhelmingly. Only signing petitions was widely done and rarely ruled out. Even attending demonstrations (a right guaranteed in the Constitution) would "never" be done by 24 percent of the respondents. Boycotting products was less objectionable and more widely practiced. According to this test, attending demonstrations and boycotting products are only marginally conventional forms of political participation. Joining strikes and occupying buildings are clearly unconventional activities for most Americans.

Source: 2000–2001 World Values Survey. The World Values Survey Association, based in Stockholm, conducts representative surveys in nations across the world. See <http://www.worldvaluessurvey.org/>.

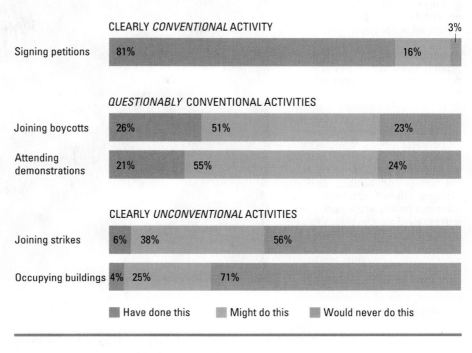

CLEARLY *CONVENTIONAL* ACTIVITY

Signing petitions 81% 16% 3%

QUESTIONABLY CONVENTIONAL ACTIVITIES

Joining boycotts 26% 51% 23%

Attending demonstrations 21% 55% 24%

CLEARLY *UNCONVENTIONAL* ACTIVITIES

Joining strikes 6% 38% 56%

Occupying buildings 4% 25% 71%

■ Have done this ■ Might do this ■ Would never do this

goes of British tea into Boston Harbor, was only the first in a long line of violent protests against British rule that eventually led to revolution. Yet we know less about unconventional than conventional participation. The reasons are twofold. First, since it is easier to collect data on conventional practices, they are studied more frequently. Second, political scientists are simply biased toward institutionalized, or conventional, politics. In fact, some basic works on political participation explicitly exclude any behavior that is "outside the system."[11] One major study of unconventional political action asked people whether they had engaged in or approved of five types of political participation other than voting: signing petitions, joining boycotts, attending demonstrations, joining strikes, and occupying buildings. As shown in Figure 7.1, of the five activities, only signing petitions was clearly regarded as conventional, in the sense that the behavior was widely practiced.

The conventionality of two other forms of behavior was questionable. Only 21 percent had ever attended a demonstration, whereas 24 percent said that they would never demonstrate. The marchers in Selma, although peaceful,

Antiwar Protest, 1968
In August 1968, thousands of youthful antiwar protesters gathered in Chicago, where the Democrats were holding their national convention. Protests against the war had already forced President Lyndon Johnson not to seek reelection. Mayor Richard J. Daley vowed that the protesters would not disturb the impending nomination of Hubert Humphrey, Johnson's vice president. Daley's police kept the youths from demonstrating at the convention, but the resulting violence did not help Humphrey, who lost to Richard Nixon in an extremely close election. When the Democratic convention returned to Chicago in 1996, the new Mayor Daley (Richard M., the former mayor's son) faced a different situation and hosted a relatively peaceful convention. *(UPI/Bettmann)*

were surely demonstrating against the established order. If we measure conventionality in terms of the proportion of people who disapprove of an action, we might argue that all demonstrations border on the unconventional. The same reasoning could be applied to boycotting products—for example, refusing to buy lettuce or grapes picked by nonunion farm workers. Demonstrations and boycotts are problem cases in deciding what is and is not conventional political participation.

The other two political activities listed in Figure 7.1 are clearly unconventional. In fact, when political activities interfere with people's daily lives (occupying buildings, for example), disapproval is nearly universal. When protesters demonstrating against the Vietnam War disrupted the 1968 Democratic National Convention in Chicago, they were clubbed by the city's police. Although the national television audience saw graphic footage of the confrontations and heard reporters' criticisms of the police's behavior, most viewers condemned the demonstrators, not the police.

The Effectiveness of Unconventional Participation

Vociferous antiabortion protests have discouraged many doctors from performing abortions, but they have not led to outlawing abortions. Does unconventional participation ever work (even when it provokes violence)? Yes. Antiwar protesters helped convince President Lyndon Johnson not to seek reelection in 1968, and they heightened public concern about U.S. participation in the Vietnam War. American college students who disrupted campuses in the late 1960s and early 1970s helped end the military draft in 1973, and although it was not one of their stated goals, they sped passage of the Twenty-sixth Amendment, which lowered the voting age to eighteen.

Antiwar Protest, 2003

In October 2003, about 50,000 people descended on Washington, D.C., traveling in about 150 buses from 140 cities, to protest the U.S. presence in Iraq. The event was cosponsored by International ANSWER (Act Now to Stop War and End Racism) and United for Peace and Justice, a coalition of more than 650 local and national groups opposing U.S. foreign policy. *(Data from Shannon McMahon, "Thousands Rally in D.C. War Protest,"* Chicago Tribune, *20 October 2003, p. 10. Photo: AFP Photo/Luke Frazza/ Getty Images)*

The unconventional activities of civil rights workers also produced notable successes. Dr. Martin Luther King, Jr., led the 1955 Montgomery bus boycott (prompted by Rosa Parks's refusal to surrender her seat to a white man), which sparked the civil rights movement. He used **direct action** to challenge specific cases of discrimination, assembling crowds to confront businesses and local governments and demanding equal treatment in public accommodations and government. The civil rights movement organized more than one thousand such newsworthy demonstrations nationwide—387 in 1965 alone.[12] And like the march in Selma, many of these protests provoked violent confrontations between whites and blacks.

Denied the usual opportunities for conventional political participation, minorities used unconventional politics to pressure Congress to pass a series of civil rights laws in 1957, 1960, 1964, and 1968—each one in some way extending national protection against discrimination by reason of race, color, religion, or national origin. (The 1964 act also prohibited discrimination in employment on the basis of sex.)

In addition, the Voting Rights Act of 1965 placed some state electoral procedures under federal supervision, protecting the registration of black voters and increasing their voting rate, especially in the South, where much of the violence occurred. Black protest activity—both violent and nonviolent—has also been credited with increased welfare support for blacks in the South.[13] The civil rights movement showed that social change can occur even when it faces violent opposition at first. In 1970, fewer than fifteen hundred blacks served as elected officials in the United States. In 2004, the number was more than nine thousand, and over four thousand Hispanics held elected office.[14] Nevertheless, racial divisions persist across the nation.

Although direct political action and the politics of confrontation can work, using them requires a special kind of commitment. Studies show that direct action appeals most to those who both distrust the political system and have a strong sense of political efficacy—the feeling that they can do something

INTERACTIVE 7.2

 Montgomery: A Victory for Civil Rights

direct action Unconventional participation that involves assembling crowds to confront businesses and local governments to demand a hearing.

to affect political decisions.[15] Whether this combination of attitudes produces behavior that challenges the system depends on the extent of organized group activity. The civil rights movement of the 1960s was backed by numerous organizations across the nation.

The decision to use unconventional behavior also depends on the extent to which individuals develop a group consciousness—identification with their group and awareness of its position in society, its objectives, and its intended course of action.[16] These characteristics were present among blacks and young people in the mid-1960s and are strongly present today among blacks and, to a lesser degree, among women. Indeed, some researchers contend that black consciousness has heightened both African Americans' distrust of the political system and their sense of individual efficacy, generating more political participation by poor blacks than by poor whites.[17] The National Organization for Women (NOW) and other women's groups have also heightened women's group consciousness, which may have contributed to their increased participation in politics in both conventional and unconventional ways.

Unconventional Participation in America and the World

Although most Americans disapprove of using certain forms of participation to protest government policies, U.S. citizens are about as likely to take direct action in politics as citizens of European democracies. Consider "Compared with What? Popular Participation in Politics," which shows how respondents in the United States compare with those in eight other countries on various modes of participation. Americans are not only about as likely as citizens in other nations to sign petitions, or demonstrate, or boycott goods, but Americans are also as likely to "discuss politics" and show "interest in politics." So compared with citizens in other nations, Americans are not markedly apathetic.

Is something wrong with a political system if citizens resort to unconventional—and often disapproved of—methods of political participation? To answer this question, we must first learn how much citizens use conventional methods of participation.

★ Conventional Participation

A practical test of the democratic nature of any government is whether citizens can affect its policies by acting through its institutions—meeting with public officials, supporting candidates, voting in elections. (See "Compared with What? Popular Participation in Politics.") If people must operate outside government institutions to influence policymaking, as civil rights workers had to do in the South, the system is not democratic. Citizens should not have to risk their life and property to participate in politics, and they should not have to take direct action to force the government to hear their views. The objective of democratic institutions is to make political participation conventional—to allow ordinary citizens to engage in relatively routine, nonthreatening behavior to get the government to heed their opinions, interests, and needs.

In a democracy, for a group to gather at a statehouse or city hall to dramatize its position on an issue—say, a tax increase—is not unusual. Such a demonstration is a form of conventional participation. The group is not powerless, and its members are not risking their personal safety by demonstrating. But violence can erupt between opposing groups demonstrating in a political setting, such as between pro-life and pro-choice groups. Circumstances, then, often determine whether organized protest is or is not conventional. In general, the less that the participants anticipate a threat, the more likely it is that the protest will be conventional.

Conventional political behaviors fall into two major categories: actions that show support for government policies and those that try to change or influence policies.

Supportive Behavior

Supportive behavior is action that expresses allegiance to country and government. Reciting the Pledge of Allegiance and flying the American flag on holidays both show support for the country and, by implication, its political system. Such ceremonial activities usually require little effort, knowledge, or personal courage; that is, they demand little initiative on the part of the citizen. The simple act of turning out to vote is in itself a show of support for the political system. Other supportive behaviors, such as serving as an election judge in a nonpartisan election or organizing a holiday parade, demand greater initiative.

At times, people's perception of patriotism moves them to cross the line between conventional and unconventional behavior. In their eagerness to support the American system, they break up a meeting or disrupt a rally of a group they believe is radical or somehow "un-American." Radical groups may threaten the political system with wrenching change, but superpatriots pose their own threat by denying to others the nonviolent means of dissent.[18]

Influencing Behavior

Citizens use **influencing behavior** to modify or even reverse government policy to serve political interests. Some forms of influencing behavior seek particular benefits from government; other forms have broad policy objectives.

Particular Benefits. Some citizens try to influence government to obtain benefits for themselves, their immediate families, or close friends. For example, citizens might pressure their alderman to rebuild the curbs on their street or vote against an increase in school taxes, especially if they have no children. Serving one's self-interest through the voting process is certainly acceptable to democratic theory. Each individual has only one vote, and no single voter can wangle particular benefits from government through voting unless a majority of the voters agree.

Political actions that require considerable knowledge and initiative are another story. Individuals or small groups who influence government officials to advance their self-interest—for instance, to obtain a lucrative government contract—may secretly benefit without others knowing. Those who quietly obtain particular benefits from government pose a serious challenge to a democracy. Pluralist theory holds that groups ought to be able to make government respond to their special problems and needs. In contrast, majoritarian theory holds that government should not do what a majority does not want it to do.

supportive behavior Action that expresses allegiance to government and country.

influencing behavior Behavior that seeks to modify or reverse government policy to serve political interests.

Compared with What?

Popular Participation in Politics

Compared with citizens in eight other nations, Americans are not noticeably apathetic when it comes to politics. Americans are most likely to sign petitions and second most likely to express interest in politics, and they are in the middle of the other country respondents on such activities as discussing politics, engaging in protest demonstrations, boycotting goods, and joining unofficial strikes.

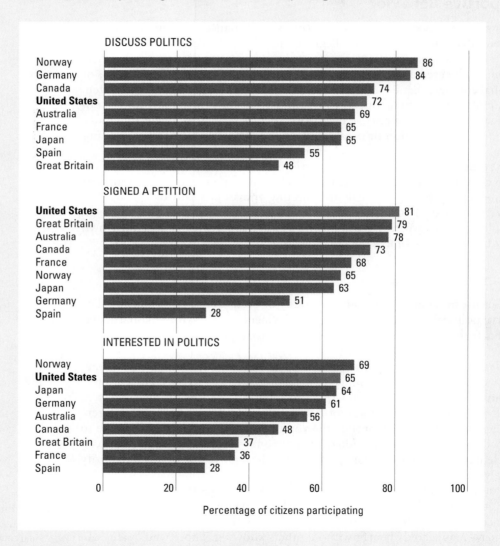

DISCUSS POLITICS

Country	
Norway	86
Germany	84
Canada	74
United States	72
Australia	69
France	65
Japan	65
Spain	55
Great Britain	48

SIGNED A PETITION

Country	
United States	81
Great Britain	79
Australia	78
Canada	73
France	68
Norway	65
Japan	63
Germany	51
Spain	28

INTERESTED IN POLITICS

Country	
Norway	69
United States	65
Japan	64
Germany	61
Australia	56
Canada	48
Great Britain	37
France	36
Spain	28

Percentage of citizens participating

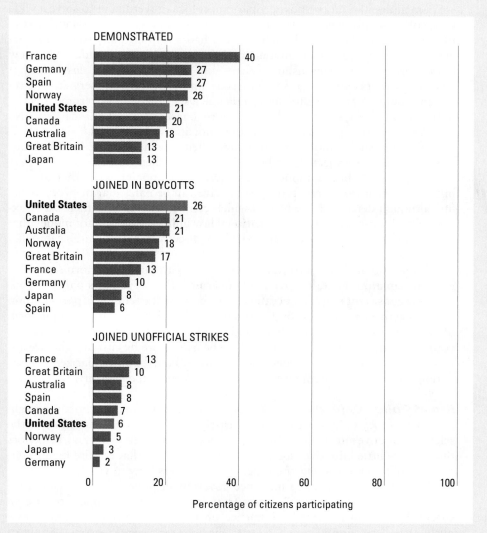

DEMONSTRATED

France	40
Germany	27
Spain	27
Norway	26
United States	21
Canada	20
Australia	18
Great Britain	13
Japan	13

JOINED IN BOYCOTTS

United States	26
Canada	21
Australia	21
Norway	18
Great Britain	17
France	13
Germany	10
Japan	8
Spain	6

JOINED UNOFFICIAL STRIKES

France	13
Great Britain	10
Australia	8
Spain	8
Canada	7
United States	6
Norway	5
Japan	3
Germany	2

Percentage of citizens participating

Source: World Values Survey, 2000–2001.

A majority of citizens might very well not want the government to do what any particular person or group seeks if it is costly to other citizens.

Citizens often ask for special services from local government. Such requests may range from contacting the city forestry department to remove a dead tree in front of a house to calling the county animal control center to deal with a vicious dog in the neighborhood. Studies of such "contacting behavior" find that it tends not to be empirically related to other forms of political activity. In other words, people who complain to city hall do not necessarily vote. Contacting behavior is related to socioeconomic status: people of higher socioeconomic status are more likely to contact public officials.[19]

Americans demand much more of their local government than of the national government. Although many people value self-reliance and individualism in national politics, most people expect local government to solve a wide range of social problems. A study of residents of Kansas City, Missouri, found that more than 90 percent thought the city had a responsibility to provide services in thirteen areas, including maintaining parks, setting standards for new home construction, demolishing vacant and unsafe buildings, ensuring that property owners clean up trash and weeds, and providing bus service. The researcher noted that "it is difficult to imagine a set of federal government activities about which there would [be] more consensus."[20] Citizens can also mobilize against a project. Dubbed the "not in my back yard," or NIMBY, phenomenon, such a mobilization occurs when citizens pressure local officials to stop undesired projects from being located near their homes.

Finally, contributing money to a candidate's campaign is another form of influencing behavior. Here, too, the objective can be particular or broad benefits, although determining which is which can sometimes be difficult. For example, as discussed in Chapter 9, national law limits the amount of money that an individual or organization can contribute directly to a candidate's campaign for president.

Several points emerge from this review of "particularized" forms of political participation. First, approaching government to serve one's particular interests is consistent with democratic theory because it encourages participation from an active citizenry. Second, particularized contact may be a unique form of participation, not necessarily related to other forms of participation such as voting. Third, such participation tends to be used more by citizens who are advantaged in terms of knowledge and resources. Fourth, particularized participation may serve private interests to the detriment of the majority.

Broad Policy Objectives.   We come now to what many scholars have in mind when they talk about political participation: activities that influence the selection of government personnel and policies. Here, too, we find behaviors that require little initiative (such as voting) and others that require high initiative (attending political meetings, persuading others how to vote).

Even voting intended to influence government policies is a low-initiative activity. Such "policy voting" differs from voting to show support or to gain special benefits in its broader influence on the community or society. Obviously, this distinction is not sharp: citizens vote for several reasons—a mix of allegiance, particularized benefits, and policy concerns. In addition to policy voting, many other low-initiative forms of conventional participation—wearing a candidate's T-shirt, watching a party convention on television, posting a bumper sticker—are also connected with elections. In the next section, we fo-

cus on elections as a mechanism for participation. For now, we simply note that voting to influence policy is usually a low-initiative activity. As we discuss later, it actually requires more initiative to *register* to vote in the United States than to cast a vote on election day. With a computer, it is even easier to e-mail members of Congress than to vote.

Other types of participation designed to affect broad policies require high initiative. Running for office requires the most (see Chapter 9). Some high-initiative activities, such as attending party meetings and working on campaigns, are associated with the electoral process; others, such as attending legislative hearings and writing letters to Congress, are not. Although many nonelectoral activities involve making personal contact, their objective is often to obtain government benefits for some group of people—farmers, the unemployed, children, oil producers. In fact, studies of citizen contacts in the United States show that about two-thirds deal with broad social issues and only one-third are for private gain.[21] Few people realize that using the court system is a form of political participation, a way for citizens to press for their rights in a democratic society. Although most people use the courts to serve their particular interests, some also use them, as we discuss shortly, to meet broad objectives. Going to court demands high personal initiative.[22] It also requires knowledge of the law or the financial resources to afford a lawyer.

People use the courts for both personal benefit and broad policy objectives. A person or group can bring **class action suits** on behalf of other people in similar circumstances. Lawyers for the National Association for the Advancement of Colored People pioneered this form of litigation in the famous school desegregation case *Brown* v. *Board of Education* (1954).[23] They succeeded in getting the Supreme Court to outlaw segregation in public schools, not just for Linda Brown, who brought the suit in Topeka, Kansas, but for all others "similarly situated"—that is, for all other black students who wanted to attend desegregated schools. Participation through the courts is usually beyond the means of individual citizens, but it has proved effective for organized groups,

class action suit A legal action brought by a person or group on behalf of a number of people in similar circumstances.

Voting in Kenya
This voter casts his ballot at a polling station near Kajiado, Kenya, south of its capital, Nairobi. The election was a referendum on proposed changes to the constitution that critics said would increase presidential power. Although backed by President Mwai Kibaki, the draft constitution was soundly defeated by the voters. *(Karel Prinsloo/AP/Wide World Photos)*

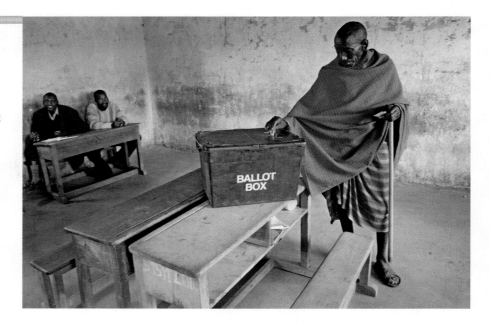

especially those that have been unable to gain their objectives through Congress or the executive branch.

Individual citizens can also try to influence policies at the national level by participating directly in the legislative process. One way is to attend congressional hearings, which are open to the public and are occasionally held outside Washington. Especially since the end of World War II, the national government has sought to increase citizen involvement in creating regulations and laws by making information on government activities available to interested parties. For example, government agencies are required to publish all proposed and approved regulations in the daily *Federal Register* and to make government documents available to citizens on request.

Conventional Participation in America

You may know someone who has testified at a congressional or administrative hearing, but the odds are that you do not. Such participation is high-initiative behavior. Relatively few people—only those with high stakes in the outcome of a decision—are willing to participate in this way. How often do Americans contact government officials and engage in other forms of conventional political participation compared with citizens in other countries?

The most common form of political behavior in most industrial democracies is voting for candidates. The rate of voting is known as **voter turnout,** the percentage of eligible voters who actually vote in a given election. Voting eligibility is hard to determine across American states, and there are different ways to estimate voter turnout.[24]* However measured, voting for candidates in the

---

voter turnout The percentage of eligible citizens who actually vote in a given election.

*Traditionally, turnout had been computed by dividing the number of voters by the voting-age population, which included noncitizens and ineligible felons. Recent research excludes these groups in estimating voter turnout and has revised the U.S. turnout rates upward by three to five points in elections since 1980.

United States is less common than it is in other countries, as demonstrated in "Compared with What? Voter Turnout in European and American Elections Since 1945" on page 213. When voting turnout in the United States over more than half a century is compared with historical patterns of voting in twenty-three other countries, the United States ranks at the *bottom* of the pack. This is a political paradox. On one hand, Americans are as likely as (or substantially more likely than) citizens in other democracies to engage in various forms of political participation. But when it comes to voting, the hand that casts the ballot, Americans rank dead last.

Other researchers noted this paradox and wrote, "If, for example, we concentrate our attention on national elections we will find that the United States is the least participatory of almost all other nations." But looking at the other indicators, they found that "political apathy, by a wide margin, is lowest in the United States. Interestingly, the high levels of overall involvement reflect a rather balanced contribution of both . . . conventional and unconventional politics."[25] Clearly, low voter turnout in the United States constitutes a puzzle, to which we will return.

★ Participating Through Voting

The heart of democratic government lies in the electoral process. Whether a country holds elections—and if so, what kind—constitutes the critical difference between democratic and nondemocratic governments. Elections institutionalize mass participation in democratic government according to the three normative principles of procedural democracy discussed in Chapter 2: electoral rules specify *who* is allowed to vote, *how much* each person's vote counts, and *how many* votes are needed to win.

Again, elections are formal procedures for making group decisions. *Voting* is the act individuals engage in when they choose among alternatives in an election. **Suffrage** and **franchise** both mean the right to vote. By formalizing political participation through rules for suffrage and for counting ballots, electoral systems allow large numbers of people, who individually have little political power, to wield great power. Electoral systems decide collectively who governs and, in some instances, what government should do.

The simple act of holding elections is less important than the specific rules and circumstances that govern voting. According to democratic theory, everyone should be able to vote. In practice, however, no nation grants universal suffrage. All countries have age requirements for voting, and all disqualify some inhabitants on various grounds: lack of citizenship, criminal record, mental incompetence, and others. What is the record of enfranchisement in the United States?

Expansion of Suffrage

The United States was the first country to provide for general elections of representatives through "mass" suffrage, but the franchise was far from universal. When the Constitution was framed, the idea of full adult suffrage was too radical to consider seriously. Instead, the framers left the issue of enfranchisement to the states, stipulating only that individuals who could vote for "the most numerous Branch of the State Legislature" could also vote for their representatives to the U.S. Congress (Article I, Section 2).

suffrage The right to vote. Also called the *franchise*.

franchise The right to vote. Also called *suffrage*.

? Can you explain why . . . the eligibility for voting in national elections varied greatly by state in early elections?

Initially, most states established taxpaying or property-holding requirements for voting. Virginia, for example, required ownership of twenty-five acres of settled land or five hundred acres of unsettled land. The original thirteen states began to lift such requirements after 1800. Expansion of the franchise accelerated after 1815, with the admission of new "western" states (Indiana, Illinois, Alabama), where land was more plentiful and widely owned. By the 1850s, the states had eliminated almost all taxpaying and property-holding requirements, thus allowing the working class—at least its white male members—to vote. Extending the vote to blacks and women took longer.

The Enfranchisement of Blacks. The Fifteenth Amendment, adopted shortly after the Civil War, prohibited the states from denying the right to vote "on account of race, color, or previous condition of servitude." However, the states of the old Confederacy worked around the amendment by reestablishing old voting requirements (poll taxes, literacy tests) that worked primarily against blacks. Some southern states also cut blacks out of politics through a cunning circumvention of the amendment. Because the amendment said nothing about voting rights in private organizations, these states denied blacks the right to vote in the "private" Democratic *primary* elections held to choose the party's candidates for the general election. Because the Democratic Party came to dominate politics in the South, the "white primary" effectively disenfranchised blacks, despite the Fifteenth Amendment. Finally, in many areas of the South, the threat of violence kept blacks from the polls.

The extension of full voting rights to blacks came in two phases, separated by twenty years. In 1944, the Supreme Court decided in *Smith* v. *Allwright* that laws preventing blacks from voting in primary elections were unconstitutional, holding that party primaries are part of the continuous process of electing public officials.[26] The Voting Rights Act of 1965, which followed Selma's Bloody Sunday by less than five months, suspended discriminatory voting tests. It also authorized federal registrars to register voters in seven southern states, where less than half of the voting-age population had registered to vote in the 1964 election. For good measure, the Supreme Court ruled in 1966 in *Harper* v. *Virginia State Board of Elections* that state poll taxes are unconstitutional.[27] Although long in coming, these actions by the national government to enforce political equality in the states dramatically increased the registration of southern blacks (see Figure 7.2).

The Enfranchisement of Women. The enfranchisement of women in the United States is a less sordid story than enfranchisement of blacks but still nothing to be proud of. Women had to fight long and hard to win the right to vote. Until 1869, women could not vote anywhere in the world.[28] American women began to organize to obtain suffrage in the mid-1800s. Known then as *suffragettes,** the early feminists initially had a limited effect on politics. Their first major victory did not come until 1869, when Wyoming, still a territory, granted women the right to vote. No state followed suit until 1893, when Colorado enfranchised women.

In the meantime, the suffragettes became more active. In 1884, they formed the Equal Rights Party and nominated Belva A. Lockwood, a lawyer

---

*The term *suffragist* applied to a person of either sex who advocated extending the vote to women, while *suffragette* was reserved primarily for women who did so militantly.

FIGURE 7.2   Voter Registration in the South, 1960, 1980, and 2000

As a result of the Voting Rights Act of 1965 and other national actions, black voter registration in the eleven states of the old Confederacy nearly doubled between 1960 and 1980. In 2000, there was very little difference between the voting registration rates of white and black voters in the Deep South.

Sources: Data for 1960 and 1980 are from U.S. Bureau of the Census, *Statistical Abstract of the United States, 1982–1983* (Washington, D.C.: U.S. Government Printing Office, 1983), p. 488; data for 2000 come from the U.S. Census Bureau, Current Population Report, P20–542, Table 3, Internet release, 27 February 2002.

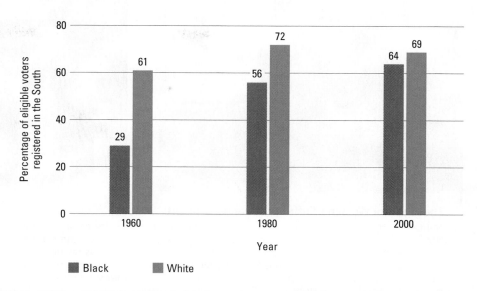

(who could not herself vote), as the first woman candidate for president.[29] Between 1896 and 1918, twelve other states gave women the vote. Most of these states were in the West, where pioneer women often departed from traditional women's roles. Nationally, the women's suffrage movement intensified, often resorting to unconventional political behaviors (marches, demonstrations), which occasionally invited violent attacks from men and even other women. In 1919, Congress finally passed the Nineteenth Amendment, which prohibits states from denying the right to vote "on account of sex." The amendment was ratified in 1920, in time for the November election.

Evaluating the Expansion of Suffrage in America. The last major expansion of suffrage in the United States took place in 1971, when the Twenty-sixth Amendment lowered the voting age to eighteen. For most of its history, the United States has been far from the democratic ideal of universal suffrage. The United States initially restricted voting rights to white male taxpayers or property owners, and wealth requirements lasted until the 1850s. Through demonstrations and a constitutional amendment, women won the franchise only two decades before World War II. Through civil war, constitutional amendments, court actions, massive demonstrations, and congressional action, blacks finally achieved full voting rights only two decades after World War II. Our record has more than a few blemishes.

But compared with other countries, the United States looks pretty democratic.[30] Women did not gain the vote on equal terms with men until 1921 in Norway; 1922 in the Netherlands; 1944 in France; 1946 in Italy, Japan, and Venezuela; 1948 in Belgium; and 1971 in Switzerland. Women are still not universally enfranchised. Among the Arab monarchies, Kuwait granted full voting rights to women in 2005. Saudi Arabia did not allow women to participate in the limited municipal elections of 2005, the first there since 1960. Of course,

The Fight for Women's Suffrage . . . and Against It

Militant suffragettes demonstrated outside the White House prior to ratification of the Nineteenth Amendment to the Constitution, which gave women the right to vote. Congress passed the proposed amendment in 1919, and it was ratified by the required number of states in time for the 1920 presidential election. Suffragettes' demonstrations were occasionally disrupted by men—and other women—who opposed extending the right to vote to women. *(Library of Congress)*

no one at all can vote in the United Arab Emirates. Comparing the enfranchisement of minority racial groups is difficult, because most other democratic nations do not have a racial makeup comparable to that in the United States. We should note, however, that the indigenous Maori population in New Zealand won suffrage in 1867, but the Aborigines in Australia were not fully enfranchised until 1961. In South Africa, blacks, who outnumber whites by more than four to one, were not allowed to vote freely in elections until 1994. With regard to voting age, nineteen of twenty-seven countries that allow free elections also have a minimum voting age of eighteen (none has a lower age), and eight have higher age requirements.

When judged against the rest of the world, the United States, which originated mass participation in government through elections, has as good a record of providing for political equality in voting rights as other democracies and a better record than many others.

Voting on Policies

Disenfranchised groups have struggled to gain voting rights because of the political power that comes with suffrage. Belief in the ability of ordinary citizens to make political decisions and to control government through the power of the ballot box was strongest in the United States during the Progressive era, which began around 1900 and lasted until about 1925. **Progressivism** was a philosophy of political reform that trusted the goodness and wisdom of individual citizens and distrusted "special interests" (railroads, corporations) and political institutions (traditional political parties, legislatures). Such attitudes have resurfaced among the followers of the Reform Party and others who find this populist outlook appealing.

progressivism A philosophy of political reform based on the goodness and wisdom of the individual citizen as opposed to special interests and political institutions.

The leaders of the Progressive movement were prominent politicians (former president Theodore Roosevelt, Senator Robert La Follette of Wisconsin) and eminent scholars (historian Frederick Jackson Turner, philosopher John Dewey). Not content to vote for candidates chosen by party leaders, the Progressives championed the **direct primary**—a preliminary election, run by the state governments, in which the voters choose the party's candidates for the general election. Wanting a mechanism to remove elected candidates from office, the Progressives backed the **recall,** a special election initiated by a petition signed by a specified number of voters. Although about twenty states provide for recall elections, this device is rarely used. Only a few statewide elected officials have actually been unseated through recall.[31] Indeed, only one state governor had ever been unseated until 2003, when California voters threw out Governor Gray Davis in a bizarre recall election that placed movie actor Arnold Schwarzenegger in the governor's mansion (see "Politics in a Changing World: Too Much Direct Democracy in California?" on page 38).

The Progressives also championed the power of the masses to propose and pass laws, approximating citizen participation in policymaking that is the hallmark of direct democracy. They developed two voting mechanisms for policymaking that are still in use:

- A **referendum** is a direct vote by the people on either a proposed law or an amendment to a state constitution. The measures subject to popular vote are known as *propositions*. Twenty-three states permit popular referenda on laws, and all but Delaware require a referendum for a constitutional amendment. Most referenda are placed on the ballot by legislatures, not voters.

- The **initiative** is a procedure by which voters can propose a measure to be decided by the legislature or by the people in a referendum. The procedure involves gathering a specified number of signatures from registered voters (usually 5 to 10 percent of the total in the state) and then submitting the petition to a designated state agency. Twenty-four states provide for some form of voter initiative.

Figure 7.3 shows the West's affinity for these democratic mechanisms. Over 350 propositions appeared on state ballots in general elections during the 1990s. In 2004 alone, voters in thirty-four states decided the outcome of 162 initiatives or referenda. Of these, citizens placed 61 on the ballot; nearly all the others were proposed by state legislatures.[32] Citizens in California led the pack, placing 16 policy measures on the ballot.[33] The definition of marriage was on the ballot in eleven states, and each state voted to define marriage as a union of a man and a woman.

At times, many politicians oppose the initiatives that citizens propose and approve. This was true, for example, of term limits. A referendum can also work to the advantage of politicians, freeing them from taking sides on a hot issue. In 1998, for example, voters in Maine repealed a state law that barred discrimination against gays and lesbians in employment, housing, and public accommodations. In so doing, it became the first state to repeal a gay rights law.[34]

What conclusion can we draw about the Progressives' legacy of mechanisms for direct participation in government? One seasoned journalist paints an unimpressive picture. He notes that an expensive "industry" developed in the 1980s that makes money circulating petitions and then managing the large sums

direct primary A preliminary election, run by the state government, in which the voters choose each party's candidates for the general election.

recall The process for removing an elected official from office.

referendum An election on a policy issue.

initiative A procedure by which voters can propose an issue to be decided by the legislature or by the people in a referendum. It requires gathering a specified number of signatures and submitting a petition to a designated agency.

FIGURE 7.3 Westward Ho!

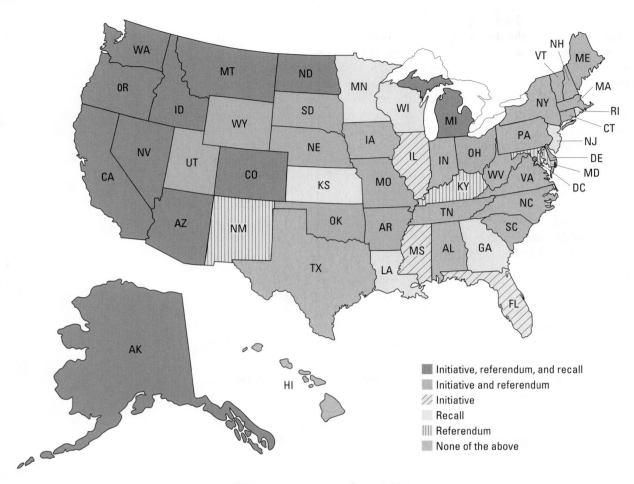

Legend:
- ■ Initiative, referendum, and recall
- ■ Initiative and referendum
- ▨ Initiative
- □ Recall
- ▥ Referendum
- ■ None of the above

This map shows quite clearly the western basis of the initiative, referendum, and recall mechanisms intended to place government power directly in the hands of the people. Advocates of "direct legislation" sought to bypass entrenched powers in state legislatures. Established groups and parties in the East dismissed them as radicals and cranks, but they gained the support of farmers and miners in the Midwest and West. The Progressive forces usually aligned with Democrats in western state legislatures to enact their proposals, often against Republican opposition.

Source: Dane M. Waters, *The Initiative and Referendum Almanac* (Durham, N.C.: Carolina Academic Press, 2003), and the National Conference on State Legislatures at <http://www.ncsl.org/programs/legman/elect/recallprovision.htm>.

of money needed to run a campaign to approve (or defeat) a referendum. In 1998, opponents of a measure to allow casino gambling on Native American land in California spent $25.8 million. This huge sum, however, pales in comparison to the $66.2 million spent during the campaign by the tribes that supported the measure. The initiative passed.[35]

Clearly, citizens can exercise great power over government policy through the mechanisms of the initiative and the referendum. What is not clear is whether these forms of direct democracy improve on the policies made by representatives elected for that purpose. On the other hand, recent research has shown that—especially in midterm elections, which are characterized by low turnout—ballot measures tend to increase voting turnout, knowledge of issues, and campaign contributions to interest groups.[36]

If the Internet had been around during their era, Progressives certainly would have endorsed it as a mechanism of direct democracy. At an elementary level, the Internet allows ordinary citizens who seek to initiate legislation to collect on petitions the thousands of signatures needed to place the proposal on the ballot.[37] At a more advanced level, the Internet encourages much closer connections between citizens and their elected and appointed government officials, as more government agencies go online. A 2003 survey of government websites found 1,603 at the state level, 48 at the national level, and 13 for federal courts.[38]

Voting for Candidates

We have saved for last the most visible form of political participation: voting to choose candidates for public office. Voting for candidates serves democratic government in two ways. First, citizens can choose the candidates they think will best serve their interests. If citizens choose candidates who are "like themselves" in personal traits or party affiliation, elected officials should tend to think as their constituents do on political issues and automatically reflect the majority's views when making public policy.

Second, voting allows the people to reelect the officials they guessed right about and to kick out those they guessed wrong about. This function is very different from the first. It makes public officials accountable for their behavior through the reward-and-punishment mechanism of elections. It assumes that officeholders are motivated to respond to public opinion by the threat of electoral defeat. It also assumes that the voters know what politicians are doing while they are in office and participate actively in the electoral process. We look at the factors that underlie voting choice in Chapter 9. Here, we examine Americans' reliance on the electoral process.

In national politics, voters seem content to elect just two executive officers—the president and vice president—and to trust the president to appoint a cabinet to round out his administration. But at the state and local levels, voters insist on selecting all kinds of officials. Every state elects a governor (and forty-five elect a lieutenant governor). Forty-two elect an attorney general; thirty-nine, a treasurer; thirty-seven, a secretary of state. The list goes on, down through superintendents of schools, secretaries of agriculture, controllers, boards of education, and public utilities commissioners. Elected county officials commonly include commissioners, a sheriff, a treasurer, a clerk, a superintendent of schools, and a judge (often several). At the local level, voters elect all but about 600 of 15,300 school boards across the nation.[39] Instead of trusting state and local chief executives to appoint lesser administrators (as we do for more important offices at the national level), we expect voters to choose intelligently among scores of candidates they meet for the first time on a complex ballot in the polling booth.

In the American version of democracy, our laws recognize no limit to voters' ability to make informed choices among candidates and thus to control government through voting. The reasoning seems to be that elections are good;

 Can you explain why . . .
Americans might be said to vote *more* than citizens in other countries?

therefore, more elections are better, and the most elections are best. By this thinking, the United States clearly has the best and most democratic government in the world because it is the undisputed champion at holding elections. The author of a study that compared elections in the United States with elections in twenty-six other democracies concluded:

> No country can approach the United States in the frequency and variety of elections, and thus in the amount of electoral participation to which its citizens have a right. No other country elects its lower house as often as every two years, or its president as frequently as every four years. No other country popularly elects its state governors and town mayors; no other has as wide a variety of nonrepresentative offices (judges, sheriffs, attorneys general, city treasurers, and so on) subject to election. . . . The average American is entitled to do far more electing—probably by a factor of three or four—than the citizen of any other democracy.[40]

However, we learn from "Compared with What? Voter Turnout in European and American Elections Since 1945" that the United States ranks at the bottom of fifteen European countries in voter turnout in national elections. How do we square low voter turnout with Americans' devotion to elections as an instrument of democratic government? To complicate matters further, how do we square low voter turnout with the findings in "Compared with What? Popular Participation in Politics" (see pages 200–201)? Americans seem to participate in politics in various ways as much as citizens in other democracies, except for voting.

★ Explaining Political Participation

As explained, political participation can be unconventional or conventional, can require little or much initiative, and can serve to support the government or influence its decisions. Researchers have found that people who take part in some form of political behavior often do not take part in others. For example, citizens who contact public officials to obtain special benefits may not vote regularly, participate in campaigns, or even contact officials about broader social issues. In fact, because particularized contacting serves individual rather than public interests, it is not even considered political behavior by some people.

This section examines some factors that affect the more obvious forms of political participation, with particular emphasis on voting. The first task is to determine how much patterns of participation vary within the United States over time.

Patterns of Participation over Time

Did Americans become more politically apathetic in the 1990s than they were in the 1960s? The answer lies in Figure 7.4, which plots several measures of participation from 1952 through 2004. The graph shows little variation over time in the percentage of citizens who worked for candidates or attended party meetings. Interest in election campaigns and persuading people how to vote have actually tended to increase. Nevertheless, except for a spurt in 1992 due

Compared with What?

Voter Turnout in European and American Elections Since 1945

Compared with turnout rates in all fifteen established members of the European Union, voter turnout for American presidential elections ranks at the bottom, and turnout for American congressional elections ranks even lower. The European data show the mean percentages of the registered electorate voting in all parliamentary elections from 1945 through 2002. The American data for all presidential and congressional elections from 1950 to 2004 show voters as percentages of the eligible voting-age population (those eighteen and older, excluding noncitizens and ineligible felons). Turnout in U.S. elections tends to average about fifteen points higher in presidential years than in congressional years. As discussed in the text, low turnout in the United States is partly due to requiring voters to register on their own initiative. The governments in virtually all the other nations automatically register eligible citizens as voters.

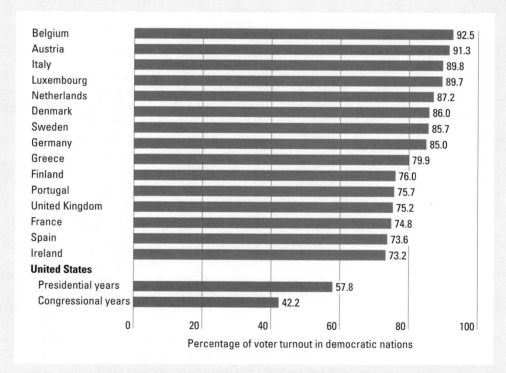

	Percentage
Belgium	92.5
Austria	91.3
Italy	89.8
Luxembourg	89.7
Netherlands	87.2
Denmark	86.0
Sweden	85.7
Germany	85.0
Greece	79.9
Finland	76.0
Portugal	75.7
United Kingdom	75.2
France	74.8
Spain	73.6
Ireland	73.2
United States	
Presidential years	57.8
Congressional years	42.2

Percentage of voter turnout in democratic nations

Sources: International IDEA, *Voter Turnout in Western Europe Since 1945* (Stockholm, Sweden: International Institute for Democracy and Electoral Assistance, 2004), p. 18; and Harold W. Stanley and Richard G. Niemi, *Vital Statistics on American Politics, 2005–2006* (Washington, D.C.: CQ Press, 2006), pp. 12–13.

FIGURE 7.4 Electoral Participation in the United States over Time

Participation patterns from five decades show that in the 1980s Americans participated in election campaigns about as much as or more than they did in the 1950s on every indicator except voting. The graph shows little variation over time in the percentage of citizens who worked on campaigns and attended party meetings. In fact, interest in election campaigns and efforts at persuasion tended to increase. Voting turnout during this period tended to decline until spurting in 1992 (when Ross Perot won 19 percent of the vote as a third candidate) and in 2004 (following the razor-close 2000 presidential election). This long-term decline in turnout runs counter to the rise in educational level, a puzzle that is discussed in the text.

Source: American National Election Surveys, University of Michigan, available at <http://www.umich.edu/~nes/nesguide/gd-index.htm>; and Harold W. Stanley and Richard G. Niemi, *Vital Statistics on American Politics, 2005–2006* (Washington, D.C.: CQ Press, 2006), Table 1.1. The percentage voting in elections is based on the eligible voter population, not simply those of voting age.

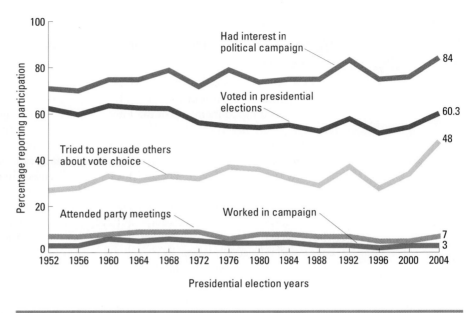

to Ross Perot's novel candidacy, voter turnout declined overall, sinking to 49 percent in 1996, before rising to a majority of the electorate in 2004. Note that *the only line that shows a downward trend before 2004 is voting in elections.* The plot has thickened: not only is voter turnout low in the United States compared with that in other countries, but turnout has basically declined over time. Moreover, while voting has decreased, other forms of participation have remained stable or even increased. What is going on? Who votes? Who does not? Why? And does it really matter?

The Standard Socioeconomic Explanation

Researchers have found that socioeconomic status is a good indicator of most types of conventional political participation. People with more education, higher incomes, and white-collar or professional occupations tend to be more aware of the effect of politics on their lives, to know what can be done to influence government actions, and to have the necessary resources (time and money) to take action. So they are more likely to participate in politics than are people of lower socioeconomic status. This relationship between socioeconomic status and conventional political involvement is called the **standard socioeconomic model** of participation.[41]

standard socioeconomic model A relationship between socioeconomic status and conventional political involvement: people with higher status and more education are more likely to participate than those with lower status.

Unconventional political behavior is related to socioeconomic status, and in much the same way. Those who protest against U.S. government policies tend to be better educated. Moreover, this relationship holds in other countries too. One scholar notes: "Protest in advanced industrial democracies is not simply an outlet for the alienated and deprived; just the opposite often occurs."[42]

In one major way, however, those who engage in unconventional political behavior differ from those who participate more conventionally: protesters tend to be younger.

Obviously, socioeconomic status does not account for all the differences in the ways people choose to participate in politics, even for conventional participation. Another important variable is age. As just noted, young people are more likely to take part in political protests, but they are less likely to participate in conventional politics. Voting rates tend to increase as people grow older, until about age sixty-five, when physical infirmities begin to lower rates again.[43]

Two other variables—race and gender—have been related to participation in the past, but as times have changed, so have those relationships. Blacks, who had very low participation rates in the 1950s, now participate at rates comparable to whites when differences in socioeconomic status are taken into account.[44] Women also exhibited low participation rates in the past, but gender differences in political participation have virtually disappeared.[45] (The one exception is in attempting to persuade others how to vote, which women are less likely to do than men.)[46] Recent research on the social context of voting behavior has shown that married men and women are more likely to vote than those of either sex living without a spouse.[47]

Of all the social and economic variables, education is the strongest single factor in explaining most types of conventional political participation. A major study on civic participation details the impact of education:

> It affects the acquisition of skills; it channels opportunities for high levels of income and occupation; it places individuals in institutional settings where they can be recruited to political activity; and it fosters psychological and cognitive engagement with politics.[48]

Figure 7.5 shows the striking relationship between level of formal education and various types of conventional political behavior. The strong link between education and electoral participation raises questions about low voter turnout in the United States, both over time and relative to other democracies. The fact is that the proportion of individuals with college degrees is greater in the United States than in other countries. Moreover, that proportion has been increasing steadily. Why, then, is voter turnout in elections so low? And why has it been dropping over time?

Low Voter Turnout in America

Economists wonder why people vote at all. In economic models of rational behavior, individuals avoid actions that have no payoff, and elections are rarely so close that an individual voter decides an outcome.[49] In contrast, political scientists wonder why citizens fail to vote. Voting is a low-initiative form of participation that can satisfy all three motives for political participation: showing allegiance to the nation, obtaining particularized benefits, and influencing broad policy. How then do we explain the decline in voter turnout in the United States, and—recalling that voting by both races in the South increased due to enfranchisement of African Americans—especially the decline in turnout in nonsouthern states? (See "Looking to the Future: Will the South Rise over the North?")

FIGURE 7.5 Effects of Education on Political Participation

Education has a powerful effect on political participation in the United States. These data from a 2004 sample show that level of education is directly related to five different forms of conventional political participation. (Respondents tend to overstate whether they voted.)

Source: This analysis was based on the 2004 National Election Study done by the Center for Political Studies, University of Michigan, and distributed by the Inter-University Consortium for Political and Social Research, Ann Arbor, Michigan.

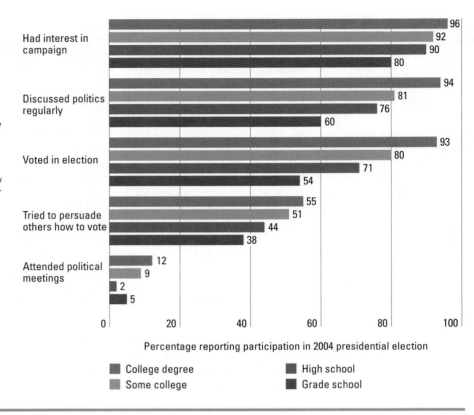

Percentage reporting participation in 2004 presidential election

■ College degree   ■ High school
■ Some college   ■ Grade school

Can you explain why . . . lowering the voting age from twenty-one to eighteen also lowered the national rate of voter turnout?

The Decline in Voting over Time. The graph of voter turnout in Figure 7.6 shows a large drop between the 1968 and 1972 elections. During this period (in 1971, actually) Congress proposed and the states ratified the Twenty-sixth Amendment, which expanded the electorate by lowering the voting age from twenty-one to eighteen. Because people younger than twenty-one are much less likely to vote, their eligibility actually reduced the overall national turnout rate (the percentage of those eligible to vote who actually vote). To increase turnout of young people, an organization called Rock the Vote was formed in 1990 within the recording industry (later incorporating the entertainment and sports communities) to mobilize young people "to create positive social and political change in their lives and communities" and "to increase youth voter turnout."[50] Despite such efforts, voting by those under age twenty-four has remained very low, but turnout rates increase as these young people age, which suggests that voting is habit forming.[51] Although young nonvoters inevitably vote more often as they grow up, observers estimate that the enfranchisement of eighteen-year-olds accounts for about one or two percentage points in the total decline in turnout since 1952. Nevertheless, that still leaves more than ten percentage points to be explained.[52]

Voter turnout has declined in most established democracies since the 1980s, but not as much as in the United States. Given that educational levels

Looking to the Future

Will the South Rise over the North?

Before the civil rights movement forced increased registration of African Americans in the eleven states of the old Confederacy, the Deep South was solidly Democratic. Contests for public office occurred in primary elections within the Democratic Party prior to the November general elections, so turnout was low in presidential elections. Two things changed that: (1) increased black registration sparked increased white registration, and (2) an increase in Republican voting by white southerners produced more party competition, which increased turnout in general elections. That explains why voting turnout in the South has increased since 1952. But why has voting turnout *decreased* in northern states over the same period? Do you expect turnout in southern states to surpass that in northern states? What might occur in the future?

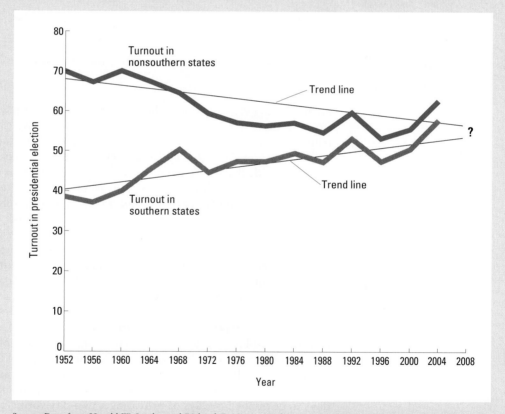

Source: Data from Harold W. Stanley and Richard G. Niemi, *Vital Statistics on American Politics, 2005–2006* (Washington, D.C.: CQ Press, 2006), Table 1.1.

FIGURE 7.6	**The Decline of Voter Turnout: An Unsolved Puzzle**

Education strongly predicts the likelihood of voting in the United States. The percentage of adult citizens with a high school education or more has grown steadily since the end of World War II, but the overall rate of voter turnout has trended downward in presidential elections since 1960—except for spikes in the voting turnout in 1992 and 2004. Why turnout has decreased as education has increased is an unsolved puzzle in American voting behavior.

Source: American National Election Surveys, University of Michigan, available at <http://www.umich.edu/~nes/nesguide/gd-index.htm>; and Harold W. Stanley and Richard G. Niemi, *Vital Statistics on American Politics, 2005–2006* (Washington, D.C.: CQ Press, 2006), Table 1.1. The percentage voting in elections is based on the eligible voter population, not the voting-age population.

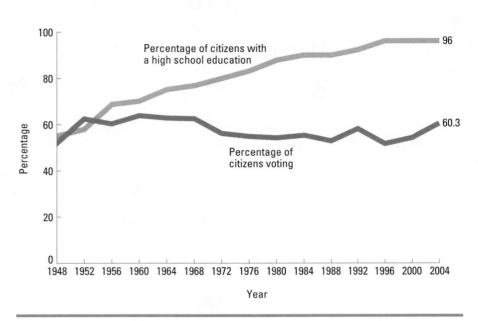

are increasing virtually everywhere, the puzzle is why turnout has decreased instead of increased. Many researchers have tried to solve this puzzle.[53] Some attribute most of the decline to changes in voters' attitudes toward politics: beliefs that government is no longer responsive to citizens, that politicians are too packaged, that campaigns are too long.[54] Another is a change in attitude toward political parties, along with a decline in the extent to which citizens identify with a political party (a topic we discuss in Chapter 8).[55] According to these psychological explanations, voter turnout in the United States is not likely to increase until the government does something to restore people's faith in the effectiveness of voting—with or without political parties. According to the age explanation, turnout in the United States is destined to remain a percentage point or two below its highs of the 1960s because of the lower voting rate of citizens younger than twenty-one.

U.S. Turnout Versus Turnout in Other Countries. Scholars cite two factors to explain the low voter turnout in the United States compared with that in other countries. First are the differences in voting laws and administrative machinery. In a few countries, voting is compulsory, and obviously turnout is extremely high. But other methods can encourage voting: declaring election days to be public holidays or providing a two-day voting period. In 1845, Congress set election day for the first Tuesday after the first Monday in November, but a new reform group—called "Why Tuesday?"—is asking Congress to change election day to a weekend.[56]

Furthermore, nearly every other democratic country places the burden of registration on the government rather than on the individual voter. This is important. Voting in the United States is a two-stage process, and the first stage

Rock the Vote: Political power for young people.

Rock the Vote is a non-profit, non-partisan organization, founded in 1990 in response to a wave of attacks on freedom of speech and artistic expression.

Rock the Vote engages youth in the political process by incorporating the entertainment community and youth culture into its activities. From actors to musicians, comedians to athletes, Rock the Vote harnesses cutting-edge trends and pop culture to make political participation cool.

Rock the Vote mobilizes young people to create positive social and political change in their lives and communities. The goal of Rock the Vote's media campaigns and street team activities is to increase youth voter turnout. Rock the Vote coordinates voter registration drives, get-out-the-vote events, and voter education efforts, all with the intention of ensuring that young people take advantage of their right to vote.

Rock the Vote's work doesn't end when the polls close. We empower young people to create change in their communities and take action on the issues they care about. Regardless of whether youth are signing petitions, running for office, contacting their elected officials, or taking up a sign in protest, they are all rocking the vote.

Rock the Vote

In 1990, a group from the recording, entertainment, and sports industries formed a nonpartisan nonprofit organization, Rock the Vote, in response to attacks on freedom of speech and artistic expression. Their website at <www.rockthevote.com> claims that the site registered 1.4 million voters in the last election. *(Reprinted with permission from Rock the Vote, Washington Office)*

(going to the proper officials to register) has required more initiative than the second stage (going to the polling booth to cast a ballot). In most American states, the registration process has been separate from the voting process in terms of both time (usually voters had to register weeks in advance of an election) and geography (often voters had to register at the county courthouse, not their polling place).[57] One researcher who studied three states (Minnesota, Maine, and Wisconsin) that allowed citizens to register and vote on the same day estimated that such practices nationwide would alone add five points to the turnout rate.[58] Moreover, registration procedures often have been obscure, requiring potential voters to call around to find out what to do. Furthermore, people who move (and younger people move more frequently) have to reregister. In short, although voting requires little initiative, registration usually has required high initiative. If we compute voter turnout on the basis of those who are registered to vote, about 80 percent of Americans vote, a figure that moves the United States to the middle (but not the top) of all democratic nations.[59]

To increase turnout, Congress in 1993 passed the so-called motor-voter law, which aimed to increase voter registration by requiring states to permit registration by mail and when obtaining or renewing a driver's license and by encouraging registration at other facilities, such as public assistance agencies. By the 1997–1998 election cycle, over half of all voter registration took place through motor vehicle agencies and other agencies specified in the motor-voter law. Although registration rose to its highest level for a congressional election since 1970, the voting rate in 1998 declined by almost 2.4 percent below the comparable 1994 election.[60]

Besides burdensome registration procedures, another factor usually cited to explain low turnout in American elections is the lack of political parties that mobilize the vote of particular social groups, especially lower-income and less educated people. American parties do make an effort to get out the vote, but neither party is as closely linked to specific groups as are parties in many other countries, where certain parties work hand in hand with specific ethnic, occupational, or religious groups. Research shows that strong party–group links can significantly increase turnout.[61] One important study claims that "changing mobilization patterns by parties, campaigns, and social movements accounts for at least half of the decline in electoral participation since the 1960s."[62] Other research suggests that although well-funded, vigorous campaigns mobilize citizens to vote, the effect depends on the type of citizens and the nature of the election. Highly educated, low-income citizens are more likely to be stimulated to vote than are less educated, high-income citizens, but lower-class citizens can be more easily mobilized to vote in presidential elections than in nonpresidential elections.[63] To these explanations for low voter turnout in the United States—the traditional burden of registration and the lack of strong party–group links—we add another. Although the act of voting requires low initiative, the process of learning about the scores of candidates on the ballot in American elections requires a great deal of initiative. Some people undoubtedly fail to vote simply because they feel inadequate to the task of deciding among candidates for the many offices on the ballot in U.S. elections.

Teachers, newspaper columnists, and public affairs groups tend to worry a great deal about low voter turnout in the United States, suggesting that it signifies some sort of political sickness—or at least that it gives us a bad mark for democracy. Some others who study elections closely seem less concerned.[64] One scholar argues:

> Turnout rates do not indicate the amount of electing—the frequency . . . , the range of offices and decisions, the "value" of the vote—to which a country's citizens are entitled. . . . Thus, although the turnout rate in the United States is below that of most other democracies, American citizens do not necessarily do less voting than other citizens; most probably, they do more.[65]

Despite such words of assurance, the nagging thought remains that turnout ought to be higher, so various organizations mount get-out-the-vote campaigns before elections. Civic leaders often back the campaigns because they value voting for its contribution to political order.

★ Participation and Freedom, Equality, and Order

As we have seen, Americans do participate in government in various ways and to a reasonable extent, compared with citizens of other countries. What is the relationship of political participation to the values of freedom, equality, and order?

Participation and Freedom

From the standpoint of normative theory, the relationship between participation and freedom is clear. Individuals should be free to participate in government and politics in the way they want and as much as they want. And they should be free not to participate as well. Ideally, all barriers to participation (such as restrictive voting registration and limitations on campaign expenditures) should be abolished, as should any schemes for compulsory voting. According to the normative perspective, we should not worry about low voter turnout because citizens should have the freedom not to vote as well as to vote.

In theory, freedom to participate also means that individuals should be able to use their wealth, connections, knowledge, organizational power (including sheer numbers in organized protests), or any other resource to influence government decisions, provided they do so legally. Of all these resources, the individual vote may be the weakest—and the least important—means of exerting political influence. Obviously, then, freedom as a value in political participation favors those with the resources to advance their own political self-interest.

Participation and Equality

The relationship between participation and equality is also clear. Each citizen's ability to influence government should be equal to that of every other citizen, so that differences in personal resources do not work against the poor or the otherwise disadvantaged. Elections, then, serve the ideal of equality better than any other means of political participation. Formal rules for counting ballots—in particular, one person, one vote—cancel differences in resources among individuals.

At the same time, groups of people who have few resources individually can combine their votes to wield political power. Various European ethnic groups exercised this type of power in the late nineteenth and early twentieth centuries, when their votes won them entry to the sociopolitical system and allowed them to share in its benefits. More recently, blacks, Hispanics, homosexuals, and those with disabilities have used their voting power to gain political recognition. However, minorities often have had to use unconventional forms of participation to win the right to vote. As two major scholars of political participation put it, "Protest is the great equalizer, the political action that weights intensity as well as sheer numbers."[66]

Participation and Order

The relationship between participation and order is complicated. Some types of participation (pledging allegiance, voting) promote order and so are encouraged

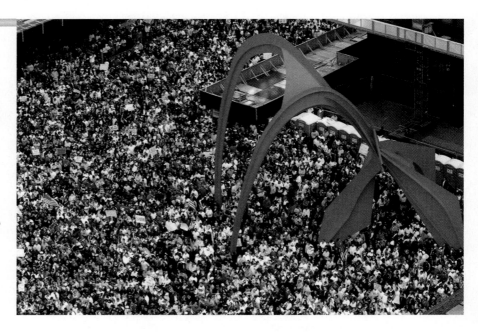

Monster Rally
A huge crowd of protesters swirled beneath Alexander Calder's giant "Flamingo" sculpture in downtown Chicago on March 10, 2006. Estimated by police at about 100,000 people, it was one of the largest pro-immigration rallies in U.S. history. The marchers favored legislation that would provide legal status for most undocumented immigrants and facilitate visits by their relatives. *(Chicago Tribune photo by Antonio Perez. All rights reserved. Used with permission.)*

by those who value order; other types promote disorder and so are discouraged. Many citizens—men and women alike—even resisted giving women the right to vote for fear of upsetting the social order by altering the traditional roles of men and women.

Both conventional and unconventional participation can lead to the ouster of government officials, but the regime—the political system itself—is threatened more by unconventional participation. To maintain order, the government has a stake in converting unconventional participation to conventional participation whenever possible. We can easily imagine this tactic being used by authoritarian governments, but democratic governments also use it. According to documents obtained after September 11, 2001, the FBI not only increased surveillance of groups with suspected ties to foreign terrorists but also began monitoring other groups that protested public policies.[67]

Popular protests can spread beyond original targets. Think about student unrest on college campuses during the Vietnam War. In private and public colleges alike, thousands of students stopped traffic, occupied buildings, destroyed property, boycotted classes, disrupted lectures, staged guerrilla theater, and behaved in other unconventional ways to protest the war, racism, capitalism, the behavior of their college presidents, the president of the United States, the military establishment, and all other institutions. (We are not exaggerating here. Students did such things at our home universities after members of the National Guard shot and killed four students at a demonstration at Kent State University in Ohio on May 4, 1970.)

Confronted by civil strife and disorder in the nation's institutions of higher learning, Congress took action. On March 23, 1971, it enacted and sent to the states the proposed Twenty-sixth Amendment, lowering the voting age to eighteen. Three-quarters of the state legislatures had to ratify the amendment before it became part of the Constitution. Astonishingly, thirty-eight states (the required number) complied by July 1, establishing a new speed record for ratification and cutting the old record nearly in half.[68] (Ironically, voting rights were not high on the list of students' demands.)

Testimony by members of Congress before the Judiciary Committee stated that the eighteen-year-old vote would "harness the energy of young people and direct it into useful and constructive channels," to keep students from becoming "more militant" and engaging "in destructive activities of a dangerous nature."[69] As one observer argued, the right to vote was extended to eighteen-year-olds not because young people demanded it but because "public officials believed suffrage expansion to be a means of institutionalizing youths' participation in politics, which would, in turn, curb disorder."[70]

★ Participation and the Models of Democracy

Ostensibly, elections are institutional mechanisms that implement democracy by allowing citizens to choose among candidates or issues. But elections also serve several other important purposes:[71]

- Elections socialize political activity. They transform what might otherwise consist of sporadic, citizen-initiated acts into a routine public function. That is, the opportunity to vote for change encourages citizens to refrain from demonstrating in the streets. This helps preserve government stability by containing and channeling away potentially disruptive or dangerous forms of mass political activity.

- Elections institutionalize access to political power. They allow ordinary citizens to run for political office or to play an important role in selecting political leaders. Working to elect a candidate encourages the campaign worker to identify problems or propose solutions to the newly elected official.

- Elections bolster the state's power and authority. The opportunity to participate in elections helps convince citizens that the government is responsive to their needs and wants, which reinforces its legitimacy.

Participation and Majoritarianism

Although the majoritarian model assumes that government responsiveness to popular demands comes through mass participation in politics, majoritarianism views participation rather narrowly. It favors conventional, institutionalized behavior—primarily voting in elections. Because majoritarianism relies on counting votes to determine what the majority wants, its bias toward equality in political participation is strong. Clearly, a class bias in voting exists because of the strong influence of socioeconomic status on turnout. Simply put, better-educated, wealthier citizens are more likely to participate in elections, and get-out-the-vote campaigns cannot counter this distinct bias.[72] Because it favors collective decisions formalized through elections, majoritarianism has little place for motivated, resourceful individuals to exercise private influence over government actions.

Majoritarianism also limits individual freedom in another way: its focus on voting as the major means of mass participation narrows the scope of conventional political behavior by defining which political actions are "orderly" and acceptable. By favoring equality and order in political participation, majoritarianism goes hand in hand with the ideological orientation of communitarianism (see Chapter 1).

Participation and Pluralism

Resourceful citizens who want the government's help with problems find a haven in the pluralist model of democracy. A decentralized and organizationally complex form of government allows many points of access and accommodates various forms of conventional participation in addition to voting. For example, wealthy people and well-funded groups can afford to hire lobbyists to press their interests in Congress. In one view of pluralist democracy, citizens are free to ply and wheedle public officials to further their own selfish visions of the public good. From another viewpoint, pluralism offers citizens the opportunity to be treated as individuals when dealing with the government, to influence policymaking in special circumstances, and to fulfill (insofar as possible in representative government) their social potential through participation in community affairs.

Summary

Terrorism is a perverse form of political action that threatens democratic government. To have "government by the people," the people must participate in politics. Conventional forms of participation—contacting officials and voting in elections—come most quickly to mind. However, citizens can also participate in politics in unconventional ways—staging sit-down strikes in public buildings, blocking traffic, and so on. Most citizens disapprove of most forms of unconventional political behavior. Yet blacks and women used unconventional tactics to win important political and legal rights, including the right to vote.

People are motivated to participate in politics for various reasons: to show support for their country, to obtain particularized benefits for themselves or their friends, or to influence broad public policy. Their political actions may demand either little political knowledge or personal initiative, or a great deal of both.

The press often paints an unflattering picture of political participation in America. Clearly, the proportion of the electorate that votes in general elections in the United States has dropped and is far below that in other nations. The United States tends to show as much citizen participation in politics as other nations, however, when a broad range of conventional and unconventional political behavior is considered. Voter turnout in the United States suffers by comparison with that of other nations because of differences in voter registration requirements. We also lack institutions (especially strong political parties) that increase voter registration and help bring those of lower socioeconomic status to the polls.

People's tendency to participate in politics is strongly related to their socioeconomic status. Education, one component of socioeconomic status, is the single strongest predictor of conventional political participation in the United States. Because of the strong effect of socioeconomic status, the political system is potentially biased toward the interests of higher-status people. Pluralist democracy, which provides many avenues for resourceful citizens to influence government decisions, tends to increase this bias. Majoritarian democracy, which relies heavily on elections and the concept of one person, one vote, offers citizens without great personal resources the opportunity to influence government decisions through elections.

Elections also serve to legitimize government simply by involving the masses in government through voting. Whether voting means anything depends on the nature of voters' choices in elections. The range of choices available is a function of the nation's political parties, the topic of the next chapter.

Internet activities and reading suggestions for this chapter are available on the *Online Study Center*

To complete the multimedia assignments for this chapter, go to AmericansGoverning.org.

Political Parties

8

(Photo by Chuck Timm/Libertarian Party of LaPorte County, Indiana)

Online Study Center
This icon will direct you to resources and activities on the website
college.hmco.com/pic/jandaupdate9e

What is "the fastest-growing political party" in the United States? The Libertarian Party, Green Party, and American Independent Party—among others—claim to be "the fastest growing" in scores of postings on the Internet. The Democratic and Republican Parties—already fully grown—stand above the controversy. These two major parties together took 99 percent of the 122,300,000 votes for president in 2004.[1] Minor parties can tout scattered electoral gains from small beginnings, but their victories pale before the massive electoral success of the Democratic Party and the Republican Party. Unlike elections in most other democracies, elections in the United States are ruled by a party duopoly.

The extent of the Democrats' and Republicans' supremacy in the electoral process can be seen in comparison with the Libertarian Party. Although its claim to be the "fastest growing" may be disputed, the Libertarian Party is conceded to be the third largest in the United States. Founded in 1971, the party embraces the libertarian philosophy set forth in Chapter 1 (see page 22). The preamble to its 2004 party platform begins, "As Libertarians, we seek a world of liberty; a world in which all individuals are sovereign over their own lives, and no one is forced to sacrifice his or her values for the benefit of others."[2] Unlike many active members in the Democratic and Republican Parties, most Libertarians seem aware of and committed to their party's platform. The national party maintains a headquarters in Washington, and its website links to party organizations in all fifty states, where the party claims some elected officials at the state and local levels. The party is also more active than any other minor party in nominating candidates to run in national elections.

Libertarian candidates for president and vice president have run in all nine presidential elections since 1972. In the 2004 national election, the party nominated far more candidates for the U.S. House (145 out of 435 up for election) and the U.S. Senate (20 out of 34) than any other minor party.[3] But despite its clear and consistent philosophy, its national and state organizations, and its record of nominating candidates, the Libertarian Party has not fared well at the polls.

No Libertarian presidential candidate ever won more than a million votes. The party's best showing was 921,300 presidential votes in 1980—the only time that a Libertarian candidate won more than 1 percent of the vote.[4] In the congressional races of 2004, all its 145 House candidates together won less than 1 percent of the total vote cast in House elections; and its 20 Senate candidates won less than 1 percent of the vote in Senate elections.[5]

No Libertarian Party candidate was ever elected to Congress. It is true that Ron Paul, the Libertarian Party presidential candidate in 1988, was elected to Congress in 1996. However, he ran in the Republican primary election, was elected as a Republican, and still serves as a Republican. Indeed, no member in Congress belongs to any third party, although two senators are independents. ★

U.S. politics is dominated by a two-party system. The Democratic and Republican Parties have dominated national and state politics for more than 125 years. Their domination is more complete than that of any pair of parties in any other democratic government. Although all democracies have some form of multiparty politics, very few have a stable two-party system, Britain being the most notable exception (see "Compared with What? Only Two to Tangle"). Most people take our two-party system for granted, not realizing that it is arguably the most distinctive feature of American politics.

Why do we have any political parties? What functions do they perform? How did we become a nation of Democrats and Republicans? Do these parties truly differ in their platforms and behavior? Are parties really necessary for democratic government, or do they just get in the way of citizens and their government? In this chapter, we will answer these questions by examining political parties, perhaps the most misunderstood element of American politics.

★ Political Parties and Their Functions

According to democratic theory, the primary means by which citizens control their government is voting in free elections. Most Americans agree that voting is important. Of those surveyed after the 2004 presidential campaign, 92 percent felt that elections make the government "pay attention to what the people think."[6] Americans are not nearly as supportive of the role played by political parties in elections, however. When asked if Ross Perot should run for president in 1996 as "head of a third party which would also run candidates in state and local races" or "by himself as an independent candidate," 60 percent of a national sample favored his running without a party.[7] Apparently, many Americans think that politics would function better without political parties.

Nevertheless, Americans are quick to condemn as "undemocratic" countries that do not regularly hold elections contested by political parties. In truth, Americans have a love-hate relationship with political parties. They believe that parties are necessary for democratic government; at the same time, they think parties are somehow obstructionist and not to be trusted. This distrust is particularly strong among younger voters. To better appreciate the role of political parties in democratic government, we must understand exactly what parties are and what they do.

What Is a Political Party?

A **political party** is an organization that sponsors candidates for political office *under the organization's name*. The italicized part of this definition is important. True political parties select individuals to run for public office through a formal **nomination** process, which designates them as the parties' official candidates. This activity distinguishes the Democratic and Republican Parties from interest groups. The AFL-CIO and the National Association of Manufacturers are interest groups. They often support candidates, but they do not nominate them to run as their avowed representatives. If they did, they would be transformed into political parties. In short, the sponsoring of candidates, designated as representatives of the organization, is what defines an organization as a party.

political party An organization that sponsors candidates for political office under the organization's name.

nomination Designation as an official candidate of a political party.

Compared with What?

Only Two to Tangle

Compared with party systems in other countries, the U.S. two-party system is unusual indeed. Most democracies have multiparty systems in which four or five parties win enough seats in the legislature to contest for government power. Even the few countries classified as having two-party systems have minor parties that regularly contest seats and win enough votes to complicate national politics. The United Kingdom is the most notable example of a country reputed to have a two-party system. The purer U.S. pattern of two-party politics shows clearly in these graphs of votes cast for party candidates running for the U.S. House compared with votes cast for party candidates running for the British House of Commons.

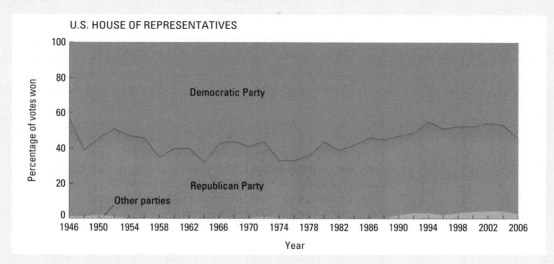

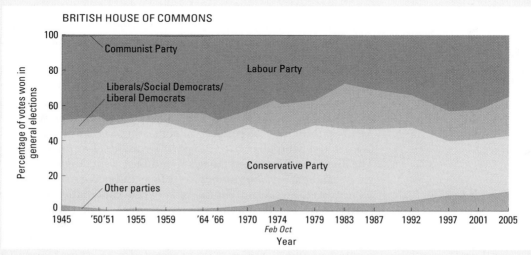

Sources: Thomas T. Mackie and Richard Rose, *The International Almanac of Electoral History,* 3rd ed. (Washington, D.C.: CQ Press, 1991); <http://www.electionguide.org/2005.htm> and <http://www.thegreenpapers.com/G06/HouseVoteByParty.phtml>.

Most democratic theorists agree that a modern nation-state cannot practice democracy without at least two political parties that regularly contest elections. In fact, the link between democracy and political parties is so firm that many people define *democratic government* in terms of competitive party politics.[8] A former president of the American Political Science Association held that even for a small nation, "democracy is impossible save in terms of parties."[9]

Party Functions

Parties contribute to democratic government through the functions they perform for the **political system**—the set of interrelated institutions that link people with government. Four of the most important party functions are nominating candidates for election to public office, structuring the voting choice in elections, proposing alternative government programs, and coordinating the actions of government officials.

Nominating Candidates. Is *any and every* American citizen qualified to hold public office? Surprisingly, a few scholars have taken this position, proposing that government positions be filled "randomly"—that is, through lotteries.[10] Most observers, however, hold that political leadership requires certain abilities (if not special knowledge or public experience) and that not just anyone should be entrusted to head the government. The question then becomes, Who should be chosen among those who offer to lead? Without political parties, voters would confront a bewildering array of self-nominated candidates, each seeking votes on the basis of personal friendships, celebrity status, or name recognition. Parties can provide a form of quality control for their nominees through the process of peer review. Party insiders, the nominees' peers, usually know the strengths and faults of potential candidates much better than average voters do and thus can judge their suitability for representing the party.

In nominating candidates, parties often do more than pass judgment on potential office seekers; sometimes they go so far as to recruit talented individuals to become candidates. In this way, parties help not only to ensure a minimum level of quality among candidates who run for office but also to raise the quality of those candidates.

Structuring the Voting Choice. Political parties help democratic government by structuring the voting choice—reducing the number of candidates on the ballot to those who have a realistic chance of winning. Established parties—those with experience in contesting elections—acquire a following of loyal voters who guarantee the party's candidates a predictable base of votes. The ability of established parties to mobilize their supporters discourages nonparty candidates from running for office and new parties from forming. Consequently, the realistic choice is between candidates offered by the major parties, reducing the amount of new information that voters need to make a rational decision. Contrast the voting decision in our stable two-party system (and the outcome) with the voter's task in the December 2003 Russian parliamentary election. Voters were confronted with more than ten parties, some newly formed for the election. Although United Russia (the main party supporting President Vladimir Putin) won only 38 percent of the popular vote, it captured almost 50 percent of the parliamentary seats.

political system A set of interrelated institutions that links people with government.

Proposing Alternative Government Programs. Parties help voters choose among candidates by proposing alternative programs of government action—the general policies their candidates will pursue if they gain office. In a stable party system, even if voters know nothing about the qualities of the parties' candidates, they can vote rationally for the candidates of the party that has policies they favor. The specific policies advocated vary from candidate to candidate and from election to election. However, the types of policies advocated by candidates of one party tend to differ from those proposed by candidates of other parties. Although there are exceptions, candidates of the same party tend to favor policies that fit their party's underlying political philosophy, or ideology.

In many countries, parties' names, such as *Conservative* and *Socialist*, reflect their political stance. The Democrats and Republicans have ideologically neutral names, but many minor parties in the United States have used their names to advertise their policies—for example, the Libertarian Party, the Socialist Party, and the Green Party.[11] The neutrality of the two major parties' names suggests that their policies are similar. This is not true. As we shall see, they regularly adopt very different policies in their platforms.

Coordinating the Actions of Government Officials. Finally, party organizations help coordinate the actions of public officials. A government based on the separation of powers, such as that of the United States, divides responsibilities for making public policy. The president and the leaders of the House and Senate are not required to cooperate with one another. Political party organizations are the major means for bridging the separate powers to produce coordinated policies that can govern the country effectively. Parties do this in two ways. First, candidates' and officeholders' political fortunes are linked to their party organization, which can bestow and withhold favors. Second, and perhaps more important in the United States, members of the same party in the presidency, the House, and the Senate tend to share political principles and thus often voluntarily cooperate in making policy.

So why do we have parties? One expert notes that successful politicians in the United States need electoral and governing majorities and that "no collection of ambitious politicians has long been able to think of a way to achieve their goals in this democracy save in terms of political parties."[12]

★ A History of U.S. Party Politics

The two major U.S. parties are among the oldest in the world. In fact, the Democratic Party, founded in 1828 but with roots reaching back to the late 1700s, has a strong claim to being the oldest party in existence. Its closest rival is the British Conservative Party, formed in 1832, two decades before the Republican Party was organized in 1854. Several generations of citizens have supported the Democratic and Republican Parties, and they are part of American history. They have become institutionalized in our political process.

The Preparty Period

Today we think of party activities as normal, even essential, to American politics. It was not always so. The Constitution makes no mention of political parties, and none existed when the Constitution was written in 1787. It was common then to refer to groups pursuing some common political interest as *factions*. Although factions were seen as inevitable in politics, they were also considered dangerous.[13] One argument for adopting the Constitution—proposed in *Federalist* No. 10 (see Chapter 3 and the appendix)—was that its federal system would prevent factional influences from controlling the government.

Factions existed even under British rule. In colonial assemblies, supporters of the governor (and thus of the Crown) were known as *Tories* or *Loyalists*, and their opponents were called *Whigs* or *Patriots*. After independence, the arguments over whether to adopt the Constitution produced a different alignment of factions. Those who backed the Constitution were loosely known as *federalists*, their opponents as *antifederalists*. At this stage, the groups could not be called parties because they did not sponsor candidates for election.

Elections then were vastly different from elections today. The Constitution provided for the president and vice president to be chosen by an **electoral college**—a body of electors who met in the capitals of their respective states to cast their ballots. Initially, in most states, the legislatures, not the voters, chose the electors (one for each senator and representative in Congress). Presidential elections in the early years of the nation, then, actually were decided by a handful of political leaders. (See Chapter 9 for a discussion of the electoral college in modern presidential politics.) Often they met in small, secret groups, called **caucuses,** to propose candidates for public office. Often these were composed of like-minded members of state legislatures and Congress. This was the setting for George Washington's election as the first president in 1789.

We can classify Washington as a federalist because he supported the Constitution, but he was not a factional leader and actually opposed factional politics. His immense prestige, coupled with his political neutrality, left Washington unopposed for the office of president, and he was elected unanimously by the electoral college. During Washington's administration, however, the political cleavage sharpened between those who favored a stronger national government and those who wanted a less powerful, more decentralized national government.

The first group, led by Alexander Hamilton, proclaimed themselves *Federalists*. The second group, led by Thomas Jefferson, called themselves *Republicans*. (Although they used the same name, they were *not* the Republicans we know today.) The Jeffersonians chose the name *Republicans* to distinguish themselves from the "aristocratic" tendencies of Hamilton's Federalists. The Federalists countered by calling the Republicans the *Democratic Republicans,* attempting to link Jefferson's party to the disorder (and beheadings) spawned by the "radical democrats" in France during the French Revolution of 1789.

The First Party System: Federalists and Democratic Republicans

Washington was reelected president unanimously in 1792, but his vice president, John Adams, was opposed by a candidate backed by the Democratic Republicans. This brief skirmish foreshadowed the nation's first major-party struggle over the presidency. Disheartened by the political split in his administration, Washington spoke out against "the baneful effects" of parties in his farewell address in 1796. Nonetheless, parties already existed in the political

electoral college A body of electors chosen by voters to cast ballots for president and vice president.

caucus A closed meeting of the members of a political party to decide questions of policy and the selection of candidates for office.

system, as Figure 8.1 shows. In the election of 1796, the Federalists supported Vice President John Adams to succeed Washington as president. The Democratic Republicans backed Thomas Jefferson for president but could not agree on a vice-presidential candidate. In the electoral college, Adams won seventy-one votes to Jefferson's sixty-eight, and both ran ahead of other candidates. At that time, the Constitution provided that the presidency would go to the candidate who won the most votes in the electoral college, with the vice presidency going to the runner-up. So Adams, a Federalist, had to accept Jefferson, a Democratic Republican, as his vice president. Obviously, the Constitution did not anticipate a presidential contest between candidates from opposing political parties.

The party function of nominating candidates emerged more clearly in the election of 1800. Both parties caucused in Congress to nominate candidates for president and vice president. The result was the first true party contest for the presidency. The Federalists nominated John Adams and Charles Pinckney; the Democratic Republicans nominated Thomas Jefferson and Aaron Burr. This time, both Democratic Republican candidates won. However, the new party organization worked too well. According to the Constitution, each elector had to vote by ballot for two persons. The Democratic Republican electors unanimously cast their two votes for Jefferson and Burr. The presidency was to go to the candidate with the most votes, but the top two candidates were tied! Although Jefferson was the party's presidential candidate and Burr its vice-presidential candidate, the Constitution empowered the House of Representatives to choose either one of them as president. After seven days and thirty-six ballots, the House decided in favor of Jefferson.

The Twelfth Amendment, ratified in 1804, prevented a repeat of the troublesome election outcomes of 1796 and 1800. It required the electoral college to vote separately for president and vice president, implicitly recognizing that parties would nominate different candidates for the two offices.

The election of 1800 marked the beginning of the end for the Federalists, who lost the next four elections. By 1820, the Federalists were no more. The Democratic Republican candidate, James Monroe, was reelected in the first presidential contest without party competition since Washington's time. (Monroe received all but one electoral vote, reportedly cast against him so that Washington would remain the only president ever elected unanimously.) Ironically, the lack of partisan competition under Monroe, in what was dubbed the "Era of Good Feelings," also fatally weakened his party, the Democratic Republicans. Lacking competition, the Democratic Republicans neglected their function of nominating candidates. In 1824, the party caucus's nominee was challenged by three other Democratic Republicans, including John Quincy Adams and Andrew Jackson, who proved to be more popular candidates among the voters in the ensuing election.

Before 1824, the parties' role in structuring the popular vote was relatively unimportant because so few people were entitled to vote. But the states began to drop restrictive requirements for voting after 1800, and voting rights for white males expanded even faster after 1815 (see Chapter 7). With the expansion of suffrage, more states began to allow the voters, rather than state legislatures, to choose the presidential electors. The 1824 election was the first in which the voters selected the presidential electors in most states. Still, the role of political parties in structuring the popular vote had not yet developed fully.

> **? Can you explain why . . .**
> President John Adams, a Federalist, had a vice president from a different political party?

FIGURE 8.1 Two-Party Systems in American History

Over time, the American party system has undergone a series of wrenching transformations. Since 1856, the Democrats and the Republicans have alternated irregularly in power, each party enjoying a long period of dominance.

Year		Democratic		National Republican / Whig	Republican
1789	Washington unanimously elected president				
1792	Washington unanimously reelected		PREPARTY PERIOD		
1796	Federalist Adams	Democratic Republican			
1800	—	Jefferson			
1804	—	Jefferson	FIRST PARTY SYSTEM		
1808	—	Madison			
1812	—	Madison			
1816	—	Monroe			
1820		Monroe	"ERA OF GOOD FEELINGS"		
1824		J. Q. Adams			
1828		Democratic Jackson		National Republican	
1832		Jackson		Whig	
1836		Van Buren		—	
1840	SECOND PARTY SYSTEM	—		Harrison	
1844		Polk			
1848		—		Taylor	
1852		Pierce		—	
1856		Buchanan			Republican
1860	Constitutional Union Southern Democrat	—			Lincoln
1864		—			Lincoln
1868		—			Grant
1872		—			Grant
1876	THIRD PARTY SYSTEM	—			Hayes
1880		—			Garfield
1884		Cleveland			—
1888	Rough Balance	—			Harrison
1892		Cleveland			—
1896		—	Populist		McKinley
1900		—			McKinley
1904		—			Roosevelt, T.
1908		—			Taft
1912	Republican Dominance	Wilson	Progressive		—
1916		Wilson			—
1920		—			Harding
1924		—			Coolidge
1928		—			Hoover
1932		Roosevelt, F. D.			—
1936		Roosevelt, F. D.			—
1940		Roosevelt, F. D.			—
1944		Roosevelt, F. D.			—
1948	Democratic Dominance	Truman	States' Rights		—
1952		—			Eisenhower
1956		—			Eisenhower
1960		Kennedy			—
1964		Johnson			—
1968		—	American Independent		Nixon
1972		—			Nixon
1976		Carter			—
1980		—	Independent		Reagan
1984		—			Reagan
1988		—			Bush, G. H. W.
1992		Clinton	Independent		—
1996		Clinton	Reform		—
2000		—	Green		Bush, G. W.
2004		—			Bush, G. W.

Although Jackson won a plurality of both the popular vote and the electoral vote in 1824, he did not win the necessary majority in the electoral college. The House of Representatives again had to decide the winner. It chose the second-place John Quincy Adams (from the established state of Massachusetts) over the voters' choice, Jackson (from the frontier state of Tennessee). The factionalism among the leaders of the Democratic Republican Party became so intense that the party split in two.

The Second Party System: Democrats and Whigs

The Jacksonian faction of the Democratic Republican Party represented the common people in the expanding South and West, and its members took pride in calling themselves simply Democrats. Jackson ran again for the presidency as a Democrat in 1828, a milestone that marked the beginning of today's Democratic Party. That election was also the first mass election in U.S. history. Although voters had directly chosen many presidential electors in 1824, the total votes cast in that election numbered fewer than 370,000. By 1828, relaxed requirements for voting (and the use of popular elections to select presidential electors in more states) had increased the vote by more than 300 percent, to more than 1.1 million.

As the electorate expanded, the parties changed. No longer could a party rely on a few political leaders in the state legislatures to control the votes cast in the electoral college. Parties now needed to campaign for votes cast by hundreds of thousands of citizens. Recognizing this new dimension of the nation's politics, the parties responded with a new method for nominating presidential candidates. Instead of selecting candidates in a closed caucus of party representatives in Congress, the parties devised the **national convention.** At these gatherings, delegates from state parties across the nation would choose candidates for president and vice president and adopt a statement of policies called a **party platform.** The Anti-Masonic Party, which was the first "third" party in American history to challenge the two major parties for the presidency, called the first national convention in 1831. The Democrats adopted the convention idea in 1832 to nominate Jackson for a second term, as did their new opponents that year, the National Republicans.

The label *National Republicans* applied to John Quincy Adams's faction of the former Democratic Republican Party. However, the National Republicans did not become today's Republican Party. Adams's followers called themselves National Republicans to signify their old Federalist preference for a strong national government, but the symbolism did not appeal to the voters, and the National Republicans lost to Jackson in 1832.

Elected to another term, Jackson began to assert the power of the nation over the states (acting more like a National Republican than a Democrat). His policies drew new opponents, who started calling him "King Andrew." A coalition made up of former National Republicans, Anti-Masons, and Jackson haters formed the Whig Party in 1834. The name referred to the English Whigs, who opposed the powers of the British throne; the implication was that Jackson was governing like a king. For the next thirty years, Democrats and Whigs alternated in the presidency. However, the issues of slavery and sectionalism eventually destroyed the Whigs from within. Although the party had won the White House in 1848 and had taken 44 percent of the vote in 1852, the Whigs were unable to field a presidential candidate in the 1856 election.

? **Can you explain why . . .**
1828 is regarded as the first mass election in history?

national convention A gathering of delegates of a single political party from across the country to choose candidates for president and vice president and to adopt a party platform.

party platform The statement of policies of a national political party.

The Current Party System: Democrats and Republicans

In the early 1850s, antislavery forces (including some Whigs and antislavery Democrats) began to organize. At meetings in Jackson, Michigan, and Ripon, Wisconsin, they recommended the formation of a new party, the Republican Party, to oppose the extension of slavery into the Kansas and Nebraska territories. This party, founded in 1854, continues as today's Republican Party.

The Republican Party entered its first presidential election in 1856. It took 33 percent of the vote, and its candidate, John Frémont, carried eleven states—all in the North. Then, in 1860, the Republicans nominated Abraham Lincoln. The Democrats were deeply divided over the slavery issue and split into two parties. The northern wing kept the Democratic Party label and nominated Stephen Douglas. The Southern Democrats ran John Breckinridge. A fourth party, the Constitutional Union Party, nominated John Bell. Breckinridge won every southern state. Lincoln took 40 percent of the popular vote and carried every northern state.

The election of 1860 is considered the first of three critical elections under the current party system.[14] A **critical election** is marked by a sharp change in the existing patterns of party loyalty among groups of voters. Moreover, this change in voting patterns, which is called an **electoral realignment,** does not end with the election but persists through several subsequent elections.[15] The election of 1860 divided the country politically between the northern states, whose voters mainly voted Republican, and the southern states, which were overwhelmingly Democratic. The victory of the North over the South in the Civil War cemented Democratic loyalties in the South.

For forty years, from 1880 to 1920, no Republican presidential candidate won even one of the eleven states of the former Confederacy. The South's solid Democratic record earned it the nickname the "Solid South." (Today's students may be puzzled, for the South has been "solid" for Republicans throughout their lifetimes. That was not true prior to 1950, and the change is addressed below.) The Republicans did not puncture the Solid South until 1920, when Warren G. Harding carried Tennessee. The Republicans won five southern states in 1928, when the Democrats ran the first Catholic candidate, Al Smith. Republican presidential candidates won no more southern states until 1952, when Dwight Eisenhower broke the pattern of Democratic dominance in the South—ninety years after that pattern had been set by the Civil War.

Eras of Party Dominance Since the Civil War

critical election An election that produces a sharp change in the existing pattern of party loyalties among groups of voters.

electoral realignment The change in voting patterns that occurs after a critical election.

two-party system A political system in which two major political parties compete for control of the government. Candidates from a third party have little chance of winning office.

The critical election of 1860 established the Democratic and Republican Parties as the dominant parties in our **two-party system.** In a two-party system, most voters are so loyal to one or the other of the major parties that independent candidates or candidates from a third party (which means any minor party) have little chance of winning office. Third-party candidates tend to be more successful at the local or state level. Since the current two-party system was established, relatively few minor-party candidates have won election to the U.S. House, even fewer have won election to the Senate, and none has won the presidency.

The voters in a given state, county, or community are not always equally divided in their loyalties between the Republicans and the Democrats. In some areas, voters typically favor the Republicans, whereas voters in other areas prefer the Democrats. When one party in a two-party system regularly enjoys support from most voters in an area, it is called the *majority party* in that area; the other is called the *minority party*. Since the inception of the current two-party system, four periods (1860–1894, 1896–1930, 1932–1964, and 1968 to the present) have characterized the balance between the two major parties at the national level.

A Rough Balance: 1860–1894. From 1860 through 1894, the Grand Old Party (or GOP, as the Republican Party is sometimes called) won eight of ten presidential elections, which would seem to qualify it as the majority party. However, some of its success in presidential elections came from its practice of running Civil War heroes and from the North's domination of southern politics. Seats in the House of Representatives are a better guide to the breadth of national support. An analysis shows that the Republicans and Democrats won an equal number of congressional elections, each controlling the chamber for nine sessions between 1860 and 1894.

A Republican Majority: 1896–1930. A second critical election, in 1896, transformed the Republican Party into a true majority party. Grover Cleveland, a Democrat, occupied the White House, and the country was in a severe depression. The Republicans nominated William McKinley, governor of Ohio and a conservative, who stood for a high tariff against foreign goods and sound money tied to the value of gold. Rather than tour the country seeking votes, McKinley ran a dignified campaign from his Ohio home.

The Democrats, already in trouble because of the depression, nominated the fiery William Jennings Bryan. In stark contrast to McKinley, Bryan advocated the free and unlimited coinage of silver, which would mean cheap money and easy payment of debts through inflation. Bryan was also the nominee of the young Populist Party, an agrarian protest party that had proposed the free-silver platform Bryan adopted. The feature "The Wizard of Oz: A Political Fable" explains that the book *The Wonderful Wizard of Oz,* which you probably know as a movie, was reportedly a Populist political fable.[16] Conservatives, especially businesspeople, were aghast at the Democrats' radical turn, and voters in the heavily populated Northeast and Midwest surged toward the Republican Party, many of them permanently. McKinley carried every northern state east of the Mississippi. The Republicans also won the House, and they retained their control of it in the next six elections.

The election of 1896 helped solidify a Republican majority in industrial America and forged a link between the Republican Party and business. In the subsequent electoral realignment, the Republicans emerged as a true majority party. The GOP dominated national politics—controlling the presidency, the Senate, and the House—almost continuously from 1896 until the Wall Street crash of 1929, which burst big business's bubble and launched the Great Depression.*

A Democratic Majority: 1932–1964. The Republicans' majority status ended in the critical election of 1932 between incumbent president Herbert Hoover and the Democratic challenger, Franklin Delano Roosevelt. Roosevelt

---

*The only break in GOP domination was in 1912, when Teddy Roosevelt's Progressive Conservative Party split from the Republicans, allowing Democrat Woodrow Wilson to win the presidency and giving the Democrats control of Congress, and again in 1916 when Wilson was reelected.

The Wizard of Oz: A Political Fable

Most Americans are familiar with *The Wizard of Oz* through the children's series or the 1939 motion picture. Some historians contend that the story was written as a political fable to promote the Populist movement around the turn of the century. Next time you see or read it, try interpreting the Tin Woodsman as the industrial worker, the Scarecrow as the struggling farmer, and the Wizard as the president, who is powerful only as long as he succeeds in deceiving the people. (Sorry, but in the book, Dorothy's ruby slippers were only silver shoes.)

The Wonderful Wizard of Oz was written by Lyman Frank Baum in 1900, during the collapse of the Populist movement. Through the Populist Party, midwestern farmers, in alliance with some urban workers, had challenged the banks, railroads, and other economic interests that squeezed farmers through low prices, high freight rates, and continued indebtedness.

The Populists advocated government ownership of railroad, telephone, and telegraph industries. They also wanted silver coinage. Their power grew during the 1893 depression, the worst in U.S. history until then, as farm prices sank to new lows, and unemployment was widespread.

In the 1894 congressional elections, the Populist Party got almost 40 percent of the vote. It looked forward to winning the presidency, and imposing the silver standard, in 1896. But in that election, which revolved around the issue of gold versus silver, Populist Democrat William Jennings Bryan lost to Republican William McKinley by ninety-five electoral votes. Bryan, a congressman from Nebraska and a gifted orator, ran again in 1900, but the Populist strength was gone.

Baum viewed these events in both rural South Dakota, where he edited a local weekly, and in urban Chicago, where he wrote *Oz*. He mourned the destruction of the fragile alliance between the midwestern farmers (the Scarecrow) and the urban industrial workers (the Tin Woodsman). Along with Bryan (the Cowardly Lion, with a roar but little else), they had been taken down the yellow brick road (the gold standard) that led nowhere. Each journeyed to Emerald City seeking favors from the Wizard of Oz (the president). Dorothy, the symbol of Everyman, went along with them, innocent enough to see the truth before the others.

promised new solutions to unemployment and the economic crisis of the Great Depression. His campaign appealed to labor, middle-class liberals, and new European ethnic voters. Along with Democratic voters in the Solid South, urban workers in the North, Catholics, Jews, and white ethnic minorities formed "the Roosevelt coalition." The relatively few blacks who voted at that time tended to remain loyal to the Republicans—"the party of Lincoln."

Roosevelt was swept into office in a landslide, carrying huge Democratic majorities with him into the House and Senate to enact his liberal activist programs. The electoral realignment reflected by the election of 1932 made the Democrats the majority party. Not only was Roosevelt reelected in 1936, 1940, and 1944, but Democrats held control of both houses of Congress in

Along the way, they met the Wicked Witch of the East, who, Baum tells us, had kept the little Munchkin people "in bondage for many years, making them slave for her night and day." She also had put a spell on the Tin Woodsman, once an independent and hard-working man, so that each time he swung his axe, it chopped off a different part of his body. Lacking another trade, he "worked harder than ever," becoming like a machine, incapable of love, yearning for a heart. Another witch, the Wicked Witch of the West, clearly symbolizes the large industrial corporations.

The small group heads toward Emerald City, where the Wizard rules from behind a papier-mâché façade. *Oz,* by the way, is the abbreviation for ounce, the standard measure for gold.

Like all good politicians, the Wizard can be all things to all people. Dorothy sees him as an enormous head. The Scarecrow sees a gossamer fairy. The Woodsman sees an awful beast, the Cowardly Lion "a ball of fire so fierce and glowing he could scarcely bear to gaze upon it."

Later, however, when they confront the Wizard directly, they see he is nothing more than "a little man, with a bald head and a wrinkled face."

"I have been making believe," the Wizard confesses. "I'm just a common man." But the Scarecrow adds, "You're more than that . . . you're a humbug."

"It was a great mistake my ever letting you into the Throne Room," admits the Wizard, a former ventriloquist and circus balloonist from Omaha.

This was Baum's ultimate Populist message. The powers-that-be survive by deception. Only people's ignorance allows the powerful to manipulate and control them. Dorothy returns to Kansas with the magical help of her silver shoes (the silver issue), but when she gets to Kansas she realizes her shoes "had fallen off in her flight through the air, and were lost forever in the desert." Still, she is safe at home with Aunt Em and Uncle Henry, simple farmers.

Source: Peter Dreier, "The Wizard of Oz: A Political Fable," *Today Journal,* 14 February 1986. Reprinted by permission of Pacific News Service, <www.pacificnews.org>.

most sessions from 1933 through 1964. The only exceptions were Republican control of the House and Senate in 1947 and 1948 (under President Truman) and in 1953 and 1954 (under President Eisenhower). The Democrats also won the presidency in seven of nine elections. Moreover, national surveys from 1952 through 1964 show that Americans of voting age consistently and decidedly favored the Democratic Party.

A Rough Balance: 1968 to the Present. Scholars agree that an electoral realignment occurred after 1964, and some attribute the realignment to the turbulent election of 1968.[17] The Republican Richard Nixon won in a very close race by winning five of the eleven southern states in the old Confederacy,

William Jennings Bryan: When Candidates Were Orators

Today, televised images of a candidate waving his hands and shouting to an audience would look silly. But candidates once had to resort to such tactics to be effective with large crowds. One of the most commanding orators around the turn of the century was William Jennings Bryan (1860–1925), whose stirring speeches extolling the virtues of the free coinage of silver were music to the ears of thousands of westerners and southern farmers. *(Library of Congress)*

while Democrat Hubert Humphrey won only one. The other five states were won by George Wallace, the candidate of the American Independent Party, made up primarily of southerners who defected from the Democratic Party. Wallace won no states outside the South.

Since 1968 Republican candidates for president have run very well in southern states. Moreover, they won seven of the ten presidential elections from 1968 to 2004 (Nixon twice, Reagan twice, and the two Bushes—father and later, his son, twice). Democratic candidates for president won only when they ran southerners (Carter and Clinton, twice). The record of party control of Congress has been more mixed since 1968. Democrats have controlled the House for thirteen of the nineteen sessions, while the parties have split control of the Senate almost evenly. From 1994 to 2006, the Republicans controlled the House and usually the Senate.

Therefore, the period since 1968 rates as a "rough balance" between the parties, much like the period from 1860 to 1894. The razor-close election of 2000 and the close election of 2004, moreover, indicate that nationally the parties are fairly even in electoral strength.

In their smashing victory in the 1994 congressional elections, however, the Republicans gained control of Congress for the first time in forty years. They retained control after the 1996 elections—the first time Republicans took both houses in successive elections since Herbert Hoover was elected in 1928. The Republican streak of congressional control ended in 2006, when Democrats won their own smashing victory in the congressional elections.

In presidential elections, moreover, the Democrats have not fared very well since Roosevelt. From 1948 to 2004, they won only six elections (Truman, Kennedy, Johnson, Carter, and Clinton twice), compared with the Republicans' nine victories (Eisenhower twice, Nixon twice, Reagan twice, and the two Bushes—father and later, his son, twice). Although Clinton in 1996 became the first Democratic president since Roosevelt to be reelected, he also became the second president to be impeached.

The North-South coalition of Democratic voters forged by Roosevelt in the 1930s has completely crumbled. Two southern scholars wrote:

> It is easy to forget just how thoroughly the Democratic party once dominated southern congressional elections. In 1950 there were no Republican senators from the South and only 2 Republican representatives out of 105 in the southern House delegation. . . . A half-century later Republicans constituted *majorities* of the South's congressional delegations—13 of 22 southern senators and 71 of 125 representatives.[18]

Although party loyalty within regions has shifted inexorably, the Democratic coalition of urban workers and ethnic minorities still seems intact, if weakened. Instead of a full realignment, we seem to be in a period of **electoral dealignment,** in which party loyalties have become less important to voters as they cast their ballots. We examine the influence of party loyalty on voting in the next chapter, after we look at the operation of our two-party system.

★ The American Two-Party System

Our review of party history in the United States has focused on the two dominant parties. But we should not ignore the special contributions of certain minor parties, among them the Anti-Masonic Party, the Populists, and the Progressives of 1912. In this section, we study the fortunes of minor, or third, parties in American politics. We also will look at why we have only two major parties, explain how federalism helps the parties survive, and describe voters' loyalty to the two major parties today.

Minor Parties in America

Minor parties have always figured in party politics in America. Most minor parties in our political history have been one of four types:[19]

■ *Bolter parties* are formed by factions that have split off from one of the major parties. Six times in the thirty-five presidential elections from the Civil War to 2004, disgruntled leaders have "bolted the ticket" and challenged their former parties.[20] Bolter parties have occasionally won significant proportions of the vote. However, with the exception of Teddy Roosevelt's Progressive Party in 1912 and the possible exception of George Wallace's American Independent Party in 1968, bolter parties have not affected the outcome of presidential elections.

■ *Farmer-labor parties* represented farmers and urban workers who believed that they, the working class, were not getting their share of society's wealth. The People's Party, founded in 1892 and nicknamed the "Populist Party," was a prime example of a farmer-labor party. The Populists won 8.5 percent of the vote in 1892 and also became the first third party since 1860 to win any electoral votes. Flushed by success, it endorsed William Jennings Bryan, the Democratic candidate, in 1896. When he lost, the party quickly faded. Farm and labor groups revived

electoral dealignment A lessening of the importance of party loyalties in voting decisions.

many Populist ideas in the Progressive Party in 1924, which nominated Robert La Follette for the presidency. Although the party won 16.6 percent of the popular vote, it carried only La Follette's home state of Wisconsin. The party died in 1925.

■ *Parties of ideological protest* go further than farmer-labor parties in criticizing the established system. These parties reject prevailing doctrines and propose radically different principles, often favoring more government activism. The Socialist Party has been the most successful party of ideological protest. Even at its high point in 1912, however, it garnered only 6 percent of the vote, and Socialist candidates for president have never won a single state. Nevertheless, the Socialist Party persists, fielding a presidential ticket again in 2004. In recent years, protest parties have tended to come from the right, arguing against government action in society. Such is the program of the Libertarian Party, which stresses freedom over order and equality. In contrast, the Green Party protests from the left, favoring government action to preserve the environment (see page 255). Together, the two parties polled less than 500,000 votes (0.4 of 1 percent) for their presidential candidates in 2004. The Libertarian candidate's share of this meager poll was three times that of the Green candidate, and Libertarian candidates for Congress also were far more plentiful and successful (see Figure 8.2).

■ *Single-issue parties* are formed to promote one principle, not a general philosophy of government. The Anti-Masonic parties of the 1820s and 1830s, for example, opposed Masonic lodges and other secret societies. The Free Soil Party of the 1840s and 1850s worked to abolish slavery. The Prohibition Party, the most durable example of a single-issue party, was founded to oppose the consumption of alcoholic beverages, but its platform for the 2004 election took other conservative positions: favoring right-to-life, limiting immigration, and urging withdrawal from the World Bank. Prohibition candidates consistently won from 1 to 2 percent of the vote in nine presidential elections between 1884 and 1916, and the party has run candidates in every presidential election since, while winning only a trickle of votes. Candidate Earl Dodge, for example, won just 1,706 votes in 2004.

America has a long history of third parties that operate on the periphery of our two-party system. Minor parties form primarily to express some voters' discontent with choices offered by the major parties and to work for their own objectives within the electoral system.[21] The Reform Party certainly reflected discontent with existing policies, but otherwise it resists classification. It did not bolt from an existing party, it did not have a farmer-labor base, it had no clear ideology, and it was not devoted to any single issue. Billionaire businessman Ross Perot created it for his 1996 presidential campaign, but Perot won only 8 percent of the vote, less than half of what he had won in 1992 as an independent. Nevertheless, the Reform Party won enough votes to qualify for some $12 million in federal funds for the 2000 campaign. Perot then turned away from the party and left others to fight for its leadership and its $12 million. By 2004, the once promising party made the ballot in only four states and won less than sixty thousand votes out of more than 122 million cast.

FIGURE 8.2 **Party Candidates for the U.S. House in the 2006 Election**

In 2006, as in recent elections, the Democratic and Republican Parties ran candidates for the House of Representatives in about 90 percent of the 435 congressional districts. Of minor parties, only the Libertarian Party, the best-organized minor party in the nation, ran candidates in more than 100 districts. In most of those districts, however, the Libertarian candidates usually got under 1 percent of the vote. All other minor parties ran fewer candidates than the Libertarians.

Sources: Thomas T. Mackie and Richard Rose, *The International Almanac of Electoral History,* 3rd ed. (Washington, D.C.: CQ Press, 1991); <www.electionguide.org/2005.htm>; *Ballot Access News,* 1 October 2006; <www.thegreenpapers.com/G06/HouseVoteByParty.html>.

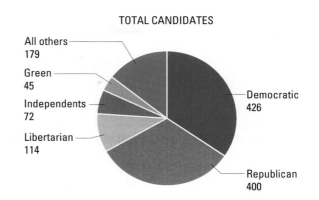

TOTAL CANDIDATES

All others 179
Green 45
Independents 72
Libertarian 114
Democratic 426
Republican 400

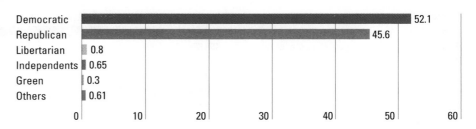

Democratic	52.1
Republican	45.6
Libertarian	0.8
Independents	0.65
Green	0.3
Others	0.61

Total percentage of the congressional vote cast for all candidates of each party in 2006

How have minor parties fared historically? As vote getters, they have not performed well. However, bolter parties have twice won more than 10 percent of the vote. More significant, the Republican Party originated in 1854 as a single-issue third party opposed to slavery in the nation's new territories. In its first election, in 1856, the party came in second, displacing the Whigs. (Undoubtedly, the Republican exception to the rule has inspired the formation of other hopeful third parties.)

As policy advocates, minor parties have a slightly better record. At times, they have had a real effect on the policies adopted by the major parties. Women's suffrage, the graduated income tax, and the direct election of senators all originated with third parties.[22] Of course, third parties may fail to win more votes simply because their policies lack popular support. The Democrats learned this lesson in 1896, when they adopted the Populists' free-silver plank in their own platform. Both their candidate and their platform went down to defeat, hobbling the Democratic Party for decades.

Most important, minor parties function as safety valves. They allow those who are unhappy with the status quo to express their discontent within the system, to contribute to the political dialogue. Surely this was the function of

Ralph Nader as the Green Party candidate in 2000, when it won 2.7 percent of the vote. (By drawing votes from Democrat Al Gore in key states, Nader also denied Gore a victory over George Bush in the closest popular vote in history.) If minor parties and independent candidates are indicators of discontent, what should we make of the numerous minor parties, detailed in Figure 8.3, which took part in the 2004 election? Not much. The number of third parties that contest elections is less important than the total number of votes they receive. Despite the presence of numerous minor parties in every presidential election,

---

FIGURE 8.3   **Candidates and Parties in the 2004 Presidential Election**

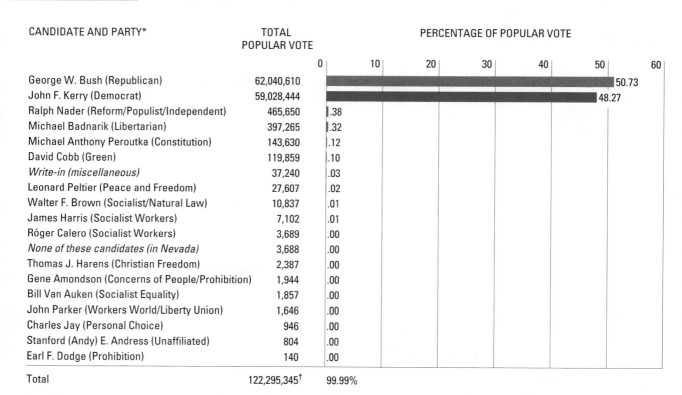

CANDIDATE AND PARTY*	TOTAL POPULAR VOTE	PERCENTAGE OF POPULAR VOTE
George W. Bush (Republican)	62,040,610	50.73
John F. Kerry (Democrat)	59,028,444	48.27
Ralph Nader (Reform/Populist/Independent)	465,650	.38
Michael Badnarik (Libertarian)	397,265	.32
Michael Anthony Peroutka (Constitution)	143,630	.12
David Cobb (Green)	119,859	.10
Write-in (miscellaneous)	37,240	.03
Leonard Peltier (Peace and Freedom)	27,607	.02
Walter F. Brown (Socialist/Natural Law)	10,837	.01
James Harris (Socialist Workers)	7,102	.01
Róger Calero (Socialist Workers)	3,689	.00
None of these candidates (in Nevada)	3,688	.00
Thomas J. Harens (Christian Freedom)	2,387	.00
Gene Amondson (Concerns of People/Prohibition)	1,944	.00
Bill Van Auken (Socialist Equality)	1,857	.00
John Parker (Workers World/Liberty Union)	1,646	.00
Charles Jay (Personal Choice)	946	.00
Stanford (Andy) E. Andress (Unaffiliated)	804	.00
Earl F. Dodge (Prohibition)	140	.00
Total	122,295,345[†]	99.99%

*Party designations vary from one state to another. Vote totals for the candidates listed include any write-in votes they received.

[†]Totals do not include the 57,230 miscellaneous write-in, blank and void votes that were compiled as one total in New York.

In addition to the candidates of the two major parties, fifteen other candidates ran in various states under banners of more than a dozen parties. All of them together, however, captured less than 1 percent of the total vote. In fact, write-in candidates won more votes than candidates of eleven parties. By law in Nevada, voters must be allowed to register their disapproval of the listed candidates by voting for "None of these candidates" as a line in the ballot. More Nevada voters voted for "None" than for Libertarian Party, Green Party, and Independent American Party presidential candidates.

Source: Federal Elections 2004: Election Results for the U.S. President, the U.S. Senate and the U.S. House of Representatives (Washington, D.C.: Federal Election Commission, May 2005).

the two major parties usually collect more than 95 percent of the vote, as they did in 2004 despite challenges from candidates of other parties.

Why a Two-Party System?

The history of party politics in the United States is essentially the story of two parties that have alternating control of the government. With relatively few exceptions, Americans conduct elections at all levels within the two-party system. Other democratic countries usually have multiparty systems—often more than three parties. Indeed, a political system with three relatively equal parties has never existed over a length of time in any country.[23] Why does the United States have only two major parties? The two most convincing answers to this question stem from the electoral system in the United States and the process of political socialization here.

In the typical U.S. election, two or more candidates contest each office, and the winner is the single candidate who collects the most votes, whether those votes constitute a majority or not. When these two principles of *single winners* chosen by a *simple plurality* of votes govern the election of the members of a legislature, the system is known as **majority representation** (despite its reliance on pluralities rather than majorities). Think about how American states choose representatives to Congress. A state entitled to ten representatives is divided into ten congressional districts, and each district elects one representative. Majority representation of voters through single-member districts is also a feature of most state legislatures.

Alternatively, a legislature might be chosen through a system of **proportional representation,** which awards legislative seats to each party in proportion to the total number of votes it wins in an election. Under this system, the state might hold a single statewide election for all ten seats, with each party presenting a rank-ordered list of ten candidates. Voters could vote for the party list they preferred, and the party's candidates would be elected from the top of each list, according to the proportion of votes won by the party. Thus, if a party got 30 percent of the vote in this example, its first three candidates would be elected.[24]

Although this form of election may seem strange, many democratic countries (for example, the Netherlands, Israel, and Denmark) use it. Proportional representation tends to produce (or perpetuate) several parties because each can win enough seats nationwide to wield some influence in the legislature. In contrast, our system of elections forces interest groups of all sorts to work within the two major parties, for only one candidate in each race stands a chance of being elected under plurality voting. Therefore, the system tends to produce only two parties. Moreover, the two major parties benefit from state laws that automatically list candidates on the ballot if their party won a sizable percentage of the vote in the previous election. These laws discourage minor parties, which usually have to collect thousands of signatures to get on a state ballot.[25]

The rules of our electoral system may explain why only two parties tend to form in specific election districts, but why do the same two parties (Democratic and Republican) operate within every state? The contest for the presidency is the key to this question. A candidate can win a presidential election only by amassing a majority of electoral votes from across the entire nation. Presidential candidates try to win votes under the same party label in each state in

majority representation The system by which one office, contested by two or more candidates, is won by the single candidate who collects the most votes.

proportional representation The system by which legislative seats are awarded to a party in proportion to the vote that party wins in an election.

order to pool their electoral votes in the electoral college. The presidency is a big enough political prize to induce parties to harbor uncomfortable coalitions of voters (southern white Protestants allied with northern Jews and blacks in the Democratic Party, for example) just to win the electoral vote and the presidential election.

The American electoral system may force U.S. politics into a two-party mold, but why must the same two parties reappear from election to election? In fact, they do not. The earliest two-party system pitted the Federalists against the Democratic Republicans. A later two-party system involved the Democrats and the Whigs. More than 135 years ago, the Republicans replaced the Whigs in what is our two-party system today. But with modern issues so different from the issues then, why do the Democrats and Republicans persist? This is where political socialization comes into play. The two parties persist simply because they have persisted. After more than one hundred years of political socialization, the two parties today have such a head start in structuring the vote that they discourage challenges from new parties. Third parties still try to crack the two-party system from time to time, but most have had little success.

The Federal Basis of the Party System

Focusing on contests for the presidency is a convenient and informative way to study the history of American parties, but it also oversimplifies party politics to the point of distortion. By concentrating only on presidential elections, we tend to ignore electoral patterns in the states, where elections often buck national trends. Even during its darkest defeats for the presidency, a party can still claim many victories for state offices. Victories outside the arena of presidential politics give each party a base of support that keeps its machinery oiled and ready for the next contest.[26]

Party Identification in America

The concept of **party identification** is one of the most important in political science. It signifies a voter's sense of psychological attachment to a party (which is not the same thing as voting for the party in any given election). Scholars measure party identification simply by asking, "Do you usually think of yourself as a Republican, a Democrat, an independent, or what?"[27] Voting is a behavior; identification is a state of mind. For example, millions of southerners voted for Eisenhower for president in 1952 and 1956 but continued to consider themselves Democrats. Across the nation, more people identify with one of the two major parties than reject a party attachment. The proportions of self-identified Republicans, Democrats, and independents (no party attachment) in the electorate since 1952 are shown in Figure 8.4. Three significant points stand out:

- The number of Republicans and Democrats combined has far exceeded the independents in every year.

- The number of Democrats has consistently exceeded that of Republicans.

- The number of Democrats has shrunk over time, to the benefit of both Republicans and independents, and the three groups are now almost equal in size.

party identification A voter's sense of psychological attachment to a party.

FIGURE 8.4   Distribution of Party Identification, 1952–2004

In every presidential election since 1952, voters across the nation have been asked, "Generally speaking, do you usually think of yourself as a Republican, a Democrat, an independent, or what?" Most voters think of themselves as either Republicans or Democrats, but the proportion of those who think of themselves as independents has increased over time. The size of the Democratic Party's majority has also shrunk. Nevertheless, most Americans today still identify with one of the two major parties, and Democrats still outnumber Republicans.

Sources: National Election Studies Guide to Public Opinion and Electoral Behavior, available at <http://www.umich.edu/~nes/nesguide/toptable/tab2a_1.htm>.

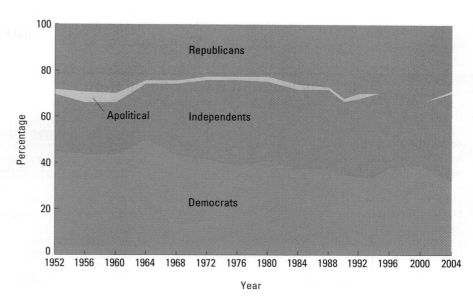

Although party identification predisposes citizens to vote for their favorite party, other factors may convince them to choose the opposition candidate. If they vote against their party often enough, they may rethink their party identification and eventually switch. Apparently, this rethinking has gone on in the minds of many southern Democrats over time. In 1952, about 70 percent of white southerners thought of themselves as Democrats, and fewer than 20 percent thought of themselves as Republicans. By 2002, white southerners were only 25 percent Democratic, whereas 35 percent were Republican and 40 percent were independent. Much of the nationwide growth in the proportion of Republicans and independents (and the parallel drop in the number of Democrats) stems from changes in party preferences among white southerners and from migration of northerners, which translated into substantial gains in the number of registered Republicans by 2002.[28]

Who are the self-identified Democrats and Republicans in the electorate? Figure 8.5 shows party identification by various social groups in 2004. The effects of socioeconomic factors are clear. People who have lower incomes and less education are more likely to think of themselves as Democrats than as Republicans. However, citizens with advanced degrees (such as college faculty) are slightly more Democratic. The cultural factors of religion and race produce even sharper differences between the parties. Jews are strongly Democratic compared with other religious groups, and African Americans are also overwhelmingly Democratic. Finally, American politics has a gender gap: more women tend to be Democrats than men, and (although not shown here) this gap seems to widen with women's greater education.[29]

The influence of region on party identification has changed over time. Because of the high proportion of blacks in the South, it is still strongly Democratic (in party identity, but not in voting because of lower turnout among low-income blacks). The north-central states have slightly more Republicans than the other regions. Despite the erosion of Democratic strength in the

---

FIGURE 8.5 **Party Identification by Social Groups**

Respondents to a 2004 election survey were grouped by seven socioeconomic criteria—income, education, religion, sex, race, region, and age—and analyzed according to their self-descriptions as Democrats, independents, or Republicans. All of these factors had some effect on party identification, with region today showing little effect. As for age, its main effect was to reduce the proportion of independents as respondents grew older. Younger citizens who tend to think of themselves as independents are likely to develop an identification with one party or the other as they mature.

Source: 2004 National Election Study, Center for Political Studies, University of Michigan.

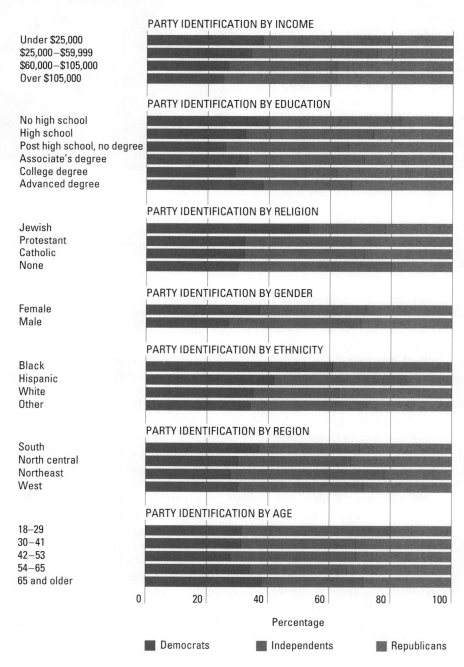

PARTY IDENTIFICATION BY INCOME

Under $25,000
$25,000–$59,999
$60,000–$105,000
Over $105,000

PARTY IDENTIFICATION BY EDUCATION

No high school
High school
Post high school, no degree
Associate's degree
College degree
Advanced degree

PARTY IDENTIFICATION BY RELIGION

Jewish
Protestant
Catholic
None

PARTY IDENTIFICATION BY GENDER

Female
Male

PARTY IDENTIFICATION BY ETHNICITY

Black
Hispanic
White
Other

PARTY IDENTIFICATION BY REGION

South
North central
Northeast
West

PARTY IDENTIFICATION BY AGE

18–29
30–41
42–53
54–65
65 and older

0   20   40   60   80   100

Percentage

■ Democrats   ■ Independents   ■ Republicans

South, we still see elements of Roosevelt's old Democratic coalition of different socioeconomic groups. Perhaps the major change in that coalition has been the replacement of white European ethnic groups by blacks, attracted by the Democrats' backing of civil rights legislation in the 1960s leading to the critical election of 1968.

Studies show that about half of all Americans adopt their parents' party. But it often takes time for party identification to develop. The youngest group of voters is most likely to be independent, but people in their mid-twenties to mid-forties, who were socialized during the Reagan and first Bush presidencies, are heavily Republican (see "Politics in a Changing World: The Changing Relationship Between Age and Party Identification"). The oldest group not only is strongly Democratic but also shows the greatest partisan commitment (fewest independents), reflecting the fact that citizens become more interested in politics as they mature.

Americans tend to find their political niche and stay there.[30] The enduring party loyalty of American voters tends to structure the vote even before an election is held, and even before the candidates are chosen. In Chapter 9, we will examine the extent to which party identification determines voting choice. But first we will explore whether the Democratic and Republican Parties have any significant differences between them.

★ Party Ideology and Organization

George Wallace, a disgruntled Democrat who ran for president in 1968 on the American Independent Party ticket, complained that "there isn't a dime's worth of difference" between the Democrats and Republicans. Humorist Will Rogers said, "I am not a member of any organized political party—I am a Democrat." Wallace's comment was made in disgust, Rogers's in jest. Wallace was wrong; Rogers was close to being right. Here we will dispel the myth that the parties do not differ significantly on issues and explain how they are organized to coordinate the activities of party candidates and officials in government.

Differences in Party Ideology

George Wallace notwithstanding, there is more than a dime's worth of difference between the two parties. In fact, the difference amounts to many billions of dollars—the cost of the different government programs each party supports. Democrats are more disposed to government spending to advance social welfare (and hence to promote equality) than are Republicans. And social welfare programs cost money, a lot of money. Republicans decry massive social spending, but they are not averse to spending billions of dollars for the projects they consider important, among them national defense. Ronald Reagan portrayed the Democrats as big spenders, but his administration spent more than $1 trillion for defense. His Strategic Defense Initiative (the missile defense program labeled "Star Wars") cost billions before it was curtailed under the Democrats.[31] Although President George W. Bush introduced a massive tax cut, he also revived spending on missile defense, backed a $400 billion increase in Medicare, and proposed building a space platform on the moon for travel to Mars. One result was a huge increase in the budget deficit and a rare *Wall Street Journal* editorial against the GOP "spending spree."[32]

Politics in a Changing World

The Changing Relationship Between Age and Party Identification

The relationship between age and party identification has changed dramatically during the past fifty years. We can visualize this change by comparing a Gallup survey in 1952 with a national survey in 2004. Both graphs show the percentage of Democratic identifiers minus the percentage of Republican identifiers for seventeen different four-year age groupings—ranging from eighteen- to twenty-one-year-olds to those eighty-two years of age and older. In 1952, the percentage of Democratic identifiers exceeded Republican identifiers by about fifteen points or more among younger and middle-aged voters, whereas

the older age groups had far more Republicans than Democrats. By 2004, this regular pattern had changed. The irregularity of the pattern in 2004 is due to the weakened relationship between age and party identification in the two eras and to relatively small numbers of respondents (sometimes under 50) on which the percentages are calculated. Nevertheless, the pattern is clear. In 2004, citizens in the middle age groups from thirty to sixty-one were more likely to be Republican, while the youngest in the electorate were strongly Democratic, along with the oldest (those who were themselves young in 1952).

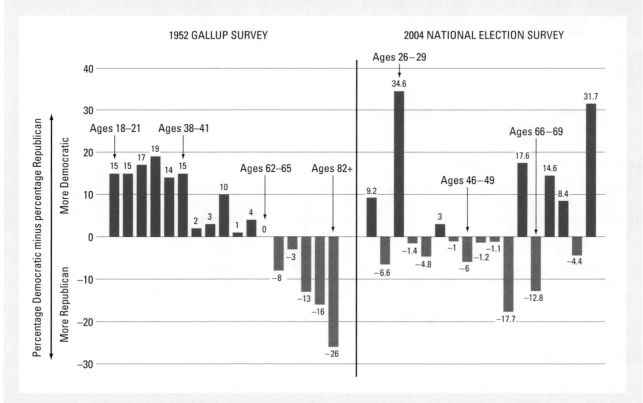

Source: Everett Carll Ladd, "Age, Generation, and Party ID," *Public Perspective* (July–August 1992): 15–16. Data for 2004 were computed from the 2004 American National Election Study.

FIGURE 8.6   Ideologies of Party Voters and Party Delegates in 2004

Contrary to what many people think, the Democratic and Republican Parties differ substantially in their ideological centers of gravity. When citizens were asked to classify themselves on an ideological scale, more Republicans than Democrats described themselves as conservative. When delegates to the parties' national conventions were asked to classify themselves, the differences between the parties grew even sharper.

Source: Katherine O. Seelye and Marjorie Connally, "Delegates Leaning to Right of G.O.P. and the Nation," *New York Times,* 29 August 2004, sec. 15, p. 14.

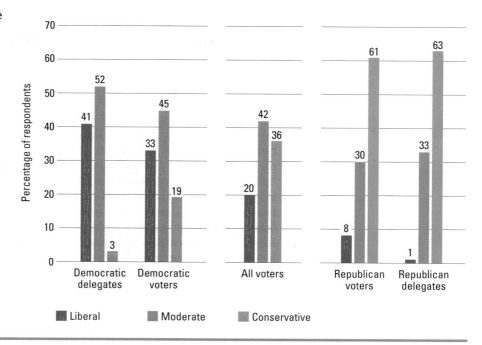

Liberal ■ Moderate ■ Conservative ■

Voters and Activists.   One way to examine the differences is to compare party voters with party activists. As shown in Figure 8.6, only 19 percent of Democratic voters described themselves as conservative, compared with 61 percent of Republican voters. As we discussed in Chapter 5, relatively few ordinary voters think about politics in ideological terms, but party activists often do. The ideological gap between the parties looms even larger when we focus on party activists on the left and right sides of Figure 8.6. Only 3 percent of the delegates to the 2004 Democratic convention described themselves as conservative, compared with 63 percent of the delegates to the Republican convention.

Platforms: Freedom, Order, and Equality.   Surveys of voters' ideological orientation may merely reflect differences in their personal self-image rather than actual differences in party ideology. For another test of party philosophy, we can look to the platforms adopted at party conventions. Although many people feel that party platforms don't matter very much, several scholars have demonstrated, using different approaches, that winning parties tend to carry out much of their platforms when in office.[33] One study matched the parties' platform statements from 1948 to 1985 against subsequent allocations of program funds in the federal budget. Spending priorities turned out to be quite closely linked to the platform emphases of the party that won control of Congress, especially if the party also controlled the presidency.[34]

Party platforms also matter a great deal to the parties' convention delegates—and to the interest groups that support the parties.[35] The wording of a platform plank often means the difference between victory and defeat for factions within a party. Delegates fight not only over ideas but also over words.

In this light, the national committees appear to be relatively useless organizations. For many years, their role was essentially limited to planning for the next party convention. The committee would select the site, invite the state parties to attend, plan the program, and so on. In the 1970s, however, the roles of the DNC and RNC began to expand—but in different ways.

In response to street rioting by Vietnam War protesters during the 1968 Democratic convention, the Democrats created a special commission to introduce party reforms. In an attempt to open the party to broader participation and weaken local party leaders' control over the process of selecting delegates, the McGovern-Fraser Commission formulated new guidelines for the selection of delegates to the 1972 Democratic convention. Included in these guidelines was the requirement that state parties take "affirmative action"—that is, see to it that their delegates included women, minorities, and young people "in reasonable relationship to the group's presence in the population of the state."[39] Many state parties rebelled at the imposition of sex, race, and age quotas. But the DNC threatened to deny seating at the 1972 convention to any state delegation that did not comply with the guidelines.

Never before had a national party committee imposed such rules on a state party organization, but it worked. Even the powerful Illinois delegation, led by Chicago mayor and Democratic Party boss Richard J. Daley, was denied seating at the convention for violating the guidelines. And overall, women, blacks, and young voters gained dramatically in representation at the 1972 Democratic convention. Although the party has since reduced its emphasis on quotas, the gains by women and blacks have held up fairly well. The representation of young people, however, has declined substantially (as the young activists grew older). Many "regular" Democrats feared that the political activists who had taken over the 1972 convention would cripple the party organization. But most challengers were socialized into the party within a decade and became more open to compromise and more understanding of the organization's need to combat developments within the Republican Party.[40]

While the Democrats were busy with *procedural* reforms, the Republicans were making *organizational* reforms.[41] The RNC did little to open up its delegate selection process; Republicans were not inclined to impose quotas on state parties through their national committee. Instead, the RNC strengthened its fundraising, research, and service roles. Republicans acquired their own building and their own computer system, and in 1976 they hired the first full-time chairperson in the history of either national party. (Until then, the chairperson had worked part time.) As RNC chairman, William Brock (formerly a senator from Tennessee) expanded the party's staff, launched new publications, held seminars, conducted election analyses, and advised candidates—things that national party committees in other countries had been doing for years. By the 2000 election, campaign finance analysts noted, American parties had become "an important source of funding in the race for the White House."[42]

The vast difference between the Democratic and Republican approaches to reforming the national committees shows in the funds raised by the DNC and RNC during election campaigns. During Brock's tenure as chairperson of the RNC, the Republicans raised three to four times as much money as the Democrats. Although the margin has narrowed, Republican Party fundraising efforts are still superior. For the 2003–2004 election cycle, the Republicans' national, senatorial, and congressional committees raised $657 million, compared with $586

million raised by the comparable Democratic committees.[43] Even though Republicans have traditionally raised more campaign money than Democrats, they no longer rely on a relatively few wealthy contributors. As a matter of fact, the Republicans received more of their funds in small contributions (less than $100), mainly through direct-mail solicitation, than the Democrats. In short, the RNC has regularly raised far more money than the DNC, from many more citizens, as part of its long-term commitment to improving its organizational services. Its efforts have also made a difference at the state and local levels. Beginning in 2002, however, significant changes occurred in how political parties could collect money to finance their activities. These campaign finance reforms are discussed in Chapter 9.

State and Local Party Organizations

At one time, both major parties were firmly anchored by powerful state and local party organizations. Big-city party organizations, such as the Democrats' Tammany Hall in New York City and the Cook County Central Committee in Chicago, were called *party machines*.

A **party machine** was a centralized organization that dominated local politics by controlling elections—sometimes by illegal means, often by providing jobs and social services to urban workers in return for their votes. The patronage and social service functions of party machines were undercut when the government expanded unemployment compensation, aid to families with dependent children, and other social services. As a result, most local party organizations lost their ability to deliver votes and thus to determine the outcome of elections. However, machines are still strong in certain areas. In Nassau County, New York, for example, suburban Republicans have shown that they can run a machine as well as urban Democrats.[44]

party machine A centralized party organization that dominates local politics by controlling elections.

? **Can you explain why . . .**
political parties have become
more important in elections?

The individual state and local organizations of both parties vary widely in strength, but recent research has found that "neither the Republican nor Democratic party has a distinct advantage with regard to direct campaign activities."[45] Whereas once both the RNC and the DNC were dependent for their funding on "quotas" paid by state parties, now the funds flow the other way. In the 2003–2004 election cycle, the national party campaign committees transferred millions of dollars to state and local parties.[46] In addition to money, state parties also received candidate training, poll data and research, and campaigning instruction.[47] The national committees have also taken a more active role in congressional campaigns.[48]

Decentralized but Growing Stronger

Although the national committees have gained strength over the past three decades, American political parties are still among the most decentralized parties in the world.[49] Not even the president can count on loyalty from the members (or even the officers) of his party. Consider the problem that confronted President Clinton after his resounding reelection in 1996. President Clinton sought legislation for authority to negotiate trade legislation that Congress could approve or disapprove but not amend. Congress had given every president since Gerald Ford this so-called fast-track authority, and Republican leaders favored it as part of their free-trade philosophy. However, organized labor feared losing jobs to other countries and opposed giving Clinton this negotiating power. Richard Gephardt, leader of the Democratic minority in the House, took labor's side and led the fight against the president on this issue. Although Clinton supposedly headed the Democratic Party, Gephardt persuaded 80 percent of House Democrats to vote against the fast-track measure, denying the president a power he dearly wanted.[50] Clinton could do nothing to discipline his disobedient party lieutenant.

The absence of centralized power has always been the most distinguishing characteristic of American political parties. Moreover, the rise in the proportion of citizens who style themselves as independents suggests that our already weak parties are in further decline.[51] But there is evidence that our political parties *as organizations* are enjoying a period of resurgence. Indeed, both national parties have "globalized" their organizations, maintaining branches in over a dozen nations.[52] Both parties' national committees have never been better funded or more active in grassroots campaign activities.[53] And more votes in Congress are being decided along party lines. (See Chapter 11 for a discussion of the rise of party voting in Congress since the 1970s.) In fact, a specialist in congressional politics has concluded, "When compared to its predecessors of the past half-century, the current majority party leadership is more involved and more decisive in organizing the party and the chamber, setting the policy agenda, shaping legislation, and determining legislative outcomes."[54] However, the American parties have traditionally been so weak that these positive trends have not altered their basic character. American political parties are still so organizationally diffuse and decentralized that they raise questions about how well they link voters to the government.

The Model of Responsible Party Government

According to the majoritarian model of democracy, parties are essential to making the government responsive to public opinion. In fact, the ideal role of parties in majoritarian democracy has been formalized in the four principles of **responsible party government:**[55]

1. Parties should present clear and coherent programs to voters.

2. Voters should choose candidates on the basis of party programs.

3. The winning party should carry out its program once in office.

4. Voters should hold the governing party responsible at the next election for executing its program.

How well do these principles describe American politics? You've learned that the Democratic and Republican platforms are different and that they are much more ideologically consistent than many people believe. So the first principle is being met fairly well.[56] To a lesser extent, so is the third principle: once parties gain power, they usually try to do what they said they would do. From the standpoint of democratic theory, the real question involves principles 2 and 4: Do voters really pay attention to party platforms and policies when they cast their ballots?[57] And if so, do voters hold the governing party responsible at the next election for delivering, or failing to deliver, on its pledges? To answer these questions, we must consider in greater detail the parties' role in nominating candidates and structuring the voters' choices in elections. At the conclusion of Chapter 9, we will return to evaluating the role of political parties in democratic government.

responsible party government A set of principles formalizing the ideal role of parties in a majoritarian democracy.

Summary

Political parties perform four important functions in a political system: nominating candidates, structuring the voting choice, proposing alternative government programs, and coordinating the activities of government officials. Political parties have been performing these functions longer in the United States than in any other country. The Democratic Party, founded in 1828, is the world's oldest political party. When the Republican Party emerged as a major party after the 1856 election, our present two-party system emerged—the oldest party system in the world.

America's two-party system has experienced three critical elections, each of which realigned the electorate for years and affected the party balance in government. The election of 1860 established the Re-publicans as the major party in the North and the Democrats as the dominant party in the South. Nationally, the two parties remained roughly balanced in Congress until the critical election of 1896. This election strengthened the link between the Republican Party and business interests in the heavily populated Northeast and Midwest and produced a surge in voter support that made the Republicans the majority party nationally for more than three decades. The Great Depression produced the conditions that transformed the Democrats into the majority party in the critical election of 1932. The presidential election of 1968 signaled the end of the Democrats' domination of national politics. Until that election, Republican candidates for president rarely ran well in the South. Since 1968, Republican candidates have won most presidential elections, and they have controlled both houses of Congress since 1994. Nevertheless, the last two presidential elections were extremely close, the two houses of Congress are closely divided, and the two parties are roughly balanced in strength.

Minor parties have not enjoyed much electoral success in America, although they have contributed ideas to the Democratic and Republican platforms. The two-party system is perpetuated in the United States by the nature of our electoral system and the political socialization process, which results in most Americans' identifying with either the Democratic or the Republican Party. The federal system of government has also helped the Democrats and Republicans survive defeats at the national level by sustaining them with electoral victories at the state level. The pattern of party identification has been changing in recent years: as more people are becoming independents and Republicans, the number of Democratic identifiers is dropping. Still, Democrats nationally outnumber Republicans by a small margin, and together they far outnumber independents.

The two major parties differ in their ideological orientations. Democratic identifiers and activists are more likely to describe themselves as liberal; Republican identifiers and activists tend to be conservative.

The party platforms also reveal substantial ideological differences. The 2004 Democratic Party platform showed a more liberal orientation by stressing equality over freedom; the Republican platform was more conservative, concentrating on freedom but also emphasizing the importance of restoring social order. Organizationally, the Republicans have recently become the stronger party at both the national and state levels, and both parties are showing signs of resurgence. Nevertheless, both parties are still very decentralized compared with parties in other countries.

In keeping with the model of responsible party government, American parties do tend to translate their platform positions into government policy if elected to power. But, as we examine in Chapter 9, it remains to be seen whether citizens pay much attention to parties and policies when casting their votes. If not, American parties do not fulfill the majoritarian model of democratic theory.

Internet activities and reading suggestions for this chapter are available on the *Online Study Center*

To complete the multimedia assignments for this chapter, go to AmericansGoverning.org.

9

Nominations, Elections, and Campaigns

(Jeff Haynes/AFP/Getty Images)

Online Study Center
This icon will direct you to resources
and activities on the website
college.hmco.com/pic/jandaupdate9e

American voters carry a heavy burden. They are asked to choose among *more* candidates for *more* offices *more* frequently than voters in any other country. Having the opportunity to choose government officials is a blessing of democracy, but learning enough about so many candidates to make informed choices is the curse of our unique and demanding electoral system.

As explained in Chapter 7, when Americans go to the polls in a general election, they are asked to decide among scores of candidates running for many different public offices at the local, state, and national levels. In the United States, an election is "general" in the sense that it includes various levels of government. In most other countries, a general election is very different and citizens have a much lighter burden in the polling booth.

Let's consider the difference between the 2004 general election in the United States and the 2006 general election in Canada. Like the United States, Canada has a federal system of government. Unlike the United States—but like most other democracies and nearly all European nations—Canada has a parliamentary, not a presidential, form of government.[1] Outlining how the Canadian government operates illustrates how most established democracies operate.

Canada is led by a prime minister chosen by members in the elected house of parliament—the House of Commons. The party controlling the House selects the prime minister. Because a parliamentary system joins the executive and legislative powers, the prime minister becomes the head of government.[2] Canadian governments are limited to five-year terms in office, but a prime minister can hold a general election earlier if the timing looks promising for the governing party. If the prime minister loses support of parliament, however, a general election is called to resolve the political problem. That's what happened to Prime Minister Paul Martin, leader of the Liberal Party, whose loss of a vote of confidence in late 2005 led to the general election in January 2006.

In Canada, general elections are not held according to a fixed calendar, so no party can prepare for them in advance. Because elections are timed to political needs (such as a vote of no confidence), the campaign period is fixed and short, but at least thirty-six days. Canada not only had a shorter election campaign in 2006 than the United States had in 2004, but it also counted its votes faster. Within hours after the polls closed, Canadians knew conclusively that the Conservative Party, led by Stephen Harper, had won a plurality of the 308 seats in the House of Commons and that Harper would be the new prime minister. The results were posted on the official "Elections Canada" website within hours after the polls closed.[3]

If Canada bases its elections on the needs of politics, we base ours on the movement of the planets. In early November, after the Earth has traveled four times around the sun, the United States holds a presidential election. The timing is entirely predictable but has little to do with political need.[4] Predictability does carry some advantages for political stability, but it also has some negative consequences. A major negative is the multiyear length of our presidential election campaigns. Presidential hopefuls in both the Democratic and Republican Parties began planning for the 2008 national election soon after the 2004 election.

In Canadian general elections, voters are asked *only* to choose among one small set of candidates running for a single seat in parliament. The election is general only in the sense that all members of the House are up for election; there are *no other offices or issues on the ballot.* This difference leaps out when comparing the ballots for the United States and Canada (see "Compared with What? The Voter's Burden in the United States and Canada").

This difference dramatically translates into enormous differences in the total votes that are cast by voters in the two countries. The 14.8 million Canadians who voted in their 2006 election cast just 14.8 million votes, all for parliamentary candidates. The 122.3 million Americans who went to the polls in 2004 cast over 1 *billion* votes—voting for president, congress, state executives, state legislatures, county executives, judges, and miscellaneous offices on their ballots. The burden of being an informed voter is much greater in the United States than in Canada. ★

In this chapter, we probe more deeply into elections in the United States. We describe the various methods that states use to count the billions of votes cast in each presidential election. We also consider the role of election campaigns and how they have changed over time. We study how candidates are nominated in the United States and the factors that are important in causing voters to favor one nominee over another. We also address these important questions: How well do election campaigns inform voters? How important is money in conducting a winning campaign? What are the roles of party identification, issues, and candidate attributes in influencing voters' choices and thus election outcomes? How do campaigns, elections, and parties fit into the majoritarian and pluralist models of democracy?

IN OUR OWN WORDS

Listen to Kenneth Janda discuss the main points and themes of this chapter.

Online Study Center
Improve Your Grade

★ The Evolution of Campaigning

Voting in free elections to choose leaders is the main way that citizens control government. As discussed in Chapter 8, political parties help structure the voting choice by reducing the number of candidates on the ballot to those who have a realistic chance of winning or who offer distinctive policies. An **election campaign** is an organized effort to persuade voters to choose one candidate over others competing for the same office. An effective campaign requires sufficient resources to acquire and analyze information about voters' interests, develop a strategy and matching tactics for appealing to these interests, deliver the candidate's message to the voters, and get them to cast their ballots.[5]

In the past, political parties conducted all phases of the election campaign. As recently as the 1950s, state and local party organizations "felt the pulse" of their rank-and-file members to learn what was important to the voters. They chose the candidates and then lined up leading officials to support them and to ensure big crowds at campaign rallies. They also prepared buttons, banners, and newspaper advertisements that touted their candidates, proudly named under the prominent label of the party. Finally, candidates relied heavily on the local precinct and county party organizations to contact voters before elections, to mention their names, to extol their virtues, and—most important—to make sure their supporters voted, and voted correctly.

INTERACTIVE 9.1

AP | *Early Election 2008*

election campaign An organized effort to persuade voters to choose one candidate over others competing for the same office.

Compared with What?

The Voter's Burden in the United States and Canada

No other country requires its voters to make as many decisions in a general election as the United States does. Compare these two facsimiles of official specimen ballots for the 2004 general election in the United States and the 2006 general election in Canada. The long U.S. ballot is just a *portion* of the one that confronted voters in the city of Evanston, Illinois. In addition to the fourteen different offices listed here, the full ballot also asked voters to check yes or no on the retention of seventy-four incumbent judges. For good measure, Evanstonians were also asked to vote on a statewide referendum. By contrast, the straightforward Canadian ballot (for the Notre-Dame-de-Grâce–Lachine district in Montreal) simply asked citizens to choose one from seven party candidates running for the House of Commons for that district. (Incidentally, the Liberal Party candidate won.) It is no wonder that voting is so complicated in the United States and so simple in Canada.

FOR THE CANADIAN HOUSE OF COMMONS

◯ Alexandre Lambert	*Bloc Québécois*
◯ Allen F. Mackenzie	*Conservative*
◯ Pierre-Albert Sévigny	*Green*
◯ Marlene Jennings	*Liberal*
◯ Earl Wertheimer	*Libertarian*
◯ Rachel Hoffman	*Marxist-Leninist*
◯ Peter Deslauriers	*New Democratic*

Today, candidates seldom rely much on political parties to conduct their campaigns. How do candidates learn about voters' interests today? By contracting for public opinion polls, not by asking the party. How do candidates plan their campaign strategy and tactics now? By hiring political consultants to devise clever sound bites (brief, catchy phrases) that will catch voters' attention on television, not by consulting party headquarters. How do candidates deliver their messages to voters? By conducting media campaigns, not by counting on party regulars to canvass the neighborhoods. Beginning with the 2004 election, presidential and congressional candidates have also relied heavily on the Internet to raise campaign funds and mobilize supporters.[6]

Increasingly, election campaigns have evolved from being party centered to being candidate centered.[7] This is not to say that political parties no longer have a role to play in campaigns, for they do. As noted in Chapter 8, the Democratic National Committee now exercises more control over the delegate selection process than it did before 1972. Since 1976, the Republicans have

United States General Election, Cook County, Illinois,
Tuesday, November 2, 2004

FOR PRESIDENT AND VICE PRESIDENT

❐ **John F. Kerry and John Edwards** — *Democrat*
❐ **George W. Bush and Dick Cheney** — *Republican*
❐ **Michael Badnarik and Richard V. Campagna** — *Libertarian*

FOR UNITED STATES SENATOR

❐ **Barack Obama** — *Democrat*
❐ **Alan Keyes** — *Republican*
❐ **Jerry Kohn** — *Libertarian*
❐ **Albert J. Franzen** — *Independent*

FOR REPRESENTATIVE IN CONGRESS
9th CONGRESSIONAL DISTRICT

❐ **Janice D. Schakowsky** — *Democrat*
❐ **Kurt J. Eckhardt** — *Republican*

FOR REPRESENTATIVE IN THE GENERAL ASSEMBLY
18th REPRESENTATIVE DISTRICT

❐ **Julie Hamos** — *Democrat*
❐ **Julianne E. Curtis** — *Republican*

**FOR COMMISSIONERS OF THE METROPOLITAN
WATER RECLAMATION DISTRICT** (vote for three)

❐ **Patricia Young** — *Democrat*
❐ **Barbara McGowan** — *Democrat*
❐ **Gloria Alitto Majewski** — *Democrat*
❐ **John Michael O'Sullivan** — *Republican*
❐ **Michael Conroy** — *Republican*
❐ **Fabian Villarreal** — *Republican*

FOR STATE'S ATTORNEY OF COOK COUNTY

❐ **Richard A. Devine** — *Democrat*
❐ **Phillip Spiwak** — *Republican*

FOR COOK COUNTY RECORDER OF DEEDS

❐ **Eugene "Gene" Moore** — *Democrat*
❐ **John H. Cox** — *Republican*

FOR CLERK OF THE CIRCUIT COURT OF COOK COUNTY

❐ **Dorothy A. Brown** — *Democrat*
❐ **Judith A. Kleiderman** — *Republican*

FOR JUDGE OF THE CIRCUIT COURT

❐ **Patrick T. Murphy** — *Democrat*

FOR JUDGE OF THE CIRCUIT COURT

❐ **Kathleen Marie Burke** — *Democrat*

FOR JUDGE OF THE CIRCUIT COURT

❐ **Laurence J. Dunford** — *Democrat*

FOR JUDGE OF THE CIRCUIT COURT

❐ **Michelle Jordan** — *Democrat*
❐ **John Joseph Coyne** — *Republican*

FOR JUDGE OF THE CIRCUIT COURT

❐ **Timothy Patrick Murphy** — *Democrat*

FOR JUDGE OF THE CIRCUIT COURT

❐ **Jeanne R. Cleveland Bernstein** — *Democrat*

greatly expanded their national organization and fundraising capacity. But whereas the parties virtually ran election campaigns in the past, now they exist mainly to support candidate-centered campaigns by providing services or funds to their candidates. Nevertheless, we will see that the party label is usually a candidate's prime attribute at election time.

Perhaps the most important change in American elections is that candidates don't campaign just to get elected anymore. It is now necessary to campaign for *nomination* as well. As we saw in Chapter 8, nominating candidates to run for office under the party label is one of the main functions of political parties. Party organizations once controlled that function. Even Abraham Lincoln served only one term in the House of Representatives before the party transferred the nomination for his House seat to someone else.[8] For most important offices today, however, candidates are no longer nominated *by* the party organization but *within* the party. That is, party leaders seldom choose candidates; they merely organize and supervise the election process by which party *voters* choose the candidates. Because almost all aspiring candidates must first win a primary election to gain their party's nomination, those who would campaign for election must first campaign for nomination.[9]

★ Nominations

The distinguishing feature of the nomination process in American party politics is that it usually involves an election by party voters. National party leaders do not choose their party's nominee for president or even its candidates for House and Senate seats. Virtually no other political parties in the world nominate candidates to the national legislature through party elections.[10] In more than half the world's parties, local party leaders choose legislative candidates, and their national party organization must usually approve these choices.

Democrats and Republicans nominate their candidates for national and state offices in varying ways across the country, because each state is entitled to make its own laws governing the nomination process. (This is significant in itself, for political parties in most other countries are largely free of laws stating how they must select their candidates.)[11] We can classify nomination practices by the types of party elections held and the level of office sought.

Nomination for Congress and State Offices

In the United States, almost all aspiring candidates for major offices are nominated through a **primary election,** a preliminary election conducted within the party to select its candidates. Forty-three states use primary elections alone to nominate candidates for all state and national offices, and primaries figure in the nomination processes of all the other states. The rules governing primary elections vary greatly by state; and they can change between elections. Hence, it is difficult to summarize the types of primaries and their incidence. Every state uses primary elections to nominate candidates for statewide office, but about ten states also use party conventions to place names on the primary ballots.[12] The nomination process, then, is highly decentralized, resting on the decisions of thousands, perhaps millions, of the party rank and file who participate in primary elections.

In both parties, only about half of the regular party voters (about one-quarter of the voting-age population) bother to vote in a given primary, although the proportion varies greatly by state and contest.[13] Early research on primary elections concluded that Republicans who voted in their primaries were more conservative than those who did not, whereas Democratic primary voters were more liberal than other Democrats. This finding led to the belief that primary voters tend to nominate candidates who are more ideologically extreme than the party as a whole would prefer. But other research, in which primary voters were compared with those who missed the primary but voted in the general election, reported little evidence that primary voters are unrepresentative of the ideological orientation of other party voters.[14] Some studies support another interpretation: although party activists who turn out for primaries and caucuses are not representative of the average party member, they subordinate their own views to select candidates "who will fare well in the general election."[15] Perhaps the most significant fact about primary elections in

primary election A preliminary election conducted within a political party to select candidates who will run for public office in a subsequent election.

American politics today is the decline in competition for party nominations. One major study found that only "about 25 percent of statewide candidates face serious primary competition."[16]

There are four major types of primary elections, and variants of each type have been used frequently across all states to nominate candidates for state and congressional offices.[17] At one end of the spectrum are **closed primaries,** in which voters must register their party affiliation to vote on that party's potential nominees. At the other end are **open primaries,** in which any voter, regardless of party registration or affiliation, can choose either party's ballot. In between are **modified closed primaries,** in which individual state parties decide whether to allow those not registered with either party to vote with their party registrants, and **modified open primaries,** in which all those not already registered with a party can choose any party ballot and vote with party registrants.

Most scholars believe that the type of primary held in a state affects the strength of its party organizations. Open primaries weaken parties more than closed primaries, for they allow voters to float between parties rather than require them to work within one. But the differences among types of primaries are much less important than the fact that our parties have primaries at all—that parties choose candidates through elections. This practice originated in the United States and largely remains peculiar to us. Placing the nomination of party candidates in the hands of voters rather than party leaders is a key factor in the decentralization of power in American parties, which contributes more to pluralist than to majoritarian democracy.[18]

Nomination for President

The decentralized nature of American parties is readily apparent in how presidential hopefuls must campaign for their party's nomination for president. Each party formally chooses its presidential and vice-presidential candidates at a national convention held every four years in the summer prior to the November election. Until the 1960s, party delegates chose their party's nominee right at the convention, sometimes after repeated balloting over several candidates who divided the vote and kept anyone from getting the majority needed to win the nomination. In 1920, for example, the Republican National Convention deadlocked over two leading candidates after nine ballots. Party leaders then met in the storied "smoke-filled room" and compromised on Warren G. Harding, who won on the tenth. Harding was not among the leading candidates and had won only a single primary (in his native Ohio). The last time that either party needed more than one ballot to nominate its presidential candidate was in 1952, when the Democrats took three ballots to nominate Adlai E. Stevenson. The Republicans that year nominated Dwight Eisenhower on only one ballot, but he won in a genuine contest with Senator Robert Taft. So Eisenhower also won his nomination on the convention floor.

Although 1952 was the last year a nominating majority was constructed among delegates inside the hall, delegates to the Democratic convention in 1960 and the Republican convention in 1964 also resolved uncertain outcomes. Since 1972, both parties' nominating conventions have simply ratified the results of the complex process for selecting the convention delegates, as described in the feature "Changes in the Presidential Nomination Process." Most minor parties, like the Green Party in 2004, still tend to use conventions to nominate their presidential candidates.

? Can you explain why . . . political parties favor closed rather than open primaries?

closed primary A primary election in which voters must declare their party affiliation before they are given the primary ballot containing that party's potential nominees.

open primary A primary election in which voters need not declare their party affiliation and can choose one party's primary ballot to take into the voting booth.

modified closed primary A primary election that allows individual state parties to decide whether they permit independents to vote in their primaries and for which offices.

modified open primary A primary election that entitles independent voters to vote in a party's primary.

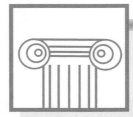

Changes in the Presidential Nomination Process

When President Lyndon Johnson abruptly announced in late March 1968 that he would not run for reelection, the door opened for his vice president, Hubert Humphrey. Humphrey felt it was too late to campaign in primaries against other candidates already in the race; nevertheless, he commanded enough support among party leaders to win the Democratic nomination. The stormy protests outside the party's national convention against the "inside politics" of his nomination led to major changes in the way both parties have nominated their presidential candidates since 1968.

Presidential Nominating Process

Until 1968

Party Dominated

The nomination decision is largely in the hands of party leaders. Candidates win by enlisting the support of state and local party machines.

Few Primaries

Most delegates are selected by state party establishments, with little or no public participation. Some primaries are held, but their results do not necessarily determine the nominee. Primaries are used to indicate candidates' "electability."

Short Campaigns

Candidates usually begin their public campaign early in the election year.

Since 1968

Candidate Dominated

Campaigns are independent of party establishments. Endorsements by party leaders have little effect on nomination choice.

Many Primaries

Most delegates are selected by popular primaries and caucuses. Nominations are determined largely by voters' decisions at these contests.

Long Campaigns

Candidates begin laying groundwork for campaigns three or four years before the election. Candidates who are not well organized at least eighteen months before the election may have little chance of winning.

Selecting Convention Delegates. No national legislation specifies how the state parties must select delegates to their national conventions. Instead, state legislatures have enacted a bewildering variety of procedures, which often differ for Democrats and Republicans in the same state. The most important distinction in delegate selection is between the presidential primary and the local caucus. In 2004, both major parties in about thirty states used primaries to select delegates to their presidential nominating conventions, and both parties in about ten states selected delegates through a combination of local caucuses and state conventions. In the remaining states, one of the two parties (usually the Democrats) used primaries, while the other (usually the Republicans) used caucuses and conventions.[19]

Until 1968

Easy Money

Candidates frequently raise large amounts of money quickly by tapping a handful of wealthy contributors. No federal limits on spending by candidates.

Limited Media Coverage

Campaigns are followed by print journalists and, in later years, by television. But press coverage of campaigns is not intensive and generally does not play a major role in influencing the process.

Late Decisions

Events early in the campaign year, such as the New Hampshire primary, are not decisive. States that pick delegates late in the year, such as California, frequently are important in selecting the nominee. Many states enter the convention without making final decisions about candidates.

Open Conventions

National party conventions sometimes begin with the nomination still undecided. The outcome is determined by maneuvering and negotiations among party factions, often stretching over multiple ballots.

Since 1968

Difficult Fundraising

Campaign contributions are limited ($1,000 per person before 2004; now $2,000), so candidates must work endlessly to raise money from thousands of small contributors. Political action committee contributions are important in primaries. Campaign spending is limited by law, both nationally and for individual states. (If candidates forgo public funds—as both Bush and John Kerry did for the primary elections in 2004—spending limits no longer apply.)

Media Focused

Campaigns are covered intensively by the media, particularly television. Media treatment of candidates plays a crucial role in determining the nominee.

"Front-Loaded"

Early events, such as the Iowa caucuses and New Hampshire primary, are important. The nomination may even be decided before many major states vote. Early victories attract great media attention, which gives winners free publicity and greater fundraising ability.

Closed Conventions

The nominee is determined before the convention, which does little more than ratify the decision made in primaries and caucuses. Convention activities focus on creating a favorable media image of the candidate for the general election campaign.

Source: Adapted from Michael Nelson (ed.), *Congressional Quarterly's Guide to the Presidency* (Washington, D.C.: CQ Press, 1989), p. 201. Copyright © 1989 Congressional Quarterly Inc. Used by permission.

A **presidential primary** is a special primary held to select delegates to attend a party's national nominating convention. Party supporters typically vote for the candidate they favor as their party's nominee for president, and candidates win delegates according to various formulas. Virtually all Democratic primaries are *proportional,* meaning that candidates win delegates in rough proportion to the votes they win. Specifically, candidates who win at least 15 percent of the vote divide the state's delegates in proportion to the percentage of their primary votes. In contrast, most Republican primaries follow the *winner-take-all* principle, which gives all the state's delegates to the candidate who wins a plurality of its vote.

The **caucus/convention** method of delegate selection has several stages. It begins with local meetings, or caucuses, of party supporters to choose delegates

presidential primary A special primary election used to select delegates to attend the party's national convention, which in turn nominates the presidential candidate.

caucus/convention A method used to select delegates to attend a party's national convention. Generally, a local meeting selects delegates for a county-level meeting, which in turn selects delegates for a higher-level meeting; the process culminates in a state convention that actually selects the national convention delegates.

Midnight Madness in New Hampshire

Once every four years, there's something to do after midnight in Dixville Notch, New Hampshire, and in nearby Hart's Landing. Both small towns (each with under forty residents) revel in the tradition of being the first to vote in the nation's first primary. In 2004, former general Wesley Clark crushed his opposition in the Democratic primary, winning a majority of the fifteen votes cast at midnight in Dixville Notch, and a plurality of the sixteen votes in Hart's Landing. Alas, Clark won only 13 percent of the primary vote in New Hampshire overall. (*Robert F. Bukaty/AP/Wide World Photos*)

? **Can you explain why . . .** convention delegates have been chosen increasingly earlier in recent election years?

front-loading States' practice of moving delegate selection primaries and caucuses earlier in the calendar year to gain media and candidate attention.

to attend a larger subsequent meeting, usually at the county level. Most delegates selected in the local caucuses openly back one of the presidential candidates. The county meetings select delegates to a higher level. The process culminates in a state convention, which selects the delegates to the national convention. In 2004, some states that planned popular primaries to select Republican delegates canceled them for lack of opposition to President George W. Bush and held caucuses instead, thus saving money.

Primary elections (which were stimulated by the Progressive movement, discussed in Chapter 7) were first used to select delegates to nominating conventions in 1912. Heralded as a party "reform," primaries spread like wildfire.[20] By 1916, a majority of delegates to both conventions were chosen through party elections, but presidential primaries soon dropped in popularity. From 1924 through 1960, rarely were more than 40 percent of the delegates to the national conventions chosen through primaries. Antiwar protests at the 1968 Democratic National Convention sparked rule changes in the national party that required more "open" procedures for selecting delegates. Voting in primaries seemed the most open procedure. By 1972, this method of selection accounted for about 60 percent of the delegates at both party conventions. Now the parties in over forty states rely on presidential primaries, which generate more than 80 percent of the delegates.[21] Because nearly all delegates selected in primaries are publicly committed to specific candidates, one can easily tell before a party's summer nominating convention who is going to be its nominee. Indeed, we have been learning the nominee's identity earlier and earlier, thanks to **front-loading** of delegate selection. This term describes the tendency during the past two decades for states to move their primaries earlier in the calendar year to gain attention from the media and the candidates (see "Looking to the Future: Happy New Year! Let's Vote!"). Some describe the phenomenon as "New Hampshire envy."[22]

Campaigning for the Nomination.

The process of nominating party candidates for president is a complex, drawn-out affair that has no parallel in

Looking to the Future

Happy New Year! Let's Vote!

In recent decades, states have tried to move ahead of other states in setting dates for primary elections to choose delegates to presidential nominating conventions. This trend is seen in the dates for the nation's first primary, traditionally held in New Hampshire. As other states moved up their primaries in a process called "front-loading" (see the text), New Hampshire, whose legislature has vowed to be first, kept ahead of the pack with support from the Democratic National Committee. For the 2008 primary, Michigan bucked the DNC and tried to move earlier than New Hampshire. (As of October 2007, Michigan's final date was not clear.) Will the trend to earlier primaries continue into the future? Do you see more costs or benefits from this trend? What might alter it?

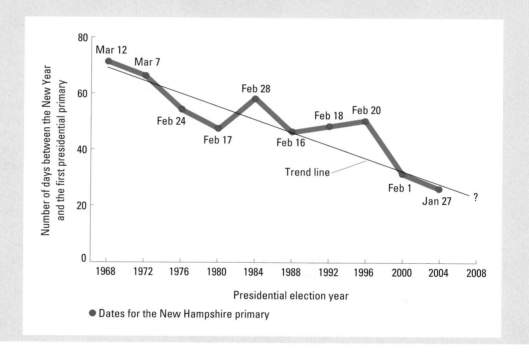

● Dates for the New Hampshire primary

any other nation.[23] Would-be presidents announce their candidacy and begin campaigning many months before the first convention delegates are selected. Soon after one election ends, prospective candidates quietly begin lining up political and financial support for their likely race nearly four years later. This early, silent campaign has been dubbed the *invisible primary*.[24]

Indeed, the invisible campaign for the presidency in 2004 began soon after the disputed 2000 election, as various presidential hopefuls in the Democratic Party contemplated their chances for capturing the party's nomination. For a time, their activities were kept in check by the likelihood that Al Gore, the 2000 Democratic presidential candidate, would seek renomination to run again in 2004. In the meantime, others began making their own plans. On November 8, 2002, Howard Dean, former governor of Vermont, took a step toward

When 2008 News Gets Old in 2007

Frontloading the process of selecting delegates to the parties' nominating conventions has led states to fix earlier dates for holding primaries and caucuses in presidential election years. Moreover, eager candidates now proclaim their candidacy more than a year before the delegate selection process even starts. Voters reading about the November 2008 election in the spring of 2007 may be turned off by such early and intense campaigning. *(Bill Schorr: © United Features Syndicate, Inc.)*

" I'M ALREADY SICK OF THE 2008 ELECTION... "

seeking the presidential nomination by creating a political action committee. A month later, Senator John Kerry announced that he would seek the nomination. Gore surprised many on December 16 when he declined to seek renomination. Before another month had passed, three other Democrats had stepped up to announce their candidacies. The 2004 primary season was becoming visible.

By historical accident, two small states, Iowa and New Hampshire, have become the testing ground of candidates' popularity with party voters. Accordingly, each basks in the media spotlight once every four years. Both state legislatures are now committed to leading the delegate selection process, ensuring their states' share of national publicity and their bids for political history. The Iowa caucuses and the New Hampshire primary have served different functions in the presidential nominating process.[25] The contest in Iowa has traditionally tended to winnow out candidates rejected by the party faithful. The New Hampshire primary, held one week later, tests the Iowa front-runners' appeal to ordinary party voters, which foreshadows their likely strength in the general election. Because voting takes little effort by itself, more citizens are likely to vote in primaries than to attend caucuses, which can last for hours. In 2004, about 7 percent of the voting-age population participated in both parties' Iowa caucuses, whereas about 30 percent voted in both New Hampshire primaries.[26]

From 1920 to 1972, New Hampshire's primary election led the nation in selecting delegates to the parties' summer conventions. But in 1972 Iowa chose its convention delegates in caucuses even earlier. Since then, Iowa and New Hampshire agreed to be first in their methods of delegate selection.[27] Pressured by other states, the Democratic National Committee ruled that in 2008 Iowa would still hold the first caucus (January 14) but Nevada could hold a caucus (January 19) before New Hampshire's first primary (January 22), while South Carolina could have the second primary (January 29). With the floodgates opened, other states defied tradition and party rules. Florida also set its primary for January 29, and Michigan moved its primary to January 15. Iowa and New Hampshire threatened to move their dates even earlier, and the DNC vowed not to seat Florida's and Michigan's delegates at the party's convention. In October 2007, the matter of which states would select delegates in January (three months later) was unresolved.

No one knows in 2007 how the 2008 delegate selection calendar will play out for presidential candidates in both parties, but reviewing past campaigns may help explain what happens. Conventional wisdom holds that a favorable showing in the Iowa caucuses helps candidates win the New Hampshire primary. Statistical analysis of the relative effects of both states' delegate selection processes from 1980 through 2000 showed that New Hampshire had a greater *direct* effect on the outcome of a contested nomination, while Iowa affected the New Hampshire results.[29] These findings certainly appeared to hold within the Democratic Party for 2004. Within the Republican Party, however, events in Iowa and New Hampshire had little effect on the outcome in 2004, for President Bush faced no real opposition to renomination.

In truth, some enterprising souls were on Republican presidential primary ballots in 2004. In New Hampshire, for example, President Bush was challenged by little-known candidates like Richard P. Bosa and Blake Ashby, among eleven others. All thirteen of Bush's challengers together won less than 7 percent of the New Hampshire primary vote.[30]

On the Democratic side, so many candidates threw their hats into the ring during the primary season that their comings and goings are hard to track. The identities and fates of the ten significant candidates who sought the Democratic presidential nomination are depicted in Figure 9.1. The earliest person to declare his candidacy for the Democratic nomination was Howard Dean. As the former governor of a very small state (Vermont) and with little national visibility, Dean was not given much chance to have an impact. An NBC News/ *Wall Street Journal* poll in January 2003 found Dean favored by only 3 percent of respondents, compared with 25 percent for Senator Joe Lieberman of Connecticut, the 2000 Democratic candidate for vice president who entered soon after Gore withdrew from the 2004 race.[31] The only others with double-digit support were Representative Dick Gephardt of Missouri (17 percent) and Senator John Kerry of Massachusetts (14 percent).

Dean quickly built his campaign around the Internet, and by spring 2003 he had raised over $1 million online, eclipsing the rate at which Democratic senator Bill Bradley raised funds online in 2000.[32] By the end of the year, Dean's campaign had raised almost $40 million, said to be a one-year record for Democratic presidential fundraising.[33] Dean was so strong in December 2003 that Bush's political advisers concluded he would be Bush's opponent in 2004.[34]

Following more than sixty days of visits to Iowa by each of the major candidates, Iowans concluded otherwise in nearly two thousand Democratic caucuses statewide on January 19. Having met the candidates and heard them speak, more Iowa caucus participants favored Kerry (38 percent) and Senator John Edwards of South Carolina (32 percent) than Howard Dean (18 percent). Attempting to energize his crestfallen supporters the evening of January 21, Dean gave a frenzied pep talk ending in an infamous scream that drew negative comments the next day across the nation and effectively terminated a brilliant campaign built around the Internet.[35]

Kerry's unexpectedly strong victory in the Iowa caucuses occurred on a Monday. The following Tuesday (January 27), Kerry won the New Hampshire primary, again taking 38 percent of the vote. According to a statewide exit poll, 56 percent of those who wanted to "defeat Bush" in November chose Kerry.[36] Since 1976, when candidate Jimmy Carter publicized the Iowa caucuses, there have been only twelve match-up contests between same-party candidates in the Iowa caucuses and the New Hampshire primary. Only five times did the Iowa

FIGURE 9.1	From Many to One: 2004 Democratic Presidential Hopefuls Dropping Out

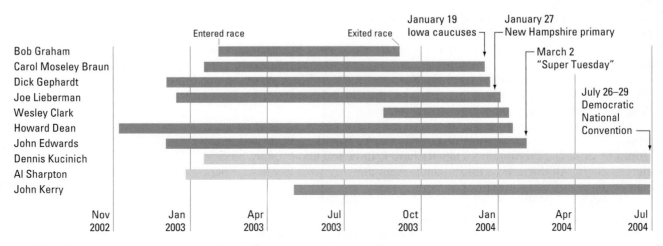

Howard Dean was the first candidate to file with the Federal Election Commission before "heir apparent" Al Gore announced on December 16, 2002, that he would not run for the 2004 Democratic presidential nomination. John Kerry also entered the race before Gore withdrew. After Gore exited, others entered. Senator Bob Graham of Florida withdrew first for lack of support, followed by former senator Carol Moseley Braun of Illinois—both leaving before any state chose delegates. Dick Gephardt withdrew after the Iowa caucuses, Joe Lieberman left after the New Hampshire primary, and General Wesley Clark from Arkansas departed soon afterward. When John Edwards withdrew after the "Super Tuesday" round of primaries on March 3, John Kerry stood without serious challenge. Although Representative Dennis Kucinich of Ohio and Reverend Al Sharpton of New York formally remained in the race, they were there for the exercise. In fact, Sharpton on March 15 actually endorsed Kerry for the nomination!

winner also win the New Hampshire primary.[37] When that occurred, the winner of both contests also won the party's nomination. In the wake of New Hampshire, Kerry won more delegates than his opponents in every state but three, as other candidates dropped out along the way (see Figure 9.1).

On March 3, Senator John Edwards withdrew from the race, meaning that Kerry effectively clinched the nomination. That was months before the July Democratic national convention, and twenty-two state parties had not yet selected their convention delegates.[38] Kerry's emergence as the Democratic presidential nominee in the first week of March broke the previous record for early nominations.[39] The new record flowed from the increased front-loading of the delegate process, and the early choice was designed to avoid "a food fight going through the spring of 2004."[40] But selecting the Democratic candidate in March eight months before the November election exposed Senator Kerry to a very long campaign fight against a sitting president, who was also sitting on over $100 million in campaign funds.

Over 24 million people (about 12 percent of the voting-age population) voted in one of the presidential primaries in 2004, and somewhat more than a half-million participated in party caucuses.[41] Requiring prospective presidential candidates to campaign before many millions of party voters in primaries and hundreds of thousands of party activists in caucus states has several consequences:

■ *When no incumbent in the White House is seeking reelection, the presidential nominating process becomes contested in both parties.* This is what occurred in 2000. In the complex mix of caucus and primary methods that states use to select convention delegates, timing and luck can affect who wins, and even an outside chance of success ordinarily attracts a half-dozen or so plausible contestants in either party lacking an incumbent president. With President Bush ineligible to run again in 2008, eleven Republicans and eight Democrats had registered as active candidates by June 2007.

■ *An incumbent president usually encounters little or no opposition for renomination within the party.* This is what happened in 2004, but challenges can occur. In 1992, President George Herbert Walker Bush faced fierce opposition for the Republican nomination from Pat Buchanan. In 1968, President Lyndon Johnson faced such hostility within the Democratic Party that he declined to seek renomination.

■ *Candidates favored by most party identifiers usually win their party's nomination.* There have been only two exceptions to this rule since 1936, when poll data first became available: Adlai E. Stevenson in 1952 and George McGovern in 1972.[42] Both were Democrats; both lost impressively in the general election. As for 2004, it depends when the poll was taken. In December 2003, most Democratic voters favored Howard Dean, but immediately after the Iowa caucuses on January 19, 2004, most voters favored John Kerry, and his margin increased following his primary victories.[43]

■ *Candidates who win the nomination do so largely on their own and owe little or nothing to the national party organization, which usually does not promote a candidate.* In fact, Jimmy Carter won the nomination in 1976 against a field of nationally prominent Democrats, although he was a party outsider with few strong connections to the national party leadership.

★ Elections

By national law, all seats in the House of Representatives and one-third of the seats in the Senate are filled in a **general election** held in early November in even-numbered years. Every state takes advantage of the national election to fill some of the nearly 500,000 state and local offices across the country, which makes the election even more "general." When the president is chosen every fourth year, the election is identified as a *presidential election.* The intervening elections are known as *congressional, midterm,* or *off-year elections.*

general election A national election held by law in November of every even-numbered year.

Presidential Elections and the Electoral College

In contrast to almost all other offices in the United States, the presidency does not go automatically to the candidate who wins the most votes. In fact, George W. Bush won the presidency in 2000 despite receiving fewer popular votes than Al Gore. Instead, a two-stage procedure specified in the Constitution decides elections for the president; it requires selection of the president by a group (college) of electors representing the states. Technically, we elect a president not in a national election but in a *federal* election.

The Electoral College: Structure. Surprising as it might seem, the term *electoral college* is not mentioned in the Constitution and is not readily found in books on American politics prior to World War II. One major dictionary defines a *college* as "a body of persons having a common purpose or shared duties."[44] The electors who choose the president of the United States became known as the electoral college largely during the twentieth century. Eventually, this term became incorporated into statutes relating to presidential elections, so it has assumed a legal basis.[45]

The Constitution (Article II, Section 1) says, "Each State shall appoint, in such Manner as the Legislature thereof may direct, a Number of Electors, equal to the whole Number of Senators and Representatives to which the State may be entitled in the Congress." Thus, each of the fifty states is entitled to one elector for each of its senators (100 total) and one for each of its representatives (435 votes total), totaling 535 electoral votes. In addition, the Twenty-third Amendment to the Constitution awarded three electoral votes (the minimum for any state) to the District of Columbia, although it elects no voting members of Congress. The total number of electoral votes therefore is 538. The Constitution specifies that a candidate needs a majority of electoral votes, or 270 today, to win the presidency. If no candidate receives a majority, the election is thrown into the House of Representatives. The House votes by state, with each state casting one vote. The candidates in the House election are the top three finishers in the general election. A presidential election has gone to the House only twice in American history, in 1800 and 1824, before a stable two-party system had developed.

Electoral votes are apportioned among the states according to their representation in Congress, which depends largely on their population. Because of population changes recorded by the 2000 census, the distribution of electoral votes among the states changed between the 2000 and 2004 presidential elections. Figure 9.2 shows the distribution of electoral votes for the 2004 election, indicating which states have lost and gained electoral votes. The clear pattern is the systemic loss of people and electoral votes in the north-central and eastern states and the gain in the western and southern states.

The Electoral College: Politics. In 1789, the first set of presidential electors was chosen under the new Constitution. Only three states chose their electors by direct popular vote; state legislatures selected electors in the others. Selection by state legislature remained the norm until 1792. Afterward, direct election by popular vote became more common, and by 1824 voters chose electors in eighteen of twenty-four states. Since 1860, all states have selected their electors through popular vote once they had entered the Union.[46] In the disputed 2000 presidential election, the Republican Florida state legislature

FIGURE 9.2 Population Shifts and Political Gains and Losses Since 1960

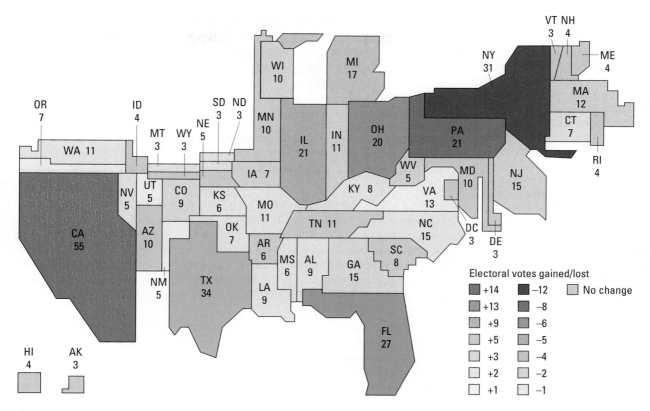

If the states were sized according to their electoral votes for the 2004 presidential election, the nation might resemble this map, on which states are drawn according to their population, based on the 2000 census. Each state has as many electoral votes as its combined representation in the Senate (always two) and the House (which depends on population). Although New Jersey is much smaller in area than Montana, New Jersey has far more people and is thus bigger in terms of "electoral geography." The coloring on this map shows the states that have gained electoral votes since 1960 (in shades of green) and those that have lost electoral votes (in shades of purple). States that have not had the number of their electoral votes changed since 1960 are blue. This map clearly reflects the drain of population (and seats in Congress) from the north-central and eastern states to the western and southern states. California, with two senators and fifty-three representatives in the 2004 election, will have fifty-five electoral votes for presidential elections through 2010, when the next census will be taken.

threatened to resolve the dispute in favor of Bush by selecting its electors itself. There was precedent to do so, but it was a pre–Civil War precedent.

Of course, the situation in Florida was itself unprecedented due to the extremely close election in 2000. Voters nationwide favored the Democratic candidate, Al Gore, by a plurality of approximately 500,000 votes out of 105

? Can you explain why . . . the presidential election is really federal and not national?

FIGURE 9.3 How America Votes

According to a study by Election Data Services, most of the registered voters in over three thousand election jurisdictions across the United States had their ballots read by optical scanning equipment in November 2004. Because such equipment is better suited to less populous jurisdictions, an even higher percentage of the nation's counties (45 percent) will count their ballots by scanning them. More populous counties tend to rely on electronic voting methods, although some experts say that electronic systems are not secure from outside entry and manipulation. In the wake of the disputed 2000 presidential election in Florida, Congress in 2002 passed the Help America Vote Act, providing funds to replace punch-card systems and mechanical lever voting machines. The number of counties relying on either punch cards or lever systems dropped from about a thousand in 2000 to under six hundred in 2004.

Source: "New Study Shows 50 Million Voters Will Use Electronic Voting System, 32 Million Still with Punch Cards in 2004," 12 February 2004, report by Election Data Services.

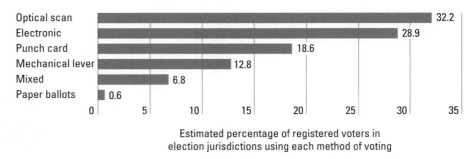

Estimated percentage of registered voters in election jurisdictions using each method of voting

million cast. But the presidential election is a *federal* election. A candidate is not chosen president by national popular vote but by a majority of the states' electoral votes. In every state but Maine and Nebraska, the candidate who wins a plurality of its popular vote—whether by 20 votes or 20,000 votes—wins *all* of the state's electoral votes. Gore and his Republican opponent, George W. Bush, ran close races in many states across the nation. Not counting Florida, Gore had won 267 electoral votes, just three short of the 270 he needed to claim the presidency.

But in Florida, which had twenty-five electoral votes in 2000, the initial vote count showed an extremely close race, with Bush ahead by the slimmest of margins. If Bush out-polled Gore by just a single vote, Bush could add its 25 electoral votes to the 246 he won in the other states, for a total of 271. That was just one more than the number needed to win the presidency. Gore trailed Bush by only about 2,000 votes, close enough to ask for a recount. But the recount proved difficult due to different ballots and different methods for counting them (see Figure 9.3). After more than a month of ballot counting, recounting, more recounting, lawsuits, court decisions—and the Republican legislature's threat to select the electors on its own to ensure Bush's victory—Bush was certified as the winner of Florida's 25 *electoral* votes by a mere 537 *popular* votes. So ended one of the most protracted, complicated, and intense presidential elections in American history.[47]

The Electoral College: Abolish It? Between 1789 and 2000, about seven hundred proposals to change the electoral college scheme were introduced in Congress.[48] Historically, polls have shown public opinion opposed to the electoral college.[49] Following the 2000 election, letters flooded into newspapers, urging anew that the system be changed.

To evaluate the criticisms, one must first distinguish between the electoral "college" and the "system" of electoral votes. Strictly speaking, the electoral college is merely the set of individuals empowered to cast a state's electoral votes. In a presidential election, voters don't actually vote for a candidate; they vote for a slate of little-known electors (their names are rarely even on the ballot) pledged to one of the candidates. Most critics hold that the founding fathers argued for a body of electors because they did not trust people to vote directly for candidates. But one scholar contends that the device of independent electors was adopted by the Constitutional Convention as a compromise between

FIGURE 9.4 The Popular Vote and the Electoral Vote

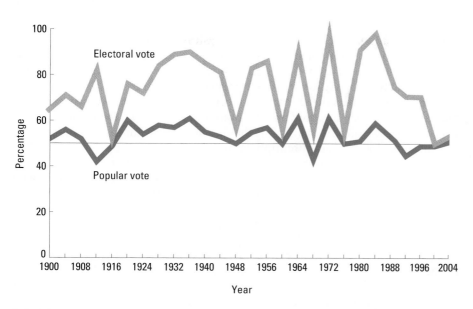

Strictly speaking, a presidential election is a federal election, not a national election. A candidate must win a majority (270) of the nation's total electoral vote (538). A candidate can win a plurality of the popular vote and still not win the presidency. Until 2000, the last time a candidate won most of the popular votes but did not win the presidency was in 1888. In every election between these two, the candidate who won a plurality of the popular vote won an even larger proportion of the electoral vote. So the electoral vote system magnified the winner's victory and thus increased the legitimacy of the president-elect. As we learned from the 2000 election, that result is not guaranteed.

Source: Harold W. Stanley and Richard G. Niemi, Vital Statistics on American Politics, 2005–2006 (Washington, D.C.: CQ Press, 2005).

those who favored having legislatures cast the states' electoral votes for president and those who favored direct popular election.[50] The electoral college allowed states to choose, and—as described in Chapter 8—all states gravitated to direct election of electors by 1860. Occasionally (but rarely), electors break their pledges when they assemble to cast their written ballots at their state capitol in December (electors who do so are called "faithless electors"). Indeed, this happened in 2004, when one of the ten Minnesota electors voted not for Democrat John Kerry, who won the state, but for his running mate, John Edwards. Electors vote by secret ballot, so no one knew which one voted for Edwards instead of Kerry.[51] Such aberrations make for historical footnotes but do not affect outcomes. Today, voters have good reason to oppose the need for a body of electors to translate their decision, and few observers defend the electoral college itself.

The more troubling criticism centers on the electoral vote *system*, which makes for a federal rather than a national election. Many reformers favor a majoritarian method for choosing the president—by nationwide direct popular vote. They argue that it is simply wrong to have a system that allows a candidate who wins the most popular votes nationally to lose the election. Until 2000, that situation had not occurred since 1888, when Grover Cleveland won the popular vote but lost the presidency to Benjamin Harrison in the electoral college. During all intervening elections, the candidate winning a plurality of the popular vote also won a majority of the electoral vote. In fact, the electoral vote generally operated to magnify the margin of victory, as Figure 9.4 shows. Some scholars argued that this magnifying effect increased the legitimacy of presidents-elect who failed to win a majority of the popular vote, which happened in the elections of Kennedy, Nixon (first time), Clinton (both times), and certainly George W. Bush (first time).

The 2000 election proved that defenders of the electoral vote system can no longer claim that a federal election based on electoral votes yields the same outcome as a national election based on the popular vote. However, three lines of argument support selecting a president by electoral votes rather than by popular vote. First, if one supports a federal form of government as embodied within the Constitution, then one may defend the electoral vote system because it gives small states more weight in the vote: they have two senators, the same as large states. Second, if one favors presidential candidates campaigning on foot and in rural areas (needed to win most states) rather than campaigning via television to the one hundred most populous market areas, then one might favor the electoral vote system.[52] Third, if one does not want to see a *nationwide* recount in a close election (multiplying by fifty the counting problems in Florida), then one might want to keep the current system. So switching to selecting the president by popular vote has serious implications, which explains why Congress has not moved quickly to amend the Constitution.

Congressional Elections

In a presidential election, the candidates for the presidency are listed at the top of the ballot, followed by the candidates for other national offices and those for state and local offices. A voter is said to vote a **straight ticket** when she or he chooses the same party's candidates for all the offices. A voter who chooses candidates from different parties is said to vote a **split ticket.** About half of all voters say they split their tickets, and the proportion of voters who chose a presidential candidate from one party and a congressional candidate from the other has varied between 15 and 30 percent since 1952.[53] In the 1970s and 1980s, the common pattern was to elect a Republican as president while electing mostly Democrats to Congress. This produced a divided government, with the executive and legislative branches controlled by different parties (see Chapter 12). In the mid-1990s, the electorate flipped the pattern, electing a Democratic president but a Republican Congress.

Until the historic 1994 election, Democrats had maintained a lock on congressional elections for decades, winning a majority of House seats since 1954 and controlling the Senate for all but six years during that period. Republicans regularly complained that inequitable districts drawn by Democrat-dominated state legislatures had denied them their fair share of seats. For example, the Republicans won 46 percent of the congressional vote in 1992 but gained only 40 percent of the seats.[54] Despite the Republicans' complaint, election specialists note that sizable discrepancies between votes won and seats won is the inevitable consequence of **first-past-the-post elections**—a British term for elections conducted in single-member districts that award victory to the candidate with the most votes. In all such elections worldwide, the party that wins the most votes tends to win more seats than projected by its percentage of the vote.* Thus in 1994, when Republicans got barely 50 percent of the House votes nationwide, they won 53 percent of the House seats. Gaining control of the House for the first time in forty years, they made no complaint. In 2004, the Republicans won 48.9 percent to the Democrats' 48.3 percent, and again

straight ticket In voting, a single party's candidates for all the offices.

split ticket In voting, candidates from different parties for different offices.

first-past-the-post elections A British term for elections conducted in single-member districts that award victory to the candidate with the most votes.

---

*If you have trouble understanding this phenomenon, think of a basketball team that scores, on average, 51 percent of the total points in all the games it plays. Such a team usually wins more than just 51 percent of its games because it tends to win the close ones.

the GOP took 53 percent of the seats for comfortable control. These recent election results reveal no evidence of Democratic malapportionment of congressional districts. Both parties have enjoyed, and suffered, the mathematics of first-past-the-post elections.

Heading into the 2006 congressional elections, Republicans feared losing one or both houses of Congress. President Bush's approval rate had declined, scandals tarred several members of Congress, and the situation in Iraq increased in violence. In a mirror image of the 1994 election, voters in 2006 replaced enough Republican incumbents with Democrats to shift control of Congress. Exit polls showed that more voters (36 to 22 percent) opposed the president than supported him. Voters who said the issues of corruption/ethics, Iraq, and the economy were "extremely important" divided 60–40 for Democratic candidates.[55]

★ Campaigns

As political scientists Barbara Salmore and Stephen Salmore have observed, election campaigns have been studied more through anecdotes than through systematic analysis.[56] These writers developed an analytical framework that emphasizes the political context of the campaign, the financial resources available for conducting the campaign, and the strategies and tactics that underlie the dissemination of information about the candidate.

The Political Context

The two most important structural factors that face each candidate planning a campaign are the office the candidate is seeking and whether he or she is the *incumbent* (the current officeholder, running for reelection) or the *challenger* (who seeks to replace the incumbent). Alternatively, both candidates can be running in an **open election,** which lacks an incumbent because of a resignation or death or constitutional requirement. Incumbents usually enjoy great advantages over challengers, especially in elections to Congress. As explained in Chapter 11, incumbents in the House of Representatives are almost impossible to defeat, historically winning more than 95 percent of the time.[57] Incumbent senators are somewhat more vulnerable. An incumbent president is also difficult to defeat—but not impossible. Democrat Jimmy Carter was defeated for reelection in 1980, as was Republican George H. W. Bush in 1992.

Every candidate for Congress must also examine the characteristics of the state or district, including its physical size and the sociological makeup of its electorate. In general, the bigger and more populous the district or state and the more diverse the electorate, the more complicated and costly the campaign. Obviously, running for president means conducting a huge, complicated, and expensive campaign. By early January 2004, 160 people staffed the Bush-Cheney national campaign headquarters in Arlington, Virginia, and 33 employees opened 14 other offices in major states.[58] Although President Bush ran as an incumbent with no opposition for renomination, his political advisers said he was already "absorbed" in his reelection campaign, launched on February 23 in a Washington speech to the Republican Governors' Association.[59] By March 2004, Senator Kerry, who had not yet selected his vice-presidential running mate, also had an elaborate campaign organization. It named fifty people to national staff positions (such as communications director, deputy press secretary,

open election An election that lacks an incumbent.

and policy analyst), listed directors in thirty states, and gave addresses for campaign offices in nine states.[60]

Despite talk about the decreased influence of party affiliation on voting behavior, the party preference of the electorate is an important factor in the context of a campaign. It is easier for a candidate to get elected when her or his party matches the electorate's preference, in part because raising the money needed to conduct a winning campaign is easier. Challengers for congressional seats, for example, get far less money from organized groups than do incumbents and must rely more on their personal funds and raising money from individual donors.[61] So where candidates represent the minority party, they have to overcome not only a voting bias but also a funding bias. Finally, significant political issues—such as economic recession, personal scandals, and war—not only affect a campaign but also can dominate it and even negate such positive factors as incumbency and the advantages of a strong economy. Bush entered the 2004 campaign as the incumbent president fighting the war on terrorism in the wake of 9/11. Ordinarily during war, an incumbent president would have a huge advantage, but many citizens opposed Bush's invasion of Iraq, and many in 2004 were unhappy with the economy, especially the loss of jobs. Kerry's campaign focused on these issues.

Financing

Regarding election campaigns, former House Speaker Thomas ("Tip") O'Neill said, "There are four parts to any campaign. The candidate, the issues of the candidate, the campaign organization, and the money to run the campaign with. Without money you can forget the other three."[62] Money pays for office space, staff salaries, cell phones, computers, travel expenses, campaign literature, and, of course, advertising in the mass media. A successful campaign requires a good campaign organization and a good candidate, but enough money will buy the best campaign managers, equipment, transportation, research, and consultants—making the quality of the organization largely a function of money.[63] So from a practical viewpoint, campaign resources boil down to campaign funds. Regulations of campaign financing for state elections vary according to the state. Campaign financing for federal elections is regulated by national legislation.

Regulating Campaign Financing. Early campaign financing laws had various flaws, and none provided for adequate enforcement. In 1971, during a period of party reform, Congress passed the Federal Election Campaign Act (FECA), which limited media spending and imposed stringent new rules for full reporting of campaign contributions and expenditures. The need for strict legislation soon became clear. In 1968, before FECA was enacted, House and Senate candidates reported spending $8.5 million on their campaigns. In 1972, with FECA in force, the same number of candidates admitted spending $88.9 million.[64]

Financial misdeeds during Nixon's 1972 reelection campaign forced major amendments to the original FECA in 1974. The new legislation created the **Federal Election Commission (FEC)**, an independent agency of six members appointed by the president with approval of the Senate. No more than three members may come from the same party, and their six-year appointments are staggered over time so that no one president appoints the entire commission.

Federal Election Commission (FEC) A bipartisan federal agency of six members that oversees the financing of national election campaigns.

The FEC is charged with enforcing limits on financial contributions to national campaigns, requiring full disclosure of campaign spending, and administering the public financing of presidential campaigns, which began with the 1976 election.

The law also limited the amounts that nonparty groups called political action committees or PACs (discussed at length in Chapter 10) could contribute to election campaigns, and it imposed limits on contributions by individuals and organizations to campaigns for federal office—that is, Congress and the presidency. The law targeted so-called **hard money** (direct contributions to candidates' election campaigns) in contrast to **soft money** (donations to party committees for buying equipment, remodeling the headquarters, or staffing regional offices). No person could contribute more than $1,000 to any candidate for federal office, but the law permitted large soft money donations to national party committees. Later, as both parties raised very large sums of soft money, that aspect of party finance became troublesome.

Some people opposed even limits on hard money contributions, viewing them as "free speech" and challenging the 1974 limits under the First Amendment. Although the Supreme Court upheld limits on contributions in 1976, it struck down limits on *spending* by individuals or organizations made independently on behalf of a national candidate—holding that such spending constituted free speech, protected under the First Amendment. It also limited the FEC to regulate only advertisements advocating a candidate's election or defeat with such words as "vote for," "vote against."[65] The 1974 FECA (with minor amendments) governed national elections for almost three decades.

As campaign spending increased, some members of Congress spoke piously about strengthening campaign finance laws but feared altering the process that elected them. In 2002 a bill introduced by Republican senator John McCain (Arizona) and Democratic senator Russell Feingold (Wisconsin) finally passed as the Bipartisan Campaign Reform Act (BCRA; pronounced "bikra"). BCRA was fiercely challenged from several sources but was upheld by the Supreme Court in 2003 and took effect for the 2004 election.

To put BCRA into perspective, we must consider it in light of the 1974 legislation, which it effectively replaced. In general, BCRA raised the old limits on individual spending. For example, the 1974 limit of $1,000 from an individual was raised to $2,000 in 2004 and indexed for inflation in future years. However, the 2002 law did not raise the $5,000 contribution limit for PACs, which many citizens thought already had too much influence in elections, and did not index PAC contributions for inflation. Here are the major BCRA limitations for 2007–2008 contributions by individuals, adjusted for inflation:

$2,300 to a specific candidate in a separate election during a two-year cycle (primaries, general, and runoff elections count as separate elections)

$10,000 per year to each state party or political committee

$28,500 per year to any national party committee

BCRA also banned large soft money contributions to political parties, which had grown over time: from $85.1 million in the 1991–1992 election cycle to $495.1 million in the 1999–2000 cycle.[66] Both parties' national committees had channeled over $200 million in soft money in 2000 to state and local party committees for registration drives and other activities not exclusively devoted to the presidential candidates but helpful to them. By outlawing large soft

? Can you explain why . . . Congress cannot limit what an individual spends independently on an election campaign?

hard money Financial contributions given directly to a candidate running for congressional office or the presidency.

soft money Financial contributions to party committees for capital and operational expenses.

money contributions, BCRA threatened both parties. It also banned organizations from running issue ads that named candidates in the weeks before an election.

No one knew how the parties' national committees would fare in the 2004 election after these reforms. Actually, both parties did quite well. They took advantage of the increased limits for hard money contribution and developed their infrastructure—especially direct mail and Internet capabilities—to raise more money from small donors. One scholar found that each national committee "had raised more money in hard dollars alone than they raised in hard and soft dollars combined in any previous election cycle."[67] Their combined total of $1.2 billion was about $164 million more than they had raised in hard and soft money for the 2000 election.[68] However, in 2007, a more conservative Supreme Court struck down BCRA's ban of issue ads run before an election, which opened the door to massive independent campaign spending by corporations, unions, and other groups and left in doubt the future of campaign spending regulations.

Public Financing of Presidential Campaigns. The 1974 FECA provided for public funding of campaigns for presidential elections but not congressional elections, and BCRA continued the distinction. A presidential candidate could qualify for public funds by raising at least $5,000 in each of twenty states from private donations no more than $250 each. The FEC matched these donations up to one-half of a preset spending limit—set in 1974 at $10 million—for each qualifying candidate. The limit for general elections was $20 million, but both limits were indexed for inflation. All major candidates for president from 1976 through 1996 accepted public funding of their primary election campaigns and thus adhered to the limitations on raising and spending campaign funds. But in 2000, wealthy publisher Steve Forbes and Texas governor George Bush both declined public funds in competing for the Republican nomination, raising and spending much more than otherwise possible.

By 2004, the public funds available to qualifying candidates for presidential primary and general election campaigns had increased to $37.3 million and $74.6 million, respectively. Like Forbes and Bush in 2000, Democrats Howard Dean and John Kerry, and President Bush (who had no meaningful opposition), declined public funds in the 2004 primaries so that they could spend more than $37.3 million. Indeed, public financing of presidential primaries became irrelevant for the 2008 election, when both parties' leading candidates announced in 2007 that they would finance their campaigns from private sources.

Both Bush and Kerry agreed to accept the $74.6 million in public funds (adjusted up from $20 million through inflation) for the 2004 general election campaign. In so doing, they were each limited to spending only that money for the election campaign. These funds went to the candidates' campaign committees, not to either party organization. Also, each major party received $14.6 million in public funds for their conventions, and each party was subject to a similar limit on spending for the presidential campaign.[69]

Because every major party nominee for president since 1976 has accepted public funds (and spending limits) for the general election, direct costs of presidential campaigns have been contained to the original FECA limit plus inflation. Total campaign spending is far more than the official limit, however. First, each national committee is permitted to spend extra millions on its conventions and on behalf of its nominees. Second, both national committees spend other millions for other campaign activities during the election cycle. According to the Federal Election Commission, all presidential candidates together in 2004 (including the ten Democrats who sought the nomination) received more than $1.02 billion for their election campaigns. This amount includes both private and public sources in the primary campaign and public funding for the general election campaign. This was 56 percent more than receipts collected during the 2000 election campaign, which occurred prior to the Bipartisan Campaign Reform Act of 2002.

National committees of the two major parties did even better, raising more than 13 percent above what they raised in 2000.[70] If BCRA did not reduce the amount of money raised for presidential campaigns, it did ban the practice of allowing national party committees to raise soft money. However, BCRA also allowed issue-advocacy groups, called **527 committees** (after Section 527 of the Internal Revenue Code, which makes them tax-exempt organizations), to spend unlimited amounts of soft money for media advertising, as long as they did not expressly advocate a candidate's election or defeat. Scholars studying campaign spending by 527 committees after BCRA found that their contributions increased from $151 million in 2002 to $424 million in 2004.[71]

Private Financing of Congressional Campaigns. One might think that a party's presidential campaign would be closely coordinated with its congressional campaigns. However, campaign funds go to the presidential candidate, not to the party, and the national committee does not run the presidential campaign. Presidential candidates may join congressional candidates in public appearances for mutual benefit, but presidential campaigns are usually isolated—financially and otherwise—from congressional campaigns.

In truth, more money was raised across the nation for all congressional campaigns in 2004 ($1.2 billion) than for the campaigns of all presidential candidates ($1.02 billion).[72] The larger number of candidates in congressional elections explains the larger sum: 2,219 candidates participated in primary and general election campaigns for the U.S. Congress in 2003–2004. Most were competing for the 435 seats in the House rather than the 34 Senate seats up for election. Nevertheless, individual Senate candidates raised relatively more money because they had to compete in larger districts (states) rather than individual House districts, which average about 675,000 people.

Future Trends in Campaign Finance. Public funding of presidential primaries faces an uncertain future. By declining public funds, the leading candidates in 2008 followed the lead of the well-financed candidates in 2004 who raised and spent more money in the primary phase. Kerry even considered declining public funds for the 2004 general election but did not, fearing the political cost of abandoning an accepted method of campaign finance. Public funding of presidential election campaigns has limited campaign expenditures and helped equalize spending by major party candidates in general elections. On the other hand, public funding has also strengthened the trend toward "personalized" presidential campaigns, because the money goes to the candidate, not to the party organization.

Private funding of congressional campaigns produces its own consequences. Under FECA, House and Senate candidates spent time seeking $1,000 contributions from individuals. Under BCRA, they now spend time seeking $2,000

527 committees Committees named after Section 527 of the Internal Revenue Code; they enjoy tax-exempt status in election campaigns if they are unaffiliated with political parties and take positions on issues, not specific candidates.

(plus adjustments for inflation).[73] Under both laws, congressional candidates—and incumbent members of Congress—must devote substantial time to raising funds from private sources.

BCRA banned the practice of raising soft money by national party committees, but national committees learned how to raise even more hard money. Moreover, BCRA also spawned the rise of issue-advocacy groups (527 committees), which raised and spent large sums during the 2004 presidential campaign.[74] Many such groups—such as MoveOn.org Voter Fund and ACT (America Coming Together)—supported Democratic agendas.[75] However, a Republican-oriented 527 committee, Swift Boat Veterans for Truth, ran ads attacking John Kerry's military record in the Vietnam War that drew considerable press coverage. Because the BCRA provisions are new, candidates experimented during the 2004 elections in raising and spending campaign funds. Politicians and scholars alike are divided about the new reforms and the impact they may have on the political system.[76]

Strategies and Tactics

In a military campaign, *strategy* is the overall scheme for winning the war, whereas *tactics* involve the conduct of localized hostilities. In an election campaign, strategy is the broad approach used to persuade citizens to vote for the candidate, and tactics determine the content of the messages and the way they are delivered.[77] Three basic strategies, which campaigns may blend in different mixes, are as follows:

- *A party-centered strategy,* which relies heavily on voters' partisan identification as well as on the party's organization to provide the resources necessary to wage the campaign

- *An issue-oriented strategy,* which seeks support from groups that feel strongly about various policies

- *A candidate-oriented strategy,* which depends on the candidate's perceived personal qualities, such as experience, leadership ability, integrity, independence, and trustworthiness[78]

The campaign strategy must be tailored to the political context of the election. Clearly, a party-centered strategy is inappropriate in a primary because all contenders have the same party affiliation. Research suggests that a party-centered strategy is best suited to voters with little political knowledge.[79] How do candidates learn what the electorate knows and thinks about politics, and how can they use this information? Candidates today usually turn to pollsters and political consultants, of whom there are hundreds.[80] Well-funded candidates can purchase a "polling package" that includes:

- A benchmark poll, which provides "campaign information about the voting preferences and issue concerns of various groups in the electorate and a detailed reading of the image voters have of the candidates in the race"

- Focus groups, consisting of ten to twenty people "chosen to represent particular target groups the campaign wants to reinforce or persuade . . . led in their discussion by persons trained in small-group dynamics," giving texture and depth to poll results

- A trend poll "to determine the success of the campaigns in altering candidate images and voting preferences"

- Tracking polls that begin in early October, "conducting short nightly interviews with a small number of respondents, keyed to the variables that have assumed importance"[81]

Professional campaign managers can use information from such sources to settle on a strategy that mixes party affiliation, issues, and images in its messages.[82] In major campaigns, the mass media disseminate these messages to voters through news coverage and advertising.

Making the News. Campaigns value news coverage by the media for two reasons: the coverage is free, and it seems objective to the audience. If news stories do nothing more than report the candidate's name, that is important, for name recognition by itself often wins elections. To get favorable coverage, campaign managers cater to reporters' deadlines and needs.[83] Getting free news coverage is yet another advantage that incumbents enjoy over challengers, for incumbents can command attention simply by announcing political decisions—even if they had little to do with them. Members of Congress are so good at this, says one observer, that House members have made news organizations their "unwitting adjuncts."[84]

Campaigns vary in the effectiveness with which they transmit their messages through the news media. Effective tactics recognize the limitations of both the audience and the media. The typical voter is not deeply interested in politics and has trouble keeping track of multiple themes supported with details. By the same token, television is not willing to air lengthy statements from candidates. As a result, news coverage is often condensed to sound bites only a few seconds long.

The media often use the metaphor of a horse race in covering politics in the United States. Ironically, evidence suggests that the national media focus more on campaign tactics and positioning than the state or local media do.[85] One longtime student of the media contends that reporters both enliven and simplify campaigns by describing them in terms of four basic scenarios: *bandwagons, losing ground, the front-runner,* and *the likely loser.*[86] Once the opinion polls show weakness or strength in a candidate, reporters dust off the appropriate story line.

The more time the press spends on the horse race, the less attention it gives to campaign issues. In fact, recent studies have found that in some campaigns, voters get more information from television ads than they do from television news.[87] Ads are more likely to be effective in low-visibility campaigns below the presidential level because the voters know less about the candidates at the outset and there is little "free" news coverage of the campaigns.[88]

Advertising the Candidate. In all elections, the first objective of paid advertising is name recognition. The next is to promote candidates by extolling their virtues. Finally, campaign advertising can have a negative objective: to attack one's opponent or play on emotions.[89] But name recognition is usually the most important. Studies show that many voters cannot recall the names of their U.S. senators or representatives, but they can recognize their names on a list—as on a ballot. Researchers attribute the high reelection rate for members of Congress mainly to high name recognition (see Chapter 11). Name recognition is the key objective during the primary season even in presidential campaigns, but other objectives become salient in advertising for the general election.

At one time, candidates for national office relied heavily on newspaper advertising; today, they overwhelmingly use the electronic media. Political ads convey more substantive information than many people believe, but the amount varies by campaign. In his comprehensive study of presidential campaign advertising, Darrell West found that political ads in presidential campaigns since 1984 contained more references to the candidates' policy positions than to their personal qualities—except for 1996 and 2004.[90] In 1996, Bill Clinton drew fire for lack of "honesty and integrity"; in 2004, John Kerry was attacked for "flip-flopping" on issues and for false "heroism" in Vietnam.

Other scholars have cautioned that the policy positions put forward in campaign ads may be misleading, however, if not downright deceptive.[91] West found that the 2004 campaign was the most negative since 1988.[92] Not all negatively toned ads qualify as *attack ads,* which advocate nothing positive. The term *contrast ads* describes those that both criticize an opponent and advocate policies of the sponsoring candidate.[93] A review of recent studies found that, ironically, both attack and contrast ads "actually carry more policy information than pure advocacy ads."[94]

The media often inflate the effect of prominent ads by reporting them as news, which means that citizens are about as likely to see controversial ads during the news as in the ads' paid time slots. Although negative ads do convey information, some studies suggest that negative ads produce low voter turnout.[95] However, recent research shows that the existing level of political mistrust is more important than the negativity of the ads.[96] Moreover, negative ads seem to work differently for challengers (who show a tendency to benefit from them) than for incumbents (who tend to do better with more positive campaigns).[97] If these findings seem confusing, that's essentially the state of research on negative ads. Researchers reviewing studies say that the connection between reality and perceptions is complex. Campaigns seen as negative by scholars are not necessarily viewed that way by voters.[98] BCRA contains a provision that was supposed to reduce negative ads in 2004: candidates must announce that they "approve" any ad run by their campaigns.[99] Ads run by independent 527 committees, however, incur no such responsibility.

Using the Internet.   The Internet is a relatively new medium for conducting election campaigns. It debuted in presidential campaigns in 1992, when Democratic candidate Jerry Brown, former governor of California, sent e-mail messages to supporters.[100] The first major candidate website appears to be that of Democratic senator Dianne Feinstein running for reelection from California in 1994. The same year, the nonpartisan Minnesota E-Democracy <www.e-democracy.org> held the first online U.S. Senate and gubernatorial candidate debates. In 1995, the Democratic National Committee created the first website for a major party. Two years later, Ted Mondale, Democratic candidate for governor of Minnesota, bought the first online banner ad. In 1998, two other major Democratic candidates made Internet firsts: Ed Garvey, running for governor of Wisconsin, posted his contributor information online; and Senator Barbara Boxer, running for reelection in California, sold campaign items online. In 2000, Democratic senator Bill Bradley raised funds online to campaign for the presidential nomination and was the first candidate to raise $1 million over the Internet; the Arizona Democratic Party held the first binding online primary election; and the Republican Party scored its own Internet first: registering 1 million activists online. Two years later in Louisiana, another Democratic candidate for governor, Claud "Buddy" Leach, announced his candidacy on the first live Internet broadcast.

Democrats pioneered Internet usage in election campaigns, and a Democrat, Howard Dean, was the first presidential candidate to use a commercial web site <www.meetup.com> to organize a meeting of campaign supporters. Using the Internet to raise large amounts of funds drew most attention, but using it to mobilize supporters was more innovative. Dean's Internet architect, Joe Trippi, also created the first presidential campaign blog for posting campaign developments, comments, and even short essays, on election politics.[101] Blogs proved effective in involving potential supporters, and virtually every 2004 candidate's web site was linked to a blog.[102] (See page 165 for more on blogs.) By 2008, presidential candidates (mainly Democrats) advertised on political blogs and were also into social-networking sites—both commercial (Facebook, MySpace) and their own (for example, Obama's MyBO and McCain's McCainSpace).

Candidates liked the Internet because it was fast, easy to use, and cheap—saving mailing costs and phone calls. During the first decade of its use in election campaigns, however, the Internet was not very productive, for relatively few people went online for political information or activity. Usage has steadily increased over the last decade. A national survey after the 2004 election asked respondents to name two sources for their news about the presidential campaign. Most (76 percent) named television, nearly half (46 percent) cited newspapers, and radio and the Internet were virtually tied at 22 and 21 percent, respectively.[103] Moreover, these scholars found that these "Online Political Citizens" are disproportionately "politically influential":

> They are seven times more likely than the general public to have attended a political rally, speech or protest in the last two to three months. They are nearly five times more likely to have contacted a politician, three times more likely to have written a letter to the editor, and three times more likely to belong to groups trying to influence public policy.[104]

When they are compared with influentials in the general public, however, online influentials have weaker ties to their local community and to long-term obligations, perhaps reflecting the relative youth of online enthusiasts.[105]

Online participants also tend to associate with like-minded partisans—except when they encounter occasional "trolls" of opposite persuasion who seek to disrupt a candidate's blog. Some observers see a dark side to the pattern of intense online debate among like-minded people, called "cyberbalkanization."[106] As one asked, "If political fragmentation is the problem, is the Internet the solution?"[107]

★ Explaining Voting Choice

Why do people choose one candidate over another? That is not easy to determine, but there are ways to approach the question. Individual voting choices can be analyzed as products of both long-term and short-term forces. Long-term forces operate throughout a series of elections, predisposing voters to choose certain types of candidates. Short-term forces are associated with particular elections; they arise from a combination of the candidates and issues

FIGURE 9.5 Effect of Party Identification on the Vote, 2004

The 2004 election showed that party identification still plays a key role in voting behavior. The chart shows the results of exit polls of thousands of voters as they left hundreds of polling places across the nation on election day. Voters were asked what party they identified with and how they voted for president. Those who identified with one of the two parties voted strongly for their party's candidate.

Source: "Survey of Voters: Who They Were," *New York Times,* 4 November 2004, p. P4.

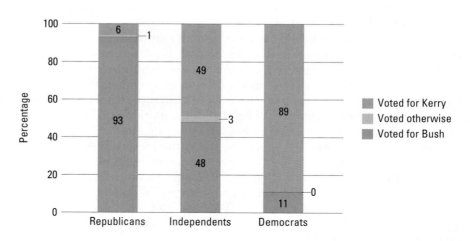

of the time. Party identification is by far the most important long-term force affecting U.S. elections. The most important short-term forces are candidates' attributes and their policy positions.

Party Identification

Ever since the presidential election of 1952, when the University of Michigan's National Election Studies began, we have known that more than half the electorate decides how to vote before the party conventions end in the summer.[108] And voters who make an early voting decision generally vote according to their party identification. Despite frequent comments in the media about the decline of partisanship in voting behavior, party identification again had a substantial effect on the presidential vote in 2004, as Figure 9.5 shows. President Bush got the votes of 93 percent of all self-described Republicans, while Senator Kerry won 89 percent of all Democrats. Independents split almost evenly between the party candidates.

This is a common pattern in presidential elections. The winner holds nearly all the voters who identify with his party. The loser holds most of his fellow Democrats or Republicans, but some percentage defects to the winner, a consequence of short-term forces—the candidates' attributes and the issues—surrounding the election. The winner usually gets most of the independents, who split disproportionately for him, also because of short-term forces. In 2004, however, independents were as split as the electorate.

In 2004, the electorate divided almost equally between the parties. But, as shown in Figure 8.4 on page 247, Democrats have consistently outnumbered Republicans over the past fifty years. Why, then, have Republican candidates won more presidential elections since 1952 than Democrats? For one thing, Democrats do not turn out to vote as consistently as Republicans do. For another, Democrats tend to defect more readily from their party. Defections are sparked by the candidates' attributes and the issues, which have usually fa-

Partying in Smaller Cities

In the past, both the Democratic and Republican Parties have held their national nominating conventions in very large cities in states with large populations. From 1932 to 2004, Chicago hosted eleven conventions, followed by Philadelphia (five) and New York (four). For 2008, both parties have chosen convention sites not in big cities and not on either coast. Democrats meet in Denver on August 25–28, and Republicans meet in Saint Paul on September 1–4. The Republican Convention is the first to be held entirely in September, which produces a very short formal campaign for the general election. The late date before a candidate is officially named also allows the Republican nominee more time to spend unlimited funds collected for the primary campaign. The Democratic nominee will have to begin spending the limited amount of public funds for the general election about a week earlier. *(left: City of Saint Paul Marketing Office; right: City of Denver Marketing Office)*

vored Republican presidential candidates since 1952. In both 1992 and 1996, however, short-term forces in presidential politics clearly benefited the Democrat Clinton, first as challenger and later as the incumbent. Entering the 2004 election campaign, President George W. Bush had a relatively low approval rating, but in the end he benefited from one major short-term force, the war on terrorism.[109]

Issues and Policies

Candidates exploit issues that they think are important to voters. Challengers usually campaign by pointing out problems—unemployment, inflation, war, civil disorders, corruption—and promising to solve them. Incumbents compile a record in office (for better or worse) and thus try to campaign on their accomplishments. In 2004, with the economy mired in a "jobless recovery" following the stock market losses in 2001 and 2002, President Bush campaigned for reelection as the "war president" fighting international terrorism after the September 11 attack on America.

His Democratic opponent, Senator John Kerry, built his campaign around economic issues: the loss of jobs to foreign countries, the high cost of health care, and huge budget deficits, which Kerry attributed to Bush's "tax cuts for the rich." He also criticized Bush for invading Iraq, which (Kerry said) was not linked to September 11 and drew resources away from the attack on terrorism. Charges made by both campaigns became nasty early—despite BCRA's requiring candidates to own up to them. What's more, the electorate was bitterly divided. In a poll taken the last week in February 2004, eight months before the November election, 38 percent of voters backed Kerry, saying they would never vote for Bush, while 33 percent favored Bush and said they would not

Bad Vote Day
Senator John Edwards, the Democratic candidate for vice president in 2004, consoles his presidential running mate, Senator John Kerry, before they deliver their concession speeches in Boston the day after the election. *(AP/Wide World Photos)*

vote for Kerry. The 29 percent uncommitted slightly favored Bush (13 to 10 percent), leaving only 6 percent truly undecided.[110] The 2004 presidential election looked like an extremely close and bitter contest. The outcome hinged on events that unfolded during the months before voting.

Candidates' Attributes

Candidates' attributes are especially important to voters who lack good information about a candidate's past performance and policy stands—which means most of us. Without such information, voters search for clues about the candidates to try to predict their behavior in office.[111] Some fall back on their personal beliefs about religion, gender, and race in making political judgments.[112] Such stereotypic thinking accounts for the patterns of opposition and support met by, among others, a Catholic candidate for president (John Kennedy), a woman candidate for vice president (Geraldine Ferraro in 1984), a black contender for a presidential nomination (Jesse Jackson in 1984 and 1988), and the first Jewish vice-presidential candidate of a major party (Joe Lieberman in 2000).

In 2004, Senator Kerry became the first Catholic candidate of a major party to run for president since 1960, but (unlike Kennedy in 1960) Kerry failed to win a majority of the Catholic vote. Voters saw Bush, a born-again Methodist, as more religious. According to exit polls, voters also overwhelmingly viewed Bush more than Kerry as a "strong leader," while Kerry was "more intelligent."

Evaluating the Voting Choice

Choosing among candidates according to their personal attributes might be an understandable approach, but it is not rational voting, according to democratic theory. According to that theory, citizens should vote according to the

the nominating process and campaigning for office offers many opportunities for organized groups outside the parties to identify and back candidates who favor their interests.[125] Although this is in keeping with pluralist theory, it is certain to frustrate majority interests on occasion.

Summary

Campaigning has evolved from a party-centered to a candidate-centered process. The successful candidate for public office usually must campaign first to win the party nomination, then to win the general election. A major factor in the decentralization of American parties is their reliance on primary elections to nominate candidates. Democratic and Republican nominations for president are no longer actually decided in the parties' national conventions but are determined in advance through the complex process of selecting delegates pledged to particular candidates. Although candidates cannot win the nomination unless they have broad support within the party, the winners can legitimately say that they captured the nomination through their own efforts and that they owe little to the party organization.

The need to win a majority of votes in the electoral college structures presidential elections. Although a candidate can win a majority of the popular vote but lose in the electoral college, that had not happened in more than one hundred years until 2000. In fact, the electoral college usually magnifies the victory margin of the winning candidate. Since World War II, Republicans have usually won the presidency, whereas Democrats have usually controlled Congress. From 1995 to 2000, the situation was reversed; Republicans controlled Congress under a Democratic president. Such divided government has interfered with party control of government.

In the general election, candidates usually retain the same staff that helped them win the nomination. The dynamics of campaign financing force candidates to rely mainly on their own resources or—in the case of presidential elections—on public funds. Party organizations now often contribute money to congressional candidates, but the candidates must still raise most of the money themselves. Money is essential in running a modern campaign for major office—for conducting polls and advertising the candidate's name, qualifications, and issue positions through the media. Candidates seek free news coverage whenever possible, but most must rely on paid advertising to get their message across. Ironically, voters also get most of their campaign information from advertisements. The trend in recent years toward negative advertising seems to work, although it may contribute to voters' distaste for politics.

Voting choice can be analyzed in terms of party identification, candidates' attributes, and policy positions. Party identification is still the most important long-term factor in shaping the voting decision, but few candidates rely on it in their campaigns. Most candidates today run personalized campaigns that stress their attributes and policies. Increased use of the Internet allows candidates even more latitude in personalizing their campaigns.

The way that nominations, campaigns, and elections are conducted in America is out of keeping with the ideals of responsible party government that fit the majoritarian model of democracy. In particular, campaigns and elections do not function to link parties strongly to voters, as the model posits. American parties are better suited to the pluralist model of democracy, which sees them as major interest groups competing with lesser groups to further their own interests. At least political parties aspire to the noble goal of representing the needs and wants of most people. As we see in the next chapter, interest groups do not even pretend as much.

Internet activities and reading suggestions for this chapter are available on the *Online Study Center*

To complete the multimedia assignments for this chapter, go to AmericansGoverning.org.

10 Interest Groups

(Tom McCarthy/PhotoEdit)

Online Study Center
This icon will direct you to resources
and activities on the website
college.hmco.com/pic/jandaupdate9e

It's every golfer's dream to play St. Andrews in Scotland. The Old Course at St. Andrews is considered to be the birthplace of the sport, and for golfers it is a shrine like no other.

During the time he was the majority leader in the House of Representatives, Tom DeLay, a Republican from the suburbs of Houston, was lucky enough to play a round at St. Andrews. But going to Scotland to play golf is not cheap. For those in DeLay's group, the golf portion of their trip came to $5,000 a person. And when they moved on to England, that wasn't cheap either. The hotel room for DeLay and his wife in London ran $790 for each of the four nights they stayed there. The plane flights (business class) for the congressman totaled $6,938.70.

Tom DeLay paid none of it.

It was Jack Abramoff who footed the bill. Jack Abramoff was a Washington lobbyist, and it was his goal to ingratiate himself with leading legislators like DeLay. Since it is illegal for legislators to take trips paid for by lobbyists, Abramoff ostensibly arranged for the travel to be paid for by a nonprofit organization sympathetic to DeLay. Yet federal investigators found that the airfare for DeLay and his wife was billed to Abramoff's American Express card.

The trip to Scotland is only one of many efforts of Abramoff that attracted the attention of the Justice Department's criminal division. Perhaps the most shocking revelation was that Abramoff had vastly overcharged a client, the Coushatta Tribe of Louisiana, which ran a casino and had hired Abramoff to protect its interests. Abramoff charged the tribe $32 million in fees, vastly out of proportion to the services he rendered. Apparently it was not enough to cheat the Coushattas; in private e-mails Abramoff called them "monkeys," "troglodytes," and "morons."

In 2006 Abramoff pled guilty to conspiracy to bribe public officials and to other charges and is now serving a six-year jail sentence. (After indictment on an unrelated matter involving Texas campaign finance law, Delay resigned from Congress.) Unfortunately, Jack Abramoff has come to represent interest group politics in Washington. Interest groups are not dishonest by nature, and few cross the line into the type of unethical and illegal behavior exhibited by Abramoff. But, as we will see, interest groups do present a challenge to our political system.[1] ★

In this chapter, we look at the central dynamic of pluralist democracy: the interaction of interest groups and government. In analyzing the process by which interest groups and lobbyists come to speak on behalf of different groups, we focus on several questions. How do interest groups form? Whom do they represent? What tactics do they use to convince policymakers that their views are best for the nation? Is the interest group system biased in favor of certain types of people? If so, what are the consequences?

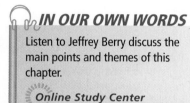

IN OUR OWN WORDS

Listen to Jeffrey Berry discuss the main points and themes of this chapter.

Online Study Center
Improve Your Grade

★ Interest Groups and the American Political Tradition

An **interest group** is an organized body of individuals who share some political goals and try to influence public policy decisions. Among the most prominent interest groups in the United States are the AFL-CIO (representing labor union members), the American Farm Bureau Federation (representing farmers), the Business Roundtable (representing big business), and Common Cause (representing citizens concerned with reforming government). Interest groups are also called **lobbies,** and their representatives are referred to as **lobbyists.**

Interest Groups: Good or Evil?

A recurring debate in American politics concerns the role of interest groups in a democratic society. Are interest groups a threat to the well-being of the political system, or do they contribute to its proper functioning? A favorable early evaluation of interest groups can be found in the writings of Alexis de Tocqueville, a French visitor to the United States in the early nineteenth century. During his travels, Tocqueville marveled at the array of organizations he found, and he later wrote that "Americans of all ages, all conditions, and all dispositions, constantly form associations."[2] Tocqueville was suggesting that the ease with which we form organizations reflects a strong democratic culture.

Yet other early observers were concerned about the consequences of interest group politics. Writing in the *Federalist* papers, James Madison warned of the dangers of "factions," the major divisions in American society. In *Federalist* No. 10, written in 1787, Madison said it was inevitable that substantial differences would develop between factions. It was only natural for farmers to oppose merchants, tenants to oppose landlords, and so on. Madison further reasoned that each faction would do what it could to prevail over other factions, that each basic interest in society would try to persuade the government

> **? Can you explain why . . .**
> the government doesn't restrict interest groups lobbying for their own selfish needs?

> *Federalist* No. 10 is available on the
> *Online Study Center*
> **General Resources**

Poster Boy for Bad Behavior
Jack Abramoff became a symbol of all that is wrong with the interest group system. His criminal behavior, including overcharging clients, laundering money, and concealing gifts to legislators, was shameful. More broadly, however, he represents a system that facilitates access for those who have the means to pay for lobbyists with the best connections to policymakers. *(AP/Wide World Photos)*

interest group An organized group of individuals that seeks to influence public policy. Also called a lobby.

lobby See interest group.

lobbyist A representative of an interest group.

stable the last few years. The most heavily organized sector of the economy today is in fact the government itself: public school teachers, postal workers, firefighters, and police have increasingly joined unions. Union leaders believe the overall decline has bottomed out and labor will make an eventual recovery as workers come to understand that they are better off with the higher wages, more generous benefits, and safer working conditions that come with union membership. More dispassionate observers believe that the decline of unionization will continue because the economy will continue to move away from the industries and occupations where unions have had the most success.

What is at stake? Union supporters say nothing less than the standard of living for working-class Americans. They point to the strike in 2003 by the United Food and Commercial Workers Union (UFCW) against major grocery chains in southern California. The chains (Safeway, Albertsons, and Ralph's) told their union employees that they wanted them to start paying for a portion of their health insurance. As a whole, American workers typically pay about $2,400 a year for their health insurance. Under the union contract, the grocery stores, which had been paying 100 percent of the insurance premiums, asked workers to agree to pay $800 a year of the cost. Union leaders responded by pointing out that full-time grocery employees made only around $27,000 a year, and if they were forced to lose part of their benefits package, their standard of living would fall.

The grocery chains argued that they had little choice but to ask for give-backs because Wal-Mart had announced plans to open up a large number of superstores, which include grocery stores within them, in southern California. Due to its massive buying power, Wal-Mart can offer groceries at a lower cost. Moreover, its work force is nonunion and costs less. Safeway and the other stores said they were fighting for their very existence. When the settlement was finally reached, it appeared to be a defeat for the union. Although current employees fared well under the contract, all new employees will start at $2.00 an hour less and receive diminished health-care benefits. For economists looking at the conflict, it is a familiar story: companies that can offer a good or service more efficiently prosper in comparison to their rivals. When unions are unable to organize all the major companies in a sector, those companies and their workers are highly vulnerable to the competition.

Sources: Labor Research Association website, <http://www.lraonline.org/charts.php?id=29>; Bureau of Labor Statistics website, <www.bls.gov/news.release/union2.nr0.htm>.

★ How Interest Groups Form

Do some people form interest groups more easily than others? Are some factions represented while others are not? Pluralists assume that when a political issue arises, interest groups with relevant policy concerns begin to lobby. Policy conflicts are ultimately resolved through bargaining and negotiation between the involved organizations and the government. Unlike Madison, who dwelled on the potential for harm by factions, pluralists believe interest groups are a good thing—that they contribute to democracy by broadening representation within the system.

An important part of pluralism is the belief that new interest groups form as a matter of course when the need arises. David Truman outlines this idea in his classic work *The Governmental Process.*[11] He says that when individuals are threatened by change, they band together in an interest group. For example, if government threatens to regulate a particular industry, the firms that compose that industry will start a trade association to protect their financial well-being. Truman sees a direct cause-and-effect relationship in all of this: existing groups stand in equilibrium until some type of disturbance (such as falling wages or declining farm prices) forces new groups to form.

Truman's thinking on the way interest groups form is like the "invisible hand" notion of laissez-faire economics: self-correcting market forces will remedy imbalances in the marketplace. But in politics, no invisible hand, no force, automatically causes interest groups to develop. Truman's disturbance theory paints an idealized portrait of interest group politics in America. In real life, people do not automatically organize when they are adversely affected by some disturbance. A good example of "nonorganization" can be found in Herbert Gans's book *The Urban Villagers.*[12] Gans, a sociologist, moved into the West End, a low-income neighborhood in Boston, during the late 1950s. The neighborhood had been targeted for urban redevelopment; the city was planning to replace old buildings with modern ones. This meant that the people living there—primarily poor Italian Americans who very much liked their neighborhood—would have to move.

Being evicted is a highly traumatic experience, so the situation in the West End certainly qualified as a bona-fide disturbance according to Truman's scheme of interest group formation. Yet the people of the West End barely put up a fight to save their neighborhood. They started an organization, but it attracted little support. Residents remained unorganized; soon they were moved, and the buildings in the neighborhood were demolished.

Disturbance theory clearly fails to explain what happened (or didn't happen) in Boston's West End. An adverse condition or change does not automatically mean that an interest group will form. What, then, is the missing ingredient? Political scientist Robert Salisbury says that the quality of interest group leadership may be the crucial factor.[13]

Interest Group Entrepreneurs

Salisbury likens the role of an interest group leader to that of an entrepreneur in the business world. An entrepreneur is someone who starts new enterprises, usually at considerable personal financial risk. Salisbury says that an **interest group entrepreneur,** or organizer, succeeds or fails for many of the same reasons a business entrepreneur succeeds or fails. The interest group entrepreneur must have something attractive to "market" in order to convince people to join.[14] Potential members must be persuaded that the benefits of joining outweigh the costs. Someone starting a new union, for example, must convince workers that the union can win them wages high enough to more than offset membership dues. The organizer of an ideological group must convince potential members that the group can effectively lobby the government to achieve their particular goals.

The development of the United Farm Workers union shows the importance of leadership in the formation of an interest group. The union is made up of men and women who pick crops in California and other parts of the country. These pickers—predominantly poor, uneducated Mexican Americans—perform backbreaking work in the hot growing season.

interest group entrepreneur
An interest group organizer or leader.

Their chronically low wages and deplorable living conditions made the farm workers prime candidates for organization into a labor union. And throughout the twentieth century, various unions tried to organize them. Yet for many reasons, including distrust of union organizers, intimidation by employers, and lack of money to pay union dues, all failed. Then, in 1962, the late Cesar Chavez, a poor Mexican American, began to crisscross the Central Valley of California, talking to workers and planting the idea of a union. Chavez had been a farm worker himself (he first worked as a picker at the age of ten), and he was well aware of the difficulties that lay ahead for his newly organized union.

After a strike against grape growers failed in 1965, Chavez changed his tactic of trying to build a stronger union merely by recruiting a larger membership. Copying the civil rights movement, Chavez and his followers marched 250 miles to the state capitol in Sacramento to demand help from the governor. The march and other nonviolent tactics began to draw sympathy from people who had no direct involvement in farming. Seeing the movement as a way to help poor members of the church, Catholic clergy were a major source of support. This support gave the charismatic Chavez greater credibility, and his followers cast him in the role of spiritual as well as political leader. At one point, he fasted for twenty-five days to show his commitment to nonviolence. Democratic senator Robert Kennedy of New York, one of the most popular politicians of the day, joined Chavez when he broke his fast at a mass conducted on the back of a flatbed truck in Delano, California.[15]

Chavez subsequently called for a boycott, and a small but significant number of Americans stopped buying grapes. The growers, who had bitterly fought the union, were finally hurt economically. Under this and other economic pressures, they eventually agreed to recognize and bargain with the United Farm Workers. The union then helped its members with the wage and benefit agreements it was able to negotiate.

Who Is Being Organized?

Cesar Chavez is a good example of the importance of leadership in the formation of a new interest group. Despite many years of adverse conditions, efforts to organize farm workers had failed. The dynamic leadership of Cesar Chavez is what seems to have made the difference.

But another important element is at work in the formation of interest groups. The residents of Boston's West End and the farm workers in California were poor, uneducated or undereducated, and politically inexperienced—factors that made it extremely difficult to organize them into interest groups. If they had been well-to-do, educated, and politically experienced, they probably would have banded together immediately. People who have money, are educated, and know how the system operates are more confident that their actions can make a difference.[16] Together, these attributes give people more incentive to devote their time and ample resources to organizing and supporting interest groups.

Every existing interest group has its own history, but the three variables just discussed can help explain why groups may or may not become fully organized. First, an adverse change or disturbance can contribute to people's awareness that they need political representation. However, this alone does not ensure that an organization will form, and organizations have formed in the absence of a disturbance. Second, the quality of leadership is critical in the organization of interest groups. Some interest group entrepreneurs are more skilled than others at convincing people to join their organizations. Third, the higher the socioeconomic level of potential members is, the more likely they are to know the value of interest groups and to participate in politics by joining them.

Finally, not all interest groups have real memberships. In this sense "group" is a misnomer; some lobbying organizations are institutions that lack members but are affected by public policy and establish lobbying offices or hire lobbyists to represent them before government. Universities and hospitals, for example, don't have members but are well represented before government. Large corporations and business trade associations are usually quite astute at understanding just how valuable it is to have lobbyists in Washington. After September 11, the General Contractors Association of New York hired the Carmen Group, a lobbying firm in Washington that works for a variety of clients. The contractors paid $500,000 to the Carmen Group to try to persuade the federal government to cover their insurance premiums while they did cleanup work at the site of the Twin Towers. The Carmen Group succeeded, and the government agreed to pay $1 billion in insurance premiums.[17]

Because wealthy and better-educated Americans are more likely to form and join lobbies, they seem to have an important advantage in the political process. Nevertheless, as the United Farm Workers' case shows, poor and uneducated people are also capable of forming interest groups. The question that remains, then, is not *whether* various opposing interests are represented but *how well* they are represented. In terms of Madison's premise in *Federalist* No. 10, are the effects of faction—in this case, the advantages of the wealthy and well educated—being controlled? Before we can answer this question about how interest groups affect the level of political equality in our society, we need to turn our attention to the resources available to interest groups.

★ Interest Group Resources

The strengths, capabilities, and influence of an interest group depend in large part on its resources. A group's most significant resources are its members, lobbyists, and money, including funds that can be contributed to political candidates. The sheer quantity of a group's resources is important, and so is the wisdom with which its resources are used.

Members

One of the most valuable resources an interest group can have is a large, politically active membership. If a lobbyist is trying to convince a legislator to support a particular bill, having a large group of members who live in the legislator's home district or state is tremendously helpful. A legislator who has not already taken a firm position on a bill might be swayed by the knowledge that voters back home are kept informed by interest groups of his or her votes on key issues. The American Association of Retired Persons (AARP) has considerable clout because it has a membership of 35 million. A critical step in the passage of President Bush's controversial Medicare drug benefit for seniors came when the AARP endorsed it in 2003. Members of Congress were clearly

Take This Membership Card and Shove It
This member of the American Association of Retired Persons is one of many who were upset when that organization endorsed the Bush administration's proposal for a Medicare prescription drug benefit. Such critics were angered because they believed the administration's bill provided little to seniors and too much to health maintenance organizations and the drug companies. Ironically, once the AARP offered a drug plan that qualified under the administration's proposal, the plan emerged as the most popular choice among Medicare recipients who chose to participate. *(Charles Krupa/AP/ Wide World Photos)*

more comfortable voting for the legislation, which contained some provisions unpopular with seniors, knowing that the AARP would be telling its members that on balance, the bill was something they should be happy with.

Members give an organization not only the political muscle to influence policy but also financial resources. The more money an organization can collect through dues and contributions, the more people it can hire to lobby government officials and monitor the policymaking process. Greater resources also allow an organization to communicate with its members more and to inform them better. And funding helps a group maintain its membership and attract new members.

Maintaining Membership.   To keep the members it already has, an organization must persuade them that it is doing a good job in its advocacy. Most lobbies use a newsletter and e-mails to keep members apprised of developments in government that relate to issues of concern to them. Interest groups use these communications as public relations tools to try to keep members believing that their lobby is playing a critical role in protecting their interests. Thus, the role the organization is playing in trying to influence government always receives prominent coverage in its newsletters and e-mails.

Business, professional, and labor associations generally have an easier time holding on to members than do citizen groups, whose basis of organization is a concern for issues not directly related to their members' jobs. In many companies, corporate membership in a trade group constitutes only a minor business expense. Big individual corporations have no memberships as such, but they often open their own lobbying offices in Washington. They have the advantage of being able to use institutional financial resources to support their lobbying; they do not have to rely on voluntary contributions. Labor unions are helped in states that require workers to affiliate with the union that is the bargaining agent with their employer. In contrast, citizen groups base their appeal on members' ideological sentiments. These groups face a difficult challenge: issues can blow hot and cold, and a particularly hot issue one year may not hold the same interest to citizens the next.

Attracting New Members.   All membership groups are constantly looking for new adherents to expand their resources and clout. Groups that rely on ideological appeals have a special problem because the competition in most policy areas is intense. People concerned about the environment, for example, can join a seemingly infinite number of local, state, and national groups.[18] The National Wildlife Federation, Environmental Defense, the Natural Resources Defense Council, Friends of the Earth, the National Audubon Society, the Wilderness Society, and the Sierra Club are just some of the national organizations that lobby on environmental issues. Groups try to distinguish themselves from competitors by concentrating on a few key issues and developing a reputation as the most involved and knowledgeable about them.[19] The Sierra Club, one of the oldest and largest environmental groups, has long had a focus on protecting national parks. Some smaller organizations, such as Defenders of Wildlife and the Rainforest Action Network, have found a sufficient number of members to support their advocacy. Organizations in a crowded policy area must differentiate themselves from the competition and then aggressively market what they have to offer to potential contributors. Indeed, these groups are like businesses—their "profits" (their members and income) depend on their management's wisdom in allocating resources and choosing which issues to address.

One common method of attracting new members is *direct mail*—letters sent to a selected audience to promote the organization and appeal for contributions. The key to direct mail is a carefully targeted audience. An organization can purchase a list of people who are likely to be sympathetic to its cause, or it can trade lists with a similar organization. A group trying to fight abortion, for instance, might use the subscription list from the conservative magazine *The Weekly Standard,* whereas a pro-choice lobby might use that of the *New Republic.* The main drawbacks to direct mail are its expense and low rate of return.

The Internet is also a tool for building a membership and even building new advocacy organizations. People with hemophilia (their blood doesn't clot adequately, and thus they are at serious risk from bleeding) were traditionally represented by the National Hemophilia Foundation (NHF). The NHF has a close relationship with drug manufacturers, which provide significant financial support to the group. This close relationship inhibited the organization from lobbying the government to force a reduction in drug prices. Through the Internet, the small and geographically dispersed community of hemophiliacs was able to organize its own independent organizations.[20]

The Free-Rider Problem.   The need for aggressive marketing by interest groups suggests that getting people who sympathize with a group's goals actually to join and support it with their contributions is difficult. Economists call this difficulty the **free-rider problem,** but we might call it, more colloquially, the "let-George-do-it problem."[21] Funding for public television stations illustrates the dilemma. Almost all agree that public television, which survives in large part through viewers' contributions, is of great value. But only a fraction

? **Can you explain why . . .** people don't join interest groups that advocate policies those same people strongly support?

free-rider problem The situation in which people benefit from the activities of an organization (such as an interest group) but do not contribute to those activities.

of those who watch public television contribute on a regular basis. Why? Because people can watch the programs whether they contribute or not. The free rider has the same access to public television as the contributor.

The same problem crops up for interest groups. When a lobbying group wins benefits, those benefits are not restricted to the members of the organization. For instance, if the U.S. Chamber of Commerce convinces Congress to enact a policy benefiting business, all businesses will benefit, not just those that actually pay the membership dues of the lobbying group. Thus, some executives may feel that their corporation doesn't need to spend the money to join the U.S. Chamber of Commerce, even though they might benefit from the group's efforts; they prefer instead to let others shoulder the financial burden.

The free-rider problem increases the difficulty of attracting paying members, but it certainly does not make the task impossible. Many people realize that if everyone decides to let someone else do it, the job simply will not get done. Millions of Americans contribute to interest groups because they are concerned about an issue or feel a responsibility to help organizations that work on their behalf. Also, many organizations offer membership benefits that have nothing to do with politics or lobbying. Business **trade associations,** for example, are a source of information about industry trends and effective management practices; they organize conventions at which members can learn, socialize, and occasionally find new customers or suppliers. An individual firm in the electronics industry may not care that much about the lobbying done by the Electronics Industries Alliance, but it may have a vital interest in the information about marketing and manufacturing that the organization provides. Successful interest groups are adept at supplying the right mix of benefits to their target constituency.

Lobbyists

Some of the money that interest groups raise is used to pay lobbyists who represent the organizations before the government. Lobbyists make sure that people in government know what their members want and that their organizations know what the government is doing. For example, when an administrative agency issues new regulations, lobbyists are right there to interpret the content and implications of the regulations for rank-and-file members. The Washington representative of an oil trade association was reading the *Federal Register* (a daily compendium of all new regulations issued by the government) as part of his daily routine when he noticed that the Federal Aviation Administration planned to issue new regulations requiring detailed flight plans by noncommercial aircraft. The policy would make rescue efforts for noncommercial planes easier, but the lobbyist realized that it could compromise the confidentiality surrounding the flights of company planes for aerial exploration for oil and gas. Anyone could obtain the filed flight plans. He notified the member companies, and their lobbying prevented the implementation of the regulations, precluding the possibility of competitors' getting hold of such secret data.[22]

Lobbyists can be full-time employees of their organization or employees of public relations or law firms who are hired on retainer (see Figure 10.3). When hiring a lobbyist, an interest group looks for someone who knows her or his way around Washington. Lobbyists are valued for their experience and their knowledge of how government operates. Often they have served in the legislative or executive branches or held a major party post—people who have

trade association An organization that represents firms within a particular industry.

firsthand experience with government. Billy Tauzin, a Republican from Louisiana who chaired the House Energy and Commerce Committee, went from that position to head the Pharmaceutical Research and Manufacturers of America, the trade group for the drug industry. Tauzin's experience as head of the committee that oversaw the drug industry and his ties to members in the House made him a prize catch for the trade group. His initial salary was reported to be around $2 million a year.[23]

> **?** **Can you explain why . . .**
> government is a training ground for lobbyists?

As Tauzin's salary suggests, the expertise on issues and connections that comes from experience in the legislative or executive branch is of great value to organizations that lobby. Capitol Hill staffers can command as much as $300,000 a year as lobbyists.[24] So lucrative is lobbying that more than 40 percent of representatives and senators who leave the Congress become employed as lobbyists.[25] Contacts with former colleagues can be invaluable. As one lobbyist said of her former associates on Capitol Hill, "They know you, and they return your phone calls."[26] Many lobbyists have a law degree and find their legal backgrounds useful in bargaining and negotiating over laws and regulations. Because of their location, many Washington law firms are drawn into lobbying. Expanding interest group advocacy has created a boon for Washington law firms. Corporations without their own Washington office rely heavily on law firms to lobby for them before the national government. Partners in the top law firms in Washington average more than $800,000 a year.[27] These firms can be quite large: lobbying powerhouse Patton Boggs employs four hundred people, half of whom are lawyers.[28]

The most common image of a lobbyist is that of an arm twister—someone who spends most of his or her time trying to convince a legislator or administrator to back a certain policy. The stereotype of lobbyists also portrays them

FIGURE 10.3 Washington's Growth Industry

Many businesses decline when the economy turns down, but the lobbying industry in Washington is recession-proof. Whatever the state of the economy, there's always reason to lobby because Congress, agencies, the White House, and the courts are always making policy decisions. As the figures indicate, more and more organizations understand that they can't afford *not* to lobby. High as these figures are, they understate the true number of lobbyists because the registration rules are somewhat ambiguous and the penalties for not registering are minor.

Source: Todd S. Purdum, "Go Ahead, Try to Stop K Street," *New York Times,* 8 January 2006, sec. 4, p. 1. Reprinted with permission.

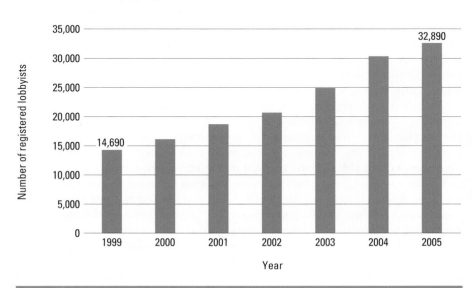

The Two Million Dollar Man
It's understandable that many members of Congress become lobbyists when they leave the House or Senate. Former representative Billy Tauzin's estimated salary of $2 million a year as a lobbyist for the Pharmaceutical Research and Manufacturers of America (PhRMA) is considerably more than the current $165,000 salary for legislators. Given the enormous stakes for drug companies in health-care legislation, it's understandable that PhRMA believes that having someone with the knowledge, skill, and connections of Tauzin is well worth the large salary. *(AP/Wide World Photos)*

as people of dubious ethics because they trade on their connections and may hand out campaign donations to candidates for office. In the last election cycle for which figures are available, lobbyists contributed $25 million in campaign donations to members of Congress. To enhance their access, many lobbyists also raise money for legislators, and in the last Congress seventy-one members listed lobbyists as treasurers of their campaigns or directors of their personal political action committees.[29] Yet lobbying is a much maligned profession.[30] The lobbyist's primary job is not to trade on favors or campaign contributions but to pass information on to policymakers. Lobbyists provide government officials and their staffs with a constant flow of data that support their organizations' policy goals. Lobbyists also try to build a compelling case for their goals, showing that the "facts" dictate that a particular change be made or avoided. What lobbyists are really trying to do, of course, is to convince policymakers that their data deserve more attention and are more accurate than those presented by opposing lobbyists.

PACs and 527s

One of the organizational resources that can make a lobbyist's job easier is a **political action committee (PAC).** PACs pool campaign contributions from group members and donate the money to candidates for political office. Under federal law, a PAC can give as much as $5,000 to a candidate for Congress for each separate election. More than four thousand PACs were active going into the 2006 election.

The greatest growth has come from corporations, which had long been prohibited from operating PACs. There has also been rapid growth in the number of nonconnected PACs, largely ideological groups that have no parent lobbying organization and are formed solely for the purpose of raising and channeling campaign funds. (Thus, a PAC can be the campaign-wing affiliate of an existing interest group or a wholly independent, unaffiliated group.) Most PACs

political action committee (PAC) An organization that pools campaign contributions from group members and donates those funds to candidates for political office.

are rather small, and 65 percent gave less than $50,000 in total contributions during the most recent two-year election cycle. Many PACs, however, are large enough to gain recognition for the issues they care about. During the 2003–2004 election cycle, PACs contributed $310 million to candidates for office, almost all of which went to congressional candidates. The National Association of Realtors had the largest PAC, with contributions of $3.7 million during the two-year cycle. Forty-eight PACs contributed at least $1 million, including the National Beer Wholesalers ($2.3 million), the International Brotherhood of Electrical Workers ($2.3 million), the American Hospital Association ($1.7 million), and FedEx ($1.5 million).[31]

Lobbyists believe that campaign contributions help significantly when they are trying to gain an audience with a member of Congress. Members of Congress and their staffers generally are eager to meet with representatives of their constituencies, but their time is limited. However, a member of Congress or staffer would find it difficult to turn down a lobbyist's request for a meeting if the PAC of the lobbyist's organization had made a significant campaign contribution in the previous election. Lobbyists also regard contributions as a form of insurance in case of issues that might arise unexpectedly. As one scholar put it, the donations are given to protect "against unforeseen future dangers as the policymaking process develops."[32]

Typically, PACs, like most other interest groups, are highly pragmatic organizations; pushing a particular political philosophy takes second place to achieving immediate policy goals.[33] Although many corporate executives strongly believe in a free-market economy, for example, their company PACs tend to hold congressional candidates to a much more practical standard. In recent elections, corporate PACs as a group have given as much as 87 percent of their contributions to incumbents (see Figure 10.4). At the same time, different sectors of the PAC universe may strongly favor one party or the other. Close to nine out of every ten dollars that unions give go to Democrats, whether they be incumbents, challengers, or open seat candidates.[34]

Critics charge that PAC contributions influence public policy, yet political scientists have not been able to document any consistent link between campaign donations and the way members of Congress vote on the floor of the House and Senate.[35] The problem is this: Do PAC contributions influence votes in Congress, or are they just rewards for legislators who would vote for the group's interests anyway because of their long-standing ideology? How do we determine the answer to this question? Simply looking for the influence of PACs in the voting patterns of members of Congress may be shortsighted; influence can also be felt before bills get to the floor of the full House or Senate for a vote. Some sophisticated research shows that PAC donations do seem to influence what goes on in congressional committees. As will be discussed in Chapter 11, committees are where the bulk of the work on legislation takes place. Lobbies with PACs have an advantage in the committee process and appear to gain influence because of the additional access they receive.[36]

During the 2004 presidential election, 527s, a new type of interest group, became highly involved in the campaign. These groups can take a stand on an issue but cannot directly contribute to candidates, nor can they explicitly endorse candidates or ask voters to specifically vote against a candidate. They are different from PACs in another important way: they can accept contributions of unlimited size. In the 2004 election, financier George Soros contributed

FIGURE 10.4   Friendship Is a Wonderful Thing

Political action committees are more practical than ideological, primarily directing their contributions to incumbents. A modest exception to this trend is so-called nonconnected PACs. These tend to be ideological citizen groups whose primary concern is promoting a broad liberal or conservative perspective. But even nonconnected PACs give almost 60 percent of their contributions to incumbents.

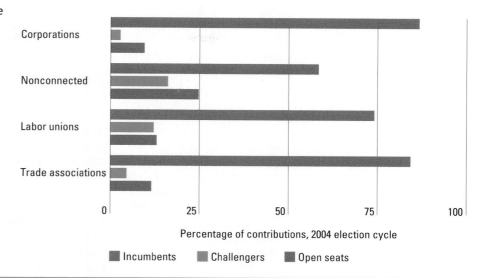

Source: Federal Election Commission, "PAC Activity Increases for 2004 Elections," 13 April 2005.

Percentage of contributions, 2004 election cycle

■ Incumbents   ■ Challengers   ■ Open seats

$23.3 million to liberal 527s.[37] Although they can't endorse a candidate, 527s can indirectly criticize candidates they don't like by emphasizing an issue that draws out the differences between those running for office. Liberal 527s like MoveOn.org and America Coming Together never said, "Vote for John Kerry," but their TV commercials criticizing President Bush's performance in office were unmistakably an effort to sway voters toward Kerry.

It is clear that the American public is suspicious of PACs and 527s. They regard such huge sums of money pouring into campaigns from interest groups as problematic. Yet there are those who defend the current system, emphasizing that individuals and organizations should have the freedom to participate in the political system through campaign donations.

★ Lobbying Tactics

When an interest group decides to try to influence the government on an issue, its staff and officers must develop a strategy, which may include several tactics aimed at various officials or offices. Together, these tactics should use the group's resources as effectively as possible.

Keep in mind that lobbying extends beyond the legislative branch. Groups can seek help from the courts and administrative agencies as well as from Congress. Moreover, interest groups may have to shift their focus from one branch of government to another. After a bill becomes a law, for example, a group that lobbied for the legislation will probably try to influence the administrative agency responsible for implementing the new law. Some policy decisions are left unresolved by legislation and are settled through regulations. Lobbies want to make sure regulatory decisions are as close to their group's preferences as possible.

We discuss three types of lobbying tactics here: those aimed at policymakers and implemented by interest group representatives (direct lobbying), those that involve group members (grassroots lobbying), and those directed at the public (information campaigns). We also examine the use of new high-tech lobbying tactics as well as cooperative efforts of interest groups to influence government through coalitions.[38]

Direct Lobbying

Direct lobbying relies on personal contact with policymakers. This interaction occurs when a lobbyist meets with a member of Congress, an agency official, or a staff member. In their meetings, lobbyists usually convey their arguments by providing data about a specific issue. If a lobbyist from a chamber of commerce, for example, meets with a member of Congress about a bill the chamber backs, the lobbyist does not say (or even suggest), "Vote for this bill, or our people in the district will vote against you in the next election." Instead, the lobbyist might say, "If this bill is passed, we're going to see hundreds of new jobs created back home." The representative has no trouble at all figuring out that a vote for the bill can help in the next election.

Personal lobbying is a day-in, day-out process. It is not enough simply to meet with policymakers just before a vote or a regulatory decision. Lobbyists must maintain contact with congressional and agency staffers, constantly providing them with pertinent data. The basic goal is to help policymakers do their job.[39] One lobbyist described his strategy in personal meetings with policymakers as rather simple and straightforward: "Providing information is the most effective tool. People begin to rely on you." Another lobbyist gave this advice: "You'd better bring good ideas and some facts, and they'd better be accurate."[40]

In their meetings with policymakers and through other tactics, lobbyists are trying to frame the issue at hand in terms most beneficial to their point of view. Is a gun-control bill before Congress a policy that would make our streets and schools safer from deranged, violent individuals who should not have access to guns—or is it a bill aimed at depriving law-abiding citizens of their constitutional right to bear arms? It is difficult for lobbyists to sharply move issue definition away from any prevailing notion of what an issue is really about, but they work hard to reshape issue definition toward their desired end.[41]

A tactic related to direct lobbying is testifying at committee hearings when a bill is before Congress. This tactic allows the interest group to put its views on record and make them widely known when the hearing testimony is published. Although testifying is one of the most visible parts of lobbying, it is generally considered window dressing. Most lobbyists believe that such testimony usually does little by itself to persuade members of Congress.

Another direct but somewhat different approach is legal advocacy. Using this tactic, a group tries to achieve its policy goals through litigation. Claiming some violation of law, a group will file a lawsuit and ask that a judge make a ruling that will benefit the organization. When the Army Corps of Engineers announced plans to permit coal companies to blast off the top of mountains to facilitate their mining, environmental groups went to court alleging a violation of the Clean Water Act. The judge agreed since the coal companies' actions would leave waste and rock deposits in adjoining streams.[42]

direct lobbying Attempts to influence a legislator's vote through personal contact with the legislator.

Grassroots Lobbying

Grassroots lobbying involves an interest group's rank-and-file members and may include people outside the organization who sympathize with its goals. Grassroots tactics, such as letter-writing campaigns and protests, are often used in conjunction with direct lobbying by Washington representatives. Letters, e-mails, faxes, and telephone calls from a group's members to their representatives in Congress or to agency administrators add to a lobbyist's credibility in talks with these officials. Policymakers are more concerned about what a lobbyist says when they know that constituents are really watching their decisions.

Group members—especially influential members (such as corporation presidents or local civic leaders)—occasionally go to Washington to lobby. But the most common grassroots tactic is letter writing. "Write your member of Congress" is not just a slogan for a civics test. Legislators are highly sensitive to the content of their mail. Interest groups often launch letter-writing campaigns through their regular publications or special alerts.[43] They may even provide sample letters and the names and addresses of specific policymakers.

If people in government seem unresponsive to conventional lobbying tactics, a group might resort to some form of political protest. A protest or demonstration, such as picketing or marching, is designed to attract media attention to an issue. Protesters hope that television and newspaper coverage will help change public opinion and make policymakers more receptive to their group's demands. Protests by advocates for the homeless in Washington have included "splashing blood on the White House gates, unrolling mats across the White House drive and declaring it a homeless shelter, [and] turning bags of cockroaches loose on the White House tour to remind onlookers of the conditions under which many poor Americans live."[44] The goal of each of these protests was to create a striking visual image that would attract media attention; if reporters covered the protest, people around the country would be exposed to the protesters' belief that the government is doing far too little to help the homeless.

grassroots lobbying Lobbying activities performed by rank-and-file interest group members and would-be members.

An Image That Angered a Nation

Demonstrations by blacks during the early 1960s played a critical role in pushing Congress to pass civil rights legislation. This photo of vicious police dogs attacking demonstrators in Birmingham, Alabama, is typical of scenes shown on network news broadcasts and in newspapers that helped build public support for civil rights legislation. *(Charles Moore/Black Star)*

The main drawback to protesting is that policymaking is a long-term, incremental process, and a demonstration is short-lived. It is difficult to sustain anger and activism among group supporters—to keep large numbers of people involved in protest after protest. A notable exception was the civil rights demonstrations of the 1960s, which were sustained over a long period. National attention focused not only on the widespread demonstrations but also on the sometimes violent confrontations between protesters and white law enforcement officers. For example, the use of police dogs and high-power fire hoses against blacks marching in Alabama in the early 1960s angered millions of Americans who saw footage of the confrontations on television. By stirring public opinion, the protests hastened the passage of the Civil Rights Act of 1964 and the Voting Rights Act of 1965.

Information Campaigns

As the strategy of the civil rights movement shows, interest groups generally feel that public backing adds strength to their lobbying efforts. And because all interest groups believe they are absolutely right in their policy orientation, they think that they will get that backing if they can only make the public aware of their position and the evidence supporting it. To this end, interest groups launch **information campaigns,** which are organized efforts to gain public backing by bringing their views to the public's attention. The underlying assumption is that public ignorance and apathy are as much a problem as the views of competing interest groups. Various means are used to combat apathy.

information campaign An organized effort to gain public backing by bringing a group's views to public attention.

Some are directed at the larger public; others are directed at smaller audiences with long-standing interest in an issue.

Public relations is one information campaign tactic. A public relations campaign might involve sending speakers to meetings in various parts of the country, producing pamphlets and handouts, taking out newspaper and magazine advertising, or establishing websites. Recently labor unions and progressives initiated a campaign critical of Wal-Mart. The huge retailer pays relatively low wages, offers limited benefits, and aggressively fights any efforts to unionize its work force. Both Wake Up Wal-Mart and Wal-Mart Watch have publicized Wal-Mart's record on its treatment of employees. In turn, Wal-Mart has fought back with a concerted public relations campaign designed to demonstrate that it is a responsible citizen in the communities where its stores are located. The company's extensive efforts to provide water and other supplies to victims of Hurricane Katrina were particularly effective at burnishing its image.[45]

Sponsoring research is another way interest groups press their cases. When a group believes that evidence has not been fully developed in a certain area, it may commission research on the subject. To publicize its belief that the government's agricultural policy unfairly favors large corporations and works against family farmers, the Environmental Working Group released a research report a week before the 2000 Iowa presidential caucuses. The report showed that nearly half of $2 billion in aid to Iowa farmers went to just 12 percent of farm owners, and many small family farms "got less money than a welfare recipient."[46] By timing the release of the report to coincide with the imminent approach of the Iowa presidential caucuses, the liberal advocacy group hoped to maximize coverage by forcing the candidates campaigning around Iowa to respond to its findings.

High-Tech Lobbying

Washington lobbies have added many high-tech tactics to their arsenals. Using such resources as direct mail, e-mail, faxes, polling, and the World Wide Web, lobbies have tried to find ways to expand their reach and increase their impact. The most conspicuous effect of high-tech lobbying is that it speeds up the political process. Using electronic communication, groups can quickly mobilize their constituents, who in turn will quickly contact policymakers about pending decisions.

As noted earlier, a great virtue of the Internet for interest groups is that it reduces the cost of communicating with members and potential members.[47] Before e-mail existed, an interest group wanting to activate its members or followers would have to turn to letters or phone calls. Mailing costs and long-distance charges quickly added up when large numbers of people needed to be contacted. MoveOn is an interesting example of an organization that has used the cost efficiency of the Internet to emerge out of nowhere to become an active participant in American national politics. Created by a married couple who had made a fortune from designing a computer screen saver depicting flying toasters, MoveOn has little in the way of organization besides its mailing list. It employs just seven individuals, but it possesses a mailing list of 1.8 million people who have shown some interest in the group. After President Bush indicated that he was prepared to go to war against Iraq in early 2003, MoveOn organized opposition to the war and raised considerable sums of money in a

join interest groups than are those who are poor.

A recent survey of interest groups is revealing, finding that "the 10 percent of adults who work in an executive, managerial, or administrative capacity are represented by 82 percent" of the organizations that in one way or another engage in advocacy on economic issues. In contrast, "organizations of or for the economically needy are a rarity." Thus, in terms of membership in interest groups, there is a profound bias in favor of those who are well off financially.[50]

Citizen Groups

Because the bias in interest group membership is unmistakable, should we conclude that the interest group system is biased overall? Before reaching that determination, we should examine another set of data. The actual population of interest groups in Washington surely reflects a class bias in interest group membership, but that bias may be modified in an important way. Some interest

MoveOn Mobilizes

Interest groups were highly mobilized for the 2006 congressional elections. The liberal organization MoveOn.org was very active, including work in the district in and around Asheville, North Carolina. Jo Hauser was one of the many volunteers who campaigned for Democratic challenger Heath Shuler. Shuler went on to defeat Republican incumbent Charles Taylor. *(AP Photo/Chuck Burton)*

Microsoft Lobbyists: Cheaper by the Dozen

For large companies like Microsoft, changes in government policies can reduce revenue by hundreds of millions or even billions of dollars. Thus, money is no object in hiring all the lobbyists who might be helpful in influencing government actions. These four Microsoft lawyers and lobbyists were defending the company at a hearing on a government complaint against the software giant. *(Rick Bowmer/AP/Wide World Photos)*

The 1970s and 1980s saw a vast increase in the number of business lobbies in Washington. Many corporations opened up Washington lobbying offices, and many trade associations headquartered elsewhere either moved to Washington or opened branch offices there.

This mobilization was partly a reaction to the success of liberal citizen groups, which business tended to view as hostile to the free enterprise system. The reaction of business also reflected the expanded scope of the national government. After the Environmental Protection Agency, the Consumer Product Safety Commission, the Occupational Safety and Health Administration, and other regulatory agencies were created, many more companies found they were affected by federal regulations. And many corporations found that they were frequently reacting to policies that were already made rather than participating in their making. They saw representation in Washington—where the policy-makers are—as critical if they were to obtain information on pending government actions soon enough to act on it. Finally, the competitive nature of business lobbying fueled the increase in business advocacy in Washington. This competition exists because legislation and regulatory decisions never seem to apply uniformly to all businesses; rather, they affect one type of business or one industry more than others.

The health-care industry is a case in point. Government regulation has become an increasingly important factor in determining health-care profits. Through reimbursement formulas for Medicare, Medicaid, and other health-care programs funded by Washington, the national government limits what providers can charge. As this regulatory influence grew, more and more health-care trade associations (like the American Hospital Association) and professional associations (like the American Nurses Association) came to view Washington lobbying as increasingly significant to the well-being of their members. In 1979 there were roughly one hundred health-related groups lobbying in Washington. A little over a decade later, there were more than seven hundred. Another decade later, the number had surpassed one thousand.[53]

FIGURE 10.5   Who Lobbies?

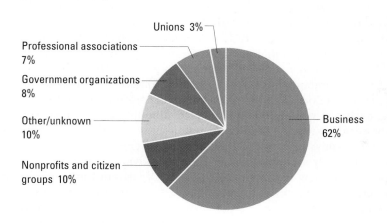

Unions 3%

Professional associations 7%

Government organizations 8%

Other/unknown 10%

Nonprofits and citizen groups 10%

Business 62%

The population of lobbying organizations in Washington is dominated by business-related organizations (individual corporations and trade associations). Such organizations not only lobby themselves but also frequently hire law firms, lobbying firms, and public relations firms to work on their behalf. These figures are drawn from a six-month period of lobby registrations with the Congress. When an organization is lobbying, it files a registration with Congress and on this form indicates what issues it is working on.

Source: Frank R. Baumgartner and Beth L. Leech, "Interest Niches and Policy Bandwagons," *Journal of Politics* 63 (November 2001): 1196.

The advantages of business are enormous. As Figure 10.5 illustrates, close to two-thirds of all organizations lobbying on all issues before the Congress are business related—either corporations or trade associations.[54] Although citizen groups do well given their numbers, the overwhelming number of business organizations and their high levels of activity point toward a real imbalance in representation of interests before government. Still, it's important to keep in mind that business is frequently divided, and much of the aggregate numerical advantage of business reflects businesses lobbying against other businesses.[55] When business is unified, as on broad corporate tax reduction measures, it can be quite influential. And on narrow issues, where only one industry is involved, it may be the only sector of the interest group community that is active.

Reform

If the interest group system is biased, should the advantages of some groups somehow be eliminated or reduced? This is hard to do. In an economic system marked by great differences in income, great differences in the degree to which people are organized are inevitable. Moreover, as Madison foresaw, limiting interest group activity is difficult without limiting fundamental freedoms. The First Amendment guarantees Americans the right to petition their government, and lobbying, at its most basic level, is a form of organized petitioning.

Still, some sectors of the interest group community may enjoy advantages that are unacceptable. If it is felt that the advantages of some groups are so great that they affect the equality of people's opportunity to be heard in the political system, then restrictions on interest group behavior can be justified on the grounds that the disadvantaged must be protected. Pluralist democracy is justified on exactly these grounds: all constituencies must have the opportunity to organize, and competition between groups as they press their case before policymakers must be fair.

Some critics charge that a system of campaign finance that relies so heavily on PACs undermines our democratic system. They claim that access to policymakers is purchased through the wealth of some constituencies. Around two-thirds of PAC contributions come from corporations, business trade associations, and professional associations.[56] It is not merely a matter of wealthy interest groups showering incumbents with donations; members of Congress aggressively solicit donations from PACs. Although observers disagree on whether PAC money actually influences policy outcomes, agreement is widespread that PAC donations give donors better access to members of Congress.

Congress took an important step in campaign finance reform with the McCain-Feingold Act in 2002. Prior to its passage, corporations, labor unions, and other organizations could donate unlimited amounts of so-called soft money to the political parties. A company or union with issues before government could give a six-figure gift to the Democratic or Republican Party, even though it could make only a modest contribution to individual candidates. As noted in Chapter 9, this new law, formally titled the Bipartisan Campaign Finance Reform Act, bans soft money contributions to national party committees. Yet 527's have emerged to present a different challenge to the campaign finance system. Although they don't contribute directly to candidates or parties, these organizations played a significant role in the last presidential election.

In the wake of the scandals involving Jack Abramoff and others and the Democrats' promise in the 2006 campaign to push for ethics reform if they captured the Congress, legislation was introduced in both houses to address a range of problems. Both houses took action to try to stop legislators from taking attractive trips paid for by lobbyists under the guise of congressional work. Rules involving gifts and entertainment were also tightened. Both houses took steps to bring transparency to the process by which lobbyists have collected contributions from their clients and then "bundled" them together in donations to legislators. (At this writing, some of the reforms await action by a conference committee to reconcile differing House and Senate bills.) At the same time, many liberal good government groups were disappointed by the Democrats' actions, believing that reform, especially in the area of campaign finance, could have gone much further.

Summary

Interest groups play many important roles in our political process. They are a means by which citizens can participate in politics, and they communicate their members' views to those in government. Interest groups differ greatly in the resources at their disposal and in the tactics they use to influence government. The number of interest groups has grown sharply in recent years.

Despite the growth and change in the nature of interest groups, the fundamental problem that Madison identified more than two hundred years ago endures. In a free and open society, groups form to pursue policies that favor them at the expense of the broader national interest. Madison hoped that the solution to the problem would come from the diversity of the population and the structure of our government.

To a certain extent, Madison's expectations have been borne out. The natural differences between groups have prevented a tyranny of any one faction. Yet the interest group system remains unbalanced, with some segments of society (particularly business, the wealthy, and the educated) considerably better organized than others. The growth of citizen groups has reduced the disparity somewhat, but significant inequalities remain in how well different interests are represented in Washington.

The inequities point to flaws in pluralist theory. There is no mechanism to automatically ensure that interest groups will form to speak for those who need representation. And when an issue arises and policymakers meet with interest groups that have a stake in the outcome, those groups may not equally represent all the constituencies that the policy changes will affect. The interest group system clearly compromises the principle of political equality stated in the maxim "one person, one vote." Formal political equality is certainly more likely to occur outside interest group politics, in elections between candidates from competing political parties, which better fits the majoritarian model of democracy.

Despite the inequities of the interest group system, little direct effort has been made to restrict interest group activity. Madison's dictum to avoid suppressing political freedoms, even at the expense of permitting interest group activity that promotes the selfish interests of narrow segments of the population, has generally guided public policy. Yet as the problem of PACs demonstrates, government has had to set some restrictions on interest groups. Where to draw the line on PAC activity remains a thorny issue because there is little consensus on how to balance the conflicting needs of our society. Congress is one institution that must try to balance our diverse country's conflicting interests. In the next chapter, we will see how difficult this part of Congress's job is.

Internet activities and reading suggestions for this chapter are available on the *Online Study Center*

To complete the multimedia assignments for this chapter, go to AmericansGoverning.org.

11

Congress

(Chip Somodevilla/Getty Images)

Online Study Center
This icon will direct you to resources
and activities on the website
college.hmco.com/pic/jandaupdate9e

Then Senate Majority Leader Bill Frist (R-Tenn.) had harsh words for Democrats in an April 2005 broadcast to churches to rally support for President Bush's judicial nominees and to raise opposition to Democratic filibusters.[1] Frist said, "Never in 214 years, never in the history of the United States Senate had a judicial nominee with majority support been denied an up-or-down vote . . . until two years ago. In the last Congress, a minority of senators denied ten of the president's judicial nominees an up-or-down vote. . . . Now we are in a new Congress, and these same senators again threaten to obstruct the vote on judges."

Any individual senator may voice opposition to having a formal vote on a bill or presidential nomination. It then takes a three-fifths vote—sixty senators—to limit debate and move on to a floor vote. These delay tactics are in keeping with the reputation of the Senate as a defense against impulsive government action. In order to rally the votes needed to end debate, senators have to lobby each other and talk over the issues. As George Washington famously put it, "We pour legislation into the senatorial saucer to cool it."

But, as then Majority Leader Frist argued, this delay can be used to make policy. Without a vote, President Bush's nominees cannot be confirmed; the outcome is the same as if a majority of senators voted against the nominees in a floor vote. The frustration for Frist and Senate Republicans was that Bush's nominees would easily have been confirmed by a majority of senators. The Republicans simply didn't have sixty votes to end the filibuster. The Senate mi-

nority leader at the time, Harry Reid (D-Nev.), argued that it was the Democratic Party's right to check the power of the president and the majority party. The Democrats felt that the ten nominees in limbo were clearly out of the ideological mainstream of American politics.

This was not the first time the filibuster was used in a battle over political ideology. In the 1940s and 1950s, for example, a conservative coalition of Republicans and southern Democrats successfully filibustered civil rights legislation. Only after the Democratic Party's landslide electoral victory in 1964 were there enough liberals in the Senate to end debate and force a vote to pass the Voting Rights Act of 1965. As the stalemate over the judicial nominees escalated, however, Frist threatened to employ a "nuclear option": he would call a vote to get rid of filibusters on judicial nominees altogether. His proposal threatened a dramatic change in Senate tradition.

With the party leadership on a collision course, mired in interest group demands over the fate of the judicial nominees, a group of fourteen senators—seven Republicans and seven Democrats—stepped in to work out a compromise. Democrats agreed that they would only filibuster nominees under "extraordinary circumstances" if Republicans would not vote to ban judicial filibusters. The day after the deal was announced, some of Bush's nominees were finally put up for a vote and confirmed. Now that Senator Frist has retired and the Democrats have a majority in the Senate, however, party leaders will undoubtedly revisit and renegotiate the filibuster again. ★

The controversy over the Senate filibuster highlights many of the forces operating in Congress: rules and traditions, partisanship, interest groups, and negotiation. In this chapter, we'll examine the procedures and norms that facilitate this kind of bargaining and compromise in the Congress. The forces of pluralism that contribute to this behavior will be discussed, as will counterpressures (such as political parties) that push legislators toward majoritarianism. We'll also focus on Congress's relations with the executive branch and analyze how the legislative process affects public policy. A starting point is to ask how the framers envisioned Congress.

★ The Origin and Powers of Congress

The framers of the Constitution wanted to keep power from being concentrated in the hands of a few, but they were also concerned with creating a Union strong enough to overcome the weaknesses of the government that had operated under the Articles of Confederation. They argued passionately about the structure of the new government. In the end, they produced a legislative body that was as much of an experiment as the new nation's democracy.

The Great Compromise

The U.S. Congress has two separate and powerful chambers: the House of Representatives and the Senate. A bill cannot become law unless it is passed in identical form by both chambers. During the drafting of the Constitution during the summer of 1787, "the fiercest struggle for power" centered on representation in the legislature.[2] The small states wanted all the states to have equal representation, and the more populous states wanted representation based on population; they did not want their power diluted. The Great Compromise broke the deadlock: the small states would receive equal representation in the Senate, but the number of each state's representatives in the House would be based on population and the House would have the sole right to originate revenue-related legislation.

As the Constitution specifies, each state has two senators, who serve six-year terms of office. Terms are staggered, so that one-third of the Senate is elected every two years. When it was ratified, the Constitution directed that senators be chosen by the state legislatures. However, the Seventeenth Amendment, adopted in 1913, provided for the direct election of senators by popular vote. From the beginning, the people have directly elected members of the House of Representatives. They serve two-year terms, and all House seats are up for election at the same time.

There are 435 members of the House of Representatives. Because each state's representation in the House is in proportion to its population, the Constitution provides for a national census every ten years; population shifts are handled by the **reapportionment** (redistribution) of seats among the states after each census is taken. Since recent population growth has been centered in the Sunbelt, California, Texas, and Florida have gained seats, while the Northeast and Midwest states have lost them. Each representative is elected from a particular congressional district within his or her state, and each district elects only one representative. The districts within a state must be roughly equal in population.

reapportionment Redistribution of representatives among the states, based on population change. The House is reapportioned after each census.

Duties of the House and Senate

Although the Great Compromise provided for considerably different schemes of representation for the House and Senate, the Constitution gives them similar legislative tasks. They share many important powers, among them the powers to declare war, raise an army and navy, borrow and coin money, regulate interstate commerce, create federal courts, establish rules for the naturalization of immigrants, and "make all Laws which shall be necessary and proper for carrying into Execution the foregoing Powers."

Of course, the constitutional duties of the two chambers are different in at least a few important ways. As noted earlier, the House alone has the right to originate revenue bills, a right that apparently was coveted at the Constitutional Convention. In practice, this power is of limited consequence because both the House and Senate must approve all bills, including revenue bills. The House of Representatives has the power of **impeachment,** the power formally to charge the president, vice president, and other "civil officers" of the national government with serious crimes. The Senate is empowered to act as a court to try impeachments, with the chief justice of the Supreme Court presiding. A two-thirds majority vote of the senators present is necessary for conviction. Prior to President Clinton's impeachment in 1998, only one sitting president, Andrew Johnson, had been impeached, and in 1868 the Senate came within a single vote of finding him guilty. Clinton was accused of both perjury and obstruction of justice concerning his relationship with a White House intern, Monica Lewinsky, but was acquitted by the Senate as well. The House Judiciary Committee voted to recommend impeachment of President Richard Nixon because of his involvement in the Watergate cover-up, but before the full House could vote, Nixon resigned from office.

The Constitution gives the Senate the power to approve major presidential appointments (such as to federal judgeships, ambassadorships, and cabinet posts) and treaties with foreign nations. The president is empowered to make treaties, but he must submit them to the Senate for approval by a two-thirds majority. Because of this requirement, the executive branch generally considers the Senate's sentiments when it negotiates a treaty. At times, a president must try to convince a doubting Senate of the worth of a particular treaty. Shortly after World War I, President Woodrow Wilson submitted to the Senate the Treaty of Versailles, which contained the charter for the proposed League of Nations. Wilson had attempted to convince the Senate that the treaty deserved its support; when the Senate refused to approve the treaty, Wilson suffered a severe setback.

Despite the long list of congressional powers stated in the Constitution, the question of what powers are appropriate for Congress has generated substantial controversy. For example, although the Constitution gives Congress the sole power to declare war, presidents have initiated military action on their own (see Chapters 12 and 20). And at times, the courts have found that congressional actions have usurped the rights of the states.

★ Electing Congress

If Americans are not happy with the job Congress is doing, they can use their votes to say so. With a congressional election every two years, the voters have frequent opportunities to express themselves.

impeachment The formal charging of a government official with "treason, bribery, or other high crimes and misdemeanors."

FIGURE 11.1 Incumbents: Life Is Good

Despite the public's dissatisfaction with Congress in general, incumbent representatives win reelection at an exceptional rate. Incumbent senators aren't quite as successful but still do well in reelection races. Voters seem to believe that their own representatives and senators don't share the same foibles that they attribute to the other members of Congress.

Sources: Norman J. Ornstein, Thomas E. Mann, and Michael J. Malbin, *Vital Statistics on Congress, 2001–2002* (Washington, D.C.: American Enterprise Institute, 2002), pp. 69–70; David Nather with John Cochran, "Still-Thin Edge Leaves GOP with a Cautious Mandate," *CQ Weekly,* 9 November 2002, pp. 2888–2893; "The 2006 Elections: Congress," *New York Times,* 9 November 2006, pp. P8–P9.

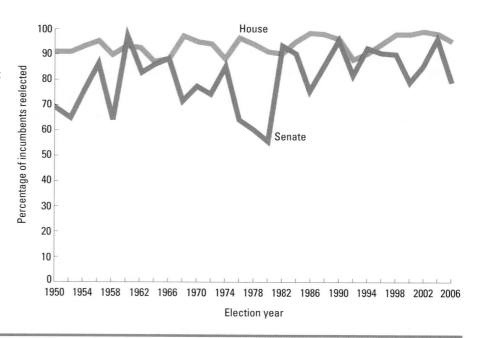

The Incumbency Effect

Congressional elections offer voters a chance to show their approval of Congress's performance, by reelecting **incumbents,** or to demonstrate their disapproval, by "throwing the rascals out." The voters do more reelecting than rascal throwing. The reelection rate is astonishingly high: in the majority of elections since 1950, more than 90 percent of all House incumbents have held on to their seats (see Figure 11.1). In the 2004 congressional elections, only nine incumbents in the House of Representatives were defeated by challengers. The percentage of incumbents winning reelection declined in 2006, when several Republican incumbents were defeated in midterm elections that many viewed as a referendum on the Bush administration. Most House elections aren't even close; in recent elections, most House incumbents have won at least 60 percent of the vote. Senate elections are more competitive, but incumbents still have a high reelection rate.[3]

These findings may seem surprising, since the public does not hold Congress as a whole in particularly high esteem. When pollsters asked a random sample of Americans if they had confidence in the Congress, only 19 percent said they had a great deal or quite a lot of confidence in the institution (see Figure 11.2).[4] One reason Americans hold Congress in disdain is that they regard it as overly influenced by interest groups. One study found that almost half of all adults would ban interest groups from contacting members of Congress, a rather extreme measure, to say the least.[5] The central role of political action committees (PACs) and lobbyists in our congressional campaign finance system reinforces the notion that interest groups have too much sway in the Congress. Nevertheless, for all their general disillusionment with the Congress,

? **Can you explain why . . .** Americans say they hate the Congress but keep reelecting their own representative?

incumbent A current officeholder.

FIGURE 11.2   Not Exactly a Vote of Confidence

Of the three major branches of the national government, Congress scores far lower in terms of public confidence than either the presidency or the Supreme Court. Only big business and health maintenance organizations (HMOs) have a lower score.

Source: Confidence in Institutions Gallup Poll, 1–4 June 2006, at <http://www.poll.gallup.com>.

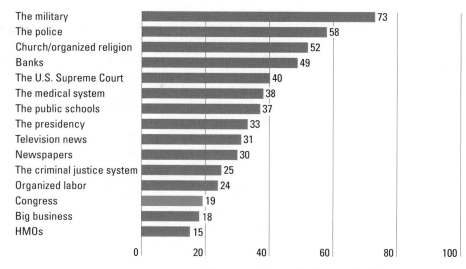

The military 73
The police 58
Church/organized religion 52
Banks 49
The U.S. Supreme Court 40
The medical system 38
The public schools 37
The presidency 33
Television news 31
Newspapers 30
The criminal justice system 25
Organized labor 24
Congress 19
Big business 18
HMOs 15

Percentage expressing "a great deal" or "quite a lot" of confidence in the institution

Americans are quick to distinguish their own members of Congress from the institution as a whole. A 2006 Gallup Poll revealed that a majority of voters believe "most members" of Congress are more focused on the needs of special interests than on constituents, but that their own member of Congress is more focused on constituents than on special interests.[6] In short, voters tend to love their own congressmen while being contemptuous of the rest of the membership. Finally, American culture has traditionally held politicians in low esteem: we don't expect much from politicians, and we react sharply to their failings.[7]

Redistricting.   One explanation for the incumbency effect centers on redistricting—the way House districts are redrawn by states after a census-based reapportionment.[8] It is entirely possible for them to draw the new districts to benefit the incumbents of one or both parties. Altering district lines for partisan advantage is commonly called **gerrymandering.**

Gerrymandering has been practiced since at least the early 1800s.[9] And with new computer software, gerrymandering is reaching new heights of precision. With an ordinary desktop computer, someone knowledgeable with the software can easily use census data and precinct voting data to manipulate boundary lines and produce districts that are optimally designed to enhance or damage a candidate or party's chances. After the 2000 census, for example, California state legislators took the solidly Republican city of San Marino out of incumbent Democrat Adam Schiff's district and put it in the adjoining district of Republican David Dreier. Instantaneously, Schiff's district became even more safely Democratic (with San Marino now gone), and Dreier's district became even more safely Republican (with San Marino now part of it). Since

gerrymandering Redrawing a congressional district to intentionally benefit one political party.

Dreier was the incumbent and not likely to lose anyway, the Democrats gave up little and gave themselves some insurance against Republican inroads.[10]

Name Recognition. Holding office brings with it some important advantages. First, incumbents develop significant name recognition among voters simply by being members of Congress. Congressional press secretaries help the name recognition advantage along through their efforts to get publicity for the activities and speeches of their bosses. The primary focus of such publicity seeking is on the local media back in the district, where the votes are. The local press is eager to cover what local members of Congress are saying about the issues.

Another resource available to members of Congress is the *franking privilege*—the right to send mail free of charge. Mailings work to make constituents aware of their legislators' names, activities, and accomplishments. Not surprisingly, legislators have taken advantage of the latest technologies to publicize their accomplishments and their availability for assisting constituencies. The individual websites of legislators can be best described as exercises in narcissism. The websites are long on public relations but short on information on how the legislator voted on recent or past legislation.[11]

Casework. Much of the work performed by the large staffs of members of Congress is **casework**—services for constituents, such as tracking down a Social Security check or directing the owner of a small business to the appropriate federal agency. Many specialists in both the Washington office and the home district or state office are employed primarily as caseworkers. Thus, the very structure of congressional offices is largely built around helping constituents. One caseworker on a staff may be a specialist on immigration, another on veterans' benefits, another on social security, and so on. Legislators devote much of their office budget to casework because they assume that when they provide assistance to a constituent, that constituent will be grateful. Not only will that person probably vote for the legislator in the next election, but he or she is also sure to tell family members and friends how helpful the representative or senator was. "Casework is all profit," says one congressional scholar.[12] The growing popularity of e-mail has made it all the easier for constituents to make a request of their legislator. A recent calculation estimates that House offices routinely receive 8,000 e-mail messages a month and Senate offices receive about 55,000.[13] Not all of these e-mails are casework related by any means, but the volume of casework requests is surely growing.

Campaign Financing. It should be clear that anyone who wants to challenge an incumbent needs solid financial backing. Challengers must spend large sums of money to run a strong campaign with an emphasis on advertising—an expensive but effective way to bring their name and record to the voters' attention. But here too the incumbent has the advantage. Challengers find raising campaign funds difficult because they have to overcome contributors' doubts about whether they can win. In the 2004 elections, incumbents raised 62 percent of all money contributed to campaigns for election to the House and the Senate. Only 16 percent went to challengers. (Those running for open seats received the rest.)[14]

PACs show a strong preference for incumbents (see Chapter 10). They tend not to want to risk offending an incumbent by giving money to a long-

casework Solving problems for constituents, especially problems involving government agencies.

shot challenger. The attitude of the American Medical Association's PAC is fairly typical. "We have a friendly incumbent policy," says its director. "We always stick with the incumbent if we agree with both candidates."[15] Over time, the financial advantage of incumbents over challengers has increased. The main reason is the "sophomore surge" as PACs rush to support the newest members when they prepare to run as incumbents for the first time.[16]

Successful Challengers.   Clearly, the deck is stacked against challengers. As one analyst put it, "The typical House challenger is in a position similar to that of a novice athlete pitted against a world-class sprinter."[17] Yet some challengers do beat incumbents. How? The opposing party and unsympathetic PACs may target incumbents who seem vulnerable because of age, lack of seniority, a scandal, or unfavorable redistricting. Some incumbents appear vulnerable because they were elected by a narrow margin, or the ideological and partisan composition of their district does not favor their holding the seat. Vulnerable incumbents also bring out higher-quality challengers—individuals who have held elective office previously and are capable of raising adequate campaign funds. Such experienced challengers are more likely to defeat incumbents than are amateurs with little background in politics.[18] The reason Senate challengers have a higher success rate than House challengers is that they are generally higher-quality candidates. Often they are governors or members of the House who enjoy high name recognition and can attract significant campaign funds because they are regarded as credible candidates.[19]

2002 and 2006 Elections.   The off-year election—the congressional election between presidential elections—is traditionally not good for the party holding the White House. As the optimism that greets a new president gives way to the realities of continuing problems, voters typically give the out party a gain of seats in the Congress. After September 11, 2001, however, the public strongly approved of President George W. Bush, and the Republicans ended up gaining five seats in the House and two in the Senate in 2002. It was only the third time since the Civil War that the party of the president gained House seats in a midterm election. The shift in public opinion toward the Republicans was, in one scholar's words, "the undeniable, if unintended, gift of Osama bin Laden."[20]

The 2006 elections could not have been more different for the Republican Party. Democrats won races around the country, taking control of both the House and the Senate for the first time since 1994. In the House, thirty-one seats switched from Republican to Democratic control, and the majority of these districts had been solidly for Bush in 2004. Democratic candidates defeated Republican incumbent senators in Pennsylvania, Ohio, Missouri, Rhode Island, Montana, and Virginia.

Two issues sealed the fate of the Republican Party. First, voters were concerned about corruption in government after several scandals involving Republican incumbents. Representative Mark Foley (R-Fla.), for example, resigned his seat after it was revealed that he sent sexually inappropriate e-mails to teenage congressional pages. Second, a majority of voters disapproved of the Bush administration's handling of the war in Iraq. Exit polls showed that independents overwhelmingly voted for the Democratic Party and cited the war in Iraq among their top concerns. Even President Bush conceded that voters were dissatisfied with the status quo; the day after the election Secretary of Defense Donald Rumsfeld resigned.

Compared with What?

Women in Legislatures

The percentage of women in the world's national legislatures differs from one country to another. The number of women does not seem to be a function of the structure of the legislature or the party system in these countries. Culture does seem to make a difference, though. This figure includes fifteen European countries as well as fifteen countries from the Americas (North America, Central America, and South America). Ranked by the percentage of women in the lower house of the national legislature, the European countries include, on average, a significantly higher percentage of women than the legislatures of countries in the Western Hemisphere.

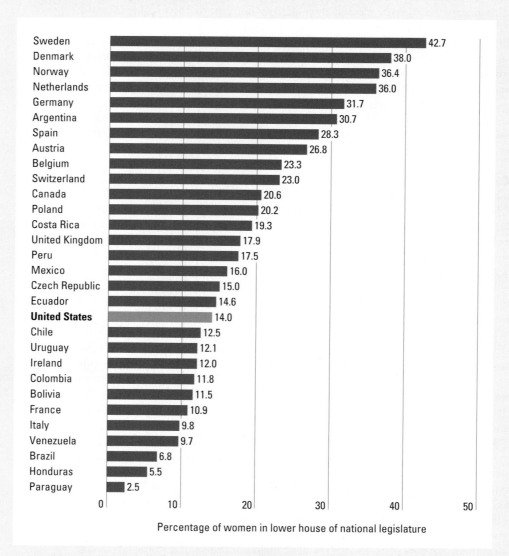

Percentage of women in lower house of national legislature

Country	Percentage
Sweden	42.7
Denmark	38.0
Norway	36.4
Netherlands	36.0
Germany	31.7
Argentina	30.7
Spain	28.3
Austria	26.8
Belgium	23.3
Switzerland	23.0
Canada	20.6
Poland	20.2
Costa Rica	19.3
United Kingdom	17.9
Peru	17.5
Mexico	16.0
Czech Republic	15.0
Ecuador	14.6
United States	**14.0**
Chile	12.5
Uruguay	12.1
Ireland	12.0
Colombia	11.8
Bolivia	11.5
France	10.9
Italy	9.8
Venezuela	9.7
Brazil	6.8
Honduras	5.5
Paraguay	2.5

Source: United Nations Development Programme, *Human Development Report 2002* (New York: Oxford University Press, 2002), pp. 239–242.

Whom Do We Elect?

The people we elect (then reelect) to Congress are not a cross-section of American society. Most members of Congress are professionals—primarily lawyers, businesspeople, and educators.[21] Although nearly a third of the American labor force works in blue-collar jobs, someone currently employed as a blue-collar worker rarely wins a congressional nomination. In contrast, members of Congress tend to be upper-class professionals, and many are millionaires.[22]

Women and minorities have long been underrepresented in elective office, although both groups have recently increased their representation in Congress significantly. For example, after the 2006 midterm elections, sixteen women will serve in the Senate. This is an historic high, but nowhere near the proportion of women to men in the population at large.[23] Other members of Congress don't necessarily ignore the concerns of women and minorities.[24] Yet many women and minorities believe that only members of their own group—people who have experienced what they have experienced—can truly represent their interests. This is a belief in **descriptive representation,** the view that a legislature should resemble the demographic characteristics of the population it represents.[25] (See "Compared with What? Women in Legislatures" for a comparison of the representation of women in the world's national legislatures.)

During the 1980s, both Congress and the Supreme Court provided support for the principle of descriptive representation for blacks and Hispanic Americans. When Congress amended the Voting Rights Act in 1982, it encouraged the states to draw districts that concentrated minorities together so that blacks and Hispanic Americans would have a better chance of being elected to office. Supreme Court decisions also pushed the states to concentrate minorities in House districts. After the 1990 census, states redrew House boundaries with the intent of creating districts with majority or near-majority minority populations. Some districts were very oddly shaped, snaking through their state to pick up

descriptive representation
A belief that constituents are most effectively represented by legislators who are similar to them in such key demographic characteristics as race, ethnicity, religion, or gender.

Politics in a Changing World

Minorities in Congress

Only forty years ago, African American and Hispanic politicians held less than 4 percent of all congressional seats. Today, African Americans make up about 8 percent of the membership of the House and Senate, while Hispanics make up about 5 percent of total members. Though gains have been steady, the representation of both groups remains well below their proportions in the population at large. Hispanics constitute 14 percent of the American population; African Americans make up almost 13 percent of the total population. Hispanics constitute over 30 percent of the population in states like California, Texas, and New Mexico, while African Americans constitute almost 30 percent of the population of southern states like Mississippi, Louisiana, and Georgia. As more minorities become involved in the political process, more will win seats in Congress, as well as state and local offices.

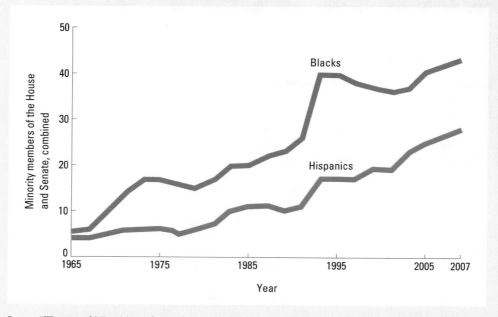

Source: "Women and Minorities in the 109th Congress," *CQ Weekly*, 31 January 2005, p. 243. Copyright © 2005 Congressional Quarterly, Inc. Reprinted with permission.

black neighborhoods in various cities but leaving adjacent white neighborhoods to other districts. This effort led to a roughly 50 percent increase in the number of blacks elected to the House (see "Politics in a Changing World: Minorities in Congress").

The effort to draw boundaries to promote the election of minorities has been considerably less effective for Hispanics. Hispanic representation is only about two-thirds that of African Americans, yet Hispanics now constitute 14.1

percent of the American population, slightly higher than the percentage of African Americans.[26] Part of the reason for this inequity is that Hispanics tend not to live in such geographically concentrated areas as do African Americans. This makes it harder to draw boundaries that will likely lead to the election of a Hispanic.

In a decision that surprised many, the Supreme Court ruled in 1993 that states' efforts to increase minority representation through **racial gerrymandering** could violate the rights of whites. In *Shaw* v. *Reno,* the majority ruled in a split decision that a North Carolina district that meandered 160 miles from Durham to Charlotte was an example of "political apartheid." (In some places, the Twelfth District was no wider than Interstate 85.) In effect, the Court ruled that racial gerrymandering segregated blacks from whites instead of creating districts built around contiguous communities.[27] In a later decision, the Supreme Court ruled that the "intensive and pervasive use of race" to protect incumbents and promote political gerrymandering violated the Fourteenth Amendment and Voting Rights Act of 1965.[28] In 2001, just before the redistricting from the 2000 census was to begin in the individual states, the Court modified its earlier decisions by declaring that race was not an illegitimate consideration in drawing congressional boundaries as long as it was not the "dominant and controlling" factor.[29]

Although this movement over time to draw districts that work to elect minorities has clearly increased the number of black and Hispanic legislators, almost all of whom are Democrats, it has also helped the Republican Party. As more Democratic-voting minorities have been packed into selected districts, this has diminished their numbers in other districts, leaving the remaining districts not merely "whiter" but also more Republican than they would have otherwise been.[30]

⭐ How Issues Get on the Congressional Agenda

The formal legislative process begins when a member of Congress introduces a *bill*, a proposal for a new law. In the House, members drop bills in the "hopper," a mahogany box near the rostrum where the Speaker presides. Senators give their bills to a Senate clerk or introduce them from the floor. But before a bill can be introduced to solve a problem, someone must perceive that a problem exists or that an issue needs to be resolved. In other words, the problem or issue somehow must find its way onto the congressional agenda. *Agenda* actually has two meanings in the vocabulary of political scientists. The first is that of a narrow, formal agenda, such as a calendar of bills to be voted on. The second meaning refers to the broad, imprecise, and unwritten agenda comprising all the issues an institution is considering. Here we use the term in the broader sense.

Many issues Congress is working on at any given time seem to have been around forever. Foreign aid, the national debt, and Social Security have come up in just about every recent session of Congress. Other issues emerge more suddenly, especially those that are the product of technological change. Genetically altered foods have recently become a controversial issue not only in the United States but around the world as well. In the Congress, consumer advocates have introduced legislation to require labeling of bioengineered food

racial gerrymandering The drawing of a legislative district to maximize the chance that a minority candidate will win election.

products. Members from farm areas have commissioned reports to show that such foods are safe. Once the technology was used to alter crops and food products, it was inevitable that Congress would have to place such a controversial issue on its agenda.[31]

New issues reach the congressional agenda in many ways. Sometimes a highly visible event focuses national attention on a problem. When it became evident that the September 11 hijackers had little trouble boarding their planes despite carrying box cutters that they would use as weapons, Congress quickly took up the issue of airport screening procedures. It decided to create a federal work force to conduct passenger and luggage screening at the nation's airports, believing the existing workers recruited by private companies were badly trained and poorly motivated. Presidential support can also move an issue onto the agenda quickly. The media attention paid to the president gives him enormous opportunity to draw the nation's attention to problems he believes need some form of government action.

Within Congress, party leaders and committee chairs have the opportunity to move issues onto the agenda, but they rarely act capriciously, seizing on issues without rhyme or reason. They often bide their time, waiting for other members of Congress to learn about an issue as they attempt to gauge the level of support for some kind of action. At times, the efforts of an interest group spark support for action, or at least awareness of an issue. When congressional leaders—or, for that matter, rank-and-file members—sense that the time is ripe for action on a new issue, they often are spurred on by the knowledge that sponsoring an important bill can enhance their own image. In the words of one observer, "Congress exists to do things. There isn't much mileage in doing nothing."[32]

★ The Dance of Legislation: An Overview

The process of writing bills and getting them enacted is relatively simple in the sense that it follows a series of specific steps. What complicates the process is the many different ways legislation can be treated at each step. Here, we examine the straightforward process by which laws are made. In the next few sections, we discuss some of the complexities of that process.

After a bill is introduced in either house, it is assigned to the committee with jurisdiction over that policy area (see Figure 11.3). A banking bill, for example, would be assigned to the Financial Services Committee in the House or to the Banking, Housing, and Urban Affairs Committee in the Senate. When a committee actively considers a piece of legislation assigned to it, the bill is usually referred to a specialized subcommittee. The subcommittee may hold hearings, and legislative staffers may do research on the bill. The original bill usually is modified or revised; if passed in some form, it is sent to the full committee. A bill approved by the full committee is reported (that is, sent) to the entire membership of the chamber, where it may be debated, amended, and either passed or defeated.

Bills coming out of House committees go to the Rules Committee before going before the full House membership. The Rules Committee attaches a rule to the bill that governs the coming floor debate, typically specifying the length of the debate and the types of amendments House members can offer. On major legislation, most rules are complex and quite restrictive in terms of any amendments that can be offered. The Senate does not have a comparable com-

FIGURE 11.3 The Legislative Process

The process by which a bill becomes law is subject to much variation. This diagram depicts the typical process a bill might follow. It is important to remember that a bill can fail at any stage because of lack of support.

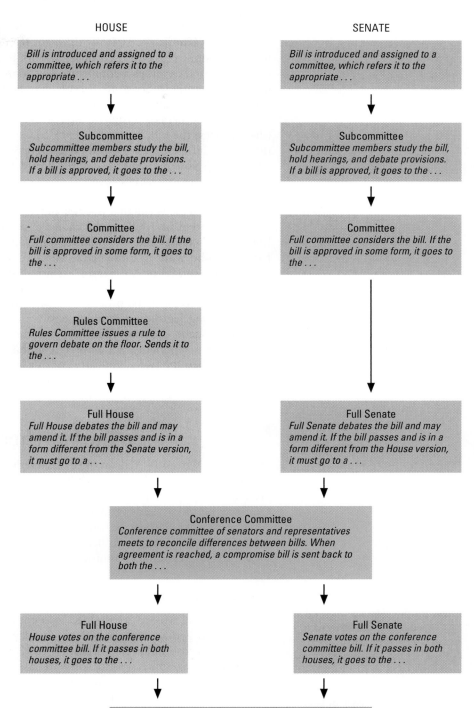

HOUSE

Bill is introduced and assigned to a committee, which refers it to the appropriate . . .

Subcommittee
Subcommittee members study the bill, hold hearings, and debate provisions. If a bill is approved, it goes to the . . .

Committee
Full committee considers the bill. If the bill is approved in some form, it goes to the . . .

Rules Committee
Rules Committee issues a rule to govern debate on the floor. Sends it to the . . .

Full House
Full House debates the bill and may amend it. If the bill passes and is in a form different from the Senate version, it must go to a . . .

SENATE

Bill is introduced and assigned to a committee, which refers it to the appropriate . . .

Subcommittee
Subcommittee members study the bill, hold hearings, and debate provisions. If a bill is approved, it goes to the . . .

Committee
Full committee considers the bill. If the bill is approved in some form, it goes to the . . .

Full Senate
Full Senate debates the bill and may amend it. If the bill passes and is in a form different from the House version, it must go to a . . .

Conference Committee
Conference committee of senators and representatives meets to reconcile differences between bills. When agreement is reached, a compromise bill is sent back to both the . . .

Full House
House votes on the conference committee bill. If it passes in both houses, it goes to the . . .

Full Senate
Senate votes on the conference committee bill. If it passes in both houses, it goes to the . . .

President
President signs or vetoes the bill. Congress can override a veto by a two-thirds majority vote in both the House and Senate.

mittee, although restrictions on the length of floor debate can be reached through unanimous consent agreements (see the "Rules of Procedure" section later in this chapter).

Even if both houses of Congress pass a bill on the same subject, the Senate and House versions are typically different from each other. In that case, a conference committee, composed of legislators from both houses, works out the differences and develops a compromise version. This version goes back to both houses for another floor vote. If both chambers approve the bill, it goes to the president for his signature or veto.

When the president signs a bill, it becomes law. If the president **vetoes** (disapproves) the bill, he sends it back to Congress with his reasons for rejecting it. The bill becomes law only if Congress overrides the president's veto by a two-thirds vote in each house. If the president neither signs nor vetoes the bill within ten days (Sundays excepted) of receiving it, the bill becomes law. There is an exception here: if Congress adjourns within the ten days, the president can let the bill die through a **pocket veto,** by not signing it.

The content of a bill can be changed at any stage of the process in either house. Lawmaking (and thus policymaking) in Congress has many access points for those who want to influence legislation. This openness tends to fit within the pluralist model of democracy. As a bill moves through the Congress, it is amended again and again, in a search for a consensus that will get it enacted and signed into law. The process can be tortuously slow, and it is often fruitless. Derailing legislation is much easier than enacting it. The process gives groups frequent opportunities to voice their preferences and, if necessary, thwart their opponents. One foreign ambassador stationed in Washington aptly described the twists and turns of our legislative process this way: "In the Congress of the U.S., it's never over until it's over. And when it's over, it's still not over."[33]

★ Committees: The Workhorses of Congress

President Woodrow Wilson once observed that "Congress in session is Congress on public exhibition, whilst Congress in its committee-rooms is Congress at work."[34] His words are as true today as when he wrote them more than one hundred years ago. A speech on the Senate floor, for example, may convince the average citizen, but it is less likely to influence other senators. Indeed, few of them may even hear it. The real nuts and bolts of lawmaking go on in the congressional committees.

The Division of Labor Among Committees

The House and Senate are divided into committees for the same reason that other large organizations are broken into departments or divisions: to develop and use expertise in specific areas. At IBM, for example, different groups of people design computers, write software, assemble hardware, and sell the company's products. Each task requires an expertise that may have little to do with the others. Likewise, in Congress, decisions on weapons systems require a special knowledge that is of little relevance to decisions on reimbursement formulas for health insurance, for example. It makes sense for some members of Congress to spend more time examining defense issues, becoming increasingly expert on the topic as they do so, while others concentrate on health matters.

veto The president's disapproval of a bill that has been passed by both houses of Congress. Congress can override a veto with a two-thirds vote in each house.

pocket veto A means of killing a bill that has been passed by both houses of Congress, in which the president does not sign the bill and Congress adjourns within ten days of the bill's passage.

Eventually, all members of Congress have to vote on each bill that emerges from the committees. Those who are not on a particular committee depend on committee members to examine the issues thoroughly, make compromises as necessary, and bring forward a sound piece of legislation that has a good chance of being passed. Each member decides individually on the bill's merits. But once it reaches the House or Senate floor, members may get to vote on only a handful of amendments (if any at all) before they must cast their yea or nay for the entire bill.

Standing Committees.   There are several different kinds of congressional committees, but the **standing committee** is predominant. Standing committees are permanent committees that specialize in a particular area of legislation—for example, the House Judiciary Committee or the Senate Environment and Public Works Committee. Most of the day-to-day work of drafting legislation takes place in the twenty standing Senate committees and twenty-one standing House committees. Typically, sixteen to twenty senators serve on each standing Senate committee, and an average of forty-two members serve on each standing committee in the House. The proportions of Democrats and Republicans on a standing committee are controlled by the majority party in each house. The majority party gives the minority a percentage of seats that, in theory, approximates the minority party's percentage in the entire chamber. However, the majority party usually gives itself enough of a cushion to ensure that it can control each committee.

With a few exceptions, standing committees are broken down further into subcommittees. For instance, the Senate Foreign Relations committee has seven subcommittees, covering different regions of the world and issues such as international economic policy and terrorism. Subcommittees exist for the same reason parent committees exist: members acquire expertise by continually working within the same fairly narrow policy area. Typically, members of the subcommittee are the dominant force in the shaping of the content of a bill.[35]

Other Congressional Committees.   Members of Congress can also serve on joint, select, and conference committees. **Joint committees** are composed of members of both the House and the Senate. Like standing committees, the four joint committees are concerned with particular policy areas. The Joint Economic Committee, for instance, analyzes the country's economic policies. Joint committees are much weaker than standing committees because they are almost always restricted from reporting bills to the House or Senate. Thus, their role is usually that of fact finding and publicizing problems and policy issues that fall within their jurisdiction.

A **select committee** is a temporary committee created for a specific purpose. Congress establishes select committees to deal with special circumstances or with issues that either overlap or fall outside the areas of expertise of standing committees. The Senate committee that investigated the Watergate scandal, for example, was a select committee, created for that purpose only.

A **conference committee** is also a temporary committee, created to work out differences between the House and Senate versions of a specific piece of legislation. Its members are appointed from the standing committees or subcommittees from each house that originally crafted and reported the legislation. Depending on the nature of the differences and the importance of the legislation, a conference committee may meet for hours or for weeks on end.

standing committee A permanent congressional committee that specializes in a particular policy area.

joint committee A committee made up of members of both the House and the Senate.

select committee A temporary congressional committee created for a specific purpose and disbanded after that purpose is fulfilled.

conference committee A temporary committee created to work out differences between the House and Senate versions of a specific piece of legislation.

The conference committee for a complex defense bill had to resolve 2,003 separate differences between the two versions.[36] When the conference committee reaches a compromise, it reports the bill to both houses, which must then either approve or disapprove the compromise; at this point they cannot amend or change it in any way. Only about 15 to 25 percent of all bills that eventually pass Congress go to a conference committee (although virtually all important or controversial bills do).[37] Committee or subcommittee leaders of both houses reconcile differences in other bills through informal negotiation.

Congressional Expertise and Seniority

Once appointed to a committee, a representative or senator has great incentive to remain on it and gain expertise over the years. Influence in Congress increases with a member's expertise. Influence also grows in a more formal way, with **seniority,** or years of consecutive service, on a committee. In their quest for expertise and seniority, members tend to stay on the same committees. However, sometimes they switch places when they are offered the opportunity to move to one of the high-prestige committees (such as Ways and Means in the House or Finance in the Senate) or to a committee that handles legislation of vital importance to their constituents.

Within each committee, the senior member of the majority party usually becomes the committee chair. Other senior members of the majority party become subcommittee chairs, whereas their counterparts from the minority party gain influence as ranking minority members. In the House and Senate combined, there are over 150 subcommittees, offering multiple opportunities for power and status. Unlike seniority, expertise does not follow simply from length of service. Ability and effort are critical factors, too.

The seniority norm has been weakened considerably since the Republican Party leadership established six-year term limits for committee and subcommittee chairs, a sharp break with the tradition of unlimited tenure as a committee chair. When the term limits went into effect in January 2005, the opening of committee chair positions led to bargains between rank-and-file members and their party leaders.[38] Senator Arlen Specter (R-Pa.), a pro-choice Republican, promised not to stop the confirmation of judges opposed to abortion if given the chairmanship of the Judiciary Committee. In the House of Representatives, Congressman Jerry Lewis (R-Calif.) donated more than $1 million to Republican candidates in 2004 and promised to push for fiscal constraint if he got the job as chair of the House Appropriations Committee. Also in the House of Representatives, Republican Party leaders took the chairmanship of the Veterans Affairs Committee away from Christopher Smith (R-N.J.) after he continually disagreed with the party leadership over the appropriate level of funding for veterans programs. Democratic Party leaders have largely adhered to the seniority system, though they have also worked to increase the representation of women, minorities, and junior members of Congress on the most prestigious congressional committees.

The way in which committees and subcommittees are led and organized within Congress is significant because much public policy decision making takes place there. The first step in drafting legislation is to collect information on the issue. Committee staffers research the problem, and committees hold hearings to take testimony from witnesses who have some special knowledge of the subject.

seniority Years of consecutive service on a particular congressional committee.

At times, committee hearings are more theatrical than informational, to draw public attention to them. When the House Judiciary Subcommittee on Administrative Law held hearings on alleged malpractice in military hospitals, for example, it did not restrict its list of witnesses to experts who had done relevant research. Instead, it called witnesses such as Dawn Lambert, a former member of the U.S. Navy, who sobbed as she told the subcommittee that she had been left sterile by a misdiagnosis and a botched operation that had left a sponge and a green marking pen inside her. It was an irresistible story for the evening news, and it brought the malpractice problem in the military to light.[39]

The meetings at which subcommittees and committees actually debate and amend legislation are called *markup sessions.* The process by which committees reach decisions varies. Many committees have a strong tradition of deciding by consensus. The chair, the ranking minority member, and others in these committees work hard, in formal committee sessions and in informal negotiations, to find a middle ground on issues that divide committee members. In other committees, members exhibit strong ideological and partisan sentiments. However, committee and subcommittee leaders prefer to find ways to overcome inherent ideological and partisan divisions so that they can build compromise solutions that will appeal to the broader membership of their house. The skill of committee leaders in assembling coalitions that produce legislation that can pass on the floor of their house is critically important. When committees are mired in disagreement, they lose power. Since jurisdictions overlap, other committees may take more initiative in their common policy area.

Oversight: Following Through on Legislation

There is general agreement in Washington that knowledge is power. For Congress to retain its influence over the programs it creates, it must be aware of how the agencies responsible for them are administering them. To that end, legislators and their committees engage in **oversight,** the process of reviewing agencies' operations to determine whether they are carrying out policies as Congress intended.

As the executive branch has grown and policies and programs have become increasingly complex, oversight has become more difficult. The sheer magnitude of executive branch operations is staggering. On a typical weekday, for example, agencies issue more than a hundred pages of new regulations. Even with the division of labor in the committee system, determining how good a job an agency is doing in implementing a program is no easy task.

Congress performs its oversight function in several different ways. The most visible is the hearing. Hearings may be part of a routine review or the by-product of information that reveals a major problem with a program or with an agency's administrative practices. After the disastrous federal response to Hurricane Katrina, congressional committees held hearings to understand why the government failed. Another way Congress keeps track of what departments and agencies are doing is by requesting reports on specific agency practices and operations. During most of the Bush administration, the Republican-controlled Congress exerted little oversight on the executive branch. After the Democrats captured the Congress in the 2006 election, committees in both houses became much more aggressive in investigating ethical lapses and policy problems in the Bush administration. Hearings were held on a range of issues, including treatment of terror suspects, the deteriorating situation in Iraq, and political firings in the Department of Justice.[40] Not

oversight The process of reviewing the operations of an agency to determine whether it is carrying out policies as Congress intended.

Brownie Under Fire
Through congressional hearings, legislators gather information, oversee the bureaucracy, and demonstrate to their constituents that they are addressing major problems of the day. Immediately after Hurricane Katrina struck the Gulf Coast in late August 2005, President George Bush praised Federal Emergency Management Agency (FEMA) director Michael Brown (aka "Brownie"). But two weeks later, the leadership of the House of Representatives formed the House Select Hurricane Katrina Committee to review the federal government's slow and ineffective response to the natural disaster. Committee members listened to testimony from Brown, pictured here, as well as to various state and local government officials. *(Joe Raedle/Getty Images)*

all oversight is so formal. A good deal of congressional oversight takes place informally, as there are ongoing contacts between committee and subcommittee leaders and agency administrators as well as between committee staffers and top agency staffers.

In the last thirty years, Congress has given itself more resources for watching over the growing federal government.[41] It has significantly expanded the staffs of individual legislators and of House and Senate committees, enhanced its analytical capabilities by creating the Congressional Budget Office, and strengthened the Government Accountability Office (GAO) and the Congressional Research Service of the Library of Congress. The quality of oversight, however, varies depending on the managerial style of the president and his relationship to his party in Congress. Congressional oversight tends to be more aggressive when the executive branch is controlled by a different political party.

Oversight is often stereotyped as a process in which angry legislators bring some administrators before the hot lights and television cameras at a hearing and proceed to dress them down for some recent scandal or mistake. Some of this does go on, but the pluralist side of Congress makes it likely that at least some members of a committee are advocates of the programs they oversee because those programs serve their constituents back home. Members of the House and Senate Agriculture Committees, for example, both Democrats and Republicans, want farm programs to succeed. Thus, most oversight is aimed at trying to find ways to improve programs and is not directed at efforts to discredit them.[42] In the last analysis, Congress engages in oversight because it is an extension of their efforts to control public policy.[43]

Majoritarian and Pluralist Views of Committees

Government by committee vests a tremendous amount of power in the committees and subcommittees of Congress—and especially their leaders. This is particularly true in the House, which has more decentralized patterns of influence than the Senate and is more restrictive about letting members amend legislation on the floor. Committee members can bury a bill by not reporting it to the full House or Senate. The influence of committee members extends even further, to the floor debate. Many of them also make up the conference committees charged with developing compromise versions of bills.

In some ways, the committee system enhances the force of pluralism in American politics. Representatives and senators are elected by the voters in their particular districts and states, and they tend to seek membership on the committees that make the decisions most important to their constituents. Members from farm areas, for example, want membership on the House and Senate Agriculture Committees. Westerners like to serve on committees that deal with public lands and water rights. Urban liberals like committees that handle social programs. As a result, committee members tend to represent constituencies with an unusually strong interest in the committee's policy area and are predisposed to write legislation favorable to those constituencies.

The committees have a majoritarian aspect as well. Although some committees have a surplus or shortage of legislators from particular kinds of districts or states, most committee members reflect the general ideological profiles of the two parties' congressional contingents. For example, Republicans on individual House committees tend to vote like all Republicans in the House. Moreover, even if a committee's views are not in line with those of the full membership, it is constrained in the legislation it writes because bills cannot become law unless they are passed by the parent chamber and the other house. Consequently, in formulating legislation, committees anticipate what other representatives and senators will accept. The parties within each chamber also have means of rewarding members who are the most loyal to party priorities. Party committees and the party leadership within each chamber make committee assignments and respond to requests for transfers from less prestigious to more prestigious committees. Those who vote in line with the party get better assignments.[44]

★ Leaders and Followers in Congress

Above the committee chairs is another layer of authority in the organization of the House and Senate. The Democratic and Republican leaders in each house work to maximize the influence of their own party while trying to keep their chamber functioning smoothly and efficiently. The operation of the two houses is also influenced by the rules and norms that each chamber has developed over the years.

The Leadership Task

Republicans and Democrats elect party leaders in both the House and Senate who are charged with overseeing institutional procedures, managing legislation, fundraising, and communicating with the press. In the House of Representatives, the majority party's leader is the **Speaker of the House,** who, gavel in hand, chairs sessions from the ornate rostrum at the front of the chamber. The Speaker is a constitutional officer, but the Constitution does not list the Speaker's duties. The majority party in the House also has a majority leader, who helps the Speaker guide the party's policy program through the legislative process, and a majority whip, who keeps track of the vote count and rallies support for legislation on the floor. The minority party is led by a minority leader who is assisted by the minority whip. Democrat Nancy Pelosi was minority leader until the 2006 election gave the Democrats a majority; Pelosi then became the first woman Speaker of the House. Both parties have special committees

Speaker of the House The presiding officer of the House of Representatives.

Rangel Takes the Reins
With the Democratic takeover of the House, a new set of chairmen took control of all the committees. Charles Rangel, who has served for close to forty years in Congress, ascended to the chairmanship of the Ways and Means Committee. Rangel is a liberal from New York City and will lead the prestigious tax writing committee in a decidedly different direction from that of his Republican predecessor. *(Alex Wong/Getty Images)*

A chart of Party Control of the Presidency and Congress is available on the

Online Study Center
General Resources

that coordinate fundraising, develop strategy, and help with the logistics of scheduling votes and making committee assignments.[45]

The Constitution makes the vice president of the United States the president of the Senate. But in practice the vice president rarely visits the Senate chamber, unless there is a possibility of a tie vote, in which case he can break the tie. The *president pro tempore* (president "for the time"), elected by the majority party, is supposed to chair the Senate in the vice president's absence, but by custom this constitutional position is entirely honorary. The title is typically assigned to the most senior member of the majority party.

The real power in the Senate resides in the **majority leader.** As in the House, the top position in the opposing party is that of minority leader. Technically, the majority leader does not preside over Senate sessions (members rotate in the president pro tempore's chair), but he or she does schedule legislation, in consultation with the minority leader. More broadly, party leaders play a critical role in getting bills through Congress. The most significant function that leaders play is steering the bargaining and negotiating over the content of legislation. When an issue divides their party, their house, the two houses, or their house and the White House, the leaders must take the initiative to work out a compromise.

Day in and day out, much of what leaders do is meet with other members of their house to try to strike deals that will yield a majority on the floor. It is often a matter of finding out whether one faction is willing to give up a policy preference in exchange for another concession. Beyond trying to engineer tradeoffs that will win votes, the party leaders must persuade others (often powerful committee chairs) that theirs is the best deal possible. Former Speaker of the House Dennis Hastert used to say, "They call me the Speaker, but . . . they really ought to call me the Listener."[46]

It is often difficult for party leaders to control rank-and-file members because they have independent electoral bases in their districts and states and receive the vast bulk of their campaign funds from nonparty sources. Contemporary party leaders are coalition builders, not autocrats. Yet party leaders can

majority leader The head of the majority party in the Senate; the second-highest-ranking member of the majority party in the House.

cult. Members of Congress resist any structural changes that might weaken their ability to gain reelection. Certainly, maintaining the prerogatives of the committee system and the dominant influence of committees over legislation and pork barrel spending has proven stubbornly resistant to significant reform.[64] Nevertheless, the growing partisanship in the Congress illustrated in Figure 11.4 represents a trend toward greater majoritarianism. As noted earlier, as both parties have become more ideologically homogeneous, there is greater unity around policy preferences. To the degree that voters correctly recognize the differences between the parties and are willing to cast their ballots on that basis, increasing majoritarianism will act as a constraint on pluralism in the Congress. Ironically, once in office legislators can weaken the incentive for their constituents to vote on the basis of ideology. The congressional system is structured to facilitate casework for those voters with a problem and to fund a certain amount of pork barrel spending. Both these characteristics of the modern Congress work to enhance each legislator's reputation in his or her district or state.

Majoritarianism isn't completely absent in Congress. The rise in party unity discussed earlier reflects the increasing success of the congressional parties in defining political debate in terms of the basic philosophical divisions between them. Still, policymaking in the House and the Senate remains more pluralistic than majoritarian in nature.

Summary

Congress writes the laws of the land and attempts to oversee their implementation. It helps to educate us about new issues as they appear on the political agenda. Most important, members of Congress represent us, working to see to it that interests from home and from around the country are heard throughout the policymaking process.

We count on Congress to do so much that criticism about how well it does some things is inevitable. However, certain strengths are clear. The committee system fosters expertise; representatives and senators who know the most about particular issues have the most influence over them. And the structure of our electoral system keeps legislators in close touch with their constituents.

Bargaining and compromise play important roles in the congressional policymaking process. Some find this disquieting. They want less deal making and more adherence to principle. This thinking is in line with the desire for a more majoritarian democracy. Others defend the current system, arguing that the United States is a large, complex nation, and the policies that govern it should be developed through bargaining among various interests.

There is no clear-cut answer to whether a majoritarian or a pluralist legislative system provides better representation for voters. Our system is a mix of pluralism and majoritarianism. It serves minority interests that might otherwise be neglected or even harmed by an unthinking or uncaring majority. At the same time, congressional parties work to represent the broader interests of the American people.

Internet activities and reading suggestions for this chapter are available on the *Online Study Center*

To complete the multimedia assignments for this chapter, go to AmericansGoverning.org.

12

The Presidency

(© Jonathan Ernst/Reuters/Corbis)

Online Study Center
This icon will direct you to resources
and activities on the website
college.hmco.com/pic/jandaupdate9e

"Most Americans want two things in Iraq: they want to see our troops win, and they want our troops to come home as soon as possible. Those are my goals as well. I will settle for nothing less than complete victory."[1] Two and a half years after the American invasion of Iraq, President Bush addressed growing concerns about the number of American casualties and a timetable for the return of American troops. "Pulling our troops out before they've achieved their purpose is not a plan for victory."

The fight against terrorism and the ongoing war in Iraq have been the defining issues of the Bush presidency. Within days of the September 11, 2001, terrorist attacks, Bush's popularity rose to 90 percent, the highest rating received by a president since Gallup started conducting popularity polls in the 1950s. In his first State of the Union address after September 11, Bush charged that states like Iraq, Iran, and North Korea "and their terrorist allies constitute an axis of evil, arming to threaten the peace of the world. By seeking weapons of mass destruction, these regimes pose a grave and growing danger. They could provide these arms to terrorists, giving them the means to match their hatred."[2] At the time of Bush's speech, Iraq had not been cooperating with U.N. weapons inspectors for almost four years. The U.S. Congress passed a resolution authorizing Bush to use military force if necessary to enforce compliance with U.N. resolutions concerning weapons inspections. The U.N. Security Council threatened "serious consequences" if Iraq did not cooperate. Iraq finally allowed weapons inspections to resume.

Despite the return of weapons inspectors, the Bush administration argued that Saddam Hussein was not fully cooperating. President Bush sought a U.N. resolution authorizing the use of force against Iraq. Several countries and key members of the U.N. Security Council—including France, Germany, Russia, and China—wanted to give weapons inspections more time and strongly opposed the use of force without U.N. approval. NATO was similarly divided, with the United States, Britain, and Spain pitted against Germany and France. Bush's threats of war with Iraq were greeted with mass popular protests at home and abroad.

Dissent in the international community and popular protest at home did not deter the Bush administration. When the U.N. Security Council would not authorize the use of force, the United States, Great Britain, and a small number of allies pursued military action on their own. In March 2003, U.S. and British forces invaded Iraq and forced Saddam Hussein from power. Only two months after the invasion, Bush declared an end to combat operations. At that time, nearly three-quarters of Americans approved of the president's handling of the situation in Iraq.[3]

Unfortunately for Bush, this moment of glory was relatively short-lived. The transition from dictatorship to democracy in Iraq proved more difficult than expected. American soldiers continue to be targeted by insurgents, who use grenade attacks, ambushes, and suicide bombings to fight against the American "occupation" of Iraq. Over thirty-five hundred American soldiers have been killed in Iraq since the start of the war. When U.S. troops uncovered no clear evidence that Iraq possessed weapons of mass destruction, the Bush administration was accused of exaggerating the evidence that Saddam Hussein was developing such weapons in order to justify military action and rally public support. In June 2004, the commission created to look into the September 11 attacks concluded that there was no "collaborative relationship" between Iraq and the Al Qaeda terrorist organization. ★

🎧 *IN OUR OWN WORDS*

Listen to Jeffrey Berry discuss the main points and themes of this chapter.

Online Study Center
Improve Your Grade

Though Bush was reelected to a second term, his approval ratings have steadily fallen.[4] A majority of Americans disapprove of his handling of Iraq. The slow federal response to aid victims of Hurricane Katrina and concerns about the deficit and illegal immigration have also chipped away at public confidence in Bush's ability to lead the country. Trust in the office has further declined with news that the Bush administration authorized the National Security Agency to eavesdrop—without a warrant—on the international telecommunications of U.S. citizens. George W. Bush's experience as president is unique, but all presidents face challenges. American presidents are expected to offer solutions to national problems, whether fighting crime or reviving a failing economy. As the nation's major foreign diplomat and commander in chief of the armed forces, they are held responsible for the security and status of America in the world. Our presidents are the focal point for the nation's hopes and disappointments.

This chapter analyzes presidential leadership, looking at how presidents try to muster majoritarian support for their domestic goals and how presidents must function today as global leaders. What are the powers of the presidency? How is the president's advisory system organized? What are the ingredients of strong presidential leadership—character, public relations, or a friendly Congress? Finally, what are the particular issues and problems that presidents face in foreign affairs?

★ The Constitutional Basis of Presidential Power

When the presidency was created, the colonies had just fought a war of independence; their reaction to British domination had focused on the autocratic rule of King George III. Thus, the delegates to the Constitutional Convention were extremely wary of unchecked power and were determined not to create an all-powerful, dictatorial presidency.

The delegates' fear of a powerful presidency was counterbalanced by their desire for strong leadership. The Articles of Confederation, which did not provide for a single head of state, had failed to bind the states together into a unified nation (see Chapter 3). In addition, the governors of the individual states had generally proved to be inadequate leaders because they had few formal powers. The new nation was conspicuously weak; its Congress had no power to compel the states to obey its legislation. The delegates knew they had to create some type of effective executive office. Their task was to provide for national leadership without allowing opportunity for tyranny.

Initial Conceptions of the Presidency

Debates about the nature of the office began. Should there be one president or a presidential council or committee? Should the president be chosen by Congress and remain largely subservient to that body? The delegates gave initial approval to a plan that called for a single executive, chosen by Congress for a seven-year term and ineligible for reelection.[5] But some delegates continued to argue for a strong president who would be elected independently of the legislative branch.

The final structure of the presidency reflected the "checks and balances" philosophy that had shaped the entire Constitution. In the minds of the dele-

Mourning the Gipper
Ronald Reagan, who served as president between 1981 and 1989, died on June 5, 2004. All living former presidents and first ladies attended a funeral service at the National Cathedral in Washington, D.C. In his eulogy, President George W. Bush noted that Reagan believed that "America was not just a place in the world but the hope of the world." Reagan had issued his own farewell to the nation ten years before his death, when he acknowledged that he suffered from Alzheimer's disease. *(Mark Wilson/Getty Images)*

gates, they had imposed important limits on the presidency through the powers specifically delegated to Congress and the courts. Those counterbalancing powers would act as checks, or controls, on presidents who might try to expand the office beyond its proper bounds.

The Powers of the President

The requirements for the presidency are set forth in Article II of the Constitution: the president must be a U.S.-born citizen, at least thirty-five years old, who has lived in the United States for a minimum of fourteen years. Article II also sets forth the responsibilities of presidents. In view of the importance of the office, the constitutional description of the president's duties is surprisingly brief and vague. This vagueness has led to repeated conflict about the limits of presidential power.

The delegates undoubtedly had many reasons for the lack of precision in Article II. One likely explanation was the difficulty of providing and at the same time limiting presidential power. Furthermore, the framers of the Constitution had no model—no existing presidency—on which to base their description of the office. And, ironically, their description of the presidency might have been more precise if they had had less confidence in George Washington, the obvious choice for the first president. According to one account of the Constitutional Convention, "when Dr. Franklin predicted on June 4 that 'the first man put at the helm will be a good one,' every delegate knew perfectly well who that first good man would be."[6] The delegates had great trust in Washington; they did not fear that he would try to misuse the office.

The major duties and powers that the delegates listed for Washington and his successors can be summarized as follows:

■ *Serve as administrative head of the nation.* The Constitution gives little guidance on the president's administrative duties. It states merely that "the executive Power shall be vested in a President of the United States of America" and that "he shall take Care that the Laws be faithfully executed." These imprecise directives have been interpreted to mean that the president is to supervise and offer leadership to various departments, agencies, and programs created by Congress. In practice, a chief executive spends much more time making policy decisions for his cabinet departments and agencies than enforcing existing policies.

- *Act as commander in chief of the military.* In essence, the Constitution names the president as the highest-ranking officer in the armed forces. But it gives Congress the power to declare war. The framers no doubt intended Congress to control the president's military power; nevertheless, presidents have initiated military action without the approval of Congress.

- *Convene Congress.* The president can call Congress into special session on "extraordinary Occasions," although this has rarely been done. He must also periodically inform Congress of "the State of the Union."

- *Veto legislation.* The president can **veto** (disapprove) any bill or resolution enacted by Congress, with the exception of joint resolutions that propose constitutional amendments. Congress can override a presidential veto with a two-thirds vote in each house.

- *Appoint various officials.* The president has the authority to appoint federal court judges, ambassadors, cabinet members, other key policymakers, and many lesser officials. Many appointments are subject to Senate confirmation.

- *Make treaties.* With the "Advice and Consent" of at least two-thirds of those senators voting at the time, the president can make treaties with foreign powers. The president is also to "receive Ambassadors," a phrase that presidents have interpreted to mean the right to recognize other nations formally.

- *Grant pardons.* The president can grant pardons to individuals who have committed "Offenses against the United States, except in Cases of Impeachment."

★ The Expansion of Presidential Power

The framers' limited conception of the president's role has given way to a considerably more powerful interpretation. In this section, we discuss how presidential power has expanded as presidents have exercised their explicit constitutional responsibilities and boldly interpreted the ambiguities of the Constitution. First, we look at the ways in which formal powers, such as veto power, have been increasingly used over time. Second, we turn to claims that presidents make about "inherent" powers implicit in the Constitution. Finally, we discuss congressional grants of power to the executive branch.

Can you explain why . . . presidential power today is so much greater than what is described in the Constitution?

veto The president's disapproval of a bill that has been passed by both houses of Congress. Congress can override a veto with a two-thirds vote in each house.

Formal Powers

The Constitution clearly involves the president in the policymaking process through his veto power, his ability to report to Congress on the state of the Union, and his role as commander in chief. Over time, presidents have become more aggressive in their use of these formal powers. Vetoes, for instance, have become much more frequent, particularly when presidents face a Congress dominated by the opposing political party. The first sixteen presidents, from Washington to Lincoln, issued a total of 59 vetoes. Dwight Eisenhower issued 181 vetoes over the course of his two terms; Ronald Reagan vetoed legislation 78 times.[7] George W. Bush is truly an exceptional case since he has vetoed only a few pieces of legislation, including a bill to expand embryonic stem cell research and one mandating a pullout of troops from Iraq. Yet his veto threats shape legislation because members of Congress anticipate vetoes and modify legislation to avoid them.[8] If a president does veto a bill and there is not enough support to override the president's veto, Congress may be forced to rewrite the bill, making concessions to the president's point of view.

Modern presidents have also taken a much more active role in setting the nation's policy agenda. The Constitution states that the president shall give Congress information on the state of the Union "from time to time." For the most part, nineteenth-century presidents sent written messages to Congress and did not publicly campaign for the passage of legislation.[9] Early-twentieth-century presidents like Woodrow Wilson began to deliver their State of the Union speeches in person before Congress, personalizing and fighting for their own policy agenda. It is now expected that the president will enter office with clear policy goals and work with his party in Congress to pass legislation.

Most controversial has been the president's use of his power as commander in chief. Several modern presidents have used their power as commander in chief to enter into foreign conflicts without appealing to Congress for a formal declaration of war.[10] The entire Vietnam War was fought without a congressional declaration of war. After the September 11 terrorist attacks, President Bush ordered retaliatory military strikes and the bombing of Taliban strongholds in Afghanistan, though Congress had never formally declared war. In mid-October 2002, the House and the Senate passed a joint resolution to authorize President Bush to use military force "as he determines to be necessary and appropriate" in order to enforce United Nations Security Council resolutions regarding Iraq.[11]

In addition, after September 11, President Bush secretly authorized the National Security Agency (NSA) to wiretap telephone calls, without a warrant, between people within the United States and people overseas with suspected links to terrorism.[12] The 1978 FISA law, however, requires intelligence agencies like the NSA to obtain a warrant from a panel of judges before wiretapping the calls of U.S. citizens. When the wiretapping was revealed, critics accused Bush of putting himself above the law. Bush argued that the Constitution designates the president as the commander in chief of the armed forces; he can disregard FISA requirements if they hinder his ability to collect the foreign intelligence necessary to protect the nation from another terrorist attack.[13] Bush administration officials also pointed to Congress's authorization for the president to use "all necessary and appropriate force against those nations, organizations, or persons" that planned the September 11 attacks.

The Inherent Powers

Several presidents have expanded the power of the office by taking actions that exceeded commonly held notions of the president's proper authority. These men justified what they had done by saying that their actions fell within the **inherent powers** of the presidency. From this broad perspective, presidential

inherent powers Authority claimed by the president that is not clearly specified in the Constitution. Typically, these powers are inferred from the Constitution.

FIGURE 12.1 Executive Orders by Subject and Decade

The content of presidential orders varies considerably depending on the priorities of the individual president and the political context. This figure shows the changes in the subject matter of executive orders from the 1940s to the 1990s. Orders were sorted into five broad categories: war/emergency powers, the establishment of presidential boards and commissions, executive branch management, defense and foreign policy, and domestic policy. Presidents started issuing many more executive orders in the area of domestic policy in the 1960s. Presidents today issue the highest percentage of executive orders in the areas of defense and foreign policy.

Source: Kenneth R. Mayer, *With the Stroke of a Pen* (Princeton, N.J.: Princeton University Press, 2001), p. 86. © 2001 Princeton University Press. Reprinted by permission of Princeton University Press.

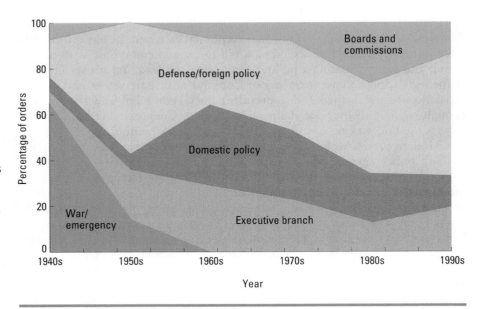

executive orders Presidential directives that create or modify laws and public policies, without the direct approval of Congress.

power derives not only from those duties clearly outlined in Article II but also from inferences that may be drawn from the Constitution.

When a president claims a power that has not been considered part of the chief executive's authority, he forces Congress and the courts either to acquiesce to his claim or to restrict it. For instance, President Bush unilaterally established military commissions to try alleged enemy combatants captured in Afghanistan and Iraq and held at the U.S. naval base at Guantánamo Bay, Cuba. In 2006, the United States Supreme Court ruled that the military commissions were illegal, and the Bush administration was forced to go to Congress for the authorization to establish new commissions with new trial procedures.[14]

When presidents succeed in claiming a new power, they leave to their successors the legacy of a permanent expansion of presidential authority. During the Civil War, for example, Abraham Lincoln instituted a blockade of southern ports, thereby committing acts of war against the Confederacy without the approval of Congress. Lincoln said the urgent nature of the South's challenge to the Union forced him to act without waiting for congressional approval. His rationale was simple: "Was it possible to lose the nation and yet preserve the Constitution?"[15] In other words, Lincoln circumvented the Constitution to save the nation. Subsequently, Congress and the Supreme Court approved Lincoln's actions. That approval gave added legitimacy to the theory of inherent powers, a theory that over time has transformed the presidency.

Today, presidents routinely issue **executive orders,** presidential directives that carry the force of law.[16] The Constitution does not explicitly grant the president the power to issue an executive order. Sometimes presidents use them to see that the laws are "faithfully executed." This was the case when Dwight Eisenhower ordered the Arkansas National Guard into service in Little Rock, Arkansas, to enforce court orders to desegregate the schools. But many times presidents issue executive orders by arguing that they may take actions in the best interest of the nation so long as the law does not directly prohibit these actions. Executive orders are issued for a wide variety of purposes, from administrative reorganization to civil rights (see Figure 12.1). For instance, Franklin Roosevelt used executive orders to centralize budget-making authority in the executive branch and to control the growing federal bureaucracy. Harry Truman issued an executive order to end racial segregation in the armed services. Bill Clinton ordered that gays and lesbians be permitted to serve (though not openly) in the military. George W. Bush used an executive order to create a White House office of faith-based and community initiatives to encourage federal government support for private and religious organizations that provide social services to fight crime and poverty.

Executive orders have become an important policymaking tool for presidents because they allow the president to act quickly and decisively, without seeking the agreement of Congress. However, it is possible, though rare, for congressional bills and court challenges to overturn executive orders. If an executive order requires federal funds, then Congress can set the terms by which funds are appropriated. Sometimes presidents announce their intention to issue an executive order and then modify the final content based on public and congressional reactions. An executive agreement is a similar tool that presidents use in foreign policy (see Chapter 20). Like executive orders, they are perceived to be within the inherent powers of the president. Unlike formal treaties with other nations, executive agreements carry the force of law but do not require Senate approval.

Congressional Delegation of Power

Presidential power grows when presidents successfully challenge Congress, but in many instances Congress willingly delegates power to the executive branch. As the American public pressures the national government to solve various problems, Congress, through a process called **delegation of powers,** gives the executive branch more responsibility to administer programs that address those problems. One example of delegation of congressional power occurred in the 1930s, during the Great Depression, when Congress gave Franklin Roosevelt's administration wide latitude to do what it thought was necessary to solve the nation's economic ills.

When Congress concludes that the government needs flexibility in its approach to a problem, the president is often given great freedom in how or when to implement policies. Richard Nixon was given discretionary authority to impose a freeze on wages and prices in an effort to combat escalating inflation. If Congress had been forced to debate the timing of the freeze, merchants and manufacturers would surely have raised their prices in anticipation of the event. Instead, Nixon was able to act suddenly, imposing the freeze without warning. (We discuss congressional delegation of authority to the executive branch in more detail in Chapter 13.)

At other times, however, Congress believes that too much power has accumulated in the executive branch, and it enacts legislation to reassert congressional authority. During the 1970s, many representatives and senators agreed that presidents were exercising power that rightfully belonged to the legislative branch, and therefore Congress's role in the American political system was declining. The most notable reaction was the enactment of the War Powers

delegation of powers The process by which Congress gives the executive branch the additional authority needed to address new problems.

Resolution (1973), which was directed at ending the president's ability to pursue armed conflict without explicit congressional approval (see Chapter 20).

★ The Executive Branch Establishment

Although we elect a single individual as president, it would be a mistake to ignore the extensive staff and resources of the entire executive branch of government. The president has a White House staff that helps him formulate policy. The vice president is another resource; his duties within the administration vary according to his relationship with the president. The president's cabinet secretaries—the heads of the major departments of the national government—play a number of roles, including the critical function of administering the programs that fall within their jurisdictions. Effective presidents think strategically about how best to use the resources available to them. Each must find ways to organize structures and processes that best suit his management style.[17]

The Executive Office of the President

The president depends heavily on key aides. They advise him on crucial political choices, devise the general strategies the administration will follow in pursuing congressional and public support, and control access to the president to ensure that he has enough time for his most important tasks. Consequently, he

Nominating Alito

The power to appoint federal court judges, with the advice and consent of the Senate, has been viewed as an indirect way for presidents to exert their influence over the course of public policy. Since the vast majority of judges keep their appointments for life ("during good behavior"), a president's appointees will often serve long after his term as president has ended. Here, President Bush introduces Samuel J. Alito, his nominee for associate justice of the Supreme Court. Despite strong Democratic opposition, Judge Alito was confirmed by a 58–42 vote in the Senate. *(© Joe Raedle/Getty Images)*

needs to trust and respect these top staffers; many in a president's inner circle of assistants are longtime associates. The president's personal staff constitutes the White House Office.

Presidents typically have a chief of staff, who may be a first among equals or, in some administrations, the unquestioned leader of the staff. H. R. Haldeman, Richard Nixon's chief of staff, played the stronger role. He ran a highly disciplined operation, frequently prodding staff members to work harder and faster. Haldeman also felt that part of his role was to take the heat for the president by assuming responsibility for many of the administration's unpopular decisions: "Every president needs a son of a bitch, and I'm Nixon's."[18] Hamilton Jordan, President Carter's chief of staff, was at the other end of the spectrum: Carter did not give him the authority to administer the White House with a strong hand.

Presidents also have a national security adviser to provide daily briefings on foreign and military affairs and longer-range analyses of issues confronting the administration. Similarly, the president has the Council of Economic Advisers to report on the state of the economy and advise the president on the best way to promote economic growth. Senior domestic policy advisers help determine the administration's basic approach to areas such as health, education, and social services.

Below these top aides are the large staffs that serve them and the president. These staffs are organized around certain specialties. Some staff members work on political matters, such as communicating with interest groups, maintaining relations with ethnic and religious minorities, and managing party affairs. One staff deals exclusively with the media, and a legislative liaison staff lobbies the Congress for the administration. The large Office of Management and Budget (OMB) analyzes budget requests, is involved in the policymaking process, and examines agency management practices. This extended White House executive establishment, including the White House Office, is known as the **Executive Office of the President.** The Executive Office employs close to 1,600 individuals and has an annual budget of nearly $374 million.[19]

No one agrees about a "right way" for a president to organize his White House staff, but scholars have identified three major advisory styles.[20] Franklin Roosevelt exemplified the first system: a competitive management style. He organized his staff so that his advisers had overlapping authority and differing points of view. Roosevelt used this system to ensure that he would get the best possible information, hear all sides of an argument, and still be the final decision maker in any dispute. Dwight Eisenhower, a former general, best exemplifies a hierarchical staff model. His staff was arranged with clear lines of authority and a hierarchical structure that mirrored a military command. This places fewer demands on presidential time and energy, since the president does not participate in the details of policy discussion. Bill Clinton had more of a collegial staffing arrangement, a loose staff structure that gave many top staffers direct access to him. Clinton himself was immersed in the details of the policymaking process and brainstormed with his advisers. He was much less likely to delegate authority to others.

Presidents tend to choose the advisory systems that best suit their personality. Most presidents use a combination of styles, learning from their predecessors. George W. Bush, for instance, set up a hierarchically organized staffing arrangement, but he initially appointed three people to be at the top of the staff hierarchy: former chief of staff Andrew Card, political strategist Karl Rove,

Executive Office of the President The president's executive aides and their staffs; the extended White House executive establishment.

and public relations adviser Karen Hughes. As the nation's first M.B.A. to be president, he surrounded himself with experienced staff members who structure his options. He is less involved in hammering out the details of policy than with formulating broad directives and overall policy vision.

Above all, a president must ensure that staff members feel comfortable telling him things he may not want to hear. Telling the president of the United States he is misguided on something is not an easy thing to do. The term *groupthink* has been used to refer to situations in which staffers reach consensus without properly considering all sides of an issue.[21] Several analysts have argued that the Johnson administration suffered from groupthink when making decisions about the Vietnam War. George Stephanopoulos, a close aide to President Clinton, acknowledged frankly in his memoirs that he was too eager to ingratiate himself with Clinton because he saw himself in a competitive position with other staff aides. In retrospect, he realizes that he should have confronted Clinton early in the 1992 campaign about his infidelity. But, says Stephanopoulos, "I needed Clinton to see me as his defender, not his interrogator, which made me, of course, his enabler."[22]

The Vice President

The most important duty of the vice president is to take over the presidency in the event of presidential death, disability, impeachment, or resignation. Traditionally, vice presidents were not used in any important advisory capacity. Before passage of the Twenty-fifth Amendment to the Constitution in 1965, vice presidents who became president due to the death of their predecessor did not even select a new vice president (see the feature "Presidential Succession" for the line of succession beyond the vice president).

Vice presidents have traditionally carried out political chores—campaigning, fundraising, and "stroking" the party faithful. This is often the case because vice-presidential candidates are chosen for reasons that have more to do with

Next in Line
Vice President Dick Cheney has been a major influence in the Bush administration. According to the Constitution, the vice president serves as president of the Senate, a largely ceremonial role except for the ability to cast tiebreaking votes. Given the almost evenly matched political parties in the Senate, Cheney has cast tiebreaking votes several times to pass Republican budget resolutions and tax amendments. Here, he meets with senior staffers in the Presidential Emergency Operations Center immediately after the September 11 terrorist attacks. *(David Bohrer/The White House)*

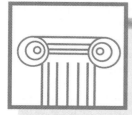

Presidential Succession

Who takes over if the president dies or is unable to carry out his duties?

According to the Constitution, the vice president succeeds the president. The continuing line of succession is most recently outlined in the Presidential Succession Act of 1947. Under this act, the vice president is followed by the Senate president pro tempore (the most senior member of the majority party) and then the Speaker of the House. The cabinet members are ordered in the line of succession according to the date their offices were established.* To succeed to the presidency, an official must meet the constitutional requirements of the office: he or she must be at least thirty-five years of age and a natural born citizen. If not, the official is passed over for the next in line.

The order of presidential succession is as follows:

- Vice President
- Speaker of the House
- President Pro Tempore of the Senate

- Secretary of State
- Secretary of the Treasury
- Secretary of Defense
- Attorney General
- Secretary of the Interior
- Secretary of Agriculture
- Secretary of Commerce
- Secretary of Labor
- Secretary of Health and Human Services
- Secretary of Housing and Urban Development
- Secretary of Transportation
- Secretary of Energy
- Secretary of Education
- Secretary of Veterans Affairs
- Secretary of Homeland Security

*Current members of the cabinet may be found at <http://www.whitehouse.gov/government/cabinet.html>.

the political campaign than with governing the nation. Presidential candidates often choose vice-presidential candidates who appeal to a different geographic region or party coalition. Sometimes they even join forces with a rival from their political primary campaign. New Englander John Kennedy chose Texan Lyndon Johnson. Conservative Ronald Reagan selected George H. W. Bush, his more moderate rival in the Republican primaries. Washington outsider Jimmy Carter chose the experienced Senator Walter Mondale as his vice-presidential running mate.

President Carter broke the usual pattern of relegating the vice president to political chores, relying heavily on Mondale. Carter was wise enough to recognize that Mondale's experience in the Senate could be of great value to him, especially because Carter had never held a national office. Al Gore played a significant role in the Clinton administration and was one of the president's most influential advisers. Dick Cheney continues the trend toward greater vice-presidential influence and involvement. Cheney came to office with impressive qualifications as a former member of the House of Representatives, presidential chief of staff, secretary of defense, and head of Halliburton, a large oil services corporation. He has been even more influential than his predecessors.[23] Cheney was placed in charge of the administration's review of national energy policy, and he chairs the president's budget review board, which rules on appeals to the Office of Management and Budget for funding of executive branch departments. Cheney has also come under intense criticism for his championing of the Iraq war. Before the American invasion, in an effort to build public support for the war, Cheney naively claimed that our troops would "be greeted as liberators." Instead, the United States has found itself in a violent quagmire.[24]

The Cabinet

INTERACTIVE 12.1

 Bush's Cabinet

The president's **cabinet** is composed of the heads of the departments of the executive branch and a small number of other key officials, such as the head of the Office of Management and Budget and the ambassador to the United Nations. The cabinet has expanded greatly since George Washington formed his first cabinet, which contained an attorney general and the secretaries of state, treasury, and war. Clearly, the growth of the cabinet to fifteen departments reflects an increase in government responsibility and intervention in areas such as energy, housing, and, most recently, homeland security.

In theory, the members of the cabinet constitute an advisory body that meets with the president to debate major policy decisions. In practice, however, cabinet meetings have been described as "vapid non-events in which there has been a deliberate non-exchange of information as part of a process of mutual nonconsultation."[25] Why is this so? First, the cabinet has become rather large. Counting department heads, other officials of cabinet rank, and presidential aides, it is a body of at least twenty people—a size that many presidents find unwieldy for the give-and-take of political decision making. Second, most cabinet members have limited areas of expertise and cannot contribute much to deliberations in policy areas they know little about. The secretary of defense, for example, would probably be a poor choice to help decide important issues of agricultural policy. Third, the president often chooses cabinet members because of their reputations or to give his cabinet some racial, ethnic, geographic, gender, or religious balance, not because they are personally close to the president or easy for him to work with.

Finally, modern presidents do not rely on the cabinet to make policy because they have such large White House staffs, which offer most of the advisory support they need. And in contrast to cabinet secretaries, who may be pulled in different directions by the wishes of the president and those of their clientele groups, staffers in the White House Office are likely to see themselves as being responsible to the president alone. Despite periodic calls for the cabinet to be a collective decision-making body, cabinet meetings seem doomed to be little more than academic exercises. In practice, presidents prefer the flexibility of ad hoc groups, specialized White House staffs, and the advisers and cabinet secretaries with whom they feel most comfortable.

More broadly, presidents use their personal staff and the large Executive Office of the President to centralize control over the entire executive branch. The vast size of the executive branch and the number and complexity of decisions that must be made each day pose a challenge for the White House. Each

Can you explain why . . . we don't have cabinet government?

cabinet A group of presidential advisers; the heads of the executive departments and other key officials.

president must be careful to appoint people to top administration positions who are not merely competent but also passionate about the president's goals and skillful enough to lead others in the executive branch to fight for the president's program instead of their own agendas.[26] Ronald Reagan was especially good at communicating to his top appointees clear ideological principles that they were to follow in shaping administration policy. To fulfill more of their political goals and policy preferences, modern presidents have given their various staffs more responsibility for overseeing decision making throughout the executive branch.[27]

★ Presidential Leadership

A president's influence comes not only from his assigned responsibilities but also from his political skills and from how effectively he uses the resources of his office. His leadership is a function of his own character and skill, as well as the political environment in which he finds himself. Does he work with a congressional majority that favors his policy agenda? Are his goals in line with public opinion? Does he have the interpersonal skills and strength of character to be an effective leader?

Table 12.1 provides a ranking of presidents based on a C-SPAN survey of fifty-eight prominent historians and professional observers of the presidency. The final score of each president is based on evaluations of characteristics such as crisis leadership, public persuasion, and administrative skill. In this section, we look at the factors that affect presidential performance—both those that reside in the person of the individual president and those that are features of the political context that he inherits. Why do some presidents rank higher than others?

A list of Presidents of the United States is available on the

Online Study Center
General Resources

TABLE 12.1 Presidential Greatness

This table provides one possible ranking of American presidents from George Washington to Bill Clinton. Survey participants were historians or observers of the presidency who rated presidents on ten scales: public persuasion, crisis leadership, economic management, moral authority, international relations, administrative skills, relations with Congress, vision/setting an agenda, pursuit of equal justice for all, and performance within the context of their time. Each subscale ranged from 0 to 100, so that the final score ranges from the lowest possible score of 0 to a perfect score of 1000.

Rank	President	Score	Rank	President	Score
1	Abraham Lincoln	900	22	Jimmy Carter	518
2	Franklin Delano Roosevelt	876	23	Gerald Ford	495
3	George Washington	842	24	William Howard Taft	491
4	Theodore Roosevelt	810	25	Richard Nixon	477
5	Harry S. Truman	753	26	Rutherford B. Hayes	477
6	Woodrow Wilson	723	27	Calvin Coolidge	451
7	Thomas Jefferson	711	28	Zachary Taylor	447
8	John F. Kennedy	704	29	James Garfield	444
9	Dwight D. Eisenhower	699	30	Martin Van Buren	429
10	Lyndon Baines Johnson	655	31	Benjamin Harrison	426
11	Ronald Reagan	634	32	Chester Arthur	423
12	James K. Polk	632	33	Ulysses S. Grant	403
13	Andrew Jackson	632	34	Herbert Hoover	400
14	James Monroe	602	35	Millard Fillmore	395
15	William McKinley	601	36	John Tyler	369
16	John Adams	598	37	William Henry Harrison	329
17	Grover Cleveland	576	38	Warren G. Harding	326
18	James Madison	567	39	Franklin Pierce	286
19	John Quincy Adams	564	40	Andrew Johnson	280
20	George H. W. Bush	548	41	James Buchanan	259
21	Bill Clinton	539			

Source: C-SPAN survey of Presidential Leadership 2000, <www.americanpresidents .org/survey/historians/overall.asp>. Copyright 2000 C-SPAN.

Presidential Character

How does the public assess which presidential candidate has the best judgment and whether a candidate's character is suitable to the office? Americans must make a broad evaluation of the candidates' personalities and leadership styles. Although it's difficult to judge, character matters. One of Lyndon Johnson's biographers argues that Johnson had trouble extricating the United States from Vietnam because of insecurities about his masculinity. Johnson wanted to make sure he "was not forced to see himself as a coward, running away from Vietnam."[28] It's hard to know for sure whether this psychological interpretation is valid. Clearer, surely, is the tie between President Nixon's character and Watergate. Nixon had such an exaggerated fear of what his "enemies" might try to do to him that he created a climate in the White House that nurtured the Watergate break-in and subsequent cover-up.

Presidential character was at the forefront of national politics when it was revealed that President Clinton engaged in a sexual relationship with Monica Lewinsky, a White House intern half his age.[29] Many argued that presidential authority is irreparably damaged when the president is perceived as personally untrustworthy or immoral. Yet despite the disgust and anger that Clinton's actions provoked, most Americans remained unconvinced that his behavior constituted an impeachable offense. The buoyant economy and the public's general satisfaction with Clinton's leadership strongly influenced the country's views on the matter. A majority of the House of Representatives voted to impeach him, on the grounds that he had committed perjury when testifying before a federal grand jury and that he had obstructed justice by concealing evidence and encouraging others to lie about his relationship with Lewinsky. But the Senate did not have the two-thirds majority necessary to convict Clinton, so he remained in office.

Scholars have identified personality traits such as strong self-esteem and emotional intelligence that are best suited to leadership positions like the American presidency.[30] In the media age, it often proves difficult to evaluate a

Mom! Dad! I Got a Great Summer Internship . . . and the Boss Likes Me a Lot!

Revelation of the affair between President Clinton and White House intern Monica Lewinsky rocked the nation. Since she had lied in a legal deposition, denying the relationship, Lewinsky was vulnerable when the special prosecutor, Kenneth Starr, began investigating her. Her lawyers eventually reached an immunity deal with Starr, and Lewinsky gave a highly detailed account of her sexual encounters with the president to the Whitewater grand jury. *(CNN/ Sygma)*

candidate's personality when everyone tries to present himself or herself in a positive light. Even so, voters repeatedly claim that they care about traits such as competence, integrity, and empathy when casting their ballots.[31] Before the Iraq war shattered his popularity, President Bush received consistently high ratings as a strong, tough, and visionary leader.[32]

The President's Power to Persuade

In addition to desirable character traits, individual presidents must have the interpersonal and practical political skills to get things done. A classic analysis of the use of presidential resources is offered by Richard Neustadt in his book *Presidential Power.* Neustadt develops a model of how presidents gain, lose, or maintain their influence. His initial premise is simple enough: "Presidential power is the power to persuade."[33] Presidents, for all their resources—a skilled staff, extensive media coverage of presidential actions, the great respect the country holds for the office—must depend on others' cooperation to get things done. Harry Truman echoed Neustadt's premise when he said, "I sit here all day trying to persuade people to do the things they ought to have sense enough to do without my persuading them. . . . That's all the powers of the President amount to."[34]

Ability in bargaining, dealing with adversaries, and choosing priorities, according to Neustadt, separates above-average presidents from mediocre ones. A president must make wise choices about which policies to push and which to put aside until he can find more support. President Nixon described such decisions as a lot like poker. "I knew when to get out of a pot," said Nixon. "I didn't stick around when I didn't have the cards."[35] The president must decide when to accept compromise and when to stand on principle. He must know when to go public and when to work behind the scenes.

A president's political skills can be important in affecting outcomes in Congress. The president must choose his battles carefully and then try to use the force of his personality and the prestige of his office to forge an agreement among differing factions. Rather than weigh in on every issue, President Bush directly lobbies members of Congress only on the issues he cares about most. "He uses his direct influence selectively," noted former Representative Rob Portman (R-Ohio). "I think that's important—you can wear out your welcome on the Hill."[36] When President Lyndon Johnson needed House Appropriations chair George Mahon (D-Tex.) to support him on an issue, he called Mahon on the phone and emphasized the value of Mahon's having a good long-term relationship with him. Speaking slowly to let every point sink in, Johnson told Mahon, "I know one thing . . . I know I'm right on this. . . . I know I mean more to you, . . . and Lubbock [Texas], . . . and your district, . . . and your State, . . . and your grandchildren, than Charlie Halleck [the Republican House leader] does."[37] In terms of getting members to vote a certain way, presidential influence is best described as taking place "at the margins." That is, presidents do not have the power to move consistently large numbers of votes one way or the other. They can, however, affect some votes—perhaps enough to affect the outcome of a closely fought piece of legislation.[38]

Neustadt stresses that a president's influence is related to his professional reputation and prestige. When a president pushes hard for a bill that Congress eventually defeats or weakens, the president's reputation is hurt. The public perceives him as ineffective or as showing poor judgment, and Congress becomes even less likely to cooperate with him in the future. President Clinton was clearly damaged by his failure to gain passage of his ambitious plan to reform the nation's health-care system. Yet presidents cannot easily avoid controversial bills, especially those meant to deliver on campaign promises. Clinton took risks with his strong support for controversial legislation such as the North American Free Trade Association and handgun control measures, and he gained considerable respect for his efforts when these bills were enacted. One scholar describes the dilemma facing presidents this way: "If they risk big, they may gain big, but they are more likely to fail big. If they choose safe strategies, there is no doubt that they will be criticized for not seeking greater yields."[39]

The President and the Public

Neustadt's analysis suggests that a popular president is more persuasive than an unpopular one. A popular president has more power to persuade because he can use his public support as a resource in the bargaining process. Members of Congress who know that the president is highly popular back home have more incentive to cooperate with the administration. If the president and his aides know that a member of Congress does not want to be seen as hostile to the president, they can apply more leverage to achieve a favorable compromise in a legislative struggle.

A familiar aspect of the modern presidency is the effort presidents devote to mobilizing public support for their programs. A president uses televised addresses (and the media coverage surrounding them), remarks to reporters, and public appearances to speak directly to the American people and convince them of the wisdom of his policies.[40] Scholars have coined the phrase "going public" to describe situations where the president "forces compliance from fellow Washingtonians by going over their heads to appeal to their constituents."[41] Rather than bargain exclusively with a small number of party and committee leaders in Congress, the president rallies broad coalitions of support as though undertaking a political campaign.

Since public opinion is a resource for modern presidents, they pay close attention to their standing in the polls. Presidents closely monitor their approval ratings or "popularity," which is a report card on how well they are performing their duties. Presidential popularity is typically at its highest during a president's first year in office. This "honeymoon period" affords the president a particularly good opportunity to use public support to get some of his programs through Congress.[42] First-term presidents who go into their reelection campaigns with low popularity ratings, as Gerald Ford and Jimmy Carter did, tend not to win reelection. Bush's 51 percent approval rating in late October 2004 was unusually low for an incumbent president winning reelection.

Several factors explain fluctuations in presidential popularity throughout a president's term. First, public approval of the job done by a president is affected by economic conditions, such as inflation and unemployment. Voters hold presidents responsible for the economy, although much of what happens there is beyond presidents' control. Second, a president is affected by major events that occur during his administration.[43] Events can cause short-term upward spikes called "rallies" in job approval ratings. Figure 12.2 graphs George W. Bush's monthly job approval ratings. In early September 2001, only 51 percent of respondents in a Gallup Poll approved of the way George W. Bush was handling his job as president. Bush's approval rate soared to 90 percent after the September 11 terrorist attacks. Also visible is the boost or "rally around the flag effect" of the March 2003 start of the war in Iraq.

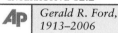

INTERACTIVE 12.2

Gerald R. Ford, 1913–2006

FIGURE 12.2   George W. Bush's Presidential Approval Ratings

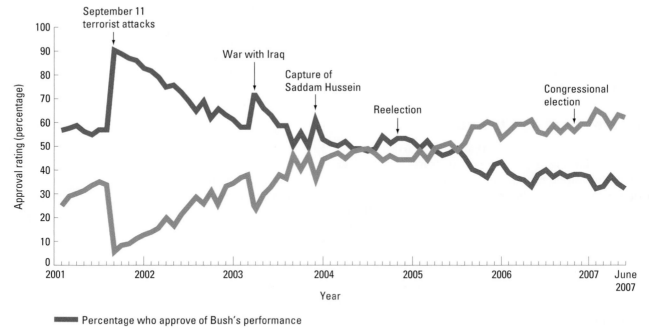

■ Percentage who approve of Bush's performance

■ Percentage who disapprove of Bush's performance

Beginning with the Truman administration, the Gallup Poll has asked, "Do you approve or disapprove of the way [the current president] is handling his job as president?" This graph presents the percentages of Americans approving and disapproving of President George W. Bush. Unlike other presidents, George W. Bush had almost no noticeable honeymoon period at the beginning of his first or second term. His ratings clearly rallied in response to foreign policy crises such as the September 11, 2001, terrorist attacks and the war with Iraq in March 2003. Movement in ratings is often a function of changes in the evaluations of moderates and members of the opposing party. Even when Bush's approval ratings plummeted below 50 percent in the population as a whole, nearly 87 percent of conservative Republicans polled said they approved of the job he was doing.

Source: Data from <www.poll.gallup.com>.

A third factor that affects approval ratings, however, is that presidents typically lose popularity when involved in a war with heavy casualties.[44] Lyndon Johnson, for example, suffered heavily during the Vietnam War. George W. Bush maintained ratings in the 80s throughout the brief Afghan war, which had few American casualties. The continued and frequent casualties after the end of official combat operations in Iraq, on the other hand, have had a decidedly negative effect on his approval ratings.

The strategy of leading by courting public opinion has considerable risks. It is not easy to move public opinion, and presidents who plan to use it as leverage in dealing with Congress are left highly vulnerable if public support for their position does not materialize. When Bill Clinton came into office, he was strongly predisposed toward governing by leading public opinion. This strategy worked poorly: he was frequently unsuccessful in rallying the public to his side on issues crucial to his administration, such as national health insurance. After his first two years in office, he told an interviewer that the problems bedeviling his presidency were due to a failure to communicate: "What I've got to do is to spend more time communicating with the American people about what we've done and where we're going."[45] Communicating with the public is crucial to a modern president's success, but so too is an ability to form bipartisan coalitions in Congress and broad interest group coalitions. Clinton's administration suffered from shortcomings in these areas as well.[46]

Presidents' obsessive concern with public opinion can be defended as a means of furthering majoritarian democracy: the president tries to gauge what the people want so that he can offer policies that reflect popular preferences. As discussed in Chapter 2, responsiveness to the public's views is a bedrock principle of democracy, and presidents should respond to public opinion as well as try to lead it.[47] Some believe that presidents are too concerned about their popularity and are unwilling to champion unpopular causes or take principled stands that may affect their poll ratings. Commenting on the presidential polls that first became widely used during his term, Harry Truman said, "I wonder how far Moses would have gone if he'd taken a poll in Egypt?"[48]

The Political Context

While character and political skill are important, the president's popularity and legislative success also depend on the wider political environment. Some presidents have the benefit of working on legislation while their own political party has a majority in both chambers of Congress. Others are fortunate to serve when the economy is good. Still others have large election victories that facilitate greater policy achievements.

Partisans in Congress. Presidents vary considerably in their ability to convince Congress to enact the legislation they send to Capitol Hill (see Figure 12.3). Generally, presidents have their greatest success in Congress during the period immediately following their inauguration, which is also the peak of their popularity. One of the best predictors of presidential success in Congress is the number of fellow partisans in Congress, particularly whether the president's party has a majority in each chamber.[49] Note the dramatic change in Clinton's fortunes in 1995, when he had to cope with a Republican Congress. Bush's success has been attributed to the fact that "the similarities of the policy approaches on Capitol Hill and in the White House let him pick his fights, because most of the time there's no need to have a fight."[50] With the Democrats now in charge of Congress, Bush's influence over legislation has declined significantly.

The American political system poses a challenge for presidents and their policy agendas because the president is elected independently of Congress. Often this leads to **divided government,** with one party controlling the White House and the other party controlling at least one house of Congress. This may seem politically schizophrenic, with the electorate saying one thing by electing a president from one party and another by its vote for legislators of the other party. This does not appear to bother the American people, however: polls often show that the public feels it is desirable for control of the government to be divided between Republicans and Democrats.[51]

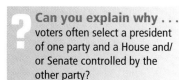

? **Can you explain why . . .** voters often select a president of one party and a House and/ or Senate controlled by the other party?

divided government The situation in which one party controls the White House and the other controls at least one house of Congress.

FIGURE 12.3 Legislative Leadership

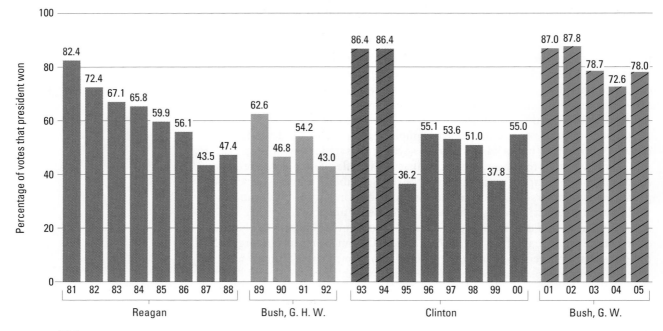

Congress controlled by president's party

Presidential success in Congress is measured as how often the president wins his way on congressional roll call votes on which he takes a clear position. In 2005, for instance, President Bush won 78 percent of the time. But overall success rates like those listed above can mask differences in presidential success across issue areas and chambers of Congress. In 2002, for instance, Bush's overall success rate was 88 percent, but he won only 67 percent of the time on issues concerning national defense or foreign policy. His success rate in the Senate was slightly higher than his success rate in the House of Representatives.

Sources: "Bush Continues His Run of Victories," *Congressional Quarterly Weekly Report*, 9 January 2006, p. 81; John Cochran, "Bush Readies Strategies for Legislative Success in 2003," *Congressional Quarterly Weekly Report*, 14 December 2002, pp. 3235–3238, 3275.

Scholars are divided about the impact of divided government.[52] Despite these differences in the scholarly literature, however, political scientists generally don't believe that divided government produces **gridlock,** a situation in which government is incapable of acting on important policy issues.[53] There is a strong tradition of bipartisan policymaking in Congress that facilitates cooperation when the government is divided. Favorable public opinion can also help a president build consensus in a highly independent legislative branch.[54]

gridlock A situation in which government is incapable of acting on important issues.

Elections. In his farewell address to the nation, Jimmy Carter lashed out at the interest groups that had plagued his presidency. Interest groups, he said, "distort our purposes because the national interest is not always the sum of all our single or special interests." Carter noted the president's singular responsibility: "The president is the only elected official charged with representing all the people."[55] Like all other presidents, Carter quickly recognized the dilemma of majoritarianism versus pluralism after he took office. The president must try to please countless separate constituencies while trying to do what is best for the whole country.

It is easy to stand on the sidelines and say that presidents should always try to follow a majoritarian path, pursuing policies that reflect the preferences of most citizens. However, simply by running for office, candidates align themselves with particular segments of the population. As a result of their electoral strategy, their identification with activists in their party, and their own political views, candidates come into office with an interest in pleasing some constituencies more than others.

As the election campaign proceeds, each candidate tries to win votes from different groups of voters through his stand on various issues. Because issue stances can cut both ways—attracting some voters but driving others away—candidates may try to finesse an issue by being deliberately vague. Candidates sometimes hope that voters will put their own interpretations on ambiguous stances. If the tactic works, the candidate will attract some voters without offending others. During the 1968 campaign, Nixon said he was committed to ending the war in Vietnam but gave few details about how he would accomplish that end. He wanted to appeal not only to those who were in favor of military pressure against the North Vietnamese but also to those who wanted quick military disengagement.[56]

But candidates cannot be deliberately vague about all issues. A candidate who is noncommittal on too many issues appears wishy-washy. And future presidents do not build their political careers without working strongly for and becoming associated with important issues and constituencies. Moreover, after the election is over, the winning candidate wants to claim that he has been given a **mandate,** or endorsement, by the voters to carry out the policy platform on which he campaigned. Newly chosen presidents make a majoritarian interpretation of the electoral process, claiming that their electoral victory is an expression of the direct will of the people. For such a claim to be credible, the candidate must have emphasized some specific issues during the campaign and offered some distinctive solutions. Candidates who win by large margins are more likely to claim mandates and ask for major policy changes.[57] Although many presidents claim that the votes they receive at the polls are expressions of support for their policy proposals, it is often difficult to document concrete evidence of broad public support for the range of specific policies a winning candidate wants to pursue.[58]

Due to the unusual circumstances surrounding the 2000 election, President George W. Bush entered office without even the illusion of a mandate. Consequently, in advocating his program, he initially emphasized national unity and bipartisanship instead of popular support. In 2004, he won the popular vote as well as a narrow electoral college victory. He interpreted his reelection as a positive referendum on his first term and a vote of confidence for his handling of foreign policy.

Political Party Systems. An individual president's election is just one in a series of contests between the major political parties in the United States. As noted in Chapter 8, American political history is marked by eras in which one

mandate An endorsement by voters. Presidents sometimes argue they have been given a mandate to carry out policy proposals.

of the major political parties tends to dominate national-level politics, consistently capturing the presidency and majorities in the Senate and House of Representatives. Scholars of the American presidency have noted that presidential leadership is shaped by the president's relationship to the dominant political party and its policy agenda.

Political scientist Stephen Skowronek argues that leadership depends on the president's place in the cycle of rising and falling political party regimes or governing coalitions.[59] Presidential leadership is determined in part by whether the president is a member of the dominant political party and whether the public policies and political philosophy associated with his party have widespread support. A president will have a greater opportunity to change public policy when he is in the majority and the opposing political party is perceived to be unable to solve major national problems. Presidents who are affiliated with the dominant political party have larger majorities in Congress and more public support for their party's policy agenda.

Presidents who come to power right after critical elections have the most favorable environment for exerting strong presidential leadership. Franklin Roosevelt, for instance, came to office when the Republican Party was unable to offer solutions to the economic crisis of the Great Depression. He enjoyed a landslide victory and large Democratic majorities in Congress, and he proposed fundamental changes in government and public policy. The weakest presidents are those, like Herbert Hoover, who are constrained by their affiliation with a political party that is perceived to stand for worn-out ideas. Democratic presidents like Truman and Johnson, who followed FDR, were also well positioned to achieve policy success and further their party program since they were affiliated with the dominant New Deal coalition. Republicans Eisenhower and Nixon faced different leadership challenges: they needed to cultivate the support of voters and legislators in both parties in order to achieve a successful legislative program.

Skowronek has argued that 1980 was a turning point for the Republican Party, when Ronald Reagan articulated the anti–New Deal philosophy that "government is not the solution but the problem." Like Hoover, Jimmy Carter was viewed as unable to offer new and creative solutions to economic and social problems. In this political context, Democrat Bill Clinton faced leadership challenges similar to those of Eisenhower and Nixon. His political success depended on bridging political philosophies to bring together members of both political parties. After his early successes Republicans were hopeful that George W. Bush could build on and strengthen the party's base.

Some presidents inherit a political climate ripe for change; others do not. As Skowronek notes, "The political conditions for presidential action can shift radically from one administration to the next, and with each change the challenge of exercising political leadership will be correspondingly altered."[60] Our evaluations of presidential greatness and success need to take the political context into account; personality and skill may be less important than historical fate.

★ The President as National Leader

With an election behind him and the resources of his office at hand, a president is ready to lead the nation. Although not every president's leadership is acclaimed, each president enters office with a general vision of how government should approach policy issues. During his term, a president spends much of his time trying to get Congress to enact legislation that reflects his general philosophy and specific policy preferences.

From Political Values . . .

Presidents differ greatly in their views of the role of government. Lyndon Johnson had a strong liberal ideology concerning domestic affairs. He believed that government has a responsibility to help disadvantaged Americans. Johnson described his vision of justice in his inaugural address:

> Justice was the promise that all who made the journey would share in the fruits of the land.
>
> In a land of wealth, families must not live in hopeless poverty. In a land rich in harvest, children just must not go hungry. In a land of healing miracles, neighbors must not suffer and die untended. In a great land of learning and scholars, young people must be taught to read and write.
>
> For [the] more than thirty years that I have served this nation, I have believed that this injustice to our people, this waste of our resources, was our real enemy. For thirty years or more, with the resources I have had, I have vigilantly fought against it.[61]

Johnson used *justice* and *injustice* as code for *equality* and *inequality*. He used them six times in his speech; he used *freedom* only twice. Johnson used his popularity, his skills, and the resources of his office to press for a "just" America—a "Great Society."

To achieve his Great Society, Johnson sent Congress an unprecedented package of liberal legislation. He launched projects such as the Job Corps (which created centers and camps offering vocational training and work experience to youths aged sixteen to twenty-one), Medicare (which provided medical care for the elderly), and the National Teacher Corps (which paid teachers to work in impoverished neighborhoods). Supported by huge Democratic majorities in Congress during 1965 and 1966, he had tremendous success getting his proposals through. Liberalism was in full swing.

In 1985, exactly twenty years after Johnson's inaugural speech, Ronald Reagan took his oath of office for the second time. Addressing the nation, Reagan reasserted his conservative philosophy. He emphasized freedom, using the term fourteen times, and failed to mention justice or equality once. In the following excerpt, we have italicized the term *freedom* for easy reference:

> By 1980, we knew it was time to renew our faith, to strive with all our strength toward the ultimate in individual *freedom* consistent with an orderly society. . . . We will not rest until every American enjoys the fullness of *freedom,* dignity, and opportunity as our birthright. . . . Americans . . . turned the tide of history away from totalitarian darkness and into the warm sunlight of human *freedom.* . . .
>
> Let history say of us, these were golden years—when the American Revolution was reborn, when *freedom* gained new life, when America reached for her best. . . . *Freedom* and incentives unleash the drive and entrepreneurial genius that are at the core of human progress. . . . From new *freedom* will spring new opportunities for growth. . . . Yet history has shown that peace does not come, nor will our *freedom* be preserved by goodwill

Different Visions

Lyndon Johnson and Ronald Reagan had strikingly different visions of American democracy and what their goals should be as president. Johnson was committed to equality for all, and major civil rights laws are among the most important legacies of his administration. He is pictured here signing the 1964 Civil Rights Act. Reagan was devoted to reducing the size of government so as to enhance freedom. He worked hard to reduce both taxes and spending. *(left: AP/Wide World Photos; right: Mark Reinstein/Uniphoto/Pictor)*

alone. There are those in the world who scorn our vision of human dignity and *freedom*. . . . Human *freedom* is on the march, and nowhere more so than in our own hemisphere. *Freedom* is one of the deepest and noblest aspirations of the human spirit. . . . America must remain *freedom's* staunchest friend, for *freedom* is our best ally. . . . Every victory for human *freedom* will be a victory for world peace. . . . One people under God, dedicated to the dream of *freedom* that He has placed in the human heart.[62]

Reagan turned Johnson's philosophy on its head, declaring that "government is not the solution to our problem. Government *is* the problem." During his presidency, Reagan worked to undo many welfare and social service programs and cut funding for programs such as the Job Corps and food stamps. By the end of his term, there had been a fundamental shift in federal spending, with sharp increases in defense spending and "decreases in federal social programs [which] served to defend Democratic interests and constituencies."[63]

Although Johnson and Reagan had well-defined political philosophies and communicated a clear vision of where they wanted to lead the country, not all presidents move strongly toward one ideological position. George W. Bush's inaugural speech in 2001 struck the themes of equality and freedom about evenly. Interestingly, he talked more about civil society and community.[64] Early in his term, Bush's rhetoric combined elements of both communitarian and traditional conservative ideologies. In his second inaugural speech, Bush followed Reagan's footsteps, using the word *freedom* twenty-seven times during his twenty-minute address.[65]

. . . to Policy Agenda

The roots of particular policy proposals, then, can be traced to the more general political ideology of the president. Presidential candidates outline that philosophy of government during their campaign for the White House as they attempt to mobilize voters and interest groups. After the election, presidents and their staffs continue to identify and track support among different kinds of voters as they decide how to translate their general philosophy into concrete legislative proposals.

When the hot rhetoric of the presidential campaign meets the cold reality of what is possible in Washington, the newly elected president must make some hard choices about what to push for during the coming term. These choices are reflected in the bills the president submits to Congress, as well as in the degree to which he works for their passage. The president's bills, introduced by his allies in the House and Senate, always receive a good deal of initial attention. In the words of one Washington lobbyist, "When a president sends up a bill, it takes first place in the queue. All other bills take second place."[66]

The president's role in legislative leadership is largely a twentieth-century phenomenon. Not until the Budget and Accounting Act of 1921 did executive branch departments and agencies have to clear their proposed budget bills with the White House. Before this, the president did not even coordinate proposals for how much the executive branch would spend on all the programs it administered. Later, Franklin D. Roosevelt required that the White House clear all major legislative proposals by an agency or department. No longer could a department submit a bill without White House support.[67]

Roosevelt's influence on the relationship between the president and Congress went far beyond this new administrative arrangement. With the nation in the midst of the Great Depression, Roosevelt began his first term in 1933 with an ambitious array of legislative proposals. During the first one hundred days Congress was in session, it enacted fifteen significant laws, including the Agricultural Adjustment Act, the act creating the Civilian Conservation Corps, and the National Industrial Recovery Act. Never before had a president demanded—and received—so much from Congress. Roosevelt's legacy was that the president would henceforth provide aggressive leadership of Congress through his own legislative program.

Chief Lobbyist

When Franklin D. Roosevelt and Harry Truman first became heavily involved in preparing legislative packages, political scientists typically described the process as one in which "the president proposes and Congress disposes." In other words, once the president sends his legislation to Capitol Hill, Congress decides what to do with it. Over time, though, presidents have become increasingly active in all stages of the legislative process. The president is expected not only to propose legislation but also to make sure that it passes.

The president's efforts to influence Congress are reinforced by the work of his legislative liaison staff. All departments and major agencies have legislative specialists as well. These department and agency people work with the White House liaison staff to coordinate the administration's lobbying on major issues.

The **legislative liaison staff** is the communications link between the White House and Congress. As a bill slowly makes its way through Congress, liaison staffers advise the president or a cabinet secretary on the problems that emerge. They specify what parts of a bill are in trouble and may have to be modified or dropped. They tell their boss what amendments are likely to be offered, which members of Congress need to be lobbied, and what the bill's chances for passage are with or without certain provisions. Decisions on how the administration will respond to such developments must then be reached. For example, when the Reagan White House realized that it was still a few votes short of victory on a budget bill in the House, it reversed its opposition

legislative liaison staff Those people who compose the communications link between the White House and Congress, advising the president or cabinet secretaries on the status of pending legislation.

Compared with What?

Presidents and Prime Ministers

In May 2005, after eight years in office, Tony Blair was reelected to a third term as Great Britain's prime minister—the first time in history that the Labour Party won three consecutive elections. Blair was reelected despite the fact that his popularity had spiraled downward in the wake of his decision to send British troops to Iraq. By early 2006, campaign finance scandals had reduced his approval rating to a mere 36 percent. "Unpopularity," Blair said, is sometimes "the cost of conviction." American presidents with such a low popularity rating would be seriously weakened in the

(Reuters/Corbis)

to a sugar price-support bill. This attracted the votes of representatives from Louisiana and Florida, two sugar-growing states, for the budget bill. The White House would not call what happened a deal, but it noted that "adjustments and considerations" had been made.[68] Still, not all demands from legislators can be met. As one legislative liaison aide noted, "One of our problems is that we have to tell people 'no' a lot."[69]

A certain amount of the president's job consists of stereotypical arm twisting—pushing reluctant legislators to vote a certain way. Yet most day-in, day-out interactions between the White House and Congress tend to be more subtle, with the liaison staff trying to build consensus by working cooperatively with legislators. When a congressional committee is working on a bill, liaison people talk to committee members individually to see what concerns they

legislative arena. The structure of the British political system, however, ensures that the prime minister will nearly always have a majority to carry out public policy no matter what his or her popular standing is.

The American political system differs from most other governments in industrialized democracies because the executive and legislative powers are separated. Most other democracies follow a parliamentary model that places executive power in a head of government (the prime minister) who also heads the legislature (the parliament). Great Britain is one example. The British prime minister is selected from Parliament by the political party that wins the most seats. Blair's 2005 victory was not a nationwide popular vote but the ability of his Labour Party to win 356 of the 646 seats in the House of Commons. The prime minister appoints a cabinet of about twenty ministers who are also members of his political party in Parliament. Thus, the prime minister is the leader of his party and of the government.

The British Parliament consists of the House of Lords and the House of Commons. Members of the House of Lords either inherit their positions or are appointed by the queen. The House of Lords can delay legislation passed by the House of Commons but not stop it. Members of the House of Commons are popularly elected. When the House of Commons passes legislation, the queen automatically gives her approval. No court can declare an act of Parliament invalid. The overwhelming influence of the House of Commons means that the British system is effectively a unicameral, or one-chamber, legislature.

Since the British prime minister is the leader of the majority party in Parliament, and British political parties are highly cohesive in voting, Britain conforms to the majoritarian model of democracy. British political parties offer clear policy alternatives, and the centralized nature of parliamentary government ensures that the majority party will be equipped to carry out its policy agenda. The British prime minister and his party are easily held accountable to voters since the majority party is clearly in charge of the legislative, executive, and administrative parts of government. American government, in contrast, conforms more to the pluralist model of democracy. The American president heads only one of three coequal branches of government. Power is dispersed, offering many access points for citizens and interest groups. American presidents are party leaders, but they are elected independent of members of Congress. Policy gridlock is a distinct possibility.

Due to his unpopularity and his long time in office, Blair succumbed to pressure from his party and resigned as prime minister in June 2007. Under the country's parliamentary form of government, the ruling Labour Party chose his replacement, one of Blair's cabinet ministers, Gordon Brown. Brown, a dour Scotsman, had served as chancellor of the exchequer (equivalent to our secretary of the treasury). British voters will have to wait until the next election if they want a change in policy in addition to a change in personnel.

have and to help fashion a compromise if some differ with the president's position. This type of quiet negotiation disappeared during the 1995–1996 session of Congress, when the new Republican majority in the House, heady with excitement at controlling the chamber for the first time in forty years, briefly let the government shut down on two occasions rather than bargain with the president. More typically, even when partisanship is running high, quiet negotiations continue.[70] For President Bush, a key task has been to keep the conservative wing of the party on board while he cuts deals with moderate Republicans and Democrats.[71]

The White House also works directly with interest groups in its efforts to build support for legislation. Presidential aides hope key lobbyists will activate the most effective lobbyists of all: the voters back home. Interest groups can quickly reach the constituents who are most concerned about a bill, using their communications network to mobilize members to write, call, or e-mail their members of Congress. There are so many interest groups in our pluralist political system that they could easily overload the White House with their demands. Consequently, except for those groups most important to the president, lobbies tend to be granted access only when the White House needs them to activate public opinion.[72]

Although much of the liaison staff's work with Congress is done in a cooperative spirit, agreement cannot always be reached. When Congress passes a bill the president opposes, he may veto it and send it back to Congress; Congress can override a veto with a two-thirds majority of those voting in each house. Presidents use their veto power sparingly, but as we noted earlier, the threat that a president will veto an unacceptable bill increases his bargaining leverage with members of Congress. We have also seen that a president's leverage with Congress is related to his standing with the American people. The ability of the president and his liaison staff to bargain with members of Congress is enhanced when he is riding high in the public opinion polls and hindered when the public is critical of his performance.[73]

Party Leader

Part of the president's job is to lead his party.[74] This is very much an informal duty, with no prescribed tasks. In this respect, American presidents are considerably different from European prime ministers, who are the formal leader of their party in the national legislature as well as the head of their government (see "Compared with What? Presidents and Prime Ministers"). In the American system, a president and members of his party in Congress can clearly take very different positions on the issues before them. When President Clinton reached agreement with Republican congressional leaders on a balanced budget deal, it provoked a great deal of controversy within the Democratic Party. Many congressional Democrats refused to join in the celebration; they thought the president had betrayed the party's ideals by trimming Medicare and taxes on the wealthy. Barney Frank (D-Mass.) expressed the liberals' anger with the president's leadership by saying, "We addressed [an envelope] to the 'Democratic president of the United States.' It came back 'addressee unknown.'"[75] Because political parties in Europe tend to have strong national organizations, prime ministers have more reason to lead the party organization. In the United States, national party committees play a relatively minor role in national politics, although they are active in raising money for their congressional candidates (see Chapter 8).

The president himself has become the "fundraiser in chief" for his party. Since presidents have a vital interest in more members of their party being elected to the House and Senate, they have a strong incentive to spend time raising money for congressional candidates. All incumbent presidents travel frequently to fundraising dinners in different states, where they are the main attraction. Donors pay substantial sums—$1,000 a ticket is common—to go to such a dinner. In addition to helping elect more members of his party, a not-so-small by-product for the president is the gratitude of legislators. It's a lot harder to say no to a president's request for help on a bill when he spoke at your fundraiser during the last election.

The President as World Leader

The president's leadership responsibilities extend beyond Congress and the nation to the international arena. Each administration tries to further what it sees as the country's best interests in its relations with allies, adversaries, and the developing countries of the world. In this role, the president must be ready to act as diplomat and crisis manager. (See "Politics in a Changing World: An International Popularity Contest.")

Foreign Relations

From the end of World War II until the late 1980s, presidents were preoccupied with containing communist expansion around the globe. Truman and Korea, Kennedy and Cuba, Johnson and Nixon and Vietnam, and Reagan and Nicaragua are just some examples of presidents and the communist crosses they had to bear. Presidents not only used overt and covert military means to fight communism but also tried to reduce tensions through negotiations. President Nixon made particularly important strides in this regard, completing an important arms control agreement with the Soviet Union and beginning negotiations with China, with which the United States had had no formal diplomatic relations.

With the collapse of communism in the Soviet Union and Eastern Europe, American presidents have entered a new era in international relations, but they are still concerned with four fundamental objectives (see Chapter 20 for a more detailed discussion of American foreign policy). First is national security, the direct protection of the United States and its citizens from external threats. National security has been highlighted since the September 11 terrorist attacks. Indeed, George W. Bush called the global war against terrorism his number one priority.[76] President Bush argued that national security may be best served by taking preemptive military action. Bush claimed that even though Iraq had not attacked us, we had the right to invade the country and topple Saddam Hussein because Iraq ostensibly possessed weapons of mass destruction and the United States could not afford to wait until Hussein used them to respond.

Second, and related, is fostering a peaceful international environment. Presidents work with international organizations like the United Nations and the North Atlantic Treaty Organization (NATO) to seek an end to regional conflicts throughout the world. In some cases, like the ongoing dispute between Palestinians and Israelis, the United States has played a central role in mediating conflict and facilitating bargaining between opposing sides. In other cases, presidents send the U.S. military to participate in multinational peacekeeping forces to ensure stability and enforce negotiated peace plans.

A third objective is the protection of U.S. economic interests. The new presidential job description places much more emphasis on managing economic relations with the rest of the world. Trade relations are an especially difficult problem because presidents must balance the conflicting interests of foreign countries (many of them allies), the interests of particular American industries, the overall needs of the American economy, and the demands of the legislative branch. President Clinton faced a particularly difficult dilemma when permanent normal trade relations with China came up for a vote in the Congress in 2000. Because of concern with human rights violations and other issues, a 1974 law required that Congress renew regular trade relations with

INTERACTIVE 12.3

 U.S. Military Interventions: Quick Strikes and Entrenched Conflicts Since the 50s

Politics in a Changing World

An International Popularity Contest

The Pew Global Attitudes Project asked voters in nine countries if they had favorable or unfavorable opinions of various political figures, including U.S. president George W. Bush, French president Jacques Chirac, British prime minister Tony Blair, and Osama bin Laden. Respondents in the United States had favorable opinions of Bush and Blair and largely unfavorable opinions of Chirac, most likely because the French president criticized the U.S.-British invasion of Iraq. Americans were not asked about the favorability of Osama bin Laden. (Blair and Chirac have since left office.)

All of the NATO members asked about bin Laden were overwhelmingly unfavorable. Respondents in predominately Muslim countries, on the other hand, held mostly favorable opinions of bin Laden and unfavorable opinions of Bush and Blair.

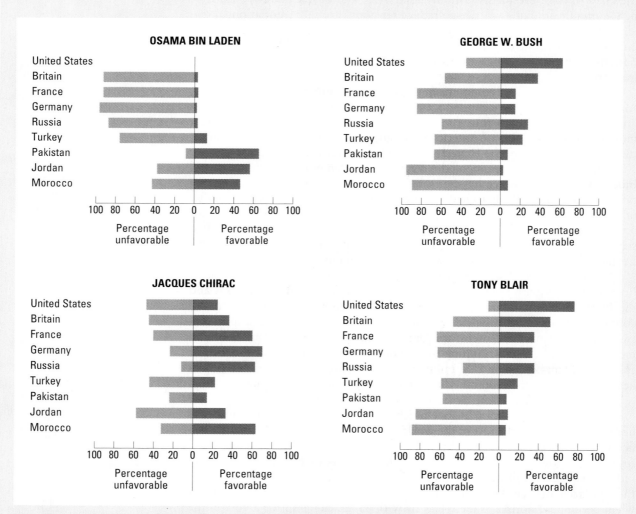

Source: Data from Pew Global Attitudes Project, "Additional Findings and Analyses: A Year After the Iraq War," <http://pewglobal.org>. Chart from "Bush vs. Bin Laden," *New York Times*, 21 March 2004. New York Times Graphics. Reprinted with permission.

From Peanuts to the Peace Prize

Former president and peanut farmer Jimmy Carter won the Nobel Peace Prize in 2002 for his continuing efforts to "find peaceful solutions to international conflicts, to advance democracy and human rights, and to promote economic and social development." Since leaving office, he has participated in activities such as election watches and the fight against tropical diseases in developing countries. Carter maintained an average approval rating of only 45 percent during his term. A little over twenty years later, 60 percent of the public claimed to retrospectively approve of his job while in office. The long-term reputations of presidents do not settle until well after their time in office. *(Bjoern Sigurdsoen/AP/Wide World Photos)*

China each year. If Congress did not pass such legislation, China would be subject to higher tariffs rather than the preferential trading rules most other U.S. trading partners received. An annual fight ensued over the legislation as critics of the Chinese regime tried to exact concessions from it as the price of renewal. As a means of promoting more trade with China and better relations with this important country, support grew for replacing the annual fight over renewal with permanent normal relations.

Many interests, especially farmers and manufacturers with goods to export to China, were intensely interested in permanent normal relations. Labor unions, worried about the price advantage that Chinese companies would have in the U.S. market because of the lower wages there, were adamantly opposed to changing the law. More Chinese imports would surely lead to fewer manufacturing jobs in the United States. Organized labor is a mainstay of the Democratic Party, and it was difficult for Clinton and congressional Democrats to work against their traditionally loyal allies. Clinton believed that increased trade was in the best long-term interests of the country and worked skillfully to push the agreement through Congress.

Finally, American presidents make foreign policy on the basis of humanitarian concerns and the promotion of democracy throughout the world. As the example of China shows, the United States may impose trade sanctions to discourage human rights violations. President Clinton sent troops to Haiti in 1994 to ensure a peaceful transition from a military dictatorship to democratically elected president Jean Bertrand Aristide. Many justified the war with Iraq as the necessary overthrow of a dictator who had brutalized and massacred many of his own people. Each president must decide the extent to which the United States should use its power to promote American ideals abroad.

Crisis Management

Periodically, the president faces a grave situation in which conflict is imminent or a small conflict threatens to explode into a larger war. Because handling such episodes is a critical part of the presidency, citizens may vote for candidates who project careful judgment. One reason for Barry Goldwater's crushing defeat in the 1964 election was his warlike image and rhetoric, which scared many Americans. Fearing that Goldwater would be too quick to resort to nuclear weapons, they voted for Lyndon Johnson instead.

A president must be able to exercise good judgment and remain cool in crisis situations. John Kennedy's behavior during the Cuban missile crisis of 1962 has become a model of effective crisis management. When the United States learned that the Soviet Union had placed missiles containing nuclear warheads in Cuba, he saw those missiles as an unacceptable threat to this country's security. Kennedy asked a group of senior aides, including top people from the Pentagon, to advise him on feasible military and diplomatic responses. Kennedy considered an invasion of Cuba and airstrikes against the missiles but eventually chose a less dangerous response: a naval blockade. He also privately signaled to Soviet leader Nikita Khrushchev that if the Soviet Union withdrew its missiles from Cuba, the United States would remove American missiles from Turkey.[77] Although the Soviet Union complied, the world held its breath for a short time over the very real possibility of a nuclear war.

What guidelines determine what a president should do in times of crisis? Drawing on a range of advisers and opinions is one. Not acting in unnecessary haste is another. A third is having a well-designed, formal review process with thorough analysis and open debate.[78] A fourth guideline is rigorously examining the reasoning underlying all options to ensure that their assumptions are valid. When President Kennedy backed a CIA plan for a rebel invasion of Cuba by expatriates hostile to Fidel Castro, he did not know that its chances for success were based on unfounded assumptions of immediate uprisings by the Cuban population.[79]

These guidelines do not guarantee against mistakes. Almost by definition, each crisis is unique. Sometimes all alternatives carry substantial risks. And almost always, time is of the essence. When Cambodia captured the American merchant ship *Mayagüez* off its coast in 1975, President Ford did not want to wait until the Cambodians moved the sailors inland, presenting little chance of rescue. So he immediately sent in the Marines. Unfortunately, forty-one American soldiers were killed, "all in vain because the American captives had shortly before the attack been released and sent across the border into Thailand."[80] Even so, Ford's decision can be defended, for he did not know what the Cambodians would do. World events are unpredictable, and in the end presidents must rely on their own judgment in crisis situations.

INTERACTIVE 12.4

 Fidel Castro: The Life of the Cuban Leader

Summary

When the delegates to the Constitutional Convention met to design the government of their new nation, they had trouble shaping the office of the president. They struggled to find a balance: an office that was powerful enough to provide unified leadership but not so strong that presidents could use their powers to become tyrants or dictators. The initial conceptions of the presidency have slowly been transformed over time, as presidents have adapted the office to meet the nation's changing needs. The trend has been to expand presidential power. Some expansion has come from presidential actions taken under claims of inherent powers. Congress has also delegated a great deal of power to the executive branch, further expanding the role of the president. The executive branch establishment has grown rapidly, and the White House has become a sizable bureaucracy.

Presidential leadership is shaped by the president's ability to bargain, persuade, and make wise choices. His influence is related to his popularity with the public because he can use his support to gain leverage with members of Congress. The president's legislative success also depends on his political party's numerical strength in Congress. Presidents who are part of a strong majority party have more resources to make bold policy changes.

New responsibilities of the presidency are particularly noticeable in the area of legislative leadership. A president is now expected to be a policy initiator for Congress, as well as a lobbyist who guides his bills through the legislative process. The presidential "job description" for foreign policy has also changed considerably. Post–World War II presidents had been preoccupied with containing the spread of communism, but with the collapse of communism in the Soviet Union and Eastern Europe, presidents pay more attention to international economic relations and security issues like terrorism.

Internet activities and reading suggestions for this chapter are available on the *Online Study Center*

To complete the multimedia assignments for this chapter, go to AmericansGoverning.org.

13

The Bureaucracy

(Spencer Platt/Getty Images)

Online Study Center
This icon will direct you to resources
and activities on the website
college.hmco.com/pic/jandaupdate9e

One of the most remarkable revelations in the wake of the September 11 attack on the United States was that six months after the tragedy the U.S. government's Immigration and Naturalization Service (INS) mailed a notice to a Venice, Florida, flight school informing it that Mohamed Atta and Marwan Al-Shehhi had been approved for student visas. Atta and Al-Shehhi were two of the hijackers who flew planes into the World Trade Center.[1] Before the attack, the Federal Aviation Administration (FAA) had received numerous warnings and had actually issued four information circulars to commercial airlines, asking them to "use caution."[2] But these bulletins sent to the airlines do not require any response, and the airlines did nothing. The FAA could have mandated changes in airline safety, such as requiring impenetrable, locked cockpit doors. The Central Intelligence Agency (CIA), which gathers intelligence outside the United States, made its share of serious mistakes too. After identifying two foreigners as being involved with Al Qaeda, it waited twenty months, until right before 9/11, before it placed these two hijackers on a federal watch list. By the time the men went on the watch list, they were already in the United States and could not be located by law enforcement officials.[3]

The solution to all these bureaucratic failings was a new bureaucracy, the Department of Homeland Security (DHS).[4] Twenty-two different federal agencies and bureaus with over 170,000 employees were merged to form this new cabinet-level department. The Department of Homeland Security has a budget of nearly $40 billion a year to carry out its mandate to protect our borders, ports, airports, and infrastructure from further terrorist attacks. Centralization was supposed to lead to increased coordination and efficiency, but many citizens and politicians complained that the new bureaucracy only made things worse. Airport passengers put up with long security lines for pat-downs and shoe scans while cargo was loaded aboard their flights without being inspected. Funds designated for first responders—local police, fire, and medical units—were being spent in low-risk rural areas instead of more populous cities.

Perhaps the most disastrous test of the new bureaucracy came when Hurricane Katrina hit the Gulf Coast and thousands of New Orleans residents were trapped within their flooded city for days before the federal government responded. Elderly citizens died in nursing homes that had not been evacuated. Thousands of poor residents were trapped in the Superdome in New Orleans with limited food and water, no working toilets, and no air conditioning. One survivor told Congress, "We saw buses, helicopters, and FEMA trucks, but no one stopped to help us. . . . We slept next to dead bodies, we slept on streets at least four times next to human feces and urine. There was garbage everywhere in the city. Fear and panic had taken over."[5] ★

INTERACTIVE 13.1

AP | *September 11: Remembering Ground Zero and Rebuilding*

bureaucracy A large, complex organization in which employees have specific job responsibilities and work within a hierarchy of authority.

bureaucrat An employee of a bureaucracy, usually meaning a government bureaucracy.

Despite their shortcomings, we must rely on bureaucracies to administer government. In this chapter we examine how bureaucracies operate and address many of the central dilemmas of American political life. Bureaucracies represent what Americans dislike about government, yet our interest groups lobby them to provide us with more of the services we desire. We say we want smaller, less intrusive government, but different constituencies value different agencies of government and fight fiercely to protect those bureaucracies' budgets. This enduring conflict once again represents the majoritarian and pluralist dimensions of American politics.

★ Organization Matters

A nation's laws and policies are administered, or put into effect, by various departments, agencies, bureaus, offices, and other government units, which together are known as its *bureaucracy*. **Bureaucracy** actually means any large, complex organization in which employees have specific job responsibilities and work within a hierarchy of authority. The employees of these government units, who are quite knowledgeable within their narrow areas, have become known somewhat derisively as **bureaucrats.**

We study bureaucracies because they play a central role in the governments of modern societies. In fact, organizations are a crucial part of any society, no matter how elementary it is. Even a preindustrial tribe is an organization. It has a clearly defined leader (a chief), senior policymakers (elders), a fixed division of labor (some hunt, some cook, some make tools), an organizational culture (religious practices, initiation rituals), and rules of governance (what kind of property belongs to families and what belongs to the tribe). How that tribe is organized is not merely a quaint aspect of its evolution; it is critical to the survival of its members in a hostile environment.

The organization of modern government bureaucracies also reflects their need to survive. The environment in which modern bureaucracies operate, filled with conflicting political demands and the ever-present threat of budget cuts, is no less hostile than that of preindustrial tribes. The way a given government bureaucracy is organized also reflects the particular needs of its clients. The bottom line, however, is that the manner in which any bureaucracy is organized affects how well it can accomplish its tasks.

Different approaches to fighting German submarines in World War II vividly demonstrate the importance of organization. At the beginning of the war German submarines, or U-boats, were sinking American merchant ships off the East Coast of America at a devastating rate. One U-boat commander wrote that his task was so easy that "all we had to do was press the button." In contrast, the British had a great deal of success in defending their ships in the North Atlantic from U-boats.

The British Navy used a highly centralized structure to quickly pool all incoming information on U-boat locations and just as quickly pass on what it had learned to commanders of antisubmarine ships and planes and to convoys. In contrast, the U.S. Navy's operations structure was decentralized, leaving top line managers to decide for themselves how to allocate their resources. No one unit was coordinating antisubmarine warfare. When the U.S. Navy finally adopted a system similar to the British Navy's, its success against the U-boats improved dramatically. In the eighteen months before it changed its

Waleed M. Alsheri   Mohammed Atta   Wail M. Alshehri   Abdulaziz Alomari   Satam M.A. al-Suqami

Ahmed Alnami   Ahmed Ibrahim A. al Haznawi   Ziad Samir al-Jarrah   Saeed Alghamdi

Khalid Almihdar   Majed Moqed   Nawaf Alhazmi   Salem Alhazmi   Hani Hanjour

Marwan Alshehhi   Ahmed Alghamdi   Mohand Alshehri   Hamza Alghamdi   Fayez Rashid

Murderers All

The trauma of the terrorist attacks on September 11, 2001, was all the more painful because of bureaucratic blunders and the inadequate funding of key bureaucracies that eased the nineteen hijackers' entry into the country. The government created a new cabinet-level agency, the Department of Homeland Security, to help the nation guard against future terrorist attacks. *(FBI/Getty Images)*

system, the Navy sank just thirty-six U-boats. In the first six months with its centralized structure, seventy-five U-boats were destroyed.[6]

Clearly, organization matters. The ways in which bureaucracies are structured to perform their work directly affect their ability to accomplish their tasks. Unfortunately, "if organization matters, it is also the case that there is no one best way of organizing."[7] Highly centralized organization, like the British Navy's approach to combating U-boats, may not always be the best approach to solving a bureaucracy's performance problems. A common complaint against Washington bureaucracies is that they devise one-size-fits-all solutions to problems. In some instances, it's surely better to give local managers the flexibility to tailor their own solutions to the unique problems they face in their community or state. The study of bureaucracy, then, centers around finding solutions to the many different kinds of problems that large government organizations face.

The Development of the Bureaucratic State

A common complaint voiced by Americans is that the national bureaucracy is too big and tries to accomplish too much. To the average citizen, the

Profiling America
One of the bureaucracy's many tasks is collecting information. Various agencies gather vitally important statistics, such as the unemployment rate and the crime rate. Each decade, the Bureau of the Census does a count of the nation's population and compiles a statistical profile of America. Much of the census is now done through the mail, but census takers still do some door-to-door work. *(Spencer Grant/PhotoEdit)*

national government may seem like an octopus—its long arms reach just about everywhere. Ironically, compared to other Western democracies, the size of the United States government is proportionally smaller (see "Compared with What? Not So Big by Comparison").

The Growth of the Bureaucratic State

American government seems to have grown unchecked since the start of the twentieth century. As one observer noted wryly, "The assistant administrator for water and hazardous materials of the Environmental Protection Agency [presides] over a staff larger than Washington's entire first administration."[8] Yet even during George Washington's time, bureaucracies were necessary. No one argued then about the need for a postal service to deliver mail or a treasury department to maintain a system of currency.

However, government at all levels (national, state, and local) grew enormously in the twentieth century, for several major reasons.[9] A principal cause of government expansion is the increasing complexity of society. George Washington did not have an assistant administrator for water and hazardous materials because he had no need for one. The National Aeronautics and Space Administration (NASA) was not necessary until rockets were invented.

Another reason government has grown is that the public's attitude toward business has changed. Throughout most of the nineteenth century, there was little or no government regulation of business. Business was generally autonomous, and any government intervention in the economy that might limit that autonomy was considered inappropriate. This attitude began to change toward the end of the nineteenth century, as more Americans became aware that the

Compared with What?

Not So Big by Comparison

When the United States is viewed against the other Western democracies, our government turns out to be relatively small. Measuring the size of government is difficult, but one way is to calculate the proportion of all of a nation's workers who are employed by their government.

The primary reason that the size of the bureaucracies in other democracies is larger in comparison to the United States is that they offer a much more extensive array of welfare and social service benefits to their citizens. These countries tend to have generous pension, health, and unemployment benefits. These benefits do not come cheaply, however; residents of the other advanced industrialized countries tend to pay much higher taxes than do Americans. There's no free lunch. In recent years, budget pressures have forced European governments to try to trim their spending.

Source: Alan R. Ball and B. Guy Peters, *Modern Politics and Government,* 7th ed. (New York: Palgrave Macmillan, 2005), p. 231.

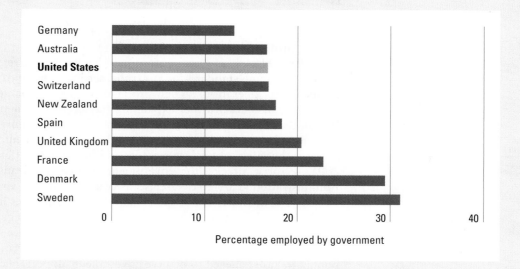

Percentage employed by government

end product of a laissez-faire approach was not always highly competitive markets that benefited consumers. Instead, businesses sometimes formed oligopolies, such as the infamous "sugar trust," a small group of companies that controlled virtually the entire sugar market.

Gradually, government intervention came to be accepted as necessary to protect the integrity of markets.[10] And if government was to police unfair business practices effectively, it needed administrative agencies. During the twentieth century, new bureaucracies were organized to regulate specific industries. Among them are the Securities and Exchange Commission (SEC), which oversees securities trading, and the Food and Drug Administration (FDA), which

Rummy Out, Gates In
After the Republicans' drubbing in the 2006 congressional elections, President Bush removed Donald Rumsfeld as secretary of defense. Rumsfeld had been widely criticized for his execution of the Iraq war. Robert Gates, former head of the CIA and president of Texas A&M University, was selected by Bush to replace Rumsfeld. Gates immediately faced intense pressure to show progress in Iraq through a "surge" in troop strength. *(© Andrew Gray/epa/Corbis)*

INTERACTIVE 13.2

 Nuclear Waste at Yucca Mountain

tries to protect consumers from unsafe food, drugs, and cosmetics. Through bureaucracies such as these, government has become a referee in the marketplace, developing standards of fair trade, setting rates, and licensing individual businesses for operation. As new problem areas have emerged, government has added new agencies, further expanding the scope of its activities. After World War II, the government created the Atomic Energy Commission—now the Nuclear Regulatory Commission—to regulate the use of nuclear materials and monitor the safety of nuclear reactors. Within months after the September 11, 2001, terrorist attacks, the government created the Transportation Security Administration (TSA) to oversee security at the nation's airports.

General attitudes about government's responsibilities in the area of social welfare have changed too. An enduring part of American culture is the belief in self-reliance. People are expected to overcome adversity on their own, to succeed on the basis of their own skills and efforts. Yet certain segments of our population are believed to deserve government support, because we either particularly value their contribution to society or have come to believe that they cannot realistically be expected to overcome adversity on their own.[11]

This belief goes as far back as the nineteenth century. The government provided pensions to Civil War veterans because they were judged to deserve financial support. Later, programs to help mothers and children were developed.[12] Further steps toward income security came in the wake of the Great Depression, when the Social Security Act became law, creating a fund that workers pay into and then collect income from during old age. In the 1960s, the government created programs like Headstart, Medicare, and Medicaid to help minorities and the poor. As the government made these new commitments, it also made new bureaucracies or expanded existing ones.

Finally, government has grown because ambitious, entrepreneurial agency officials have expanded their organizations and staffs to take on added responsibilities.[13] Each new program leads to new authority, and larger budgets and staffs are necessary to support that authority.

Can We Reduce the Size of Government?

Even incumbent candidates for Congress and the presidency typically "run against the government." For many Americans, government is unpopular: they have little confidence in its capabilities and feel that it wastes money and is out of touch with the people. They want a smaller government that costs less and performs better.

Most of the national government is composed of large bureaucracies, so if government is to become smaller, bureaucracies will have to be eliminated or reduced in size. Everyone wants to believe that we can shrink government just by eliminating unnecessary bureaucrats. Although efficiencies can be found, serious budget cuts also require serious reductions in programs. Not surprisingly, presidents and members of Congress face opposition when they try to cut specific programs. As discussed in Chapter 17, the national government often engages in a bit of a shell game, modestly reducing the number of bureaucrats (which is popular) without reducing government programs (which is politically risky). The government often turns over the former bureaucrats' jobs to nonprofit or private contractors who do the same job but are not technically government employees (see "Looking to the Future: Downsizing the Federal Bureaucracy?").[14]

Beneath the common rhetoric that government needs to be smaller and more efficient, serious efforts to contract the bureaucracy have varied considerably. Ideological differences between the two parties and the gyrating size of the national budget deficit have shaped the debate. During the 1980s, President Reagan preached smaller government and made a concerted effort to reduce domestic social programs. He had only modest success, and his most ambitious proposals, like abolishing the Department of Education, didn't come close to passage by Congress. At the same time, budget deficits ballooned, in part because of the large tax cuts Congress enacted at his request. The budget deficits, in turn, made it difficult to expand government and frustrated the Democrats, who wanted to restore the domestic program cuts Reagan succeeded in getting passed.

The sharp economic growth during the Clinton years led to large budget surpluses. Republican strength in Congress frustrated Clinton's effort to expand the role of government with a large-scale reform of the nation's healthcare delivery system. George W. Bush inherited the Clinton era surpluses, but within two years of his election, the downturn in the economy, the 2001 tax cut, and the war on terrorism ate up the surplus, and large budget deficits reappeared. The deficit continues to rise as the war in Iraq, the new Medicare prescription drug benefit, an orgy of congressional earmarks (special projects for legislators' home districts and states), and many other factors push federal spending ever higher.

Unlike Ronald Reagan, George W. Bush didn't emphasize downsizing government as he campaigned for president. Surely to his surprise, the conservative Republican found that the bureaucracy was growing during his time in office. Most significant, the attack on September 11 and the continuing threat of terrorism led to the creation of the Department of Homeland Security and the expansion of defense- and other security-related agencies. Accounting

Looking to the Future

Downsizing the Federal Bureaucracy?

At first glance it may seem that the federal government is shrinking. As the accompanying graph illustrates, the number of bureaucrats working for the national government has changed little in recent years. At the same time, the American population has grown significantly, roughly 30 percent since 1975. Thus, our federal work force has effectively shrunk as a percentage of the American population. Possibly the federal government has simply become more efficient, using computers and other technologies to do more with fewer employees, just as American industry has done. Yet since employment by state and local governments has grown by a roughly proportionate amount in relation to the growth of the population, this explanation seems unconvincing. Most of the same technologies and new efficiencies available to the federal government are also available to the cities and states.

As noted in the text, there has been pressure on Washington to restrict its

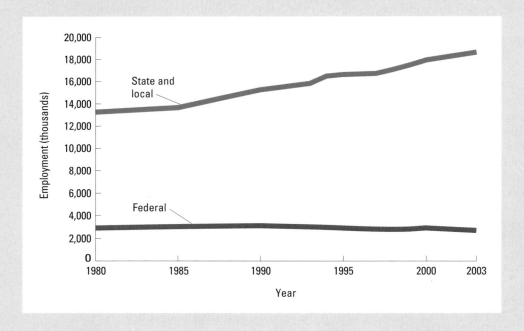

scandals that inflated corporate profits and misled investors at large companies like Enron and WorldCom led to the new Public Company Accounting Oversight Board.

The creation of new agencies masks some of the evolutionary changes in the bureaucracy. Often new agencies absorb other agencies, which are then terminated. When the Interstate Commerce Commission was ended, many of its functions were moved to the newly created Surface Transportation Board.[15]

growth, while at the same time Americans remain interested in preserving the services and benefits of the many programs and agencies of the national government. These are contradictory desires: it takes people—bureaucrats—to run government programs. Although there are areas where government has reduced its role and jobs have truly been eliminated, the way policymakers have generally addressed this dilemma of "small government, large services" is to *devolve* responsibilities onto state and local government. One mechanism has been block grants. In the area of community development, for example, the federal government folded many different programs, each for a specific purpose (such as water and sewer construction, urban renewal, and neighborhood development), into one funding instrument, the Community Development Block Grant program. Cities are given a fixed amount of money that they can use for any mix of community development projects. One consequence of block grants is that the national government needs fewer bureaucrats to oversee a large funding program than it does to administer a large number of categorical programs, each with its own grant procedures and substantive requirements. Conversely, state and local governments need more bureaucrats because of the increasing responsibilities devolved on them.

Another manifestation of devolution is the increasing use of nonprofits to carry out government programs. In 1996, for example, President Clinton and the Congress agreed on legislation to alter welfare fundamentally. The new program, Temporary Assistance for Needy Families (TANF), established strict time limits on how long welfare recipients could receive financial support. TANF placed greater emphasis on giving adults on welfare the job skills or education they need so they can get a job. But virtually none of the individual programs across the country for training welfare recipients is run directly by the federal government. Instead, they are administered mostly by nonprofits. The employees of a nonprofit like the Transitional Work Corporation in Philadelphia are paid through a government contract for training welfare recipients, but they don't show up in government employment statistics. The number of nonprofits in the United States has skyrocketed, while the number of federal employees has ostensibly remained relatively stable.

Looking to the future, many questions emerge. One is whether the fight against terrorism and an aggressive foreign and defense policy will continue to lead to a larger federal government. The Department of Homeland Security merged agencies but also created new positions. Congress recently reorganized the gathering of national intelligence by creating a director of national intelligence, with a staff of five hundred.

Second, the budget deficit ballooned because of an economic downturn, tax cuts, hurricane relief, and the war in Iraq. Members of Congress don't have the money to spend on new government services and continue to debate cuts in entitlement programs to manage the deficit. State and local governments are also strapped for cash. Is it possible that Americans will become less hostile to taxes and signal a willingness to pay for more services and, indirectly, to pay for more bureaucrats to provide those services?

Sources: Statistical Abstract of the United States, available at <http://www.census.gov/prod/2005pubs/06statab/stlocgov.pdf> and <http://www.census.gov/prod/2005pubs/06statab/fedgov.pdf>.

The Department of Homeland Security has many new components, but much of it is an amalgam of other agencies, like the Coast Guard, the Customs Service, and the Federal Emergency Management Agency. The new department was seen as a means of better coordinating many of the nation's security-related bureaucracies.

The tendency for big government to endure reflects the tension between majoritarianism and pluralism. Even when the public as a whole wants a smaller

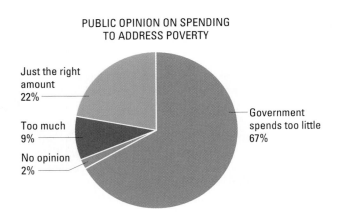

FIGURE 13.1   **Give More to the Poor!**

PUBLIC OPINION ON SPENDING
TO ADDRESS POVERTY

Just the right amount
22%

Too much
9%

No opinion
2%

Government spends too little
67%

According to the U.S. Census Bureau, about 37 million Americans live in poverty. Most Americans expect the government to do something about it. In September 2005, the Gallup organization asked respondents whether the federal government is spending too much, too little, or just the right amount of money to address the issue of poverty. A two-thirds majority said the government was spending too little. How the bureaucracy should spend the money is another question.

Source: Raksha Arora, "Americans Dissatisfied with Government's Efforts on Poverty," 25 October 2005, <http://poll.gallup.com>.

IDEAlog.org

Do you prefer a bigger government with more services or smaller government with fewer services? After reading this chapter, would you still give the same answer? Take IDEAlog's self-test.

national government, that sentiment can be undermined by the strong desire of different segments of society for government to continue performing some valuable function for them. Lobbies that represent these segments work strenuously to convince Congress and the administration that certain agencies' funding is vital and that any cuts ought to come out of other agencies' budgets. At the same time, those other agencies are also working to protect themselves and to garner support.

★ Bureaus and Bureaucrats

We often think of the bureaucracy as a monolith. In reality, the bureaucracy in Washington is a disjointed collection of departments, agencies, bureaus, offices, and commissions—each a bureaucracy in its own right.

The Organization of Government

By examining the basic types of government organizations, we can better understand how the executive branch operates. In our discussion, we pay particular attention to the relative degree of independence of these organizations and to their relationship with the White House.

Departments.   The biggest units of the executive branch are **departments**, covering broad areas of government responsibility. As noted in Chapter 12, the secretaries (heads) of the departments, along with a few other key officials, form the president's cabinet. The current cabinet departments are State, Treasury, Defense, Interior, Agriculture, Justice, Commerce, Labor, Health and Human Services, Housing and Urban Development, Transportation, Energy, Education, Veterans Affairs, and Homeland Security (see Figure 13.2). Each of these massive organizations is broken down into subsidiary agencies, bureaus, offices, and services.

department The biggest unit of the executive branch, covering a broad area of government responsibility. The heads of the departments, or secretaries, form the president's cabinet.

FIGURE 13.2 Bureaucrats at Work

The size of the cabinet departments varies dramatically. That
more than 1 million civilian
employees are employed in
the departments of Defense,
Homeland Security, and Veterans Affairs is a reflection of the
centrality of national security
and war in recent American
history. At the opposite end
of the spectrum is the tiny
Department of Education, with
fewer than 5,000 employees,
despite the common rhetoric
about the need to improve
education.

*Source: Statistical Abstract of the United
States, 2006, available at <http://
www.census.gov/prod/2005pubs/
06statab/fedgov.pdf>.*

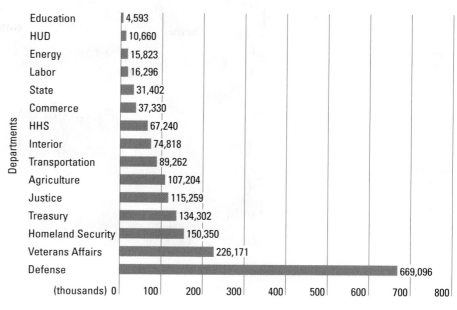

Departments	Number of civilian employees, 2003
Education	4,593
HUD	10,660
Energy	15,823
Labor	16,296
State	31,402
Commerce	37,330
HHS	67,240
Interior	74,818
Transportation	89,262
Agriculture	107,204
Justice	115,259
Treasury	134,302
Homeland Security	150,350
Veterans Affairs	226,171
Defense	669,096

Independent Agencies. Within the executive branch are many **independent agencies** that are not part of any cabinet department. They stand alone
and are controlled to varying degrees by the president. Some, among them
the CIA, are directly under the president's control. Others, such as the Federal
Communications Commission, are structured as **regulatory commissions.**
Each commission is run by a small number of commissioners (usually an odd
number, to prevent tie votes) appointed to fixed terms by the president. Some
commissions were formed to guard against unfair business practices. Others
were formed to protect the public from unsafe products. Although presidents
don't have direct control over these regulatory commissions, they can strongly
influence their direction through their appointments of new commissioners.

Government Corporations. Finally, Congress has also created a small
number of **government corporations.** The services these executive branch
agencies perform theoretically could be provided by the private sector, but
Congress has decided that the public is better served by these organizations'
having some link with the government. For example, the national government
maintains the postal service as a government corporation because it feels that
Americans need low-cost, door-to-door service for all kinds of mail, not just
for profitable routes or special services. In some instances, the private sector
does not have enough financial incentive to provide an essential service. This is
the case with the financially troubled Amtrak train line.

independent agency An
executive agency that is not part of
a cabinet department.

regulatory commission
An agency of the executive branch of
government that controls or directs
some aspect of the economy.

government corporation
A government agency that performs
services that might be provided by the
private sector but that either involve
insufficient financial incentive or are
better provided when they are somehow linked with government.

Gonzales Under Fire
Attorney General Alberto Gonzales came under fire from the press and from Democrats who believed he was excessively partisan in administering the Justice Department. He was accused of placing strict loyalty to the Republican Party ahead of appropriate experience in personnel decisions. President Bush responded that Gonzales had done nothing wrong and that charges against him were partisan. Gonzales, however, resigned in August 2007.
(© Ron Sachs/CNP/Corbis)

The Civil Service

The national bureaucracy is staffed by nearly 2.9 million civilian employees, who account for about 2 percent of the U.S. work force.[16] Americans have a tendency to stereotype all government workers as faceless paper pushers, but the public sector work force is actually quite diverse. Government workers include forest rangers, FBI agents, typists, foreign service officers, computer programmers, policy analysts, public relations specialists, security guards, librarians, administrators, engineers, plumbers, and people from literally hundreds of other occupations. (For the gender balance of different government departments and agencies, see Figure 13.3.)

An important feature of the national bureaucracy is that most of its workers are hired under the requirements of the **civil service.** The civil service was created after the assassination of President James Garfield, who was killed by an unbalanced and dejected job seeker. Congress responded by passing the Pendleton Act (1883), which established the Civil Service Commission (now the Office of Personnel Management). The objective of the act was to reduce patronage—the practice of filling government positions with the president's political allies or cronies. The civil service fills jobs on the basis of merit and sees to it that workers are not fired for political reasons. Over the years, job qualifications and selection procedures have been developed for most government positions.

The tidal wave of criticism of the federal bureaucracy—that it's unresponsive, too big, and too inefficient—has raised concerns that the government has become a less appealing place to work. As one study concluded, "The federal bureaucracy became the symbol of big government's problems—rarely of its success."[17] The quality of the civil service could decline as agencies may find fewer superior candidates for job openings. Surveys do find that younger people seem less interested in working for the government, preferring private sector employment instead.[18] Still, research demonstrates that along a range of indicators, the quality of civil servants has not declined over time.[19]

civil service The system by which most appointments to the federal bureaucracy are made, to ensure that government jobs are filled on the basis of merit and that employees are not fired for political reasons.

FIGURE 13.3 — Gender Diversity in the Federal Work Force

The Equal Employment Opportunity Commission (EEOC) monitors the percentage of women and minorities across federal departments and agencies. Departments like Homeland Security and agencies like NASA are overwhelmingly male. Others, such as the Department of Health and Human Services and the Social Security Administration, have more female employees. The balance of men and women is largely a function of the required training (fewer women major in math and science) and the constituencies of each department.

Source: Annual Report on the Federal Work Force, Fiscal Year 2004, available at <www.eeoc.gov/federal/fsp2004/profiles/index.htm>.

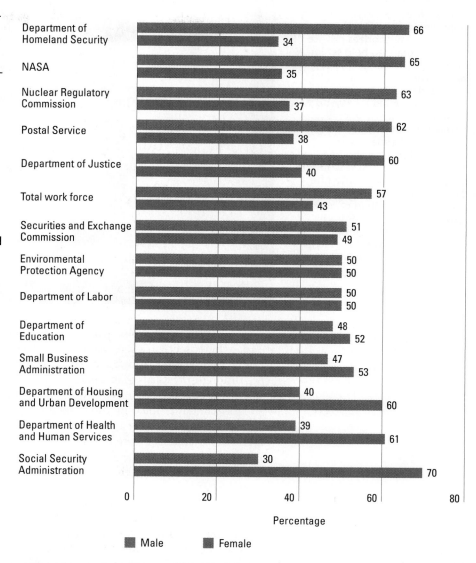

Presidential Control over the Bureaucracy

Civil service and other reforms have effectively insulated the vast majority of government workers from party politics. An incoming president can appoint only about 7,000 people to jobs in his administration, less than 1 percent of all executive branch employees. These presidential appointees fill the top policy-making positions in government, and about 800 of his appointees require Senate confirmation.[20] Each new president, then, establishes an extensive personnel review process to find appointees who are both politically compatible and qualified in their field. Although the president selects some people from his

Too Many Choices?

The Medicare Prescription Drug, Improvement, and Modernization Act of 2003 authorizes private insurance plans to help senior citizens pay for prescription drugs. The Bush administration argued that private provision of benefits would be a good deal for the elderly and all taxpayers. But many seniors were overwhelmed by the number of choices and had trouble filling their prescriptions when the plan went into effect. The program is also projected to cost much more than originally expected. Members of both parties in Congress have promised to revisit the issue in the near future. *(Tim Boyle/Getty Images)*

campaign staff, most political appointees have not been campaign workers. Instead, cabinet secretaries, assistant secretaries, agency heads, and the like tend to be drawn directly from business, universities, and government itself.

Although presidents can appoint top administrators who are ideologically compatible with their own philosophy, there are some limits to this partisanship. A major scandal erupted in 2007 when it was revealed that the Department of Justice fired eight U.S. attorneys because Republican administrators there believed those attorneys were not aggressive enough in pursuing cases damaging to Democratic constituencies.

Presidents find that the bureaucracy is not always as responsive as they might like, for several reasons. Principally, pluralism can pull agencies in a direction other than that favored by the president. The Department of Transportation may want to move toward more support for mass transit, but politically it cannot afford to ignore the preferences of highway builders. An agency administrator must often try to broker a compromise between conflicting groups rather than pursue a position that holds fast and true to the president's ideology. Bureaucracies must also follow—at least in general terms—the laws governing the programs they are entrusted with, even if the president doesn't agree with some of those statutes.

Even with the constraints imposed by interest group preferences and by what the statutes require, presidents still have considerable influence over agency policymaking.[21] They appoint administrators sympathetic to their policy goals who work to adapt the president's philosophy to both pending issues and new initiatives. Presidential aides review agency policymaking to ensure that it is in line with their preferences, often setting up a process requiring agencies to submit draft regulations to a White House office like the Office of Management and Budget. As will be explored in the next section, in varying degrees agencies have the authority to set policy under the laws passed by Congress authorizing an agency to administer a program.

Congress always has the prerogative to override regulations that it doesn't like or that it feels distort its intent. When a president faces a Congress controlled by the opposition party, this constraint is more significant. When his own party also controls both houses, it is much easier for him to implement regulations that are in line with his preferences. Whatever party controls Congress, the White House and agency administrators have an incentive to consult with committee chairs to minimize conflict and gain a sense of what might provoke a hostile response on the part of a committee overseeing a particular agency.[22] A committee can punish an agency by cutting its budget, altering a key program, or (for Senate committees) holding up confirmation of a nominee to a top agency post.

Every president, along with every administration, has a different level of attention to the details of policymaking. The Bush administration has been criticized for a lack of interest in the activities of some of its departments and agencies and for three major bureaucratic failures.[23] First, questions have been raised about the war in Iraq, from the quality of intelligence information before the war to the ability of the United States Army to train a viable Iraqi security force.[24] Second, the federal government's response to Hurricane Katrina was marked by inadequate planning, miscommunication, and an inability to provide adequate assistance to hurricane victims. Finally, during the implementation of the Medicare drug benefit program in January 2006, a large number of seniors were temporarily denied prescription drug coverage because Medicare databases had not been updated.[25] Governors declared health-care emergencies, and more than twenty states paid millions of dollars to cover these individuals while the federal government resolved the confusion. This string of recent crises has only heightened public awareness of the critical role of bureaucracy in the policymaking process.

INTERACTIVE 13.3

 Iraq Election: What's Next?

★ Administrative Policymaking: The Formal Processes

Many Americans wonder why agencies sometimes actually make policy rather than merely carry it out. Administrative agencies are, in fact, authoritative policymaking bodies, and their decisions on substantive issues are legally binding on the citizens of this country.

Administrative Discretion

What are executive agencies set up to do? To begin with, cabinet departments, independent agencies, and government corporations are creatures of Congress. Congress creates a new department or agency by enacting a law that describes the organization's mandate, or mission. As part of that mandate, Congress grants the agency the authority to make certain policy decisions. Congress recognized long ago that it has neither the time nor the technical expertise to make all policy decisions. Ideally, it sets general guidelines for policy and expects agencies to act within those guidelines. The latitude that Congress gives agencies to make policy in the spirit of their legislative mandate is called **administrative discretion.**

Critics of the bureaucracy frequently complain that agencies are granted too much discretion because Congress commonly gives vague directives in its

? **Can you explain why . . .** agencies make policy rather than just carry out the policies that Congress sets?

administrative discretion
The latitude that Congress gives agencies to make policy in the spirit of their legislative mandate.

initial enabling legislation. Congress charges agencies with protecting "the public interest" but leaves them to determine on their own what policies best serve the public. Critics believe that members of Congress delegate too much of their responsibility for difficult policy choices to appointed administrators.

Congress often is vague about its intent when setting up a new agency or program. At times, a problem is clear-cut but the solution is not; yet Congress is under pressure to act. So it creates an agency or program to show that it is concerned and responsive, but it leaves to administrators the work of developing specific solutions. For example, the 1934 legislation that established the Federal Communications Commission (FCC) recognized a need for regulation in the burgeoning radio industry. The growing number of stations and overlapping frequencies would soon have made it impossible to listen to the radio. But Congress avoided tackling several sticky issues by giving the FCC the ambiguous directive that broadcasters should "serve the public interest, convenience, and necessity."[26]

When agency directives are vague, bureaucrats work out the policy details. For instance, Congress gives the FCC the power to fine broadcasters for violating decency standards. The FCC's operating definition for "indecent" is language or material that is offensive "as measured by community standards."[27] Some cases of indecency are fairly straightforward: the FCC fined CBS stations after the singer Janet Jackson's "wardrobe malfunction" caused accidental exposure during the 2004 Super Bowl halftime show. But even after the Super Bowl controversy, members of Congress could not agree on a more concrete definition of indecency; they only agreed to increase the amount of fines for violations of the current law. Affected industries often have an interest in maintaining administrative discretion. After the 2004 Super Bowl incident, the National Cable and Telecommunications Association announced a $250 million campaign to educate consumers about channel-blocking tools; they did not want lawmakers to give the FCC the power to regulate cable and satellite.[28]

Congress grants the broadest discretion to those agencies that are involved in domestic and global security. Both the FBI and the CIA have enjoyed a great deal of freedom from formal and informal congressional constraints because of the legitimate need for secrecy in their operations. The National Security Agency was formed to centralize the work of breaking foreign codes and protecting sensitive government information systems. The NSA also monitors foreign communications. After September 11, President Bush directed the National Security Agency to wiretap telephone conversations between people within the United States and people overseas who have suspected links with terrorists, without first obtaining a warrant as required by the 1978 Foreign Intelligence Surveillance Act. NSA bureaucrats followed the secret orders of the president, without the knowledge of members of Congress.[29] (For more on this controversy, see Chapters 1 and 4.)

Rule Making

rule making The administrative process that results in the issuance of regulations by government agencies.

regulations Administrative rules that guide the operation of a government program.

Agencies exercise their policymaking discretion through formal administrative procedures, usually rule making. **Rule making** is the administrative process that results in the issuance of regulations.[30] **Regulations** are rules that guide the operation of government programs. When an agency issues regulations, it is using the discretionary authority granted to it by Congress to implement a program or policy enacted into law.

Because they are authorized by congressional statutes, regulations have the effect of law. The policy content of regulations is supposed to follow from the intent of enabling legislation. After Congress enacted the Nutrition Labeling and Education Act, for example, the Food and Drug Administration (FDA) drew up regulations to implement the policy guidelines set forth in the law. One part of the law says that producers of foods and food supplements can make health claims for their products only when "significant scientific agreement" exists to support those claims. Following that principle, the FDA proposed regulations requiring manufacturers of vitamins and dietary supplements to substantiate the health claims they make for their products on their labels. Clearly, the FDA was following the intent of a law enacted by Congress.

Regulations are first published as proposals, to give all interested parties an opportunity to comment on them and try to persuade the agency to adopt, alter, or withdraw them. When the FDA issued its proposed regulations on vitamins and health supplements, the industry fought them vigorously. Aware that many of their health claims could not be substantiated and that it would be expensive to finance scientific studies to try to prove their assertions, the manufacturers asked Congress for relief. Although it was responsible for the legislation authorizing the regulations, Congress passed a one-year moratorium on the proposed rules. Congress seemed to want to have it both ways, ensuring the integrity of food and drugs while protecting the business interests of industry constituents. When the moratorium expired, however, the FDA announced plans to reissue the regulations.[31]

The regulatory process is controversial because regulations often require individuals and corporations to act against their own self-interest. In this case, the producers of vitamins and dietary supplements resented the implication that they were making false claims and reminded policymakers that they employ many people to make products that consumers want. However, the FDA must balance its desire not to put people out of work through overregulation with its concern that people not be misled or harmed by false labeling.

> **? Can you explain why . . .**
> Americans want less red tape, but bureaucracies keep producing more and more regulations?

★ Administrative Policymaking: Informal Politics

When an agency is considering a new regulation and all the evidence and arguments have been presented, how does an administrator reach a decision? Because policy decisions typically address complex problems that lack a single satisfactory solution, these decisions rarely exhibit mathematical precision and efficiency.

The Science of Muddling Through

In his classic analysis of policymaking, "The Science of Muddling Through," Charles Lindblom compared the way policy might be made in the ideal world with the way it is formulated in the real world.[32] The ideal, rational decision-making process, according to Lindblom, begins with an administrator's tackling a problem by ranking values and objectives. After clarifying the objectives, the administrator thoroughly considers all possible solutions to the problem. He or she comprehensively analyzes alternative solutions, taking all relevant factors into account. Finally, the administrator chooses the alternative that

When It Rains It Pours
The Federal Emergency Management Agency (FEMA) came under fire when
the federal government was slow to help the victims of Hurricane Katrina.
Bureaucrats at the FEMA command center in Washington, D.C., shown
here, were uncertain about conditions on the ground in New Orleans, not
knowing the extent of the flooding or the number of residents who needed
to be evacuated. *(left: Tim Sloan/AFP/Getty Images; right: Marko Georgiev/
Getty Images)*

appears to be the most effective means of achieving the desired goal and solving the problem.

Lindblom claims that this "rational-comprehensive" model is unrealistic.
Policymakers have great difficulty defining precise values and goals. Administrators at the U.S. Department of Energy, for example, want to be sure that
supplies of home heating oil are sufficient each winter. At the same time, they
want to reduce dependence on foreign oil. Obviously, the two goals are not
fully compatible. How should these administrators decide which goal is more
important? And how should they relate them to the other goals of the nation's
energy policy?

Real-world decision making parts company with the ideal in another way:
the policy selected cannot always be the most effective means to the desired
end. Even if a tax at the gas pump is the most effective way to reduce gasoline
consumption during a shortage, motorists' anger would make this theoretically
"right" decision politically difficult. So the "best" policy is often the one on
which most people can agree. However, political compromise may mean that
the government is able to solve only part of a problem.

Finally, critics of the rational-comprehensive model point out that policymaking can never be based on truly comprehensive analyses. A secretary of
energy cannot possibly find the time to read a comprehensive study of all alternative energy sources and relevant policy considerations for the future. A
truly thorough investigation of the subject would produce thousands of pages
of text. Instead, administrators usually rely on short staff memos that outline
a limited range of feasible solutions to immediate problems. Time is of the
essence, and problems are often too pressing to wait for a complete study. In
short, policymaking tends to be characterized by **incrementalism,** with policies and programs changing bit by bit, step by step. Decision makers are constrained by competing policy objectives, opposing political forces, incomplete

incrementalism Policymaking
characterized by a series of decisions,
each instituting modest change.

information, and the pressures of time. They choose from a limited number of feasible options that are almost always modifications of existing policies rather than wholesale departures from them.

Because policymaking proceeds by means of small modifications of existing policies, it is easy to assume that incrementalism describes a process that is intrinsically conservative, sticking close to the status quo. Yet even if policymaking moves in small steps, those steps may all be in the same direction. Over time, a series of incremental changes can significantly alter a program.[33]

The Culture of Bureaucracy

How an agency makes decisions and performs its tasks is greatly affected by the people who work there: the bureaucrats. Americans often find their interactions with bureaucrats frustrating because bureaucrats are inflexible (they go by the book) or lack the authority to get things done. Top administrators too can become frustrated with the bureaucrats who work for them.

Why do people act bureaucratically? Individuals who work for large organizations cannot help but be affected by the culture of bureaucracy.[34] Modern bureaucracies develop explicit rules and standards to make their operations more efficient and guarantee fair treatment for their clients.

But within each organization, **norms** (informal, unwritten rules of behavior) also develop and influence the way people act on the job. Norms at the IRS, for example, have long encouraged an adversarial relationship with taxpayers. Officials reinforced this tendency within the agency by ranking district offices according to the amount of money they collected from the public. To make sure their offices met their expected quotas, district supervisors sometimes looked the other way when agents blatantly harassed citizens or even subtly encouraged them to pursue illegal tactics to force citizens to pay up. This picture of the internal operations of the IRS emerged from a hearing before the Senate Finance Committee in 1997. After mistreated taxpayers aired their grievances on nationwide television and agents testified about flagrant abuses by the IRS, acting commissioner Michael P. Dolan began dismantling the quota system and apologized to the American people for the agency's transgressions.[35]

To change norms and improve customer service throughout the government, the Clinton administration adopted the Reinventing Government initiative. Bureaucracies were encouraged to adopt the business philosophy known as total quality management (or TQM). First developed as a means of improving manufacturing processes, TQM emphasizes listening to the customer, relying on teamwork, focusing on continually improving quality, breaking down barriers between parts of organizations, and engaging in participatory management.[36] Many agencies developed new ways to treat their clients with efficiency and respect.

Bureaucracies are often influenced in their selection of policy options by the prevailing customs, attitudes, and expectations of the people working within them. Departments and agencies commonly develop a sense of mission, where a particular objective or a means for achieving it is emphasized. The Army Corps of Engineers, for example, is dominated by engineers who define the agency's objective as protecting citizens from floods by building dams. There could be other objectives, and there are certainly other methods of achieving this one,

norms An organization's informal, unwritten rules that guide individual behavior.

but the engineers promote the solutions that fit their conception of what the agency should be doing.

Strong as the culture of bureaucracies may be, agency leaders recognize the danger of antagonizing the White House and congressional overseers. Administrators may override the prevailing pattern of behavior to please political superiors. Prior to the war against Saddam Hussein, the CIA was under pressure to produce evidence demonstrating that Iraq had weapons of mass destruction, President Bush's primary argument for going to war. Even though normally cautious CIA analysts had serious doubts about the evidence they had seen, the agency issued a classified report for the president indicating that Iraq had resumed efforts to build nuclear weapons.[37]

Bureaucrats go by the book because the "book" is actually the law they administer, and they are obligated to enforce the law. The regulations under those laws are often broad standards intended to cover a range of behavior. Yet sometimes those laws and regulations don't seem to make sense. Take the case of Tommy McCoy, who was the batboy for the Savannah Cardinals, a farm team for the Major League Atlanta Braves. An investigator for the Department of Labor discovered that Tommy was only fourteen years old and was working at night games. Child labor laws forbid fourteen-year-olds from working past 7:00 P.M. on school nights, and the Department of Labor inspector threatened to fine the team unless they stopped employing Tommy. The Cardinals went to bat for Tommy, scheduling a "Save Tommy's Job" night at the stadium. The publicity about Tommy's imminent firing made the Department of Labor look ridiculous. When ABC News asked Secretary of Labor Robert Reich to comment on the situation, he knew he was facing a public relations disaster. But when he asked his staff how they could permit Tommy to keep his job, he was told, "There's nothing we can do. The law is the law."[38]

Reich overrode his staff, deciding that new regulations would exempt batboys and batgirls. That may seem to be a happy ending to a story of a bureaucracy gone mad, but it's not that simple. Child labor laws are important. Before this country had such laws, children were exploited in factories that paid them low wages and subjected them to unsanitary working conditions. The exploitation of child labor is still a problem in many parts of the world. It made sense for Congress to pass a law to forbid child labor abuses, and it made sense for the Department of Labor to write a blanket regulation that forbids work after 7:00 P.M. for all children age fourteen and under. The alternative was to try to determine an evening curfew for every type of job that a youngster might have. Although Reich's exemption made sense from a public relations point of view, it was nonsensical as public policy. How about kids working as peanut vendors at the Cardinals' games? Why didn't Reich write a new regulation exempting them as well? And if he wrote an exemption for children who worked for a baseball team, how about children who scoop ice cream at the local creamery? Why should Tommy McCoy be treated with favoritism?

Bureaucrats often act bureaucratically because they are trying to apply the laws of this country in a manner that treats everyone equally. Sometimes, as in the case of Tommy McCoy, equal application of the law doesn't seem to make sense. Yet it would be unsettling if government employees interpreted rules as they please. Americans expect to be treated equally before the law, and bureaucrats work with that expectation in mind.

★ Problems in Implementing Policy

The development of policy in Washington is the end of one phase of the policymaking cycle and the beginning of another. After policies have been developed, they must be implemented. **Implementation** is the process of putting specific policies into operation. Ultimately, bureaucrats must convert policies on paper into policies in action. It is important to study implementation because policies do not always do what they were designed to do.

Implementation may be difficult because the policy to be carried out is not clearly stated. Policy directives to bureaucrats sometimes lack clarity and leave them with too much discretion. We have already mentioned the example of the FCC enforcing standards of "decency." Implementation can also be problematic because of the sheer complexity of some government endeavors. Take, for example, the government's Superfund program to clean up toxic waste sites. When the EPA cleans up a site itself, the cleanup takes an average of eight years to complete. Yet this is not a program that works badly because of irresponsible administrators. Superfund cleanups pose complex engineering, political, and financial problems. Inevitably, regional EPA offices and key actors on the local level must engage in considerable negotiations at each stage of the process.[39] The more organizations and levels of government that are involved, the more difficult it is to coordinate implementation.

The federal response to Hurricane Katrina in late August 2005 illustrates the difficulties of policy implementation, particularly when bureaucracy must respond rapidly to a crisis.[40] As noted in the introduction to Chapter 4, Katrina was a natural disaster of major proportions, causing over $150 billion in damage and killing over 1,300 people in Mississippi, Louisiana, and Alabama. The hurricane triggered the flooding of New Orleans, the nation's thirty-fifth largest city. Poor residents of New Orleans had lacked the means to evacuate the city before the storm and remained trapped for days without food and water.

Though the Bush administration was warned about the impending hurricane, senior officials failed to appoint an executive branch officer to take charge of the disaster before the storm hit the coast.[41] With no clear chain of command, bureaucrats at all levels of government—state, local, and federal—had a difficult time sharing information about storm damage and coordinating relief. Responsibility for natural disaster relief falls within the jurisdiction of the Federal Emergency Management Agency (FEMA), an independent agency that became one of the four major branches of the Department of Homeland Security (DHS) in 2003. Three days after the storm, DHS secretary Michael Chertoff could not find out how many people were stranded in the Convention Center in downtown New Orleans. Estimates ranged from 1,500 to 15,000. Nor could he find out how many buses had evacuated people seeking refuge at the Superdome. State and local officials had trouble locating FEMA chief Michael Brown by phone or e-mail in the days after the disaster.

Brown, an attorney and former official in the Arabian Horse Association, had no experience in emergency management prior to his appointment to lead FEMA in 2003. He resigned a little over a week after the storm hit. On his way out, he blamed Louisiana governor Kathleen Blanco and New Orleans mayor C. Ray Nagin for infighting and the absence of local evacuation plans.[42] Congressional investigations revealed confusion and a distinct lack of communication among all of the major players. Members of Congress blamed the Bush administration. "The president is still at his ranch, the vice president is still

implementation The process of putting specific policies into operation.

fly fishing in Wyoming, the president's chief of staff [Andrew Card] is in Maine. . . . They should have had better leadership. It is disengagement."[43] In sum, the federal response to Hurricane Katrina was marked by ineffective leadership, a lack of clear objectives, and the absence of well-established procedures for the delivery of government support.

Obstacles to effective implementation can create the impression that nothing the government does succeeds, but programs can and do work. Problems in implementation demonstrate why patience and continual analysis are necessary ingredients of successful policymaking. To return to a term we used earlier, implementation is by its nature an *incremental* process, in which trial and error eventually lead to policies that work. After the disastrous response to Hurricane Katrina, the federal government was ready for Hurricane Rita, which hit the coast of Texas almost a month later, on September 24, 2005.[44] Two days before Rita, the homeland security secretary named a federal officer to be in charge, FEMA officials were in touch with state and local government officials, and National Guard and active military troops were readied for duty. FEMA sent search-and-rescue teams to Texas, stockpiled water and ice, and fueled up buses for evacuation and rescue.

★ Reforming the Bureaucracy: More Control or Less?

As we saw at the beginning of this chapter, organization matters. How bureaucracies are designed directly affects how effective they are in accomplishing their tasks. People in government constantly tinker with the structure of bureaucracies, trying to find ways to improve their performance. Administrative reforms have taken many different approaches as criticism of government has mounted.

In recent years three basic approaches to reforming the bureaucracy have attracted the most attention. First, advocates of *deregulation* envision eliminating layers of bureaucracy and reducing the rules that govern business markets with the market forces of supply and demand. Let consumer preferences dictate what products and services are offered. A second approach is directed at waste and inefficiency in government and promotes *competition* so that government services are offered by the lowest bidder from the public or private sector. Instead of a bureaucracy having a monopoly over a particular task, create incentives for that bureaucracy to continually find ways of doing the job more cheaply, thus saving the taxpayers money. Third, a range of reforms focus on measuring agency performance. Instituting clear *performance standards* and holding bureaucrats accountable for meeting those standards should improve the quality and efficiency of government services.[45]

Deregulation

regulation Government intervention in the workings of a business market to promote some socially desired goal.

deregulation A bureaucratic reform by which the government reduces its role as a regulator of business.

Many people believe that government is too involved in **regulation,** intervening in the natural working of business markets to promote some social goal. For example, government might regulate a market to ensure that products pose no danger to consumers. Through **deregulation,** the government reduces its role and lets the natural market forces of supply and demand take over. Conservatives have championed deregulation because they see freedom in the marketplace as the best route to an efficient and growing economy. Indeed, nothing

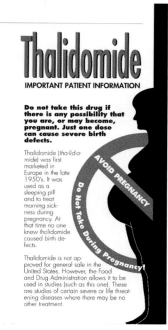

The Return of Thalidomide

The United States was spared the thalidomide disaster because of the skepticism of Frances Kelsey, a Food and Drug Administration doctor who refused to allow thalidomide to be prescribed here. In 1997, however, the FDA decided to permit the use of thalidomide to treat leprosy, although the dangers to pregnant women remain. Shown here is an adult thalidomide victim, as well as one of the FDA stickers designed to prevent women from taking this drug during pregnancy. *(left: Don Jones/Gamma Liaison; right: Dept. of Health & Human Services/FDA)*

is more central to capitalist philosophy than the belief that the free market will efficiently promote the balance of supply and demand. Considerable deregulation took place in the 1970s and 1980s, notably in the airline, trucking, financial services, and telecommunications industries.

In telecommunications, for example, consumers used to have no choice in choosing a long-distance vendor—one could call on the Bell system or not call at all. After an out-of-court settlement broke up the Bell system in 1982, AT&T was awarded the right to sell the long-distance services that had previously been provided by that system, but it now had to face competition from other long-distance carriers, like MCI and Sprint. Consumers have benefited from the competition, and, more recently, competition opened up for local phone service as well.

Deciding on an appropriate level of deregulation is particularly difficult for health and safety issues. Companies within a particular industry may legitimately claim that health and safety regulations are burdensome, making it difficult for them to earn sufficient profits or compete effectively with foreign manufacturers. But the FDA's drug licensing procedures illustrate the potential danger of deregulating such policy areas. The thorough and lengthy process that the FDA uses to evaluate drugs has as its ultimate validation the thalidomide case. The William S. Merrill Company purchased the license to market this sedative, already available in Europe, and filed an application with the FDA in 1960. The company then began a protracted fight with an FDA bureaucrat,

Dr. Frances Kelsey, who was assigned to evaluate the thalidomide application. She demanded that the company abide by all FDA drug testing requirements, despite the fact that the drug was already in use in other countries. She and her superiors resisted pressure from the company to bend the rules a little and expedite approval. Before Merrill had conducted all the FDA tests, news came pouring in from Europe that some women who had taken thalidomide during pregnancy were giving birth to babies without arms, legs, or ears. Strict adherence to government regulations protected Americans from the same tragic consequences.

Nevertheless, the pharmaceutical industry has been highly critical of the FDA, claiming that its licensing procedures are so complex that drugs of great benefit are kept from the marketplace for years, with people suffering from diseases and denied access to new treatments.[46] In response to industry critics and in an effort to address the urgency of the AIDS crisis, the FDA has issued new rules expediting the availability of experimental drugs and more generally has adopted a somewhat speedier timetable for clinical tests of new drugs. In legislation passed in 1997, Congress stipulated that patients with any life-threatening illness, not just AIDS or cancer, can have their doctors petition to use a drug still under investigation by the FDA. In addition, new drugs and vaccines designed for diseases with no effective treatment can be placed on an FDA fast-track list for quicker review.[47]

The conflict over how far to take deregulation reflects the traditional dilemma of choosing between freedom and order. A strong case can be made for deregulated business markets, in which free and unfettered competition benefits consumers and promotes productivity. The strength of capitalist economies comes from the ability of individuals and firms to compete freely in the marketplace, and the regulatory state places restrictions on this freedom. But without regulation, nothing ensures that marketplace participants will act responsibly.

Competition and Outsourcing

Conservative critics of government have long complained that bureaucracies should act more like businesses, meaning they should try to emulate private sector practices that promote efficiency and innovation. Many recent reformers advocate something more drastic: unless bureaucracies can demonstrate that they are as efficient as the private sector, turn those agencies' functions over to the private sector. Underlying this idea is the belief that competition will make government more dynamic and more responsive to changing environments, and will weaken the ability of labor unions to raise wages beyond those of nonunion employees.[48]

The most widespread adaptation of competitive bidding to administer government programs has come in the area of social services. Over time government welfare programs have increasingly emphasized social services—giving people training and noncash support—rather than income maintenance (cash support). Social services are labor intensive, and state and local governments have found it efficient to outsource programs to nongovernmental organizations, principally nonprofit organizations like community health centers and elderly day-care centers. Recently, for-profit companies have started to compete for the grants and contracts that the government awards through competitive grants or bidding. For example, the for-profit company Maximus holds a contract from the state of Connecticut to manage the state's program for providing child-care slots to poor families seeking such assistance.[49]

The Bush administration has mounted the most extensive effort to bring **competition and outsourcing** to the national government. Regulations were adopted in 2003 that will eventually allow private sector competition for hundreds of thousands of government jobs. If government agencies included in this plan can offer the lowest-priced services and meet other requirements set forth in the contract to be bid on, they can keep those positions. Recognizing that the Bush plan is antagonistic toward them, labor unions fought the plan as it was going through administrative rule making. Some concessions were made to unions, but the basic policy was left intact.[50]

Performance Standards

Another approach to improving the bureaucracy's performance is to focus on performance: To what degree does any individual agency accomplish the objectives that have been set for it? In this view, each agency is held accountable for reaching quantifiable goals each year or budget cycle. Under such a system, congressional and White House overseers examine each agency to see if it meets its objectives, and they reward or punish agencies accordingly. As one analyst noted, this is a philosophy of "*making* the managers manage."[51]

A major initiative to hold agencies accountable for their performance is the **Government Performance and Results Act.** Passed by Congress, it requires each agency to identify specific goals, adopt a performance plan, and develop quantitative indicators of agency progress in meeting its goals.[52] The law requires that agencies publish reports with performance data on each measure established. In addition, the Office of Management and Budget under the Bush administration surveys individual programs (such as food stamps, the space shuttle, or the college work study program) and rates them as "effective," "adequate," or "ineffective."[53] The Bush administration also provides quarterly ratings of each cabinet department and major agency according to how well it fulfills the president's management agenda, from financial performance to work force planning.[54]

Despite the value of improved accountability and more extensive data on how well programs are working, performance management is not without its problems. Since agencies set their own goals and know they'll be judged on meeting them, they may select indicators where they know they'll do best. Should an agency running a job training program emphasize its success in the number of people it enrolls or the success rate of its graduates? If it chooses the success rate of its graduates—how many are holding jobs six or twelve months after the training ends—will the agency be tempted to be more selective in who it takes into the program? That is, it may "cream" the applicant pool, rejecting those with the least education or most problematic record. But those are the people most in need of assistance to succeed in the job market. In short, performance-based management runs the risk of perverting an agency's incentives toward what it can achieve rather than what would be most valuable to achieve.[55]

Despite the relative appeal of these different approaches to improving the bureaucracy, each has serious shortcomings. There is no magic bullet. The commitment of the government to solve a problem is far more important than

competition and outsourcing Procedures that allow private contractors to bid for jobs previously held exclusively by government employees.

Government Performance and Results Act A law requiring each government agency to implement quantifiable standards to measure its performance in meeting stated program goals.

management techniques.[56] Still, to return to a theme that we began with, organization does matter. Trying to find ways of improving the bureaucracy is important because bureaucracies affect people's lives, and enhancing their performance, even at the margins, has real consequences.

Summary

As the scope of government activity has grown during the twentieth and early twenty-first centuries, so too has the bureaucracy. The executive branch has evolved into a complex set of departments, independent agencies, and government corporations. The way in which the various bureaucracies are organized matters a great deal because their structure affects their ability to carry out their tasks.

Through the administrative discretion granted them by Congress, these bodies make policy decisions through rules that have the force of law. In making policy choices, agency decision makers are influenced by their external environment, especially the White House, Congress, and interest groups. Internal norms and the need to work cooperatively with others both inside and outside their agencies also influence decision makers.

The most serious charge facing the bureaucracy is that it is unresponsive to the will of the people. In fact, the White House, Congress, interest groups, and public opinion act as substantial controls on the bureaucracy. Still, to many Americans, the bureaucracy seems too big, too costly, and too intrusive. Reducing the size and scope of bureaucratic activity is difficult because pluralism characterizes our political system. The entire executive branch may appear too large, and each of us can point to agencies that we believe should be reduced or eliminated. Yet each bureaucracy has its supporters. The Department of Agriculture performs vital services for farmers. Unions care a great deal about the Department of Labor. Scholars want the National Science Foundation protected. And home builders do not want Housing and Urban Development programs cut back. Bureaucracies survive because they provide important services to groups of people, and those people—no matter how strong their commitment to shrinking the government—are not willing to sacrifice their own benefits.

Plans for reforming the bureaucracy to make it work better are not in short supply. Broad-scale reforms include deregulation, competition and outsourcing, and performance standards. Each has merits and offers plausible mechanisms for improving government efficiency and responsiveness. Each has shortcomings as well, and advocates often overlook the tradeoffs and problems associated with these reforms. Yet it is important to keep trying to find ways of improving government because most people continue to believe that the overall management of bureaucracies is poor and that government needs to be more customer-driven.

Internet activities and reading suggestions for this chapter are available on the *Online Study Center*

To complete the multimedia assignments for this chapter, go to AmericansGoverning.org.

14

The Courts

(Robert C. Shaff/Pictor)

Online Study Center
This icon will direct you to resources and activities on the website
college.hmco.com/pic/jandaupdate9e

"Are you saying what I think you're saying?" asked a disbelieving Governor George W. Bush in the early morning hours of November 8, 2000. "Let me make sure I understand. You're calling me back to retract your concession?"

"You don't have to get snippy about it!" replied Vice President Al Gore. Just forty-five minutes earlier, Gore had conceded the closely contested presidential race to Bush. "Circumstances have changed since I first called you," said Gore. "The state of Florida is too close to call."[1]

The 2000 presidential election hinged on the results in Florida. Bush maintained a narrow lead of 1,725 votes, so narrow as to cast in doubt the true winner. Gore was ahead in the national popular vote by more than 300,000 votes of the more than 100 million cast. But elections for president do not hinge on the popular vote; they depend on the electoral college vote (see Chapter 10). Florida would cast all of its twenty-five electoral votes for the candidate who won the most popular votes in that state.

If Bush kept his razor-thin lead in Florida, he would have 271 electoral votes, just one more than the minimum to claim victory. If Gore moved into the lead in Florida, he would be the victor, with 292 electoral votes.

On the day after the election, William Daley, Gore's campaign chairman, declared: "Until the results in Florida are official, our campaign continues."[2] The campaign continued in a new venue: the courts. Judges in the United States exercise enormous power. By transforming the electoral dispute into a legal dispute, the campaign for the presidency moved to the judicial branch, where different rules and actors would achieve resolution.

Democrats immediately dispatched a planeload of lawyers to Florida to consider their options. Republican lawyers soon followed. Over the next thirty-six days, teams of lawyers on both sides would parry and thrust in a rash of lawsuits in state and federal courts and rely on the separate and overlapping allocation of power between state and nation to resolve the presidential election. ★

IN OUR OWN WORDS

Listen to Jerry Goldman discuss the main points and themes of this chapter.

Online Study Center
Improve Your Grade

Florida was now in the spotlight. Given the small margin of victory—fewer than 2,000 votes—Florida's election law required a recount. The recount produced a much slimmer margin—930 votes—but a similar outcome for Bush. A surprising number of votes for president had been disallowed, however, because voters had cast votes for two or more candidates (these are called overvotes) or for no candidate at all (these are called undervotes). Many of these disallowed ballots were cast in counties with large Democratic majorities. With the margin of victory paper-thin, reasoned the Democrats, it was possible that errors in the vote-counting process could reverse the results. Moreover, overseas absentee ballots still had not been tallied. There were enough such ballots to cast the results one way or the other. Since members of the military, who tend to support Republican candidates, cast many of these ballots, counting the overseas ballots could bolster the Bush lead.

Given the fast-approaching deadline established by the Florida legislature to report, or "certify," the results officially, the Democrats protested the vote counting in court. The Democratic strategy was to assert that all the votes had not been counted and that the obligation of government was to count every vote. The Republicans replied that every legitimate vote had been counted—twice—and Bush was the winner both times. Florida state law permits hand recounts. The Gore team seized on this approach, focusing on a few select counties, to determine whether the overvotes or undervotes signaled an intent to support one candidate or another. In largely Democratic Palm Beach and Broward counties, local officials ordered a complete hand recount of all the votes.

Threatened with the possibility that a full hand recount could reverse the result of the original count and machine recount, the Bush team requested that federal courts stop the hand recount. The lengthy hand recount process, they argued, would violate the conditions in Florida state law for officially certifying the results. The Democrats, looking at the same Florida voting rules, argued in the Florida courts that the state law was riddled with inconsistencies and that the overall policy was to determine the intent of the voters, even if that effort took additional time.

Through a fast-paced series of legal cases, the matter reached the Florida Supreme Court. Its seven justices (all Democratic appointees), in an effort to harmonize conflicting state voting statutes, ruled unanimously to include the hand recounts and to push back the time required for the state to certify the election outcome. To Republicans, this action was a blatant attempt to rewrite the rulebook after the game was over. When the new deadline for certification arrived and with some hand recounts still under way, Florida elected officials (who were Republicans) certified George W. Bush as the winner by 537 votes. Meanwhile, the Bush team had sought and won review in the Supreme Court of the United States, arguing that the Florida Supreme Court rewrote the rules by improperly extending the certification deadline. Within a few days, the

Supreme Court unanimously declined to review the major issue of the recount. Instead, it set aside the Florida Supreme Court decision and requested a clarifying ruling with regard to possible conflicts with federal law and the U.S. Constitution.[3]

The Democrats were down but not out. Although the *protest* period ended with the official certification of the vote, Florida law permitted candidates to *contest* the election results following certification. In a new lawsuit, the Gore team sought a complete hand recount of all votes in the disputed counties. Following a marathon court hearing, a Florida trial judge denied the request for a hand recount. Not yet finished, the Democrats appealed once more to the Florida Supreme Court. In a breathtaking 4–3 decision, the Florida justices ordered an immediate, complete manual recount for all ballots in the state where no vote for president was recorded by machine, a total of 45,000 votes out of more than 6 million votes cast. It also ordered the inclusion of additional undervotes for Gore, reducing Bush's lead to 193 votes.[4]

With their margin of victory eroding with every decision, the Republicans countered with another appeal to the Supreme Court of the United States. Acting on an emergency request, the deeply divided Court temporarily halted the recount on the ground that such action would produce irreparable harm; it also set the case for a hearing.[5] In this round of arguments, the Bush team maintained that the vote recount procedures were standardless—they varied within and across counties—and therefore violated the Constitution's Fourteenth Amendment guarantee of equal protection. The Gore team argued the importance of counting every vote and deferred to the wisdom of the Florida courts.

Just one day after hearing arguments, the justices acted decisively and controversially when the Supreme Court invoked its role as umpire in the extra-inning game of presidential politics. While in substantial agreement (7–2) that the state vote-counting procedures violated the equal protection guarantee of the Fourteenth Amendment, the justices split 5–4 on the remedy. The majority (all conservatives) declared that the time had run out on the recounting of disputed votes. The minority (moderates and liberals) maintained that the recounts should have continued.[6] In words that reflected the sharp partisan tone of the Court's action, dissenting Justice John Paul Stevens wrote:

> Although we may never know with complete certainty the identity of the winner of this year's Presidential election, the identity of the loser is perfectly clear. It is the Nation's confidence in the judge as an impartial guardian of the rule of law.

The following day, Vice President Al Gore made his third and final telephone call to Governor George W. Bush, conceding the election while strongly disagreeing with the Supreme Court's ruling. The game was over. (A year after the 2000 presidential race, a comprehensive and impartial review concluded that George Bush would have won the election had all the uncounted Florida ballots been tallied.[7])

This extraordinary election illustrates the powerful role of the judiciary in American politics. A surprisingly assertive (and conservative) Supreme Court majority ended the controversy and short-circuited a constitutional crisis, avoiding a drawn-out battle in Congress regarding the proper winner of the 2000 election. In the name of the Constitution, the justices trumped the Florida courts, raising the specter that the nation's highest court acted out of partisanship rather than impartiality.

The power of the courts to shape public policy, including the extraordinary circumstance of the 2000 election, creates a difficult problem for democratic theory. According to that theory, the power to make law and the power to determine the outcome of elections reside only in the people or their elected representatives. When judges undo the work of elected majorities (as some have charged they did in the 2000 election), they risk depriving the people of the right to make the laws or to govern themselves.

Court rulings—especially Supreme Court rulings—extend far beyond any particular case. Judges are students of the law, but they remain human beings. They have their own opinions about the values of freedom, order, and equality. And although all judges are constrained by statutes and precedents from imposing their personal will on others through their decisions, some judges are more prone than others to interpreting the law in the light of those beliefs.

America's courts are deeply involved in the life of the country and its people. Some courts, such as the Supreme Court, make fundamental policy decisions vital to the preservation of freedom, order, and equality. Through checks and balances, the elected branches link the courts to democracy, and the courts link the elected branches to the Constitution. But does this system work? Can the courts exercise political power within the pluralist model? Or are judges simply sovereigns in black robes, making decisions independent of popular control? In this chapter, we examine these questions by exploring the role of the judiciary in American political life.

★ National Judicial Supremacy

Section 1 of Article III of the Constitution creates "one supreme Court." The founders were divided on the need for other national courts, so they deferred to Congress the decision to create a national court system. Those who opposed the creation of national courts believed that such a system would usurp the authority of state courts.[8] Congress considered the issue in its first session and, in the Judiciary Act of 1789, gave life to a system of federal (that is, national) courts that would coexist with the courts in each state but be independent of them. Federal judges would also be independent of popular influences because the Constitution provided for their virtual lifetime appointment.

In the early years of the Republic, the federal judiciary was not a particularly powerful branch of government. It was especially difficult to recruit and keep Supreme Court justices. They spent much of their time as individual traveling judges ("riding circuit"); disease and poor transportation were everyday hazards. The justices met as the Supreme Court only for a few weeks in February and August.[9] John Jay, the first chief justice, refused to resume his duties in 1801 because he concluded that the Court could not muster the "energy, weight, and dignity" to contribute to national affairs.[10] Several distinguished statesmen refused appointments to the Court, and several others, including Oliver Ellsworth, the third chief justice, resigned. But a period of profound change began in 1801 when President John Adams appointed his secretary of state, John Marshall, to the position of chief justice.

Judicial Review of the Other Branches

Shortly after Marshall's appointment, the Supreme Court confronted a question of fundamental importance to the future of the new republic: If a law enacted

Chief Justice John Marshall

John Marshall (1755–1835) clearly ranks as the Babe Ruth of the Supreme Court. Both Marshall and the Bambino transformed their respective games and became symbols of their institutions. Scholars now recognize both men as originators—Marshall of judicial review and Ruth of the modern age of baseball. *(The National Portrait Gallery/ Smithsonian Institution/Art Resource)*

by Congress conflicts with the U.S. Constitution, which should prevail? The question arose in the case of *Marbury* v. *Madison* (1803), which involved a controversial series of last-minute political appointments.

The case began in 1801, when an obscure Federalist, William Marbury, was designated a justice of the peace in the District of Columbia. Marbury and several others were appointed to government posts created by Congress in the last days of John Adams's presidency, but the appointments were never completed. The newly arrived Jefferson administration had little interest in delivering the required documents; qualified Jeffersonians would welcome the jobs.

To secure their jobs, Marbury and the other disgruntled appointees invoked an act of Congress to obtain the papers. The act authorized the Supreme Court to issue orders against government officials. Marbury and the others sought such an order in the Supreme Court against the new secretary of state, James Madison, who held the crucial documents.

Marshall observed that the act of Congress that Marbury invoked to sue in the Supreme Court conflicted with Article III of the U.S. Constitution, which did not authorize such suits. In February 1803, the Court delivered its opinion.*

Must the Court follow the law or the Constitution? The High Court held, in Marshall's forceful argument, that the Constitution was "the fundamental and paramount law of the nation" and that "an act of the legislature, repugnant to the constitution, is void." In other words, when an act of the legislature conflicts with the Constitution—the nation's highest law—that act is invalid. Marshall's argument vested in the judiciary the power to weigh the validity of congressional acts:

> It is emphatically the province and duty of the judicial department to say what the law is. Those who apply the rule to particular cases, must of necessity expound and interpret that rule. . . . So if a law be in opposition to the constitution; if both the law and the constitution apply to a particular case, so that the court must either decide that case conformably to the law, disregarding the constitution; or conformably to the constitution, disregarding the law; the court must determine which of these conflicting rules governs the case. This is of the very essence of judicial duty.[11]

The decision in *Marbury* v. *Madison* established the Supreme Court's power of **judicial review**—the power to declare congressional acts invalid if they violate the Constitution.[†] Subsequent cases extended the power to cover presidential acts as well.[12]

Marshall expanded the potential power of the Supreme Court to equal or exceed the power of the other branches of government. Should a congressional

judicial review The power to declare congressional (and presidential) acts invalid because they violate the Constitution.

---

*Courts publish their opinions in volumes called reporters. Today, the *United States Reports* is the official reporter for the U.S. Supreme Court. For example, the Court's opinion in the case of *Brown* v. *Board of Education* is cited as 347 U.S. 483 (1954). This means that the opinion in *Brown* begins on page 483 of Volume 347 in *United States Reports*. The citation includes the year of the decision, in this case, 1954.

Before 1875, the official reports of the Supreme Court were published under the names of private compilers. For example, the case of *Marbury* v. *Madison* is cited as 1 Cranch 137 (1803). This means that the case is found in Volume 1, compiled by reporter William Cranch, starting on page 137, and that it was decided in 1803.

†The Supreme Court had earlier upheld an act of Congress in *Hylton* v. *United States* (3 Dallas 171 [1796]). *Marbury* v. *Madison* was the first exercise of the power of a court to invalidate an act of Congress.

act (or, by implication, a presidential act) conflict with the Constitution, the Supreme Court claimed the power to declare the act void. The judiciary would be a check on the legislative and executive branches, consistent with the principle of checks and balances embedded in the Constitution. Although Congress and the president may sometimes wrestle with the constitutionality of their actions, judicial review gave the Supreme Court the final word on the meaning of the Constitution. The exercise of judicial review—an appointed branch's checking of an elected branch in the name of the Constitution—appears to run counter to democratic theory. But in more than two hundred years of practice, the Supreme Court has invalidated only about 160 provisions of national law. Only a small number have had great significance for the political system.[13] (In recent years, the Court has voided an exceptional number of national laws, including provisions of the Brady gun-control law, the Violence Against Women Act, the Americans with Disabilities Act, and the Age Discrimination in Employment Act; and the entire Communications Decency Act, Religious Freedom Restoration Act, Indian Land Consolidation Act, Gun-Free School Zones Act, and Bipartisan Campaign Reform Act.) The Constitution provides mechanisms to override judicial review (constitutional amendments) and to control excesses of the justices (impeachment), but these steps are more theoretical than practical. In addition, the Court can respond to the continuing struggle among competing interests (a struggle that is consistent with the pluralist model) by reversing itself.

Judicial Review of State Government

The establishment of judicial review of national laws made the Supreme Court the umpire of the national government. When acts of the national government conflict with the Constitution, the Supreme Court can declare those acts invalid. But suppose state laws conflict with the Constitution, national laws, or federal treaties: Can the U.S. Supreme Court invalidate them as well?

The Court answered in the affirmative in 1796. The case involved a British creditor who was trying to collect a debt from the state of Virginia.[14] Virginia law canceled debts owed to British subjects, yet the Treaty of Paris (1783), in which Britain formally acknowledged the independence of the colonies, guaranteed that creditors could collect such debts. The Court ruled that the Constitution's supremacy clause (Article VI), which embraces national laws and treaties, nullified the state law.

The states continued to resist the yoke of national supremacy. Advocates of strong states' rights conceded that the supremacy clause obligates state judges to follow the Constitution when state law conflicts with it; however, they maintained that the states were bound only by their own interpretation of the Constitution. The Supreme Court said no, ruling that it had the authority to review state court decisions calling for the interpretation of national law.[15] National supremacy required the Supreme Court to impose uniformity on national law; otherwise, the Constitution's meaning would vary from state to state. The people, not the states, had ordained the Constitution, and the people had subordinated state power to establish a viable national government. In time, the Supreme Court would use its judicial review power in nearly 1,200 instances to invalidate state and local laws, on issues as diverse as abortion, the death penalty, the rights of the accused, and reapportionment.[16]

Compared with What?

The Many Ways of Judicial Review

The U.S. Constitution does not explicitly give the Supreme Court the power of judicial review. In a controversial interpretation, the Court inferred this power from the text and structure of the Constitution. Other countries, trying to avoid political controversy over the power of their courts to review legislation, explicitly define that power in their constitutions. This is a noticeable fact in the design of post–World War II democratic political institutions. For example, Japan's constitution, inspired by the American model, went beyond it in providing that "the Supreme Court is the court of last resort with power to determine the constitutionality of any law, order, regulation, or official act."

The basic objection to the American form of judicial review is an unwillingness to place federal judges, who are usually appointed for life, above representatives elected by the people. Some constitutions explicitly deny judicial review. For example, Article 84 of the Belgian constitution (revised in 1994) firmly asserts that "the authoritative interpretation of laws is solely the prerogative of the Legislative authority."

The logical basis of judicial review—that government is responsible to a higher authority—can take interesting forms in other countries. In some, judges can invoke an authority higher than the constitution—God, an ideology, or a code of ethics. For example, both Iran and Pakistan provide

for an Islamic review of all legislation. (Pakistan also has the American form of judicial review.)

By 2000, about seventy countries—mostly in Western Europe, Latin America, Africa, and the Far East—had adopted some form of judicial review. Australia, Brazil, Canada, India, and Japan give their courts a full measure of judicial review power. Australia and Canada come closest to the American model of judicial review, but the fit is never exact. And wherever courts exercise judicial review, undoing it requires extraordinary effort. For example, the federal parliament in Australia has no recourse after a law is declared unconstitutional by its high court but to redraft the offending act in a manner prescribed by the court. In the United States, overruling judicial review by the Supreme Court would require a constitutional amendment.

Governments with a tradition of judicial review share some common characteristics: stability, competitive political parties, distribution of power (akin to separation of powers), a tradition of judicial independence, and a high degree of political freedom. Is judicial review the cause or the consequence of these characteristics? More likely than not, judicial review contributes to stability, judicial independence, and political freedom. And separation of powers, judicial independence, and political freedom contribute to the effectiveness of judicial review.

The Exercise of Judicial Review

These early cases, coupled with other historic decisions, established the components of judicial review:

- The power of the courts to declare national, state, and local laws invalid if they violate the Constitution

Some constitutional courts possess extraordinary power compared with the American model. The German constitutional court, for example, has the power to rectify the failure of the nation's lawmakers to act. In 1975, the German constitutional court nullified the legalization of abortion and declared that the government had a duty to protect unborn human life against all threats. The court concluded that the German constitution required the legislature to enact legislation protecting the fetus.

Some judges take their power at face value. South Africa created a constitutional court in 1995 and gave it powers on a par with the legislative and executive branches. In its first major decision, the court's eleven appointed justices abolished the death penalty, a decades-old practice that placed South Africa among the nations with the highest rate of capital punishment. "Everyone, including the most abominable of human beings, has a right to life, and capital punishment is therefore unconstitutional," declared the court's president.

The Supreme Court of India offers an extreme example of judicial review. In 1967, the court held that the Indian parliament could not change the fundamental rights sections of the country's constitution, even by constitutional amendment. The parliament then amended the constitution to secure its power to amend the constitution. The Supreme Court upheld the amendment but declared that any amendments that attacked the "basic structure" of the constitution would be invalid. In India, the Supreme Court is truly supreme.

Switzerland's Supreme Federal Tribunal is limited by the country's constitution to ruling on the constitutionality of cantonal laws (the Swiss equivalent of our state laws). It lacks the power to nullify laws passed by the national assembly. Through a constitutional initiative or a popular referendum, the Swiss people may exercise the sovereign right to determine the constitutionality of federal law. In Switzerland, the people are truly supreme.

In 2003, British prime minister Tony Blair moved to create an American-style supreme court and an independent commission to appoint its judges. Britain's highest judges (known as Law Lords) were both legislators in the House of Lords and judges. No other constitutional democracy makes its legislature the highest court. By imposing this separation of powers, Britain's judicial system would be decoupled from political control. This new Supreme Court of the United Kingdom will start work in 2009 and occupy its own building. But there are no plans to confer on the new high court the American power of judicial review, that is, the power to declare acts of Parliament void. Britain regards Parliament as supreme, and the new court will not challenge its primacy. Nevertheless, a worldwide consensus has emerged that the judiciary has become the safeguard of democracy and the rule of law, particularly in new democracies.

Sources: Henry J. Abraham, *The Judicial Process,* 7th ed. (New York: Oxford University Press, 1998), pp. 229–334; Chester J. Antineau, *Adjudicating Constitutional Issues* (London: Oceana, 1985), pp. 1–6; Jerold L. Waltman and Kenneth M. Holland, *The Political Role of Law Courts in Modern Democracies* (New York: St. Martin's Press, 1988), pp. 46, 99–100; Robert L. Hardgrave, Jr., and Stanley A. Kochanek, *India: Government and Politics in a Developing Nation,* 5th ed. (New York: Harcourt Brace Jovanovich, 1993), p. 102; Howard W. French, "South Africa's Supreme Court Abolishes Death Penalty," *New York Times,* 7 June 1995, p. A3; C. Neal Tate, *Comparative Judicial Systems* (Washington, D.C.: CQ Press, 2004); Warren Hoge, "Blair Seeks a Supreme Court Modeled on the U.S. Version," *New York Times,* 15 June 2003, p. 16; C. Neal Tate and Torbjorn Vallinder, *The Global Expansion of Judicial Power* (New York: New York University Press, 1995); Nathan J. Brown, "Judicial Review and the Arab World," *Journal of Democracy* 9 (October 1998).

■ The supremacy of national laws or treaties when they conflict with state and local laws

■ The role of the Supreme Court as the final authority on the meaning of the Constitution

This political might—the power to undo decisions of the representative branches of the national and state governments—lay in the hands of appointed

Can you explain why . . .
the Supreme Court's power to invalidate unconstitutional laws might be construed as antidemocratic?

judges, that is, people who were not accountable to the electorate. Did judicial review square with democratic government?

Alexander Hamilton had foreseen and tackled the problem in *Federalist* No. 78. Writing during the ratification debates surrounding the adoption of the Constitution (see Chapter 3), Hamilton maintained that despite the power of judicial review, the judiciary would be the weakest of the three branches of government because it lacked the strength of the sword or the purse. The judiciary, wrote Hamilton, had "neither FORCE nor WILL, but merely judgment."

Although Hamilton was defending legislative supremacy, he argued that judicial review was an essential barrier to legislative oppression.[17] He recognized that the power to declare government acts void implied the superiority of the courts over the other branches. But this power, he contended, simply reflects the will of the people, declared in the Constitution, as opposed to the will of the legislature, expressed in its statutes. Judicial independence, guaranteed by lifetime tenure and protected salaries, frees judges from executive and legislative control, minimizing the risk of their deviating from the law established in the Constitution. If judges make a mistake, the people or their elected representatives have the means to correct the error, through constitutional amendments and impeachment.

Their lifetime tenure does free judges from the direct influence of the president and Congress. And although mechanisms to check judicial power are in place, these mechanisms require extraordinary majorities and are rarely used. When they exercise the power of judicial review, then, judges can and occasionally do operate counter to majoritarian rule by invalidating the actions of the people's elected representatives. (See "Compared with What? The Many Ways of Judicial Review" for a discussion of the nature of judicial review in other governments, democratic and nondemocratic.)

★ The Organization of Courts

The American court system is complex, partly as a result of our federal system of government. Each state runs its own court system, and no two states' courts are identical. In addition, we have a system of courts for the national government. The national, or federal, courts coexist with the state courts (see Figure 14.1). Individuals fall under the jurisdiction of both court systems. They can sue or be sued in either system, depending mostly on what their case is about. Litigants file nearly all cases (99 percent) in state courts.[18] State trial courts receive on average one civil, domestic relations, criminal, juvenile, or traffic case for every three citizens. The volume of state court cases continues to rise at about 1 percent a year.[19]

Can you explain why . . .
the number of state court cases continues to rise?

Some Court Fundamentals

Courts are full of mystery to citizens uninitiated in their activities. Lawyers, judges, and seasoned observers understand the language, procedures, and norms associated with legal institutions. Let's start with some fundamentals.

Criminal and Civil Cases. A crime is a violation of a law that forbids or commands an activity. Criminal laws are created, amended, and repealed by state legislatures. These laws and the punishments for violating them are recorded in each state's penal code. Some crimes—murder, rape, arson—are on

FIGURE 14.1 The Federal and State Court Systems, 2006–2007

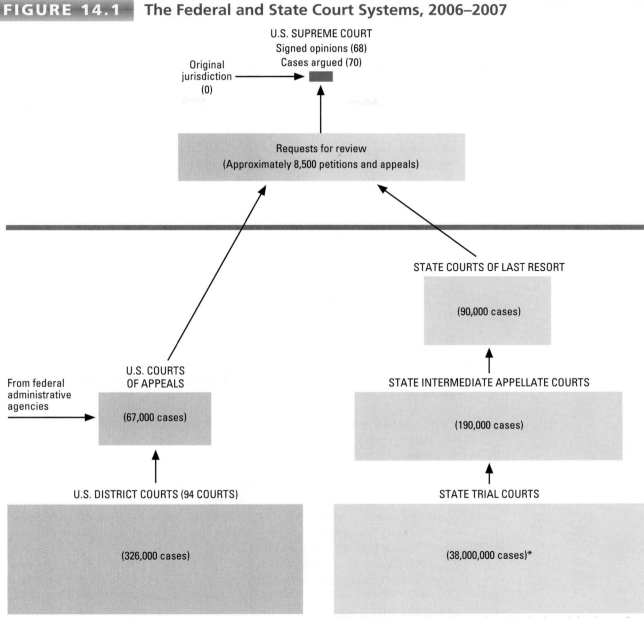

U.S. SUPREME COURT
Signed opinions (68)
Cases argued (70)

Original jurisdiction (0)

Requests for review
(Approximately 8,500 petitions and appeals)

STATE COURTS OF LAST RESORT

(90,000 cases)

U.S. COURTS OF APPEALS

From federal administrative agencies

(67,000 cases)

STATE INTERMEDIATE APPELLATE COURTS

(190,000 cases)

U.S. DISTRICT COURTS (94 COURTS)

(326,000 cases)

STATE TRIAL COURTS

(38,000,000 cases)*

* Note: If this box were shown in proportion to the other boxes below the gray line, the actual size would be approximately 3 feet wide × 1 foot high.

The federal courts have three tiers: district courts, courts of appeals, and the Supreme Court. The Supreme Court was created by the Constitution; all other federal courts were created by Congress. State courts dwarf federal courts, at least in terms of case load. There are more than one hundred state cases for every federal case filed. The structure of state courts varies from state to state; usually, there are minor trial courts for less serious cases, major trial courts for more serious cases, intermediate appellate courts, and supreme courts. State courts were created by state constitutions.

Sources: John Roberts, "The 2006 Year-End Report on the Federal Judiciary," 1 January 2007, available at <http://www.supremecourtus.gov/publicinfo/year-end/2006year-endreport.pdf>; "Federal Court Management Statistics 2005," available at <http://www.uscourts.gov/fcmstat/index.html>; Court Statistics Project, "State Court Caseload Statistics, 2005" (National Center for State Courts, 2005), available at <http://www.ncsconline.org/d_research/csp/2005_files/state%court%20caseload %20statistics%202005.pdf>.

the books of every state. Others—marijuana use, for example—are considered crimes in certain states but not all. Because crime is a violation of public order, the government prosecutes **criminal cases.** Maintaining public order through the criminal law is largely a state and local function. Criminal cases brought by the national government represent only a small fraction of all criminal cases prosecuted in the United States. In theory, the national penal code is limited by the principle of federalism. The code is aimed at activities that fall under the delegated and implied powers of the national government, enabling the government, for example, to criminalize tax evasion or the use of computers and laser printers to counterfeit money, bank checks, or even college transcripts.

Fighting crime is popular, and politicians sometimes outbid one another in their efforts to get tough on criminals. National crime-fighting measures have begun to usurp areas long viewed to be under state authority. Since 1975, Congress has added hundreds of new federal criminal provisions covering a wide range of activities once thought to be within the states' domain, including carjacking, willful failure to pay child support, and crossing state lines to engage in gang-related street crime.[20]

Courts decide both criminal and civil cases. **Civil cases** stem from disputed claims to something of value. Disputes arise from accidents, contractual obligations, and divorce, for example. Often the parties disagree over tangible issues (possession of property, custody of children), but civil cases can involve more abstract issues too (the right to equal accommodations, compensation for pain and suffering). The government can be a party to civil disputes, called on to defend its actions or to allege wrongdoing.

Procedures and Policymaking. Most civil and criminal cases never go to trial. In most criminal cases, the defendant's lawyer and the prosecutor **plea-bargain,** negotiating the severity and number of charges to be brought against the defendant. In a civil case, one side may only be using the threat of a lawsuit to exact a concession from the other. Often the parties *settle* (or resolve between themselves), because of the uncertainties involved in litigation. Though rare, settlement can occur even at the level of the Supreme Court. And sometimes, the initiating parties (the plaintiffs in civil cases) may simply abandon their efforts, leaving disputes unresolved.

When cases are neither settled nor abandoned, they end with an *adjudication,* a court judgment resolving the parties' claims and enforced by the government. When trial judges adjudicate cases, they may offer written reasons to support their decisions. When the issues or circumstances of cases are novel, judges may publish *opinions,* explanations justifying their rulings.

Judges make policy in two different ways. The first is through their rulings on matters that no existing legislation addresses. Such rulings set precedents that judges rely on in future, similar cases. We call this body of rules the **common, or judge-made, law.** The roots of the common law lie in the English legal system. Contracts, property, and torts (injuries or wrongs to the person or property of another) are common-law domains. The second area of judicial lawmaking involves the application of statutes enacted by legislatures. The judicial interpretation of legislative acts is called *statutory construction.* The proper application of a statute is not always clear from its wording. To determine how a statute should be applied, judges look for the legislature's intent, reading reports of committee hearings and debates. If these sources do not clarify the statute's meaning, the court does so. With or without legislation to

criminal case A court case involving a crime, or violation of public order.

civil case A court case that involves a private dispute arising from such matters as accidents, contractual obligations, and divorce.

plea bargain A defendant's admission of guilt in exchange for a less severe punishment.

common (judge-made) law Legal precedents derived from previous judicial decisions.

guide them, judges look to the relevant opinions of higher courts for authority to decide the issues before them.

The federal courts are organized in three tiers, as a pyramid. At the bottom of the pyramid are the **U.S. district courts,** where litigation begins. In the middle are the **U.S. courts of appeals.** At the top is the Supreme Court of the United States. To *appeal* means to take a case to a higher court. The courts of appeals and the Supreme Court are appellate courts; with few exceptions, they review only cases that have already been decided in lower courts. Most federal courts hear and decide a wide array of civil and criminal cases.

The U.S. District Courts

There are ninety-four federal district courts in the United States. Each state has at least one district court, and no district straddles more than one state.[21] In 2006, there were 678 full-time federal district judgeships, and they received over 326,000 new criminal and civil cases.[22]

The district courts are the entry point for the federal court system. When trials occur in the federal system, they take place in the federal district courts. Here is where witnesses testify, lawyers conduct cross-examinations, and judges and juries decide the fate of litigants. More than one judge may sit in each district court, but each case is tried by a single judge, sitting alone. U.S. magistrate-judges assist district judges, but they lack independent judicial authority. Magistrate-judges have the power to hear and decide minor offenses and conduct preliminary stages of more serious cases. District court judges appoint magistrate-judges for eight-year (full-time) or four-year (part-time) terms. In 2006, there were 503 full-time and 45 part-time magistrate-judges.[23]

Sources of Litigation.   Today, the authority of U.S. district courts extends to the following:

- Federal criminal cases, as defined by national law (for example, robbery of a nationally insured bank or interstate transportation of stolen securities)

- Civil cases, brought by individuals, groups, or the government, alleging violation of national law (for example, failure of a municipality to implement pollution-control regulations required by a national agency)

- Civil cases brought against the national government (for example, a vehicle manufacturer sues the motor pool of a government agency for its failure to take delivery of a fleet of new cars)

- Civil cases between citizens of different states when the amount in controversy exceeds $75,000 (for example, when a citizen of New York sues a citizen of Alabama in a U.S. district court in Alabama for damages stemming from an auto accident that occurred in Alabama)

U.S. district court A court within the lowest tier of the three-tiered federal court system; a court where litigation begins.

The U.S. Courts of Appeals

All cases resolved in a U.S. district court and all decisions of federal administrative agencies can be appealed to one of the twelve regional U.S. courts of appeals. These courts, with 167 full-time judgeships, received nearly 67,000 new cases in 2006.[24] Each appeals court hears cases from a geographical area

U.S. court of appeals A court within the second tier of the three-tiered federal court system, to which decisions of the district courts and federal agencies may be appealed for review.

known as a *circuit*. The U.S. Court of Appeals for the Seventh Circuit, for example, is located in Chicago; it hears appeals from the U.S. district courts in Illinois, Wisconsin, and Indiana. The United States is divided into twelve circuits.*

Appellate Court Proceedings. Appellate court proceedings are public, but they usually lack courtroom drama. There are no jurors, witnesses, or cross-examinations; these are features only of the trial courts. Appeals are based strictly on the rulings made and procedures followed in the trial courts. Suppose, for example, that in the course of a criminal trial, a U.S. district judge allows the introduction of evidence that convicts a defendant but was obtained under questionable circumstances. The defendant can appeal on the ground that the evidence was obtained in the absence of a valid search warrant and so was inadmissible. The issue on appeal is the admissibility of the evidence, not the defendant's guilt or innocence. If the appellate court agrees with the trial judge's decision to admit the evidence, the conviction stands. If the appellate court disagrees with the trial judge and rules that the evidence is inadmissible, the defendant must be retried without the incriminating evidence or be released.

The courts of appeals are regional courts. They usually convene in panels of three judges to render judgments. The judges receive written arguments known as *briefs* (which are also sometimes submitted in trial courts). Often the judges hear oral arguments and question the lawyers to probe their arguments.

Precedents and Making Decisions. Following review of the briefs and, in many appeals, oral arguments, the three-judge panel meets to reach a judgment. One judge attempts to summarize the panel's views, although each judge remains free to disagree with the judgment or the reasons for it. When an appellate opinion is published, its influence can reach well beyond the immediate case. For example, a lawsuit turning on the meaning of the Constitution produces a ruling, which then serves as a **precedent** for subsequent cases; that is, the decision becomes a basis for deciding similar cases in the future in the same way. Thus, judges make public policy to the extent that they influence decisions in other courts. Although district judges sometimes publish their opinions, it is the exception rather than the rule. At the appellate level, however, precedent requires that opinions be written.

Making decisions according to precedent is central to the operation of our legal system, providing continuity and predictability. The bias in favor of existing decisions is captured by the Latin expression *stare decisis,* which means "let the decision stand." But the use of precedent and the principle of **stare decisis** do not make lower-court judges cogs in a judicial machine. "If precedent clearly governed," remarked one federal judge, "a case would never get as far as the Court of Appeals: the parties would settle."[25]

Judges on the courts of appeals direct their energies to correcting errors in district court proceedings and interpreting the law (in the course of writing opinions). When judges interpret the law, they often modify existing laws. In effect, they are making policy. Judges are politicians in the sense that they ex-

precedent A judicial ruling that serves as the basis for the ruling in a subsequent case.

stare decisis Literally, "let the decision stand"; decision making according to precedent.

*The thirteenth court, the U.S. Court of Appeals for the Federal Circuit, is not a regional court. It specializes in appeals involving patents, contract claims against the national government, and federal employment cases.

ercise political power, but the black robes that distinguish judges from other politicians signal constraints on their exercise of power.

Uniformity of Law. Decisions by the courts of appeals ensure a measure of uniformity in the application of national law. For example, when similar issues are dealt with in the decisions of different district judges, the decisions may be inconsistent. The courts of appeals harmonize the decisions within their region so that laws are applied uniformly.

The regional character of the courts of appeals undermines uniformity somewhat because the courts are not bound by the decisions of other circuits. A law may be interpreted differently in different courts of appeals. For example, the Internal Revenue Code imposes identical tax burdens on similar individuals. But thanks to the regional character of the courts of appeals, national tax laws may be applied differently throughout the United States. The percolation of cases up through the federal system of courts virtually guarantees that at some point, two or more courts of appeals, working with similar sets of facts, are going to interpret the same law differently. However, the problem of conflicting decisions in the intermediate appellate courts can be corrected by review in the Supreme Court, where policymaking, not error correction, is the paramount goal.

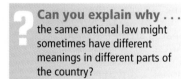

Can you explain why . . . the same national law might sometimes have different meanings in different parts of the country?

★ The Supreme Court

Above the west portico of the Supreme Court building are inscribed the words EQUAL JUSTICE UNDER LAW. At the opposite end of the building, above the east portico, are the words JUSTICE THE GUARDIAN OF LIBERTY. The mottos reflect the Court's difficult task: achieving a just balance among the values of freedom, order, and equality. Consider how these values came into conflict in two controversial issues the Court has faced.

Flag burning as a form of political protest pits the value of order, or the government's interest in maintaining a peaceful society, against the value of freedom, including the individual's right to vigorous and unbounded political expression. In two flag-burning cases, the Supreme Court affirmed constitutional protection for unbridled political expression, including the emotionally charged act of desecrating a national symbol.[26] Because under a pluralist system no decision is ever truly final, the flag-burning decisions hardly quelled the demand for laws to punish flag desecration. In 2006, Congress inched ever so close to a constitutional amendment banning flag desecration. The proposal passed by more than two-thirds vote in the House but failed by a single vote in the Senate.

School desegregation pits the value of equality against the value of freedom. In *Brown v. Board of Education* (1954), the Supreme Court carried the banner of racial equality by striking down state-mandated segregation in public schools. The decision helped launch a revolution in race relations in the United States. The justices recognized the disorder their decision would create in a society accustomed to racial bias, but in this case, equality clearly outweighed freedom. Twenty-four years later, the Court was still embroiled in controversy over equality when it ruled that race could be a factor in university admissions (to diversify the student body).[27] Having secured equality for blacks, the Court in 2003 faced the charge by white students who sought admission to

A list of Justices of the Supreme Court Since 1900 is available on the

Online Study Center
General Resources

INTERACTIVE 14.1

 Flag Fight: Free Speech or Felony

INTERACTIVE 14.2

 U.S. Supreme Court

The Supreme Court, 2006 Term: The Lineup

The justices of the Supreme Court of the United States. Seated are (*left to right*) Anthony Kennedy, John Paul Stevens, Chief Justice John Roberts, Antonin Scalia, and David Souter. Standing are Stephen Breyer, Clarence Thomas, Ruth Bader Ginsburg, and Samuel Alito. (*© Brooks Kraft/Corbis*)

IDEAlog.org

Do you support or oppose affirmative action? After reading the material here, would your answer be the same? Take IDEAlog's self-test.

the University of Michigan that it was denying whites the freedom to compete for admission. A slim Court majority concluded that the equal protection clause of the Fourteenth Amendment did not prohibit the narrowly tailored use of race as *a* factor in law school admissions but rejected the automatic use of racial categories to award fixed points toward undergraduate admissions.[28]

The Supreme Court makes national policy. Because its decisions have far-reaching effects on all of us, it is vital that we understand how it reaches those decisions. With this understanding, we can better evaluate how the Court fits within our model of democracy.

Access to the Court

There are rules of access that must be followed to bring a case to the Supreme Court. Also important is a sensitivity to the justices' policy and ideological preferences. The notion that anyone can take a case all the way to the Supreme Court is true only in theory, not fact.

The Supreme Court's cases come from two sources. A few arrive under the Court's **original jurisdiction,** conferred by Article III, Section 2, of the Constitution, which gives the Court the power to hear and decide "all Cases affecting Ambassadors, other public Ministers and Consuls, and those in which a State shall be Party." Cases falling under the Court's original jurisdiction are tried and decided in the Court itself; the cases begin and end there. For example, the Court is the first and only forum in which legal disputes between states are resolved. It hears few original jurisdiction cases today, however, usually referring them to a special master, often a retired judge, who reviews the parties' contentions and recommends a resolution that the justices are free to accept or reject.

original jurisdiction The authority of a court to hear a case before any other court does.

appellate jurisdiction The authority of a court to hear cases that have been tried, decided, or reexamined in other courts.

Most cases enter the Supreme Court from the U.S. courts of appeals or the state courts of last resort. This is the Court's **appellate jurisdiction.** These cases have been tried, decided, and reexamined as far as the law permits in other federal or state courts. The Court exercises judicial power under its appellate jurisdiction only because Congress gives it the authority to do so. Con-

FIGURE 14.2 Access to and Decision Making in the U.S. Supreme Court, 2006 Term

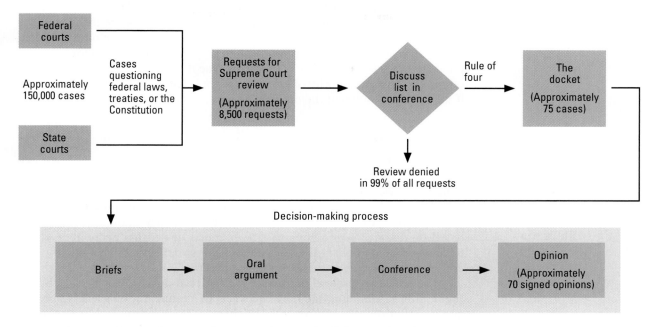

State and national appeals courts churn out thousands of decisions each year. Only a fraction end up on the Supreme Court's docket. This chart sketches the several stages leading to a decision from the High Court.

Source: John G. Roberts, Jr., "The 2006 Year-End Report on the Federal Judiciary," *Third Branch: Newsletter of the Federal Courts,* available at <www.uscourts.gov/ttb/jan07ttb/appendix/index.html>.

gress may change (and, perhaps, eliminate) the Court's appellate jurisdiction. This is a powerful but rarely used weapon in the congressional arsenal of checks and balances.

Litigants in state cases who invoke the Court's appellate jurisdiction must satisfy two conditions. First, the case must have reached the end of the line in the state court system. Litigants cannot jump at will from a state to the national arena of justice. Second, the case must raise a **federal question,** that is, an issue covered by the Constitution, federal laws, or national treaties. But even cases that meet both of these conditions do not guarantee review by the Court.

Since 1925, the Court has exercised substantial (today, nearly complete) control over its **docket,** or agenda (see Figure 14.2). The Court selects a handful of cases (fewer than one hundred) for full consideration from the eight thousand or more requests filed each year. These requests take the form of petitions for *certiorari,* in which a litigant seeking review asks the Court "to become informed" of the lower-court proceeding. For the vast majority of cases, the Court denies the petition for *certiorari,* leaving the decision of the lower court undisturbed. No explanations accompany these denials, so they have little or no value as Court rulings.

The Court grants a review only when four or more justices agree that a case warrants full consideration. This unwritten rule is known as the **rule of four.**

federal question An issue covered by the U.S. Constitution, national laws, or U.S. treaties.

docket A court's agenda.

rule of four An unwritten rule that requires at least four justices to agree that a case warrants consideration before it is reviewed by the U.S. Supreme Court.

With advance preparation by their law clerks, who screen petitions and prepare summaries, all nine justices make these judgments at secret conferences held twice a week.[29] During the conferences, justices vote on previously argued cases and consider which new cases to add to the docket. The chief justice circulates a "discuss list" of worthy petitions. Cases on the list are then subject to the rule of four. Though it takes only four votes to place a case on the docket, it may ultimately take an enormous leap to garner a fifth, and deciding, vote on the merits of the appeal. This is especially true if the Court is sharply split ideologically. Thus, a minority of justices in favor of an appeal may oppose review if they are not confident the outcome will be to their satisfaction.[30]

The Solicitor General

Why does the Court decide to hear certain cases but not others? The best evidence scholars have adduced suggests that agenda setting depends on the individual justices, who vary in their decision-making criteria, and on the issues raised by the cases. Occasionally, justices weigh the ultimate outcome of a case when granting or denying review. At other times, they grant or deny review based on disagreement among the lower courts or because delay in resolving the issues would impose alarming economic or social costs.[31] The solicitor general plays a vital role in the Court's agenda setting.

The **solicitor general** represents the national government before the Supreme Court, serving as the hinge between an administration's legal approach and its policy objectives. Appointed by the president, the solicitor general is the third-ranking official in the U.S. Department of Justice (after the attorney general and the deputy attorney general).

By a razor-thin vote in 2001, the Senate confirmed President George W. Bush's nomination of Theodore B. Olson as his solicitor general. Olson had rescued Bush's presidential bid by arguing before the justices in December 2000 that the ballot counting in Florida should stop. (Olson resigned in 2004.) Today, the solicitor general is Paul D. Clement.

The solicitor general's duties include determining whether the government should appeal lower-court decisions; reviewing and modifying, when necessary, the briefs filed in government appeals; and deciding whether the government should file an **amicus curiae brief**[*] in any appellate court.[32] The objective is to create a cohesive program for the executive branch in the federal courts.

Solicitors general play two different, and occasionally conflicting, roles. First, they are advocates for the president's policy preferences; second, as officers of the Court, they traditionally defend the institutional interests of the national government.

Solicitors general usually act with considerable restraint in recommending to the Court that a case be granted or denied review. By recommending only cases of general importance, they increase their credibility and their influence.

By carefully selecting the cases it presses, the solicitor general's office usually maintains a very impressive record of wins in the Supreme Court. Solicitors general are a "formidable force" in the process of setting the Supreme Court's

solicitor general The third-highest official of the U.S. Department of Justice, and the one who represents the national government before the Supreme Court.

amicus curiae brief A brief filed (with the permission of the court) by an individual or group that is not a party to a legal action but has an interest in it.

---

[*]*Amicus curiae* is Latin for "friend of the court." Amicus briefs can be filed with the consent of all the parties or with the permission of the court. They allow groups and individuals who are not parties to the litigation but have an interest in it to influence the court's thinking and, perhaps, its decision.

agenda.[33] Their influence in bringing cases to the Court and arguing them there has earned them the informal title of "the tenth justice."

Decision Making

Once the Court grants review, attorneys submit written arguments (briefs). Oral arguments, typically limited to thirty minutes for each side, usually follow. From October through April, the justices spend four hours a day, five or six days a month, hearing arguments. Experience seems to help. Like the solicitor general, seasoned advocates enjoy a greater success rate, regardless of the party they represent.[34] The justices like crisp, concise, conversational presentations; they disapprove of attorneys who read from a prepared text. Some justices are aggressive, relentless questioners who frequently interrupt the lawyers; others are more subdued. In a 1993 free speech case, an attorney who offered an impassioned plea on the facts of the case was soon "awash in a sea of judicial impatience that at times seemed to border on anger. . . . 'We didn't take this case to determine who said what in the cafeteria,'" snapped one justice.[35]

Court protocol prohibits the justices from addressing one another directly during oral arguments, but they often debate obliquely through the questions they pose to the attorneys. The justices reach no collective decision at the time of oral arguments. They reach a tentative decision only after they have met in conference.

Our knowledge of the dynamics of decision making on the Supreme Court is all secondhand. Only the justices attend the Court's Wednesday and Friday conferences. By tradition, the justices first shake hands prior to conference and to going on the bench, a gesture of harmony. The handshaking was introduced by Melville Fuller when he was chief justice from 1888 to 1910.[36] The chief justice then begins the presentation of each case with a discussion of it and his vote, which is followed by a discussion and vote from each of the other justices, in order of their seniority on the Court. Justice Antonin Scalia, who

"Who would have thought that under the hat sat Justice Stephen G. Breyer? How about that—a judicial cat!"

Taking a break from his judicial duties, Justice Stephen G. Breyer read Dr. Seuss's "Oh, the Places You'll Go!" to elementary school students in the Supreme Court library on March 3, 2003, to celebrate what would have been the ninety-ninth birthday of Theodor Geisel, who wrote as Dr. Seuss. *(Evan Vucci/AP/Wide World Photos)*

"So three lawyers approach the bar . . . "

Justice Anthony Kennedy enjoys a light moment with his clerks. Justices assign a range of responsibilities to their four clerks, from memo preparation to opinion drafting. The typical clerkship lasts a year, though it may seem longer at times because of the demanding work schedule. Despite the absence of overtime pay, there is no shortage of applications from the best graduates of the best law schools. *(Photo by David Hume Kennerly/Getty Images)*

joined the Court in 1986, remarked that "not much conferencing goes on." By *conferencing*, Scalia meant efforts to persuade others to change their view by debating points of disagreement. "To call our discussion of a case a conference," he said, "is really something of a misnomer. It's much more a statement of the views of each of the nine Justices, after which the totals are added and the case is assigned" for an opinion.[37]

Judicial Restraint and Judicial Activism. How do the justices decide how to vote on a case? According to some scholars, legal doctrines and previous decisions explain their votes. This explanation, which is consistent with the majoritarian model, anchors the justices closely to the law and minimizes the contribution of their personal values. This view is embodied in the concept of **judicial restraint,** which maintains that legislators, not judges, should make the laws. Judges are said to exercise judicial restraint when they hew closely to statutes and previous cases in reaching their decisions. Other scholars contend that the value preferences and resulting ideologies of the justices provide a more powerful interpretation of their voting.[38] This view is embodied in the concept of **judicial activism,** which maintains that judges should interpret laws loosely, using their power to promote their preferred social and political goals. Judges are said to be activists when they are likely to interpret existing laws and rulings with little regard to precedent and to interject their own values into court decisions, a pattern more consistent with the pluralist model.

The terms *judicial restraint* and *judicial activism* describe different relative degrees of judicial assertiveness. Judges acting according to an extreme model of judicial restraint would never question the validity of duly enacted laws but would defer to the superiority of other government institutions in construing the laws. Judges acting according to an extreme model of judicial activism would be an intrusive and ever-present force that would dominate other government institutions. Actual judicial behavior lies somewhere between these two extremes.

judicial restraint A judicial philosophy whereby judges adhere closely to statutes and precedents in reaching their decisions.

judicial activism A judicial philosophy whereby judges interpret existing laws and precedents loosely and interject their own values in court decisions.

FIGURE 14.3 Measuring Judicial Activism

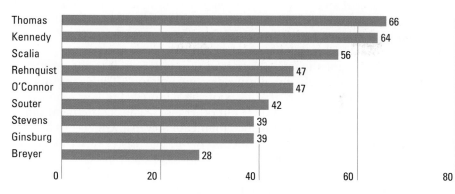

Votes to strike down congressional acts, 1994–2005 (percentage)

The terms *activism* and *restraint* are not tied to a particular ideology. They simply describe a behavior. Conservatives and liberals are equally capable of exercising activism or restraint. One measure of activism is the extent to which judges are inclined to strike down congressional acts. Of course, judicial invalidation of legislation may be appropriate, but that requires an examination of the reasons behind a particular vote. From 1994 through 2005, the Supreme Court led by Chief Justice William Rehnquist confronted sixty-four congressional acts that the justices voted to uphold or strike down. This figure shows that the more conservative justices during this period tended to greater activism than the more liberal justices.

Source: Data from Paul Gewirtz and Chad Golder, "So Who Are the Activists?" *New York Times,* 6 July 2005, p. A19.

In recent history, many activist judges have tended to support liberal values, thus linking judicial activism with liberalism. But the critical case of *Bush* v. *Gore* suggests to many critics that conservative jurists can also be judicial activists, promoting their preferred political goals. Had a majority deferred to the Florida courts on the issue of the recount, the decision would have been hailed as an example of judicial restraint. But overturning the Florida courts and delivering a victory for the Republicans has labeled the majority in *Bush* v. *Gore* as conservative judicial activists (see also Figure 14.3).

Judgment and Argument.   The voting outcome is the **judgment,** the decision on who wins and who loses. The justices often disagree not only on the winner and loser, but also on the reasons for their judgment. This should not be surprising, given nine independent minds and issues that can be approached in several ways. Voting in the conference does not end the justices' work or resolve their disagreements. Votes remain tentative until the Court issues an opinion announcing its judgment.

After voting, the justices in the majority must draft an opinion setting out the reasons for their decision. The **argument** is the kernel of the opinion—its logical content, as distinct from supporting facts, rhetoric, and procedures. If all justices agree with the judgment and the reasons supporting it, the opinion is unanimous. Agreement with a judgment for different reasons from those set forth in the majority opinion is called a **concurrence.** Or a justice can **dissent** if she or he disagrees with a judgment. Both concurring and dissenting opinions may be drafted, in addition to the majority opinion.

The Opinion.   After the conference, the chief justice or most senior justice in the majority (in terms of years of service on the Court) decides which justice will write the majority opinion. He or she may consider several factors in assigning the crucial opinion-writing task, including the prospective author's workload, expertise, public opinion, and (above all) ability to hold the majority together. (Remember that the votes are only tentative at this point.) On the one hand, if the drafting justice holds an extreme view on the issues in a case

judgment The judicial decision in a court case.

argument The heart of a judicial opinion; its logical content separated from facts, rhetoric, and procedure.

concurrence The agreement of a judge with the Court's majority decision, for a reason other than the majority reason.

dissent The disagreement of a judge with a majority decision.

and is not able to incorporate the views of more moderate colleagues, those justices may withdraw their votes. On the other hand, assigning a more moderate justice to draft an opinion could weaken the argument on which the opinion rests. Opinion-writing assignments can also be punitive. Justice Harry Blackmun once commented, "If one's in the doghouse with the Chief [former Chief Justice Warren Burger], he gets the crud."[39]

Opinion writing is the justices' most critical function. It is not surprising, then, that they spend much of their time drafting opinions. The justices usually call on their law clerks—top graduates of the nation's elite law schools—to help them prepare opinions and carry out other tasks. The commitment can be daunting. With the exception of Justice John Paul Stevens, who writes his own first drafts of opinions, all of the justices rely on their clerks to shoulder substantial responsibilities, including the initial drafts of opinions.[40]

The writing justice distributes a draft opinion to all the justices, who then read it and circulate their criticisms and suggestions. An opinion may have to be rewritten several times to accommodate colleagues who remain unpersuaded by the draft. Justice Felix Frankfurter was a perfectionist; some of his opinions went through thirty or more drafts. Justices can change their votes, and perhaps alter the judgment, until the decision is officially announced. Often, the most controversial cases pile up as coalitions on the Court vie for support or sharpen their criticisms. When the Court announces a decision, the justices who wrote the opinion read or summarize their views in the courtroom.

Justices in the majority frequently try to muffle or stifle dissent to encourage institutional cohesion. Since the mid-1940s, however, unity has been more difficult to obtain.[41] Gaining agreement from the justices today is akin to negotiating with nine separate law firms. It may be more surprising that the justices ever agree. In 2006, for example, the Court spoke without dissent in more than half of its cases. The conservative shift occasioned by the appointments of Roberts and Alito has infused cohesion among dissenters, who have tended to join a single opinion. And the Court's genteel etiquette appears strained as once collegial justices voice their views publicly and forcefully from the bench.[42]

The justices remain aware of the slender foundation of their authority, which rests largely on public respect. That respect is tested whenever the Court ventures into controversial areas. Banking, slavery, and Reconstruction policies embroiled the Court in the nineteenth century. Freedom of speech and religion, racial equality, the right to privacy, the 2000 election, and the extent of presidential power have led the Court into controversy in the last sixty years.

Strategies on the Court

The Court is more than the sum of its formal processes. The justices exercise real political power. If we start with the assumption that the justices attempt to stamp their own policy views on the cases they review, we should expect typical political behavior from them. Cases that reach the Supreme Court's docket pose difficult choices. Because the justices are grappling with conflict on a daily basis, they probably have well-defined ideologies that reflect their values. Scholars and journalists have attempted to pierce the veil of secrecy that shrouds the Court from public view and analyze the justices' ideologies.[43]

The beliefs of most justices can be located on the two-dimensional model of political values discussed in Chapter 1 (see Figure 1.2). Liberal justices, such as John Paul Stevens and Ruth Bader Ginsburg, choose freedom over order and equality over freedom. Conservative justices—Antonin Scalia and Clarence

Deal
Chief Justice John G. Roberts, Jr., greets newest colleague, Associate Justice Samuel A. Alito. Both Roberts and Alito possess strong conservative credentials. Their appointments were a consequence of Republican victories in the 2004 elections. The Court has now shifted in a more conservative direction.
(© Tim Sloan/AFP/Getty Images)

Thomas, for example—choose order over freedom and freedom over equality. These choices translate into clear policy preferences.

As in any other group of people, the justices also vary in their intellectual ability, advocacy skills, social graces, temperament, and other characteristics. For example, Chief Justice Charles Evans Hughes (1930–1941) had a photographic memory and came to each conference armed with well-marked copies of Supreme Court opinions. Few justices could keep up with him in debates. Then, as now, justices argue for the support of their colleagues, offering information in the form of drafts and memoranda to explain the advantages and disadvantages of voting for or against an issue. And justices make occasional, if not regular, use of friendship, ridicule, and appeals to patriotism to mold their colleagues' views.

A justice might adopt a long-term strategy of encouraging the appointment of like-minded colleagues to marshal additional strength on the Court. Chief Justice (and former president) William Howard Taft, for example, bombarded President Warren G. Harding with recommendations and suggestions whenever a Court vacancy was announced. Taft was especially determined to block the appointment of anyone who might side with the "dangerous twosome," Justices Oliver Wendell Holmes and Louis D. Brandeis. Taft said he "must stay on the court in order to prevent the Bolsheviki from getting control."[44]

The Chief Justice

The chief justice is only one of nine justices, but he has several important functions based on his authority. Apart from his role in forming the docket and directing the Court's conferences, the chief justice can also be a social leader, generating solidarity within the group. Sometimes a chief justice can embody intellectual leadership. Finally, the chief justice can provide policy leadership, directing the Court toward a general policy position. Perhaps only John Marshall could lay claim to possessing social, intellectual, and policy leadership.

Warren E. Burger, who resigned as chief justice in 1986, was reputed to be a lackluster leader in all three areas.[45]

When presiding at the conference, the chief justice can control the discussion of issues, although independent-minded justices are not likely to acquiesce to his views. Moreover, justices today rarely engage in a debate of the issues in the conference. Rather, they use their law clerks as ambassadors between justices' chambers and, in effect, "run the Court without talking to one another."[46]

★ Judicial Recruitment

Neither the Constitution nor national law imposes formal requirements for appointment to the federal courts. Once appointed, district and appeals judges must reside in the district or circuit to which they are appointed.

The president appoints judges to the federal courts, and all nominees must be confirmed by majority vote in the Senate. Congress sets, but cannot lower, a judge's compensation. In 2007, salaries were as follows:

Chief justice of the Supreme Court	$212,100
Associate Supreme Court justices	203,000
Courts of appeals judges	175,100
District judges	165,200
Magistrate-judges	151,984

By comparison, in 2005 the average salary of a state supreme court judge was $134,788. The average for a state trial judge was $116,347.[47] Annual compensation for equity partners in major law firms now exceeds $700,000. Today, Supreme Court clerks entering private practice earn more than the justices who hired them. No wonder some lawyers find the judicial path unappealing.

In more than half the states, the governor appoints the state judges, often in consultation with judicial nominating commissions. In many of these states, voters decide whether the judges should be retained in office. Other states select their judges by partisan, nonpartisan, or (rarely) legislative election.[48] In some states, nominees must be confirmed by the state legislature. Contested elections for judgeships are unusual. In Chicago, where judges are elected, even highly publicized and widespread criminal corruption in the courts failed to unseat incumbents. Most voters paid no attention whatsoever.

The Appointment of Federal Judges

The Constitution states that federal judges shall hold their commission "during good Behaviour," which in practice means for life.* A president's judicial appointments, then, are likely to survive his administration, providing a kind of political legacy. The appointment power assumes that the president is free to identify candidates and appoint judges who favor his policies. President Franklin D. Roosevelt had appointed nearly 75 percent of all sitting federal judges by the end of his twelve years in office. In contrast, President Ford appointed fewer than 13 percent in his three years in office. Presidents Reagan

---

*Only twelve federal judges have been impeached. Of these, seven were convicted in the Senate and removed from office. Three judges were impeached by the Senate in the 1980s. In 1992, Alcee Hastings became the first such judge to serve in Congress.

and George H. W. Bush together appointed more than 60 percent of all federal judges. During his administration, President Clinton appointed more than 40 percent of the 852 federal judges at all levels.

Judicial vacancies occur when sitting judges resign, retire, or die. Vacancies also arise when Congress creates new judgeships to handle increasing caseloads. In both cases, the president nominates a candidate, who must be confirmed by the Senate. Under President George W. Bush, the head of the Office of White House Counsel, Harriet Miers, and her staff are deeply involved in this screening process. The president also has the help of the Justice Department, primarily through its Office of Legal Policy, which screens candidates before the formal nomination, subjecting serious contenders to FBI investigation. The White House and the Justice Department have formed a Judicial Selection Committee as part of this vetting process. The White House and the Senate vie for control in the approval of district and appeals court judges.

The "Advice and Consent" of the Senate.

For district and appeals court vacancies, the nomination "must be acceptable to the home state senator from the president's party"[49] (or to the state's House delegation from the president's party if no senator is from the president's party). The Judicial Selection Committee consults extensively with home state senators from which the appointment will be made.[50] Senators' influence is greater for appointments to district court than for appointments to the court of appeals.

This practice, called **senatorial courtesy,** forces presidents to share the nomination power with members of the Senate. The Senate will not confirm a nominee who is opposed by the senior senator from the nominee's state if that senator is a member of the president's party. The Senate does not actually reject the candidate. Instead, the chairman of the Senate Judiciary Committee, which reviews all judicial nominees, will not schedule a confirmation hearing, effectively killing the nomination.

Although the Justice Department is still sensitive to senatorial prerogatives, senators can no longer submit a single name to fill a vacancy. The department searches for acceptable candidates and polls the appropriate senator for her or his reaction to them. President George H. W. Bush asked Republican senators to seek more qualified female and minority candidates. Bush made progress in developing a more diverse bench, and President Clinton accelerated the change.[51] President George W. Bush has a better track record appointing women and minorities to the bench than did either his father or Ronald Reagan, but he still lags behind Clinton. Ideology remains the dominant motivating force behind judicial appointments.[52]

The Senate Judiciary Committee conducts a hearing for each judicial nominee. The chairman exercises a measure of control in the appointment process that goes beyond senatorial courtesy. If a nominee is objectionable to the chairman, he or she can delay a hearing or hold up other appointments until the president and the Justice Department find an alternative. Such behavior does not win a politician much influence in the long run, however. So committee chairmen of the president's party are usually loath to place obstacles in a president's path, especially when they may want presidential support for their own policies and constituencies.

Beginning with the Carter administration, judicial appointments below the Supreme Court have proved a new battleground, with a growing proportion of nominees not confirmed and increasing delays in the process. These appointments were once viewed as presidential and party patronage, but that

senatorial courtesy A norm under which a nomination must be acceptable to the home state senator from the president's party.

old-fashioned view has given way to a focus on the president's policy agenda through judicial appointments. This perspective has enlarged the ground on which senators have opposed judicial nominees to include matters of judicial policy (for example, abortion) and theory (for example, delving into a nominee's approach when interpreting the meaning of a statute). Beginning in 2003, Democratic senators used the filibuster to prevent confirmation votes for judicial candidates they deemed "outside the mainstream." This behavior provoked ire from the majority Republicans, who threatened to end the filibuster practice entirely. The parties reached an uneasy compromise in 2005 to invoke a judicial filibuster only for "extraordinary circumstances," thus ending its use to scuttle most presidential nominations.

The American Bar Association. The American Bar Association (ABA), the biggest organization of lawyers in the United States, has been involved in screening candidates for the federal bench since 1946.[53] Its role is defined by custom, not law. At the president's behest, the ABA's Standing Committee on the Federal Judiciary routinely rates prospective appointees using a three-value scale: "well qualified," "qualified," and "not qualified." The association no longer has advance notice of possible nominees, but it continues to evaluate the professional qualifications of nominees after they have been nominated. Those assessments have been used to buttress nominations during confirmation hearings.

Recent Presidents and the Federal Judiciary

Since the presidency of Jimmy Carter, chief executives have tended—more or less—to make appointments to the federal courts that are more diverse in racial, ethnic, and gender terms than in previous administrations (see Figure 14.4). President Bill Clinton took the lead on diversity. For the first time in history, more than half of the president's judicial appointments were women or minorities. Clinton's chief judge selector, Assistant Attorney General Eleanor Acheson, followed through on Clinton's campaign pledge to make his appointees "look like America."

The racial and ethnic composition of the parties themselves helps to explain much of the variation between the appointments of presidents of different parties. It seems clear that political ideology, not demographics, lies at the heart of judicial appointments. Reagan and George H. W. Bush sought nominees with particular policy preferences who would leave their stamp on the judiciary well into the twenty-first century; they appointed a third of all judges sitting today. Clinton was animated by the same goal; he appointed more than a quarter of all judges sitting today.[54] When it comes to ideological preferences as revealed by judicial choices, Carter's judges take the cake. A review of more than 25,000 federal court decisions from 1968 to 1995 concluded that Carter-appointed judges were the most liberal, whereas Reagan- and Bush-appointed judges were the least liberal. (Carter had an advantage in his efforts to mold the bench because his appointees were reviewed by a Democratic-led Senate. Reagan, George H. W. Bush, Clinton, and George W. Bush contended with a Senate in the hands of the opposing party for part of their administrations.) Clinton-appointed judges are somewhat less liberal than Carter's but decidedly more liberal than the legacy of Nixon, Ford, Reagan, or George H. W. Bush.[55] And George W. Bush's judges are among the most conservative on record when

FIGURE 14.4 Diversity on the Federal Courts

To what extent should the courts reflect the diverse character of the population? President Jimmy Carter sought to make the federal courts more representative of the population by appointing more blacks, Hispanics, and women. Ronald Reagan's appointments reflected neither the lawyer population nor the population at large. George H. W. Bush's appointments were somewhat more representative than Reagan's on race and gender criteria. Clinton's nominees represented a dramatic departure in appointments, especially in terms of race and gender. George W. Bush has made more Hispanic appointments than any of his predecessors, but he has appointed a smaller percentage of blacks and women than Clinton did.

Sources: The Federal Judges Biographical Database, available at <http://www.fjc.gov/public/home.nsf/>; United States Census 2000, available at <http://www.census.gov/main/www/cen2000.html>.

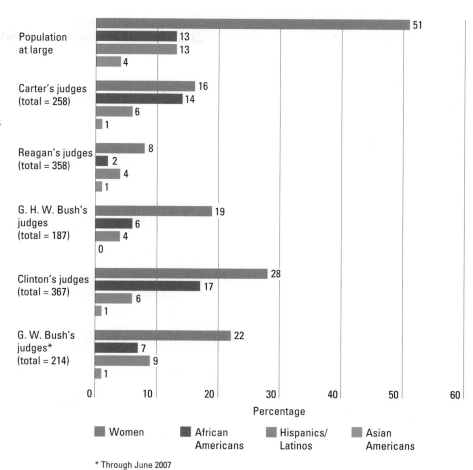

it comes to civil rights and liberties.[56] One general rule seems clear: presidents are likely to appoint judges who share similar values.

Appointment to the Supreme Court

The announcement of a vacancy on the High Court usually causes quite a stir. Campaigns for Supreme Court seats are commonplace, although the public rarely sees them. Hopefuls contact friends in the administration and urge influential associates to do the same on their behalf. Some candidates never give up hope. Judge John J. Parker, whose nomination to the Court was defeated in 1930, tried in vain to rekindle interest in his appointment until he was well past the age—usually the early sixties—that appointments are made.[57]

The president is not shackled by senatorial courtesy when it comes to nominating a Supreme Court justice. However, appointments to the Court attract more intense public scrutiny than do lower-level appointments, effectively

FIGURE 14.5 "But enough about you, Judge; let's hear what I have to say"

With few exceptions, senators consumed more time than Alito during the question-and-answer sessions. Here is a summary from just one day of hearings. With only two exceptions, senators of both parties offered more words (and presumably consumed more time) than the candidate they were examining. With live media feeds in the hearing room and stage lighting in place, it should not come as a surprise that senators felt compelled to do most of the talking.

Source: "Questions and Answers," *New York Times,* 11 January 2006, p. A21. Reprinted with permission.

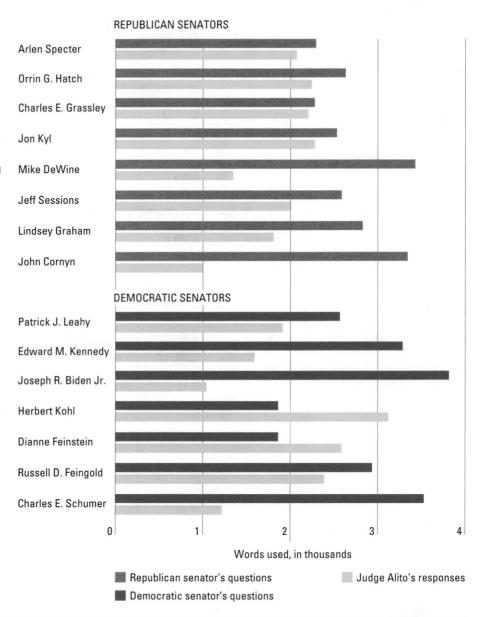

REPUBLICAN SENATORS

Arlen Specter
Orrin G. Hatch
Charles E. Grassley
Jon Kyl
Mike DeWine
Jeff Sessions
Lindsey Graham
John Cornyn

DEMOCRATIC SENATORS

Patrick J. Leahy
Edward M. Kennedy
Joseph R. Biden Jr.
Herbert Kohl
Dianne Feinstein
Russell D. Feingold
Charles E. Schumer

Words used, in thousands

■ Republican senator's questions   ▨ Judge Alito's responses
■ Democratic senator's questions

narrowing the president's options and focusing attention on the Senate's advice and consent.

Of the 155 men and 3 women nominated to the Court, 11 names have been withdrawn and 25 have failed to receive Senate confirmation. (Seven confirmed justices declined to serve!)[58] Only 6 such fumbles have occurred since 1900. The last one was George W. Bush's nomination of Harriet Miers in 2005 to fill the vacancy created by the retirement of Sandra Day O'Connor. Miers, who was White House counsel, withdrew her candidacy after coming under withering criticism, largely from conservatives, for her lack of clarity on issues likely to come before the Court.

The most important factor in the rejection of a nominee is partisan politics. Thirteen candidates lost their bids for appointment because the presidents who nominated them were considered likely to become lame ducks: the party in control of the Senate anticipated victory for its candidate in an upcoming presidential race and sought to deny the incumbent president an important political appointment.[59]

Eighteen of the twenty-four successful Supreme Court nominees since 1950 have had prior judicial experience in federal or state courts. This tendency toward "promotion" from within the judiciary may be based on the idea that a judge's previous opinions are good predictors of his or her future opinions on the High Court. After all, a president is handing out a powerful lifetime appointment, so it makes sense to want an individual who is sympathetic to his views. Federal or state court judges holding lifetime appointments are likely to state their views frankly in their opinions. In contrast, the policy preferences of High Court candidates who have been in legal practice or in political office can only be guessed at, based on the conjecture of professional associates or on speeches they have given to local Rotary Clubs, on the floor of a legislature, and elsewhere.

After a vacancy drought of more than eleven years, President George W. Bush put his stamp on the Supreme Court with two appointments in 2005. He nominated federal judge John G. Roberts, Jr., in July 2005 to replace Associate Justice Sandra Day O'Connor (after the withdrawal of Harriet Miers). But with the death of Chief Justice William H. Rehnquist in September, Bush withdrew Roberts's nomination as associate justice and resubmitted him for the position of chief justice. Roberts was confirmed 78–22. Democrats were evenly split: 22 for and 22 against. Bush then nominated federal judge Samuel A. Alito for the seat vacated by O'Connor. His confirmation hearing was far more contentious (see Figure 14.5), with the Democrats aiming to paint him as "outside the mainstream." The effort failed, as did a last-minute call to filibuster the nomination. Alito was confirmed by the Senate by a narrow margin, 58–42 (nearly all Democrats were opposed), and he took his seat as the 110th justice in January 2006.

★ The Consequences of Judicial Decisions

Judicial rulings represent the tip of the iceberg in terms of all the legal conflicts and disputes that arise in this country. Most cases never surface in court. The overwhelming majority of lawsuits end without a court judgment. Many civil cases are settled, or the parties give up, or the courts dismiss the suits because they are beyond the legitimate bounds of judicial resolution. Most criminal cases end in a plea bargain, with the defendant admitting his or her guilt in exchange for a less severe punishment. Only about 10 percent of criminal cases in the federal district courts are tried; an equally small percentage of civil cases are adjudicated.

Furthermore, the fact that a judge sentences a criminal defendant to ten years in prison or a court holds a company liable for billions in damages does not guarantee that the defendant will lose his or her freedom or the company will give up any assets. In the case of the criminal defendant, the road of seeking an appeal following trial and conviction is well traveled and, if nothing else, serves to delay the day when he or she must go to prison. In civil cases as well, an appeal may be filed to delay the day of reckoning.

Supreme Court Rulings: Implementation and Impact

When the Supreme Court makes a decision, it relies on others to implement it, to translate policy into action. How a judgment is implemented depends in good measure on how it was crafted. Remember that the justices, in preparing their opinions, must work to hold their majorities together, to gain greater, if not unanimous, support for their arguments. This forces them to compromise in their opinions, to moderate their arguments, which introduces ambiguity into many of the policies they articulate. Ambiguous opinions affect the implementation of policy. For example, when the Supreme Court issued its unanimous order in 1955 to desegregate public school facilities "with all deliberate speed,"[60] judges who opposed the Court's policy dragged their feet in implementing it. In the early 1960s, the Supreme Court prohibited prayers and Bible reading in public schools. Yet state court judges and attorneys general reinterpreted the High Court's decision to mean that only compulsory prayer or Bible reading was unconstitutional and that state-sponsored voluntary prayer or Bible reading was acceptable.[61]

Because the Supreme Court confronts issues freighted with deeply felt social values or fundamental political beliefs, its decisions have influence beyond the immediate parties in a dispute. The Court's decision in *Roe* v. *Wade*, legalizing abortion, generated heated public reaction. The justices were barraged with thousands of angry letters. Groups opposing abortion vowed to overturn the decision; groups favoring the freedom to obtain an abortion moved to protect the right they had won. Within eight months of the decision, more than two dozen constitutional amendments had been introduced in Congress, although none managed to carry the extraordinary majority required for passage. Still, the antiabortion faction achieved a modest victory with the passage of a provision forbidding the use of national government funds for abortions except when the woman's life is in jeopardy. (Since 1993, the exception has also included victims of rape or incest.)

Abortion opponents have also directed their efforts at state legislatures, hoping to load abortion laws with enough conditions to discourage women from terminating their pregnancies. For example, one state required that women receive detailed information about abortions, then wait at least twenty-four hours before consenting to the procedure. The information listed every imaginable danger associated with abortion and included a declaration that fathers are liable to support their children financially. A legal challenge to these new restrictions reached the Supreme Court, and in 1989, it abandoned its strong defense of abortion rights.[62] The Court continued to support a woman's right to abortion, but in yet another legal challenge in 1992, it recognized the government's power to further limit the exercise of that right.[63] In 2000, in a 5–4 vote, it struck down a state law banning late-term abortions. But in 2007, the Roberts Court reversed course and in a 5–4 vote upheld a nearly identical federal late-term abortion ban.[64]

? Can you explain why . . . racial school segregation persisted for nearly two decades after the Court declared it illegal in *Brown* v. *Board of Education* (1954)?

IDEAlog.org

What are your views on abortion? Take IDEAlog's self-test.

Public Opinion and the Supreme Court

Democratic theorists have a difficult time reconciling a commitment to representative democracy with a judiciary that is not accountable to the electorate yet has the power to undo legislative and executive acts. The difficulty may simply be a problem for theorists, however. The policies coming from the Supreme Court, although lagging years behind public opinion, rarely seem out of line with the public's ideological choices.[65] Surveys in several controversial areas reveal that an ideologically balanced Court seldom departs from majority sentiment or trends.[66]

The evidence supports the view that the Supreme Court reflects public opinion at least as often as other elected institutions. In a comprehensive study comparing 146 Supreme Court rulings with nationwide opinion polls from the mid-1930s through the mid-1980s, the Court reflected public opinion majorities or pluralities in more than 60 percent of its rulings.[67] There are at least three explanations for this consistency. First, the modern Court has shown deference to national laws and policies, which typically echo national public opinion. Second, the Court moves closer to public opinion during periods of crisis. And third, rulings that reflect the public view are subject to fewer changes than rulings that depart from public opinion. The fit is not perfect, however. The Court parted company with public opinion in a third of its rulings. For example, it has clearly defied the wishes of the majority for decades on the issue of school prayer. Most Americans today do not agree with the Court's position. And so long as much of the public continues to want prayer in schools, the controversy will continue.

Finally, the evidence also supports the view that the Court seldom influences public opinion. Americans have little factual knowledge of the Court. According to a 2002 survey, nearly two-thirds of all Americans can't name a single justice, although two-thirds can correctly identify the Rice Krispies characters "Snap, Crackle, and Pop."[68] It is not surprising that the Court enjoys only moderate popularity and that its decisions are not much noticed by the public. With few exceptions, there is no evidence of shifting public opinion before and after a Supreme Court ruling.[69]

The Court's decision in *Bush* v. *Gore* will provide critics with fodder for years to come. However, the public seems content with the outcome and realistic in its assessment of the process by which it was reached. As recently as 2005, the Gallup Poll showed that nearly six out of ten Americans are much more likely to approve than disapprove of the job the Supreme Court is doing.[70] Following the 2000 presidential election, polling organizations documented a large gap in the Court's approval ratings between Democrats and Republicans. But time seems to have healed that wound, and today there is virtually no difference in support for the Court across political party affiliation. So despite the barrage of criticism, the Court weathered the controversial 2000 presidential election with no sustainable damage to its integrity.[71]

The judicial process is imperfect, so it is not surprising that the Court will continue to step into minefields of public criticism. In 2005 the Court ruled that the Constitution did not forbid a city from taking private property for private development.[72] The outrage across the ideological spectrum was enormous and immediate. State legislatures and courts acted swiftly to give greater protection to private property. This was strong evidence that the Court's measured opinion was out of step with conventional wisdom.

IDEAlog.org
Do you believe that public schools should allow or ban prayers? Take IDEAlog's self-test.

★ The Courts and Models of Democracy

How far should judges stray from existing statutes and precedents? Supporters of the majoritarian model would argue that the courts should adhere to the letter of the law, that judges must refrain from injecting their own values into their decisions. If the law places too much (or not enough) emphasis on equality or order, the elected legislature, not the courts, can change the law. In contrast, those who support the pluralist model maintain that the courts are a policymaking branch of government. It is thus legitimate for the individual values and interests of judges to mirror group interests and preferences and for judges to attempt consciously to advance group interests as they see fit. However, when, where, and how to proceed are difficult for judges at all levels to determine (see "Politics in a Changing World: The Right to Die").

The argument that our judicial system fits the pluralist model gains support from a legal procedure called a **class action.** A class action is a device for assembling the claims or defenses of similarly situated individuals so that they can be heard in a single lawsuit. A class action makes it possible for people with small individual claims and limited financial resources to aggregate their claims and resources and thus make a lawsuit viable. The class action also permits the case to be tried by representative parties, with the judgment binding on all. Decisions in class action suits can have broader impact than decisions in other types of cases. Since the 1940s, class action suits have been the vehicles through which groups have asserted claims involving civil rights, legislative apportionment, and environmental problems. For example, schoolchildren have sued (through their parents) under the banner of class action to rectify claimed racial discrimination on the part of school authorities, as in *Brown* v. *Board of Education.*

Abetting the class action is the resurgence of state supreme courts' fashioning policies consistent with group preferences. Informed Americans often look to the U.S. Supreme Court for protection of their rights and liberties. In many circumstances, that expectation is correct. But state courts may serve as the staging areas for legal campaigns to change the law in the nation's highest court. They also exercise substantial influence over the policies that affect citizens daily, including the rights and liberties enshrined in state constitutions, statutes, and common law.[73]

Furthermore, state judges need not look to the U.S. Supreme Court for guidance on the meaning of certain state rights and liberties. If a state court chooses to rely solely on national law in deciding a case, that case is reviewable by the U.S. Supreme Court. But a state court can avoid review by the U.S. Supreme Court by basing its decision solely on state law or by plainly stating that its decision rests on both state and federal law. If the U.S. Supreme Court is likely to render a restrictive view of a constitutional right and the judges of a state court are inclined toward a more expansive view, the state judges can use the state ground to avoid Supreme Court review. In a period when the nation's highest court is moving in a decidedly conservative direction, some state courts have become safe havens for liberal values. And individuals and groups know where to moor their policies.

The New Jersey Supreme Court has been more aggressive than most other state supreme courts in following its own liberal constitutional path. It has gone further than the U.S. Supreme Court in promoting equality at the expense

? **Can you explain why . . .** the U.S. Supreme Court may be powerless to review certain decisions made by state supreme courts?

class action A procedure by which similarly situated litigants may be heard in a single lawsuit.

of freedom by prohibiting discrimination against women by private employers and by striking down the state's public school financing system, which had perpetuated vast disparities in public education within the state. The court has also preferred freedom over order in protecting the right to terminate life-support systems and in protecting free speech against infringement.[74] The New Jersey judges have charted their own path, despite the similarity in language between sections of the New Jersey Constitution and the U.S. Constitution. And the New Jersey judges have parted company with their national cousins even when the constitutional provisions at issue were identical.[75]

For example, the U.S. Supreme Court ruled in 1988 that warrantless searches of curbside garbage are constitutionally permissible. Both the New Jersey Constitution and the U.S. Constitution bar unreasonable searches and seizures. Yet in a 1990 decision expanding constitutional protections, the New Jersey court ruled that police officers need a search warrant before they can rummage through a person's trash. The court claimed that the New Jersey Constitution offers a greater degree of privacy than the U.S. Constitution. Because the decision rested on an interpretation of the state constitution, the existence of a similar right in the national charter had no bearing. The New Jersey court cannot act in a more restrictive manner than the U.S. Supreme Court allows, but it can be—and is—less restrictive.[76] State supreme courts can turn to their own state constitutions to "raise the ceiling of liberty above the floor created by the federal Bill of Rights."[77]

When judges reach decisions, they pay attention to the views of other courts—and not just those above them in the judicial hierarchy. State and federal court opinions are the legal storehouse from which judges regularly

Politics in a Changing World

The Right to Die

In June 1997, the Supreme Court ended its long silence on the constitutionality of a right to suicide, rejecting two separate challenges to state laws prohibiting assisted suicide. In 1996, the U.S. Court of Appeals for the Ninth Circuit relied on the Supreme Court's abortion decisions to strike down a Washington State law against aiding or abetting suicide. The circuit court reasoned from the High Court's abortion rulings that the Fourteenth Amendment's due process clause protects the individual's right "to define one's own concept of existence, of meaning, of the universe, and of the mystery of life." The Supreme Court, however, in *Washington* v. *Glucksberg*, unanimously rejected the circuit court's reasoning, in no uncertain terms. Chief Justice Rehnquist's opinion for the Court stressed that suicide is not a "fundamental right" that is "deeply rooted in our legal tradition." Unlike abor-

tion, suicide has been all but universally condemned in the law.

In another 1996 decision, the U.S. Court of Appeals for the Second Circuit adopted a different line of reasoning to invalidate a New York law banning physician-assisted suicide. The court held that the law violated the Fourteenth Amendment's equal protection clause because it treated those who needed a physician's help to administer lethal doses of prescription drugs (which is criminalized by law) differently from those who can demand removal of life-support systems (which is allowed under prior Supreme Court cases). In June 1997, the Supreme Court unanimously rejected this argument in *Vacco* v. *Quill*. Chief Justice Rehnquist's opinion for the Court held that the New York law does not result in similar cases being treated differently. It creates no suspect classifications; anyone

draw their ideas. Often the issues that affect individual lives—property, family, contracts—are grist for state courts, not federal courts. For example, when a state court faces a novel issue in a contract dispute, it will look at how other state courts have dealt with the problem. (Contract disputes are not a staple of the federal courts.) And if courts in several states have addressed an issue and the direction of the opinion is largely one-sided, the weight and authority of those opinions may move the court in that direction.[78] Courts that confront new issues with cogency and clarity are likely to become leaders of legal innovation.

State courts have become renewed arenas for political conflict, with litigants, individually or in groups, vying for their preferred policies. The multiplicity of the nation's court system, with overlapping state and national responsibilities, provides alternative points of access for individuals and groups to present and argue their claims. This description of the courts fits the pluralist model of government.

Terminiello's speech was far more incendiary than Walter Chaplinsky's. Yet the Supreme Court struck down Terminiello's conviction on the ground that provocative speech, even speech that stirs people to anger, is protected by the First Amendment. "Freedom of speech," wrote Justice William O. Douglas in the majority opinion, "though not absolute . . . is nevertheless protected against censorship or punishment, unless shown likely to produce a clear and present danger of a serious substantive evil that rises far above public inconvenience, annoyance, or unrest."

This broad view of protection brought a stiff rebuke in Justice Jackson's dissenting opinion:

> The choice is not between order and liberty. It is between liberty with order and anarchy without either. There is danger that, if the court does not temper its doctrinaire logic with a little practical wisdom, it will convert the constitutional Bill of Rights into a suicide pact.[39]

The times seem to have caught up with the idealism that Jackson criticized in his colleagues. In *Cohen v. California* (1971), a nineteen-year-old department store worker expressed his opposition to the Vietnam War by wearing a jacket in the hallway of a Los Angeles county courthouse emblazoned with the words FUCK THE DRAFT. STOP THE WAR. The young man, Paul Cohen, was charged in 1968 under a California statute that prohibits "maliciously and willfully disturb[ing] the peace and quiet of any neighborhood or person [by] offensive conduct." He was found guilty and sentenced to thirty days in jail. On appeal, the U.S. Supreme Court reversed Cohen's conviction.

The Court reasoned that the expletive he used, while provocative, was not directed at anyone in particular; besides, the state presented no evidence that the words on Cohen's jacket would provoke people in "substantial numbers" to take some kind of physical action. In recognizing that "one man's vulgarity is another's lyric," the Supreme Court protected two elements of speech: the emotive (the expression of emotion) and the cognitive (the expression of ideas).[40]

The Supreme Court will confront these kinds of questions again as challenges to intimidating speech on the World Wide Web make their way through the nation's legal system. In 1996, Congress passed the Communications Decency Act, which made it a crime for a person knowingly to circulate "patently offensive" sexual material to Internet sites accessible to those under eighteen years old. Is this an acceptable way to protect children from offensive material or is it a muzzle on free speech? A federal court quickly declared the act unconstitutional. In an opinion of over 200 pages, the court observed that "just as the strength of the Internet is chaos, so the strength of our liberty depends on the chaos and cacophony of the unfettered speech the First Amendment protects."[41]

The Supreme Court upheld the lower court's ruling in June 1997 in *Reno v. ACLU*.[42] Its nearly unanimous opinion was a broad affirmation of free speech rights in cyberspace, arguing that the Internet was more analogous to print media than to television, and thus even indecent material on the Internet was entitled to First Amendment protection.

New forms of expression driven by the computer and the Internet confront traditional barriers in the form of copyright. And true to the pluralist model, interest groups have succeeded in extending copyright protections, but at what price for free expression? (See "Looking to the Future: 'FREE THE MOUSE': Mickey Remains Behind Copyright Bars.")

Looking to the Future

"FREE THE MOUSE": Mickey Remains Behind Copyright Bars

Walt Disney created a cartoon character, Steamboat Willie, in 1928 that begat Mickey Mouse, and Mickey Mouse begat the Disney Corporation. Disney followed a creative path familiar to most of us: he used information created by others and gave it his own spin. He built a vast empire by bringing fairy tales to life. Disney applied for and received a copyright for his work. The U.S. Constitution gives Congress the power to issue copyrights and patents. A copyright grants an exclusive right, that is, a monopoly, to publish and sell one's work. Many types of work come under the copyright umbrella today, including books, drama, dance, music, sound recordings, pictures, photographs, sculpture, architecture, computer programs, and, of course, movies.

New works and forms of expression arise from modifying existing works and forms of expression. By relying on existing works—in other words, our common culture—we generate new knowledge. Copyrighting a work encourages creation by granting a limited-time monopoly. And anyone who has played the game Monopoly knows that monopolies can be very rewarding. The framers of the Constitution understood this concept, and that's why they insisted that "to promote the Progress of Science and useful Arts," copyrights shall be granted "for limited times." When the limited term expired, a work would enter the public domain and become fair game for others to exploit in new works,

Copyright Terms

Year	Minimum years	Maximum years
1790	14	28
1831	28	42
1909	28	56
1976	Life of author plus 50 years	
1998	Life of author plus 70 years	

Free Speech Versus Order: Obscenity. The Supreme Court has always viewed obscene material—in words, music, books, magazines, and films—as being outside the bounds of constitutional protection, which means that states may regulate or even ban obscenity. However, difficulties arise in determining what is obscene and what is not. In *Roth* v. *United States* (1957), Justice William J. Brennan, Jr., outlined a test for judging a work as obscene: "Whether to the average person, applying contemporary community standards, the dominant theme of the material taken as a whole appeals to prurient interest."[43] (*Prurient* means having a tendency to incite lustful thoughts.) Yet a definition of obscenity has proved elusive; no objective test seems adequate. Justice Potter Stewart will long be remembered for his solution to the problem of iden-

just as Disney had done. But the field of play has changed, limiting the works that enter the public domain and thus constraining free expression.

The first copyright laws granted a limited term of fourteen years of protection. Over two centuries, Congress has amended the copyright statutes to extend the period of protection. Today, that protection extends to the life of the creator plus seventy years. As a result, works that would flow into the common culture—and serve as the basis of new forms of expression—remain under copyright protection. When the copyright for Mickey Mouse was about to expire, and thus allow Mickey to enter the public sphere, the Disney Corporation, along with other media companies, pushed Congress to grant another extension to the copyright laws.

Just about every person under age twenty understands the ease with which computing technology and the Internet allow works to be copied, shared, and molded into new forms of expression. "Rip Mix Burn" has become a mantra to the digerati. Continuing the age-old creative process in the digital world generates a new and profound set of copyright restrictions on the use of digital copies. Restricting information use limits creativity and undermines the very creativity that Walt Disney employed when he made Mickey Mouse and his great classic films.

The ever-expanding copyright protections were challenged as an unconstitutional departure from the Constitution's command that copyrights extend only for limited times. By constantly extending the terms of copyright, argued the petitioners in *Eldred* v. *Ashcroft,* Congress had violated the spirit and perhaps the letter of the Constitution. The Supreme Court considered this novel argument in 2002.

The challenge to the law, the Sonny Bono Copyright Term Extension Act of 1998, failed. It might be bad public policy for Congress to repeatedly extend copyright protection, but it was not the Supreme Court's responsibility to correct bad policies, only unconstitutional ones. Works that might have entered the public domain now have another monopoly lease. And if the past is any predictor of the future, current copyright giants will seek to extend copyright protection when it appears that their works are headed once again for the public domain.

"Free the Mouse" became the rallying cry for a political movement that aims to support and nurture free resources. As philosopher Richard Stallman observed, "free not in the sense of 'free beer' but free in the sense of 'free speech.'" A resource is "free," wrote Professor Lawrence Lessig, "if (1) one can use it without the permission of anyone else; or (2) the permission one needs is granted neutrally." "So understood," continued Lessig, "the question for our generation is not whether the market or the state will control a resource, but whether that resource shall remain free."

Sources: Eldred v. *Ashcroft,* 537 U.S. 186 (2003); Robert S. Boynton, "The Tyranny of Copyright," *New York Times Magazine,* 25 January 2003; Lawrence Lessig, *The Future of Ideas* (New York: Random House, 2001), p. 12.

---

tifying obscene materials. He declared that he could not define it. "But," he added, "I know it when I see it."[44]

In *Miller* v. *California* (1973), its most recent major attempt to clarify constitutional standards governing obscenity, the Court declared that a work—a play, film, or book—is obscene and may be regulated by the government if (1) the work taken as a whole appeals to prurient interests, (2) the work portrays sexual conduct in a patently offensive way, and (3) the work taken as a whole lacks serious literary, artistic, political, or scientific value.[45] Local community standards govern application of the first and second prongs of the *Miller* test.

Freedom of the Press

The First Amendment guarantees that government "shall make no law . . . abridging the freedom . . . of the press." Although the free press guarantee was originally adopted as a restriction on the national government, the Supreme Court has held since 1931 that it applies to state and local governments as well.

The ability to collect and report information without government interference was (and still is) thought to be essential to a free society. The print media continue to use and defend the freedom conferred on them by the framers. However, the electronic media have had to accept some government regulation stemming from the scarcity of broadcast frequencies (see Chapter 6).

Defamation of Character. Libel is the written defamation of character.* A person who believes his or her name and character have been harmed by false statements in a publication can institute a lawsuit against the publication and seek monetary compensation for the damage. Such a lawsuit can impose limits on freedom of expression; at the same time, false statements impinge on the rights of individuals. In a landmark decision in *New York Times* v. *Sullivan* (1964), the Supreme Court declared that freedom of the press takes precedence—at least when the defamed individual is a public official.[46] The Court unanimously agreed that the First Amendment protects the publication of all statements—even false ones—about the conduct of public officials, except statements made with actual malice (with knowledge that they are false or in reckless disregard for their truth or falsity). Citing John Stuart Mill's 1859 treatise *On Liberty,* the Court declared that "even a false statement may be deemed to make a valuable contribution to public debate, since it brings about the 'clearer perception and livelier impression of truth, produced by its collision with error.'"

Three years later, the Court extended this protection to apply to suits brought by any public figure, whether a government official or not. **Public figures** are people who assume roles of prominence in society or thrust themselves to the forefront of public controversies, including officials, actors, writers, and television personalities. These people must show actual malice on the part of the publication that printed false statements about them. Because the burden of proof is so great, few plaintiffs prevail. And freedom of the press is the beneficiary.

What if the damage inflicted is not to one's reputation but to one's emotional state? Government seeks to maintain the prevailing social order, which prescribes proper modes of behavior. Does the First Amendment restrict the government in protecting citizens from behavior that intentionally inflicts emotional distress? This issue arose in a parody of a public figure in *Hustler* magazine. The target was the Reverend Jerry Falwell, a Baptist televangelist who founded the Moral Majority and organized conservative Christians into a political force. The parody had Falwell—in an interview—discussing a drunken, incestuous rendezvous with his mother in an outhouse, saying, "I always get sloshed before I go out to the pulpit." Falwell won a $200,000 award for "emotional distress." The magazine appealed, and the Supreme Court confronted the issue of social order versus free speech in 1988.[47]

public figures People who assume roles of prominence in society or thrust themselves to the forefront of public controversy.

---

*Slander is the oral defamation of character. The durability of the written word usually means that libel is a more serious accusation than slander.

Shock Jock Rocks
To his legions of loyal fans, shock radio DJ Howard Stern is a superstar. But Stern's obscene and sexually provocative language on FM stations made him an outcast. So he abandoned his longtime FM home for satellite, hosting his brand of talk radio in 2006 on Sirius Satellite Radio. Government can impose speech restrictions on the limited AM and FM frequencies, but free speech is virtually unfettered when it comes to satellite transmission. *(Getty Images)*

In a unanimous decision, the Court overturned the award. In his sweeping opinion for the Court, Chief Justice William H. Rehnquist gave wide latitude to the First Amendment's protection of free speech. He observed that "graphic depictions and satirical cartoons have played a prominent role in public and political debate" throughout the nation's history and that the First Amendment protects even "vehement, caustic, and sometimes unpleasantly sharp attacks." Free speech protects criticism of public figures, even if the criticism is outrageous and offensive.

Prior Restraint and the Press. As discussed above, in the United States, freedom of the press has primarily meant protection from prior restraint, or censorship. The Supreme Court's first encounter with a law imposing prior restraint on a newspaper was in *Near* v. *Minnesota* (1931).[48] In Minneapolis, Jay Near published a scandal sheet in which he attacked local officials, charging that they were in league with gangsters.[49] Minnesota officials obtained an injunction to prevent Near from publishing his newspaper, under a state law that allowed such action against periodicals deemed "malicious, scandalous, and defamatory."

The Supreme Court struck down the law, declaring that prior restraint places an unacceptable burden on a free press. Chief Justice Charles Evans Hughes forcefully articulated the need for a vigilant, unrestrained press: "The fact that the liberty of the press may be abused by miscreant purveyors of scandal does not make any the less necessary the immunity of the press from previous restraint in dealing with official misconduct." Although the Court acknowledged that prior restraint may be permissible in exceptional circumstances, it did not specify those circumstances, nor has it yet done so.

Consider another case, which occurred during a war, a time when the tension between government-imposed order and individual freedom is often at a peak. In 1971, Daniel Ellsberg, a special assistant in the Pentagon's Office of International Security Affairs, delivered portions of a classified U.S. Department of Defense study to the *New York Times* and the *Washington Post*. By making the documents public, he hoped to discredit the Vietnam War and thereby end it. The U.S. Department of Justice sought to restrain the *Times* and the *Post* from publishing the documents, which became known as the Pentagon Papers, contending that their publication would prolong the war and embarrass the government. The case was quickly brought before the Supreme Court, which delayed its summer adjournment to hear oral arguments.

Three days later, in a 6–3 decision in *New York Times* v. *United States* (1971), the Court concluded that the government had not met the heavy burden of proving that immediate, inevitable, and irreparable harm would follow publication of the documents.[50] The majority expressed its view in a brief, unsigned opinion; individual and collective concurring and dissenting views added nine additional opinions to the decision. Two justices maintained that the First Amendment offers absolute protection against government censorship, no matter what the situation. But the other justices left the door ajar for the imposition of prior restraint in the most extreme and compelling of circumstances. The result was hardly a ringing endorsement of freedom of the press or a full affirmation of the public's right to all the information that is vital to the debate of public issues.

Freedom of Expression Versus Maintaining Order. The courts have consistently held that freedom of the press does not override the requirements of law enforcement. A grand jury called on a Louisville, Kentucky, reporter who had researched and written an article about drug-related activities to identify people he had seen in possession of marijuana or in the act of processing it. The reporter refused to testify, maintaining that freedom of the press shielded him from this inquiry. In a closely divided decision, the Supreme Court in 1972 rejected this position.[51] The Court declared that no exception, even a limited one, is permissible to the rule that all citizens have a duty to give their government whatever testimony they are capable of giving.

Consider the 1988 case of a St. Louis high school principal who deleted articles on divorce and teenage pregnancy from the school's newspaper on the grounds that the articles invaded the privacy of students and families who were the focus of the stories. Three student editors filed suit in federal court, claiming that the principal had violated their First Amendment rights. They argued that the principal's censorship interfered with the newspaper's function as a public forum, a role protected by the First Amendment. The principal maintained that the newspaper was just an extension of classroom instruction and thus was not protected by the First Amendment.

In a 5–3 decision, the Supreme Court upheld the principal's actions in sweeping terms. Educators may limit speech within the confines of the school curriculum, including speech that might seem to bear the approval of the school, provided their actions serve any "valid educational purpose." Student expression beyond school property took a hit in 2007 when an increasingly conservative Supreme Court upheld the suspension of a high school student who had displayed a banner ("Bong Hits 4 Jesus") at an outside school event. School officials may prohibit speech, wrote Chief Justice John G. Roberts, Jr., if it could be interpreted as promoting illegal drug use.[52]

The Rights to Assemble Peaceably and to Petition the Government

The final clause of the First Amendment states that "Congress shall make no law . . . abridging . . . the right of the people peaceably to assemble, and to petition the Government for a redress of grievances." The roots of the right of petition can be traced to the Magna Carta, the charter of English political and civil liberties granted by King John at Runnymede in 1215. The right of peaceable assembly arose much later. The framers meant that the people have the right to assemble peaceably *in order to* petition the government. Today, however, the right to assemble peaceably is equated with the right to free speech and a free press, independent of whether the government is petitioned. Precedent has merged these rights and made them indivisible.[53] Government cannot prohibit peaceful political meetings and cannot brand as criminals those who organize, lead, and attend such meetings.[54]

The clash of interests in cases involving these rights illustrates the continuing nature of the effort to define and apply fundamental principles. The need for order and stability has tempered the concept of freedom. And when freedom and order conflict, the justices of the Supreme Court, who are responsible only to their consciences, strike the balance. Such clashes are certain to occur again and again. Freedom and order conflict when public libraries become targets of community censors, when religious devotion interferes with military service, and when individuals and groups express views or hold beliefs at odds with majority sentiment.

The Right to Bear Arms

The Second Amendment declares:

> A well-regulated militia being necessary to the security of a free State, the right of the people to keep and bear arms shall not be infringed.

This amendment has created a hornet's nest of problems for gun-control advocates and their opponents. Gun-control advocates assert that the amendment protects the right of the states to maintain *collective* militias. Gun-use advocates assert that the amendment protects the right of *individuals* to own and use guns. There are good arguments on both sides.

Federal firearms regulations did not come into being until Prohibition, so the Supreme Court had little to say on the matter before then. In 1939, however, a unanimous Court upheld a 1934 federal law requiring the taxation and registration of machine guns and sawed-off shotguns. The Court held that the Second Amendment protects a citizen's right to own ordinary militia weapons; sawed-off shotguns did not qualify for protection.[55]

Restrictions on gun ownership (for example, registration and licensing) have passed constitutional muster. However, outright prohibitions on gun ownership (for example, a ban on handguns) might run afoul of the amendment. After all, Madison and others supported the amendment based on the view that armed citizens provided a bulwark against tyranny. However, some scholars argue that modern circumstances should confine the amendment to the preservation of state militias, relinquishing the right of individuals to possess modern lethal weapons.[56]

★ Applying the Bill of Rights to the States

The major purpose of the Constitution was to structure the division of power between the national government and the state governments. Even before it was amended, the Constitution set some limits on both the nation and the states with regard to citizens' rights. It barred both governments from passing **bills of attainder,** laws that make an individual guilty of a crime without a trial. It also prohibited them from enacting **ex post facto laws,** laws that declare an action a crime after it has been performed. And it barred both nation and states from impairing the **obligation of contracts,** the obligation of the parties in a contract to carry out its terms.

Although initially the Bill of Rights seemed to apply only to the national government, various litigants pressed the claim that its guarantees also applied to the states. In response to one such claim, Chief Justice John Marshall affirmed what seemed plain from the Constitution's language and "the history of the day" (the events surrounding the Constitutional Convention): the provisions of the Bill of Rights served only to limit national authority. "Had the framers of these amendments intended them to be limitations on the powers of the state governments," wrote Marshall, "they would have . . . expressed that intention."[57]

Change came with the Fourteenth Amendment, which was adopted in 1868. The due process clause of that amendment is the linchpin that holds the states to the provisions of the Bill of Rights.

The Fourteenth Amendment: Due Process of Law

> *Section 1.* . . . No State shall make or enforce any law which shall abridge the privileges or immunities of citizens of the United States; nor shall any State deprive any person of life, liberty, or property, without due process of law.

Most freedoms protected in the Bill of Rights today function as limitations on the states. And many of the standards that limit the national government serve equally to limit state governments. The changes have been achieved through the Supreme Court's interpretation of the due process clause of the Fourteenth Amendment: "nor shall any State deprive any person of life, liberty, or property, without due process of law." The clause has two central meanings. First, it requires the government to adhere to appropriate procedures. For example, in a criminal trial, the government must establish the defendant's guilt beyond a reasonable doubt. Second, it forbids unreasonable government action. For example, at the turn of the twentieth century, the Supreme Court struck down a state law that forbade bakers from working more than sixty hours a week. The justices found the law unreasonable under the due process clause.[58]

The Supreme Court has used the first meaning of the due process clause as a sponge, absorbing or incorporating the procedural specifics of the Bill of Rights and spreading or applying them to the states. The history of due process cases reveals that unlikely litigants often champion constitutional guarantees and that freedom is not always the victor.

bill of attainder A law that pronounces an individual guilty of a crime without a trial.

ex post facto law A law that declares an action to be criminal after it has been performed.

obligation of contracts The obligation of the parties to a contract to carry out its terms.

The Fundamental Freedoms

In 1897, the Supreme Court declared that the states are subject to the Fifth Amendment's prohibition against taking private property without providing just compensation.[59] The Court reached that decision by absorbing the prohibition into the due process clause of the Fourteenth Amendment, which explicitly applies to the states. Thus, one Bill of Rights protection—but only that one—applied to both the states and the national government, as illustrated in Figure 15.1. In 1925, the Court assumed that the due process clause protected the First Amendment speech and press liberties from impairment by the states.[60]

The inclusion of other Bill of Rights guarantees within the due process clause faced a critical test in *Palko* v. *Connecticut* (1937).[61] Frank Palko had been charged with homicide in the first degree. He was convicted of second-degree murder, however, and sentenced to life imprisonment. The state of Connecticut appealed and won a new trial; this time, Palko was found guilty of first-degree murder and sentenced to death. Palko appealed the second conviction on the ground that it violated the protection against double jeopardy guaranteed to him by the Fifth Amendment. This protection applied to the states, he contended, because of the Fourteenth Amendment's due process clause.

The Supreme Court upheld Palko's second conviction. In his opinion for the majority, Justice Benjamin N. Cardozo formulated principles that were to guide the Court's actions for the next three decades. He reasoned that some Bill of Rights guarantees, such as freedom of thought and speech, are fundamental and that these fundamental rights are absorbed by the Fourteenth Amendment's due process clause and are therefore applicable to the states. These rights are essential, argued Cardozo, because "neither liberty nor justice would exist if they were sacrificed." Trial by jury and other rights, although valuable and important, are not essential to liberty and justice and therefore are not absorbed

---

FIGURE 15.1   **The Selective Incorporation of the Bill of Rights**

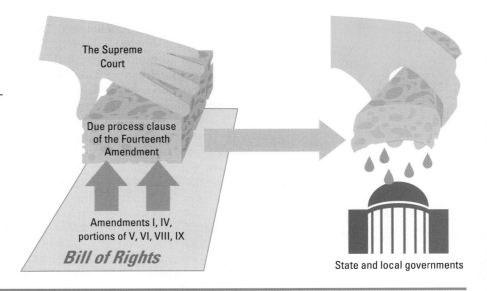

The Supreme Court has used the due process clause of the Fourteenth Amendment as a sponge, absorbing most—but not all—of the provisions in the Bill of Rights and applying them to state and local governments. All provisions in the Bill of Rights apply to the national government.

The Supreme Court

Due process clause of the Fourteenth Amendment

Amendments I, IV, portions of V, VI, VIII, IX

Bill of Rights

State and local governments

by the due process clause. "Few would be so narrow or provincial," Cardozo claimed, "as to maintain that a fair and enlightened system of justice would be impossible" without these other rights. In other words, only certain provisions of the Bill of Rights—the "fundamental" provisions—were absorbed selectively into the due process clause and made applicable to the states. Because protection against double jeopardy was not one of them, Palko died in Connecticut's gas chamber in 1938.

The next thirty years saw slow but perceptible change in the standard for determining whether a Bill of Rights guarantee was fundamental. The reference point changed from the idealized "fair and enlightened system of justice" in *Palko* to the more realistic "American scheme of justice" thirty years later.[62] Case after case tested various guarantees that the Court found to be fundamental. By 1969, when *Palko* was finally overturned, the Court had found most of the Bill of Rights applicable to the states.

Criminal Procedure: The Meaning of Constitutional Guarantees

"The history of liberty," remarked Justice Felix Frankfurter, "has largely been the history of observance of procedural safeguards."[63] The safeguards embodied in the Fourth through Eighth Amendments to the Constitution specify how government must behave in criminal proceedings. Their application to the states has reshaped American criminal justice in the past thirty years in two stages. The first stage was the judgment that a guarantee asserted in the Bill of Rights also applied to the states. The second stage required that the judiciary give specific meaning to the guarantee. The courts could not allow the states to define guarantees themselves without risking different definitions from state to state—and thus differences among citizens' rights. If rights are fundamental, their meaning cannot vary. But life is not quite so simple under the U.S. Constitution. The concept of federalism is sewn into the constitutional fabric, and the Supreme Court has recognized that there may be more than one way to prosecute the accused while heeding his or her fundamental rights.

Consider, for example, the right to a jury trial in criminal cases, which is guaranteed by the Sixth Amendment. This right was made obligatory for the states in *Duncan* v. *Louisiana* (1968). The Supreme Court later held that the right applied to all nonpetty criminal cases—those in which the penalty for conviction was more than six months' imprisonment.[64] But the Court did not require that state juries have twelve members, the number required for federal criminal proceedings. The Court permits jury size to vary from state to state, although it has set the minimum number at six. Furthermore, it has not imposed on the states the federal requirement of a unanimous jury verdict. As a result, even today, many states do not require unanimous verdicts for criminal convictions. Some observers question whether criminal defendants in these states enjoy the same rights as defendants in unanimous-verdict states.

In contrast, the Court left no room for variation in its definition of the fundamental right to an attorney, also guaranteed by the Sixth Amendment. Clarence Earl Gideon was a penniless vagrant accused of breaking into and robbing a pool hall. (The "loot" he was charged with taking was mainly change from vending machines.) Because Gideon could not afford a lawyer, he asked the state to provide him with legal counsel for his trial. The state refused and subsequently convicted Gideon and sentenced him to five years in the

Florida State Penitentiary. From his cell, Gideon appealed to the U.S. Supreme Court, claiming that his conviction should be struck down because the state had denied him his Sixth Amendment right to counsel. (Gideon was also without counsel in this appeal; he filed a handwritten "pauper's petition" with the Court after studying law texts in the prison library. When the Court agreed to consider his case, he was assigned a prominent Washington attorney, Abe Fortas, who later became a Supreme Court justice.)[65]

In its landmark decision in *Gideon* v. *Wainwright* (1963), the Court set aside Gideon's conviction and extended to defendants in state courts the Sixth Amendment right to counsel.[66] The state retried Gideon, who this time had the assistance of a lawyer, and the court found him not guilty.

In subsequent rulings that stretched over more than a decade, the Court specified at which points in the course of criminal proceedings a defendant is entitled to a lawyer (from arrest to trial, appeal, and beyond). These pronouncements are binding on all states. In state as well as federal proceedings, the government must furnish legal assistance to those who do not have the means to hire their own attorney.

During this period, the Court also came to grips with another procedural issue: informing suspects of their constitutional rights. Without this knowledge, procedural safeguards are meaningless. Ernesto Miranda was arrested in Arizona in connection with the kidnapping and rape of an eighteen-year-old woman. After the police questioned him for two hours and the woman identified him, Miranda confessed to the crime. An Arizona court convicted him on the basis of that confession—although he was never told that he had the right to counsel and the right not to incriminate himself. Miranda appealed his conviction, which was overturned by the Supreme Court in 1966.[67]

The Court based its decision in *Miranda* v. *Arizona* on the Fifth Amendment privilege against self-incrimination. According to the Court, the police had forced Miranda to confess during in-custody questioning, not with physical force but with the coercion inherent in custodial interrogation without counsel. The Court said that warnings are necessary to dispel that coercion. The Court does not require warnings if a person is only held in custody without being questioned or is only questioned without being arrested. But in *Miranda*, the Court found the combination of custody and interrogation sufficiently intimidating to require warnings before questioning. These statements are known today as the **Miranda warnings:**

- You have the right to remain silent.

- Anything you say can be used against you in court.

- You have the right to talk to a lawyer of your own choice before questioning.

- If you cannot afford to hire a lawyer, a lawyer will be provided without charge.

In each area of criminal procedure, the justices have had to grapple with two steps in the application of constitutional guarantees to criminal defendants: the extension of a right to the states and the definition of that right. In *Duncan*, the issue was the right to jury trial, and the Court allowed variation in all states. In *Gideon,* the Court applied the right to counsel uniformly in all states. Finally, in *Miranda*, the Court declared that all governments—national,

IDEAlog.org

Should confessions from defendants be barred when suspects were not read their constitutional rights? Take IDEAlog's self-test.

Miranda **warnings** Statements concerning rights that police are required to make to a person before he or she is subjected to in-custody questioning.

state, and local—have a duty to inform suspects of the full measure of their constitutional rights. In one of its most important cases in 2000, the Court reaffirmed this protection in a 7–2 decision, holding that *Miranda* had "announced a constitutional rule" that Congress could not undermine through legislation.[68]

The problems in balancing freedom and order can be formidable. A primary function of government is to maintain order. What happens when the government infringes on individuals' freedom for the sake of order? Consider the guarantee in the Fourth Amendment: "The right of the people to be secure in their persons, houses, papers, and effects, against unreasonable searches and seizures, shall not be violated." The Court made this right applicable to the states in *Wolf* v. *Colorado* (1949).[69] Following the reasoning in *Palko,* the Court found that the core of the amendment—security against arbitrary police intrusion—is a fundamental right and that citizens must be protected from illegal searches by state and local governments. But how? The federal courts had long followed the **exclusionary rule,** which holds that evidence obtained from an illegal search and seizure cannot be used in a trial. If that evidence is critical to the prosecution, the case dissolves. But the Court refused to apply the exclusionary rule to the state courts. Instead, it allowed the states to decide on their own how to handle the fruits of an illegal search. The decision in *Wolf* stated that obtaining evidence by illegal means violated the Constitution and that states could fashion their own rules of evidence to give effect to this constitutional decree. The states were not bound by the exclusionary rule.

The justices considered the exclusionary rule again twelve years later, in *Mapp* v. *Ohio.*[70] An Ohio court had found Dolree Mapp guilty of possessing obscene materials after an admittedly illegal search of her home for a fugitive. The Ohio Supreme Court affirmed her conviction, and she appealed to the U.S. Supreme Court. Mapp's attorneys argued for a reversal based primarily on freedom of expression, contending that the First Amendment protected the confiscated materials. However, the Court elected to use the decision in *Mapp* to give meaning to the constitutional guarantee against unreasonable search and seizure. In a 6–3 decision, the justices declared that "all evidence obtained by searches and seizures in violation of the Constitution is, by [the Fourth Amendment], inadmissible in a state court." Ohio had convicted Mapp illegally; the evidence should have been excluded.

The decision was historic. It placed the exclusionary rule under the umbrella of the Fourth Amendment and required all levels of government to operate according to the provisions of that amendment. Failure to do so could result in the dismissal of criminal charges against guilty defendants.

Mapp launched a divided Supreme Court on a troubled course of determining how and when to apply the exclusionary rule. For example, the Court has continued to struggle with police use of sophisticated electronic eavesdropping devices and searches of movable vehicles. In each case, the justices have confronted a rule that appears to handicap the police and to offer freedom to people whose guilt has been established by the illegal evidence. In the Court's most recent pronouncements, order has triumphed over freedom.

The struggle over the exclusionary rule took a new turn in 1984, when the Court reviewed *United States* v. *Leon.*[71] In this case, the police obtained a search warrant from a judge on the basis of a tip from an informant of unproved reliability. The judge issued a warrant without firmly establishing probable cause to believe the tip. The police, relying on the warrant, found large

exclusionary rule The judicial rule that states that evidence obtained in an illegal search and seizure cannot be used in trial.

quantities of illegal drugs. The Court, by a vote of 6–3, established the **good faith exception** to the exclusionary rule. The justices held that the state could introduce at trial evidence seized on the basis of a mistakenly issued search warrant. The exclusionary rule, argued the majority, is not a right but a remedy against illegal police conduct. The rule is costly to society. It excludes pertinent valid evidence, allowing guilty people to go unpunished and generating disrespect for the law. These costs are justifiable only if the exclusionary rule deters police misconduct. Such a deterrent effect was not a factor in *Leon:* the police acted in good faith. Hence, the Court decided, there is a need for an exception to the rule.

The Court recognized another exception in 2006. When police search a home with a warrant, they have been required to "knock and announce" before entering. But the Supreme Court held that when the police admittedly fail to "knock and announce," the evidence obtained from such a search may still be admitted into evidence, thus creating a new exception to the exclusionary rule. The case was a close one: decided 5 to 4 with Justice Scalia writing the majority opinion and implying that the exclusionary rule should not be applied in other illegal search circumstances.[72] As a more conservative coalition takes shape, the exclusionary rule will come under close scrutiny as the preference for order outweighs the value in freedom.

The USA-Patriot Act

More than fifty years ago, Justice Robert H. Jackson warned that exceptional protections for civil liberties might convert the Bill of Rights into a suicide pact. The national government decided, after the September 11 terrorist attacks, to forgo some liberties in order to secure greater order, through bipartisan passage of the USA-Patriot Act. This landmark law greatly expanded the ability of law enforcement and intelligence agencies to tap phones, monitor Internet traffic, and conduct other forms of surveillance in pursuit of terrorists. In 2006, Congress extended with a few minor changes sixteen expiring provisions of the act.

Shortly after the bill became law, then Attorney General John Ashcroft declared: "Let the terrorists among us be warned: If you overstay your visas, even by one day, we will arrest you. If you violate a local law, we will hope that you will, and work to make sure that you are, put in jail and kept in custody as long as possible. We will use every available statute. We will seek every prosecutorial advantage. We will use all our weapons within the law and under the Constitution to protect life and enhance security for America."[73]

In this shift toward order, civil libertarians worry. "These new and unchecked powers could be used against American citizens who are not under criminal investigation," said Gregory T. Nojeim, associate director of the American Civil Liberties Union's Washington office.[74]

The USA-Patriot Act runs over three hundred pages. Some parts engender strong opposition; others are benign. More than 150 communities have passed resolutions denouncing the act as an assault on civil liberties. Consider one of the key provisions: Section 215, dealing with rules for searching private records such as you might find in the library, video store, or doctor's office. Prior to the act, the government needed, at minimum, a warrant issued by a judge and probable cause to access such records. (Foreign intelligence information could justify a warrantless search, but judges still reviewed the exception.) Now, under

good faith exception An exception to the Supreme Court exclusionary rule, holding that evidence seized on the basis of a mistakenly issued search warrant can be introduced at trial if the mistake was made in good faith, that is, if all the parties involved had reason at the time to believe that the warrant was proper.

IDEAlog.org

Do you believe that the USA-Patriot Act is needed to protect the country from terrorism? Take IDEAlog's self-test.

the USA-Patriot Act, the government need only certify without substantiation that its search protects against terrorism, which turns judicial oversight into a rubber stamp. With the bar lowered, more warrantless searches are likely to follow. In 2005, the FBI conducted more than 3,500 such searches of U.S. citizens and legal residents, a significant jump from previous years.[75] To complicate matters, a gag order bars the person turning over the records to disclose the search to anyone. You may never know that your records were searched. In a fig leaf to civil libertarians, the renewed provision allows those served with such gag orders to challenge them in court after a year's wait. But in order to prevail they must prove that the government acted in "bad faith."[76]

Detainees and the War on Terrorism

In June 2004, the Supreme Court addressed some of the difficult issues in the war on terrorism in two cases in which war detainees had been designated "enemy combatants." President Bush maintained that the detainees were not entitled to basic legal requirements such as attorneys or hearings and that his actions could not be reviewed in the courts. The Supreme Court rejected his position. Regardless of the location of their detention—hundreds of foreign detainees are being held at a naval base in Guantánamo Bay, Cuba—the Court said they are entitled to challenge their designation as "enemy combatants" before a federal judge or other neutral decision maker.[77]

INTERACTIVE 15.2

 Inside Guantánamo

In a second case, a Saudi Arabian resident, who was born in the United States and thus a citizen, was picked up on an Afghan battlefield and detained as an enemy combatant. In an 8–1 vote, the Court declared that he is entitled by the due process clause of the Fifth Amendment to a "meaningful opportunity" to contest the basis for his detention. In blunt language, Justice Sandra Day O'Connor, speaking for herself and three other justices, rebuffed the president's claim: "We have long since made clear that a state of war is not a blank check for the President when it comes to the rights of the Nation's citizens."[78]

INTERACTIVE 15.3

 The Geneva Conventions

In 2006, the Court rejected by a vote of 5 to 3 the president's claim of unbounded authority in the creation and use of military commissions for enemy combatants imprisoned at Guantánamo Bay, Cuba. In *Hamdan* v. *Rumsfeld*, the justices held that the commissions were unauthorized by Congress and that they violated a provision of international law. The opinion rebuking presidential authority also established minimum procedures for any future commissions. Shortly thereafter, the Bush administration complied with the decision by announcing that terror suspects held by the United States would have a right to basic legal and human protections under international law. In 2007, the Court granted review to determine whether Guantánamo detainees have constitutional protections.[79]

★ The Ninth Amendment and Personal Autonomy

The enumeration in the Constitution, of certain rights, shall not be construed to deny or disparage others retained by the people.

The working and history of the Ninth Amendment remain an enigma; the evidence supports two different views: the amendment may protect rights that are not enumerated, or it may simply protect state governments against the assumption of power by the national government.[80] The meaning of the amendment was not an issue until 1965, when the Supreme Court used it to protect privacy, a right that is not enumerated in the Constitution.

Controversy: From Privacy to Abortion

In *Griswold* v. *Connecticut* (1965), the Court struck down, by a vote of 7–2, a seldom-enforced Connecticut statute that made the use of birth control devices a crime.[81] Justice Douglas, writing for the majority, asserted that the "specific guarantees in the Bill of Rights have penumbras [partially illuminated regions surrounding fully lit areas]" that give "life and substance" to broad, unspecified protections in the Bill of Rights. Several specific guarantees in the First, Third, Fourth, and Fifth Amendments create a zone of privacy, Douglas argued, and this zone is protected by the Ninth Amendment and is applicable to the states by the due process clause of the Fourteenth Amendment.

Three justices gave further emphasis to the relevance of the Ninth Amendment, which, they contended, protects fundamental rights derived from those specifically enumerated in the first eight amendments. This view contrasted sharply with the position expressed by the two dissenters, Justices Black and Stewart. In the absence of some specific prohibition, they argued, the Bill of Rights and the Fourteenth Amendment do not allow judicial annulment of state legislative policies, even if those policies are abhorrent to a judge or justice.

Griswold established the principle that the Bill of Rights as a whole creates a right to make certain intimate, personal choices, including the right of married people to engage in sexual intercourse for reproduction or pleasure. This zone of personal autonomy, protected by the Constitution, was the basis of a 1973 case that sought to invalidate state antiabortion laws. But rights are not absolute, and in weighing the interests of the individual against the interests of the government, the Supreme Court found itself caught up in a flood of controversy that has yet to subside.

In *Roe* v. *Wade* (1973), the Court, in a 7–2 decision, declared unconstitutional a Texas law making it a crime to obtain an abortion except for the purpose of saving the woman's life.[82]

Justice Harry A. Blackmun, who wrote the majority opinion, could not point to a specific constitutional guarantee to justify the Court's ruling. Instead, he based the decision on the right to privacy protected by the due process clause of the Fourteenth Amendment. In effect, state abortion laws were unreasonable and hence unconstitutional. The Court declared that in the first three months of pregnancy, the abortion decision must be left to the woman and her physician. In the interest of protecting the woman's health, states may restrict but not prohibit abortions in the second three months of pregnancy. Finally, in the last three months of pregnancy, states may regulate or even prohibit abortions to protect the life of the fetus, except when medical judgment determines that an abortion is necessary to save the woman's life. In all, the Court's ruling affected the laws of forty-six states.

The dissenters—Justices Byron R. White and Rehnquist—were quick to assert what critics have frequently repeated since the decision: the Court's judgment was directed by its own dislikes, not by any constitutional compass. In the absence of guiding principles, they asserted, the majority justices simply substituted their views for the views of the state legislatures whose abortion

? Can you explain why . . . there is a constitutional right to privacy even though the word *privacy* is never mentioned in the Constitution?

Anguished Voices; Angry Voices
Every year on January 22, demonstrators gather on the plaza outside the U.S. Supreme Court building to protest the Court's 1973 abortion decision, *Roe* v. *Wade.* The justices and the public remain divided on abortion. In 1992, the Court upheld a woman's right to choose abortion, but it also upheld new restrictions on the exercise of that right. *(left: Tim Sloan/AFP/Getty Images; right: Ron Sachs/Corbis Sygma)*

IDEAlog.org

What are your views on abortion? Would your view differ after reading this material? Take IDEAlog's self-test.

regulations they invalidated.[83] In a 1993 television interview, Blackmun insisted that "*Roe* versus *Wade* was decided . . . on constitutional grounds."[84] It was as if Blackmun were trying, by sheer force of will, to turn back twenty years' worth of stinging objections to the opinion he had crafted.

The composition of the Court shifted under President Ronald Reagan. His elevation of Rehnquist to chief justice in 1986 and his appointment of Scalia in 1986 and Kennedy in 1988 raised new hope among abortion foes and old fears among advocates of choice.

A perceptible shift away from abortion rights materialized in *Webster* v. *Reproductive Health Services* (1989). The case was a blockbuster, attracting voluminous media coverage. In *Webster,* the Supreme Court upheld the constitutionality of a Missouri law that denied the use of public employees or publicly funded facilities in the performance of an abortion unless the woman's life was in danger.[85] Furthermore, the law required doctors to perform tests to determine whether fetuses twenty weeks and older could survive outside the womb. This was the first time that the Court upheld significant government restrictions on abortion.

The justices issued five opinions, but no single opinion captured a majority. Four justices (Blackmun, Brennan, Thurgood Marshall, and John Paul Stevens) voted to strike down the Missouri law and hold fast to *Roe.* Four justices (Kennedy, Rehnquist, Scalia, and White) wanted to overturn *Roe* and return to the states the power to regulate abortion. The remaining justice, Sandra Day O'Connor, avoided both camps. Her position was that state abortion restrictions are permissible provided they are not "unduly burdensome." She voted with the conservative plurality to uphold the restrictive Missouri statute on the ground that it did not place an undue burden on women's rights. But she declined to reconsider (and overturn) *Roe.*

The Court has since moved cautiously down the road toward greater government control of abortion. In 1990, the justices split on two state parental notification laws. The Court struck down a state requirement that compelled unwed minors to notify both parents before having an abortion. In another case, however, the Court upheld a state requirement that a physician notify one parent of a pregnant minor of her intent to have an abortion. In both cases, the justices voiced widely divergent opinions, revealing a continuing division over abortion.[86]

The abortion issue pits freedom against order. The decision to bear or beget children should be free from government control. Yet government has a legitimate interest in protecting and preserving life, including fetal life, as part of its responsibility to maintain an orderly society. Rather than choose between freedom and order, the majority on the Court has loosened constitutional protections of abortion rights and cast the politically divisive issue into the state legislatures, where elected representatives can thrash out the conflict.

Many groups defending or opposing abortion have now turned to state legislative politics to advance their policies. This approach will force candidates for state office to debate the abortion issue and then translate electoral outcomes into legislation that restricts or protects abortion. If the abortion issue is deeply felt by Americans, pluralist theory would predict that the strongest voices for or against abortion will mobilize the greatest support in the political arena.

With a clear conservative majority, the Court seemed poised to reverse *Roe* in 1992. But a new coalition—forged by Reagan and Bush appointees O'Connor, Souter, and Kennedy—reaffirmed *Roe* yet tolerated additional restrictions on abortions. In *Planned Parenthood* v. *Casey*, a bitterly divided bench opted for the O'Connor "undue burden" test. Eight years later, in 2000, O'Connor sided with a coalition of liberal and moderate justices in a 5–4 decision striking down a Nebraska law that had banned so-called partial-birth abortion, illustrating the Court's continuing and deep division on the abortion issue.[87]

Let's view the abortion controversy through our lens of value conflicts. Presidents try to appoint justices whose values coincide with their own. Justices appointed by conservative presidents Reagan and George H. W. Bush weakened abortion as a constitutional right, putting more weight on order. President Clinton's appointees (Ruth Bader Ginsburg and Stephen G. Breyer) fulfilled his liberal campaign promise to protect women's access to abortion from further assault, putting more weight on freedom. President George W. Bush's conservative appointees—John G. Roberts, Jr., and Samuel A. Alito, Jr.—have tipped the balance toward order. In 2007, the Court by a 5–4 vote upheld a federal law banning partial-birth abortion.[88] The law was nearly identical to the one struck down by the Court years before. Today, order trumps freedom. But an ideological shift in the White House, coupled with key departures from the Court, may yet produce a different result.

Personal Autonomy and Sexual Orientation

The right-to-privacy cases may have opened a Pandora's box of divisive social issues. Does the right to privacy embrace private homosexual acts between consenting adults? Consider the case of Michael Hardwick, who was arrested in 1982 in his Atlanta bedroom while having sex with another man. In a standard approach to prosecuting homosexuals, Georgia charged him under a state criminal statute with the crime of sodomy, which means oral or anal intercourse. The police said that they had gone to his home to arrest him for failing to pay

Adam and Eve or Adam and Steve?

Protesters against gay marriage rallied outside the Massachusetts State House in Boston as state legislators contemplated amending the state constitution in 2004 to ban such unions. The state's highest court had ruled that only full, equal marriage rights for gay couples satisfied the state constitution. The amendment effort failed. *(Ramin Talaie/Corbis)*

a fine for drinking in public. Although the prosecutor dropped the charges, Hardwick sued to challenge the law's constitutionality. He won in the lower courts, but the state pursued the case.

The conflict between freedom and order lies at the core of the case. "Our legal history and our social traditions have condemned this conduct uniformly for hundreds and hundreds of years," argued Georgia's attorney. Constitutional law, he continued, "must not become an instrument for a change in the social order." Hardwick's attorney, a noted constitutional scholar, said that government must have a more important reason than "majority morality to justify regulation of sexual intimacies in the privacy of the home." He maintained that the case involved two precious freedoms: the right to engage in private sexual relations and the right to be free from government intrusion in one's home.[89]

More than half the states have eliminated criminal penalties for private homosexual acts between consenting adults. The rest still outlaw homosexual sodomy, and many outlaw heterosexual sodomy as well. As a result, homosexual rights groups and some civil liberties groups followed Hardwick's case closely. Fundamentalist Christian groups and defenders of traditional morality expressed deep interest in the outcome too.

In a bitterly divided ruling in 1986, the Court held in *Bowers* v. *Hardwick* that the Constitution does not protect homosexual relations between consenting adults, even in the privacy of their own homes.[90] The logic of the findings in the privacy cases involving contraception and abortion would seem to have compelled a finding of a right to personal autonomy—a right to make personal choices unconstrained by government—in this case as well. But the 5–4 majority maintained that only heterosexual choices—whether and whom to marry, whether to conceive a child, whether to have an abortion—fall within the zone of privacy established by the Court in its earlier rulings. "The Judiciary necessarily takes to itself further authority to govern the country without express constitutional authority" when it expands the list of fundamental rights not rooted in the language or design of the Constitution, wrote Justice White, the author of the majority opinion.

The arguments on both sides of the privacy issue are compelling. This makes the choice between freedom and order excruciating for ordinary citizens and Supreme Court justices alike. At the conference to decide the merits of the *Hardwick* case, Justice Lewis Powell cast his vote to extend privacy rights to homosexual conduct. Later, he joined with his conservative colleagues, fashioning a new majority. Four years after the *Hardwick* decision, Powell revealed another change of mind: "I probably made a mistake," he declared, speaking of his decision to vote with the conservative majority.[91]

Justice White's majority opinion was reconsidered in 2003 when the Court considered a challenge to a Texas law that criminalized homosexual but not heterosexual sodomy. This time, in *Lawrence and Garner* v. *Texas,* a new coalition of six justices viewed the issue in a different light. May a majority use the power of government to enforce its views on the whole society through the criminal law? Speaking through Justice Kennedy, the Court observed "an emerging awareness that liberty gives substantial protection to adult persons in deciding how to conduct their private lives in matters pertaining to sex." Since the Texas law furthered no legitimate state interest but intruded into the intimate personal choices of individuals, the law was void. Kennedy along with four other justices then took the unusual step of reaching back in time to declare that the *Bowers* decision was wrong and should be overruled.[92]

Justice Antonin Scalia, joined by Chief Justice Rehnquist and Justice Clarence Thomas, issued a stinging dissent. Scalia charged the majority with "signing on to the homosexual agenda" aimed at eliminating the moral opprobrium traditionally attached to homosexual conduct. The consequence is that the Court would be departing from its role of ensuring that the democratic rules of engagement are observed. He continued:

> What Texas has chosen to do is well within the range of traditional democratic action, and its hand should not be stayed through the invention of a brand-new "constitutional right" by a Court that is impatient of democratic change. It is indeed true that "later generations can see that laws once thought necessary and proper in fact serve only to oppress," . . . and when that happens, later generations can repeal those laws. But it is the premise of our system that those judgments are to be made by the people, and not imposed by a governing caste that knows best.[93]

The challenge of democracy calls for the democratic process to sort out value conflicts whenever possible. And, according to Scalia, the majority has moved from its traditional responsibility of umpiring the system to favoring one side over another in the struggle between freedom and order.

Issues around sexual orientation have shifted toward the states, where various groups continue to assert their political power. At one point, the Hawaii courts were poised to be the first in the nation to approve gay marriages. But this effort failed when the state legislature voted to put a state constitutional amendment on the ballot reaffirming traditional marriage. The amendment passed. In anticipation of state-approved same-sex unions, Congress moved affirmatively in 1996 to bar the effects of homosexual marriage through passage of the Defense of Marriage Act. President Clinton signed the bill into law. The law defines marriage as a union between people of opposite sexes and declares that states are not obliged to recognize gay marriages performed elsewhere. (The Constitution's full faith and credit clause would otherwise impose a duty on all the states to enforce the legal acts of every other state.) The law does not ban such unions; it only protects states from having to recognize homosexual marriage sanctioned by other states. Forty-three restrict marriage to persons of the opposite sex, and twenty-six states have included a state constitutional clause that bars recognition of same-sex marriage.

Some states have been innovators in legitimizing homosexuality. In 2000, the Vermont legislature approved same-sex "unions" but not same-sex marriages. The difference between a union and a marriage may prove to be a distinction without a difference. In 2003, the highest court in Massachusetts mandated the state legislature to acknowledge homosexual marriage as a fundamental right under its state constitution. Today Massachusetts is the only state where same-sex marriage is permitted. (In 2006, the Massachusetts court limited its decision by ruling that gay couples who live in states where such marriages are prohibited cannot marry in Massachusetts.) These actions should encourage groups for and against such intimate choices to push or oppose similar legislation in their own states.

The pluralist model provides one solution for groups dissatisfied with rulings from the nation's highest court. State courts and state legislatures have demonstrated their receptivity to positions that are probably untenable in the federal courts. However, state-by-state decisions offer little comfort to Americans who believe the U.S. Constitution protects them in their most intimate decisions and actions, regardless of where they reside.

IDEAlog.org

Do you support a constitutional amendment that would bar marriages between gay and lesbian couples? Take IDEAlog's self-test.

★ Summary

When they established the new government of the United States, the states and the people compelled the framers, through the Bill of Rights, to protect their freedoms. In interpreting these ten amendments, the courts, especially the Supreme Court, have taken on the task of balancing freedom and order.

The First Amendment protects several freedoms: freedom of religion, freedom of speech and of the press, and the freedom to assemble peaceably and to petition the government. The establishment clause demands government neutrality toward religions and between the religious and the nonreligious. According to judicial interpretations of the free-exercise clause, religious beliefs are inviolable, but the Constitution does not protect antisocial actions in the name of religion. Extreme interpretations of the religion clauses could bring the clauses into conflict with each other.

Freedom of expression encompasses freedom of speech, freedom of the press, and the right to assem-

ble peaceably and to petition the government. Freedom of speech and freedom of the press have never been held to be absolute, but the courts have ruled that the Bill of Rights gives the people far greater protection than other freedoms. Exceptions to free speech protections include some forms of symbolic expression, fighting words, and obscenity. Press freedom has enjoyed broad constitutional protection because a free society depends on the ability to collect and report information without government interference. The rights to assemble peaceably and to petition the government stem from the guarantees of freedom of speech and of the press. Each freedom is equally fundamental, but the right to exercise them is not absolute.

The adoption of the Fourteenth Amendment in 1868 extended the guarantees of the Bill of Rights to the states. The due process clause became the vehicle for applying specific provisions of the Bill of Rights—one at a time, case after case—to the states. The designation of a right as fundamental also called for a

★ The Civil War Amendments

The Civil War amendments were adopted to provide freedom and equality to black Americans. The Thirteenth Amendment, ratified in 1865, provided that

> neither slavery nor involuntary servitude . . . shall exist within the United States, or any place subject to their jurisdiction.

The Fourteenth Amendment was adopted three years later. It provides first that freed slaves are citizens:

> All persons born or naturalized in the United States, and subject to the jurisdiction thereof, are citizens of the United States and of the State wherein they reside.

As we saw in Chapter 15, it also prohibits the states from abridging the "privileges or immunities of citizens of the United States" or depriving "any person of life, liberty, or property, without due process of law." The amendment then goes on to guarantee equality under the law, declaring that no state shall

> deny to any person within its jurisdiction the equal protection of the laws.

The Fifteenth Amendment, adopted in 1870, added a measure of political equality:

> The right of citizens of the United States to vote shall not be denied or abridged by the United States or by any State on account of race, color, or previous condition of servitude.

American blacks were thus free and politically equal—at least according to the Constitution. But for many years, the courts sometimes thwarted the efforts of the other branches to protect their constitutional rights.

Congress and the Supreme Court: Lawmaking Versus Law Interpreting

In the years after the Civil War, Congress went to work to protect the rights of black citizens. In 1866, lawmakers passed a civil rights act that gave the national government some authority over the treatment of blacks by state courts. This legislation was a response to the **black codes,** laws enacted by the former slave states to restrict the freedom of blacks. For example, vagrancy and apprenticeship laws forced blacks to work and denied them a free choice of employers. One section of the 1866 act that still applies today grants all citizens the right to make and enforce contracts; the right to sue others in court (and the corresponding ability to be sued); the duty and ability to give evidence in court; and the right to inherit, purchase, lease, sell, hold, or convey property. Later, in the Civil Rights Act of 1875, Congress attempted to guarantee blacks equal access to public accommodations (parks, theaters, and the like).

Although Congress enacted laws to protect the civil rights of black citizens, the Supreme Court weakened some of those rights. In 1873, the Court ruled that the Civil War amendments had not changed the relationship between the state and national governments.[6] State citizenship and national citizenship remained separate and distinct. According to the Court, the Fourteenth Amendment did not obligate the states to honor the rights guaranteed by U.S. citizenship.

black codes Legislation enacted by former slave states to restrict the freedom of blacks.

In subsequent years, the Court's decisions narrowed some constitutional protections for blacks. In 1876, the justices limited congressional attempts to protect the rights of blacks.[7] A group of Louisiana whites had used violence and fraud to prevent blacks from exercising their basic constitutional rights, including the right to assemble peaceably. The justices held that the rights allegedly infringed on were not nationally protected rights and that therefore Congress was powerless to punish those who violated them. On the very same day, the Court ruled that the Fifteenth Amendment did not guarantee all citizens the right to vote; it simply listed grounds that could not be used to deny that right.[8] And in 1883, the Court struck down the public accommodations section of the Civil Rights Act of 1875.[9] The justices declared that the national government could prohibit only *government* action that discriminated against blacks; private acts of discrimination or acts of omission by a state were beyond the reach of the national government. For example, a person who refused to serve blacks in a private club was outside the control of the national government because the discrimination was a private—not a governmental—act. The Court refused to see racial discrimination as an act that the national government could prohibit. In many cases, the justices tolerated racial discrimination. In the process, they abetted **racism,** the belief that there are inherent differences among the races that determine people's achievement and that one's own race is superior to and thus has a right to dominate others.

The Court's decisions gave the states ample room to maneuver around civil rights laws. In the matter of voting rights, for example, states that wanted to bar black men from the polls simply used nonracial means to do so. One popular tool was the **poll tax,** first imposed by Georgia in 1877. This was a tax of $1 or $2 on every citizen who wanted to vote. The tax was not a burden for most whites. But many blacks were tenant farmers, deeply in debt to white merchants and landowners; they had no extra money for voting. Other bars to black suffrage included literacy tests, minimum education requirements, and a grandfather clause that restricted suffrage to men who could establish that their grandfathers were eligible to vote before 1867 (three years before the Fifteenth Amendment declared that race could not be used to deny individuals the right to vote).[10] White southerners also used intimidation and violence to keep blacks from the polls.

The Roots of Racial Segregation

From well before the Civil War, **racial segregation** had been a way of life in the South: blacks lived and worked separately from whites. After the war, southern states began to enact Jim Crow laws to reinforce segregation. (*Jim Crow* was a derogatory term for a black person.) Once the Supreme Court took the teeth out of the Civil Rights Act of 1875, such laws proliferated. They required blacks to live in separate (generally inferior) areas and restricted them to separate sections of hospitals; separate cemeteries; separate drinking and toilet facilities; separate schools; and separate sections of trains, jails, and parks.

In 1892, Homer Adolph Plessy, who was seven-eighths Caucasian, took a seat in a "whites-only" car of a Louisiana train. He refused to move to the car reserved for blacks and was arrested. Plessy argued that Louisiana's law mandating racial segregation on its trains was an unconstitutional infringement on both the privileges and immunities guaranteed by the Fourteenth Amendment and its equal protection clause. The Supreme Court disagreed. The majority in *Plessy* v. *Ferguson* (1896) upheld state-imposed racial segregation.[11] They based

racism A belief that human races have distinct characteristics such that one's own race is superior to, and has a right to rule, others.

poll tax A tax of $1 or $2 on every citizen who wished to vote, first instituted in Georgia in 1877. Although it was no burden on most white citizens, it effectively disenfranchised blacks.

racial segregation Separation from society because of race.

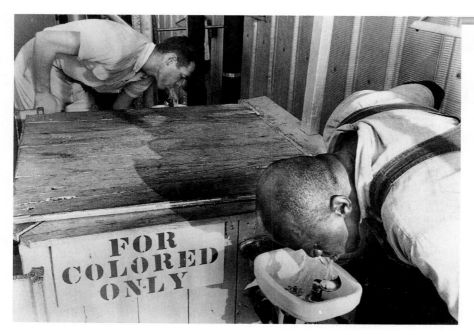

Separate and Unequal
The Supreme Court gave constitutional protection to racial separation on the theory that states could provide "separate but equal" facilities for blacks. But racial separation meant unequal facilities, as these two water fountains dramatically illustrate. The Supreme Court struck a fatal blow against the separate-but-equal doctrine in its landmark 1954 ruling in *Brown* v. *Board of Education*. (Corbis-Bettmann)

their decision on what came to be known as the **separate-but-equal doctrine,** which held that separate facilities for blacks and whites satisfied the Fourteenth Amendment as long as they were equal.

Three years later, the Supreme Court extended the separate-but-equal doctrine to the schools.[12] The justices ignored the fact that black educational facilities (and most other "colored-only" facilities) were far from equal to those reserved for whites.

By the end of the nineteenth century, legal racial segregation was firmly entrenched in the American South. Although constitutional amendments and national laws to protect equality under the law were in place, the Supreme Court's interpretation of those amendments and laws rendered them ineffective. Several decades would pass before any change was discernible.

★ The Dismantling of School Segregation

Denied the right to vote and to be represented in the government, blacks sought access to power through other parts of the political system. The National Association for the Advancement of Colored People (NAACP), founded in 1909 by W. E. B. Du Bois and others, both black and white, with the goal of ending racial discrimination and segregation, took the lead in the campaign for black civil rights. The plan was to launch a two-pronged legal and lobbying attack on the separate-but-equal doctrine: first by pressing for fully equal facilities for blacks, then by proving the unconstitutionality of segregation. The process would be a slow one, but the strategies involved did not require a large organization or heavy financial backing; at the time, the NAACP had neither.*

---

*In 1939, the NAACP established an offshoot, the NAACP Legal Defense and Education Fund, to work on legal challenges while the parent organization concentrated on lobbying.

separate-but-equal doctrine
The concept that providing separate but equivalent facilities for blacks and whites satisfies the equal protection clause of the Fourteenth Amendment.

Pressure for Equality . . .

By the 1920s, the separate-but-equal doctrine was so deeply ingrained in American law that no Supreme Court justice would dissent from its continued application to racial segregation. But a few Court decisions offered hope that change would come. In 1935, Lloyd Gaines graduated from Lincoln University, a black college in Missouri, and applied to the state law school. The law school rejected him because he was black. Missouri refused to admit blacks to its all-white law school; instead, the state's policy was to pay the costs of blacks admitted to out-of-state law schools. With the support of the NAACP, Gaines appealed to the courts for admission to the University of Missouri Law School. In 1938, the U.S. Supreme Court ruled that he must be admitted.[13] Under the *Plessy* ruling, Missouri could not shift to other states its responsibility to provide an equal education for blacks.

Later cases helped reinforce the requirement that segregated facilities must be equal in all major respects. One was brought by Heman Sweatt, again with the help of the NAACP. The all-white University of Texas Law School had denied Sweatt entrance because of his race. A federal court ordered the state to provide a black law school for him; the state responded by renting a few rooms in an office building and hiring two black lawyers as teachers. Sweatt refused to attend the school and took his case to the Supreme Court.[14]

The Court ruled on *Sweatt* in 1950. The justices unanimously found that the facilities were inadequate: the separate "law school" provided for Sweatt did not approach the quality of the white state law school. The University of Texas had to give Sweatt full student status. But the Court avoided reexamining the separate-but-equal doctrine.

. . . and Pressure for Desegregation

These decisions suggested to the NAACP that the time was right for an attack on segregation itself. In addition, public attitudes toward race relations were slowly changing from the predominant racism of the nineteenth and early twentieth centuries toward greater tolerance. Black groups had fought with honor—albeit in segregated military units—in World War II. Blacks and whites were working together in unions and in service and religious organizations. Social change and court decisions suggested that government-imposed segregation was vulnerable.

President Harry S Truman risked his political future with his strong support of blacks' civil rights. In 1947, he established the President's Committee on Civil Rights. The committee's report, issued later that year, became the agenda for the civil rights movement during the next two decades. It called for national laws prohibiting racially motivated poll taxes, segregation, and brutality against minorities and for guarantees of voting rights and equal employment opportunity. In 1948, Truman ordered the **desegregation** (the dismantling of authorized racial segregation) of the armed forces.

In 1947, the U.S. Department of Justice had begun to submit briefs to the courts in support of civil rights. The department's most important intervention probably came in *Brown* v. *Board of Education*.[15] This case was the culmination of twenty years of planning and litigation on the part of the NAACP to invalidate racial segregation in public schools.

Linda Brown was a black child whose father had tried to enroll her in a white public school in Topeka, Kansas. The white school was close to Linda's

desegregation The ending of authorized segregation, or separation by race.

home; the walk to the black school meant that she had to cross a dangerous set of railroad tracks. Brown's request was refused because of Linda's race. A federal district court found that the black public school was equal in quality to the white school in all relevant respects; therefore, according to the *Plessy* doctrine, Linda was required to go to the black public school. Brown appealed the decision.

Brown v. *Board of Education* reached the Supreme Court in late 1951. The justices delayed argument on the sensitive case until after the 1952 national election. *Brown* was merged with four similar cases into a class action, a device for combining the claims or defenses of similar individuals so that they can be tried in a single lawsuit (see Chapter 14). The class action was supported by the NAACP and coordinated by Thurgood Marshall, who would later become the first black justice to sit on the Supreme Court. The five cases squarely challenged the separate-but-equal doctrine. By all tangible measures (standards for teacher licensing, teacher-pupil ratios, library facilities), the two school systems in each case—one white, the other black—were equal. The issue was legal separation of the races.

On May 17, 1954, Chief Justice Earl Warren, who had only recently joined the Court, delivered a single opinion covering four of the cases. Warren spoke for a unanimous Court when he declared that "in the field of public education the doctrine of 'separate but equal' has no place. Separate educational facilities are inherently unequal,"[16] depriving the plaintiffs of the equal protection of the laws. Segregated facilities generate in black children "a feeling of inferiority . . . that may affect their hearts and minds in a way unlikely ever to be undone."[17] In short, the nation's highest court found that state-imposed public school segregation violated the equal protection clause of the Fourteenth Amendment.

A companion case to *Brown* challenged the segregation of public schools in Washington, D.C.[18] Segregation there was imposed by Congress. The equal protection clause protected citizens only against state violations; no equal

INTERACTIVE 16.1

Brown v. Board of Education

protection clause restrained the national government. It was unthinkable for the Constitution to impose a lesser duty on the national government than on the states. In this case, the Court unanimously decided that the racial segregation requirement was an arbitrary deprivation of liberty without due process of law, a violation of the Fifth Amendment. In short, the concept of liberty encompassed the idea of equality.

The Court deferred implementation of the school desegregation decisions until 1955. Then, in *Brown* v. *Board of Education II*, it ruled that school systems must desegregate "with all deliberate speed" and assigned the task of supervising desegregation to the lower federal courts.[19]

Some states quietly complied with the *Brown* decree. Others did little to desegregate their schools. And many communities in the South defied the Court, sometimes violently. Some white business and professional people formed "white citizens' councils." The councils put economic pressure on blacks who asserted their rights by foreclosing on their mortgages and denying them credit at local stores. Georgia and North Carolina resisted desegregation by paying tuition for white students attending private schools. Virginia and other states ordered that desegregated schools be closed.

This resistance, along with the Supreme Court's "all deliberate speed" order, placed a heavy burden on federal judges to dismantle what was the fundamental social order in many communities.[20] Gradual desegregation under *Brown* was in some cases no desegregation at all. In 1969, a unanimous Supreme Court ordered that the operation of segregated school systems stop "at once."[21]

Two years later, the Court approved several remedies to achieve integration, including busing, racial quotas, and the pairing or grouping of noncontiguous school zones. In *Swann* v. *Charlotte-Mecklenburg County Schools*, the Supreme Court affirmed the right of lower courts to order the busing of children to ensure school desegregation.[22] But these remedies applied only to **de jure segregation,** government-imposed segregation (for example, government assignment of whites to one school and blacks to another within the same community). Court-imposed remedies did not apply to **de facto segregation,** segregation that is not the result of government action (for example, racial segregation resulting from residential patterns).

The busing of schoolchildren came under heavy attack in both the North and the South. Desegregation advocates saw busing as a potential remedy in many northern cities, where schools had become segregated as white families left the cities for the suburbs. This "white flight" had left inner-city schools predominantly black and suburban schools almost all white. Public opinion strongly opposed the busing approach, and Congress sought to impose limits on busing as a remedy to segregation. In 1974, a closely divided Court ruled that lower courts could not order busing across school district boundaries unless each district had practiced racial discrimination or school district lines had been deliberately drawn to achieve racial segregation.[23] This ruling meant an end to large-scale school desegregation in metropolitan areas.

de jure segregation
Government-imposed segregation.

de facto segregation
Segregation that is not the result of government influence.

★ The Civil Rights Movement

Although the NAACP concentrated on school desegregation, it also made headway in other areas. The Supreme Court responded to NAACP efforts in the late 1940s by outlawing whites-only primary elections in the South, declaring them to be in violation of the Fifteenth Amendment. The Court also declared segregation on interstate bus routes to be unconstitutional and desegregated restaurants and hotels in the District of Columbia. Despite these and other decisions that chipped away at existing barriers to equality, states still were denying black citizens political power, and segregation remained a fact of daily life.

Dwight D. Eisenhower, who became president in 1953, was not as concerned about civil rights as his predecessor had been. He chose to stand above the battle between the Supreme Court and those who resisted the Court's decisions. He even refused to reveal whether he agreed with the Court's decision in *Brown* v. *Board of Education.* "It makes no difference," Eisenhower declared, because "the Constitution is as the Supreme Court interprets it."[24]

Eisenhower did enforce school desegregation when the safety of schoolchildren was involved, but he appeared unwilling to do much more to advance racial equality. That goal seemed to require the political mobilization of the people—black and white—in what is now known as the **civil rights movement.**

Black churches served as the crucible of the movement. More than places of worship, they served hundreds of other functions. In black communities, the church was "a bulletin board to a people who owned no organs of communication, a credit union to those without banks, and even a kind of people's court."[25] Some of its preachers were motivated by fortune, others by saintliness. One would prove to be a modern-day Moses.

INTERACTIVE 16.2

AP | *Black History Month*

Civil Disobedience

Rosa Parks, a black woman living in Montgomery, Alabama, sounded the first call to action. That city's Jim Crow ordinances were tougher than those in other southern cities, where blacks were required to sit in the back of the bus while whites sat in the front, both races converging as the bus filled with passengers. In Montgomery, bus drivers had the power to define and redefine the floating line separating blacks and whites: drivers could order blacks to vacate an entire row to make room for one white or order blacks to stand even when some seats were vacant. Blacks could not walk through the white section to their seats in the back; they had to leave the bus after paying their fare and reenter through the rear.[26] In December 1955, Parks boarded a city bus on her way home from work and took an available seat in the front of the bus; she refused to give up her seat when the driver asked her to do so and was arrested and fined $10 for violating the city ordinance.

Montgomery's black community responded to Parks's arrest with a boycott of the city's bus system. A **boycott** is a refusal to do business with a company or individual as an expression of disapproval or a means of coercion. Blacks walked or carpooled or stayed at home rather than ride the city's buses. As the bus company moved close to bankruptcy and downtown merchants suffered from the loss of black business, city officials began to harass blacks, hoping to frighten them into ending the boycott. But Montgomery's black citizens now had a leader, a charismatic twenty-six-year-old Baptist minister named Martin Luther King, Jr.

King urged the people to hold out, and they did. A year after the boycott began, a federal court ruled that segregated transportation systems violated the equal protection clause of the Constitution. The boycott had proved to be an effective weapon.

civil rights movement The mass mobilization during the 1960s that sought to gain equality of rights and opportunities for blacks in the South and to a lesser extent in the North, mainly through nonviolent, unconventional means of participation.

boycott A refusal to do business with a firm, individual, or nation as an expression of disapproval or as a means of coercion.

When Leaders Confer

Martin Luther King, Jr., was a Baptist minister who believed in the principles of nonviolent protest practiced by India's Mohandas (Mahatma) Gandhi. This photograph captures King at a meeting with President Lyndon Johnson and other civil rights leaders in the White House cabinet room on March 18, 1966. King later joked that he was instructed to reach the White House south gate by "irregular routes," chuckling that he "had to sneak in the back door." King, who won the Nobel Peace Prize in 1964, was assassinated in 1968 in Memphis, Tennessee. *(LBJ Library/Photo by Yoichi R. Okamoto)*

INTERACTIVE 16.3

 I Have a Dream

In 1957, King helped organize the Southern Christian Leadership Conference (SCLC) to coordinate civil rights activities. He was totally committed to nonviolent action to bring racial issues into the light. To that end, he advocated **civil disobedience,** the willful but nonviolent breach of unjust laws.

One nonviolent tactic was the sit-in. On February 1, 1960, four black freshmen from North Carolina Agricultural and Technical College in Greensboro sat down at a whites-only lunch counter. They were refused service by the black waitress, who said, "Fellows like you make our race look bad." The young men stayed all day and promised to return the next morning to continue what they called a "sit-down protest." Other students soon joined in, rotating shifts so that no one missed classes. Within two days, eighty-five students had flocked to the lunch counter. Although abused verbally and physically, the students would not move. Finally, they were arrested. Soon people held similar sit-in demonstrations throughout the South and then in the North.[27] The Supreme Court upheld the actions of the demonstrators, although the unanimity that had characterized its earlier decisions was gone. (In this decision, three justices argued that even bigots had the right to call on the government to protect their property interests.)[28]

The Civil Rights Act of 1964

civil disobedience The willful but nonviolent breach of laws that are regarded as unjust.

In 1961, a new administration, headed by President John F. Kennedy, came to power. At first Kennedy did not seem to be committed to civil rights. But his stance changed as the movement gained momentum and as more and more whites became aware of the abuse being heaped on sit-in demonstrators, freedom riders (who protested unlawful segregation on interstate bus routes), and those who were trying to help blacks register to vote in southern states. Volunteers were being jailed, beaten, and even killed for advocating activities among blacks that whites took for granted.

In late 1962, President Kennedy ordered federal troops to ensure the safety of James Meredith, the first black to attend the University of Mississippi. In early 1963, Kennedy enforced the desegregation of the University of Alabama. In April 1963, television viewers were shocked to see civil rights marchers in Birmingham, Alabama, attacked with dogs, fire hoses, and cattle prods. (The idea of the Birmingham march was to provoke confrontations with white officials in an effort to compel the national government to intervene on behalf of blacks.) Finally, in June 1963, Kennedy asked Congress for legislation that would outlaw segregation in public accommodations.

Two months later, Martin Luther King, Jr., joined in a march on Washington, D.C. The organizers called the protest "A March for Jobs and Freedom," signaling the economic goals of black America. More than 250,000 people, black and white, gathered peaceably at the Lincoln Memorial to hear King speak. "I have a dream," the great preacher extemporized, "that my little children will one day live in a nation where they will not be judged by the color of their skin but by the content of their character."[29]

Congress had not yet enacted Kennedy's public accommodations bill when he was assassinated on November 22, 1963. His successor, Lyndon B. Johnson, considered civil rights his top legislative priority. Within months, Congress enacted the Civil Rights Act of 1964, which included a vital provision barring segregation in most public accommodations. This congressional action was in part a reaction to Kennedy's death. But it was also almost certainly a response to the brutal treatment of blacks throughout the South.

Congress had enacted civil rights laws in 1957 and 1960, but they dealt primarily with voting rights. The 1964 act was the most comprehensive legislative attempt ever to erase racial discrimination in the United States. Among its many provisions, the act

> **Can you explain why . . .** some people would argue that the 1964 Civil Rights Act had a wider impact than *Brown* v. *Board of Education*?

- Entitled all persons to "the full and equal enjoyment" of goods, services, and privileges in places of public accommodation, without discrimination on the grounds of race, color, religion, or national origin (the inclusion of "national origin" or place of birth would set in motion plans for immigration reform the following year)

- Established the right to equality in employment opportunities

- Strengthened voting rights legislation

- Created the Equal Employment Opportunity Commission (EEOC) and charged it with hearing and investigating complaints of job discrimination*

- Provided that funds could be withheld from federally assisted programs administered in a discriminatory manner

---

*Since 1972, the EEOC has had the power to institute legal proceedings on behalf of employees who allege that they have been victims of illegal discrimination.

The last of these provisions had a powerful effect on school desegregation when Congress enacted the Elementary and Secondary Education Act in 1965. That act provided for billions of federal dollars for the nation's schools; the threat of losing that money spurred local school boards to formulate and implement new plans for desegregation.

The 1964 act faced an immediate constitutional challenge. Its opponents argued that the Constitution does not forbid acts of private discrimination—the position the Supreme Court itself had taken in the late nineteenth century. But this time, a unanimous Court upheld the law, declaring that acts of discrimination impose substantial burdens on interstate commerce and thus are subject to congressional control.[30] In a companion case, Ollie McClung, the owner of a small restaurant, had refused to serve blacks. McClung maintained that he had the freedom to serve whomever he wanted in his own restaurant. The justices, however, upheld the government's prohibition of McClung's racial discrimination on the ground that a substantial portion of the food served in his restaurant had moved in interstate commerce.[31] Thus, the Supreme Court vindicated the Civil Rights Act of 1964 by reason of the congressional power to regulate interstate commerce rather than on the basis of the Fourteenth Amendment. Since 1937, the Court had approved ever-widening authority to regulate state and local activities under the commerce clause. It was the most powerful basis for the exercise of congressional power in the Constitution.

President Johnson's goal was a "great society." Soon a constitutional amendment and a series of civil rights laws were in place to help him meet his goal:

- The Twenty-fourth Amendment, ratified in 1964, banned poll taxes in primary and general elections for national office.

- The Economic Opportunity Act of 1964 provided education and training to combat poverty.

- The Voting Rights Act of 1965 empowered the attorney general to send voter registration supervisors to areas in which fewer than half the eligible minority voters had been registered. This act has been credited with doubling black voter registration in the South in only five years.[32]

- The Fair Housing Act of 1968 banned discrimination in the rental and sale of most housing.

The Continuing Struggle over Civil Rights

In the decades that followed, it became clear that civil rights laws on the books do not ensure civil rights in action. In 1984, for example, the Supreme Court was called on to interpret a law forbidding sex discrimination in schools and colleges that receive financial assistance from the national government: Must the entire institution comply with the regulations, or only those portions of it that receive assistance?

In *Grove City College* v. *Bell,* the Court ruled that government educational grants to students implicate the institution as a recipient of government funds; therefore, it must comply with government nondiscrimination provisions. However, only the specific department or program receiving the funds (in Grove City's case, the financial aid program), not the whole institution, was barred from discriminating.[33] Athletic departments rarely receive such government funds, so colleges had no obligation to provide equal opportunity for women in their sports programs.

The *Grove City* decision had widespread effects because three other important civil rights laws were worded similarly. The implication was that any law barring discrimination on the basis of race, sex, age, or disability would be applicable only to programs receiving federal funds, not to the entire institution. So a university laboratory that received federal research grants could not discriminate, but other departments that did not receive federal money could. The effect of *Grove City* was to frustrate enforcement of civil rights laws. In keeping with pluralist theory, civil rights and women's groups shifted their efforts to the legislative branch.

Congress reacted immediately, exercising its lawmaking power to check the law-interpreting power of the judiciary. Congress can revise national laws to counter judicial decisions; in this political chess game, the Court's move is hardly the last one. Legislators protested that the Court had misinterpreted the intent of the antidiscrimination laws, and they forged a bipartisan effort to make that intent crystal clear: if any part of an institution gets federal money, no part of it can discriminate. Their work led to the Civil Rights Restoration Act, which became law in 1988 despite a presidential veto by Ronald Reagan.

Although Congress tried to restore and expand civil rights enforcement, the Supreme Court weakened it again. The Court restricted minority contractor **set-asides** of state public works funds, an arrangement it had approved in 1980. (A set-aside is a purchasing or contracting provision that reserves a certain percentage of funds for minority-owned contractors.) The five-person majority held that past societal discrimination alone cannot serve as the basis for rigid quotas.[34]

Buttressed by Republican appointees, the Supreme Court continued to narrow the scope of national civil rights protections in a string of decisions that suggested the ascendancy of a new conservative majority more concerned with freedom than equality.[35] To counter the Court's changing interpretations of civil rights laws, liberals turned to Congress to restore and enlarge earlier Court decisions by writing them into law. The result was a comprehensive new civil rights bill. The Civil Rights Act of 1991 reversed or altered twelve Court decisions that had narrowed civil rights protections. The new law clarified and expanded earlier legislation and increased the costs to employers for intentional, illegal discrimination. Continued resentment generated by equal outcomes policies would move the battle back to the courts, however.

Racial Violence and Black Nationalism

Increased violence on the part of those who demanded their civil rights and those who refused to honor them marked the middle and late 1960s. Violence against civil rights workers was confined primarily to the South, where volunteers continued to work for desegregation and to register black voters. Among the atrocities that incensed even complacent whites were the bombing of dozens of black churches; the slaying of three young civil rights workers in Philadelphia, Mississippi, in 1964 by a group of whites, among them deputy sheriffs; police violence against demonstrators marching peacefully from Selma, Alabama, to Montgomery in 1965; and the assassination of Martin Luther King, Jr., in Memphis in 1968.

Black violence took the form of rioting in northern inner cities. Civil rights gains had come mainly in the South. Northern blacks had the vote and were not subject to Jim Crow laws, yet most lived in poverty. Unemployment was high, opportunities for skilled jobs were limited, and earnings were low. The

set-aside A purchasing or contracting provision that reserves a certain percentage of funds for minority-owned contractors.

segregation of blacks into the inner cities, although not sanctioned by law, was nevertheless real; their voting power was minimal because they constituted a small minority of the northern population. The solid gains made by southern blacks added to their frustration. Beginning in 1964, northern blacks took to the streets, burning and looting. Riots in 168 cities and towns followed King's assassination in 1968, and many were met with violent responses from urban police forces and the National Guard.

The lack of progress toward equality for northern blacks was an important factor in the rise of the black nationalist movement in the 1960s. The Nation of Islam, or Black Muslims, called for separation from whites rather than integration and for violence in return for violence. Malcolm X was their leading voice, until he distanced himself from the Muslims shortly before his assassination by fellow Muslims in 1965. The militant Black Panther Party generated fear with its denunciation of the values of white America. In 1966, Stokely Carmichael, then chairman of the Student Nonviolent Coordinating Committee (SNCC), called on blacks to assert, "We want black power," in their struggle for civil rights. Organizations that had espoused integration and nonviolence now argued that blacks needed power more than white friendship.

The movement had several positive effects. Black nationalism instilled and promoted pride in black history and black culture. By the end of the decade, U.S. colleges and universities were beginning to institute black studies programs. More black citizens were voting than ever before, and their voting power was evident: increasing numbers of blacks were winning election to public office. In 1967, Cleveland's voters elected Carl Stokes, the first black mayor of a major American city. And by 1969, black representatives formed the Congressional Black Caucus. These achievements were incentives for other groups that also faced barriers to equality.

★ Civil Rights for Other Minorities

Recent civil rights laws and court decisions protect members of all minority groups. The Supreme Court underscored the breadth of this protection in an important decision in 1987.[36] The justices ruled unanimously that the Civil Rights Act of 1866 (known today as Section 1981) offers broad protection against discrimination to all minorities. Previously, members of white ethnic groups could not invoke the law in bias suits. Under the 1987 decision, members of any ethnic group can recover money damages if they prove they have been denied a job, excluded from rental housing, or subjected to another form of discrimination prohibited by the law. The 1964 Civil Rights Act offers similar protections but specifies strict procedures for filing suits that tend to discourage litigation. Moreover, the remedies in most cases are limited. In job discrimination, for example, back pay and reinstatement are the only remedies. Section 1981 has fewer hurdles and allows litigants to seek punitive damages (damages awarded by a court as additional punishment for a serious wrong). In some respects, then, the older law is a more potent weapon than the newer one in fighting discrimination.

Clearly, the civil rights movement has had an effect on all minorities. Here we examine the civil rights struggles of four groups: Native Americans, immigrant groups (the largest of which are Latinos), the disabled, and homosexuals.

Native Americans

During the eighteenth and nineteenth centuries, the U.S. government took Indian lands, isolated Native Americans on reservations, and denied them political and social rights. The government's dealings with the Indians were often marked by violence and broken promises. The agencies responsible for administering Indian reservations kept Native Americans poor and dependent on the national government.

The national government switched policies at the beginning of the twentieth century, promoting assimilation instead of separation. The government banned the use of native languages and religious rituals; it sent Indian children to boarding schools and gave them non-Indian names. In 1924, Indians received U.S. citizenship. Until that time, they had been considered members of tribal nations whose relations with the U.S. government were determined by treaties. The Native American population suffered badly during the Great Depression, primarily because the poorest Americans were affected most severely but also because of the inept administration of Indian reservations. (Today, Indians make up less than 1 percent of the population.) Poverty persisted on the reservations well after the Depression was over, and Indian land holdings continued to shrink through the 1950s and into the 1960s—despite signed treaties and the religious significance of portions of the lands they lost. In the 1960s, for example, a part of the Hopi Sacred Circle, which is considered the source of all life in the Hopi tribal religion, was strip-mined for coal.

Anger bred of poverty, unemployment, and frustration with an uncaring government exploded in militant action in late 1969, when several American Indians seized Alcatraz Island, an abandoned island in San Francisco Bay. The group cited an 1868 Sioux treaty that entitled them to unused federal lands; they remained on the island for a year and a half. In 1973, armed members of the American Indian Movement seized eleven hostages at Wounded Knee, South Dakota, the site of an 1890 massacre of two hundred Sioux (Lakota) by U.S. cavalry troops. They remained there, occasionally exchanging gunfire with federal marshals, for seventy-one days, until the government agreed to examine the treaty rights of the Oglala Sioux.[37]

In 1946, Congress enacted legislation establishing an Indian claims commission to compensate Native Americans for land that had been taken from them. In the 1970s, the Native American Rights Fund and other groups used that legislation to win important victories in the courts. The tribes won the return of lands in the Midwest and in the states of Oklahoma, New Mexico, and Washington. In 1980, the Supreme Court ordered the national government to pay the Sioux $117 million plus interest for the Black Hills of South Dakota, which had been stolen from them a century before. Other cases, involving land from coast to coast, are still pending.

The special status accorded Indian tribes in the Constitution has proved attractive to a new group of Indian leaders. Some of the 557 recognized tribes have successfully instituted casino gambling on their reservations, even in the face of state opposition to their plans. The tribes pay no taxes on their profits, which has helped them make gambling a powerful engine of economic growth for themselves and has given a once impoverished people undreamed-of riches and responsibilities. Congress has allowed these developments, provided that the tribes spend their profits on Indian assistance programs.

It is important to remember that throughout American history, Native Americans have been coerced physically and pressured economically to assimilate into the mainstream of white society. The destiny of Native Americans as viable groups with separate identities depends in no small measure on curbing their dependence on the national government.[38] The wealth created by casino gambling and other ventures funded with gambling profits may prove to be Native Americans' most effective weapon for regaining their heritage.

Immigrant Groups

The Statue of Liberty stands at the entrance to New York harbor, a gift from the people of France to commemorate the centennial of the United States. It is an icon of the United States in the world, capturing the belief that this country is a beacon of liberty for countless immigrants far and wide. We are a nation of immigrants. But the truth is more complex. Until 1965, the laws that governed immigration were rooted in invidious discrimination. Liberty's beacon drew millions of undocumented or illegal immigrants. Efforts to stem this tide brought unanticipated consequences, but further reform has failed to stop the flow of illegal immigrants to these shores.

For most of the first half of the twentieth century, immigration rules established a strict quota system that gave a clear advantage to Northern and Western Europeans and guaranteed that few Southern or Eastern Europeans, Asians, Africans, and Jews would enter the country by legal means. This was akin to the same unjustified discrimination that had subjugated blacks since the end of the Civil War. In the same spirit that championed civil rights for African Americans, a once reluctant Congress changed the rules to end discrimination on the basis of national origin. In 1965, President Lyndon Johnson signed a new immigration bill into law at the Statue of Liberty. Henceforth, the invidious quota system was gone; everyone was supposed to have an equal chance of immigrating to the United States. Upon signing the bill, Johnson remarked that there was nothing revolutionary about the law. "It will not reshape the structure of our daily lives or add importantly to either our wealth or our power." Within a few years, Johnson's prediction proved fundamentally wrong.

One purpose of the new law was to reunite families. It gave preference to relatives of immigrants already here, but since the vast majority of these legal immigrants came from Northern or Western Europe, the expectation was that reuniting families would continue the earlier preferences. Another provision gave preference in much smaller numbers to immigrants with much needed skills, such as doctors and engineers. It never occurred to the law's designers that African doctors, Indian engineers, Philippine nurses, or Chinese software programmers would be able to immigrate. Word trickled out to those newly eligible to come. Once here, these immigrants petitioned for their relatives to come. And those family members petitioned for yet others. As a result of this "chain migration," entire extended families established themselves in the United States, and the law did nothing to staunch the flow of illegal immigrants.

The demand for cheap labor in agriculture and manufacturing proved an enticing lure to many of the poor with access to America's southern border. The personal risk in crossing the border illegally was often outweighed by the possible gain in employment and a new, though illegal, start. There was no risk of imprisonment, merely a return to south of the border and perhaps another attempt to cross into a "promised land." During the post-1965 period, millions of men and women chose personal risk for the possibility of a better future.

FIGURE 16.1 Illegal Immigrants in the United States, 2005

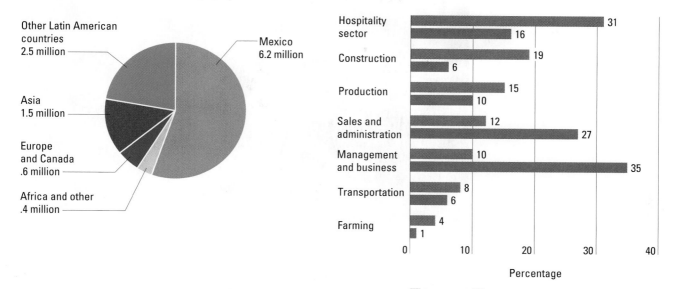

ILLEGAL IMMIGRANTS BY COUNTRY OF ORIGIN

Other Latin American countries 2.5 million

Mexico 6.2 million

Asia 1.5 million

Europe and Canada .6 million

Africa and other .4 million

JOBS HELD BY ILLEGAL IMMIGRANTS AND NATIVES

Hospitality sector — 31 / 16
Construction — 19 / 6
Production — 15 / 10
Sales and administration — 12 / 27
Management and business — 10 / 35
Transportation — 8 / 6
Farming — 4 / 1

Percentage

■ Illegal   ■ Native

In 2005, there were 37 million foreign-born people living in America. Of this number, 11.1 million (or 30 percent) were unauthorized, that is, illegal, immigrants. The pie chart on the left shows the country of origin for these unauthorized immigrants. The bar graph on the right depicts the employment of illegal immigrants compared to other (i.e., native) workers.

Source: Pew Hispanic Center, "The Size and Characteristics of Unauthorized Migrant Population in the U.S." (March 7, 2006), as seen in *Wall Street Journal,* 24 May 2006, p. A4.

In 1986, Congress sought to fix a system that by all accounts was broken. It sought to place the burden of enforcement on employers by imposing fines for hiring undocumented workers and then by offering amnesty to resident illegal immigrants who were in the United States for at least five years. But lax government enforcement and ease in obtaining falsified worker documents such as a "green card" doomed the enforcement strategy. Illegal immigrants continued to enter the United States, the majority from Mexico and Latin America (see Figure 16.1).

By 2006, politicians were ready for another round of reform, motivated by over 11 million illegal immigrants in the United States (triple the number since the last reform effort twenty years earlier); state and local governments in border states that were hit hard for the cost of public services (for example, health and education) for illegals; and the threat to national security in a post-9/11 world posed by porous, unguarded borders.

While the public is opposed to illegal immigrants obtaining driver's licenses or health care, it is important to note that in 2005, illegal immigrants paid an

Laboring Without Illegals
In May 2006 a half million immigrants and their supporters took a day off to rally in Los Angeles (and other cities) in opposition to proposed immigration law reforms. One aim was to impress the importance of immigrant labor to the lives of Americans. President Bush has been sympathetic to the immigrant community, but he has yet to win over skeptical and skittish members of his party in Congress. *(David McNew/Getty Images)*

estimated $7 billion in Social Security taxes with little or nothing in return from the government.

Taking a lesson from the civil rights struggle for African Americans, immigrant organizers in 2006 publicly voiced their opposition to new legislation that would fence off large sections of the U.S.-Mexican border and make illegal aliens criminals who face penalties in excess of a year in prison. Immigrants from a wide range of ethnic communities responded with large-scale, peaceful protests across the United States. Their point was to demonstrate their quest for legal status and their deep resistance to the concept that their mere presence was to be taken as a criminal act. But a major overhaul of immigration policy orchestrated by the Bush administration and Senate Democrats failed in 2007. Republicans abandoned the president as conservative critics abetted by talk radio programs insisted on labeling the effort a form of amnesty for lawbreakers. For their part, Democrats brought the bill to the Senate floor without committee hearings, hoping that any bill would be better than no bill. Sen. Edward M. Kennedy (D-Mass.), the bill's chief Democratic architect, said many senators "voted their fears, not their hopes."

Many Latinos have a rich and deep-rooted heritage in America, but until the 1920s, that heritage was largely confined to the southwestern states, particularly California. Then, unprecedented numbers of Mexican immigrants came to the United States in search of employment and a better life. Businesspeople who saw in them a source of cheap labor welcomed them. Many Mexicans became farm workers; others settled mainly in crowded, low-rent, inner-city districts in the Southwest, forming their own barrios, or neighborhoods, within the cities, where they maintained the customs and values of their homeland.

Like blacks who had migrated to northern cities, most new Latino immigrants found poverty and discrimination. And like poor blacks and Native Americans, they suffered disproportionately during the Great Depression.

About one-third of the Mexican American population (mainly those who had been migratory farm workers) returned to Mexico during the 1930s.

World War II gave rise to another influx of Mexicans, who this time were primarily courted to work farms in California. But by the late 1950s, most farm workers—blacks, whites, and Hispanics—were living in poverty. Latinos who lived in cities fared little better. Yet millions of Mexicans continued to cross the border into the United States, both legally and illegally. The effect was to depress wages for farm labor in California and the Southwest.

In 1965, Cesar Chavez led a strike of the United Farm Workers union against growers in California. The strike lasted several years and eventually, in combination with a national boycott, resulted in somewhat better pay, working conditions, and housing for farm workers.

In the 1970s and 1980s, the Latino population continued to grow, and it continues to grow rapidly. (See "Looking to the Future: White or Black? Try Moreno, Trigueño, or Indio.") The 20 million Latinos living in the United States in the 1970s were still mainly Puerto Rican and Mexican American, but they were joined by immigrants from the Dominican Republic, Colombia, Cuba, and Ecuador. Although civil rights legislation helped them to an extent, they were among the poorest and least educated groups in the United States. Their problems were similar to those faced by other nonwhites, but most also had to overcome the further difficulty of learning and using a new language.

One effect of the language barrier is that voter registration and voter turnout among Hispanics are lower than among other groups. The creation of nine Hispanic-majority congressional districts ensured a measure of representation. These majority minority districts remain under scrutiny as a result of Supreme Court decisions prohibiting race-based districting. Also, voter turnout depends on effective political advertising, and Hispanics have not been targeted as often as other groups with political messages in Spanish. But despite these stumbling blocks, Hispanics have started to exercise a measure of political power.

Hispanics occupy positions of power in national and local arenas. Hispanics or Latinos constitute nearly 13 percent of the population and 4 percent of Congress. The 109th Congress (2005–2007) convened with a diverse group of twenty-six members of Hispanic descent, twenty-four in the House and two in the Senate. The National Hispanic Caucus of State Legislators, which has over three hundred members, is an informal bipartisan group dedicated to voicing and advancing issues affecting Hispanic Americans.

Disabled Americans

Minority status is not confined to racial and ethnic groups. After more than two decades of struggle, 43 million disabled Americans gained recognition in 1990 as a protected minority with the enactment of the Americans with Disabilities Act (ADA).

The law extends the protections embodied in the Civil Rights Act of 1964 to people with physical or mental disabilities, including people with AIDS, alcoholism, and drug addiction. It guarantees them access to employment, transportation, public accommodations, and communication services.

The roots of the disabled rights movement stem from the period after World War II. Thousands of disabled veterans returned to a country and a society that

Looking to the Future

White or Black? Try Moreno, Trigueño, or Indio

In 2003, Hispanics edged past blacks as the nation's largest minority group. And the gap will widen far into the century. The extraordinary growth in the Hispanic population is a result of higher birthrates and a decade-long wave of immigrants. This growth will continue as more immigrants seek opportunities in the United States and as birthrates for Hispanics continue to outpace birthrates for blacks. Indeed, it is estimated that "Hispanics may constitute up to 25 percent of the U.S. population by 2050. These changes are driven not just by immigration but also by fertility. In 2002, fertility rates in the United States were estimated at 1.8 for non-Hispanic whites, 2.1 for blacks, and 3.0 for Hispanics."

This change may signal a shift with symbolic and practical consequences. In symbolic terms, American attitudes have frequently been characterized by "black" and "white." Now that Hispanics have overtaken blacks in population, viewing American issues in racial terms may recede and more sensitivity to the needs of a growing Hispanic population will take on greater importance. In practical terms, there is wisdom in the old saying that "the joint that squeaks the loudest gets the grease." Demands by Hispanic leaders may overcome competing claims by black leaders, provided citizens vote. But one-quarter of all Hispanics living in the United States are not citizens. And more than half of the Spanish-speaking population resides in Texas, California, and New York. Those who command more votes in key elections will likely hold sway.

Multiculturalism is now a feature of the decennial census. Starting in 2000, respondents were allowed to choose more than one race for identification. Moreover, Hispanics—a cultural and ethnic classification—could elect any race. The problem of racial or ethnic categorization has stumped the Census Bureau. Almost half the Hispanic respondents in the 2000 Census refused to identify themselves by any of the five standard racial categories: white, black, Asian, American Indian, or Alaska Native and natives of Hawaii or the Pacific Islands. Only 2 percent of Hispanics chose black, and 48 percent chose white. The remaining 50 percent of Hispanics chose "some other race" and added such disparate identities as Mayan, Tejano, and mestizo.

Take the example of Cuban American Rene Goderich. He identifies himself as white, although he would describe himself as "jabao," a Cuban term for a light-skinned mulatto. "Over here there's no 'jabao' or 'mulatto,' so I say I'm white. We're all mixed."

What political consequences might flow from the predicted doubling of the Hispanic population by 2050? Would allegiance to a single political party strengthen or weaken Hispanics' influence?

were insensitive to their needs. Institutionalization seemed the best way to care for the disabled, but this approach came under increasing fire as the disabled and their families sought care at home.

Advocates for the disabled found a ready model in the existing civil rights laws. Opponents argued that the changes mandated by the 1990 law (such as access for those confined to wheelchairs) could cost billions of dollars, but sup-

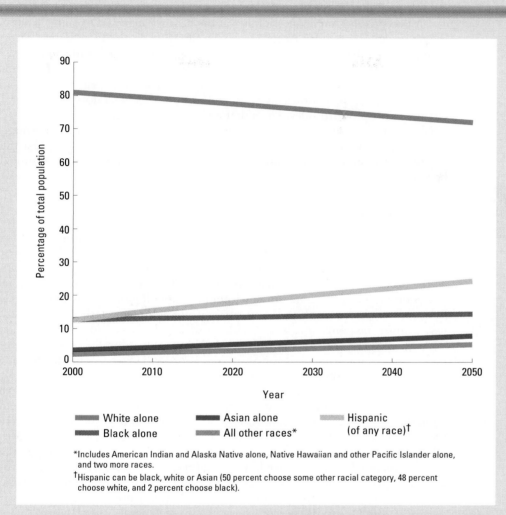

White alone

Black alone

Asian alone

All other races*

Hispanic
(of any race)†

*Includes American Indian and Alaska Native alone, Native Hawaiian and other Pacific Islander alone,
and two more races.

†Hispanic can be black, white or Asian (50 percent choose some other racial category, 48 percent
choose white, and 2 percent choose black).

Sources: Lynette Clemetson, "Hispanics Now Largest Minority, Census Shows," *New York Times,* 22 January 2003,
p. A4; Mireya Navarro, "Going Beyond Black and White, Hispanics Choose 'Other,'" *New York Times,* 9 November
2003; data from U.S. Census Bureau, 2004, "U.S. Interim Projections by Age, Sex, Race, and Hispanic Origin," available at <http://www.census.gov/ipc/www/usinterimproj/>; Samuel P. Huntington, "The Hispanic Challenge," *Foreign
Policy,* March 2004, p. 34.

porters replied that the costs would be offset by an equal or greater reduction
in federal aid to disabled people, who would rather be working.

The law's enactment set off an avalanche of job discrimination complaints
filed with the national government's discrimination watchdog agency, the
EEOC. By 2005, the EEOC had received almost 220,000 ADA-related complaints. Curiously, most complaints came from already employed people, both

previously and recently disabled. They charged that their employers failed to provide reasonable accommodations as required by the new law. The disabilities cited most frequently were back problems, mental illness, heart trouble, neurological disorders, and substance abuse.[39]

A deceptively simple question lies at the heart of many ADA suits: What is the meaning of *disability*? According to the EEOC, a disability is "a physical or mental impairment that substantially limits one or more major life activities." This deliberately vague language has thrust the courts into the role of providing needed specificity, a path that politicians have feared to tread.[40]

A change in the nation's laws, no matter how welcome, does not ensure a change in people's attitudes. Laws that end racial discrimination do not extinguish racism, and laws that ban biased treatment of the disabled cannot mandate their acceptance. But civil rights advocates predict that bias against the disabled, like similar biases against other minorities, will wither as the disabled become full participants in society.

Homosexual Americans

June 27, 1969, marked the beginning of an often overlooked movement for civil rights in the United States. On that Friday evening, plainclothes officers of the New York City police force raided a gay bar in Greenwich Village known as the Stonewall Inn. The police justified the raid because of their suspicions that Stonewall had been operating without a proper liquor license. In response, hundreds of citizens took to the streets in protest. Violent clashes and a backlash against the police involving hundreds of people ensued for several nights, during which cries of "Gay power!" and "We want freedom!" could be heard. The event became known as the Stonewall Riots and served as the touchstone for the gay liberation movement in the United States.[41]

Stonewall led to the creation of several political interest groups that have fought for the civil liberties and civil rights of members of the gay and lesbian communities. One in particular, the National Gay and Lesbian Task Force (NGLTF), successfully lobbied the U.S. Civil Service Commission in 1973 to allow gay people to serve in public employment. More recently, in 1999, the NGLTF founded the Legislative Lawyering Program, designed to work for progressive legislation at both the federal and state levels. Another organization, the Human Rights Campaign, founded in 1980, today boasts a membership of over 360,000. One of its current priorities is to seek passage of an employment nondiscrimination act to prevent U.S. citizens from being fired from their jobs for being gay.

Although once viewed as being on the fringe of American society, the gay community today maintains a visible presence in national politics. Two openly gay members serve in the U.S. House of Representatives (110th Congress): Barney Frank (D-Mass.) and Tammy Baldwin (D-Wisc.). But gay and lesbian issues seem less paramount than other issues to the American public. In the 2004 election, the economy and the Iraq war were more important to voters than homosexual marriage.[42] Financial support for candidates and groups favoring gay and lesbian rights has declined since 2000.[43]

Gays and lesbians have made significant progress since the early 1970s, but they still have a long way to go to enjoy the complete menu of civil rights now written into laws that protect other minority groups. In addition to some of the

Going to the Chapel
Julie and Hillary Goodridge, along with daughter Annie, were the first gay couple to obtain a marriage license from Boston registrar Judith A. McCarthy in May 2004. After affirming the truth of the information they provided and paying the requisite fee, they headed to the altar. Armed with their license, a minister pronounced the couple "fully and legally married." Alas, marital bliss ran out for the Goodridges two years later. They filed for divorce in 2006. *(Boston Globe Staff Photo/David L. Ryan)*

civil liberties concerns noted in Chapter 15, gays and lesbians are still unable to serve openly in the U.S. military, despite attempts by the Clinton administration, and later, the Bush administration, to improve conditions through its "don't ask, don't tell" policy, which some observers maintain has actually made things worse for homosexuals in uniform. Because domestic partner benefits are not recognized uniformly across the United States, same-sex partners are unable to take full advantage of laws that allow citizens to leave their personal estates to family members. And finally, they often cannot sign onto their partner's health-care plans (except when company policies allow it); heterosexual couples enjoy this employment benefit almost without exception.

The demand for equality found a new voice in 2003 when the highest court in Massachusetts held, in a 4–3 ruling, that same-sex couples have a state constitutional right to the "protections, benefits, and obligations of civil marriage." The majority rested its holding on the Massachusetts constitution, which affirms the dignity and equality of all individuals. The justices acknowledged that the Massachusetts constitution is more protective of equality and liberty than the federal Constitution, enabling actions that the U.S. Supreme Court might be unwilling or unable to take.[44]

The decision challenged the state legislature, which sought a compromise to avoid an affirmation of homosexual marriage. The High Court rejected this maneuver, setting the stage for a state constitutional amendment limiting marriages to unions between a man and a woman. At least thirty-seven states prohibit recognition of marriages between gay couples. Only residents of states that recognize the validity of homosexual marriage may legally marry today in Massachusetts. But it will be years before the lengthy amendment process runs its course.

A 2000 Supreme Court decision, *Boy Scouts of America* v. *Dale*, illustrates both the continuing legal struggles of gays and lesbians for civil rights and the

IDEAlog.org
Do you support a constitutional amendment that would bar marriages between gay and lesbian couples? Take IDEAlog's self-test.

modern conflict between freedom and equality. James Dale began his involvement in scouting in 1978 and ten years later achieved the esteemed rank of Eagle Scout. In 1989, he applied to and was accepted for the position of assistant scoutmaster of Troop 73 in New Jersey. Shortly after, in 1990, the Boy Scouts revoked Dale's membership in the organization when it learned that he had become a campus activist with the Rutgers University Lesbian/Gay Alliance. The Boy Scouts argued that because homosexual conduct was inconsistent with its mission, the organization enjoyed the right to revoke his membership. Dale argued that the Scouts' actions violated a New Jersey law that prohibited discrimination on the basis of sexual orientation in places of public accommodation. The Court resolved this conflict in a narrow 5–4 decision and sided with the Scouts. The majority opinion, authored by Chief Justice William H. Rehnquist, maintained that New Jersey's public accommodations law violated the Boy Scouts' freedom of association, outweighing Dale's claim for equal treatment. The dissenters, led by Justice John Paul Stevens, maintained that equal treatment outweighed free association. They reasoned that allowing Dale to serve as an assistant scoutmaster did not impose serious burdens on the Scouts or force the organization "to communicate any message that it does not wish to endorse."[45]

★ Gender and Equal Rights: The Women's Movement

Together with unconventional political activities such as protests and sit-ins, conventional political tools such as the ballot box and the lawsuit have brought minorities in America a measure of equality. The Supreme Court, once responsible for perpetuating inequality for blacks, has expanded the array of legal tools available to all minorities to help them achieve social equality. Women, too, have benefited from this change.

Protectionism

Until the early 1970s, laws that affected the civil rights of women were based on traditional views of the relationship between men and women. At the heart of these laws was **protectionism**—the notion that women must be sheltered from life's harsh realities. Thomas Jefferson, author of the Declaration of Independence, believed that "were our state a pure democracy there would still be excluded from our deliberations women, who, to prevent deprivation of morals and ambiguity of issues, should not mix promiscuously in gatherings of men."[46] And "protected" they were, through laws that discriminated against them in employment and other areas. With few exceptions, women were also "protected" from voting until early in the twentieth century.

The demand for women's rights arose from the abolition movement and later was based primarily on the Fourteenth Amendment's prohibition of laws that "abridge the privileges or immunities of citizens of the United States." However, the courts consistently rebuffed challenges to protectionist state laws. In 1873, the Supreme Court upheld an Illinois statute that prohibited women from practicing law. The justices maintained that the Fourteenth Amendment had no bearing on a state's authority to regulate admission of members to the bar.[47]

protectionism The notion that women must be protected from life's cruelties; until the 1970s, the basis for laws affecting women's civil rights.

Protectionism reached a peak in 1908, when the Court upheld an Oregon law limiting the number of hours women could work.[48] The decision was rife with assumptions about the nature and role of women, and it gave wide latitude to laws that "protected" the "weaker sex." It also led to protectionist legislation that barred women from working more than forty-eight hours a week and from working at jobs that required them to lift more than thirty-five pounds. (The average work week for men was sixty hours or longer.) In effect, women were locked out of jobs that called for substantial overtime (and overtime pay) and were shunted to jobs that men believed suited their abilities.

Protectionism can take many forms. Some employers hesitate to place women at risk in the workplace. Some have excluded women of child-bearing age from jobs that involve exposure to toxic substances that could harm a developing fetus. Usually such jobs offer more pay to compensate for their higher risk. Although they too face reproductive risks from toxic substances, men have faced no such exclusions.

In 1991, the Supreme Court struck down a company's fetal protection policy in strong terms. The Court relied on amendments to the 1964 Civil Rights Act providing for only a very few, narrow exceptions to the principle that unless some workers differ from others in their ability to work, they must be treated the same as other employees. "In other words," declared the majority, "women as capable of doing their jobs as their male counterparts may not be forced to choose between having a child and having a job."[49]

Political Equality for Women

With a few exceptions, women were not allowed to vote in this country until 1920. In 1869, Francis and Virginia Minor sued a St. Louis, Missouri, registrar for not allowing Virginia Minor to vote. In 1875, the Supreme Court held that the Fourteenth Amendment's privileges and immunities clause did not confer the right to vote on all citizens or require that the states allow women to vote.[50]

The decision clearly slowed the movement toward women's suffrage, but it did not stop it. In 1878, Susan B. Anthony, a women's rights activist, convinced a U.S. senator from California to introduce a constitutional amendment requiring that "the right of citizens of the United States to vote shall not be denied or abridged by the United States or by any State on account of sex." The amendment was introduced and voted down several times over the next twenty years. Meanwhile, as noted in Chapter 7, a number of states, primarily in the Midwest and West, did grant limited suffrage to women.

The movement for women's suffrage became a political battle to amend the Constitution. In 1917, police arrested 218 women from twenty-six states when they picketed the White House, demanding the right to vote. Nearly one hundred went to jail, some for days and others for months. The movement culminated in the adoption in 1920 of the **Nineteenth Amendment,** which gave women the right to vote. Its wording was that first suggested by Anthony.

Meanwhile, the Supreme Court continued to act as the benevolent protector of women. Women entered the work force in significant numbers during World War I and did so again during World War II, but they received lower wages than the men they replaced. Again, the justification was the "proper" role of women as mothers and homemakers. Because society expected men to be the principal providers, it followed that women's earnings were less important to the family's support. This thinking perpetuated inequalities in the

? Can you explain why . . . some women in the United States were able to vote many years before the adoption of the Nineteenth Amendment in 1920?

Nineteenth Amendment
The amendment to the Constitution, adopted in 1920, that ensures women of the right to vote.

workplace. Economic equality was closely tied to social attitudes. Because society expected women to stay at home, the assumption was that they needed less education than men did. Therefore, they tended to qualify only for low-paying, low-skilled jobs with little chance for advancement.

Prohibiting Sex-Based Discrimination

The movement to provide equal rights to women advanced a step with the passage of the Equal Pay Act of 1963. That act required equal pay for men and women doing similar work. However, state protectionist laws still had the effect of restricting women to jobs that men usually did not want. Where employment was stratified by sex, equal pay was an empty promise. To remove the restrictions of protectionism, women needed equal opportunity for employment. They got it in the Civil Rights Act of 1964 and later legislation.

The objective of the Civil Rights Act of 1964 was to eliminate racial discrimination in America. The original wording of Title VII of the act prohibited employment discrimination based on race, color, religion, and national origin— but not gender. In an effort to scuttle the provision during House debate, Democrat Howard W. Smith of Virginia proposed an amendment barring job discrimination based on sex. Smith's intention was to make the law unacceptable; his effort to ridicule the law brought gales of laughter to the debate. But Democrat Martha W. Griffiths of Michigan used Smith's strategy against him. With her support, Smith's amendment carried, as did the act.[51] Congress extended the jurisdiction of the EEOC to cover cases of invidious sex discrimination, or **sexism.**

Subsequent women's rights legislation was motivated by the pressure for civil rights, as well as by a resurgence of the women's movement, which had subsided in 1920 after the adoption of the Nineteenth Amendment. One particularly important law was Title IX of the Education Amendments of 1972, which prohibited sex discrimination in federally aided education programs. Another boost to women came from the Revenue Act of 1972, which provided tax credits for child-care expenses. In effect, the act subsidized parents with young children so that women could enter or remain in the work force. However, the high-water mark in the effort to secure women's rights was the equal rights amendment, as we shall explain shortly.

In 2007, a conservative Supreme Court tightened the rules over pay discrimination lawsuits under Title VII.[52] The case involved a woman who did not learn of the pay disparity with sixteen men in her office until years later, because salary information is secret. But the law required her to file a complaint within 180 days of pay setting. The 5–4 decision prompted a bitter oral dissent by Justice Ruth Bader Ginsburg.

Stereotypes Under Scrutiny

After nearly a century of protectionism, the Supreme Court began to take a closer look at gender-based distinctions. In 1971, it struck down a state law that gave men preference over women in administering the estate of a person who died without naming an administrator.[53] The state maintained that the law reduced court workloads and avoided family battles; however, the Court dismissed those objections, because they were not important enough to justify

sexism Invidious sex discrimination.

making gender-based distinctions between individuals. Two years later, the justices declared that paternalism operated to "put women not on a pedestal, but in a cage."[54] They then proceeded to strike down several laws that either prevented or discouraged departures from traditional sex roles. In 1976, the Court finally developed a workable standard for reviewing such laws: gender-based distinctions are justifiable only if they serve some important government purpose.[55]

The objective of the standard is to dismantle laws based on sexual stereotypes while fashioning public policies that acknowledge relevant differences between men and women. Perhaps the most controversial issue is the idea of *comparable worth,* which requires employers to pay comparable wages for different jobs, filled predominantly by one sex or the other, that are of about the same worth to the employer. Absent new legislation, the courts remain reluctant and ineffective vehicles for ending wage discrimination.[56]

The courts have not been reluctant to extend to women the *constitutional* guarantees won by blacks. In 1994, the Supreme Court extended the Constitution's equal protection guarantee by forbidding the exclusion of potential jurors on the basis of their sex. In a 6–3 decision, the justices held that it is unconstitutional to use gender, and likewise race, as a criterion for determining juror competence and impartiality. "Discrimination in jury selection," wrote Justice Harry A. Blackmun for the majority, "whether based on race or on gender, causes harm to the litigants, the community, and the individual jurors who are wrongfully excluded from participation in the judicial process."[57] The 1994 decision completed a constitutional revolution in jury selection that began in 1986 with a bar against juror exclusions based on race.

In 1996, the Court spoke with uncommon clarity when it declared that the men-only admissions policy of the Virginia Military Institute (VMI), a state-supported military college, violated the equal protection clause of the Fourteenth Amendment. Virginia defended the school's policy on the ground that it was preserving diversity among America's educational institutions.

In an effort to meet women's demands to enter VMI—and to stave off continued legal challenges—Virginia established a separate-but-equal institution called the Virginia Women's Institute for Leadership (VWIL). The program was housed at Mary Baldwin College, a private liberal arts college for women, and students enrolled in VWIL received the same financial support as students at VMI.

The presence of women at VMI would require substantial changes in the physical environment and the traditional close scrutiny of the students. Moreover, the presence of women would alter the manner in which cadets interacted socially. Was the uniqueness of VMI worth preserving at the expense of women who could otherwise meet the academic, physical, and psychological stress imposed by the VMI approach?

In a 7–1 decision, the High Court voted no. Writing for a six-member majority in *United States* v. *Virginia,* Justice Ruth Bader Ginsburg applied a demanding test she labeled "skeptical scrutiny" to official acts that deny individuals rights or responsibilities based on their sex. "Parties who seek to defend gender-based government action," she wrote, "must demonstrate an 'exceedingly persuasive justification' for that action." Ginsburg declared that "women seeking and fit for a VMI-quality education cannot be offered anything less, under the State's obligation to afford them genuinely equal protection." Ginsburg went on to note that the VWIL program offered no cure for the "opportunities and advantages withheld from women who want a VMI education and can make the grade."[58] The upshot is that distinctions based on sex are almost as suspect as distinctions based on race.

Three months after the Court's decision, VMI's board of directors finally voted 9–8 to admit women. This ended VMI's distinction as the last government-supported single-sex school. However, school officials made few allowances for women. Buzz haircuts and fitness requirements remained the standard for all students. "It would be demeaning to women to cut them slack," declared VMI's superintendent.[59]

The Equal Rights Amendment

Policies protecting women, based largely on gender stereotypes, have been woven into the legal fabric of American life. This protectionism has limited the freedom of women to compete with men socially and economically on an equal footing. However, the Supreme Court has been hesitant to extend the principles of the Fourteenth Amendment beyond issues of race. When judicial interpretation of the Constitution imposes a limit, then only a constitutional amendment can overcome it.

The National Women's Party, one of the few women's groups that did not disband after the Nineteenth Amendment was enacted, introduced the proposed **equal rights amendment (ERA)** in 1923. The ERA declared that "equality of rights under the law shall not be denied or abridged by the United States or any State on account of sex." It remained bottled up in committee in every Congress until 1970, when Representative Martha Griffiths filed a discharge petition to bring it to the House floor for a vote. The House passed the ERA, but the Senate scuttled it by attaching a section calling for prayer in the public schools.

A national coalition of women's rights advocates generated enough support to get the ERA through Congress in 1972. Its proponents then had seven years to get the amendment ratified by thirty-eight state legislatures, as required by the Constitution. By 1977, they were three states short of that goal, and three states had rescinded their earlier ratification. Then, in an unprecedented action, Congress extended the ratification deadline. It didn't help. The ERA died in 1982, still three states short of adoption.

Why did the ERA fail? There are several explanations. Its proponents mounted a national campaign to generate approval, while its opponents organized state-based anti-ERA campaigns. ERA proponents hurt their cause by exaggerating the amendment's effects; such claims only gave ammunition to the amendment's opponents. For example, the puffed-up claim that the amendment would make wife and husband equally responsible for their family's financial support caused alarm among the undecided. As the opposition grew stronger, especially from women who wanted to maintain their traditional role, state legislators began to realize that supporting the amendment involved risk. Given the exaggerations and counter-exaggerations, lawmakers ducked. Because it takes an extraordinary majority to amend the Constitution, it takes only a committed minority to thwart the majority's will.

Despite its failure, the movement to ratify the ERA produced real benefits. It raised the consciousness of women about their social position, spurred the formation of the National Organization for Women (NOW) and other large

equal rights amendment (ERA) A failed constitutional amendment introduced by the National Women's Party in 1923, declaring that "equality of rights under the law shall not be denied or abridged by the United States or any State on account of sex."

organizations, contributed to women's participation in politics, and generated important legislation affecting women.[60]

The failure to ratify the ERA stands in stark contrast to the quick enactment of many laws that now protect women's rights. Such legislation had little audible opposition. If years of racial discrimination called for government redress, then so did years of gender-based discrimination. Furthermore, laws protecting women's rights required only the amending of civil rights bills or the enactment of similar bills.

Some scholars argue that for practical purposes, the Supreme Court has implemented the equivalent of the ERA through its decisions. It has struck down distinctions based on sex and held that stereotyped generalizations about sexual differences must fall.[61] In recent rulings, the Court has held that states may require employers to guarantee job reinstatement to women who take maternity leave, that sexual harassment in the workplace is illegal, and that the existence of a hostile work environment may be demonstrated by a reasonable perception of abuse rather than by proven psychological injury.[62]

But the Supreme Court can reverse its decisions, and legislators can repeal statutes. Without an equal rights amendment, argue some feminists, the Constitution will continue to bear the sexist imprint of a document written by men for men. Until the ERA becomes part of the Constitution, said feminist Betty Friedan, "We are at the mercy of a Supreme Court that will interpret equality as it sees fit."[63]

★ Affirmative Action: Equal Opportunity or Equal Outcome?

In his vision of a Great Society, President Johnson linked economic rights with civil rights and equality of outcome with equality of opportunity. "Equal opportunity is essential, but not enough," he declared. "We seek not just legal equity but human ability, not just equality as a right and a theory but equality as a fact and equality as a result."[64] This commitment led to affirmative action programs to expand opportunities for women, minorities, and the disabled.

Affirmative action is a commitment by a business, employer, school, or other public or private institution to expand opportunities for women, blacks, Hispanic Americans, and members of other minority groups. Affirmative action aims to overcome the effects of present and past discrimination. It embraces a range of public and private programs, policies, and procedures, including special recruitment, preferential treatment, and quotas in job training and professional education, employment, and the awarding of government contracts. The point of these programs is to move beyond equality of opportunity to equality of outcome.

Establishing numerical goals (such as designating a specific number of places in a law school for minority candidates or specifying that 10 percent of the work on a government contract must be subcontracted to minority-owned companies) is the most aggressive form of affirmative action, and it generates more debate and opposition than any other aspect of the civil rights movement. Advocates claim that such goal setting for college admissions, training programs, employment, and contracts will move minorities, women, and the disabled out of their second-class status. President Johnson explained why aggressive affirmative action was necessary:

affirmative action Any of a wide range of programs, from special recruitment efforts to numerical quotas, aimed at expanding opportunities for women and minority groups.

You do not take a person who for years has been hobbled by chains, liberate him, bring him up to the starting line of a race, and then say, "You are free to compete with all the others," and still justly believe that you have been completely fair. Thus, it is not enough just to open the gates of opportunity; all our citizens must have the ability to walk through those gates.[65]

Arguments for affirmative action programs (from increased recruitment efforts to quotas) tend to use the following reasoning: certain groups have historically suffered invidious discrimination, denying them educational and economic opportunities. To eliminate the lasting effects of such discrimination, the public and private sectors must take steps to provide access to good education and jobs. If the majority once discriminated to hold groups back, discriminating to benefit those groups is fair. Therefore, quotas are a legitimate means to provide a place on the ladder to success.[66]

Affirmative action opponents maintain that quotas for designated groups necessarily create invidious discrimination (in the form of reverse discrimination) against individuals who are themselves blameless. Moreover, they say, quotas lead to admission, hiring, or promotion of the less qualified at the expense of the well qualified. In the name of equality, such policies thwart individuals' freedom to succeed.

Government-mandated preferential policies probably began in 1965 with the creation of the Office of Federal Contract Compliance. Its purpose was to ensure that all private enterprises doing business with the federal government complied with nondiscrimination guidelines. Because so many companies do business with the federal government, a large portion of the American economy became subject to these guidelines. In 1968, the guidelines required "goals and timetables for the prompt achievement of full and equal employment opportunity." By 1971, they called for employers to eliminate "underutilization" of minorities and women, which meant that employers had to hire minorities and women in proportion to the government's assessment of their availability.[67]

Preferential policies are seldom explicitly legislated. More often, such policies are the result of administrative regulations, judicial rulings, and initiatives in the private sector to provide a remedial response to specific discrimination or to satisfy new legal standards for proving nondiscrimination. Quotas or goals enable administrators to assess changes in hiring, promotion, and admissions policies. Racial quotas are an economic fact of life today. Employers engage in race-conscious preferential treatment to avoid litigation. Cast in value terms, equality trumps freedom. Do preferential policies in other nations offer lessons for us? See "Compared with What? How India Struggles with Affirmative Action" to learn the answer.

Reverse Discrimination

The Supreme Court confronted an affirmative action quota program for the first time in *Regents of the University of California* v. *Bakke.*[68] Allan Bakke, a thirty-five-year-old white man, had twice applied for admission to the University of California Medical School at Davis. He was rejected both times. As part of the university's affirmative action program, the school had reserved sixteen places in each entering class of one hundred for qualified minority applicants in an effort to redress long-standing and unfair exclusion of minorities from the medical profession. Bakke's academic qualifications exceeded those of all of the minority students admitted in the two years his applications were rejected. Bakke contended, first in the California courts and then in the Supreme Court, that he was excluded from admission solely on the basis of his race. He argued that the equal protection clause of the Fourteenth Amendment and the Civil Rights Act of 1964 prohibited this reverse discrimination.

The Court's decision in *Bakke* contained six opinions and spanned 154 pages, but no opinion commanded a majority. Despite the confusing multiple opinions, the Court struck down the school's rigid use of race, thus admitting Bakke, and it approved of affirmative action programs in education that use race as a *plus* factor (one of many such factors) but not as the *sole* factor. Thus, the Court managed to minimize white opposition to the goal of equality (by finding for Bakke) while extending gains for racial minorities through affirmative action.

True to the pluralist model, groups opposed to affirmative action continued their opposition in federal courts and state legislatures. They met with some success. The Supreme Court struck down government-mandated set-aside programs in the U.S. Department of Transportation.[69] Lower federal courts took this as a signal that other forms of affirmative action were ripe for reversal.

By 2003—twenty-five years after *Bakke*—the Supreme Court reexamined affirmative action in two cases, both challenging aspects of the University of Michigan's racial preferences policies. In *Gratz* v. *Bollinger,* the Court considered the university's undergraduate admissions policy, which conferred 20 points automatically to members of favored groups (100 points guaranteed admission). In a 6–3 opinion, Chief Justice William H. Rehnquist argued that such a policy violated the equal protection clause because it lacked the narrow tailoring required for permissible racial preferences and it failed to provide for individualized consideration of each candidate.[70] In the second case, *Grutter* v. *Bollinger,* the Court considered the University of Michigan's law school admissions policy, which gave preference to minority applicants with lower GPAs and standardized test scores over white applicants. This time, the Court, in a 5–4 decision authored by Justice Sandra Day O'Connor, held that the equal protection clause did not bar the school's narrowly tailored use of racial preferences to further a compelling interest that flowed from a racially diverse student body.[71] Since each applicant is judged individually on his or her merits, race remains only one among many factors that enters into the admissions decision.

The issue of race-based classifications in education arose again in 2007 when parents challenged voluntary school integration plans based on race.[72] Chief Justice John G. Roberts, Jr., writing for the 5–4 majority on a bitterly divided bench, invalidated the plans, declaring that the programs were "directed only to racial balance, pure and simple," which the equal protection clause of the Fourteenth Amendment forbids. "The way to stop discrimination on the basis of race is to stop discriminating on the basis of race," he said.

Justice Anthony Kennedy, who cast the fifth and deciding vote, wrote separately to say that achieving racial diversity and avoiding racial isolation were "compelling interests" that schools could constitutionally pursue as long as they "narrowly tailored" their programs to avoid racial labeling and sorting of individual children. Kennedy's opinion, and his key role as the "swing" vote, will likely determine the design of such programs to pass legal muster. In a broader sense, Kennedy's vote may prove to be the most important vote in a growing number of 5-to-4 decisions.

Compared with What?

How India Struggles with Affirmative Action

Americans are not alone in their disagreements over affirmative action. Controversies, even bloodshed, have arisen in other countries where certain groups of citizens are treated preferentially by the government over others. One study found several common patterns among countries that had enacted preferential policies. Although begun as temporary measures, preferential policies tended to persist and even to expand to include more groups. The policies usually sought to improve the situation of disadvantaged groups as a whole, but they often benefited the better-off members of such groups more so than the worse-off members. Finally, preferential policies tended to increase antagonisms among different groups within a country.

Of course, there were variations across countries in terms of who benefited from such policies, what types of benefits were bestowed, and even the names the policies were given. In India, such policies carry the label "positive discrimination." But that isn't the only way India differs from the United States when it comes to preferential policies.

Although India is the world's largest democracy, its society is rigidly stratified into groups called castes. Although the government forbade caste-based discrimination, members of the lower castes (the lowest being the Dalits, or "untouchables") were historically restricted to the least prestigious and lowest-paying jobs. To improve their status, India has set aside government jobs for the lower castes, who make up half of India's population of 1 billion. India now reserves 27 percent of government jobs for the lower castes and an additional 23 percent for untouchables and remote tribe members. Gender equality has also improved since a 1993 constitutional amendment that set aside one-third of all seats

Justice Stephen G. Breyer, writing for the minority, and speaking from the bench, used pointed language, declaring: "This is a decision that the Court and the nation will come to regret." A sign of growing frustration among the justices is the increased frequency with which they have read their dissents aloud, a tactic used to express great distress with the majority opinion.

The Politics of Affirmative Action

A comprehensive review of nationwide surveys conducted over the past twenty-five years reveals an unsurprising truth: that blacks favor affirmative action programs and whites do not. The gulf between the races was wider in the 1970s than it is today, but the moderation results from shifts among blacks, not whites. Perhaps the most important finding is that "whites' views have remained essentially unchanged over twenty-five years."[73]

How do we account for the persistence of equal outcomes policies? A majority of Americans have consistently rejected explicit race or gender preferences for the awarding of contracts, employment decisions, and college admis-

in local government councils for women. By 2004, 900,000 women had been elected to public office, and 80,000 of them now lead local governing bodies.

Positive discrimination in India has intensified tensions between the lower and upper castes. In 1990, soon after the new quotas were established, scores of young upper-caste men and women set themselves ablaze in protest. And when Indian courts issued a temporary injunction against the positive discrimination policies, lower-caste terrorists bombed a train and killed dozens of people.

In the latest effort to extend its quota system, the Indian government has proposed setting aside 27 percent of the places in the nation's most competitive universities and some elite medical colleges to members of the "other backward castes." This proposal has been met with strikes and protests. One student protester wore a T-shirt that read: "My merit is my caste. What is yours?"

India's experience with positive discrimination has implications for majoritarian and pluralist models of democracy. All governments broker conflict to varying degrees. Under a majoritarian model, group demands could lead quickly to conflict and instability because majority rule leaves little room for compromise. A pluralist model allows different groups to get a piece of the pie. By parceling out benefits, pluralism mitigates disorder in the short term. But in the long term, repeated demands for increased benefits can spark instability. A vigorous pluralist system should provide acceptable mechanisms (legislative, executive, bureaucratic, judicial) to vent such frustrations and yield new allocations of benefits.

Sources: Trudy Rubin, "Will Democracy Survive in India?" *The Record* (Bergen County, N.J.), 19 January 1998, p. A12; Alex Spillius, "India's Old Warriors to Launch Rights Fight," *Daily Telegraph,* 20 October 1997, p. 12; Robin Wright, "World's Leaders: Men, 187, Women, 4," *Los Angeles Times,* 30 September 1997, p. A1; "Indian Eunuchs Demand Government Job Quotas," *Agence France Presse,* 22 October 1997; Juergen Hein and M. V. Balaji, "India's First Census of New Millennium Begins on February 9," *Deutsche Presse-Agentur,* 7 February 2001; Gillian Bowditch, "You Can Have Meritocracy or Equality, but Not Both," *Sunday Times,* Features Section: Scotland News, 19 January 2003, p. 21; Press Trust of India, "About a Million Women Elected to Local Bodies in India," 10 February 2004; Somini Sengupta, "Quotas to Aid India's Poor vs. Push for Meritocracy," *New York Times,* 23 May 2006, p. A3.

sions, regardless of the groups such preferences benefit. Nevertheless, preference policies have survived and thrived under both Democrats and Republicans because they are attractive. They encourage unprotected groups to strive for inclusion. The list of protected groups includes African Americans, Hispanic Americans, Native Americans, Asian Pacific Americans, and Subcontinent Asian Americans.[74] Politicians have a powerful motive—votes—to expand the number of protected groups and the benefits such policies provide.

Recall that affirmative action programs began as temporary measures, ensuring a jump-start for minorities shackled by decades or centuries of invidious discrimination. For example, forty years ago, minority racial identity was a fatal flaw on a medical or law school application. Today it is viewed as an advantage, encouraging applicants to think in minority-group terms. Thinking in group terms and conferring benefits on such ground generates hostility from members of the majority, who see the deck stacked against them for no other reason than their race. It is not surprising that affirmative action has become controversial, since many Americans view it as a violation of their individual freedom.

Diversity vs. Racism

On June 23, 2003, the Supreme Court handed down two affirmative action decisions that signaled the affirmation and continuation of racial preference policies. Such policies are permissible provided that they are "narrowly tailored" to meet "a compelling interest." Racial diversity in higher education is now such a compelling interest. But to these protesters, *diversity* is simply a code word for reverse racism. This view won a majority in 2007 when the Court struck down voluntary public school integration plans. Justice Anthony Kennedy cast the critical vote but wrote separately to suggest that achieving racial diversity was a "compelling interest" that government policies could legitimately address. But which policies and under what circumstances? It may take years to sort out the answers. *(Alex Wong/Getty Images)*

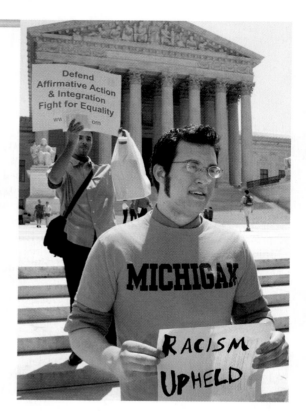

Recall Lyndon Johnson's justification for equal outcomes policies. Though free to compete, a person once hobbled by chains cannot run a fair race. Americans are willing to do more than remove the chains. They will support special training and financial assistance for those who were previously shackled. The hope is that such efforts will enable once-shackled runners to catch up with those who have forged ahead. But Americans stop short at endorsing equal outcomes policies because they predetermine the results of the race.[75]

The conflict between freedom and equality will continue as other individuals and groups continue to press their demands through litigation and legislation. The choice will depend on whether and to what extent Americans still harbor deep-seated racial prejudice.

IDEAlog.org

Do you support or oppose affirmative action programs for racial minorities? Take IDEAlog's self-test.

Summary

Americans want equality, but they disagree on the extent to which government should guarantee it. At the heart of this conflict is the distinction between equal opportunities and equal outcomes. Today, immigrant groups are vocal advocates for a share of the American dream, including tax-paying illegal immigrants and their children who may require health care and public education. Their quest follows the long path toward equality forged by African Americans.

Congress enacted the Civil War amendments—the Thirteenth, Fourteenth, and Fifteenth Amendments—to provide full civil rights to black Americans. In the late nineteenth century, however, the Supreme Court interpreted the amendments very narrowly, declaring that they did not restrain individuals from denying civil rights to blacks and that they did not apply to the states. The Court's rulings had the effect of denying the vote to most blacks and of institutionalizing racism, making racial segregation a fact of daily life.

Through a series of court cases spanning two decades, the Court slowly dismantled segregation in the schools. The battle for desegregation culminated in the *Brown* cases in 1954 and 1955, in which a now-supportive Supreme Court declared segregated schools to be inherently unequal and therefore unconstitutional. The Court also ordered the desegregation of all schools and upheld the use of busing to do so.

Gains in other spheres of civil rights came more slowly. The motivating force was the civil rights movement, led by Martin Luther King, Jr., until his assassination in 1968. King believed strongly in civil disobedience and nonviolence, strategies that helped secure for blacks equality in voting rights, public accommodations, higher education, housing, and employment opportunity.

Civil rights activism and the civil rights movement worked to the benefit of all minority groups—in fact, they benefited all Americans. Native Americans obtained some redress for past injustices. Immigrant groups press government for a stake in the American experience as they work in jobs that few citizens will do to gain a better life. Latinos have come to recognize the importance of group action to achieve economic and political equality. Disabled Americans won civil rights protections enjoyed by African Americans and others. And civil rights legislation removed the protectionism that was, in effect, legalized discrimination against women in education and employment. Homosexuals aim to follow the same path, but their quest for equality has been trumped by occasional conflicts with freedom.

Despite legislative advances in the area of women's rights, the states did not ratify the equal rights amendment. Still, the struggle for ratification produced several positive results, heightening awareness of women's roles in society and mobilizing their political power. And legislation and judicial rulings implemented much of the amendment's provisions in practice. The Supreme Court now judges sex-based discrimination with "skeptical scrutiny," meaning that distinctions based on sex are almost as suspect as distinctions based on race.

Government and business instituted affirmative action programs to counteract the results of past discrimination. These provide preferential treatment for women, minorities, and the disabled in a number of areas that affect individuals' economic opportunity and well-being. In effect, such programs discriminate to remedy earlier discrimination. But in a major reversal beginning in 2007, government acts of racial discrimination, however well-intentioned, are out-of-bounds for all but the most compelling reasons. When programs make race the determining factor in awarding contracts, offering employment, or granting admission to educational institutions, the courts will be increasingly skeptical of their validity. However, the politics of affirmative action suggest that such programs are likely to remain persistent features on our political landscape.

We can guarantee equal outcomes only if we restrict the free competition that is an integral part of equal opportunity. Many Americans object to policies that restrict individual freedom, such as quotas and set-asides that arbitrarily change the outcome of the race. The challenge of pluralist democracy is to balance the need for freedom with demands for equality.

KEY CASES

Plessy v. *Ferguson* (racial segregation constitutional)
Brown v. *Board of Education* (racial segregation unconstitutional)
Brown v. *Board of Education II* (racial desegregation implementation)
Boy Scouts of America v. *Dale* (association rights, Boy Scouts vs. gays)
United States v. *Virginia* (gender equality)
Regents of the University of California v. *Bakke* (affirmative action, 1978)

Gratz v. *Bollinger* (affirmative action, 2003)
Grutter v. *Bollinger* (affirmative action, 2003)

Internet activities and reading suggestions for this chapter are available on the *Online Study Center*

To complete the multimedia assignments for this chapter, go to AmericansGoverning.org.

17 Policymaking

(Mingasson/Liaison/Getty Images)

Although she has good office skills, Deidra Everett has had a lot of trouble finding a job. At 440 pounds, her weight is a problem for employers. When she receives a call for an interview, she says that she's overweight to see if that's going to be a problem. Deidra says that often the response is, "You know the job I was calling you about? I'm really thinking it isn't something you'd be interested in."

Deidra isn't just a little on the heavy side. She's obese. And obesity is a serious problem in the United States. Thirty percent of adults in America (around 60 million people) are obese. They're not all as big as Deidra, but based on the government's Centers for Disease Control body mass index (weight in relation to height), there is an epidemic of obesity in the United States.

The obesity problem has many manifestations, but discrimination against very fat people is one of the less visible, less discussed symptoms. The job discrimination that Deidra Everett faces is easy enough to explain. An employee is a representative of his or her organization, and for many people an obese person isn't pleasing to look at. Employers worry that they will present a bad image. But even in back office jobs, where there is no personal interaction between the worker and customers or clients, employers show hesitation in hiring obese people. Other workers may feel uncomfortable around an obese person; as uncomfortable as it is to acknowledge, a lot of people just don't like to look at those who are badly overweight.

Such hiring practices are discrimination, plain and simple, and such practices damage obese people beyond the economic consequences of not being able to earn a paycheck. Moreover,

the problems of obese people extend far beyond problems in finding a job. If you're badly overweight, it's difficult to go to the movies, fly on a plane, see a game at the ballpark, or even sit in a college classroom, all because you are too large for the seats.

These are terrible problems, and those who encounter them largely suffer in silence. Most pertinent to our discussion here, these problems are not political issues—at least not yet. By and large, all of these problems of discrimination against obese people are ignored by those who could do something to ameliorate them. No one is asking business leaders and government policymakers to stop the discrimination, and, thus, they're under no pressure to act.

Yet obesity is not being ignored. As a health matter, it has become an issue. There is a substantial public health sector in the United States, and doctors, nutritionists, and other health experts have pushed for programs to educate people about healthy eating habits and exercise. A few states have restricted the sale of soda and candy in schools, and others may follow suit. A handful of consumer advocates have threatened to file lawsuits, charging fast-food companies with making consumers vulnerable to obesity-related illnesses.[1]

Other public policy proposals spring not from worry about the well-being of those who are obese but from financial concerns. Some advocate recalibrating insurance policies so that obese people pay a higher rate, one commensurate with their greater health risks and, thus, the higher medical costs they incur. Proponents ask whether this is really any different from charging more to smokers or teenage drivers.[2]

Insurance companies have no trouble mobilizing so they can try to get policymakers to pay attention to a problem that they believe is being ignored. Insurance companies are already organized—they have substantial resources and can easily afford to employ public policy specialists, researchers, and lobbyists who can work to gain policymakers' attention. In our pluralist system, they have every reason to be active and vocal in the policymaking process.

Obese people are not organized; they're not even close to being organized. There may be 60 million obese adults by government standards, but only 5,000 belong to their leading advocacy group, the National Association to Advance Fat Acceptance.[3] As we learned in Chapter 10 on interest groups, there are many reasons that people don't join organizations designed to promote those individuals' interests. For voluntary organizations, a major reason is the free-rider problem: Why donate money when others are willing to do it? In the case of obese people, though, there is another problem. Many of those who are obese blame themselves for the discrimination they encounter; they have such a poor self-image that they believe they deserve what has befallen them. And someone who feels at fault sees no reason to support an advocacy group to fight on his or her behalf.

Maybe someday this will change. Maybe someday the Rosa Parks of obese people will light the fire that catalyzes political mobilization. Maybe someday science will demonstrate convincingly that obesity is not symptomatic of any psychological predisposition or condition, and public attitudes will become more accepting. Maybe. And maybe not. What is clear is that pushing new issues onto the political agenda is difficult. Getting those in government to understand that a problem is a *political issue* is truly a challenge. ★

IN OUR OWN WORDS

Listen to Jeffrey Berry discuss the main points and themes of this chapter.

Online Study Center
Improve Your Grade

This chapter looks at this process of agenda building as part of a broader examination of the public policy process. Previous chapters have focused on individual institutions of government. Here we look at government more broadly and ask how policymaking takes place across institutions. We first identify different types of public policies and then analyze the stages in the policymaking process. Because different institutions and different levels of government (national, state, and local) frequently work on the same issues, policymaking is often fragmented. How can better coordination be achieved?

★ Government Purposes and Public Policies

In Chapter 1, we noted that virtually all citizens are willing to accept limitations on their personal freedom in return for various benefits of government. We defined the major purposes of government as maintaining order, providing public benefits, and promoting equality. Different governments place different values on each broad purpose, and those differences are reflected in their public policies. A **public policy** is a general plan of action adopted by a government to solve a social problem, counter a threat, or pursue an objective.

At times, governments choose not to adopt a new policy to deal with a troublesome situation; instead, they just muddle through, hoping the problem

public policy A general plan of action adopted by the government to solve a social problem, counter a threat, or pursue an objective.

A Failing Grade, with Lots of Room for Improvement
Policymaking emerges through the exchange of ideas and plans for action. One argument for diversity in government is that policy outcomes will more adequately reflect the needs of the diverse American population. Here, U.S. representative Sheila Jackson Lee (D-Tex.) and other members of the Congressional Black Caucus respond to the congressional report on the federal response to Hurricane Katrina. The Congressional Black Caucus sponsored legislation to help the largely African American population of New Orleans rebuild its community. *(Alex Wong/Getty Images)*

will go away or diminish in importance. This too is a policy decision because it amounts to choosing to maintain the status quo. Sometimes government policies are carefully developed and effective. Sometimes they are hastily drawn and ineffective, even counterproductive. But careful planning is no predictor of success. Well-constructed policies may result in total disaster, and quick fixes may work just fine.

Whatever their form and effectiveness, however, all policies have this in common: they are the means by which government pursues certain goals in specific situations. People disagree about public policies because they disagree about one or more of the following elements: the goals government should have, the means it should use to meet them, and how the situation at hand should be perceived.

★ The Policymaking Process

When people in and outside government disagree on goals, that disagreement is often rooted in a basic difference in values. As emphasized throughout this book, such value conflict is often manifested as disputes pitting freedom versus order or freedom versus equality. The roots of the values we hold can run deep, beginning with childhood socialization as the values of parents are transmitted to their children. Disputes involving values are in many ways the hardest to bridge since they reflect a basic worldview and go to the core of one's sense of right and wrong.

The problem of illegal drugs illustrates how different core values lead us to prefer different public policies. Everyone is in agreement that government should address the problems created by drugs. Yet there are sharply contrasting views of what should be done. Recall from Chapter 1 that libertarians put individual freedom above all else and want to limit government as much as possible. Many libertarians argue that drugs should be decriminalized; if people want to take drugs, they should be free to do so, just as they are free to drink alcohol if they want. If drugs were decriminalized, they could be sold openly, the prices would fall dramatically, and the crime associated with illegal drugs would largely evaporate. Conservatives' value system places considerable emphasis on order. In their mind, a decent, safe, and civilized society does not allow people to debase themselves through drug abuse, and the government should punish those who violate the law. Liberals place greater emphasis on treatment as a policy option. They regard drug addiction as a medical or emotional problem and believe that government should offer the services that addicts can use to stop their self-destructive behavior. Liberals value equality, and their view on this issue is that government should be expansive so that it can help people in need. Many drug offenders are impoverished because of their spending on drugs and cannot pay for private treatment (see "Compared with What? European Youth Say Throw the Book at Drug Dealers, Treat Users").

Types of Policies

Although values underlie choices, analysis of public policy does not usually focus explicitly on core beliefs. Political scientists often try to categorize public policy choices by their objectives. That is, in the broad scheme of things, what are policymakers trying to do by choosing a particular policy direction? One common purpose is to allocate resources so that some segment of society can receive a service or benefit. We can call these **distributive policies.** Consider budgetary earmarks for colleges and universities. In the 2003 budget, Congress distributed over $2 billion in grants for specific projects at particular colleges and universities. The University of Southern California received a $6.8 million grant to create a virtual reality simulation to help train soldiers for combat situations they may face on the battlefield some day. The same budget contained $1.7 million for a project at the University of Missouri to study ways to improve the cultivation of shiitake mushrooms. Some projects seem vital while others are derided as "pork barrel."[4]

Distributional policies are not all projects or new buildings. Some are social programs designed to help some disadvantaged group in society. What distributional policies have in common is that all of us pay through our taxes to support those who receive the benefit, presumably because that benefit works toward the common good, such as stronger security, a better-trained work force, or even more bountiful (and cheaper) mushrooms (see Figure 17.1). In contrast, **redistributional policies** are explicitly designed to take resources from one sector of society and transfer them to another (reflecting the core value of greater equality). In a rather unusual redistributional proposal in Seattle, Washington, proponents of early childhood education programs succeeded in getting an initiative on a citywide ballot that would have added a 10 cent tax on every cup of espresso sold in the city. The new revenues brought in by this tax were to fund early childhood programs, and, as such, the plan was to redistribute revenues from espresso drinkers to families with small children. The voters rejected the initiative, and no such redistribution took place.[5]

A broader, more far-reaching redistributive tax plan was put forth in 2003 by the Republican governor of Alabama, Bob Riley. Alabama is unusual in that it taxes the wealthy at an effective rate of only 3 percent, one of the lowest rates among the fifty states. At the other end of the spectrum, it begins taxing citizens when they reach just $4,600 in income and then taxes the poorest Alabamians at an effective tax rate of 12 percent. The reason to compare the

distributive policies Government policies designed to confer a benefit on a particular institution or group.

redistributional policies Policies that take government resources, such as tax funds, from one sector of society and transfer them to another.

Compared with What?

European Youth Say Throw the Book at Drug Dealers, Treat Users

Drug use is common in Europe, as it is in the United States. Attitudes and laws in some European countries are more liberal than others, notably in the Netherlands, where so-called soft drugs like hashish and marijuana are effectively legal and can be purchased at some coffee shops. Young people in Europe, as in the United States, are drawn more to drugs than their elders are. Yet their attitudes are decidedly mixed when it comes to what to do about drugs because European youth are far from libertarian in their attitudes. When pollsters asked those between the ages of fifteen and twenty-four in fifteen Western European countries what they thought the most effective ways of tackling drug-related problems are, a substantial percentage of respondents

wanted drug dealers punished. Yet their conservatism relating to the source of drugs did not seem to extend to the matter of what to do with those who abused drugs. Leniency seemed more the answer here: only 22 percent cited "tougher measures against drug users" as one of their top three solutions to the drug problem. When it comes to drug users, they appear to be more liberal, seeing drug use as an illness requiring treatment. Interestingly, the permissiveness toward drugs in the Netherlands has not resulted in differing policy views by young people there. The youth in that country are no more liberal on what to do about drugs than are young people from elsewhere in Europe.

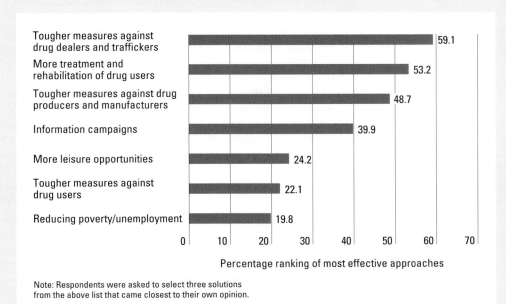

Note: Respondents were asked to select three solutions from the above list that came closest to their own opinion.

Source: Eurobarometer, special survey, 27 April–10 June 2002.

FIGURE 17.1 Little Room for Maneuver

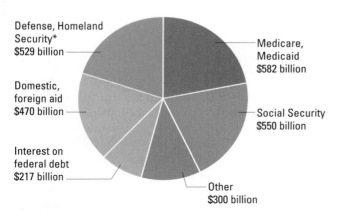

Defense, Homeland Security* $529 billion

Domestic, foreign aid $470 billion

Interest on federal debt $217 billion

Medicare, Medicaid $582 billion

Social Security $550 billion

Other $300 billion

*Excludes supplemental funding for Iraq, Afghanistan

Passing the budget is one of the most contentious policy decisions for lawmakers. There's not much money to go around. Most of government revenue is already committed to paying for interest on the federal deficit, defense and homeland security, and entitlement programs like Medicare and Social Security. The amount available for "discretionary" spending—everything from college financial aid to farm subsidies to secretary salaries—is a mere one-sixth of government spending. This pie chart shows estimated government spending in 2006 according to the Congressional Budget Office.

Source: Jackie Calmes, "Budget Wish Lists Come and Go, But Entitlements Outweigh All," *Wall Street Journal,* 3 February 2006, p. A1.

effective rate—what people actually pay as opposed to the stated tax rate—is that there are many deductions and exceptions in the tax code, such as taxing investment income lower than salaried income. Wealthy people have more deductions and more investment income. Alabama schools reflect the revenue problems produced by its tax code: the state ranks dead last in per capita expenditures per student. Governor Riley pushed a new tax code designed to be redistributive, giving tax relief to poor and working-class Alabamians while taxing the wealthy at a higher rate. Also, some of the new revenue was not to be redistributed to those at the lower end of the income scale but was to be put into the state's schools. Under the state's constitution, a tax change must be approved by the voters, and a statewide referendum was held on Riley's plan. The redistribution plan was defeated: many lower-income Alabamians were not persuaded that a conservative Republican was really going to help them. The antitax coalition also ran a more persuasive and much better-funded campaign.[6] (For public opinion on federal taxes, see Figure 17.2.)

Another basic policy approach is **regulation.** In Chapter 13, we noted that regulations are the rules that guide the operation of government programs. When regulations apply to business markets, they are an attempt to structure the operations of that market in a particular way. Government intersperses itself as a referee, setting rules as to what kinds of companies can participate in what kinds of market activities. Trucking is a case in point. The United States used to restrict the entrance of Mexican trucks into this country, barring them from traveling more than twenty miles into the United States. Truckers would have to unload their cargo at a transfer station, where it would be placed on an American carrier that would take the merchandise to its destination. The United States said it forbade Mexican trucks from traveling on their own to wherever their cargo was headed because they weren't always safe and they polluted more than American trucks. An international trade panel determined, however, that these regulatory rules violated the North American Free Trade

regulation Government intervention in the workings of a business market to promote some socially desired goal.

FIGURE 17.2 Who Is Paying Their Fair Share?

Do most Americans think that federal income taxes are fair? It depends on who is paying. According to opinion polls, nearly half of Americans think that poor people pay too much and that the middle class pays just the right amount. Over two-thirds of those polled say that rich people and corporations pay too little in federal taxes.

Source: April 2006 Gallup Poll, reported at <http://poll.gallup.com>.

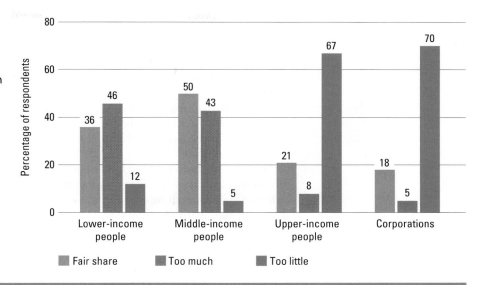

Agreement. In response, Congress passed a new law providing for inspection stations at border crossings to ensure that the Mexican trucks were safe and that their drivers met the same licensing standards as American drivers.

Americans disagree as to the degree to which markets should be free and open, relying on a minimal amount of government supervision. Others believe that markets usually need close supervision because competitive pressures can lead individual businesses to cut corners on the safety of their products or the integrity of their conduct. On the one hand, the decisions on how to regulate or whether to reduce regulation (to *deregulate*) may involve many technical questions and seem to be matters best left to the experts who work for the relevant bureaucratic agencies. What, for example, is the minimum amount of tire tread that should be required for trucks entering the United States? On the other hand, regulation and deregulation are subject to the same pulls and pushes of the political process as distributional and redistributional policies. In the case of the Mexican trucks, the restrictive regulations were largely the product of lobbying by American trucking firms and the Teamsters union, which wanted to preserve business for themselves.[7]

This framework of distributional, redistributional, and regulatory policies is rather general, and there are surely policy approaches that don't fit neatly into one of these categories.[8] As you will see in Chapter 20, some kinds of foreign policies, such as the regulation of international trade, fit this framework better than other issues, like national security. Nevertheless, this framework is a useful prism to examine public policymaking. Understanding the broad purposes of public policy allows a better evaluation of the tools necessary to attain these objectives.

Public Policy Tools

Just as there are different objectives in public policy, there are different ways of achieving those objectives. If the goal is to redistribute wealth, there are different approaches that can accomplish the same goal. As in the Alabama referendum, one way is to tax the wealthy more and tax working-class people less. A more politically palatable approach may be simply to institute more tax exemptions for working-class people so their effective tax rate drops. An example would be a child tax credit of $500 for those with incomes below $35,000. This is still redistributive, since a higher percentage of the state's overall revenue must come from those with a higher income who do not receive the deductions.

One of the most basic of policy tools are *incentives*. A fundamental element of human behavior is that we can be induced to do certain things if the rewards become substantial enough. We should all give to charity because we're generous and caring people. To promote more charity, the government provides taxpayers who file an itemized tax return a substantial tax credit for donating to a nonprofit with charitable status. For a taxpayer with a marginal tax rate of 30 percent, a donation of $1,000 to the local United Way effectively costs her only $700. (The deduction for this taxpayer is 30 percent of the $1,000, or $300.) Although we can all agree that charity is a good thing, there's no free lunch. When incentives come in the form of money saved by those who take advantage of the incentive, it constitutes a *tax expenditure*. Since government loses revenue on the charity deduction, it is effectively spending those funds and must make up revenue elsewhere. This tax expenditure is quite substantial: Americans give $300 billion a year in charity.[9]

The flip side of incentives are *disincentives*—policies that discourage particular behavior. A tax on pollution, for example, is a disincentive for a factory to continue using the same (high-polluting) manufacturing process. State taxes on cigarettes are meant to discourage smoking. In some cases, the threat of government disincentives is enough to spur private resolution of a problem. For instance, members of the House Government Reform Committee held a series of hearings in early 2005 in which they summoned Major League Baseball players to testify about steroid use in professional sports. Lawmakers introduced legislation that would curb the use of steroids and other performance-enhancing drugs by instituting more rigid drug testing and imposing tough penalties on players caught using these drugs. When baseball team owners and players agreed to institute their own tougher policy on steroid use, members of Congress backed off.[10]

Much of what policymakers want to accomplish cannot be done through a set of incentives or disincentives. Often government must provide a service or program. That is, rather than coaxing or discouraging behavior, it must take responsibility itself to establish a program. The largest expenditures of government—for health care, education, social services, and defense—come from direct payments of government to its employees or vendors.

Finally, a common policy tool is to set rules. Much of what government does in the form of regulation is to set rules as to what various businesses or individuals can do in the marketplace. To preserve the integrity of pensions, government agencies set rules to try to ensure that companies protect such funds so that money is available when employees retire. What kind of investments can pension funds be invested in? How much pension money can a company

FIGURE 17.3   The Policymaking Process

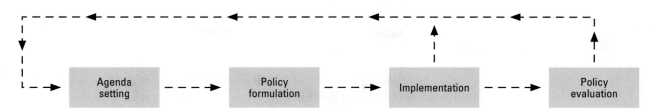

This model, one of many possible ways to depict the policymaking process, shows four policymaking stages. Feedback on program operations and performance from the last two stages stimulates new cycles of the process.

---

invest in its own stock? Rules are set on such matters. Each day the federal government issues new or revised rules on a variety of policy questions.

Whatever the policy objectives of government, the main tools are thus incentives and disincentives, direct provision of services, and rule setting. They are often combined to achieve a particular goal, and over time one approach may fall out of favor and another may be tried. Policies aimed at specific problems are not static; means, goals, and situations change.

A Policymaking Model

Clearly, different approaches to solving policy problems affect the policymaking process, but common patterns do underlie most processes. Political scientists have produced many models of the policymaking process to distinguish the different types of policy. They also distinguish different stages of the policymaking process and try to identify patterns in the way people attempt to influence decisions and in the way decisions are reached.

We can separate the policymaking process into four stages: agenda setting, policy formulation, implementation, and policy evaluation.[11] Figure 17.3 shows the four stages in sequence. Note, however, that the process does not end with policy evaluation. As you will see, policymaking is a circular process; the end of one phase is really the beginning of another.

Agenda Setting.   **Agenda setting** is the part of the process in which problems are defined as political issues. Many problems confront Americans in their daily lives, but government is not actively working to solve them all. Consider Social Security, for example. Today the old-age insurance program seems a hardy perennial of American politics, but it was not created until the New Deal. The problem of poverty among the elderly did not suddenly arise during the 1930s—there had always been poor people of all ages—but that is when inadequate income for the elderly was defined as a political problem. During this time, people began arguing that it was government's responsibility to create a system of income security for the aged rather than leaving old people to fend for themselves.

When the government begins to consider acting on an issue it has previously ignored, we say that the issue has become part of the political agenda.

agenda setting The stage of the policymaking process during which problems get defined as political issues.

Politics in a Changing World

Legislating Life and Death

In 1990, at the age of twenty-seven, Terri Schiavo suffered severe brain damage when her heart stopped for several minutes. Doctors told her husband Michael that she was in a "persistent vegetative state" with no chance of recovery. Michael Schiavo claimed that his wife would not want to be kept alive in such a condition and asked that her feeding tube be removed. Terri's parents, Bob and Mary Schindler, disagreed. They disputed Michael's account of their daughter's wishes and insisted that Terri

(Getty Images)

Usually when we use *agenda* in this context, we are simply referring to the entire set of issues before all the institutions of government. (There is no formal list of issues for the entire political system; the concept of an agenda for the system is merely a useful abstraction.)

Why does an existing social problem become redefined as a political problem? There is no single reason; many different factors can stimulate new thinking about a problem. Sometimes highly visible events or developments push issues onto the agenda. Examples are great calamities (such as a terrible oil spill, showing a need for safer tankers), the effects of technology (such as air pollution, requiring clean-air regulations), or irrational human behavior (such as airline hijackings, pointing to the need for greater airport security).[12] The probability that a certain problem will move onto the agenda is also affected by who controls the government and by broad ideological shifts. (See "Politics in a Changing World: Legislating Life and Death.") Presidential and congressional candidates run for office promising to put neglected issues on the policy

would get better with further rehabilitative therapy. In 1998, Michael Schiavo began a legal battle in the Florida state courts to have his wife's feeding tube removed.

Florida judges repeatedly ruled in favor of Michael Schiavo. The Schindlers, devout Catholics, turned to interest groups for support. Conservative groups such as the National Right to Life Committee and Operation Rescue put Terri's story on their websites. The Schindlers' position was promoted by the Vatican and disabled rights groups. Once the Florida state legislature and then Florida governor Jeb Bush stepped in on behalf of the Schindlers, national politicians, including President George Bush, began to take a stand.

By mid-March 2005, the Schindlers had no further recourse in the Florida state court system. They sought help from members of Congress. Former House majority leader Tom DeLay wrote that "our values must define our laws, not the other way around. If our laws don't prevent a helpless, disabled woman, capable of rehabilitation, from being starved and parched to death by an estranged husband . . . then our laws are meaningless." Over the weekend of March 20–21, House and Senate Republicans agreed on a bill to allow the Schindlers to file a complaint in the Florida federal court system. President Bush rushed to Washington from Texas to sign the bill into law. But the federal courts ended up ruling against the Schindlers. Terri Schiavo's feeding tube was removed, and she died on March 31.

Schiavo's official autopsy confirmed that she had minimal brain functioning at the time of her death. Public reaction to the congressional intervention was harsh. Over three-quarters of Americans believe that when a patient has irreversible brain damage, his or her spouse should be allowed to make the decision to end the patient's life. Eighty-two percent of Americans said that Congress and the president should "stay out of it." When asked why members of Congress intervened, two-thirds of respondents said that congressional motives had more to do with "politics" than with "values and principles."

The Schiavo case illustrates how the policy agenda is shaped by interest groups and the ideology of those who control government. The Schindlers' cause meshed with the beliefs of the right-to-life movement and conservative politicians. But the example also shows the volatility of the policy process where social issues are concerned: politicians and interest groups may want to legislate, but public opinion may be too divided or (as in this case) too opposed to their preferences.

Sources: Jeffrey Birnbaum, "The Forces that Set the Agenda," *Washington Post,* 24 April 2005, p. B1; Frank Newport, "The Terri Schiavo Case in Review," *Gallup Poll,* 1 April 2005, <http://poll.gallup.com>; Seth Stern, "2005 Legislative Summary: Schiavo Intervention," *CQ Weekly,* 2 January 2006, p. 48.

agenda. The political parties also take up new issues to promote their candidates for office and respond to public opinion.

Technology is one of the major factors explaining the rise of new issues. New discoveries and applications emerge quickly, and government finds itself without a policy to regulate adequately the problems produced by new products brought to market. The technology allowing individuals to download music from websites went quickly from the minds of computer programmers to the active transmittal of digital music. File-sharing programs from companies like Kazaa and Grokster allow individuals to copy music files from other computers to their own machine. Since popular music is protected by copyright, someone downloading a song by Nelly or Coldplay and not paying for it is violating the law. The temptation has been too great, however, and large numbers of people, especially younger Americans, have developed a rationale as to why file sharing is not stealing. In the fall of 2003, with neither Congress nor an administrative agency responding to the problem, the big recording companies

Vicious 12-Year-Old Criminal. Lock Her Up
After Brianna LaHara used a file-sharing program to download some Mariah Carey songs from the Internet, the twelve-year-old was sued by the recording industry because she paid nothing for the tunes. Brianna's mother agreed to a $2,000 out-of-court settlement, but some file-sharing companies quickly offered to reimburse her. (Splash News and Picture Agency)

like Warner Music, Bertelsmann, and EMI sued 261 individuals who had downloaded music files onto their computers. In a celebrated case, the mother of a twelve-year-old music downloader, Brianna LaHara, quickly agreed to an out-of-court settlement, paying $2,000 to the record companies for her daughter's transgressions. This prompted some in Congress to propose restraints against such record company suits, but the legislation received a chilly reception from many legislators who believed that it was important to stand up for the property rights of music companies and performers.[13]

Political scientists analyze the agenda of a particular political institution over time to try to understand political change. In looking at Congress, for example, the number of hearings held on different issue areas can be measured over time to document how some sectors of society succeed in getting their concerns addressed. As Figure 17.4 illustrates, change over time can be quite significant. Health care has always been of critical importance, but the government's role in health policy has expanded significantly, and Congress spends more and more time on an array of health matters.[14] One of the sharpest trends is the increased amount of time and resources that Congress has devoted to quality-of-life issues, such as environmental protection and consumer protection. Such issues involve protecting wildlife and wilderness, ensuring the integrity of markets so that consumers are not taken advantage of, establishing the rights of vulnerable segments of society, and reforming the procedures of government so that it works better.[15]

Part of the politics of agenda building is not just which new issues emerge and which issues decline in visibility, but the way the substantive problem at the heart of an issue is conceived. **Issue definition** is the way we think about a problem.[16] As individuals, our conception of an issue is influenced by our own values and the way we see the political world. However, issue definition is

issue definition Our conception of the problem at hand.

FIGURE 17.4   A Changing Agenda

The general stability of the political system should not obscure the very real changes in the composition of the political agenda. Just after World War II, environment, health, law and family, international affairs, and space and technology accounted for less than 10 percent of the congressional agenda. A half-century later, they constituted 35 percent of the agenda.

Source: Frank R. Baumgartner and Christine Mahoney, "Social Movements, the Rise of New Issues, and the Public Agenda," in *Routing the Opposition: Social Movements, Public Policy, and Democracy,* ed. David S. Meyer, Valerie Jenness, and Helen Ingram (Minneapolis: University of Minnesota Press, 2005). Copyright 2005 by the Regents of the University of Minnesota. Reprinted with permission.

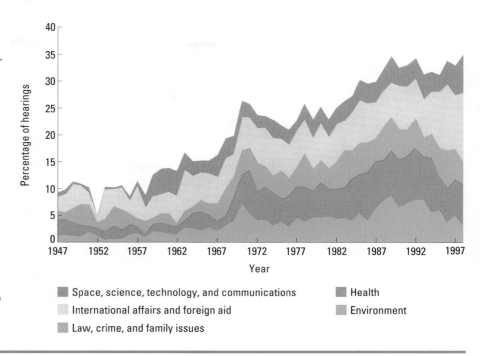

strongly shaped by interest groups and politicians as they try to cast their views in an advantageous light. For example, the pro-life movement was very successful in casting late-term abortions as partial birth abortions. This issue definition evokes a gruesome image of the actual procedure, and the opponents of abortion have succeeded in gaining widespread use of this term. Those on the other side of the issue prefer that these abortions be referred to as late-term abortions or by a more neutral-sounding medical term. This example illustrates not only how important issue definition is, but also that not everyone accepts the same definition.

When interest groups believe that it would be better if an issue of concern were defined differently, they can try to change it.[17] In the language of Washington, they can try to change the spin on the story. This is hard to do, however, because there is no coordinating mechanism that determines how we define problems. Even a wealthy group that can buy a lot of advertising has an uphill struggle to change the way a problem is broadly perceived. For most issues, issue definition remains relatively constant over time, changing in incremental ways, if at all.[18]

When an issue definition is changed by some outside event or technological breakthrough, the political implications can be dramatic. During the 1990s, a number of public policies were changed to allow for some deregulation of the electricity business. But the new century brought with it massive fraud at Enron, a Houston-based electricity broker; a huge spike in energy costs in California (deriving in large part from industry-induced shortages); and a huge power failure in the Midwest and East in the summer of 2003, due in part to aging equipment on a power grid that companies had little incentive to upgrade. The policy solutions being debated now place less emphasis on deregulation.

Policy Formulation. **Policy formulation** is the stage of the policymaking process in which formal policy proposals are developed and officials decide whether to adopt them. The most obvious kind of policy formulation is the proposal of a measure by the president or the development of legislation by Congress. Administrative agencies also formulate policy, through the regulatory process. Courts formulate policy, too, when their decisions establish new interpretations of the law. We usually think of policy formulation as a formal process with a published document (a statute, regulation, or court opinion) as the final outcome. In some instances, however, policy decisions are not published or otherwise made explicit. Presidents and secretaries of state may not always fully articulate their foreign policy decisions, for example, because they want some wiggle room for adapting policy to changing conditions.

Although policy formulation is depicted in Figure 17.3 as one stage, it can actually take place over several separate stages. For example, the Americans with Disabilities Act was enacted by Congress to protect the civil rights of those who are blind, deaf, wheelchair bound, otherwise physically disabled, or mentally ill. Then the Architectural and Transportation Barriers Compliance Board issued administrative regulations specifying standards for complying with the act. For instance, at least 5 percent of the tables in a restaurant must be accessible to those with disabilities, and at least half the drinking fountains on every floor in an office building must be accessible to those in wheelchairs.[19] In addition, the Justice Department issued guidelines for those who want to bring legal complaints against the government for failing to implement the act properly.[20]

As noted in Chapter 13, policy formulation tends to be *incremental*. As policies are being debated, the starting point is the existing policy in that area, and if new policy is adopted, it is usually a modification of what was in place previously. Figure 17.3 depicts how this process works. At the very end of the Clinton administration, the Forest Service adopted a new set of regulations that banned the construction of new roads into one-third of all the national forests. This change effectively banned any logging in these areas because roads are necessary to take the timber out.[21] On one level, this new departure was important because it marked a change in the way the Forest Service calculated the costs and benefits of logging versus the preservation of wilderness. On another level, however, this policy had its roots in policies on wilderness formulated in the late 1970s by the Carter administration.[22] In another twist, shortly after taking office, the Bush administration modified the Clinton rules, instituting a new regulation that allowed each forest plan to be reviewed on a case-by-case basis. Thus, the ban in these forests could be lifted if officials in Washington believed more logging (and road building) was warranted.[23]

Keep in mind that policy formulation is only the development of proposals designed to solve a problem. Some issues reach the agenda and stimulate new proposals but then fail to win enactment because political opposition mobilizes. In the early 1980s, for example, a movement arose to freeze the development of nuclear weapons. Although a freeze resolution gained significant support in Congress, it never gained enough votes to pass. The nuclear freeze movement quickly withered away and disappeared from sight. Thus, the move from proposal to policy requires the approval of some authoritative, policymaking body.

policy formulation The stage of the policymaking process during which formal proposals are developed and adopted.

Implementation.   Policies are not self-executing; **implementation** is the process by which they are carried out. When regulations are issued by agencies in Washington, some government bodies must then put those policies into effect. This may involve notifying the intended targets of agency actions of new or changed regulations. In the case of the Americans with Disabilities Act, for example, the owners of office buildings would probably not have repositioned their water fountains simply because Washington published new regulations. Administrative bodies at the regional, state, or local level had to inform them of the rules, give them a timetable for compliance, communicate the penalties for noncompliance, be available to answer questions that emerged, and report to Washington on how well the regulations were working.

Some policy programs encounter more practical difficulties than others. In 2003, President Bush signed into law the Medicare Prescription Drug, Improvement, and Modernization Act, expanding Medicare to offer prescription drug coverage for senior citizens. According to the new law, a number of private companies are authorized to sell insurance plans offering prescription drug coverage to senior citizens. Over 30 million seniors are enrolled in the new program.

Implementation of the new Medicare program was marked by several problems. First, every county within every state offers a different type and number of prescription drug plans. Many seniors had difficulty sorting out their options. And seniors who made a decision were often waiting well over thirty minutes to reach a customer service representative to sign up for a prescription plan.[24] To make matters worse, federal officials found that some insurers were publishing misleading information about which prescription drugs would be covered and which would not. In addition, as noted in Chapter 13, when the law finally went into effect in January 2006, some senior citizens could not get their medication because Medicare databases had not been adequately updated. State governments stepped in to pay for medication for these individuals while state and federal bureaucrats sorted out the problems. In another computer glitch, premiums that were supposed to be withheld from Social Security checks were not, with the result that seniors were being billed directly by drug companies for months of premiums with threats to drop their coverage altogether.[25]

The drug plan falls under the jurisdiction of the Centers for Medicare and Medicaid Services (CMS) in the Department of Health and Human Services. Mike Leavitt, the secretary of Health and Human Services, acknowledged the need for better data transmission of patient information to private companies and for more surveillance to ensure that private companies are complying with the law.[26] Over time, however, administrators have made changes and improved their management of the program and seniors' overall satisfaction with it has grown.

Although it may sound highly technical, implementation is very much a political process. It involves a great deal of bargaining and negotiation among different groups of people in and out of government. The difficulty of implementing complex policies in a federal system, with multiple layers of government, that is also a pluralistic system, with multiple competing interests, seems daunting. Yet there are incentives for cooperation, not the least of which is to avoid blame if a policy fails. (We will discuss coordination in more detail later in the chapter.)

implementation The process of putting specific policies into operation.

No Pressure, Kids, but If You Fail This Test We May Lose Our Funding

The No Child Left Behind Act requires all states to systematically test their students. Schools with a significant percentage of students failing to pass the tests can lose funding. Consequently, the stakes are high when the tests approach, and students, like these middle schoolers in Indianapolis, are pushed hard by their teachers to prepare for the exams. *(© 2004, Washington Post photo by Michael Dobbs. Reprinted with permission.)*

? Can you explain why . . . the end of the policymaking process is also the beginning?

policy evaluation Analysis of a public policy so as to determine how well it is working.

feedback Information received by policymakers about the effectiveness of public policy.

Policy Evaluation. How does the government know whether a policy is working? In some cases, success or failure may be obvious, but at other times, experts in a specific field must tell government officials how well a policy is working. **Policy evaluation** is the analysis of the results of public policy. Although there is no one method of evaluating policy, evaluation tends to draw heavily on approaches used by academics, including cost-effectiveness analysis and various statistical methods designed to provide concrete measurements of program outcomes. Although technical, the studies can be quite influential in decisions on whether to continue, expand, alter, reduce, or eliminate programs. The continuing stream of negative evaluations of programs designed to bring jobs to the unemployed has clearly reduced political support for such policies.[27]

Evaluation is part of the policymaking process because it helps to identify problems and issues that arise from current policy. In other words, evaluation studies provide **feedback** to policymakers on program performance. (The dotted line in Figure 17.3 represents a feedback loop. Problems that emerge during the implementation stage also provide feedback to policymakers.) Feedback can be positive or negative.[28] When Congress enacted welfare reform in 1996, its intent was to reduce poor families' dependence on government. The new program, known as Temporary Assistance for Needy Families (TANF), set strict limits on the amount of time any family can receive a welfare check and created incentives for those on welfare to gain more education or job training. Numerous evaluation studies were subsequently launched to evaluate just how well different aspects of the new program were working.[29] Much of the feedback was positive; notably striking was a reduction in the number of people receiving welfare. The positive feedback led President Bush to propose new revisions to TANF to require states to lower even further the percentage of people on welfare at any one time.[30] Critics argued that the reduction in welfare rolls was a consequence of a buoyant economy and that those left on welfare are the least capable of working.

Frequently program evaluations reveal shortcomings in a program. Such negative feedback can isolate policies that need to be changed. The ambitious No Child Left Behind Act, passed by Congress at President Bush's urging in 2001, mandated improvements in schools' performance. Schools whose students don't score high enough on standardized tests can lose funding after receiving a warning. As soon as the first round of testing was completed under the new requirements, individual schools with significant percentages of students falling below the required performance thresholds were easily identified. Yet an evaluation providing feedback that a program is failing doesn't mean that problem will be solved. After the first round of testing, some states, including Colorado and Michigan, reduced the performance standard for their students rather than risk eventually losing their funding under No Child Left Behind.[31] The states' changes solved the immediate political problem, but they didn't address the underlying learning issues that lead students to perform poorly on math and reading tests.

Feedback, positive or negative, reflects the dynamic nature of policymaking. By drawing attention to emerging problems, policy evaluation influences the political agenda. The end of the process—evaluating whether the policy is being implemented as it was envisioned when it was formulated—is the beginning of a new cycle of public policymaking.

★ Fragmentation and Coordination

The policymaking process encompasses many different stages and includes many different participants at each stage. Here we examine some forces that pull the government in different directions and make problem solving less coherent than it might otherwise be. In the next section, we look at some structural elements of American government that work to coordinate competing and sometimes conflicting approaches to the same problems.

Multiplicity and Fragmentation

A single policy problem may be attacked in different and sometimes competing ways by government for many reasons. At the heart of this **fragmentation** of policymaking is the fundamental nature of government in America. The separation of powers divides authority among the branches of the national government, and federalism divides authority among the national, state, and local levels of government. These multiple centers of power are, of course, a primary component of pluralist democracy. Different groups try to influence different parts of the government; no one entity completely controls policymaking.

Fragmentation is often the result of many different agencies being created at different times to address different problems. Over time, however, as those problems evolve and mutate, they can become more closely related even as the different agencies do little or nothing to try to coordinate their efforts. In the earlier chapter on bureaucracy, we noted that many of the intelligence and operational failures associated with the September 11 disaster could be traced in

fragmentation In policymaking, the phenomenon of attacking a single problem in different and sometimes competing ways.

part to the lack of coordination between various security-related agencies. In the area of border and transportation security, for example, responsibility was split among the Immigration and Naturalization Service, the Transportation Security Agency, the Customs Service, the Coast Guard, the Federal Protective Services, and other agencies. In other words, lots of agencies were in charge of border and transportation security, but no one was in charge of all those agencies.

The formation of the cabinet-level Department of Homeland Security in 2002 was an attempt to create a centralized administrative structure to overcome policy fragmentation in this area. Left out of the new department, however, were the FBI and the CIA, each a critical component of the government's effort to protect our borders from those who would do this country harm. These agencies were simply too powerful in their own right, and Congress would not have gone along with incorporating them into the new department.

Congress is also characterized by a diffusion of authority. For instance, at the time the Department of Homeland Security was created, sixty-one House and Senate committees and subcommittees possessed some degree of jurisdiction over the agencies that were incorporated into the new organization.[32] Congressional committees jealously guard their prerogatives and ardently fight reorganizations that will reduce their authority.[33]

Foreign policy may be marked by considerable policy fragmentation as well. As commander in chief of the armed forces, the president must work with members of Congress, who have the power to declare war and authorize funding for foreign policy. There can also be differences in approach and opinion within the executive branch. For instance, members of President Bush's state department and defense department had sharply different views of how to proceed before and during the war in Iraq.[34] And officials in Washington had trouble coordinating with military officials on the ground in Iraq after the war started, as evidenced by conflicting opinions about whether the United States should have immediately disbanded the Iraqi army.[35]

As we'll discuss below, the multiplicity of institutional participants is partly the product of the complexity of public policy issues. Controlling illegal drugs is not one problem but a number of different, interrelated problems. Drug treatment questions, for example, have little in common with questions related to the smuggling of drugs into the country. Still, the responsibilities of agencies and committees do overlap. Why are responsibilities not parceled out more precisely to clarify jurisdictions and eliminate overlap? Such reorganizations create winners and losers, and agencies fearing the loss of jurisdiction over an issue become highly protective of their turf.

The Pursuit of Coordination

How does the government overcome fragmentation so that it can make its public policies more coherent? Coordination of different elements of government is not impossible, and fragmentation often creates a productive pressure to rethink jurisdictions.

One common response to the problem of coordination is the formation of interagency task forces within the executive branch. Their common goal is to develop a broad policy response that all relevant agencies will endorse. Such task forces include representatives of all agencies claiming responsibility for a particular issue. They attempt to forge good policy as well as goodwill among competing agencies. President Lyndon Johnson's expansive War on Poverty incorporated several new policy initiatives that cut across many existing departments and agencies. He relied heavily on interagency task forces to work through the jurisdictional issues among different parts of government and to make a range of decisions about program design and administration.

The Office of Management and Budget (OMB) also fosters coordination within the executive branch. OMB can do much more than review budgets and look for ways to improve management practices. The Reagan administration used OMB to clear regulations before they were proposed publicly by the administrative agencies. It initiated OMB's regulatory review role to centralize control of the executive branch. Various presidents have modified this approach in different ways to suit their needs. President Clinton gave his departments and agencies greater latitude and used centralized clearance more sparingly. President George W. Bush moved in the opposite direction, expanding the office in OMB that reviews regulations, thus centralizing more power in the White House.[36]

As illustrated with the case of homeland security, reorganization of disparate parts of government working in related areas is a fundamental approach to enhancing coordination. Despite the obstacles that administrators trying to protect their turf put up, reorganization across agencies is possible. The involvement and commitment of the president is often critical as his status and willingness to expend political capital can put reorganizations on the agenda and push them forward.

Reorganizations within a single agency are easier to accomplish, though not simple by any means. A highly visible problem, a scandal, or a critical report (forms of negative feedback) can catalyze agency restructuring and minimize the ability of managers within that agency to work against changes they oppose. The Federal Emergency Management Agency (FEMA) was an independent agency formed in 1979 to unify the nation's disaster response programs. In 2002, FEMA was one of the many agencies incorporated into the Department of Homeland Security. This reorganization resulted in budget cuts for FEMA as well as the departure of many experienced FEMA employees. Rather than work directly with the White House, FEMA officials had to request resources by going through the DHS bureaucracy. As we have already discussed in previous chapters, the nation's new disaster response bureaucracy was put to the test by Hurricane Katrina, and it failed miserably. There was little coordination between FEMA officials, DHS officials, the White House, and state and local politicians. After Katrina, politicians moved to change the structure of FEMA; some even argued that FEMA should be abolished and a new emergency preparedness agency built from scratch.

Over its history, Congress has repeatedly made efforts to promote greater coordination among all its disparate, decentralized parts. As noted in Chapter 11, the Republican Party leadership has tried to increase party cohesion by awarding committee chairmanships on the basis of loyalty to the party program rather than seniority. Even so, it is difficult to achieve consensus in the area of budgeting, where individual committee preferences have to be balanced with overall budget goals. As agendas change with the emergence of new issues, the overlap in committee jurisdictions worsens. As noted above, many committees and subcommittees can claim some jurisdiction over the same problem.

Since the power of individual committee chairs makes it difficult for the House and the Senate to make significant reorganizations of their committee systems, reorganization often comes about incrementally. Individual chairs try to expand their jurisdictions, or conflict erupts between committees and new jurisdictional boundaries are negotiated.[37] At the beginning of 2001, the Republican leadership in the House reorganized the Banking Committee and the Commerce Committee. The Commerce Committee had long held jurisdiction over the securities and insurance industries. Changes in the financial services industry have led to many conglomerates' doing business in banking, securities, and insurance rather than in just one of these fields. To provide greater coordination in these areas, the Banking Committee was given jurisdiction over securities and insurance to go along with its authority over banking; it was renamed the Financial Services Committee. The Commerce Committee was left with a narrower (but still substantial) jurisdiction.[38]

Finally, the policy fragmentation created by federalism may be solved when an industry asks the national government to develop a single regulatory policy. Often the alternative is for that industry to try to accommodate the different regulatory approaches used in various states. Although an industry may prefer no regulation at all, it generally prefers one master to fifty.

The effect of pluralism on the problem of coordination is all too evident. In a decentralized, federal system of government with large numbers of interest groups, fragmentation is inevitable. Beyond the structural factors is the natural tendency of people and organizations to defend their base of power. Government officials understand, however, that mechanisms of coordination are necessary so that fragmentation does not overwhelm policymaking. Mechanisms such as interagency task forces, reorganizations, and White House review can bring some coherence to policymaking.

Government by Policy Area

Another counterweight to the fragmentation of a pluralist system with many different parts of government, each making policy, and many different sets of participants with differing objectives, is the working relationships that develop among these participants. We noted earlier that policy formulation takes place across different institutions. Participants from these institutions do not patiently wait their turn as policymaking proceeds from one institution to the next. Rather, they try to influence policy at whatever stage they can. Suppose that Congress is considering amendments to the Clean Air Act. Because Congress does not function in a vacuum, the other parts of government that will be affected by the legislation participate in the process too. The Environmental Protection Agency (EPA) has an interest in the outcome because it will have to administer the law. The White House is concerned about any legislation that affects such vital sectors of the economy as the steel and coal industries. As a result, officials from both the EPA and the White House work with members of Congress and the appropriate committee staffs to try to ensure that their interests are protected. At the same time, lobbyists representing corporations, trade associations, and environmental groups do their best to influence Congress, agency officials, and White House aides. Trade associations might hire public relations firms to sway public opinion toward their industry's point of view. Experts from think tanks and universities might be asked to testify at hearings or to serve in an informal advisory capacity in regard to the technical, economic, and social effects of the proposed amendments.

The various individuals and organizations that work in a particular policy area form a loosely knit community. More specifically, those "who share expertise in a policy domain and who frequently interact constitute an issue network."[39] The boundaries and membership of an **issue network** are hardly precise, but in general terms, such networks include members of Congress, committee staffers, agency officials, lawyers, lobbyists, consultants, scholars, and public relations specialists. Overall, a network can be quite large. One study identified over twelve hundred interest groups that had some contact with government officials in Washington in relation to health care over a five-year period.[40] But the real working relationships develop in specific policy areas, not throughout the entire policy community. The drug companies and their trade groups work with legislators and administrators on issues involving pharmaceuticals. Insurance companies work on other issues with other officials. It is within these more limited networks that ongoing working relationships emerge. Although network participants try to reach consensual agreements that an agency or congressional committee can act on, conflict within a network is common. On a regulatory issue, environmental or consumer groups may be lined up against an industry. It is common for different parts of an industry to have conflicting views on an issue. It is often the case, for example, that small businesses have different views on regulatory matters than the large corporations in the same field have.

The common denominator in a network is not the same political outlook but policy expertise. One must have the necessary expertise to enter the community of activists and politicians that influence policymaking in an issue area. Expertise has always been important, but "more than ever, policymaking is becoming an intramural activity among expert issue watchers."[41]

Consider Medicare, for example. The program is crucial to the health of the elderly, and with millions of baby boomers rapidly approaching retirement age, it needs to be restructured to make sure there will be enough money available to care for them all. But to enter the political debate on this issue requires specialized knowledge. What is the difference between a "defined benefit" and a "defined contribution," or between a "provider-sponsored organization" and a "health maintenance organization"? Which needs to be reformed first: "Medicare Part A" or "Medicare Part B"? Without getting into "portability" or "capitated" arrangements, is it better to have "medical savings accounts" or "fee-for-service" plans?[42]

The members of an issue network speak the same language. They can participate in the negotiation and compromise of policymaking because they can offer concrete, detailed solutions to the problems at hand. They understand the substance of policy, the way Washington works, and one another's viewpoints.

In a number of ways, issue networks promote pluralist democracy. They are open systems, populated by a wide range of interest groups. Decision making is not centralized in the hands of a few key players; policies are formulated in a participatory fashion. But there is still no guarantee that all relevant interests are represented, and those with greater financial resources have an advantage. Nevertheless, issue networks provide access to government for a diverse set of competing interests and thus further the pluralist ideal.

For those who prefer majoritarian democracy, however, issue networks are an obstacle to achieving their vision of how government should operate.[43] The technical complexity of contemporary issues makes it especially difficult for the public at large to exert control over policy outcomes. When we think of the complexity of issues such as nuclear power, toxic wastes, air pollution, poverty, and drug abuse, it is easy to understand why majoritarian democracy is so

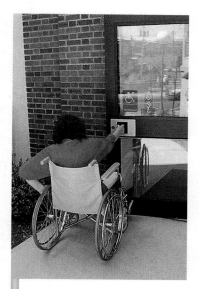

Opening the Door to Access
Implementation of the Americans with Disabilities Act was enormously challenging, as regulations written in Washington had to be put into effect in every community across the country. Policymaking is incremental and step-by-step. The access section of the law has been successfully implemented in office buildings, grocery stores, post offices, restaurants, shopping malls, banks, and many other kinds of facilities. *(Mulvehill/ The Image Works)*

issue network A shared-knowledge group consisting of representatives of various interests involved in some particular aspect of public policy.

difficult to achieve. The more complex the issue is, the more elected officials must depend on a technocratic elite for policy guidance. And technical expertise is a chief characteristic of participants in issue networks.

At first glance, having technical experts play a key role in policymaking may seem highly desirable. After all, who but the experts should be making decisions about toxic wastes? This works to the advantage of government bureaucracies, which are full of people hired for their technical expertise. But governmental dependence on technocrats also helps interest groups, which use policy experts to maximize their influence with government. Seen in this light, issue networks become less appealing. Interest groups—at least those with which we do not personally identify—are seen as selfish. They pursue policies that favor their constituents rather than the national interest.

Although expertise is an important factor in bringing interest groups into the decision-making process, it is not the only one. Americans have a fundamental belief that government should be open and accessible to "the people." If some constituency has a problem, they reason, government ought to listen to it. However, the practical consequence of this view is a government that is open to interest groups.

Finally, although issue networks promote pluralism, keep in mind that majoritarian influences on policymaking are still significant. The broad contours of public opinion can be a dominant force on highly visible issues. Policymaking on civil rights, for example, has been sensitive to shifts in public opinion. Elections, too, send messages to policymakers about the most widely discussed campaign issues. What issue networks have done, however, is facilitate pluralist politics in policy areas in which majoritarian influences are weak.[44]

★ The Nonprofit Sector

Community-based organizations are important participants in the policymaking process. Though they are not officially part of the government, these organizations may receive government funds and use them to implement a government program. With a largely volunteer work force, they provide social services and offer the government valuable feedback about policy implementation at the local level. These organizations are **nonprofits.** Nonprofits are neither governmental organizations nor private sector organizations, and, as the term *nonprofit* denotes, they may not distribute profits to shareholders or to anyone else.[45]

There are many different types of nonprofits, but when we use the term, we are usually referring to organizations that are considered "public charities" by the Internal Revenue Service. They are not charities in the sense that they necessarily have to distribute money or goods to the needy; rather, they perform some public good. The greatest number of nonprofits are involved in social services (see Figure 17.5). Social service nonprofits might distribute meals, offer after-school activities to low-income children, administer shelters for abused women or runaway children, or provide hospice care for the terminally ill.

Such organizations include the Salvation Army, a nonprofit with 60,000 employees that provides services to 30 million people a year, as well as smaller organizations like the Genesis Women's Shelter in Dallas, where women and their children can find safe haven from an abusive situation at home; Beyond Shelter, a Los Angeles organization that works to find housing for the homeless

Can you explain why . . .
government doesn't always do what the experts tell it to do?

nonprofits Organizations that are not part of government or business and cannot distribute profits to shareholders or to anyone else.

FIGURE 17.5 America's Nonprofit Sector

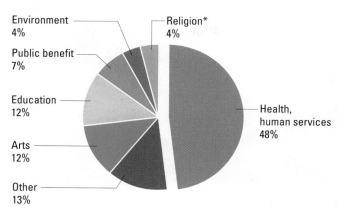

Environment
4%

Public benefit
7%

Education
12%

Arts
12%

Other
13%

Religion*
4%

Health,
human services
48%

Of all nonprofits large enough to file a tax return, close to half work in the fields of human services or health care. Overall, the sector has grown sharply, expanding by 64 percent between 1987 and 1997. Nonprofits employ 9 percent of the nation's work force.

Source: Jeffrey M. Berry with David F. Arons, *A Voice for Nonprofits* (Washington, D.C.: Brookings Institution, 2003), p. 5. Reprinted by permission.

*"Religion" is religion-related nonprofits and excludes individual congregations.

and provides social services to them; and the Transitional Work Corporation of Philadelphia, which offers job training to hard-core unemployed.[46] Nonprofits offer vitally important services, and all communities are highly dependent on them. As one scholar notes, they are "the glue that holds civil society together."[47]

Not all the nonprofits that qualify as public charities are social service providers. Other nonprofits include symphony orchestras, PTAs, Little Leagues, museums, and foundations. All of these groups provide something valuable to society by engaging people in their communities, offering them a chance to appreciate art, creating opportunities for volunteering, and providing recreation to children and adults alike. These activities enrich society, and it's important to design policies to encourage people to become involved in nonprofits. Nonprofits are rewarded for these valuable endeavors with tax deductibility for donors. Individuals who contribute money to public charity nonprofits can deduct that money from their taxable income. This tax break encourages people to give money because government is essentially subsidizing the contribution. (Recall the earlier discussion of tax expenditures—tax provisions that cause a loss of government revenue.)

The typical nonprofit is supported by a mix of private and government funds. One of the advantages for government from using nonprofits to administer social service programs is that substantial amounts of funding come from contributions made by individuals. Although the government is subsidizing those contributions through the tax deductibility of donations, it benefits by not having to pay for all those services itself.

The government also gets more social services than would be the case if there were no nonprofits and the government had to provide more direct services through its bureaucracies at the national, state, and local levels. Government is under substantial pressure to keep expenditures down. Indeed, nonprofits are growing in importance because government has found it desirable to shift more administration of social services to this sector. This allows elected officials to appear to cut the size of government by reducing the

? Can you explain why . . . government programs aren't always administered by the government?

Curious George Takes a Job
The nonprofit group Helping Hands trains capuchin monkeys to help people who are paralyzed. Monkeys can turn lights on and off, put on a CD, and warm up food in the microwave. It costs roughly $35,000 to train each monkey, but no fee is charged to the recipients of their services. *(Melanie Stetson Freeman/The Christian Science Monitor via Getty Images)*

number of bureaucrats while at the same time not angering people who depend on social services.[48]

Nonprofits are also inexpensive ways to deliver services because they make considerable use of volunteer labor. America is a nation of volunteers; a recent survey showed that 56 percent of the adult population, well over 100 million people, volunteered. On average, volunteers contribute 3.5 hours a week, and much of this volunteering is channeled through nonprofits.[49] It's not clear what percentage of this volunteering is devoted to helping paid staff deliver social services, but it is an enormously significant means of support in our social welfare system. A primary reason that people volunteer for nonprofits is that they find it meaningful and rewarding to help others.

Nonprofits may sound too good to be true, and in a sense they are because they can't do all that we might like them to. Policymakers have often claimed that the nonprofit sector could provide the safety net that protects Americans when they are in serious need of support. President Reagan said that his budget cuts wouldn't damage the safety net because philanthropy and nonprofits would fill the gap. His assurances were overly optimistic. During any recession, states must make significant budget cuts. This, in turn, means that many nonprofits have their state funding cut and find themselves struggling to deliver the same level of services they were offering before the recession hit.[50]

Given the importance of nonprofits in providing social services, it's clear that they have a role to play in developing policy as well as in implementing it. In many policy areas, they've become part of the policymaking communities that dominate the debate over the political issues relevant to their concerns.

Summary

Underlying policy choices are basic values—the core beliefs about how government should work. But values must be translated into policy choices. The basic objectives of government tend to be distributional, redistributional, and regulatory. To achieve a policy objective, those in government usually rely on one or more of the most basic tools or approaches: incentives and disincentives, direct provision of services, or rule setting.

Although there is much variation in the policymaking process, we can conceive of it as consisting of four stages. The first stage is agenda setting, the process by which problems become defined as political issues worthy of government attention. Once people in government feel that they should be doing something about a problem, an attempt at policy formulation will follow. All three branches of the national government formulate policy. Once policies have been formulated and ratified, administrative units of government must implement them. Finally, once policies are being carried out, they need to be evaluated. Implementation and program evaluation influence agenda building because program shortcomings become evident during these stages. Thus, the process is really circular, with the end often marking the beginning of a new round of policymaking.

Our policymaking system is also characterized by forces that push it toward fragmentation and by institutional structures intended to bring some element of coordination to government. The multiplicity of participants in policymaking, the diffusion of authority within both Congress and the executive branch, the separation of powers, and federalism are chief causes of conflict and fragmentation in policymaking.

To try to reduce fragmentation, presidents and congressional leaders have pushed for various reforms designed to bring greater coordination to policymaking and program implementation. Presidents continually tinker with the organization of the executive branch, reorganizing agencies and offices within the constraints of political feasibility. Coordination of the budgetary process comes from the Office of Management and Budget and from the budget committees of Congress. In varying degrees, presidents have also relied on central clearance of proposed agency regulations.

The fragmentation of government accentuates the forces of pluralism. The structure of the policymaking process facilitates the participation of interest groups. This in turn works in favor of well-organized, aggressive constituencies and against the broader but more passive public at large. There are certainly majoritarian counterweights to the advantages to pluralism inherent in the structure of our government, but such forces as public opinion and political party stands work best on national issues of great concern to the public. On the mundane, day-to-day issues of government, pluralism is aided by the complexity of public policy and the fragmentation of responsibility.

Internet activities and reading suggestions for this chapter are available on the *Online Study Center*

To complete the multimedia assignments for this chapter, go to AmericansGoverning.org.

18

Economic Policy

(© Copyright 2006, The Nasdaq Stock Market, Inc. Reprinted with permission.)

Online Study Center
This icon will direct you to resources and activities on the website
college.hmco.com/pic/jandaupdate9e

"Return to Spender," proclaimed the *Wall Street Journal*'s editorial against spending billions following Hurricane Katrina in 2005. Lashing out against the president and party it supported in the 2004 election, the paper said, "For five years the White House has let Congress spend at will, declining to veto even a single bill, though many have arrived at his desk with billions of dollars more than he requested."[1] The *Journal* editorialized against the GOP again in early 2006: "When Republicans took control of the purse strings in 1995, the federal budget was $1.5 trillion. It is now $2.55 trillion—or $5 million a minute."[2] Three weeks later, the *Journal* took after President Bush after he unveiled his fiscal 2007 budget: "The only thing worse than Mr. Bush's spending record is the clucking on Capitol Hill deploring it."[3]

This was not a new line of criticism from the *Journal*. Two months before President Bush's 2004 State of the Union address, it published an editorial, "The GOP's Spending Spree," that charged, "Elected in 1994 as the party of limited government, Republicans seem to have abandoned any effort to limit spending. Worse, the current Republican President has shown no inclination to control it either."[4] The *Journal* was only echoing the voices of other conservatives, such as Dick Armey, former House Republican leader and head of Citizens for a Sound Economy, who said, "I'm upset about the deficit, and I'm upset about spending. There's no way I can pin that on the Democrats. Republicans own the town now."[5]

According to the budget that President Bush proposed in 2007, federal spending in 2008 would exceed revenues by $187 billion, the seventh deficit since 2002. The recurring annual budget deficits had raised the accumulated public debt at the end of 2006 to more than *$4.9 trillion* (that's $4,900,000,000,000), over 45 percent of which was held by foreigners (for example, in Japan and China) who could stop financing the operation of our government.[6] On top of the record budget deficit, the U.S. trade deficit in 2005 soared to a new record—with Americans purchasing $818 billion more in goods and services than they were selling to foreigners.[7] (See "Looking to the Future: Another Year Older and Deeper in Debt?") Clearly, serious economic problems were threatening the U.S. economy—not to mention Bush's reelection in 2004. Why didn't the president take steps to solve those problems?

Of course, President Bush did not want record deficits during his administration, and he did not want to be known as a big spender on government. He wanted a healthy domestic economy with high employment, but many jobs were lost to the global economy (see the introduction to Chapter 20). Can the president be blamed for failing to control the American economy? How much control of the domestic economy can government really exercise through the judicious use of economic theory? How much is it influenced by events that lie outside presidential control? More concretely, how is the national budget formulated, and why did the deficit grow so large and prove so difficult to control against spending appetites of Congress? What effects do government taxing and spending policies have on the economy and on economic equality? We address these questions in this chapter. As we shall see, no one person or organization controls the American economy; multiple actors have a voice in economic conditions. And not all of these actors are public—or American. ★

★ Theories of Economic Policy

Government attempts to control the economy rely on theories about how the economy responds to government taxing and spending policies. How policymakers tax and spend depends on their beliefs about how the economy functions and the proper role of government in the economy. The American economy is so complex that no policymaker knows exactly how it works. Policymakers rely on economic theories to explain its functioning, and there are nearly as many theories as there are economists. Unfortunately, different theories (and economists) often predict different outcomes. One source of differing predictions is the different assumptions that underlie competing economic theories. Another problem is the differences between abstract theories and the real world. Still, despite the disagreement among economists, a knowledge of basic economics is necessary to understand how government approaches public policy.[8]

We are concerned here with economic policy in a market economy—one in which the prices of goods and services are determined through the interaction of sellers and buyers (that is, through supply and demand). This kind of economy is typical of the consumer-dominated societies of Western Europe and the United States. A nonmarket economy relies on government planners to determine both the prices of goods and the amounts that are produced. The old Soviet economy is a perfect example. In a nonmarket economy, the government owns and operates the major means of production.

Market economies are loosely called *capitalist economies:* they allow private individuals to own property; sell goods for profit in free, or open, markets; and accumulate wealth, called *capital.* Market economies often exhibit a mix of government and private ownership. For example, Britain has had more government-owned enterprises (railroads, broadcasting, and housing) than has the United States. Competing economic theories differ largely on how free they say the markets should be—in other words, on government's role in directing the economy.

Laissez-Faire Economics

The French term *laissez faire,* introduced in Chapter 1 and discussed again in Chapter 13, describes the absence of government control. The economic doctrine of laissez faire likens the operation of a free market to the process of natural selection. Economic competition weeds out the weak and preserves the strong. In the process, the economy prospers, and everyone eventually benefits.

Advocates of laissez-faire economics are fond of quoting Adam Smith's *The Wealth of Nations.* In this 1776 treatise, Smith argued that each individual, pursuing his own selfish interests in a competitive market, was "led by an invisible hand to promote an end which was no part of his intention." Smith's "invisible hand" has been used for two centuries to justify the belief that the narrow pursuit of profits serves the broad interests of society.[9] Strict advocates of laissez faire maintain that government interference with business tampers with the laws of nature, obstructing the workings of the free market. Mainstream economists today favor market principles but do recognize that "governments can sometimes improve market outcomes."[10]

Looking to the Future

Another Year Older and Deeper in Debt?

Looking toward the future about three decades off (if you are age twenty now, you will be age fifty then), what do you see as the debt picture facing the United States? Over the past decade, an increasing share of the national debt of over $4.8 trillion has been acquired by foreigners, while Americans are increasingly buying more goods and services from other countries than they are selling to them. As shown by the dips in the lines, these trends can be altered, but will they be? What could cause either trend to change, thus reducing our foreign obligations?

Sources: Data from Table 16–6: "Foreign Holdings of Federal Debt," *Budget of the United States, Fiscal Year 2008: Analytical Perspectives* (Washington, D.C.: U.S. Government Printing Office, 2007); "U.S. Trade in Goods and Services, Balance of Payments (BOP) Basis," from the U.S. Census Bureau, Foreign Trade Division, available from <http://www.census.gov/foreign-trade/statistics/historical/gands.txt>, accessed 27 April 2006.

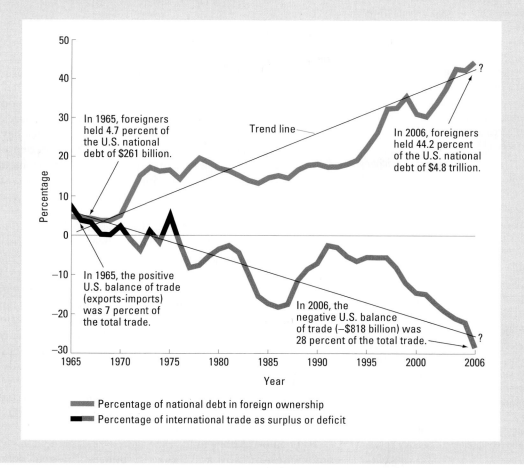

In 1965, foreigners held 4.7 percent of the U.S. national debt of $261 billion.

Trend line

In 2006, foreigners held 44.2 percent of the U.S. national debt of $4.8 trillion.

In 1965, the positive U.S. balance of trade (exports-imports) was 7 percent of the total trade.

In 2006, the negative U.S. balance of trade (−$818 billion) was 28 percent of the total trade.

Percentage of national debt in foreign ownership
Percentage of international trade as surplus or deficit

Economists Getting Data for Predictions

The forecast you get depends on the economist you ask. *(Reprinted by permission, Tribune Media Service)*

THE ECONOMISTS

economic depression A period of high unemployment and business failures; a severe, long-lasting downturn in a business cycle.

inflation An economic condition characterized by price increases linked to a decrease in the value of currency.

business cycles Expansions and contractions of business activity, the first accompanied by inflation and the second by unemployment.

aggregate demand The money available to be spent for goods and services by consumers, businesses, and government.

productive capacity The total value of goods and services that can be produced when the economy works at full capacity.

gross domestic product (GDP) The total value of the goods and services produced by a country during a year.

Keynesian theory An economic theory stating that the government can stabilize the economy—that is, can smooth business cycles—by controlling the level of aggregate demand, and that the level of aggregate demand can be controlled by means of fiscal and monetary policies.

fiscal policies Economic policies that involve government spending and taxing.

Keynesian Theory

One problem with laissez-faire economics is its insistence that government should do little about **economic depression** (a period of high unemployment and business failures) or raging **inflation** (price increases that decrease the value of currency). Inflation is ordinarily measured by the consumer price index (CPI), explained in the feature "The Consumer Price Index." Since the beginning of the Industrial Revolution, capitalist economies have suffered through many cyclical fluctuations. The United States has experienced more than fifteen of these **business cycles**—expansions and contractions of business activity, the first stage accompanied by inflation and the second stage by unemployment. No one had a theory that really explained these cycles until the Great Depression of the 1930s.

That was when John Maynard Keynes, a British economist, theorized that business cycles stem from imbalances between aggregate demand and productive capacity. **Aggregate demand** is the income available to consumers, business, and government to spend on goods and services. **Productive capacity** is the total value of goods and services that can be produced when the economy is working at full capacity. The value of the goods and services actually produced is called the **gross domestic product (GDP)**. When demand exceeds productive capacity, people are willing to pay more for available goods, which leads to price inflation. When productive capacity exceeds demand, producers cut back on their output of goods, which leads to unemployment. When many people are unemployed for an extended period, the economy is in a depression. Keynes theorized that government could stabilize the economy (and smooth out or eliminate business cycles) by controlling the level of aggregate demand.

Keynesian theory holds that aggregate demand can be adjusted through a combination of fiscal and monetary policies.[11] **Fiscal policies,** which are enacted by the president and Congress, involve changes in government spending and taxing. When demand is too low, according to Keynes, government should

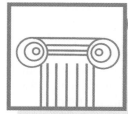

The Consumer Price Index

Inflation in the United States is usually measured in terms of the consumer price index (CPI), which is calculated by the U.S. Bureau of Labor Statistics (BLS). The CPI is based on prices paid for food, clothing, shelter, transportation, medical services, and other items necessary for daily living. Data are collected from eighty-seven areas across the country, from over fifty thousand homes and more than twenty thousand businesses. The CPI is thoroughly reviewed about every ten years, most recently in 1998. Moreover, the BLS has since made many adjustments in the index.

The CPI is not a perfect measure of inflation. For example, it does not differentiate between inflationary price increases and other price increases. An automobile bought in 1997 is not the same as one bought in 2007. Any price increase for the same model reflects an improved product as well as a decrease in the value of the dollar. Another problem is the CPI's delay in reflecting changes in buying habits. VCRs were around for several years before they were included among the hundreds of items in the index; DVD players were still not listed in 2006.

These are minor issues compared with the changing weight given to the cost of housing. Before 1983, the cost of purchasing and financing a home accounted for 26 percent of the CPI, which neglected the reality that few people buy a home every year—and many people rent. Since 1983, the BLS figured the cost of renting equivalent housing as only 15 percent of the CPI.

In recent years, the BLS has released a "core" CPI that excludes the costs of food and energy, which fluctuate more widely than what has become known as the standard or "headline" CPI.

The government incorporates the standard CPI in cost-of-living adjustments for civil service and military pension payments and Social Security benefits. Moreover, union wage contracts with private businesses are often indexed (tied) to the CPI. As the CPI tends to rise each year, so do payments that are tied to it. In this way, CPI indexing promotes both the growth of government spending and inflation itself. The United States is one of the few nations that also ties its tax brackets to a price index, which reduces government revenues by eliminating the effect of inflation on taxpayer incomes.

Despite its faults, the CPI is at least a consistent measure of prices, and it is likely to continue as the basis for adjustments to wages, benefits, and payments affecting millions of people.

Sources: Bureau of Labor Statistics, *BLS Handbook of Methods,* Chapter 17, "The Consumer Price Index," <http://www.bls.gov/opub/hom/homch17_a.htm>; David S. Moore, *Statistics: Concepts and Controversies,* 2nd ed. (New York: Freeman, 1985), pp. 239–241; and Floyd Norris, "On Wall Street, the Inflation View Is Rosier Than It Is on Main Street," *New York Times,* 25 February 2006, p. B3. Unfortunately, the CPI captures costs of goods better than costs of services, such as medical care, insurance, and education. Thus, many citizens complain of rising prices while the CPI stays low. See Jon E. Hilsenrath, "America's Pricing Paradox," *Wall Street Journal,* 16 May 2003, p. B1.

either spend more itself, hiring people and thus giving them money, or cut taxes, giving people more of their own money to spend. When demand is too great, the government should either spend less or raise taxes, giving people less money to spend. **Monetary policies,** which are largely determined by the Federal Reserve Board, involve changes in the money supply and operate less directly on the economy. Increasing the amount of money in circulation increases aggregate demand and thus increases price inflation. Decreasing the money supply decreases aggregate demand and inflationary pressures.

Despite some problems with the assumptions of Keynesian theory, capitalist countries have widely adopted it in some form.[12] At one time or another, virtually all have used the Keynesian technique of **deficit financing**—spending in excess of tax revenues—to combat an economic slump. The objective of deficit financing, which can also occur through cutting taxes, is to inject extra money into the economy to stimulate aggregate demand in the short run. Most deficits are financed with funds borrowed through the issuing of government bonds, notes, or other securities. The theory holds that deficits can be paid off with budget surpluses after the economy recovers.

Because Keynesian theory requires government to play an active role in controlling the economy, it runs counter to laissez-faire economics. Before Keynes, no administration in Washington would shoulder responsibility for maintaining a healthy economy. In 1946, the year Keynes died, Congress passed an employment act establishing "the continuing responsibility of the national government to . . . promote maximum employment, production and purchasing power." It also created the **Council of Economic Advisers (CEA)** within the Executive Office of the President to advise the president on maintaining a stable economy. The CEA normally consists of three economists (usually university professors) appointed by the president with Senate approval. Aided by a staff of about twenty-five people (mostly economists), the CEA helps the president prepare his annual economic report, also a provision of the 1946 act. The chair of the CEA is usually a prominent spokesperson for the administration's economic policy.

The Employment Act of 1946, which reflected Keynesian theory, had a tremendous effect on government economic policy. Many people believe it was the primary source of "big government" in America. Even Richard Nixon, a conservative president, admitted that "we are all Keynesians now," by accepting government responsibility for the economy.

Monetary Policy

Although most economists accept Keynesian theory in its broad outlines, they depreciate its political utility. Some especially question the value of fiscal policies in controlling inflation and unemployment. They argue that government spending programs take too long to enact in Congress and to implement through the bureaucracy. As a result, jobs are created not when they are needed but years later, when the crisis may have passed and government spending needs to be reduced.

Also, government spending is easier to start than to stop because the groups that benefit from spending programs tend to defend them even when they are no longer needed. A similar criticism applies to tax policies. Politically, it is much easier to cut taxes than to raise them. In other words, Keynesian the-

monetary policies Economic policies that involve control of, and changes in, the supply of money.

deficit financing The Keynesian technique of spending beyond government income to combat an economic slump. Its purpose is to inject extra money into the economy to stimulate aggregate demand.

Council of Economic Advisers (CEA) A group that works within the executive branch to provide advice on maintaining a stable economy.

Changing Fed Heads
Ben S. Bernanke strides confidently to President Bush's announcement of his nomination to head the Federal Reserve Board, followed by outgoing chairman Alan Greenspan. Greenspan had served as Fed Head for more than eighteen years before leaving office in early 2006 just short of age eighty. During his long tenure, Greenspan drew praise for guiding the economy through troubled times. *(Doug Mills/The New York Times)*

ory requires that governments be able to begin and end spending quickly and to cut and raise taxes quickly. But in the real world, these fiscal tools are easier to use in one direction than the other.

Recognizing these limitations of fiscal policies, **monetarists** argue that government can control the economy's performance simply by controlling the nation's money supply.[13] Monetarists favor a long-range policy of small but steady growth in the amount of money in circulation rather than frequent manipulation of monetary policies.

Monetary policies in the United States are under the control of the **Federal Reserve System,** which acts as the country's central bank. Established in 1913, the Fed is not a single bank but a system of banks. At the top of the system is the board of governors, seven members appointed by the president for staggered terms of fourteen years. The president designates one member of the board to be its chairperson, who serves a four-year term that extends beyond the president's term of office. This complex arrangement was intended to make the board independent of the president and even of Congress. An independent board, the reasoning went, would be able to make financial decisions for the nation without regard to their political implications.[14]

The Fed controls the money supply, which affects inflation, in three ways. Most important, the Fed can sell and buy government securities (such as U.S. Treasury bonds) on the open market. When the Fed sells securities, it takes money out of circulation, thereby making money scarce and raising the interest rate. When the Fed buys securities, the process works in reverse, lowering interest rates. The Fed also sets a target for the *federal funds rate*, which banks charge one another for overnight loans and which is usually cited when newspapers write, "The Fed has decided to lower [or raise] interest rates." Less frequently (for technical reasons), the Fed may change its *discount rate,* the interest rate that member banks have to pay to borrow money from a Federal

monetarists Those who argue that government can effectively control the performance of an economy only by controlling the supply of money.

Federal Reserve System The system of banks that acts as the central bank of the United States and controls major monetary policies.

Reserve bank. Finally, the Fed can change its *reserve requirement,* which is the amount of cash that member banks must keep on deposit in their regional Federal Reserve bank. An increase in the reserve requirement reduces the amount of money banks have available to lend.[15]

Basic economic theory holds that interest rates should be raised when the economy is growing too quickly (this restricts the flow of money, thus avoiding inflation) and lowered when the economy is sluggish (thus increasing the money flow to encourage spending and economic growth). Historically, the Fed has adjusted interest rates to combat inflation rather than to stimulate economic growth.[16] (A former Fed chairman once said its task was "to remove the punch bowl when the party gets going.")[17] That is, the Fed would dampen economic growth before it leads to serious inflation.

Accordingly, some charge that the Fed acts to further interests of the wealthy (who fear rampant inflation) more than interests of the poor (who fear widespread unemployment). Why so? Although all classes of citizens complain about increasing costs of living, inflation usually harms upper classes (creditors) more than lower classes (debtors). To illustrate, suppose someone borrows $20,000, to be repaid after ten years, during which the inflation rate was 10 percent. When the loan is due, the $20,000 borrowed is "worth" only $18,000. Debtors find the cheaper money easier to raise, while creditors are paid less than the original value of their loan. Hence, wealthy people fear severe inflation, which can erode the value of their saved wealth. As one Federal Reserve bank bluntly states: "Debtors gain when inflation is unexpectedly high, and creditors gain when it is unexpectedly low."[18]

Although the president is formally responsible for the state of the economy and although voters hold him accountable, the president neither determines interest rates (the Fed does) nor controls spending (Congress does). In this respect, all presidents since 1913 have had to work with a Fed made independent of both the president and Congress, and all have had to deal with the fact that Congress ultimately controls spending. These restrictions on presidential authority are consistent with the pluralist model of democracy, but a president held responsible for the economy may not appreciate that theoretical argument.

Although the Fed's economic policies are not perfectly insulated from political concerns, they are sufficiently independent that the president is not able to control monetary policy without the Fed's cooperation. This means that the president cannot be held completely responsible for the state of the economy, although traditionally most Americans have held him almost totally responsible. In fact, political scientists who study presidential elections suggest that economic conditions play an important, though not always decisive, role in determining which candidate wins. Naturally, a strong economy favors the incumbent party. When people are optimistic about the economic future and feel that they are doing well, they typically see no reason to change the party controlling the White House. But when conditions are bad or worsening, voters often decide to seek a change.

The Fed's activities are essential parts of the government's overall economic policy, but they lie outside the direct control of the president—and directly in the hands of the chairman of the Federal Reserve Board. This makes the Fed chairman a critical player in economic affairs and can create problems in coordinating economic policy. For example, the president might want the Fed to lower interest rates to stimulate the economy, but the Fed might resist

? Can you explain why . . . a president is not directly responsible for the nation's interest rates?

for fear of inflation. Such policy clashes can pit the chair of the Federal Reserve Board directly against the president. So presidents typically court the Fed chair, even one who served a president of the other party.

Originally appointed by President Reagan in 1987, Alan Greenspan served as chairman of the Federal Reserve Board until 2006 and—despite his elliptical manner of speaking—gained enormous respect for his performance.[19] During the stock market boom in the late 1990s, the Fed—and Greenspan—oversaw an economy with low inflation, low unemployment, *and* strong growth. Many on Wall Street and in Washington attributed such extraordinary economic conditions to his stewardship. When the stock market collapsed in early 2001, however, Greenspan drew criticism for inflating the stock bubble by issuing optimistic economic assessments.[20] Others praised him for combating the effects of the bubble's bursting by lowering interest rates a dozen times within two years after the collapse. Greenspan himself suggested that globalization helped him control inflation: the overall supply of labor abroad prevented workers at home from demanding higher wages.[21] Greenspan has been succeeded by Ben S. Bernanke, who was appointed by President Bush and took office in early 2006.

Supply-Side Economics

When Reagan came to office in 1981, he embraced a school of thought called **supply-side economics** to deal with the double-digit inflation that the nation was experiencing. Keynesian theory argues that inflation results when consumers, businesses, and governments have more money to spend than there are goods and services to buy. The standard Keynesian solution is to reduce demand (for example, by increasing taxes). Supply-siders argue that inflation can be lowered more effectively by increasing the supply of goods (that is, they stress the supply side of the economic equation). Specifically, they favor tax cuts to stimulate investment (which leads to the production of more goods) and less government regulation of business (again, to increase productivity—which they hold will yield more, not less, government revenue). Supply-siders also argue that the rich should receive larger tax cuts than the poor because the rich have more money to invest. The benefits of increased investment will then "trickle down" to working people in the form of additional jobs and income.

In a sense, supply-side economics resembles laissez-faire economics because it prefers fewer government programs and regulations, and less taxation. Supply-siders believe that government interferes too much with the efforts of individuals to work, save, and invest. Inspired by supply-side theory, Reagan proposed (and got) massive tax cuts in the Economic Recovery Tax Act of 1981. The act reduced individual tax rates by 23 percent over a three-year period and cut the marginal tax rate for the highest income group from 70 to 50 percent. Reagan also launched a program to deregulate business. According to supply-side theory, these actions would generate extra government revenue, making spending cuts unnecessary to balance the budget. Nevertheless, Reagan also cut funding for some domestic programs, including Aid to Families with Dependent Children. Contrary to supply-side theory, he also proposed hefty increases in military spending. This blend of tax cuts, deregulation, cuts in spending for social programs, and increases in spending for defense became known, somewhat disparagingly, as *Reaganomics*.

supply-side economics
Economic policies aimed at increasing the supply of goods (as opposed to decreasing demand); consist mainly of tax cuts for possible investors and less regulation of business.

FIGURE 18.1 Budget Deficits and Surpluses over Time

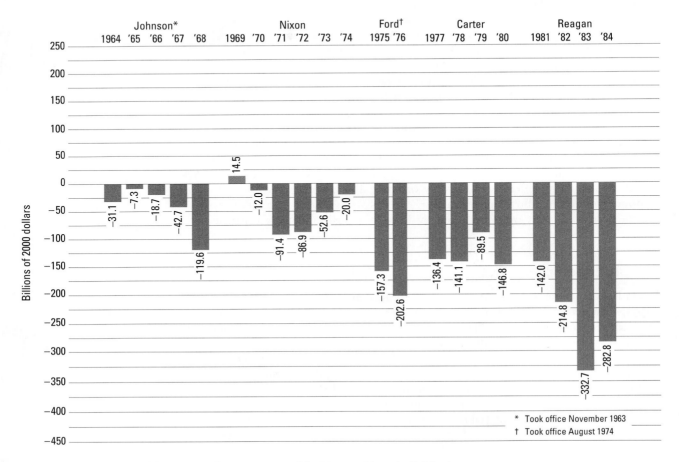

In his first inaugural address, President Reagan said, "You and I, as individuals, can, by borrowing, live beyond our means, but only for a limited period of time. Why, then, should we think that collectively, as a nation, we're not bound by that same limitation?" But borrow he did. Reagan's critics charged that the budget deficits under his administration—more than $1.3 trillion—exceeded the total deficits of all previous presidents. But this charge does not take inflation into account. A billion dollars in the 2000s is worth much less than it was a century ago, or even ten years ago.

How well did Reaganomics work? Although it reduced inflation and unemployment (aided by a sharp decline in oil prices) and worked largely as expected in the area of industry deregulation, Reaganomics failed massively to reduce the budget deficit. Contrary to supply-side theory, the 1981 tax cut was accompanied by a massive drop in tax revenues. Shortly after taking office, Reagan promised that his economic policies would balance the national budget by 1984. In fact, lower tax revenues and higher defense spending produced the

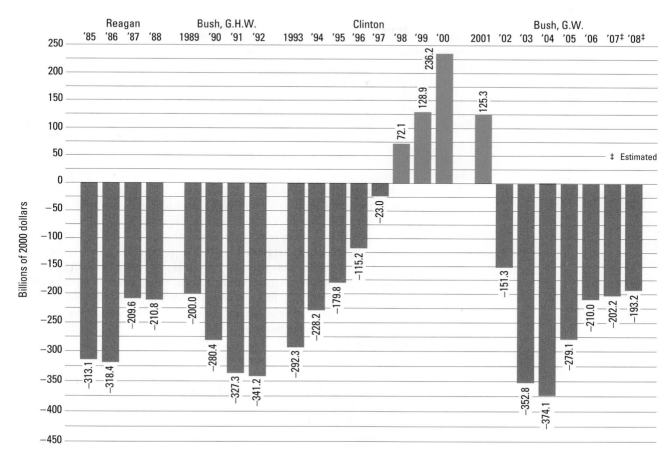

A fairer way to calculate deficits and surpluses is in constant dollars—dollars whose value is standardized to a given year. This chart shows the actual deficits and surpluses in 2000 dollars incurred under administrations from Johnson to George W. Bush. Even computed this way, the deficits were enormous under Reagan, George H. W. Bush, and even during Clinton's early years. Budget deficits were eventually eliminated under Clinton and replaced by surpluses. Deficits appeared again under George W. Bush.

Source: Executive Office of the President, *Budget of the United States Government, Fiscal Year 2008: Historical Tables* (Washington, D.C.: U.S. Government Printing Office, 2007), pp. 25–26.

largest budget deficits ever, as shown in Figure 18.1.[22] Budget deficits continued until 1998, when a booming U.S. economy generated the first budget surplus since 1969. Economist Gregory Mankiw, who became head of President Bush's Council of Economic Advisers, said that history failed to confirm the main conjecture of supply-side economics: that lower tax revenues would raise tax revenues: "When Reagan cut taxes after he was elected, the result was less tax revenue, not more."[23]

★ Public Policy and the Budget

To most people the national budget is B-O-R-I-N-G. To national politicians, it is an exciting script for high drama. The numbers, categories, and percentages that numb normal minds cause politicians' nostrils to flare and their hearts to pound. The budget is a battlefield on which politicians wage war over the programs they support.

Control of the budget is important to members of Congress because they are politicians, and politicians want to wield power, not watch someone else wield it. Also, the Constitution established Congress, not the president, as the "first branch" of government and the people's representatives. Unfortunately for Congress, the president has emerged as the leader in shaping the budget. Although Congress often disagrees with presidential spending priorities, it has been unable to mount a serious challenge to presidential authority by presenting a coherent alternative budget.

Today, the president prepares the budget, and Congress approves it. This was not always the case. Before 1921, Congress prepared the budget under its constitutional authority to raise taxes and appropriate funds. The budget was formed piecemeal by enacting a series of laws that originated in the many committees involved in the highly decentralized process of raising revenue, authorizing expenditures, and appropriating funds. Executive agencies even submitted their budgetary requests directly to Congress, not to the president. No one was responsible for the big picture—the budget as a whole. The president's role was essentially limited to approving revenue and appropriations bills, just as he approved other pieces of legislation.

Congressional budgeting (such as it was) worked well enough for a nation of farmers, but not for an industrialized nation with a growing population and an increasingly active government. Soon after World War I, Congress realized that the budget-making process needed to be centralized. With the Budget and Accounting Act of 1921, it thrust the responsibility for preparing the budget onto the president. The act established the Bureau of the Budget to help the president write "his" budget, which had to be submitted to Congress each January. Congress retained its constitutional authority to raise and spend funds, but now Congress would begin its work with the president's budget as its starting point. And all executive agencies' budget requests had to be funneled for review through the Bureau of the Budget (which became the Office of Management and Budget in 1970); those consistent with the president's overall economic and legislative program were incorporated into the president's budget.

The Nature of the Budget

The national budget is complex. But its basic elements are not beyond understanding. We begin with some definitions. The *Budget of the United States Government* is the annual financial plan that the president is required to submit to Congress at the start of each year. It applies to the *next* **fiscal year,** the interval the government uses for accounting purposes. Currently, the fiscal year runs from October 1 to September 30. The budget is named for the year in which it *ends,* so the FY 2007 budget that Bush submitted in early 2006 applies to the twelve months from October 1, 2006, to September 30, 2007.

Broadly, the budget defines **budget authority** (how much government agencies are authorized to spend on programs); **budget outlays,** or expenditures

fiscal year (FY) The twelve-month period from October 1 to September 30 used by the government for accounting purposes. A fiscal year budget is named for the year in which it ends.

budget authority The amounts that government agencies are authorized to spend for their programs.

budget outlays The amounts that government agencies are expected to spend in the fiscal year.

(how much agencies are expected to spend); and **receipts** (how much is expected in taxes and other revenues). President Bush's FY 2007 budget contained authority for expenditures of $2,739 billion, but it provided for outlays of $2,770 billion (including some previous obligations). His budget also anticipated receipts of $2,416 billion, leaving an estimated *deficit* of $354 billion—the difference between receipts and outlays.

When the U.S government runs a deficit, it borrows funds on a massive scale to finance its operation that fiscal year, thus limiting the supply of loadable funds for business investment. The former head of Bush's Council of Economic Advisers wrote in his best-selling economics textbook, "Because investment is important for long-run economic growth, government budget deficits reduce the economy's growth rate."[24] As described in this chapter's opening vignette, the long-run impact of Bush's budget deficits worried fiscal conservatives, who complained about the "GOP spending spree." But the Bush administration seemed unconcerned; Vice President Dick Cheney reportedly told the secretary of the treasury, "Reagan proved deficits don't matter."[25]

Indeed, economists seemed more concerned about the accumulated government debt, not the annual deficit.[26] A deficit in the annual budget is different from the **public debt,** which represents the accumulated sum of borrowing (mainly to finance past annual deficits) that remains to be paid to lenders outside the government.[27] The public debt in 2006 was a staggering $4.8 *trillion*, and of this amount, more than 45 percent was held by institutions or individuals in other countries.[28] If foreign lenders were to stop financing America's governmental annual deficit and national debt, the economy could suffer a serious blow, a prospect discussed frequently in financial pages, especially in the *Wall Street Journal*.[29]

Preparing the President's Budget

Bush's FY 2007 budget, with appendixes, was thousands of pages long and weighed several pounds. (The president's budget document contains more than numbers. It also explains individual spending programs in terms of national needs and agency objectives, and it analyzes proposed taxes and other receipts.) Each year, the publication of the president's budget is anxiously awaited by reporters, lobbyists, and political analysts eager to learn his plans for government spending in the coming year.

The budget that the president submits to Congress each winter is the end product of a process that begins the previous spring under the supervision of the **Office of Management and Budget.** The OMB is located within the Executive Office of the President and is headed by a director appointed by the president with the approval of the Senate. The OMB, with a staff of more than five hundred, is the most powerful domestic agency in the bureaucracy, and its director, who attends meetings of the president's cabinet, is one of the most powerful figures in government.

The OMB initiates the budget process each spring by meeting with the president to discuss the economic situation and his budgetary priorities. It then sends broad budgeting guidelines to every government agency and requests their initial projection of how much money they will need for the next fiscal year. The OMB assembles this information and makes recommendations to the president, who then develops more precise guidelines describing how much each is likely to get. By summer, the agencies are asked to prepare budgets based on

receipts For a government, the amount expected or obtained in taxes and other revenues.

public debt The accumulated sum of past government borrowing owed to lenders outside the government.

Office of Management and Budget (OMB) The budgeting arm of the Executive Office; prepares the president's budget.

the new guidelines. By fall, they submit their formal budgets to the OMB, where budget analysts scrutinize agency requests, considering both their costs and their consistency with the president's legislative program. A lot of politicking goes on at this stage, as agency heads try to circumvent the OMB by pleading for their pet projects with presidential advisers and perhaps even the president himself.

Political negotiations over the budget may extend into the early winter—and often until it goes to the printer. The voluminous document looks very much like a finished product, but the figures it contains are not final. In giving the president the responsibility for preparing the budget in 1921, Congress simply provided itself with a starting point for its own work. And even with this head start, Congress has a hard time disciplining itself to produce a coherent, balanced budget.

Passing the Congressional Budget

The president's budget must be approved by Congress. Its process for doing so is a creaky conglomeration of traditional procedures overlaid with structural reforms from the 1970s, external constraints from the 1980s, and changes introduced by the 1990 Budget Enforcement Act. The cumbersome process has had difficulty producing a budget according to Congress's own timetable.

The Traditional Procedure: The Committee Structure. Traditionally, the tasks of budget making were divided among a number of committees, a process that has been retained. Three types of committees are involved in budgeting:

- **Tax committees** are responsible for raising the revenues to run the government. The Ways and Means Committee in the House and the Finance Committee in the Senate consider all proposals for taxes, tariffs, and other receipts contained in the president's budget.

- **Authorization committees** (such as the House Armed Services Committee and the Senate Banking, Housing, and Urban Affairs Committee) have jurisdiction over particular legislative subjects. The House has about twenty committees that can authorize spending, and the Senate about fifteen. Each pores over the portions of the budget that pertain to its area of responsibility. However, in recent years, power has shifted from the authorization committees to the appropriations committees.

- **Appropriations committees** decide which of the programs approved by the authorization committees will actually be funded (that is, given money to spend). For example, the House Armed Services Committee might propose building a new line of tanks for the army, and it might succeed in getting this proposal enacted into law. But the tanks will never be built unless the appropriations committees appropriate funds for that purpose. Thirteen distinct appropriations bills are supposed to be enacted each year to fund the nation's spending.

Two serious problems are inherent in a budgeting process that involves three distinct kinds of congressional committees. First, the two-step spending process (first authorization, then appropriation) is complex; it offers wonderful opportunities for interest groups to get into the budgeting act in the spirit of pluralist democracy. Second, because one group of legislators in each house

tax committees The two committees of Congress responsible for raising the revenue with which to run the government.

authorization committees Committees of Congress that can authorize spending in their particular areas of responsibility.

appropriations committees Committees of Congress that decide which of the programs passed by the authorization committees will actually be funded.

plans for revenues and many other groups plan for spending, no one is responsible for the budget as a whole. In the 1970s, Congress added a new committee structure that combats the pluralist politics inherent in the old procedures and allows budget choices to be made in a more majoritarian manner, by votes in both chambers. In the 1980s, Congress tried to force itself to balance the budget by setting targets. In the 1990s, Congress introduced some belt-tightening reforms and passed important tax increases that led to a balanced budget. In the early 2000s, Congress allowed some reforms to lapse and cut taxes, recreating budget deficits. Here is a brief account of these developments.

Reforms of the 1970s: The Budget Committee Structure.

Congress surrendered considerable authority in 1921 when it gave the president the responsibility of preparing the budget. During the next fifty years, attempts by Congress to regain control of the budgeting process failed because of jurisdictional squabbles between the revenue and appropriations committees. The Budget and Impoundment Control Act of 1974 fashioned a political solution to these squabbles while adding a new element. All the tax and appropriations committees (and chairpersons) were retained, but new House and Senate budget committees were superimposed over the old committee structure. The **budget committees** supervise a comprehensive budget review process, aided by the Congressional Budget Office. The **Congressional Budget Office (CBO)**, with a staff of more than two hundred, has acquired a budgetary expertise equal to that of the president's OMB, so it can prepare credible alternative budgets for Congress.

At the heart of the 1974 reforms was a timetable for the congressional budgeting process. The budget committees are supposed to propose an initial budget resolution that sets overall revenue and spending levels, broken down into twenty-one different "budget functions," such as national defense, agriculture, and health. By April 15, both houses are supposed to have agreed on a single budget resolution to guide their work on the budget during the summer. The appropriations committees are supposed to begin drafting the thirteen appropriations bills by May 15 and complete them by June 30. Throughout, the levels of spending set by majority vote in the budget resolution are supposed to constrain pressures by special interests to increase spending.

Congress implemented this basic process in 1975, and it worked reasonably well for the first few years. Congress was able to work on and structure the budget as a whole rather than in pieces. But the process broke down during the Reagan administration, when the president submitted annual budgets with huge deficits. The Democratic Congress adjusted Reagan's spending priorities away from the military and toward social programs, but it refused to propose a tax increase to reduce the deficit without the president's cooperation. At loggerheads with the president, Congress encountered increasing difficulty in enacting its budget resolutions according to its own timetable.

Lessons of the 1980s: Gramm-Rudman.

In 1985, Republican senators Phil Gramm of Texas and Warren Rudman of New Hampshire were joined by Democrat Ernest Hollings of South Carolina in a drastic proposal to force a balanced budget by gradually eliminating the deficit. Soon known simply as **Gramm-Rudman,** this act mandated that the budget deficit be lowered to a specified level each year until the budget was balanced by FY 1991. If Congress did not meet the deficit level in any year, the act would trigger across-the-board

budget committees One committee in each house of Congress that supervises a comprehensive budget review process.

Congressional Budget Office (CBO) The budgeting arm of Congress, which prepares alternative budgets to those prepared by the president's OMB.

Gramm-Rudman Popular name for an act passed by Congress in 1985 that, in its original form, sought to lower the national deficit to a specified level each year, culminating in a balanced budget in FY 1991. New reforms and deficit targets were agreed on in 1990.

budget cuts. In 1986, the first year under Gramm-Rudman, Congress failed to meet its deficit target. Unable to make the deficit meet the law again in 1987, Congress and the president simply changed the law to match the deficit. Gramm-Rudman showed that Congress lacked the will to force itself to balance the budget by an orderly plan of deficit reduction.

INTERACTIVE 18.1

 Balancing a State Budget

Reforms of the 1990s: Balanced Budgets. When the 1990 recession threatened another huge deficit for FY 1991, Congress and President George H. W. Bush agreed on a new package of reforms and deficit targets in the **Budget Enforcement Act (BEA)** of 1990. Instead of defining annual deficit targets, the BEA defined two types of spending: **mandatory spending** and **discretionary spending.** Spending is mandatory for programs that have become **entitlements** (such as Social Security and veterans' pensions), which provide benefits to individuals legally entitled to them (see Chapter 19) and cannot be reduced without changing the law. This is not true of discretionary spending, which consists of expenditures authorized by annual appropriations, such as for the military. For the first time, the law established **pay-as-you-go** restrictions on mandatory spending: any proposed expansion of an entitlement program must be offset by cuts to another program or by a tax increase. Similarly, any tax cut must be offset by a tax increase somewhere else or by spending cuts.[30] Also for the first time, the law imposed limits, or *caps,* on discretionary spending. To get the Democratic Congress to pass the BEA, President George H. W. Bush accepted some modest tax increases—despite having vowed at the 1988 Republican National Convention: "Read my lips: no new taxes." Consequently, he faced a rebellion from members of his own party in Congress, who bitterly opposed the tax increase. Indeed, the tax hike may have cost him reelection in 1992.

Bush paid a heavy price for the BEA, but the 1990 law did limit discretionary spending and slowed unfinanced entitlements and tax cuts. Clinton's 1993 budget deal, which barely squeaked by Congress, made even more progress in reducing the deficit. It retained the limits on discretionary spending and the pay-as-you-go rules from the 1990 act and combined spending cuts and higher revenues to cut the accumulated deficits from 1994 to 1998 by $500 billion. The 1993 law worked better than expected, and the deficit declined to $22 billion in 1997.[31]

The 1990 and 1993 budget agreements, both of which encountered strong opposition in Congress, helped pave the way for the historic **Balanced Budget Act (BBA)** that President Clinton and Congress negotiated in 1997. The BBA accomplished what most observers thought was beyond political possibility. It not only led to the balanced budget it promised but actually produced a budget surplus ahead of schedule—the first surplus since 1969.

After annual budget deficits were eliminated during the Clinton administration, the parties differed sharply in the 2000 presidential campaign over what to do with the budget surplus. Republicans advocated large across-the-board tax cuts to return money to taxpayers (and to maintain spending discipline in the federal government). Democrats targeted unmet social needs, such as Social Security reform, prescription drug coverage for the elderly, and universal health coverage for children.

Backsliding in the 2000s: Deficits Return. Most observers agree that the caps on discretionary spending and pay-as-you-go requirements for increases in mandatory spending and taxes, which were established by the 1990

Budget Enforcement Act (BEA) A 1990 law that distinguished between mandatory and discretionary spending.

mandatory spending In the Budget Enforcement Act of 1990, expenditures required by previous commitments.

discretionary spending In the Budget Enforcement Act of 1990, authorized expenditures from annual appropriations.

entitlements Benefits to which every eligible person has a legal right and that the government cannot deny.

pay-as-you-go In the Budget Enforcement Act of 1990, the requirement that any tax cut or expansion of an entitlement program must be offset by a tax increase or other savings.

Balanced Budget Act (BBA) A 1997 law that promised to balance the budget by 2002.

Budget Enforcement Act, helped balance the budget entering 2000.[32] However, many in Congress resented these restrictions on their freedom to make fiscal decisions, regarding the restrictions as unnecessary given the budget surpluses that occurred in 1998 through 2001 (see Figure 18.1). Accordingly, Congress allowed the caps on discretionary spending and the pay-as-you-go requirements to expire at the end of 2002.[33] Since 2002, the government has run budget deficits, not surpluses.

In his inaugural address, President George W. Bush pledged to "reduce taxes, to recover the momentum of our economy and reward the effort and enterprise of working Americans." His pledge fit with his philosophy of limited government and with his belief in the ability of wealthy capitalists to create jobs. Entering Bush's presidency, however, the economy slowed and projected surpluses dwindled. In his overall tax reform package (see page 572), Bush proposed giving tax rebates of $300 to individuals and $600 to families to stimulate the economy. Beginning in July 2001, approximately 131 million checks were mailed to taxpayers. Most observers agreed that Bush's immediate tax cuts stimulated the economy, at least in the short run. Even columnists at the *Wall Street Journal,* however, worried that "taxes will go up significantly" during the next decade as "a Republican president with a Republican Congress is proving unwilling or unable to restrain spending even as it continues to cut taxes."[34]

★ Tax Policies

So far, we have been concerned mainly with the spending side of the budget, for which appropriations must be enacted each year. The revenue side of the budget is governed by overall tax policy, which is designed to provide a continuous flow of income without annual legislation. A major text on government finance says that tax policy is sometimes changed to accomplish one or more of several objectives:

Interactive 18.2

Taxes

- To adjust overall revenue to meet budget outlays

- To make the tax burden more equitable for taxpayers

- To help control the economy by raising taxes (thus decreasing aggregate demand) or by lowering taxes (thus increasing demand)[35]

If those were the only objectives, the tax code might be simple. It is complex because tax policy is also used to advance social goals (such as home ownership through the deduction for mortgage interest) or to favor certain industries. To accommodate such deductions and incentives, the tax code (which is available over the Internet) runs over seven thousand pages.[36] Nearly 95 percent of the government revenue in FY 2007 was expected from three major sources: individual income taxes (45 percent), Social Security payments (37 percent), and corporate income taxes (11 percent).[37] Because the income tax accounts for most government revenue, discussion of tax policy usually focuses on that source.

Tax Reform

Tax reform proposals are usually so heavily influenced by interest groups looking for special benefits that they end up working against their original purpose.[38]

We Gave at the Bureaucracy
You are looking inside the Brookhaven Service Center in New York, one of the ten centers operated by the Internal Revenue Service to process tax forms and taxpayer requests. This is the aptly titled "extracting and sorting area." *(Lisa Qinones/Black Star)*

However, Reagan's proposals in the 1980s met with relatively few major changes, and in 1986 Congress passed one of the most sweeping tax reform laws in history. The new policy reclaimed a great deal of revenue by eliminating many deductions for corporations and wealthy citizens. That revenue was supposed to pay for a general reduction in tax rates for individual citizens. By eliminating many tax brackets, the new tax policy approached the idea of a flat tax—one that requires everyone to pay at the same rate.

A flat tax has the appeal of simplicity, but it violates the principle of **progressive taxation,** under which the rich pay proportionately higher taxes than the poor. The ability to pay has long been a standard of fair taxation, and surveys show that citizens favor this idea in the abstract.[39] In practice, however, they have different opinions, as we will see. Nevertheless, most democratic governments rely on progressive taxation to redistribute wealth and thus promote economic equality.

In general, the greater the number of tax brackets, the more progressive a tax can be, for higher brackets can be taxed at higher rates. Before Reagan's tax reforms of 1986, there were fourteen tax brackets, ranging from 11 percent to 50 percent. His reforms created only two rates: 15 and 28 percent. In 1990, George H. W. Bush violated his campaign pledge of "no new taxes" by creating a third tax rate, 31 percent, for those with the highest incomes. In 1993, Clinton created a fourth level, 40 percent, moving toward a more progressive tax structure, although still less progressive than before 1986. Both presidents acted to increase revenue to reduce a soaring deficit.

Campaigning for president, George W. Bush promised to cut taxes. Soon after his election, he got Congress to pass a complex $1.35 trillion tax cut. The 2001 law, amended in 2003, created six brackets: 10, 15, 25, 28, 33, and 35 percent. With more brackets, the new structure might seem more progressive, but the income levels triggering the rates changed. For example, in 2000 a "head of household" paid 39.6 percent of income over $288,350; in 2003, the

? Can you explain why . . .
a flat tax may not be a fair tax?

progressive taxation A system of taxation whereby the rich pay proportionately higher taxes than the poor; used by governments to redistribute wealth and thus promote equality.

Compared with What?

Tax Burdens in Thirty Countries

All nations tax their citizens, but some nations impose a heavier tax burden than do others. This graph compares tax burdens in 2002 in thirty countries as a percentage of gross domestic product (GDP), which is the market value of goods produced inside the country by workers, businesses, and government. The percentages encompass national, state, and local taxes and social security contributions. By this measure,

the U.S. government extracts less in taxes from its citizens than do the governments of almost every other democratic nation. At the top of the list stand Sweden and Denmark, well known as states that provide heavily for social welfare. Despite its low ranking in tax burden, the United States also supports the world's largest military force, to which it allocates about 3 percent of its GDP, or nearly 10 percent of its total tax receipts.

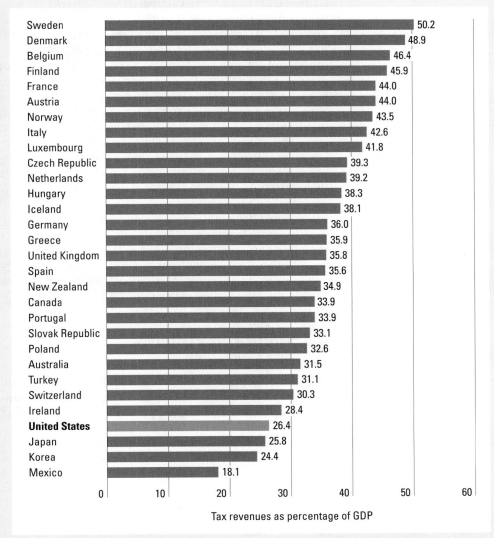

Country	Tax revenues as percentage of GDP
Sweden	50.2
Denmark	48.9
Belgium	46.4
Finland	45.9
France	44.0
Austria	44.0
Norway	43.5
Italy	42.6
Luxembourg	41.8
Czech Republic	39.3
Netherlands	39.2
Hungary	38.3
Iceland	38.1
Germany	36.0
Greece	35.9
United Kingdom	35.8
Spain	35.6
New Zealand	34.9
Canada	33.9
Portugal	33.9
Slovak Republic	33.1
Poland	32.6
Australia	31.5
Turkey	31.1
Switzerland	30.3
Ireland	28.4
United States	26.4
Japan	25.8
Korea	24.4
Mexico	18.1

Tax revenues as percentage of GDP

Source: OECD in Figures: Statistics on the Member Countries, 2005 Edition (Paris: Organization for Economic Cooperation and Development, 2005). Available at <http://www.oecd.org/document/34/0,2340,en_2649_201185_2345918_1_1_1_1,00.html>.

same taxpayer paid only 35 percent of income over the higher inflation-adjusted figure of $326,450.[40] Intended to stimulate the economy, the tax cuts also reduced the revenue needed to match government spending. Expectations of reduced revenues account only in part for the projected budget deficits shown in Figure 18.1.[41] Two other major factors were the downturn in the economy following the 2001 collapse in the stock market and unanticipated expenses for homeland defense and military action following the September 11 attack on America.

Comparing Tax Burdens

No one likes to pay taxes, so politicians find it popular to criticize the agency that collects taxes: the Internal Revenue Service. The income tax itself—and taxes in general—are also popular targets for U.S. politicians who campaign on getting government off the backs of the people. Is the tax burden on U.S. citizens truly too heavy? Compared with what? One way to compare tax burdens is to examine taxes over time in the same country; another is to compare taxes in different countries at the same time. By comparing taxes over time in the United States, we find that the total tax burden on U.S. citizens has not grown since the 1970s. Middle-income families paid about 20 percent of their income in federal income taxes and about 10 percent in state and local taxes into the 2000s.[42] The largest increases have come in social security taxes, which have risen steadily to pay for the government's single largest social welfare program: aid to the elderly (see Figure 18.2 and Chapter 19).

Another way to compare tax burdens is to examine tax rates in different countries. By nearly two to one, more respondents in a post-2000 national survey thought that Americans pay a higher percentage of their income in taxes than citizens in Western Europe.[43] They were flat wrong. Despite Americans' complaints about high taxes, the U.S. tax burden is not large compared with that of other democratic nations. As shown in "Compared with What? Tax Burdens in Thirty Countries," Americans' taxes are quite low in general compared with those in twenty-nine other democratic nations. Primarily because they provide their citizens with more generous social benefits (such as health care and unemployment compensation), almost every democratic nation taxes more heavily than the United States does.[44]

★ Spending Policies

The national government now spends over $2 trillion every year. Where does the money go? Figure 18.2 breaks down the $2.8 trillion in proposed outlays in President Bush's FY 2007 budget, by eighteen major governmental functions. The largest amount (22 percent of the total budget) was earmarked for Social Security.

Until FY 1993, national defense accounted for most spending under these categories, but military spending dropped into second place after the collapse of communism. Medicare and health, the third and fifth largest categories, together account for over 25 percent of all budgetary outlays, which underscores the importance of controlling the costs of health care. The fourth largest, income security, encompasses various programs that provide a social safety net, including unemployment compensation, food for low-income parents and children, help for the blind and disabled, and assistance for the homeless. The

FIGURE 18.2 Federal Spending in 2007, by Function

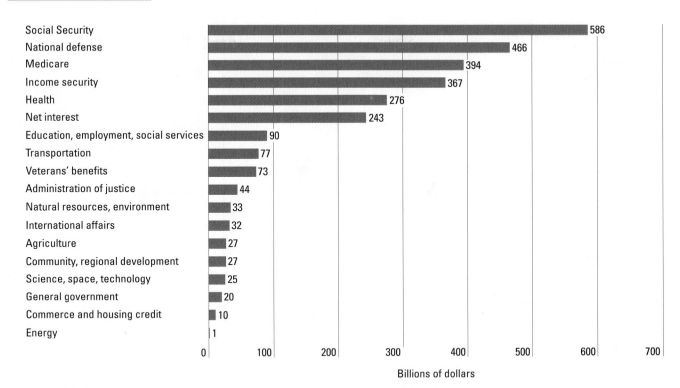

Federal budget authorities and outlays are organized into about twenty categories, some of which are mainly for bookkeeping purposes. This graph shows expected outlays for each of eighteen substantive functions for the year 2007 in President Bush's FY 2007 budget. The final budget differed somewhat from this distribution because Congress amended some of the president's spending proposals. The graph makes clear the huge differences among spending categories. Nearly 40 percent of government outlays are for Social Security and income security—that is, payments to individuals. Health costs (including Medicare) account for 25 percent more, more than national defense, and net interest consumes about 9 percent. This leaves relatively little for transportation, agriculture, justice, science, and energy—matters often regarded as important centers of government activity—which fall under the heading of "discretionary spending."

Source: Executive Office of the President, *Budget of the United States Government, Analytical Perspectives, Fiscal Year 2007* (Washington, D.C.: U.S. Government Printing Office, 2006), Table 25-8.

sixth largest category is interest on the accumulated national debt, which alone consumes about 9 percent of all national government spending.

To understand current expenditures, consider national expenditures over time, as in Figure 18.3. The effect of World War II is clear: spending for national defense rose sharply after 1940, peaked at about 90 percent of the budget in 1945, and fell to about 30 percent in peacetime. The percentage for defense rose again in the early 1950s, reflecting rearmament during the Cold War with the Soviet Union. Thereafter, defense's share of the budget decreased steadily

FIGURE 18.3 National Government Outlays over Time

This chart plots the percentage of the annual budget devoted to four major expense categories over time. It shows that significant changes have occurred in national spending since 1940. During World War II, defense spending consumed more than 80 percent of the national budget. Defense again accounted for most national expenditures during the Cold War of the 1950s. Since then, the military's share of expenditures has declined, while payments to individuals (mostly in the form of Social Security benefits) have increased dramatically. Also, as the graph shows, the proportion of the budget paid in interest on the national debt has increased substantially since the 1970s.

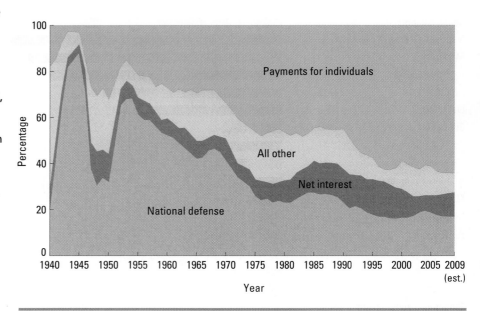

Source: Executive Office of the President, *Budget of the United States Government, Fiscal Year 2007: Historical Tables* (Washington, D.C.: U.S. Government Printing Office, 2006).

(except for the bump during the Vietnam War in the late 1960s). This trend was reversed by the Carter administration in the 1970s and then shot upward during the Reagan presidency. Defense spending decreased under George H. W. Bush and continued to decline under Clinton. Following the September 11 attack, President George W. Bush increased military spending 22 percent in FY 2003 over 2001.

Government payments to individuals (e.g., Social Security checks) consistently consumed less of the budget than national defense until 1971. Since then, payments to individuals have accounted for the largest portion of the national budget, and they have been increasing. Net interest payments also increased substantially during the years of budget deficits. Pressure from payments for national defense, individuals, and interest on the national debt has squeezed all other government outlays.

One might expect government expenditures to increase steadily, if only because of price inflation. In fact, national spending has barely outstripped inflation over fifty years. Figure 18.4 graphs government receipts and outlays as a percentage of gross domestic product (GDP), which eliminates the effect of inflation. It shows that national spending was about 20 percent of GDP in the early 1950s and only slightly more than that in 2007.

There are two major explanations for the general trend of increasing government spending. One is bureaucratic, the other political.

incremental budgeting
A method of budget making that involves adding new funds (an increment) onto the amount previously budgeted (in last year's budget).

Incremental Budgeting . . .

The bureaucratic explanation for spending increases involves **incremental budgeting:** bureaucrats, in compiling their funding requests for the following year,

FIGURE 18.4 Government Outlays and Receipts as a Percentage of GDP

In this graph, outlays and receipts are each expressed as a percentage of GDP. The area between the two lines represents years of surpluses or (more often) deficits. Because the graph portrays outlays and receipts in the context of economic growth (as some economists favor), it makes the deficit look less alarming.

Source: Executive Office of the President, *Budget of the United States Government, Fiscal Year 2007: Historical Tables* (Washington, D.C.: U.S. Government Printing Office, 2007), Table 1.3.

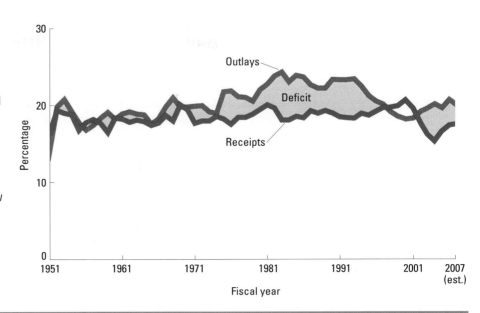

traditionally ask for the amount they got in the current year plus some incremental increase to fund new projects. Because Congress has already approved the agency's budget for the current year, it pays little attention to the agency's current size (the largest part of its budget) and focuses instead on the extra money (the increment) requested for the next year. As a result, few agencies are ever cut back, and spending continually goes up.

Incremental budgeting generates bureaucratic momentum that continually raises spending. Once an agency is created, it attracts a clientele that defends its existence and supports its requests for extra funds year after year. Because budgeting is a two-step process, agencies that get cut back in the authorizing committees sometimes manage (assisted by their interest group clientele) to get funds restored in the appropriations committees—and if not in the House, then perhaps in the Senate. Often appropriations committees approve spending for a specific purpose, known as an **earmark.** One watchdog organization identified 9,963 earmarks for pet projects worth $29 billion in 2006—for example, $150,000 for a Bulgarian-Macedonian cultural center in Pittsburgh.[45] The practice of earmarking funds for "congressional pork" greatly increased since the early 1990s.[46] In 2007, the new Democratic Congress vowed to end earmarks but only partially succeeded. Incremental budgeting and the congressional budget-making process itself are ideally suited to pluralist politics.

. . . and Uncontrollable Spending

Certain government programs are effectively immune to budget reductions because they have been enacted into law and are enshrined in politics. For example, Social Security legislation guarantees certain benefits to program participants when they retire. Medicare and veterans' benefits also entitle citizens to

earmarks Federal funds appropriated by Congress for use on local projects.

certain payments. Because these payments have to be made under existing law, they represent **uncontrollable outlays.** In Bush's FY 2007 budget, almost two-thirds of all budget outlays were uncontrollable or relatively uncontrollable—mainly payments to individuals under Social Security, Medicare, and public assistance; interest on the public debt; and farm price supports. About half of the rest went for defense, leaving less than 20 percent for domestic discretionary spending.

To be sure, Congress could change the laws to abolish entitlement payments, and it does modify them through the budgeting process. But politics argues against large-scale reductions. What spending cuts would be acceptable to or even popular with the public? At the most general level, voters favor cutting government spending, but they tend to favor maintaining "government programs that help needy people and deal with important national problems."[47] Substantial majorities favor spending the same or even more on Social Security, Medicare, education, job training, programs for poor children, and the military. In fact, when a national poll asked whether respondents favored "increasing, decreasing, or keeping about the same level" of government spending for sixteen different purposes—highways, AIDS research, welfare, public schools, big city schools, crime, child care, homeland security, terrorism, unemployment insurance, protecting the environment, poor people, working poor, Social Security, border security, and foreign aid—respondents favored increasing or keeping about the same level of spending for *every* purpose![48] Support was strongest (45 percent) for cutting foreign aid, which makes up only about 1 percent of the budget and thus would not offer much savings.

In truth, a perplexed Congress, trying to reduce the budget deficit, faces a public that favors funding most programs at even higher levels than those favored by most lawmakers.[49] Moreover, spending for the most expensive of these programs—Social Security and Medicare—is uncontrollable. Americans have grown accustomed to certain government benefits, but they do not like the idea of raising taxes to pay for them.

★ Taxing, Spending, and Economic Equality

As we noted in Chapter 1, the most controversial purpose of government is to promote equality, especially economic equality. Economic equality comes about only at the expense of economic freedom, for it requires government action to redistribute wealth from the rich to the poor. One means of redistribution is government tax policy, especially the progressive income tax. The other instrument for reducing inequalities is government spending through welfare programs. The goal in both cases is not to produce equality of outcome; it is to reduce inequalities by helping the poor.

The national government introduced an income tax in 1862 to help finance the Civil War. That tax was repealed in 1871, and the country relied on revenue from tariffs on imported goods to finance the national government. The tariffs acted as a national sales tax imposed on all citizens, and many manufacturers—themselves taxed at the same rate as a laborer—grew rich from undercutting foreign competition.[50] A new political movement, the Populists (see Chapter 7), decried the inequities of wealth and called for a more equitable form of taxation, an income tax. An income tax law passed in 1894 was declared unconstitutional by the Supreme Court the next year. The Democratic Party and the

uncontrollable outlay
A payment that government must make by law.

Populists accused the Court of defending wealth against equal taxation and called for amending the Constitution to permit an income tax in their 1896 platforms. A bill to do so was introduced in 1909 and ratified in 1913 as the Sixteenth Amendment.

The Sixteenth Amendment gave the government the power to levy a tax on individual incomes, and it has done so every year since 1914.[51] From 1964 to 1981, people who reported taxable incomes of $100,000 or more paid a top marginal tax rate of 70 percent (except during the Vietnam War, when the rate peaked a little higher), whereas those with lower incomes paid taxes at progressively lower rates. (Figure 18.5 shows how the top rate has fluctuated over the years.) At about the same time, the government launched the War on Poverty as part of President Johnson's Great Society initiative. His programs and their successors are discussed at length in Chapter 19. For now, let us look at the overall effect of government spending and tax policies on economic equality in America.

Government Effects on Economic Equality

We begin by asking whether government spending policies have any measurable effect on income inequality. Economists refer to a government payment to individuals through Social Security, unemployment insurance, food stamps, and other programs, such as agricultural subsidies, as a **transfer payment.** Transfer payments need not always go to the poor. In fact, one problem with the farm program is that the wealthiest farmers have often received the largest subsidies.[52] Nevertheless, most researchers have determined that transfer payments have had a definite effect on reducing income inequality.

A study of the poverty-reducing effects of taxes and transfer payments from 1979 to 2002 found that government policies cut the poverty rate almost in half for the years studied. For example, 20 percent of the population was below or at the poverty rate in 2002 based on income before taxes and transfer payments, but only 10.6 percent was at or below that rate after the government policies were figured into their situation.[53]

According to the principle of progressive taxation, tax rates are supposed to take more revenue from the rich than from the poor. Did that happen more at some times than others? A study of tax rates in 1979 (before the Reagan tax cuts), in 1989 (after the cuts), and in 2001 (after Clinton raised the rates) concluded, "The progressivity of federal tax rates varied substantially over the period."[54] In 1979, the 20 percent of households in the top income level paid 27.5 percent of their income in taxes, compared with 8.0 percent for the lowest income quintile—that is, the wealthy paid 3.4 times more than the poor. But with the lower top tax rate in 1989, the wealthy paid only 3.0 times more. After Clinton raised the top rate, the wealthiest 20 percent paid 4.4 times more in 2001 than the poorest 20 percent.[55]

Although the effective rates have varied during the recent past, the wealthy were always taxed at higher rates than the poor, in line with the principle of progressive taxation. The Bush administration, however, thought the wealthy were taxed too heavily. The chairman of Bush's Council of Economic Advisers complained, "The income tax is paid almost entirely by the well-to-do."[56] In fact, the richest 1 percent of taxpayers do pay about 37 percent of all federal income taxes.[57] Perhaps they are paying so much because they are *making* so much. If the richest 1 percent of all taxpayers take in 18 percent of all income

transfer payment A payment by government to an individual, mainly through Social Security or unemployment insurance.

FIGURE 18.5 The Ups and Downs of National Tax Rates

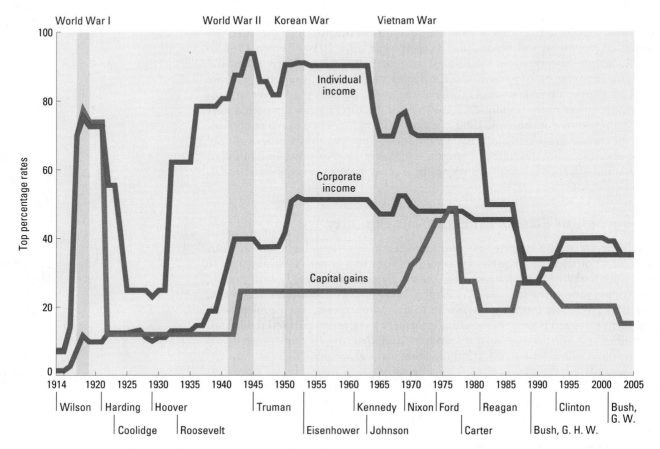

In 1913, the Sixteenth Amendment empowered the national government to collect taxes on income. Since then, the government has levied taxes on individual and corporate income and on capital gains realized by individuals and corporations from the sale of assets, such as stocks or real estate. Typically, incomes above certain levels are taxed at higher rates than incomes below those levels. This chart, which lists only the maximum tax rates, shows that these top tax rates have fluctuated wildly over time, from less than 10 percent to more than 90 percent. (They tend to be highest during periods of war.) During the Reagan administration, the maximum individual income tax rate fell to the lowest level since the Coolidge and Hoover administrations in the late 1920s and 1930s. The top rate increased slightly for 1991, to 31 percent, as a result of a law enacted in 1990, and jumped to 39.6 percent for 1994 under Clinton's 1993 budget package. The top rate was reduced in stages to 35 percent by Bush's tax plans in 2001 and 2003.

Source: Wall Street Journal, 18 August 1986, p. 10. Reprinted by permission of the Wall Street Journal, Dow Jones & Company, Inc., 1986. All rights reserved. Additional data from the Tax Policy Center, which reports tax brackets for individual years at <www.taxpolicycenter.org>, and from Brown, Kaplan & Liss, LLP.

in the nation (which they do), some think that they should pay twice that percentage in taxes (which they do).[58]

However, the national income tax is only part of the story. In some cases, poorer citizens pay a larger share of their income in taxes than wealthier citizens. How can people in the lowest income group pay a higher percentage of their income in taxes than do those in the very highest group? The answer has to do with the combination of national, state, and local tax policies. Only the national income tax is progressive, with rates rising as income rises. The national payroll tax, which funds Social Security and Medicare, is highly regressive: its effective rate decreases as income increases beyond a certain point. Everyone pays Social Security at the same rate: 12.4 percent in 2006—but employers typically pay half, so the effective rate for taxpayers is usually 6.2 percent. However, this tax is levied on only the first $94,200 of a person's income (in 2006), and there is no Social Security tax at all on wages over that amount. So the effective rate of the Social Security tax is higher for lower-income groups than for the very top group. In fact, 98 percent of employees in the lowest 20 percent (who usually work for hourly wages) paid more payroll tax than income tax, compared with only 3 percent of employees in the upper 20 percent (who usually work for salaries).[59]

Most state and local sales taxes are equally regressive. Poor and rich usually pay the same flat rate on their purchases. But the poor spend almost everything they earn on purchases, which are taxed, whereas the rich are able to save. A study showed that the effective sales tax rate for the lowest-income group was thus about 7 percent, whereas that for the top 1 percent was only 1 percent.[60]

In general, the nation's tax policies at all levels have historically favored not only those with higher incomes, but also the wealthy—those who draw income from capital (wealth) rather than labor—for example:

- There is no national tax at all on investments in certain securities, including municipal bonds (issued by local governments for construction projects).

- The tax on earned income (salaries and wages) is withheld from paychecks by employers under national law; the tax on unearned income (interest and dividends) is not.

- The tax on income from the sale of real estate or stocks (called *capital gains*) has typically been lower than the highest tax on income from salaries. (Bush's 2003 tax cuts further reduced these rates to 15 percent, so income from selling property or from receiving stock dividends is taxed at 15 percent, while income from salaries is subject to a cap of 35 percent.)

Effects of Taxing and Spending Policies over Time

In 1966, at the beginning of President Johnson's Great Society programs, the poorest fifth of American families received 4 percent of the nation's income after taxes, whereas the richest fifth received 46 percent. In 2004, after many billions of dollars had been spent on social programs, the income gap between the rich and poor had actually *grown*, as illustrated in Figure 18.6. This is true despite the fact that many households in the lowest category had about one-third more earners, mainly women, going to work, and that the average American

Can you explain why . . . lower-income people pay a higher percentage of their income taxes than higher-income people do?

FIGURE 18.6 Distribution of Family Income over Time

Over the past four decades, the 20 percent of U.S. families with the highest incomes received over 45 percent of all income, and their share has increased over time. This distribution of income is one of the most unequal among Western nations. At the bottom end of the scale, the poorest 20 percent of families received less than 5 percent of total family income, and their share has decreased over time.

Sources: For the 1966 data, see Joseph A. Pechman, *Who Paid the Taxes, 1966–1985?* (Washington, D.C.: Brookings Institution, 1985), p. 74; the 2004 data come from the U.S. Census Bureau at <http://www.census.gov/hhes/www/income/effect2004/effect2004.html>.

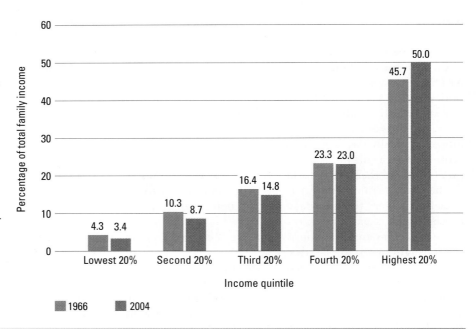

worked ninety-three more hours (two full work weeks) per year in 2000 than in 1989.[61]

In a capitalist system, some degree of inequality is inevitable. Is there some mechanism that limits how much economic equality can be achieved and prevents government policies from further equalizing income, no matter what is tried? To find out, we can look to other democracies to see how much equality they have been able to sustain. A study of household inequality in eighteen developed countries found that the United States had the most unequal distribution of income. The median income of U.S. households in the top ninetieth percentile had 5.64 times the median income of the bottom tenth percentile. Italy was next most unequal, with the top group of Italians having 4.68 times the income of the bottom. The average ratio for all nations was 3.83.[62] Other studies also show that our society has more economic inequality than other advanced nations.[63] The question is, why?

Democracy and Equality

Although the United States is a democracy that prizes political equality for its citizens, its record in promoting economic equality is not as good. In fact, its distribution of wealth—which includes not only income but also ownership of savings, housing, automobiles, stocks, and so on—is strikingly unequal. According to the Federal Reserve, the wealthiest 1 percent of American families control about 33 percent of the nation's household wealth (property, stock holdings, bank accounts).[64] Moreover, the distribution of wealth among ethnic groups is alarming. The typical white family has an annual income almost 1.5 times that of both blacks and Hispanics.[65] If democracy means government "by the people," why aren't the people sharing more equally in the nation's wealth? If one of the supposed purposes of government is to promote equality, why are government policies not working that way?

One scholar theorizes that interest group activity in a pluralist democracy distorts government's efforts to promote equality. His analysis of pluralism sees "corporations and organized groups with an upper-income slant as exerting political power over and above the formal one-man-one-vote standard of democracy."[66] Even Clinton's budget for FY 1998, which was ostensibly designed to cut taxes for the middle class, produced large tax savings for the top income group and numerous tax breaks for interest groups.[67] As you learned in Chapters 10 and 17, the pluralist model of democracy rewards those groups that are well organized and well funded.

What would happen if national tax policy were determined according to principles of majoritarian rather than pluralist democracy? Perhaps not much, if public opinion is any guide. The people of the United States are not eager to redistribute wealth by increasing the only major progressive tax, the income tax. If national taxes must be raised, Americans favor a national sales tax over increased income taxes.[68] But a sales tax is a flat tax, paid by rich and poor at the same rate, and it would have a regressive effect on income distribution, promoting inequality. The public also prefers a weekly $10 million national lottery to an increase in the income tax.[69] Because the poor are willing to chance more of their income on winning a fortune through lotteries than are rich people, lotteries (run by about forty states) also contribute to wealth inequality.[70]

Majoritarians might argue that most Americans fail to understand the inequities of the national tax system, which hides regressiveness in sales taxes and

Under the Overpass
Tax cuts are not likely to help this homeless family living under I-95 near Miami, Florida.
(Christopher Brown/Stock Boston)

Social Security taxes. According to a national survey, Americans in the highest income categories (earning over $150,000 a year) understand the tax system much better than those at the lower income levels.[71] In Alabama, for example, income above $4,600 for a family of four went untaxed—meaning that most poor and all rich paid the same income tax, and the state relied mainly on sales and property taxes. In 2003, the conservative Republican governor of Alabama proposed a more progressive system of higher tax rates, mainly on the wealthy, only to have voters reject his reforms 2 to 1.[72] A black preacher and advocate of tax reform said that his parishioners like the regressive sales tax because they pay it in small increments.[73]

So majoritarians cannot argue that the public demands "fairer" tax rates that take from richer citizens to help poorer ones. If the public did, the lowest-income families might receive a greater share of the national income than they do. Instead, economic policy is determined mainly through a complex process of pluralist politics that returns nearly half the national income to only 20 percent of the nation's families.

Summary

There are conflicting theories about how market economies work best. Laissez-faire economics holds that the government should keep its hands off the economy. Keynesian theory holds that government should take an active role in dealing with inflation and unemployment, using fiscal and monetary policies to produce desired levels of aggregate demand. Monetarists believe fiscal policies are unreliable; they opt instead to use the money supply to affect aggregate demand. Supply-side economists, who had an enormous influence on economic policy during the Reagan administration, focus on controlling the supply of goods and services rather than the demand for them. The remarkable growth of the U.S. economy in the mid- to late 1990s led economists of all schools to question some of their key principles. And the continuing process of globalization has eroded any government's ability to manage its own economy completely.

Congress alone prepared the budget until 1921, when it thrust the responsibility onto the president. After World War II, Congress tried unsuccessfully to regain control of the process. Later, Congress managed to restructure the process under the House and Senate budget committees. The new process worked well until it confronted the huge budget deficits of the 1980s. Because so much of the budget involves military spending and uncontrollable payments to individuals, balancing the budget by reducing what remains—mainly spending for nonentitlement domestic programs—was regarded as impossible. Unwilling to accept responsibility for passing a tax increase, Congress passed the Gramm-Rudman deficit-reduction law in 1985. Under that law, deficits were to be reduced in stages, through automatic across-the-board cuts if necessary, until the budget was balanced by FY 1991. The deficit problem proved so intractable, however, that Congress had to amend the law in 1987 to extend the deadline to 1993—and the budget still wasn't balanced. When the Republicans gained control of Congress in 1995, they abandoned the informal policy of incremental budgeting and drastically cut spending on discretionary programs. New restrictions on spending came later during the Clinton administration.

President George H. W. Bush promised "no new taxes" when campaigning for office in 1988, but he needed revenue to cut huge deficits and had to accept a 1990 law that raised the income tax. It also modified the budgeting procedure to help meet deficit targets, but Bush suffered in his reelection campaign for breaking his pledge. The 1990 act also amended Reagan's 1986 tax reform bill, which had drastically reduced the number of tax brackets to two. The 1990 law added a third bracket, at 31 percent, still much lower than the top rate before Reagan's reforms. In 1993, President Clinton won approval for a fourth bracket, at 40 percent. Responding to increased revenue and a hold on spending, the deficit declined. Aided by a growth economy, Clinton engineered taxing and spending changes in 1997 that produced a budget surplus in FY 1998—the first since 1969. The budget surplus disappeared in FY 2002, after President George W. Bush cut taxes and increased spending to combat terrorism.

Despite public complaints about high taxes, current U.S. tax rates are lower than those in most other major countries and lower than they have been since the Great Depression of the 1930s. But even with the heavily progressive tax rates of the past, the national tax system has done little to redistribute income. Government transfer payments to individuals have helped reduce some income inequalities, but the distribution of income is less equal in the United States than in most major Western nations.

Pluralist democracy as practiced in the United States has allowed well-organized, well-financed interest groups to manipulate taxing and spending policies to their benefit. The result is that a larger and poorer segment of society is paying the price. Taxing and spending policies in the United States are tipped in the direction of freedom rather than equality.

Internet activities and reading suggestions for this chapter are available on the *Online Study Center*

To complete the multimedia assignments for this chapter, go to AmericansGoverning.org.

19

Domestic Policy

(Jonathan Nourok/PhotoEdit)

Online Study Center
This icon will direct you to resources
and activities on the website
college.hmco.com/pic/jandaupdate9e

The drug crisis in the United States has long conjured up images of cocaine addiction, marijuana busts, and "just say no" campaigns. More recently, however, the nation has become attuned to a different dimension of the drug issue altogether. Ask politicians about today's drug crisis, and they are as likely to talk with you about people like Harlene Kopp, Robert and Sara Bergeon, and Jane Roberts as they are to discuss a pusher in the back alley.

Harlene Kopp is a retired widow in her seventies who lives in Evanston, Illinois. Without a drug plan as part of her health insurance coverage, she was forced to fill her twenty monthly prescriptions out of her own limited financial resources and personal creativity. One drug alone, Prilosec, which she uses for a stomach ailment, sets her back over $1,000 per year. Without a state aid program and free samples from her doctor, she would be unable to get by. Even so, "It's not easy living these days," she says.[1]

Just up the lakeshore from Harlene, in south Milwaukee, Wisconsin, live Robert and Sarah Bergeon. A retired couple (he is seventy-two and she is seventy-one), the Bergeons spend approximately $6,500 per year on prescription drugs to control Sarah's heart disease and diabetes and to keep Robert's gout and high blood pressure in check. That amount may not seem like much until one considers that the Bergeons' annual family income is only $21,000. To help finance their monthly prescription drug costs, Robert works part time at a local grocery store and sometimes skips taking some of his own medications. They consider themselves solid citizens. According to Robert, "We both worked hard all of our lives and never asked for help from anyone." But now, he says, "It's stressful

and it's scary. I don't want to see anybody else go through this."[2]

Jane Roberts of Pasadena, Texas, is eighty-three years old and lives on a $500 per month Social Security check. She spends $150 of that amount on drugs for her diabetes, glaucoma, and high blood pressure. She relies on her children to pay for several of her monthly bills; were it not for them, she says, "I guess I'd be in the soup line."[3]

As the 1990s ended and the new century began, elected officials and candidates on the campaign trail began to pay greater attention to the growing cost of prescription drugs. The development of new medicines has been both a blessing and a curse for the nation's elderly. These drugs do help to extend and improve the quality of life for many aging Americans. However, that improved health has come at an increasing cost, which sometimes forces seniors to choose between filling a prescription and paying their other bills.

These growing concerns led politicians of both major political parties to call for adding a prescription drug benefit to the nation's Medicare program. After hearing promises for at least two election cycles that such a plan would be forthcoming, it appeared that seniors were finally granted their wish with the passage in 2003 of the Medicare Prescription Drug, Improvement, and Modernization Act. Or were they?

Supporters of the legislation hailed it as an important success.[4] The Senate majority leader, Republican Bill Frist, himself a doctor, drew on his own experience and noted: "As a physician, I've written hundreds of prescriptions that I knew would go unfilled because patients simply would not be able to afford them. With this bill, that would change." Senator Kent Conrad, a Democrat from North Dakota, was less enthusiastic but supportive nonetheless: "There are a lot of terrible things in this bill, [but] the only thing worse would have been not passing it. It is a beginning."

Critics expressed outrage, but for varied reasons.[5] Senator Edward Kennedy (D-Mass.) claimed that the bill "cynically uses the elderly's need for prescription drugs as a Trojan horse to reshape Medicare." The law, Kennedy believed, would "unravel" the nation's primary health-care program for the elderly. In contrast, fiscal conservatives, such as Senator Judd Gregg (R-N.H.), scoffed at the bill's $400 billion price tag, which soon proved well below the expected cost. The new estimate places the price tag at $788 billion over the next ten years.[6] Other critics envisioned an explosion of possible choices, which would confound and confuse the elderly. "This is the largest tax increase that one generation has put on another generation in the history of this country," Gregg argued. The main purpose of the bill, he said, was "to get us through the next election."

Whether Harlene Kopp, the Bergeons, or Jane Roberts will see their drug burdens eased by this addition to Medicare, known as Plan D, remains to be seen. It went into effect in January 2006. (We take up this topic again later in the chapter.) ★

IN OUR OWN WORDS

Listen to Jerry Goldman discuss the main points and themes of this chapter.

Online Study Center
Improve Your Grade

public policy A general plan of action adopted by the government to solve a social problem, counter a threat, or pursue an objective.

General plans of action adopted by government to solve a social problem, counter a threat, or pursue an objective, that is, a **public policy,** often appear promising or frightening in theory, but what matters most is how they behave in practice. Medicare Plan D is a textbook example that is both promising and frightening but with little information so far on the workings of the program. In Chapter 17 we examined the policymaking process in general; in this chapter we look at specific domestic social policies, that is, government plans of action targeting concerns internal to the United States. These are among the most enduring and costly programs that the government has launched on behalf of its citizens. Four key questions guide our inquiry: What are the origins and politics of specific domestic policies? What are the effects of these policies once they are implemented? Why do some policies succeed and others fail? Finally, are disagreements about policy really disagreements about values?

Public policies sometimes seem as numerous as fast-food restaurants, offering something for every appetite and budget. Despite this wide range of policies worth exploring, we focus our efforts in this chapter on a few key areas: Social Security, public assistance, health care, and education. These policies deserve special consideration for four reasons. First, government expenditures in these areas represent more than half the national budget and roughly one-tenth of our gross domestic product (GDP), the total market value of all goods and services produced in this country during a year. All citizens ought to know how their resources are allocated and why. Second, one goal of social welfare policies is to alleviate some consequences of economic inequality. Nevertheless, poverty remains a fixture of American life, and we must try to understand why. Third, these policies pose some vexing questions involving the conflicts between freedom and order and between freedom and equality. Fourth, despite increasing concerns about terrorism, social welfare issues (along with the economy) have remained at the forefront of the nation's agenda. In the 2000 presidential election, education, the economy, health care, and Social Security (in that order) were the most influential issues in helping voters choose among the candidates.[7] Although concerns about national security have increased since the September 11, 2001, attacks on the United States, domestic issues such as health and education continued to animate lists of the public's top concerns in anticipation of the 2006 midterm congressional elections.[8]

This chapter concentrates on policies based on the authority of the national government to tax and spend for the general welfare. But it is important to recognize that state and local governments play a vital role in shaping and directing the policies that emanate from Washington. It is not an understatement to say that the success of several national domestic initiatives depends in large part on the capacities of governments at lower levels to effectively carry them out.

IDEAlog.org
Should the government try to improve the standard of living for poor Americans? Take IDEAlog's self-test.

★ The Development of the American Welfare State

The most controversial purpose of government is to promote social and economic equality. To do so may conflict with the freedom of some citizens because it requires government action to redistribute income from rich to poor. This choice between freedom and equality constitutes the modern dilemma of government; it has been at the center of many conflicts in U.S. public policy since World War II. On one hand, most Americans believe that government should help the needy. On the other hand, they do not want to sacrifice their own standard of living to provide government handouts to those whom they may perceive as shiftless and lazy.

At one time, governments confined their activities to the minimal protection of people and property—to ensuring security and order. Now, almost every modern nation may be characterized as a **welfare state,** serving as the provider and protector of individual well-being through economic and social programs. **Social welfare programs** are government programs designed to provide the minimum living conditions necessary for all citizens. Income for the elderly, health care, public assistance, and education are among the concerns addressed by government social welfare programs.

Social welfare policy is based on the premise that society has an obligation to provide for the basic needs of its members. The term *welfare state* describes this protective role of government. Moreover, the public wants government to shoulder some of this responsibility. In two recent national surveys, a vast majority of Americans agreed that money and wealth should be more evenly distributed and that the federal government is spending too little money to combat poverty.[9]

America today is far from being a welfare state on the order of Germany or Great Britain; those nations provide many more medical, educational, and unemployment benefits to their citizens than does the United States. However, the United States does have several social welfare functions. To understand American social welfare policies, you must first understand the significance of a major event in U.S. history—the Great Depression—and the two presidential plans that extended the scope of the government, the New Deal and the Great Society. The initiatives that flowed from those presidential programs dominated national policy until changes in the 1980s and 1990s produced retrenchment and significant reforms in important aspects of the American welfare state.

welfare state A nation in which the government assumes responsibility for the welfare of its citizens by providing a wide array of public services and redistributing income to reduce social inequality.

social welfare programs Government programs that provide the minimum living standards necessary for all citizens.

A Human Tragedy
The Great Depression idled millions of able-bodied Americans. By 1933, when President Herbert Hoover left office, about one-fourth of the labor force was out of work. Private charities were swamped with the burden of feeding the destitute. The hopeless men pictured here await a handout from a wealthy San Francisco matron known as the "White Angel" who provided resources for a bread line. *(Culver Pictures)*

INTERACTIVE 19.1

AP *The Great Crash: October 29, 1929*

Great Depression The longest and deepest setback the American economy has ever experienced. It began with the stock market crash on October 24, 1929, and did not end until the start of World War II.

The Great Depression

Throughout its history, the U.S. economy has experienced alternating good times and hard times, generally referred to as business cycles (see Chapter 18). The **Great Depression** was by far the longest and deepest setback that the American economy has ever experienced. It began with the stock market crash on October 24, 1929, a day known as Black Thursday, and did not end until the start of World War II. By 1932, one out of every four U.S. workers was unemployed, and millions more were underemployed. (To put that number into perspective, during the period 2001–2003, which included an economic recession and significant fiscal crises in the American states, U.S. unemployment never exceeded 6.5 percent.) No other event, with the exception of World War II, perhaps, has had a greater effect on the thinking and the institutions of government in the twentieth and twenty-first centuries than the Great Depression.

In the 1930s, the forces that had stemmed earlier business declines were no longer operating. There were no more frontiers, no growth in export markets, no new technologies to boost employment. Unchecked, unemployment spread like an epidemic, and the crisis fueled itself. Workers who lost their source of income could no longer buy the food, goods, and services that kept the economy going. Thus, private industry and commercial farmers tended to produce more than they could sell profitably. Closed factories, surplus crops, and idle workers were the consequences.

The industrialized nations of Europe were also hit hard. The value of U.S. exports fell, and the value of imports increased; this led Congress to impose high tariffs, which strangled trade and fueled the Depression. From 1929 to 1932, more than 44 percent of the nation's banks failed when unpaid loans exceeded the value of bank assets. Farm prices fell by more than half in the same period. Marginal farmers lost their land, and tenant farmers succumbed to mechanization. The uprooted—tens of thousands of dispossessed farm families—headed West with their possessions atop their cars and trucks in a hopeless quest for opportunity. Author John Steinbeck described the plight of these desperate poor in his Pulitzer Prize–winning novel *The Grapes of Wrath* (1939).

The New Deal

In his speech accepting the presidential nomination at the 1932 Democratic National Convention, Franklin Delano Roosevelt, then governor of New York, made a promise: "I pledge you, I pledge myself to a new deal for the American people." Roosevelt did not specify the contents of his **New Deal,** but the term was later applied to measures Roosevelt's administration undertook to stem the Depression. Some scholars regard these measures as the most imaginative burst of domestic policy in the nation's history. Others see them as the source of massive government growth without matching benefits.

President Roosevelt's New Deal had two phases. The first, which ended in 1935, was aimed at boosting prices and lowering unemployment through programs like the Civilian Conservation Corps (CCC), which provided short-term jobs for young men. The second phase, which ended in 1938, was aimed at aiding the forgotten people: the poor, the aged, unorganized working men and women, and farmers. The hallmark of this second phase is the Social Security program.

Poverty and unemployment persisted despite the best efforts of Roosevelt and his massive Democratic majorities in Congress. By 1939, 17 percent of the work force (more than 9 million people) were still unemployed. Only World War II was able to provide the economic surge needed to yield lower unemployment and higher prices, the elusive goals of the New Deal.

Roosevelt's overwhelming popularity did not translate into irresistibly popular policy or genuine popularity for government. Public opinion polls revealed that Americans were divided over New Deal policies through the early 1940s. Eventually, the New Deal became the status quo, and Americans grew satisfied with it. But Americans remained wary of additional growth in the power of the national government.[10]

Economists still debate whether the actual economic benefits of the New Deal reforms outweighed their costs. It is clear, however, that New Deal policies initiated a long-range trend toward government expansion. And another torrent of domestic policymaking burst forth three decades later.

The Great Society

John F. Kennedy's election in 1960 brought to Washington a corps of public servants sensitive to the needs of the poor and minorities. This raised expectations that national government policies would benefit these groups. But Kennedy's razor-thin margin of victory was far from a mandate to improve the plight of the poor and dispossessed.

In the aftermath of Kennedy's assassination in November 1963, his successor, Lyndon Baines Johnson, received enormous support for a bold policy

New Deal The measures advocated by the Roosevelt administration to alleviate the Depression.

program designed to foster equality. After winning the 1964 presidential election in a landslide over his opponent, Barry Goldwater, LBJ entered 1965 committed to pushing an aggressive and activist domestic agenda. In his 1965 State of the Union address, President Johnson offered his own version of the New Deal: the **Great Society,** a broad array of programs designed to redress political, social, and economic inequality. In contrast to the New Deal, few, if any, of Johnson's programs were aimed at short-term relief; most were targeted at chronic ills requiring a long-term commitment by the national government.

A vital element of the Great Society was the **War on Poverty.** The major weapon in this war was the Economic Opportunity Act (1964); its proponents promised that it would eradicate poverty in ten years. The act encouraged a variety of local community programs to educate and train people for employment. Among them were college work-study programs, summer employment for high school and college students, loans to small businesses, a domestic version of the Peace Corps (called VISTA, for Volunteers in Service to America), educational enrichment and nutrition for preschoolers through Head Start, and legal services for the poor. It offered opportunity: a hand up rather than a handout.

The act also established the Office of Economic Opportunity (OEO), which was the administrative center of the War on Poverty. Its basic strategy was to involve the poor themselves in administering antipoverty programs, in the hope that they would know which programs would best serve their needs. The national government channeled money directly to local community action programs. This approach avoided the vested interests of state and local government bureaucrats and political machines. But it also led to new local controversies by shifting the control of government funds from local politicians to other groups. (In one notorious example, the Blackstone Rangers, a Chicago street gang, received funds for a job-training program.)

The War on Poverty eventually faded as funding was diverted to the Vietnam War. Although it achieved little in the way of income redistribution, it did lead to one significant change: it made the poor aware of their political power. Some candidates representing the poor ran for political office, and officeholders paid increased attention to this segment of the population. These citizens also found that they could use the legal system to their benefit. For example, with assistance from the OEO, low-income litigants were successful in striking down state laws requiring a minimum period of residency before people could receive public assistance.[11]

Retrenchment and Reform

Despite the declining national poverty rate that ensued after the passage of major domestic legislation of the 1960s, in subsequent years critics seized on the perceived shortcomings of the growing American welfare state. Perhaps these counterarguments were the predictable result of the high standards that LBJ and his team had set, such as their promise to eliminate poverty in a decade. The fact that poverty still persisted (even though it had declined) and had become more concentrated in areas that the Great Society had targeted (inner cities and rural areas) suggested to some observers that the Johnson effort was a failure. In the War on Poverty, these critics claimed, poverty had won.

Those arguments began to take hold in the latter part of the 1970s and in part helped Ronald Reagan capture the White House in 1980. Reagan's overwhelming victory and his landslide reelection in 1984 forced a reexamination

Great Society President Lyndon Johnson's broad array of programs designed to redress political, social, and economic inequality.

War on Poverty A part of President Lyndon Johnson's Great Society program, intended to eradicate poverty within ten years.

of social welfare policy. In office, the president professed support for the "truly needy" and for preserving a "reliable safety net of social programs," by which he meant the core programs begun in the New Deal. Nevertheless, his administration abolished several social welfare programs and redirected others.

In a dramatic departure from his predecessors (Republicans as well as Democrats), Reagan shifted emphasis from economic equality to economic freedom. He questioned whether government alone should continue to be responsible for guaranteeing the economic and social well-being of less fortunate citizens. And he maintained that to the extent that government should bear this responsibility, state and local governments could do so more efficiently than the national government.

The Congress, controlled by Democrats, blocked some of Reagan's proposed cutbacks, and many Great Society programs remained in force, although with less funding. Overall spending on social welfare programs (as a proportion of the gross national product) fell to about mid-1970s levels. But the dramatic growth in the promotion of social welfare that began with the New Deal ended with the Reagan administration. It remained in repose during George H. W. Bush's term in the White House.

After Bush's term in office, the rest of the 1990s produced important reforms to the American welfare state. Recognizing persistent concerns that federal welfare policy made recipients dependent on government rather than helping them to live independent lives, President Bill Clinton entered office in 1993 hoping to reform the system while simultaneously protecting the basic fabric that was the nation's safety net. Charting that middle course suited Clinton's political tendencies. It also became absolutely necessary after 1994 when Republicans took control of Congress. By the end of Clinton's two terms, important reforms emerged in public assistance, which we describe later in the chapter. And the George W. Bush administration has led the greatest expansion of welfare benefits for seniors with the passage of the Medicare drug program.

★ Social Security

Insurance is a device for protecting against loss. Since the late nineteenth century, there has been a growing tendency for governments to offer **social insurance,** which is government-backed protection against loss by individuals, regardless of need. The most common forms of social insurance offer health protection and guard against losses from worker sickness, injury, and disability; old age; and unemployment. The first example of social insurance in the United States was workers' compensation. Beginning early in the twentieth century, most states created systems of insurance that compensated workers who lost income because they were injured in the workplace.

Social insurance benefits are distributed to recipients without regard to their economic status. Old-age benefits, for example, are paid to workers—rich or poor—provided that they have enough covered work experience and have reached the required age. Thus, social insurance programs are examples of entitlements. Today, national entitlement programs consume about half of every dollar of government spending; the largest entitlement program is **Social Security.**

As a general concept, Social Security is social insurance that provides economic assistance to people faced with unemployment, disability, or old age. In most social insurance programs, employees and employers contribute to a fund

social insurance A government-backed guarantee against loss by individuals without regard to need.

Social Security Social insurance that provides economic assistance to persons faced with unemployment, disability, or old age. It is financed by taxes on employers and employees.

from which employees later receive payments. If you examine your end-of-year W2 wage and tax statement from your employer, you should be able to find your contributions to two specific programs for social insurance in the United States: Social Security and Medicare. The Social Security tax, which was assessed at a rate of 6.20 percent for the first $94,200 of wages earned in 2006, supports disability, survivors', and retirement benefits. The Medicare tax finances much (but not all) of the Medicare program and was assessed at 1.45 percent of all wages in 2006.[12]

Origins of Social Security

Compared with its international peers, the idea of Social Security came late to the United States. As early as 1883, Germany enacted legislation to protect workers against the hazards of industrial life. Most European nations adopted old-age insurance after World War I; many provided income support for the disabled and income protection for families after the death of the principal wage earner. In the United States, however, the needs of the elderly and the unemployed were left largely to private organizations and individuals. Although twenty-eight states had old-age assistance programs by 1934, neither private charities nor state and local governments—nor both together—could cope with the prolonged unemployment and distress that resulted from the Great Depression. It became clear that a national policy was necessary to deal with a national crisis.

The first important step came on August 14, 1935, when President Franklin Roosevelt signed the **Social Security Act,** which remains the cornerstone of the modern American welfare state. The act's framers developed three approaches to the problem of dependence. The first provided social insurance in the form of old-age and surviving-spouse benefits and cooperative state-national unemployment assistance. To ensure that the elderly did not retire into poverty, it created a program to provide income to retired workers. Its purpose was to guarantee that the elderly would have a reliable base income after they stopped working. (Most Americans equate Social Security with this part of the Social Security Act.) An unemployment insurance program, financed by employers, was also created to provide payments for a limited time to workers who were laid off or dismissed for reasons beyond their control.

The second approach provided aid to the destitute in the form of grants-in-aid to the states. The act represented the first permanent national commitment to provide financial assistance to the needy aged, needy families with dependent children, the blind, and (since the 1950s) the permanently and totally disabled. By the 1990s, the disabled category had grown to include those who are learning disabled and those who are drug and alcohol dependent.

The third approach provided health and welfare services through federal aid to the states. Included were health and family services for disabled children and orphans and vocational rehabilitation for the disabled.

How Social Security Works

Social Security Act The law that provided for Social Security and is the basis of modern American social welfare.

Although the Social Security Act encompasses many components, when most people think of "Social Security" they have the retirement security element of the law in mind. Specifically, revenues for old-age retirement security go into their own *trust fund* (each program contained in the Social Security Act has a separate fund). The fund is administered by the Social Security Administration, which became an independent government agency in 1995. Trust fund revenue can be spent only for the old-age benefits program. Benefits, in the form of monthly payments, begin when an employee reaches retirement age, which today is sixty-five. (People can retire as early as age sixty-two but with reduced benefits.) The age at which full benefits are paid is now sixty-seven for persons born in 1938 or later.

Many Americans believe that each person's Social Security contributions are set aside specifically for his or her retirement, like a savings account.[13] But Social Security doesn't operate quite like that. Instead, the Social Security taxes collected today pay the benefits of today's retirees with surpluses held over, in theory at least, to help finance the retirement of future generations. Thus, Social Security (and social insurance in general) is not a form of savings; it is a pay-as-you-go tax system. Today's workers support today's elderly and other program beneficiaries.

When the Social Security program began, it had many contributors and few beneficiaries. The program could thus provide relatively large benefits with low taxes. In 1937, for example, the tax rate was 1 percent, and the Social Security taxes of nine workers supported each beneficiary. As the program matured and more people retired or became disabled, the ratio of workers to recipients decreased. In 2006, the Social Security system paid benefits of $546 billion to 50 million people and collected tax revenue from 162 million, a ratio of roughly 3.2 workers for every beneficiary. By 2030, the ratio will decline to just over two workers for every beneficiary.[14]

The solvency of the Social Security program will soon be tested. As the baby-boom generation retires beginning in about 2010, politicians will face an inevitable dilemma: lower benefits and generate the ire of retirees or raise taxes and generate the ire of taxpayers. To put off this day of reckoning, policymakers built up the trust funds' assets in anticipation of the growth in the number of retirees. But based on projections of the most recent report of the trustees of the Social Security system, the program's assets will be exhausted by 2041 under intermediate economic and demographic assumptions (see Figure 19.1), or by 2030 if a more high-cost scenario pans out.[15]

At one time, federal workers, members of Congress, judges, and even the president were omitted from the Social Security system. Today there are few exceptions. Because the system is a tax program, not a savings program, universal participation is essential. If participation were not compulsory, revenue would be insufficient to provide benefits to current retirees. Government—the only institution with the authority to coerce—requires all employees and their employers to contribute, thereby imposing restrictions on freedom.

People who currently pay into the system will receive retirement benefits financed by future participants. As with a pyramid scheme or a chain letter, success depends on the growth of the base. If the birthrate remains steady or grows, future wage earners will be able to support today's contributors when they retire. If the economy expands, there will be more jobs, more income, and a growing wage base to tax for increased benefits to retirees. But suppose the birthrate falls, or mortality declines, or unemployment rises and the economy falters? Then contributions could decline to the point at which benefits exceed revenues. The pyramidal character of Social Security is its Achilles' heel.

? Can you explain why . . . many younger Americans fear they will never get any Social Security benefits, even though they have been paying into the system?

Day of Reckoning

Social Security tax revenues now exceed benefits paid out. But after 2017, benefits paid out will begin to exceed revenues flowing into the program from taxes. With bankruptcy of the system looming so predictably, the debate over change boils down to two questions that politicians politely decline to answer: How soon will the national government change the current system, and how much will it change it?

Source: Annual Report of the Board of Trustees of the Federal Old-Age and Survivors Insurance and Disability Insurance Trust Funds, 2006, available at <http://www.ssa.gov/OACT/TR/TR06/>.

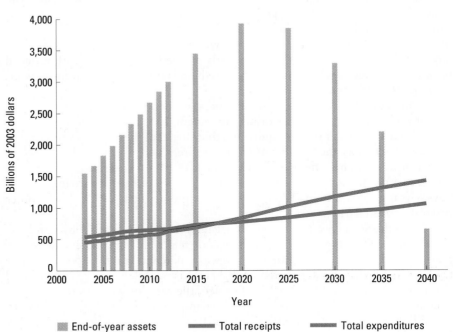

Who Pays? Who Benefits?

"Who pays?" and "Who benefits?" are always important questions in government policymaking, and they continue to shape Social Security policy. In 1968, the Republican Party platform called for automatic increases in Social Security payments as the cost of living rose. The theory was simple: as the cost of living rises, so should retirement benefits; otherwise, benefits are paid in "shrinking dollars" that buy less and less. Cost-of-living adjustments (COLAs) became a political football in 1969 as Democrats and Republicans tried to outdo each other by suggesting larger increases for retirees. The result was a significant expansion in benefits, far in excess of the cost of living. The beneficiaries were the retired, who were beginning to flex their political muscle. Politicians knew that alienating this constituency could lose them an election.[16]

In 1972, Congress adopted automatic adjustments in benefits and in the dollar amount of contributors' wages subject to tax, so that revenue would expand as benefits grew. This approach set Social Security on automatic pilot. When most economists criticized the COLA as overly generous, Congress tempered it. The 2006 COLA is 4.1 percent.

When stagflation (high unemployment coupled with high inflation) took hold in the 1970s, it jeopardized the entire Social Security system. Stagflation produced an economic vise: unemployment meant a reduction in revenue; high inflation meant automatically growing benefits. This one-two punch drained Social Security Trust Fund reserves to critically low levels in the late 1970s and early 1980s. Meanwhile, other troubling factors were becoming clear. A lower birthrate meant that in the future fewer workers would be available to support the pool of retirees. And the number of retirees would grow as average life

Welfare German Style
Rolf John was a sixty-four-year-old retired banker who suffered from depression and lived in Florida supported by $2,400 a month in government payments. There was nothing unusual about this but for the fact that John was a German citizen. "Florida Rolf," who lived in a gated community steps from the beach, became a symbol of a dysfunctional German welfare system. News coverage forced the government to curtail payments to Germans living abroad. John returned to Germany but sued for reinstatement of his checks. He vowed to return to Florida in an effort to overcome his depression. (© BILD-Zeitung/Andreas Thelen)

spans lengthened and the baby-boom generation retired. Higher taxes, an unpopular political move, loomed as one alternative. Another was to pay for Social Security out of general revenues—that is, income taxes. Social Security would then become a public assistance program, similar to welfare, which some people believed would deal a political blow to the program. In 1983, shortly before existing Social Security benefit funds would have become exhausted, Congress and President Reagan agreed to a solution that called for two painful adjustments: increased taxes and reduced benefits.

Social Security Reform

The changes enacted in 1983 prolonged the life of the Social Security system. However, future economic conditions will determine its success or failure. Concern over the future survival of Social Security is reflected in public opinion polls. For example, in a nationwide poll conducted in January 2006, 51 percent of adults said that they did not believe Social Security would have the money available to provide the benefits they expect in retirement.[17]

In the 2000 and 2004 presidential election campaigns, both major parties sought to capitalize on Social Security reform as an issue. The Republicans argued that if the system is not changed, the country will be faced with "three bitter choices": raising taxes, reducing benefits, or adding to the national debt. As an alternative, Republicans proposed a plan that would allow individual workers to invest their own payroll taxes in the stock market in hopes of earning a higher rate of return than currently paid to the Social Security Trust Funds. However, people who wanted to stay in the current Social Security system could choose to do so.[18]

The Democrats also proposed a private investment program, but theirs would be in addition to the existing program rather than a part or a reform of it. Called Retirement Savings Plus, the Democrats' program would have "let Americans save and invest on top of the foundation of Social Security's guaranteed benefit. Under this plan, the federal government would match individual contributions with tax credits, with the hardest pressed working families getting the most assistance."[19]

The positions of both parties illustrate how each side, in attempting to extend the life of the Social Security program, emphasized different values. The Republicans relied more on choice and freedom as values in their proposed reforms. The Democrats' reference to fairness and to greater help for the neediest Americans clearly indicates a commitment to greater equality as a value.

Meaningful reforms to the Social Security program did not materialize in the four years after the 2000 national election season. The vanishing of federal budget surpluses and financial scandals that rocked investor confidence in the nation's stock market put plans for major reforms, which were both expensive and relied on private investments, on hold. Despite no concrete progress on policy reforms, a federally appointed bipartisan commission did offer some guidance regarding the program's future.

Named by President Bush on May 2, 2001, the President's Commission to Strengthen Social Security issued its report in December of that same year. The commission offered three approaches for helping the program to achieve fiscal sustainability. Each plan embraced the concept of personal retirement accounts, which the commission believed would provide individuals with greater freedom and improved retirement security.[20] Following his 2004 reelection bid, President Bush used his hard-earned political capital to implement personal retirement accounts as a necessary fix for Social Security. Despite all the hoopla, speeches, and town hall meetings, the effort proved a failure.

IDEAlog.org

Should the government invest Social Security taxes in the stock market? Take IDEAlog's self-test.

★ Public Assistance

Most people mean **public assistance** when they use the terms *welfare* or *welfare payments;* it is government aid to individuals who demonstrate a need for that aid. Although much public assistance is directed toward those who lack the ability or the resources to provide for themselves or their families, the poor are not the only recipients of welfare. Corporations, farmers, and college students are among the many recipients of government aid in the form of tax breaks, subsidized loans, and other benefits.

Public assistance programs instituted under the Social Security Act, in contrast to the retirement security components of the law, are known today as *categorical assistance programs.* They include (1) old-age assistance for the needy elderly not covered by old-age pension benefits, (2) aid to the needy blind, (3) aid to needy families with dependent children, and (4) aid to the totally and permanently disabled. Adopted initially as stop-gap measures during the Great Depression, these programs have become **entitlements**—benefits to which every eligible person has a legal right and that the government cannot deny. They are administered by the states, but the bulk of the funding comes from the national government's general tax revenues. Because the states also contribute to the funding of their public assistance programs, the benefits and some of the standards that define eligibility can vary widely from state to state.

public assistance Government aid to individuals who can demonstrate a need for that aid.

entitlements Benefits to which every eligible person has a legal right and that the government cannot deny.

Poverty in the United States

Until 1996, the national government imposed national standards on state welfare programs. It distributed funds to each state based on the proportion of its population that was living in poverty. That proportion is determined on the basis of a federally defined **poverty level,** or poverty threshold, which is the minimum cash income that will provide for a family's basic needs. The poverty level varies by family size and is calculated as three times the cost of a minimally nutritious diet for a given number of people over a given time period. (The threshold is computed in this way because research suggests that poor families of three or more persons spend approximately one-third of their income on food.*) Policymakers have considered different approaches to determine how much a family of four needs to live in the United States. One formula would be the sum of five different monthly expenses: food, housing, health care, transportation, and personal expenses. Such an approach would likely increase the poverty level and thus put more families below its threshold.[21] Politicians have been reluctant to act on such a change.

The poverty level is fairly simple to apply, but it is only a rough measure for distinguishing the poor from the nonpoor. Using it is like using a wrench as a hammer: it works, but not very well. We attach importance to the poverty level figure, despite its inaccuracies, because measuring poverty is a means of measuring how the American promise of equality stands up against the performance of our public policies.

The poverty rate in the United States has declined since the mid-1960s. It rose slightly in the 1980s, then declined again after that. In 2005, the U.S. Census Bureau calculated that 37 million people, or roughly 12.6 percent of the population, were living in poverty in the United States.[22] Poverty was once a condition of old age. Social Security changed that. Today, poverty is still related to age, but in the opposite direction: it is largely a predicament of the young. In 2004, nearly 18 percent of persons under eighteen years of age were in poverty, compared with about 10 percent of people over sixty-five.[23]

Another trend in the United States, which we describe in "Politics in a Changing World: The Feminization of Poverty," is the concentration of poverty in households headed by single women. Researchers have labeled this trend toward greater poverty among women the **feminization of poverty,** as a growing percentage of all poor Americans are women or dependents of women.[24]

The poverty level is adjusted each year to reflect changes in consumer prices. One measure, the poverty *threshold*, determines the number of people who live below the threshold. (A second measure, the poverty *guideline*, determines the income level at which families qualify for government assistance.) In 2005, the poverty threshold for a family of four was a cash income below $19,971.[25] This is income *before* taxes. If the poverty threshold were defined as disposable income (income *after* taxes), the proportion of the population categorized as living in poverty would increase. Some critics believe that factors other than income should be considered in computing the poverty level. Assets (home, cars, possessions), for example, are excluded from the definition.

Can you explain why . . . the adoption of a more realistic formula to determine the poverty rate has proved unpopular with officeholders?

poverty level The minimum cash income that will provide for a family's basic needs; calculated as three times the cost of a market basket of food that provides a minimally nutritious diet.

feminization of poverty The term applied to the fact that a growing percentage of all poor Americans are women or the dependents of women.

---

*Although it has been the source of endless debate, today's definition of poverty retains remarkable similarity to its precursors. As early as 1795, a group of English magistrates "decided that a minimum income should be the cost of a gallon loaf of bread, multiplied by three, plus an allowance for each dependent." See Alvin L. Schorr, "Redefining Poverty Levels," *New York Times,* 9 May 1984, p. 27.

Politics in a Changing World

The Feminization of Poverty

When we examine the composition of poor families, especially over the past few decades, we observe a dramatic and disturbing trend: one in every two poor Americans resides in a family in which a woman is the sole householder, or head of the household. Thirty years ago, only one in every four poor people lived in such a family. What accounts for this dramatic upward shift in the proportion of female-headed poor families?

The twentieth century brought extraordinary changes for women. Women won the right to vote and to own property, and they gained a measure of legal and social equality (see Chapter 16). But increases in the rates of divorce, marital separation, and adolescent pregnancy have cast more women into the head-of-household role, a condition that tends to push women and children into poverty. Caring for children competes with women's ability to work. Affordable child care is out of reach for many single parents. In the absence of a national child-care policy, single women with young children face limited employment opportunities and lower wages in comparison to full-time workers. These factors and others contribute to the feminization of poverty—the fact that a growing percentage of all poor Americans are women or the dependents of women.

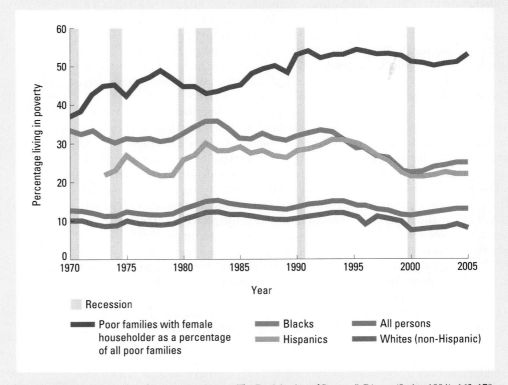

Sources: Barbara Ehrenreich and Frances Fox Piven, "The Feminization of Poverty," *Dissent* (Spring 1984): 162–170; Harrell R. Rodgers, Jr., *Poor Women, Poor Families: The Economic Plight of America's Female-Headed Households,* 2nd ed. (Armonk, N.Y.: M. E. Sharpe, 1990); U.S. Census Bureau, *Poverty in the United States: 2004,* Table 3, available at <http://www.census.gov/hhes/www/poverty/poverty05/table4.pdf>, accessed 24 June 2007.

Also, the computation fails to take into account noncash benefits such as food stamps, health benefits (Medicaid), and subsidized housing. Presumably, the inclusion of these noncash benefits as income would reduce the number of individuals seen as living below the poverty level.

The use of the poverty line as a social indicator reflects a fundamental ambiguity in the notion of equality. Consider, for example, that greater equality of incomes can be achieved in two completely different ways: those lowest in the income distribution could be raised up by increasing their income, or those at the top could be brought down by the government's taking a greater share of their income. Doing the latter alone would not help the worst off at all if the money taken from the wealthiest were not transferred to the poorest. Using a concept like the poverty threshold, which reflects a social commitment that no citizen should live below a certain standard, helps ensure that our progress toward equality does improve the absolute condition of the least well off among us.

Welfare Reform

It is relatively easy to draw a portrait of the poor. It is much more difficult to craft policies that move them out of destitution. Critics of social welfare spending, led by libertarian scholar Charles Murray, argue that antipoverty policies have made poverty more attractive by removing incentives to work. They believe that policies aimed at providing for the poor have actually promoted poverty.

Another explanation, proposed by liberal thinker William Julius Wilson, maintains that the failure of government policies to reduce poverty rests on changes in racial attitudes. In the 1960s, racial barriers kept the black middle class in the same urban neighborhoods as poor blacks. Their presence provided social stability, role models, and strong community institutions and businesses. Then the decline of racial barriers allowed middle-class blacks to move out of the inner cities. As a result, the inner cities became increasingly poor and increasingly dependent on welfare.[26]

The 1990s represented an important turning point in this ongoing debate. In the 1992 and 1996 elections, candidates for all offices turned up the rhetoric regarding the future of public assistance to the poor. In 1996, the Republican-led Congress sought a fundamental revision of the welfare system and managed to enlist the president in their cause. When President Clinton signed the **Temporary Assistance for Needy Families Act (TANF)** into law on August 22, 1996, he joined forces with the Republican-led Congress "to end welfare as we know it." The act abolished the sixty-one-year-old Aid to Families with Dependent Children (AFDC) program, which since the 1930s had provided a federal guarantee of cash assistance that had kept millions of citizens afloat during difficult times.

Critics of AFDC had complained that for some recipients, floating had become a way of life and that government aid discouraged individuals from swimming on their own. Although originally established with widowed mothers in mind, at a time when divorce and out-of-wedlock births were rare, AFDC grew rapidly beginning in the 1960s as divorce and single motherhood increased (see Figure 19.2). By the time AFDC was abolished, 4 million adults and almost 9 million children were on the welfare rolls, and 24 million Americans were receiving food stamps. The end of AFDC significantly changed the lives of more than one-fifth of American families.

Temporary Assistance for Needy Families Act (TANF)
A 1996 national act that abolished the longtime welfare policy, AFDC (Aid for Families with Dependent Children). TANF gives the states much more control over welfare policy.

Under the new plan, adult recipients of welfare payments have to become employed within two years. The law places the burden of job creation on the states. Families can receive no more than a total of five years of benefits in a lifetime, and the states can set a lower limit. Even before signing the bill, Clinton had granted waivers permitting states to offer extensions beyond the five-year limit, as long as recipients continue to look for work. Republicans countered that such waivers effectively undermined the law.[27]

Nonetheless, for the 328 House members and 74 senators who voted for the bill (Republicans heavily in favor, Democrats split), devolving power to the states proved a prime force in the reform effort. President Clinton's own desire to permit states to act as laboratories for welfare reform provided ample ammunition for advocates of change. When the bill was signed into law, some forty-five states had already begun experimenting with their welfare systems.[28] Clinton and others had heaped praise on such experiments as Wisconsin's "W-2" plan ("Wisconsin Works"), which Republican governor Tommy Thompson put into effect in 1997. Its pilot program had some success in dropping the state's welfare caseload, but long-run assessment remains years away. George W. Bush appointed Thompson his secretary of health and human services. Thompson left in 2005 to seek a Republican bid for the presidency.

How has the welfare reform bill of 1996 affected the states? As envisioned, there are now fifty new welfare systems under the plan of federal block, or lump-sum, grants to the states. Initially, at least, some state officials were concerned by the stringent work requirements imposed by the new law and confused by some of its provisions. The extent to which states would be able to count job training as work is an issue that state and federal officials have de-

---

| **FIGURE 19.2** | **Families on Welfare, 1955–2007** |

Beginning in the 1950s, the number of families on welfare skyrocketed as divorce and single motherhood increased. The welfare rolls stabilized during the late 1970s and 1980s but again lurched upward in the early 1990s. The sharp decline at the end of the 1990s represents the "end of welfare as we know it" by legislation and the demand for workers fueled by a strong domestic economy in the 1990s, reaching a new stability through 2007.

Source: U.S. Department of Health and Human Services, "Cash Assistance for Needy Families—AFDC and TANF," available at <http://www.acf.hhs.gov/programs/ofa/caseload/caseloadindex.htm>.

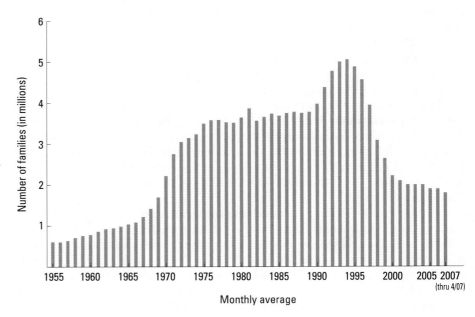

bated since 1996. As in any other complicated piece of domestic legislation, the process of writing regulations and offering guidance to help states implement the law has consumed significant time. Overall, though, despite their several specific complaints, state leaders generally have been pleased with the increased flexibility that TANF has provided when compared to policy on the books prior to 1996.

In terms of funding, federal support for the law was implemented through a block grant to the states totaling $16.5 billion per year. It ran until 2002. TANF's future then remained in limbo while Congress considered revisions to the law. The reauthorization legislation was finally enacted in 2006 and will extend TANF through 2010. Changes include new grants to support healthy marriages and responsible fatherhood, projects supported by the Bush administration.[29]

What about welfare recipients themselves? How have they fared under the law? Now that TANF has begun to build up a track record, during a time period that included a national economic recession (something that observers noted would provide a strong test of the law's ability to provide assistance to the needy), some general results have begun to emerge.

Most clearly, as Figure 19.2 illustrates, the number of families on welfare has declined and remained relatively low when compared to the pre-TANF period. And the good news is that large numbers of former welfare recipients have been able to find steady work. Actual totals vary by study, but generally it appears that roughly 60 percent are now employed at any given time.[30] Also, one of the biggest fears of TANF's critics, that employers would find former welfare recipients undesirable employees and that there would be few jobs available in major urban areas, appears not to have materialized.[31] Supporters of the law have cheered these results and celebrated specific success stories of people who have moved from welfare to work.

Other findings are less promising and raise issues that members of Congress have been considering as they debate how to reauthorize TANF. Despite former welfare recipients' increased levels of employment, most have not been able to find jobs that pay good wages and offer valuable benefits, such as health care. Studies have consistently found that these jobs pay between $6.00 and $8.50 per hour, and they often require workers to travel great distances (such as long commutes from urban centers to the suburbs), which creates added stress as parents need to secure child care during their long workday commutes. One source of confusion among TANF recipients and state officials alike has been the extent to which recipients still maintain eligibility for other federal programs, such as Medicaid, even as they move into full-time employment. Reaching out to individuals as they make the transition from welfare to work, to help make them aware of these opportunities, has been a challenge for policymakers and private or nonprofit contractors on the front lines who are implementing the law.[32]

The most recent national economic recession of 2001 provided an important test for TANF. While policymakers continued to point to relatively low TANF case loads in 2001 and 2002 as good news, others voiced concern. A track record of work experience may have helped some former welfare recipients to weather the recession's storm better (it is easier to find employment if one can document a successful history of work), which may have contributed to keeping the case loads relatively low.

But rising national unemployment combined with low TANF participation signaled for some observers a sort of perfect storm that threatened the poor.

Lacking employment and access to public assistance, many families may have found themselves in especially dire circumstances. Drawing on government data, the Children's Defense Fund sounded this alarm in its report "The Unprotected Recession," which documented increasing numbers of female-headed households and children with no access to employment or TANF income during 2001.[33]

★ Health Care

It is hard to imagine a modern welfare state that does not protect the health of its population. Yet the United States is the only major industrialized nation without a universal health-care system. Rather, the United States has what is perhaps best described as a patchwork system of care designed to cover different segments of the population—but not all citizens in the nation. In addition to private insurance, which many Americans receive as a benefit of employment, government programs to provide health care include Medicare, primarily for the elderly; Medicaid, for the qualifying poor; and the State Children's Health Insurance Program (SCHIP), for children in needy families. This chapter discusses only Medicare and Medicaid.

Cost and Access

Nearly everyone maintains that the U.S. health-care system needs fixing. To better understand the American patchwork system of health care and possibilities for future reforms, it is important to consider two issues that have animated the nation's health-care debate for several years: access to care and cost.

First, many Americans have no health insurance. In 2007, nearly 47 million people in America, roughly 16 percent of all Americans, had no health insurance. That total was higher than the 15.2 percent figure the Census Bureau had calculated for the previous year, but it was still below the most recent peak of 16.3 percent from 1998.[34]

Like all other statistics, the actual number of uninsured people depends a great deal on how one decides to measure the condition of being uninsured. Using data from 1998, the most recent year that comparable numbers were available, a recent study from the Congressional Budget Office offered a more nuanced look at the issue. If one defines being uninsured as lacking insurance for the entire year, then between 21 and 31 million people were uninsured in the United States in 1998. The numbers jumped to between 56 and 59 million if the definition of uninsured was broadened to include people who lacked insurance at any time during the year. Nearly 60 percent of the people were covered by health insurance for some or all of 2004. However, the proportion was about 0.5 percent lower than in 2003.[35]

Access to health care depends on more than simply having insurance coverage. Even with private or public health insurance of some kind, several million Americans who live in rural areas are unable to receive health care because they lack easy access to doctors or hospitals. During the past forty years, for example, the gap in the number of active physicians in rural areas (fewer than 10,000 people) versus larger urban centers (metropolitan areas of more than 1 million people) has grown. In 1950, the urban-to-rural physician ratio was 2.6 to 1, and by 1998 that difference had widened to 3.6 to 1.[36]

IDEAlog.org

Do you believe that health care is a government responsibility? Take IDEAlog's self-test.

The second major issue confronting the nation's health-care system is cost. Overall, the health-care sector is a significant portion of the U.S. economy. In 2005, public and private spending on health care reached an all-time high of $2 trillion, which was more than 16 percent of GDP.[37] Given the aging of the American population and the development of newer medical technologies, those numbers are projected to increase in the future. By 2014, for example, health care is expected to account for 18.7 percent of GDP.[38] Looking at the factors driving these increasing costs, the fastest-growing segment of the nation's health-care bill is in the area of prescription drugs.

Among advanced industrial nations, the United States spends the largest proportion of its economy on health care. In 2005, it spent more than other nations with comprehensive systems of coverage, including Switzerland (11.6 percent of GDP), Germany (10.9 percent), Canada (9.9 percent), and France (10.5 percent).[39] These numbers have raised concerns for some observers who note that the benefits to the entire nation of higher health-care spending may be elusive (see "Compared with What? Health Spending and Its Possible Effects").

The two central problems of health care, access and cost, give rise to two key goals and a familiar dilemma. First, any reform should democratize health care—that is, it should make health care available to more people, ideally everyone. But by providing broad access to medical care, we will increase the amount we spend on such care. Second, any reform must control the ballooning cost of health care. But controlling costs requires restricting the range of procedures and providers available to patients. Thus, the health-care issue goes to the heart of the modern dilemma of government: we must weigh greater equality in terms of universal coverage and cost controls against a loss of freedom in markets for health care and in choosing a doctor.

The dilemma of controlling costs without inhibiting the freedom to choose one's doctor applies not just to public health care. The same financial pressures affecting Medicare and Medicaid have also affected privately provided health coverage. Over the past quarter of a century, the health insurance industry has undergone tremendous change.

Most Americans used to carry what was called catastrophic care insurance, which provided hospital coverage for serious illnesses only. As the cost of medical care ballooned, numerous scholars and health-care providers realized that preventing illness through regular physical examinations and appropriate lifestyle changes was far cheaper than curing illnesses after onset. Thus, health insurance providers began to offer extended coverage of routine, preventive care in return for limiting an individual's freedom to choose when and what type of medical specialist to see.

These new types of insurance fell into two main categories: health maintenance organizations (HMOs) or preferred provider organizations (PPOs). In either case, insurance benefits now covered routine office visits for preventive care (sometimes with a modest copayment by the patient) in return for restricted access to more expensive, specialized care. The success of these new plans, and the transformation of the health-care industry, is reflected in the following facts: in 1993, 55 percent of insured Americans carried traditional, catastrophic coverage; 22 percent used HMOs; and 14 percent used PPOs. By 2000, 34 percent of those insured carried HMO coverage, 31 percent were enrolled in PPOs, and 25 percent carried traditional catastrophic coverage.[40]

Compared with What?

Health Spending and Its Possible Effects

In 2004, the United States spent more than 16 percent of its GDP (the total market value of all goods and services produced in this country during the year) on health care.[1] This amount was substantially more than any other large-population nation. Most of American health-care spending was in the private sector. Public health spending is far less, both as a proportion of the GDP and in comparison to other nations.

What does health spending achieve? Measures of health spending outcomes are too numerous for inclusion here. Let's focus on just one: longevity. With only one exception noted here (Mexico), life expec-

tancy in large-population nations reveals very little variation. Female babies born in Mexico in 2004 can expect to live on average to age seventy-seven. In contrast, also for 2004, babies born in Japan can expect to live to eighty-five, and those born in Australia are likely to reach age eighty-three. Despite the fact that Americans outspend other nations on health care, the payoff in life expectancy has not yet been realized.

---

1. Cynthia Smith, Cathy Cowan, Stephen Heffler, and Aaron Catlin, "National Health Spending in 2004: Recent Slowdown Led by Prescription Drug Spending," *Health Affairs* 25/1 (January–February 2006): 186–196.

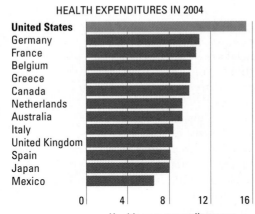

HEALTH EXPENDITURES IN 2004

Health care expenditures as percentage of gross domestic product

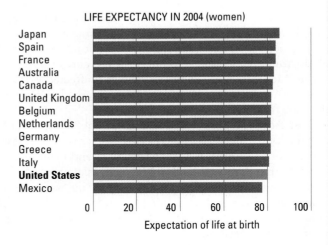

LIFE EXPECTANCY IN 2004 (women)

Expectation of life at birth

Sources: Left figure: Organization for Economic Cooperation and Development, "Health at a Glance: OECD Indicators 2003," Chart 1, accessed 24 June 2006 at <http://www.oecd.org/document/124/0,3343,en_2649_34587_2671576 _1_1_1_1,00.html>. Right figure: U.S. Census Bureau, *Statistical Abstract of the United States, 2005* (Washington, D.C.: U.S. Government Printing Office, 2006), Table 1318, accessed 12 February 2006 at <http://www.census.gov/prod/ 2005pubs/06statab/intlstat.pdf>.

Speech/label text in cartoon: "KEEP YOUR EYE ON THE BEST CARD FOR YOU!...", "PICK THE WRONG CARD, AND YOU LOSE...", "BOY, THIS IS WAY MORE CONFUSING THAN THAT @!!☆☆ BUTTERFLY BALLOT...", "NEW! MEDICARE CARD INFORMATION BOOTH and 70-CARD MONTE GAME"

Dazed and Confused Seniors
Medicare Plan D provides a cornucopia of prescription drug plans for seniors. Rather than have the government operate a single plan, the Bush administration's idea was to create a market for insurance companies to compete with each other for the premiums paid by seniors. Now with upwards of thirty to forty plans available in some communities, the choices and options have proved overwhelming to many of the elderly. *(Jeff Parker © 2004 Florida Today/Caglecartoons.com)*

Medicare

In 1962, the Senate considered extending Social Security benefits to provide hospitalization and medical care for the elderly. Democratic senator Russell Long of Louisiana opposed the extension and declared, "We are not staring at a sweet old lady in bed with her kimono and nightcap. We are looking into the eyes of the wolf that ate Red Riding Hood's grandma."[41] Long was concerned that costs would soar without limit. Other opponents echoed the fears of the American Medical Association (AMA), which saw virtually any form of government-provided medical care as a step toward government control of medicine. Long and his compatriots won the battle that day. Three years later, however, on the heels of Lyndon Johnson's sweeping victory in the 1964 presidential election, the Social Security Act was amended to provide **Medicare,** a health insurance program for all people aged sixty-five and older.

As early as 1945, public opinion had clearly supported some form of national health insurance, and President Harry Truman proposed such a program during his administration. However, that idea became entangled in Cold War politics—the growing crusade against communism in America.[42] The AMA, representing the nation's physicians, mounted and financed an all-out campaign to link national health insurance (so-called socialized medicine) with socialism; the campaign was so successful that the prospect of a national health-care policy vanished.

Both proponents and opponents of national health insurance tried to link their positions to deeply rooted American values: advocates emphasized equality and fairness; opponents stressed individual freedom. In the absence of a clear mandate on the kind of insurance (publicly funded or private) the public

Medicare A health insurance program serving primarily persons sixty-five and older.

wanted, the AMA was able to exert its political influence to prevent any national insurance at all.[43]

By 1960, however, the terms of the debate had changed. It no longer focused on the clash between freedom and equality. Now the issue of health insurance was cast in terms of providing assistance to the aged, and a groundswell of support forced it onto the national agenda.[44]

The Democratic victory in 1964 and the advent of President Johnson's Great Society made some form of national health-care policy almost inevitable. On July 30, 1965, with Harry Truman at his side in the former president's hometown of Independence, Missouri, Johnson signed a bill that provided a number of health benefits to the elderly and the poor. Fearful of the AMA's power to punish its opponents, rather than pushing for a comprehensive program such as the one Truman had advocated while in office, the Democrats in 1965 confined their efforts to a compulsory hospitalization insurance plan for the elderly (known today as Part A of Medicare). In addition, the bill contained a version of an alternative Republican plan that called for voluntary government-subsidized insurance to cover physicians' fees (known today as Part B of Medicare).

Medicare was designed as a health insurance program for the elderly, and today 85 percent of the program's beneficiaries are aged sixty-five and older. A small portion of two other groups can also qualify for the program even though they might not have reached retirement age: those who are disabled, who make up 14 percent of the beneficiary pool, and a small number (less than 1 percent) of citizens who suffer from end-stage renal disease, a kidney disorder. In 2005, 43 million people were enrolled in the program at a total cost of roughly $330 billion.[45]

Medicare is compulsory insurance that covers certain hospital services for people aged sixty-five and older. Workers pay a tax; and for certain parts of the program other than Part A, retirees pay premiums deducted from their Social Security payments. Payments for necessary services are made by the national government directly to participating hospitals and other qualifying facilities. Citizens who enjoy Medicare coverage may also possess or purchase private insurance for additional services that the program may not cover or may cover only in less generous ways. Seniors who receive health insurance as part of their employment retirement packages, for example, are not required to give up those benefits because of Medicare; they can enjoy coverage from both Medicare and their private plans.

The program still contains its original components, Part A and Part B, but over the years Medicare has also expanded to cover more kinds of services and to provide program participants with additional health-care options. Today, Part A essentially pays for care in facilities, such as inpatient hospital visits, care in skilled nursing facilities, hospice, and some home health care. Part B pays for doctors' services and outpatient hospital care. Services under Part A come at no cost to beneficiaries, but Part B services require participants to pay a premium of 25 percent; the remaining cost of Part B is picked up by the federal government.

Taken together, Part A and Part B are referred to as the Original Medicare Plan. Because that plan may not cover all services that program participants may desire, and because some may not have access to additional health insurance options as a part of their private retirement packages, the Medicare program has expanded to attempt to meet additional health-care needs. The

Looking to the Future

Are the Social Security and Medicare Programs Sustainable?

Taken together, Social Security and Medicare account for over one-third of federal spending. Currently, Social Security tax revenues exceed benefits paid out to retirees. But some time after 2015, benefits paid out will begin to exceed revenues flowing into the program from taxes. (See Figure 19.1.) And policymakers are still assessing the long-term impact that the recently enacted Medicare prescription drug plan will have on that program; one estimate from the federal Centers for Medicare and Medicaid Services puts the total cost at $534 billion over roughly the next decade alone.

Nearly everyone seems to agree that Social Security and Medicare face significant challenges to their futures. But reforming these programs, which citizens and politicians alike see as bedrocks of the nation's social safety net, will not be easy. Consider three potential options: (1) cut Social Security and Medicare benefits to existing and future recipients; (2) increase payroll taxes to fund benefits at current levels; or (3) give future beneficiaries more control over the money they contribute to the Social Secu-

rity Trust Fund, which could include investing their Social Security dollars in the stock market.

The first two options face high political hurdles. The third would require a major infusion of new funding to make the transition from the current program to a new investor-based approach that would not compromise current benefit levels. Elected officials face a dual challenge then: how to craft a reform strategy that is both technically sound and politically palatable to the nation's citizens? At this point it is anyone's guess.

What factors have placed Social Security and Medicare in such a precarious position for the long run? Why do the politics associated with these two programs make any reform difficult?

Sources: Annual Report of the Board of Trustees of the Federal Old-Age and Survivors Insurance and Disability Insurance Trust Funds, 2005, accessed at <http://www.ssa.gov/OACT/TR/> on 12 February 2006; statement of Rick Foster, Chief Actuary, Centers for Medicare and Medicaid Services, testimony before the House Committee on Ways and Means, 24 March 2004, accessed at <http://waysandmeans.house.gov/hearings.asp?formmode=view&id=1303> on 3 May 2004.

program now offers a series of supplemental plans known as Medigap plans that are run by private insurance companies and that seniors pay for through a premium, which varies by type of plan.

The most recent change in Medicare occurred in 2003 with the passage of the Medicare Prescription Drug, Improvement, and Modernization Act. The controversial bill squeaked through the House of Representatives after a late-night roll call vote, which Republican leaders left open for nearly three hours (rather than the customary fifteen minutes typically allowed to complete a roll call) to provide them with time to persuade members to switch their votes in support of the bill. At 5:50 A.M., when the vote had finally closed, the bill passed by a margin of 220 to 215. That success deflated a filibuster that Democrats in the Senate had planned; three days after the House vote, the bill cleared the Senate on a tally of 54 to 44.

Rather than a single program with simple rules, the new drug plan encouraged private insurers to offer competing plans. In some locations, seniors may have the option of thirty or more plans from which to choose, each with a different combination of costs, deductibles, participating pharmacies, and formularies (covered medications). It should come as no surprise that only a small proportion of seniors have signed up for any plan, since the list of different plans, options, and prices was overwhelming. And those who did make the choice early on faced confusion and frustration when attempting to fill their prescriptions at the start of 2006. It remains to be seen whether more seniors will pick a plan. In the meantime, simply sorting out the tangle of rules and regulations is the order of the day.

Like other aspects of Medicare, the costs of the program continue to increase at rates in excess of the cost of living (see "Looking to the Future: Are the Social Security and Medicare Programs Sustainable?"). Consequently, government has sought to contain those costs. One previous attempt at cost containment, in addition to several new devices designed to promote competition in the recent prescription drug law, makes use of economic incentives in the hospital treatment of Medicare patients. The plan seems to have had the desired economic benefits, but it raises questions about possibly endangering the health of elderly patients.

Previously, Medicare payments to hospitals were based on the length of a patient's stay: the longer the stay, the more revenue the hospital earned. This approach encouraged longer, more expensive hospital stays because the government was paying the bill. In 1985, however, the government switched to a new payment system under which hospitals are paid a fixed fee based on the patient's diagnosis. If the patient's stay costs more than the fee schedule allows, the hospital pays the difference. If the hospital treats a patient for less than the fixed fee, the hospital reaps a profit. This new system provides an incentive for hospitals to discharge patients sooner, perhaps in some cases before they are completely well.

Medicaid

In addition to Medicare, another important part of the nation's health-care patchwork is **Medicaid,** which is the nation's main program to provide health care to Americans with low incomes. Like Medicare, this program was also the product of Lyndon Johnson's Great Society effort; it passed as yet another amendment to the Social Security Act. In 1965, the program was relatively small and enrolled 4 million people at an annual cost of $0.4 billion. By 2006, it had grown to become the single largest public program in the nation, enrolling more than 63 million people at a cost of $311 billion.[46]

The program's scope is quite vast. According to one author, "Medicaid has now overtaken Medicare in both enrollment and spending to become the largest health insurance program in the United States. It insures one-fifth of the nation's children and pays for one-third of all childbirths. It finances nearly 40 percent of all long-term care expenses, more than one-sixth of all drug costs, and half of states' mental health services. It is . . . the 'workhorse' of the U.S. health system."[47]

Although Medicaid is designed primarily to cover citizens with low incomes, the pool of potentially eligible people can vary significantly across the country. That is because, unlike Medicare, which is solely a federal program,

Medicaid A need-based comprehensive medical and hospitalization program.

Medicaid is jointly run and financed by the federal government and the states. Federal law defines a certain minimum level of benefits that states must offer through Medicaid, but states have much leeway to determine income levels and other criteria to define eligibility.

This sharing of cost and administration in the American federal system can leave some Medicaid beneficiaries in challenging circumstances. For example, citizens who might be eligible for Medicaid services in one state may lose eligibility if they move elsewhere. Also, because Medicaid expenditures are typically one of the top expenses in state budgets (usually just ahead of or behind spending on education), benefits are frequently cut when states experience difficult budgetary situations, as has occurred since 2001. In fiscal year 2003, for example, in order to contain Medicaid costs, eighteen states reported restricting eligibility, fifteen reduced benefits, and fifteen increased the copayments required of program participants.[48]

Medicaid participants essentially fall into four groups: children under age twenty-one (31.1 million in 2006), adults (16.2 million), those who are blind and disabled (9.7 million), and those aged sixty-five and over (6.1 million).[49] Don't be confused by that last group. Senior citizens qualify for Medicare, but they can also participate in Medicaid if their incomes fall below a certain level. Finally, although their numbers are relatively small compared to other participants in the program, those who are blind and disabled and the elderly account for over half of Medicaid expenditures. Thus, the cost of the program appears to be driven by the high cost of medical care for these two groups, rather than other factors.[50]

★ Elementary and Secondary Education

Although it is no less important, education is unlike the other public policies discussed in this chapter given that responsibility for children's schooling resides primarily in state and local governments in the United States. Since Horace Mann introduced mandatory public schooling in Massachusetts in the second quarter of the nineteenth century, public elementary and secondary schools have been a highly visible part of local government. And at no time in the nation's history has the federal government contributed more than 10 percent to finance the nation's K–12 education bill; today, as it has for many years, Washington's contribution hovers around 7 percent. Although federal policy in education dates back to the earliest days of the nation, significant national involvement in education has been more recent.

Concerns Motivating Change

Two main factors, related to freedom, order, and equality, have prompted greater federal involvement in the nation's elementary and secondary schools during the last half century.

Equity. The overriding and persistent concern has been educational equity. An important part of Lyndon Johnson's Great Society was the traditional American belief that social and economic equality could be attained through equality of educational opportunity. The justices of the U.S. Supreme Court argued as much in their landmark decision in *Brown* v. *Board of Education* (1954).

Legislatively, the **Elementary and Secondary Education Act of 1965 (ESEA),** yet another product of the Great Society, was the first major federal effort to address educational equity in a systematic way. The law, which has been re-authorized periodically since its original enactment, provided direct national government aid to local school districts in order to improve the educational opportunities of the economically disadvantaged.

The ESEA began as a relatively short bill of around thirty pages in 1965, but it has grown to encompass hundreds of pages and dozens of federal programs, with nearly all devoted to improving educational opportunities for disadvantaged groups. The original law focused on economic disadvantage; later iterations recognized more explicitly other groups, such as students for whom English is a second language and Native American students. A separate law altogether, the Individuals with Disabilities Education Act (IDEA), which originally passed with a different name in the 1970s, is designed to improve educational opportunities for students of all ages (elementary school through college and graduate school) with physical or other disabilities.

Despite the efforts of federal policy, the promised improvements in educational, and thus social and economic, equality have been elusive. Differences in student achievement between advantaged and disadvantaged groups have declined since the 1960s. However, as data from the 2005 National Assessment of Educational Progress, a federally sponsored test also known as the "nation's report card," show, significant gaps still remain in key subject areas such as reading and math.[51] These test score gaps are important because they tend to correlate with future educational and economic opportunities.[52]

National Security and Prosperity.

Concern over educational achievement is not limited to issues of social equality at home. In an increasingly competitive global economy with fewer barriers to international investment and plant relocation, countries are competing to offer—and attract—highly educated and skilled workers. Thus, a desire to keep the United States competitive with other nations, both economically and militarily, is one reason that politicians, business leaders, and American citizens more generally see education as a key public policy area.

In fact, the connection between national security and federal education policy is not recent. It dates back at least as far as the 1950s when the Eisenhower administration supported and helped to push into law the National Defense Education Act of 1958 (NDEA). The law is typically considered to be a response to the Soviet Union's launch of a tiny satellite known as *Sputnik*, the first such craft to orbit the Earth. This Soviet success, which many interpreted to mean that the United States was losing the "brain race" against its rival, set off calls for improving the nation's stock of scientists and engineers, as well as its cadre of foreign language speakers, to counter the communist threat around the globe. Funding from the NDEA supported efforts in all of these areas at the elementary, secondary, and postsecondary levels.

A desire to improve American economic competitiveness has been the most recent force prompting greater efforts to improve the nation's education system. These concerns date back to the 1970s, when state governors became increasingly attuned to the link between their own states' economic fortunes and the quality of their schools. These state-level concerns foreshadowed subsequent debates at the national level that forged a similar link between the competitiveness of the entire nation and the educational preparation of the country's young people.

Elementary and Secondary Education Act of 1965 (ESEA) The federal government's primary law to assist the nation's elementary and secondary schools. It emerged as part of President Lyndon Johnson's Great Society program.

These state- and national-level concerns coalesced in a famous report entitled *A Nation at Risk,* which was released in 1983 by the National Commission on Excellence in Education. The commission was the brainchild of the nation's second secretary of education, Terrell Bell. The report, along with improved data comparing American students with their international counterparts, through projects such as the Trends in International Mathematics and Science Study (TIMSS), created significant momentum for public officials at all levels of government to support improving the nation's schools.

Values and Reform

At the center of the current debate over education is the dilemma of freedom versus equality. The American belief in equality is heavily weighted toward equality of opportunity, and equality of opportunity depends on equal access to a good education. Thus, several advocates suggest that important components of any future reforms must include measures to provide better teachers and funding commensurate with educational needs in the nation's urban and rural areas.

At the same time, the American belief in freedom is perhaps nowhere expressed more vigorously than in the freedom to choose both where to live and what one's children will be taught in school. Advocates of this view see greater educational success tied to plans to increase educational opportunities for students and their parents. Popular among these proposals are charter schools, which are public schools of choice that have been freed from several state and local regulations. (Since 1991, forty-one states, plus the District of Columbia and Puerto Rico, enacted some sort of charter school law.) Others would go still further and support school voucher programs, which would enable parents to choose to send their children to any school—public or private, secular or religious—at taxpayer expense. Choice would not only improve opportunities for these parents and children, proponents argue, but would also provide a jolt of competition that would improve public schools more generally.

As the national and international challenges we face grow in technological and scientific sophistication, the dilemmas of education reform will become more pressing. The questions of who will pay for reform, who will benefit, and how best to improve student learning have all come to a head in the most recent reauthorization of the ESEA known as the **No Child Left Behind Act of 2001 (NCLB).**

The No Child Left Behind Act of 2001

In 2000, Republican candidate George W. Bush made education one of the most important issues in his campaign for the White House.[53] Once in office, Bush wasted no time in offering up his vision to reform the Elementary and Secondary Education Act. The fact that Bush and his team pressed the issue, even after the attacks on the United States of 9/11, illustrated the importance that the president placed on achieving significant education reform in his first year in office. The president's persistence and the efforts of key Democrats and Republicans in Congress eventually paid off, and by December the Congress had passed the No Child Left Behind Act of 2001. With much fanfare, President Bush signed the measure into law in January 2002.

Although Bush, members of Congress, and observers in the press called the bill a historic breakthrough, it actually extended several initiatives that the

INTERACTIVE 19.2

 Nearly 2 Million Scores Left Behind

No Child Left Behind Act of 2001 (NCLB) The latest reauthorization of the Elementary and Secondary Education Act.

previous reauthorization of the ESEA from 1994 had set in motion. Most significant among NCLB's numerous components is the law's requirement that states guarantee that all of their students are performing at proficient levels in reading and math by 2014. Along the way, schools will have to show that they are making what the law calls Adequate Yearly Progress among all student groups, be they economically disadvantaged, weak in English language skills, or disabled. Schools need to demonstrate that progress through annual testing in reading and math for students in grades 3 through 8 and then once again in tests administered in grades 10, 11, or 12.

The law also includes several other provisions to help schools and to offer more public school choices to parents whose children attend schools that persistently fail to meet Adequate Yearly Progress targets. In an effort to improve the nation's stock of classroom teachers, NCLB also calls on school districts to hire only highly qualified teachers in the core subjects of reading and math. Beyond these prescriptive provisions in the law, NCLB does provide for some added flexibility with how districts and states use federal funds across a variety of programs. And most critical, because education is still primarily a state and local function in the United States, the law leaves it up to states to develop and define the standards to measure educational proficiency in reading and math. That has led some critics of the law to fear that states will simply water down their standards to prevent large numbers of their schools and students from being defined as needing improvement.

The No Child Left Behind Act became law in 2002 and faced reauthorization in 2007. While the law has increased tensions among federal, state, and local education officials, these leaders tend to share common educational goals for the nation: that American students need to learn more reading and math and that achievement gaps between students need to be eliminated. That unified vision has prevented any group from pushing for major changes to the law. The reauthorization gives the Democratic-controlled Congress a chance to demonstrate its commitment to low-income children by increased funding beyond previous levels and above the amount requested by President Bush. Still, Congress has yet to fund NCLB to the levels it agreed to in 2001 when the law passed.

★ Benefits and Fairness

As we have seen, the national government provides many Americans with benefits. There are two kinds of benefits: cash, such as a retiree's Social Security check, and noncash, such as food stamps. Some benefits are conditional. **Means-tested benefits** impose an income test to qualify. For example, free or low-cost school lunch programs and Pell college grants are available to households that have an income that falls below a designated threshold. **Non-means-tested benefits** impose no such income test; benefits such as Medicare and Social Security are available to all, regardless of income.

Some Americans question the fairness of non-means-tested benefits. After all, benefits are subsidies, and some people need them more than others do. If the size of the benefit pie remains fixed, imposing means tests on more benefits has real allure. For example, all elderly people now receive the same basic Medicare benefits, regardless of their income. Fairness advocates maintain that the affluent elderly should shoulder a higher share of Medicare costs, shifting more benefits to the low-income elderly.

? **Can you explain why . . .** even very rich people are eligible for some government benefits?

means-tested benefits
Conditional benefits provided by government to individuals whose income falls below a designated threshold.

non-means-tested benefits
Benefits provided by government to all citizens, regardless of income; Medicare and Social Security are examples.

If the idea of shifting benefits gains support in the future, reform debates will focus on the income level below which a program will apply. Thus, the question of fairness is one more problem for policymakers to consider as they try to reform social insurance, public assistance, health-care, and education programs.

Summary

In this chapter, we have examined several different domestic policies—general plans of action adopted by the government to solve a social problem, counter a threat, or pursue an objective within the country's own borders. Often, disagreements about public policy are disagreements about values. Some of the oldest and most costly domestic policies, such as Social Security and Medicare, pose choices between freedom and equality.

Many domestic policies that provide benefits to individuals and promote economic equality were instituted during the Great Depression. Today, the government plays an active role in providing benefits to the poor, the elderly, and the disabled. The object of these domestic policies is to alleviate conditions that individuals are powerless to prevent. This is the social welfare function of the modern state. The call for health-care reform is a reflection of the modern dilemma of democracy: universal coverage and cost controls versus a loss of freedom in health-care choices.

Government confers benefits on individuals through social insurance and public assistance. Social insurance is not based on need; public assistance (welfare) hinges on proof of need. In one form of social insurance—old-age benefits—a tax on current workers pays retired workers' benefits. Aid for the poor, by contrast, comes from the government's general tax revenues.

Programs to aid the elderly and the poor have been gradually transformed into entitlements, or rights that accrue to eligible persons. These government programs have reduced poverty among some groups, especially the elderly. However, poverty retains a grip on certain segments of the population. Social and demographic changes have feminized poverty, and there is little prospect of reversing that trend soon.

Bill Clinton and a Republican-led Congress reformed the welfare system. The biggest entitlement program (Aid to Families with Dependent Children, or AFDC) is gone. Thanks to Temporary Assistance for Needy Families (TANF), individual state programs will substitute for a single national policy. Work requirements and time limits on welfare may break the cycle of dependency, but the reforms run the risk of endangering the neediest among us. Time and experience will tell whether this grand experiment will produce better outcomes.

In contrast to social insurance and public assistance programs, significant federal involvement in education is of relatively recent origin, dating from the Great Society initiatives of the 1960s. Even today, education remains largely a state and local endeavor, with the federal government providing less than 10 percent of the funds for primary and secondary education. Traditionally, the federal government's education policy has centered around providing equal access to a good education for all Americans. That goal of achieving educational equity still remains important. With efforts such as the No Child Left Behind Act, we can see how policymakers have begun to link equity with educational excellence. In short, financial equity in education has little meaning if students do not achieve at comparable levels.

Some government subsidy programs provide means-tested benefits, for which eligibility hinges on income. Non-means-tested benefits are available to all, regardless of income. As the demand for such benefits exceeds available resources, policymakers have come to question their fairness. Subsidies for rich and poor alike are the basis for a broad national consensus. A departure from that consensus in the name of fairness may very well be the next challenge of democracy.

20

Global Policy

(© Chris Helgren/Reuters/Corbis)

Online Study Center
This icon will direct you to resources
and activities on the website
college.hmco.com/pic/jandaupdate9e

Etch-A-Sketch is no longer made in Bryan, Ohio. In 1960, the Ohio Art Company began manufacturing the Etch-A-Sketch drawing toy and continued for forty years.[1] Providing about one hundred union jobs, the company was the leading industry in Bryan, a town of 8,000. Then in 2000, the company shifted production to Shenzhen, China, where the same toy is now made by workers earning far less money under harsher working conditions.[2] Etch-A-Sketch became just one more plaything for China, which now makes 80 percent of all toys sold in America.[3]

Union workers with low skills in small American towns are not alone in losing jobs abroad. IBM announced plans to move work done by almost 5,000 programmers in Poughkeepsie, Raleigh, Dallas, Boulder, and elsewhere in the United States to India, China, and other countries that can supply high-tech workers at far lower cost.[4] IBM's plan, called "Global Sourcing," reflects a general flight of technology jobs from American companies in a pattern known as "offshore outsourcing."[5] The Information Technology Association of America projected a net loss of 20,000 jobs in information software and services through 2008 to "offshore" locations.[6]

The flight of manufacturing and technology jobs to developing nations with lower labor costs is not just America's problem. Thompson, the French electronics company and maker of RCA television sets (once made in America), became a minority partner with China's TCL International Holdings, which can make sets for a few dollars less.[7] In northern Italy, where family firms have manufactured high-quality cloth and leather goods for 600 years, business has been lost to Chinese companies offering lower price and comparable quality. Now once-proud Italian companies are shifting production to China.[8] Even Mexico, whose low wages attracted American companies to relocate there at the cost of American jobs, has itself lost work and markets to China—for example, in making Christmas ornaments.[9] In 2003, China overtook Mexico to become the No. 2 exporter of goods to the United States (just behind Canada).

Under globalization, free trade among nations with free markets was supposed to generate a "win-win" outcome for both developed and developing nations. As reported in the *Wall Street Journal,* the "free trade axiom" held that

> when a rich country sends blue-collar jobs overseas, it creates opportunities back home for workers to move up the skill ladder [creating better jobs for those lost]. The more recent corollary was that sending service jobs overseas would do the same for white-collar workers at home.[10]

Globalization dominated the agenda of the 2006 World Economic Forum in Davos, Switzerland. Hundreds of top business and political leaders discussed policies to deal with global problems under such themes as "The Emergence of China and India," "The Challenging Economic Landscape," and "New Mindsets and Changing Attitudes."[11] Surprisingly, *globalization* in an economic context rarely appeared in President Bush's speeches. A senior aide said, "It makes him uncomfortable," because "globalization sounds like the creation of a lot of rules that may restrict the president's choice, that dilute American influence."[12] As leader of a sovereign nation—and the world's greatest military power—President Bush liked to pick and choose his relationships with other nations.

Indeed, Bush *never* used *globalization* in his five State of the Union addresses from 2002 to

2006, although he did mention "global" in two contexts (referring to global "trade" and "economy" in 2006, and global "war" and "treaties" in 2003). In contrast, President Clinton in his last State of the Union address (2000) described "globalization" as "the central reality of our time," repeated the term in three places, and mentioned "global" five times. How can we characterize these different worldviews of our two most recent presidents? How might their different views affect our relations with other nations? ★

IN OUR OWN WORDS

Listen to Kenneth Janda discuss the main points and themes of this chapter.

Online Study Center
Improve Your Grade

The ideological framework in Chapter 1, which runs through this book, was devised for analyzing ideological attitudes in domestic politics. One can adapt it to international affairs, as shown in Figure 20.1. Actions that Bush took in Afghanistan after September 11, 2001, might place him in the International Liberals category for his readiness to build an ad hoc international coalition prior to taking action against Al Qaeda. But that placement would only reflect his tactical decision to deal with that particular situation. More broadly, the president's strategy—as demonstrated in the Iraqi war—was to act unilaterally if necessary to serve his view of America's interests. Accordingly, President Bush fits better in the International Libertarian category. President Clinton was more of an International Liberal.

FIGURE 20.1 **A Two-Dimensional Framework of International Ideologies**

As in Figure 1.2 in Chapter 1, the four ideological types here are defined by the values that they favor in balancing the values of freedom and order and freedom and equality in international affairs. In this typology, however, order is tied to the defense of national sovereignty within the traditional nation-state system of international relations.

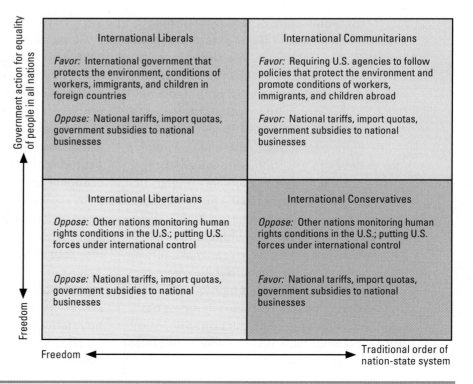

Although the president is held accountable for U.S. foreign affairs, many other actors are involved. We begin our discussion of global policy by establishing the constitutional bases of governmental authority for making American foreign policy in the military, economic, and social arenas.

★ Making Foreign Policy: The Constitutional Context

A nation's **foreign policy** is its general plan to defend and advance national interests, especially its security against foreign threats. The Constitution uses the word *foreign* in only five places. Four are in the section dealing with Congress, which is entrusted to "regulate commerce among foreign nations"; to "regulate the value . . . of foreign coin"; to approve any gift or title to a government official "from any king, prince, or foreign state"; and to approve "any compact or agreement" between a state and "a foreign power" in time of war. The fifth mention gives the courts jurisdiction over cases arising "between a state . . . and foreign states." The Constitution never uses *foreign* in its article describing the executive branch, and yet the presidency has emerged as the dominant actor in foreign policy. Why?

Constitutional Bases of Presidential Authority in Foreign Policy

One must read between the lines of the Constitution to understand how presidents have derived their authority in foreign policy. The Constitution creates the executive in Article II, which provides that the president:

■ is commander in chief of the armed forces.

■ has the power to make treaties (subject to the consent of the Senate).

■ appoints U.S. ambassadors and the heads of executive departments (also with the advice and consent of the Senate).

■ receives (or refuses to receive) ambassadors from other countries.

Over time, the president has parlayed these constitutional provisions—plus laws passed by Congress, Supreme Court decisions, and precedents created by bold action and political acceptance—to emerge as the leading actor in American foreign policy. But as in a play, there are other actors in the foreign policy drama, and Congress plays a strong supporting role—sometimes even upstaging the star performer.

Constitutional Bases of Congressional Authority in Foreign Policy

As noted above, Congress already claims most uses of the word *foreign* in the Constitution, and, as in the case of the presidency, the Constitution gives Congress additional powers in foreign policy without mentioning the term. Specifically, the Constitution establishes that the Congress is empowered to:

■ legislate.

■ declare war.

foreign policy The general plan followed by a nation in defending and advancing its national interests, especially its security against foreign threats.

- raise revenue and dispense funds.

- support, maintain, govern, and regulate the army and navy.

- call out the state militias to repel invasions.

- regulate commerce with foreign nations.

- define and punish piracy and offenses against the law of nations.

The most salient power for foreign policy on this list is the power to declare war, but Congress has used this power only five times. It has relied more on its other powers to influence foreign policy. Using its legislative power, Congress can involve the nation in programs of international scope or limit the actions of the executive branch. Probably most important, Congress has used the power of the purse to provide funds for the activities it supports—and to prohibit funds for those it opposes. The Constitution also ascribes some powers to the Senate alone, which has made the U.S. Senate the leading chamber of Congress on foreign policy issues. The Constitution requires that the Senate:

- give advice and consent to treaties made by the president.

- give advice and consent to the appointment of ambassadors and various other public officials involved in foreign policy.

The Senate has used its special powers to check presidential initiatives in foreign policy. Whereas only the president can *make* treaties, the Senate can *break* treaties—in the sense of rejecting those made by the president.

The Senate and Major Treaties. In truth, the Senate rarely defeats a treaty, having defeated only twenty-one of the thousands it has considered.[13] Some of the defeats have been historically significant, however, establishing the Senate as a force in foreign policy. A hard-hearted Senate demonstrated its veto power to Democratic President Woodrow Wilson in 1919. At the end of World War I, Wilson proposed and championed a plan for an international organization—the League of Nations—to eliminate future wars. To enter the League, however, Wilson's treaty had to be approved by two-thirds of the Senate. Wilson, an idealistic, international liberal, was opposed by a group of mostly Republican, internationally conservative senators. After eight months of debate, the Senate rejected his treaty and the United States never joined the League of Nations. Some attribute the weakness of the League of Nations, which failed to prevent a second world war, to the absence of the United States.

In the early days of World War II, President Franklin D. Roosevelt and British Prime Minister Winston Churchill revived Wilson's idea for collective security and proposed a new international organization—the United Nations—after the war. By the time the U.N. treaty went to the Senate in the summer of 1945, Roosevelt had died. It fell to President Harry Truman, also a Democrat and mindful of Wilson's failure with the League of Nations, to win acceptance of the U.N. treaty by a Republican-controlled Senate. In public hearings on the treaty, several representatives of isolationist groups spoke against it, fearing loss of American sovereignty to a world government.[14] But by then, both parties in Congress widely accepted U.S. international involvement, and Republican Senator Arthur H. Vandenberg, chair of the Foreign Relations Committee, led his party and the Senate to approve the treaty by a vote of 89 to 2 after only five days of debate. Without the Senate's approval, the United States would not have entered the United Nations.

The twenty-first and most recent treaty rejection by the Senate occurred on October 13, 1999, on the Comprehensive Nuclear Test Ban Treaty. This treaty, signed by President Clinton in 1996, would have effectively outlawed all nuclear weapons testing. Almost all arms control agreements since Eisenhower's administration have been proposed by presidents of both parties and opposed by conservatives in Congress from both parties. True to form, the Nuclear Test Ban Treaty failed to get the required two-thirds majority. All Democratic senators voted for it, and all but four Republicans voted against.[15]

Governmental leaders around the world reacted angrily to the defeat of a treaty that had been decades in the making. One overseas newspaper editorialized, "If the United States, the sole superpower, refuses stubbornly to ratify a global nuclear test ban treaty that will make the world safer for all, why on earth would any other country want to do it?"[16] In the United States, however, Senator Jon Kyl (R-Ariz.) said that the treaty rejection shows "that our constitutional democracy, with its shared powers and checks and balances, is alive and well."[17]

Skirting the Senate Through Executive Agreements.

An **executive agreement** is a pact between heads of countries concerning their joint activities. The Supreme Court has ruled that executive agreements are within the inherent powers of the president and have the legal status of treaties.[18] Executive agreements must conform to the Constitution, existing treaties, and the laws of Congress.[19] Like treaties, executive agreements have the force of law; unlike treaties, they do not require Senate approval. Until 1972 the texts of these agreements did not even have to be reported to Congress. Legislation passed that year required the president to send copies to the House and Senate Foreign Relations committees. This requirement has not seriously affected the use of executive agreements, which has escalated dramatically, outnumbering treaties by about ten to one since the 1930s.[20]

Most executive agreements deal with minor bureaucratic business that would not interest a busy Senate. On occasion, presidents have resorted to executive agreements on important issues that were unlikely to win Senate consent. In 1992, President George H. W. Bush negotiated an accord with Canada and Mexico that facilitated free trade among the three countries by reducing national tariffs on imported goods. This plan, which reflected a free-market international libertarian ideology, was widely favored by economists but bitterly opposed by trade protectionists and international conservatives.

Instead of proposing the arrangement as a treaty, President Bush framed it as an executive agreement: the North American Free Trade Agreement (NAFTA). He had to send the agreement to Congress for enabling legislation, but it required only simple majorities in both houses to pass.[21] President Clinton inherited the pending NAFTA legislation when he succeeded Bush. Clinton, who touted himself a "new Democrat," was closer to Bush on free trade than to the traditional core of the Democratic Party. Bucking organized labor, which feared losing jobs to Mexico, he shepherded NAFTA through passage with more support from Republicans than from Democrats. In 1993, President Clinton signed the NAFTA agreement negotiated by President George H. W. Bush.

In 2004, President George W. Bush signed CAFTA—the Central American Free Trade Agreement—with Costa Rica, the Dominican Republic, El Salvador, Guatemala, Honduras, and Nicaragua. Similar to NAFTA, it drew similar criticisms but was approved in 2005 after a close vote in the Senate and an even closer vote in the House.

> **? Can you explain why . . .**
> NAFTA was not framed as an international treaty?

executive agreement
A pact between the heads of two countries.

Constitutional Roots of Statutory Powers in Foreign Policy

Within the framework of the powers the Constitution grants to the executive, Congress has conferred other responsibilities to the presidency through laws—and creative presidents have expanded on these grants of authority. For example, Congress has allowed the presidency certain leeway on the use of *discretionary funds*—large sums of cash that may be spent on unforeseen needs to further the national interest. Similarly, the president's *transfer authority,* or the reprogramming of funds, allows him to take money that Congress has approved for one purpose and spend it on something else. The executive branch also has control over the disposal of excess government stocks, including surplus or infrequently used equipment. The Central Intelligence Agency (CIA) has been an important beneficiary of excess stock disposal.

As commander in chief of the armed forces, several presidents have committed American troops in emergency situations, thus involving the United States in undeclared wars. America's undeclared wars, police actions, and similar interventions have outnumbered its formal, congressionally declared wars by about forty to one. Since the last declared war ended in 1945, over 100,000 American members of the military have died in locations ranging from Korea and Vietnam to Grenada, Somalia, Afghanistan, and Iraq.

Reacting to casualties from the undeclared Vietnam War, Congress passed the War Powers Resolution in 1973 over Nixon's veto. It required that the president "consult" with Congress in "every possible instance" before involving U.S. troops in hostilities and notify Congress within forty-eight hours of committing troops to a foreign intervention. If troops are deployed, they may not stay for more than sixty days without congressional approval (although the president may take up to thirty days more to remove them "safely"). Some critics of the legislation claimed that it did not restrict presidential power as much as extend a free hand to wage war for up to sixty days.[22] The actual impact of the War Powers Resolution is probably quite minimal. Nixon's successors in the White House (like Nixon) have all questioned its constitutionality, and no president has ever been punished for violating its provisions.

After September 11, 2001, President George W. Bush had to work within the War Powers Resolution to build his "global coalition against terrorism." That posed no problem. Congress promptly and overwhelmingly voted on September 14 to authorize the president to "use all necessary and appropriate force against those nations, organizations or persons he determines planned, authorized, committed or aided the terrorist attacks . . . or harbored such organizations or persons."[23] Bush relied on this Joint Resolution to attack Al Qaeda in Afghanistan and to defeat the Taliban regime there in late 2001.

A year later, Congress was not as quick to support the president's use of military force against Saddam Hussein. Bush again sought authorization through a Joint Resolution in October 2002. It began with a series of "whereas" clauses (e.g., "Whereas in 1998 Congress concluded that Iraq's continuing weapons of mass destruction programs threatened vital United States interests and international peace and security") and then authorized the president

> to use the Armed Forces of the United States as he determines to be necessary and appropriate in order to (1) defend the national security of the United States against the continuing threat posed by Iraq; and (2) enforce all relevant United Nations Security Council Resolutions regarding Iraq.

Although the resolution passed with strong support in both chambers, it was opposed by more than half the Democrats in the House and nearly half in the Senate.

As presidents have expanded their role in the foreign policy drama, the Senate sought to enlarge its part, interpreting quite broadly its power to "advise and consent" on presidential appointments to offices involved in foreign affairs. Senators have used confirmation hearings to prod the administration for more acceptable appointments. In March 2005, President Bush nominated John Bolton, a controversial State Department official, as U.S. ambassador to the United Nations—which Bolton had publicly criticized. With Bolton's confirmation uncertain, President Bush bypassed the Senate by installing him as U.N. ambassador under a "recess appointment" to expire when a new Congress convened in January 2007. Facing a new Senate held by Democrats, Bolton resigned. He was replaced by diplomat Zalmay Khalilzad, who was quickly confirmed.

★ Making Foreign Policy: Organization and Cast

Although American foreign policy originates within the executive branch, the organizational structure for policymaking is created and funded by Congress and is subject to congressional oversight. When the United States acquired its superpower status after World War II, Congress overhauled the administration of foreign policy with the 1947 National Security Act, which established three new organizations—the Department of Defense, the National Security Council, and the CIA—to join the Department of State in the organizational structure. Following 9/11, new legislation sought to coordinate the intelligence activities of all three new organizations.

The Department of State

During its very first session in 1789, Congress created the Department of Foreign Affairs as the government's first executive department. Within two months, it was renamed the State Department, as it has remained.[24] The State Department helps formulate American foreign policy and then executes and monitors it throughout the world. The department's head, the secretary of state, is the highest-ranking official in the cabinet; he is also, in theory at least, the president's most important foreign policy adviser. However, some chief executives, like John Kennedy, preferred to act as their own secretary of state and appointed relatively weak figures to the post. Others, such as Dwight Eisenhower, appointed stronger individuals (John Foster Dulles) to the post. Presidents often come to the Oval Office promising to rely on the State Department and its head to play a leading role in formulating and carrying out foreign policy. The reality that emerges is usually somewhat different and prompts analysts to bemoan the chronic weakness of the department.[25]

In nominating former general Colin L. Powell to be his secretary of state, President Bush implied that the State Department would play a greater role than usual in foreign policy. General Powell, a former chairman of the Joint Chiefs of Staff, formulated what became known as the Powell doctrine: "Define your objective. Bring massive force to bear. Take on only those battles you are sure you can win, and line up public support before you start."[26] As secretary of state, however, Powell found himself supporting a war in Iraq that was arguably short on ground troops, and he found his preference for multilateral negotiations clashing with the unilateral militaristic positions of others in the Bush administration.[27] Powell resigned his office in late 2004. Condoleezza Rice, longtime Bush adviser and head of the National Security Council, was confirmed as secretary of state in January 2005.

Like other executive departments, the State Department is staffed by political appointees and permanent employees selected under the civil service merit system. Political appointees include deputy secretaries and undersecretaries of state and some—but not all—ambassadors. Permanent employees include approximately four thousand foreign service officers, at home and abroad, who staff and service U.S. embassies and consulates throughout the world. They have primary responsibility for representing America to the rest of the world and caring for American citizens and interests abroad. Although the foreign service is highly selective (fewer than two hundred of the fifteen thousand candidates who take the annual examination are appointed), the State Department is often charged with lacking initiative and creativity. Critics claim that bright young foreign service officers quickly realize that conformity is the best path to career advancement.[28]

The State Department also lacks a strong domestic constituency to exert pressure in support of its policies. The Department of Agriculture, by contrast, can mobilize farmers to support its activities, and the Department of Defense can count on help from defense industries and veterans' groups. In a pluralist democracy, the lack of a natural constituency is a serious drawback for an agency or department. Exacerbating this problem is the changing character of global political issues. As economic and social issues emerge in foreign affairs, executive agencies with pertinent domestic policy expertise have become more involved in shaping global policy.

The Department of Defense

In 1947, Congress replaced two venerable cabinet-level departments—the War Department and the Department of the Navy—with the Department of Defense, intending to promote unity and coordination among the armed forces and to provide the modern bureaucratic structure needed to manage America's greatly expanded peacetime military. In keeping with the U.S. tradition of civilian control of the military, the new department was given a civilian head—the secretary of defense—a cabinet member with authority over the military. Later reorganizations of the department (in 1949 and 1958) have given the secretary greater budgetary powers; control of defense research; and the authority to transfer, abolish, reassign, and consolidate functions among the military services.

The role of the defense secretary depends on the individual's vision of the job and willingness to use the tools available. Strong secretaries, including Robert McNamara (under Kennedy and Johnson), Melvin Laird (under Nixon), James Schlesinger (under Nixon and Ford), and Caspar Weinberger (under Reagan), wielded significant power. President George W. Bush chose Donald Rumsfeld, an experienced government official who had previously served as secretary of defense under President Ford. When Powell was secretary of state, Rumsfeld and Powell engaged in a continuing feud over planning and handling the Iraqi war.[29] Rumsfeld was criticized over the prolonged conflict in Iraq, which led to the Republican losses in the 2006 election. After the election, Bush replaced Rumsfeld with Robert M. Gates, former director of the CIA.

Below the secretary are the civilian secretaries of the army, navy, and air force; below them are the military commanders of the individual branches of the armed forces, who make up the Joint Chiefs of Staff. The Joint Chiefs meet to coordinate military policy among the different branches; they also serve as the primary military advisers to the president, the secretary of defense, and the National Security Council, helping to shape policy positions on matters such as alliances, plans for nuclear and conventional war, and arms control and disarmament.

The National Security Council

The National Security Council (NSC) is made up of a group of advisers who help the president mold a coherent approach to foreign policy by integrating and coordinating details of domestic, foreign, and military affairs that relate to national security. The statutory members of the NSC include the president, the vice president, and the secretaries of state and defense. NSC discussions can cover a wide range of issues, such as how to deal with changes in Eastern Europe or the formulation of U.S. policy in the Middle East. In theory, at least, NSC discussions offer the president an opportunity to solicit advice and allow key participants in the foreign policy–making process to keep abreast of the policies and capabilities of other departments.

In practice, the role played by the NSC has varied considerably under different presidents. Truman and Kennedy seldom met with it; Eisenhower and Nixon brought it into much greater prominence. During the Nixon administration, the NSC was critically important in making foreign policy. Much of this importance derived from Nixon's reliance on Henry Kissinger, his assistant for national security affairs (the title of the head of the NSC staff). President George W. Bush nominated as head of the NSC Condoleezza Rice, a former professor of political science at Stanford, who had served on the NSC under Bush's father and was George W.'s top national security adviser during his presidential campaign. Rice, Bush said, "can explain foreign policy matters to me in a way I can understand."[30] At the NSC, she played a major role in formulating Bush's national security strategy after September 11.[31] After President Bush elevated Rice to secretary of state, her deputy on the National Security Council, Stephen J. Hadley, was appointed to replace her.

The Intelligence Community

Conducting an effective foreign policy requires accurate information—termed "intelligence" in international affairs.[32] Raw data on foreign countries, observations of politics abroad, and inside information are merged into finished intelligence for policymakers through activities spread across sixteen agencies in the executive branch known as the **Intelligence Community**.[33] Of these agencies listed in the photo caption on page 626, the two most prominent are the Central Intelligence Agency (CIA) and the National Security Agency (NSA). The CIA is an independent agency, while the NSA is part of the Department of Defense (DOD), as is the National Reconnaissance Office (NRO); the National Geospatial-Intelligence Agency (NGA); the Defense Intelligence Agency (DIA);

Intelligence Community
Sixteen agencies in the executive branch that conduct the various intelligence activities that make up the total U.S. national intelligence effort.

Pieces of Intelligence

The Office of the Director of National Intelligence is charged with coordinating the intelligence operations of all sixteen agencies whose seals are arrayed here in two rows in alphabetical order: (*top row*) Air Force Intelligence, Army Intelligence, Central Intelligence Agency, Coast Guard Intelligence, Defense Intelligence Agency, Department of Energy, Department of Homeland Security, Department of State; (*bottom row*) Department of the Treasury, Drug Enforcement Administration, Federal Bureau of Investigation, Marine Corps Intelligence, National Geospatial-Intelligence Agency, National Reconnaissance Office, National Security Agency, and Navy Intelligence. (*Office of the Director of National Intelligence*)

and the intelligence operations of the Army, Navy, Marine Corps, Coast Guard, and Air Force—which explains why 80 percent of the intelligence budget is controlled by the DOD.[34]

Many attributed the 9/11 attack on America to a failure of intelligence, and Congress created an independent commission to investigate the charge. Known as the 9/11 Commission, its 2004 report proposed sweeping reorganization of intelligence agencies and responsibilities. How well these reforms will work remains to be seen, but a brief account of the three main elements sets the stage for evaluation.

The Director of National Intelligence.

Responding to the 9/11 Report, Congress passed the Intelligence Reform and Terrorism Prevention Act of 2004. It amended the 1947 National Security Act, restructured the Intelligence Community (IC), and created an Office of Director of National Intelligence to coordinate all intelligence activities. The law also stripped the title of director of central intelligence (DCI) from the head of the CIA, who would now only head that agency. The new director of national intelligence (DNI) assumed all the coordinating functions of the DCI and became the principal adviser to the president and the National Security Council. The DNI also oversees and directs the National Intelligence Program.

The first director of national intelligence, John D. Negroponte, took office in 2005 and soon clashed with then director of the CIA, Porter Goss, over his reluctance to transfer CIA personnel and resources to the DNI.[35] Some observers doubted that the Office of Director of National Intelligence had enough clout to manage the more powerful spy agencies—such as the CIA and NSA—it supposedly supervised. Negroponte left in 2007 for a lesser rank at the State Department. Admiral John Michael McConnell replaced him.

The Central Intelligence Agency.

Before World War II, the United States had no permanent agency specifically charged with gathering intelligence about the actions and intentions of foreign powers. After the war, when America began to play a much greater international role and feared the spread of communism, Congress created the Central Intelligence Agency to collect information and to draw on intelligence activities in other departments and agencies.

Most material obtained by the CIA comes from readily available sources: statistical abstracts, books, and newspapers. The agency's Intelligence Directorate is responsible for these overt (open) activities in collecting and processing information. The CIA's charter also empowers it "to perform such other functions and duties related to intelligence affecting the national security as the National Security Council shall direct." This vague clause has been used to justify the agency's covert (secret) activities undertaken in foreign countries by its Operations Directorate. These activities have included espionage, coups, assassination plots, wiretaps, interception of mail, and infiltration of protest groups.

Covert operations raise both moral and legal questions for a democracy. Allen Dulles, President Eisenhower's CIA director, once called these operations "an essential part of the free world's struggle against communism." Are they equally important in a post–Cold War world? Can they be reconciled with the principle of checks and balances in American government? When government engages in clandestine actions, are the people able to hold their government accountable for its actions? Prior to the September 11 terrorist attack, one analyst argued that "the Cold War may be over, but the U.S. need for accurate information about the world remains acute."[36]

After September 11, some accused the CIA of neglecting covert intelligence activities (such as infiltrating terrorist organizations abroad), and blame centered on Director George J. Tenet, who had led the CIA since 1997. But President Bush trusted Tenet, who had mobilized the agency for the successful war in Afghanistan.[37] Tenet said it was a "slam dunk case" that Iraq had weapons of mass destruction.[38] When the U.S. chief weapons inspector failed to find major stockpiles of weapons of mass destruction and said, "Clearly, the intelligence that we went to war on was inaccurate, wrong," Tenet's position deteriorated.[39]

Tenet resigned in the summer of 2004. President Bush's replacement, Porter Goss (chair of the House Intelligence Committee and former CIA agent) lasted only nineteen months before resigning in May 2006 after losing his power struggle with Negroponte. Bush promptly nominated Negroponte's second-in-command, Air Force General Michael V. Hayden and former director of the National Security Agency, to head the CIA. The CIA usually had a civilian head, and General Hayden was confirmed over opposition. Although Hayden drew criticism for actions while head of the NSA, the electronic surveillance organization, in 2007 he ordered release of "the family jewels"—a disturbing 700-page report on domestic wiretapping, spying on journalists and protesters, and failed assassination plots in the 1960s and 1970s.[40]

The National Security Agency. Created in 1952, the National Security Agency today conducts SIGINT—SIGnals INTelligence—using supercomputers, satellites, and other high-tech equipment for *foreign* (outside the United States) electronic intelligence surveillance. (This activity contrasts with the CIA's focus on HUMINT—HUMan INTelligence.) NSA's work is highly secret; the joke is that NSA stands for "No Such Agency." Although it keeps a lower profile than the CIA, NSA has more employees and a much larger budget. Located in the Defense Department, its directors have always been high-ranking military officers. Lieutenant General Michael Hayden headed NSA for two years before leaving in April 2005 to assist Negroponte in the Office of Director of National

Intelligence, with promotion to general. He was succeeded by another lieutenant general, Keith B. Alexander. While head of NSA, Hayden acquiesced in secret electronic eavesdropping on U.S. citizens without court warrants (see page 2) and then vigorously defended the program when it became public.[41] In May 2006, *USA Today* revealed that NSA had also secretly collected billions of *domestic* (not foreign) phone call records of millions of Americans from AT&T, Verizon, and BellSouth.[42] This activity appeared to conflict with NSA's mission and jeopardized General Hayden's Senate confirmation as head of the CIA.

The Intelligence Community is less communal than feudal. As witnessed in the clash between Negroponte (DNI) and Goss (CIA), agencies jealously guard their turf. On the horizon, moreover, is a brewing conflict between the Department of Defense and DNI over covert intelligence operations, which were traditionally done by the CIA. However, Secretary Rumsfeld at DOD charged a Special Operations Command—outside the control of the DNI—to conduct secret counterterrorism activities cloaked as military missions.[43] With DOD already spending 80 percent of the intelligence budget, members of both parties in Congress were worried that the military would dominate the spy world, especially with a weakened civilian CIA.

Other Parts of the Foreign Policy Bureaucracy

Government agencies outside the Intelligence Community provide input to making foreign policy. Due to globalization and the interdependence of social, environmental, and economic issues with political matters, many departments and agencies other than those described above now find themselves involved in global policy. For some, foreign affairs constitute their chief concern. The Agency for International Development (AID) oversees aid programs to nations around the globe. In doing so, AID works with a full range of other departments and agencies, including the Defense Department, the CIA, the Peace Corps, and the Department of Agriculture.

Other departments and agencies primarily concerned with domestic issues have become more active in the foreign policy arena. For example, the Department of Agriculture provides agricultural assistance to other countries and promotes American farm products abroad. The Department of Commerce tries to expand overseas markets for nonagricultural U.S. goods. In addition, the Department of Commerce administers export control laws to prevent other nations from gaining access to American technologies connected with national security (such as computers and military equipment). As trade has become a more important aspect of foreign policy, the role of the Commerce Department in promoting American business abroad has also grown. The Department of Energy monitors nuclear weapons programs internationally and works with foreign governments and international agencies such as the International Atomic Energy Agency to coordinate international energy programs. Recently it has also supported American energy companies trying to do business abroad.

An array of government corporations, independent agencies, and quasi-governmental organizations also participate in the foreign policy arena. These include the National Endowment for Democracy, an independent nonprofit organization, funded by Congress, to promote democracy in other countries; the Export-Import Bank, a government corporation that subsidizes the export of American products; and the Overseas Private Investment Corporation, an independent agency that helps American companies invest abroad.

This list of bureaucratic entities with foreign policy interests is by no means exhaustive, but it does suggest the complexity of the foreign policy–making machinery. Furthermore, as social and economic issues become more prominent on the global policy agenda, we can expect an increase in the involvement of agencies not traditionally preoccupied with foreign policy. Finally, states and localities have also begun to pay attention to international matters. Most state governments now have separate offices, bureaus, or divisions for promoting the export of state goods and attracting overseas investment into their state.[44] All this suggests that the line between domestic and foreign policy will become even more blurred.

★ A Review of U.S. Foreign Policy

Presidents come to office with an ideological orientation for interpreting and evaluating international events, and they tend to be more internationalist than isolationist in their orientation. Presidents also tend to fill the offices of secretary of state, secretary of defense, national security adviser, and director of the CIA with individuals who are tuned to the presidential wavelength. However, presidents must accept advice and receive consent from members of Congress, who tend to be more isolationist in their orientations. The political result is the nation's foreign policy. Of course, foreign policies change according to presidential and congressional views of "national interests" and according to whatever actions are thought appropriate for defending and advancing those interests. In examining America's role in foreign affairs, it is helpful to structure the review in terms of presidents and the shorthand labels attached to the nation's policies during their administrations.

Emerging from Isolationism

For most of the nineteenth century, American interests were defined by the Monroe Doctrine of 1823, in which the United States rejected European intervention in the Western Hemisphere and agreed not to involve itself in European politics. Throughout the 1800s, U.S. presidents practiced a policy of **isolationism,** or withdrawal from the political entanglements of Europe. American isolationism was never total, however. As the nineteenth century wore on, the United States expanded from coast to coast and became a regional power that was increasingly involved in Pacific and Latin American nations. Still, America's defense establishment and foreign policy commitments remained limited.

World War I was the United States' first serious foray into European politics. The idealistic rhetoric that surrounded our entry into the war in 1917—"to make the world safe for democracy"—cloaked America's effort to advance its interest in freedom of the seas. Such moralism (see page 389) has often characterized America's approach to international politics, and it was certainly reflected in Wilson's plan for U.S. entry into the League of Nations. When the Senate failed to ratify the treaty needed for entry, America's brief moment of internationalism ended. Until World War II, America continued to define its security interests narrowly and needed only a small military establishment to defend them.

World War II dramatically changed America's orientation toward the rest of the world. The United States emerged from the war a superpower, and its national security interests extended across the world. The country also confronted

isolationism A foreign policy of withdrawal from international political affairs.

The Same in Any Language

These three World War I posters (from Germany, Great Britain, and the United States) were used to persuade men to join the army. Interestingly, all employed the same psychological technique: pointing at viewers to make each individual feel the appeal personally. *(Photosearch)*

INTERACTIVE 20.1

AP *D-Day: Invasion of Normandy*

Cold War A prolonged period of adversarial relations between the two superpowers, the United States and the Soviet Union. During the Cold War, which lasted from the late 1940s to the late 1980s, many crises and confrontations brought the superpowers to the brink of war, but they avoided direct military conflict with each other.

containment The basic U.S. policy toward the Soviet Union during the Cold War, according to which the Soviets were to be contained within existing boundaries by military, diplomatic, and economic means, in the expectation that the Soviet system would decay and disintegrate.

North Atlantic Treaty Organization (NATO) An organization including nations of Western Europe, the United States, and Canada, created in 1949 to defend against Soviet expansionism.

a new rival: its wartime ally, the Soviet Union. In the fight against Hitler, the Soviets overran much of Eastern Europe. After the war, the Soviets solidified their control over these lands, spreading their communist ideology. To Americans, Soviet communism aimed to destroy freedom, and the prospect of Soviet expansion in Europe threatened international order. European conflicts had drawn the United States into war twice in twenty-five years. American foreign policy experts believed that the Soviets, if left unchecked, might soon do it again.

Cold War and Containment

To frustrate Soviet expansionist designs, Americans prepared to wage a new kind of war: not an actual shooting war, or "hot war," but a **Cold War,** characterized by suspicion, rivalry, mutual ideological revulsion, and a military buildup between the two superpowers, but no shooting. The United States waged its Cold War on a policy of **containment,** or holding Soviet power in check.[45]

The policy of containment had military, economic, and political dimensions. Militarily, the United States committed itself to high defense expenditures, including maintaining a large fighting force with troops stationed around the world. Economically, the United States backed the establishment of an international economic system that relied on free trade, fixed currency exchange rates, and America's ability to act as banker for the world. This system, plus an aid program to rebuild Europe (the Marshall Plan), fueled recovery and reduced the economic appeal of communism. Politically, the United States forged numerous alliances against Soviet aggression. The first treaty of alliance (1949) created the **North Atlantic Treaty Organization (NATO),** dedicated to the defense of member countries in Europe and North America. In addition, the

United States tried to use international institutions such as the United Nations as instruments of containment. Because the Soviets had veto power in the U.N. Security Council, the United States was rarely able to use the United Nations as anything more than a sounding board to express anti-Soviet feelings.

In the first decades of the Cold War, the United States relied on its weapons superiority to implement a policy of nuclear deterrence. It discouraged Soviet expansion by threatening to use nuclear weapons to retaliate against Soviet power, which had also acquired nuclear capabilities. By the late 1960s, both nations had enough weapons to destroy each other. This led to a MAD (mutual assured destruction) situation: a first strike from either nation would result in the complete annihilation of both sides.

In the 1950s and 1960s, many countries in the developing world were seeking independence from colonial control by Western nations, and the Soviets were paying close attention to these developing nations. They offered to help forces involved in these "wars of national liberation," that is, wars fought to end colonialism. To counter the Soviets, the United States followed policies aimed at **nation building:** strengthening the opponents of communism in newly emerging nations (the so-called Third World) by promoting democratic reforms and shoring up their economies.

Vietnam and the Challenge to the Cold War Consensus

Soviet support for wars of national liberation conflicted with American nation building in Vietnam. There, the United States tried to strengthen noncommunist institutions in South Vietnam to prevent a takeover by Soviet-backed forces from North Vietnam and their communist allies in the south, the Viet Cong. The Cold War turned hot in Vietnam by the mid-1960s. Over 58,000 American lives were lost before the United States withdrew in 1973. The Vietnam War badly damaged the Cold War consensus on containment, both abroad and at home. Some American critics charged that the government lacked the will to use enough military force to win. Others argued that America relied on military force to solve what were really political problems. Still others objected that America was intervening in a civil war rather than blocking Soviet expansion. In short, Americans disagreed passionately on what to do in Vietnam and how to do it. After signing a peace agreement in 1973, the United States pulled its forces out of Vietnam, and in 1975, north and south were joined under a communist regime.

As the war in Vietnam wore on, President Nixon and his chief foreign policy adviser (and later secretary of state), Henry Kissinger, overhauled American foreign policy under the **Nixon Doctrine.** Now the United States would intervene only where "it makes a real difference and is considered in our interest."[46] A student of European diplomatic history, Kissinger believed that peace prevailed when the great nations maintained a balance of power among themselves. Nixon and Kissinger sought to create a similar framework for peace among the world's most powerful nations. To this end, they pursued a policy of **détente** (a relaxing of tensions between rivals) with the Soviet Union and ended decades of U.S. hostility toward communist China. The brief period of détente saw the conclusion of a major arms agreement, the Strategic Arms Limitation Treaty (SALT I), in 1972. This pact limited the growth of strategic nuclear weapons. The thaw in the Cold War also witnessed greater cooperation between the United States and the Soviet Union in other spheres, including a joint space mission.

nation building A policy once thought to shore up Third World countries economically and democratically, thereby making them less attractive targets for Soviet opportunism.

Nixon Doctrine Nixon's policy, formulated with assistance from Henry Kissinger, that restricted U.S. military intervention abroad absent a threat to its vital national interests.

détente A reduction of tensions. This term is particularly used to refer to a reduction of tensions between the United States and the Soviet Union in the early 1970s during the Nixon administration.

President Jimmy Carter's stance on foreign policy from 1977 to 1979 differed substantially from that of his predecessors. He downplayed the Soviet threat, seeing revolutions in Nicaragua and Iran as products of internal forces, not Soviet involvement. In contrast to Nixon and Kissinger, Carter was criticized as being overly idealistic. He emphasized human rights, admonishing both friends and enemies with poor human rights records. He usually leaned toward open rather than secret diplomacy. Nonetheless, his greatest foreign policy achievement—peace between Egypt and Israel—resulted from closed negotiations he arranged between Egyptian president Anwar Sadat and Israeli premier Menachem Begin at Camp David.

In many ways, Carter's foreign policy reflected the influence of the Vietnam syndrome—a crisis of confidence that resulted from America's failure in Vietnam and the breakdown of the Cold War consensus about America's role in the world. For example, his administration deemphasized the use of military force but could offer no effective alternatives in late 1979 when Iranians took American diplomats hostage and when the Soviets invaded Afghanistan.

The End of the Cold War

Carter's successor, Ronald Reagan, came to the Oval Office in 1981 untroubled by the Vietnam syndrome. He believed that the Soviets were responsible for most of the evil in the world. Attributing instability in Central America, Africa, and Afghanistan to Soviet meddling, he argued that the best way to combat the Soviet threat was to renew and demonstrate American military strength—a policy of **peace through strength.** Increased defense spending focused on major new weapons systems, such as the Strategic Defense Initiative (dubbed the "Star Wars" program), a new space-based missile defense system. The Reagan administration argued that its massive military buildup was both a deterrent and a bargaining chip to use in talks with the Soviets. During this period, the Cold War climate once again grew chilly. Things changed when Mikhail Gorbachev came to power in the Soviet Union in 1985. Gorbachev wished to reduce his nation's commitments abroad so it could concentrate on needed domestic reforms. By the end of Reagan's second term, the United States and the Soviet Union had concluded agreements outlawing intermediate-range nuclear forces (the INF Treaty) and providing for a Soviet military pullout from Afghanistan.[47]

In 1989, only months after Reagan left office, the Berlin Wall was torn down, symbolizing the end of the Cold War. The conventional view is that the Cold War ended and America won.[48] Some believe that communism collapsed because of Reagan's policies. Others insist that the appeal of Western affluence, Gorbachev's own new thinking, and a shared interest in overcoming the nuclear threat led to the end of the Cold War.[49] Still others argue that both superpowers had lost by spending trillions of dollars on defense while neglecting other sectors of their economies.[50] Regardless of its explanation, the end of the Soviet threat raised the question about what would shape American foreign policy.

Foreign Policy Without the Cold War

In 1990, soon after George H. W. Bush became president, Saddam Hussein invaded Kuwait. Not only did Iraq attack an American friend, but it also threatened the U.S. supply of oil. Bush emphasized multilateral action, building a

peace through strength
Reagan's policy of combating communism by building up the military, including aggressive development of new weapons systems.

coalition of nations that included America's Western allies, Eastern European nations, many Arab states, and other developing countries. The United States also won approval for actions against Iraq from the U.N. Security Council. During the Cold War, the Security Council usually proved ineffective because the U.S. and U.S.S.R. could veto the other's action. However, the two superpowers cooperated against Saddam in this post–Cold War crisis. After the coalition launched its counterattack in January 1991, the war lasted less than two months. By the end of February 1991, Iraqi troops were driven out of Kuwait and into Iraq, but the ceasefire left Saddam Hussein in power.

Iraq's invasion of Kuwait constituted a visible, vital threat to U.S. interests and galvanized Americans in support of President Bush's military action to repel the invasion. President Clinton, who came to the White House in 1993 with no foreign policy experience, enjoyed no galvanizing challenge and struggled to provide clear, coherent foreign policy leadership. Clinton's presidential campaign emphasized domestic concerns, but he soon found that messy crises in Somalia, Bosnia, Haiti, and then Kosovo absorbed much of his time. His administration replaced the Cold War policy of containment with a policy of **enlargement and engagement.** "Enlargement" meant increasing the number of democracies with market economies and also adding to the membership of NATO. "Engagement" meant rejecting isolationism and striving to achieve greater flexibility in a chaotic global era. But critics worried that the policy did not provide adequate guidelines about when, where, and why the United States should be engaged.[51] Even when Clinton acted with NATO to stop the genocidal violence in Kosovo, his policy was criticized. Nevertheless, Clinton himself drew praise for his efforts to end the fighting in Northern Ireland and for working to broker a peaceful end to the Israeli-Palestinian conflict.

The Hot War on Terrorism

Entering the presidency in 2001, George W. Bush had something in common with Bill Clinton: no foreign policy experience. The attack on America on September 11, 2001, transformed Bush's presidency, testing him in foreign affairs as no other previous president had been tested.[52] Addressing Congress on September 20, he vowed, "I will not yield; I will not rest; I will not relent in waging this struggle for freedom and security for the American people." That speech set forth Bush's plans—as leader of the world's only remaining superpower—for eliminating the threat to order posed by international terrorism. Bush implied that the sovereignty of other nations would not limit the United States from acting as world policeman to eliminate terrorism.

Bush made international affairs the centerpiece of his administration.[53] He also presided over a brilliant campaign against Al Qaeda in Afghanistan. As documented in *Bush at War,* by Pulitzer Prize–winning reporter Bob Woodward, the United States did not strike back quickly and blindly at Al Qaeda after September 11.[54] The president and his advisers spent three weeks lining up international support and planning for a military response before launching airstrikes on October 7. Although the United States led the assault against the Al Qaeda network, it headed a truly international coalition against terrorism. The war in Afghanistan (which cost very few U.S. casualties) was effectively over by December 6. On December 20, Hamid Karzai arrived in Kabul to head an interim government with British Royal Marines in the vanguard of a United Nations force.

enlargement and engagement Clinton's policy, following the collapse of communism, of increasing the spread of market economies and increasing the U.S. role in global affairs.

Flushed with genuine success in Afghanistan, President Bush announced in September 2002 a new doctrine of **preemptive action:** "to act alone, if necessary, to exercise our right of self-defense by acting preemptively against . . . terrorists to prevent them from doing harm against our people and our country."[55] Bush explicitly scrapped the doctrine of containment in 2003 as invoked in his controversial doctrine of preemption and launched war on Iraq.[56]

In contrast to the two-month war in Afghanistan, the war in Iraq dragged on for more than three years, cost thousands of American lives, and produced little success apart from toppling Saddam Hussein. No weapons of mass destruction were destroyed (or found), and Iraq remained a place of violent death with an unstable government, dismal oil production, and crumbling infrastructure. Moreover, there was no timetable for removing U.S. troops. American public opinion turned against the president on Iraq three years after the war began. In May 2003, when Bush had declared that "combat operations were over," 74 percent of the public approved of the way he was handling the situation in Iraq. In May 2006, his approval fell to 29 percent.[57]

President Bush, nevertheless, defended his decision to invade Iraq. His 2006 *National Security Strategy* stated, "We choose to deal with challenges now rather than leaving them for future generations. We fight our enemies abroad instead of waiting for them to arrive in our country."[58] In *Plan of Attack*, Bob Woodward's book on the decision to invade Iraq, Bush is quoted as saying, "I am prepared to risk my presidency to do what I think is right."[59] Bush told Woodward that "it would take about ten years to understand the impact and true significance of the war." History may yet prove him right, but citizens at home and people abroad have doubts. Some see Bush's policy of preemptive action as heralding an "American Empire."[60] Citizens in many foreign countries turned against Bush's twist in American foreign policy (see "Compared with What? Disapproval of Bush's Foreign Policy and U.S. Global Leadership").[61]

From Foreign Policy to Global Policy

The end of the Cold War and the process of globalization have resulted in a fundamental shift in the nature of foreign policy. For the first time, U.S. foreign policy has taken on a truly *global* focus. We apply the term **global policy,** like *foreign policy,* to a general plan to defend and advance national interests, but global policy embraces a broader view of national interests. Whereas foreign policy focuses on security against foreign threats (mainly military but also economic threats), global policy adds social and environmental concerns to matters of national interest. Whereas foreign policy typically deals with disputes between leaders, ideologies, or states, global policy confronts more silent, cumulative effects of billions of individual choices made by people everywhere around the globe. Inevitably, global policy requires global action. The players are no longer competing alliances among nations but international organizations that cooperate on a worldwide scale.

Even the Reagan administration, which claimed credit for ending the Cold War, did not do well on issues outside the East-West confrontation. Until the mid-1960s, nations in the U.N. General Assembly had usually supported U.S. positions in their votes. As the United Nations expanded its membership to include many newly independent states, however, the United States and its Western European allies frequently found themselves outvoted. Under Reagan, the United States reduced its commitment to international institutions such as the United Nations and the World Court when they acted in ways that ran counter

preemptive action The policy of acting against a nation or group that poses a severe threat to the United States before waiting for the threat to occur; sometimes called the "Bush doctrine."

global policy Like foreign policy, it is a plan for defending and advancing national interests, but—unlike foreign policy—it includes social and environmental concerns among national interests.

Compared with What?

Disapproval of Bush's Foreign Policy and U.S. Global Leadership

People in ten Atlantic countries and the United States were asked in 2005 about their feelings toward President Bush's "handling of international policies" and toward the United States exerting "strong leadership in world affairs." This chart shows the percentage in each country that *disapproved* of Bush's policies and thought it *undesir-* *able* that the United States lead in world affairs. Two facts stand out: (1) respondents in all eleven nations were more negative about Bush's policies than about U.S. leadership, and (2) respondents in all countries but the United States had majorities or substantial minorities opposed to U.S. leadership in world affairs.

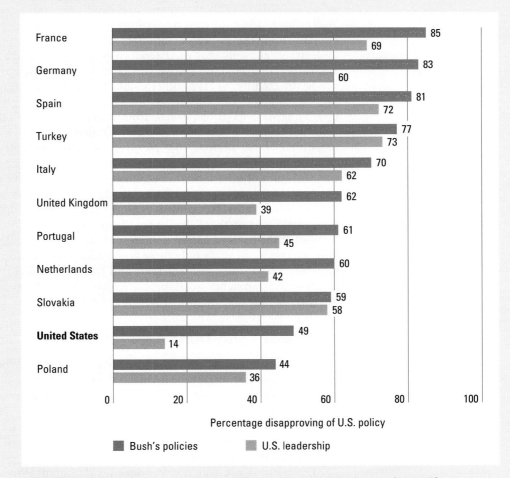

Source: "Transatlantic Trends Overview 2005," available at <http://www.transatlantictrends.org/>. The surveys were taken in May and June 2005. These were the questions: "Do you approve or disapprove of the way the President of the United States George W. Bush is handling international policies?" and "How desirable is it that the United States exert strong leadership in world affairs?"

to American interests. For example, the United States began to drag its feet on paying its U.N. assessments, briefly withdrew from the International Labor Organization, and rejected the jurisdiction of the World Court in cases involving U.S. activities in Nicaragua.

The United States did act as a world leader under President George H. W. Bush during the Gulf War. When the international political agenda shifted toward issues such as world trade, world poverty, the environment, human rights, and emerging democracy, American leadership was less evident—and less accepted. After the Cold War ended, other goals, such as promoting economic prosperity and preserving environmental quality, received increased attention as important components of our national interest. Since the September 11, 2001, terrorist attacks, military action has again assumed prominence in international affairs, but this was added on top of other global problems.[62]

★ Global Policy Issue Areas

Global issues like world poverty and environmental degradation have always existed, and they have moved up on national policy agendas because of globalization, the increased interdependence among nations. Nations today understand not only that their economies are tied to one another, but that the air we breathe, the illnesses we contract, and even the climate we experience can be affected by events in other countries. In addition to terrorism, globalization (according to one author) involves fighting five other festering wars: against illegal international trade, drugs, arms, transportation of aliens, and theft of intellectual property.[63] Consequently, global policy deals with **intermestic issues**—those that blend international and domestic concerns. Because global policy requires global action, domestic policies and practices become subject to policies and rules of international organizations. Conservative opponents of international organizations regard this global interaction as compromising their nation's sovereignty. Not only does global policy present different challenges to policymaking, but those challenges threaten the very concept of sovereignty that lies at the basis of national interest in traditional foreign policy. In this section, we choose to study only three broad topics within global interdependence: investment and trade, human rights and foreign aid, and the environment. International approaches to all topics involve salient threats to the sovereignty of the nations that take on global policies.

Investment and Trade

At the end of World War II, the United States dominated the world's economy. Half of all international trade involved the United States, and the dollar played a key role in underwriting economic recovery in Europe and Asia. America could not expect to retain the economic dominance it enjoyed in the late 1940s and 1950s, but it was able to invest heavily abroad even through the 1970s, prompting European concern that both profits and control of European-based firms would drain away to America.

During the Cold War, the economically dominant United States often made tactical use of economic policy in foreign policy. To shore up anti-Soviet forces in Western Europe and Japan, the United States lowered trade barriers for those countries. Meanwhile, the United States forbade the export to communist countries of products with possible military uses.[64] These policies were thought to

intermestic issues Issues in which international and domestic concerns are mixed.

Get the Lead Out
China produces 80 percent of the toys sold in the United States, including the popular Thomas and Friends Wooden Railway Toys—over 1.5 billion sold. In June 2007 China's RC2 Corporation warned parents to stop children from playing with these toys, which were painted with lead, a toxin dangerous to children if chewed or swallowed. The U.S. Consumer Product Safety Commission, which issued the recall, said that Chinese products accounted for 65 percent of all products recalled in 2007. As global trade increases, so does the problem of ensuring that goods sold in the United States meet U.S. manufacturing standards. (© Ryan Pyle/Corbis)

produce security gains that outweighed their economic costs. In the 1980s, however, a combination of tax cuts and increases in defense spending created gaping deficits in the federal budget. These deficits were partly financed by selling U.S. treasury obligations to foreigners. As they bought up American government debt, the value of the dollar soared, making American goods very expensive on the world market and foreign goods relatively cheap. The result was a shift in our balance of trade: the United States began to import more than it exported. And we continued to borrow heavily. With the recession in the late 1980s and declining interest rates, foreign firms became less interested in investing in the United States. The flow of foreign capital into the United States slowed, deepening American economic problems.

An increasingly severe problem is American dependence on oil imports. In 1960, the United States produced 7 million barrels of oil a day (more than Saudi Arabia and all the Persian Gulf states combined) and met over 80 percent of its own needs.[65] Due to increasing demand for oil and decreasing domestic supply, the United States today imports about two-thirds of the oil it consumes (see "Politics in a Changing World: Growing Dependency on Foreign Oil"). As other nations (especially China) increased their oil consumption, the price climbed from $30 per barrel in 2004 to over $70 in 2006. The increase in oil prices led to increased gasoline prices and inflationary pressures.

As the United States became entangled in the global web of international finance, it became more closely tied to other countries through international trade. In 1970, the value of U.S. foreign trade came to 11.2 percent of the nation's GDP; by 2004, it had reached 25 percent.[66] As foreign trade became more important to the American economy, policymakers faced alternative responses. Among them are free trade, fair trade, managed trade, and protectionism.

A true **free-trade** policy would allow for the unfettered operation of the free market—nations would not impose tariffs or other barriers to keep foreign goods from being sold in their countries. All trading partners would benefit under free trade, which would allow the principle of **comparative advantage** to work unhindered. According to this principle, all trading nations gain when

free trade An economic policy that allows businesses in different nations to sell and buy goods without paying tariffs or other limitations.

comparative advantage
A principle of international trade that states that all nations will benefit when each nation specializes in those goods that it can produce most efficiently.

Politics in a Changing World

Growing Dependence on Foreign Oil

In 1960, the United States supplied nearly all its petroleum needs from its own oil wells. By 1995, the United States imported more oil from foreign sources than it produced. In 1960, the United States accounted for 46 percent of the world's oil consumption of 21 million barrels. Despite doubling its own use by 2004, the U.S. share dropped to 25 percent of the world's use of over 82 million barrels. As demand for oil rose across the world, so did oil prices, leading to increased costs for our increasing energy needs.

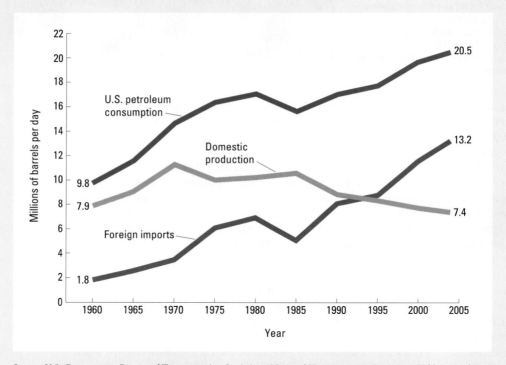

Source: U.S. Government, Bureau of Transportation Statistics, "National Transportation Statistics," Table 4–1, <http://www.bts.gov/publications/national_transportation_statistics/>.

INTERACTIVE 20.2

 Oil Dependency

INTERACTIVE 20.3

AP *War Over ANWR*

each produces goods it can make comparatively cheaply and then trades them to obtain funds for the items it can produce only at a comparatively higher cost.

Although the United States has not embraced a pure form of free trade, it has generally favored a liberal international trade regime in the last decades of the twentieth century. (In this case, the word *liberal* is used in its classic sense to mean "free.") American critics of free-trade policies complain that free trade has too often been a one-way street. America's trading partners could sell their goods in the United States while restricting their own markets through an ar-

Free Trade Means Free Speech
At its core, "free trade" means no tariffs on imported goods—which includes steel from China. During President Bush's fundraising visit to Pittsburgh in December 2003, protesters urged the president to keep the tariffs on foreign steel that he had imposed earlier. Nevertheless, Bush ended the tariffs under pressure from the World Trade Organization and from U.S. manufacturers who favored cheaper steel. *(Jeff Swensen/ Getty Images)*

ray of tariffs and nontariff barriers (NTBs)—regulations that make importation of foreign goods difficult or impossible by outlining stringent criteria that an imported product must meet in order to be offered for sale. The Japanese, for example, have been criticized for excessive use of NTBs. In one instance, American-made baby bottles were barred from the Japanese market because the bottles provided gradation marks in ounces as well as centiliters.[67]

Although the United States has sought to make trade freer by reducing tariff and nontariff barriers, Americans want more than freedom in the world market; they want order too. Policymakers committed to the idea of **fair trade** have worked to create order through international agreements outlawing unfair business practices. These practices include bribery; pirating intellectual property such as software, CDs, and films; and "dumping," a practice in which a country sells its goods below cost in order to capture the market for its products in another country. The World Trade Organization (WTO) was created in 1995 to regulate trade among member nations. Headquartered in Geneva, Switzerland, it has a staff of six hundred to administer trade agreements signed by its 149 member nations and ratified in their parliaments. According to the WTO, "These agreements are the legal ground-rules for international commerce. Essentially, they are contracts, guaranteeing member countries important trade rights. They also bind governments to keep their trade policies within agreed limits."[68] Originally, conservatives in the United States feared that the WTO's dispute settlement authority could be used to erode America's sovereignty and international trading position. Indeed, the WTO has ruled that some U.S. laws have violated its regulations, but the rulings were highly technical and with limited impact. For example, in early 2000, the WTO ruled against certain tax breaks to American exporters, and the United States offered to change its tax laws.[69] More recently, the WTO has been criticized also from the left for its secretive decision making and for neglecting labor rights and environmental concerns in making purely business decisions.[70]

Free trade and fair trade are not the only approaches to trade that American policymakers consider. America began the 1980s as the world's leading

> **?** **Can you explain why . . .**
> "free trade" is not necessarily "fair trade"?

fair trade Trade regulated by international agreements outlawing unfair business practices.

creditor and ended the decade as the world's leading debtor. For years the nation has run up huge balance-of-payments deficits with other nations. The largest of these deficits has been with Japan, but the U.S. debt to China has grown almost as large.[71] The trade acts mentioned above are ways the United States has tried to redress trade imbalances. Another method is **managed trade,** in which the government intervenes in trade policy in order to achieve a specific result, a clear departure from a free-trade system.

Domestic political pressure often bears on trade issues. Although free traders claim that the principle of comparative advantage ensures that eliminating trade barriers would make everyone better off in the long run, their opponents argue that imports threaten American industries and jobs. To guard against these hazards, **protectionists** want to retain barriers to free trade. For example, most unions and many small manufacturers opposed NAFTA. They believed that if tariffs were removed, Mexico, with its low labor costs, would be able to undersell American producers and thus run them out of business or force them to move their operations to Mexico. Either alternative threatened American jobs. At the same time, many Americans were eager to take advantage of new opportunities in a growing Mexican market for goods and services. They realized that protectionism can be a double-edged sword. Countries whose products are kept out of the United States retaliate by refusing to import American goods. And protectionism enormously complicates the process of making foreign policy. It is a distinctly unfriendly move toward nations that may be our allies.

Human Rights, Poverty, and Foreign Aid

NATO's campaign against ethnic cleansing in the Balkans in the late 1990s made clear that the Western democracies would go to war to protect human rights. This is especially true of America, which has long championed democracy and human rights. Support for moral ideals such as freedom, democracy, and human rights fits well with U.S. interests. These elements of liberal democracy permeate our political culture, and we relate better to nations that share them. But the relationship between America's human rights policy goals and its economic policy goals has often been problematic.

The ten big emerging markets (BEMs) that seem especially promising for U.S. investments and trade are the Chinese economic area (the People's Republic of China, Taiwan, and Hong Kong), Indonesia, India, South Korea, Mexico, Brazil, Argentina, South Africa, Turkey, and Poland. These nations have large areas and populations, are growing rapidly, are influential in their region, and buy the types of goods and services America has to sell. The Commerce Department took the lead in helping American businesses win contracts in these nations.[72] But engagement with these countries raises questions that go beyond America's economic interests. Some of the BEMs have dubious records in the areas of human rights, workers' rights, and child labor. Some are lax about environmental standards, intellectual property protection, or nuclear nonproliferation. To what extent should development of commercial ties with these nations override other policy objectives?

In addition to granting nations favorable trade terms, the United States can use other economic tools to pursue its policy objectives. These include development aid, debt forgiveness, and loans with favorable credit terms (see Figure 20.2). Assistance to developing countries also takes the form of donations of

managed trade Government intervention in trade policy in order to achieve a specific result.

protectionists Those who wish to prevent imports from entering the country and therefore oppose free trade.

FIGURE 20.2 Aid to Developing Countries

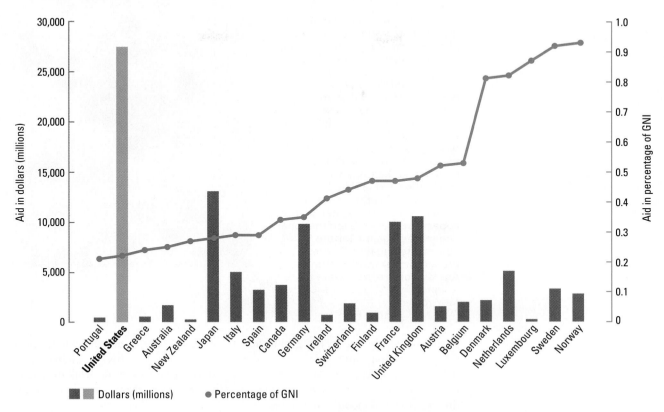

This graph compares U.S. aid to developing countries in 2005 with aid given by the other twenty-one member countries of the Development Assistance Committee of the Organization of Economic Cooperation and Development (OECD). These figures are reported for Official Development Assistance, a standard measure of grants and loans to a designated list of recipient nations. The data show the amount of aid in absolute dollars given by each country and the amount of aid as a percentage of the country's gross national income (GNI), with the nations ranked from most to least on percentage of GNI. Although the United States gave the most in dollars to assist developing countries, it gave almost the least (slightly more than Portugal) in percentage of national income.

Source: Organization for Economic Cooperation and Development, Reference DAC Statistical Tables, updated 14 April 2006, available at <http://www.oecd.org/document/11/0,2340,en_2649_34447 _1894347_1_1_1,00.html>.

American goods, which directly benefits the American businesses that supply the products. Inequality between rich nations and poor nations is growing. Figures show an increasing gap in income between the industrialized states of the North and the nonindustrialized states of the South.[73] This income gap between nations provokes arguments in international politics, just as issues of social inequality motivate those who favor social equality for minorities in domestic politics. Many people believe it is unjust for the developed world to enjoy great

A Case for the International Criminal Court?

The world was shocked at seeing this photo (among many others) of prisoner abuse in Iraqi detention facilities run by the United States in 2004. President Bush said he was appalled and disgusted at such photos and vowed that any soldiers involved in prisoner abuse would be prosecuted by the U.S. military. As discussed in the text, this is the type of behavior that might be taken to the International Criminal Court—had the United States joined the court and had it not initiated prosecution on its own. Indeed, in 2006 the United States appeared before the international Committee Against Torture to defend itself against charges brought under the Convention Against Torture, a separate treaty it signed in 1987. *(Courtesy of The New Yorker)*

wealth while people in the global South, or Third World, are deprived. Sheer self-interest may also motivate policymakers to address this problem. Great disparities in wealth between the developed and developing nations may lead to political instability and disorder, and thus threaten the interests of the industrially developed democracies.

In times of fiscal austerity, foreign aid is an easy target for budget cuts. Foreign aid tends to be unpopular, partly because recipients do not vote in American elections and because American citizens overestimate what the nation spends on aid. In repeated national surveys, about half the respondents believe that at least 15 percent of the federal budget went to foreign aid. Half also think it would be appropriate to devote 5 percent of the budget to foreign aid and that 3 percent would be too little. In actuality, far less than 1 percent of the federal budget goes to foreign aid.[74] Figure 20.2 shows how America's aid to developing countries stacks up against the contributions of other developed nations.

Late in his administration, Clinton signed a treaty to establish the International Criminal Court, the world's first standing court with jurisdiction over individuals charged with genocide and other crimes against humanity. Conservatives and the armed services feared that American troops abroad could be vulnerable to prosecution as a result of military operations. George W. Bush not only failed to submit the treaty to the Senate but also announced that he "unsigned" it in 2002 when the sixtieth nation ratified the treaty and the International Criminal Court became a reality.[75] In 2005, ninety-nine countries—but not the United States—were members.[76] Moreover, the United States suspended military assistance to thirty-five of the member nations for not pledging immunity to Americans if brought before the court.[77]

The Environment

Environmental issues pose new and vexing challenges for foreign policy makers. The value conflict of freedom versus order, which we have seen in domestic politics, surfaced in the international arena. In the prototypical example, wealthy industrialized nations, which polluted the world environment in the process of industrializing, tell Third World nations that *they* cannot burn fossil fuels to develop themselves because that would further pollute the environment. Leaders in developing countries do not appreciate limits on their freedom to industrialize—limits that serve the developed world's definition of global order.

The United States, as the richest, most powerful nation on Earth, often drew attacks from developed and underdeveloped nations alike for claiming special privileges in international agreements widely accepted by other nations. The 1992 United Nations Conference on Environment and Development in Rio de Janeiro, popularly known as the Earth Summit, illustrates the new issues in global politics and the problematic position of the United States. The Earth Summit produced the Biodiversity Treaty, which aimed at conserving the Earth's diverse biological resources through development of national strategies for conservation, creation of protected areas, and protection of ecosystems and natural habitats. President George H. W. Bush feared that the Biodiversity Treaty placed too many limits on U.S. patent rights in biotechnology and failed to protect U.S. intellectual property rights, so he refused to sign it. In the administration's view, the measures proposed at Rio would threaten the U.S. economy. Although Clinton signed the treaty and sent it to the Senate, the Senate did not vote on it, so the United States is not a party to the treaty.

A similar problem occurred with the 1997 understanding on global warming worked out by 170 nations in Kyoto, Japan. It committed three dozen industrialized nations to reducing their combined greenhouse gas emissions by at least 5 percent of their 1990 levels by 2012. In late 2000, when the United States proposed counting its forest lands as carbon sinks (based on the fact that trees capture gas emissions) to help meet its target of 7 percent reduction, the treaty talks failed. The industrialized nations in Europe had no forests and instead had to reduce greenhouse gases at the source: mainly tailpipes and smokestacks.[78] A representative for the European Union rejected the American proposal, saying, "We didn't come here to trade away the work done at Kyoto."[79] So even in the Clinton administration, which was more receptive to international concerns about the environment, domestic politics prevented that round of talks on controlling global warming from succeeding. The Bush administration studiously deemphasized global warming during its early years, but in 2007 the President backed "a long-term global goal" for lowering greenhouse gas emissions, recognizing the problem.[80]

 Can you explain why . . . the United States does not observe the 1992 Biodiversity Treaty, although the president signed it?

★ The Public and Global Policy

The president and Congress have always considered public opinion when making foreign policy: both had to face the public's wrath if blamed for policy failures. Historically, the public has paid little attention to traditional concerns of foreign policy—alliances, military bases abroad, and general diplomacy.[81] Except for issues of war and peace, other matters of national security, and the spread of communism, public opinion on foreign policy seldom affected domestic politics in any major way.

Today, globalization has made nations more interdependent in economic and social spheres, and major events in other countries can have a direct impact on life in the United States. If gangsters in Russia and China cooperate with mobs in Nigeria and Italy, the United States will soon experience an increase in smuggled aliens, drugs, and counterfeit goods.[82] The globalized media immediately communicate foreign affairs to the American audience. If the economy collapses in Asian countries, Wall Street reacts literally within hours. Accordingly, one might expect the U.S. public to pay much more attention to foreign affairs now than it did thirty years ago. Alas, this is not so.

The Public and the Majoritarian Model

To assess the state of public knowledge of and interest in foreign affairs, we draw on a 2004 survey by the Chicago Council on Foreign Relations, the ninth in a series begun in 1974.[83] The CCFR interviewed a random sample of 1,195 Americans and 450 knowledgeable individuals selected from Congress, academia, business, the media, labor unions, and religious organizations. The study permits comparisons of public attitudes over time and comparisons of public opinion with leaders' opinions. Immediately after 9/11, the 2002 survey showed a spike in the percentage of the public that was "very interested" in news of other countries, rising to 62 percent above the range of 44 to 53 in previous surveys. The 2004 survey, however, found a return to pre-9/11 levels, with only 53 percent being "very interested" in foreign news.[84] The 2004 survey asked specifically about globalization: whether "the increasing connections of our economy with others around the world" is "mostly good or mostly bad for the United States." Most of the public (64 percent) thought that globalization was mostly good, while 87 percent of the leaders thought it was mostly good for the United States. But 78 percent of the public—versus only 41 percent of the leaders—thought "protecting jobs of American workers" was "very important."[85] Only 14 percent of the public and 29 percent of U.S. leaders thought it was a "very important" goal to help "bring a democratic form of government to other nations"—a cornerstone of President Bush's foreign policy (see Chapter 1).

The majoritarian model of democracy posits that a nation's foreign policy should conform to public opinion. In a major study of influences on U.S. foreign policy, however, two scholars find that public opinion has little unique effect on foreign policy; the most important direct effect comes from internationally minded business organizations and their leaders.[86] This finding fits instead with the pluralist model of democracy.

Interest Groups and the Pluralist Model

What would be the nature of policies in a global society made under the pluralist model, in which government responds to competing groups? Ordinary citizens can become interested in foreign affairs when they learn how events in foreign lands can affect their economic interests or values. Often citizens learn from the more knowledgeable leaders of groups to which they belong. Both labor and business leaders in the auto industry may urge their followers to favor import restrictions on Japanese cars. Church leaders may warn of religious

WTO Toasts the Third World
Farmers in Third World countries contend that farmers in developed nations are aided by government subsidies, keeping farmers in poor countries from competing in international trade. This contention prompted protests that disrupted the September 2003 meeting of the World Trade Organization in Cancún, Mexico. *(© 2001 by permission of Chip Bok and Creators Syndicate, Inc.)*

persecution abroad. Aroused citizens often have their positions argued to law-makers in Washington by group representatives.

As described in Chapter 10, thousands of interest groups maintain offices in Washington. Even foreign firms, groups, and governments have hired lobbying firms to represent their interests in the U.S. capital. The influence of these groups varies with the issue. Interest groups are more effective at maintaining support for the status quo than at bringing about policy changes.[87] Because global policies often respond to new events abroad, one might expect these policies to form with little impact from interest groups. However, lobbying is also more effective when it deals with noncrisis issues of little importance to the public at large and can take place behind the scenes. Because the public has little interest in foreign affairs, interest groups can wield a great deal of influence on global policies outside matters of national security.

Passage of the 2000 China trade bill illustrates the pluralist model in action. The bill's roots can be traced to the presidency of Ronald Reagan, who favored free trade with China as a strategy for breaking down its communist system. President Clinton endorsed the idea and made the China trade bill a centerpiece of his administration. Early in his 2000 presidential campaign, Governor George W. Bush came out in support of the bill and urged Republicans in Congress to support it, saying, "This trade agreement is the work of 13 years and of three administrations" (one of which was his father's).[88]

The bill itself embodied a comprehensive 250-page agreement characterized by technical and complex provisions. The U.S. objective was to change the balance of trade with China: we bought large amounts of Chinese goods, but the Chinese bought little from the United States. For its part, China agreed to phase out import quotas and to reduce its tariffs on U.S. goods from 24.6 to 9.4 percent. In return, the United States promised (1) to support China's entry into the World Trade Organization (WTO) and (2) to ask Congress to extend normal trade relations (NTR) status to China on a permanent basis. China already had NTR status (China enjoyed the same trade terms as other nations), but it was extended on an annual basis, each year producing debate about whether the communist nation deserved such status.[89]

Are you asleep yet? Well, the China trade bill certainly did not keep the public awake. At the height of Congress's attention to the bill, only 46 percent of respondents in a national survey said that they had heard about it.[90] It was the kind of technical, complex bill that interested only certain segments of the public with a real or symbolic stake in the outcome, such as trade groups, human rights groups, specific businesses, labor unions, and lawyers (always lawyers). Lobbying on all sides was intense. Those favoring the bill included the Business Roundtable, the major lobbying arm of big business, and the U.S. Chamber of Commerce, which asked small-business executives in swing districts to pitch the deal to their House members. The Business Coalition for U.S.-China Trade gave weekly awards for grassroots campaigning efforts, and one winner was the Electronics Industry Alliance, which gave free T-shirts to those who signed a letter supporting the bill and supplied their zip code for electronic mass mailing to their representative in Congress.[91]

Those opposed to the bill included most labor unions, which denied that they wanted only to protect American jobs. They opposed the China trade bill, they said, because it did nothing to protect the rights and safety of Chinese workers. Incidentally, lax labor standards in China could invite U.S. companies to relocate there.[92] Opposition also came from religious groups, which argued that China "tortures and kills priests and nuns," and from human rights groups, which denounced "Slave State Red China."[93]

The bill passed the House in late May 2000 by a surprisingly large margin of 237 to 197. This bill, backed by a Democratic president, was supported by about 75 percent of Republicans and opposed by 65 percent of Democrats. (It cleared the Senate in September by a vote of 83 to 15, with both parties supporting it about equally.) Although the Bush administration in 2006 still favored trade with China, it faced in China a stronger economic and military rival than policymakers envisioned when the trade bill passed.[94]

Passage of the China trade bill clearly fit the pluralist model of democracy, not the majoritarian model. The public knew little about the bill, and those who did were divided about its merits.[95] But interested groups openly competed in presenting their arguments to members of Congress, which then decided the issue. As one seasoned reporter put it, "Members vote their districts": that is, they vote their districts if their constituents have an interest, and a trade bill is a singular foreign policy measure because the question of jobs gained and lost commands attention from lawmakers and constituents not much concerned about the rest of the world.[96]

Summary

The ideological orientations of key players on the stage affect the nation's global policy. The president is the leading actor, but Congress, and especially the U.S. Senate, have strong supporting roles. With shared responsibility among Congress, the executive branch, and various agencies, foreign policy can change from drama to farce if the cast is not reading from the same script. For two decades following World War II, from which America emerged as a superpower, there was a clear consensus: communism was the threat, and the goal was to contain Soviet expansion. The Vietnam War challenged that consensus, and Democrats and Republicans began to argue over foreign policy. In the post–Cold War era, international issues and domestic concerns became more closely entwined as a result of globalization, and foreign policy became embraced within broader issues of global policy. Strict notions of national sovereignty eroded as international organizations emerged to deal with global policies.

The September 11, 2001, terrorist attacks on America shifted attention back to military options for dealing with international threats. Although most American citizens want broad international backing for military action, the public supported President George W. Bush's 2003 invasion of Iraq (aided by British troops) to eliminate the threat from Saddam Hussein's weapons of mass destruction. When no such weapons were found after Hussein's defeat, the Bush administration was accused of acting with incorrect intelligence. *The 9/11 Commission Report* severely criticized the performance of the CIA, FBI, and Intelligence Community in the war on terrorism and proposed sweeping reforms that culminated in the creation of a director of national intelligence.

Global policy embraces more than military actions. Globalization has involved the nation more deeply than ever in international investments and foreign trade—especially as the U.S. government depends increasingly on foreign investments and the nation incurs increasing deficits in foreign trade. Issues of human rights and poverty in other countries are now linked more specifically to U.S. foreign aid, which tends to be lower (as a percentage of gross national income) than aid given by other developed countries. Environmental issues, such as global warming, often pit the United States (as the largest source of gaseous emissions) against other countries in negotiating and implementing international treaties (such as the Kyoto Treaty) to deal with worldwide health threats.

Generally, the majoritarian model of democratic policymaking does not fit well with foreign policy, and even less with global policy, because most citizens do not pay much attention to foreign affairs. Opinion leaders are closely attuned to globalization, however, and global policy tends to be hammered out on the anvil of competing groups, according to the pluralist model.

Internet activities and reading suggestions for this chapter are available on the *Online Study Center*

To complete the multimedia assignments for this chapter, go to AmericansGoverning.org.

Appendix

The Declaration of Independence, July 4, 1776
The Constitution of the United States of America

The Articles of Confederation, *Federalist* No. 10, *Federalist* No. 51, Presidents of the United States, Justices of the Supreme Court Since 1900, and Party Control of the Presidency and Congress, 1901–2007, are available on the

Online Study Center
General Resources

THE DECLARATION OF INDEPENDENCE, JULY 4, 1776

The unanimous Declaration of the thirteen United States of America

When in the course of human events, it becomes necessary for one people to dissolve the political bands which have connected them with another, and to assume, among the powers of the earth the separate and equal station to which the Laws of Nature and of Nature's God entitle them, a decent respect to the opinions of mankind requires that they should declare the causes which impel them to the separation.

We hold these truths to be self-evident, that all men are created equal, that they are endowed by their Creator with certain unalienable rights, that among these are life, liberty, and the pursuit of happiness. That to secure these rights, governments are instituted among men, deriving their just powers from the consent of the governed. That whenever any form of government becomes destructive of these ends, it is the right of the people to alter or to abolish it, and to institute new government, laying its foundation on such principles, and organizing its power in such form, as to them shall seem most likely to effect their safety and happiness. Prudence, indeed, will dictate that governments long established should not be changed for light and transient causes; and accordingly all experience hath shown, that mankind are more disposed to suffer, while evils are sufferable, than to right themselves by abolishing the forms to which they are accustomed. But when a long train of abuses and usurpations, pursuing invariably the same object evinces a design to reduce them under absolute despotism, it is their right, it is their duty, to throw off such government, and to provide new guards for their future security. Such has been the patient sufferance of these Colonies; and such is now the necessity which constrains them to alter their former systems of government. The history of the present King of Great Britain is a history of repeated injuries and usurpa-

tions, all having in direct object the establishment of an absolute tyranny over these States. To prove this, let facts be submitted to a candid world.

He has refused his assent to laws, the most wholesome and necessary for the public good.

He has forbidden his governors to pass laws of immediate and pressing importance, unless suspended in their operation till his assent should be obtained; and, when so suspended, he has utterly neglected to attend to them.

He has refused to pass other laws for the accommodation of large districts of people, unless those people would relinquish the right of representation in the legislature, a right inestimable to them, and formidable to tyrants only.

He has called together legislative bodies at places unusual, uncomfortable, and distant from the depository of their public records, for the sole purpose of fatiguing them into compliance with his measures.

He has dissolved representative houses repeatedly, for opposing, with manly firmness, his invasions on the rights of the people.

He has refused for a long time, after such dissolutions, to cause others to be elected; whereby the legislative powers, incapable of annihilation, have returned to the people at large for their exercise; the State remaining, in the meantime exposed to all the dangers of invasions from without and convulsions within.

He has endeavored to prevent the population of these States; for that purpose obstructing the laws for naturalization of foreigners; refusing to pass others to encourage their migration hither, and raising the conditions of new appropriations of lands.

He has obstructed the administration of justice, by refusing his assent to laws for establishing judiciary powers.

He has made judges dependent on his will alone, for the tenure of their offices, and the amount and payment of their salaries.

He has erected a multitude of new offices, and sent hither swarms of officers to harass our people, and eat out their substance.

He has kept among us, in times of peace, standing armies, without the consent of our legislatures.

He has affected to render the military independent of and superior to the civil power.

He has combined with others to subject us to a jurisdiction foreign to our constitution, and unacknowledged by our laws; giving his assent to their acts of pretended legislation:

For quartering large bodies of armed troops among us;

For protecting them, by a mock trial, from punishment for any murders which they should commit on the inhabitants of these states;

For cutting off our trade with all parts of the world;

For imposing taxes on us without our consent;

For depriving us, in many cases, of the benefits of trial by jury;

For transporting us beyond seas, to be tried for pretended offenses;

For abolishing the free system of English laws in a neighboring province, establishing therein an arbitrary government, and enlarging its boundaries, so as to render it at once an example and fit instrument for introducing the same absolute rule into these Colonies;

For taking away our Charters, abolishing our most valuable laws, and altering fundamentally the forms of our governments;

For suspending our own Legislatures, and declaring themselves invested with power to legislate for us in all cases whatsoever.

He has abdicated government here, by declaring us out of his protection and waging war against us.

He has plundered our seas, ravaged our coasts, burned our towns, and destroyed the lives of our people.

He is at this time transporting large armies of foreign mercenaries to complete the works of death, desolation, and tyranny, already begun with circumstances of cruelty and perfidy scarcely paralleled in the most barbarous ages, and totally unworthy the head of a civilized nation.

He has constrained our fellow-citizens taken captive on the high seas to bear arms against their country, to become the executioners of their friends and brethren, or to fall themselves by their hands.

He has excited domestic insurrection among us, and has endeavored to bring on the inhabitants of our frontiers the merciless Indian savages, whose known rule of warfare is an undistinguished destruction of all ages, sexes, and conditions.

In every stage of these oppressions we have petitioned for redress in the most humble terms: our repeated petitions have been answered only by repeated injury. A prince whose character is thus marked by every act which may define a tyrant, is unfit to be the ruler of a free people.

Nor have we been wanting in our attentions to our British brethren. We have warned them, from time to time, of attempts by their Legislature to extend an unwarrantable jurisdiction over us. We have reminded them of the circumstances of our emigration and settlement here. We have appealed to their native justice and magnanimity, and we have conjured them by the ties of our common kindred to disavow these usurpations, which would inevitably interrupt our connections and correspondence. They too have been deaf to the voice of justice and of consanguinity. We must, therefore, acquiesce in the necessity, which denounces our separation, and hold them, as we hold the rest of mankind, enemies in war, in peace friends.

We, therefore, the Representatives of the United States of America, in General Congress assembled, appealing to the Supreme Judge of the world for the rectitude of our intentions, do, in the name, and by the authority of the good people of these Colonies, solemnly publish and declare, That these United Colonies are, and of right ought to be, FREE AND INDEPENDENT STATES; that they are absolved from all allegiance to the British Crown, and that all political connection between them and the State of Great Britain is, and ought to be, totally dissolved; and that, as Free and Independent States they have full power to levy war, conclude peace, contract alliances, establish commerce, and do all other acts and things which independent States may of right do. And for the support of this declaration, with a firm reliance on the protection of Divine Providence, we mutually pledge to each other our lives, our fortunes and our sacred honor.

JOHN HANCOCK
and fifty-five others

THE CONSTITUTION OF THE UNITED STATES OF AMERICA*

[Preamble: outlines goals and effect]

We the people of the United States, in order to form a more perfect Union, establish Justice, insure domestic Tranquility, provide for the common defence, promote the general Welfare, and secure the Blessings of Liberty to ourselves and our Posterity, do ordain and establish this Constitution for the United States of America.

ARTICLE I
[The legislative branch]

[Powers vested]

Section 1   All legislative Powers herein granted shall be vested in a Congress of the United States, which shall consist of a Senate and a House of Representatives.

[House of Representatives: selection, term, qualifications, apportionment of seats, census requirement, exclusive power to impeach]

Section 2   The House of Representatives shall be composed of Members chosen every second Year by the people of the several States, and the Electors in each State shall have the Qualifications requisite for Electors of the most numerous Branch of the State Legislature.

No person shall be a Representative who shall not have attained to the Age of twenty five Years, and been seven Years a Citizen of the United States, and who shall not, when elected, be an Inhabitant of that State in which he shall be chosen.

Representatives and direct Taxes shall be apportioned among the several States which may be included within this Union, according to their respective numbers, *which shall be determined by adding to the whole Number of free Persons, including those bound to Service for a Term of Years and excluding Indians not taxed, three-fifths of all other Persons.* The actual Enumeration shall be made within three Years after the first Meeting of the Congress of the United States, and within every subsequent Term of ten Years, in such Manner as they shall by Law direct. The number of Representatives shall not exceed one for every thirty Thousand, but each State shall have at Least one Representative; *and until such enumeration shall be made, the State of New Hampshire shall be entitled to choose three, Massachusetts eight, Rhode Island and Providence Plantations one, Connecticut five, New York six, New Jersey four, Pennsylvania eight, Delaware one, Maryland six, Virginia ten, North Carolina five, South Carolina five, and Georgia three.*

When vacancies happen in the Representation from any State, the Executive Authority thereof shall issue Writs of Election to fill such Vacancies.

The House of Representatives shall chuse their Speaker and other Officers; and shall have the sole Power of Impeachment.

[Senate: selection, term, qualifications, exclusive power to try impeachments]

Section 3   The Senate of the United States shall be composed of two Senators from each State, *chosen by the Legislature thereof,* for six years; and each Senator shall have one Vote.

Immediately after they shall be assembled in Consequence of the first Election, they shall be divided as equally as may be into three Classes. The Seats of the Senators of the first Class shall be vacated at the Expiration of the second Year, of the second Class at the expiration of the fourth Year, and of the third Class at the expiration of the sixth Year, so that one-third may be chosen every second Year; *and if Vacancies happen by Resignation or otherwise, during the Recess of the Legislature of any State, the Executive thereof may make temporary Appointments until the next meeting of the legislature, which shall then fill such Vacancies.*

No person shall be a Senator who shall not have attained to the Age of thirty Years, and been nine Years a Citizen of the United States, and who shall not, when elected, be an Inhabitant of that State for which he shall be chosen.

The Vice-President of the United States shall be President of the Senate, but shall have no Vote, unless they be equally divided.

The Senate shall choose their other officers, and also a President pro tempore, in the absence of the Vice-President, or when he shall exercise the Office of President of the United States.

The Senate shall have the sole Power to try all impeachments. When sitting for that purpose, they shall be on Oath or Affirmation. When the President of the United States is tried, the Chief Justice shall preside: and no Person shall be convicted without the Concurrence of two-thirds of the members Present.

Judgment in Cases of Impeachment shall not extend further than to removal from the Office, and disqualification to hold and enjoy any Office of honor, Trust or Profit under the United States: but the Party convicted shall nevertheless be liable and subject to Indictment, Trial, Judgment and Punishment, according to Law.

[Elections]

Section 4   The Times, Places and Manner of holding Elections for Senators and Representatives shall be prescribed in each State by the Legislature thereof; but the Congress may

---

*Passages no longer in effect are printed in italic type.

at any time by Law make or alter such regulations, except as to the Places of chusing Senators.

The Congress shall assemble at least once in every Year, and such meeting *shall be on the first Monday in December, unless they shall by Law appoint a different Day.*

[Powers and duties of the two chambers: rules of procedure, power over members]

Section 5   Each House shall be the Judge of the Elections, Returns and Qualifications of its own Members, and a Majority of each shall constitute a Quorum to do Business; but a smaller Number may adjourn from day to day, and may be authorized to compel the Attendance of absent Members, in such Manner, and under such Penalties as each House may provide.

Each House may determine the Rules of its proceedings, punish its Members for disorderly behaviour, and with the Concurrence of two thirds, expel a Member.

Each House shall keep a Journal of its Proceedings, and from time to time publish the same, excepting such Parts as may in their Judgment require Secrecy; and the Yeas and Nays of the Members of either House on any question shall, at the Desire of one fifth of those Present, be entered on the Journal.

Neither House, during the Session of Congress, shall, without the Consent of the other, adjourn for more than three days, nor to any other Place than that in which the two Houses shall be sitting.

[Compensation, privilege from arrest, privilege of speech, disabilities of members]

Section 6   The Senators and Representatives shall receive a Compensation for their services, to be ascertained by Law, and paid out of the Treasury of the United States. They shall in all Cases, except Treason, Felony and Breach of the Peace, be privileged from Arrest during their Attendance at the Session of their respective Houses, and in going to and returning from the same; and for any Speech or Debate in either House, they shall not be questioned in any other Place.

No Senator or Representative shall, during the Time for which he was elected, be appointed to any civil office under the Authority of the United States, which shall have been created, or the Emoluments whereof shall have been increased, during such time; and no Person holding any Office under the United States, shall be a Member of either House during his Continuance in Office.

[Legislative process: revenue bills, approval or veto power of president]

Section 7   All bills for raising Revenue shall originate in the House of Representatives; but the Senate may propose or concur with Amendments as on other Bills.

Every Bill which shall have passed the House of Representatives and the Senate, shall, before it become a Law, be presented to the President of the United States; if he approve he shall sign it, but if not he shall return it with Objections to that House in which it originated, who shall enter the Objections at large on their journal, and proceed to reconsider it. If after such Reconsideration two thirds of that House shall agree to pass the Bill, it shall be sent, together with the Objections, to the other House, by which it shall likewise be reconsidered, and, if approved by two thirds of that house, it shall become a Law. But in all such Cases the Votes of both houses shall be determined by yeas and Nays, and the Names of the Persons voting for and against the Bill shall be entered on the journal of each House respectively. If any Bill shall not be returned by the President within ten Days (Sundays excepted) after it shall have been presented to him, the Same shall be a Law, in like Manner as if he had signed it, unless the Congress by their Adjournment prevent its Return, in which Case it shall not be a Law.

Every Order, Resolution, or Vote to which the Concurrence of the Senate and House of Representatives may be necessary (except on a question of Adjournment) shall be presented to the President of the United States; and before the Same shall take Effect, shall be approved by him, or being disapproved by him, shall be repassed by two thirds of the Senate and House of Representatives, according to the Rules and Limitations prescribed in the Case of a Bill.

[Powers of Congress enumerated]

Section 8   The Congress shall have Power

To lay and collect Taxes, Duties, Imposts, and Excises, to pay the Debts and provide for the common Defence and general Welfare of the United States; but all Duties, Imposts and Excises shall be uniform throughout the United States;

To borrow Money on the credit of the United States;

To regulate Commerce with foreign Nations, and among the several States, and with the Indian tribes;

To establish an uniform Rule of Naturalization, and uniform Laws on the subject of Bankruptcies throughout the United States;

To coin Money, regulate the Value thereof, and of foreign Coin, and fix the Standard of Weights and Measures;

To provide for the Punishment of counterfeiting the Securities and current Coin of the United States;

To establish Post Offices and post Roads;

To promote the Progress of Science and useful Arts by securing for limited Times to Authors and Inventors the exclusive Right to their respective Writings and Discoveries;

To constitute Tribunals inferior to the supreme Court;

To define and punish Piracies and Felonies committed on the high Seas, and offenses against the Law of Nations;

To declare War, grant Letters of Marque and Reprisal, and make Rules concerning Captures on Land and Water;

To raise and support Armies, but no Appropriation of Money to that Use shall be for a longer Term than two Years;

To provide and maintain a Navy;

To make rules for the Government and Regulation of the land and naval Forces;

To provide for calling forth the Militia to execute the Laws of the Union, suppress Insurrections, and repel Invasions;

To provide for organizing, arming, and disciplining the Militia, and for governing such Part of them as may be employed in the Service of the United States, reserving to the States respectively the Appointment of the Officers, and the Authority of training the Militia according to the discipline prescribed by Congress;

To exercise exclusive Legislation in all Cases whatsoever, over such District (not exceeding ten Miles square) as may, by cession of particular States, and the Acceptance of Congress, become the Seat of Government of the United States, and to exercise like Authority over all places purchased by the Consent of the Legislature of the State in which the Same shall be, for Erection of Forts, Magazines, Arsenals, dock-Yards, and other needful Buildings;—And

[Elastic clause]

To make all Laws which shall be necessary and proper for carrying into Execution the foregoing Powers, and all other powers vested by this Constitution in the Government of the United States, or in any Department or Officer thereof.

[Powers denied Congress]

Section 9 *The Migration or Importation of such persons as any of the States now existing shall think proper to admit, shall not be prohibited by the Congress prior to the Year 1808; but a Tax or duty may be imposed on such Importation, not exceeding $10 for each Person.*

The Privilege of the Writ of Habeas Corpus shall not be suspended, unless when in Cases of Rebellion or Invasion the public Safety may require it.

No Bill of Attainder or ex post facto Law shall be passed.

No Capitation, or other direct, Tax shall be laid, unless in Proportion to the Census or Enumeration herein before directed to be taken.

No Tax or Duty shall be laid on Articles exported from any State.

No Preference shall be given by any Regulation of Commerce or Revenue to the Ports of one State over those of another; nor shall Vessels bound to, or from, one State, be obliged to enter, clear, or pay Duties in another.

No Money shall be drawn from the Treasury, but in Consequence of Appropriations made by Law; and a regular Statement and Account of the receipts and Expenditures of all public Money shall be published from time to time.

No Title of Nobility shall be granted by the United States: And no Person holding any Office or Profit or trust under them, shall, without the Consent of the Congress, accept of any present, Emolument, Office, or Title, of any kind whatever, from any King, Prince, or foreign State.

[Powers denied the states]

Section 10 No State shall enter into any Treaty, Alliance, or Confederation; grant Letters of Marque and Reprisal; coin Money; emit Bills of Credit; make any Thing but gold and silver Coin a Tender in Payment of Debts; pass any Bill of Attainder, ex post facto law, or Law impairing the obligation of Contracts, or grant any Title of Nobility.

No State shall, without the Consent of Congress, lay any Imposts or Duties on Imports or Exports, except what may be absolutely necessary for executing its inspection Laws: and the net Produce of all duties and imposts, laid by any State on Imports or Exports, shall be for the Use of the Treasury of the United States; and all such Laws shall be subject to the Revision and Controul of the Congress.

No State shall, without the consent of Congress, lay any Duty of Tonnage, keep Troops or Ships of War in time of Peace, enter into any Agreement or Compact with another State, or with a foreign Power, or engage in War, unless actually invaded, or in such imminent Danger as will not admit of delay.

ARTICLE II
[The executive branch]

[The president: power vested, term, electoral college, qualifications, presidential succession, compensation, oath of office]

Section 1 The executive Power shall be vested in a President of the United States of America. He shall hold his office during the Term of four Years, and, together with the Vice President, chosen for the same Term, be elected as follows:

Each State shall appoint, in such Manner as the Legislature thereof may direct, a Number of Electors, equal to the whole Number of Senators and Representatives to which the State may be entitled in the Congress; but no Senator or Representative, or Person holding an Office of Trust or Profit under the United States, shall be appointed an Elector.

The Electors shall meet in their respective States, and vote by Ballot for two Persons, of whom one at least shall not be an inhabitant of the same State with themselves. And they shall make a List of all the Persons voted for, and of the Number of Votes for each: which List they shall sign and certify, and transmit sealed to the Seat of Government of the United States, directed to the President of the Senate. The President of the Senate shall, in the presence of the Senate and House of Representatives, open all the Certificates, and the Votes shall then be counted. The Person having the greatest Number of Votes shall be the President, if such Number be a Majority of the whole number of Electors appointed; and if there be more than one who have such Majority, and have an equal Number of Votes, then the House of Representatives shall immediately chuse by Ballot one of them for President; and if no Person have a Majority, then from the five highest on the List said House shall in like Manner chuse the President. But in chusing the President the Votes shall be taken by States, the Representation from each State having one Vote; a quorum for this purpose shall consist of a Member or Members from two thirds of the States, and a Majority of all the States shall be necessary to a Choice. In every Case, after the Choice of the President, the person having the greatest Number of Votes of the Electors shall be the Vice President. But if there should remain two or more who have equal Votes, the Senate shall chuse from them by Ballot the Vice President.

The Congress may determine the Time of chusing the Electors and the Day on which they shall give their Votes; which Day shall be the same throughout the United States.

No person except a natural born Citizen, or a Citizen of the United States at the time of the Adoption of this Constitution, shall be eligible to the Office of President; neither shall any Person be eligible to that Office who shall not have attained to the age of thirty-five Years, and been fourteen Years a Resident within the United States.

In cases of the Removal of the President from Office or of his Death, Resignation, or Inability to discharge the Powers and Duties of the said Office, the same shall devolve on the Vice President, and the Congress may by law provide for the case of Removal, Death, Resignation, or inability, both of the President and Vice President, declaring what Officer shall then act as President, and such Officer shall act accordingly, until the Disability be removed, or a President shall be elected.

The President shall, at stated Times, receive for his Services, a Compensation, which shall neither be increased nor diminished during the Period for which he shall have been elected, and he shall not receive within that Period any other emolument from the United States, or any of them.

Before he enter on the Execution of his Office, he shall take the following Oath or Affirmation:—"I do solemnly swear (or affirm) that I will faithfully execute the Office of the President of the United States, and will to the best of my Ability preserve, protect and defend the Constitution of the United States."

[Powers and duties: as commander in chief, over advisers, to pardon, to make treaties and appoint officers]

Section 2   The President shall be Commander in Chief of the Army and Navy of the United States, and of the Militia of the several States, when called into the actual service of the United States; he may require the Opinion, in writing, of the principal Officer in each of the executive Departments, upon any Subject relating to the Duties of their respective Offices, and he shall have Power to grant Reprieves and Pardons for Offences against the United States, except in Cases of Impeachment.

He shall have Power, by and with the Advice and Consent of the Senate, to make Treaties, provided two-thirds of the Senators present concur; and he shall nominate, and by and with the Advice and Consent of the Senate, shall appoint Ambassadors, other public Ministers and Consuls, Judges of the supreme Court, and all other Officers of the United States, whose Appointments are not herein otherwise provided for, and which shall be established by Law: but

Congress may by Law vest the Appointment of such inferior Officers, as they think proper, in the President alone, in the courts of Law, or in the Heads of Departments.

The President shall have Power to fill up all Vacancies that may happen during the Recess of the Senate, by granting Commissions which shall expire at the end of their next Session.

[Legislative, diplomatic, and law-enforcement duties]

Section 3   He shall from time to time give to the Congress Information of the State of the Union, and recommend to their Consideration such Measures as he shall judge necessary and expedient; he may, on extraordinary Occasions, convene both Houses, or either of them, and in Case of Disagreement between them, with Respect to the Time of Adjournment, he may adjourn them to such Time as he shall think proper; he shall receive Ambassadors and other public Ministers; he shall take Care that the Laws be faithfully executed, and shall Commission all the Officers of the United States.

[Impeachment]

Section 4   The President, Vice President and all civil Officers of the United States shall be removed from Office on Impeachment for, and on Conviction of, Treason, Bribery, or other high Crimes and Misdemeanors.

ARTICLE III
[The judicial branch]

[Power vested; Supreme Court; lower courts; judges]

Section 1   The judicial Power of the United States shall be vested in one supreme Court, and in such inferior Courts as the Congress may from time to time ordain and establish. The Judges, both of the supreme and inferior Courts, shall hold their Offices during good Behaviour, and shall, at stated Times, receive for their Services a Compensation which shall not be diminished during their Continuance in Office.

[Jurisdiction; trial by jury]

Section 2   The judicial Power shall extend to all Cases, in Law and Equity, arising under this Constitution, the Laws of the United States, and Treaties made, or which shall be made, under their Authority;—to all Cases affecting Ambassadors, other public Ministers and Consuls;—to all Cases of admiralty and maritime Jurisdiction;—to Controversies to which the United States shall be a Party;—to controversies between two or more States;—*between a State and Citizens of another State;*—between Citizens of different States— between Citizens of the same State claiming Lands under grants of different States, and between a State, or the Citizens thereof, and foreign States, Citizens or Subjects.

In all cases affecting Ambassadors, other public Ministers and Consuls, and those in which a State shall be Party, the supreme Court shall have original Jurisdiction. In all the other Cases before mentioned, the supreme Court shall have appellate Jurisdiction, both as to Law and Fact, with such Exceptions, and under such Regulations, as the Congress shall make.

The Trial of all Crimes, except in cases of Impeachment, shall be by Jury; and such Trial shall be held in the State where said Crimes shall have been committed; but when not committed within any State, the Trial shall be at such Place or Places as the Congress may by Law have directed.

[Treason: definition, punishment]

Section 3   Treason against the United States shall consist only in levying War against them, or in adhering to their Enemies, giving them Aid and Comfort. No Person shall be convicted of Treason unless on the Testimony of two Witnesses to the same overt Act, or on confession in open Court.

The Congress shall have power to declare the Punishment of Treason, but no Attainder of Treason shall work Corruption of Blood, or Forfeiture except during the Life of the Person attainted.

ARTICLE IV
[States' relations]

[Full faith and credit]

Section 1   Full Faith and Credit shall be given in each State to the public Acts, Records, and judicial Proceedings of every other State. And the Congress may by general laws prescribe the Manner in which such Acts, Records, and Proceedings shall be proved, and the Effect thereof.

[Interstate comity, rendition]

Section 2   The Citizens of each State shall be entitled to all Privileges and Immunities of Citizens in the several States.

A Person charged in any State with Treason, Felony, or other Crime, who shall flee from Justice, and be found in another State, shall on Demand of the executive Authority of the State from which he fled, be delivered up, to be removed to the State having Jurisdiction of the Crime.

No person held to Service or Labor in one State, under the Laws thereof, escaping into another, shall, in consequence of any Law or Regulation therein, be discharged from such Service or Labor, but shall be delivered up on Claim of the Party to whom such Service or Labor may be due.

[New states]

Section 3   New States may be admitted by the Congress into this Union; but no new State shall be formed or erected within the Jurisdiction of any other State; nor any State be formed by the Junction of two or more States, or parts of States, without the Consent of the Legislatures of the States concerned as well as of the Congress.

The Congress shall have Power to dispose of and make all needful Rules and Regulations respecting the Territory or other Property belonging to the United States; and nothing in this Constitution shall be so construed as to Prejudice any Claims of the United States, or of any particular State.

[Obligations of the United States to the states]

Section 4   The United States shall guarantee to every State in this Union a Republican Form of Government, and shall protect each of them against Invasion; and on Application of the Legislature, or of the Executive (when the Legislature cannot be convened), against domestic Violence.

ARTICLE V
[Mode of amendment]

The Congress, whenever two-thirds of both Houses shall deem it necessary, shall propose Amendments to this Constitution, or, on the Application of the Legislatures of two-thirds of the several States, shall call a Convention for proposing Amendments, which, in either Case, shall be valid to all Intents and Purposes, as part of this Constitution, when ratified by the legislatures of three-fourths of the several States, or by Conventions in three-fourths thereof, as the one or the other Mode of Ratification may be proposed by the Congress; Provided *that no Amendment which may be made prior to the Year One thousand eight hundred and eight shall in any Manner affect the first and fourth clauses in the Ninth Section of the first Article;* and that no State, without its Consent, shall be deprived of its equal suffrage in the Senate.

ARTICLE VI
[Prior debts, supremacy of Constitution, oaths of office]

All Debts contracted and Engagements entered into, before the Adoption of this Constitution, shall be as valid against the United States under this Constitution, as under the Confederation.

This Constitution, and the Laws of the United States which shall be made in Pursuance thereof; and all Treaties made, or which shall be made, under the Authority of the United States, shall be the supreme Law of the Land; and the judges in every State shall be bound thereby, anything in the Constitution or Laws of any State to the Contrary notwithstanding.

The Senators and Representatives before mentioned, and the Members of the several State Legislatures, and all executive and judicial Officers, both of the United States and of the several States, shall be bound by Oath or Affirmation to support this Constitution; but no religious test shall ever be required as a Qualification to any Office or public Trust under the United States.

ARTICLE VII
[Ratification]

The ratification of the Conventions of nine States shall be sufficient for the Establishment of this Constitution between the States so ratifying the Same.

Done in Convention by the Unanimous Consent of the States present, the seventeenth day of September in the Year of our Lord one thousand seven hundred and eighty-seven and of the Independence of the United States of America the twelfth. In WITNESS whereof We have hereunto subscribed our Names.

GEORGE WASHINGTON
and thirty-seven others

Amendments to the Constitution

[The first ten amendments—the Bill of Rights—were adopted in 1791.]

AMENDMENT I
[Freedom of religion, speech, press, assembly]

Congress shall make no law respecting an establishment of religion, or prohibiting the free exercise thereof; or abridging the freedom of speech, or of the press; or the right of the people peaceably to assemble, and to petition the Government for a redress of grievances.

AMENDMENT II
[Right to bear arms]

A well-regulated militia being necessary to the security of a free State, the right of the people to keep and bear arms shall not be infringed.

AMENDMENT III
[Quartering of soldiers]

No Soldier shall, in time of peace, be quartered in any house without the consent of the Owner, nor in time of war, but in a manner to be prescribed by law.

AMENDMENT IV
[Searches and seizures]

The right of the people to be secure in their persons, houses, papers, and effects, against unreasonable searches and seizures, shall not be violated, and no Warrants shall issue but upon probable cause, supported by Oath or affirmation, and particularly describing the place to be searched, and the persons or things to be seized.

AMENDMENT V
[Rights of persons: grand juries, double jeopardy, self-incrimination, due process, eminent domain]

No person shall be held to answer for a capital, or otherwise infamous crime, unless on a presentment or indictment of a Grand Jury, except in cases arising in the land or naval forces, or in the Militia, when in actual service in time of War or public danger; nor shall any person be subject for the same offense to be twice put in jeopardy of life or limb; nor shall be compelled in any criminal case to be a witness against himself, nor be deprived of life, liberty, or property, without due process of law; nor shall private property be taken for public use without just compensation.

AMENDMENT VI
[Rights of accused in criminal prosecutions]

In all criminal prosecutions, the accused shall enjoy the right to a speedy and public trial, by an impartial jury of the State and district wherein the crime shall have been committed, which district shall have been previously ascertained by law, and to be informed of the nature and cause of the accusation; to be confronted with the witnesses against him; to have compulsory process for obtaining Witnesses in his favor, and to have the assistance of counsel for his defence.

AMENDMENT VII
[Civil trials]

In Suits at common law, where the value in controversy shall exceed twenty dollars, the right of trial by jury shall be preserved, and no fact tried by a jury shall be otherwise reexamined in any Court of the United States, than according to the rules of the common law.

AMENDMENT VIII
[Punishment for crime]

Excessive bail shall not be required, nor excessive fines imposed, nor cruel and unusual punishments inflicted.

AMENDMENT IX
[Rights retained by the people]

The enumeration in the Constitution, of certain rights, shall not be construed to deny or disparage others retained by the people.

AMENDMENT X
[Rights reserved to the states]

The powers not delegated to the United States by the Constitution, nor prohibited by it to the States, are reserved to the States respectively, or to the people.

AMENDMENT XI
[Suits against the states; adopted 1798]

The Judicial power of the United States shall not be construed to extend to any suit in law or equity, commenced or prosecuted against one of the United States by Citizens of another state, or by Citizens or Subjects of any Foreign State.

AMENDMENT XII

[Election of the president; adopted 1804]

The electors shall meet in their respective States, and vote by ballot for President and Vice-President, one of whom, at least, shall not be an inhabitant of the same state with themselves; they shall name in their ballots the person voted for as President, and in distinct ballots the person voted for as Vice-President, and they shall make distinct lists of all persons voted for as President, and of all persons voted for as Vice-President, and of the number of votes for each, which lists they shall sign and certify, and transmit sealed to the seat of government of the United States, directed to the President of the Senate;—the President of the Senate shall, in the presence of the Senate and House of Representatives, open all the certificates and the votes shall then be counted;—the person having the greatest number of votes for President shall be the President, if such number be a majority of the whole number of electors appointed; and if no person have such majority, then from the persons having the highest numbers not exceeding three on the list of those voted for as President, the House of Representatives shall choose immediately, by ballot, the President. But in choosing the President, the votes shall be taken by States, the representation from each State having one vote; a quorum for this purpose shall consist of a member or members from two-thirds of the States, and a majority of all the States shall be necessary to a choice. And if the House of Representatives shall not choose a President whenever the right of choice shall devolve upon them, before *the fourth day of March* next following, then the Vice-President shall act as President, as in the case of the death or other constitutional disability of the President.—The person having the greatest number of votes as Vice-President shall be the Vice-President, if such number be a majority of the whole number of electors appointed; and if no person have a majority, then from the two highest numbers on the list the Senate shall choose the Vice-President; a quorum for the purpose shall consist of two-thirds of the whole number of Senators, and a majority of the whole number shall be necessary to a choice. But no person constitutionally ineligible to the office of President shall be eligible to that of Vice-President of the United States.

AMENDMENT XIII

[Abolition of slavery; adopted 1865]

Section 1   Neither slavery nor involuntary servitude, except as a punishment for crime whereof the party shall have been duly convicted, shall exist within the United States, or any place subject to their jurisdiction.

Section 2   Congress shall have power to enforce this article by appropriate legislation.

AMENDMENT XIV

[Adopted 1868]

[Citizenship rights; privileges and immunities; due process; equal protection]

Section 1   All persons born or naturalized in the United States, and subject to the jurisdiction thereof, are citizens of the United States and of the State wherein they reside. No State shall make or enforce any law which shall abridge the privileges or immunities of citizens of the United States; nor shall any State deprive any person of life, liberty, or property, without due process of law; nor deny to any person within its jurisdiction the equal protection of the laws.

[Apportionment of representation]

Section 2   Representatives shall be apportioned among the several States according to their respective numbers, counting the whole number of persons in each State, excluding Indians not taxed. But when the right to vote at any election for the choice of Electors for President and Vice-President of the United States, Representatives in Congress, the Executive and Judicial officers of a State, or the members of the Legislature thereof, is denied to any of the male inhabitants of such State, being twenty-one years of age and citizens of the United States, or in any way abridged, except for participation in rebellion, or other crime, the basis of representation therein shall be reduced in the proportion which the number of such male citizens shall bear to the whole number of male citizens twenty-one years of age in such State.

[Disqualification of Confederate officials]

Section 3   No person shall be a Senator or Representative in Congress, or Elector of President and Vice-President, or hold any office, civil or military, under the United States, or under any State, who, having previously taken an oath, as a member of Congress, or as an officer of the United States, or as a member of any State legislature, or as an executive or judicial officer of any State, to support the Constitution of the United States, shall have engaged in insurrection or rebellion against the same, or given aid or comfort to the enemies thereof. Congress may, by a vote of two-thirds of each house, remove such disability.

[Public debts]

Section 4   The validity of the public debt of the United States, authorized by law, including debts incurred for payment of pensions and bounties for services in suppressing insurrection or rebellion, shall not be questioned. But neither the United States nor any State shall assume or pay any debt or obligation incurred in aid of insurrection or rebellion against the United States, or any claim for the loss of emancipation of any slave; but all such debts, obligations, and claims shall be held illegal and void.

[Enforcement]

Section 5   The Congress shall have power to enforce, by appropriate legislation, the provisions of this article.

AMENDMENT XV
[Extension of right to vote; adopted 1870]

Section 1   The right of citizens of the United States to vote shall not be denied or abridged by the United States or by any State on account of race, color, or previous condition of servitude.

Section 2   The Congress shall have power to enforce this article by appropriate legislation.

AMENDMENT XVI
[Income tax; adopted 1913]

The Congress shall have power to lay and collect taxes on incomes, from whatever source derived, without apportionment among the several States, and without regard to any census or enumeration.

AMENDMENT XVII
[Popular election of senators; adopted 1913]

Section 1   The Senate of the United States shall be composed of two Senators from each State, elected by the people thereof, for six years; and each Senator shall have one vote. The electors in each State shall have the qualifications requisite for electors of the most numerous branch of the State legislatures.

Section 2   When vacancies happen in the representation of any State in the Senate, the executive authority of such State shall issue writs of election to fill such vacancies: Provided, that the Legislature of any State may empower the executive thereof to make temporary appointments until the people fill the vacancies by election as the Legislature may direct.

Section 3   This amendment shall not be so construed as to affect the election or term of any Senator chosen before it becomes valid as part of the Constitution.

AMENDMENT XVIII
[Prohibition of intoxicating liquors; adopted 1919, repealed 1933]

Section 1   After one year from the ratification of this article the manufacture, sale or transportation of intoxicating liquors within, the importation thereof into, or the exportation thereof from the United States and all territory subject to the jurisdiction thereof, for beverage purposes, is hereby prohibited.

Section 2   The Congress and the several States shall have concurrent power to enforce this article by appropriate legislation.

Section 3   This article shall be inoperative unless it shall have been ratified as an amendment to the Constitution by the legislatures of the several States, as provided by the Constitution, within seven years from the date of the submission thereof to the States by the Congress.

AMENDMENT XIX
[Right of women to vote; adopted 1920]

Section 1   The right of citizens of the United States to vote shall not be denied or abridged by the United States or by any State on account of sex.

Section 2   The Congress shall have power to enforce this article by appropriate legislation.

AMENDMENT XX
[Commencement of terms of office; adopted 1933]

Section 1   The terms of the President and Vice-President shall end at noon on the 20th day of January, and the terms of Senators and Representatives at noon on the 3d day of January, of the years in which such terms would have ended if this article had not been ratified; and the terms of their successors shall then begin.

Section 2   The Congress shall assemble at least once in every year, and such meetings shall begin at noon on the 3d day of January, unless they shall by law appoint a different day.

[Extension of presidential succession]

Section 3   If, at the time fixed for the beginning of the term of the President, the President-elect shall have died, the Vice-President-elect shall become President. If a President shall not have been chosen before the time fixed for the beginning of his term, or if the President-elect shall have failed to qualify, then the Vice-President-elect shall act as President until a President shall have qualified; and the Congress may by law provide for the case wherein neither a President-elect nor a Vice-President-elect shall have qualified, declaring who shall then act as President, or the manner in which one who is to act shall be selected, and such persons shall act accordingly until a President or Vice-President shall have qualified.

Section 4   The Congress may by law provide for the case of the death of any of the persons from whom the House of Representatives may choose a President whenever the right of choice shall have devolved upon them, and for the case of the death of any of the persons from whom the Senate may choose a Vice-President whenever the right of choice shall have devolved upon them.

Section 5   Sections 1 and 2 shall take effect on the 15th day of October following the ratification of this article.

Section 6   This article shall be inoperative unless it shall have been ratified as an amendment to the Constitution by the Legislatures of three-fourths of the several States within seven years from the date of its submission.

AMENDMENT XXI
[Repeal of Eighteenth Amendment; adopted 1933]

Section 1   The eighteenth article of amendment to the Constitution of the United States is hereby repealed.

Section 2   The transportation or importation into any State, Territory, or Possession of the United States for delivery or use therein of intoxicating liquors, in violation of the laws thereof, is hereby prohibited.

Section 3   This article shall be inoperative unless it shall have been ratified as an amendment to the Constitution by conventions in the several States, as provided in the Constitution, within seven years from the date of submission thereof to the States by the Congress.

AMENDMENT XXII
[Limit on presidential tenure; adopted 1951]

Section 1   No person shall be elected to the office of President more than twice, and no person who has held the office of President, or acted as President, for more than two years of a term to which some other person was elected President shall be elected to the office of President more than once. But this article shall not apply to any person holding the office of President when this article was proposed by the Congress, and shall not prevent any person who may be holding the office of President, or acting as President, during the term within which this article becomes operative from holding the office of President or acting as President during the remainder of such term.

Section 2   This article shall be inoperative unless it shall have been ratified as an amendment to the Constitution by the legislatures of three-fourths of the several States within seven years from the date of its submission to the States by the Congress.

AMENDMENT XXIII
[Presidential electors for the District of Columbia; adopted 1961]

Section 1   The District constituting the seat of Government of the United States shall appoint in such manner as the Congress may direct:

A number of electors of President and Vice President equal to the whole number of Senators and Representatives in Congress to which the District would be entitled if it were a State, but in no event more than the least populous State; they shall be in addition to those appointed by the States, but they shall be considered for the purposes of the election of President and Vice President, to be electors appointed by a State; and they shall meet in the District and

perform such duties as provided by the twelfth article of amendment.

Section 2   The Congress shall have the power to enforce this article by appropriate legislation.

AMENDMENT XXIV
[Poll tax outlawed in national elections; adopted 1964]

Section 1   The right of citizens of the United States to vote in any primary or other election for President or Vice President, for electors for President or Vice President, or for Senator or Representative in Congress, shall not be denied or abridged by the United States or any State by reason of failure to pay any poll tax or other tax.

Section 2   The Congress shall have the power to enforce this article by appropriate legislation.

AMENDMENT XXV
[Presidential succession; adopted 1967]

Section 1   In case of the removal of the President from office or of his death or resignation, the Vice President shall become President.

[Vice-presidential vacancy]

Section 2   Whenever there is a vacancy in the office of the Vice President, the President shall nominate a Vice President who shall take office upon confirmation by a majority vote of both Houses of Congress.

Section 3   Whenever the President transmits to the President pro tempore of the Senate and the Speaker of the House of Representatives his written declaration that he is unable to discharge the powers and duties of his office, and until he transmits to them a written declaration to the contrary, such powers and duties shall be discharged by the Vice President as Acting President.

[Presidential disability]

Section 4   Whenever the Vice President and a majority of either the principal officers of the executive departments or of such other body as Congress may by law provide, transmit to the President pro tempore of the Senate and the Speaker of the House of Representatives their written declaration that the President is unable to discharge the powers and duties of his office, the Vice President shall immediately assume the powers and duties of the office as Acting President.

Thereafter, when the President transmits to the President pro tempore of the Senate and the Speaker of the House of Representatives his written declaration that no inability exists, he shall resume the powers and duties of his office unless the Vice President and a majority of either the principal officers of the executive department(s) or of such other body as Congress may by law provide, transmit within four days to the President pro tempore of the Senate and the Speaker of the House of Representatives their written declaration that the President is unable to discharge the powers and duties of his office. Thereupon Congress shall decide the issue, assembling within forty-eight hours for that purpose if not in session. If the Congress, within twenty-one days after receipt of the latter written declaration, or, if Congress is not in session, within twenty-one days after Congress is required to assemble, determines by two-thirds vote of both Houses that the President is unable to discharge the powers and duties of his office, the Vice President shall continue to discharge the same as Acting President; otherwise, the President shall resume the powers and duties of his office.

AMENDMENT XXVI
[Right of eighteen-year-olds to vote; adopted 1971]

Section 1   The right of citizens of the United States, who are eighteen years of age or older, to vote shall not be denied or abridged by the United States or by any State on account of age.

Section 2   The Congress shall have power to enforce this article by appropriate legislation.

AMENDMENT XXVII
[Congressional pay raises; adopted 1992]

No law, varying the compensation for the services of the Senators and Representatives shall take effect, until an election of Representatives shall have intervened.

⭐ Glossary

administrative discretion The latitude that Congress gives agencies to make policy in the spirit of their legislative mandate. (13)

affirmative action Any of a wide range of programs, from special recruitment efforts to numerical quotas, aimed at expanding opportunities for women and minority groups. (16)

agenda building The process by which new issues are brought into the political limelight. (10)

agenda setting The stage of the policymaking process during which problems get defined as political issues. (17)

aggregate demand The money available to be spent for goods and services by consumers, businesses, and government. (18)

amicus curiae brief A brief filed (with the permission of the court) by an individual or group that is not a party to a legal action but has an interest in it. (14)

anarchism A political philosophy that opposes government in any form. (1)

appellate jurisdiction The authority of a court to hear cases that have been tried, decided, or reexamined in other courts. (14)

appropriations committees Committees of Congress that decide which of the programs passed by the authorization committees will actually be funded. (18)

argument The heart of a judicial opinion; its logical content separated from facts, rhetoric, and procedure. (14)

Articles of Confederation The compact among the thirteen original states that established the first government of the United States. (3)

attentive policy elites Leaders who follow news in specific policy areas. (6)

authorization committees Committees of Congress that can authorize spending in their particular areas of responsibility. (18)

autocracy A system of government in which the power to govern is concentrated in the hands of one individual. Also called monarchy. (2)

Balanced Budget Act (BBA) A 1997 law that promised to balance the budget by 2002. (18)

bill of attainder A law that pronounces an individual guilty of a crime without a trial. (15)

Bill of Rights The first ten amendments to the Constitution. They prevent the national government from tampering with fundamental rights and civil liberties, and emphasize the limited character of national power. (3)

bimodal distribution A distribution (of opinions) that shows two responses being chosen about as frequently as each other. (5)

black codes Legislation enacted by former slave states to restrict the freedom of blacks. (16)

block grants Grants-in-aid awarded for general purposes, allowing the recipient great discretion in spending the grant money. (4)

blog A form of newsletter, journal, or "log" of thoughts for public reading, usually devoted to social or political issues and often updated daily. The term derives from we**blog**. (6)

boycott A refusal to do business with a firm, individual, or nation as an expression of disapproval or as a means of coercion. (16)

budget authority The amounts that government agencies are authorized to spend for their programs. (18)

budget committees One committee in each house of Congress that supervises a comprehensive budget review process. (18)

Budget Enforcement Act (BEA) A 1990 law that distinguished between mandatory and discretionary spending. (18)

budget outlays The amounts that government agencies are expected to spend in the fiscal year. (18)

bureaucracy A large, complex organization in which employees have specific job responsibilities and work within a hierarchy of authority. (13)

bureaucrat An employee of a bureaucracy, usually meaning a government bureaucracy. (13)

business cycles Expansions and contractions of business activity, the first accompanied by inflation and the second by unemployment. (18)

cabinet A group of presidential advisers; the heads of the executive departments and other key officials. (12)

capitalism The system of government that favors free enterprise (privately owned businesses operating without government regulation). (1)

casework Solving problems for constituents, especially problems involving government agencies. (11)

categorical grants Grants-in-aid targeted for a specific purpose by either formula or project. (4)

caucus A closed meeting of the members of a political party to decide questions of policy and the selection of candidates for office. (8)

caucus/convention A method used to select delegates to attend a party's national convention. Generally, a local meeting selects delegates for a county-level meeting, which in turn selects delegates for a higher-level meeting; the process culminates in a state convention that actually selects the national convention delegates. (9)

checks and balances A government structure that gives each branch some scrutiny of and control over the other branches. (3)

citizen group Lobbying organization built around policy concerns unrelated to members' vocational interests. (10)

civil case A court case that involves a private dispute arising from such matters as accidents, contractual obligations, and divorce. (14)

civil disobedience The willful but nonviolent breach of laws that are regarded as unjust. (16)

civil liberties Freedoms guaranteed to individuals. (15)

civil rights Powers or privileges guaranteed to individuals and protected from arbitrary removal at the hands of government or individuals. (15, 16)

civil rights movement The mass mobilization during the 1960s that sought to gain equality of rights and opportunities for blacks in the South and to a lesser extent in the North, mainly through nonviolent, unconventional means of participation. (16)

civil service The system by which most appointments to the federal bureaucracy are made, to ensure that government jobs are filled on the basis of merit and that employees are not fired for political reasons. (13)

class action A procedure by which similarly situated litigants may be heard in a single lawsuit. (14)

class action suit A legal action brought by a person or group on behalf of a number of people in similar circumstances. (7)

clear and present danger test A means by which the Supreme Court has distinguished between speech as the advocacy of ideas, which is protected by the First Amendment, and speech as incitement, which is not protected. (15)

closed primary A primary election in which voters must declare their party affiliation before they are given the primary ballot containing that party's potential nominees. (9)

cloture The mechanism by which a filibuster is cut off in the Senate. (11)

coalition building The banding together of several interest groups for the purpose of lobbying. (10)

Cold War A prolonged period of adversarial relations between the two superpowers, the United States and the Soviet Union. During the Cold War, which lasted from the late 1940s to the late 1980s, many crises and confrontations brought the superpowers to the brink of war, but they avoided direct military conflict with each other. (20)

commerce clause The third clause of Article I, Section 8, of the Constitution, which gives Congress the power to regulate commerce among the states. (4)

common (judge-made) law Legal precedents derived from previous judicial decisions. (14)

communism A political system in which, in theory, ownership of all land and productive facilities is in the hands of the people, and all goods are equally shared. The production and distribution of goods are controlled by an authoritarian government. (1)

communitarians Those who are willing to use government to promote both order and equality. (1)

comparative advantage A principle of international trade that states that all nations will benefit when each nation specializes in those goods that it can produce most efficiently. (20)

competition and outsourcing Procedures that allow private contractors to bid for jobs previously held exclusively by government employees. (13)

concurrence The agreement of a judge with the Court's majority decision, for a reason other than the majority reason. (14)

confederation A loose association of independent states that agree to cooperate on specified matters. (3)

conference committee A temporary committee created to work out differences between the House and Senate versions of a specific piece of legislation. (11)

Congressional Budget Office (CBO) The budgeting arm of Congress, which prepares alternative budgets to those prepared by the president's OMB. (18)

congressional campaign committee An organization maintained by a political party to raise funds to support its own candidates in congressional elections. (8)

conservatives Those who are willing to use government to promote order but not equality. (1)

constituents People who live and vote in a government official's district or state. (11)

containment The basic U.S. policy toward the Soviet Union during the Cold War, according to which the Soviets were to be contained within existing boundaries by military, diplomatic, and economic means, in the expectation that the Soviet system would decay and disintegrate. (20)

conventional participation Relatively routine political behavior that uses institutional channels and is acceptable to the dominant culture. (7)

cooperative federalism A view that holds that the Constitution is an agreement among people who are citizens of both state and nation, so there is much overlap between state powers and national powers. (4)

Council of Economic Advisers (CEA) A group that works within the executive branch to provide advice on maintaining a stable economy. (18)

county governments The government units that administer a county. (4)

criminal case   A court case involving a crime, or violation of public order. (14)

critical election   An election that produces a sharp change in the existing pattern of party loyalties among groups of voters. (8)

Declaration of Independence   Drafted by Thomas Jefferson, the document that proclaimed the right of the colonies to separate from Great Britain. (3)

de facto segregation   Segregation that is not the result of government influence. (16)

deficit financing   The Keynesian technique of spending beyond government income to combat an economic slump. Its purpose is to inject extra money into the economy to stimulate aggregate demand. (18)

de jure segregation   Government-imposed segregation. (16)

delegate   A legislator whose primary responsibility is to represent the majority view of his or her constituents, regardless of his or her own view. (11)

delegation of powers   The process by which Congress gives the executive branch the additional authority needed to address new problems. (12)

democracy   A system of government in which, in theory, the people rule, either directly or indirectly. (2)

democratic socialism   A socialist form of government that guarantees civil liberties such as freedom of speech and religion. Citizens determine the extent of government activity through free elections and competitive political parties. (1)

democratization   A process of transition as a country attempts to move from an authoritarian form of government to a democratic one. (2)

department   The biggest unit of the executive branch, covering a broad area of government responsibility. The heads of the departments, or secretaries, form the president's cabinet. (13)

deregulation   A bureaucratic reform by which the government reduces its role as a regulator of business. (13)

descriptive representation   A belief that constituents are most effectively represented by legislators who are similar to them in such key demographic characteristics as race, ethnicity, religion, or gender. (11)

desegregation   The ending of authorized segregation, or separation by race. (16)

détente   A reduction of tensions. This term is particularly used to refer to a reduction of tensions between the United States and the Soviet Union in the early 1970s during the Nixon administration. (20)

direct action   Unconventional participation that involves assembling crowds to confront businesses and local governments to demand a hearing. (7)

direct lobbying   Attempts to influence a legislator's vote through personal contact with the legislator. (10)

direct primary   A preliminary election, run by the state government, in which the voters choose each party's candidates for the general election. (7)

discretionary spending   In the Budget Enforcement Act of 1990, authorized expenditures from annual appropriations. (18)

dissent   The disagreement of a judge with a majority decision. (14)

distributive policies   Government policies designed to confer a benefit on a particular institution or group. (17)

divided government   The situation in which one party controls the White House and the other controls at least one house of Congress. (12)

docket   A court's agenda. (14)

dual federalism   A view that holds that the Constitution is a compact among sovereign states, so that the powers of the national government and the states are clearly differentiated. (4)

earmarks   Federal funds appropriated by Congress for use on local projects. (11, 18)

economic depression   A period of high unemployment and business failures; a severe, long-lasting downturn in a business cycle. (18)

elastic clause   The last clause in Section 8 of Article I of the Constitution, which gives Congress the means to execute its enumerated powers. This clause is the basis for Congress's implied powers. Also called the *necessary and proper clause*. (4)

election campaign   An organized effort to persuade voters to choose one candidate over others competing for the same office. (9)

electoral college   A body of electors chosen by voters to cast ballots for president and vice president. (3, 8)

electoral dealignment   A lessening of the importance of party loyalties in voting decisions. (8)

electoral realignment   The change in voting patterns that occurs after a critical election. (8)

Elementary and Secondary Education Act of 1965 (ESEA)   The federal government's primary law to assist the nation's elementary and secondary schools. It emerged as part of President Lyndon Johnson's Great Society program. (19)

elite theory   The view that a small group of people actually makes most of the important government decisions. (2)

enlargement and engagement   Clinton's policy, following the collapse of communism, of increasing the spread of market economies and increasing the U.S. role in global affairs. (20)

entitlements   Benefits to which every eligible person has a legal right and that the government cannot deny. (18, 19)

enumerated powers   The powers explicitly granted to Congress by the Constitution. (3)

equality of opportunity   The idea that each person is guaranteed the same chance to succeed in life. (1, 16)

equality of outcome   The concept that society must ensure that people are equal, and governments must design policies to redistribute wealth and status so that economic and social equality is actually achieved. (1, 16)

equal rights amendment (ERA)   A failed constitutional amendment introduced by the National Women's Party in 1923, declaring that "equality of rights under the law shall not be denied or abridged by the United States or any State on account of sex." (16)

establishment clause   The first clause in the First Amendment, which forbids government establishment of religion. (15)

exclusionary rule   The judicial rule that states that evidence obtained in an illegal search and seizure cannot be used in trial. (15)

executive agreement   A pact between the heads of two countries. (20)

executive branch   The law-enforcing branch of government. (3)

Executive Office of the President   The president's executive aides and their staffs; the extended White House executive establishment. (12)

executive orders   Presidential directives that create or modify laws and public policies, without the direct approval of Congress. (12)

ex post facto law   A law that declares an action to be criminal after it has been performed. (15)

extraordinary majority   A majority greater than the minimum of 50 percent plus one. (3)

fair trade   Trade regulated by international agreements outlawing unfair business practices. (20)

Federal Communications Commission (FCC)   An independent federal agency that regulates interstate and international communication by radio, television, telephone, telegraph, cable, and satellite. (6)

Federal Election Commission (FEC)   A bipartisan federal agency of six members that oversees the financing of national election campaigns. (9)

federalism   The division of power between a central government and regional governments. (3, 4)

federal question   An issue covered by the U.S. Constitution, national laws, or U.S. treaties. (14)

Federal Reserve System   The system of banks that acts as the central bank of the United States and controls major monetary policies. (18)

feedback   Information received by policymakers about the effectiveness of public policy. (17)

feminization of poverty   The term applied to the fact that a growing percentage of all poor Americans are women or the dependents of women. (19)

fighting words   Speech that is not protected by the First Amendment because it inflicts injury or tends to incite an immediate disturbance of the peace. (15)

filibuster   A delaying tactic, used in the Senate, that involves speechmaking to prevent action on a piece of legislation. (11)

first-past-the-post election   A British term for elections conducted in single-member districts that award victory to the candidate with the most votes. (9)

fiscal policies   Economic policies that involve government spending and taxing. (18)

fiscal year (FY)   The twelve-month period from October 1 to September 30 used by the government for accounting purposes. A fiscal year budget is named for the year in which it ends. (18)

527 committees   Committees named after Section 527 of the Internal Revenue Code; they enjoy tax-exempt status in election campaigns if they are unaffiliated with political parties and take positions on issues, not specific candidates. (9)

foreign policy   The general plan followed by a nation in defending and advancing its national interests, especially its security against foreign threats. (20)

formula grants   Categorical grants distributed according to a particular set of rules, called a formula, that specify who is eligible for the grants and how much each eligible applicant will receive. (4)

fragmentation   In policymaking, the phenomenon of attacking a single problem in different and sometimes competing ways. (17)

franchise   The right to vote. Also called *suffrage*. (7)

freedom from   Immunity, as in *freedom from want*. (1)

freedom of   An absence of constraints on behavior, as in *freedom of speech* or *freedom of religion*. (1)

free-exercise clause   The second clause in the First Amendment, which prevents the government from interfering with the exercise of religion. (15)

free-expression clauses   The press and speech clauses of the First Amendment. (15)

free-rider problem   The situation in which people benefit from the activities of an organization (such as an interest group) but do not contribute to those activities. (10)

free trade   An economic policy that allows businesses in different nations to sell and buy goods without paying tariffs or other limitations. (20)

front-loading   States' practice of moving delegate selection primaries and caucuses earlier in the calendar year to gain media and candidate attention. (9)

gatekeepers   Media executives, news editors, and prominent reporters who direct the flow of news. (6)

general election   A national election held by law in November of every even-numbered year. (9)

gerrymandering Redrawing a congressional district to intentionally benefit one political party. (11)

globalization The increasing interdependence of citizens and nations across the world. (1)

global policy Like foreign policy, it is a plan for defending and advancing national interests, but—unlike foreign policy—it includes social and environmental concerns among national interests. (20)

good faith exception An exception to the Supreme Court exclusionary rule, holding that evidence seized on the basis of a mistakenly issued search warrant can be introduced at trial if the mistake was made in good faith, that is, if all the parties involved had reason at the time to believe that the warrant was proper. (15)

government The legitimate use of force to control human behavior; also, the organization or agency authorized to exercise that force. (1)

government corporation A government agency that performs services that might be provided by the private sector but that involve either insufficient financial incentive or are better provided when they are somehow linked with government. (13)

Government Performance and Results Act A law requiring each government agency to implement quantifiable standards to measure its performance in meeting stated program goals. (13)

Gramm-Rudman Popular name for an act passed by Congress in 1985 that, in its original form, sought to lower the national deficit to a specified level each year, culminating in a balanced budget in FY 1991. New reforms and deficit targets were agreed on in 1990. (18)

grant-in-aid Money provided by one level of government to another to be spent for a given purpose. (4)

grassroots lobbying Lobbying activities performed by rank-and-file interest group members and would-be members. (10)

Great Compromise Submitted by the Connecticut delegation to the Constitutional Convention of 1787, and thus also known as the Connecticut Compromise, a plan calling for a bicameral legislature in which the House of Representatives would be apportioned according to population and the states would be represented equally in the Senate. (3)

Great Depression The longest and deepest setback the American economy has ever experienced. It began with the stock market crash on October 24, 1929, and did not end until the start of World War II. (19)

Great Society President Lyndon Johnson's broad array of programs designed to redress political, social, and economic inequality. (19)

gridlock A situation in which government is incapable of acting on important issues. (12)

gross domestic product (GDP) The total value of the goods and services produced by a country during a year. (18)

hard money Financial contributions given directly to a candidate running for congressional office or the presidency. (9)

home rule The right to enact and enforce legislation locally. (4)

horse race journalism Election coverage by the mass media that focuses on which candidate is ahead rather than on national issues. (6)

impeachment The formal charging of a government official with "treason, bribery, or other high crimes and misdemeanors." (11)

implementation The process of putting specific policies into operation. (13, 17)

implied powers Those powers that Congress needs to execute its enumerated powers. (3, 4)

incremental budgeting A method of budget making that involves adding new funds (an increment) onto the amount previously budgeted (in last year's budget). (18)

incrementalism Policymaking characterized by a series of decisions, each instituting modest change. (13)

incumbent A current officeholder. (11)

independent agency An executive agency that is not part of a cabinet department. (13)

inflation An economic condition characterized by price increases linked to a decrease in the value of the currency. (18)

influencing behavior Behavior that seeks to modify or reverse government policy to serve political interests. (7)

information campaign An organized effort to gain public backing by bringing a group's views to public attention. (10)

infotainment A mix of information and diversion oriented to personalities or celebrities, not linked to the day's events, and usually unrelated to public affairs or policy; often called "soft news." (6)

inherent powers Authority claimed by the president that is not clearly specified in the Constitution. Typically, these powers are inferred from the Constitution. (12)

initiative A procedure by which voters can propose an issue to be decided by the legislature or by the people in a referendum. It requires gathering a specified number of signatures and submitting a petition to a designated agency. (7)

Intelligence Community Sixteen agencies in the executive branch that conduct the various intelligence activities that make up the total U.S. national intelligence effort. (20)

interest group An organized group of individuals that seeks to influence public policy. Also called a *lobby*. (2, 10)

interest group entrepreneur An interest group organizer or leader. (10)

intermestic issues Issues in which international and domestic concerns are mixed. (20)

invidious discrimination Discrimination against persons or groups that works to their harm and is based on animosity. (16)

isolationism A foreign policy of withdrawal from international political affairs. (20)

issue definition Our conception of the problem at hand. (17)

issue framing The way that politicians or interest group leaders define an issue when presenting it to others. (5)

issue network A shared-knowledge group consisting of representatives of various interests involved in some particular aspect of public policy. (17)

joint committee A committee made up of members of both the House and the Senate. (11)

judgment The judicial decision in a court case. (14)

judicial activism A judicial philosophy whereby judges interpret existing laws and precedents loosely and interject their own values in court decisions. (14)

judicial branch The law-interpreting branch of government. (3)

judicial restraint A judicial philosophy whereby judges adhere closely to statutes and precedents in reaching their decisions. (14)

judicial review The power to declare congressional (and presidential) acts invalid because they violate the Constitution. (3, 14)

Keynesian theory An economic theory stating that the government can stabilize the economy—that is, can smooth business cycles—by controlling the level of aggregate demand, and that the level of aggregate demand can be controlled by means of fiscal and monetary policies. (18)

laissez faire An economic doctrine that opposes any form of government intervention in business. (1)

legislative branch The lawmaking branch of government. (3)

legislative liaison staff Those people who compose the communications link between the White House and Congress, advising the president or cabinet secretaries on the status of pending legislation. (12)

liberalism The belief that states should leave individuals free to follow their individual pursuits. Note that this differs from the definition of *liberal*. (1)

liberals Those who are willing to use government to promote equality but not order. (1)

libertarianism A political ideology that is opposed to all government action except as necessary to protect life and property. (1)

libertarians Those who are opposed to using government to promote either order or equality. (1)

lobby See *interest group*.

lobbyist A representative of an interest group. (10)

majoritarian model of democracy The classical theory of democracy in which government by the people is interpreted as government by the majority of the people. (2)

majority leader The head of the majority party in the Senate; the second-highest-ranking member of the majority party in the House. (11)

majority representation The system by which one office, contested by two or more candidates, is won by the single candidate who collects the most votes. (8)

majority rule The principle—basic to procedural democratic theory—that the decision of a group must reflect the preference of more than half of those participating; a simple majority. (2)

managed trade Government intervention in trade policy in order to achieve a specific result. (20)

mandate A requirement that a state undertake an activity or provide a service, in keeping with minimum national standards. (4)

mandate An endorsement by voters. Presidents sometimes argue they have been given a mandate to carry out policy proposals. (12)

mandatory spending In the Budget Enforcement Act of 1990, expenditures required by previous commitments. (18)

market-driven journalism Both reporting news and running commercials geared to a target audience defined by demographic characteristics. (6)

mass media The means employed in mass communication; often divided into print media and broadcast media. (6)

means-tested benefits Conditional benefits provided by government to individuals whose income falls below a designated threshold. (19)

media event A situation that is so "newsworthy" that the mass media are compelled to cover it. Candidates in elections often create such situations to garner media attention. (6)

Medicaid A need-based comprehensive medical and hospitalization program. (19)

Medicare A health insurance program serving primarily persons sixty-five and older. (19)

minority rights The benefits of government that cannot be denied to any citizens by majority decisions. (2)

***Miranda* warnings** Statements concerning rights that police are required to make to a person before he or she is subjected to in-custody questioning. (15)

modified closed primary A primary election that allows individual state parties to decide whether they permit independents to vote in their primaries and for which offices. (9)

modified open primary A primary election that entitles independent voters to vote in a party's primary. (9)

monetarists Those who argue that government can effectively control the performance of an economy only by controlling the supply of money. (18)

monetary policies Economic policies that involve control of, and changes in, the supply of money. (18)

municipal governments The government units that administer a city or town. (4)

national committee A committee of a political party composed of party chairpersons and party officials from every state. (8)

national convention A gathering of delegates of a single political party from across the country to choose candidates for president and vice president and to adopt a party platform. (8)

national sovereignty "A political entity's externally recognized right to exercise final authority over its affairs." (1)

nation building A policy once thought to shore up Third World countries economically and democratically, thereby making them less attractive targets for Soviet opportunism. (20)

necessary and proper clause The last clause in Section 8 of Article I of the Constitution, which gives Congress the means to execute its enumerated powers. This clause is the basis for Congress's implied powers. Also called the *elastic clause.* (3)

New Deal The measures advocated by the Roosevelt administration to alleviate the Depression. (19)

New Jersey Plan Submitted by the head of the New Jersey delegation to the Constitutional Convention of 1787, a set of nine resolutions that would have, in effect, preserved the Articles of Confederation by amending rather than replacing them. (3)

newsworthiness The degree to which a news story is important enough to be covered in the mass media. (6)

Nineteenth Amendment The amendment to the Constitution, adopted in 1920, that ensures women of the right to vote. (16)

Nixon Doctrine Nixon's policy, formulated with assistance from Henry Kissinger, that restricted U.S. military intervention abroad absent a threat to its vital national interests. (20)

No Child Left Behind Act of 2001 (NCLB) The latest reauthorization of the Elementary and Secondary Education Act. (19)

nomination Designation as an official candidate of a political party. (8)

non-means-tested benefits Benefits provided by government to all citizens, regardless of income; Medicare and Social Security are examples. (19)

nonprofits Organizations that are not part of government or business and cannot distribute profits to shareholders or to anyone else. (17)

normal distribution A symmetrical bell-shaped distribution (of opinions) centered on a single mode, or most frequent response. (5)

norms An organization's informal, unwritten rules that guide individual behavior. (13)

North Atlantic Treaty Organization (NATO) An organization including nations of Western Europe, the United States, and Canada, created in 1949 to defend against Soviet expansionism. (20)

obligation of contracts The obligation of the parties to a contract to carry out its terms. (15)

Office of Management and Budget (OMB) The budgeting arm of the Executive Office; prepares the president's budget. (18)

oligarchy A system of government in which power is concentrated in the hands of a few people. (2)

open election An election that lacks an incumbent. (9)

open primary A primary election in which voters need not declare their party affiliation and can choose one party's primary ballot to take into the voting booth. (9)

order The rule of law to preserve life and protect property. Maintaining order is the oldest purpose of government. (1)

original jurisdiction The authority of a court to hear a case before any other court does. (14)

oversight The process of reviewing the operations of an agency to determine whether it is carrying out policies as Congress intended. (11)

parliamentary system A system of government in which the chief executive is the leader whose party holds the most seats in the legislature after an election or whose party forms a major part of the ruling coalition. (11)

participatory democracy A system of government where rank-and-file citizens rule themselves rather than electing representatives to govern on their behalf. (2)

party conference A meeting to select party leaders and decide committee assignments, held at the beginning of a session of Congress by Republicans or Democrats in each chamber. (8)

party identification A voter's sense of psychological attachment to a party. (8)

party machine A centralized party organization that dominates local politics by controlling elections. (8)

party platform The statement of policies of a national political party. (8)

pay-as-you-go In the Budget Enforcement Act of 1990, the requirement that any tax cut or expansion of an entitlement program must be offset by a tax increase or other savings. (18)

peace through strength Reagan's policy of combating communism by building up the military, including aggressive development of new weapons systems. (20)

plea bargain   A defendant's admission of guilt in exchange for a less severe punishment. (14)

pluralist model of democracy   An interpretation of democracy in which government by the people is taken to mean government by people operating through competing interest groups. (2)

pocket veto   A means of killing a bill that has been passed by both houses of Congress, in which the president does not sign the bill and Congress adjourns within ten days of the bill's passage. (11)

police power   The authority of a government to maintain order and safeguard citizens' health, morals, safety, and welfare. (1)

policy entrepreneurs   Citizens, members of interest groups, or public officials who champion particular policy ideas. (4)

policy evaluation   Analysis of a public policy so as to determine how well it is working. (17)

policy formulation   The stage of the policymaking process during which formal proposals are developed and adopted. (17)

political action committee (PAC)   An organization that pools campaign contributions from group members and donates those funds to candidates for political office. (10)

political agenda   A list of issues that need government attention. (6)

political equality   Equality in political decision making: one vote per person, with all votes counted equally. (1, 2)

political ideology   A consistent set of values and beliefs about the proper purpose and scope of government. (1)

political participation   Actions of private citizens by which they seek to influence or support government and politics. (7)

political party   An organization that sponsors candidates for political office under the organization's name. (8)

political socialization   The complex process by which people acquire their political values. (5)

political system   A set of interrelated institutions that links people with government. (8)

poll tax   A tax of $1 or $2 on every citizen who wished to vote, first instituted in Georgia in 1877. Although it was no burden on most white citizens, it effectively disenfranchised blacks. (16)

poverty level   The minimum cash income that will provide for a family's basic needs; calculated as three times the cost of a market basket of food that provides a minimally nutritious diet. (19)

precedent   A judicial ruling that serves as the basis for the ruling in a subsequent case. (14)

preemption   The power of Congress to enact laws by which the national government assumes total or partial responsibility for a state government function. (4)

preemptive action   The policy of acting against a nation or group that poses a severe threat to the United States before waiting for the threat to occur; sometimes called the "Bush doctrine." (20)

presidential primary   A special primary election used to select delegates to attend the party's national convention, which in turn nominates the presidential candidate. (9)

primary election   A preliminary election conducted within a political party to select candidates who will run for public office in a subsequent election. (9)

prior restraint   Censorship before publication. (15)

procedural democratic theory   A view of democracy as being embodied in a decision-making process that involves universal participation, political equality, majority rule, and responsiveness. (2)

productive capacity   The total value of goods and services that can be produced when the economy works at full capacity. (18)

program monitoring   Keeping track of government programs; usually done by interest groups. (10)

progressive taxation   A system of taxation whereby the rich pay proportionately higher taxes than the poor; used by governments to redistribute wealth and thus promote equality. (18)

progressivism   A philosophy of political reform based on the goodness and wisdom of the individual citizen as opposed to special interests and political institutions. (7)

project grants   Categorical grants awarded on the basis of competitive applications submitted by prospective recipients to perform a specific task or function. (4)

proportional representation   The system by which legislative seats are awarded to a party in proportion to the vote that party wins in an election. (8)

protectionism   The notion that women must be protected from life's cruelties; until the 1970s, the basis for laws affecting women's civil rights. (16)

protectionists   Those who wish to prevent imports from entering the country and therefore oppose free trade. (20)

public assistance   Government aid to individuals who can demonstrate a need for that aid. (19)

public debt   The accumulated sum of past government borrowing owed to lenders outside the government. (18)

public figures   People who assume roles of prominence in society or thrust themselves to the forefront of public controversy. (15)

public goods   Benefits and services, such as parks and sanitation, that benefit all citizens but are not likely to be produced voluntarily by individuals. (1)

public opinion   The collected attitudes of citizens concerning a given issue or question. (5)

public policy A general plan of action adopted by the government to solve a social problem, counter a threat, or pursue an objective. (17, 19)

racial gerrymandering The drawing of a legislative district to maximize the chance that a minority candidate will win election. (11)

racial segregation Separation from society because of race. (16)

racism A belief that human races have distinct characteristics such that one's own race is superior to, and has a right to rule, others. (16)

reapportionment Redistribution of representatives among the states, based on population change. The House is reapportioned after each census. (11)

recall The process for removing an elected official from office. (7)

receipts For a government, the amount expected or obtained in taxes and other revenues. (18)

redistributional policies Policies that take government resources, such as tax funds, from one sector of society and transfer them to another. (17)

redistricting The process of redrawing political boundaries to reflect changes in population. (4)

referendum An election on a policy issue. (7)

regulation Government intervention in the workings of a business market to promote some socially desired goal. (13, 17)

regulations Administrative rules that guide the operation of a government program. (13)

regulatory commission An agency of the executive branch of government that controls or directs some aspect of the economy. (13)

representative democracy A system of government where citizens elect public officials to govern on their behalf. (2)

republic A government without a monarch; a government rooted in the consent of the governed, whose power is exercised by elected representatives responsible to the governed. (3)

republicanism A form of government in which power resides in the people and is exercised by their elected representatives. (3)

responsible party government A set of principles formalizing the ideal role of parties in a majoritarian democracy. (8)

responsiveness A decision-making principle, necessitated by representative government, that implies that elected representatives should do what the majority of people wants. (2)

restraint A requirement laid down by act of Congress, prohibiting a state or local government from exercising a certain power. (4)

rights The benefits of government to which every citizen is entitled. (1)

rule making The administrative process that results in the issuance of regulations by government agencies. (13)

rule of four An unwritten rule that requires at least four justices to agree that a case warrants consideration before it is reviewed by the U.S. Supreme Court. (14)

school district The government unit that administers elementary and secondary school programs. (4)

select committee A temporary congressional committee created for a specific purpose and disbanded after that purpose is fulfilled. (11)

self-interest principle The implication that people choose what benefits them personally. (5)

senatorial courtesy A norm under which a nomination must be acceptable to the home state senator from the president's party. (14)

seniority Years of consecutive service on a particular congressional committee. (11)

separate-but-equal doctrine The concept that providing separate but equivalent facilities for blacks and whites satisfies the equal protection clause of the Fourteenth Amendment. (16)

separation of powers The assignment of lawmaking, law-enforcing, and law-interpreting functions to separate branches of government. (3)

set-aside A purchasing or contracting provision that reserves a certain percentage of funds for minority-owned contractors. (16)

sexism Invidious sex discrimination. (16)

skewed distribution An asymmetrical but generally bell-shaped distribution (of opinions); its mode, or most frequent response, lies off to one side. (5)

social contract theory The belief that the people agree to set up rulers for certain purposes and thus have the right to resist or remove rulers who act against those purposes. (3)

social equality Equality in wealth, education, and status. (1)

social insurance A government-backed guarantee against loss by individuals without regard to need. (19)

socialism A form of rule in which the central government plays a strong role in regulating existing private industry and directing the economy, although it does allow some private ownership of productive capacity. (1)

Social Security Social insurance that provides economic assistance to persons faced with unemployment, disability, or old age. It is financed by taxes on employers and employees. (19)

Social Security Act The law that provided for Social Security and is the basis of modern American social welfare. (19)

social welfare programs   Government programs that provide the minimum living standards necessary for all citizens. (19)

socioeconomic status   Position in society, based on a combination of education, occupational status, and income. (5)

soft money   Financial contributions to party committees for capital and operational expenses. (9)

solicitor general   The third-highest official of the U.S. Department of Justice, and the one who represents the national government before the Supreme Court. (14)

sovereignty   The quality of being supreme in power or authority. (4)

Speaker of the House   The presiding officer of the House of Representatives. (11)

special districts   Government units created to perform particular functions, especially when those functions are best performed across jurisdictional boundaries. (4)

split ticket   In voting, candidates from different parties for different offices. (9)

stable distribution   A distribution (of opinions) that shows little change over time. (5)

standard socioeconomic model   A relationship between socioeconomic status and conventional political involvement: people with higher status and more education are more likely to participate than those with lower status. (7)

standing committee   A permanent congressional committee that specializes in a particular policy area. (11)

stare decisis   Literally, "let the decision stand"; decision making according to precedent. (14)

states' rights   The idea that all rights not specifically conferred on the national government by the U.S. Constitution are reserved to the states. (4)

straight ticket   In voting, a single party's candidates for all the offices. (9)

strict scrutiny   A standard used by the Supreme Court in deciding whether a law or policy is to be adjudged constitutional. To pass strict scrutiny, the law or policy must be justified by a "compelling governmental interest," as well as being the least restrictive means for achieving that interest. (15)

substantive democratic theory   The view that democracy is embodied in the substance of government policies rather than in the policymaking procedure. (2)

suffrage   The right to vote. Also called the *franchise*. (7)

supply-side economics   Economic policies aimed at increasing the supply of goods (as opposed to increasing demand); consist mainly of tax cuts for possible investors and less regulation of business. (18)

supportive behavior   Action that expresses allegiance to government and country. (7)

supremacy clause   The clause in Article VI of the Constitution that asserts that national laws take precedence over state and local laws when they conflict. (3)

tax committees   The two committees of Congress responsible for raising the revenue with which to run the government. (18)

television hypothesis   The belief that television is to blame for the low level of citizens' knowledge about public affairs. (6)

Temporary Assistance for Needy Families Act (TANF)   A 1996 national act that abolished the longtime welfare policy, AFDC (Aid for Families with Dependent Children). TANF gives the states much more control over welfare policy. (19)

terrorism   Premeditated, politically motivated violence perpetrated against noncombatant targets by subnational groups or clandestine agents. (7)

totalitarianism   A political philosophy that advocates unlimited power for the government to enable it to control all sectors of society. (1)

trade association   An organization that represents firms within a particular industry. (10)

transfer payment   A payment by government to an individual, mainly through Social Security or unemployment insurance. (18)

trustee   A representative who is obligated to consider the views of constituents but is not obligated to vote according to those views if he or she believes they are misguided. (11)

two-party system   A political system in which two major political parties compete for control of the government. Candidates from a third party have little chance of winning office. (8)

two-step flow of communication   The process in which a few policy elites gather information and then inform their more numerous followers, mobilizing them to apply pressure to government. (6)

uncontrollable outlay   A payment that government must make by law. (18)

unconventional participation   Relatively uncommon political behavior that challenges or defies established institutions and dominant norms. (7)

universal participation   The concept that everyone in a democracy should participate in governmental decision making. (2)

U.S. court of appeals   A court within the second tier of the three-tiered federal court system, to which decisions of the district courts and federal agencies may be appealed for review. (14)

U.S. district court   A court within the lowest tier of the three-tiered federal court system; a court where litigation begins. (14)

veto The president's disapproval of a bill that has been passed by both houses of Congress. Congress can override a veto with a two-thirds vote in each house. (11, 12)

Virginia Plan A set of proposals for a new government, submitted to the Constitutional Convention of 1787; included separation of the government into three branches, division of the legislature into two houses, and proportional representation in the legislature. (3)

voter turnout The percentage of eligible citizens who actually vote in a given election. (7)

War on Poverty A part of President Lyndon Johnson's Great Society program, intended to eradicate poverty within ten years. (19)

watchdog journalism Journalism that scrutinizes public and business institutions and publicizes perceived misconduct. (6)

welfare state A nation in which the government assumes responsibility for the welfare of its citizens by providing a wide array of public services and redistributing income to reduce social inequality. (19)

 # References

Chapter 1 / Freedom, Order, or Equality? / pages 1–27

1. James Risen and Eric Lichtblau, "Bush Lets U.S. Spy on Callers Without Courts," *New York Times*, 16 December 2005, p. A1.
2. David Johnston and Neil A. Lewis, "Defending Spy Program, Administration Cites Law," *New York Times*, 23 December 2005, p. A18; letter from William. E. Moschella, Assistant Attorney General, to Dennis Hastert, Speaker of the House, dated 1 April 2005.
3. Johnston and Lewis, "Defending Spy Program, Administration Cites Law"; Neil King, Jr., "Wiretap Furor Widens Republican Divide," *Wall Street Journal*, 22 December 2005, p. A4; Jon Van, "Phone Giants Mum on Spying," *Chicago Tribune*, 29 December 2005, p. 1; Eric Lichtblau, "F.B.I. Watched Activist Groups, New Files Show," *New York Times*, 20 December 2005, p. 1; James Risen and Eric Lichtblau, "Spying Program Snared U.S. Calls," *New York Times*, 21 December 2005, p. 1.
4. Center for Political Studies, Institute for Social Research, *American National Election Study*, 2000 (Ann Arbor: University of Michigan Press, 2001).
5. David Easton, *The Political System* (New York: Knopf, 1953), p. 65.
6. Thomas Biersteker and Cynthia Weber (eds.), *State Sovereignty as Social Construct* (Cambridge: Cambridge University Press, 1996), p. 12. For distinctions among four different types of sovereignty, see Stephen D. Krasner, "Abiding Sovereignty," *International Political Science Review* 22 (July 2001): 229–251.
7. William T. R. Fox and Annette Baker Fox, "International Politics," in *International Encyclopedia of the Social Sciences* (New York: The Macmillan Company and the Free Press, 1968), 8:50–53.
8. Judith Miller, "Sovereignty Isn't So Sacred Anymore," *New York Times*, 18 April 1999, Section 4, p. 4.
9. Stephanie Strom, "Fund for Wartime Slaves Set Up in Japan," *New York Times*, 30 November 2000, p. A14.
10. Roger Cohen, "A European Identity: National-State Losing Ground," *New York Times*, 14 January 2000, p. A3.
11. Jess Bravin, "U.S. to Pull Out of World Court on War Crimes," *Wall Street Journal*, 6 May 2002, p. A4.
12. Charles M. Madigan and Colin McMahon, "A Slow, Painful Quest for Justice," *Chicago Tribune*, 7 September 1999, pp. 1, 8.
13. Tom Hundley, "Europe Seeks to Convert U.S. on Death Penalty," *Chicago Tribune*, 26 June 2000, p. 1; Salim Muwakkil, "The Capital of Capital Punishment," *Chicago Tribune*, 12 July 1999, p. 18.
14. Liberalism constitutes a nebulous doctrine for theorists. Louis Hartz, in his classic *The Liberal Tradition in America* (New York: Harcourt, Brace & World, 1955), says it is an "even vaguer term" than *feudalism* (pp. 3–4). David G. Smith calls it "too ecumenical and too pluralistic to be called, properly, an ideology" in *The International Encyclopedia of the Social Sciences* (New York: Macmillan and Free Press, 1968), 9:276. More recently, Robert Eccleshall admitted that "in everyday usage," liberalism "often stands for little more than a collection of values and principles which no decent person would reject," but then proceeds to find substance in an "incoherent

doctrine." In *Political Ideologies: An Introduction*, 3rd ed. (London: Routledge, 2003), p. 18.
15. Karl Marx and Friedrich Engels, *Critique of the Gotha Programme* (New York: International Publishers, 1938), p. 10. Originally written in 1875 and published in 1891.
16. See the argument in Amy Gutman, *Liberal Equality* (Cambridge: Cambridge University Press, 1980), pp. 9–10.
17. See John H. Schaar, "Equality of Opportunity and Beyond," in *Equality, NOMOS IX*, ed. J. Roland Pennock and John W. Chapman (New York: Atherton Press, 1967), pp. 228–249.
18. Lyndon Johnson, "To Fulfill These Rights," commencement address at Howard University, 4 June 1965, available at <http://www.hpol.org/record.asp?id=54>.
19. Jean Jacques Rousseau, *The Social Contract and Discourses*, trans. G. D. H. Cole (New York: Dutton, 1950), p. 5.
20. Pew Research Center for the People and the Press, survey conducted by Princeton Survey Research Associates International, 7–11 December 2005.
21. Michael A. Lev, "Vicious Crimes Taking Root in China's Changing Society," *Chicago Tribune*, 5 November 2000, pp. 1, 13.
22. Centers for Disease Control and Prevention, *HIV/AIDS Surveillance Report for December 2005* (Atlanta, Ga.: Centers for Disease Control, 2006).
23. Milton Friedman, *Capitalism and Freedom* (Chicago: University of Chicago Press, 1962).
24. Joseph Khan, "Anarchism, the Creed That Won't Stay Dead," *New York Times*, 5 August 2000, p. A15.
25. The communitarian category was labeled "populist" in the first four editions of this book. We have relabeled it for two reasons. First, we believe that *communitarian* is more descriptive of the category. Second, we recognize that the term *populist* has been used increasingly to refer to the political styles of candidates such as Pat Buchanan and Ralph Nader. In this sense, a populist appeals to mass resentment against those in power. Given the debate over what *populist* really means, we have decided to use *communitarian*, a less familiar term with fewer connotations. See Michael Kazin, *The Populist Persuasion: An American History* (New York: Basic Books, 1995).
26. The communitarian movement was founded by a group of ethicists and social scientists who met in Washington, D.C., in 1990 at the invitation of sociologist Amitai Etzioni and political theorist William Galston to discuss the declining state of morality and values in the United States. Etzioni became the leading spokesperson for the movement. See his *Rights and the Common Good: The Communitarian Perspective* (New York: St. Martin's Press, 1995), pp. iii–iv. The communitarian political movement should be distinguished from communitarian thought in political philosophy, which is associated with theorists such as Alasdair MacIntyre, Michael Sandel, and Charles Taylor, who wrote in the late 1970s and early 1980s. In essence, communitarian theorists criticized liberalism, which stressed freedom and individualism, as excessively individualistic. Their fundamental critique was that liberalism slights the values of community life. See Allen E. Buchanan, "Assessing the Communitarian Critique of Liberalism," *Ethics* 99 (July 1989): 852–882, and Patrick Neal and David Paris, "Liberalism and the Communitarian Critique: A Guide for the Perplexed," *Canadian Journal of Political Science* 23 (September 1990): 419–439. Communitarian philosophers attacked

liberalism over the inviolability of civil liberties. In our framework, such issues involve the tradeoff between freedom and order. Communitarian and liberal theorists differ less concerning the tradeoff between freedom and equality. See William R. Lund, "Communitarian Politics and the Problem of Equality," *Political Research Quarterly* 46 (September 1993): 577–600. But see also Susan Hekman, "The Embodiment of the Subject: Feminism and the Communitarian Critique of Liberalism," *Journal of Politics* 54 (November 1992): 1098–1119.

27. Etzioni, *Rights and the Common Good*, p. iv, and Etzioni, "Communitarian Solutions/What Communitarians Think," *Journal of State Government* 65 (January–March 1992): 9–11. For a critical review of the communitarian program, see Jeremiah Creedon, "Communitarian Manifesto," *Utne Reader* (July–August 1992): 38–40.

28. Etzioni, "Communitarian Solutions/What Communitarians Think," p. 10. Dana Milbank, "Catch-word for Bush Ideology; 'Communitarianism' Finds Favor," *Washington Post*, 1 February 2001, p. A1. See also Lester Thurow, "Communitarian vs. Individualistic Capitalism," in Etzioni, *Rights and the Common Good*, pp. 277–282. Note, however, that government's role in dealing with issues of social and economic inequality is far less developed in communitarian writings than is its role in dealing with issues of order. In the same volume, an article by David Osborne, "Beyond Left and Right: A New Political Paradigm" (pp. 283–290), downplays the role of government in guaranteeing entitlements.

29. Mike Allen, "Bush Plans Values-Based Initiative to Rev Up Agenda," *Washington Post*, 29 July 2001.

30. Etzioni, *Rights and the Common Good*, p. 17.

31. Ibid., p. 22.

32. On the philosophical similarities and differences between communitarianism and socialism, see Alexander Koryushkin and Gerd Meyer (eds.), *Communitarianism, Liberalism, and the Quest for Democracy in Post-Communist Societies* (St. Petersburg: St. Petersburg University Press, 1999).

Chapter 2 / Majoritarian or Pluralist Democracy? / pages 28–50

1. Somini Sengupta, "U.S. Gives India Applause, Pakistan a Pat on the Back," *New York Times*, 5 March 2006, p. 11.

2. Transcript of the joint press conference available from the White House at <http://www.whitehouse.gov/news/releases/2006/03/20060304-2.html>.

3. Kim Barker, "An Ex-Playboy Aligns with Puritans," *Chicago Tribune*, 9 March 2006, p. 11.

4. Kenneth Janda, "What's in a Name? Party Labels Across the World," in *The CONTA Conference: Proceedings of the Conference of Conceptual and Terminological Analysis of the Social Sciences*, ed. F. W. Riggs (Frankfurt: Indeks Verlage, 1982), pp. 46–62.

5. American National Election Study of 2004.

6. Richard F. Fenno, Jr., *The President's Cabinet* (New York: Vintage, 1959), p. 29.

7. Robert A. Dahl, *Democracy and Its Critics* (New Haven, Conn.: Yale University Press, 1989), pp. 13–23.

8. Jeffrey M. Berry, Kent E. Portney, and Ken Thomson, *The Rebirth of Urban Democracy* (Washington, D.C.: Brookings Institution, 1993).

9. Jean Jacques Rousseau, *The Social Contract* (1762; reprint, Hammondsworth, England: Penguin, 1968), p. 141.

10. Berry, Portney, and Thomson, *Rebirth*, p. 77.

11. See James A. Stimson, Michael B. MacKuen, and Robert S. Erikson, "Dynamic Representation," *American Political Science Review* 89 (September 1995): 543–565; and G. Bingham Powell, Jr., "The Chain of Responsiveness," *Journal of Democracy* 15 (October 2004): 91–105.

12. "Americans Remain Less Inclined to Look to Government Than Citizens of Other Industrial Democracies," *Public Perspective* 9 (February–March 1998): 32; Dietrich Rueschemeyer, "Address Inequality," *Journal of Democracy* 15 (October 2004): 76–90.

13. See Robert A. Dahl, "What Political Institutions Does Large-Scale Democracy Require?" *Political Science Quarterly* 120 (2005): 187–197.

14. Shaun Bowler and Todd Donovan, "The Initiative Process," in *Politics in the American States*, 8th ed., ed. Virginia Gray and Russell L. Hanson (Washington, D.C.: CQ Press, 2004), pp. 129–156; Thomas E. Cronin, *Direct Democracy* (Cambridge, Mass.: Harvard University Press, 1989), p. 47.

15. Kenneth Janda, "Do Our People's Republics Work?" *Newsday*, 6 August 2003.

16. Richard J. Ellis, *Democratic Delusions* (Lawrence: University of Kansas Press, 2002); Elisabeth R. Gerber, *The Populist Paradox: Interest Group Influence and the Promise of Direct Legislation* (Princeton, N.J.: Princeton University Press, 1999).

17. Initiative and Referendum Institute, "General Election Post Election Report," November 2002, available at <http://www.iandrinstitute.org/>.

18. "Ireland Votes to Drop Death Penalty, Join International Court," *Deutsche Presse-Agentur*, 8 June 2001.

19. Jack Citrin, "Who's the Boss? Direct Democracy and Popular Control of Government," in *Broken Contract?* ed. Stephen C. Craig (Boulder, Colo.: Westview Press, 1996), p. 271.

20. "Reform: More Direct Democracy," *Public Perspective* 9 (February–March 1998): 45.

21. American National Election Study, 2004.

22. John R. Hibbing and Elizabeth Theiss-Morse, *Stealth Democracy: Americans' Beliefs About How Government Should Work* (New York: Cambridge University Press, 2002), p. 2.

23. Ibid., p. 7.

24. Benjamin I. Page and Robert Y. Shapiro, *The Rational Public* (Chicago: University of Chicago Press, 1992), p. 387. See also Arthur Lupia and Mathew D. McCubbins, *The Democratic Dilemma* (Cambridge: Cambridge University Press, 1998).

25. Robert A. Dahl, *Pluralist Democracy in the United States* (Chicago: Rand McNally, 1967), p. 24.

26. Jeffrey M. Berry, *The New Liberalism* (Washington, D.C.: Brookings Institution, 1999).

27. See Theda Skocpol, *Diminished Democracy* (Norman: University of Oklahoma Press, 2003); Matthew A. Crenson and Benjamin Ginsberg, *Downsizing Democracy* (Baltimore: Johns Hopkins University Press, 2002).

28. Robert D. Putnam, *Bowling Alone* (New York: Simon & Schuster, 2000).

29. The classic statement on elite theory is C. Wright Mills, *The Power Elite* (New York: Oxford University Press, 1956).

30. Robert A. Dahl, *Who Governs?* (New Haven, Conn.: Yale University Press, 1961).

31. Clarence N. Stone, *Regime Politics* (Lawrence: University of Kansas Press, 1989).

32. Peter Bachrach and Morton S. Baratz, "Two Faces of Power," *American Political Science Review* 56 (December 1962): 947–952; John Gaventa, *Power and Powerlessness* (Urbana: University of Illinois Press, 1980).

33. Diane Renzulli, *Capitol Offenders* (Washington, D.C.: Center for Public Integrity, 2002).

34. David Beetham, Sarah Bracking, Iain Kearton, and Stuart Weir, *International IDEA Handbook on Democracy Assessment* (New York: Kluwer Law International, 2002).

35. Kevin Watkins, *Human Development Report 2005* (New York: United Nations Human Development Programme, 2005), p. 20.

36. Freedom House, *Annual Global Survey of Political Rights and Civil Liberties 2006* (New York: Freedom House, 2006).

37. *Africa Demos* 3 (May 1996): 1, 27; Michael Bratton and Nicholas van de Walle, "Popular Protest and Political Reform in Africa," *Comparative Politics* 24 (July 1992): 419–442.

38. Abraham Diskin, Hanna Diskin, and Reuven Y. Hazan, "Why Democracies Collapse: The Reasons for Democratic Failure and Success," *International Political Science Review* 26 (July 2005): 291–309.

39. Nazif M. Shahrani, "War, Factionalism, and the State in Afghanistan," *American Anthropologist* 104 (September 2002): 715–722.

40. See Fareed Zakaria, *The Future of Freedom* (New York: Norton, 2003). The classic treatment of the conflict between freedom and order in democratizing countries is Samuel P. Huntington, *Political Order in Changing Societies* (New Haven, Conn.: Yale University Press, 1968).

41. Henry Teune, "The Consequences of Globalization on Local Democracy: An Assessment" (paper delivered at the International Political Science Association, Durban, South Africa, July 2003); *Human Development Report 2002: Deepening Democracy in a Fragmented World* (New York: United Nations, 2002), pp. 51–61. See also Yi Feng, *Democracy, Governance, and Economic Performance: Theory and Evidence* (Cambridge, Mass.: MIT Press, 2003), pp. 296–299.

42. Tony Smith, *America's Mission: The United States and the Worldwide Struggle for Democracy in the Twentieth Century* (Princeton, N.J.: Princeton University Press, 1994).

43. See Thomas L. Friedman, *Longitudes and Attitudes: The World After September 11* (New York: Farrar, Straus & Giroux, 2002).

44. Steven R. Weisman, "Bush Defends His Goal of Spreading Democracy to the Mideast," *New York Times*, 27 January 2006, p. A9.

45. PIPA/Knowledge Networks and Chicago Council on Foreign Relations Poll, "Americans on Democratization and U.S. Foreign Policy," 15–21 September 2005.

46. Susan J. Pharr and Robert D. Putnam (eds.), *Disaffected Democracies* (Princeton, N.J.: Princeton University Press, 2000).

47. Rita Jalai and Seymour Martin Lipset, "Racial and Ethnic Conflicts: A Global Perspective," *Political Science Quarterly* 107 (Winter 1992–1993): 588.

48. E. E. Schattschneider, *The Semi-Sovereign People* (New York: Holt, Rinehart, & Winston, 1960), p. 35.

49. See Jack Dennis and Diana Owen, "Popular Satisfaction with the Party System and Representative Democracy in the United States," *International Political Science Review* 22 (2001): 399–415. They attribute a lack of satisfaction with democracy to breakdowns in the U.S. political party system.

50. Ellis, *Democratic Delusions*, p. 43.

Chapter 3 / The Constitution / pages 51–90

1. Introductory speech by President V. Giscard d'Estaing to the Convention on the Future of Europe, 28 February 2002, available at <http://european-convention.eu.int/dynadoc.asp?lang=EN&Content=DOCSPEE>.

2. Letter from George Washington to James Madison, 31 March 1787, available at <http://gwpapers.virginia.edu/documents/constitution/1787/madison3.html>.

3. The website for the European Constitutional Convention is <http://european-convention.eu.int/>.

4. Elaine Sciolino, "French No Vote on Constitution Rattles Europe," *New York Times*, 31 May 2005.

5. Guenter Burghardt, "The Development of the European Constitution from the U.S. Point of View" (lecture in the Framework of the Forum Constitutionis Europae, Walter Hallstein Institute for European Constitutional Law, Humboldt University, Berlin, 6 June 2002), available at <http://www.eurunion.org/News/speeches/2002/020606ENGgb.htm>.

6. Samuel Eliot Morison, *Oxford History of the American People* (New York: Oxford University Press, 1965), p. 172.

7. Richard Walsh, *Charleston's Sons of Liberty: A Study of the Artisans, 1763–1789* (Columbia: University of South Carolina Press, 1959).

8. Mary Beth Norton, *Liberty's Daughters* (Boston: Little, Brown, 1980), pp. 155–157.

9. Morison, *Oxford History*, p. 204.

10. David McCullough, *John Adams* (New York: Simon & Schuster, 2001).

11. John Plamentz, *Man and Society*, rev. ed., ed. M. E. Plamentz and Robert Wokler, Vol. 1: *From the Middle Ages to Locke* (New York: Longman, 1992), pp. 216–218.

12. Pauline Maier, *American Scripture: Making the Declaration of Independence* (New York: Knopf, 1997), pp. 133–134.

13. Joseph Ellis, *American Sphinx: The Character of Thomas Jefferson* (New York: Vintage Books, 1998), p. 59.

14. Charles H. Metzger, *Catholics and the American Revolution: A Study in Religious Climate* (Chicago: Loyola University Press, 1962).

15. Extrapolated from U.S. Department of Defense, *Selected Manpower Statistics, FY 1982* (Washington, D.C.: U.S. Government Printing Office, 1983), Table 2–30, p. 130; and U.S. Bureau of the Census, *1985 Statistical Abstract of the United States* (Washington, D.C.: U.S. Government Printing Office, 1985), Tables 1 and 2, p. 6.

16. McCullough, *John Adams*, pp. 165–385.

17. Joseph T. Keenan, *The Constitution of the United States* (Homewood, Ill.: Dow-Jones-Irwin, 1975).

18. David P. Szatmary, *Shays' Rebellion: The Making of an Agrarian Insurrection* (Amherst: University of Massachusetts Press, 1980), pp. 82–102.

19. As cited in Morison, *Oxford History*, p. 304.

20. "The Call for the Federal Constitutional Convention, Feb. 21, 1787," in Edward M. Earle (ed.), *The Federalist* (New York: Modern Library, 1937), p. 577.

21. Robert H. Jackson, *The Struggle for Judicial Supremacy* (New York: Knopf, 1941), p. 8.

22. John Dickinson of Delaware, as quoted in Morison, *Oxford History*, p. 270.

23. Catherine Drinker Bowen, *Miracle at Philadelphia* (Boston: Little, Brown, 1966), p. 122.

24. Forrest McDonald, *Novus Ordo Seclorum: The Intellectual Origins of the Constitution* (Lawrence: University Press of Kansas, 1985), pp. 205–209.

25. Donald S. Lutz, "The Preamble to the Constitution of the United States," *This Constitution* 1 (September 1983): 23–30.

26. Charles O. Jones, "The Separated Presidency—Making It Work in Contemporary Politics," in *The New American Political System*, 2nd ed., ed. Anthony King (Washington, D.C.: American Enterprise Institute, 1990).

27. Charles A. Beard, *An Economic Interpretation of the Constitution of the United States* (New York: Macmillan, 1913).

28. Leonard W. Levy, *Constitutional Opinions* (New York: Oxford University Press, 1986), p. 101.

29. Robert E. Brown, *Charles Beard and the Constitution* (Princeton, N.J.: Princeton University Press, 1956); Levy, *Constitutional Opinions*, pp. 103–104; Forrest McDonald, *We the People: Economic Origins of the Constitution* (Chicago: University of Chicago Press, 1958).

30. Compare Eugene D. Genovese, *The Political Economy of Slavery: Studies in the Economics and Society of the Slave South* (Middletown, Conn.: Wesleyan University Press, 1989), and Robert William Fogel, *Without Contract or Consent: The Rise and Fall of American Slavery* (New York: Norton, 1989).

31. Robert A. Goldwin, letter to the editor, *Wall Street Journal*, 30 August 1993, p. A11.

32. Bernard Bailyn, *Faces of Revolution: Personalities and Themes in the Struggle for American Independence* (New York: Knopf, 1990), pp. 221–222.

33. Walter Berns, *The First Amendment and the Future of Democracy* (New York: Basic Books, 1976), p. 2.

34. Herbert J. Storing (ed.), *The Complete Anti-Federalist*, 7 vols. (Chicago: University of Chicago Press, 1981).

35. Alexis de Tocqueville, *Democracy in America*, ed. J. P. Mayer and Max Lerner (1835–1839, reprint, New York: Harper & Row, 1966), p. 102.

36. Russell L. Caplan, *Constitutional Brinkmanship: Amending the Constitution by National Convention* (New York: Oxford University Press, 1988), p. 162.

37. Richard L. Berke, "1789 Amendment Is Ratified but Now the Debate Begins," *New York Times*, 8 May 1992, p. A1.

38. The interpretation debate is fully explored in John H. Garvey and T. Alexander Aleinikoff, *Modern Constitutional Theory: A Reader*, 2nd ed. (Minneapolis, Minn.: West Publishing Co., 1991). A classic statement on judicial decision making, composed before he became a member of the U.S. Supreme Court in 1932, is Benjamin N. Cardozo's *The Nature of the Judicial Process* (New Haven, Conn.: Yale University Press, 1921).

39. International Institute for Democracy (ed.), *The Rebirth of Democracy: Twelve Constitutions of Central and Eastern Europe*, 2nd ed. rev. (Amsterdam: Council of Europe, 1996).

40. Jerold L. Waltman, *Political Origins of the U.S. Income Tax* (Jackson: University Press of Mississippi, 1985), p. 10.

Chapter 4 / Federalism / pages 91–123

1. Dan Baum, "When Katrina Hit, Where Were the Police?" *New Yorker*, 9 January 2006, available at <http://www.newyorker.com/fact/content/articles/060109fa_fact>.

2. Evan Thomas, "How Bush Blew It," *Newsweek*, 19 September 2005, available at <http://www.msnbc.msn.com/id/9287434/site/newsweek/>.

3. As part of a major government restructuring that took place after September 11, FEMA lost its independent status and became a subdepartment under the Department of Homeland Security. September 11 profoundly changed the list of priorities in the United States, as terrorism replaced natural disasters as a clear and present danger. Unfortunately, these situations require different measures. What is good for fighting terrorism may be inadequate for handling natural catastrophes.

4. Actual testimony from affected people, from "The Storm," *Frontline-PBS*, 22 November 2005, available at <http://www.pbs.org/wgbh/pages/frontline/storm/view>.

5. William H. Stewart, *Concepts of Federalism* (Lanham, Md.: University Press of America, 1984).

6. Martha Derthick, *Keeping the Compound Republic: Essays on American Federalism* (Washington, D.C.: Brookings Institution Press, 2001), p. 153.

7. Edward Corwin, "The Passing of Dual Federalism," *University of Virginia Law Review* 36 (1950): 1–24.

8. See Daniel J. Elazar, *The American Partnership* (Chicago: University of Chicago Press, 1962); Morton Grodzins, *The American System* (Chicago: Rand McNally, 1966).

9. James T. Patterson, *The New Deal and the States: Federalism in Transition* (Princeton, N.J.: Princeton University Press, 1969).

10. See, for example, Eric Lichtblau and Adam Liptak, "Bush Presses On in Legal Defense for Wiretapping," *New York Times*, 28 January 2006, p. A1.

11. *South Carolina v. Katzenbach*, 383 U.S. 301 (1966).

12. *McCulloch v. Maryland*, 4 Wheat. 316 (1819).

13. *Dred Scott v. Sandford*, 19 How. 393, 426 (1857).

14. Raoul Berger, *Federalism: The Founders' Design* (Norman: University of Oklahoma Press, 1987), pp. 61–62.

15. *United States v. Lopez*, 514 U.S. 549 (1995).

16. *Printz v. United States*, 521 U.S. 898 (1997).

17. *United States v. Morrison*, 120 S. Ct. 1740 (2000).

18. *Lawrence and Garner v. Texas*, 539 U.S. 558 (2003). This decision overturned *Bowers v. Hardwick*, 478 U.S. 186 (1986).

19. *Atkins v. Virginia*, 536 U.S. 304 (2002).

20. *Roper v. Simmons*, 343 U.S. 551 (2005).

21. Historical Tables, *Budget of the United States Government*, FY2005 (Washington, D.C.: U.S. Government Printing Office, 2006), Table 12.1.

22. Ibid., Table 12.3 (adjusted to 1996 dollars).

23. *South Dakota v. Dole*, 483 U.S. 203 (1987).

24. Jonathan D. Silver, "Clinton Signs Lower Drunk Driving Limit; States That Don't Adopt 0.08 Rule Would Lose Federal Highway Aid," *Pittsburgh Post-Gazette*, 24 October 2000, p. A1.

25. Terry Sanford, *Storm over the States* (New York: McGraw-Hill, 1967).

26. Quoted in Cynthia J. Bowling and Deil S. Wright, "Public Administration in the Fifty States: A Half-Century Administrative Revolution," *State and Local Government Review* 30 (Winter 1998): 52.

27. David M. Hedge, *Governance and the Changing American States* (Boulder, Colo.: Westview Press, 1998).

28. Cynthia J. Bowling and Deil S. Wright, "Change and Continuity in State Administration: Administrative Leadership Across Four Decades," *Public Administration Review* 58 (September–October 1998): 431.

29. Paul Manna, "Federalism, Agenda Setting, and the Development of Federal Education Policy, 1965–2001" (Ph.D. diss., University of Wisconsin, 2003).

30. Ronald Reagan, "Statement on Signing Executive Order Establishing the Presidential Advisory Committee on Federalism," 1981 *Public Papers of the President* 341, 8 April 1981.

31. W. John Moore, "Stopping the States," *National Journal*, 21 July 1990, p. 1758.

32. Congressional Preemption of State Laws and Regulations, United States House of Representatives, Committee on Government Reform—Minority Staff, Special Investigations Division (June 2006), available at <http://www.democrats.reform.house.gov/Documents/20060606095331-23055.pdf>.

33. Lorianne Denne, "Food Labeling Bill Is a Fine Idea—But Scary, Too," *Puget Sound Business Journal*, 12 November 1990, sec. 1, p. 13; Elaine S. Povich, "New Food Labeling Rules Get Stuck in States-Rights Dispute," *Chicago Tribune*, 23 March 1990, Business Section, p. 1.

34. U.S. Bureau of the Census, *Statistical Abstract of the United States: 2004*, Table 128, available at <www.census.gov/prod/2004pubs/03statab/health.pdf>; National Governors' Association, *Policy Positions*, July 2000, <http://www.nga.org/Pubs/Policies/HR/hr16.asp>; Vernon Smith, "States Undertaking Medicaid Cost Containment Strategies [slide]," *Medicaid Eligibility Milestones, 1965–2001*, 6 December 2002, <http://www.ncsl.org/programs/health/forum/chairs/NOLA/rowland/index.html>.

35. "Unfunded Federal Mandates," *Congressional Digest* (March 1995): 68.

36. "50-State Update: Analysis Details State Costs of Federal Mandates," *National Conference of State Legislatures News*, 7 April 2004 (updated 12 May 2004), available at <http://www.ncsl.org/programs/press/2004/pr040407.htm>, accessed 29 January 2006.

37. Ibid.

38. Report to the Chairman, Subcommittee on Oversight of Government Management, the Federal Workforce, and the District of Columbia, Committee on Governmental Affairs,

U.S. Senate, *Unfunded Mandates: Analysis of Reform Act Coverage*, United States General Accounting Office, May 2004, p. 22. Available at <http://www.gao.gov/new.items/d04637.pdf>, accessed 29 January 2006.

39. William T. Gormley, Jr., "An Evolutionary Approach to Federalism in the U.S." (paper presented at the annual meeting of the American Political Science Association, 2001), p. 8.

40. Paul L. Posner, *The Politics of Unfunded Mandates: Whither Federalism?* (Washington, D.C.: Georgetown University Press, 1998), p. 54.

41. C. David Kotok, "Cheney Lends a Hand in Iowa, Vice President Rallies GOP Voters: A Day with the V.P.," *Omaha World Herald*, 1 November 2002, p. 1A; Raymond Hernandez, "Bush Swings Through Three States to Build Support for the GOP," *New York Times*, 1 November 2002, p. A27; James Harding, "Bush Finds Time for Diplomacy on Campaign Trail," *Financial Times* (London), 25 October 2002, p. 10; John Broder, "The 2006 Elections: Democrats Take Senate," *New York Times*, 10 November 2006 (online edition).

42. CNN, "Texas House Paralyzed by Democratic Walkout," 19 May 2002, <http://www.cnn.com/2003/allpolitics/05/13/texas.legislature/>; R. Jeffrey Smith, "DeLay, FAA Roles in Texas Redistricting Flap Detailed," *Washington Post*, 12 July 2003, p. A3; Karen Masterson, "Transportation Investigator Says Agency Erred in Seeking Democrats," *Houston Chronicle*, 16 July 2003, p. A6.

43. U.S. Department of Justice, "Guidance Concerning Redistricting in Retrogression Under Section 5 of the Voting Rights Act 42 U.S.C., 1973c," *Federal Register*, 18 January 2001. Also available at <http://www.usdoj.gov/crt/voting/sec_5/fedregvoting.pdf>; David E. Rosenbaum, "Fight over Political Map Centers on Race," *New York Times*, 21 February 2002, p. A20.

44. U.S. Census Bureau, *2002 Census of Governments*. Available at <http://www.census.gov/govs/www/cog2002.html>.

45. Nancy Burns, *The Formation of American Local Governments: Private Values in Public Institutions* (New York: Oxford University Press, 1994), pp. 11–13.

46. State Tax Actions 2006: Executive Summary, *National Conference of State Legislatures*, April 2007, available at <http://www.ncsl.org/programs/fiscal/sta06sum.htm>, accessed 22 June 2006.

47. CNN, "Sniper Attacks: A Trail of Terror," 2002, <http://www.cnn.com/SPECIALS/2002/sniper/>.

48. Bowling and Wright, "Public Administration in the Fifty States," pp. 57–58.

49. Alabama, Alaska, Arizona, California, Colorado, Connecticut, Delaware, Florida, Georgia, Idaho, Illinois, Indiana, Iowa, Louisiana, Maine, Maryland, Massachusetts, Michigan, Minnesota, Mississippi, Missouri, Nevada, New Hampshire, New Jersey, New Mexico, New York, North Carolina, North Dakota, Ohio, Oklahoma, Oregon, Pennsylvania, Rhode Island, South Carolina, Utah, Vermont, Washington, West Virginia, and Wisconsin. Information available at SIDOAmerica.org, <http://www.sidoamerica.org/aboutus.htm>, accessed 29 January 2006.

50. SIDO maintains a presence at <http://www.sidoamerica.org/>.

51. *Crosby v. National Foreign Trade Council*, 530 U.S. 363 (2000); Terrence Guay, "Local Government and Global Politics: The Implications of Massachusetts' 'Burma Law,'" *Political Science Quarterly* 115 (Fall 2000): 353–376.

52. *U.S. Term Limits v. Thornton*, 514 U.S. 779 (1995).

53. Ann L. Griffiths and Karl Nerenberg (eds.), *Handbook of Federal Countries* (Montreal and Kingston, Canada: McGill–Queens University Press, 2005).

54. Ronald L. Watts, *Comparing Federal Systems*, 2nd ed. (Montreal and Kingston, Canada: McGill–Queen's University Press, 1999), p. 4.

Chapter 5 / Public Opinion and Political Socialization / pages 124–156

1. William J. Kole, "Austrian Stadium Terminates Schwarzenegger Marquee," *Chicago Tribune*, 27 December 2005, p. 2.

2. Jenifer Warren and Maura Dolan, "Tookie Williams Is Executed," *Los Angeles Times*, 13 December 2005.

3. "Killer's Advocates Vow Funeral 'Befitting a Statesman,'" *Chicago Tribune*, 14 December 2005, p. 29.

4. Gallup Poll conducted 5–7 May 2006, reported by Jeffrey M. Jones, "Two in Three Favor Death Penalty for Convicted Murderers," 1 June 2006, *The Gallup Poll*, <http://poll.gallup.com>.

5. Warren Weaver, Jr., "Death Penalty a 300-Year Issue in America," *New York Times*, 3 July 1976.

6. *Furman v. Georgia*, 408 U.S. 238 (1972).

7. *Gregg v. Georgia*, 248 U.S. 153 (1976).

8. U.S. Department of Justice, Bureau of Justice Statistics, "Number of Persons Executed in the U.S. 1930–2004," <http://www.ojp.usdoj.gov/bjs/glance/tables/exetab.htm>; and the Death Penalty Information website, "Number of Executions by State and Region Since 1976," <http://www.deathpenaltyinfo.org>.

9. Gallup Poll, 2–5 May 2005.

10. Frank Zimring, "Capital Punishment," Microsoft Encarta Online Encyclopedia 2003, <http://encarta.msn.com>.

11. Ibid.

12. Death Penalty Information website, "Number of Executions by State and Region Since 1976," <http://www.deathpenaltyinfo.org>.

13. E. Wayne Carp, "If Pollsters Had Been Around During the American Revolution" (letter to the editor), *New York Times*, 17 July 1993, p. 10.

14. "Government by the People," results of the 2001 Henry J. Kaiser Family Foundation/Public Perspective Polling and Democracy Survey, <http://www.ropercenter.uconn.edu/pp_poll_dem.html>.

15. Sidney Verba, "The Citizen as Respondent: Sample Surveys and American Democracy," *American Political Science Review* 90 (March 1996): 3.

16. Linda Lyons, "The Gallup Brain: Prayer in Public Schools," Gallup News Service, 10 December 2002, <http://www.gallup.com/poll/tb/religvalue/20021210b.asp>.

17. Warren E. Miller and Santa A. Traugott, *American National Election Studies Sourcebook, 1952–1986* (Cambridge, Mass.: Harvard University Press, 1989), pp. 94–95; Richard Niemi, John Mueller, and Tom Smith, *Trends in Public Opinion: A Compendium of Survey Data* (Westport, Conn.: Greenwood Press, 1989), p. 19.

18. Tom W. Smith and Paul B. Sheatsley, "American Attitudes Toward Race Relations," *Public Opinion* 7 (October–November 1984): 15.

19. Ibid., p. 83.

20. Steven A. Peterson, *Political Behavior: Patterns in Everyday Life* (Newbury Park, Calif.: Sage, 1990), pp. 28–29. For the importance of early learning for political attitudes, see also Jon A. Krosnick and Duane F. Alwin, "Aging and Susceptibility to Attitude Change," *Journal of Personality and Social Psychology* 57 (1989): 416–423.

21. Paul Allen Beck, "The Role of Agents in Political Socialization," in *Handbook of Political Socialization Theory and Research*, ed. Stanley Allen Renshon (New York: Free Press, 1977), pp. 117–118; see also James G. Gimpel, J. Celeste Lay, and Jason E. Schuknecht, *Cultivating Democracy: Civic Environments and Political Socialization in America* (Washington, D.C.: Brookings Institution Press, 2003).

22. W. Russell Neuman, *The Paradox of Mass Politics: Knowledge and Opinion in the American Electorate* (Cambridge,

Mass.: Harvard University Press, 1986), pp. 113–114. See also Richard G. Niemi and Jane Junn, *Civic Education: What Makes Students Learn* (New Haven, Conn.: Yale University Press, 1998). Niemi and Junn found that a favorable home environment (for example, having reading and reference material at home) related significantly to factual knowledge in a high school civics test.

23. M. Kent Jennings and Richard G. Niemi, *The Political Character of Adolescence: The Influence of Families and Schools* (Princeton, N.J.: Princeton University Press, 1974), p. 39. See also Stephen E. Frantzich, *Political Parties in the Technological Age* (New York: Longman, 1989), p. 152. Frantzich presents a table showing that more than 60 percent of children in homes in which both parents have the same party preference will adopt that preference. When parents are divided, the children tend to be divided among Democrats, Republicans, and independents.

24. In a panel study of parents and high school seniors in 1965 and in 1973, some years after their graduation, Jennings and Niemi found that 57 percent of children shared their parents' party identification in 1965, but only 47 percent did by 1973. See Jennings and Niemi, *Political Character*, pp. 90–91. See also Robert C. Luskin, John P. McIver, and Edward G. Carmines, "Issues and the Transmission of Partisanship," *American Journal of Political Science* 33 (May 1989): 440–458. They found that children are more likely to shift between partisanship and independence than to "convert" to the other party. When conversion occurs, it is more likely to be based on economic issues than on social issues.

25. Robert D. Hess and Judith V. Torney, *The Development of Political Attitudes in Children* (Chicago: Aldine, 1967). But other researchers disagree. See Jerry L. Yeric and John R. Todd, *Public Opinion: The Visible Politics* (Itasca, Ill.: F. E. Peacock, 1989), pp. 45–47, for a summary of the issues. For a critical evaluation of the early literature on political socialization, see Pamela Johnston Conover, "Political Socialization: Where's the Politics?" in *Political Science: Looking to the Future*, Volume 3: *Political Behavior*, ed. William Crotty (Evanston, Ill.: Northwestern University Press, 1991), pp. 125–152.

26. David Easton and Jack Dennis, *Children in the Political System* (New York: McGraw-Hill, 1969).

27. Jarol B. Manheim, *The Politics Within* (New York: Longman, 1982), pp. 83, 125–151.

28. Niemi and Junn, *Civic Education*.

29. Edith J. Barrett, "The Political Socialization of Inner-City Adolescents" (paper prepared for presentation at the annual meeting of the American Political Science Association, Washington, D.C., September 1993).

30. M. Kent Jennings, "Political Knowledge over Time and Across Generations," *Public Opinion Quarterly* 60 (Summer 1996): 239, 241.

31. Janie S. Steckenrider and Neal E. Cutler, "Aging and Adult Political Socialization: The Importance of Roles and Transitions," in *Political Learning in Adulthood: A Sourcebook of Theory and Research*, ed. Roberta S. Sigel (Chicago: University of Chicago Press, 1989), pp. 56–88.

32. See Robert Huckfeldt and John Sprague, *Citizens, Politics, and Social Communication* (Cambridge: Cambridge University Press, 1995), Chapter 7. The authors' study of voting in neighborhoods in South Bend, Indiana, found that residents who favored the minority party were acutely aware of their minority status.

33. Theodore M. Newcomb et al., *Persistence and Social Change: Bennington College and Its Students After Twenty-Five Years* (New York: Wiley, 1967); Duane F. Alwin, Ronald L. Cohen, and Theodore M. Newcomb, *Political Attitudes over the Life Span: The Bennington Women After Fifty Years* (Madison: University of Wisconsin Press, 1991).

34. M. Kent Jennings and Gregory Marcus, "Yuppie Politics," *Institute of Social Research Newsletter* (August 1986).

35. See Roberta S. Sigel (ed.), *Political Learning in Adulthood: A Sourcebook of Theory and Research* (Chicago: University of Chicago Press, 1989).

36. Pew Center for the People and the Press, "Public's News Habits Little Changed by September 11," 9 June 2002, <http://people-press.org/reports/display.php3?ReportID=156>.

37. Other scholars have analyzed opinion on abortion using six questions from the General Social Survey. See R. Michael Alvarez and John Brehm, "American Ambivalence Toward Abortion Policy," *American Journal of Political Science* 39 (1995): 1055–1082; Elizabeth Adell Cook, Ted G. Jelen, and Clyde Wilcox, *Between Two Absolutes: Public Opinion and the Politics of Abortion* (Boulder, Colo.: Westview Press, 1992).

38. Although some people view the politics of abortion as "single-issue" politics, the issue has broader political significance. In their book on the subject, Cook, Jelen, and Wilcox say, "Although embryonic life is one important value in the abortion debate, it is not the only value at stake." They contend that the politics is tied to alternative sexual relationships and traditional roles of women in the home, which are "social order" issues. See *Between Two Absolutes*, pp. 8–9.

39. Ibid., p. 50.

40. The increasing wealth in industrialized societies may or may not be replacing class conflict with conflict over values. See the exchange between Ronald Inglehart and Scott C. Flanagan, "Value Change in Industrial Societies," *American Political Science Review* 81 (December 1987): 1289–1319.

41. Earl Black and Merle Black, *The Vital South* (Cambridge, Mass.: Harvard University Press, 1992), and *The Rise of Southern Republicans* (Cambridge, Mass.: Harvard University Press, 2002); David Lublin, *The Republican South: Democratization and Partisan Change* (Princeton, N.J.: Princeton University Press, 2004); Nicholas Valentino and David O. Sears, "Old Times There Are Not Forgotten: Race and Partisan Realignment in the Contemporary South," *American Journal of Political Science* 49 (2005): 672–688.

42. Nathan Glazer, "The Structure of Ethnicity," *Public Opinion* 7 (October–November 1984): 4.

43. See the U.S. Census Bureau, "2004 Population Profile of the United States: Dynamic Version," <http://www.census.gov/population/www/pop-profile/profiledynamic.html>.

44. Ibid.

45. Ibid.

46. Michael Dawson, *Black Visions: The Roots of Contemporary African American Political Ideologies* (Chicago: University of Chicago Press, 2001), and *Behind the Mule* (Princeton, N.J.: Princeton University Press, 1994); John Garcia, *Latino Politics in America* (Lanham, Md.: Rowman and Littlefield, 2003); Pei-te Lien, *The Making of Asian America Through Political Participation* (Philadelphia: Temple University Press, 2001); Wendy Tam, "Asians—A Monolithic Voting Bloc?" *Political Behavior* 17 (1995): 223–249; Katherine Tate, *Black Faces in the Mirror: African Americans and Their Representatives in the U.S. Congress* (Princeton, N.J.: Princeton University Press, 2003).

47. Glazer, "Structure of Ethnicity," p. 5.

48. National Election Study for 2004, an election survey conducted by the Center for Political Studies at the University of Michigan.

49. See David C. Leege and Lyman A. Kellstedt (eds.), *Rediscovering the Religious Factor in American Politics* (Armonk, N.Y.: M. E. Sharpe, 1993); and the Pew Center for the People and the Press, "Religion and Politics: Contention and Consensus," 24 July 2003, <http://people-press.org/reports/display.php3?ReportID=189>.

50. Some scholars have argued that Americans are not as polarized as the news media would have us think. See Morris P. Fiorina, *Culture Wars? The Myth of a Polarized America* (Longman, 2004).

51. Jeffrey M. Jones, "Understanding Americans' Support for the Death Penalty," Gallup News Service, 3 June 2003, <http://www.gallup.com/poll/tb/religvalue/20030603c.asp>.

52. Paul Abramson, John Aldrich, and David Rohde, *Change and Continuity in the 2000 Elections* (Washington, D.C.: CQ Press, 2002), p. 101.

53. John Robinson, "The Ups and Downs and Ins and Outs of Ideology," *Public Opinion* 7 (February–March 1984): 12.

54. For a more positive interpretation of ideological attitudes within the public, see William G. Jacoby, "The Structure of Ideological Thinking in the American Electorate," *American Journal of Political Science* 39 (1995): 314–335. Jacoby analyzes data for the 1984 and 1988 elections and concludes "that there is a systematic, cumulative structure underlying liberal–conservative thinking in the American public" (p. 315).

55. Quoted in Marjorie Connelly, "A 'Conservative' Is (Fill in the Blank)," *New York Times*, 3 November 1996, sec. 4, p. 5.

56. Angus Campbell, Philip E. Converse, Warren E. Miller, and Donald E. Stokes, *The American Voter* (New York: Wiley, 1960), Chapter 10.

57. Connelly, "A 'Conservative' Is (Fill in the Blank)."

58. See William G. Jacoby, "Levels of Conceptualization and Reliance on the Liberal–Conservative Continuum," *Journal of Politics* 48 (May 1986): 423–432. We also know that certain political actors, such as delegates to national party conventions, hold far more consistent and durable beliefs than does the general public. See M. Kent Jennings, "Ideological Thinking Among Mass Publics and Political Elites," *Public Opinion Quarterly* 56 (Winter 1992): 419–441.

59. National Election Study, 2004.

60. However, citizens can have ideologically consistent attitudes toward candidates and perceptions about domestic issues without thinking about politics in explicitly liberal and conservative terms. See Jacoby, "The Structure of Ideological Thinking."

61. Pamela Johnston Conover, "The Origins and Meaning of Liberal–Conservative Self-identifications," *American Journal of Political Science* 25 (November 1981): 621–622, 643.

62. A relationship between liberalism and political tolerance was found by John L. Sullivan et al., "The Sources of Political Tolerance: A Multivariate Analysis," *American Political Science Review* 75 (March 1981): 102. See also Robinson, "Ups and Downs," pp. 13–15.

63. Herbert Asher, *Presidential Elections and American Politics*, 5th ed. (International Thomson Publishing Group, 1997). Asher also constructs a two-dimensional framework, distinguishing between "traditional New Deal" issues and "new lifestyle" issues.

64. John E. Jackson, "The Systematic Beliefs of the Mass Public: Estimating Policy Preferences with Survey Data," *Journal of Politics* 45 (November 1983): 840–865.

65. Milton Rokeach also proposed a two-dimensional model of political ideology grounded in the terminal values of freedom and equality. See *The Nature of Human Values* (New York: Free Press, 1973), especially Chapter 6. Rokeach found that positive and negative references to the two values permeate the writings of socialists, communists, fascists, and conservatives and clearly differentiate the four bodies of writing from one another (pp. 173–174). However, Rokeach built his two-dimensional model around only the values of freedom and equality; he did not deal with the question of freedom versus order.

66. William S. Maddox and Stuart A. Lilie, *Beyond Liberal and Conservative: Reassessing the Political Spectrum* (Washington, D.C.: Cato Institute, 1984), p. 68. From 1993 to 1996, the Gallup Organization, in conjunction with CNN and USA Today, asked national samples two questions: (1) whether individuals or government should solve our country's problems, and (2) whether the government should promote traditional values. Gallup constructed a similar ideological typology from responses to these questions and found a similar distribution of the population into four groups. See Gallup's "Final Top Line" for 12–15 January 1996, pp. 30–31.

67. See Neuman, *Paradox*, p. 81. See also Aaron Wildavsky, "Choosing Preferences by Constructing Institutions: A Cultural Theory of Preference Formation," *American Political Science Review* 81 (March 1987): 13.

68. The same conclusion was reached in a major study of British voting behavior. See Hilde T. Himmelweit et al., *How Voters Decide* (New York: Academic Press, 1981), pp. 138–141. See also Wildavsky, "Choosing Preferences," p. 13.

69. In our framework, opposition to abortion is classified as a communitarian position. However, the communitarian movement led by Amitai Etzioni adopted no position on abortion (personal communication from Vanessa Hoffman by e-mail, in reply to a query of 5 February 1996).

70. Michael X. Delli Carpini and Scott Keeter, *What Americans Know About Politics and Why It Matters* (New Haven, Conn.: Yale University Press, 1996).

71. Ibid., p. 269. For more on this topic, see Scott L. Althaus, *Collective Preferences in Democratic Politics: Opinion Surveys and the Will of the People* (New York: Cambridge University Press, 2003).

72. Carpini and Keeter, *What Americans Know*, p. 271.

73. There is evidence that the educational system and parental practices hamper the ability of women to develop their political knowledge. See Linda L. M. Bennett and Stephen Earl Bennett, "Enduring Gender Differences in Political Interests," *American Politics Quarterly* 17 (January 1989): 105–122.

74. Neuman, *Paradox*, p. 81.

75. Stephan Lewandowsky, Werner Stritzke, Klaus Oberauer, and Michael Morales, "Memory for Fact, Fiction, and Misinformation: The Iraq War 2003," *Psychological Science* 16 (March 2005): 190–195.

76. Benjamin I. Page and Robert Y. Shapiro, *The Rational Public* (Chicago: University of Chicago Press, 1992).

77. Ibid., p. 45.

78. Ibid., p. 385. The argument for a rational quality in public opinion by Page and Shapiro was supported by Stimson's massive analysis of swings in the liberal–conservative attitudes of the U.S. public from 1956 to 1990. Analyzing more than one thousand attitude items, he found that the public mood had already swung away from liberalism when Ronald Reagan appeared on the scene to campaign for president as a conservative. See James A. Stimson, *Public Opinion in America: Moods, Cycles, and Swings* (Boulder, Colo.: Westview Press, 1992), and *Tides of Consent: How Public Opinion Shapes American Politics* (Cambridge: Cambridge University Press, 2004). But for a more cynical view of citizen competence, see Althaus, *Collective Preferences*, and James Kuklinski and Paul Quirk, "Reconsidering the Rational Public," in *Elements of Reason*, ed. A. Lupia, M. McCubbins, and S. Popkin (Cambridge: Cambridge University Press, 2000), pp. 153–182.

79. Self-interest is often posed as the major alternative to choice based on general orientations such as political ideology and moral values. A significant literature exists on the limitations of self-interest in explaining political life. See Jane J. Mansbridge (ed.), *Beyond Self-Interest* (Chicago: University of Chicago Press, 1990). A literature is also developing on the role of emotions in the process of political judgment. See G. E. Marcus, W. R. Neuman, and M. Mackuen, *Affective Intelligence and Political Judgment* (Chicago: University of

Chicago Press, 2000), and George E. Marcus, *The Sentimental Citizen: Emotion in Democratic Politics* (University Park, Pa.: Pennsylvania State University Press, 2002).

80. See, for example, Richard D. Dixon et al., "Self-Interest and Public Opinion Toward Smoking Policies," *Public Opinion Quarterly* 55 (1991): 241–254; David O. Sears and Jack Citrin, *Tax Revolt: Something for Nothing in California* (Cambridge, Mass.: Harvard University Press, 1985); Robin Wolpert and James Gimpel, "Self-Interest, Symbolic Politics, and Public Attitudes Toward Gun Control," *Political Behavior* 20 (1998): 241–262.

81. Wildavsky, "Choosing Preferences," pp. 3–21.

82. Henry Brady and Paul Sniderman, "Attitude Attribution: A Group Basis for Political Reasoning," *American Political Science Review* 79 (1985): 1061–1078; Samuel Popkin, *The Reasoning Voter*, 2nd ed. (Chicago: University of Chicago Press, 1994); P. Sniderman, R. Brody, and P. Tetlock, *Reasoning and Choice* (Cambridge: Cambridge University Press, 1991). Psychologists have tended to emphasize the distorting effects of heuristics. See D. Kahneman, P. Slovic, and A. Tversky (eds.), *Judgment Under Uncertainty: Heuristics and Biases* (Cambridge: Cambridge University Press, 1982), and R. Nisbett and L. Ross, *Human Inference: Strategies and Shortcomings of Social Judgment* (Englewood Cliffs, N.J.: Prentice-Hall, 1980).

83. Political psychologists refer to beliefs that guide information processing as opinion "schemas." See Pamela Johnston Conover and Stanley Feldman, "How People Organize the Political World: A Schematic Model," *American Journal of Political Science* 28 (February 1984): 95–127; M. Lodge and K. M. McGraw, *Political Judgment: Structure and Process* (Ann Arbor: University of Michigan Press, 1995). For an excellent review of schema structures in contemporary psychology, especially as they relate to political science, see Reid Hastie, "A Primer of Information-Processing Theory for the Political Scientist," in *Political Cognition*, ed. Richard R. Lau and David O. Sears (Hillsdale, N.J.: Erlbaum, 1986), pp. 11–39.

84. Pew Center for the People and the Press, "Religion and Politics."

85. J. Kuklinski and N. L. Hurley, "On Hearing and Interpreting Political Messages," *Journal of Politics* 56 (1994): 729–751.

86. On framing, see William Jacoby, "Issue Framing and Public Opinion on Government Spending," *American Journal of Political Science* 44 (October 2000): 750–767; James N. Druckman, "The Implications of Framing Effects for Citizen Competence," *Political Behavior* 23 (September 2001): 225–253; and "Political Preference Formation: Competition, Deliberation, and the (Ir)relevance of Framing Effects," *American Political Science Review* 98 (November 2004): 671–686. On political spin, see Lawrence Jacobs and Robert Y. Shapiro, *Politicians Don't Pander* (Chicago: University of Chicago Press, 2000).

87. Benjamin I. Page, Robert Y. Shapiro, and Glenn R. Dempsey, "What Moves Public Opinion?" *American Political Science Review* 81 (March 1987): 23–43.

88. Michael Margolis and Gary A. Mauser, *Manipulating Public Opinion: Essays on Public Opinion as a Dependent Variable* (Pacific Grove, Calif.: Brooks/Cole, 1989).

Chapter 6 / The Media / pages 157–189

1. Jim Rutenberg, "Cable's War Coverage Suggests a New 'Fox Effect' on Television Journalism," *New York Times*, 16 April 2003, p. B9; Alex R. Jones, "Fox News Moves from the Margins to the Mainstream," *New York Times*, 1 December 2002, sec. 4, p. 4; Scott Collins, *Crazy like a Fox: The Inside Story of How Fox News Beat CNN* (New York: Portfolio, 2004).

2. David Kirkpatrick, "Mr. Murdoch's War," *New York Times*, 7 April 2003, pp. C1, C7.

3. Rutenberg, "Cable's War Coverage."

4. Ibid.; Jones, "Fox News Moves from the Margins."

5. Joe Flint, "Playing the Underdog Helps Fox News Stay on Top of CNN," *Wall Street Journal*, 15 January 2003, pp. B1, B12.

6. Survey taken in April 2002 and reported in "Public's News Habits Little Changed by September 11," *Survey Report*, Pew Research Center for the People and the Press, 29 September 2003, available at <people-press.org/reports/display.php3?PageID=613>.

7. Frank Newport and Joseph Carroll, "Are the News Media too Liberal?" *Poll Analysis*, Gallup News Service, 8 October 2003, available at <gallup.com>. A study found that "exposure to Fox news induced 3 to 8 percent of its non-Republican viewers to start voting for the Republican party." See Stefano DellaVigna and Ethan Kaplan, "The Fox News Effect: Media Bias and Voting," unpublished paper dated 30 October 2005 and posted by an author at <http://emlab.berkeley.edu/users/sdellavi/>.

8. Mark Jurkowitz, "Public Wants War News Neutral, Sort of," *Chicago Tribune*, 15 July 2003, sec. 2, p. 2, which reprints a story from the *Boston Globe*.

9. Kirkpatrick, "Mr. Murdoch's War"; Joe Flint, "Fox News Expands Radio Offering in Bid to Duplicate Its TV Success," *Wall Street Journal*, 29 September 2003, p. 1.

10. David McKnight, "'A World Hungry for a New Philosophy': Rupert Murdoch and the Rise of Neo-Liberalism," *Journalism Studies* 4 (2003): 347–358.

11. S. N. D. North, *The Newspaper and Periodical Press* (Washington, D.C.: U.S. Government Printing Office, 1884), p. 27. This source provides much of the information reported here about newspapers and magazines before 1880.

12. Editor & Publisher, *International Year Book*, 2004 (New York: Editor & Publisher, 2004), p. xi.

13. In 1950, a total of 1,772 daily papers had a circulation of 53.8 million; in 2003, a total of 1,456 newspapers had a circulation of 55.2 million—while the population increased from 151 million in 1950 to about 280 million in 2003. See Harold W. Stanley and Richard G. Niemi (eds.), *Vital Statistics on American Politics 2005–2006* (Washington, D.C.: CQ Press, 2006), p. 175; Editor & Publisher, *International Year Book*.

14. On framing in the media, see Stephen D. Reese, Oscar H. Gandy, Jr., and August E. Grant (eds.), *Framing Public Life: Perspectives on Media and Our Understanding of the Social World* (Mahwah, N.J.: Erlbaum, 2001). More generally on how leaders mediate public deliberation on issues, see Doris A. Graber, *Media Power in Politics*, 7th ed. (Washington, D.C.: CQ Press, 2005).

15. David Barker and Kathleen Knight, "Political Talk Radio and Public Opinion," *Public Opinion Quarterly* 64 (Summer 2000): 149–170; David C. Barker, *Rushed to Judgment: Talk Radio, Persuasion, and American Political Behavior* (New York: Columbia University Press, 2003).

16. Dana R. Ulloth, Peter L. Klinge, and Sandra Eells, *Mass Media: Past, Present, Future* (St. Paul, Minn.: West, 1983), p. 278.

17. Douglas Ahers, "News Consumption and the New Electronic Media," *Harvard International Journal of Press/Politics* 11 (Winter 2006): 29–52.

18. John December, Neil Randall, and Wes Tatters, *Discover the World Wide Web with Your Sportster* (Indianapolis, Ind.: Sams.net Publishing, 1995), pp. 11–12.

19. Katharine Q. Seelye, Jacques Steinberg, and David F. Gallagher, "Bloggers as News Media Trophy Hunters," *New York Times*, 14 February 2005, p. C1; and Bill Carter, "Post-Mortem of a Broadcast Disaster," *New York Times*, 11 January 2005, p. C1.

20. Jonathan Glater, "At a Suit's Core: Are Bloggers Reporters, Too?" *New York Times*, 17 March 2005, p. C1.
21. Katharine Q. Seelye, "Take That, Mr. Newsman!" *New York Times*, 1 January 2006, p. C1.
22. Joe Hagan, "Miller Retires from Times, but Not Quietly," *Wall Street Journal*, 10 November 2005, p. B1.
23. Katie Hafner and Matt Richtel, "U.S. Is Pressing Google for Data on Searches," *New York Times*, 20 January 2006, p. 1.
24. Howard W. French, "Chinese Censors and Web Users Match Wits," *New York Times*, 4 March 2005, p. A8; and Tom Zeller, Jr., "China, Still Winning Against the Web," *New York Times*, 15 January 2006, sec. 4, p. 4.
25. Kevin J. Delaney, "Google to Launch Service in China," *Wall Street Journal*, 25 January 2006, p. B2.
26. Amy Schatz, "Tech Firms Defend China Web Policies," *Wall Street Journal*, 16 February 2006, p. A2.
27. World Bank, *World Development Report 2002: Building Institutions for Markets* (New York: Oxford University Press, 2002), Chapter 10.
28. Pew Research Center, Survey Report of 8 June 2004, "News Audiences Increasingly Politicized: Online News Audience Larger, More Diverse," available at <http://people-press.org/reports/print.php3?PageID=841>.
29. Doris A. Graber, *Mass Media and American Politics*, 7th ed. (Washington, D.C.: CQ Press, 2005), pp. 98–101. See also W. Lance Bennett, *News: The Politics of Illusion*, 3rd ed. (White Plains, N.Y.: Longman, 1996), Chapter 2.
30. John H. McManus, *Market Driven Journalism: Let the Citizen Beware?* (Thousand Oaks, Calif.: Sage, 1994), p. 85.
31. David D. Kurplus, "Bucking a Trend in Local Television News," *Journalism* 4 (2003): 77–94.
32. Joe Flint, "Viacom to Split, Create 2 Companies," *Wall Street Journal*, 15 June 2005, p. B5.
33. Ellen Gray, "Same anchor, different show" (May 22, 2007), at http://www.philly.com/dailynews/columnists/ellen)_gray/20070522_Ellen_Gray_Same_anchor_different_show.html.
34. Thomas E. Patterson, "Doing Well and Doing Good: How Soft News and Critical Journalism Are Shrinking the News Audience and Weakening Democracy—and What News Outlets Can Do About It" (Cambridge, Mass.: Harvard University, Joan Shorenstein Center for Press, Politics, and Public Policy, 2000), pp. 2–5.
35. Learning from soft news was argued by Matthew A. Baum, "Sex, Lies, and War: How Soft News Brings Foreign Policy to the Inattentive Public," *American Political Science Review* 96 (2002): 91–110. The study that found otherwise was by Markus Prior, "Any Good News in Soft News? The Impact of Soft News Preferences on Political Knowledge," *Political Communication* 20 (2003): 149–171.
36. Ted Koppel, "And Now, a Word for Our Demographic," *New York Times*, 29 January 2006, sec. 4, p. 16; and Katharine Q. Seelye, "Hands-On Readers," *New York Times*, 4 July 2005, p. C1.
37. "The State of the News Media," *An Annual Report on American Journalism 2005*, available at <http://stateofthenewsmedia.org/2005/narrative_networktv_audience.asp?cat=3&m>.
38. Kelvin Childs, "End the Cross-Owner Ban," *Editor & Publisher*, 28 June 1997, p. 11.
39. Jonathan R. Laing, "Harvest Time: After Years of Stumbles, News Corp.'s Big Bets Finally Pay Off," *Barron's*, 20 October 2003, pp. 28–31.
40. Graber, *Mass Media and American Politics*, pp. 43–47.
41. Matthew Rose and Joe Flint, "Behind Media-Ownership Fight, an Old Power Struggle Is Raging," *Wall Street Journal*, 15 October 2003, p. 1.
42. Jennifer Lee, "On Minot, N.D., Radio, a Single Corporate Voice," *New York Times*, 31 March 2003, p. C7.
43. Jim Rutenberg with Micheline Maynard, "TV News That Looks Local, Even If It's Not," *New York Times*, 2 June 2003, pp. C1, C9.
44. For a clear summary of very complex developments, see Robert B. Horowitz, "Communications Regulations in Protecting the Public Interest," in *The Institutions of American Democracy: The Press*, ed. Geneva Overholser and Kathleen Hall Jamieson (New York: Oxford University Press, 2005), pp. 284–302.
45. Mark Crispin Miller, "Free the Media," *Nation*, 3 June 1996, pp. 9–15; see also Stephen Labaton, "It's a World of Media Plenty. Why Limit Ownership?" *New York Times*, 12 October 2003, sec. 4, p. 4.
46. Jim Rutenberg, "Fewer Media Owners, More Media Choices," *New York Times*, 2 December 2002, p. C1.
47. Jared Sandberg, "Federal Judges Block Censorship on the Internet," *Wall Street Journal*, 13 June 1996, p. B1.
48. Robert Entman, *Democracy Without Citizens: Media and the Decay of American Politics* (New York: Oxford University Press, 1989), pp. 103–108.
49. John Leland, "Why the Right Rules the Radio Waves," *New York Times*, 8 December 2003, sec. 4, p. 7.
50. For an alternative view of the functions of the media, see Graber, *Mass Media and American Politics*, pp. 5–12.
51. Martha Joynt Kumar, "The President and the News Media," in *The President, the Public, and the Parties*, 2nd ed. (Washington, D.C.: CQ Press, 1997), p. 119. In March 2005, Garrett M. Graff was issued a daily pass to attend the White House briefing for the purpose of contributing to his blog on journalists. See Katharine Q. Seelye, "White House Approves Pass for Bloggers," *New York Times*, 7 March 2005, p. C5.
52. Warren Weaver, "C-Span on the Hill: 10 Years of Gavel to Gavel," *New York Times*, 28 March 1989, p. 10; Francis X. Clines, "C-Span Inventor Offers More Politics Up Close," *New York Times*, 31 March 1996, p. 11.
53. Jon Garfunkel, "The New Gatekeepers Part 1: Changing the Guard," in *Civilities: Media Structures Research* (4 April 2005), available at <http://civilities.net/The NewGatekeepers-Changing>.
54. Bennett, *News: The Politics of Illusion*, p. 26.
55. Quote attributed to Sandra Mims Rowe, president of the American Society of Newspaper Editors, in Janny Scott, "A Media Race Enters Waters Still Uncharted," *New York Times*, 1 February 1998, p. 1.
56. Bill Kovach, "The Brewing Backlash," *Chicago Tribune*, 1 February 1998, sec. 2, p. 1; and Scott, "A Media Race Enters Waters Still Uncharted."
57. Graber, *Mass Media and American Politics*, p. 253. See also Janet Hook, "Most of Us Don't Have a Clue About How Congress Works," *Chicago Tribune*, 10 June 1993, sec. 1, p. 17.
58. Stephen J. Farnsworth and S. Robert Lichter, "*The Nightly News Nightmare* Revisited: Network Television's Coverage of the 2004 Presidential Election," paper prepared for presentation at the annual meeting of the American Political Science Association (Washington, D.C.: 2005); and "Contest Lacks Content," *Media Tenor* 1 (2005): 12–15.
59. Ibid., p. 24.
60. Pew Research Center, " News Audiences Increasingly Politicized: Online News Audience Larger, More Diverse," *Survey Report*. The survey was taken 19 April to 12 May and released on 8 June 2004.
61. Ibid.
62. Ibid.
63. W. Russell Neuman, Marion R. Just, and Ann N. Crigler, *Common Knowledge: News and the Construction of Political Meaning* (Chicago: University of Chicago Press, 1992), p. 10. See also Debra Gersh Hernandez, "Profile of the News Consumer," *Editor & Publisher*, 18 January 1997, pp. 6, 7. Respondents who said that newspapers were their primary source of information correctly answered more factual questions than those who used other media. For a more optimistic assessment

of television's instructional value, see Doris A. Graber, *Processing Politics: Learning from Television in the Internet Age* (Chicago: University of Chicago Press, 2001), esp. pp. 120–128. Another negative note is sounded by Alan B. Krueger, "Economic Scene," *New York Times*, 1 April 2004, p. C2.

64. James N. Druckman, "Media Matter: How Newspapers and Television News Cover Campaigns and Influence Voters," *Political Communication* 22 (October–December 2005): 463–481. For a complementary study finding that television news has little effect on campaign learning, see Stephen C. Craig, James G. Kane, and Jason Gainous, "Issue-Related Learning in a Gubernatorial Campaign: A Case Study," *Political Communication* 22 (October–December 2005): 483–503.

65. Stephen J. Farnsworth and S. Robert Lichter, *Nightly News Nightmare: Network Television's Coverage of U.S Presidential Elections, 1988–2000* (Lanham, Md.: Rowman & Littlefield, 2003), p. 6.

66. Ibid., p. 113.

67. William P. Eveland, Jr., Andrew F. Hayes, Dhavan V. Shah, and Nojin Kwak, "Understanding the Relationship Between Communication and Political Knowledge: A Model Comparison Approach Using Panel Data," *Political Communication* 22 (October–December 2005): 423–446.

68. Laurence Parisot, "Attitudes About the Media: A Five-Country Comparison," *Public Opinion* 10 (January–February 1988): 60.

69. Farnsworth and Lichter, *Nightly News Nightmare*, pp. 16–21, consider three models of media influence: (1) "hypodermic needle"—quick effect, like a shot; (2) "minimal effects"—the two-step flow, which may work only as the media focus on the activity; and (3) "more-than-minimal effects," primarily through setting the agenda for discussion.

70. Alessandra Stanley, "Reporters Turn from Deference to Outrage," *New York Times*, 5 September 2005, p. A14.

71. Graber, *Media Power in Politics*, pp. 278–279.

72. Daniel J. Wakin, "Report Calls Networks' Election Night Coverage a Disaster," *New York Times*, 3 February 2001, p. A8.

73. Maxwell McCombs, "The Agenda-Setting Function of the Press," in Overholser and Jamieson, *Institutions of American Democracy*, pp. 156–168.

74. Danilo Yanich, "Kids, Crime, and Local TV News," a report of the Local TV News Media Project (Newark: University of Delaware, January 2005). See also Jeremy H. Lipschultz and Michael L. Hilt, *Crime and Local Television News: Dramatic, Breaking, and Live from the Scene* (Mahwah, N.J.: Erlbaum, 2002).

75. Lipschultz and Hilt, p. 2.

76. Lawrie Mifflin, "Crime Falls, but Not on TV," *New York Times*, 6 July 1997, sec. 4, p. 4.

77. W. Russell Neuman, "The Threshold of Public Attention," *Public Opinion Quarterly* 54 (Summer 1990): 159–176.

78. David E. Harrington, "Economic News on Television: The Determinants of Coverage," *Public Opinion Quarterly* 53 (Spring 1989): 17–40.

79. John Tierney, "Talk Shows Prove Key to White House," *New York Times*, 21 October 2002, p. A13.

80. Doris Graber reviews some studies of socially undesirable effects on children and adults in *Processing Politics*, pp. 91–95.

81. Richard Zoglin, "Is TV Ruining Our Children?" *Time*, 5 October 1990, p. 75. Moreover, much of what children see is advertisements. See "Study: Almost 20% of Kid TV Is Ad-Related," *Chicago Tribune*, 22 April 1991, p. 11. See also Stephen Seplow and Jonathan Storm, "Reviews Mixed on Television's Effect on Children," *St. Paul Pioneer Press*, 28 December 1997, p. 9A; and Nell Minow, "Standards for TV Language Rapidly Going Down the Tube," *Chicago Tribune*, 7 October 2003, sec. 5, p. 2.

82. John J. O'Connor, "Soothing Bromides? Not on TV," *New York Times*, 28 October 1990, Arts & Leisure section, pp. 1,

35. Some people watched *The X-Files* because it involved sinister government activities. See Alanna Nash, "Confused or Not, the X-Philes Keep Coming," *New York Times*, 11 January 1998, p. 41.

83. Douglas Kellner, *Television and the Crisis of Democracy* (Boulder, Colo.: Westview Press, 1990), p. 17.

84. James Fallows, *Breaking the News: How the Media Undermine American Democracy* (New York: Pantheon Books, 1996).

85. Katharaine Q. Seelye, "Survey on News Media Finds Wide Displeasure," *New York Times*, 27 June 2005, p. C5.

86. See Bernard Goldberg, *Bias: A CBS Insider Exposes How the Media Distort the News* (Washington, D.C.: Regnery Publishing, 2002), and Ann Coulter, *Slander: Liberal Lies About the American Right* (New York: Crown, 2002).

87. See Eric Alterman, *What Liberal Media? The Truth About Bias and the News* (New York: Basic Books, 2003); and Al Franken, *Lies and the Liars Who Tell Them . . . a Fair and Balanced Look at the Right* (New York: Penguin, 2003).

88. Pew Research Center of the People and the Press, "Bottom-Line Pressures Now Hurting Coverage, Say Journalists," press release, 23 May 2004, <http://people-press.org/reports/>.

89. Farnsworth and Lichter, "The Nightly News Nightmare Revisited," p. 31.

90. William G. Mayer, "Why Talk Radio Is Conservative," *Public Interest* (Summer 2004): pp. 86–103.

91. *The People, the Press, and Their Leaders* (Washington, D.C.: Times-Mirror Center for the People and the Press, 1995). See also Pew Research Center, "Self Censorship: How Often and Why," survey of nearly 300 journalists and news executives in February–March 2000, released on 30 April 2000.

92. Stanley and Niemi, *Vital Statistics on American Politics*, p. 199.

93. Maura Clancey and Michael J. Robinson, "General Election Coverage: Part I," *Public Opinion* 7 (December–January 1985): 54. Some journalists take their watchdog role seriously. See Pew Research Center, "Striking the Balance, Audience Interests, Business Pressures and Journalists' Values," 30 March 1999, at <http://people-press.org/reports/display.php3?ReportID=67>.

94. Todd Shields, "Media Accentuates the Negative," *Editor & Publisher*, 27 November 2000, p. 12.

95. Bob Kemper, "Bush: No Iraqi Link to Sept. 11," *Chicago Tribune*, 18 September 2003, pp. 1–6.

96. Steven Kull and others, "Misperceptions, the Media, and the Iraq War," Program on International Policy Attitudes (PIPA), 2 October 2003, available at <www.PIPA.org>.

97. Barbie Zelizer, David Park, and David Gudelunas, "How Bias Shapes the News: Challenging *The New York Times'* Status as a Newspaper of Record on the Middle East," *Journalism* 3 (2002): 303.

98. W. Lance Bennett and William Serrin, "The Watchdog Role," in Overholser and Jamieson, *Institutions of American Democracy*, pp. 169–188.

99. For a historical account of efforts to determine voters' preferences before modern polling, see Tom W. Smith, "The First Straw? A Study of the Origin of Election Polls," *Public Opinion Polling* 54 (Spring 1990): 21–36. See also Susan Herbst, *Numbered Voices: How Opinion Polling Has Shaped American Politics* (Chicago: University of Chicago Press, 1993), Chapter 4.

100. William Schneider and I. A. Lewis, "Views on the News," *Public Opinion* 8 (August–September 1985): 6–11, 58–59. For similar findings from a 1994 study, see Times-Mirror Center for the People and the Press, "Mixed Message About Press Freedom on Both Sides of the Atlantic," press release, 16 March 1994, p. 65. See also Thomas E. Patterson, "News Decisions: Journalists as Partisan Actors," paper presented at the 1996 Annual Meeting of the American Political Science Association, p. 21.

101. Pew Research Center for the People and the Press, News Interest Final Topline, 1–5 February 2006, available at <http://people-press.org/reports/display.php3?ReportID=270>.

Chapter 7 / Participation and Voting / pages 190–225

1. Remarks by the president and special envoy to Iraq, Ambassador Bremer, at a photo opportunity in the Oval Office, 27 October 2003.
2. Scott Atran, "Genesis of Suicide Terrorism," *Science,* 7 March 2003, pp. 1534–1539. A penetrating review of several books on terrorist attacks is provided by Nichole Argo, "The Role of Social Context in Terrorist Attacks," *Chronicle of Higher Education,* 3 February 2006, p. B15.
3. Remark attributed to Bruce Hoffman by Nicholas Lemann, "What Terrorists Want," *New Yorker,* 29 October 2001.
4. U.S. Department of State, "Patterns of Global Terrorism 2001" (Washington, D.C.: U.S. Department of State, May 2002), p. 17. The definition is contained in Title 22 of the U.S. Code, Section 2656f(d). On the problem of defining terrorism, see Walter Laquer, *No End to War: Terrorism in the 21st Century* (New York: Continuum International, 2003), esp. the appendix.
5. Stephen J. Hedges, "U.S. Left to Box with Bombers' Shadows," *Chicago Tribune,* 28 October 2003, pp. 1, 5. A columnist also contended that the terrorists feared less the American occupation of Iraq than that the Americans would change Iraq into a democratic nation. Tom Friedman, "It's No Vietnam," *New York Times,* 30 October 2003, p. A29.
6. Lou Nichel and Dan Herbeck, *American Terrorist: Timothy McVeigh and the Oklahoma City Bombing* (New York: HarperCollins, 2001), pp. 350–354.
7. M. Margaret Conway, *Political Participation in the United States,* 3rd ed. (Washington, D.C.: CQ Press, 2000), p. 3.
8. See Robert L. Snow, *The Militia Threat: Terrorists Among Us* (New York: Plenum, 1999). Kathryn Westcott, "Militias 'in Retreat,'" *BBC News Online,* 11 May 2001, available at <http://news.bbc.co.uk/1/hi/world/americas/1325330.stm>.
9. Michael Lapsky, "Protest as a Political Resource," *American Political Science Review* 62 (December 1968): 1145.
10. William E. Schmidt, "Selma Marchers Mark 1965 Clash," *New York Times,* 4 March 1985.
11. See Sidney Verba and Norman H. Nie, *Participation in America: Political Democracy and Social Equality* (New York: Harper & Row, 1972), p. 3.
12. Jonathan D. Casper, *Politics of Civil Liberties* (New York: Harper & Row, 1972), p. 90.
13. David C. Colby, "A Test of the Relative Efficacy of Political Tactics," *American Journal of Political Science* 26 (November 1982): 741–753. See also Frances Fox Piven and Richard Cloward, *Poor People's Movements* (New York: Vintage, 1979).
14. Raoul V. Mowatt, "Voting Act Heralded 35 Years Later," *Chicago Tribune,* 5 August 2000, p. 5; U.S. Department of Commerce, *Statistical Abstract of the United States 2006* (Washington, D.C.: U.S. Government Printing Office, 2005), Tables 403–404.
15. Stephen C. Craig and Michael A. Magiotto, "Political Discontent and Political Action," *Journal of Politics* 43 (May 1981): 514–522. But see Mitchell A. Seligson, "Trust Efficacy and Modes of Political Participation: A Study of Costa Rican Peasants," *British Journal of Political Science* 10 (January 1980): 75–98, for a review of studies that came to different conclusions.
16. Arthur H. Miller et al., "Group Consciousness and Political Participation," *American Journal of Political Science* 25

(August 1981): 495. See also Susan J. Carroll, "Gender Politics and the Socializing Impact of the Women's Movement," in *Political Learning in Adulthood: A Sourcebook of Theory and Research,* ed. Roberta S. Sigel (Chicago: University of Chicago Press, 1989), p. 307.
17. Richard D. Shingles, "Black Consciousness and Political Participation: The Missing Link," *American Political Science Review* 75 (March 1981): 76–91. See also Lawrence Bobo and Franklin D. Gilliam, Jr., "Race, Sociopolitical Participation, and Black Empowerment," *American Political Science Review* 84 (June 1990): 377–393; and Jan Leighley, "Group Membership and the Mobilization of Political Participation," *Journal of Politics* 58 (May 1996): 447–463.
18. See James L. Gibson, "The Policy Consequences of Political Intolerance: Political Repression During the Vietnam War Era," *Journal of Politics* 51 (February 1989): 13–35. Gibson found that individual state legislatures reacted quite differently in response to antiwar demonstrations on college campuses, but the laws passed to discourage dissent were not related directly to public opinion within the state.
19. See Verba and Nie, *Participation in America,* p. 69. Also see John Clayton Thomas, "Citizen-Initiated Contacts with Government Agencies: A Test of Three Theories," *American Journal of Political Science* 26 (August 1982): 504–522; and Elaine B. Sharp, "Citizen-Initiated Contacting of Government Officials and Socioeconomic Status: Determining the Relationship and Accounting for It," *American Political Science Review* 76 (March 1982): 109–115.
20. Elaine B. Sharp, "Citizen Demand Making in the Urban Context," *American Journal of Political Science* 28 (November 1984): 654–670, esp. pp. 654, 665.
21. Verba and Nie, *Participation in America,* p. 67; Sharp, "Citizen Demand Making," p. 660.
22. See Joel B. Grossman et al., "Dimensions of Institutional Participation: Who Uses the Courts and How?" *Journal of Politics* 44 (February 1982): 86–114; Frances Kahn Zemans, "Legal Mobilization: The Neglected Role of the Law in the Political System," *American Political Science Review* 77 (September 1983): 690–703.
23. *Brown v. Board of Education,* 347 U.S. 483 (1954).
24. See Michael P. MacDonald and Samuel L. Popkin, "The Myth of the Vanishing Voter," *American Political Science Review* 95 (December 2001): 963–974.
25. Max Kaase and Alan Marsh, "Political Action: A Theoretical Perspective," in *Political Action: Mass Participation in Five Western Democracies,* ed. Samuel H. Barnes and Max Kaase (Beverly Hills, Calif.: Sage, 1979), p. 168.
26. *Smith v. Allwright,* 321 U.S. 649 (1944).
27. *Harper v. Virginia State Board of Elections,* 383 U.S. 663 (1966).
28. Everett Carll Ladd, *The American Polity* (New York: Norton, 1985), p. 392.
29. Gorton Carruth and associates (eds.), *The Encyclopedia of American Facts and Dates* (New York: Crowell, 1979), p. 330. For an eye-opening account of women's contributions to politics before gaining the vote, see Robert J. Dinkin, *Before Equal Suffrage: Women in Partisan Politics from Colonial Times to 1920* (Westport, Conn.: Greenwood Press, 1995).
30. Ivor Crewe, "Electoral Participation," in *Democracy at the Polls: A Comparative Study of Competitive National Elections,* ed. David Butler, Howard R. Penniman, and Austin Ranney (Washington, D.C.: American Enterprise Institute, 1981), pp. 219–223.
31. Thomas E. Cronin, *Direct Democracy: The Politics of Initiative, Referendum, and Recall* (Cambridge, Mass.: Harvard University Press, 1989), p. 127.
32. John G. Matsusaka, "2004 Initiatives and Referendums," in *Book of the States 2005* (Lexington, Ky.: Council of State Governments, 2005), pp. 281–290.

33. Ibid.

34. "Gay Rights Law Faces Reversal in Maine Vote," *Chicago Tribune*, 11 January 1998, p. 16.

35. David S. Broder, *Democracy Derailed: Initiative Campaigns and the Power of Money* (New York: Harcourt, 2000), and David S. Broder, "A Snake in the Grass Roots," *Washington Post*, 26 March 2000, pp. B1–B2.

36. Caroline J. Tolbert, Ramona S. McNeal, and Daniel A. Smith, "Enhancing Civic Engagement: The Effect of Direct Democracy on Political Participation and Knowledge," *State Politics and Policy Quarterly* 3 (Spring 2003): 23–41. For a more critical look at initiatives as undermining representative government, see Bruce E. Cain and Kenneth P. Miller, "The Populist Legacy: Initiatives and the Undermining of Representative Government," in *Dangerous Democracy? The Battle over Ballot Initiatives in America*, ed. Larry J. Sabato, Howard R. Ernst, and Bruce A. Larson (Lanham, Md.: Rowman & Littlefield, 2001), pp. 33–62. For the role of interest groups in ballot issue campaigns, see Robert M. Alexander, *Rolling the Dice with State Initiatives* (Westport, Conn.: Praeger, 2002).

37. For the impact of the Internet on ballot measures (not all good), see Richard J. Ellis, *Democratic Delusions: The Initiative Process in America* (Lawrence: University of Kansas Press, 2002), esp. pp. 198–203.

38. Darrell M. West, "State and Federal E-Government in the United States, 2003," *Brown Policy Reports* (September 2003), available at <www.insidepolitics.org>. Also see Elaine Ciulla Kamarack and Joseph S. Nye, Jr. (eds.), *Governance.com: Democracy in the Information Age* (Washington, D.C.: Brookings Institution Press, 2002).

39. Data on the elected state officials come from *The Book of the States 2003* (Lexington, Ky.: Council of State Governments, 2003), p. 201. Estimates of the number of elected school board members come from *Chicago Tribune*, 10 March 1985.

40. Crewe, "Electoral Participation," p. 232. A rich literature has grown to explain turnout across nations. See Pippa Norris, *Democratic Phoenix: Reinventing Political Activism* (Cambridge: Cambridge University Press, 2002), Chapter 3; Mark N. Franklin, "The Dynamics of Electoral Participation," in *Comparing Democracies 2: New Challenges in the Study of Elections and Voting*, ed. Lawrence LeDuc, Richard G. Niemi, and Pippa Norris (London: Sage, 2002), pp. 148–168.

41. Verba and Nie, *Participation in America*, p. 13.

42. Russell J. Dalton, *Citizen Policies*, 3rd ed. (New York: Seven Bridges, 2002), pp. 67–68.

43. For a concise summary of the effect of age on voting turnout, see William H. Flanigan and Nancy H. Zingale, *Political Behavior of the American Electorate*, 10th ed. (Washington, D.C.: CQ Press, 2002), pp. 44–46.

44. Ibid., pp. 46–47.

45. M. Margaret Conway, Gertrude A. Steuernagel, and David W. Ahern, *Women and Political Participation: Cultural Change in the Political Arena* (Washington, D.C.: CQ Press, 1997), pp. 79–80.

46. Ronald B. Rapoport, "The Sex Gap in Political Persuading: Where the 'Structuring Principle' Works," *American Journal of Political Science* 25 (February 1981): 32–48. Perhaps surprisingly, research fails to show any relationship between a wife's role in her marriage and her political activity. See Nancy Burns, Kay Lehman Schlozman, and Sidney Verba, "The Public Consequences of Private Inequality: Family Life and Citizen Participation," *American Political Science Review* 91 (June 1997): 373–389.

47. Bruce C. Straits, "The Social Context of Voter Turnout," *Public Opinion Quarterly* 54 (Spring 1990): 64–73.

48. Sidney Verba, Kay Lehman Scholzman, and Henry E. Brady, *Voice and Equality: Civic Voluntarism in American Politics* (Cambridge, Mass.: Harvard University Press, 1995), p. 433.

49. Stephen J. Dubner and Steven D. Levitt, "Why Vote"? *New York Times Magazine*, 6 November 2005, pp. 30–31.

50. Obtained on 11 July 1996, from "Rock the Vote" home page at <www.rockthevote.org>.

51. See Eric Pultzer, "Becoming a Habitual Voter: Inertia, Resources, and Growth in Young Adulthood," *American Political Science Review* (March 2002): 41–56; Alan S. Gerber, Donald P. Green, and Ron Shachar, "Voting May Be Habit-Forming: Evidence from a Randomized Field Experiment," *American Journal of Political Science* (July 2003): 540–550; and David Dreyer Lassen, "The Effect of Information on Voter Turnout: Evidence from a Natural Experiment," *American Journal of Political Science* 49 (January 2005): 103–118.

52. Stephen D. Shaffer, "A Multivariate Explanation of Decreasing Turnout in Presidential Elections, 1960–1976," *American Journal of Political Science* 25 (February 1981): 68–95; Paul R. Abramson and John H. Aldrich, "The Decline of Electoral Participation in America," *American Political Science Review* 76 (September 1981): 603–620. However, one scholar argues that this research suffers because it looks only at voters and nonvoters in a single election. When the focus shifts to people who vote sometimes but not at other times, the models do not fit so well. See M. Margaret Conway and John E. Hughes, "Political Mobilization and Patterns of Voter Turnout" (paper prepared for delivery at the annual meeting of the American Political Science Association, Washington, D.C., September 1993).

53. Apparently Richard A. Brody was the first scholar to pose this problem as a puzzle. See his "The Puzzle of Political Participation in America," in *The New American Political System*, ed. Anthony King (Washington, D.C.: American Enterprise Institute, 1978), pp. 287–324. Since then, a sizable literature has attempted to explain the decline in voter turnout in the United States. One scholar contends that postindustrial societies experience a "ceiling effect" that blunts increased voting due to increased education; see Norris, *Democratic Phoenix*, Chapter 3. Another finds that the perceived importance of electoral contests and the closeness of the vote are the major factors explaining differences in turnout; see Franklin, "The Dynamics of Electoral Participation," pp. 148–168.

54. See Jack Doppelt and Ellen Shearer, *America's No-Shows: Non-voters* (Washington, D.C.: Medill School of Journalism, 2001); Thomas E. Patterson, *The Vanishing Voter* (New York: Vintage Books, 2003).

55. Some scholars argue that Americans generally have become disengaged from social organizations (not just political parties), becoming more likely to act "alone" than to participate in group activities. See Robert D. Putnam, *Bowling Alone: The Collapse and Revival of American Community* (New York: Simon & Schuster, 2000).

56. Steve Ivey, "Election Day Would Draw More Voters on Weekend, Group Says," *Chicago Tribune*, 8 November 2005, p. 12.

57. The negative effect of registration laws on voter turnout is argued in Frances Fox Piven and Richard Cloward, "Government Statistics and Conflicting Explanations of Nonvoting," *PS: Political Science and Politics* 22 (September 1989): 580–588. Their analysis was hotly contested in Stephen Earl Bennett, "The Uses and Abuses of Registration and Turnout Data: An Analysis of Piven and Cloward's Studies of Nonvoting in America," *PS: Political Science and Politics* 23 (June 1990): 166–171. Bennett showed that turnout declined 10 to 13 percent after 1960, despite efforts to remove or lower legal hurdles to registration. For their reply, see Frances Fox Piven and Richard Cloward, "A Reply to Bennett," *PS: Political Science and Politics* 23 (June 1990): 172–173. You can see that reasonable people can disagree on this matter. Moreover, cross-national research has found that compulsory voter

registration (not voluntary, as in the United States) did not increase turnout across nations. See Franklin, "The Dynamics of Electoral Participation," p. 159.

58. Mark J. Fenster, "The Impact of Allowing Day of Registration Voting on Turnout in U.S. Elections from 1960 to 1992: A Research Note," *American Politics Quarterly* 22 (January 1994): 74–87.

59. David Glass, Peverill Squire, and Raymond Wolfinger, "Voter Turnout: An International Comparison," *Public Opinion* 6 (December–January 1984): 52. Wolfinger says that because of the strong effect of registration on turnout, most rational choice analyses of voting would be better suited to analyzing turnout of only registered voters. See Raymond E. Wolfinger, "The Rational Citizen Faces Election Day," *Public Affairs Report* 6 (November 1992): 12.

60. Federal Election Commission, *The Impact of the National Voter Registration Act of 1993 on the Administration of Elections for Federal Office 1997–1998* (Washington, D.C.: Federal Election Commission, 1999), available at <http://www.fec.gov/pages/9798NVRAexec.htm>.

61. Recent research finds that "party contact is clearly a statistically and substantively important factor in predicting and explaining political behavior." See Peter W. Wielhouwer and Brad Lockerbie, "Party Contacting and Political Participation, 1952–1990" (paper prepared for delivery at the annual meeting of the American Political Science Association, Chicago, 1992), p. 14. Of course, parties strategically target the groups that they want to see vote in elections. See Peter W. Wielhouwer, "Strategic Canvassing by Political Parties, 1952–1990," *American Review of Politics* 16 (Fall 1995): 213–238.

62. Steven J. Rosenstone and John Mark Hansen, *Mobilization, Participation, and Democracy in America* (New York: Macmillan, 1993), p. 213.

63. See Robert A. Jackson, "Voter Mobilization in the 1986 Midterm Election," *Journal of Politics* 55 (November 1993): 1081–1099; Kim Quaile Hill and Jan E. Leighley, "Political Parties and Class Mobilization in Contemporary United States Elections," *American Journal of Political Science* 40 (August 1996): 787–804.

64. See Charles Krauthammer, "In Praise of Low Voter Turnout," *Time,* 21 May 1990, p. 88. Krauthammer says, "Low voter turnout means that people see politics as quite marginal to their lives, as neither salvation nor ruin. . . . Low voter turnout is a leading indicator of contentment." A major study in 1996 that compared 1,000 likely nonvoters with 2,300 likely voters found that 24 percent of the nonvoters, versus 5 percent of likely voters, said they "hardly ever" followed public affairs. See Dwight Morris, "No-Show '96: Americans Who Don't Vote," summary report to the Medill News Service and WTTW Television, Northwestern University School of Journalism, 1996. For a critical view of nonvoting, see Patterson, *The Vanishing Voter,* pp. 11–13.

65. Crewe, "Electoral Participation," p. 262.

66. Barnes and Kaase, *Political Action,* p. 532.

67. Eric Lichtblau, "F.B.I. Watched Activist Groups, New Files Show," *New York Times,* 20 December 2005, p. 1.

68. *1971 Congressional Quarterly Almanac* (Washington, D.C.: CQ Press, 1972), p. 475.

69. Benjamin Ginsberg, *The Consequences of Consent: Elections, Citizen Control, and Popular Acquiescence* (Reading, Mass.: Addison-Wesley, 1982), p. 13.

70. Ibid., pp. 13–14.

71. Ibid., pp. 6–7.

72. Some people have argued that the decline in voter turnout during the 1980s served to increase the class bias in the electorate because people of lower socioeconomic status stayed home. But later research has concluded that "class bias has not increased since 1964" (Jan E. Leighley and Jonathan Nagler, "Socioeconomic Class Bias in Turnout, 1964–1988:

The Voters Remain the Same," *American Political Science Review* 86 [September 1992]: 734). Nevertheless, Rosenstone and Hansen, in *Mobilization, Participation, and Democracy in America,* say, "The economic inequalities in political participation that prevail in the United States today are as large as the racial disparities in political participation that prevailed in the 1950s. America's leaders today face few incentives to attend to the needs of the disadvantaged" (p. 248).

Chapter 8 / Political Parties / pages 226–258

1. *Federal Elections 2004: Election Results for the U.S. President, the U.S. Senate and the U.S. House of Representatives* (Washington, D.C.: Federal Election Commission, May 2005), p. 5.

2. Adopted in convention at Atlanta, Georgia, in May 2004 and available at <http://www.lp.org/issues/platform_all.shtml>.

3. Counts of Libertarian Party congressional candidates in 2004 were compiled from election data in Clerk of the House of Representatives, *Statistics of the Presidential and Congressional Election of November 2, 2004* (Washington, D.C., 2005); and *Federal Elections 2004.*

4. The Ultimate Third Party Encyclopedia at <http://www.thirdpartywatch.com/encyclopedia/index.php?title=Libertarian_Party>.

5. *Statistics of the Presidential and Congressional Election of November 2, 2004,* pp. 65–67.

6. Center for Political Studies of the Institute for Social Research, *American National Election Study 2004* (Ann Arbor: University of Michigan, 2005).

7. David W. Moore, "Perot Supporters: For the Man, Not a Third Party," *Gallup Organization Newsletter Archive,* 7 August 1995; the Gallup Organization's web page at <www.gallup.com/newsletter/aug95/>.

8. See, for example, Peter Mair, "Comparing Party Systems," in *Comparing Democracies 2: New Challenges in the Study of Elections and Voting,* ed. Lawrence LeDuc, Richard G. Niemi, and Pippa Norris (London: Sage, 2002), pp. 88–107.

9. E. E. Schattschneider, *Party Government* (New York: Holt, 1942).

10. See Lyn Carson and Brian Martin, *Random Selection in Politics* (Westport, Conn.: Praeger, 1999). They say: "The assumption behind random selection in politics is that just about anyone who wishes to be involved in decision making is capable of making a useful contribution, and that the fairest way to ensure that everyone has such an opportunity is to give them an equal chance to be involved" (p. 4).

11. See James M. Snyder, Jr., and Michael M. Ting, "An Informational Rationale for Political Parties," *American Journal of Political Science* 46 (January 2002): 90–110. They formalize the argument that political parties acquire "brand names" that help voters make sense of politics.

12. John H. Aldrich, *Why Parties? The Origin and Transformation of Political Parties in America* (Chicago: University of Chicago Press, 1995), p. 296.

13. See John Kenneth White and Daniel M. Shea (eds.), *New Party Politics: From Jefferson and Hamilton to the Information Age* (Boston: Bedford/St. Martin's, 2000), for essays on the place of political parties in American history.

14. See Jerome M. Clubb, William H. Flanigan, and Nancy H. Zingale, *Partisan Realignment: Voters, Parties, and Government in American History* (Beverly Hills, Calif.: Sage, 1980), p. 163. Once central to the analysis of American politics, the concept of critical elections has been discounted by some scholars in recent years. See Larry M. Bartels, "Electoral Continuity and Change," *Electoral Studies* 17 (September 1998): 301–326; and David R. Mayhew, *Electoral Realignments: A Critique of an American Genre* (New Haven, Conn.: Yale University Press, 2002). However, the concept has been

defended by other scholars. See Peter F. Nardulli, "The Concept of a Critical Realignment, Electoral Behavior, and Political Change," *American Political Science Review* 89 (March 1995): 10–22; and Normal Schofield, Gary Miller, and Andrew Martin, "Critical Elections and Political Realignments in the USA: 1860–2000," *Political Studies* 51 (2003): 217–240.

15. See Gerald M. Pomper, "Classification of Presidential Elections," *Journal of Politics* 29 (August 1967): 535–566. See also Walter Dean Burnham, *Critical Elections and the Mainsprings of American Politics* (New York: Norton, 1970). Decades later, an update of Gerald Pomper's analysis of presidential elections through 1996 determined that 1960, 1964, and 1968 all had realigning characteristics. See Jonathan Knuckley, "Classification of Presidential Elections: An Update," *Polity* 31 (Summer 1999): 639–653.

16. For more extensive treatments, see Henry M. Littlefield, "The Wizard of Oz: Parable on Populism," *American Quarterly* 16 (Spring 1964): 47–58; and David B. Parker, "The Rise and Fall of *The Wonderful Wizard of Oz* as a 'Parable on Populism,'" *Journal of the Georgia Association of Historians* 15 (1994): 49–63.

17. In "Realignment in Presidential Politics: South and North?" (paper prepared for The Citadel Symposium on Southern Politics, March 4–5, 2004), William Crotty argues that a political realignment definitely occurred in the South around 1968 that affected presidential politics and national voting behavior.

18. Earl Black and Merle Black, *The Rise of Southern Republicans* (Cambridge, Mass.: Harvard University Press, 2002), pp. 2–3.

19. The discussion that follows draws heavily on Austin Ranney and Willmoore Kendall, *Democracy and the American Party System* (New York: Harcourt, Brace, 1956), Chapters 18, 19. For later analyses of multiparty politics in America, see Steven J. Rosenstone, Roy L. Behr, and Edward H. Lazarus, *Third Parties in America: Citizen Response to Major Party Failure*, 2nd ed. (Princeton, N.J.: Princeton University Press, 1996); and John F. Bibby and L. Sandy Maisel, *Two Parties—or More?* (Boulder, Colo.: Westview Press, 1998).

20. The seven candidates who bolted from their former parties and ran for president on a third-party ticket were Theodore Roosevelt (1912), Robert La Follette (1924), Henry A. Wallace (1948), Strom Thurmond (1948), George Wallace (1968), John Anderson (1980), and Pat Buchanan (2000). Thurmond and both Wallaces had been Democrats; the others had originally been elected to office as Republicans. Note that Harry Truman won reelection in 1948 despite facing opposition from former Democrats running as candidates of other parties.

21. J. David Gillespie, *Politics at the Periphery: Third Parties in a Two-Party America* (Columbia: University of South Carolina Press, 1993). Surveys of public attitudes toward minor parties are reported in Christian Coller, "Trends: Third Parties and the Two-Party System," *Public Opinion Quarterly* 60 (Fall 1996): 431–449. For a spirited defense of having a strong third party in American politics, see Theodore J. Lowi, "Toward a More Responsible Three-Party System: Deregulating American Democracy," in *The State of the Parties*, 4th ed., ed. John C. Green and Rick Farmer (Lanham, Md.: Rowman & Littlefield, 2003), pp. 354–377.

22. Rosenstone, Behr, and Lazarus, *Third Parties in America*, p. 8.

23. In his study of party systems, Jean Blondel noticed that most three-party systems had two major parties and a much smaller third party, which he called two-and-a-half-party systems. (Britain, for example, has two major parties—Labour and Conservative—and a smaller Social Democratic Party. Germany has followed a similar pattern.) Blondel said, "While it would seem theoretically possible for three-party systems to exist in which all three significant parties were of about equal size, there are in fact no three-party systems of this kind among Western democracies." He concluded that "genuine three-party systems do not normally occur because they are essentially transitional, thus unstable, forms of party systems." See his "Types of Party System," in *The West European Party System*, ed. Peter Mair (New York: Oxford University Press, 1990), p. 305.

24. See Douglas J. Amy, *Real Choices, New Voices: The Case for Proportional Representation in the United States*, 2nd ed. (New York: Columbia University Press, 2002).

25. The most complete report of these legal barriers is contained in monthly issues of *Ballot Access News*, whose website is <www.ballot-access.org/>. State laws and court decisions may systematically support the major parties, but the U.S. Supreme Court seems to hold a more neutral position toward major and minor parties. See Lee Epstein and Charles D. Hadley, "On the Treatment of Political Parties in the U.S. Supreme Court, 1900–1986," *Journal of Politics* 52 (May 1990): 413–432; E. Joshua Rosenkranz, *Voter Choice 96: A 50-State Report Card on the Presidential Elections* (New York: New York University School of Law, Brennan Center for Justice, 1996), p. 24.

26. See James Gimpel, *National Elections and the Autonomy of American State Party Systems* (Pittsburgh, Pa.: University of Pittsburgh Press, 1996).

27. Measuring the concept of party identification has had its problems. For insights into the issues, see R. Michael Alvarez, "The Puzzle of Party Identification," *American Politics Quarterly* 18 (October 1990): 476–491; and Donald Philip Green and Bradley Palmquist, "Of Artifacts and Partisan Instability," *American Journal of Political Science* 34 (August 1990): 872–902.

28. Rhodes Cook, "GOP Shows Dramatic Growth, Especially in the South," *Congressional Quarterly Weekly Report*, 13 January 1996, pp. 97–100.

29. Susan Page, "Highly Educated Couples Often Split on Candidates," *USA Today*, 18 December 2002, pp. 1–2.

30. Two scholars on voting behavior describe partisanship as "the feeling of sympathy for and loyalty to a political party that an individual acquires—sometimes during childhood—and holds through life, often with increasing intensity." See William H. Flanigan and Nancy H. Zingale, *Political Behavior of the American Electorate*, 10th ed. (Washington, D.C.: CQ Press, 2002), p. 60.

31. Bill Keller, "As Arms Buildup Eases, U.S. Tries to Take Stock," *New York Times*, 14 May 1985; Ed Gillespie and Bob Schellhas, *Contract with America* (New York: Times Books, 1994), p. 107.

32. "The GOP's Spending Spree," *Wall Street Journal*, 25 November 2003, p. A18.

33. See, for example, Gerald M. Pomper, *Elections in America* (New York: Dodd, Mead, 1968); Benjamin Ginsberg, "Election and Public Policy," *American Political Science Review* 70 (March 1976): 41–50; Jeff Fishel, *Presidents and Promises* (Washington, D.C.: CQ Press, 1985).

34. Ian Budge and Richard I. Hofferbert, "Mandates and Policy Outputs: U.S. Party Platforms and Federal Expenditures," *American Political Science Review* 84 (March 1990): 111–131.

35. See Terri Susan Fine, "Economic Interests and the Framing of the 1988 and 1992 Democratic and Republican Party Platforms," *American Review of Politics* 16 (Spring 1995): 79–93.

36. James Dao, "Platform Is Centrist, like G.O.P.'s, but Differs in Details," *New York Times*, 14 August 2000, pp. A1, A16.

37. Robert Harmel and Kenneth Janda, *Parties and Their Environments: Limits to Reform?* (New York: Longman, 1982), pp. 27–29. See also John Huber and Ronald Inglehart, "Expert Interpretations of Party Space and Party Locations in 42 Societies," *Party Politics* 1 (January 1995): 73–111; and Alan Ware, *Political Parties and Party Systems* (New York: Oxford University Press, 1996), Chapter 1.

38. See Ralph M. Goldman, *The National Party Chairmen and Committees: Factionalism at the Top* (Armonk, N.Y.: M. E. Sharpe, 1990). The subtitle is revealing.

39. William Crotty and John S. Jackson III, *Presidential Primaries and Nominations* (Washington, D.C.: CQ Press, 1985), p. 33.

40. Debra L. Dodson, "Socialization of Party Activists: National Convention Delegates, 1972–1981," *American Journal of Political Science* 34 (November 1990): 1119–1141.

41. Phillip A. Klinkner, "Party Culture and Party Behavior," in *The State of the Parties*, 3rd ed., ed. Daniel M. Shea and John C. Green (Lanham, Md.: Rowman & Littlefield, 1999), pp. 275–287; Phillip A. Klinkner, *The Losing Parties: Out-Party National Committees, 1956–1993* (New Haven, Conn.: Yale University Press, 1994).

42. Anthony Corrado, Sarah Barclay, and Heitor Gouvea, "The Parties Take the Lead: Political Parties and the Financing of the 2000 Presidential Election," in *The State of the Parties*, 4th ed., ed. John C. Green and Rick Farmer (Lanham, Md.: Rowman & Littlefield, 2003), p. 97; Klinkner, *The Losing Parties*.

43. "Political MoneyLine," Money in Politics Database at <http://www.tray.com/cgi-win/ x_partysummary.exe?DoFn=&sYR=2004>.

44. Dan Barry, "Republicans on Long Island Master Science of Politics," *New York Times*, 8 March 1996, p. A1S. Recent research suggests that when both major parties have strong organizations at the county level, the public has more favorable attitudes toward the parties. See John J. Coleman, "Party Organization Strength and Public Support for Parties," *American Journal of Political Science* 40 (August 1996): 805–824.

45. John Frendreis, Alan R. Gitelson, Gregory Flemming, and Anne Layzell, "Local Political Parties and Legislative Races in 1992," in Shea and Green, *The State of the Parties*, p. 139.

46. Robin Kolodny and Diana Dwyre, "The Committee Shuffle: Major Party Spending in Congressional Elections," in Green and Farmer, *The State of the Parties*, p. 124. Political Money-Line reports that each party transferred about $40 million more to its party affiliates than it received from them in the 2003–2004 election cycle.

47. Raymond J. La Raja, "State Parties and Soft Money: How Much Party Building?" in Green and Farmer, *The State of the Parties*, p. 146.

48. Robert Biersack, "Hard Facts and Soft Money: State Party Finance in the 1992 Federal Elections," in Shea and Green, *The State of the Parties*, p. 114.

49. See the evidence presented in Harmel and Janda, *Parties and Their Environments*, Chapter 5.

50. See John M. Broder and Lizette Alvarez, "President and Party Sound like Couple in Need of Therapy," *New York Times*, 15 November 1997, pp. A1, A8.

51. Martin P. Wattenberg, *The Decline of American Political Parties, 1952–1994* (Cambridge, Mass.: Harvard University Press, 1996).

52. Taylor Dark III, "The Rise of a Global Party? American Party Organizations Abroad," *Party Politics* 9 (March 2003): 241–255.

53. In 1996, the Democratic National Committee mounted an unprecedented drive to organize up to 60,000 precinct captains in twenty states, while the new Republican candidate for U.S. senator from Illinois, Al Salvi, fired his own campaign manager and replaced him with someone from the National Republican Senatorial Campaign Committee. See Sue Ellen Christian, "Democrats Will Focus on Precincts," *Chicago Tribune*, 29 June 1996; Michael Dizon, "Salvi Fires Top Senate Race Aides," *Chicago Tribune*, 24 May 1996, sec. 2, p. 3.

54. Barbara Sinclair, "The Congressional Party: Evolving Organizational, Agenda-Setting, and Policy Roles," in *The Parties Respond: Changes in American Parties and Campaigns*, 3rd ed., ed. L. Sandy Maisel (Boulder, Colo.: Westview Press, 1998), p. 227.

55. The model is articulated most clearly in a report by the American Political Science Association, "Toward a More Responsible Two-Party System," *American Political Science Review* 44 (September 1950): Part II. See also Gerald M. Pomper, "Toward a More Responsible Party System? What, Again?" *Journal of Politics* 33 (November 1971): 916–940. See also the seven essays in the symposium "Divided Government and the Politics of Constitutional Reform," *PS: Political Science and Politics* 24 (December 1991): 634–657.

56. Within the American states, parties also differ on policies, but to varying degrees. See John H. Aldrich and James S. Coleman Battista, "Conditional Party Government in the States," *American Journal of Political Science* 46 (January 2002): 164–172.

57. Recent research finds that voters do differentiate between policies backed by the president and by congressional candidates. See David R. Jones and Monika L. McDermott, "The Responsible Party Government Model in House and Senate Elections," *American Journal of Political Science* 48 (January 2004): 1–12.

Chapter 9 / Nominations, Elections, and Campaigns / pages 259–295

1. See Arend Lijphart, *Patterns of Democracy: Government Forms and Performance in Thirty-Six Countries* (New Haven, Conn.: Yale University Press, 1999), pp. 116–121. Of Lijphart's thirty-six democracies, only six have had presidential forms of government at some time in their history, while Colombia, Costa Rica, Venezuela, and the United States have been consistently presidential.

2. The Canadian parliament has a Senate, but it is an appointive body with limited legislative powers—like the British House of Lords.

3. Elections Canada is the nonpartisan agency responsible for the conduct of federal elections and referendums. See <http:// www.elections.ca/>.

4. For a philosophical discussion of "temporal properties" of American elections, see Dennis F. Thompson, "Election Time: Normative Implications of the Electoral Process in the United States," *American Political Science Review* 98 (February 2004): 51–64.

5. This is essentially the framework for studying campaigns set forth in Barbara C. Salmore and Stephen A. Salmore, *Candidates, Parties, and Campaigns: Electoral Politics in America*, 2nd ed. (Washington, D.C.: CQ Press, 1989).

6. Adam Nagourney, "Internet Injects Sweeping Change into U.S. Politics," *New York Times*, 2 April 2006, pp. 1 and 17.

7. David Menefree-Libey, *The Triumph of Campaign-Centered Politics* (New York: Chatham House, 2000).

8. Stephen E. Frantzich, *Political Parties in the Technological Age* (New York: Longman, 1989), p. 105.

9. "It is probable that no nation has ever experimented as fully or as fitfully with mechanisms for making nominations as has the United States," say William J. Keefe and Marc J. Hetherington, *Parties, Politics, and Public Policy in America*, 9th ed. (Washington, D.C.: CQ Press, 2003), p. 59.

10. Michael Gallagher, "Conclusion," in *Candidate Selection in Comparative Perspective: The Secret Garden of Politics*, ed. Michael Gallagher and Michael Marsh (London: Sage, 1988), p. 238. See also Malcolm E. Jewell, "Primary Elections," in *International Encyclopedia of Elections*, ed. Richard Rose (Washington, D.C.: CQ Press, 2000), p. 224. See Krister Lundell, "Determinants of Candidate Selection: The Degree of Centralization in Comparative Perspective," *Party Politics* 10 (January 2004): 25–47.

11. Kenneth Janda, "Adopting Party Law," in *Political Parties and Democracy in Theoretical and Practical Perspectives* (a series of research papers published by the National Democratic Institute for International Affairs, Washington, D.C., 2005).

12. *The Book of the States, 2003* (Lexington, Ky.: Council of State Governments, 2003), pp. 295–296.

13. In the 2004 Democratic New Hampshire primary, for example, the 23 percent turnout was the highest since 1960, but in the nineteen other states that held primaries through March 2, the turnout was the third lowest since 1960. See Katharine Q. Seelye, "Democratic Primaries' Turnout Is Said Not to Have Been Strong," *New York Times,* 10 March 2004, p. A17.

14. See John G. Geer, "Assessing the Representativeness of Electorates in Presidential Elections," *American Journal of Political Science* 32 (November 1998): 929–945; Barbara Norrander, "Ideological Representativeness of Presidential Primary Voters," *American Journal of Political Science* 33 (August 1989): 570–587.

15. James A. McCann, "Presidential Nomination Activists and Political Representation: A View from the Active Minority Studies," in *In Pursuit of the White House: How We Choose Our Presidential Nominees,* ed. William G. Mayer (Chatham, N.J.: Chatham House, 1996), p. 99.

16. James M. Snyder, Jr., Stephen Ansolabehere, John Mark Hansen, and Shigeo Hirano, "The Decline of Competition in U.S. Primary Elections, 1908–2004" (unpublished paper, MIT, Cambridge, Mass., June 2005), p. 22.

17. Talar Aslanian et al., "Recapturing Voter Intent: The Nonpartisan Primary in California" (capstone seminar report, Pepperdine University, April 2003), Appendix C, available at <publicpolicy.pepperdine.edu/academics/mpp/capstone/primary.pdf>.

18. Lawrence LeDuc, "Democratizing Party Leadership Selection," *Party Politics* 7 (May 2001): 323–341.

19. See "The Green Papers" web site at <www.thegreenpapers.com> for information on state methods of delegate selection in 2004.

20. Alan Ware, *The American Direct Primary: Party Institutionalization and Transformation in the North* (Cambridge: Cambridge University Press, 2002). Ware argues that the primary system resulted less from the reform movement than the unwieldy nature of the caucus/convention system for nominating candidates.

21. Harold W. Stanley and Richard G. Niemi, *Vital Statistics on American Politics, 1999–2000* (Washington, D.C.: CQ Press, 2000), p. 62. According to state-by-state delegate totals in "The Green Papers" website, 15 percent of the delegates to the 2004 Democratic presidential nominating convention were selected through the caucus/convention system.

22. William G. Mayer and Andrew E. Busch, *The Front-Loading Problem in Presidential Nominations* (Washington, D.C.: Brookings Institution, 2004), p. 23.

23. See Rhodes Cook, *The Presidential Nominating Process: A Place for Us?* (Lanham, Md.: Rowman & Littlefield, 2004), Chapter 5. Nations that have copied the American model have experienced mixed results. See James A. McCann, "The Emerging International Trend Toward Open Presidential Primaries," in *The Making of the Presidential Candidates 2004,* ed. William G. Mayer (Lanham, Md.: Rowman & Littlefield, 2004), pp. 265–293.

24. Arthur T. Hadley, *The Invisible Primary* (Englewood Cliffs, N.J.: Prentice-Hall, 1976). For a test of some of Hadley's assertions, see Emmett H. Buell, Jr., "The Invisible Primary," in Mayer, *In Pursuit of the White House,* pp. 1–43. More recently, see Cook, *The Presidential Nominating Process,* pp. 83–89.

25. Gary R. Orren and Nelson W. Polsby (eds.), *Media and Mo-*

mentum: The New Hampshire Primary and Nomination Politics (Chatham, N.J.: Chatham House, 1987), p. 23.

26. These figures, calculated for voting eligible population (VEP), come from <elections.gmu.edu/Voter_Turnout_2004_Primaries.htm>. VEP is lower than voting age population (VAP), because VEP excludes those ineligible to vote, usually noncitizens and felons.

27. Richard L. Berke, "Two States Retain Roles in Shaping Presidential Race," *New York Times,* 29 November 1999, p. 1; Leslie Wayne, "Iowa Turns Its Presidential Caucuses into a Cash Cow, and Milks Furiously," *New York Times,* 5 January 2000, p. A16. See also Adam Nagourney, "Iowa Worries About Losing Its Franchise," *New York Times,* 18 January 2004, sec. 4, p. 3.

28. Christopher Cooper, "Early Voting May Clip Iowa's Role," *Wall Street Journal,* 5 May 2007, p. A4.

29. William G. Mayer, "The Basic Dynamics of the Contemporary Nomination Process: An Expanded View," in Mayer, *The Making of the Presidential Candidates 2004,* pp. 107–109.

30. Results for the 2004 Republican primary in New Hampshire are available at <www.thegreenpapers.com/P04/NH-R.phtml>.

31. NBC News/*Wall Street Journal* Poll of 1,002 adults conducted by the polling organizations of Peter Hart (D) and Robert Teeter (R), 10–12 January 2004. Asked of Democrats and of non-Democrats who said they would vote in a Democratic presidential primary. Available at <www.pollingreport.com/wh04dem.htm>.

32. Robert J. Klotz, *The Politics of Internet Communication* (Lanham, Md.: Rowman & Littlefield, 2004), pp. 77–78.

33. Glen Justice, "Dean Raises $14 Million and Sets Record, Aides Say," *New York Times,* 30 December 2003, p. A17.

34. Richard Stevenson, "Bush's Advisers Focus on Dean as Likely Opponent Next Year," *New York Times,* 11 December 2003, pp. A1, A27.

35. See Brian Faler, "Dean Leaves Legacy of Online Campaign," *Washington Post,* 20 February 2004, p. A12.

36. David E. Rosenbaum and Janet Elder, "Kerry Support Found Across Wide Range of Democrats," *New York Times,* 29 January 2004, p. A18.

37. See the table "Campaign's First Stops No Guarantee of Victory," *Chicago Tribune,* 1 January 2004, p. 18.

38. John Harwood and Jacob M. Schlesinger, "Kerry Finds Himself in Enviable Position," *New York Times,* 4 March 2004, p. A4.

39. "Looking Back: Heading Up the Ticket," *New York Times,* 15 March 2000, p. A18. This chart portrays the times at which candidates were selected from 1972 to 2000. Before 1972, one or both candidates were not effectively chosen until the summer nominating conventions.

40. Adam Nagourney, "Democrats' Plan for Early Nominee May Be Costly," *New York Times,* 1 January 2004, p. 1.

41. Turnout for presidential primaries comes from the Federal Election Commission at <http://www.fec.gov/pubrec/fe2004/federalelections2004.shtml>. Turnout of 595,529 in the Democratic caucuses comes from <www.dos.state.pa.us/election_reform/lib/election_reform/2004_Democratic_Caucus_Turnout_Statistics.doc>.

42. See James R. Beniger, "Winning the Presidential Nomination: National Polls and State Primary Elections, 1936–1972," *Public Opinion Quarterly* 40 (Spring 1976): 22–38.

43. A FOX News/Opinion Dynamics Poll of registered Democrats on 21–22 January 2004 found Kerry favored over Dean by 29 to 17 percent. A poll on 4–5 February by the same firm found Kerry favored by 54 to 7 percent.

44. *The American Heritage Dictionary of the English Language,* 4th ed. (Boston: Houghton Mifflin, 2000), p. 362. Indeed, the entry on "Electoral College" in the 1989 *Oxford English*

Dictionary does not note any usage in American politics up to 1875, when it cites a reference in connection with the Germanic Diet.

45. References to the electoral college in the U.S. Code can be found through the Legal Information Institute website, <http://www4.law.cornell.edu/uscode/3/ch1.html>.

46. Michael Nelson, *Congressional Quarterly's Guide to the Presidency* (Washington, D.C.: CQ Press, 1989), pp. 155–156. Colorado selected its presidential electors through the state legislature in 1876, but that was the year it entered the Union.

47. Who would have become president if the 538 electoral votes had been divided equally, at 269 each? According to the Constitution, the House of Representatives would have chosen the president, for no candidate had a majority. One way to avoid tied outcomes in the future is to create an odd number of electoral votes. To do this, one scholar proposes making the District of Columbia a state. That would give Washington three electoral votes—the same number as it has now without congressional representation. The Senate would increase to 102 members, while the House would remain fixed at 435. (Presumably, Washington's seat would come from one of the other states after decennial reapportionment.) This clever solution would produce an electoral college of 537, an odd number that could not produce a tie between two candidates. See David A. Crockett, "Dodging the Bullet: Election Mechanics and the Problem of the Twenty-third Amendment," *PS: Political Science & Politics* 36 (July 2003): 423–426.

48. Shlomo Slonim, "The Electoral College at Philadelphia: The Evolution of an Ad Hoc Congress for the Selection of a President," *Journal of American History* 73 (June 1986): 35. For a recent critique and proposal for reform, see David W. Abbott and James P. Levine, *Wrong Winner: The Coming Debacle in the Electoral College* (New York: Praeger, 1991). For a reasoned defense, see Walter Berns (ed.), *After the People Vote: A Guide to the Electoral College* (Washington, D.C.: American Enterprise Institute, 1992).

49. Gallup News Service, "Americans Have Historically Favored Changing Way Presidents Are Elected," *Poll Releases,* 10 November 2000, available at <www.gallup.com/poll/releases/pr001110.asp>. See also Frank Newport, "Americans Support Proposal to Eliminate Electoral College System," *Poll Releases,* 5 January 2001, available at <www.gallup.com/poll/releases/pr010105.asp>.

50. Walter Berns (ed.), *After the People Vote: A Guide to the Electoral College* (Washington, D.C.: American Enterprise Institute, 1992), pp. 45–48. The framers had great difficulty deciding how to allow both the people and the states to participate in selecting the president. This matter was debated on twenty-one different days before they compromised on the electoral college, which, Slonim says, "in the eyes of its admirers . . . represented a brilliant scheme for successfully blending national and federal elements in the selection of the nation's chief executive" ("The Electoral College at Philadelphia," p. 58).

51. Observers suspect that the vote for Edwards instead of Kerry was cast by error. See <http://news.minnesota.publicradio.org/features/2004/12/13_ap_electors/>.

52. See Alexis Simendinger, James A. Barnes, and Carl M. Cannon, "Pondering a Popular Vote," *National Journal,* 18 November 2000, pp. 3650–3656.

53. Harold W. Stanley and Richard G. Niemi, *Vital Statistics on American Politics, 1999–2000* (Washington, D.C.: CQ Press, 2000), p. 133.

54. Rhodes Cook, "House Republicans Scored a Quiet Victory in '92," *Congressional Quarterly Weekly Report,* 17 April 1993, p. 966.

55. "Centrists Deliver for Democrats," Pew Research Center for the People & the Press (8 November 2006), <http://pewresearch.org/obdeck/?ObDeckID=88>.

56. Salmore and Salmore, *Candidates, Parties, and Campaigns,* p. 1.

57. See Edward I. Sidlow, *Challenging the Incumbent: An Underdog's Undertaking* (Washington, D.C.: CQ Press, 2004), for the engaging account of the unsuccessful 2000 campaign by a young political scientist, Lance Pressl, against the most senior Republican in the House, Phil Crane, in Illinois' Sixth District. Sidlow's book invites readers to ponder what the high reelection rate of incumbents means for American politics.

58. Elisabeth Bumiller and Richard W. Stevenson, "Aides Say Bush Is Already Absorbed in 2004 Race," *New York Times,* 11 January 2004, p. 19.

59. Jeff Zeleny, "Bush Jumps into Fray, Jabs Kerry, Democrats," *Chicago Tribune,* 24 February 2004, pp. 1, 10.

60. Obtained from <www.gwu.edu/~action/2004/kerry/kerrorg.html>, the Democracy in Action website maintained by George Washington University.

61. See Peter L. Francia et al., *The Financiers of Congressional Elections* (New York: Columbia University Press, 2003).

62. Quoted in E. J. Dionne, Jr., "On the Trail of Corporation Donations," *New York Times,* 6 October 1980.

63. Salmore and Salmore, *Candidates, Parties, and Campaigns,* p. 11. See also David Himes, "Strategy and Tactics for Campaign Fund-Raising," in *Campaigns and Elections: American Style,* ed. James A. Thurber and Candice J. Nelson (Boulder, Colo.: Westview Press, 1995), pp. 62–77.

64. Federal Election Commission, "The First Ten Years: 1975–1985" (Washington, D.C.: Federal Election Commission, 14 April 1985), p. 1.

65. Michael J. Malbin, "Assessing the Bipartisan Campaign Reform Act," in *The Election After Reform: Money, Politics and the Bipartisan Campaign Reform Act,* ed. Michael J. Malbin (Rowman & Littlefield, forthcoming).

66. Center for Responsive Politics, at <http://www.opensecrets.org/softmoney/softglance.asp>.

67. Anthony Corrado, "Party Finance in the Wake of BCRA: An Overview," in Malbin, *The Election After Reform.*

68. Ibid.

69. Federal Election Commission, "Adjustment to National Convention Entitlements," *Record* 30 (May 2004): 15.

70. Federal Election Commission, "Party Financial Activity Summarized for the 2004 Election Cycle," press release, 14 March 2005.

71. Steve Weissman and Ruth Hassan, "BCRA and the 527 Groups," in Malbin, *The Election After Reform.*

72. Federal Election Commission, "Congressional Candidates Spend $1.16 billion during 2003–04," press release, 9 June 2005.

73. For a concise and comprehensive account of the BCRA's history and provisions, see Joseph E. Cantor, "Campaign Financing," *CRS Issue Brief for Congress,* 15 December 2003.

74. Glen Justice, "Advocacy Groups Allowed to Raise Unlimited Funds," *New York Times,* 19 February 2004, pp. 1, 21.

75. Jeanne Cummings, "A Hard Sell on Soft Money," *Wall Street Journal,* 2 December 2003, p. A4; Paul Singer, "Regulators Scrutinize Non-Party Spending," *Chicago Tribune,* 17 February 2004, pp. 1, 14.

76. Thomas E. Mann, "Linking Knowledge and Action: Political Science and Campaign Finance Reform," *Perspectives on Politics* 1 (March 2003): 69–83.

77. David A. Dulio, "Strategic and Tactical Decisions in Campaigns," in *Guide to Political Campaigns in America,* ed. Paul S. Herrnson (Washington, D.C.: CQ Press, 2005), pp. 231–243.

78. Salmore and Salmore, *Candidates, Parties, and Campaigns,* p. 11.

79. According to Brian F. Schaffner and Matthew J. Streb, less

educated respondents are less likely to express a vote preference when party labels are not available. See "The Partisan Heuristic in Low-Information Elections," *Public Opinion Quarterly* 66 (Winter 2002): 559–581.

80. See the "Marketplace: Political Products and Services" section in monthly issues of the magazine *Campaigns and Elections.* These classified ads list scores of names, addresses, and telephone numbers for people who supply "political products and services"—from "campaign schools" to "voter files and mailing lists." For an overview, see Philip Kotler and Neil Kotler, "Political Marketing: Generating Effective Candidates, Campaigns, and Causes," in *Handbook of Political Marketing,* ed. Bruce I. Newman (Thousand Oaks, Calif.: Sage, 1999), pp. 3–18.

81. Salmore and Salmore, *Candidates, Parties, and Campaigns,* pp. 115–116. See also Eric W. Rademacher and Alfred J. Tuchfarber, "Preelection Polling and Political Campaigns," in Newman, *Handbook of Political Marketing,* pp. 197–221.

82. Bruce I. Newman, "A Predictive Model of Voter Behavior," in Newman, *Handbook of Political Marketing,* pp. 259–282. For studies on campaign consultants at work, see James A. Thurber and Candice J. Nelson (eds.), *Campaign Warriors: The Role of Political Consultants in Elections* (Washington, D.C.: Brookings Institution Press, 2000).

83. James Warren, "Politicians Learn Value of Sundays—Too Well," *Chicago Tribune,* 22 October 1990, p. 1.

84. Timothy E. Cook, *Making Laws and Making News: Media Strategies in the U.S. House of Representatives* (Washington, D.C.: Brookings Institution, 1989). Subsequent research into media effects on Senate and House elections finds that in low-information elections, which characterize House more than Senate elections, the media coverage gives an advantage to incumbents, particularly among independent voters. See Robert Kirby Goidel, Todd G. Shields, and Barry Tadlock, "The Effects of the Media in United States Senate and House Elections: A Comparative Analysis" (paper presented at the annual meeting of the American Political Science Association, Washington, D.C., September 1993).

85. Julianne F. Flowers, Audrey A. Haynes, and Michael H. Crispin, "The Media, the Campaign, and the Message," *American Journal of Political Science* 47 (April 2003): 259–273.

86. Ann N. Crigler, Marion R. Just, and Timothy E. Cook, "Local News, Network News and the 1992 Presidential Campaign" (paper presented at the annual meeting of the American Political Science Association, Washington, D.C., September 1993), p. 9.

87. Stephen Ansolabehere and Shanto Iyengar, *Going Negative: How Political Advertisements Shrink and Polarize the Electorate* (New York: Free Press, 1995), p. 145.

88. Darrell M. West, *Air Wars: Television Advertising in Election Campaigns, 1952–2004,* 4th ed. (Washington, D.C.: CQ Press, 2005), p. 48.

89. Ted Brader, "Striking a Responsive Chord: How Political Ads Motivate and Persuade Voters by Appealing to Emotions," *American Journal of Political Science* 49 (April 2005): 388–405.

90. Ibid., p. 152.

91. This theme runs throughout Kathleen Hall Jamieson's *Dirty Politics: Deception, Distraction, and Democracy* (New York: Oxford University Press, 1992). See also John Boiney, "You Can Fool All of the People . . . Evidence on the Capacity of Political Advertising to Mislead" (paper presented at the annual meeting of the American Political Science Association, Washington, D.C., September 1993).

92. West, *Air Wars,* p. 79.

93. Kathleen Hall Jamieson, Paul Waldman, and Susan Sheer, "Eliminate the Negative? Categories of Analysis for Political Advertisements," in *Crowded Airwaves: Campaign Advertising in Elections,* ed. James A. Thurber, Candice J. Nelson, and David A. Dulio (Washington, D.C.: Brookings Institution Press, 2000), p. 49.

94. David A. Dulio, Candice J. Nelson, and James A. Thurber, "Summary and Conclusions," in Thurber, Nelson, and Dulio, *Crowded Airwaves,* p. 172.

95. Ansolabehere and Iyengar, *Going Negative,* p. 112.

96. West, however, takes issue with the Ansolabehere and Iyengar analysis [note 87], saying that turnout is more dependent on mistrust than on negativity of ads. See West, *Air Wars,* pp. 71–72.

97. Richard R. Lau and Gerald M. Pomper, "Effectiveness of Negative Campaigning in U.S. Senate Elections," *American Journal of Political Science* 46 (January 2002): 47–66.

98. Lee Sigelman and Mark Kugler, "Why Is Research on the Effects of Negative Campaigning So Inconclusive? Understanding Citizens' Perceptions of Negativity," *Journal of Politics* 65 (February 2003): 142–160.

99. Jeanne Cummings, "Attacking Is Riskier in 2004 Campaign," *Wall Street Journal,* 23 March 2004, p. A4.

100. The information on early campaign websites comes from Jill Zuckerman, "Candidates Spin Web of Support on Cybertrail," *Chicago Tribune,* 3 December 2003, p. 13.

101. Jeanne Cummings, "Behind Dean Surge: A Gang of Bloggers and Webmasters," *Wall Street Journal,* 14 October 2003, pp. A1, A14.

102. Lee Gomes, "Blogs Have Become Part of Media Machine That Shapes Politics," *Wall Street Journal,* 23 February 2004, p. B1; Christopher Conkey, "Checking Out Candidates' Sites," *Wall Street Journal,* 16 March 2004, p. D3.

103. Pew Research Center for the People and the Press, "Voters Liked Campaign 2004, but Too Much 'Mud-Slinging,'" survey reports, 11 November 2004.

104. Ibid., p. 15.

105. Ibid., p. 34.

106. Amy Harmon, "Politics of the Web: Meet, Greet, Segregate, Meet Again," *New York Times,* 25 January 2004, sec. 4, p. 16.

107. William A. Galston, "If Political Fragmentation Is the Problem, Is the Internet the Solution?" in *The Civic Web: Online Politics and Democratic Values,* ed. David M. Anderson and Michael Cornfield (Lanham, Md.: Rowman & Littlefield, 2003), pp. 35–44.

108. See the website for the National Election Studies at <http://www.umich.edu/~nes/nesguide/nesguide.htm>.

109. Patricia Conley, "The Presidential Race of 2004: Strategy, Outcome, and Mandate," in *A Defining Moment: The Presidential Election of 2004,* ed. William Crotty (Armonk, N.Y.: M. E. Sharpe, 2005), pp. 131–132.

110. Pew Research Center, "Three-in-Ten Voters Open to Persuasion," survey report, 3 March 2004, available at <people-press.org>.

111. Pamela Johnston Conover and Stanley Feldman, "Candidate Perception in an Ambiguous World: Campaigns, Cues, and Inference Processes," *American Journal of Political Science* 33 (November 1989): 912–940.

112. Kira Sanbonmatsu, "Gender Stereotypes and Vote Choice," *American Journal of Political Science* 46 (January 2002): 20–34. Sanbonmatsu contends that some voters have a "baseline preference" for men or women candidates and that women are more likely to hold the preference than men. See also Kathleen A. Dolan, *Voting for Women: How the Public Evaluates Women Candidates* (Boulder, Colo.: Westview Press, 2004).

113. See Herbert F. Weisberg and Clyde Wilcox (eds.), *Models of Voting in Presidential Elections: The 2000 U.S. Election* (Stanford: Stanford University Press, 2004), for a set of

studies explaining voting behavior in the presidential election.

114. Michael M. Gant and Norman R. Luttbeg, *American Electoral Behavior* (Itasca, Ill.: Peacock, 1991), pp. 63–64. Ideology appears to have played little role in the 2000 election. See William G. Jacoby, in Weisberg and Wilcox, *Models of Voting in Presidential Elections*, pp. 103–104.

115. Richard E. Cohen, "How They Measured Up," *National Journal*, 28 February 2004, pp. 630–633.

116. For studies of campaign effects in different countries and settings, see David M. Farrell and Rüdiger Schmitt-Beck (eds.), *Do Political Campaigns Matter? Campaign Effects in Elections and Referendums* (London: Routledge, 2002).

117. The Institute of Politics, Harvard University, *Campaign for President: The Managers Look at 2004* (Lanham, Md.: Rowman & Littlefield, 2006), p. 139.

118. These figures come from the Center for Media and Public Affairs, which monitored television news coverage throughout the 2000 presidential campaign. See CMPA, "Journalists Monopolize TV Election News," press release, 30 October 2000, available at <www.cmpa.com/pressrel/electpr10.htm>.

119. Matthew A. Baum, "Talking the Vote: Why Presidential Candidates Hit the Talk Show Circuit," *American Journal of Political Science* 49 (April 2005): 213–234.

120. "Bush, Dem. TV Adv. Near Equal," 25 March 2004, Wisconsin Advertising Project, available at <polisci.wisc.edu/tvadvertising/>.

121. The Center for Responsive Politics, "'04 Elections Expected to Cost Nearly $4 Billion," press release, 21 October 2004, posted on the Internet; CBC News, "U.S. Presidential Campaign Spending Triples," Canadian Broadcasting Corporation, report of 1 November 2004, posted on the Internet.

122. David M. Halbfinger and Jim Rutenberg, "Frantic Presidential Race Ends with a Flood of Ads," *New York Times*, 1 November 2004, pp. 1 and 22.

123. Katharine Q. Seelye, "Moral Values Cited as a Defining Issue of the Election," *New York Times*, 4 November 2004, p. P4.

124. John Harwood and Jeanne Cummings, "Debates Take Center Stage," *Wall Street Journal*, 15 October 2004, p. A4.

125. See Peter Kobrak, *Cozy Politics: Political Parties, Campaign Finance, and Compromised Governance* (Boulder, Colo.: Lynne Rienner, 2002), for an indictment of the flow of money in politics from interest groups untempered by the aggregating influence of political parties.

Chapter 10 / Interest Groups / pages 296–325

1. This account draws primarily on reporting by the *Washington Post*. See R. Jeffrey Smith, "DeLay Airfare Was Charged to Lobbyist's Credit Card," *Washington Post*, 24 April 2005, p. A01; R. Jeffrey Smith, "The DeLay-Abramoff Money Trail," *Washington Post*, 31 December 2005, p. A01; Susan Schmidt and James V. Grimaldi, "Abramoff Pleads Guilty to 3 Counts," *Washington Post*, 4 January 2005, p. A01.

2. Alexis de Tocqueville, *Democracy in America, 1835–1839*, ed. Richard D. Heffner (New York: Mentor Books, 1956), p. 79.

3. *The Federalist Papers* (New York: Mentor Books, 1961), p. 79.

4. Ibid., p. 78.

5. See Robert A. Dahl, *A Preface to Democratic Theory* (Chicago: University of Chicago Press, 1956), pp. 4–33.

6. The poll was taken by the Pew Research Center for the People and the Press, 1–5 February 2006; available at <http://www.pollingreport.com/politics.htm>.

7. Jeffrey H. Birnbaum, "Lobbyists Foresee Business as Usual," *Washington Post*, 19 March 2006, p. A1.

8. This discussion follows from Jeffrey M. Berry and Clyde Wilcox, *The Interest Group Society*, 4th ed. (New York: Longman, forthcoming).

9. John Simons and John Harwood, "For the Tech Industry, Market in Washington Is Toughest to Crack," *Wall Street Journal*, 5 March 1998, p. A1.

10. Rebecca Adams, "Federal Regulations Face Assault on Their Foundation," *CQ Weekly*, 10 August 2002, p. 2183.

11. David B. Truman, *The Governmental Process* (New York: Knopf, 1951).

12. Herbert Gans, *The Urban Villagers* (New York: Free Press, 1962).

13. Robert H. Salisbury, "An Exchange Theory of Interest Groups," *Midwest Journal of Political Science* 13 (February 1969): 1–32.

14. See Mancur Olson, Jr., *The Logic of Collective Action* (New York: Schocken, 1968).

15. Peter Matthiessen, *Sal Si Puedes* (New York: Random House, 1969); John G. Dunne, *Delano*, rev. ed. (New York: Farrar, Strauss & Giroux, 1971).

16. Kay Lehman Schlozman, Benjamin I. Page, Sidney Verba, and Morris P. Fiorina, "Inequalities of Political Voice," in *Inequality and American Democracy*, ed. Lawrence R. Jacobs and Theda Skocpol (New York: Russell Sage Foundation, 2005), pp. 19–87.

17. Jeffrey H. Birnbaum, "Clients' Rewards Keep K Street Lobbyists Thriving," *Washington Post*, 14 February 2006, p. A01.

18. Ronald G. Shaiko, *Voices and Echoes for the Environment* (New York: Columbia University Press, 1999).

19. Christopher J. Bosso, *Environment, Inc.* (Lawrence: University Press of Kansas, 2005).

20. Lori A. Brainard and Patricia D. Siplon, "Cyberspace Challenges to Mainstream Nonprofit Health Organizations," *Administration and Society* 34 (May 2002): 141–175.

21. See Olson, *Logic*.

22. Edward O. Laumann and David Knoke, *The Organizational State* (Madison: University of Wisconsin Press, 1987), p. 3, cited in Robert H. Salisbury, "The Paradox of Interest Groups in Washington—More Groups, Less Clout," in *The New American Political System*, 2nd ed., ed. Anthony King (Washington, D.C.: American Enterprise Institute, 1990), p. 226.

23. William M. Welch, "Tauzin Switches Sides from Drug Industry Overseer to Lobbyist," *USA Today*, 15 December 2004.

24. Berry and Wilcox, *The Interest Group Society*, forthcoming.

25. *Congressional Revolving Doors* (Washington, D.C.: Public Citizen, 2005), p. 6.

26. Jeffrey H. Birnbaum, *The Lobbyists* (New York: Times Books, 1992), pp. 128–129.

27. Berry and Wilcox, *The Interest Group Society*, forthcoming.

28. From Findlaw at <http://www.infirmation.com/shared/search/partners-compare.tcl?city=Washington&base_per_hour_p=t>.

29. Brody Mullins, "Growing Role for Lobbyists: Raising Funds for Lawmakers," *Wall Street Journal*, 27 January 2006, p. A1.

30. Rogan Kersh, "Corporate Lobbyists as Political Actors: A View from the Field," in *Interest Group Politics*, 6th ed., ed. Allan J. Cigler and Burdett A. Loomis (Washington, D.C.: CQ Press, 2002), pp. 225–248.

31. Federal Election Commission, "PAC Activity Increases for 2004 Elections," 13 April 2005, available at <http://www.fec.gov/press/press2005/20050412pac/PACFinal2004.html>.

32. Rogan Kersh, "To Donate or Not to Donate?" (paper delivered at the annual meeting of the American Political Science Association, Philadelphia, August 2003), p. 2.

33. On how different PACs approach the tradeoff between pragmatism and ideology, see Robert Biersack, Paul S. Herrnson, and Clyde Wilcox (eds.), *After the Revolution* (Needham Heights, Mass.: Allyn & Bacon, 1999).

34. Federal Election Commission, "PAC Activity Increases for 2004 Elections."

35. Stephen Ansolabehere, John de Figueredo, and James M. Snyder, Jr., "Why Is There So Little Money in U.S. Politics?" *Journal of Economic Perspectives* 17 (Winter 2003): 161–181; Mark Smith, *American Business and Political Power* (Chicago: University of Chicago Press, 2000), pp. 115–141.

36. Marie Hojnacki and David Kimball, "PAC Contributions and Lobbying Access in Congressional Committees," *Political Research Quarterly* 54 (March 2001): 161–180; John R. Wright, "Contributions, Lobbying, and Committee Voting in the U.S. House of Representatives," *American Political Science Review* 84 (June 1990): 417–438; Richard L. Hall and Frank W. Wayman, "Buying Time: Money Interests and the Mobilization of Bias in Congressional Committees," *American Political Science Review* 84 (September 1990): 797–820.

37. Center for Responsive Politics, <http://www.opensecrets.org/527s/527contribs.asp?cycle=2004>.

38. On tactics generally, see Beth L. Leech, *Conflict and Cooperation: Interest Group Lobbying Strategies in Washington* (Princeton, N.J.: Princeton University Press, forthcoming).

39. Richard L. Hall and Alan V. Deardorff, "Lobbying as Legislative Subsidy," *American Political Science Review* 100 (February 2006): 69–84.

40. Berry and Wilcox, *The Interest Group Society,* forthcoming.

41. Beth L. Leech, Frank R. Baumgartner, Jeffrey M. Berry, Marie Hojnacki, and David C. Kimball, "Organized Interests and Issue Definition in Policy Debates," in Cigler and Loomis, *Interest Group Politics,* pp. 275–292.

42. Eric Pianin, "For Environmentalists, Victories in the Courts," *Washington Post,* 27 January 2003, p. A3.

43. Kenneth M. Goldstein, *Interest Groups, Lobbying, and Participation in America* (Cambridge: Cambridge University Press, 1999).

44. Douglas R. Imig, *Poverty and Power* (Lincoln: University of Nebraska Press, 1996), p. 88.

45. Clay Risen, "Store Lobby," *New Republic,* 25 July 2005, pp. 10–11.

46. Bruce Ingersoll, "Iowa Farm Aid Helped Rich Most, Study Says," *Wall Street Journal,* 14 January 2000, p. A2.

47. Christopher J. Bosso and Michael Thomas Collins, "Just Another Tool?" in Cigler and Loomis, *Interest Group Politics,* p. 97.

48. Lynette Clemetson, "Protest Groups Using Updated Tactics to Spread Antiwar Message," *New York Times,* 15 January 2003; Chris Taylor and Karen Tumulty, "MoveOn's Big Moment," available at <http://www.cnn.com/2003/ALLPOLITICS/11/17/timep.moveon.tm/>.

49. Kevin Hula, "Rounding Up the Usual Suspects: Forging Interest Group Coalitions in Washington" (paper delivered at the annual meeting of the Midwest Political Science Association, Chicago, April 1993), p. 29.

50. Kay Lehman Schlozman, Traci Burch, and Samuel Lampert, "Still an Upper-Class Accent?" (paper delivered at the annual meeting of the American Political Science Association, September 2004), pp. 16 and 25.

51. Such nonprofits have obstacles created by their status as tax-deductible public charities. See Jeffrey M. Berry with David F. Arons, *A Voice for Nonprofits* (Washington, D.C.: Brookings Institution, 2003).

52. Jeffrey M. Berry, *The New Liberalism* (Washington, D.C.: Brookings Institution, 1999), pp. 120–130.

53. Jonathan Rauch, *Demosclerosis* (New York: Times Books, 1991), p. 91. The latter figure is interpolated from Rauch and Michael T. Heaney, "Coalitions and Interest Group Influence over Health Care Policy" (paper delivered at the annual meeting of the American Political Science Association, Philadelphia, August 2003), p. 16.

54. Frank R. Baumgartner and Beth L. Leech, "Interest Niches and Policy Bandwagons," *Journal of Politics* 63 (November 2001): 1196.

55. Smith, *American Business and Political Power.*

56. Federal Election Commission, "PAC Activity Increases for 2004 Elections."

Chapter 11 / Congress / pages 326–357

1. The text of Frist's "statement for family research council telecast" may be found at his website: <http://frist.senate.gov>.

2. Clinton Rossiter, *1787: The Grand Convention* (New York: Mentor, 1968), p. 158.

3. Norman J. Ornstein, Thomas E. Mann, and Michael J. Malbin, *Vital Statistics on Congress, 2001–2002* (Washington, D.C.: AEI Press, 2002), pp. 75–76.

4. Lydia Saad, "Military Still Tops in Public Confidence," 7 June 2006, The Gallup Poll, <http://poll. gallup.com>.

5. John R. Hibbing and Elizabeth Theiss-Morse, *Stealth Democracy* (New York: Cambridge University Press, 2002), pp. 96–97.

6. "Congress and the Public," Gallup Poll, 6–8 January 2006, <http://poll.gallup.com>.

7. John R. Hibbing and Elizabeth Theiss-Morse, "What the Public Dislikes About Congress," in *Congress Reconsidered,* 6th ed., ed. Lawrence C. Dodd and Bruce I. Oppenheimer (Washington, D.C.: CQ Press, 1997), pp. 61–80.

8. Alan Abramowitz, Brad Alexander, and Matthew Gunning, "Incumbency, Redistricting, and the Decline of Competition in U.S. House Elections," *Journal of Politics* 68 (February 2006): 75–88.

9. Gary W. Cox and Jonathan N. Katz, *Elbridge Gerry's Salamander* (Cambridge: Cambridge University Press, 2002).

10. John Harwood, "House Incumbents Tap Census, Software to Get a Lock on Seats," *Wall Street Journal,* 19 June 2002, p. A1.

11. Katharine Q. Seelye, "Congress Online: Much Sizzle, Little Steak," *New York Times,* 24 June 2003, p. A16.

12. Morris P. Fiorina, as cited in Roger H. Davidson and Walter J. Oleszek, *Congress and Its Members,* 9th ed. (Washington, D.C.: CQ Press, 2004), p. 143.

13. "Congress Struggles with Flood of E-mail," *New York Times,* 19 March 2001, p. A16.

14. Federal Election Commission, available at <http://www.fec.gov/press2004/20050103canstat/overviewpost2004.pdf>.

15. Larry Sabato, *PAC Power* (New York: Norton, 1984), p. 72.

16. Stephen Ansolabehere and James M. Snyder, Jr., "Money and Office: The Sources of the Incumbency Advantage in Congressional Campaign Finance," in *Continuity and Change in House Elections,* ed. David W. Brady, John F. Cogan, and Morris P. Fiorina (Stanford, Calif.: Stanford University Press, 2000), pp. 65–86.

17. Paul S. Herrnson, *Congressional Elections,* 3rd ed. (Washington, D.C.: CQ Press, 2000), p. 231.

18. Gary C. Jacobson and Samuel Kernell, *Strategy and Choice in Congressional Elections* (New Haven, Conn.: Yale University Press, 1983). See also Walter J. Stone and L. Sandy Maisel, "The Not-So-Simple Calculus of Winning: Potential U.S. House Candidates' Nomination and General Election Prospects," *Journal of Politics* 65 (November 2003): 951–977.

19. Jonathan S. Krasno, *Challengers, Competition, and Reelection* (New Haven, Conn.: Yale University Press, 1994).

20. Gary C. Jacobson, "Terror, Terrain, and Turnout: Explaining the 2002 Midterm Election," *Political Science Quarterly* 118 (Spring 2003): 1.

21. Gregory Giroux, "A Touch of Gray on Capitol Hill," *CQ Weekly,* 28 January 2005, p. 240.

22. Jonathan D. Salant, "43% of Incoming Freshman Congressmen Are Millionaires," *Boston Globe,* 25 December 2002, p. A23.

23. Giroux, "A Touch of Gray on Capitol Hill."

24. See Beth Reingold, *Representing Women* (Chapel Hill, N.C.: University of North Carolina Press, 2000); Michele L. Swers, *The Difference Women Make* (Chicago: University of Chicago Press, 2002).

25. Hanna Fenichel Ptikin, *The Concept of Representation* (Berkeley: University of California Press, 1967), pp. 60–91; Jane Mansbridge, "Should Blacks Represent Blacks and Women Represent Women? A Contingent 'Yes,'" *Journal of Politics* 61 (1999): 628–657.

26. See the Census Bureau website at <http://www.census.gov/population/www/pop-profile/profiledynamic.html>.

27. *Shaw v. Reno,* 509 U.S. 630 (1993).

28. *Bush v. Vera,* 116 S. Ct. 1941 (1996).

29. *Easley v. Cromartie,* 532 U.S. 234 (2001).

30. See David Lublin, *The Paradox of Representation* (Princeton, N.J.: Princeton University Press, 1997). See, *contra,* Kenneth W. Shotts, "Does Racial Redistricting Cause Conservative Policy Outcomes?" *Journal of Politics* 65 (2003): 216–226.

31. Adriel Bettelheim, "Reluctant Congress Drafted into Bioengineering Battle," *CQ Weekly,* 22 April 2000, pp. 938–944.

32. John W. Kingdon, *Agendas, Alternatives, and Public Policies,* 2nd ed. (New York: HarperCollins, 1995), p. 38; see also Glen Krutz, "Issues and Institutions: 'Winnowing' in the U.S. Congress," *American Journal of Political Science* 49 (April 2005): 313–326.

33. David Shribman, "Canada's Top Envoy to Washington Cuts Unusually Wide Swath," *Wall Street Journal,* 29 July 1985, p. 1.

34. Woodrow Wilson, *Congressional Government* (Boston: Houghton Mifflin, 1885), p. 79.

35. Richard L. Hall and C. Lawrence Evans, "The Power of Subcommittees," *Journal of Politics* 52 (May 1990): 342.

36. Lawrence D. Longley and Walter J. Oleszek, *Bicameral Politics* (New Haven, Conn.: Yale University Press, 1989), p. 10.

37. Ibid., p. 4.

38. Veronika Oleksyn, "Seniority, Loyalty and Political Needs Shape Makeup of Committee," *CQ Weekly,* 11 April 2005, p. 894; Allison Stevens, "More Power to the Senate's Majority Leader?" *CQ Weekly,* 6 November 2004, p. 2605.

39. Philip M. Boffey, "Lawmakers Vow a Legal Recourse for Military Malpractice Victims," *New York Times,* 9 July 1985, p. A14.

40. Dan Eggen and Paul Kane, "2 Former Aides to Bush Get Subpoenas," *Washington Post,* 14 June 2007, p. A01; Lolita Blakdor, "Pace to Lose Post as Joint Chiefs Head," *Washington Post,* 9 June 2007.

41. Joel D. Aberbach, *Keeping a Watchful Eye* (Washington, D.C.: Brookings Institution, 1990), p. 44.

42. Ibid., pp. 162–183.

43. John D. Huber and Charles R. Shipan, *Deliberate Discretion?* (New York: Cambridge University Press, 2002).

44. Gary W. Cox and Mathew D. McCubbins, *Legislative Leviathan* (Berkeley: University of California Press, 1993); Keith Krehbiel, *Information and Legislative Organization* (Ann Arbor: University of Michigan Press, 1992).

45. To learn about the occupants and agenda of our current political party leaders and committees, go to <www.house.gov> and click on "leadership offices."

46. Jonathan Franzen, "The Listener," *New Yorker,* 6 October 2003, p. 85.

47. Cox and McCubbins, *Legislative Leviathan.*

48. Charles O. Jones, *The United States Congress* (Homewood, Ill.: Dorsey Press, 1982), p. 322.

49. See Keith Krehbiel, *Pivotal Politics* (Chicago: University of Chicago Press, 1998).

50. Gary W. Cox and Mathew D. McCubbins, *Setting the Agenda: Responsible Party Government in the U.S. House of Representatives* (New York: Cambridge University Press, 2005).

51. These ideological views affect policy outcomes as well as the structure of the institution itself. See Nelson Polsby, *How Congress Evolves: Social Bases of Institutional Change* (New York: Oxford University Press, 2004).

52. James Sterling Young, *The Washington Community* (New York: Harcourt, Brace, 1964).

53. For the importance of reelection as a motivation for members of Congress, see David Mayhew, *Congress: The Electoral Connection,* 2nd ed. (New Haven, Conn.: Yale University Press, 2004).

54. See John Cochran, "The Influence Implosion," *CQ Weekly,* 16 January 2006, p. 174; Susan Ferrechio, "2005 Legislative Summary: House Ethics Investigations," *CQ Weekly,* 2 January 2006, p. 31.

55. Isaiah Poole, "Abramoff Plea Bargain Shakes GOP," *CQ Weekly,* 6 January 2006, p. 138.

56. Richard F. Fenno, Jr., *Home Style* (Boston: Little, Brown, 1978), p. xii.

57. Ibid., p. 32.

58. Louis I. Bredvold and Ralph G. Ross (eds.), *The Philosophy of Edmund Burke* (Ann Arbor: University of Michigan Press, 1960), p. 148.

59. For an alternative and more highly differentiated set of representation models, see Jane Mansbridge, "Rethinking Representation," *American Political Science Review* 97 (November 2003): 515–528.

60. Warren E. Miller and Donald E. Stokes, "Constituency Influence in Congress," *American Political Science Review* 57 (March 1963): 45–57.

61. Sheryl Gay Stolberg, "Ease a Little Guilt, Provide Some Jobs: It's Pork on the Hill," *New York Times,* 20 January 2003, p. A1; Michael Crowley, "Under-Cut," *New Republic,* 25 February 2002, pp. 10–12.

62. Jonathan Kaplan, "Hill Leaders May Be Pressed to Give Up Pet Projects," *The Hill,* 25 January 2006, p. 1; for a running tally of pork projects, see the Citizens Against Government Waste website at <http://www.cagw.org>.

63. Stolberg, "Ease a Little Guilt."

64. E. Scott Adler, *Why Congressional Reforms Fail* (Chicago: University of Chicago Press, 2002); Eric Schickler, *Disjointed Pluralism* (Princeton, N.J.: Princeton University Press, 2001).

Chapter 12 / The Presidency / pages 358–391

1. Speech at the United States Naval Academy, Annapolis, Maryland, 30 November 2005; the text of Bush's speech may be found at <http://www.whitehouse.gov>.

2. The text of Bush's 2002 State of the Union address may be found at <http://www.whitehouse.gov>.

3. Lydia Saad, "From Vietnam to Iraq: How Americans Have Rated the President," *Gallup Poll,* 4 November 2003, <http://poll.gallup.com>.

4. See Jeffrey M. Jones, "Bush Finishes 19th Quarter in Office on Low Note: Quarterly Average Only in 18th Percentile," *Gallup Poll,* 21 October 2005, and "Independents, Moderate Republicans Lead Decline in Bush Ratings," *Gallup Poll,* 8 November 2005, <http://poll.gallup.com>.

5. Clinton Rossiter, *1787: The Grand Convention* (New York: Mentor, 1968), p. 148.

6. Ibid., pp. 190–191.

7. Lyn Ragsdale, *Vital Statistics on the Presidency: Washington to Clinton* (Washington, D.C.: CQ Press, 1996), p. 396.

8. Charles Cameron, *Veto Bargaining: Presidents and the Politics of Negative Power* (Cambridge: Cambridge University Press, 2000).

9. Jeffrey Tulis, *The Rhetorical Presidency* (Princeton, N.J.: Princeton University Press, 1987).

10. Louis Fisher, *Presidential War Power* (Lawrence: University Press of Kansas, 1995); Donald R. Kelley (ed.), *Divided Power: The Presidency, Congress, and the Formation of American Foreign Policy* (Fayetteville, Ark.: University of Arkansas Press, 2005); Andrew Rudalevige, *The New Imperial Presidency: Renewing Presidential Power After Watergate* (Ann Arbor: University of Michigan Press, 2005); Arthur M. Schlesinger, Jr., *War and the American Presidency* (New York: W. W. Norton, 2004), and *The Imperial Presidency* (New York: Houghton Mifflin, 2004).

11. Text of Joint Resolution to Authorize Use of Military Force Against Iraq, *Congressional Quarterly Weekly Report*, 12 October 2002, p. 2697.

12. James Risen and Eric Lichtblau, "Bush Lets U.S. Spy on Callers Without Courts," *New York Times*, 16 December 2005, p. A1; Lauren Etter, "Is Someone Listening to Your Phone Calls?" *Wall Street Journal*, 7 January 2006, p. A5.

13. Keith Perine, "Imbalance of Power in War on Terror," *CQ Weekly*, 27 February 2006, p. 542.

14. *Hamdan v. Rumsfeld*, 548 U.S. ___ (2006).

15. Wilfred E. Binkley, *President and Congress*, 3rd ed. (New York: Vintage, 1962), p. 155.

16. William G. Howell, *Power Without Persuasion: The Politics of Direct Presidential Action* (Princeton, N.J.: Princeton University Press, 2003); Kenneth R. Mayer, *With the Stroke of a Pen: Executive Orders and Presidential Power* (Princeton, N.J.: Princeton University Press, 2001); Adam Warber, *Executive Orders and the Modern Presidency* (Boulder, Colo.: Lynne Rienner, 2005).

17. See Peri Arnold, *Making the Managerial Presidency*, 2nd ed. (Lawrence: University of Kansas Press, 1998); Bradley H. Patterson, *The White House Staff* (Washington, D.C.: Brookings Institution Press, 2000); James Pfiffner (ed.), *The Managerial Presidency*, 2nd ed. (College Station: Texas A&M University Press, 1999).

18. Jeb Stuart Magruder, *An American Life* (New York: Atheneum, 1974), p. 58, quoted in Benjamin I. Page and Mark Petracca, *The American Presidency* (New York: McGraw-Hill, 1983), p. 171.

19. *Statistical Abstract of the United States, 1999*, available at <www.census.gov/prod/99pubs/99statab/sec10.pdf>.

20. Richard Tanner Johnson, *Managing the White House* (New York: Harper & Row, 1974); John P. Burke, *The Institutional Presidency* (Baltimore: Johns Hopkins University Press, 1992).

21. Irving Janus, *Victims of Groupthink: A Psychological Study of Foreign Policy Decisions and Fiascoes* (Boston: Houghton Mifflin, 1972); Andrew Rudalevige, "The Structure of Leadership: Presidents, Hierarchies, and Information Flow," *Presidential Studies Quarterly* 35 (June 2005): 333–360.

22. George Stephanopoulos, *All Too Human* (Boston: Back Bay Books, 1999), p. 61.

23. Karen Hult, "The Bush White House in Comparative Perspective," in *The George W. Bush Presidency*, ed. Fred I. Greenstein (Baltimore: Johns Hopkins University Press, 2003), pp. 51–77.

24. Transcript of "Meet the Press," Dick Cheney guest, Tim Russert moderator, <http://www.msnbc.com/id/3080244/>.

25. Edward Weisband and Thomas M. Franck, *Resignation in Protest* (New York: Penguin, 1975), p. 139, quoted in Thomas E. Cronin, *The State of the Presidency*, 2nd ed. (Boston: Little, Brown, 1980), p. 253.

26. David E. Lewis, "Staffing Alone: Unilateral Action and the Politicization of the Executive Branch," *Presidential Studies Quarterly* 35 (September 2005): 496–514. For an excellent discussion of Lincoln's appointment of his political rivals to his cabinet, see Doris Kearns Goodwin, *Team of Rivals* (New York: Simon & Schuster, 2005).

27. Terry M. Moe, "The Politicized Presidency," in *The New Direction in American Politics*, ed. John E. Chubb and Paul E. Peterson (Washington, D.C.: Brookings Institution, 1985), pp. 235–271.

28. Doris Kearns, *Lyndon Johnson and the American Dream* (New York: Signet, 1977), p. 363.

29. See Merrill McLoughlin (ed.), *The Impeachment and Trial of President Clinton: The Official Transcripts, from the House Judiciary Committee Hearings to the Senate Trial* (New York: Random House, 1999); Richard Posner, *An Affair of State* (Cambridge, Mass.: Harvard University Press, 1999); Jeffrey Toobin, *A Vast Conspiracy* (New York: Touchstone, 1999).

30. James David Barber, *Presidential Character*, 4th ed. (Englewood Cliffs, N.J.: Prentice Hall, 1992); Fred I. Greenstein, *The Presidential Difference: Leadership Style from FDR to Clinton* (Princeton, N.J.: Princeton University Press, 2000); David G. Winter, "Things I've Learned About Personality from Studying Political Leadership at a Distance," *Journal of Personality* 73/3 (2005): 557–584.

31. Donald Kinder, "Presidential Character Revisited," in *Political Cognition*, ed. Richard Lau and David O. Sears (Hillsdale, N.J.: Erlbaum, 1986), pp. 233–255; W. E. Miller and J. M. Shanks, *The New American Voter* (Cambridge, Mass.: Harvard University Press, 1996).

32. "Presidential Ratings—Personal Characteristics," <http://www.poll.gallup.com>.

33. Richard E. Neustadt, *Presidential Power* (New York: Wiley, 1980), p. 10.

34. Ibid., p. 9.

35. Chad Roedemeier, "Nixon Kept Softer Self Off Limits, Tape Shows," *Boston Globe*, 8 July 2000, p. A4.

36. Joseph Schatz, "Presidential Support Vote Study: With a Deft and Light Touch, Bush Finds Ways to Win," *Congressional Quarterly Weekly Report*, 10 December 2004, p. 2904.

37. Terry Sullivan, "I'll Walk Your District Barefoot" (paper delivered at the MIT Conference on the Presidency, Cambridge, Mass., 29 January 2000), p. 6.

38. George C. Edwards III, *At the Margins* (New Haven, Conn.: Yale University Press, 1989). See also Jon R. Bond and Richard Fleisher, *The President in the Legislative Arena* (Chicago: University of Chicago Press, 1990).

39. Bert Rockman, "Leadership Style and the Clinton Presidency," in *The Clinton Presidency: First Appraisals*, ed. Colin Campbell and Bert A. Rockman (Chatham, N.J.: Chatham House, 1996), p. 328.

40. See Stephen J. Farnsworth, *The Mediated Presidency: Television News and Presidential Governance* (Rowman and Littlefield, 2005); and Lori Cox Han and Diane J. Heith (eds.), *In the Public Domain: Presidents and the Challenges of Public Leadership* (Albany, N.Y.: State University of New York Press, 2005).

41. Samuel Kernell, *Going Public: New Strategies of Presidential Leadership*, 3rd ed. (Washington, D.C.: CQ Press, 1997), p. 2.

42. Richard A. Brody, *Assessing the President* (Stanford, Calif.: Stanford University Press, 1991), pp. 27–44; Gary C. Jacobson, "The Bush Presidency and the American Electorate," in *The George W. Bush Presidency*, ed. Fred I. Greenstein (Baltimore: Johns Hopkins University Press, 2003), pp. 197–227.

43. Paul Brace and Barbara Hinckley, *Follow the Leader* (New York: Basic Books, 1992); Richard Brody, "President Bush and the Public," in Greenstein, *The George W. Bush Presidency*, pp. 228–244; George C. Edwards III and Tami Swenson, "Who Rallies? The Anatomy of a Rally Event," *Journal of Politics* 59 (February 1997): 200–212; George C. Edwards, *The Public Presidency: The Pursuit of Popular Support* (New York: St. Martin's Press, 1983).

44. Richard C. Eichenberg and Richard J. Stoll, *The Political Fortunes of War: Iraq and the Domestic Standing of President*

George W. Bush (London: The Foreign Policy Centre, 2004), p. 8.

45. George C. Edwards III, "Frustration and Folly: Bill Clinton and the Public Presidency," in Campbell and Rockman, *The Clinton Presidency,* p. 255.

46. Mark A. Peterson, "Clinton and Organized Interests: Splitting Friends, Unifying Enemies," in *The Clinton Legacy,* ed. Colin Campbell and Bert A. Rockman (New York: Chatham House, 2000), pp. 140–168.

47. Jeffrey E. Cohen, *Presidential Responsiveness and Public Policy-Making* (Ann Arbor: University of Michigan Press, 1999); Lawrence C. Jacobs and Robert Y. Shapiro, *Politicians Don't Pander* (Chicago: University of Chicago Press, 2000).

48. David McCullough, *Truman* (New York: Simon & Schuster, 1992), p. 914.

49. Jon Bond and Richard Fleisher, *The President in the Legislative Arena;* Mark Peterson, *Legislating Together* (Cambridge, Mass.: Harvard University Press, 1990).

50. Joseph Schatz, "Presidential Support Vote Study," p. 2904.

51. "Two Cheers for United Government," *American Enterprise* 4 (January–February 1993): 107–108. Political scientists do not agree about whether voters intentionally try to elect divided government. See, for example, Barry Burden and David C. Kimball, *Why Americans Split Their Tickets* (Ann Arbor: University of Michigan Press, 2004); Morris Fiorina, *Divided Government,* 2nd ed. (Needham Heights, Mass.: Allyn & Bacon, 1996); and Gary C. Jacobson, *The Electoral Origins of Divided Government* (Boulder, Colo.: Westview Press, 1990).

52. David R. Mayhew, *Divided We Govern* (New Haven, Conn.: Yale University Press, 1991); David R. Mayhew, "The Return to Unified Government Under Clinton: How Much of a Difference in Lawmaking?" in *The New American Politics,* ed. Bryan D. Jones (Boulder, Colo.: Westview Press, 1995), pp. 111–121; see Jon Bond and Richard Fleisher (eds.), *Polarized Politics: Congress and the President in a Partisan Era* (Washington, D.C.: CQ Press, 2000).

53. See Sarah H. Binder, "The Dynamics of Legislative Gridlock, 1947–96," *American Political Science Review* 93 (September 1999): 519–534.

54. See Charles O. Jones, *The Presidency in a Separated System,* 2nd ed. (Washington, D.C.: Brookings Institution, 2005).

55. "Prepared Text of Carter's Farewell Address," *New York Times,* 15 January 1981, p. B10.

56. Benjamin I. Page, *Choices and Echoes in Presidential Elections* (Chicago: University of Chicago Press, 1978).

57. Patricia Conley, *Presidential Mandates: How Elections Shape the National Agenda* (Chicago: University of Chicago Press, 2001).

58. Robert A. Dahl, "Myth of the Presidential Mandate," *Political Science Quarterly* 105 (Fall 1990): 355–372.

59. Stephen Skowronek, *The Politics Presidents Make,* 2nd ed. (Cambridge, Mass.: Harvard University Press, 1997).

60. Stephen Skowronek, "Presidential Leadership in Political Time," in *The Presidency in the Political System,* 6th ed., ed. Michael Nelson (Washington, D.C.: CQ Press, 2000), p. 164; Stephen Skowronek, "Leadership by Definition: First Term Reflections on George W. Bush's Political Stance," *Perspectives on Politics* 3 (December 2005): 817–831.

61. *Public Papers of the President, Lyndon B. Johnson, 1965,* vol. 1 (Washington, D.C.: U.S. Government Printing Office, 1966), p. 72.

62. "Transcript of Second Inaugural Address by Reagan," *New York Times,* 22 January 1985, p. 72.

63. Kevin Phillips, *The Politics of Rich and Poor* (New York: Random House, 1990), p. 88.

64. See the text of Bush's inaugural address at <http://janda.org/politxts/Inaugural%20Addresses/Bush.001.htm>.

65. David E. Sanger, "A Speech About Nothing, Something, Everything," *New York Times,* 23 January 2005, sec. 4, p. 5.

66. John W. Kingdon, *Agendas, Alternatives, and Public Policies* (Boston: Little, Brown, 1984), p. 25.

67. Richard E. Neustadt, "Presidency and Legislation: The Growth of Central Clearance," *American Political Science Review* 48 (September 1954): 641–671.

68. Seth King, "Reagan, in Bid for Budget Votes, Reported to Yield on Sugar Prices," *New York Times,* 27 June 1981, p. A1.

69. Barbara Sinclair, "The President as Legislative Leader," in Campbell and Rockman, *The Clinton Legacy,* p. 75.

70. Roger H. Davidson and Colton C. Campbell, "The Senate and the Executive," in *Esteemed Colleagues,* ed. Burdett A. Loomis (Washington, D.C.: Brookings Institution, 2000), pp. 194–219.

71. "Special Report," *CQ Weekly,* 16 December 2000, pp. 2842–2856.

72. Jeffrey M. Berry and Kent E. Portney, "Centralizing Regulatory Control and Interest Group Access: The Quayle Council on Competitiveness," in *Interest Group Politics,* 4th ed., ed. Allan J. Cigler and Burdett A. Loomis (Washington, D.C.: CQ Press, 1994), pp. 319–347.

73. The extent to which popularity affects presidential influence in Congress is difficult to determine with any precision. For an overview of this issue, see Jon R. Bond, Richard Fleisher, and Glen S. Katz, "An Overview of the Empirical Findings on Presidential-Congressional Relations," in *Rivals for Power,* ed. James A. Thurber (Washington, D.C.: CQ Press, 1996), pp. 103–139.

74. For a history of the relationship between presidents and the American party system, see Sidney Milkis, "Executive Power and Political Parties," in *The Executive Branch,* ed. Joel Aberbach and Mark Peterson (New York: Oxford University Press, 2005), pp. 379–418.

75. George Hager, "Clinton, GOP Congress Strike Historic Budget Agreement," *Congressional Quarterly Weekly Report,* 3 May 1997, p. 996.

76. For an inside account of the Bush administration's response to September 11, see Bob Woodward, *Bush at War* (New York: Simon & Schuster, 2002). For an account of the decision to go to war with Iraq, see Bob Woodward, *Plan of Attack* (New York: Simon & Schuster, 2004).

77. Ernest R. May and Philip D. Zelikow (eds.), *The Kennedy Tapes: Inside the White House During the Cuban Missile Crisis* (Cambridge, Mass.: Harvard University Press, 1997), pp. 498–499, 501, 512–513, 663–666.

78. John P. Burke and Fred I. Greenstein, *How Presidents Test Reality* (New York: Russell Sage Foundation, 1989).

79. Richard E. Neustadt and Ernest R. May, *Thinking in Time* (New York: Free Press, 1986), p. 143.

80. Theodore J. Lowi, *The Personal President* (Ithaca, N.Y.: Cornell University Press, 1985), p. 185.

Chapter 13 / The Bureaucracy / pages 392–418

1. Mark Potter and Rich Phillips, "Six Months After Sept. 11, Hijackers Visa Approval Letters Received," available at <http://edition.cnn.com/2002/US/03/12/inv.flight.school.visas>.

2. Seymour M. Hersh, "Missed Messages," *New Yorker,* 3 June 2002, p. 41.

3. Jeff Gerth, "C.I.A. Chief Won't Name Officials Who Failed to Add Hijackers to Watch List," *New York Times,* 15 May 2003, p. A18.

4. For details, see Martin Kady II, "Provisions of Homeland Security Creation," *Congressional Quarterly Weekly,* 15 February 2003, p. 417.

5. New Orleans resident Patricia Thompson, quoted in "A Failure of Initiative," the final report of the House Select

Bipartisan Committee to Investigate the Preparation for and Response to Hurricane Katrina, <http://Katrina.house.gov>.

6. Malcolm Gladwell, "The Talent Myth," *New Yorker,* 22 July 2002, p. 32.

7. James Q. Wilson, *Bureaucracy* (New York: Basic Books, 1989), p. 25.

8. Bruce D. Porter, "Parkinson's Law Revisited: War and the Growth of American Government," *Public Interest* 60 (Summer 1980): 50.

9. See generally Ballard C. Campbell, *The Growth of American Government* (Bloomington: Indiana University Press, 1995).

10. See generally Marc Allen Eisner, *Regulatory Politics in Transition,* 2nd ed. (Baltimore: Johns Hopkins University Press, 2000).

11. See Anne Schneider and Helen Ingram, "Social Construction of Target Populations: Implications for Politics and Policy," *American Political Science Review* 87 (June 1993): 334–347.

12. Theda Skocpol, *Protecting Soldiers and Mothers: The Political Origins of Social Policy in the United States* (Cambridge, Mass.: Harvard University Press, 1992), and *Social Policy in the United States* (Princeton, N.J.: Princeton University Press, 1995).

13. Paul C. Light, *Thickening Government* (Washington, D.C.: Brookings Institution, 1995), and "Fact Sheet on the Continued Thickening of Government," Brookings Institution, July 2004, <http://www.brookings.edu/views/papers/light/20040723.htm>. For an account of bureaucratic entrepreneurs at the turn of the twentieth century, see Daniel P. Carpenter, *The Forging of Bureaucratic Autonomy: Reputations, Networks, and Policy Innovation in Executive Agencies, 1862–1928* (Princeton, N.J.: Princeton University Press, 2001).

14. Paul C. Light, *The True Size of Government* (Washington, D.C.: Brookings Institution, 1999).

15. David E. Lewis, "The Politics of Agency Termination: Confronting the Myth of Agency Immortality," *Journal of Politics* 64 (February 2002): 89–107.

16. *Statistical Abstract of the United States, 2003.* The source material is available at <http://www.census.gov/prod/2003pubs/02statab/stlocgov.pdf> and <http://www.census.gov/prod/2003pubs/02statab/labor.pdf>.

17. Joel D. Aberbach and Bert A. Rockman, *In the Web of Politics* (Washington, D.C.: Brookings Institution, 2000), p. 162.

18. Gregory B. Lewis and Sue A. Frank, "Who Wants to Work for the Government?" *Public Administration Review* 62 (July–August 2002): 395–404.

19. Aberbach and Rockman, *In the Web of Politics.*

20. *Staffing a New Administration: A Guide to Personnel Appointments in a Presidential Transition* (Washington, D.C.: Brookings Institution, 2000), available at <http://www.appointee.brookings.edu/resourcecenter/journalismguide.pdf>.

21. Terry M. Moe, "The Presidency and the Bureaucracy: The Presidential Advantage," in *The Presidency and the Political System,* 7th ed., ed. Michael Nelson (Washington, D.C.: CQ Press, 2003), pp. 425–457; David Lewis, *Presidents and the Politics of Agency Design: Political Insulation in the United States Government Bureaucracy, 1946–1997* (Stanford, Calif.: Stanford University Press, 2003).

22. Though formally located within the executive branch, the bureaucracy is "caught in the middle" between the Congress and the president. See Barry Weingast, "Caught in the Middle: The President, Congress, and the Political-Bureaucratic System," in *The Executive Branch,* ed. J. Aberbach and M. Peterson (New York: Oxford University Press, 2005), pp. 312–343.

23. John Cochran, "Debacles, DeLay, and Disarray," *CQ Weekly,* 3 October 2005, p. 2636.

24. James Fallows, "Why Iraq Has No Army," *Atlantic Monthly* 296 (December 2005): 60–77; Anne Plummer, Tim Starks,

and Mary Speck, "Pushback Grows over Bush and War," *CQ Weekly,* 22 December 2005, p. 3386.

25. Kate Schuler, "New Medicare Drug Plan Gets Off to Rocky Start," *CQ Weekly,* 30 January 2006, p. 267.

26. Doris A. Graber, *Mass Media and American Politics,* 3rd ed. (Washington, D.C.: CQ Press, 1989), p. 51.

27. Amol Sharma and Jennifer Dlouhy, "A New Indecency Standard: Lost in Terminal Vagueness?" *CQ Weekly,* 10 July 2004, p. 1668.

28. Amol Sharma, "2005 Legislative Summary: Broadcast Indecency Penalties," *CQ Weekly,* 2 January 2006, p. 55.

29. Lauren Etter, "Is Someone Listening to Your Phone Calls?" *Wall Street Journal,* 7 January 2006, p. A5; James Risen and Eric Lichtblau, "Bush Lets U.S. Spy on Callers Without Courts," *New York Times,* 16 December 2005, p. A1.

30. Cornelius M. Kerwin, *Rulemaking: How Government Agencies Write Law and Make Policy,* 3rd ed. (Washington, D.C.: CQ Press, 2003); Cass Sunstein, *After the Rights Revolution: Reconceiving the Regulatory State* (Cambridge, Mass.: Harvard University Press, 2005); William West, "Administrative Rule Making: An Old and Emergent Literature," *Public Administration Review* 65 (November–December 2005): 655–668.

31. Marian Burros, "F.D.A. Is Again Proposing to Regulate Vitamins and Supplements," *New York Times,* 15 June 1993, p. A25. For a general discussion of the relationship between the FDA and members of Congress, see Charles Shipan, "Regulatory Regimes, Agency Actions, and the Conditional Nature of Congressional Influence," *American Political Science Review* 98 (August 2004): 467–480.

32. Charles E. Lindblom, "The Science of Muddling Through," *Public Administration Review* 19 (Spring 1959): 79–88.

33. Andrew Weiss and Edward Woodhouse, "Reframing Incrementalism: A Constructive Response to the Critics," *Policy Sciences* 25 (August 1992): 255–273.

34. "Bureaucratic culture" is a particularly slippery concept but can be conceived of as the interplay of artifacts, values, and underlying assumptions. See Irene Lurie and Norma Riccucci, "Changing the 'Culture' of Welfare Offices," *Administration and Society* 34 (January 2003): 653–677; and Marissa Martino Golden, *What Motivates Bureaucrats?* (New York: Columbia University Press, 2000).

35. "Battles with the IRS," *Congressional Quarterly Weekly Report,* 27 September 1997, p. 2299; "IRS Overhaul," *Congressional Quarterly Weekly Report,* 20 December 1997, p. 3119.

36. A good, short introduction to TQM in government is James E. Swiss, "Adapting Total Quality Management to Government," *Public Administration Review* 52 (July–August 1992): 356–362.

37. David S. Cloud, "Case for War Relied on Selective Intelligence," *Wall Street Journal,* 5 June 2003, p. A4; Paul R. Pillar, "Intelligence, Policy, and the War in Iraq," *Foreign Affairs* 85 (March–April 2006): 15–27.

38. Robert B. Reich, *Locked in the Cabinet* (New York: Vintage, 1998), pp. 115–118.

39. Thomas W. Church and Robert T. Nakamura, *Cleaning Up the Mess* (Washington, D.C.: Brookings Institution, 1993).

40. Ronald Daniels (ed.), *On Risk and Disaster: Lessons from Hurricane Katrina* (Philadelphia: University of Pennsylvania Press, 2006); Saundra Schneider, "Administrative Breakdowns in Governmental Response to Hurricane Katrina," *Public Administration Review* 65 (September–October 2005): 515–516.

41. Spencer Hsu and Amy Goldstein, "Administration Faulted on Katrina," *Washington Post,* 2 February 2006, p. A5.

42. Spencer Hsu, "Brown Defends FEMA's Efforts," *Washington Post,* 28 September 2005, p. A1.

43. Representative Thomas Davis (R-Va.) quoted by Eric Lipton, "White House Knew of Levee's Failure on Night of Storm," *New York Times*, 10 February 2006, p. A1.

44. Spencer Hsu and Steve Hendrix, "Hurricanes Katrina and Rita Were like Night and Day," *Washington Post*, 25 September 2005, p. A1.

45. See Donald Kettl et al., *Managing for Performance: A Report on Strategies for Improving the Results of Government* (Washington, D.C.: Brookings Institution, 2006); Paul Light, "The Tides of Reform Revisited: Patterns in Making Government Work, 1945–2002," *Public Administration Review* 66 (January 2006): 6–19.

46. Peter H. Stone, "Ganging Up on the FDA," *National Journal*, 18 February 1995, pp. 410–414.

47. Lori Nitschke, "Senate Bill Aims to Speed Review of Drugs, Medical Devices by FDA," *Congressional Quarterly Weekly Report*, 27 September 1997, p. 2312.

48. See generally E. S. Savas, *Privatization and Public-Private Partnerships* (New York: Chatham House, 2000).

49. Steven Rathgeb Smith, "Social Services," in *The State of Nonprofit America*, ed. Lester M. Salamon (Washington, D.C.: Brookings Institution and Aspen Institute, 2002), p. 165.

50. John D. McKinnon, "Bush Outsourcing Rules May Help Placate Unions," *Wall Street Journal*, 29 May 2003, p. A6.

51. Donald F. Kettl, "The Global Revolution in Public Management: Driving Themes, Missing Links," *Journal of Policy Analysis and Management* 16 (1997): 448.

52. Beryl A. Radin, *Beyond Machiavelli: Policy Analysis Comes of Age* (Washington, D.C.: Georgetown University Press, 2000), pp. 168–169.

53. The OMB posts its ratings on its "expectmore.gov" website. To learn about the OMB's Program Assessment and Rating Tool (PART), go to its website at <http://www.whitehouse.gov/omb/part/index.html>. Results are posted at <http://www.whitehouse.gov/omb/expectmore>.

54. The President's Management Agenda homepage is located at <http://www.whitehouse.gov/results/agenda/scorecard.html>; the specific standards for success are located at <http://www.whitehouse.gov/results/agenda/standards.pdf>.

55. See Carolyn J. Heinrich, "Outcomes-Based Performance in the Public Sector," *Public Administration Review* 62 (November–December 2002): 712–725; and David Hirschmann, "Thermometers or Sauna? Performance Measurement and Democratic Assistance in the United States Agency for International Development (USAID)," *Public Administration* 80 (2002): 235–255.

56. See Amahai Glazer and Lawrence S. Rothenberg, *Why Government Succeeds and Why It Fails* (Cambridge, Mass.: Harvard University Press, 2001).

Chapter 14 / The Courts / pages 419–454

1. David Von Drehle, "The Night That Would Not End," *Washington Post*, 9 November 2000, p. A1.

2. Sara Fritz, Bill Adair, and David Ballingrud, "Florida Finish," *St. Petersburg Times*, 8 November 2000, p. 3A.

3. *Bush* v. *Palm Beach County Canvassing Board*, 531 U.S. 70 (2000).

4. *Gore and Lieberman* v. *Harris*, 772 So.2d 1243 (8 December 2000, as corrected 14 December 2000).

5. *Bush* v. *Gore*, No. 00-949 (00A504) (granting a stay in SC00-2431). 531 U.S. 1046 (2000) (December 9, 2000).

6. *Bush* v. *Gore*, 531 U.S. 98 (2000).

7. National Opinion Research Center, *Florida Ballots Project*, <www.norc.uchicago.edu/fl/index.asp>.

8. Felix Frankfurter and James M. Landis, *The Business of the Supreme Court* (New York: Macmillan, 1928), pp. 5–14; Julius Goebel, Jr., *Antecedents and Beginnings to 1801*, vol. 1 of *The History of the Supreme Court of the United States* (New York: Macmillan, 1971).

9. Maeva Marcus (ed.), *The Justices on Circuit, 1795–1800*, vol. 3 of *The Documentary History of the Supreme Court of the United States, 1789–1800* (New York: Columbia University Press, 1990).

10. Robert G. McCloskey, *The United States Supreme Court* (Chicago: University of Chicago Press, 1960), p. 31.

11. *Marbury* v. *Madison*, 1 Cranch 137 at 177, 178 (1803).

12. Interestingly, the term *judicial review* dates only to 1910; it was apparently unknown to Marshall and his contemporaries. Robert Lowry Clinton, *Marbury* v. *Madison and Judicial Review* (Lawrence: University Press of Kansas, 1989), p. 7.

13. Lee Epstein et al., *The Supreme Court Compendium*, 3rd ed. (Washington, D.C.: CQ Press, 2003), Table 2-15.

14. *Ware* v. *Hylton*, 3 Dallas 199 (1796).

15. *Martin* v. *Hunter's Lessee*, 1 Wheat. 304 (1816).

16. Epstein et al., *The Supreme Court Compendium*, Table 2-16.

17. Garry Wills, *Explaining America: The Federalist* (Garden City, N.Y.: Doubleday, 1981), pp. 127–136.

18. *State Justice Institute News* 4 (Spring 1993): 1.

19. Court Statistics Project, *Examining the Work of State Courts, 2004* (National Centers for State Courts, 2005). Available at <http://www.ncsconline.org/D_Research/csp/2004_Files/EWOverview_final_2.pdf>, accessed 10 February 2006.

20. William P. Marshall, "Federalization: A Critical Overview," *DePaul Law Review* 44 (1995): 722–723.

21. Charles Alan Wright, *Handbook on the Law of Federal Courts*, 3rd ed. (St. Paul, Minn.: West, 1976), p. 7.

22. Table 6.1, "U.S. District Courts, Civil and Criminal Cases Filed, Terminated, Pending," available at <http://www.uscourts.gov/judicialfactsfigures/Table601.pdf>, accessed 6 July 2006.

23. Table 1.1, Total Judicial Officers: Courts of Appeals, District Courts, Bankruptcy Courts, available at <http://www.uscourts.gov/judicialfactsfigures/Table101.pdf>, accessed 6 July 2006.

24. Table 2.1, "Appeals Filed, Terminated, Pending—Summary (Excludes Federal Circuit)," available at <http://www.uscourts.gov/judicialfactsfigures/Table201.pdf>, accessed 6 July 2006.

25. Linda Greenhouse, "Precedent for Lower Courts: Tyrant or Teacher?" *New York Times*, 29 January 1988, p. B7.

26. *Texas* v. *Johnson*, 491 U.S. 397 (1989); *United States* v. *Eichman*, 496 U.S. 310 (1990).

27. *Regents of the University of California* v. *Bakke*, 438 U.S. 265 (1978).

28. *Grutter* v. *Bollinger*, 539 U.S. 244 (2003); *Gratz* v. *Bollinger*, 539 U.S. 306 (2003).

29. "Reading Petitions Is for Clerks Only at High Court Now," *Wall Street Journal*, 11 October 1990, p. B7.

30. H. W. Perry, Jr., *Deciding to Decide: Agenda Setting in the United States Supreme Court* (Cambridge, Mass.: Harvard University Press, 1991); Linda Greenhouse, "Justice Delayed; Agreeing Not to Agree," *New York Times*, 17 March 1996, sec. 4, p. 1.

31. Perry, *Deciding to Decide*; Gregory A. Caldiera and John R. Wright, "The Discuss List: Agenda Building in the Supreme Court," *Law and Society Review* 24 (1990): 807.

32. Doris M. Provine, *Case Selection in the United States Supreme Court* (Chicago: University of Chicago Press, 1980), pp. 74–102.

33. Perry, *Deciding to Decide*, p. 286.

34. Kevin T. McGuire, "Repeat Players in the Supreme Court: The Role of Experienced Lawyers in Litigation Success," *Journal of Politics* 57 (1995): 187–196.

35. Michael Kirkland, "Court Hears 'Subordinate' Speech Debate," 1 December 1993, NEWSNET News Bulletin Board.

The oral argument in the case, *Waters* v. *Churchill*, can be found at <http://www.oyez.org/oyez/audio/632/argument.smil>.

36. William H. Rehnquist, "Remarks of the Chief Justice: My Life in the Law Series," *Duke Law Journal* 52 (2003): 787–805.

37. "Rising Fixed Opinions," *New York Times*, 22 February 1988, p. 14. See also Linda Greenhouse, "At the Bar," *New York Times*, 28 July 1989, p. 21.

38. Jeffrey A. Segal and Harold J. Spaeth, *The Supreme Court and the Attitudinal Model* (Cambridge: Cambridge University Press, 1993).

39. Stuart Taylor, Jr., "Lifting of Secrecy Reveals Earthy Side of Justices," *New York Times*, 22 February 1988, p. A16.

40. Richard A. Posner, "The Courthouse Mice," *The New Republic*, 12 June 2006, available at <http://www.tnr.com/doc.mhtml?i=20060612&s=posner061206>.

41. Thomas G. Walker, Lee Epstein, and William J. Dixon, "On the Mysterious Demise of Consensual Norms in the United States Supreme Court," *Journal of Politics* 50 (1988): 361–389.

42. Linda Greenhouse, "Roberts Is at Court's Helm, but He Isn't Yet in Control," *New York Times*, 2 July 2006, sec. 1, p. 1. See also John P. Kelsh, "The Opinion Delivery Practices of the United States Supreme Court, 1790–1945," *Washington University Law Quarterly* 77 (1999): 137–181. For more on the Roberts Court, see Linda Greenhouse, "Oral Dissents Give Ginsberg New Voice," *New York Times*, 31 May 2007, p. A1; Jeffrey Toobin, "Five to Four," *The New Yorker*, 25 June 2007, pp. 35–37.

43. See, for example, Walter F. Murphy, *Elements of Judicial Strategy* (Chicago: University of Chicago Press, 1964); Bob Woodward and Scott Armstrong, *The Brethren* (New York: Simon & Schuster, 1979).

44. Henry J. Abraham, *Justices and Presidents: A Political History of Appointments to the Supreme Court*, 2nd ed. (New York: Oxford University Press, 1985), pp. 183–185.

45. Stephen L. Wasby, *The Supreme Court in the Federal Judicial System*, 3rd ed. (Chicago: Nelson-Hall, 1988), p. 241.

46. Greenhouse, "At the Bar," p. 21.

47. National Center for State Courts, "Survey of Judicial Salaries," Vol. 30, No. 1, available at <www.ncsconline.org> (salaries as of April 2005).

48. Lawrence Baum, *American Courts: Process and Policy*, 3rd ed. (Boston: Houghton Mifflin, 1994), pp. 114–129.

49. Tajuana D. Massie, Thomas G. Hansford, and David R. Songer, "The Timing of Presidential Nominations to Lower Federal Courts," *Political Research Quarterly* 57/1: 145–154.

50. Sheldon Goldman et al., "W. Bush Remaking the Judiciary: Like Father Like Son?" *Judicature* 86 (May–June 2003): 282–309.

51. Paul Barrett, "More Minorities, Women Named to U.S. Courts," *Wall Street Journal*, 23 December 1993, p. B1; Sheldon Goldman and Elliot Slotnick, "Clinton's Second Term Judiciary: Picking Judges Under Fire," *Judicature* 82 (May–June 1999): 264–284.

52. Kenneth L. Manning and Robert A. Carp, "The Decision-Making Ideology of George W. Bush's Judicial Appointees: An Update" (paper presented at the 2004 annual meeting of the American Political Science Association, Chicago, Illinois, 2–5 September 2004).

53. Wasby, *Supreme Court*, pp. 107–110.

54. Goldman et al., "W. Bush Remaking the Judiciary," p. 298 (Table 1).

55. Ronald Stidham, Robert A. Carp, and Donald R. Songer, "The Voting Behavior of Judges Appointed by President Clinton" (paper presented at the annual meeting of the Southwestern Political Science Association, Houston, Texas, March 1996). See also Susan B. Haire, Martha Anne Humphries, and Donald R. Songer, "The Voting Behavior of Clinton's Courts of Appeals Appointees," *Judicature* 84 (March–April 2001): 274–281.

56. Robert A. Carp, Ronald Stidham, and Kenneth L. Manning, "The Voting Behavior of George W. Bush's Judges: How Sharp a Turn to the Right?" in *Principles and Practice of American Politics: Classic and Contemporary Readings*, 3rd ed., ed. Samuel Kernell and Steven S. Smith (Washington, D.C.: CQ Press, 2006), forthcoming.

57. Peter G. Fish, "John J. Parker," in *Dictionary of American Biography*, supp. 6, 1956–1980 (New York: Scribner's, 1980), p. 494.

58. Information from the *US Senate*, "Supreme Court Nominations" available at <http://www.senate.gov/pagelayout/reference/nominations/Nominations.htm>, accessed 12 February 2006.

59. *Congressional Quarterly's Guide to the U.S. Supreme Court*, 2nd ed. (Washington, D.C.: CQ Press, 1990), pp. 655–656.

60. *Brown* v. *Board of Education II*, 349 U.S. 294 (1955).

61. Charles A. Johnson and Bradley C. Canon, *Judicial Policies: Implementation and Impact* (Washington, D.C.: CQ Press, 1984).

62. *Webster* v. *Reproductive Health Services*, 492 U.S. 490 (1989).

63. *Planned Parenthood* v. *Casey*, 505 U.S. 833 (1992).

64. *Stenberg* v. *Carhart*, 530 U.S. 914 (2000); *Gonzales* v. *Carhart*, 550 U.S. ___ (2007).

65. Alexander M. Bickel, *The Least Dangerous Branch* (Indianapolis, Ind.: Bobbs-Merrill, 1962); Robert A. Dahl, "Decision-Making in a Democracy: The Supreme Court as a National Policy-Maker," *Journal of Public Law* 6 (1962): 279.

66. William Mishler and Reginald S. Sheehan, "The Supreme Court as a Countermajoritarian Institution? The Impact of Public Opinion on Supreme Court Decisions," *American Political Science Review* 87 (1993): 87–101.

67. Thomas R. Marshall, *Public Opinion and the Supreme Court* (Boston: Unwin Hyman, 1989).

68. The Polling Company, <www.pollingcompany.com>, 19 April 2002.

69. Marshall, *Public Opinion and the Supreme Court*, pp. 192–193; Gerald N. Rosenberg, *The Hollow Hope: Can Courts Bring About Social Change?* (Chicago: University of Chicago Press, 1991).

70. Gallup Poll, 12–15 September 2005, available at *Gallup Brain*, <http://brain.gallup.com>, accessed 18 February 2006.

71. Jeffrey M. Jones, "Nearly 6 in 10 Approve of Supreme Court," *Social Issues & Policy*, Gallup Poll News Service (17 June 2003).

72. *Kelo* v. *City of New London*, 545 U.S. ___ (2005).

73. William J. Brennan, Jr., "State Supreme Court Judge Versus United States Supreme Court Justice: A Change in Function and Perspective," *University of Florida Law Review* 19 (1966): 225.

74. G. Alan Tarr and M. C. Porter, *State Supreme Courts in State and Nation* (New Haven, Conn.: Yale University Press, 1988), pp. 206–209.

75. John B. Wefing, "The Performance of the New Jersey Supreme Court at the Opening of the Twenty-first Century: New Cast, Same Script," *Seton Hall Law Review* 32 (2003): 769.

76. Dennis Hevesi, "New Jersey Court Protects Trash from Police Searches," *New York Times*, 19 July 1990, p. A9.

77. Kermit L. Hall, "The Canon of American Constitutional History in Comparative Perspective" (keynote address to the Supreme Court Historical Society, Washington, D.C., 16 February 2001).

78. Baum, *American Courts*, pp. 319–347.

Chapter 15 / Order and Civil Liberties / pages 455–491

1. "Dressed for Protest: Controversial T-Shirt Stirs Up Freedom of Speech Debate," *Washington Post*, 18 March 2003, p. C13.

2. Learned Hand, *The Bill of Rights* (Boston: Atheneum, 1958), p. 1.

3. Richard E. Berg-Andersson, "Of Liberties, Rights and Powers (Part One): Just How Far Is Too Far—for Both Governments and Persons?" The Green Papers Commentary, <http://www.thegreenpapers.com/PCom/?20060427-0>, accessed 9 May 2006.
4. Leonard W. Levy, *The Establishment Clause: Religion and the First Amendment* (New York: Macmillan, 1986); Leo Pfeffer, *Church, State, and Freedom* (Boston: Beacon Press, 1953); Leonard W. Levy, "The Original Meaning of the Establishment Clause of the First Amendment," in *Religion and the State*, ed. James E. Wood, Jr. (Waco, Tex.: Baylor University Press, 1985), pp. 43–83.
5. "U.S. Stands Alone in Its Embrace of Religion," Pew Research Center for the People and the Press, Washington, D.C., 19 December 2002.
6. *Reynolds* v. *United States*, 98 U.S. 145 (1879).
7. *Everson* v. *Board of Education*, 330 U.S. 1 (1947).
8. *Board of Education* v. *Allen*, 392 U.S. 236 (1968).
9. *Lemon* v. *Kurtzman*, 403 U.S. 602 (1971).
10. *Agostini* v. *Felton*, 96 U.S. 552 (1997).
11. *Zelman* v. *Simmons-Harris*, 536 U.S. 639 (2002).
12. *Lynch* v. *Donnelly*, 465 U.S. 668 (1984).
13. *Van Orden* v. *Perry*, 545 U.S. ___ (2005).
14. *McCreary County* v. *ACLU of Kentucky*, 545 U.S. ___ (2005).
15. *Engle* v. *Vitale*, 370 U.S. 421 (1962).
16. *Abington School District* v. *Schempp*, 374 U.S. 203 (1963).
17. *Lee* v. *Weisman*, 505 U.S. 577 (1992).
18. *Sante Fe Independent School District* v. *Doe*, 530 U.S. 290 (2000), quoting *West Virginia Board of Education* v. *Barnette*, 319 U.S. 624, 638 (1943).
19. Michael W. McConnell, "The Origins and Historical Understanding of the Free Exercise of Religion," *Harvard Law Review* 103 (1990): 1409.
20. *Sherbert* v. *Verner*, 374 U.S. 398 (1963).
21. McConnell, "Origins and Historical Understanding."
22. *Employment Division* v. *Smith*, 494 U.S. 872 (1990).
23. *Church of the Lukumi Babalu Aye* v. *Hialeah*, 508 U.S. 520 (1993).
24. *City of Boerne* v. *Flores*, 95 U.S. 2074 (1997).
25. *Gonzales* v. *O Centro Espírita Beneficente União do Vegetal*, 546 U.S. ___ (2006).
26. Laurence Tribe, *Treatise on American Constitutional Law*, 2nd ed. (St. Paul, Minn.: West, 1988), p. 566.
27. Zechariah Chafee, *Free Speech in the United States* (Cambridge, Mass.: Harvard University Press, 1941).
28. Leonard W. Levy, *The Emergence of a Free Press* (New York: Oxford University Press, 1985).
29. Mark Twain, *Following the Equator* (Hartford, Conn.: American Publishing, 1897).
30. *Brandenburg* v. *Ohio*, 395 U.S. 444 (1969).
31. *Schenck* v. *United States*, 249 U.S. 47 (1919).
32. *Abrams* v. *United States*, 250 U.S. 616 (1919).
33. *Gitlow* v. *New York*, 268 U.S. 652 (1925).
34. *Dennis* v. *United States*, 341 U.S. 494 (1951).
35. *Brandenburg* v. *Ohio*, 395 U.S. 444 (1969).
36. *Tinker* v. *Des Moines Independent County School District*, 393 U.S. 503, at 508 (1969).
37. *Barber* v. *Dearborn Public Schools*, 286 F. Supp. 2d 847, 857 (E.D. Mich., 2003).
38. *Chaplinsky* v. *New Hampshire*, 315 U.S. 568 (1942).
39. *Terminiello* v. *Chicago*, 337 U.S. 1, 37 (1949).
40. *Cohen* v. *California*, 403 U.S. 15 (1971).
41. *ACLU* v. *Reno*, 929 F. Supp. 824 (E.D. Penn., 1996).
42. *Reno* v. *ACLU*, 521 U.S. 844 (1997).
43. *Roth* v. *United States*, 354 U.S. 476 (1957).
44. *Jacobellis* v. *Ohio*, 378 U.S. 184 (1964).
45. *Miller* v. *California*, 413 U.S. 15 (1973).
46. *New York Times* v. *Sullivan*, 376 U.S. 254 (1964).
47. *Hustler Magazine* v. *Falwell*, 485 U.S. 46 (1988).
48. *Near* v. *Minnesota*, 283 U.S. 697 (1931).
49. For a detailed account of *Near*, see Fred W. Friendly, *Minnesota Rag* (New York: Random House, 1981).
50. *New York Times* v. *United States*, 403 U.S. 713 (1971).
51. *Branzburg* v. *Hayes*, 408 U.S. 665 (1972).
52. *Hazelwood School District* v. *Kuhlmeier*, 484 U.S. 260 (1988); *Morse* v. *Frederick*, 551 U.S. ___ (2007).
53. *United States* v. *Cruikshank*, 92 U.S. 542 (1876); *Constitution of the United States of America: Annotated and Interpreted* (Washington, D.C.: U.S. Government Printing Office, 1973), p. 1031.
54. *DeJonge* v. *Oregon*, 299 U.S. 353 (1937).
55. *United States* v. *Miller*, 307 U.S. 174 (1939).
56. Laurence H. Tribe and Michael C. Dorf, *On Reading the Constitution* (Cambridge, Mass.: Harvard University Press, 1991), p. 10.
57. *Barron* v. *Baltimore*, 32 U.S. (7 Pet.) 243 (1833).
58. *Lochner* v. *New York*, 198 U.S. 45 (1905).
59. *Chicago B&Q Railroad* v. *Chicago*, 166 U.S. 226 (1897).
60. *Gitlow* v. *New York*, 268 U.S. 652, 666 (1925).
61. *Palko* v. *Connecticut*, 302 U.S. 319 (1937).
62. *Duncan* v. *Louisiana*, 391 U.S. 145 (1968).
63. *McNabb* v. *United States*, 318 U.S. 332 (1943).
64. *Baldwin* v. *New York*, 399 U.S. 66 (1970).
65. Anthony Lewis, *Gideon's Trumpet* (New York: Random House, 1964).
66. *Gideon* v. *Wainwright*, 372 U.S. 335 (1963).
67. *Miranda* v. *Arizona*, 384 U.S. 436 (1966).
68. *Dickerson* v. *United States*, 530 U.S. 428 (2000).
69. *Wolf* v. *Colorado*, 338 U.S. 25 (1949).
70. *Mapp* v. *Ohio*, 367 U.S. 643 (1961).
71. *United States* v. *Leon*, 468 U.S. 897 (1984).
72. *Hudson* v. *Michigan*, 547 U.S. ___ (2006).
73. Liane Hansen, "Voices in the News This Week," *NPR Weekend Edition*, 28 October 2001 (NEXIS transcript).
74. Dan Eggen, "Tough Anti-Terror Campaign Pledged: Ashcroft Tells Mayors He Will Use New Law to Fullest Extent," *Washington Post*, 26 October 2001, p. A1.
75. "Security: FBI Sought 3,500 Records Without Subpeonas," *National Journal's Technology Daily*, 1 May 2006, accessed 11 May 2006.
76. Michael Sandler, "Anti-Terrorism Law on Final Tack," *CQ Weekly*, 3 March 2006, p. 600.
77. *Rasul* v. *Bush*, 542 U.S. ___ (2004).
78. *Hamdi* v. *Rumsfeld*, 542 U.S. ___ (2004).
79. *Hamdan* v. *Rumsfeld*, 548 U.S. ___ (2006); *Boumedine* v. *Bush* (06-1195) and *Odah* v. *United States* (06-1196) (cert. Granted 29 June 2007).
80. Paul Brest, *Processes of Constitutional Decision-making* (Boston: Little, Brown, 1975), p. 708.
81. *Griswold* v. *Connecticut*, 381 U.S. 479 (1965).
82. *Roe* v. *Wade*, 410 U.S. 113 (1973).
83. See John Hart Ely, "The Wages of Crying Wolf: A Comment on *Roe* v. *Wade*," *Yale Law Journal* 82 (1973): 920.
84. Interview with Justice Harry Blackmun, ABC, *Nightline*, 2 December 1993.
85. *Webster* v. *Reproductive Health Services*, 492 U.S. 490 (1989).
86. *Hodgson* v. *Minnesota*, 497 U.S. 417 (1990); *Ohio* v. *Akron Center for Reproductive Health*, 497 U.S. 502 (1990).
87. *Steinberg* v. *Carhart*, 530 U.S. 914 (2000).
88. *Gonzales* v. *Carhart*, 550 U.S. ___ (2007).
89. Stuart Taylor, "Supreme Court Hears Case on Homosexual Rights," *New York Times*, 1 April 1986, p. A24.
90. *Bowers* v. *Hardwick*, 478 U.S. 186 (1986).
91. Linda Greenhouse, "Washington Talk: When Second Thoughts Come Too Late," *New York Times*, 5 November 1990, p. A9.
92. *Lawrence and Garner* v. *Texas*, 539 U.S. 558 (2003).
93. Ibid.

Chapter 16 / Equality and Civil Rights / pages 492–527

1. Nina Bernstein, "100 Years in the Back Door, Out the Front," *New York Times*, 21 May 2006, sec. 4, p. 4, quoted in Aristide Zolberg, *A Nation by Design: Immigration Policy in the Fashioning of America* (New York: Russell Sage, 2006).
2. Jack Citrin, "Affirmative Action in the People's Court," *Public Interest* 122 (1996): 40–41; Sam Howe Verhovek, "In Poll, Americans Reject Means but Not Ends of Racial Diversity," *New York Times*, 14 December 1997, sec. 1, p. 1; National Election Studies Guide to Public Opinion and Electoral Behavior, "Aid to Blacks and Minorities, 1970–1998," available at <www.umich.edu/~nes/nesguide/toptable/tab4b_4.htm>.
3. David W. Moore, "Americans Today Are Dubious About Affirmative Action," *Gallup Poll Monthly* (March 1995): 36–38; Charlotte Steeh and Maria Krysan, "Affirmative Action and the Public, 1970–1995," *Public Opinion Quarterly* 60 (1996): 128–158; Gallup Poll, 25–28 October 2000: "Would you vote . . . for or against a law which would allow your state to give preferences in job hiring and school admission on the basis of race?" For, 13 percent; against, 85 percent; no opinion, 2 percent.
4. *Gallup Brain* question: "Do you generally favor or oppose affirmative action programs for racial minorities?" 12–15 June 2003: For, 58 percent; against, 34 percent; don't know/refused, 8 percent. 6–26 June 2005: For, 50 percent; against, 42 percent, don't know/refused, 8 percent. Available at <http://brain.gallup.com/>, accessed 8 March 2006.
5. *Regents of the University of California v. Bakke*, 438 U.S. 265, 407 (1978).
6. *The Slaughterhouse Cases*, 83 U.S. 36 (1873).
7. *United States v. Cruikshank*, 92 U.S. 542 (1876).
8. *United States v. Reese*, 92 U.S. 214 (1876).
9. *Civil Rights Cases*, 109 U.S. 3 (1883).
10. Mary Beth Norton et al., *A People and a Nation: A History of the United States,* 3rd ed. (Boston: Houghton Mifflin, 1990), p. 490.
11. *Plessy v. Ferguson*, 163 U.S. 537 (1896).
12. *Cummings v. County Board of Education*, 175 U.S. 528 (1899).
13. *Missouri ex rel. Gaines v. Canada*, 305 U.S. 337 (1938).
14. *Sweatt v. Painter*, 339 U.S. 629 (1950).
15. *Brown v. Board of Education*, 347 U.S. 483 (1954).
16. Ibid., 347 U.S. 483, 495 (1954).
17. Ibid., 347 U.S. 483, 494 (1954).
18. *Bolling v. Sharpe*, 347 U.S. 497 (1954).
19. *Brown v. Board of Education II*, 349 U.S. 294 (1955).
20. Jack W. Peltason, *Fifty-Eight Lonely Men*, rev. ed. (Urbana: University of Illinois Press, 1971).
21. *Alexander v. Holmes County Board of Education*, 396 U.S. 19 (1969).
22. *Swann v. Charlotte-Mecklenburg County Schools*, 402 U.S. 1 (1971).
23. *Milliken v. Bradley*, 418 U.S. 717 (1974).
24. Richard Kluger, *Simple Justice* (New York: Knopf, 1976), p. 753.
25. Taylor Branch, *Parting the Waters: America in the King Years, 1955–1963* (New York: Simon & Schuster, 1988), p. 3.
26. Ibid., p. 14.
27. Ibid., p. 271.
28. *Bell v. Maryland*, 378 U.S. 226 (1964).
29. Norton et al., *People and a Nation*, p. 943.
30. *Heart of Atlanta Motel v. United States*, 379 U.S. 241 (1964).
31. *Katzenbach v. McClung*, 379 U.S. 294 (1964).
32. But see Abigail M. Thernstrom, *Whose Vote Counts? Affirmative Action and Minority Voting Rights* (Cambridge, Mass.: Harvard University Press, 1987).
33. *Grove City College v. Bell*, 465 U.S. 555 (1984).
34. *Richmond v. J. A. Croson Co.*, 488 U.S. 469 (1989).
35. *Martin v. Wilks*, 490 U.S. 755 (1989); *Wards Cove Packing Co. v. Atonio*, 490 U.S. 642 (1989); *Patterson v. McLean Credit Union*, 491 U.S. 164 (1989); *Price Waterhouse v. Hopkins*, 490 U.S. 228 (1989); *Lorance v. AT&T Technologies*, 490 U.S. 900 (1989); and *EEOC v. Arabian American Oil Co.*, 499 U.S. 244 (1991).
36. *Saint Francis College v. Al-Khazraji*, 481 U.S. 604 (1987).
37. Dee Brown, *Bury My Heart at Wounded Knee: An Indian History of the American West* (New York: Holt, Rinehart & Winston, 1971).
38. Francis Paul Prucha, *The Great Father: The United States Government and the American Indian*, vol. 2 (Lincoln: University of Nebraska Press, 1984).
39. "Americans with Disabilities Act of 1990 (ADA) FY 1992–FY 2005," *The U.S. Equal Employment Opportunity Commission;* information available at <http://www.eeoc.gov/stats/ada-charges.html>, accessed 8 March 2006.
40. Lisa J. Stansky, "Opening Doors," *ABA Journal* 82 (1996): 66–69.
41. "Stonewall and Beyond: Lesbian and Gay Culture," Columbia University Libraries exhibition, 25 May to 17 September 1994, available at <www.columbia.edu/cu/libraries/events/sw25/>.
42. See, generally, *PS: Political Science and Politics* 38 (April 2005 issue).
43. "Gay/Lesbian Rights: Long-Term Contribution Trends," <http://www.opensecrets.org/industries/indus.asp?Ind=J7300>, accessed 30 May 2006.
44. *Goodridge & Others v. Department of Public Health*, 440 Mass. 309 (2003); *Opinions of the Justices to the Senate*, 440 Mass. 1201 (2004).
45. *Boy Scouts of America v. Dale*, 530 U.S. 610 (2000).
46. Cited in Martin Gruberg, *Women in American Politics* (Oshkosh, Wisc.: Academic Press, 1968), p. 4.
47. *Bradwell v. Illinois*, 83 U.S. 130 (1873).
48. *Muller v. Oregon*, 208 U.S. 412 (1908).
49. *International Union, United Automobile, Aerospace and Agricultural Implement Workers of America v. Johnson Controls, Inc.*, 499 U.S. 187 (1991).
50. *Minor v. Happersett*, 88 U.S. 162 (1875).
51. John H. Aldrich et al., *American Government: People, Institutions, and Policies* (Boston: Houghton Mifflin, 1986), p. 618.
52. *Ledbetter v. Goodyear Tire and Rubber Company*, 550 U.S. ___ (2007).
53. *Reed v. Reed*, 404 U.S. 71 (1971).
54. *Frontiero v. Richardson*, 411 U.S. 677 (1973).
55. *Craig v. Boren*, 429 U.S. 190 (1976).
56. Paul Weiler, "The Wages of Sex: The Uses and Limits of Comparable Worth," *Harvard Law Review* 99 (1986): 1728; Paula England, *Comparable Worth: Theories and Evidence* (New York: Aldine de Gruyter, 1992).
57. *J.E.B. v. Alabama ex rel. T.B.*, 511 U.S. 127 (1994).
58. *United States v. Virginia*, slip op. 94–1941 and 94–2107 (decided 26 June 1996).
59. Mike Allen, "Defiant V.M.I. to Admit Women but Will Not Ease Rules for Them," *New York Times*, 22 September 1996, sec. 1, p. 1.
60. Jane J. Mansbridge, *Why We Lost the ERA* (Chicago: University of Chicago Press, 1986).
61. Melvin I. Urofsky, *A March of Liberty* (New York: Knopf, 1988), p. 902.
62. *Harris v. Forklift Systems*, 510 U.S. 17 (1993).
63. *Time*, 6 July 1987, p. 91.
64. *Facts on File* 206B2, 4 June 1965.
65. As quoted in Melvin I. Urofsky, *A Conflict of Rights: The Supreme Court and Affirmative Action* (New York: Scribner's, 1991), p. 17.

66. Ibid., p. 29.
67. Thomas Sowell, *Preferential Policies: An International Perspective* (New York: Morrow, 1990), pp. 103–105.
68. *Regents of the University of California v. Bakke*, 438 U.S. 265 (1978).
69. *Adarand Constructors, Inc. v. Peña*, 518 U.S. 200 (1995).
70. *Gratz v. Bollinger*, 539 U.S. 244 (2003).
71. *Grutter v. Bollinger*, 539 U.S. 306 (2003).
72. *Parents Involved in Community Schools v. Seattle School District No. 1*, 551 U.S. ___ (2007).
73. Stephen Earl Bennett et al., *Americans' Opinions About Affirmative Action* (Cincinnati, Ohio: University of Cincinnati, Institute for Policy Research, 1995), p. 4; Lawrence Bobo, "Race and Beliefs About Affirmative Action," in *Racialized Politics: The Debate About Racism in America*, ed. David O. Sears, Jim Sidanius, and Lawrence Bobo (Chicago: University of Chicago Press, 2000).
74. For example, see the eligibility standards of the Small Business Administration for "small disadvantaged business," <www.sba.gov/sdb/indexaboutsdb.html>, accessed 30 May 2006.
75. Seymour Martin Lipset, "Two Americas, Two Systems: Whites, Blacks, and the Debate over Affirmative Action," *New Democrat* (May–June 1995): 9–15, available at <http://www.ndol.org/documents/May95TND.pdf>.

Chapter 17 / Policymaking / pages 528–553

1. Adriel Bettelheim, "Obesity on the Docket," *CQ Weekly*, 20 March 2006, p. 756.
2. See Carey Goldberg, "Fat People Say an Intolerant World Condemns Them on First Sight," *New York Times*, 5 November 2000, p. 28; Ceci Connolly, "Public Policy Targeting Obesity," *Washington Post*, 10 August 2003, p. A01.
3. Goldberg, "Fat People Say"; visit the NAAFA website at <http://www.naafa.org>.
4. Jeffrey Brainard and Anne Marie Borrego, "Academic Pork Barrel Tops $2-Billion for the First Time," *Chronicle of Higher Education*, 26 September 2003, pp. A18–A21.
5. "Espresso Tax Is Defeated," *New York Times*, 18 September 2003, p. A17.
6. Jason Zengerle, "Not a Prayer," *New Republic*, 22 September 2003, pp. 13–15.
7. Steven Greenhouse, "Mexican Trucks Gain Approval to Haul Cargo Throughout U.S.," *New York Times*, 28 November 2002, p. A1.
8. This typology is adapted from Theodore Lowi's classic article, "American Business, Public Policy Case Studies, and Political Theory," *World Politics* 16 (July 1964): 677–715.
9. Sally Beatty, "Americans Set Record for Giving," *Wall Street Journal*, 25 June 2007, p. A2.
10. Isaiah J. Poole, "2005 Legislative Summary: Steroids Regulation," *CQ Weekly*, 2 January 2006, p. 51.
11. The policymaking process can be depicted in many ways. Another approach, a bit more elaborate than this, is described in James E. Anderson, *Public Policymaking*, 5th ed. (Boston: Houghton Mifflin, 2003), p. 28.
12. Roger W. Cobb and Charles D. Elder, *Participation in American Politics*, 2nd ed. (Baltimore, Md.: Johns Hopkins University Press, 1983), p. 14.
13. Frank Ahrens, "File-Sharing Companies Offer to Pay Girl's Settlement," *Washington Post*, 11 September 2003, p. E5; "Lawmakers Weigh in on File Sharing," Reuters newswire, 17 September 2003.
14. Frank R. Baumgartner and Beth L. Leech, "Where Is the Public in Public Policy?" (paper presented at the conference Political Participation: Building a Research Agenda, Princeton University, October 2000).
15. Jeffrey M. Berry, *The New Liberalism* (Washington, D.C.: Brookings Institution, 1999).
16. Beth L. Leech, Frank R. Baumgartner, Jeffrey M. Berry, Marie Hojnacki, and David C. Kimball, "Organized Interests and Issue Definition in Policy Debates," in *Interest Group Politics*, 6th ed., ed. Allan J. Cigler and Burdett A. Loomis (Washington, D.C.: CQ Press, 2002), pp. 275–292.
17. William H. Riker, *The Art of Political Manipulation* (New Haven, Conn.: Yale University Press, 1986).
18. Leech et al., "Organized Interests and Issue Definition in Policy Debates."
19. Robert Pear, "U.S. Proposes Rules to Bar Obstacles for the Disabled," *New York Times*, 22 January 1991, p. A1.
20. Peter C. Bishop and Augustus J. Jones, Jr., "Implementing the Americans with Disability Act: Assessing the Variables of Success," *Public Administration Review* 53 (March–April 1993): 126.
21. Douglas Jehl, "Road Ban Set for One-Third of U.S. Forests," *New York Times*, 5 January 2001, p. A1.
22. Jeffrey M. Berry, "Effective Advocacy for Nonprofits" (paper presented at the Urban Institute, Washington, D.C., September 2000), pp. 8–9.
23. Douglas Jehl, "Bush Will Modify Ban on New Roads in Federal Lands," *New York Times*, 4 May 2001, p. A1.
24. Robert Pear, "Deadline Near, Jams Are Seen for Drug Plan," *New York Times*, 24 April 2006, p. A1.
25. Ibid., p. A14.
26. Kate Schuler, "New Medicare Drug Plan Gets Off to Rocky Start," *CQ Weekly*, 30 January 2006, p. 267.
27. Margaret Weir, *Politics and Jobs* (Princeton, N.J.: Princeton University Press, 1992).
28. Frank R. Baumgartner and Bryan D. Jones, "Positive and Negative Feedback in Politics," in *Policy Dynamics*, ed. Frank R. Baumgartner and Bryan D. Jones (Chicago: University of Chicago Press, 2002), pp. 3–28.
29. See, for example, Rebecca Blank and Ron Haskins (eds.), *The New World of Welfare* (Washington, D.C.: Brookings Institution, 2003).
30. Bill Swindell, "Welfare Overhaul Legislation Tops GOP 'Must-Do' List of 107th Congress Holdovers," *CQ Weekly*, 8 February 2003, p. 355.
31. Sam Dillon, "States Are Relaxing Education Standards to Avoid Sanctions from Federal Law," *New York Times*, 22 May 2003, p. A25; Patrick McQuinn, *No Child Left Behind and the Transformation of Federal Education Policy, 1965–2005* (Lawrence, Kans.: University Press of Kansas, 2006).
32. Derek Willis, "Turf Battles Could Lie Ahead in Fight to Oversee Homeland Department," *CQ Weekly*, 16 November 2002, p. 3006.
33. E. Scott Adler, *Why Congressional Reforms Fail* (Chicago: University of Chicago Press, 2002).
34. Bob Woodward, *Plan of Attack* (New York: Simon & Schuster, 2004).
35. James Fallows, "Why Iraq Has No Army," *Atlantic Monthly* 296 (December 2005): 60–77.
36. Jacob M. Schlesinger, "White House Plans Overhaul of Regulations," *Wall Street Journal*, 20 March 2002, p. A3; "Memorandum for the President's Management Council," Office of Management and Budget, 20 September 2001, available at <http://www.whitehouse.gov/omb/inforeg/oira_review-process.html>.
37. David C. King, *Turf Wars* (Chicago: University of Chicago Press, 1997).
38. Karen Foerstel with Alan K. Ota, "Early Grief for GOP Leaders in New Committee Rules," *CQ Weekly*, 6 January 2001, pp. 11–12.
39. Jeffrey M. Berry, *The Interest Group Society*, 3rd ed. (New York: Longman, 1997), p. 187.
40. Michael T. Heaney, "Coalitions and Interest Group Influence over Health Care Policy" (paper delivered at the annual

meeting of the American Political Science Association, Philadelphia, August 2003), p. 16.

41. Hugh Heclo, "Issue Networks and the Executive Establishment," in *The New American Political System,* ed. Anthony King (Washington, D.C.: American Enterprise Institute, 1978), p. 105.

42. Steve Langdon, "On Medicare, Negotiators Split over Policy, Not Just Figures," *Congressional Quarterly Weekly Report,* 22 February 1997, pp. 488–490.

43. For a general argument in favor of more citizen involvement in governing, see Harry C. Boyte, "Reframing Democracy: Governance, Civic Agency, and Politics," *Public Administration Review* 65 (September 2005): 536–546.

44. U.S. foreign policy appears to be much more influenced by experts and organized interests than by general public opinion. See Lawrence R. Jacobs and Benjamin I. Page, "Who Influences U.S. Foreign Policy?" *American Political Science Review* 99 (February 2005): 107–123.

45. See Peter Frumkin, *On Being Nonprofit* (Cambridge, Mass.: Harvard University Press, 2002), pp. 1–28.

46. Jeffrey M. Berry with David F. Arons, *A Voice for Nonprofits* (Washington, D.C.: Brookings Institution, 2003), pp. 1–2; for information about the Salvation Army, one of the world's largest nonprofits, see <http//www.salvationarmyusa.org>.

47. William Gorham, "Foreword," in *Nonprofits and Government,* ed. Elizabeth T. Boris and C. Eugene Steuerle (Washington, D.C.: Urban Institute, 1999), p. xi. But the poor and marginalized recipients of the services of nonprofits are not encouraged to participate in policymaking. See Jeffrey M. Berry, "Nonprofits and Civic Engagement," *Public Administration Review* 65 (September 2005): 568–578.

48. Paul C. Light, *The True Size of Government* (Washington, D.C.: Brookings Institution, 1999); and "Fact Sheet on the New True Size of Government," Center for Public Service, Brookings Institution, 5 September 2003, <www.brookings.edu/gs/cps/light20030905.htm>.

49. Murray S. Weitzman, Nadine T. Jalandoni, Linda M. Lampkin, and Thomas H. Pollak, *The New Nonprofit Almanac and Desk Reference* (San Francisco: Jossey-Bass, 2002), p. 69.

50. Paul Light, *Sustaining Nonprofit Performance* (Washington, D.C.: Brookings Institution, 2004).

Chapter 18 / Economic Policy / pages 554–585

1. "Return to Spender," *Wall Street Journal,* 27 September 2005, p. A18.

2. "The Keepers of K Street," *Wall Street Journal,* 17 January 2006, p. A16.

3. "St. Augustine's Budget," *Wall Street Journal,* 7 February 2006, p. A26.

4. "The GOP's Spending Spree," *Wall Street Journal,* 25 November 2003, p. A18.

5. Jackie Calmes and John D. McKinnon, "Widening Deficit Is Posing a Risk to Bush's Agenda," *Wall Street Journal,* 30 January 2004, pp. A1, A4.

6. Phillip Day and Hae Won Choi, "Asian Central Banks Consider Alternatives to Big Dollar Holdings," *Wall Street Journal,* 5 February 2004, p. A1. To be precise, the U.S. Department of the Treasury reported the debt held by the public on 25 June 2007 as $4,950,662,396,067.18. If one counts intragovernmental holdings in the debt, the total is over $8.9 trillion. Go to <http://www.treasurydirect.gov/NP/NPGateway>.

7. U.S. Census Bureau, "Foreign Trade Statistics: Top Trading Partners—Total Trade, Exports, Imports, January–December 2006," at <http://www.census.gov/foreign-trade/statistics/highlights/top/top0612.html>.

8. You won't learn basic economics in this chapter. For a quick summary of "ten principles of economics," see N. Gregory Mankiw, *Principles of Economics,* 3rd ed. (Mason, Ohio: Thomson South-Western, 2004), pp. 3–14. Mankiw served as chairman of the Council of Economic Advisers under President Bush.

9. Dan Usher, in *Political Economy* (Malden, Mass.: Blackwell Publishing, 2003), offers this interpretation of Adam Smith's "invisible hand" metaphor: "Self-interested people are guided by market-determined prices to deploy the resources of the world to produce what people want to consume. This assertion, made commonplace by repetition, is so extraordinary and so completely counter-intuitive that it cannot be strictly and unreservedly true. A central task of economics is to show when the assertion is true, when public intervention in the economy might be helpful, and when markets are best left alone because public intervention is likely to do more harm than good" (p. xiv).

10. Two of the ten principles of economics that Mankiw cites in *Principles of Economics* are "#6: Markets are usually a good way to organize economic activity," and "#7: Governments can sometimes improve market outcomes" (pp. 9–11).

11. Paul Peretz, "The Politics of Fiscal and Monetary Policy," in *The Politics of American Economic Policy Making,* 2nd ed., ed. Paul Peretz (Armonk, N.Y.: M. E. Sharp, 1996), pp. 101–113.

12. Shaun P. Hargraves Heap, "Keynesian Economics," in *Routledge Encyclopedia of International Political Economy,* Vol. 2, ed. R. J. Barry Jones (London: Routledge, 2001), pp. 877–878.

13. Kathleen R. McNamara, "Monetarism," in Jones, *Routledge Encyclopedia of International Political Economy,* pp. 1035–1037.

14. See Allan H. Meltzer, *A History of the Federal Reserve,* Vol. 1, *1913–1951* (Chicago: University of Chicago Press, 2003). Meltzer writes that the leading banks in 1913 were privately owned institutions with public responsibilities. Fears were that they would place their interests above the public interest, but there was also concern about empowering government to control money. "President Woodrow Wilson offered a solution that appeared to reconcile competing public and private interests. He proposed a public-private partnership with semiautonomous, privately funded reserve banks supervised by a public board" (p. 3).

15. See the discussion of Federal Reserve policy actions in John B. Taylor, *Economics,* 4th ed. (Boston: Houghton Mifflin, 2004), Chapter 32.

16. Greg Ip and Jon E. Hilsenrath, "Having Defeated Inflation, Fed Girds for New Foe: Falling Prices," *Wall Street Journal,* 19 May 2003, p. A1.

17. The quote, attributed to William McChesney Martin, Jr., is in Martin Mayer, *The Fed* (New York: Free Press, 2001), p. 165.

18. Federal Reserve Bank of San Francisco, *Weekly Letter 96–08,* 23 February 1996.

19. David Martin, "The Economical Poet," *Chicago Tribune,* 21 July 2002, sec. 2, p. 9.

20. Peter G. Gosselin, "Is Fed Chief Greenspan Part of the Problem Too?" *Cleveland Plain Dealer,* 22 July 2002, p. A6.

21. Greg Ip, "Greenspan's Final Act: Calculating the Impact of Globalization on Inflation," *Wall Street Journal,* 9 January 2006, p. A2.

22. Jonathan Rauch, Lawrence J. Haas, and Bruce Stokes, "Payment Deferred," *National Journal,* 14 May 1988, p. 1256.

23. Mankiw, *Principles of Economics,* pp. 170–171.

24. Ibid., p. 577.

25. William Neikirk, "Budget Deficits Have Weight," *Chicago Tribune,* 8 February 2004, sec. 2, pp. 1–6.

26. Ibid.; David Leonhardt, "That Big Fat Budget Deficit. Yawn," *New York Times,* 8 February 2004, sec. 3, p. 1.

27. If one includes intragovernmental loans, the public debt on 27 April 2006 was over $8.3 trillion dollars. See <http://www.publicdebt.treas.gov/opd/opdpdodt.htm>. This larger sum is sometimes called the "national debt."

28. Executive Office of the President, *Budget of the United States Government, Fiscal Year 2005; Analytical Perspectives* (Washington, D.C.: U.S. Government Printing Office, 2004), p. 235. Many financial analysts think that the national debt seriously understates the *real* debt by several trillion dollars. See the website operated by the Institute for Truth in Accounting: <www.truthinaccounting.org>.

29. See, for example, these articles: Christopher Rhoads et al., "A Growing Global Unease," *Wall Street Journal,* 22 January 2004, pp. A10–11; Phillip Day and Hae Won Choi, "Asian Central Banks Consider Alternatives to Big Dollar Holdings," *Wall Street Journal,* 5 February 2004, pp. A1, A8; David Wessel, "U.S. to Rest of the World: Charge It!" *Wall Street Journal,* 12 February 2004, p. A2.

30. For a concise discussion of the 1990 budget reforms, see James A. Thurber, "Congressional-Presidential Battles to Balance the Budget," in *Rivals for Power: Presidential-Congressional Relations,* ed. James A. Thurber (Washington, D.C.: CQ Press, 1996), pp. 196–202.

31. For a brief account of presidential attempts, from Carter to Clinton, to deal with budget deficits, see Alexis Simendinger, David Baumann, Carl M. Cannon, and John Maggs, "Sky High," *National Journal,* 7 February 2004, pp. 370–373.

32. Ibid., p. 377; Concord Coalition, "Budget Process Reform: An Important Tool for Fiscal Discipline, but Not a Magic Bullet," *Issue Brief,* 5 February 2004.

33. Concord Coalition, "Budget Process Reform," p. 3.

34. David Wessel, "There Is No Denying the Math: Taxes Will Rise," *Wall Street Journal,* 20 November 2003, p. A2.

35. Richard A. Musgrave and Peggy B. Musgrave, *Public Finance in Theory and Practice,* 2nd ed. (New York: McGraw-Hill, 1976), p. 42.

36. If you can spare 24 megabytes of storage, you can download the complete text of the U.S. Internal Revenue Code, Title 26 of the U.S. Code, at <http://www.fourmilab.ch/uscode/26usc/>. If you print the tax code, expect more than 7,500 pages.

37. Office of Management and Budget, "Overview of the President's 2007 Budget," Table S-8, available at <http://www.whitehouse.gov/omb/budget/fy2007/budget.html>.

38. David Cay Johnston, "Talking Simplicity, Building a Maze," *New York Times,* 15 February 2004, Money and Business section, pp. 11, 14.

39. Michael L. Roberts, Peggy A. Hite, and Cassie F. Bradley, "Understanding Attitudes Toward Progressive Taxation," *Public Opinion Quarterly* 58 (Summer 1994): 167–168. See also David W. Moore and Frank Newport, "Public Lukewarm on Flat Tax," *Gallup Poll Monthly* (January 1996): 18–20. And a *Gallup/CNN/USA Today* Poll, 6–7 April 1999, found that 66 percent of respondents said "upper-income people" paid "too little" in taxes while 51 percent said "lower-income people" paid "too much."

40. See individual "Tax Facts" at <http://www.taxpolicycenter.org>.

41. Jill Barshay, "'Case of the Missing Revenue' Is Nation's Troubling Mystery," *CQ Weekly,* 17 January 2004, p. 144.

42. Iris J. Lav, "Taxes on Middle-Income Families Are Declining" (Washington, D.C.: Center on Budget and Policy Priorities, release of 10 January 2001).

43. Pew Research Center for the People and the Press, "Economic Inequality Seen as Rising, Boom Bypasses Poor," *Survey Report,* 21 June 2001.

44. Spending as percentage of GDP is a common way of measuring social welfare benefits, but it is not the only way. If spending is measured by dollars per capita, the United States, with a very high GDP, rates much more favorably. See Christopher Howard, "Is the American Welfare State Unusually Small?" *PS: Political Science and Politics* 36 (July 2003): 411–416.

45. Bob Deans, "Watchdog: Wasteful Spending Bloats U.S. Budget by $29 Billion," *Chicago Tribune,* 6 April 2006, p. 7.

46. Jackie Calmes, "In Search of Presidential Earmarks," *Wall Street Journal,* 21 February 2006, p. A6.

47. Times-Mirror Center for the People and the Press, "Voter Anxiety Dividing GOP: Energized Democrats Backing Clinton," press release, 14 November 1995, p. 88.

48. These questions were asked in the 2002 American National Election Survey conducted by the Survey Research Center at the University of Michigan.

49. Fay Lomax Cook et al., *Convergent Perspectives on Social Welfare Policy: The Views from the General Public, Members of Congress, and AFDC Recipients* (Evanston, Ill.: Center for Urban Affairs and Policy Research, Northwestern University, 1988), Table 4–1.

50. Cynthia Crossen, "Not Too Long Ago, Some People Begged for an Income Tax," *Wall Street Journal,* 4 June 2003, p. B1.

51. B. Guy Peters, *The Politics of Taxation: A Comparative Perspective* (Cambridge, Mass.: Basil Blackwell, 1991), p. 228.

52. Elizabeth Becker, "U.S. Subsidizes Companies to Buy Subsidized Cotton," *New York Times,* 4 November 2003, p. C1.

53. Lawrence Mishel, Jared Bernstein, and Sylvia Allegretto, *The State of Working America, 2004–2005* (Ithaca, N.Y.: Cornell University Press, 2005), pp. 338–340.

54. Ibid., p. 79.

55. Ibid., p. 62.

56. Attributed to R. Glenn Hubbard and quoted in Edmund L. Andrews, "Fight Looms over Who Bears the Biggest Tax Burden," *New York Times,* 14 January 2003, pp. C1, C8.

57. Ibid.; David Wessel, "Behind Tax Debate, Issues of Ethics and Economics," *Wall Street Journal,* 2 January 2003, p. 1.

58. For income shares in 1999, see Lawrence Mishel, Jared Bernstein, and Heather Boushey, *The State of Working America, 2002–2003* (Ithaca, N.Y.: Cornell University Press, 2003), p. 86. For income shares in 2001, see David Cay Johnston, "Top 1% in '01 Lost Income, but Also Paid Lower Taxes," *New York Times,* 27 September 2003, pp. B1, B2.

59. Congressional Budget Office, "Effective Tax Rates, 1997–2000" (August 2003), published by the Tax Policy Center on 16 February 2004 at <www.taxpolicycenter.org/TaxFacts> under "Historic Payroll Tax Rates."

60. Joseph A. Pechman, *Who Paid the Taxes, 1966–1985?* (Washington, D.C.: Brookings Institution, 1985), p. 80. See also Mishel, Bernstein, and Boushey, *The State of Working America, 2002–2003,* p. 66.

61. Mishel, Bernstein, and Boushey, *The State of Working America,* p. 118.

62. Ibid., p. 411.

63. For a general discussion, see Vita Tanzi and Ludger Schuknecht, *Public Spending in the Twentieth Century: A Global Perspective* (Cambridge: Cambridge University Press, 2000), pp. 94–98.

64. Keith Bradsher, "Gap in Wealth in U.S. Called Widest in West," *New York Times,* 17 April 1995, p. 1; Dave Hage, "Gap Between the Rich and Poor Spurs New Questions," *Minneapolis Star Tribune,* 24 July 2005, pp. AA1, AA5; and Christopher Conkey, "Wealthiest American Families Add to Their Share of U.S. Net Worth," *Wall Street Journal,* 5 April 2006, p. A4.

65. U.S. Bureau of the Census, *Statistical Abstract of the United States 2005* (Washington, D.C.: U.S. Government Printing Office, 2005), Table 674.

66. Benjamin I. Page, *Who Gets What from Government?* (Berkeley: University of California Press, 1983), p. 213.

67. David Wessel, "Budget Seeks to Raise U.S. Living Standards

and Reduce Inequality," *Wall Street Journal*, 7 February 1997, p. 1; David Cay Johnston, "'97 Middle-Class Tax Relief Benefits Wealthy First," *New York Times*, 4 May 1997, p. 17; Lizette Alvarez, "Buried in the Tax-Cut Bill, Dozens of Breaks for Small Interest Groups," *New York Times*, 29 June 1997, p. 12.

68. A 2003 survey reported 36 percent of respondents favoring changing from an income tax to a flat-rate tax, with only 32 percent opposed; cited in Robert J. Blendon et al., "Tax Uncertainty: A Divided America's Uninformed View of the Federal Tax System," *Brookings Review* 21 (Summer 2003): 28–31. Data from the National Conference of State Legislatures show that states raised income taxes by $8.2 billion from 1990 through 1993, which had a greater impact on wealthy than on poor residents. But from 1994 to 1997, the states reduced income taxes by $9.8 billion. In contrast, sales and excise taxes, which weigh more on those with lower incomes, were raised by $11.7 billion from 1990 through 1993 and cut by only $200 million from 1994 to 1997. See David Cay Johnston, "Taxes Are Cut, and Rich Get Richer," *New York Times*, 5 October 1997, p. 16.

69. James Sterngold, "Muting the Lotteries' Perfect Pitch," *New York Times*, national edition, 14 July 1996, sec. 4, p. 1.

70. "Taxes: What's Fair?" *Public Perspective* 7 (April–May 1996): 40–41. Similar findings were found in experiments involving undergraduate students in advanced tax classes at two public universities; see Roberts, Hite, and Bradley, "Understanding Attitudes Toward Progressive Taxation."

71. Blendon et al., "Tax Uncertainty."

72. Jason White, "Taxes and Budget," *State of the States: 2004* (Washington, D.C.: Pew Center on the States, 2004), p. 30.

73. Shailagh Murray, "Seminar Article in Alabama Sparks Tax-Code Revolt," *Wall Street Journal*, 12 February 2003, pp. A1, A8.

Chapter 19 / Domestic Policy / pages 586–615

1. Katherine Hobson, "A Prescription for Poverty," *US News and World Report*, 3 June 2002, p. 82.

2. Joan Raymond and Anne Belli Gesalman, "Why Drugs Cost So Much," *Newsweek*, 25 September 2000, p. 22.

3. Ibid.

4. Robert Pear, "Sweeping Medicare Change Wins Approval in Congress; President Claims a Victory," *New York Times*, 26 November 2003, p. A1.

5. Ibid.

6. Sarah Lueck, "Medicare's Cost of Drug Benefit Will Be Lower Than Expected," *Wall Street Journal*, 2 May 2006, p. A4.

7. "Education: A Vital Issue in Election 2000," 2 October 2000, available at <gallup.com/poll /releases/pr001002.asp>.

8. The Polling Report, "Problems and Priorities," accessed 6 January 2004 at <http://www.pollingreport.com/prioriti.htm>.

9. Gallup Poll, 10–12 January 2003, sample size of 1,002, available at *Gallup Brain*, <http://brain.gallup.com/>; Gallup Poll, 8–11 September 2005, sample size of 1,005, available at *Gallup Brain*, <http://brain.gallup.com/>.

10. Linda L. M. Bennett and Stephen Earl Bennett, *Living with Leviathan: Americans Coming to Terms with Big Government* (Lawrence: University Press of Kansas, 1990), pp. 21–24.

11. *Shapiro* v. *Thompson*, 394 U.S. 618 (1969).

12. Information available at the website of the U.S. Social Security Administration, <http://www.ssa.gov/OACT/COLA/cbb.html> and <http://www.ssa.gov/OACT/ProgData/taxRates.html>.

13. Paul C. Light, *Artful Work: The Politics of Social Security Reform* (New York: Random House, 1985), p. 63.

14. *Annual Report of the Board of Trustees of the Federal Old-Age and Survivors Insurance and Disability Insurance Trust Funds*, 2007, accessed 24 June 2007, available at <http://www.ssa.gov/OACT/TR/TR07/tr07.pdf/>.

15. Ibid.

16. Martha Derthick, *Policymaking for Social Security* (Washington, D.C.: Brookings Institution, 1979), pp. 346–347.

17. The Polling Report, "Social Security," available at <http://www.pollingreport.com/social.htm>, accessed 21 January 2006.

18. *Retirement Security and Quality Health Care: Our Pledge to America*, n.d., available at <www.rnc.org/2000/2000platform5>.

19. *The 2000 Democratic National Platform: Prosperity, Progress, and Peace* (Washington, D.C.: Democratic National Committee, 2000), p. 6.

20. President's Commission to Strengthen Social Security, *Strengthening Social Security and Creating Personal Wealth for All Americans* (December 2001), accessed 7 January 2004 at <http://www.csss.gov/>.

21. Louis Uchitelle, "Devising New Math to Define Poverty," *New York Times*, 18 October 1999, p. A1.

22. U.S. Census Bureau, *Poverty in the United States: 2004* (Washington, D.C.: U.S. Government Printing Office, 2005), and accompanying press release, accessed 21 January 2006 at <http://www.census.gov/hhes/www/poverty04.html>.

23. Ibid.

24. U.S. Census Bureau, U.S. Department of Commerce, *Current Population Reports: Money Income and Poverty Status in the United States, 1989*, Series P-60, No. 168, pp. 5–7 (Washington, D.C.: U.S. Government Printing Office, 1990); U.S. Census Bureau, *Poverty in the United States*, 1992 Series P-60, No. 185, p. xvii (Washington, D.C.: U.S. Government Printing Office, 1993); U.S. Census Bureau, *Poverty in the United States: 2002*, accessed 7 January 2004 at <http://www.census.gov/hhhs/www/poverty02.html>.

25. U.S. Census Bureau, "Poverty Thresholds 2005," <http://www.census.gov/hhes/www/poverty/threshld/thres05.html>.

26. William Julius Wilson, *The Truly Disadvantaged: The Inner City, the Underclass, and Public Policy* (Chicago: University of Chicago Press, 1987).

27. Francis X. Clines, "Clinton Signs Bill Cutting Welfare," *New York Times*, 23 August 1996, p. A1.

28. Peter T. Kilborn, "With Welfare Overhaul Now Law, States Grapple with the Consequences," *New York Times*, 23 August 1996, p. A10.

29. Martha Coven, "An Introduction to TANF," revised 22 November 2005, accessed 21 January 2006 from the Center on Budget and Policy Priorities website at <http://www.cbpp.org/1-22-02tanf2.htm>; Fact Sheet: President Bush Signs the Deficit Reduction Act, accessed 24 June 2006 from the White House website <http:www.whitehouse.gov/news/releases/2006/02/20060208-9.html>.

30. Ibid.

31. Alan Weil and Kenneth Feingold (eds.), *Welfare Reform: The Next Act* (Washington, D.C.: Urban Institute, 2002).

32. Coven, "An Introduction to TANF"; Weil and Feingold, *Welfare Reform.*

33. Children's Defense Fund, "The Unprotected Recession: Record Numbers of Families Have No Work and No Welfare in 2001," accessed 22 January 2006 at <http://www.childrensdefense.org/pdf/noworknowelfare.pdf>.

34. Robert Pear, "Without Health Benefits, a Good Life Turns Fragile," *New York Times*, 5 March 2007, p. A1. Data from the U.S. Census Bureau, press release, 30 August 2005, accessed 21 January 2006 at <http://www.census.gov/Press-Release/www/releases/archives/income_wealth/005647.html>.

35. Carmen DeNavas-Walt, Bernadette D. Proctor, and Cheryl Hill Lee, U.S. Census Bureau, Current Population Reports, P60-229, *Income, Poverty, and Health Insurance Coverage in the United States: 2004* (Washington, D.C.: U.S. Government Printing Office, 2005). Accessed 21 January 2006 at <http://www.census.gov/prod/2005pubs/p60-229.pdf>.

36. Ratios computed from Centers for Medicare and Medicaid

Services, "Table 2.6: Active Physicians per 100,000 Persons by Location, 1950–1998 [slide]," *The CMS Chart Series,* accessed 3 December 2003 at <http://cms.hhs.gov/charts/default.asp>.

37. Cynthia Smith, Cathy Cowan, Stephen Heffler, and Aaron Catlin, "National Health Spending in 2004: Recent Slowdown Led by Prescription Drug Spending," *Health Affairs* 25/1 (January–February 2006): 186–196.

38. Centers for Medicare and Medicaid Services, "National Health Expenditures as a Share of Gross Domestic Product (GDP) [slide]" and "The Nation's Health Dollar, CY 2000 [slide]," *The CMS Chart Series,* accessed 3 December 2003 at <http://cms.hhs.gov/charts/default.asp>.

39. Organization for Economic Cooperation and Development, "Health at a Glance: OECD Indicators 2005, Chart 3.7. Health Expenditure as a Percentage of GDP, 2003," accessed 21 January 2006 at <http://www.oecd.org/document/11/0,2340,en_2825_495642_16502667_1_1_1_1,00.html#TOC>.

40. Chris Chambers, *Americans Largely Satisfied with Own Health Care, and HMO Users Only Slightly Less Satisfied Than Those with Other Forms of Health Care Coverage,* accessed 20 September 2000 at <http://www.gallup.com/poll/releases/pr000920.asp>.

41. Derthick, *Policymaking,* p. 335.

42. Paul Starr, *The Social Transformation of American Medicine* (New York: Basic Books, 1982), pp. 279–280.

43. Ibid., p. 287.

44. Theodore Marmor, *The Politics of Medicare* (Chicago: Aldine, 1973).

45. Centers for Medicare & Medicaid Services, 2003 Compendium, <http://www.cms.hhs.gov/researchers/pubs/datacompendium/2003/03pg2.pdf>.

46. Ibid.

47. Alan Weil, "There's Something About Medicaid," *Health Affairs* 22 (January–February 2003): 13.

48. Vernon Smith for the National Conference of State Legislatures, "Figure 18. States Undertaking Medicaid Cost Containment Strategies, FY2002 vs. FY2003 [slide]," *Medicaid Eligibility Milestones 1965–2001,* 6 December 2002, accessed 24 July 2003 at <http://www.ncsl.org/programs/health/forum/chairs/NOLA/rowland/index.htm>.

49. Centers for Medicare and Medicaid Services, *2005 CMS Statistics,* "Table 11: Medicaid and SCHIP Enrollment," accessed 22 January 2006 at <http://www.cms.hhs.gov/MedicareMedicaidStatSupp/downloads/2005_CMS_Statistics.pdf>.

50. Centers for Medicare and Medicaid Services, *2005 CMS Statistics,* "Table 34: Medicaid/Payments by Eligibility Status," accessed 22 January 2006 at <http://www.cms.hhs.gov/MedicareMedicaidStatSupp/downloads/2005_CMS_Statistics.pdf>.

51. *The Nation's Report Card* (2003), accessed 22 January 2006 at <http://nces.ed.gov/nationsreportcard/>.

52. Christopher Jencks and Meredith Phillips (eds.), *The Black-White Test Score Gap* (Washington, D.C.: Brookings Institution Press, 1998).

53. Paul Manna, "Federalism, Agenda Setting, and the Development of Federal Education Policy, 1965–2001" (Ph.D. diss., University of Wisconsin–Madison, 2003).

Chapter 20 / Global Policy / pages 616–647

1. Joseph Kahn, "An Ohio Town Is Hard Hit as Leading Industry Moves to China," *New York Times,* 7 December 2003, p. 8.

2. Joseph Kahn, "Ruse in Toyland: Chinese Workers' Hidden Woe," *New York Times,* 7 December 2003.

3. Ibid.

4. William M. Bulkeley, "IBM to Export Highly Paid Jobs to India, China," *Wall Street Journal,* 15 December 2003, p. B1. Concerning the economic contest between India and China, see Yasheng Huang and Tarun Khanna, "Can India Overtake China?" *Foreign Policy* (July–August 2003): 74–81.

5. Ibid.; Steve Lohr, "Offshore Jobs in Technology: Opportunity or a Threat?" *New York Times,* 22 December 2003, p. C1.

6. Nancy Brigham, "Outsourcing High-Tech Jobs: Why Benign Neglect Isn't Working, and Why It Matters," *Working Papers* (May 2005), p. 2, at <http://www.cpsr.org/pubs/workingpapers/1/Brigham>.

7. Eric A. Taub, "For a Few Dollars Less, TV Making Moves to Asia," *New York Times,* 22 December 2003, p. C1.

8. Christopher Rhoads, "Threat from China Starts to Unravel Italy's Cloth Trade," *Wall Street Journal,* 17 December 2003, p. 1; Mark Landler and Ian Fisher, "Italy's Once-Plucky Little Factories Now Complicate Its Battle with 'Made in China,'" *New York Times,* 14 May 2006, p. A8.

9. Hugh Dellios, "Ornament-Makers Try to Hang On," *Chicago Tribune,* 22 December 2003, p. 1.

10. Bob Davis, "Migration of Skilled Jobs Abroad Unsettles Global-Economy Fans," *Wall Street Journal,* 26 January 2004, p. 1.

11. The Annual Report of the 2006 World Economic Forum is available at <http://www.weforum.org/pdf/summitreports/am2006/default.htm>.

12. David E. Sanger, "While America Sells Security, China Is Buying Its Dollars," *New York Times,* 7 December 2003, sec. 4, p. 3.

13. The official Senate website lists twenty-one having been rejected, including the 1999 nuclear test ban treaty: <http://www.senate.gov/artandhistory/history/common/briefing/Treaties.htm>.

14. "Pros and Cons Testify at Charter Hearings," *Life,* 30 July 1945, pp. 22–23.

15. *Congressional Quarterly Weekly Report,* 16 October 1999, p. 2477. See also R. W. Apple, "The G.O.P. Torpedo," *New York Times,* 14 October 1999, p. 1.

16. Barbara Crossette, "Around the World, Dismay over Senate Vote on Treaty," *New York Times,* 15 October 1999, p. A1. The article quotes *The Straits Times of Singapore.*

17. Chuck McCutcheon, "Treaty Vote a 'Wake-Up Call,'" *Congressional Quarterly Weekly Report,* 16 October 1999, p. 2435.

18. *United States* v. *Curtiss-Wright Export Corporation,* 299 U.S. 304 (1936); *United States* v. *Belmont,* 301 U.S. 324 (1937). Jack C. Plano and Roy Olton, *The International Relations Dictionary* (New York: Holt, Rinehart and Winston, 1969), p. 149.

19. Plano and Olton, *The International Relations Dictionary,* p. 149.

20. Lyn Ragsdale, *Vital Statistics on the Presidency* (Washington, D.C.: CQ Press, 1998), pp. 317–319. After 1984, government reports eliminated the clear distinction between treaties and executive agreements, making it difficult to determine the ratio. Indeed, other nations have criticized the reluctance of the United States to sign binding treaties. See Barbara Crossette, "Washington Is Criticized for Growing Reluctance to Sign Treaties," *New York Times,* 4 April 2002, p. A5.

21. Ragsdale, *Vital Statistics on the Presidency,* p. 298.

22. These critics included both conservative Republican senator Barry Goldwater of Arizona and liberal Democratic senator Thomas Eagleton of Missouri. Eagleton's feelings were succinctly summarized in the title of his book: *War and Presidential Power: A Chronicle of Congressional Surrender* (New York: Liveright, 1974).

23. Miles A. Pomper, "In for the Long Haul," *CQ Weekly Report,* 15 September 2001, p. 2118.

24. Richard Morris (ed.), *Encyclopedia of American History: Bicentennial Edition* (New York: Harper & Row, 1976), p. 146.

25. Duncan Clarke, "Why State Can't Lead," *Foreign Policy* 66 (Spring 1987): 128–142. See also Steven W. Hook, "Domestic Obstacles to International Affairs: The State Department Under Fire at Home," *PS: Political Science and Politics* 36 (January 2003): 23–29.

26. Kenneth T. Walsh, "The Next Powell Doctrine," *U.S. News and World Report,* 14 April 1997, p. 9.

27. Todd S. Purdum, "Embattled, Scrutinized, Powell Soldiers On," *New York Times,* 25 July 2002, pp. A1, A5.

28. Harry Crosby [pseudonym], "Too at Home Abroad: Swilling Beer, Licking Boots and Ignoring the Natives with One of Jim Baker's Finest," *Washington Monthly* (September 1991): 16–20.

29. See Steven R. Weisman, "The Battle Lines Start in Washington," *New York Times,* 27 April 2003, sec. 4, p. 2; Gerald F. Seib and Carla Anne Robbins, "Powell-Rumsfeld Feud Now Hard to Ignore," *Wall Street Journal,* 25 April 2003, p. A4.

30. Elaine Sciolino, "Compulsion to Achieve: Condoleezza Rice," *New York Times,* 18 December 2000, p. 1.

31. David E. Sanger, "Bush to Outline Doctrine of Striking First," *New York Times,* 20 September 2002, p. 1.

32. From "The Intelligence Cycle" in the *CIA Factbook,* available at <http://www.cia.gov/cia/publications/facttell/intelligence_cycle.html>.

33. The Intelligence Community was defined in the Intelligence Reform and Terrorism Prevention Act of 2004. See <http://www.intelligence.gov/>.

34. Merle D. Kellerhals, Jr., "Negroponte Nominated to Become Director of National Intelligence," 17 February 2005, an announcement of the U.S. Department of State, International Information Programs, <http://usinfo.state.gov/mena/Archive/2005/Feb/17-172501.html>.

35. Greg Miller, "CIA Chief's Ouster Points to Larger Issues: Problems Plague the Nation's Spy Services—Despite or Even Because of Intended Reforms," *Los Angeles Times,* 7 May 2006, <http://www.latimes.com/news/nationworld/nation/la-na-cia7may07,0,2458645,print.story>.

36. Loch K. Johnson, "Now That the Cold War Is Over, Do We Need the CIA?" in *The Future of American Foreign Policy,* ed. Charles Kegley and Eugene Wittkopf (New York: St. Martin's Press, 1992), p. 306.

37. David S. Cloud, "Caught Off-Guard by Terror, the CIA Fights to Catch Up," *Wall Street Journal,* 14 April 2002, p. 1.

38. Quoted in Bob Woodward, *Plan of Attack* (New York: Simon & Schuster, 2004), p. 249; and David S. Cloud, "Tenet's Mission: Devising an Exit Strategy," *Wall Street Journal,* 28 January 2004, p. A4.

39. Bob Kemper, "Bush De-emphasizes Weapons Claim," *Chicago Tribune,* 28 January 2004, p. 9.

40. Stephen J. Hedges and John Crewdson, "Bungled Plots, Wire Taps, Leaks," *Chicago Tribune,* 27 June 2007, p. 1.

41. Elisabeth Bumiller and Carl Hulse, "C.I.A. Pick Names as White House Takes up Critics," *New York Times,* 8 May 2006, pp. A1, A21.

42. Leslie Cauley, "NSA Has Massive Database of Americans' Phone Calls," *USA Today,* 11 May 2006, p. 1.

43. Eric Schmitt, "Clash Foreseen Between C.I.A. and Pentagon," *New York Times,* 10 May 2006, pp. A1, A19.

44. Dag Ryen, "State Action in a Global Framework," in *The Book of the States* (Lexington, Ky.: Council of State Governments, 1996), pp. 524–536.

45. X [George F. Kennan], "The Sources of Soviet Conduct," *Foreign Affairs* 25 (July 1947): 575.

46. Richard M. Nixon, *U.S. Foreign Policy for the 1970s: A New Strategy for Peace* (Washington, D.C.: U.S. Government Printing Office, 1970), p. 2.

47. Thomas Halverson, *The Last Great Nuclear Debate: NATO and Short-Range Nuclear Weapons in the 1980s* (New York: St. Martin's Press, 1995).

48. See, for example, Francis Fukuyama, *The End of History and the Last Man* (New York: Free Press, 1992).

49. Daniel Deudney and C. John Ikenberry, "Who Won the Cold War?" *Foreign Policy* 87 (Summer 1992): 128–138.

50. See, for example, Paul Kennedy, *Preparing for the Twenty-first Century* (New York: Random House, 1993), especially Chapter 13.

51. Richard H. Ullman, "A Late Recovery," *Foreign Policy* 101 (Winter 1996): 76–79; James M. McCormick, "Assessing Clinton's Foreign Policy at Midterm," *Current History* (November 1995): 370–374; Michael Mandelbaum, "Foreign Policy as Social Work," *Foreign Affairs* (January–February 1996): 16–32.

52. Frank Bruni, "Bush, and His Presidency, Are Transformed," *New York Times,* 22 September 2001, p. 1.

53. David E. Sanger, "On the Job, Bush Has Mastered Diplomacy 101, His Aides Say," *New York Times,* 22 May 2002, p. 1.

54. Bob Woodward, *Bush at War* (New York: Simon & Schuster, 2002). Woodward was given access to contemporaneous notes taken during more than fifty meetings of the National Security Council and other personal notes, memos, and so on from participants in planning the war in Afghanistan.

55. The 19 September 2002 document is "The National Security Strategy of the United States." Extracts were published in the *New York Times,* 20 September 2002, p. A10. The full version is at <http://usinfo.state.gov/topical/pol/terror/secstrat.htm>.

56. In a news conference, Bush said, "After Sept. 11, the doctrine of containment just doesn't hold any water, as far as I'm concerned." Quoted in the *New York Times,* 1 February 2003, p. A8.

57. Adam Nagourney and Megan Thee, "Poll Gives Bush Worst Marks Yet on Major Issues," *New York Times,* 10 May 2006, pp. A1, A18. Poll results are at <http://nytimes.com/ref/us/polls_index.html>.

58. The National Security Strategy of the United States of America, March 2006. Available at <http://www.whitehouse.gov/nsc/nss/2006/>.

59. Bob Woodward, *Plan of Attack: The Definitive Account of the Decision to Invade Iraq* (New York: Simon & Schuster, 2004), p. 443.

60. Ivo H. Daalder and James M. Lindsay, "American Empire, Not 'If' But 'What Kind,'" *New York Times,* 10 May 2003, p. A19; R. C. Longworth, "Why a Unilateral America Frightens Its Historical Allies," *Chicago Tribune,* 16 March 2003, sec. 2, p. 1; Emmanuel Todd, *After the Empire: The Breakdown of the American Order* (New York: Columbia University Press, 2003); Harry Turtledove, *American Empire: The Victorious Opposition* (New York: Random House, 2003); Noam Chomsky, *Hegemony or Survival: America's Quest for Global Dominance (The American Empire Project)* (New York: Holt, 2003).

61. For a list of sins of contemporary American foreign policy, see Loch K. Johnson and Kiki Caruson, "The Seven Deadly Sins of American Foreign Policy," *PS: Political Science and Politics* 36 (January 2003): 5–10.

62. See Joseph S. Nye, "U.S. Power and Strategy After Iraq," *Foreign Affairs* (July–August 2003): 60–73. For a contrasting view, see Grenville Byford, "The Wrong War," *Foreign Affairs* (July–August 2002): 34–43.

63. See Moisés Naím, "The Five Wars of Globalization," *Foreign Policy* (January–February 2003): 29–37. For problems in combating terrorism, see Thomas Homer-Dixon, "The Rise of Complex Terrorism," *Foreign Policy* (January–February 2002): 52–62.

64. Michael Mastanduno, "Trade Policy," in *U.S. Foreign Policy: The Search for a New Role,* ed. Robert J. Art and Seyom Brown (New York: Macmillan, 1993), p. 142.

65. U.S. Government, Energy Information Administration, available at <http://www.eia.doe.gov/emeu/aer/txt/ptb1105.html>.

66. Statistics derived from Office of Trade and Economic Analysis, International Trade Administration, U.S. Department of Commerce, "GDP & U.S. International Trade in Goods and Services, 1973–2002," available at <http://www.ita.doc.gov/industry/otea/>.

67. "Hills, in Japan, Stirs a Baby-Bottle Dispute," *New York Times,* 14 October 1989, p. 35.

68. Information available as of 1 February 2004 from the World Trade Organization's website at <http://www.WTO.org/>.

69. "WTO Rules Against U.S. Dumping Laws," *Wall Street Journal,* 7 June 2000, p. A2.

70. R. C. Longworth, "WTO Deserves Some but Not All of the Criticism It's Getting," *Chicago Tribune,* 2 December 1999, p. 25.

71. Andrew Higgins, "As China Surges, It Also Proves a Buttress to American Strength," *Wall Street Journal,* 30 January 2004, pp. A1, A8.

72. John Stremlau, "Clinton's Dollar Diplomacy," *Foreign Policy* 97 (Winter 1995): 18–35.

73. R. C. Longworth, "A 'Grotesque' Gap," *Chicago Tribune,* 12 July 1999, p. 1.

74. Steven Kull, "What the Public Knows That Washington Doesn't," *Foreign Policy* 101 (Winter 1995–1996): 102–115.

75. Barbara Crossette, "War Crimes Tribunal Becomes Reality, Without U.S. Role," *New York Times,* 12 April 2002, p. A3; Neil A. Lewis, "U.S. Rejects All Support for New Court on Atrocities," *New York Times,* 7 May 2002, p. A9.

76. See <http://www.globalsolutions.org/programs/law_justice/faqs/ataglance.html>.

77. Elizabeth Becker, "U.S. Suspends Aid to 35 Countries over New International Court," *New York Times,* 2 July 2003, p. A8.

78. Andrew C. Revkin, "U.S. Move Improves Chance for Global Warming Treaty," *New York Times,* 20 November 2000, p. A6.

79. Ray Moseley, "Climate Meeting Extended a Day amid Controversy," *Chicago Tribune,* 25 November 2000, p. 3.

80. Sheryl Gay Stolberg, "Bush Proposes Goal to Reduce Greenhouse Gas," *New York Times,* 1 June 2007, p. 1.

81. See Paul R. Brewer, Kimberly Gross, Sean Aday, and Lars Willnat, "International Trust and Public Opinion About World Affairs," *American Journal of Political Science* 48 (January 2004): 93, 109. They say, "Most Americans see the realm of international relations as resembling the 'state of nature' described by Hobbes. Put more simply, they see it as a 'dog-eat-dog' world" (p. 105).

82. Joseph Kahn and Judith Miller, "Getting Tough on Gangsters, High Tech and Global," *New York Times,* 15 December 2000, p. A7.

83. Marshall M. Bouton (ed.), *Global Views 2004: American Public Opinion and U.S. Foreign Policy, 2004* (Chicago: Chicago Council on Foreign Relations, 2004).

84. Report available at <http://www.ccfr.org/globalviews2004/sub/usa.htm>, p. 1.

85. Ibid.; these comparative data are contained in the report of leaders' opinions, p. 8.

86. Lawrence R. Jacobs and Benjamin I. Page, "Who Influences U.S. Foreign Policy?" *American Political Science Review* 99 (February 2005): 107–123.

87. Charles Kegley and Eugene Wittkopf, *American Foreign Policy: Pattern and Process,* 4th ed. (New York: St. Martin's Press, 1991), pp. 272–273.

88. Alison Mitchell, "Bush, Invoking 3 Presidents, Casts 'Vote' for China Trade," *New York Times,* 18 May 2000, p. 1.

89. Lori Nitschke, "White House in Full Battle Mode in Final Push for China NTR," *Congressional Quarterly Weekly Report,* 18 March 2000, pp. 606–609.

90. "Voter Preferences Vacillate: Gender Gaps on the Candidates, Guns, China, and Missile Defense," news release, Pew Research Center for the People and the Press, 11 May 2000, p. 37.

91. Helene Cooper, "Eclectic Grass-Roots Campaigns Emerge on China Trade," *Wall Street Journal,* 13 March 2000, p. A48.

92. Steven Greenhouse, "Unions Deny Stand over Trade Policy Is Protectionism," *New York Times,* 24 April 2000, p. 1.

93. Cooper, "Eclectic Grass-Roots Campaigns," p. A48.

94. Neil King, Jr., and Marc Champion, "Policy Convergence on China," *Wall Street Journal,* 4 May 2006, p. A4.

95. "Voter Preferences Vacillate," p. 37.

96. Adam Clymer, "House Vote on China Trade: The Politics Was Local," *New York Times,* 27 May 2000, p. A3.

★ Index of References

★ Index